Encyclopedia
of the
American Constitution

Editorial Board

Encyclopedia
of the
American Constitution

LEONARD W. LEVY, Editor-in-Chief
Claremont Graduate School, Claremont, California

KENNETH L. KARST, Associate Editor
University of California, Los Angeles

DENNIS J. MAHONEY, Assistant Editor
Claremont Graduate School, Claremont, California

MACMILLAN PUBLISHING COMPANY
A Division of Macmillan, Inc.
NEW YORK

Collier Macmillan Publishers
LONDON

74131

Macmillan Publishing Company
A Division of Macmillan, Inc.
866 Third Avenue, New York, NY 10022

Collier Macmillan Canada, Inc.

Printed in the United States of America

printing number
1   2   3   4   5   6   7   8   9   10

Library of Congress Catalog in Publication Data

Encyclopedia of the American Constitution.

Includes index.
1. United States—Constitutional Law—Dictionaries.
I. Levy, Leonard Williams, 1923–   II. Karst,
Kenneth L.   III. Mahoney, Dennis J.
KF4548.E53   1986   342.73′023′03   86–3038
ISBN 0–02–918610–2   347.3022303

STAFF:

Charles E. Smith, *Publisher*

Elly Dickason, *Project Editor*

Morton I. Rosenberg, *Production Manager*

Joan Greenfield, *Designer*

JACKSON, ANDREW
(1767–1845)

Andrew Jackson, the seventh President of the United States, was the son of Irish immigrant parents who had settled in the South Carolina backcountry. Drifting to North Carolina after the Revolutionary war, he read enough law to gain admission to the bar. When only twenty-one he was appointed prosecuting attorney for the Western District at Nashville. There he built a flourishing practice, married, and became a leading planter-aristocrat. In 1796 he was elected a delegate to the CONSTITUTIONAL CONVENTION of Tennessee, then was chosen the new state's first representative in Congress. His service there was brief and undistinguished; it was followed by appointment to the Tennessee Superior Court, where he sat for six years, retiring in 1804. In the factional brawls of Tennessee politics Jackson won a reputation for hot-blooded courage. He killed an adversary in a celebrated duel and barely escaped with his own life in another.

Jackson rose to national fame during the War of 1812. It was mainly an Indian war on the southwest frontier. As major general of the Tennessee militia, Jackson defeated the Creeks and then imposed a humiliating treaty. In 1814 he was commissioned major general in the United States Army and was entrusted with the defense of the Gulf country from Mobile to New Orleans. He defeated the British in the Battle of New Orleans, the last and the greatest victory of the war; and although it occurred after the peace treaty was signed, the victory made Jackson a national hero. Criticized by a local citizen for refusing to lift martial law after the battle, Jackson arrested him; and when a federal judge, Dominick Hall, issued a writ of HABEAS CORPUS for the citizen, Jackson arrested the judge as well. Upon his release Judge Hall hauled the errant general into court. Jackson pleaded "the law of necessity" in his defense and got off with a thousand dollar fine. He paid, yet bristled at the alleged injustice until finally, in 1844 a Democratic Congress returned the fine with interest.

Jackson had a more serious scrape with the law in 1818. In command of an army ordered to suppress Indian disturbances along the Spanish border, he invaded Florida, executed two British subjects for stirring up the Seminoles, and captured Pensacola together with other Spanish posts. President JAMES MONROE disavowed the general's conquest, said it was unauthorized, and ordered surrender of the posts. Two cabinet officers wished to punish Jackson. Not only had he violated orders, he had violated the Constitution by making war on Spain, a power reserved to Congress. When Congress convened, a sensational month-long debate occurred in the House of Representatives on resolutions condemning Jackson for his behavior and recommending legislation to prohibit invasion of foreign territory without the consent of Congress except in direct pursuit of a defeated enemy. The resolutions failed. Jackson insisted he had acted within the broad confines of his orders. Monroe, while admitting none of this, conceded that Jackson had acted honorably on his own responsibility.

In 1822 the Tennessee legislature nominated Jackson for President. At first no one took the nomination seriously; it was obviously a stratagem of the General's political friends to avail themselves of his popularity in order to regain control of the state government. But the candidacy of "the military hero" caught fire in 1824. Jackson emerged from the election with a plurality of the popular vote; but since no candidate received a majority of the electoral vote the final choice was referred to the House, and there the influence of HENRY CLAY led to the election of JOHN QUINCY ADAMS. Jackson and his party immediately accused Adams and Clay of a "corrupt bargain." Trailing clouds of democratic rhetoric the Jacksonian politicians forged a powerful coalition that elected Old Hickory President in 1828.

The new President, though in wretched health, was a man of distinguished bearing, fascinating manners, resolute character, and still uncertain politics. In his first annual message to Congress, he called for constitutional amendments to limit the President to a single term of four or six years and, in a case like the 1824 election, to transfer the choice from the House to the people. Nothing came of this, of course. Jackson extended the old republican idea of "rotation in office" to the federal civil service, thereby laying the basis for wholesale partisan removals and appointments. He called for Indian removal. Reiterating his support for a "judicious tariff," he seemed as little inclined to back southern demands for reform as to make war on the AMERICAN SYSTEM. He pledged himself to extinguish the debt; and rather than reduce the tariff when that was accomplished, he proposed to distribute the surplus revenue to the states for works of INTERNAL IMPROVEMENTS. Finally, he pointedly raised the question of the constitutionality of the BANK OF THE UNITED STATES, whose charter would expire in 1836.

Congress responded quickly to Jackson's call for legislation to remove eastern Indian tribes west of the Mississippi. For many years he had regarded the policy of treating with the Indians "an absurdity." Now as President he sided with Georgia's policy of extending the laws of the state to Indians within its borders. When the Supreme Court in WORCESTER v. GEORGIA ruled against Georgia and upheld the Cherokee claim to federal protection, Jackson reputedly declared, "John Marshall has made his decision, now let him enforce it." The President, certainly, had no intention of coercing Georgia. By a mixture of force and persuasion he got the Cherokee and other tribes to cede their lands and migrate westward under the terms of the Removal Act. (See CHEROKEE INDIAN CASES, 1831–1832.)

Indian removal upon the pain of subjection to state authorities was the first indication of the sweeping denationalization of public policy that came to characterize the Jackson administration. Seeking to return the government to "that simple machine which the Constitution created," he struck at federal aid and planning of internal improvements by vetoing the MAYSVILLE ROAD BILL. Finding the bill unconstitutional because of its "purely local character," he nevertheless went on to express opposition to any general system of internal improvements; and after Congress adjourned he pocket-vetoed two improvement bills that could not be dismissed on local grounds. Jackson thereafter signed many improvement bills, mostly of the "pork barrel" variety, yet he repeatedly denounced the "sinister" policy matured by previous administrations and boasted of overthrowing it.

In 1832 Jackson again struck at the foundations of national authority when he vetoed the bill to recharter the Bank. The veto message adroitly combined the democratic appeals of western agrarianism with the STATES' RIGHTS prejudices of the South. On the question of constitutionality Jackson rejected the result of forty years' experience and placed his own independent judgment above that of Congress and the Supreme Court. "The opinion of the judges has no more authority over Congress than the opinion of Congress has over the judges," Jackson declared, "and on that point the president is independent of both." This was radical doctrine. In the eyes of opposition leaders, who would soon call themselves Whigs, it presaged a government of men, not of laws. (See JACKSON'S VETO OF THE BANK BILL.)

Not all of his actions were denationalizing in tendency, however. JACKSON'S PROCLAMATION TO THE PEOPLE OF SOUTH CAROLINA, condemning that state's NULLIFICATION of the protective tariff in 1832, was boldly nationalistic. Jackson ridiculed nullification as an "absurdity," defended the constitutionality of the tariff, and set forth the theory of the supremacy and indivisibility of the Union. The Constitution had created a national union, a government of "one people," to which had been committed sovereign powers heretofore belonging to the state governments; and no state could violate this union or secede from it without dissolving the whole. A month later, as South Carolina persisted in its course, Jackson called upon Congress for additional powers to enforce the revenue laws, including use of the army, navy, and militia if necessary. Congress enacted the FORCE ACT, as it was called. Use of force was averted, however, because South Carolina accepted the terms of Henry Clay's

Compromise Tariff and rescinded the ordinance of nullification.

Jackson was the first President to exercise strong, independent leadership in domestic affairs. The Bank veto, while shrinking congressional powers, expanded the President's. Overwhelmingly reelected in 1832, Jackson took his victory as a mandate to destroy the Bank. He proceeded on his own responsibility to remove the government deposits from the Bank, placing them in so-called pet banks operating under state charters. Congress had delegated authority over the government deposits to the secretary of the treasury. When that officer, William Duane, refused to remove the deposits, Jackson fired him and appointed a willing accomplice, ROGER B. TANEY, in his place. Congress convened in an uproar in December 1833. The opposition led by Clay called on the President for a paper he was known to have read to his cabinet outlining the removal policy. Jackson peremptorily refused to forward the paper on the grounds that communications to cabinet officers were privileged. (See EXECUTIVE PRIVILEGE.) Clay then introduced two resolutions censuring the President, as well as the new treasury secretary, for assuming powers "not conferred by the constitution and laws, but in derogation of both." The old issue of banking policy virtually disappeared as the opposition concentrated on the new issue of executive tyranny. The Senate, though not the House, adopted Clay's resolutions. Jackson was furious. He returned a lengthy "Protest" in which he argued that the entire executive power rested in the President, that he alone could decide how the laws should be executed, and that regardless of acts of Congress his authority to direct and remove subordinates was absolute. Congress, moreover, could not censure him; it could only impeach him. The Senate indignantly refused to enter the Protest in its journal. This bitter conflict finally came to an end in 1837, as Jackson's presidency expired, when the Senate voted to expunge the censure from the journal.

The relationship between Jackson's presidency and the Constitution was complex and confused. In the nullification crisis he placed the preservation of the Union above extravagant states' rights claims. Thirty years later, in a much deeper crisis of Union, ABRAHAM LINCOLN had no need to search for higher ground than Jackson had provided in his most famous state paper. But Jackson's presidency also gave renewed vigor to ideas of STRICT CONSTRUCTION and states' rights. It reversed the twenty-year trend toward consolidation in the general government and returned power to the states. Finally, Jackson magnified the power of the presidency at the expense of Congress. Exploiting popular democratic sentiments, he appealed to the will of the people, which he also claimed to embody, against the will of Congress. He vetoed more bills than all his predecessors combined; he was the first to employ the POCKET VETO and used it seven times. Paradoxically, his actions weakened the office. After him every President was thrown on the defensive; none would be reelected until Lincoln and none would serve two terms until ULYSSES S. GRANT. The Supreme Court, too, was challenged, for Jackson shook the ground from under the emerging consensus that the Court was the final arbiter of the Constitution. The appointment of his friend Taney as Chief Justice in 1835 terrified the Whigs, who feared that it would extend Jackson's baneful influence far into the future.

Jackson retired to his home, The Hermitage, near Nashville, and resumed the life of the planter. The patriarch of the Democratic party, he continued to influence its leaders and policies. He died at the Hermitage on June 8, 1845.

MERRILL D. PETERSON

Bibliography

BASSETT, JOHN S. and JAMESON, J. FRANKLIN, EDS. 1926–1935 *The Correspondence of Andrew Jackson,* 7 Vols. Washington: American Historical Association.

JAMES, MARQUIS 1938 *The Life of Andrew Jackson.* Indianapolis: Bobbs-Merrill.

REMINI, ROBERT 1977 *Andrew Jackson and the Course of American Empire, 1767–1821.* New York: Harper & Row.

_____ 1981 *Andrew Jackson and the Course of American Freedom, 1822–1832.* New York: Harper & Row.

RICHARDSON, J. D., ED. 1896 *A Compilation of the Messages and Papers of the Presidents,* Vol. II. Washington: Government Printing Office.

JACKSON, HOWELL E.
(1832–1895)

Howell Edmunds Jackson, a native of Tennessee, was appointed to the Supreme Court by BENJAMIN HARRISON in 1893. Although a Democrat, Jackson had Whig antecedents and had long been a vigorous exponent of the "New South" creed. He led the conservative opposition to repudiation of the Tennessee debt in the 1870s and represented some of the region's most prominent corporations in his law practice. GROVER CLEVELAND appointed him to a Sixth Circuit judgeship in 1886. His opinions in cases on the INTERSTATE COMMERCE ACT and the SHERMAN ANTITRUST ACT underscored his solicitude for big business.

Jackson's Supreme Court career lasted about a year and a half. Poor health precluded his participation in UNITED STATES V. E. C. KNIGHT CO. (1895) and IN RE DEBS (1895), two of the most important cases decided during his tenure. But Jackson sat with an equally divided Court at the second hearing of POLLOCK V. FARMERS LOAN & TRUST CO. (1895). His eloquent dissent, in which he insisted that the invalidation of the income tax was "the most disastrous blow ever struck at the constitutional power of Congress," remains his most famous opinion. It also sparked an enduring controversy over which, if any, of the Justices switched his vote between hearings.

CHARLES W. MCCURDY

Bibliography

SCHIFFMAN, IRVING 1970 Escaping the Shroud of Anonymity: Justice Howell Edmunds Jackson and the Income Tax Case. *Tennessee Law Review* 37:334–348.

JACKSON, ROBERT H.
(1892–1954)

The orderly, middle-class world of Jamestown, New York, the economic calamity of the Great Depression, and the horrors of Nazi Germany—these were the crucial experiences that shaped the jurisprudence of Robert Houghwout Jackson, the only Supreme Court Justice to serve both as SOLICITOR GENERAL and ATTORNEY GENERAL of the United States, and the last to learn his law initially through the old-fashioned apprentice method.

Appointed to the Court by FRANKLIN D. ROOSEVELT in 1941 and facing the most important constitutional issues of the post-Depression era—the scope of federal economic management and the nationalization of the BILL OF RIGHTS—Jackson helped to accelerate the former but resisted the latter. In alliance with his close friend and colleague FELIX FRANKFURTER, he often found himself locked in combat between 1941 and 1954 with Justices HUGO L. BLACK and WILLIAM O. DOUGLAS, the ideological leaders of the Court's liberal block.

Few Justices in the Court's history articulated a more robust version of economic nationalism than Justice Jackson who, despite his small-town heritage and solicitude for independent entrepreneurship, supported consistently the expansion of federal ECONOMIC REGULATION and the growth of an integrated national marketplace, which soon became dominated by giant CORPORATIONS. Jackson wrote a sweeping

validation of congressional authority under the COMMERCE CLAUSE in WICKARD V. FILBURN (1942), and he also used that provision absent federal law in *H. P. Hood & Sons v. DuMond* (1949) to strike down state regulations that insulated local economic activities from the rigors of interstate competition.

The crisis of the Great Depression convinced Jackson of the dangers of both *laissez-faire* and economic Balkanization. His later confrontation with Nazism when he served as chief American prosecutor at Nuremberg persuaded him of the dangers posed to human freedom by the growth of a monolithic police state. His firm commitment to economic nationalism never wavered, except near the end of his life in situations where the federal government began to employ the COMMERCE CLAUSE in an effort to regulate more than traditional economic activities. A year before his death, for example, Jackson narrowly construed a federal anticrime statute, voting to sustain the dismissal of INDICTMENTS for failure to register as dealers in gambling machines in *United States v. Five Gambling Devices* (1953). In the course of making their arrests in the case, FBI agents had stormed into a Tennessee country club and seized slot machines that were not shown to have been transported in interstate commerce. Jackson read into the statute a requirement of such a showing.

Jackson's fears of expanded federal police controls became so pronounced that he resisted efforts to attack RACIAL DISCRIMINATION by means of the criminal and civil provisions of the Reconstruction-era CIVIL RIGHTS ACTS, especially where these efforts threatened to undermine the autonomy of local law enforcement officials, such as SCREWS V. UNITED STATES (1945) and *Collins v. Hardyman* (1951). He also opposed federal judicial intervention under the FOURTEENTH AMENDMENT to correct local abuses in the administration of criminal justice. Although he interpreted the FOURTH AMENDMENT strictly as to federal SEARCHES AND SEIZURES, as in his dissent in BRINEGAR V. UNITED STATES (1949), he refused to extend the EXCLUSIONARY RULE to state criminal prosecutions, and he exhibited broad toleration for local police practices that shocked other members of the Court. "Local excesses or invasions of liberty," he wrote, "are more amenable to political correction," a point of view which no doubt surprised Mississippi Negroes and many state criminal suspects who endured the third degree. Even Frankfurter broke with Jackson on these issues, for example, in IRVINE V. CALIFORNIA (1954).

Jackson's small-town roots and his fear of mass-based political movements such as Nazism colored his views of other CIVIL LIBERTIES issues as well. He often defended the lone individual against the repressive machinery of the state, but he thoroughly distrusted people in groups, especially well-organized, zealous minorities who threatened to disrupt what Jackson regarded as the community's peace, stability, and proper order. The Constitution, he believed, prohibited West Virginia officials from imposing a mandatory flag salute observance on the children of Jehovah's Witnesses. (See FLAG SALUTE CASES.) The federal government, likewise, could not convict without a finding of criminal intent, condemn for TREASON without substantial proof, or hold a hapless ALIEN indefinitely on Ellis Island without charging him with a specific crime. "This man, who seems to have led a life of unrelieved insignificance," he wrote angrily, in SHAUGHNESSY V. UNITED STATES EX REL. MEZEI (1953) (dissenting opinion), "must have been astonished to find himself suddenly putting the Government of the United States in such fear that it was afraid to tell him why it was afraid of him. . . . No one can make me believe that we are that far gone."

Yet Jackson did not believe that the Constitution gave cadres of Jehovah's Witnesses the right to distribute their religious literature in defiance of local ordinances prohibiting house-to-house canvassing and ringing doorbells. "I doubt if only the slothfully ignorant wish repose in their homes," he wrote sarcastically in *Martin v. City of Struthers* (1943), responding to Justice Black's opinion upholding the Witnesses' claim, "or that the forefathers intended to open the door to such forced 'enlightenment' as we have here." A similar loathing for collective political behavior informed his attitude toward the Communist party which, like the Nazi organizations condemned at Nuremberg, he equated with a conspiracy against the social order in a concurring opinion in *Dennis v. United States* (1951).

Jackson's belief in the fragility of the political system also made him a conservative on most FREEDOM OF SPEECH issues, witness his dissenting opinion in KUNZ V. NEW YORK (1950). He objected, for instance, to the specific law upheld in the famous Illinois GROUP LIBEL case, BEAUHARNAIS V. ILLINOIS (1952), but he acknowledged the state's "commendable desire to reduce sinister abuses of our freedom of expression—abuses which I have had occasion to learn can tear society apart, brutalize its dominant elements, and persecute, even to extermination, its minorities."

Witty, combative, and gifted with an eloquent prose style, Jackson remained a person of many paradoxes: the rugged individualist who helped to fashion the New Deal's welfare state; the two-fisted prosecutor who wished to be the disinterested judge; and the economic nationalist who distrusted the growth of centralized, bureaucratic authority.

MICHAEL E. PARRISH

Bibliography

GERHART, EUGENE C. 1958 *America's Advocate: Robert H. Jackson.* Indianapolis: Bobbs-Merrill.
JAFFE, LOUIS L. 1955 Mr. Justice Jackson. *Harvard Law Review* 68:940–998.
WHITE, G. EDWARD 1976 The Dilemmas of Robert Jackson. Pages 230–250 in White, *The American Judicial Tradition: Profiles of Leading American Judges.* New York: Oxford University Press.

JACKSON v. GEORGIA

See: Capital Punishment Cases, 1972

JACKSON v. METROPOLITAN EDISON CO.
419 U.S. 345 (1974)

In the WARREN COURT years, the STATE ACTION doctrine was progressively weakened as a limitation on the FOURTEENTH AMENDMENT; more and more "private" conduct fell under the Amendment's reach. The *Jackson* decision illustrates how the BURGER COURT called a halt to this trend, limiting the substantive scope of the Amendment by giving new life to the state action limitation.

Metropolitan Edison turned off Jackson's supply of electricity, asserting that she had not paid her bill. She sued for damages and injunctive relief under federal CIVIL RIGHTS laws, claiming PROCEDURAL DUE PROCESS rights to NOTICE, hearing, and an opportunity to pay any amounts due the company. The lower courts denied relief, holding that the company's conduct did not amount to state action. The Supreme Court affirmed, 6–3, in an opinion by Justice WILLIAM H. REHNQUIST, systematically rejecting a series of arguments supporting the contention that state action was present in the case.

The fact of state regulation was held insufficient to constitute state action. As in MOOSE LODGE NO. 107 V. IRVIS (1972), there was no showing of a "close nexus" between the company's no-hearing policy and the state. The approval by the state's public utilities commission of the company's tariff, stating the right to terminate service for nonpayment, was held insufficient to demonstrate explicit state approval of the no-hearing policy. Where *Moose Lodge* had relied on the absence of a monopoly under a state liquor license, *Jackson* characterized *Moose Lodge* as a near-monopoly case and said there was no showing of a connection between the utility's monopoly status and its no-hearing policy. Finally, the Court rejected the notion that Metropolitan Edison was performing a "public function" by supplying electricity, saying there had been no delegation to the company of a power "traditionally associated with sovereignty." The latter comment looked forward to the Court's decision in FLAGG BROS., INC. V. BROOKS (1978).

Justice WILLIAM J. BRENNAN dissented without reaching the merits. Justices WILLIAM O. DOUGLAS and THURGOOD MARSHALL dissented on the merits, pointing out how the majority was departing from the teaching of the Warren Court—something that Justice Rehnquist likely did not need to have explained. *Jackson* did more than reverse currents in the various individual streams of state action DOCTRINE (public functions, monopolies, state encouragement). By taking up each of these arguments separately and rejecting them one by one, the Court also implicitly abandoned the approach of BURTON V. WILMINGTON PARKING AUTHORITY (1961), which had called for determining state action questions by looking at the totality of circumstances in a particular case.

KENNETH L. KARST

JACKSON'S PROCLAMATION TO THE PEOPLE OF SOUTH CAROLINA
(December 10, 1832)

On November 24, 1832, a state convention adopted the SOUTH CAROLINA ORDINANCE OF NULLIFICATION declaring that the federal tariff acts of 1828 and 1832 were "null, void, and no law, nor binding upon this State, its officers or citizens." Sixteen days later President ANDREW JACKSON responded with a proclamation directed at the people of South Carolina, rather than at the state government. Jackson declared the NULLIFICATION ordinance "incompatible with the existence of the Union, contradicted expressly by the letter of the Constitution, unauthorized by its spirit, inconsistent with every principle on which it was founded, and destructive of the great object for which it was formed." After a detailed and withering analysis of the legality and constitutionality of the ordinance,

Jackson turned to the question of SECESSION, which South Carolina threatened if the tariffs were enforced in that state. Jackson warned the people of South Carolina that "Disunion by armed force is TREASON" and that on their heads "may fall the punishment" for that crime. Congress subsequently modified the tariffs but also passed the FORCE ACT authorizing the use of military power to enforce federal laws. South Carolina then repealed its Nullification Ordinance, but in a final flurry of defiance passed an ordinance purporting to nullify the Force Act.

PAUL FINKELMAN

Bibliography
FREEHLING, WILLIAM W. 1965 *Prelude to Civil War: The Nullification Controversy in South Carolina, 1816–1836.* New York: Harper & Row.

JACKSON'S VETO OF THE BANK OF THE UNITED STATES BILL
(July 10, 1832)

The first Bank of the United States was chartered in 1791 despite Jeffersonian opposition. In 1811 its charter expired, but in 1815 the bank was rechartered, with little opposition, as the Second Bank of the United States. The Supreme Court in McCULLOCH V. MARYLAND (1819) upheld the constitutionality of the bank. In 1832 Congress extended the charter of the Second Bank. For a variety of reasons President ANDREW JACKSON opposed the extension. In his veto message Jackson asserted, more emphatically than previous Presidents, the necessity of exercising the presidential VETO POWER on constitutional grounds, rather than on grounds of policy or expediency. Jackson rejected *McCulloch*, arguing that "Mere PRECEDENT is a dangerous source of authority," which should not decide "questions of constitutional power except where the acquiescence of the people and the States can be considered as well settled." Furthermore, Jackson believed Supreme Court opinions "ought not to control the coordinate authorities of this Government." Rather, each branch of the government must "be guided by its own opinion of the Constitution" because a public official swears to support the Constitution "as he understands it, and not as it is understood by others." Jackson argued that the Bank was neither a necessary nor a proper subject for congressional legislation, and so he felt constitutionally obligated to veto the bill.

PAUL FINKELMAN

Bibliography

REMINI, ROBERT V. 1967 *Andrew Jackson and the Bank War: A Study in the Growth of Presidential Power.* Norton Essays in American History. New York: Norton.

JACOBELLIS v. OHIO
378 U.S. 184 (1964)

The Supreme Court reversed Jacobellis's conviction for possessing and exhibiting an obscene motion picture, finding the movie not obscene under ROTH V. UNITED STATES (1957). Justice WILLIAM J. BRENNAN's plurality opinion announced two significant constitutional developments and presaged a third. First, in any case raising the issue whether a work was obscene, the Court would determine independently whether the material was constitutionally protected. Second, in judging the material's appeal to prurient interests against "contemporary community standards," courts were to apply a national standard, not the standards of the particular local community from which the case arose. Finally, purporting to apply standards based on *Roth* and foreshadowing his opinion in MEMOIRS V. MASSACHUSETTS (1965), Brennan noted that a work could not be proscribed unless it was " 'utterly' without social importance."

Jacobellis is best known, however, for Justice POTTER J. STEWART's concurring opinion. Contending that only hard-core pornography constitutionally could be proscribed, Stewart declined to define the material that term included, stating only, "I know it when I see it."

KIM McLANE WARDLAW

JACOBS, IN RE
98 N.Y. 98 (1885)

This exceptionally influential decision, cited hundreds of times by state and federal courts, reflected laissez-faire principles against government regulation of the economy. New York in 1884 enacted a statute to improve the public health by penalizing the manufacture of cigars on the same floor of tenement houses where people lived. Jacobs, a tenement occupant prosecuted under the statute, somehow retained WILLIAM M. EVARTS, "the Prince of the American Bar," whose powerful defense of free enterprise convinced the New York Court of Appeals to decide unanimously against the constitutionality of the regulation. Judge Robert Earl, drawing heavily on Evarts's argument, larded his opinion with polemics against state infringement on liberty and property conducted under the pretext of the POLICE POWER. The constitutional basis of the opinion is not clear because Earl stopped short of invoking the DOCTRINE of FREEDOM OF CONTRACT, but the rhetoric of SUBSTANTIVE DUE PROCESS as a limitation on LEGISLATIVE POWER to regulate the economy stands out. "Under the mere guise of police regulations," Earl said, "personal rights and private property cannot be arbitrarily invaded," and JUDICIAL REVIEW determines whether the legislative power exceeded the limits. The court found that the state plainly had not passed a health law but had trampled personal liberty.

LEONARD W. LEVY

JACOBSON v. MASSACHUSETTS
197 U.S. 11 (1905)

A Massachusetts statute required VACCINATION of a town's inhabitants when health authorities so ordered. For the Supreme Court, Justice JOHN MARSHALL HARLAN concluded the regulation was within the POLICE POWER of the commonwealth and violated no federal constitutional right.

The FIRST AMENDMENT was not then interpreted to apply to the states. Jacobson relied on the liberty guaranteed by the FOURTEENTH AMENDMENT's DUE PROCESS clause, although his objection to vaccination was religious. Harlan concluded that SUBSTANTIVE DUE PROCESS implied no absolute right to control one's body. Justices DAVID BREWER and RUFUS PECKHAM dissented.

RICHARD E. MORGAN

JAMES v. BOWMAN
190 U.S. 127 (1903)

A provision of the FORCE ACTS, passed to protect FIFTEENTH AMENDMENT guarantees, forbade bribery or intimidation to prevent the exercise of VOTING RIGHTS. Bowman, a private citizen, was indicted for preventing several blacks from voting in a Kentucky congressional election. Justice DAVID BREWER for a 6–2 Supreme Court, relying mainly on UNITED STATES V. REESE (1876), declared that the amendment applied to abridgments of the right to vote by the federal government or by a state on account of race; it did not reach private actions. A congressional measure purporting to punish "purely individual action," said Brewer, could not be sustained as an enforcement of the Fifteenth Amendment's prohibition against STATE ACTION abridging the right to vote on account of race. Further, the statute was not limited to RACIAL DISCRIMINATION denying the right to vote. Congress had not relied on its power under Article I to regulate federal elections.

DAVID GORDON

JAMES v. VALTIERRA
402 U.S. 137 (1971)

The California state constitution required voter approval in a local REFERENDUM for the building of public low-rent housing projects. The Supreme Court, 5–3, sustained this requirement against an EQUAL PROTECTION attack.

Justice HUGO L. BLACK wrote for the majority. It was not the business of the courts to analyze governmental structures to see whether they disadvantaged one group or another. In any case, advocates of low-rent housing had not been singled out for disadvantage; California required referenda for the adoption of a number of kinds of legislation. Black distinguished HUNTER V. ERICKSON (1969), which had struck down a similar referendum requirement imposed on fair housing laws. Here no RACIAL DISCRIMINATION was shown.

Justice THURGOOD MARSHALL, for the dissenters, argued that discrimination "between 'rich' and 'poor' as such" was forbidden, quoting Justice JOHN MARSHALL HARLAN's dissent in DOUGLAS V. CALIFORNIA (1963). "[S]ingling out the poor to bear a burden not placed on any other class of citizens tramples the values that the FOURTEENTH AMENDMENT was designed to protect."

KENNETH L. KARST

(SEE ALSO: *Wealth Discrimination; Indigent.*)

JAPANESE AMERICAN CASES
Hirabayashi v. United States
320 U.S. 81 (1943)
Korematsu v. United States
323 U.S. 214 (1944)
Ex parte Endo
323 U.S. 283 (1944)

For more than a month after the Japanese attack on Pearl Harbor in December 1941, no one of high authority in the armed services or elsewhere in the national government suggested seriously that persons of Japanese ancestry should be moved away from the West Coast. The Army's historian wrote that in February and March of 1942 the military estimates were that "there was no real threat of a Japanese invasion" of the area. Yet by March 1942 a program was fully underway to remove about 120,000 persons from their West Coast homes and jobs and place them in internment camps in the interior of the country. About 70,000 of these people were citizens of the United States; two out of every five people sent to the camps were under the age of fifteen or over fifty. All were imprisoned for an indefinite time without any individualized determination of grounds for suspicion of disloyalty, let alone charges of unlawful conduct, to be held in custody until their loyalty might be determined. (See PREVENTIVE DETENTION.) The basis for their imprisonment was a single common trait—their Japanese ancestry.

The military services came to discover the "military necessity" of relocating the Japanese Americans in response to pressure from the West Coast congressional delegations and from other political leaders in the region—including, to his later regret, EARL WARREN, then attorney general of California. These politicians were responding, in turn, to a clamor from certain newspapers and labor unions, along with (as U.S. Attorney General FRANCIS BIDDLE later listed them) "the American Legion, the California Joint Immigration Committee, the Native Sons and Daughters of the Golden West, the Western Growers Protective Association, the California Farm Bureau Federation [and] the Chamber of Commerce of Los Angeles." The groups' campaign was aided by newspaper accounts of American military defeats and Japanese atrocities in the early days of the war, and by false reports of sabotage at Pearl Harbor. Anti-Asian racism, long a feature of California, now had a focus. In Hawaii, which *had* been attacked, no evacuation was proposed; persons of Japanese ancestry constituted almost one third of that territory's population. On the West Coast, Japanese Americans barely exceeded one percent of the population; thus, no political force resisted the mixture of fear, racism, and greed. "The Japanese race is an enemy race," said General John DeWitt in his official report to the War Department. Once the Army urged wholesale evacuation, the opposition of Biddle and the Justice Department was unavailing. President FRANKLIN D. ROOSEVELT sided with the Army, and the evacuation began.

The program, first established by EXECUTIVE ORDER 9066 and then partly ratified by Congress, called for three measures in "military areas"—that is, the entire West Coast. First, persons of Japanese descent were placed under curfew at home from 8:00 P.M. to 6:00 A.M. Second, they would be excluded from "military areas" upon military order. Third, they would be "relocated" in internment camps until their "loyalty" could be determined. The loyalty-determining process was leisurely; as late as the spring of 1945 some 70,000 persons remained in the camps.

The three parts of the program, all of which raised serious constitutional problems, were considered separately by the Supreme Court in three cases: *Hirabayashi v. United States* (1943), *Korematsu v. United States* (1944), and *Ex Parte Endo* (1944).

The *Hirabayashi* case offered the Court a chance to rule on the validity of both the curfew and the exclusion orders. A young American citizen was charged with violating the curfew and refusing to report to a control station to be evacuated from Seattle, where he lived. He was convicted on both counts, and sentenced to three months of imprisonment. In June 1943 the Supreme Court unanimously upheld the curfew violation conviction, and said that it need not consider the validity of the exclusion order, because the two sentences were to run concurrently.

Not until December 1944 did the Court reach the other parts of the evacuation program. In *Korematsu*, the Court divided 6–3 in upholding an order excluding an American citizen from his home town, San Leandro, California. On the same day, the Court in *Endo* avoided deciding on the constitutional validity of internment. Instead, it concluded that the act of Congress ratifying the evacuation program had not authorized prolonged detention of a citizen whose loyalty was conceded. The Court assumed that some brief detention was implicitly authorized as an incident of an exclusion program aimed at preventing espionage and sabotage. Any further detention would have to rest on an assumption the Court was unwilling to make: that citizens were being detained because of their ancestry, in response to community hostility. Justice OWEN ROBERTS, concurring in the result, found congressional authority for internment in the appropriation of funds to operate the camps. Reaching the constitutional issues the majority had avoided, he concluded the Endo's detention violated "the guarantees of the BILL OF RIGHTS . . . and especially the guarantee of DUE PROCESS OF LAW."

The Japanese American cases have made two positive contributions to the development of egalitarian constitutional doctrine. The *Hirabayashi* and *Korematsu* opinions were links in a chain of precedent leading to the Supreme Court's recognition that the Fifth Amendment's due process clause contains a guarantee of equal protection as a substantive limit on the conduct of the national government. (See BOLLING V. SHARPE, 1954; EQUAL PROTECTION OF THE LAWS.) And *Korematsu* first announced the principle that legal restrictions on the civil rights of a racial group are "suspect." (See SUSPECT CLASSIFICATIONS.) Even so, these decisions deserve Eugene Rostow's epithet: "a disaster." The Supreme Court's evasion of issues, its refusal to examine the factual assumptions underlying the "military necessity" of evacuation—in short, its failures to perform as a court—are easier to forgive than to excuse. There is little comfort in the fact that the Court's *Hirabayashi* and *Korematsu* opinions were authored by Justices celebrated as civil libertarians.

Chief Justice HARLAN FISKE STONE wrote for a unanimous Court in *Hirabayashi*, approaching the validity of the curfew not so much as a question about the liberties of a citizen but as a question about congressional power. The WAR POWERS, of course, are far-reaching; they include, as Justices often repeat, "the power to wage war successfully." Thus, for Stone, the only issue before the Court was whether there was "a RATIONAL BASIS" for concluding that the curfew was necessary to protect the country against espionage and sabotage in aid of a threatened invasion. As to that necessity, the Chief Justice said: "We cannot close our eyes to the fact, demonstrated by experience, that in time of war residents having ethnic affiliations with an invading enemy may be a greater source of danger than those of a different ancestry." There was no effort to examine into the likelihood of invasion, or to specify what experience demonstrated the "fact" assumed. The one hard fact was that no sabotage or espionage had been committed by persons of Japanese ancestry at the time of the Hawaii attack or afterward. (California's Attorney General Warren had been equal to that challenge, however: ". . . that is the most ominous sign in our whole situation. It convinces me more than perhaps any other factor that the sabotage we are to get, the fifth column activities that we are to get, are timed just like Pearl Harbor was timed. . . .")

Another question remained: Why impose wholesale restrictions on persons of Japanese ancestry, when Germans and Italians were being investigated individually? Here the Court took refuge in a presumption: "We cannot say that the war-making branches of the Government did not have ground for believing that in a critical hour [disloyal] persons could not readily be isolated and separately dealt with. . . ." This is the classical language of "rational basis" review; government officials have made a factual determination, and a court "cannot say" they are mistaken. That standard of review serves well enough to test the reasonableness of a congressional conclusion that some type of activity substantially affects INTERSTATE COMMERCE. It is utterly inappropriate to test the justification for selectively imposing restrictions on a racial minority.

Justice HUGO L. BLACK began his opinion for the majority in *Korematsu* by recognizing this difference. Racial distinctions, he said, were "immediately suspect," and must be subjected to "the most rigid scrutiny." Following that pronouncement, however, all judicial scrutiny of the racial discrimination at hand was abandoned. The opinion simply quoted the "We cannot say" passage from the *Hirabayashi* opinion; stated, uncritically, the conclusions of the military authorities; observed that "war is an aggregation of hardships"; and—unkindest cut—concluded that "Citizenship has its responsibilities as well as its privileges."

Justice Roberts, dissenting, argued that Korematsu had been subjected to conflicting orders to leave the military area and to stay put, a plain due process violation. It was left to Justice FRANK MURPHY—in his finest hour—to expose the absence of imperial clothing. He demonstrated how the "military" judgment of the necessity for evacuation had departed from subjects in which Army officers were expert and had embarked on breathtaking sociological generalization: the Japanese American community were "a large, unassimilated, tightly knit racial group, bound to an enemy nation by strong ties of race, culture, custom and religion" (quoting General DeWitt).

Decades later, Peter Irons discovered in government archives irrefutable evidence that government officers had deliberately misled the Supreme Court on questions directly related to the claim of military necessity for the evacuations. In response to this evidence, in the mid-1980s federal district courts set aside the convictions of Gordon Hirabayashi, Fred Korematsu, and Minoru Yasui (whose conviction had been affirmed along with Hirabayashi's).

Justice ROBERT H. JACKSON, dissenting in *Korematsu*, said, in effect: There is nothing courts can do to provide justice in this case, or in any case in which the military and the President are determined to take action in wartime; yet we should not lend our approval to this action, lest we create a precedent for similar extraconstitutional action in the future. Of all the oft-noted ironies of the Japanese American cases, this topsy-turvy prediction may be the most ironic of all. *Korematsu* as a judicial precedent has turned out to provide a strong doctrinal foundation for the Supreme Court's vigorous defense of racial equality in the years

since mid-century. The disaster of the Japanese American cases was not doctrinal. It was instead the betrayal of justice there and then for Gordon Hirabayashi, Fred Korematsu, Minoru Yasui, and some 120,000 other individuals—and thus for us all.

KENNETH L. KARST

Bibliography

GRODZINS, MORTON 1949 *Americans Betrayed: Politics and the Japanese Evacuation.* Chicago: University of Chicago Press.

IRONS, PETER 1983 *Justice at War.* New York: Oxford University Press.

ROSTOW, EUGENE V. 1949 The Japanese American Cases—A Disaster. *Yale Law Journal* 54:489–533.

JAY, JOHN
(1745–1829)

John Jay was a major figure during the Revolutionary era. Born into one of colonial New York's leading families, he was aristocratic in appearance, well educated, and a hard worker with a precise and orderly mind. He graduated from King's College in 1764, was admitted to the bar four years later, and soon had a prosperous practice. He early took an interest in the constitutional debate between England and the American colonies; although uneasy about the radical implication of some of the resistance to imperial policies in the 1770s, he nevertheless was a firm patriot. He served as a member of the New York Committee of Correspondence and in the Provincial Congress, as well as in the first and second Continental Congresses in Philadelphia. In 1776 he returned to New York to help draft a state constitution (1777) and to become New York's first chief justice. His major interests, however, lay in the field of diplomacy: he became the United States Minister to Spain in 1779 and later joined BENJAMIN FRANKLIN and JOHN ADAMS in Paris to negotiate the treaty of 1783 that recognized American independence and formally ended the fighting with Great Britain.

Returning to the United States in 1784 Jay assumed the position of secretary of foreign affairs under the ARTICLES OF CONFEDERATION. Unhappy over the weakness of the central government during the 1780s, he sympathized with the movement to create a new constitution that would strengthen the power of the federal government over the states. Jay was not a member of the CONSTITUTIONAL CONVENTION OF 1787, but he strongly advocated adoption of the Constitution in the closely contested ratification struggle in New York the following year. Joining forces with ALEXANDER HAMILTON and JAMES MADISON, Jay contributed several pieces (#2–#5 and, after a bout with illness, #64) to THE FEDERALIST. In these essays Jay warned that failure to adopt the new government would probably lead to the dissolution of the Union and the creation of separate confederacies. He also stressed that only through the creation of a strong and energetic central government could the discord and jealousies of the various states be brought under control and the territorial integrity of the United States be protected from foreign encroachment.

Shortly after becoming President, GEORGE WASHINGTON appointed Jay the first Chief Justice of the United States, a position he held from 1789 to 1795. Two main themes ran through Jay's decisions. The first stressed the supremacy of the newly created national government. CHISHOLM V. GEORGIA (1793) involved the constitutional question of whether a state could be sued in a federal court by a citizen of a different state without its permission, thus limiting its SOVEREIGNTY. The question had been raised during the debate over ratification, and the supporters of the Constitution had given assurances that such suits would not be allowed. Nevertheless, under Jay's leadership the Court handed down an affirmative decision, couched in extremely nationalistic terms. Jay stressed the role of the people of the United States in the creation of the Union, and deemphasized the powers and sovereignty of the states. A very controversial decision, *Chisholm* was vitiated when reaction to it culminated in the adoption of the ELEVENTH ADMENDMENT.

While riding circuit in 1793 Jay delivered a dissenting opinion in WARE V. HYLTON, arguing that a Virginia statute sequestering prerevolutionary debts of British creditors was invalid because it had been nullified by the Treaty of Paris (1783) which specifically indicated that such debts would be honored. The case was appealed in 1796, and the Supreme Court, from which Jay had already resigned, adopted the former Chief Justice's reasoning and reversed the lower court's decision. In another important case, *Glass v. The Sloop Betsy* (1794), the Supreme Court overturned a Maryland District Court ruling that allowed French consuls in America to function as prize courts and dispose of prizes captured by French privateers. Writing for the Court, Jay concluded that United States sovereignty required that these cases be handled by American courts.

Jay's other major concern as Chief Justice was to protect the independence of the Supreme Court by insisting on a strict SEPARATION OF POWERS. He re-

jected various attempts to incorporate the Court into the activities of the legislative and executive branches. For example, when Congress passed an act that required the circuit courts to review the applications of military invalids for pensions, Jay, while riding circuit in New York, declared that "neither the Legislative nor Executive branch can constitutionally assign to the Judicial any duties but such as are properly judicial and to be performed in a judicial manner." This position was upheld a short time later by the United States Circuit Court of Pennsylvania, in what has become known as HAYBURN'S CASE (1792), when the constitutionality of the law was actually challenged. Jay also rejected occasional requests from the President and Secretary of the Treasury Alexander Hamilton for ADVISORY OPINIONS on controversial matters, arguing that the Supreme Court should render opinions only in actual lawsuits brought by contending parties.

Jay was never happy serving on the Court. He thought the circuit riding duties too arduous. He also believed the Court lacked "the energy, weight and dignity which are essential to its affording due support to the national government." Hoping to return to a more active political life, he was defeated in a bid to become governor of New York in 1792. In 1794, while still holding the position of Chief Justice, he went on a special diplomatic mission to try to resolve existing controversies with Great Britain. The result was the controversial but successful JAY'S TREATY. Resigning his post on the Court, Jay became governor of New York in 1795 for two terms. Following the Jeffersonian successes in 1800 he declined reappointment as Chief Justice of the United States Supreme Court and retired from public life.

RICHARD E. ELLIS

Bibliography
MONAGHAN, FRANK 1935 *John Jay.* Indianapolis: Bobbs-Merrill.
MORRIS, RICHARD B. 1967 *John Jay, the Nation and the Court.* Boston: Boston University Press.

JAY BURNS BAKING COMPANY v. BRYAN

See: *Burns Baking Co. v. Bryan*

JAY COURT

See: Supreme Court, 1789–1801

JAY'S TREATY
8 Stat. 116 (1795)

Although obligated by the treaty that ended the Revolutionary War to evacuate its military posts in the Northwest Territory, the British government held the posts, established new ones, and, in 1793, began a policy of encouraging Indian depredations against American settlers in the territory. At the same time, the British fleet, then at war with France, began seizing American ships that called at French ports.

In April 1794, President GEORGE WASHINGTON appointed Chief Justice JOHN JAY envoy extraordinary to Britain to negotiate for neutral shipping rights and evacuation of the Northwest Territory. The treaty Jay negotiated in London and signed in November 1794 provided for both; but it also made many concessions to the British, especially at the expense of Western settlers. Several questions were left to be decided by joint commissions, which would require appropriated funds for their operation.

The congressional debate on Jay's Treaty raised constitutional issues that endure to the present day. Republicans in the House of Representatives, led by ALBERT GALLATIN, objected to a treaty with the force of supreme law that required appropriation of money but from the making of which the House was excluded. They attempted to hold the TREATY POWER hostage to the spending power.

After the treaty was ratified, during the debate on the appropriation, Gallatin induced the House to request from the President documents related to the negotiations. Washington refused to comply, invoking EXECUTIVE PRIVILEGE in order that "the boundaries fixed by the Constitution between the different departments should be preserved."

DENNIS J. MAHONEY

Bibliography

COMBS, JERALD A. 1970 *The Jay Treaty: Political Battleground of the Founding Fathers.* Berkeley: University of California Press.

JEFFERSON, THOMAS
(1743–1826)

Thomas Jefferson, statesman, philosopher, architect, champion of freedom and enlightenment, was United States minister to France when the federal CONSTITUTIONAL CONVENTION met in 1787. Long an advocate of a strengthened confederation, he applauded the convention and anxiously awaited the result of its deliberations. On seeing the roster of delegates, he exclaimed to his diplomatic colleague and friend JOHN ADAMS, "It is really an assembly of demigods." Jefferson soon made the Constitution the polestar of his politics, aligning its principles with those of aspiring American democracy, with momentous consequences for the future of the republic.

Educated for the law in his native Virginia, tutored by GEORGE WYTHE, young Jefferson was a keen student of the English constitution. Like a good Whig, he traced the venerable rights and liberties of Englishmen back to Saxon foundations. The degeneration under George III turned on the system of minsterial influence to corrupt the Parliament. This upset the balance of king, lords, and Commons upon which the freedom and order of the constitution depended; and it threatened, Jefferson came to believe, tyranny for America. He was thus led in his first published work, *A Summary View of the Rights of British America* (1774), to repudiate the political authority of the mother country over the colonies. When he penned the DECLARATION OF INDEPENDENCE two years later, he placed the American claim not in the prescriptive guarantees of the English constitution but on the Lockean ground of the NATURAL RIGHTS of man. In recoil from the treacheries of an unwritten constitution, he concluded with the mass of American patriots that a CONSTITUTION should be written; in this and other ways he sought to secure the supremacy of FUNDAMENTAL LAW over statutory law, which was the great failure of the English constitution. Finally, Jefferson entered upon the search for a new system of political balance consonant with American principles and capable of breaking the classic cycle of liberty, corruption, and tyranny, thereby ensuring the permanence of free government.

Jefferson's constitutional theory first found expression in the making of the VIRGINIA CONSTITUTION OF 1776. In June, while he was drafting the Declaration of Independence for Congress, Jefferson also drafted a plan of government for Virginia and sent it to the revolutionary convention meeting in Williamsburg. The work of framing a new government, he wrote, was "the whole object of the present controversy." In his mind, the relationship of one state paper to the other was that of theory to practice, principle to application. Endeavoring to reach all the great objects of public liberty in the constitution, he included a number of fundamental reforms in Virginia society and government. The constitution adopted at Williamsburg contained none of these reforms, however. Jefferson at once became its severest critic, not only because of its conservative character but also because it failed to meet the test of republican legitimacy. The "convention" that adopted it, as he observed, was the revolutionary successor of the House of Burgesses, elected in April to perform the ordinary business of government. It could not, therefore, frame a supreme law, a law binding on government itself. Jefferson was groping toward the conception of constituent SOVEREIGNTY, in which the government actually arises from "the consent of the governed" through the constitution-making authority of the people. Thus it was that he proposed a form of popular ratification of the constitution—a radical notion at that time. He also proposed, and included in his plan, a provision for amendment by the consent of the people in two-thirds of the counties. This proposal was unprecedented. Jefferson made the omission of any provision for constitutional change a leading count in his indictment of the Virginia frame of government.

Jefferson returned to Virginia in 1776, served his state as a legislative reformer, then as wartime governor, and reentered Congress in the fall of 1783. Turning his attention to the problems of the confederation, he followed his young friend JAMES MADISON in advocating the addition of new congressional powers to raise revenue and regulate FOREIGN COMMERCE. He persuaded Congress to try the provision of the ARTICLES OF CONFEDERATION for an interim executive in the form of a committee of the states, thereby overcoming the dilemma of a congress in perpetual session, which was one source of its debility, or virtual obliteration of the government of the United States. The plan promptly collapsed under trial. Congress seemed as incapable of exercising the powers it already had as it was of obtaining new powers from the states. Jefferson was no "strict constructionist" where the Articles were concerned. In the case of the LAND ORDINANCE OF 1784 for the government of the western territory, he prevailed upon Congress to adopt a bold nation-building measure without a stitch of constitutional authority.

Jefferson's congressional career ended in May 1784, when he was appointed minister plenipotentiary to join BENJAMIN FRANKLIN and John Adams, in Paris, on the commission to negotiate treaties of amity and commerce with European states. He had helped reformulate policy on this subject in Congress. The policy concerned trade, of course; but it also concerned the strength and character of the confederation. Although the front door to congressional commercial regulation was closed, the back door was open through the power of Congress to negotiate treaties. "The moment these treaties are concluded the JURISDICTION of Congress over the commerce of the states springs into existence, and that of particular states is suppressed," Jefferson wrote. Only in treating with foreign nations could the United States act as "one Nation," and so acting not only expand trade abroad but strengthen the bonds of union at home. Indeed, Jefferson asserted that the latter was his "primary object." His hopes were quickly disappointed, however. The European courts, with two or three exceptions, rebuffed the American overtures for freer trade; and as the various state legislatures undertook to regulate foreign trade, Jefferson's political objective was undermined. He reluctantly concluded with Madison and other nationalists that there was no alternative to the outright grant of commercial power to Congress. It was the logic of commercial policy, basically, that led Jefferson to support the federal convention.

Jefferson's position in France, where he had succeeded Franklin as minister, conditioned his response to the new constitution in opposite ways. On the one hand, he had seen the infant republic jeered, kicked, and scoffed at from London to Algiers, all respect for its government annihilated from the universal opinion of its feebleness and incompetence. He had been frustrated in commercial diplomacy even at Versailles; and he and Adams had gone begging to Dutch bankers to keep the confederation afloat. A stronger government, more national in character, with higher tone and energy, was therefore necessary to raise the country's reputation in Europe. On the other hand, Jefferson pondered the new constitution in Paris, where tyranny, not anarchy, was the problem, where the drama of the French Revolution had just begun, and where he had come to recognize the inestimable blessings of American liberty. Learning of SHAYS' REBELLION, which terrified Adams in London, Jefferson declared philosophically, "I like a little rebellion now and then. It is like a storm in the atmosphere." In this spirit, reading the convention's plan in November, he thought the delegates had overreacted to the insurrection in Massachusetts and set up "a kite to keep the hen yard in order." He was staggered, too, by the boldness of the work, a wholly new frame of government, when he had looked for reinvigorating amendments to the Articles.

But the more Jefferson studied the Constitution the more he liked it. He had two main objections. The perpetual reeligibility of the chief magistrate aroused monarchical fears in his mind. Most of the evils of European governments were traceable to their kings, he said; and an American president reeligible every fourth year would soon become a king, albeit an elective one. The fears were little felt at home, however, chiefly because of the universal confidence in GEORGE WASHINGTON, whose election to the first office was a foregone conclusion. So, increasingly, Jefferson concentrated on his second objection, the omission of a BILL OF RIGHTS. In this, of course, he was supported by the mass of anti-Federalists. At first he unwittingly played into their game of using the demand for a bill of rights to delay or defeat RATIFICATION OF THE CONSTITUTION. His suggestion in a private letter that four states withhold their assent until the demand was met contributed to the initial rejection of the Constitution in North Carolina. Actually, Jefferson always wanted speedy adoption by the necessary nine states; and when he learned of the Massachusetts plan of unconditional ratification with recommended amendments, he backed this approach. Meanwhile, in a lengthy correspondence, he converted Madison, the Federalist leader, to the cause of a bill of rights. Acknowledging the inconveniences and imperfections of all such parchment guarantees and conceding the theoretical objection to denying powers that had not been granted, he nevertheless insisted "that a bill of rights is what the people are entitled to against every government on earth, general or particular, and what no just government should refuse, or rest on inference."

Jefferson returned from France in 1789 and became secretary of state in the Washington administration. Great issues of foreign and domestic policy, which struck to the bedrock of principle, soon brought him into conflict with treasury secretary ALEXANDER HAMILTON. The conflict symbolized the rising opposition, first in the government, then in the country at large, between two nascent POLITICAL PARTIES, Republican and Federalist. The Constitution itself became an issue in February 1791, on Hamilton's plan to incorporate a national bank. After Washington received the bank bill from Congress, where Madison had pointedly questioned its constitutionality, he asked the secretaries for their opinions. Jefferson returned a brisk 2,200-word brief against the bill. No power to incorporate a bank had been delegated to Congress. None could be found among the ENUMERATED POWERS, nor could it be fairly inferred from either of the general clauses appealed to by the bank's advocates. The power of Congress to provide for the GENERAL WELFARE was only the power to lay taxes for that purpose; the NECESSARY AND PROPER CLAUSE, unless construed strictly, would "swallow up all the DELEGATED POWERS, and reduce the whole to one power." The bank bill, he concluded, would breach the limits of the Constitution, trample on the

laws of the states, and open "a boundless field of power, no longer susceptible to definition." Washington, however, was persuaded by Hamilton's opinion founded on the doctrine of IMPLIED POWERS and signed the bill. The issue of congressional power was reargued a year later on Hamilton's Report on Manufactures. No legislation resulted, but Jefferson told the President that on the principles of the report Congress could tax and spend without limit on the apology of aiding the general welfare. The deeper grounds of division involved matters of morals, interests, and politics; but because policies were debated in constitutional terms, the question of who was loyal to the Constitution—whether it was best served by strict or loose construction, by STATES' RIGHTS or national consolidation, whether it ought to be viewed as a superintending rule of political action or as a point of departure for vigorous statesmanship—became a major issue between the parties.

The general doctrine of states' rights had been present from the beginning of the controversy, but only in 1798, when Jefferson was vice-president, did it become firmly associated in his mind with the preservation of the Constitution, the Union, and republican liberty. (See UNION, THEORIES OF.) All were threatened, in his opinion, by the ALIEN AND SEDITION ACTS enacted during the war crisis with France. Under the pretense of saving the country from Jacobins and incendiaries, the Federalists, he believed, aimed by these laws to cripple or destroy the Republican party. Because of the danger of criminal prosecution, the delusion of public opinion, and Federalist control of the government, including the courts, the usual means of opposition were ineffectual; so Jefferson turned to the state legislatures as the point of protest and resistance. There was nothing novel in the proceeding. As early as 1790 the Virginia assembly had protested against the allegedly unconstitutional acts of the federal government; in fact, opposition of this kind had been contemplated, and approved, in THE FEDERALIST #28. But the resolutions secretly drafted by Jefferson, and adopted by the Kentucky legislature in November, offered an authoritative theory of "state interposition" that was destined to have great influence. (See VIRGINIA AND KENTUCKY RESOLUTIONS.) The Kentucky Resolutions set forth the theory of the Constitution as a compact among the states. Acts beyond the delegated powers were unconstitutional and void; and since the contracting parties had created no ultimate arbiter, each state had "an equal right to judge for itself, as well of infractions as of the mode and measure of redress." How far Jefferson meant to go was unclear. He called for NULLIFICATION of the oppressive laws; but rather than cause overt state defiance of federal authority, his aim was to arouse opposition opinion through the legislatures to force repeal of the laws. When this political strategy failed, he got Kentucky, as well as Virginia, to renew its protest in 1799, again to no avail. Nevertheless, Jefferson always believed that the Virginia and Kentucky Resolutions were crucial to "the revolution of 1800" that elevated him to the presidency. They had saved the party and the freedom of the political process upon which victory at the polls depended. To this extent, certainly, the resolutions strengthened principles of freedom and self-government under the Constitution. But in appealing to states' rights and state resistance—interposition or nullification or SECESSION—Jefferson struck a course potentially as dangerous to the Constitution and the Union as the odious laws were to civil and political liberty.

Jefferson entered the presidency pledged to return the government to the original principles of the Constitution. These principles included, first, the protection of the state governments in all their rights as the primary jurisdictions of domestic affairs; second, a frugal and simple administration of the federal government; and third, a sharp contradiction of executive power and influence, which had threatened to "monarchize" the Constitution. Such principles were likely to prove embarrassing to the President's leadership. The story of the administration became the story of how Jefferson escaped, evaded, or overcame the restraints of his own first principles in order to provide the strong leadership the country required.

Jefferson's first test concerned the judiciary. He had always favored an independent judiciary as the guardian of individual rights against legislative and executive tyranny. But in "the crisis of '98" the courts became the destroyers rather than the guardians of the liberties of the citizen. The power of this partisan judiciary had been increased by the JUDICIARY ACT OF 1801 passed in the waning hours of the Adams administration. The Federalists, Jefferson believed, had retired to the judiciary as a stronghold from which to assail his administration; and he promptly called for repeal of the Judiciary Act. This was done, although it involved the abolition of judgeships held on GOOD BEHAVIOR tenure. The case of MARBURY v. MADISON (1803) arose at the same time. It, too, was significant primarily in its political character, as a duel between the President and the new Chief Justice, JOHN MARSHALL. Jefferson, who disliked his Virginia cousin, objected to the decision not because the

Court asserted the ultimate power to interpret the Constitution, for in fact it did not go that far, but because Marshall traveled out of the case, pretending to a JURISDICTION he then disclaimed, in order to slap the chief magistrate for violating constitutional rights.

With regard to JUDICIAL REVIEW, Jefferson consistently held to the theory of "tripartite balance," under which each of the coordinate branches of government had the equal right to decide questions of constitutionality for itself. This equality of decisional power was as necessary to maintaining the constitutional SEPARATION OF POWERS, in his view, as the doctrine of states' rights was to preserving the division of authority in the federal system. Under the theory he considered the Sedition Act, which had expired, unconstitutional from the beginning and pardoned those still suffering its penalties. The idea of governmental adaptation and change through construction of the Constitution was repugnant to Jefferson. Even more repugnant was the idea of vesting the ultimate authority of interpretation in a court whose members had no accountability to the people. But Jefferson, though he held the judiciary at bay, was unwilling to push his principles to conclusion and left the foundations of judicial power undisturbed for Marshall to build upon later.

Jefferson overcame the restraints of his whiggish view of executive power by capitalizing on his personal magnetism and influence as a party leader. In FOREIGN AFFAIRS, the principal field of the general government, he had generally taken a more expansive view. Yet the foreign affairs triumph of his administration, the LOUISIANA PURCHASE, became a constitutional crisis for him. While other Republicans easily discovered legal warrant for the treaty, he could not. It was "an act beyond the Constitution," and there was nothing for the President and Congress to do but "throw themselves on the country for doing them unauthorized, what we know they would have done for themselves had they been in a situation to do it." So he drafted a constitutional amendment—"an act of indemnity"—to sanction the treaty retroactively. "I had rather ask an enlargement of power from the nation," he wrote to a Virginia senator, "than to assume it by construction which would make our powers boundless. Our peculiar security is in the possession of a written Constitution. Let us not make it a blank paper by construction." Congress was less scrupulous, however, and when it declined to follow him, he acquiesced. A revolution in the Union perforce became a revolution in the Constitution as well. He found justification for other executive actions—in foreign affairs, in the suppression of the Burr Conspiracy—above and beyond the law. "It is," he wrote, "incumbent on those only who accept of great charges, to risk themselves on great occasions, when the safety of the nation, or some of its very high interests are at stake." In Jefferson's thinking, actions of this kind, which were exceptional and uncodified, were preferable to false and frivolous constructions of the Constitution, which permanently corrupted it. Yet he took little comfort from the theory of "higher obligation" in the case of the Louisiana Purchase.

In retirement at Monticello from 1809 until his death seventeen years later, Jefferson repeatedly confronted the problem of constitutional preservation and change. He knew there could be no preservation without change, no constructive change without preservation. He knew, as he wrote in again championing reform of the Virginia constitution, "that laws and institutions must go hand in hand with the progress of the human mind." And he did not hesitate to declare again his belief, formed in 1789 in the shadow of the Bastille, that each generation, representing a new constituent majority, should make its own constitution. Change should occur, fundamentally, by CONSTITUTIONAL CONVENTION. Next to that, it should occur by regular amendment. As President he had advocated the TWELFTH AMENDMENT, approved in 1804, and several others that were stillborn. Now, from Monticello, he advocated amendments authorizing federal INTERNAL IMPROVEMENTS, the direct election of the president, and the two-term limitation on the president. Nothing happened. Finally, not long before his death, he "despair[ed] of ever seeing another amendment to the Constitution," and observed, "Another general convention can alone relieve us." Thus in the nation, as in the state, he appealed to both lawmaking and constitution-making authorities to keep the fundamental law responsive to new conditions and new demands.

Jefferson continued to the end to reject constitutional change by construction or interpretation. In the wake of the Panic of 1819, which threw his affairs into hopeless disorder, he reacted sharply against the course of consolidation in the general government, above all the bold nationalism of the Supreme Court. "The judiciary of the United States is the subtle corps of sappers and miners constantly working under ground to undermine the foundations of our confederated fabric," he wrote in 1820. "They are construing our constitution from a co-ordination of a general and special government to a general and supreme one. This will lay all things at their feet." Only by combining the revolutionary theory of "constituent sover-

eignty" with the rule of "strict construction" would it be possible, Jefferson believed, to maintain constitutional government on the republican foundations of "the consent of the governed."

MERRILL D. PETERSON

Bibliography

BOYD, JULIAN P., ED. 1950–1974 *The Papers of Thomas Jefferson.* 19 Vols. to date. Princeton, N.J.: Princeton University Press.

LEVY, LEONARD W. 1963 *Jefferson and Civil Liberties: The Darker Side.* Cambridge, Mass.: Harvard University Press.

LIPSCOMB, A. A. and BERGH, A. E., EDS. 1904 *The Writings of Thomas Jefferson.* 20 Vols. Washington, D.C.: Thomas Jefferson Memorial Association.

MALONE, DUMAS 1948–1982 *Jefferson and His Times.* 6 Vols. to date. Boston: Little, Brown.

PETERSON, MERRILL D. 1970 *Thomas Jefferson and the New Nation: A Biography.* New York: Oxford University Press.

JENCKS ACT
71 Stat. 595 (1957)

In *Jencks v. United States*, in June 1957, the Supreme Court, speaking through Justice WILLIAM J. BRENNAN, reversed the conviction of a labor leader, Clinton E. Jencks, charged with perjury for falsely swearing he was not a communist. The five-man majority held that reports filed by FBI-paid informants alleging Jencks's participation in Communist party activities should have been available to his counsel when requested. The majority ruled that the prosecution must either disclose to the defense statements made by government witnesses or drop the case.

Justice TOM C. CLARK wrote a near-inflammatory dissent contending that unless Congress nullified the decision, "those intelligence agencies of our government engaged in law enforcement may as well close up shop." The decision, he warned, would result in a "Roman holiday" for criminals to "rummage" through secret files. Congress seized upon Clark's dissent and a Jencks Act was quickly passed, amending the United States Code. In sharply restricting the Court's decision, the measure provided that a defendant in a criminal case could, following testimony by a government witness, request disclosure of a pretrial statement made by that witness, so long as the statement was written and signed by the witness or was a transcription of an oral statement made at the time the statement was given. Other requested material was to be screened by the trial judge for relevance, with the judge given the right to delete unrelated matters. In subsequent challenges, raised in *Rosenberg v. United States* (1959) and *Palermo v. United States* (1959), the Justices upheld the law, carefully conforming to its provisions.

PAUL L. MURPHY

Bibliography

NOTE 1958 The Jencks Legislation: Problems in Prospect. *Yale Law Journal* 67:674–699.

JENIFER, DANIEL OF ST. THOMAS
(1723–1790)

Daniel of St. Thomas Jenifer signed the Constitution as a Maryland delegate to the CONSTITUTIONAL CONVENTION OF 1787. The most national-minded of Maryland's delegates, he quarreled often with LUTHER MARTIN. His late arrival on July 2 permitted approval of equal votes for the states in the Senate.

DENNIS J. MAHONEY

JENKINS v. ANDERSON
447 U.S. 231 (1980)

The Fifth Amendment allows a criminal defendant to remain silent during his trial and prevents the prosecution from commenting on his silence, in order to prevent the jury from drawing adverse inferences. In *Jenkins* the defendant surrendered to the police two weeks after killing a man and claimed that he had acted in self-defense. When he told that self-defense story at his trial, the prosecutor countered that he would have surrendered immediately had he killed in self-defense. After conviction the defendant, seeking HABEAS CORPUS relief, argued that the use of his prearrest silence violated his RIGHT AGAINST SELF-INCRIMINATION and fundamental fairness. The Supreme Court, like the federal courts below, denied relief. Justice LEWIS F. POWELL, for a 7–2 Court, ruled that the use of prearrest silence to impeach a defendant's credibility, if he testifies in his own defense, does not violate any constitutional rights. Powell's murky reasoning provoked Justices THURGOOD MARSHALL and WILLIAM J. BRENNAN, dissenting, to declare that a duty to incriminate oneself now replaced the right to remain silent. Powell had supported no such duty, but he rejected a "right to commit perjury," which no one claimed. His opinion weakened the right to remain silent.

LEONARD W. LEVY

JENSEN, MERRILL
(1905–1980)

Author and editor of many books on American colonial and revolutionary history, Merrill Monroe Jensen is best known for his challenge of the traditional interpretation of the ARTICLES OF CONFEDERATION as an inadequate form of government whose weaknesses required that it be replaced by the Constitution of 1787. Jensen argued in his most influential books, *The Articles of Confederation* (1940) and *The New Nation* (1950), that the American Revolution was as much a political and social upheaval as the winning of independence from Great Britain and that the Articles of Confederation were the logical result of the democratic philosophy of the DECLARATION OF INDEPENDENCE and the state constitutions of the 1770s. Jensen also contended that the Articles' weaknesses were exaggerated both by the Federalists of 1787–1788, who actually supported the Constitution as a check on the democratic tendencies of which the Articles were the clearest expression, and by most historians.

RICHARD B. BERNSTEIN

JIM CROW LAWS

See: Segregation; Separate-but-Equal Doctrine

JOHNS, UNITED STATES v.
105 S. Ct. 881 (1985)

This case continued a trend of decisions by which the automobile exception to the FOURTH AMENDMENT's SEARCH WARRANT requirement expands without discernible limits. Warrantless AUTOMOBILE SEARCHES were first tolerated because a culprit might suddenly drive away with the evidence of his guilt before a warrant could be obtained. That possibility became the basis of holdings that if a vehicle can constitutionally be searched at the time it is found or stopped, it can be impounded and searched later; and if the vehicle can be searched, sealed containers found within may be opened and searched, too. In *Johns* the Court ruled that if officers unload the containers and store them, instead of searching them on the spot, three days later the containers may be opened without a warrant and any contraband that may be found can be introduced in EVIDENCE. Only Justices WILLIAM J. BRENNAN and THURGOOD MARSHALL dissented from the OPINION OF THE COURT by Justice SANDRA DAY O'CONNOR.

LEONARD W. LEVY

(SEE ALSO: *Chambers v. Maroney; United States v. Ross.*)

JOHNSON, ANDREW
(1808–1875)

Born in 1808, Andrew Johnson became a Tennessee legislator in 1833, congressman in 1843, governor in 1853, United States senator in 1856, Tennessee's military governor in 1862, vice-president of the United States in March 1865, and, on ABRAHAM LINCOLN's death in April 1865, President. Early in his career Johnson mixed STRICT CONSTRUCTION and STATES' RIGHTS views with an unusually warm nationalism, stern loyalty to the Democratic party (until the Civil War: Johnson returned to the Democratic allegiance in late 1866), and a remarkable devotion to white supremacy. By 1860 Johnson's sponsorship of homestead legislation (see HOMESTEAD ACT) and frontier-style campaign rhetoric had won him a reputation as a latter-day Jacksonian.

In the 1860–1861 winter, Johnson, the only slave-state senator who refused to follow his state into SECESSION, openly counseled Tennesseans against seceding. For his temerity he had to flee to Washington. In the Senate, Johnson, achieving at last his homestead goal, won Republicans' appreciation also for supporting Lincoln's and Congress's policies on TEST OATHS, military arrests of civilians, confiscation, emancipation, and Reconstruction. Johnson insisted that the Constitution's WAR POWERS and TREASON clauses authorized the nation, not to coerce a state, but to punish disloyal individuals directly. This believer in a fixed, state-on-top, race-ordered FEDERALISM in 1862 accepted from Lincoln assignment as Tennessee's military governor, a position unknown to the Constitution or statutes, supportable only from the most flexible contemporary ideas on national primacy under martial law.

As military governor, Johnson employed test oaths and troops against alleged pro-Confederates, sometimes purging unfriendly government officeholders and officials of private CORPORATIONS, to rebuild local and state governments. Johnson's policies helped the Republican-War Democratic "Union" coalition win Tennessee in 1864. That party named Johnson its vice-presidential candidate in order to attract the support of other Unionists in the reconquered South and bor-

der states, who seemed to be educable on race. Then, just as the Confederacy's collapse made Reconstruction an immediate concern, Johnson became President.

Although no specific Reconstruction statute constrained him, the 1861–1862 CONFISCATION ACTS, the 1862 test oath act, and the 1865 FREEDMEN'S BUREAU law limited and defined executive actions. Johnson arrogated to himself an unprecedented right to enforce them selectively or not at all in order to further his Reconstruction policy. (For a modern parallel, see IMPOUNDMENT OF FUNDS.)

That policy (announced May 29, 1865, for North Carolina and later for other states) he based on the war powers (but Johnson later insisted that the end of hostilities cut off this source of authority) and on the GUARANTEE CLAUSE: the same authorities Lincoln and Congress employed in wartime Reconstructions (later Johnson insisted that the guarantee clause did not justify a national interest in state residents' CIVIL RIGHTS). Without authority from statute, he appointed a provisional (that is, military) governor for every defeated state, who, with Army help, initiated elections for a CONSTITUTIONAL CONVENTION among qualified voters, including ex-rebels Johnson amnestied and pardoned. The convention was to renounce secession and ratify the THIRTEENTH AMENDMENT. Johnson secretly counseled his provisional governors to appoint officials who could swear to required test oaths and even, as Lincoln had advised publicly, to grant suffrage to token Negroes. But no states obeyed their creator; several only very reluctantly ratified the Thirteenth Amendment, balking at its enforcement clause.

In "reconstructing" thirteen states, Johnson had the largest federal patronage opportunity in American history, especially with respect to postal and tax officers, traditional nuclei of political parties. He filled these influential offices with pardoned ex-Confederates who could not subscribe to the required test oaths, exempting them from the stipulation, thus returning power to recent rebels. Johnson canceled prosecutions under the confiscation laws and inhibited the work of the Freedmen's Bureau, thereby blighting blacks' prospects for a secure economic base. "Johnson" state and local officers, including judges, state attorneys, and police encouraged lawsuits against the Bureau and Army officers for alleged assaults and trespasses and for violating the BLACK CODES. Johnson did not protect his harassed military personnel under the HABEAS CORPUS ACT of 1863. In April 1866, he proclaimed that peace existed everywhere in the

South and that all federal Reconstruction authority ended.

His policies made the security of blacks, white Unionists, and federal officials woefully uncertain and seriously distorted the Constitution's CHECKS AND BALANCES. Johnson insisted that Congress should admit delegates-elect from the Southern states, though conceding that Congress had independent authority (Article I, section 5, on CONGRESSIONAL MEMBERSHIP) to judge the qualifications of its members; he reiterated that the nation had no right to intervene in those states and assigned the Army to police them. Johnson unprecedentedly enlarged the VETO POWER. His stunning vetoes of bills on CIVIL RIGHTS, the Freedmen's Bureau, and military Reconstruction, among others, antagonized even congressmen sympathetic to his views. His vetoes invoked the decision in EX PARTE MILLIGAN (1866), paid tribute to the STATE POLICE POWER, and decried the centralized military despotism he claimed to discern in these bills. But Johnson appealed also to the lowest race views of the time. And he never dealt with the question, with which congressmen at least tried to grapple, of individuals' remedies when the states failed to treat them equally in civil and criminal relationships. The President's decision to campaign in the fall 1866 elections against the party that had elected him, his opposition to the FOURTEENTH AMENDMENT (public disapprobation by a President of a proposed amendment was itself unprecedented), and his intemperate attacks against leading congressmen further alienated many persons.

Johnson rejected the idea of an adaptable Constitution and of a federal duty to seek more decent race relations. There was no halfway house between the centralization he insisted was occurring and a total abandonment of any national interest in the rights of its citizens, who were also state citizens. Johnson's rigidity reflected his heightening racism and his yearning for an independent nomination for the presidency in 1868 from Democrats and the most conservative Republicans.

Johnson himself destroyed his presidential prospects. After obeying the TENURE OF OFFICE ACT by suspending (August 1867) Secretary of War EDWIN M. STANTON, Johnson decided, upon the Senate's nonconcurrence (February 1868), to violate that law. He ousted Stanton and named ULYSSES S. GRANT as interim secretary. Republican congressmen in 1867 had shied away from IMPEACHMENT but in February 1868 the House (128–74, 15 not voting) impeached Johnson for "high crimes and misdemeanors," an offense undefined in the few earlier American impeachments, es-

pecially as to whether the "high crimes" had to be criminally indictable (Article I, section 2; Article II, sections 2, 4; Article III, section 2). Contemporary legal scholar JOHN NORTON POMEROY held that indictability was not a prerequisite for impeachability, conviction, and removal from office. The impeachment committee's charges (Articles I–X) nevertheless stressed largely indictable offenses, including Johnson's obstructions of the military Reconstruction Tenure of Office, and Army Appropriations Acts. Article XI was a catch-all to attract senators who did not hold with indictability as a minimum for impeachability. (See ARTICLES OF IMPEACHMENT, JOHNSON.)

From February through May 1868 the President's able counsel HENRY STANBERY, by insisting on indictability as the test of impeachability, confused senators who formed the court in the impeachment trial. Johnson, at last restraining his intemperateness, now enforced the military reconstruction law and other statutes he had vetoed. He replaced Grant as secretary of war with John M. Schofield, who, though conservative on race, was trusted on Capitol Hill. The Republican majority, wedded to checks and balances, hesitated to subordinate the presidency by convicting and removing Johnson. The House "managers" of the trial harassed witnesses and journalists, outraging some Republican senators. And 1868 was an election year. Johnson, his hopes for a nomination destroyed, must leave office by March 1869. These factors combined to leave Johnson unconvicted by a single Senate vote, 35–19.

Johnson was not the victim of a Radical Republican conspiracy but was the architect of his own remarkably successful effort to thwart improvements in race equality. He won because he exploited men's lowest race fears, cloaking them in glorifications of states' rights. His return to Congress in 1875 as a Tennessee senator (he died later that year), when sentiment was rising even among Republicans to dump the Negro, symbolized his triumph.

HAROLD M. HYMAN

Bibliography

BENEDICT, MICHAEL L. 1973 *The Impeachment and Trial of Andrew Johnson.* New York: Norton.

BERGER, RAOUL 1973 *Impeachment: Constitutional Problems.* Cambridge, Mass.: Harvard University Press.

SEFTON, JAMES 1980 *Andrew Johnson and the Uses of Constitutional Power.* Boston: Little, Brown.

TREFOUSSE, HANS L. 1975 *Impeachment of a President: Andrew Johnson, the Blacks, and Reconstruction.* Knoxville: University of Tennessee Press.

JOHNSON, LYNDON B.
(1908–1973)

Lyndon Baines Johnson was a strong President whose performance was tempered by an affectionate reverence for the constitutional system as a whole. He exploited the cumulative precedents for presidential leadership and authority in domestic, foreign, and military policy; protected presidential power against congressional intrusion while working with vigor to carry Congress with him; and turned the office over to his successor intact. Jointly with Congress, he extended federal power greatly in CIVIL RIGHTS, education, and welfare. He appointed the first black Supreme Court Justice, THURGOOD MARSHALL; but Johnson's attempt to assure liberal leadership beyond his term by the nomination of ABE FORTAS as Chief Justice failed when Fortas withdrew in 1968.

All this tells us little of how the American constitutional process actually operated in the turbulent, creative, and tragic days between November 22, 1963, and January 20, 1969. The agenda Lyndon Johnson confronted was unique. Aside from the urgent need to unify the nation and establish his legitimacy in the wake of JOHN F. KENNEDY's assassination, he faced simultaneous protracted crises at home and abroad: a crisis in race relations and a disintegrating position in Southeast Asia. WOODROW WILSON and FRANKLIN D. ROOSEVELT had also confronted both urgent domestic problems and war; but the course of events permitted them to be dealt with in sequence. Johnson faced them together and they stayed with him to the end.

By personality and conviction, Johnson was a man driven to grapple with problems. But he also carried into office a passionate moral vision of an American society of equal opportunity—a vision he proved capable of translating into LEGISLATION, above all in the fields of civil rights, education, and medical care. The CIVIL RIGHTS ACT OF 1964, the VOTING RIGHTS ACT OF 1965, and the Fair Housing and Federal Jury Reform Acts of 1968 were major results of his crusade for racial equality. The ELEMENTARY AND SECONDARY EDUCATION ACT and HEALTH INSURANCE FOR THE AGED ACT (MEDICARE) of 1965 were outstanding among dozens of acts passed in both fields. In carrying the religious constituencies on the Education Act, Johnson displayed skill bordering on wizardry. As proportions of gross national product, social welfare outlays of the federal government rose dramatically between 1964 and 1968 while national security outlays rose only slightly. This was possible because of an average real growth rate of 4.8 percent in the American economy.

Johnson had been a man of the Congress for some thirty years before assuming the presidency. No President ever came to responsibility with a deeper and more subtle working knowledge of the constitutional tensions between Congress and the President, and of the requirement of generating a partnership out of that tension, issue by issue. But Johnson knew from experience that, on domestic issues, a President's time for leading Congress and achieving major legislative results was short. From his first days as President, Johnson expected Congress would, in the end, mobilize to frustrate one of his initiatives and then progressively reduce or end his primacy. He was, therefore, determined to use his initial capital promptly. Although momentum slowed after mid-1965, Johnson proved capable of carrying Congress on significant domestic legislation virtually to the end of his term.

Johnson was opportunistic in the best sense. He exploited the Congress elected with him in November 1964; but he also channeled the powerful waves of popular feeling in the wake of the assassinations of John Kennedy, MARTIN LUTHER KING, JR., and ROBERT F. KENNEDY into support for his legislative program.

Johnson believed the presidency was the central repository of the nation's ideals and the energizing agent for change in the nation's policy. He understood the advantage a President enjoys relative to a fragmented Congress: the power to initiate. He brought into the White House every constructive idea he could mobilize from both private life and the bureaucracies, setting in motion some one hundred task forces, sixty within the government, forty made up of outside experts. Where possible, he also engaged members of Congress in the drafting of legislation at an early stage in the hope that their subsequent interest and support would be more energetic.

Johnson also understood that in domestic affairs there was little a President could constitutionally do on his own. His was primarily a license to persuade. He used the conventional levers of presidential influence in dealing with Congress. But his most effective instrument was his formidable power of persuasion, based on knowledge of individual members and a sensitive perception of the possibility of support from each on particular issues. He spent far more time with members of Congress than any President before or since—face to face, by telephone, or in group meetings at the White House.

Johnson judged that he had come to responsibility at a rare, transient interval of opportunity for social progress. Therefore, he used up his capital and achieved much. He left Washington with a sense of how much more he would have liked to have done; but he also realized that the nation was determined to pause and catch its breath rather than continue to plunge forward. Nevertheless, the programs initiated in Johnson's time continued to expand in the 1970s. As Ralph Ellison, the black novelist, said, Johnson will perhaps be recognized as "the greatest American President for the poor and for Negroes . . . a very great honor indeed."

But all did not go smoothly with the Great Society. In 1965, five days after the signing of the Voting Rights Act, rioting broke out in Watts, and riots in urban ghettoes continued for three years. Despite vigorous and imaginative efforts, these problems proved relatively unyielding although violence subsided in 1968 as it became increasingly clear that the costs were primarily borne by the black community. Moreover, as new welfare programs moved from law to administration, resistance gradually built up both to their cost and to intrusions on state and local authority. Although significant modifications in the Great Society programs were made in the 1970s and 1980s, it seems unlikely that the basic extensions of public policy in civil rights, education, and welfare will be withdrawn.

Although Johnson led public opinion and drove Congress in domestic affairs, he conducted the war in Southeast Asia with a reserve that did not match the nation's desire for a prompt resolution of the conflict. Johnson's relations with the Congress on the VIETNAM WAR thus differed markedly from his approach on domestic policy. HARRY S. TRUMAN had decided, with the agreement of the congressional leadership, to resist the invasion of South Korea on the basis of his powers as COMMANDER-IN-CHIEF. Johnson preferred the precedents of the Middle East and Formosa Resolutions which he, when Democratic leader in the Senate, had recommended to DWIGHT D. EISENHOWER. He followed that course in the Tonkin Gulf Resolution in 1964. Despite later controversy over the resolution, the record of the Senate debate indicates that its members understood the solemn constitutional step they were taking. Johnson consulted the bipartisan leadership and received their unanimous support on July 27, 1965, before announcing the next day that he had ordered substantial forces to Vietnam—a decision which, at the time, had overwhelming popular as well as congressional support. The possibilities of a formal DECLARATION OF WAR or new congressional mandate were examined and rejected on the ground that they might have brought into effect possible secret military agreements between North Vietnam and other communist powers.

Johnson's determination to consult with and to carry the Congress in 1964 and 1965 was real. But he knew that legislative support at the initiation of hostilities would not prevent members of Congress, disciplined by changes in public opinion, from later opposing him. In the end, he was convinced, the primary responsibility under the Constitution in matters of war and peace rested with the President; and he accepted the implications of that judgment, including the possibility that support for his decision would fade and leave him, like some of his predecessors, lonely and beleaguered.

Johnson made his decision when the entrance of North Vietnamese regular units into South Vietnam had created a crisis, compounded by the Malaysian confrontation instigated by Indonesia with Chinese support. The choice before him was to accept defeat or to fight. He chose to fight because, in his view, the Southeast Asia Treaty (SEATO) reflected authentic United States interests in Asia; a failure to honor the treaty would weaken the credibility of American commitments elsewhere; and the outcome of withdrawal would not be peace but a wider war.

The strategy Johnson adopted was gradually to reduce communist military capabilities within South Vietnam; to use air power against the lines of supply; to impose direct costs on North Vietnam by attacks on selected targets in the Hanoi area; and to support the South Vietnamese in their efforts to create a strong military establishment and to build a viable economy and a democratic political system. His objective was to convince North Vietnam that the takeover of South Vietnam was beyond its military and political grasp and that the costs of continuing the effort were excessive. From the beginning to the end of his administration, Johnson was in virtually continuous diplomatic contact with the North Vietnamese. Protracted formal negotiations began in April 1968 in the wake of the Tet offensive, during which the communist cause suffered a severe military setback but gained ground in American public opinion.

Johnson's cautious strategy in Vietnam conformed to the views of neither the hawkish majority in American public opinion and the Congress, nor the dovish minority. Johnson realized that his conduct of the war was unpopular and that public support had eroded; the nation resisted a protracted engagement with limited objectives and mounting casualties. He nevertheless held to his strategy and resisted those who advocated decisive military action on the ground outside South Vietnam. As Commander-in-Chief, Johnson was determined to conduct the war in a way that minimized the chance of a large engagement with Chinese Communist or Soviet forces. The memory of Chinese Communist entrance into the KOREAN WAR may well have played an important part in Johnson's determination; and he knew that he would be judged in history, in part, on whether his assessment of the risks of a more decisive course of action was correct. Johnson's strategy may also have been affected by two other considerations: a determination to maintain the momentum of his domestic initiatives; and fear that an all-out mobilization might regenerate an undifferentiated anticommunism, with disruptive consequences for foreign policy and McCarthyite implications at home.

The tension between impatient public opinion and Johnson's cautious strategy led to a quasi-constitutional crisis in the early months of 1968. The bipartisan unity of the American foreign policy establishment, which began in 1940, ended, for a generation at least, in 1968. Johnson's distinguished outside advisers, who had been united in November 1967 in support of Johnson's Vietnam policy, were hopelessly divided four months later.

Many complex factors contributed to the schism, but in part it was the product of conflicting images. For Johnson and others who had foreseen the Tet offensive and acted to frustrate it, the communist military failure was apparent, and Johnson's March 31 bombing reduction and proposal to negotiate were designed to exploit a position of relative strength. For those to whom the offensive was a shock and a demonstration of the futility of the American effort, Johnson's negotiation initiative seemed an admission of defeat. Johnson's simultaneous announcement of his decision not to seek reelection may have strengthened the latter image in the public mind.

Thus, Johnson left to his successor a greatly improved military, political, and economic situation in Southeast Asia, a weary and discouraged majority of Americans, and a divided foreign policy establishment in addition to an ardent minority that had been advocating withdrawal from Vietnam for several years.

The antiwar crusaders challenged Johnson's assessment on multiple grounds, among them: the importance of American interests in Southeast Asia; the legality and morality of the war itself; and the belief that Vietnamese nationalism was overwhelmingly on the side of the communists. Johnson weighed carefully the antiwar views, but he remained convinced to the end of his life that his assessment of the issues at stake was correct. He was less sure that his cautious military strategy had been correct.

There was a great deal more to Johnson's foreign policy than the war in Southeast Asia. He stabilized NATO in the wake of French withdrawal from its unified military command; saw the Dominican Republic through a crisis in 1965 to a period of economic and social progress under democracy; and encouraged regional cohesion in Latin America, Africa, and Asia.

Like all American Presidents in the nuclear age, Johnson consciously bore an extraconstitutional responsibility to the human race to minimize the risk of nuclear war. He sought to normalize relations with the Soviet Union; he carried forward efforts to tame nuclear weapons through the Non-proliferation and Outer Space treaties; and he laid the foundation for strategic arms limitation talks.

But the central fact of his administration was the convergence of war and social revolution that resulted in an accelerated inflation rate and yielded four years of antiwar demonstrations and burning ghettoes against a backdrop of prosperity and social reform. Johnson was required, at the request of the governor of Michigan, to send regular Army units to suppress riots in Detroit in July 1967; and troops had to be deployed again in Washington, D.C., in April 1968 after the assassination of Martin Luther King, Jr.

In 1967, after reading the results of a poll assessing his presidency, Johnson said: "In this job you must set a standard for making decisions. Mine is: 'What will my grandchildren think of my administration when I'm buried under the tree at the Ranch, in the family graveyard.' I believe they will be proud of two things: what I have done for the Negro and in Asia. But right now I've lost twenty points on the race issue, fifteen on Vietnam." As Lyndon Johnson's voice repeats many times each day on a tape played at the LBJ Library, ". . . it is for the people themselves and their posterity to decide."

W. W. ROSTOW

Bibliography

BURNS, JAMES MCGREGOR 1968 *To Heal and to Build: The Programs of Lyndon B. Johnson.* New York: McGraw-Hill.

JOHNSON, LYNDON B. 1971 *The Vantage Point.* New York: Holt, Rinehart & Winston.

MCPHERSON, HARRY 1972 *A Political Education.* Boston: Little, Brown.

MUELLER, JOHN E. 1973 *War, Presidents and Public Opinion.* New York: Wiley.

REDFORD, EMMETTE S. and BLISSETT, MARLAN 1981 *Organizing the Executive Branch: The Johnson Presidency.* Chicago: University of Chicago Press.
ROSTOW, W. W. 1972 *The Diffusion of Power.* New York: Macmillan.

JOHNSON, REVERDY
(1796–1876)

A leading constitutional lawyer and Maryland Unionist, Reverdy Johnson argued numerous important Supreme Court cases, including *Seymour v. McCormick* (1854), DRED SCOTT V. SANDFORD (1857), and UNITED STATES V. CRUIKSHANK (1876). At President ABRAHAM LINCOLN's request Johnson published a rebuttal to Chief Justice ROGER B. TANEY's opinion in *Ex parte Merryman* (1861), in which Johnson argued that the President had authority to suspend HABEAS CORPUS. Johnson approved the use of Negro troops and as a senator (1854–1859; 1863–1868) voted for the THIRTEENTH AMENDMENT. However, Johnson broke with Lincoln over the suppression of civilians in Maryland and war aims. Johnson believed that the Confederate states had never been legally out of the Union, and thus once the rebellion was militarily suppressed, the states should be allowed to resume their antebellum status. Johnson opposed LOYALTY OATHS and was President ANDREW JOHNSON's leading Senate supporter during the IMPEACHMENT trial.

PAUL FINKELMAN

Bibliography
STEINER, BERNARD C. 1914 *Life of Reverdy Johnson.* Baltimore: Norman, Remington Co.

JOHNSON, THOMAS
(1732–1819)

Thomas Johnson served in Maryland's colonial House of Delegates and was a member of committees to instruct delegates to the STAMP ACT CONGRESS and to draft a protest against the TOWNSHEND ACTS. He sat in the Continental Congress but was absent when the DECLARATION OF INDEPENDENCE was signed. He was a member of the convention that drafted Maryland's revolutionary constitution (1776) and served as its first governor (1777–1779). Johnson served in Congress from 1781 to 1787 and was a judge of the special federal court to settle a boundary dispute between New York and Massachusetts. He supported RATIFICATION OF THE CONSTITUTION in the state convention of 1788.

His longtime friend, President GEORGE WASHINGTON, offered Johnson a district judgeship in 1789, but Johnson accepted instead the chief judgeship of the Maryland General Court. When JOHN RUTLEDGE resigned in 1791, Washington appointed Johnson to the Supreme Court.

Serving only fourteen months on the Court, Johnson took part in no major decision. He sat for a single term (during which the JAY COURT heard only four cases) and wrote a single short opinion. In 1793, plagued by illness and fatigued by circuit duty, he resigned and was replaced by WILLIAM PATERSON.

DENNIS J. MAHONEY

JOHNSON, WILLIAM
(1771–1834)

Justice William Johnson of Charleston, South Carolina, was THOMAS JEFFERSON's first appointee to the Supreme Court. Johnson was the son of a blacksmith and revolutionary patriot. After attending Princeton and reading law with CHARLES COTESWORTH PINCKNEY, Johnson was elected to serve three terms in the state legislature as a member of the new Republican party. During his third term he became speaker of the House. In 1799, he was elected to the state's highest court, and on March 22, 1804, he was appointed to the Supreme Court, where he served until his death. Of all the fifteen Justices who sat on the MARSHALL COURT, Johnson was, at least to 1830, the most independent and vocal in advancing opinions different from those of Chief Justice JOHN MARSHALL. In treating the accountability of the members of the Court, the distribution of the national power among the three branches, the powers reserved to the states, and VESTED RIGHTS, Johnson often found himself in disagreement with the majority of the Marshall Court. At the time of his appointment, Johnson objected to Marshall's practice of rendering unaminous opinions. He felt that the judicial role required freedom of expression, and he fought to revive the practice of SERIATIM OPINIONS. "Few minds," he protested in a separate opinion in 1816, "are accustomed to the same habit of thinking. . . ." From his advent until 1822, Johnson wrote twelve of twenty-four CONCURRING OPINIONS and sixteen of thirty-two DISSENTING OPINIONS. Toward the end of his career, new Justices joined the Court who agreed with Johnson and frequently spoke out separately with him. Johnson succeeded in establishing the right to dissent, so important in later years.

Johnson also ran into conflict with other members of the Court concerning the allocation of power among the branches of the national government. Like the rest of the Marshall Court, he believed that a strong national government was vital to national unity, and he was willing to delegate broad powers to the government. However, he believed that Congress should be the chief recipient of these powers, and he was willing to construe more narrowly the powers of the judiciary and the President, as he did, for example, in *United States v. Hudson and Goodwin*. In relation to Congress, Johnson made assertions of broad power that surpassed even those of Marshall. For a unanimous Court, in *Anderson v. Dunn*, Johnson upheld Congress's LEGISLATIVE CONTEMPT POWER, and in so doing defended the legislative discretion. Every grant of congressional power draws with it "others, not expressed, but vital to its exercise; not substantive and independent, indeed, but auxiliary and subordinate." Johnson thought IMPLIED POWERS were essential to a responsive government that served the needs of the people. Securities against the abuse of discretion rested on accountability and appeals to the people. Individual liberty stood in little danger "where all power is derived from the people, and at the feet of the people, to be resumed again only at their will."

Johnson's conception of FEDERALISM was in many ways quite modern. In broadly construing powers of Congress, he looked on these less as limitations on the states than as means of strengthening national unity and improving the lot of individuals. In a separate opinion in GIBBONS V. OGDEN, Johnson wrote that where the language of the Constitution leaves room for interpretation, the judges should consult its overriding purpose: "to unite this mass of wealth and power for the protection of the humblest individual: his rights civil and political, his interests and prosperity, are the sole end; the rest are nothing but means." Chief among the means was "the independence and harmony of the states." As Justice Johnson knew from experience, some collisions between state and federal government was inevitable; the only remedy where two governments claimed power over the same individuals was a "frank and candid co-operation for the general good."

Finally, on the rights of property, Johnson showed somewhat less reverence than did the rest of the Court. Toward the end of his career, Johnson lost some of his esteem for a powerful judiciary enforcing property rights against the states, and he began to look to the states for economic and social regulation. In OGDEN V. SAUNDERS Johnson spoke for the majority. He argued that the CONTRACT CLAUSE did not prohibit "insolvent debtor laws" as applied to contracts made subsequent to the laws' enactment. In *Ogden* Johnson objected to construing that contract clause literally. He argued that contracts should receive a "relative, and not a positive interpretation: for the rights of all should be held and enjoyed to the good of the whole." Johnson seemed to foresee the notion of STATE POLICE POWERS when he insisted that the states had the power to regulate the "social exercise" of rights.

In winning tolerance for dissenting opinions and in contributing creatively and prophetically to the body of constitutional doctrine, William Johnson won a niche as an outstanding member of the early Court.

DONALD G. MORGAN

Bibliography

MORGAN, DONALD G. 1954 *Justice William Johnson: The First Dissenter.* Columbia: University of South Carolina Press.

JOHNSON, WILLIAM SAMUEL
(1727–1819)

Dr. William Samuel Johnson signed the Constitution as a Connecticut delegate to the CONSTITUTIONAL CONVENTION OF 1787. A lawyer and educator, he had already served his state as a legislator and judge. Johnson, a conciliator respected by all delegates, formally proposed the Connecticut Compromise (GREAT COMPROMISE). He also proposed the words defining the extent of the JUDICIAL POWER OF THE UNITED STATES, inserting the key phrase, "all cases arising under *the Constitution and* laws of the United States," and he chaired the Committee on Style. Johnson helped keep the Convention from dissolving in the heat of factional dispute. He was later a United States senator (1789–1791).

DENNIS J. MAHONEY

JOHNSON v. AVERY
393 U.S. 483 (1969)

In a 7–2 decision, the Supreme Court, through Justice ABE FORTAS, upheld the right of state prisoners to receive the assistance of fellow convicts in the preparation of writs. The Court overturned a Tennessee prison rule aimed at abolishing the "jailhouse lawyer" practice by which a few convicts, relatively skilled at writ-writing, achieved a position of power among the inmates. Because the rule might have the effect of denying the poor and illiterate the right of HABEAS CORPUS, Tennessee was ordered either to abolish the rule or to provide alternative legal assistance for prisoners wishing to seek postconviction review of their cases.

DENNIS J. MAHONEY

JOHNSON v. LOUISIANA
406 U.S. 356 (1972)
APODACA v. OREGON
406 U.S. 404 (1972)

In DUNCAN V. LOUISIANA (1968) the Supreme Court declared that every criminal charge must be "confirmed by the unanimous suffrage of twelve jurors," and in WILLIAMS V. FLORIDA (1970) the Court found little reason to believe that a jury of six people functions differently from a jury of twelve "particularly if the requirement of unanimity is retained." Justice BYRON R. WHITE, the Court's spokesman in these cases, also wrote its opinion in *Johnson* and for a plurality of four Justices in *Apodaca;* he found nothing constitutionally defective in verdicts by a "heavy" majority vote and no constitutional mandate for verdicts by unanimous vote. The Court upheld the laws of two states that permitted verdicts of 9–3 and 10–2 respectively. These 1972 cases, according to the dissenters, diminished the BURDEN OF PROOF beyond REASONABLE DOUBT and made convictions possible by a preponderance of jurors.

For centuries the standard of proof of guilt beyond reasonable doubt was inextricably entwined with the principle of a unanimous verdict, creating a hedge against jury bias. The requirement of JURY UNANIMITY had meant that a single juror might veto all others, thwarting an overwhelming majority. Accordingly, Johnson contended that DUE PROCESS OF LAW, by embodying the standard of proof beyond a reasonable doubt, required unanimous verdicts and that three jurors who possessed such doubt in his case showed that his guilt was not proved beyond such doubt. White answered that no basis existed for believing that the majority jurors would refuse to listen to the doubts of the minority. Yet Johnson's jurors, who were "out" for less than twenty minutes, might have taken a poll before deliberating, and if nine had voted for a guilty verdict on the first ballot, they might have returned the verdict without the need of considering the minority's doubts. The dissenters saw the jury as an entity incapable of rendering a verdict by the undisputed standard of proof beyond a reasonable doubt if any juror remained unconvinced. The Court majority saw the jury as twelve individuals, nine of whom could decide the verdict if they were satisfied beyond a reasonable doubt, regardless of minority views.

If the prosecution's burden of proving guilt beyond a reasonable doubt does not change when a 9–3 verdict is permissible, verdicts returned by a nine-juror majority ought to be the same as those returned by unanimous juries of twelve. In fact, the 9–3 system yields a substantially higher conviction ratio and substantially fewer hung juries by which defendants avoid conviction, thus substantially lowering the prosecution's burden of proof.

Johnson also contended that Louisiana's complicated three-tier system of juries—unanimous verdicts of twelve in some cases, unanimous verdicts of five in others, and 9–3 verdicts in still others—denied him the EQUAL PROTECTION OF THE LAWS. In fact, the standard of proof varied with the crime, but White rejected the equal protection argument, claiming instead that Louisiana's three-tier scheme was "not invidious" because it was rational: it saved time and money. The Court hardly considered whether it diluted justice.

In *Apodaca,* the 10–2 verdict came under attack from an argument that the FOURTEENTH AMENDMENT extended to the states the same standard as prevailed in federal courts, where unanimity prevails. Four Justices, led by White, would have ruled that the SIXTH AMENDMENT does not require unanimous verdicts even in federal trials; four, led by Justice WILLIAM O. DOUGLAS, believed that because the amendment embodies the requirement of unanimous jury verdicts, no state can permit a majority verdict. LEWIS F. POWELL's opinion was decisive. He concurred with the Douglas wing to save the unanimous verdict in federal criminal trials and with the White wing to allow nonunanimous verdicts for states wanting them. In *Apodaca,* White contradictorily conceded that the reasonable doubt standard "has been rejected in *Johnson v. Louisiana.*" Douglas proved, contrary to White, that the use of the nonunanimous jury altered the way the jury functioned, stacking it against the defendant. He interpreted the majority opinions as reflecting "a 'law and order' judicial mood."

LEONARD W. LEVY

(SEE ALSO: *Jury Size.*)

Bibliography
LEVY, LEONARD W. 1974 *Against the Law: The Nixon Court and Criminal Justice.* Pages 276–298. New York: Harper & Row.

JOHNSON v. ZERBST
304 U.S. 458 (1938)

Defendants who neither sought nor were offered counsel were convicted in a federal court. The Supreme Court held that the SIXTH AMENDMENT requires counsel in all federal criminal proceedings unless the right is waived. This HOLDING is mainly of historical interest, but the case retains remarkable vitality and is often cited because of its definition of WAIVER. Starting with the proposition that there is "every reasonable presumption against 'waiver,'" the Court declared: "A waiver is ordinarily an intelligent relinquishment or abandonment of a known right or privilege."

Johnson's strong suspicion of waiver of the RIGHT TO COUNSEL is reiterated in many decisions. In *Von Moltke v. Gillies* (1948) the Supreme Court established a duty of the trial judge "to investigate [waiver of counsel] as long and as thoroughly as the 'circumstances of the case before him demand." The Court has also said that waiver must affirmatively appear on the record and will not be presumed from a silent record.

Although the Court's definition of waiver applies to all FUNDAMENTAL RIGHTS, and although *Johnson* is cited in FOURTH AMENDMENT and Fifth Amendment cases, the definition has been rigorously applied only in the right to counsel context that spawned it.

BARBARA ALLEN BABCOCK

JOINT ANTI-FASCIST REFUGEE COMMITTEE v. MCGRATH
341 U.S. 123 (1951)

Five members of the VINSON COURT dealt a setback to the HARRY S. TRUMAN administration's anticommunist crusade by condemning the procedures through which the ATTORNEY GENERAL of the United States listed certain organizations as "totalitarian, fascist, communist or subversive" under the President's Executive Order of 1947 creating a LOYALTY-SECURITY PROGRAM for all federal employees. Three organizations designated as "communist" by the attorney general complained that they had been stigmatized without an opportunity for a hearing at which they could rebut the government's presumption. Justice HAROLD H. BURTON concluded that the executive order did not permit the attorney general to make arbitrary, EX PARTE findings without a hearing. In separate concurring opinions, four Justices concluded that the President's order may have authorized such *ex parte* proceedings, but did so in violation of the DUE PROCESS clause. Justice HUGO L. BLACK also condemned the list as a violation of the FIRST AMENDMENT and as a BILL OF ATTAINDER. Justice STANLEY F. REED, for three dissenters, said the attorney general's actions were appropriate "to guard the Nation from espionage, subversion and SEDITION."

MICHAEL E. PARRISH

JOINT COMMITTEE ON RECONSTRUCTION

In December 1865, Congress by CONCURRENT RESOLUTION created the Joint Committee of Fifteen on Reconstruction to provide a deliberative body for consideration of Reconstruction policy, because Republicans refused to accept President ANDREW JOHNSON's "Restoration" as an accomplished fact. All legislation directly affecting Reconstruction was referred to it.

The majority report of the Joint Committee (1866), prepared by Senator WILLIAM P. FESSENDEN (Republican, Maine), rejected punitive theories of Reconstruction as "profitless abstractions" and repudiated the lenient policies of President Johnson and congressional Democrats. The Committee's Republican majority insisted that only Congress had final power to regularize the constitutional status of the seceded states. The Democratic minority report countered that the states were entitled to immediate readmission and self-government. The Joint Committee fashioned the FOURTEENTH AMENDMENT as a compendium of Republican Reconstruction objectives as of the summer of 1866: freedmen's CITIZENSHIP and voting, equality before the law and assurance of DUE PROCESS for freedmen, Confederate disfranchisement, repudiation of the Confederate war debt, denial of compensation for slaves, and confirmation of the Union debt. When the inadequacy of the Fourteenth Amendment as a comprehensive Reconstruction measure became apparent, Republican committee members drafted the first MILITARY RECONSTRUCTION ACT, which created legal machinery for beginning the process of congressional Reconstruction.

WILLIAM M. WIECEK

Bibliography
KENDRICK, BENJAMIN B. 1914 *The Journal of the Joint Committee of Fifteen on Reconstruction.* New York: Columbia University Press.

JOINT RESOLUTIONS

Joint resolutions, unlike CONCURRENT RESOLUTIONS, have the force of law and require the signature of the President to be enacted. They are therefore subject to the VETO POWER. A joint resolution may be used when a permanent statutory enactment is inappropriate. Joint resolutions may be used to issue a DECLARATION OF WAR, to end a STATE OF WAR, to annex territory, or to extend the effective life of previously enacted legislation.

As part of the AMENDING PROCESS, joint resolutions are used to propose constitutional amendments. Such resolutions require a two-thirds vote in each house, but not the President's signature.

DENNIS J. MAHONEY

JONES v. ALFRED H. MAYER CO.
392 U.S. 409 (1968)

This opinion contains important interpretations of a CIVIL RIGHTS statute and of Congress's power to prohibit private discrimination. Jones alleged that the defendants had refused to sell him a home because he was black. He brought an action under section 1982 of Title 42, United States Code, a remnant of the CIVIL RIGHTS ACT OF 1866, which states in part that all citizens shall have the same right as white citizens to purchase property.

Because Jones relied on a federal law to challenge private discrimination, and because the Supreme Court found that section 1982 encompassed Jones's claim, the case raised the question whether the Constitution grants Congress authority to outlaw private discrimination. The degree to which Congress may do so under the FOURTEENTH AMENDMENT has been a recurring unsettled question. (See UNITED STATES V. GUEST, 1966.) In *Jones,* Justice POTTER STEWART's opinion for the Court avoided that complex matter by sustaining section 1982's applicability to private behavior under Congress's THIRTEENTH AMENDMENT power to eliminate slavery. But even this HOLDING generated tension with the Court's nineteenth-century pronouncements on Congress's power to reach private discrimination.

In the CIVIL RIGHTS CASES (1883) the Court seemed to concede that the Thirteenth Amendment vests in Congress power to abolish all badges or incidents of slavery. (See BADGES OF SERVITUDE.) In that case, however, the Court viewed those badges or incidents narrowly and limited Congress's role in defining them. In striking down the CIVIL RIGHTS ACT OF 1875, a provision barring discrimination in PUBLIC ACCOMMODATIONS, the Court commented, "It would be running the slavery argument into the ground" to make it apply to every act of private discrimination in the field of public accommodations. In *Jones,* however, the Court acknowledged Congress's broad discretion not merely to eliminate the badges or incidents of slavery but also to define the practices constituting them.

Jones thus granted Congress virtually unlimited power to outlaw private RACIAL DISCRIMINATION. In later cases, *Jones* provided support for Congress's power to outlaw private racial discrimination in contractual relationships. Section 1981, another remnant of the Civil Rights Act of 1866, confers on all persons the same right "enjoyed by white citizens" to make and enforce contracts, to be parties or witnesses in lawsuits, and to be protected by law in person and property. RUNYON V. MCCRARY (1976) held section 1981 to prohibit the exclusion of blacks from private schools, and *Johnson v. Railway Express Agency, Inc.* (1974) held it to prohibit discrimination in employment.

As Justice JOHN MARSHALL HARLAN's dissent noted, *Jones*'s interpretation of section 1982 established it, more than a hundred years after its enactment, as a fair housing law discovered within months of passage of the CIVIL RIGHTS ACT OF 1968, which itself contained a detailed fair housing provision. (See OPEN HOUSING LAWS.) In finding that section 1982 reaches private discrimination not authorized by state law, *Jones* offers a questionable interpretation of the 1866 act's structure and manipulates legislative history. Whether a candid opinion could support *Jones*'s interpretation of section 1982 remains a subject of debate.

THEODORE EISENBERG

Bibliography
CASPER, GERHARD 1968 *Jones v. Mayer:* Clio, Bemused and Confused Muse. *Supreme Court Review* 1968:89–132.
FAIRMAN, CHARLES 1971 *Reconstruction and Reunion 1864–88: Part One.* Volume 6 of *The Oliver Wendell Holmes Devise History of the Supreme Court of the United States.* New York: Macmillan.

JONES v. SECURITIES & EXCHANGE COMMISSION
298 U.S. 1 (1936)

Although unimportant as a matter of constitutional law, *Jones* has significance in constitutional history. The Court's decision and the tone of Justice GEORGE SUTHERLAND's opinion for the majority helped convince President FRANKLIN D. ROOSEVELT that the Court was prejudiced against the New Deal. A Wall Street manipulator had withdrawn a securities offering on learning that the Securities and Exchange Commission was investigating his fraud. The commission had continued its investigation, raising the question whether it had exceeded its statuory authority. Sutherland called its action arbitrary, inquisitional, odious, and comparable to Star Chamber procedure. Justices BENJAMIN N. CARDOZO, LOUIS D. BRANDEIS, and HARLAN FISKE STONE answered Sutherland's charges and defended the commission. The opinion of the Court hardened Roosevelt's attitude toward it, culminating in his court-packing plan of 1937.

LEONARD W. LEVY

JONES v. VAN ZANDT

See: Fugitive Slavery

JONES v. WOLF

See: Religious Liberty

JOSEPH BURSTYN, INC. v. WILSON

See: Burstyn, Inc. v. Wilson

JUDGE PETERS, UNITED STATES v.
5 Cranch 115 (1809)

This case bears historical significance as an episode in defiance, expressed in NULLIFICATION and bordering on rebellion, by a state against the United States courts. The state was Pennsylvania, which suggests that doctrines of state sovereignty have never been merely sectional. The case was the occasion of Chief Justice JOHN MARSHALL's first nationalist opinion, but more important is the fact that Pennsylvania successfully thwarted the federal courts, exposing their helplessness in enforcing their writs, until a President of the Virginia dynasty unhesitatingly backed the judiciary, still Federalist-dominated, against the political machine of his own party in Pennsylvania.

The case originated during the Revolution as the result of a dispute between the state and Gideon Olmstead over the proceeds from the sale of a captured enemy ship. A state court denied Olmstead's claim, but a prize court established by Congress ruled in his favor; the state court refused to obey the federal order and the state treasurer retained the money. Litigation went on for years. In 1803 Judge RICHARD PETERS of the United States District court in Philadelphia decided in favor of Olmstead in his suit against the treasurer's estate, which held the money for the state. The state legislature, invoking the ELEVENTH AMENDMENT, resolved that Peters had "illegally usurped" JURISDICTION and instructed the governor to protect the rights of the state. In 1808 Olmstead, then in his eighties, obtained from the Supreme Court an order against Peters to show cause why a WRIT OF MANDAMUS should not be issued compelling him to enforce his decision of 1803. The judge stated that the state legislature had commanded the governor "to call out an armed force" to prevent the execution of a federal process. Peters asked for a resolution of the issue by the supreme tribunal of the nation, saying that he had withheld process to avoid a conflict between the state and federal governments.

In 1809, at a time when New England was disobeying the EMBARGO ACTS, Marshall, speaking for the Court, declared:

If the legislatures of the several states may, at will, annul the judgments of the courts of the United States, and destroy the rights acquired under those judgements, the constitution itself becomes a solemn mockery, and the nation is deprived of the means of enforcing its laws by the instrumentality of its own tribunals. So fatal a result must be deprecated by all; and the people of Pennsylvania, not less than the citizens of every other state, must feel a deep interest in resisting principles so destructive of the Union, and in averting consequences so fatal to themselves.

(That passage was quoted by the Court in the 1950s and 1960s in cases involving southern defiance of federal orders commanding DESEGREGATION.) The Court awarded a "peremptory mandamus" against Peters, but neither he nor Marshall could force the state to comply.

The state governor called out the militia, and the state legislature, supporting him, announced that "*as guardians of the State rights,* we cannot permit an infringement of those rights by an unconstitutional exercise of power in the United States Courts." Those actions were not the only reply to Marshall's declaration that the Eleventh Amendment did not apply inasmuch as the suit had not been commenced against the state. Pennsylvania also denied that the Supreme Court had appellate powers over the state courts or that it was the final arbiter in a dispute between the United States and any state. When a federal marshal attempted to execute Peters's judgment, 1400 men of the state militia opposed him; he summoned a federal *posse comitatus* of 2,000 men, but to avoid bloodshed fixed the day for service in three weeks. At this juncture, while the papers in the country were still carrying news about Federalist New England's defiance of the EMBARGO ACTS, the Democratic governor of Pennsylvania turned to the Democratic national administration for support. "The issue is in fact come to this," said *The Aurora,* the administration newspaper in Philadelphia, "whether the Constitution of the United States is to remain in force or to become a dead letter. . . . The decree of the Court must be obeyed." President JAMES MADISON, mindful of the repercussions of the case, chastised the state governor. "The Executive," he replied, "is not only unauthorized to prevent the execution of a decree sanctioned by the Supreme Court of the United States, but is expressly enjoined, by statute, to carry into effect any such decree, where opposition may be made to it."

The incipient rebellion immediately collapsed. The state withdrew its militia and appropriated the money to pay Olmstead. In the aftermath of the affair, the United States arrested and tried the commanding general of the state militia and eight of his officers for having obstructed the federal marshal. A federal jury convicted them in a trial before Justice BUSHROD WASHINGTON, who sentenced the defendants to fines and imprisonment, but the President pardoned them. Eleven state legislatures adopted resolutions condemning Pennsylvania's resistance to the federal courts. Every southern state rejected Pennsylvania's doctrines of STATES' RIGHTS. That northern state had also proposed the establishment of "an impartial tribunal" to settle disputes between "the general and state governments." The legislature of Virginia replied that "a tribunal is already provided by the Constitution of the United States, *to wit:* the Supreme Court, more eminently qualified . . . to decide the disputes aforesaid . . . than any other tribunal which could be erected." In a few years, however, Virginia would be playing Pennsylvania's tune. (See MARTIN V. Hunt-

er's Lessee, 1816.) The supremacy of the Supreme Court had by no means been established yet.

LEONARD W. LEVY

Bibliography

HIGGINBOTHAM, SANFORD W. 1952 *The Keystone in the Democratic Arch: Pennsylvania Politics 1800–1816.* Pages 177–204. Harrisburg: Pennsylvania Historical and Museum Commission.

TREACY, KENNETH W. 1957 The Olmstead Case, 1778–1809. *Western Political Quarterly* 10:675–691.

WARREN, CHARLES 1923 *The Supreme Court in American History,* 3 vols. Vol. I:375–387. Boston: Little, Brown.

JUDGMENT

The judgment of a court is its conclusion or sentence of the law applied to the facts of a case. It is the court's final determination of the rights of the parties to the case. A judgment, once entered (unless successfully appealed), is conclusive as to the rights of the parties and ordinarily may not be challenged either in a future suit by the same parties or in a collateral proceeding. The judgment is essentially equivalent to the DECISION of the court. Judgments in EQUITY and admiralty cases are called "decrees"; judgments in criminal and ecclesiastical cases are called "sentences."

DENNIS J. MAHONEY

(SEE ALSO: *Res Judicata; Habeas Corpus; Final Judgment Rule.*)

JUDICIAL ACTIVISM AND JUDICIAL RESTRAINT

"Judicial activism" and "judicial restraint" are terms used to describe the assertiveness of judicial power. In no sense unique to the Supreme Court or to cases involving some construction of the Constitution, they are editorial summations of how different courts and different judges conduct themselves.

The user of these terms ("judicial activism" and "judicial restraint") presumes to locate the relative assertiveness of particular courts or individual judges between two theoretical extremes. The extreme model of judicial activism is of a court so intrusive and ubiquitous that it virtually dominates the institutions of government. The antithesis of such a model is a court that decides virtually nothing at all: it strains to find reasons why it lacks JURISDICTION; it avows deference to the superiority of other departments or agencies in construing the law; it finds endless reasons why the constitutionality of laws cannot be examined. It is a model of government virtually without useful recourse to courts as enforcers of constitutional limits.

The uses of "judicial activism" and "judicial restraint," however, are not entirely uniform. Often the terms are employed noncommittally, that is, merely as descriptive shorthand to identify some court or judge as more activist or more restrained than some other, or more than the same court formerly appeared to be. In this sense, the usage is neither commendatory nor condemnatory. Especially with reference to the Supreme Court, however, the terms are also used polemically. The user has a personal or professional view of the "right" role of the Court and, accordingly, commends or condemns the Court for conforming to or straying from that right role. Indeed, an enduring issue of American constitutional law has centered on this lively controversy of right role; procedurally and substantively, how activist or how restrained ought the Supreme Court to be in its use of the power of constitutional JUDICIAL REVIEW?

Ought that Court to confront the constitutionality of the laws as speedily as opportunity affords, the better to furnish authoritative guidance and settle political controversy in keeping with its unique competence and function as the chief constitutional court of the nation? Or ought it, rather, to eschew any unnecessary voluntarism, recognizing that all participants in government are as bound as the Court to observe the Constitution and that the very insularity of the Supreme Court from representative government is a powerful reason to avoid the appearance of constitutional arrogance or constitutional monopoly? In brief, what degree of strict necessity should the Supreme Court require as a condition of examining the substantive constitutionality of government acts or government practices?

Substantively, the issues of "proper" activism or proper restraint are similar. When the constitutionality of governmental action is considered, what predisposition, if any, ought the Supreme Court to bring to bear? Should it take a fairly strict view of the Constitution and, accordingly, hold against the constitutionality of each duly contested governmental act unless the consistency of that act with the Constitution can be demonstrated virtually to anyone's satisfaction? Or, to the contrary, recognizing its own fallibility and the shared obligation of Congress (and the President and every member of every state legislature) fully to respect the Constitution as much as judges are bound to respect it, should the Court hold against the constitutionality of what other departments of government have enacted only when virtually no reasonable per-

son could conclude that the act in question is consistent with the Constitution?

Disputes respecting the Supreme Court's procedural judicial activism (or restraint) and substantive judicial activism (or restraint) are thus of recurring political interest. Most emphatically is this the case with regard to judicial review of the constitutionality of legislation, as distinct from nonconstitutional judicial review. For here, unlike activism on nonconstitutional issues (such as the interpretation of statutes), the consequences of an adverse holding on the merits are typically difficult to change. An act of Congress, held inapplicable to a given transaction, need only be approved in modified form to "reverse" the Supreme Court's impression. On the other hand, a holding that the statute did cover the transaction but in presuming to do so was unconstitutional is a much more nearly permanent boundary. It may be overcome only by extraordinary processes of amending the Constitution itself (a recourse successfully taken during two centuries only four times), or by a reconsideration and overruling by the Supreme Court itself (an eventuality that has occurred about 130 times). Thus, the special force of adjudication of constitutionality, being of the greatest consequence and least reversibility, has made the proper constitutional activism (or proper restraint) of the Supreme Court itself a central question.

An appraisal of the Supreme Court in these terms involves two problems: the activism (or restraint) with which the Court rations the judicial process in developing or in avoiding occasions to decide constitutional claims; and the activism (or restraint) of its STANDARDS OF REVIEW when it does decide such claims.

The Supreme Court's own description of its proper role in interpreting the Constitution is one of strict necessity and of last resort. In brief, the Court has repeatedly held that the Constitution itself precludes the Court from considering constitutional issues unless they are incidental to an actual CASE OR CONTROVERSY that meets very stringent demands imposed by Article III. In addition, the Court holds that prudence requires the complete avoidance of constitutional issues in any case in which the rights of the litigants can be resolved without reference to such an issue.

In 1982, in VALLEY FORGE CHRISTIAN SCHOOLS v. AMERICANS UNITED, Justice WILLIAM H. REHNQUIST recapitulated the Court's conventional wisdom. Forswearing any judicial power generally to furnish advice on the Constitution, and denying that the Supreme Court may extend its jurisdiction more freely merely because constitutional issues are at stake, he declared: "The constitutional power of federal courts cannot be defined, and indeed has no substance, without reference to the necessity to 'adjudge the legal rights of litigants in actual controversies.' " Even when the stringent prerequisites of jurisdiction have been fully satisfied, moreover, "[t]he power to declare the rights of individuals and to measure the authority of governments, this Court said 90 years ago, 'is legitimate only in the last resort, and as a necessity in the determination of real, earnest, and vital controversy.' " For emphasis, he added, "The federal courts were simply not constituted as ombudsmen of the general welfare. [Such a philosophy] has no place in our constitutional scheme."

In so declaring, Justice Rehnquist was relying substantially upon a similar position adopted by Chief Justice JOHN MARSHALL in MARBURY V. MADISON (1803). Explaining that the Court's determination of constitutional questions was but an incident of its duty to pass upon legal questions raised in the due course of litigation, in no respect different from its duty when some statutory issue or COMMON LAW question might likewise be presented in a case, Marshall had insisted: "The province of the Court is, solely, to decide on the rights of individuals," and not to presume any larger role.

Accordingly, though a constitutional issue may be present, if the dispute in which it arises does not otherwise meet conventionally strict standards of STANDING, RIPENESS, genuine adverseness of parties, or sufficient factual concreteness to meet the demands of a justiciable case or controversy as required by Article III, the felt urgency or gravity of the constitutional question can make no difference. In steering a wide course around the impropriety of deciding constitutional questions except as incidental to a genuine adversary proceeding, moreover, the Court has also declared that it will not entertain COLLUSIVE SUITS. As Marshall declared in *Marbury*, "it never was the thought that, by means of a friendly suit, a party beaten in the legislature could transfer to the courts an inquiry as to the constitutionality of a legislative act." Similarly, if during the course of genuine litigation the grievance has become moot in light of subsequent events, it must then be dismissed insofar as there remains no necessity to address the original issue.

When, moreover, all requisites of conventional, genuine litigation remain such that adjudication of the parties' rights is an unavoidable judicial duty, the Court has still insisted that it should determine whether the case can be disposed of without addressing any issue requiring it to render an interpretation of the Constitution itself. Accordingly (within the conventional wisdom), even with respect to disputes properly before it, well within its jurisdiction and prominently featuring a major, well-framed, well-contested constitutional question, the Supreme Court may still refuse to address that question. In his famous concurring opinion in ASHWANDER V. TENNESSEE VALLEY AUTHORITY (1936), Justice LOUIS D. BRANDEIS insisted that constitutional questions were to be decided only as a last resort: "When the validity of an act of Congress is drawn in question, and even if a serious doubt of constitutionality is raised, it is a cardinal principle that this Court will first ascertain whether a construction of the statute is fairly possible by which the question may be avoided." Indeed, Brandeis continued, the Court will not "pass upon a constitutional question although properly presented by the record, if there is also present some other ground upon which the case may be disposed of." Moreover, though there may be no other ground, if the constitutional question arises at the instance of a public official, "the challenge by a public official interested only in the performance of his official duty will not be entertained." Even when the issue is raised by a private litigant, his challenge to the constitutionality of a statute will not be heard "at the instance of one who has availed himself of its benefits."

Self-portrayals of the Court as a wholly reluctant constitutional tribunal that is not an oracle of constitutional proclamation but a court of law that will face constitutional questions only when a failure to do so would involve it as a tribunal in an unconstitutional oppression of a litigant go even further. A litigant may have much at stake, and nothing except his reliance upon some clause in the Constitution may remain to save him from jeopardy. Still, if the clause in the Constitution is deemed not to yield objective criteria adequate to guide its application by the Court, the Court may decline to attempt to fix any meaning for the clause on the basis that it is nonjusticiable. (See POLITICAL QUESTIONS.) Similarly, if the relief requested should require the Court to consider an order against the Congress itself, an order the Court cannot be confident would be obeyed and which it is without resources otherwise to enforce, it may refuse to consider the case. Identically, if an adjudication of the constitutional question, though otherwise imperative to the litigant's case, might involve conflict with the President respecting decisions already made, communicated to, and relied upon by other governments, the case may also be regarded as nonjusticiable.

In rough outline, then, these are the principal elements of the orthodoxy of extreme judicial restraint.

Consistent with them, even when the Court does adjudicate a constitutional question, its decision is supposed to be "no broader than is required by the precise facts." Anything remotely resembling an advisory opinion or a gratuitous judicial utterance respecting the meaning of the Constitution is to be altogether avoided.

Although this combination of Article III requirements and policies has characterized a large part of the Court's history (most substantially when the constitutional questions involved acts of Congress or executive action), the Court's practice has not, in fact, been at all uniform. Collusive suits have sometimes been entertained, and the constitutional issues at once examined. Public officials sometimes have been deemed to have sufficient standing to press constitutional questions, though they have had no more than an official interest in the matter. Holdings on the Constitution occasionally have been rendered in far broader terms than essential to decide the case, often for the advisory guidance of other judges or for the benefit of state or local officials. When the constitutional issue seemed clear enough and strongly meritorious, parties placed in positions of advantage solely by force of the very condition of which they later complained on constitutional grounds have not always been estopped from securing a decision. On occasion when third parties would be unlikely or unable to raise a constitutional claim on their own behalf, moreover, other litigants deemed suitable to represent their claim have been allowed to proceed on the merits of the constitutional issues. And some utterly moot cases have been decided on the merits of their constitutional questions on the paradoxical explanation that unless the moot cases were treated as still lively, then conceivably the merits of the constitutional issues would forever elude judicial review. Indeed, the nation's most famous case, *Marbury v. Madison,* was in many respects an example of extreme procedural activism despite its disclaimer of strict necessity.

At issue in Marbury's case was the question of the Supreme Court's power to hear the case in the first instance, within its ORIGINAL JURISDICTION, rather than merely on appeal. The statute William Marbury relied upon to demonstrate his right to commence his action in the Supreme Court was altogether unclear as to whether it authorized his suit to begin in the Supreme Court. Avoidance of the necessity of examining the constitutionality of the statute was readily available merely by construing the statute as not providing for original jurisdiction: an interpretation thus making clear that Marbury had sued in the wrong court, resulting in his case's being dismissed for lack

of (statutory) jurisdiction and obviating any need to say anything at all about the constitutionality of an act of Congress.

Rather than pursue that course, however, Chief Justice Marshall "actively" interpreted the act of Congress, that is, he interpreted it to draw into issue its very constitutionality and then promptly resolved that issue by holding the act unconstitutional. Beyond that, rather than be content to dismiss the case for lack of either statutory or constitutional jurisdiction, the Chief Justice also (and quite gratuitously) addressed every other question raised by the complaint, including Marbury's right to the public office he sought, the appropriateness of the remedy he asked for, the illegality of the secretary of state's refusal to give it to him, and the lack of immunity from such suits by the secretary of state. Each of these other issues was of substantial controversy. Several of them raised substantial constitutional questions. Marshall resolved all in an opinion most of which was purely advisory, that is, of no necessity in light of the ultimate holding, which was that the Court was (constitutionally) without power (jurisdiction) to address the merits of the case at all. Marshall addressed all these questions on the basis of a factual record supplied principally on affidavit of his own brother. Still, Marshall, far from recusing himself on that account or on account of his own participation as the secretary of state who failed to deliver Marbury's commission, fully participated in the case, voted, and wrote the opinion for the Court. In these many respects, the case of *Marbury v. Madison* was an extraordinary example of extreme procedural activism. Its resemblance to what the Court has otherwise said (as in the Brandeis *Ashwander* guidelines or the *Valley Forge* case) is purely ironic. Indeed, the unstable actual practices of the Court which has so often described its institutional role in constitutional adjudication as one of the utmost procedural restraint, while not uniformly adhering to that description, have contributed to the Court's great controversiality in American government.

As we have seen, procedural activism (and restraint) has consisted principally of two parts. The first part is the rigor or lack of rigor with which the Court has interpreted the limitation in Article III of the Constitution, according to which the use of the judicial power can operate solely on "cases and controversies." The second part is the extent to which the Court has also adopted a number of purely self-denying ordinances according to which it will decline to adjudicate the merits of a constitutional claim in any case in which a decision can be reached on some other ground.

In contrast, substantive activism (and restraint) has consisted principally of three parts, each reflecting the extent to which the Court has interpreted the Constitution either aggressively to invalidate actions taken by other departments of government, or diffidently to acquiesce in these actions. The first part pertains to the Court's substantive interpretations of the ENUMERATED and IMPLIED POWERS of the other departments of the national government, that is, the powers vested by Article I in Congress and the powers vested by Article II in the President. The second part pertains to the Court's interpretation of the Constitution as implicitly withdrawing from state governments a variety of powers not explicitly forbidden to them by the Constitution. And the third part pertains to the Court's interpretations of those clauses in the Constitution that impose positive restrictions on the national and the state governments, principally the provisions in Article I, sections 9 and 10, in the BILL OF RIGHTS, and in the FOURTEENTH AMENDMENT. Although there may be no a priori reason to separate the substantive activism and restraint of the Supreme Court into these three particular categories, it is nonetheless practically useful to do so: overall, the Court has responded to them quite distinctly. Indeed, in practice, despite very great differences among particular Justices, the general tendency has been to develop a constitutional jurisprudence of selective activism and selective restraint.

In respect to constitutional challenges to acts of Congress for consistency with Article I's enumeration of affirmative powers, the Court's standard of review has generally been one of extraordinary restraint. With the exception of the first three and a half decades of the twentieth century, the Court has largely deferred to Congress's own suppositions respecting the scope of its powers. During the first seventy-five years of the Constitution, for instance, only two acts of Congress were held not to square with the Constitution. During the most recent forty years (a period of intense and extremely far-reaching national legislation), again but two acts have been held to fail for want of enumerated or implied constitutional authorization. Indeed, even when the comparison is enlarged to include cases challenging acts of Congress not merely for want of enacting authority but rather because they were alleged to transgress specific prohibitions (for example, the FIRST AMENDMENT restriction that Congress shall make no law abridging the FREEDOM OF SPEECH), still the record overall is one of general diffidence and restraint. Over the entirety of the Court's history, scarcely more than 120 acts of Congress have been held invalid.

An influential rationale for such restraint toward acts of Congress was set forth in 1893, in an essay by JAMES BRADLEY THAYER that Justice FELIX FRANKFURTER subsequently identified as uniquely influential on his own thinking as a judicial conservative. Thayer admonished the judiciary to bear in mind that the executive and legislative departments of the national government were constitutionally equal to the judiciary, that they were equivalently bound by oath of office to respect the Constitution, and that each was a good deal more representative of the people than the life-tenured members of the Supreme Court. Accordingly, Thayer urged, the Court should test the acts of coordinate national departments solely according to a rule of "clear error." In brief, such acts were to be examined not to determine whether their constitutionality necessarily conformed to the particular interpretation which the judges themselves might independently have concluded was the most clearly correct interpretation of the Constitution. Rather, such acts should be sustained unless they depended on an interpretation of constitutional power that was itself manifestly unreasonable, that is, an interpretation *clearly* erroneous.

Thayer's rule provided a strong political rationale for extreme judicial deference in respect to enumerated and implied national powers. Of necessity, however, it also tended practically to the enlistment of the judiciary less as an independent guardian of the Constitution (at least in respect to the scope of enumerated and implied powers) than as an institution tending to validate claims of national authority against state perspectives on the proper boundaries of FEDERALISM. It is a thesis that has periodically attracted criticism on that account, but it does not stand as the sole explanation for the general restraint reflected in the Supreme Court's permissive construction of national legislative and executive powers. Rather, without necessarily assuming that Congress and the President possess a suitably reliable detachment to be the presumptive best judges of their respective powers, decades before the appearance of Thayer's essay the Supreme Court had already expressed a separate rationale: a judicial rule of BROAD CONSTRUCTION respecting enumerated national powers.

The most durable expression of that rule is reported in a famous OBITER DICTUM by Chief Justice John Marshall. In MCCULLOCH V. MARYLAND (1819), Marshall emphasized to his own colleagues, the federal judges: "We must never forget, that it is a *constitution* we are expounding." In full context, Marshall plainly meant that it was a Constitution for the future as well as for the present, for a nation then quite small and new but expected to become much more considerable. To meet these uncertain responsibilities, Congress would require flexibility and legislative latitude. Thus, powers granted to it by the Constitution should be read generously.

The point was expanded upon more than a century later by Justice OLIVER WENDELL HOLMES, in MISSOURI V. HOLLAND (1920), defending the judiciary's predisposition to interpret the TREATY POWER very deferentially: "When we are dealing with words that also are a constituent act, like the Constitution of the United States, we must realize that they have called into life a being the development of which could not have been foreseen completely by the most gifted of its begetters. . . . [I]t has taken a century and has cost their successors much sweat and blood to prove that they created a nation." This rule of generous construction, like Thayer's rule of "clear error," tends to support a judicial policy of substantive interpretative restraint. And while not free of criticism on its own account (as federalism critics will tend to fault it as unfaithful to their view of the extent to which substantive legislative authority was meant to be reserved to the states), it is not contingent upon doubtful assumptions respecting the capacity of the President or of the Congress fairly to assess the scope of powers they are given by the Constitution. Arguably, it is as well that this policy of judicial restraint not be made to rest on such assumptions. Although reference to the early constitutional history of the United States tends to support Thayer's thesis (early members of Congress included many persons who had participated in the shaping of the Constitution and who frequently debated proposed legislation in terms of its consistency with that Constitution), two centuries of political change have weakened its suppositions considerably. Persons serving in Congress are far removed from the original debates over enumerated powers; the business of Congress is vastly greater than it once was; the electorate is itself vastly enlarged beyond the limited numbers of persons originally eligible to vote; and such attention as may be given within Congress to issues of constitutionality is understandably likely to be principally political in its preoccupations rather than cautious and detached. Thus, the Marshall rule of generous construction in respect to national powers, rather than the Thayer proposal (of yielding to not-unreasonable interpretations by Congress), tends more strongly to anchor the general policy of judicial restraint in this area. (When the issue had been one of conflict between Congress and the President, on the other hand, the Court has tended to defer to the position of Congress as first among equals.)

In contrast, there is less evidence of a consistent policy of substantive judicial restraint in the Supreme Court's examination of state laws and state acts. Here, to the contrary, the role of the Court has emphatically been significantly more activist, procedurally as well as substantively. The Court will more readily regard the review of governmental action as within the JUDICIAL POWER OF THE UNITED STATES in the litigation of state laws. A principal example is the ease with which state TAXPAYER SUITS impugning state laws on federal constitutional grounds will be deemed reviewable in the Supreme Court, when in most instances an equivalently situated federal taxpayer is deemed to have inadequate standing in respect to an act of Congress. In addition, the Court has interpreted the Constitution to create a judicial duty to determine the constitutionality of certain kinds of state laws, though the clauses relied upon do not themselves expressly confer such a judicial duty (or power) and speak, rather, solely of some preemptive power in Congress to determine the same matter. For instance, the COMMERCE CLAUSE provides merely that Congress shall have power to regulate commerce among the several states. But in the absence of congressional regulation, the Court has actively construed the clause as directing the federal courts themselves to determine, by their own criteria, whether state statutes so unreasonably or discriminatorily burden INTERSTATE COMMERCE that they should be deemed invalid by the courts as an unconstitutional trespass upon a field of regulation reserved to Congress.

Here also the rationales have differed, and indeed not every Supreme Court Justice has embraced either rationale. (Justice HUGO L. BLACK, for instance, preferring a constitutional jurisprudence of "literal" interpretation, generally declined to find any basis in the commerce clause for judicial intervention against state statutes.) In part, the substantive activism of the Court has been explained by a "political marketplace" calculus that is the obverse of Thayer's rule for deference to Congress. According to this view, as the state legislatures are not equal departments to the Supreme Court (in the sense that Congress is an equal department), and as national interests are not necessarily as well represented in state assemblies as state interests are said to be represented in Congress (insofar as members of Congress are all chosen from state-based constituencies), there are fewer built-in political safeguards in state legislatures than in Congress. To the extent of these differences, it is said that there is correspondingly less reason for courts to assume that state legislatures will have acted with appropriate sensitivity to federal constitutional questions and, accordingly, that there is more need for closer judicial attention to their acts. The sheer nonuniformity of state legislation may be of such felt distress to overriding needs for greater uniformity in a nation with an increasingly integrated economy that a larger measure of judicial activism in adjudicating the constitutional consistency of state legislation may be warranted in light of that fact. Something of this thought may lie behind Justice Holmes's view respecting the relative importance of constitutional review itself: "I do not think the United States would come to an end if we lost our power to declare an Act of Congress void. I do think the Union would be imperiled if we could not make that declaration as to the laws of the several states." Finally, more activist substantive review of state laws has been defended on the view that, assuming Congress itself may presume to substitute a uniform rule or otherwise forbid states to legislate in respect to certain matters, the frequency with which state statutes may be adopted and the resulting interference they may impose upon matters of national importance prior to any possibility of corrective congressional action require that the federal courts exercise an interim and activist responsibility of their own. In any event, this much is clear. In respect to substantive standards of constitutional review and challenges to state laws on grounds that they usurp national authority, the overall position of the Supreme Court has been that of an activist judiciary in umpiring the boundaries of federalism.

Finally, and most prominently within the last half-century, selective judicial activism has made its strongest appearance in the judicial review of either federal or state laws that, in the Court's view, bear adversely on one or more of the following three subjects: participation in the political process, specific personal rights enumerated in the Bill of Rights, and laws adversely affecting "DISCRETE AND INSULAR MINORITIES." The scope of these respective activist exceptions (to the general rule of procedural and substantive restraint) is still not entirely settled. Indeed, each is itself somewhat unstable. Nonetheless, the indication of more aggressive, judicially assertive constitutional intervention in all three areas was strongly suggested in a footnote to UNITED STATES V. CAROLENE PRODUCTS CO. (1938). There, the Court suggested that the conventional "presumption of constitutionality" would not obtain, and that "searching judicial inquiry" would be applied to the review of laws that, on their face, appeared "to be within a

specific prohibition of the Constitution," or to "restrict those political processes which can ordinarily be expected to bring about the repeal of undesirable legislation," or to bear heavily on "discrete and insular minorities" suffering from prejudice likely to lead to their neglect in the legislative process.

In respect to the first of these categories, however, it is doubtful whether the standards applied by the Supreme Court should be defined as unconventionally activist at all. To the extent that a constitutional provision explicitly forbids a given kind of statute, its mere application by the Court scarcely seems exceptional. To the contrary, it would require an extreme version of "restraint" to do otherwise.

The second category (principally concerned with limitations on voting eligibility or with varieties of unfairness in REPRESENTATION) is differently reasoned. The Court has assumed generally that deference is ordinarily due the constitutional interpretations of legislative bodies because they are themselves representatives of the people (who have the greatest stake in the Constitution). But if the law in question itself abridges the representative character of the legislatures, it tends by that fact to undermine the entire foundation of judicial restraint in respect to all other legislative acts. As it tends thereby also to reduce the efficacy of the legislative process to repeal improvident legislation, such representation-reducing statutes ought to be severely questioned.

The third category (such legislation as bears adversely on insular and discrete minorities) has emerged as by far the most controversial and unstable example of modern judicial activism. Its theory of justification is one of rationing the activism of constitutional review inversely, again in keeping with the perceived "market failure" of representative government. And, up to a point, it is quite straightforward in keeping with that theory. Thus, when the numbers of a particular class are few and their financial resources insignificant, and when the class upon whom a law falls with great force is not well-connected but, to the contrary, seems left out of account in legislative processes (by prejudices entrenched within legislatures), the resulting market place failure of political power or ordinary empathy is felt to leave a gap to be filled by exceptional judicial solicitude.

The paradigm case for such activism is that of legislation adversely affecting blacks, when challenged on grounds of inconsistency with the EQUAL PROTECTION clause of the Fourteenth Amendment. On its face, the equal protection clause provides no special standards of justification that race-related legislation must satisfy that other kinds of adverse legislative classifications need not meet. Nonetheless, on quite sound historical grounds, race-related legislation was singled out for exceptional judicial activism by the WARREN COURT. Although many of the Warren Court decisions remain of enduring controversy, it is generally conceded that the Court's STRICT SCRUTINY of such race-based laws was itself consistent with the special preoccupation of the Fourteenth Amendment with that subject. Thus, as early as 1873, in the SLAUGHTER-HOUSE CASES, the Court had observed: In the light of the history of [the THIRTEENTH, Fourteenth, and FIFTEENTH] AMENDMENTS, and the pervading purpose of them, [it] is not difficult to give a meaning to [the equal protection clause]. The existence of laws in the states where the newly emancipated negroes resided, which discriminated with gross injustice and hardship against them as a class, was the evil to be remedied by this clause, and by it such laws are forbidden."

As this historical Civil War basis for that one exception was left behind, the Supreme Court plied an increasingly complicated sociology of political marketplace failure to explain an equivalent interventionism on a much broader front. Thus, gender-based laws, laws restricting ALIENS vis-à-vis citizens, and laws restricting minors vis-à-vis adults came also to be examined much more stringently under the equal protection clause than laws adversely affecting particular businesses, particular classes of property owners, certain groups of taxpayers, or others. The determination of "adequate representation" (whether direct or vicarious), the conjecture as to whether such legislative classifications were based on "stereotypes" rather than real differences, and ultimately the tentative extension of equal protection activism even to require a variety of state support for poor persons, produced unstable and largely unsustainable pluralities within the Supreme Court.

Indeed, the difficulties of selective activism in this area have been the principal object of contemporary criticism in American constitutional law. The most serious questions have been addressed to the apparent tendency of the Court to adjust its own interpretations of the Constitution not according simply to its own best understanding of that document, but rather according to its perceptions respecting the adequacy of representative government. Given the fact that far more cases compete for the opportunity to be determined by the Supreme Court than its own resources can permit it to hear, the Court might be expected to pursue a course of selective procedural activism according to which it would more readily entertain cases and more readily reach the merits of constitu-

tional claims it should consider not to have been adequately considered elsewhere because of built-in weaknesses of representative government. On the other hand, it remains much more problematic why the Court should utilize its impressions respecting the adequacies of representative government twice over: once to determine which cases to review, and again to determine whether the Constitution has in fact been violated.

Descriptions of judicial activism and judicial restraint in constitutional adjudication are, of course, but partial truths. In two centuries of judicial review, superintended by more than one hundred Justices who have served on the Supreme Court and who have interpreted a Constitution highly ambiguous in much of its text, consistency has not been institutional but personal. Individual judges have maintained strongly diverse notions of the "proper" judicial role, and the political process of APPOINTMENT OF SUPREME COURT JUSTICES has itself had a great deal to do with the dominant perspectives of that role from time to time. Here, only the most prominent features of judicial activism and judicial restraint have been canvassed.

It is roughly accurate to summarize that in respect to interpreting the Constitution, procedurally the Supreme Court has usually exercised great restraint. Subject to some notable exceptions, it has eschewed addressing the constitutional consistency of acts of government to a dramatically greater degree of self-denial than it has exercised in confronting other kinds of legal issues seeking judicial resolution. Substantively, the Court has been predisposed to the national government in respect to the powers of that government: except for the early twentieth century, Thayer's law, requiring a showing of "clear error," has been the dominant motif. In respect to the states, on the other hand, the Court has been actively more interventionist, construing the Constitution to enforce its own notions of national interest in the absence of decisions by Congress. And, most controversially in recent decades, it has been unstably activist in deciding whether it will interpret the Constitution more as an egalitarian set of imperatives than as a document principally concerned with commerce, federalism, the SEPARATION OF POWERS, and the protection of explicitly protected liberties.

WILLIAM W. VAN ALSTYNE

Bibliography

BICKEL, ALEXANDER M. 1962 *The Least Dangerous Branch: The Supreme Court at the Bar of Politics.* Indianapolis: Bobbs-Merrill.

ELY, JOHN H. 1980 *Democracy and Distrust: A Theory of Judicial Review.* Cambridge, Mass.: Harvard University Press.
JACKSON, ROBERT H. 1941 *The Struggle for Judicial Supremacy.* New York: Knopf.
THAYER, JAMES B. 1893 "The Origin and Scope of the American Doctrine of Constitutional Law." *Harvard Law Review* 7:129.
WECHSLER, HERBERT 1959 "Toward Neutral Principles of Constitutional Law." *Harvard Law Review* 73:1.

JUDICIAL CODE

The Judicial Code of the United States is an official collection and codification of laws governing the federal judiciary and federal court procedures. Codified as Title 28 of the UNITED STATES CODE, the Judicial Code is an exercise of the Article I power of Congress to make such laws as it deems NECESSARY AND PROPER for carrying into execution the broad and ill-defined powers vested in the judiciary by Article III of the Constitution.

The present code, enacted in 1948, is the lineal descendant of the original JUDICIARY ACT OF 1789, the judiciary portions of the REVISED STATUTES of 1877, and the Judicial Code of 1911. It is an effort by judicial, legislative, and legal experts to rearrange, update, and improve the many laws dealing with the federal judicial system. Additions and improvements are periodically made by Congress, and integrated into the structural scheme of the code. The code itself is divided into six main parts, with numerous subdivisions, each relating to a particular subject matter. Among the more important subjects covered by the code are: the organization, personnel, and administration of the federal courts, including the SUPREME COURT; the JURISDICTION conferred by Congress on these various courts, including the Supreme Court; provisions for determining the proper VENUE for instituting a case in a UNITED STATES DISTRICT COURT, and provisions governing the REMOVAL to a federal court of a case instituted in a state court; and the procedures to be followed in various kinds of federal court proceedings.

The 1948 revision and recodification have been both highly praised and highly criticized. Criticism has often been focused on the provisions dealing with the jurisdiction of the federal district courts, for it is the exercise of that jurisdiction that most directly affects the delicate and controversial federal–state court relationships. Concern for these relationships led the American Law Institute to undertake a major study

of the Judicial Code, culminating in a 1968 proposal to revise substantial portions of the code. Specifically, the institute suggested major modifications and limitations respecting district courts' DIVERSITY-OF-CITIZENSHIP JURISDICTION, as well as clarifications of FEDERAL QUESTION JURISDICTION and ADMIRALTY AND MARITIME JURISDICTION, and changes as to venue and removal of actions from state courts. Some of the institute's proposals bore legislative fruit and influenced judicial thinking. But the major proposals have lain fallow, and in some respects they have been outmoded by the passage of time and the birth of new tensions in the JUDICIAL SYSTEM.

Controversy about some of the Judicial Code's provisions is endless, especially those that concern the scope and exercise of the diversity jurisdiction of the federal courts. Such controversy reflects the historic and perhaps unresolvable concern that, as Chief Justice EARL WARREN once said, "we achieve a proper jurisdictional balance between the Federal and State court systems, assigning to each system those cases most appropriate in the light of the basic principles of FEDERALISM."

EUGENE GRESSMAN

Bibliography
CURRIE, DAVID P. 1968–1969 The Federal Courts and the American Law Institute. *University of Chicago Law Review* 36:1–49, 268–337.
WECHSLER, HERBERT 1948 Federal Jurisdiction and the Revision of the Judicial Code. *Law and Contemporary Problems* 13:216–243.

JUDICIAL IMMUNITY

In *Randall v. Brigham* (1869) the Supreme Court endorsed the principle of judicial immunity. Under doctrine "as old as the law," Justice STEPHEN J. FIELD wrote for the Court, judges of courts of general jurisdiction are immune from suit for judicial acts "unless perhaps where the acts, in excess of JURISDICTION, are done maliciously or corruptly." In *Bradley v. Fisher* (1872) Justice Field, again writing for the Court, extended *Randall*'s standard for protecting judges to preclude liability for all judicial acts except "acts where no jurisdiction whatever" existed and illustrated the difference between acts "in excess of jurisdiction" and acts clearly without jurisdiction. A probate judge acts clearly without jurisdiction when he tries a criminal case. A judge who improperly holds an act to be a crime or sentences a defendant to more than the statutory maximum merely acts in excess of jurisdiction. *Bradley* also disavowed the suggestion in *Randall* that a malicious or corrupt motive might affect a judge's immunity.

The Civil War Amendments, ratified at about the time *Randall* and *Bradley* were decided, led many years later to a vast growth in individual constitutional protections. This development caused both a reexamination and an eventual reaffirmation of judicial immunity. Because actions against state officials for constitutional violations are brought under SECTION 1983, TITLE 42, UNITED STATES CODE, the scope of judicial immunity from suit for constitutional violations has been defined mainly in answer to the question whether judges may be sued under section 1983.

The unequivocal language of section 1983 led some lower courts to find judges subject to suit. In TENNEY V. BRANDHOVE (1951), however, the Supreme Court held that Congress did not intend section 1983 to overturn the traditional immunity of legislators from suit. Although judicial immunity was less firmly established at COMMON LAW than was legislative immunity, *Tenney* led courts to conclude that judges, like legislators, are immune from suit under section 1983. In PIERSON V. RAY (1967), with limited discussion of the issue, the Supreme Court adopted this view in holding a judge immune from suit for convicting defendants under a statute later found to be unconstitutional.

In STUMP V. SPARKMAN (1978) the Court reaffirmed the immunity in a case that presented extreme facts. Without a hearing and without NOTICE to the victim, the defendant judge had granted a mother's petition to have her daughter sterilized. Because granting the petition was found to be a judicial act and because no state law or decision expressly denied the judge authority to grant the petition, the judge was immune.

There are, however, some limits to judicial immunity. In *Pulliam v. Allen* (1984) the Supreme Court held that state judges are not immune from section 1983 actions seeking injunctive relief or from awards of attorney's fees. In both O'SHEA V. LITTLETON (1974) and IMBLER V. PACHTMAN (1976) the Court suggested that judges are not immune from criminal prosecutions for violating constitutional rights.

A SEPARATION OF POWERS question lurks in the background of the judicial immunity DOCTRINE. Courts might well invalidate a federal statute that imposed liability on federal judges in what the courts believed to be inappropriate circumstances. Because the Court has been relatively generous in protecting its judicial colleagues from liability, and because most activity concerning judicial immunity involves actions

against state judges under section 1983, the potential separation of powers issue goes largely unnoticed.

THEODORE EISENBERG

Bibliography

NOTE 1969 Liability of Judicial Officers under Section 1983. *Yale Law Journal* 79:322–337.

JUDICIAL LEGISLATION

The term "judicial legislation" appears to be something of an oxymoron, as the Constitution clearly assigns the principal task of LEGISLATION to the Congress. The Constitution does, of course, give the President a role in the legislative process through the VETO POWER and through his power to recommend legislation to Congress that "he shall judge necessary and expedient." The Framers explicitly rejected, however, a similar role for the judiciary. Several attempts to create a council of revision, composed of the executive and members of the Supreme Court, to review the constitutionality of proposed legislation, were defeated in the CONSTITUTIONAL CONVENTION. The most effective arguments against including the Court in a council of revision were derived from considerations of the SEPARATION OF POWERS. ELBRIDGE GERRY, for example, remarked that including members of the Supreme Court in a revisory council "was quite foreign from the nature of the office," because it would not only "make them judges of the policy of public measures" but would also involve them in judging measures they had a direct hand in creating. Assigning ultimate legislative responsibility to the Congress apparently reflected the Framers' belief that, in popular forms of government, primary lawmaking responsibility should be lodged with the most representative branches of the government. In JAMES MADISON's words, "the people are the only legitimate fountain of power."

Justice FELIX FRANKFURTER expressed the same view in his concurring opinion in *American Federation of Labor v. American Sash and Door Co.* (1949). "Even where the social undesirability of a law may be convincingly urged," he said, "invalidation of the law by a court debilitates popular democratic government. . . . Such an assertion of JUDICIAL POWER deflects responsibility from those on whom in a democratic society it ultimately rests—the people." Frankfurter continued his brief for judicial restraint by arguing that because the powers exercised by the Supreme Court are "inherently oligarchic" they should "be exercised with rigorous self-restraint." The

Court, Frankfurter laconically concluded, "is not saved from being oligarchic because it professes to act in the service of humane ends."

The modern Supreme Court is not so easily deterred as Frankfurter was by charges of oligarchy. Since the landmark BROWN V. BOARD OF EDUCATION decision in 1954, the Court has actively and overtly engaged in the kind of lawmaking and policymaking that in previous years was regarded as exclusively the province of the more political branches of government. William Swindler explained the Court's transition from judicial deference to judicial activisim in these terms: "If the freedom of government to act was the basic principle evolving from the Hughes-Stone decade, from 1937–1946, the next logical question—to be disposed of by the WARREN COURT—was the obligation created by the Constitution itself, to compel action in the face of inaction. This led in turn to the epochal decisions in *Brown v. Board of Education*, BAKER V. CARR, and GIDEON V. WAINWRIGHT."

Some scholars have argued that it was the identification of EQUAL PROTECTION rights as class rights and the attendant necessity of fashioning classwide remedies for class injuries that gave the real impetus to the Court's JUDICIAL ACTIVISM in the years immediately following *Brown*. The Court, in other words, effectively legislated under its new-molded EQUITY powers. (See INSTITUTIONAL LITIGATION.)

The Court's legislative role is usually justified in terms of its power of JUDICIAL REVIEW. But judicial review—even if it be regarded as a necessary inference from the fact of a written constitution—is not a part of the powers explicitly assigned to the Court by the Constitution. The Court made its boldest claim for the legitimacy of judicial legislation in COOPER V. AARON (1958). Justice WILLIAM J. BRENNAN, writing an opinion signed by all the members of the Court, outlined the basic constitutional argument for JUDICIAL SUPREMACY. Brennan recited "some basic constitutional propositions which are settled doctrine," and which were derived from Chief Justice JOHN MARSHALL's argument in MARBURY V. MADISON (1803). First is the proposition, contained in Article VI of the Constitution, that the Constitution is the supreme law of the land (see SUPREMACY CLAUSE); second is Marshall's statement that the Constitution is "the fundamental and paramount law of the nation"; third is Marshall's declaration that "[i]t is emphatically the province and duty of the judicial department to say what the law is." Justice Brennan concluded that *Marbury* therefore "declared the basic principle that the federal judiciary is supreme in the exposition of the law of the Constitution, and that principle has ever since been respected by this Court and the Country as a permanent and indispensable feature of our constitutional system. It follows that the interpretation of the FOURTEENTH AMENDMENT enunciated by this Court in the Brown Case is the supreme law of the land. . . ." The defect of Brennan's argument, of course, is that it confounds the Constitution with constitutional law.

Marshall did indeed say that the Constitution was "the fundamental and paramount law of the nation," and that any "ordinary legislative acts" "repugnant to the constitution" were necessarily void. But when Marshall wrote the famous line relied upon by Brennan that "it is emphatically the province and duty of the judicial department to say what the law is," he was referring not to the Constitution but to "ordinary legislative acts." In order to determine the law's conformity with the Constitution it is first necessary to know what the law is. And once the law is ascertained it is also necessary to determine whether the law is in conformity with the "paramount law" of the Constitution. This latter, of course, means that "in some cases" the Constitution itself "must be looked into by the judges" in order to determine the particular disposition of a case. But Marshall was clear that the ability of the Court to interpret the Constitution was incident to the necessity of deciding a law's conformity to the Constitution, and not a general warrant for CONSTITUTIONAL INTERPRETATION or judicial legislation. Marshall was emphatic in his pronouncement that "the province of the court is, solely, to decide on the rights of individuals."

"It is apparent," Marshall concluded, "that the framers of the constitution contemplated that instrument as a rule for the government of courts, as well as of the legislature." As he laconically noted in the peroration of his argument, "it is also not entirely unworthy of observation, that in declaring what shall be the supreme law of the land, the constitution itself is first mentioned; and not the laws of the United States generally, but those only which shall be made in pursuance of the constitution, have that rank." For Marshall, Brennan's assertion that the Court's decision in *Brown* was "the supreme law of the land" would indeed make "written constitutions absurd" because it would usurp the "original right" of the people to establish their government on "such principles" that must be "deemed fundamental" and "permanent." If the Supreme Court were indeed to sit as a "continuing constitutional convention," any written Constitution would certainly be superfluous since, under the circumstances there would be no "rule for the government of courts." After all, by parity of reasoning, if one were to accept Brennan's argument, it would also be necessary to hold that the Court's decision in DRED SCOTT V. SANDFORD (1857) was the supreme law of the land. But *Dred Scott* gave way because forces other than the Supreme Court decided that it was a decision not "pursuant" to the "fundamental and paramount law" of the nation. As John Agresto has cogently remarked; "If Congress can mistake the meaning of the text [of the Constitution], which is what the doctrine of judicial review asserts, so, of course, can the Court. And if it be said that it is more dangerous to have interpretive supremacy in the same body that directs the nation's public policy—that is, Congress—then (especially in this age of pervasive judicial direction of political and social life) an independent judicial interpretive power is equally fearsome for exactly the same reasons."

In SWANN V. CHARLOTTE-MECKLENBURG BOARD OF EDUCATION (1971) the Court was confronted with the question of the federal judiciary's equity powers under the equal protection clause of the Fourteenth Amendment. At issue was whether the Court could uphold SCHOOL BUSING as a "remedy for state-imposed segregation in violation of Brown I." As part of the CIVIL RIGHTS ACT OF 1964 the Congress had included in Title IV a provision that "nothing herein shall empower any official or court . . . to issue any order seeking to achieve a racial balance in any school by requiring the transportation of pupils or students from one school to another . . . or otherwise enlarge the existing power of the court to insure compliance with constitutional standards." Chief Justice WARREN E. BURGER, writing for a unanimous Court, remarked that on its face this section of Title IV is only "designed to foreclose any interpretation of the Act as expanding the *existing* powers of federal courts to enforce the Equal Protection Clause. There is no suggestion of an intention to restrict those powers or withdraw from courts their historic equitable remedial powers." According to Burger these equity powers flow directly from the Fourteenth Amendment—despite the fact that section 5 of the Amendment gives Congress explicit enforcement authority, an authority that was mistakenly restricted by the Court in the SLAUGHTERHOUSE CASES (1873) and the CIVIL RIGHTS CASES (1883).

A serious question arises, however, concerning Burger's claim that forced busing is one of the "historic" equity powers of the Court. It was never asserted as such by the Court prior to 1964, and as late as two years *after* the *Swann* decision it was still being

described by Justice LEWIS F. POWELL as "a novel application of equitable power—not to mention a dubious extension of constitutional doctrine." Congress's response to *Swann*, the Equal Educational Opportunity and Transportation of Students Act of 1972, contained restrictions similar to those included in Title IV. These provisions suffered the same fate as the Title IV provisions, only now the Court was able to use *Swann* as authority for its ruling.

The *Swann* rationale derives equity powers directly from the Constitution. But the way in which the Court exercises its equity powers is indistinguishable from legislation. Thus, in effect, the Court now derives what is tantamount to legislative power from the Constitution. Because this power rests upon an interpretation of the Constitution, no act of Congress can overturn or modify the interpretation. Many scholars argue that if the Congress were to attempt to curtail the Court's power to order forced busing under the exceptions clause, the Court would be obligated, under the *Swann* reasoning, to declare such an attempt unconstitutional, because the Court's obligation to require busing as a remedy for equal protection violations is derived directly from the Constitution.

Judicial legislation incident to statutory interpretation is less controversial, for the Congress can overturn any constructions of the Court by repassing the legislation in a way that clarifies congressional intent. The interpretation of statutes necessarily involves the judiciary in legislation. In many instances the courts must engage in judicial legislation in order to say what the law is. In years past the Court's sense of judicial deference confined such judicial legislation to what Justice OLIVER WENDELL HOLMES called the "interstices" of the law. It was generally believed that the plain language of the statute should be the controlling factor in statutory construction and that extrinsic aids to construction such as legislative history should be used only where they were necessary to avoid a contradictory or absurd result.

The courts are not always the aggressive agents in the process of judicial legislation. In recent years courts have acted to fill the void created by Congress's abdication of legislative responsibility. Many statutes passed by Congress are deliberately vague and imprecise; indeed, the Congress in numerous instances charges administrative agencies and courts to supply the necessary details. This delegation of authority to administrative agencies with provisions for judicial oversight of the administrative process has contributed to the judiciary's increased participation in judicial legislation. This tendency was intensified by the

Court's decision in IMMIGRATION AND NATURALIZATION SERVICE V. CHADHA (1983), holding the LEGISLATIVE VETO unconstitutional. Congress had for years used the single-house legislative veto as a device for overseeing the activities of administrative agencies. But, as Judge Carl McGowan has noted, "the question inevitably recurs as to whether judicial review is an adequate protection against the abdication by Congress of substantive policy making in favor of broad delegation of what may essentially be the power to make laws and not merely to administer them."

The volume of litigation calling for "legislation" on the part of the courts also increases in proportion with the liberalization of the rules of STANDING. In previous years the Court's stricter requirements for standing were merely a recognition that the province of the judiciary, in the words of John Marshall quoted earlier, "was solely to decide on the rights of individuals, not to inquire how the executive, or executive officers, perform duties in which they have a discretion." Liberalized rules of standing tend to produce what Court of Appeals Judge Atonin Scalia has called "an overjudicialization of the process of self-governance." Judge Scalia reminds us of the question posed by Justice Frankfurter—whether it is wise for a self-governing people to give itself over to the rule of an oligarchic judiciary. James Bradley Thayer wrote more than eighty-five years ago that "the exercise of [judicial review], even when unavoidable, is always attended with a serious evil, namely, that the correction of legislative mistakes comes from the outside, and the people thus lose the political experience, and the moral education and stimulus that comes from fighting the question out in the ordinary way, and correcting their own errors. The tendency of a common and easy resort to this great function, now lamentably too common, is to dwarf the political capacity of the people, and to deaden its sense of moral responsibility."

If, on the other hand, the processes of democracy are unsuited for protecting democratic ends—if, that is, in the words of Jesse Choper, it is necessary for the Supreme Court generally to act "contrary to the popular will" to promote "the precepts of democracy"—then the question whether the American people can be a self-governing people is indeed a serious one. It was once thought that constitutional majorities could rule safely in the interest of the whole of society—that constitutional government could avoid the formation of majority faction. Today many scholars—and often the Supreme Court itself—simply assume that the majority will always be a factious majority seeking to promote its own interest at the expense

of the interest of the minority. This requires that the judiciary intervene not only in the processes of democracy but also as the virtual representatives of the interest of those who are said to be permanently isolated from the majoritarian political process. If American politics is indeed incapable of forming nonfactious majorities—and America has never had such a monolithic majority—then the American people should give itself over honestly and openly to "government by judiciary," for if constitutional government is impossible, then so too is the possibility of self-governance.

EDWARD J. ERLER

(SEE ALSO: *Judicial Policymaking; Judicial Review and Democracy.*)

Bibliography

AGRESTO, JOHN   1984   *The Supreme Court and Constitutional Democracy.* Ithaca, N.Y.: Cornell University Press.
ERLER, EDWARD J.   1985   Sowing the Wind: Judicial Oligarchy and the Legacy of *Brown v. Board of Education. Harvard Journal of Law and Public Policy* 8:399–426.
LEVY, LEONARD W.   1967   Judicial Review, History, and Democracy. Pages 1–42 in Leonard W. Levy, ed., *Judicial Review and the Supreme Court.* New York: Harper & Row.
SWINDLER, WILLIAM   1969   *Court and Constitution in the 20th Century.* Indianapolis: Bobbs-Merrill.

JUDICIAL POLICYMAKING

Judicial policymaking and related terms—JUDICIAL ACTIVISM, judicial creativity, and JUDICIAL LEGISLATION—emphasize that judges are not mere legal automatons who simply "discover" or "find" definite, preexisting principles and rules, as the declaratory or oracular conception of the judicial function insisted, but are often their makers. As Justice OLIVER WENDELL HOLMES remarked, they often exercise "the sovereign prerogative of choice," and they "can and do legislate." Indeed, that is why the Supreme Court has often been viewed as "a continuing constitutional convention."

Policymaking is deciding what is to be done by choosing among possible actions, methods, or principles for determining and guiding present and future actions or decisions. Courts, especially high appellate courts such as the SUPREME COURT, often make such choices, establishing new rules and principles, and thus are properly called policymakers. That was emphasized by CHARLES EVANS HUGHES's famous rhetorical exaggeration, "The Constitution is what the judges say it is," and by his remark that a federal statute finally means what the Court, as ultimate interpreter of congressional LEGISLATION, says it means.

The persistent "declaratory" conception of the judicial role, a view critics derided as MECHANICAL JURISPRUDENCE, and simplistic notions of the SEPARATION OF POWERS principle long obscured the reality of judicial policymaking. Today it is widely recognized that, as C. Herman Pritchett has explained, "judges are inevitably participants in the process of public policy formulation; that they do in fact 'make law'; that in making law they are necessarily guided in part by their personal conceptions of justice and public policy; that written law requires interpretation which involves the making of choices; that the rule of STARE DECISIS is vulnerable because precedents are typically available to support both sides in a controversy."

As a system of social control, law must function largely through general propositions rather than through specific directives to particular persons. And that is especially true of the Constitution. The Framers did not minutely specify the national government's powers or the means for executing them: as Chief Justice JOHN MARSHALL said, the Constitution "is one of enumeration, rather than of definition." Many of its most important provisions are indeterminate and open-textured. They are not self-interpreting, and thus judges must read specific meanings into them and determine their applicability to particular situations, many of which their authors could not have anticipated.

Among the Constitution's many ambiguous, undefined, pregnant provisions are those concerning CRUEL AND UNUSUAL PUNISHMENT; DOUBLE JEOPARDY; DUE PROCESS OF LAW; EQUAL PROTECTION OF THE LAWS; ESTABLISHMENT OF RELIGION; excessive BAIL and fines; EX POST FACTO LAWS; FREEDOM OF SPEECH, press, assembly, and religion; life, liberty, and property; the power to regulate commerce among the several states; and unreasonable SEARCHES AND SEIZURES. Also undefined by the Constitution are such fundamental conceptions as FEDERALISM, JUDICIAL REVIEW, the RULE OF LAW, and the separation of powers. Small wonder, then, that Justice ROBERT H. JACKSON plaintively remarked that the Court must deal with materials nearly as enigmatic as the dreams of Pharaoh which Joseph had to interpret; or that Chief Justice EARL WARREN emphasized that the Constitution's words often have "an iceberg quality, containing beneath their surface simplicity submerged complexities which go to the very heart of our constitutional form of government."

Because the Constitution embodies in its ambiguous provisions both common and conflicting community ideals, the Supreme Court serves, as Edward H. Levi has said, as "a forum for the discussion of policy in the gap of ambiguity," which allows the infusion into constitutional law of new meanings and new ideas as situations and people's ideas change. That is the process which Justice FELIX FRANKFURTER described as "the evolution of social policy by way of judicial application of the Delphic provisions of the Constitution." Brief accounts of some notable Supreme Court decisions reveal their policymaking features.

Although the Constitution nowhere explicitly grants Congress the power to incorporate a national bank, the Supreme Court in MCCULLOCH V. MARYLAND (1819) held that power to be implied by the Constitution's NECESSARY AND PROPER CLAUSE. That clause empowers Congress, in executing its various enumerated powers, to make all laws for that purpose which are "necessary and proper." But those ambiguous words are not further defined by the Constitution.

In making its *McCulloch* decision, the Court chose between two historic, diametrically opposed interpretations. The narrow, STATES' RIGHTS, STRICT CONSTRUCTION, Jeffersonian interpretation of the clause was restrictive and limited Congress to legislation that was "absolutely necessary," that is, literally indispensable. The opposing interpretation, which the Court adopted, was the broad, nationalist, loose constructionist, Hamiltonian view that "necessary and proper" were equivalent to "convenient and useful" and thus were facilitative, not restrictive. The bank, declared the Court, was a convenient and useful means to legitimate ends and thus was constitutional.

Viewed broadly as the great implied powers case and the "fountainhead of national powers," *McCulloch* laid down the Hamiltonian doctrine as the authoritative rule of construction to be followed in interpreting Congress's various undefined powers. Subsequently, on that foundation, Congress erected vast superstructures of regulatory and social service legislation. The profound policy considerations underlying the Court's choices are highlighted by the contrast between Jefferson's warning that the dangerous Hamiltonian doctrine would give Congress a boundless field of undefined powers, and Chief Justice Marshall's emphasis upon the "pernicious, baneful," narrow construction which would make the national government's operations "difficult, hazardous, and expensive" and would reduce the Constitution to "a splendid bauble."

The RIGHT TO PRIVACY was recognized by the Supreme Court in GRISWOLD V. CONNECTICUT (1965). There, and in other cases, the Court variously discerned the "roots" of that right, which is not explicitly mentioned in the Constitution, in the FIRST, FOURTH, Fifth, NINTH, and FOURTEENTH AMENDMENTS and in "the penumbras of the BILL OF RIGHTS." Later, in ROE V. WADE (1973), the Court included a woman's right to an abortion in the right of privacy, and, in the detailed manner characteristic of legislation, divided the pregnancy term into three periods and prescribed specific rules governing each. Balancing a woman's interests against a state's interests during these three periods, the Court held that any decision regarding abortion during the first was solely at the discretion of the woman and her physician. But it further ruled that a state's interests in protecting maternal health, maintaining medical standards, and safeguarding potential human life—interests growing in substantiality as the pregnancy term extended—justified greater state regulation later. Thus, state regulations relating to maternal health and medical standards would be permissible in the second period, and more stringent state regulations, even extending to prohibition of abortion, would be permissible in the third period in the interest of safeguarding potential life.

The protests by dissenting Justices in the *Griswold* and *Roe* cases emphasized the judicial policymaking which those decisions revealed. The *Griswold* dissenters objected that no right of privacy could be found "in the Bill of Rights, in any other part of the Constitution, or in any case ever before decided by this Court." And dissenters in *Roe* complained that the Court's decision was "an improvident and extravagant exercise of the power of JUDICIAL REVIEW"; that the Court had fashioned "a new constitutional right for pregnant mothers"; and that the Court's "conscious weighing of competing factors" and its division of the pregnancy term into distinct periods were "far more appropriate to a legislative judgement than to a judicial one."

The Supreme Court's "REAPPORTIONMENT revolution" remedied long-standing discriminations against urban and metropolitan areas in favor of rural areas, by requiring states to reapportion their legislatures in conformity with the rule that legislative districts must be as nearly of equal population as is practicable.

That rule is not found in any constitutional provision specifically addressed to legislative apportionment, for none exists. It is a Court-created rule which clearly demonstrates the leeway for policymaking that open-ended constitutional provisions give the Court. Equal population, the Court said in WESBERRY V. SANDERS (1964), is required for congressional districts by "the command" of Article I, section 2, of the Constitution, that representatives "be chosen by the People" of the states; and is required for state legislative

districts, the Court held in REYNOLDS V. SIMS (1964), by "the clear and strong command" of the FOURTEENTH AMENDMENT's equal protection clause, forbidding states to deny to any persons "the equal protection of the laws."

Courtesy may ascribe the Court's rule to CONSTITUTIONAL INTERPRETATION; but candor ascribes it to judicial policymaking. The dissenting Justices' objections in these cases made that clear. They included complaints that the Court had frozen one political theory of REPRESENTATION into the Constitution; had failed to exercise judicial self-restraint; had decided questions appropriate only for legislative judgment; had violated the separation of powers doctrine; and had excluded numerous important considerations other than population.

Supreme Court overruling decisions, in which it rejects its earlier positions for those later thought more fitting, often strikingly exemplify judicial policymaking. In MAPP V. OHIO (1961) the Court imposed upon state courts its judicially created EXCLUSIONARY RULE making illegally obtained evidence inadmissible in court. It overruled WOLF V. COLORADO (1949) which, in deference to state policies, had held an exclusionary rule not essential for due process of law.

Some overruling decisions illustrate "the victory of dissent," when earlier dissenting Justices' views in time became the law. Thus in GIDEON V. WAINWRIGHT (1963) the Court applied its rule that indigent defendants in all state felony trials must have court-appointed counsel. Overruling BETTS V. BRADY (1942), the Court adopted Justice Black's dissenting position from it, thus repudiating its *Betts* pronouncement that such appointment was "not a fundamental right, essential to a fair trial."

According to the Court in BARRON V. BALTIMORE (1833), the Bill of Rights—the first ten amendments—limits the national government but not the states. But the Court, by its INCORPORATION DOCTRINE, has read nearly all the specific guarantees of the Bill of Rights into the due process clause of the Fourteenth Amendment which provides simply that no state shall "deprive any person of life, liberty, or property, without due process of law." The incorporation has been called selective because the Court, proceeding case by case, has incorporated those guarantees which it considers "fundamental" and "of the very essence of a scheme of ORDERED LIBERTY."

Selective incorporation has involved two kinds of Supreme Court policymaking: adopting the FUNDAMENTAL RIGHTS standard for guiding incorporation, and making the separate decisions incorporating particular Bill of Rights guarantees. Thus the Court, applying its open-textured rule, has given specific meaning to "the vague contours" of the due process clause. And it has become "a perpetual censor" over state actions, invalidating those that violate fundamental rights and liberties.

Clearly the Supreme Court is more than just a legal body: the Justices are also "rulers," sharing in the quintessentially political function of authoritatively allocating values for the American polity. Representing a coordinate branch of the national government, they address their mandates variously to lawyers, litigants, federal and state legislative, executive, and judicial officials, and to broader concerned "publics." Concerning their role, no sharp line can be drawn between law and politics in the broad sense. They do not expound a prolix or rigid legal code, but rather a living Constitution "intended to be adapted to the various *crises* of human affairs," as Chief Justice Marshall said in the *McCulloch* case. And the Justices employ essentially COMMON LAW judicial techniques: they are inheritors indeed, but developers too— "weavers of the fabric of constitutional law"—as Chief Justice Hughes observed. The nature of the judicial process and the growth of the law are intertwined. The Constitution, itself the product of great policy choices, is both the abiding Great Charter of the American polity and the continual focus of clashing philosophies of law and politics among which the Supreme Court must choose: "We are very quiet there," said Justice Holmes plaintively, "but it is the quiet of a storm center, as we all know."

HOWARD E. DEAN

Bibliography

CARDOZO, BENJAMIN N. 1921 *The Nature of the Judicial Process.* New Haven, Conn.: Yale University Press.
LEVI, EDWARD H. 1948 *An Introduction to Legal Reasoning.* Chicago: University of Chicago Press.
MILLER, ARTHUR SELWYN 1978 *The Supreme Court: Myth and Reality.* Westport, Conn.: Greenwood Press.
MURPHY, WALTER F. 1964 *Elements of Judicial Strategy.* Chicago: University of Chicago Press.
PRITCHETT, C. HERMAN 1969 The Development of Judicial Research. Pages 27–42 in Joel B. Grossman and Joseph Tanenhaus, eds., *Frontiers of Judicial Research.* New York: Wiley.

JUDICIAL POWER OF THE UNITED STATES

"[T]he legislative, executive, and judicial powers, of every well constructed government," said JOHN MARSHALL in OSBORN v. BANK OF THE UNITED STATES (1824), "are co-extensive with each other; . . . [t]he executive department may constitutionally execute every law which the Legislature may constitutionally make, and the judicial department may receive from the legislature the power of construing every such law." The ARTICLES OF CONFEDERATION fell far short of this model. Not only was there no federal executive with authority to enforce congressional measures against individuals, but, apart from a cumbersome procedure for resolving interstate disputes, Congress was authorized to establish courts only for the trial of crimes committed at sea and for the determination of "appeals in all cases of captures." The remedy for these shortcomings was one of the major accomplishments of the Constitution adopted in 1789. As Article II gave the country a President with the obligation to "take care that the Laws be faithfully executed," Article III provided for a system of federal courts that more than satisfied Marshall's conditions for a "well constructed government."

Article III consists of three brief sections. The first describes the tribunals that are to exercise federal judicial power and prescribes the tenure and compensation of their judges. The second lists the types of disputes that may be entrusted to federal courts, specifies which of these matters are to be determined by the SUPREME COURT in the first instance, and guarantees TRIAL BY JURY in criminal cases. The third defines and limits the crime of TREASON.

"The judicial Power of the United States," Article III declares, "shall be vested in one Supreme Court, and in such inferior Courts as the Congress may from time to time ordain and establish." The text itself indicates that the Supreme Court was the only tribunal the Constitution required to be established, and the debates of the CONSTITUTIONAL CONVENTION demonstrate that the latter words embodied a deliberate compromise.

In fact, however, Congress created additional courts at the very beginning, in the JUDICIARY ACT OF 1789. Since 1911 the basic system has consisted of the UNITED STATES DISTRICT COURTS—at least one in every state—in which most cases are first tried; a number of regional appellate courts now called the UNITED STATES COURTS OF APPEALS; and the Supreme Court itself, which functions largely as a court of last resort. From time to time, moreover, Congress has created specialized courts with JURISDICTION to determine controversies involving relatively limited subjects. All this lies well within Congress's broad discretion under Article III to determine what lower courts to create and how to allocate judicial business among them. Specialization at the highest level, however, seems precluded; Congress can no more divide the powers of "one Supreme Court" among two or more bodies than abolish it altogether.

"The Judges, both of the supreme and inferior Courts," section 1 continues, "shall hold their Offices during GOOD BEHAVIOUR and shall, at stated Times, receive for their Services, a Compensation, which shall not be diminished during their Continuance in Office." Under the second section of Article II the judges have always been appointed by the President subject to Senate confirmation; under the fourth section of that article they may be removed from office on IMPEACHMENT and conviction of "Treason, Bribery, or other high Crimes and Misdemeanors." The central purpose of the tenure and salary provisions, as ALEXANDER HAMILTON explained in THE FEDERALIST #78, was to assure judicial independence.

The Supreme Court has repeatedly enforced the tenure and salary provisions. In EX PARTE MILLIGAN (1867), for example, the Court held even the Civil War no excuse for submitting civilians to military trials in states where the civil courts were open, and in *O'Donoghue v. United States* (1933), it held that the Great Depression did not justify reducing judicial salaries.

On a number of occasions, however, the Court has permitted matters within the judicial power to be determined by LEGISLATIVE COURTS whose judges do not possess tenure and salary guarantees. State courts may decide Article III cases, as the Framers of the Constitution clearly contemplated; the tenure and salary provisions do not apply to the TERRITORIES or to the DISTRICT OF COLUMBIA, where there is no SEPARATION OF POWERS requirement; Article III did not abolish the traditional COURT-MARTIAL for military offenses; federal magistrates may make initial decisions in Article III cases provided they are subject to unlimited reexamination by tenured judges.

Early in the twentieth century the Supreme Court appeared to give judicial blessing to the numerous quasi-judicial bodies that have grown up since the creation of the Interstate Commerce Commission in 1887, although scholars have debated heatedly whether there is any satisfactory way to distinguish them from the nontenured trial courts plainly forbidden by Article III. That these developments did not mean the effective end of the tenure and salary requirements, however, was made clear in 1982, when the Court in NORTHERN PIPE LINE CONSTRUCTION CO. V. MARATHON PIPE LINE CO. invalidated a statute empowering judges with temporary commissions to exercise virtually the entire jurisdiction of the district courts in BANKRUPTCY cases. Where to draw this line promises to be a continuing problem.

The power to be vested in federal courts is the "judicial power," and the various categories of matters that fall within this power are all described as CASES OR CONTROVERSIES—"Cases," for example, "arising under this Constitution," and "Controversies to which the United States shall be a Party." From the beginning the Supreme Court has taken this language as a limitation: federal courts may not resolve anything but "cases" and "controversies," and those terms embrace only judicial functions.

Thus, for example, when President GEORGE WASHINGTON asked the Justices for legal advice respecting the United States' neutrality during hostilities between England and France, they declined to act "extra-judicially"; and when Congress directed them to advise the war secretary concerning veterans' pensions, five Justices sitting on circuit refused, saying the authority conferred was "not of a judicial nature" (HAYBURN'S CASE, 1792). Washington's request for advice did not begin to resemble the ordinary lawsuit, but later decisions have invoked the "case" or "controversy" limitation to exclude federal court consideration of matters far less remote from the normal judicial function. The essential requirement, the Court has emphasized, is a live and actual dispute between adversary parties with a real stake in the outcome.

One dimension of this principle is the doctrine of RIPENESS or prematurity: the courts are not to give advice on the mere possibility that it might be of use in the future. Occasionally the Court has appeared to require a person to violate a law in order to test its constitutionality—causing one commentator to remark that "the only way to determine whether the subject is a mushroom or a toadstool, is to eat it." The DECLARATORY JUDGMENT ACT, passed to mitigate this hardship, has generally been applied to allow preenforcement challenges when the intentions of the parties are sufficiently firm, and it has been held consistent with the "Case" or "Controversy" requirement.

At the opposite end of the spectrum is the MOOTNESS doctrine, which ordinarily forbids litigation after death or other changed circumstances deprive the issue of any further impact on the parties. A series of debatable decisions essentially dating from *Moore v. Ogilvie* (1969), however, has relaxed the mootness DOCTRINE, especially in CLASS ACTIONS, so as to permit persons with no remaining interest to continue litigating issues deemed "capable of repetition, yet evading review."

The "case or controversy" requirement has also been held to forbid the decision of COLLUSIVE SUITS, and to preclude the courts from exercising the discretion of an administrator, as by reviewing de novo the decision to grant a broadcasting license. The most important remaining element of that requirement, however, is the constitutional dimension of the doctrine of STANDING to sue.

While standing has been aptly characterized as one of the most confused areas of federal law, its constitutional component was simply stated in *Warth v. Seldin* (1975): "[t]he Article III power exists only to redress or otherwise to protect against injury to the complaining party." Injury in this context is hardly self-defining, but it plainly requires something more than intellectual or emotional "interest in a problem." This principle puts under a serious cloud the periodic congressional attempts to authorize "any person" to obtain judicial relief against violations of environmental or other laws. On the other hand, other aspects of the standing doctrine are not of constitutional dimension and thus do not preclude Congress from conferring standing on anyone injured by governmental action.

One of the principal points of contention of the law of standing has been the right of federal taxpayers to challenge the constitutionality of federal spending programs. When a taxpayer attacked expenditures for maternal health on the ground that they exceeded the powers granted Congress by Article I, the Court in FROTHINGHAM V. MELLON (1923) found no standing: "the taxpayer's interest in the moneys of the treasury . . . is shared with millions of others, is comparatively minute and indeterminable, and the effect upon future taxation, of any payment out of the funds, so remote, fluctuating, and uncertain, that no basis is afforded for an appeal to the preventive powers of a court of EQUITY."

Although the apparent reference to equitable discretion made it uncertain that the Court was saying taxpayer suits were not "cases or controversies" within Article III, the remainder of the passage suggests that the taxpayer could not show the constitutionally required injury because it was uncertain that a victory would mean reduced taxes. Nevertheless, in FLAST V. COHEN (1968) the Court allowed a federal taxpayer to challenge expenditures for church-related education as an ESTABLISHMENT OF RELIGION in violation of the FIRST AMENDMENT. Unlike the taxpayer in *Frothingham*, who "was attempting to assert the States' interest in their legislative prerogatives," the plaintiff in *Flast* asserted "a federal taxpayer's interest in being free of taxing and spending in contravention of specific constitutional limitations," for one purpose of the establishment clause was to prevent taxation

for religious ends. Whether the distinction was of constitutional scope the Court did not say; interestingly, the taxpayer opinions have tended to avoid entirely the traditional constitutional inquiry into the existence of an injury that will be redressed if the plaintiff's claim prevails.

Underlying the constitutional "case or controversy" limitation are a variety of policy concerns. The first group relates to reducing the risk of erroneous decisions. Concrete facts enable judges to understand the practical impact of their holdings; adverse parties help to assure that arguments on both sides will be considered; as argued by FELIX FRANKFURTER, "the ADVISORY OPINION deprives CONSTITUTIONAL INTERPRETATION of the judgment of the legislature upon facts." A second group of reasons focuses upon strengthening the Court's institutional position. Lawmaking by appointed judges is least difficult to reconcile with democratic principles when it is the inevitable by-product of the stock business of judging; the courts should not squander their power of moral suasion or multiply conflicts with other branches by deciding unnecessary legal questions. Third, and of considerable importance, is a concern for the separation of powers. The courts are not to exercise a general superintendence over the activities of the other branches.

The costs of the "case or controversy" limitation include the delay, uncertainty, and disruption incident to determining the constitutionality of legislation only in the course of subsequent litigation, and the danger that some legislative and executive actions may escape JUDICIAL REVIEW entirely. Whether the latter is cause for concern has much to do with one's perception of the function and importance of judicial review itself; it seems reasonable to expect that perception to influence the definition of a "case" or "controversy."

In addition to restricting federal courts to the decision of "cases" and "controversies" of a judicial nature, section 2 of Article III enumerates those categories of "cases" and "controversies" to which the "judicial Power shall extend." As the former limitation serves the interests of separating federal powers, the latter serves those of FEDERALISM. In accord with the spirit of the TENTH AMENDMENT the Supreme Court has held that Congress may not give the federal courts jurisdiction over disputes of types not listed in Article III. John Marshall set the tone in cutting down to constitutional size a statute providing for jurisdiction over cases involving ALIENS in HODGSON V. BOWERBANK in 1809: "Turn to the article of the constitution of the United States, for the statutes cannot extend the jurisdiction beyond the limits of the constitution."

Article III's provision that federal judicial power "shall extend to" certain classes of cases and controversies has generally been taken to mean that it shall embrace nothing else. From the text alone one might think it even more plain that federal courts *must* be given jurisdiction over all the matters listed, for section 1 commands that the federal judicial power "shall be vested" in federal courts. Indeed, Justice JOSEPH STORY suggested just such an interpretation in MARTIN V. HUNTER'S LESSEE in 1816. This conclusion, however, was unnecessary to the decision, contrary to the understanding of the First Congress, and inconsistent with both earlier and later decisions of the Supreme Court.

Article III, in other words, has been read to mean only that Congress may confer jurisdiction over the enumerated cases, not that it must do so. This arguably unnatural construction has been defended by reference to the limited list of controversies over which the Supreme Court has original jurisdiction, the explicit congressional power to make exceptions to the Supreme Court's appellate authority, and the compromise at the Constitutional Convention permitting Congress not to establish inferior courts at all.

This is not to say, however, that Congress has unfettered authority to deny the courts jurisdiction, for all powers of Congress are subject to limitations found elsewhere in the Constitution. A statute depriving the courts of authority to determine cases filed by members of a particular racial group, for instance, would be of highly doubtful vitality under the modern interpretation of the Fifth Amendment DUE PROCESS clause, and one part of Marshall's reasoning in MARBURY V. MADISON (1803) supports an argument that closing all federal and state courts to free-speech claims would defeat the substantive right itself. Proposals to remove entire categories of constitutional litigation from the ken of one or more federal courts often follow controversial judicial decisions. Out of respect for the tradition of CHECKS AND BALANCES, however, such bills are seldom enacted; we have so far been spared the constitutional trauma of determining the extent to which they may validly be adopted.

The cases and controversies within federal judicial power fall into two categories: those in which jurisdiction is based upon the nature of the dispute and those in which it is based upon the identity of the parties. In the first category are three kinds of disputes: those "arising under this Constitution, the Laws of the United States, and Treaties made, or which shall be made, under their Authority"; those "of ADMIRALTY AND MARITIME JURISDICTION"; and those involving competing land claims "under Grants of different States." The provision last quoted is of minor importance; the second formed the staple business of the district courts throughout their early history; the first fulfills Marshall's condition for a "well constructed government" and is by any measure the most critical ingredient of federal jurisdiction today.

The provision for jurisdiction in cases arising under the Constitution and other federal laws has two essential purposes: to promote uniformity in the interpretation of federal law, and to assure the vindication of federal rights. The First Congress sought to accomplish the second of these goals by providing, in section 25 of the 1789 Judiciary Act, for Supreme Court review of state-court decisions denying federal rights; the additional uniformity attendant upon review of state decisions *upholding* federal claims was not provided until 1914. In sustaining section 25, the opinion in *Martin v. Hunter's Lessee* demonstrated the difficulty of achieving Article III's purpose without Supreme Court review of state courts: while plaintiffs might be authorized to file federal claims directly in federal courts and defendants to remove state court actions to federal courts on the basis of federal defenses, it was not easy to see how a state court opposing removal "could . . . be compelled to relinquish the jurisdiction" without some federal court reviewing the state court decision.

Conversely, although Congress failed to give federal trial courts general jurisdiction of federal question cases until 1875, Marshall made clear as early as 1824, in *Osborn v. Bank of the United States,* that it had power to do so. Supreme Court review alone was no more an adequate protection for federal rights, Marshall argued, than was exclusive reliance on litigation beginning in federal trial courts. As the latter would leave claimants without remedy against a recalcitrant state court, the former would give a state tribunal the critical power to shape the factual record beyond assurance of federal appellate correction.

The *Osborn* opinion also settled that jurisdiction of a federal trial court over a case arising under federal law was not defeated by the presence of additional issues dependent upon state law. In a companion case, indeed, the Court upheld jurisdiction over a suit by the national bank on notes whose validity and interpretation were understood to depend in substantial part upon nonfederal law: it was enough that the plaintiff derived its existence and its right to contract from the act of Congress incorporating it. The courts have not followed this broad approach, however, in determining whether FEDERAL QUESTION JURISDICTION lies under general *statutory* provisions; when the federal ingredient of a claim is remote from the actual controversy, as in a dispute over ownership of land whose title is remotely derived from a federal land grant, the district courts lack statutory jurisdiction.

In the contract dispute discussed in *Osborn*, federal and state law were bound together in the resolution of a single claim; in such a case, as HENRY HART and Herbert Wechsler said, "a federal trial court would . . . be unable to function as a court at all" if its jurisdiction did not extend to state as well as federal matters. In the interest of "judicial economy," however, as the Supreme Court put it in *United Mine Workers v. Gibbs* (1966), jurisdiction over a case arising under federal law embraces not only a plaintiff's federal claim but also any claims under state law based on the same facts. This so-called PENDENT JURISDICTION doctrine, however, is inapplicable when the Supreme Court reviews a state court decision. With one exception, in such a case the Court may review only federal and not state questions, as the Court held in *Murdock v. Memphis* (1875); for to reverse a state court in the interpretation of its own law would be a major incursion into state prerogatives not required by the purposes for which Supreme Court review was provided.

A corollary of the *Murdock* principle is that a state court decision respecting state law often precludes the Supreme Court from reviewing even federal questions in the same case. If a state court concludes, for example, that a state law offends both federal and state constitutions, the Supreme Court cannot reverse the state law holding; thus, however it may decide the federal issue, it cannot alter the outcome of the case. This independent and ADEQUATE STATE GROUND for the state court decision means there is no longer a live case or controversy between the parties over the federal question. In light of this relation between state and federal issues, *Martin* itself announced the sole exception to the *Murdock* rule: when the state court has interpreted state law in such a way as to frustrate the federal right itself—as by holding that a contract allegedly impaired in violation of the CONTRACT CLAUSE never existed—a complete absence of power to review the state question would mean the Court's authority to protect federal rights "may be evaded at pleasure."

"The most bigoted idolizers of state authority," wrote Alexander Hamilton in *The Federalist* #80, "have not thus far shown a disposition to deny the National Judiciary the cognizance of maritime causes"; for such cases "so generally depend upon the law of nations, and so commonly affect the rights of foreigners, that they fall within the considerations which are relative to the public peace." Jurisdiction

over what Article III refers to as "Cases of admiralty, and maritime Jurisdiction" has been vested by statute in the district courts since 1789. Today federal admiralty jurisdiction extends, as the Court stated in another context in *The Daniel Ball* (1871), to all waters forming part of "a continued highway over which commerce is or may be carried on with other states or foreign countries."

Not everything occurring on navigable waters, however, is a proper subject of admiralty jurisdiction; in denying jurisdiction of claims arising out of an airplane crash in Lake Erie, the Supreme Court made clear that the case must "bear a significant relationship to traditional maritime activity . . . involving navigation and commerce on navigable waters." Conversely, the relation of an activity to maritime concerns may bring it within admiralty cognizance even if it occurs on land. Marine insurance contracts, for example, are within the jurisdiction although both made and to be performed on land. Similarly, the Court has acquiesced in Congress's provision for jurisdiction over land damage caused by vessels on navigable waters.

Because an additional purpose of federal judicial power over maritime cases is understood to have been to provide a uniform law to govern the shipping industry, the Supreme Court also held in *Southern Pacific Company v. Jensen* (1917) that Article III empowers the federal courts to develop a "general maritime law" binding even on state courts, and that Congress may supplement this law with statutes under its authority to adopt laws "necessary and proper" to the powers of the courts. Indeed the Court has held that this aspect of the judicial power, like the legislative authority conferred by the commerce clause of Article I, has an implicit limiting effect upon state law. Not only does state law that contradicts federal law yield under the SUPREMACY CLAUSE, but, as the Court said in rejecting the application of a state workers' compensation law to longshoremen in the case last cited, no state law is valid if it "interferes with the proper harmony and uniformity" of the general maritime law "in its international and interstate relations."

The remaining authorization of federal court jurisdiction protects parties whose fortunes the Framers were for various reasons unwilling to leave wholly at the mercy of state courts. Many of these categories involve government litigation: "Controversies to which the United States shall be a Party; . . . between two or more States; between a State and Citizens of another State, . . . and between a State, or the Citizens thereof, and foreign States, Citizens or Subjects." A federal forum for the national government itself protects against possible state hostility; federal jurisdiction over interstate conflicts provides not only a neutral forum but also a safeguard against what Hamilton in *The Federalist* #80 called "dissentions and private wars"; that "the union will undoubtedly be answerable to foreign powers, for the conduct of its members," was an additional reason for jurisdiction over disputes involving foreign countries as well as the related jurisdiction over "Cases affecting Ambassadors, other public Ministers and Consuls."

The most interesting issue concerning these provisions has been that of SOVEREIGN IMMUNITY. In CHISHOLM V. GEORGIA (1793), ignoring the assurances of prominent Framers like James Madison and Alexander Hamilton as well as the common law tradition that the king could not be sued without his consent, the Supreme Court relied largely on the text of Article III to hold that the power over "Controversies . . . between a State and Citizens of another State" included those in which the state was an unwilling defendant. Obviously, as the Justices pointed out, this was true of the parallel authority over "Controversies . . . between two or more States," and Justice JAMES WILSON added his understanding that the English tradition was a mere formality, since consent to sue was given as a matter of course.

Whether this decision was right or wrong as an original matter, within five years it was repudiated by adoption of the ELEVENTH AMENDMENT, which provides that "[t]he Judicial power of the United States shall not be construed to extend to any suit in law or equity, commenced or prosecuted against one of the United States by Citizens or Subjects of any Foreign State." Notably, the amendment does not mention admiralty cases, suits by foreign countries, suits against a state by its own citizens under federal law, or suits against the United States. Nevertheless the Supreme Court, taking the amendment as casting doubt on the reasoning underlying *Chisholm*, has denied jurisdiction in all of these instances. The best explanation has been that, although not excepted by the amendment, they are outside the power conferred by Article III itself. One state may still sue another, however, and the United States may sue a state. The Court has found such jurisdiction "essential to the peace of the Union" and "inherent in the constitutional plan." Why this is not equally true of a suit by a state against the United States has never been satisfactorily explained.

At least since the 1824 decision in *Osborn v. Bank of the United States*, however, both the Eleventh Amendment and its related immunities have been construed to allow certain actions against state or federal officers even though the effect of the litigation is the same as if the government itself had been named defendant. The theoretical explanation that the officer cannot be acting for the state when he does what the Constitution forbids is inconsistent with the substantive conclusion, often reached in the same cases, that his action is attributable to the state for purposes of the FOURTEENTH AMENDMENT. A more principled explanation is that suits against officers are necessary if the Constitution is to be enforced at all; the response is that those who wrote the amendment could not have intended to allow it to be reduced to a hollow shell.

In any event, the *Osborn* exception has not been held to embrace all suits against government officers. At one time it was said generally that an officer could be prevented from acting but could not be ordered to take affirmative action such as paying off a government obligation, for if he was not acting for the state he had no authority to reach into its treasury. The simplicity of this distinction was shattered, however, by opinions acknowledging the availability of a WRIT OF MANDAMUS to compel an officer to perform a nondiscretionary duty. The more recent formulation in EDELMAN V. JORDAN (1974), which essentially distinguishes between prospective and retrospective relief, seems difficult to reconcile with the language of the Constitution, with its apparent purposes, or with the fiction created to support the *Osborn* rule.

Even when the government is itself a party, it may consent to be sued, and the books are filled with a confusing and incomplete array of statutes allowing suits against the United States. Some judges and scholars have argued that suits against consenting states are inconsistent with the language of the amendment, which declares them outside the judicial power; the Court's persuasive explanation has been that, like venue and personal jurisdiction, immunity is a privilege waivable by the party it protects (*Clark v. Barnard,* 1883). More debatable was the Court's decision in *Parden v. Terminal Railway* (1964) that a state had "waived" its immunity by operating a railroad after passage of a federal statute making "every" interstate railway liable for injuries to its employees; in *Edelman v. Jordan,* retreating from this conclusion, the Court emphasized that "[c]onstructive consent is not a doctrine commonly associated with the surrender of constitutional rights." Still later, however, in FITZPATRICK V. BITZER (1976) the Court held that Congress had power to override a state's immunity in legislating to enforce the Fourteenth Amendment, although it has never suggested that that amendment allowed Congress to ignore other constitutional limitations, such as the BILL OF RIGHTS.

The two remaining categories of disputes within federal judicial power are "controversies . . . between Citizens of different States" and between state citizens and "Citizens or Subjects" of "foreign States." Once again the reasons for federal jurisdiction are generally said to be the avoidance of state-court bias and of interstate or international friction. In contrast not only to the admiralty cases but also to those between states, federal jurisdiction based solely on the diverse citizenship of the parties does not carry with it authority to make substantive law. Absent a federal statute, the Court held in ERIE RAILROAD V. TOMPKINS (1938), "the law to be applied . . . is the law of the State." Later cases such as *Textile Workers Union v. Lincoln Mills* (1957) have qualified the effect though not the principle of this decision by finding in silent statutes implicit authorization to the federal courts to make law. An occasional decision has upheld FEDERAL COMMON LAW, without the pretense of statutory authority, on matters mysteriously found to be "intrinsically federal"; an example was the Court's refusal in *Banco Nacional de Cuba v. Sabbatino* (1964) to look behind official acts of foreign governments. (See ACT OF STATE DOCTRINE.)

In early decisions the Supreme Court took a narrow view of what constituted a controversy between citizens of different states for purposes of the statute implementing this provision of Article III. More recently, however, the Court has generously interpreted the power of Congress to confer DIVERSITY JURISDICTION on the federal courts. And as early as the mid-nineteenth century, recognizing that corporations can be the beneficiaries or victims of state court prejudice without regard to the citizenship of those who compose them, the Court effectively began to treat corporations as citizens by employing the transparent fiction of conclusively presuming that the individuals whose citizenship was determinative were citizens of the state of incorporation.

The best known decision involving the diversity jurisdiction was DRED SCOTT V. SANDFORD (1857), in which three Justices took the position that a black American descended from slaves could never be a state citizen for diversity purposes because he could not be a citizen of the United States. Questionable enough at the time, this conclusion was repudiated by the Fourteenth Amendment's provision that all persons born in this country are citizens of the United States "and of the state wherein they reside." Nevertheless the courts have held that only American citizens are "Citizens of . . . States" within Article III, and conversely that only foreign nationals are "Citizens or Subjects" of "foreign States."

"In all Cases involving Ambassadors, other public Ministers and Consuls, and those in which a state shall be Party," Article III, Section 2 provides, "the supreme Court shall have ORIGINAL JURISDICTION. In all the other Cases before mentioned, the supreme Court shall have APPELLATE JURISDICTION, both as to Law and Fact, with such Exceptions, and under such Regulations as the Congress shall make."

Original jurisdiction is the power to determine a dispute in the first instance; appellate jurisdiction, the power to review a decision already made. *Marbury v. Madison* (1803) held that Congress had no power to give the Supreme Court original jurisdiction of a case to which neither a diplomat nor a state was a party; a contrary result, Chief Justice Marshall argued, would make the constitutional distribution between original and appellate jurisdiction "mere surplusage." This reasoning is not especially convincing, and the converse is not true; in COHENS V. VIRGINIA in 1821 Marshall himself conceded that Congress could give the Court appellate jurisdiction over cases for which Article III provided original jurisdiction. *Cohens* also held that the Supreme Court had original authority not over all Article III cases in which a state happened to be a party but only over those "in which jurisdiction is given, because a state is a party," and thus not over a federal question case between a state and one of its own citizens. Inconsistently, however, the Court allowed the United States to sue a State in the Supreme Court in *United States v. Texas* (1892).

Marbury's implicit conclusion that the exceptions clause quoted above does not allow Congress to tamper with the original jurisdiction strongly suggests that the enumeration of original cases is a minimum as well as a maximum, and the Court has described as "extremely doubtful" the proposition that Congress may deprive it of original power over state or diplomat cases; yet the Court has concluded that it has discretion not to entertain cases within its original jurisdiction.

Unlike the original jurisdiction provision, that giving the Court appellate authority in "all the other" Article III cases contains an explicit escape valve: "with such Exceptions . . . as the Congress shall make." In *The Federalist* #81, Hamilton explained that this clause permitted Congress to limit review of facts decided by juries, but he did not say this was its sole objective. From the beginning Congress has denied the Court jurisdiction over entire classes of controversies within the constitutional reach of appellate power—such as federal criminal cases, most of which were excluded from appellate cognizance for many years even if constitutional issues were presented. The Court itself accepted this particular limitation as early as *United States v. More* (1805), without questioning its constitutionality. Moreover, when Congress repealed a statute under which a pending case attacking the Reconstruction Act had been filed, the Court in EX PARTE MCCARDLE (1869) meekly dismissed the case, observing that "the power to make exceptions to the appellate jurisdiction of this court is given by express words."

As the *McCardle* opinion noted, however, other avenues remained available for taking similar cases to the Supreme Court, and three years later the Court made clear in *United States v. Klein* (1872) that Congress could not under the guise of limiting jurisdiction effectively dictate the result of a case by directing dismissal if the Court should find for the plaintiff. Respected commentators have contended that the Supreme Court must retain appellate authority over certain constitutional questions, arguing that the exceptions clause cannot have been intended, in Henry Hart's words, to "destroy the essential role of the Supreme Court in the constitutional plan." The persuasiveness of this position depends on one's perceptions of the function of judicial review. (See JUDICIAL SYSTEM.)

In order for the Court in *Marbury v. Madison* to dismiss an action that it found Congress had authorized, it had first to conclude that it had the right to refuse to obey an unconstitutional act of Congress. Marshall's argument that this power was "essentially attached to a written constitution" is contradicted by much European experience; and his assertion that choosing between the Constitution and a statute was an inescapable aspect of deciding cases begged the question, for the Constitution might have required the courts to accept Congress's determination that a statute was valid. For the same reason one may object to his reliance on Article VI's requirement that judges swear to support the Constitution: one does not offend that oath by enforcing an unconstitutional statute if that is what the Constitution requires.

The SUPREMACY CLAUSE of Article VI is no better support; the contrasting reference to "Treaties made, or which shall be made" in the same clause strongly suggests that the phrase "laws . . . which shall be made in Pursuance of" the Constitution, also invoked by Marshall, was meant to deny supremacy to acts adopted under the Articles of Confederation, not to those that were invalid. Most promising of the provisions brought forward in *Marbury* was Article III's extension of judicial power to "Cases . . . arising under this Constitution"; as Marshall said, it could scarcely have been "the intention of those who gave

this power, to say that in using it the constitution should not be looked into." Yet even here the case is not airtight. For while Article III provides for jurisdiction in constitutional cases, it is Article VI that prescribes the force to be given the Constitution; and while the latter article plainly gives the Constitution precedence over conflicting *state* laws, it appears to place *federal* statutes on a par with the Constitution itself.

Nevertheless the *Marbury* decision should be regarded as neither a surprise nor a usurpation. Though Marshall did not say so, judicial review had a substantial history before *Marbury*, and despite occasional scholarly denials it seems clear that most of the Framers expected that the courts would refuse to enforce unconstitutional acts of Congress. Moreover, there is force to Marshall's argument that a denial of this power would effectively undermine the express written limitations on congressional power; the natural reluctance to assume that the Framers meant to leave the fox in charge of the chickens lends credence to the conclusion that judicial review is implicit in the power to decide constitutional cases or in the substantive constitutional limitations themselves.

In fact the *Marbury* opinion espouses two distinct theories of judicial review that have opposite implications for a number of related issues, some of which have been discussed above. If, as Marshall at one point seemed to suggest, judicial review is only an incidental by-product of the need to resolve pending cases, it is no cause for constitutional concern if Congress eliminates the Supreme Court's jurisdiction over First Amendment cases, or if no one has standing to attack a federal spending program. If, on the other hand, as argued elsewhere in *Marbury*, judicial review is essential to a plan of constitutional checks and balances, one may take a more restrictive view of Congress's power to make exceptions to the appellate jurisdiction, and perhaps a broader view of what constitutes a case or controversy as well.

Dissenting from the assertion of judicial authority over legislative reapportionment cases in BAKER V. CARR (1962), Justice Felix Frankfurter argued for a broad exception to judicial review of both federal and state actions: even unconstitutional acts could not be set aside if they presented POLITICAL QUESTIONS. Some have attempted to trace this notion to *Marbury* itself, where the Court did say that "[q]uestions in their nature political" were beyond judicial ken. The context suggests, however, that Marshall meant only that the Court would respect actions taken by other branches of government within their legitimate authority, and Louis Henkin has shown that most later decisions using "political question" language can be so explained.

The Court itself, however, spoke in *Baker* of a general "political question" doctrine preventing decision of the merits when, among other things, there was "a lack of judicially discoverable and manageable standards for resolving" a "political" issue. A number of lower courts relied on such a doctrine in refusing to decide the legality of the VIETNAM WAR. While the doctrine as so conceived appears at cross-purposes with the checks-and-balances aspect of *Marbury*, nothing in that decision bars a finding that a particular constitutional provision either gives absolute discretion to a nonjudicial branch (such as the power to recognize foreign governments) or makes an exception to Article III's grant of the judicial power itself (as, arguably, in the case of impeachment).

In most respects, then, Article III amply satisfies Marshall's conditions for a "well constructed government." Though the governmental immunities associated with the Eleventh Amendment may seem anachronistic today, unsympathetic judicial interpretation has blunted their interference with the enforcement of federal law. Decisions since the 1950s have generally rejected Justice Frankfurter's broad conception of the political question. Thus with rare exceptions the federal judiciary, as Marshall insisted, may be given authority to construe every federal law; and the extension of judicial power to controversies between citizens of different states means that the federal courts may often be given power to apply state law as well. Though increased mobility has led to serious efforts to repeal the statutory basis for the diversity jurisdiction, it served an important function in the past and conceivably may become more important in the future. Moreover, the Framers were farsighted enough to assure federal judges the independence necessary to do their appointed job. The weakest point in the system is the arguable authority of Congress to take away all or a substantial part of the Supreme Court's appellate power in constitutional cases; for such an authority undermines other elements of the system of checks and balances that the Framers so carefully constructed.

DAVID P. CURRIE

Bibliography

BICKEL, ALEXANDER   1962   *The Least Dangerous Branch.* Pages 111–199. Indianapolis: Bobbs-Merrill.

BORCHARD, EDWIN   1928   *Hearings on H.R. 5623 before the Subcommittee of the Senate Committee on the Judiciary.* 70th Cong., 1st Sess., pp. 75–76.

FARRAND, MAX (ED.)   1911   *Records of the Federal Convention of 1787.* Vol. 1, pp. 119–129. New Haven, Conn.: Yale University Press.

HART, HENRY and WECHSLER, HERBERT   1973   *The Federal Courts and the Federal System.* Pages 309–418, 833–1103. Mineola, N.Y.: Foundation Press.

HENKIN, LOUIS   1976   Is There a "Political Question" Doctrine? *Yale Law Journal* 85:597–625.

JUDICIAL RESTRAINT

See: Judicial Activism and Restraint

JUDICIAL REVIEW

Judicial review, in its most widely accepted meaning, is the power of courts to consider the constitutionality of acts of other organs of government when the issue of constitutionality is germane to the disposition of lawsuits properly pending before the courts. This power to consider constitutionality in appropriate cases includes the courts' authority to refuse to enforce, and in effect invalidate, governmental acts they find to be unconstitutional.

Judicial review is America's most distinctive contribution to CONSTITUTIONALISM. Although courts have exercised judicial review almost from the beginning of American constitutional government, the question of the legitimacy of that JUDICIAL POWER has often provoked controversy as well as recurrent charges that American judges usurped the authority. Nearly two centuries of exercises of and popular acquiescence in the power have quieted the storms over its basic justifiability in recent decades, but vehement controversy continues regarding the proper scope and authority of judicial rulings on constitutionality. Moreover, particular exercises of judicial review continue to stir passionate political debates, as they have from the beginning.

The classic justification for judicial review was set forth by Chief Justice JOHN MARSHALL in MARBURY V. MADISON (1803). Marshall relied on general principles and constitutional text. His arguments from principle are not compelling. For example, his unchallengeable assertion that the Constitution was designed to establish a limited government does not demonstrate that *courts* should enforce those limitations. Constitutions prescribing limits on government had been adopted before 1803, as many have been since; but relatively few look to the judiciary for enforcement. Similarly, the fact that judges take an oath to support the Constitution does not imply judicial review, for the Constitution requires the oath of all federal and state officers. Far more persuasive are Marshall's references to two passages of the constitutional text. First, Article III lists cases "arising under the Constitution" as one of the subjects included within the JUDICIAL POWER OF THE UNITED STATES, suggesting that constitutional questions can give rise to judicial rulings. Second, the SUPREMACY CLAUSE of Article VI lists the Constitution first as among the legal sources that "shall be the supreme Law of the Land."

Although the inferences derivable from the constitutional text are not unchallengeable, they provide the strongest available support for Marshall's justification for judicial review. True, Article VI is specifically addressed only to state judges, for the "supreme Law of the Land" clause is followed by the statement that "Judges in every State shall be bound thereby, any Thing in the Constitution or Laws of any State to the Contrary notwithstanding." Still, the CONSTITUTIONAL CONVENTION debates and federal LEGISLATION, ever since Section 25 of the JUDICIARY ACT OF 1789, have contemplated Supreme Court review of state court rulings on constitutional questions, and it is surely plausible to argue that the Supreme Court's authority on review would be no less than that of state judges obeying the command of the supremacy clause.

Federal court review of state court judgments is an especially plausible aspect of judicial review, for it is a typical policing technique to maintain the delineations of governing authority in federal systems. That strand of judicial review is common in other federal schemes as well, as in Switzerland and Australia. Yet even federal systems are conceivable without judicial review. Thus, nationalists at the Constitutional Convention initially urged reliance on the congressional veto and on military force to curb excesses by the states. The supremacy clause, and its reliance on routine judicial power to enforce federalistic restraints, stemmed from suggestions by states' rights forces at the convention.

Judicial review in the interest of FEDERALISM has played an important role in the United States; some observers, indeed, view it as the most essential function of judicial review. As Justice OLIVER WENDELL HOLMES once put it: "I do not think the United States would come to an end if we lost our power to declare an Act of Congress void. I do think the Union would be imperiled if we could not make that declaration as to the laws of the several States." The supremacy clause goes a long way toward assuring this protection of the Union; but it provides less compelling justification for judicial review of congressional acts.

The constitutional text cited by John Marshall supports judicial review in all its aspects in a more basic sense. Article III and Article VI both reflect the premise central to judicial review—the premise that the Constitution is to be considered a species of law and accordingly cognizable in courts of law. Judicial review is essentially the judicial enforceability of constitutional norms, and viewing the Constitution as law rather than mere policy or precatory adjuration is the keystone of the more persuasive argument that the American constitutional scheme was designed to rely on judges, not merely troops or political restraints, to enforce constitutional limits.

This view of the Constitution as law—the view central to the argument for giving courts a major role in constitutional enforcement—made it relevant for Marshall to state that it was "emphatically the province and duty of the judicial department to say what the law is," and to describe judicial review as an outgrowth of the normal task of judges: to adjudicate the cases before them on the basis of all relevant rules of law, rules that include those stemming from the Constitution. And that in turn made it plausible for him to say that, where a statute and the Constitution conflict, the courts must enforce the superior Constitution and "disregard" the statute. That, to Marshall, was "of the very essence of judicial duty."

Even if Marshall's views of the Constitution as law and of the "judicial duty" were unanswerable, charges of usurpation would not be stilled. Whatever the strength of the inferences from Articles III and VI, it is undeniable that the power of judicial review is not explicitly granted by the Constitution—in contrast to the constitutions of the nations that, in modern times, have embraced systems similar to the American scheme of judicial review, such as West Germany, Italy, India, and Japan. Defenders of judicial review have accordingly sought to find added support for Marshall's conclusion in historical understandings and practices. None of the sources relied on, however, conveys overwhelming force.

For example, it is true that Marshall's argument was to a considerable extent anticipated by ALEXANDER HAMILTON in THE FEDERALIST #78; but Hamilton's essay was after all only a propagandistic defense of the Constitution during the ratification debates. Similarly, the arguments from historical practice are inconclusive at best. The much invoked statement by EDWARD COKE in BONHAM'S CASE (1610)—that "the COMMON LAW will controul Acts of Parliament, [and] adjudge them to be utterly void" when they are "against common right and reason"—was inconsistent with British practice at the time and thus is not even respectable OBITER DICTUM. More relevant was the APPELLATE JURISDICTION of the PRIVY COUNCIL over colonial courts; but invalidation of legislation through that route was rare and unpopular. And the much debated alleged PRECEDENTS in the practice of state courts during the years immediately following independence hardly establish a well-entrenched practice of judicial review in the era of the ARTICLES OF CONFEDERATION. The preconstitutional examples that withstand scrutiny are few and controversial, and in any event it is not clear that many delegates at the Constitutional Convention knew about the scattered actual or alleged instances of invalidation of state laws by state judges.

Nor do the statements in the Constitutional Convention and the state ratification debates provide iron-clad proof that judicial review was intended by the Framers. While it is true that most of the statements addressing the issue supported such a judicial power, it is equally true that only a minority of speakers at the Constitution framing and ratifying conventions expressed their views. The most important statements at the Constitutional Convention came during the discussion of the council of revision proposal—a proposal that the Justices join with the President in exercising the VETO POWER. That proposal was rejected, partly on grounds supporting the legitimacy of judicial review. Thus, LUTHER MARTIN, in criticizing "the association of the Judges with the Executive" as a "dangerous innovation," argued that, "as to the Constitutionality of laws, that point will come before the Judges in their proper official character. In this character they have a negative on the laws. Join them with the Executive in the Revision and they will have a double negative."

Some scholars have argued, questionably, that judicial review was so normal a judicial function that it was taken for granted by the Framers. HENRY M. HART and Herbert Wechsler claimed to find clear support in the Convention debates: "The grant of judicial power was to include the power, where necessary in the decision of cases, to disregard state or federal statutes found to be unconstitutional. Despite the curiously persisting myth of usurpation, the Convention's understanding on this point emerges from its records with singular clarity." But with regard to original intent, EDWARD S. CORWIN's Senate testimony on the 1937 Court-packing plan still represents a fair summary of the state of the record. Corwin stated that the "people who say the framers intended [judicial review] are talking nonsense," but he added that "people who say they did not intend it are talking nonsense." As Leonard W. Levy commented after

noting Corwin's assessment that there is "great uncertainty" on the issue: "A close textual and contextual examination of the evidence will not result in an improvement on these propositions."

Most important in the search for preconstitutional bases for judicial review authority is probably the late-eighteenth-century prevalence of general ideas conducive to the acceptance of the power asserted in *Marbury v. Madison.* The belief in written CONSTITUTIONS to assure LIMITED GOVERNMENT was hardly an American invention, but Americans had an unusually extensive experience with basic, HIGHER LAW documents of government, from royal charters to state constitutions and the Articles of Confederation. Yet it is possible to have constitutions without judicial review: to say that a government cannot exceed constitutional limits does not demonstrate who is to decide. It bears reiterating, then, that viewing a constitution as a species of "law" was the vital link between constitutionalism and judicial competence to decide constitutional issues. Moreover, the view that the Constitution was an act of the people rather than of the state governments helped provide an ideology congenial to Marshall's insistence that the courts could, in the name of the people, refuse to enforce the acts of the people's representatives.

Accepting the persuasiveness of Marshall's core argument is not tantamount to endorsing all of the alleged implications of judicial review that are pervasive in the late twentieth century. Marshall's stated view of the role of courts in constitutional cases was a relatively modest one; after nearly two centuries of exercise of judicial review by courts, and especially the Supreme Court, the scope and binding effect of judicial rulings are far broader. Most of Marshall's argument was largely defensive, designed to undergird judicial competence and authority to adjudicate issues of constitutionality. He insisted that the Constitution is "a rule for the government of *courts* as well as the legislature" and concluded that "*courts*, as well as other departments, are bound by that instrument." Modern perceptions, by contrast, often view the courts as playing a superior or supreme role in CONSTITUTIONAL INTERPRETATION. Claims of JUDICIAL SUPREMACY and sometimes even exclusiveness are widespread in scholarly statements and popular understandings. The extent to which such impressions are justifiable continues to give rise to sharp controversy.

Marshall's claims about judicial competence and authority were closely tied to a tripartite theory of government reflecting the SEPARATION OF POWERS. He did not deny that other branches, including the

President in the exercise of the veto power and Congress in enacting legislation, could and—under the oath to support the Constitution emphasized in *Marbury* itself—presumably must consider issues of constitutionality. Marshall's argument that courts *also* have competence to take the Constitution into account in their work was essentially a "me too" position. Modern variants on justifications for judicial review—and a number of statements from the modern Supreme Court itself—lend stronger support than anything in Marshall's reasoning to a "me superior" or even a "me only" view.

Nearly from the beginning, Presidents have taken issue with Supreme Court rulings. THOMAS JEFFERSON insisted that "nothing in the Constitution has given [the judges] a right to decide for the Executive, more than to the Executive to decide for them." And he argued that considering "the judges as the ultimate arbiters of all constitutional questions" was "a very dangerous doctrine indeed, and one which would place us under the despotism of an oligarchy." Similarly, ANDREW JACKSON insisted, in vetoing the bill to recharter the Bank of the United States in 1832, that MCCULLOCH V. MARYLAND (1819) did not preclude his action: "Mere precedent is a dangerous source of authority, and should not be regarded as deciding questions of constitutional power except where the acquiescence of the people and the States can be considered as well settled." Similar statements are found in the utterances of later Presidents, from ABRAHAM LINCOLN to FRANKLIN D. ROOSEVELT and beyond.

John Marshall was no doubt unhappy with the political statements of Jeffersonians and Jacksonians. Clearly, he would have preferred ready acceptance of his Court's glosses on the Constitution by all governmental officials and the entire nation. But nothing in the stances of the leaders of his day or since was in sharp conflict with anything in *Marbury v. Madison.* Jefferson, Jackson, and their successors did not deny the binding effect of the judges' constitutional rulings in the cases before them. But the Presidents insisted on their right to disagree with the principles underlying the Court decision. As Lincoln said in the course of his debates with STEPHEN A. DOUGLAS, he did not propose that after Dred Scott had been held to be a slave by the Court—in DRED SCOTT V. SANDFORD (1857)—"we, as a mob, will decide him to be free." But, he added, "we nevertheless do oppose that decision as a political rule which shall be binding on the voter, to vote for nobody who thinks it wrong, which shall be binding on the members of Congress or the President to favor no measure that does not actually

concur with the principles of that decision. [We] propose so resisting it as to have it reversed if we can, and a new judicial rule established upon this subject."

Does it follow that, if such presidential statements are consistent with *Marbury v. Madison,* the scheme sketched by Marshall in 1803 contemplated never-ending chaos—a state of chaos in which the political branches of the national government, and the states as well, might forever disagree with the principles of Supreme Court decisions, in which the only way to implement the Court's principles would be to bring the resisting parties to court in multiple lawsuits, in which no constitutional question would ever be settled? Not necessarily, and certainly not in American experience. Judicial review has not meant that the Supreme Court's reasoning ends all constitutional debate, but neither has it meant endless litigation and dispute over every constitutional issue. Yet the reasons for the growing role of the Supreme Court in settling constitutional issues rest less on any legal principle underlying judicial review than on considerations stemming from institutional arrangements and from prudence. The only arguable basis in *Marbury* itself for viewing the courts as the ultimate arbiters of constitutional issues is Marshall's ambiguous statement that it is "emphatically the province and duty of the judicial department to say what the law is." That statement establishes judicial competence, as noted; but its ambiguity also may provide the basis for arguments for a special judicial expertise in constitutional matters and for a de facto judicial supremacy. Marshall's statement is not so strong, however, as a similar one from Hamilton, in *The Federalist* #78: "The interpretation of laws is the proper and peculiar province of the courts."

The widely observable phenomenon that a Court interpretation of the Constitution has significance beyond the parties to a particular lawsuit rests on other, stronger bases. A central one is that, to the extent a disputed constitutional issue arises in a lawsuit, and to the extent that the Supreme Court is the highest court in the judicial hierarchy, a Supreme Court interpretation is final. Technically, it is final only with respect to the parties in the case, to be sure; but the Court gives general reasons in resolving specific controversies, and the Justices normally operate under a system of PRECEDENT and STARE DECISIS. Similarly situated parties not before the Court in the particular case ordinarily recognize that, other things being equal, the Court will adhere to precedent, will apply the same rule to them if litigation ensues, and accordingly choose not to engage in needless litigation.

Basically, then, the reason that the courts generally

and the Supreme Court in particular wield such vast influence in Americans' understanding of their Constitution is that most constitutional issues can and do arise in lawsuits; and once they do, the courts, with the Supreme Court at the apex, do have the final say. As a result, most potential opponents of Court rulings follow the course implied in Lincoln's First Inaugural Address. Lincoln did not deny that Supreme Court decisions "must be binding in any case upon the parties to a suit as to the object of that suit" and "are also entitled to very high respect and consideration in all parallel cases by all other departments of the Government." He added: "And while it is obviously possible that such decision may be erroneous in any given case, still the evil effect following it, being limited to that particular case, with a chance that it may be overruled or never become a precedent for other cases, can better be borne than could the evil of a different practice." From that position, Herbert Wechsler's rhetorical question plausibly follows: When the chance that a judicial ruling "may be overruled and never become a precedent for other cases . . . has been exploited and has run its course, with reaffirmation rather than REVERSAL of decision, has not the time arrived when its acceptance is demanded, without insisting on repeated litigation? The answer here, it seems to me, must be affirmative, both as to a necessary implication of our constitutional tradition and to avoid the greater evils that will otherwise ensue." Wechsler's admonition, it should be noted, is one of prudence, not of any necessary legal mandate stemming from the *Marbury* rationale.

Beginning in the late twentieth century, however, the Supreme Court has repeatedly claimed a greater import for its exercises of judicial review than anything clearly set forth in *Marbury*. A major example came in one of the cases stemming from the school DESEGREGATION controversy, COOPER V. AARON (1958). The opinion in that case, signed by each of the Justices, provides the strongest judicial support for a view widely held by the public—that the Court is the ultimate, the supreme interpreter of the Constitution. Rejecting the premise of the actions of the legislature and of the governor of Arkansas in that case—that they were not bound by the ruling in BROWN V. BOARD OF EDUCATION (1954)—the Court purported to "recall some basic constitutional propositions which are settled doctrine." The Justices quoted Article VI and Marshall's "province and duty of the judicial department" passage in *Marbury* and added: "This decision declared the basic principle that the federal judiciary is supreme in the exposition of the law of the Constitution. [It] follows that the interpreta-

tion of the Fourteenth Amendment enunciated by this Court in the *Brown* case is the supreme law of the land, and Article VI of the Constitution makes it of binding effect on the States. [Every] state legislator and executive and judicial officer is solemnly committed by oath taken pursuant to Article VI, 3, 'to support this Constitution.' "

Similar statements have surfaced in other controversial cases in recent years, especially in BAKER V. CARR (1962) (referring to the "responsibility of this Court as ultimate interpreter of the Constitution") and POWELL V. MCCORMACK (1969) ("[It] is the responsibility of this Court to act as the ultimate interpreter of the Constitution. *Marbury v. Madison.*"). The Court in these cases was no doubt marshaling all possible rhetorical force in efforts to ward off actual or potential resistance from the states or from other branches of the federal government; but these broad modern assertions no doubt also reflect widespread popular understandings of the "ultimate" role of the Court, understandings bolstered by the nation's general acceptance of that role, despite frequent and continuing disagreements with particular decisions.

From the relatively modest assertions of the judicial review power in *Marbury v. Madison*, nearly two centuries of history have brought the Court increasingly close to the self-announced dominant role in constitutional interpretation it set forth in *Cooper v. Aaron*. That does not mean that Supreme Court interpretations are entitled to immunity from criticism, popular or academic. Nor does it signify the end of all political restraints on the Court, restraints stemming from the same Constitution that Marshall relied on in defending judicial review. Judges may be subjected to congressional IMPEACHMENT and Congress may arguably curtail the federal courts' JURISDICTION in constitutional cases. (See JUDICIAL SYSTEM.) But both weapons, though frequently brandished, have rarely been used. Moreover, the constitutional AMENDING PROCESS, albeit difficult to invoke, is available to overturn unpopular Court rulings. More significant, the composition of the Court as well as its size rest with the political branches, and the President's nominating role, together with the Senate's in confirmation, have been major safeguards against judges deviating too far from the national consensus. Despite these potential and actual checks, however, the Supreme Court's role in American government has outgrown both the view that it is the weakest branch and Marshall's own delineation of the judicial review power. What ALEXIS DE TOCQUEVILLE recognized over a century and a half ago has become ever more true since he wrote: "Scarcely any question arises in the United States which does not become, sooner or later, a subject of judicial debate."

Even though historical exercises of judicial review and popular acquiescence have largely stilled the outcries that the federal courts usurped the power to consider the constitutionality of legislation, the core arguments on behalf of the legitimacy of judicial review, summarized by Marshall in *Marbury v. Madison*, continue to generate controversial implications. Two especially important and recurrent modern debates involve arguments reaching back all the way to *Marbury*. The first issue is whether courts should strain to avoid decisions on controversial constitutional issues by invoking such devices as the POLITICAL QUESTION doctrine. The second issue concerns the proper sources of constitutional adjudication: Must courts limit themselves to "interpretation" of the Constitution, or are "noninterpretive" decisions also legitimate?

Courts confident about the legitimacy of judicial review may tend to exercise that power assertively; judges in doubt about the underpinnings of that authority may shrink from exercising the power to invalidate legislative acts and may indeed seek to escape altogether from rulings on the merits in constitutional cases. The connection between views of legitimacy and modern exercises (or nonexercises) of judicial review is illustrated by an exchange between LEARNED HAND and Herbert Wechsler. Hand insisted that there was "nothing in the United States Constitution that gave courts any authority to review the decisions of Congress" and that the text "gave no ground for inferring that the decisions of the Supreme Court [were] to be authoritative upon the Executive and the Legislature." He found the sole justification for judicial review in the practical need "to prevent the defeat of the venture at hand"—to keep constitutional government from foundering. Wechsler retorted: "I believe the power of the courts is grounded in the language of the Constitution and is not a mere interpolation."

These contending positions have contrasting implications. Thus, Hand concluded that "since this power is not a logical deduction from the structure of the Constitution but only a practical condition upon its successful operation, it need not be exercised whenever a court sees, or thinks it sees, an invasion of the Constitution. It is always a preliminary question how importunately the occasion demands an answer." Wechsler countered that there was no such broad discretion to decline constitutional adjudication in a case properly before a court: "For me, as for anyone who finds the judicial power anchored in the Constitution, there is no such escape from the judicial obligation;

the duty cannot be attenuated in this way." (That "duty," he cautioned, was "not that of policing or advising legislatures or executives," but rather simply "to decide the litigated case [in] accordance with the law.")

It is true that courts do often abstain from deciding constitutional questions pressed upon them. There is no question about the legitimacy of that phenomenon to the extent that courts rely on nonconstitutional, narrower grounds of decision in disposing of a case. Nor is there any doubt that courts need not—and under the *Marbury* rationale may not—decide constitutional issues if they are not properly presented in a case because, for example, the litigation does not square with the CASE AND CONTROVERSY requirement of Article III. But twentieth-century courts have occasionally gone beyond such justifiable ABSTENTIONS to claim a more general and more questionable authority to resort to considerations of prudence in refusing to issue rulings on the merits even though a case falls within the contours of Article III and even though congressional statutes appear to confer obligatory jurisdiction on the courts.

Some commentators have defended judicial resort to the "passive virtues"; others have attacked such refusals to adjudicate as often unprincipled and illegitimate. The controversy about the political question doctrine is illustrative. To the extent that the doctrine rests on constitutional interpretation, as it does under its strand regarding what the Court in *Baker v. Carr* (1962) called "a textually demonstrable constitutional commitment of the issue to a coordinate political department," it is undoubtedly legitimate. But the courts have often gone beyond that concern to refuse adjudication on the ground of a lack of judicially "manageable standards" and on the basis of even broader, wholly prudential considerations as well. Wechsler argued that, in political question cases, "the only proper judgment that may lead to an abstention from decision is that the Constitution has committed the determination of the issues to another agency of government than the courts. [What] is involved is in itself an act of constitutional interpretation, to be made and judged by standards that should govern the interpretive process generally. That, I submit, is *toto caelo* [by all heaven] different from a broad discretion to abstain or intervene." ALEXANDER M. BICKEL strongly disagreed, insisting that "only by means of a play on words can the broad discretion that the courts have in fact exercised be turned into an act of constitutional interpretation." He saw the political question doctrine as something different from the interpretive process—"something greatly more flexible, something of prudence, not construction and not principle."

To the extent that the Supreme Court rests largely on discretionary, prudential concerns in refusing to adjudicate—as, for example, it appears to have done in holding federalistic restraints on congressional power largely nonjusticiable in GARCIA V. SAN ANTONIO METROPOLITAN TRANSIT AUTHORITY (1985)—it raises questions of legitimacy under *Marbury v. Madison*. Courts deriving their authority from a premise that the Constitution is law, as the *Marbury* argument does, are not authorized to resort to discretionary abstention devices not justified by law. As Marshall himself pointed out in COHENS V. VIRGINIA (1821): "We have no more right to decline the exercise of jurisdiction which is given, than to usurp that which is not given." But discretionary devices of self-limitation have become commonplace in judicial behavior, as a result of glosses articulated by modern judges rather than because of anything in the Constitution itself or in Marshall's reasoning. (See COMITY.)

There is a second modern issue, especially pervasive and controversial, in which the rationale of *Marbury v. Madison* affects debates about judicial review: Are the courts bound to limit themselves to "interpretations" of the Constitution in exercising judicial review? Marshall's reasoning in *Marbury* suggests that "noninterpretive" rulings are illegitimate. A justification that derives judicial review from the existence of a written constitution and from the premise that the Constitution is a species of law implies that the courts are confined by the Constitution in delineating constitutional norms. And courts indeed almost invariably purport to rest their constitutional rulings on "interpretations" of the basic document.

But modern academic commentary is sharply divided on this issue. Most scholars who insist on "interpretation" as the sole legitimate ingredient of constitutional rulings do not argue for a narrow, strict interpretation based solely on a literal reading of the constitutional text or a specific basis in the Framers' intent. But their "broad interpretivist" position does insist that constitutional rulings must rest on a clear nexus to—and plausible inference from—the Constitution's text, history, or structure. The "noninterpretivist" critics of that position emphasize the many opaque and open-ended phrases in the Constitution and the changing interpretations of these phrases over the years. They claim that the Court's behavior cannot be squared with even a broad interpretivist position and argue that the Court has always relied on extraconstitutional norms. These critics insist that "noninterpretivist" decision making is justified not only by the history of the Court's elaborations of such vague yet pervasive concepts as SUBSTANTIVE DUE PROCESS but also by the appropriate role of courts in American constitutional democracy. The noninterpretivist literature accordingly abounds with suggestions of sources courts might rely on in the search for fundamental, judicially enforceable values—sources that range from moral philosophy to contemporary political consensus and analogies to literary and scriptural analyses.

The interpretivist arguments that draw in part on Marshall's justification for judicial review have difficulty explaining the Court's performance in "reinterpreting" the Constitution in light of changing societal contexts. The noninterpretivist position has difficulty squaring its arguments with the *Marbury* view of the Constitution as a species of law. That position has difficulty as well in articulating limits on the legitimate ingredients of constitutional decision making that safeguard adequately against excessive judicial subjectivism—against the specter reflected in Learned Hand's fear of being "ruled by a bevy of Platonic Guardians." Whether constitutional decision making by judges can continue to contribute to the flexibility and durability of the Constitution without deteriorating into merely politicized and personalized rulings that risk subverting the legitimacy of constitutional government is the central and unresolved challenge confronting modern judicial review.

GERALD GUNTHER

Bibliography

BICKEL, ALEXANDER M. 1962 *The Least Dangerous Branch: The Supreme Court at the Bar of Politics.* Indianapolis: Bobbs-Merrill.

ELY, JOHN H. 1980 *Democracy and Distrust: A Theory of Judicial Review.* Cambridge, Mass.: Harvard University Press.

GREY, THOMAS 1975 Do We Have an Unwritten Constitution? *Stanford Law Review* 27:703–718.

GUNTHER, GERALD 1964 The Subtle Vices of the "Passive Virtues": A Comment on Principle and Expediency in Judicial Review. *Columbia Law Review* 64:1–25.

HAND, LEARNED 1958 *The Bill of Rights.* Cambridge, Mass.: Harvard University Press.

HART, HENRY M., JR. and WECHSLER, HERBERT 1973 Pages 1–241 in Paul Bator, Paul Mishkin, David Shapiro, and Herbert Wechsler, eds., *The Federal Courts and the Federal System,* 2nd ed. Mineola, N.Y.: Foundation Press.

LEVY, LEONARD W. 1967 Judicial Review, History, and Democracy: An Introduction. Pages 1–42 in Leonard W. Levy, ed., *Judicial Review and the Supreme Court: Selected Essays.* New York: Harper & Row.

MCCLOSKEY, ROBERT G. 1960 *The American Supreme Court.* Chicago: University of Chicago Press.

McLaughlin, Andrew C. 1935 *A Constitutional History of the United States.* New York: Appleton-Century-Crofts.

Perry, Michael J. 1982 *The Constitution, the Courts, and Human Rights: An Inquiry into the Legitimacy of Constitutional Policymaking by the Judiciary.* New Haven, Conn.: Yale University Press.

Wechsler, Herbert 1961 *Principles, Politics, and Fundamental Law.* Cambridge, Mass.: Harvard University Press.

———— 1965 The Courts and the Constitution. *Columbia Law Review* 65:1001–1014.

JUDICIAL REVIEW AND DEMOCRACY

The American ideal of democracy lives in constant tension with the American ideal of JUDICIAL REVIEW in the service of individual liberties. It is a tension that sometimes erupts in crisis. THOMAS JEFFERSON planned a campaign of IMPEACHMENTS to rid the bench, and particularly the Supreme Court, of Federalist judges. The campaign collapsed when the impeachment of Associate Justice SAMUEL CHASE failed in the Senate. FRANKLIN D. ROOSEVELT, frustrated by a Court majority that repeatedly struck down New Deal economic measures, tried to "pack" the Court with additional Justices. That effort was defeated in Congress, though the attempt may have persuaded some Justices to alter their behavior. In recent years there have been movements in Congress to deprive federal courts of JURISDICTION over cases involving such matters as abortion, SCHOOL BUSING, and school prayer (see RELIGION IN PUBLIC SCHOOLS)—topics on which the Court's decisions have angered strong and articulate constituencies.

The problem is the resolution of what Robert Dahl called the Madisonian dilemma. The United States was founded as a Madisonian system, one that allows majorities to govern wide and important areas of life simply because they are majorities, but that also holds that individuals have some freedoms that must be exempt from majority control. The dilemma is that neither the majority nor the minority can be trusted to define the proper spheres of democratic authority and individual liberty.

It is not at all clear that the Founders envisaged a leading role for the judiciary in the resolution of this dilemma, for they thought of the third branch as relatively insignificant. Over time, however, Americans have come to assume that the definition of majority power and minority freedom is primarily the func-

tion of the judiciary, most particularly the function of the Supreme Court. This assumption places a great responsibility upon constitutional theory. America's basic method of policymaking is majoritarian. Thus, to justify exercise of a power to set at naught the considered decisions of elected representatives, judges must achieve, in ALEXANDER BICKEL's phrase, "a rigorous general accord between JUDICIAL SUPREMACY and democratic theory, so that the boundaries of the one could be described with some precision in terms of the other." At one time, an accord was based on the understanding that judges followed the intentions of the Framers and ratifiers of the Constitution, a legal document enacted by majorities, though subject to alteration only by supermajorities. A conflict between democracy and judicial review did not arise because the respective areas of each were specified and intended to be inviolate. Though this obedience to original intent was occasionally more pretense than reality, the accord was achieved in theory, and that theory stated an ideal to which courts were expected to conform. That is no longer so. Many judges and scholars now believe that the courts' obligations to intent are so highly generalized and remote that judges are in fact free to create the Constitution they think appropriate to today's society. The result is that the accord no longer stands even theoretically. The increasing perception that this is so raises the question of what elected officials can do to reclaim authority they regard as wrongfully taken by the judiciary.

There appear to be two possible responses to a judiciary that has overstepped the limits of its legitimate authority. One is political, the other intellectual. It seems tolerably clear that political responses are of limited usefulness, at least in the short run. Impeachment and Court-packing, having failed in the past, are unlikely to be resorted to again. Amending the Constitution to correct judicial overreaching is such a difficult and laborious process (requiring either two-thirds of both houses of Congress or an application for a convention by the legislatures of two-thirds of the states, followed, in either case, by ratification by three-fourths of the states) that it is of little practical assistance. It is sometimes proposed that Congress deal with the problem by removing federal court jurisdiction, using the exceptions clause of Article III of the Constitution in the case of the Supreme Court. The constitutionality of this approach has been much debated, but, in any case, it will often prove not feasible. Removal of all federal court jurisdiction would not return final power either to Congress or to state legislatures but to fifty state court systems. Thus, as a practical matter, this device could not be used as to any subject where national uniformity of constitutional law is necessary or highly desirable. Moreover, jurisdiction removal does not vindicate democratic governance, for it merely shifts ultimate power to different groups of judges. Democratic responses to judicial excesses probably must come through the replacement of judges who die or retire with new judges of different views. But this is a slow and uncertain process, the accidents of mortality being what they are and prediction of what new judges will do being so perilous.

The fact is that there exist few, if any, usable and effective techniques by which federal courts can be kept within constitutional bounds. A Constitution that provides numerous CHECKS AND BALANCES between President and Congress provides little to curb a judiciary that expands its powers beyond the allowable meaning of the Constitution. Perhaps one reason is that the Framers, though many of them foresaw that the Supreme Court would review laws for constitutionality, had little experience with such a function. They did not remotely foresee what the power of judicial review was capable of becoming. Nor is it clear that an institutional check—such as Senator ROBERT LA FOLLETTE's proposal to amend the Constitution so that Congress could override a Supreme Court decision by a two-thirds majority—would be desirable. Congress is less likely than the Court to be versed in the Constitution. La Follette's proposal could conceivably wreak as much or more damage to the Court's legitimate powers as it might accomplish in restraining its excesses. That must be reckoned at least a possibility with any of the institutional checks just discussed and is probably one of the reasons that they have rarely been used. In this sense, the Court's vulnerability is one of its most important protections.

If a political check on federal courts is unlikely to succeed, the only rein left is intellectual, the widespread acceptance of a theory of judicial review. After almost two centuries of constitutional adjudication, we appear to be further than ever from the possession of an adequate theory.

In the beginning, there was no controversy over theory. JOSEPH STORY, who was both an Associate Justice of the Supreme Court and the Dane Professor of Law at Harvard, could write in his *Commentaries on the Constitution of the United States,* published in 1833, that "I have not the ambition to be the author of any new plan of interpreting the theory of the Constitution, or of enlarging or narrowing its powers by ingenious subtleties and learned doubts." He thought that the job of constitutional judges was to interpret:

"The first and fundamental rule in the interpretation of all instruments is, to construe them according to the sense of the terms and the intention of the parties."

The performance of the courts has not always conformed to this interpretivist ideal. In the last decade or so of the nineteenth century and the first third of the twentieth the Supreme Court assiduously protected economic liberties from federal and state regulation, often in ways that could not be reconciled with the Constitution. The case that stands as the symbol of that era of judicial adventurism is LOCHNER V. NEW YORK (1905), which struck down the state's law regulating maximum hours for bakers. That era ended when Franklin D. Roosevelt's appointments remade the Court, and *Lochner* is now generally regarded as discredited.

But, if the Court stopped defending economic liberties without constitutional justification in the mid-1930s, it began in the mid-1950s to make other decisions for which it offered little or no constitutional argument. It had been generally assumed that constitutional questions were to be answered on grounds of historical intent, but the Court began to make decisions that could hardly be, and were not, justified on that basis. Existing constitutional protections were expanded and new ones created. Sizable minorities on the Court indicated a willingness to go still further. The widespread perception that the judiciary was re-creating the Constitution brought the tension between democracy and judicial review once more to a state of intellectual and political crisis.

Much of the new judicial power claimed cannot be derived from the text, structure, or history of the Constitution. Perhaps because of the increasing obviousness of this fact, legal scholars began to erect new theories of the judicial role. These constructs, which appear to be accepted by a majority of those who write about constitutional theory, go by the general name of noninterpretivism. They hold that mere interpretation of the Constitution may be impossible and is certainly inadequate. Judges are assigned not the task of defining the meanings and contours of values found in the historical Constitution but rather the function of creating new values and hence new rights for individuals against majorities. These new values are variously described as arising from "the evolving morality of our tradition," our "conventional morality" as discerned by "the method of philosophy," a "fusion of constitutional law and moral theory," or a HIGHER LAW of "unwritten NATURAL RIGHTS." One author has argued that, since "no defensible criteria" exist "to assess theories of judicial review," the judge should enforce his conception of the good. In all cases, these theories purport to empower judges to override majority will for extraconstitutional reasons.

Judges have articulated theories of their role no less removed from interpretation than those of the noninterpretivist academics. Writing for the Court in GRISWOLD V. CONNECTICUT (1965), Justice WILLIAM O. DOUGLAS created a constitutional RIGHT OF PRIVACY that invalidated the state's law against the use of contraceptives. He observed that many provisions of the BILL OF RIGHTS could be viewed as protections of aspects of personal privacy. These provisions were said to add up to a zone of constitutionally secured privacy that did not fall within any particular provision. The scope of this new right was not defined, but the Court has used the concept in a series of cases since, the most controversial being ROE V. WADE (1973). (See JUDICIAL ACTIVISM AND SELF-RESTRAINT.)

A similar strategy for the creation of new rights was outlined by Justice WILLIAM J. BRENNAN in a 1985 address. He characterized the Constitution as being pervasively concerned with human dignity. From this, Justice Brennan drew a more general judicial function of enhancing human dignity, one not confined by the clauses in question and, indeed, capable of nullifying what those clauses reveal of the Framers' intentions. Thus, the address states that continued judicial tolerance of CAPITAL PUNISHMENT causes us to "fall short of the constitutional vision of human dignity." For that reason, Justice Brennan continues to vote that capital punishment violates the Constitution. The potency of this method of generalizing from particular clauses, and then applying the generalization instead of the clauses, may be seen in the fact that it leads to a declaration of the unconstitutionality of a punishment explicitly assumed to be available three times in the Fifth Amendment to the Constitution and once again, some seventy-seven years later, in the FOURTEENTH AMENDMENT. By conventional methods of interpretation, it would be impossible to use the Constitution to prohibits that which the Constitution explicitly assumes to be lawful.

Because noninterpretive philosophies have little hard intellectual structure, it is impossible to control them or to predict from any inner logic or principle what they may require. Though it is regularly denied that a return to the judicial function as exemplified in *Lochner v. New York* is underway or, which comes to the same thing, that decisions are rooted only in the judges' moral predilections, it is difficult to see what else can be involved once the function of searching for the Framers' intent is abandoned. When con-

stitutional adjudication proceeds in a noninterpretive manner, the Court necessarily imposes new values upon the society. They are new in the sense that they cannot be derived by interpretation of the historical Constitution. Moreover, they must rest upon the moral predilections of the judge because the values come out of the moral view that most of us, by definition (since we voted democratically for a different result), do not accept.

This mode of adjudication makes impossible any general accord between judicial supremacy and democratic theory. Instead, it brings the two into head-on conflict. The Constitution specifies certain liberties and allocates all else to democratic processes. Noninterpretivism gives the judge power to invade the province of democracy whenever majority morality conflicts with his own. That is impossible to square either with democratic theory or the concept of law. Attempts have, nonetheless, been made to reconcile, or at least to mitigate, the contradiction. One line of argument is that any society requires a mixture of principle and expediency, that courts are better than legislatures at discerning and formulating principle, and hence may intervene when principle has been inadequately served by the legislative process. Even if one assumes that courts have superior institutional capacities in this respect, which is by no means clear, the conclusion does not follow. By placing certain subjects in the legislative arena, the Constitution holds that the tradeoff between principle and expediency we are entitled to is what the legislature provides. Courts have no mandate to impose a different result merely because they would arrive at a tradeoff that weighed principle more heavily or that took an altogether different value into account.

A different reconciliation of democracy and noninterpretive judicial review begins with the proposition that the Supreme Court is not really final because popular sentiment can in the long run cause it to be overturned. As we know from history, however, it may take decades to overturn a decision, so that it will be final for many people. Even then an overruling probably cannot be forced if a substantial minority ardently supports the result.

To the degree, then, that the Constitution is not treated as law to be interpreted in conventional fashion, the clash between democracy and judicial review is real. It is also serious. When the judiciary imposes upon democracy limits not to be found in the Constitution, it deprives Americans of a right that is found there, the right to make the laws to govern themselves. Moreover, as courts intervene more frequently to set aside majoritarian outcomes, they teach the lesson that democratic processes are suspect, essentially unprincipled and untrustworthy.

The main charge against a strictly interpretive approach to the Constitution is that the Framers' intentions cannot be known because they could not foresee the changed circumstances of our time. The argument proves too much. If it were true, the judge would be left without any law to apply, and there would be no basis for judicial review.

But that is not what is involved. From the text, the structure, and the history of the Constitution we can usually learn at least the core values the Framers intended to protect. Interpreting the Constitution means discerning the principle the Framers wanted to enact and applying it to today's circumstances. As John Hart Ely put it, interpretivism holds that "the work of the political branches is to be invalidated only in accord with an inference whose starting point, whose underlying premise, is fairly discoverable in the Constitution. That the complete inference will not be found there—because the situation is not likely to have been foreseen—is generally common ground."

This, of course, requires that constitutional DOCTRINE evolve over time. Most doctrine is merely the judge-made superstructure that implements basic constitutional principles, and, because circumstances change, the evolution of doctrine is inevitable. The FOURTH AMENDMENT was framed by men who did not foresee electronic surveillance, but judges may properly apply the central value of that amendment to electronic invasions of personal privacy. The difference between this method and that endorsed by Justices Douglas and Brennan lies in the level of generality employed. Adapting the Fourth Amendment requires the judge merely to recognize a new method of governmental search of one's property. The Justices, on the other hand, create a right so general that it effectively becomes a new clause of the Constitution, one that gives courts no guidance in its application. Modifying doctrine to preserve a value already embedded in the Constitution is an enterprise wholly different in nature from creating new values.

The debate over the legitimate role of the judiciary is likely to continue for some years. Noninterpretivists have not as yet presented an adequate theoretical justification for a judiciary that creates rather than interprets the Constitution. The task of interpretation is often complex and difficult, but it remains the only model of the judicial role that achieves an accord between democracy and judicial review.

ROBERT H. BORK

Bibliography

AGRESTO, JOHN 1984 *The Supreme Court and Constitutional Democracy.* Ithaca, N.Y.: Cornell University Press.

BICKEL, ALEXANDER M. 1962 *The Least Dangerous Branch: The Supreme Court at the Bar of Politics.* Indianapolis: Bobbs-Merrill.

BORK, ROBERT H. 1985 Styles in Constitutional Theory. *South Texas Law Journal* 26:383–395.

CHOPER, JESSE 1980 *Judicial Review and the National Political Process.* Chicago: University of Chicago Press.

ELY, JOHN HART 1980 *Democracy and Distrust: A Theory of Judicial Review.* Cambridge, Mass.: Harvard University Press.

LEVY, LEONARD W., ed. 1967 *Judicial Review and the Supreme Court.* New York: Harper & Row.

JUDICIAL STRATEGY

That judges shape much public policy is a fact of political life. The significant questions are how, how often, how effectively, and how wisely they influence policy. Each of these inquiries poses normative as well as empirical problems. Here we shall be concerned only with legitimate strategies that a Justice of the United States Supreme Court can employ to maximize his or her influence. We shall focus mainly on marshalling the Court.

A Justice, like any strategist, must coordinate limited resources to achieve goals. He or she must make choices—about goals and priorities among goals and also about means to achieve those goals. Intelligent choices among means depend in part on accurate assessments of the resources the Justice controls and of the limitations that others may impose on use of those resources.

The Justices can order litigants, including government officials, to act or not act in specified ways. Less tangibly, judges also have the prestige of their office, supported by a general cultural ethos of respect for the RULE OF LAW. In particular, a Justice has a powerful weapon, an opinion—a document that will be widely distributed by the Government Printing Office and several private firms. That opinion will justify— well or poorly—a particular decision and, explicitly or implicitly, the public policy it supports.

A Justice's power is limited by the nature of judicial institutions. Judges lack self-starters. Someone has to bring a case to them. Furthermore, while they can hold acts of other public officials constitutional or unconstitutional and so allow or forbid particular policies, it is much more difficult for judges to compel government to act. The Supreme Court can rule that blacks are entitled to vote, but it cannot force Congress to pass a CIVIL RIGHTS law to make that right effective. Moreover, the Court can hear only a limited number of cases. It depends on thousands of state and federal judges to carry out its jurisprudence. And no Justice plays an *official* role in selecting, retaining, or promoting judges.

Second, a Supreme Court Justice needs the agreement of at least four colleagues. And each Justice can write a separate opinion, dissenting or concurring, in any case.

Third, and more broadly, the Court is dependent on Congress and the President for appropriations and enforcement of decisions. Each of these branches has other important checks: The House can impeach and the Senate can then remove a Justice. Congress can increase the size of the Court, remove at least part of its APPELLATE JURISDICTION, propose constitutional amendments to erase the effects of decisions or strike at judicial power itself, and use its access to mass media to challenge the Court's prestige. The President can even more effectively attack the Court's prestige, and he can persuade Congress to use any of its weapons against the Justices. He can also choose new judges who, he hopes, will change the course of CONSTITUTIONAL INTERPRETATION.

Fourth, state officials can influence public opinion to pressure Congress and the President. State officers can also drag their heels in carrying out judicial decisions and select judges who are hostile to the Court's jurisprudence.

Fifth, leaders of interest groups can pressure elected officials at all levels of government. And when judicial decisions threaten or support their values, these people seldom hesitate to apply whatever political leverage is in their self-interest.

Commentators—journalists and social scientists as well as law professors—constitute a sixth check. If judges make law, EDWARD S. CORWIN said, so do commentators. Justices who want their jurisprudence to endure must look not only to immediate reactions but also to the future. What commentators write may influence later generations of voters, lawyers, and public officials.

A Justice confronts these limitations simultaneously, and each of these groups will include a range of opinion. Any ruling will elate some and infuriate others, and the political power of various factions is likely to vary widely. In short, problems of synchronizing activities are always present and are typically complex.

The first audience a Justice must convince is composed of other Justices. The most obvious way of having one's views accepted by one's colleagues is to have colleagues who agree with one's views. Thus ability to influence the recruiting process is a difficult but fruitful means of maximizing influence. (See APPOINTMENT OF SUPREME COURT JUSTICES.) Justices who cannot choose their colleagues must consider how to persuade them.

Although treating others with courtesy may never change a vote or modify an opinion, it does make it more likely that others will listen. When others listen, intellectual capacity becomes critical. The Justice who knows "the law," speaks succinctly, writes clearly, and analyzes wisely gains distinct advantages.

Practical experience can be a valuable adjunct. Logic is concerned with relations among propositions, not with their desirability or social utility. According to WILLIAM O. DOUGLAS, several Justices were converted to Chief Justice EARL WARREN's position in BROWN V. BOARD OF EDUCATION (1954) because of his vast political experience. Strength of character is also crucial. Although neither learned nor gifted as a writer, Warren led the Court and the country through a constitutional revolution. It was his "passion for justice," his massive integrity, Douglas also recalled, that made Warren such a forceful leader. "Is it right?" was his typical question, not "Do earlier decisions allow it?"

In another sense, intellect alone is unlikely to suffice. Justices are all apt to be intelligent, strong-willed people with divergent views about earlier rulings as well as public policy. They are also apt to differ about the Court's proper roles in the political system—in sum, about fundamentals of jurisprudence. At that level of dispute, it is improbable that one Justice, no matter how astute and eloquent, will convert another.

Facing disagreements that cannot be intellectually reconciled, a Justice may opt for several courses. Basically, he can negotiate with his colleagues or go it alone. Most often, it will be prudent to negotiate. Like policymaking, negotiation, even bargaining, is a fact of judicial life. Writing the opinion of the Court requires "an orchestral, not a solo performance." All Justices can utilize their votes and freedom to write separate opinions. The value of each depends upon the circumstances. If the Court divides 4–4, the ninth Justice, in effect, decides the case. On the other hand, when the Court votes 8–0, the ninth Justice's ability to negotiate will depend almost totally on his capacity to write a separate opinion that, the others fear, would undermine their position.

To be effective, negotiations must be restrained and sensitive. Justices are likely to sit together for many years. Driving a hard bargain today may damage future relations. The mores of the Court forbid trading of votes. The Justices take their oaths of office seriously; and, while reality pushes them toward accommodation, they are not hagglers in a market, peddling their views.

The most common channels of negotiating are circulation of draft opinions, comments on those drafts, and private conversations. A Justice can nudge others, especially the judge assigned the task of producing the OPINION OF THE COURT, by suggesting additions, deletions, and rephrasings. In turn, to retain a majority, the opinion writer must be willing to accede to many suggestions, even painful ones, as he tries to persuade the Court to accept the core of his reasoning. OLIVER WENDELL HOLMES once complained that "the boys generally cut one of the genitals" out of his drafts, and he made no claim to have restored their manhood.

Drafts and discussions of opinions can and do change votes, even outcomes. Sometimes those changes are not in the intended direction. After reading FELIX FRANKFURTER's dissent in BAKER V. CARR (1961), TOM C. CLARK changed his vote, remarking that if those were the reasons for dissenting he would join the majority.

Although the art of negotiation is essential, a Justice should not wish to appear so malleable as to encourage efforts to dilute his jurisprudence. He would much prefer a reputation of being reasonable but tough-minded. He thus might sometimes find it wise to stand alone rather than even attempt compromise. It is usually prudent for a Justice, when with the majority, to inject as many of his views as possible into the Court's opinion, and when with the minority to squeeze as many hostile ideas as possible out of the Court's opinion. There are, however, times when both conscience and prudence counsel standing alone, appealing to officials in other governmental processes or to future judges to vindicate his jurisprudence.

Although Justices have very limited authority to make the other branches of government act, they are not powerless. Judges can often find more in a statute than legislators believe they put there. OBITER DICTA in an opinion can also prod other officials to follow the "proper" path. The Court might even pursue a dangerous course that might push a reluctant President to carry out its decisions lest he seem either indifferent to the rule of law or unprotective of federal power against state challenges.

Lobbying with either branch is also possible. Indeed, judicial lobbying has a venerable history running back to JOHN JAY. Advice delivered through third parties may have been even more common. Over time, however, expectations of judicial conduct have risen so that even a hint of such activity triggers an outcry. Thus a judge must heavily discount the benefits of direct or indirect contacts by the probability of their being discovered.

The most obvious weapon that a Justice has against unwelcome political action is the ability to persuade his colleagues to declare that action unconstitutional or, if it comes in the shape of a federal statute or EXECUTIVE ORDER, to disarm it by interpretation. These are the Court's ultimate weapons, and their overuse or use at the wrong time might provoke massive retaliation.

A Justice must therefore consider more indirect means. Delay is the tactic that procedural rules most readily permit. The Justices can deny a WRIT OF CERTIORARI, dismiss an APPEAL, REMAND the case for clarification, order reargument, or use a dozen other tactics to delay deciding volatile disputes until the political climate changes.

Under other circumstances, it might be more prudent for a Justice to move the Court step by step. Gradual erosion of old rules and accretion of new ones may win more adherents than sudden statements of novel DOCTRINES. The Court's treatment of segregation provides an excellent illustration. If MISSOURI EX REL. GAINES V. CANADA (1938) had struck down SEPARATE BUT EQUAL, the Court could never have made the decision stick. Indeed, years later, when it excommunicated Jim Crow, enforcement created a generation of litigation that still continues.

Strategy is concerned with efficient utilization of scarce resources to achieve important objectives. Its domain is that of patience and prudence, not of wisdom in choosing among goals nor of courage in fighting for the right. The messages that a study of judicial strategy yields are: A web of checks restrains a judge's power; and If he or she wishes to maximize his or her ability to do good, a judge must learn to cope with those restrictions, to work within and around them, and to conserve available resources for the times when he or she must, as a matter of conscience, directly challenge what he or she sees as a threat to the basic values of constitutional democracy.

WALTER F. MURPHY

Bibliography

BICKEL, ALEXANDER M. 1957 *The Unpublished Opinions of Mr. Justice Brandeis.* Cambridge, Mass.: Harvard University Press.

———— 1961 The Passive Virtues. *Harvard Law Review* 75:40–79.

DOUGLAS, WILLIAM O. 1980 *The Court Years, 1939–1975.* New York: Random House.

KLUGER, RICHARD 1976 *Simple Justice.* New York: Knopf.

MURPHY, BRUCE 1982 *The Brandeis/Frankfurter Connection.* New York: Oxford University Press.

MURPHY, WALTER F. 1964 *Elements of Judicial Strategy.* Chicago: University of Chicago Press.

O'BRIEN, DAVID M. 1986 *Storm Center: The Supreme Court in American Politics.* New York: Norton.

JUDICIAL SUPREMACY

Stripped of the partisan rhetoric that usually surrounds important decisions of the Supreme Court, debate about judicial supremacy raises a fundamental question: Who is the final, authoritative interpreter of the Constitution? The response of judicial supremacy is that courts perform that function and other officials are bound not only to respect judges' decisions in particular cases but also, in formulating future public policy, to follow the general principles judges have laid down.

JUDICIAL REVIEW does not necessarily entail or logically imply judicial supremacy. One can, as THOMAS JEFFERSON did, concede the legitimacy of courts' refusing on constitutional grounds to enforce statutes and EXECUTIVE ORDERS and still deny either that officials of a coordinate branch must obey a decision or follow its rationale in the future. This view, called "departmentalism," sees the three branches of the national government as equal in CONSTITUTIONAL INTERPRETATION: Each department has authority to interpret the Constitution for itself, but its interpretations do not bind the other two.

There are other possible answers to the basic question: Congress, the President, the states, or the people. A claim for the states presupposes the Constitution to be a compact among sovereign entities who reserved to themselves authority to construe their obligations. Such was Jefferson's assertion in the KENTUCKY RESOLUTIONS (1798), and it echoed down decades of dreary debates on NULLIFICATION and SECESSION. The Civil War settled the matter, though some southern states briefly tried to resurrect nullification to oppose BROWN V. BOARD OF EDUCATION (1954).

A claim for the President as the ultimate, authoritative interpreter smacks too much of royalty for the idea to have been seriously maintained. On the other hand, Presidents have frequently and effectively defended their independent authority to interpret the Constitution for the executive department.

A case for the people as the final, authoritative interpreter permeates the debate. American government rests on popular consent. The people can elect officials to amend the Constitution or create a new constitution and so shape basic political arrangements as well as concrete public policies. Jefferson advocated constitutional conventions as a means of popular judging between conflicting departmental interpretations.

Although even JAMES MADISON rejected Jefferson's solution, indirect appeals to the people as the ultimate interpreters are reflected in claims to the supremacy of a popularly elected legislature. On the other hand, in THE FEDERALIST #78, ALEXANDER HAMILTON rested his argument for judicial review on the authority of the people who have declared their will in the Constitution. Judicial review, he argued, does not imply that judges are superior to legislators but that "the power of the people is superior to both."

Although JOHN MARSHALL partially incorporated this line of reasoning in MARBURY V. MADISON (1803), neither he nor Hamilton ever explicitly asserted that the Supreme Court's interpretation of the Constitution was binding on other branches of the federal government. One might, however, infer that conclusion from Marshall's opinions in *Marbury* and in *McCulloch v. Maryland* (1819), where he expressly claimed supremacy as far as state governments were concerned.

We know little of the Framers' attitudes toward judicial supremacy. In *The Federalist* #51, Madison took a clear departmentalist stand, as he did in the First Congress. In 1788 Madison wrote a friend that the new Constitution made no provision for settling differences among departments' interpretations: "[A]nd as ye Courts are generally the last in making the decision, it results to them by refusing or not refusing to execute a law, to stamp it with its final character. This makes the Judiciary Dept paramount in fact to the Legislature, which was never intended and can never be proper."

In the Senate in 1802, however, GOUVERNEUR MORRIS argued that the judges derived their power to decide on the constitutionality of laws "from authority higher than this Constitution. They derive it from the constitution of man, from the nature of things, from the necessary progress of human affairs. The decision of the Supreme Court is and, of necessity, must be final."

What turns a brief for judicial review into one for judicial supremacy is, of course, the claim of finality. Partially, that claim rests on the notion that interpretation of law is a uniquely judicial function (and, by its own terms, the Constitution is "the supreme law"); partially, on the ambiguity of the Constitution about the interpretive authority of other branches; and partially on the need for a supreme arbiter to assure the supremacy and uniform interpretations of the Constitution. The claim also rests on the belief that judges, because they are protected from popular pressures, are more apt to act fairly and coherently than elected officials. "It is only from the Supreme Court," CHARLES EVANS HUGHES once asserted, "that we can obtain a sane, well-ordered interpretation of the Constitution." The Court itself has seldom explicitly claimed judicial supremacy and has never articulated a full argument for it vis-à-vis Congress or the President. Indeed, through such DOCTRINES as the presumption of constitutionality and POLITICAL QUESTIONS, the Court often defers to interpretations by other departments.

The first modern, categorical claim by the Court to supremacy came in COOPER V. AARON (1958), where the Justices said that "the federal judiciary is supreme in the exposition of the law of the Constitution," and thus that *Brown v. Board of Education* was "the supreme law of the land." But *Cooper* involved state officials as did BAKER V. CARR (1962), where the Court first referred to itself as the "ultimate interpreter of the Constitution." Still, it was not until POWELL V. MCCORMACK (1969) that the Court so designated itself in a dispute involving Congress, an assertion the Justices repeated about the President in UNITED STATES V. NIXON (1974) and about both in IMMIGRATION AND NATURALIZATION SERVICE V. CHADHA (1983). *Powell,* however, addressed only the authority of the House to exclude a duly elected member and it did not require that he be readmitted or be given back pay. *Nixon* upheld a SUBPOENA to a President whose political situation was already desperate. What would have happened to the Court's claim as "ultimate interpreter" had it faced a politically secure chief executive in *Nixon* or tried to force Congress to take action in *Powell* might well have produced examples of departmentalism, as did Jefferson's refusal to obey Marshall's subpoena in UNITED STATES V. BURR (1807). And early congressional reactions to *Chadha's* declaring the LEGISLATIVE VETO unconstitutional have been mixed. Formally as well as informally, Congress has continued the practice, though in a more guarded fashion and on a smaller scale.

Although the constitutional text does not require judicial supremacy, Congress and the President have usually gone along with the Court's constitutional interpretations. Yet the exceptions have been sufficiently frequent and important that it is difficult to demonstrate a firm tradition requiring coordinate federal branches to accept the Court's doctrines. In matters strictly judicial—whether or not courts will enforce particular statutes—judges have been supreme, though subject to checks regarding JURISDICTION and appointment of new personnel. The other branches, however, have frequently denied that they have an obligation, when setting policy, to follow the Court's constitutional interpretations.

There is a stronger argument for a duty of enforcing a judicial decision in a particular case. Certainly where the government has brought the case to the courts, an obligation to obey is obvious, as even Jefferson admitted. Where, however, the government is the defendant, the matter is much more complicated, especially when a court commands an official to perform a positive action. Jefferson and ANDREW JACKSON said they had no duty to obey such orders; ABRAHAM LINCOLN acted as if he did not; and FRANKLIN D. ROOSEVELT was prepared to ignore the GOLD CLAUSE CASES (1934) had they been decided against the government.

Typically, Congress and the President acquiesce in judicial interpretations of the Constitution because they agree with the results of judicial decisions, or fear public opinion, or recognize the difficulty of securing a congressional response. Often, too, the Justices reinforce Congress's tendency toward inertia by not pressing a claim to supremacy. Always hovering in the background of any department's assertion of supremacy is the possibility of an appeal to "the people" through the AMENDING PROCESS. Yet even such an appeal, when directed against the Court's jurisprudence, implies an admission of the tactical if not theoretical superiority of the Court as constitutional interpreter.

WALTER F. MURPHY

Bibliography

CORWIN, EDWARD S. 1914 *Marbury v. Madison* and the Doctrine of Judicial Review. *Michigan Law Review* 12:538–572.

FISHER, LOUIS 1985 Constitutional Interpretation by Members of Congress. *North Carolina Law Review* 63:701–741.

MIKVA, ABNER J. 1983 How Well Does Congress Support and Defend the Constitution? *North Carolina Law Review* 61:587–611.

MURPHY, WALTER F.; FLEMING, JAMES E.; and HARRIS, WILLIAM F., II 1986 *American Constitutional Interpretation.* Chaps. 6–7. Mineola, N.Y.: Foundation Press.

JUDICIAL SYSTEM, FEDERAL

The charter of the federal judicial system is Article III of the Constitution, authorizing the creation of federal tribunals vested with the JUDICIAL POWER OF

THE UNITED STATES, that is, the authority to adjudicate a specifically enumerated set of CASES AND CONTROVERSIES. Article III also specifies the method of appointment of federal judges and lays down rules designed to guard their independence.

The Framers, mindful of the problems that the absence of a national judiciary had caused under the ARTICLES OF CONFEDERATION, easily agreed that there must be a national Supreme Court with power to assure the uniformity and supremacy of federal law. But the Framers were divided over the question whether further provision should be made for national courts. Some favored the creation of a complete system of federal courts. Some thought that this would unnecessarily narrow the preexisting general JURISDICTION of the state courts; they argued that national interests could be sufficiently protected by providing for Supreme Court review of state court decisions involving questions of federal law. This division was settled by a compromise: Article III itself mandates that there shall be "one Supreme Court"; but beyond this the federal judicial power is simply vested in "such inferior Courts as the Congress may from time to time ordain and establish."

Article III specifies that the Supreme Court (and whatever inferior federal courts Congress may establish) are to be courts of a strictly limited jurisdiction: they may adjudicate only nine enumerated categories of cases. Some of these were included because they touch on issues of national interest: most important, cases "arising under" the Constitution and laws of the United States (the FEDERAL QUESTION JURISDICTION); cases of ADMIRALTY AND MARITIME JURISDICTION; and cases to which the United States is a party. Federal courts were also empowered to decide certain controversies implicating the nation's FOREIGN AFFAIRS (for example, disputes affecting ambassadors and other alien parties; cases arising under treaties). The remaining categories authorize the federal courts to engage in interstate umpiring in cases where it was feared that parochial interests would prevail in the state courts. Examples are controversies between states, between a state and a citizen of another state, and between citizens of different states.

Article III's specification that the judicial power consists of adjudicating "cases" or "controversies" itself embodies a fundamental political decision: the national courts were to exercise only a judicial power. Thus the CONSTITUTIONAL CONVENTION OF 1787 repeatedly and explicitly rejected a variety of proposals to allow federal courts or judges to participate as advisers or revisers in the legislative process or to render ADVISORY OPINIONS; their authority was to be limited to "cases of a judiciary nature." On the other hand, the historical evidence establishes the Framers' understanding that the grant of the judicial power was to include the authority, where necessary to the lawful decision of a case properly within a court's jurisdiction, to disregard federal or state statutes found to be unconstitutional. This power of JUDICIAL REVIEW, occasionally challenged as a usurpation because it is not explicitly mentioned in Article III, has been settled since MARBURY V. MADISON (1803).

Besides defining the outer bounds of the federal judicial power, Article III protects federal judges from political pressures by guaranteeing tenure during GOOD BEHAVIOR without reduction in compensation.

Article III is not self-executing; it needs LEGISLATION to bring it to life, most particularly because Congress must determine whether there should be "inferior" federal courts and what should be the scope of their jurisdiction. It is to this task that the First Congress turned in its twentieth enactment: the seminal JUDICIARY ACT OF 1789. Obeying the Constitution's command, the act constituted a Supreme Court, consisting of a CHIEF JUSTICE and five associates. Next, the act, establishing a tradition persisting without interruption to this day, took up the constitutional option to create a system of federal courts of ORIGINAL JURISDICTION. The structure created was curious, but survived for a century. The country was divided into districts (at least one for each state), with a district court manned by a district judge. In addition, the country was divided into circuits (originally three), each with another trial court—a CIRCUIT COURT —manned not by its own judges but by two Supreme Court Justices (sitting "on circuit") and a district judge.

Only a fraction of the constitutional potential for original federal court jurisdiction was exploited by the first Judiciary Act, attesting to the clear contemporaneous understanding of the Constitution that it is for Congress to determine which (if any) of the cases and controversies encompassed by the federal judicial power should be adjudicated in the first instance in a lower federal (rather than a state) court. (The modest original jurisdiction of the Supreme Court, limited to controversies where a state is a party and certain cases involving foreign diplomats, is thought to flow "directly" from the Constitution and thus represents a special case.) The district courts were given the jurisdiction most clearly felt to be a national one: authority to adjudicate admiralty cases. In a controversial decision, the First Congress set a precedent by opening the circuit courts to some cases involving controversies between citizens of different states and involving

ALIENS. The federal trial courts were also granted jurisdiction over most civil suits brought by the United States and over the then negligible federal criminal caseload. Notably, the act did not give the federal trial courts jurisdiction over cases "arising under" federal law, leaving these to be adjudicated in the state courts.

The appellate structure of the new court system was rudimentary. Federal criminal cases were left without direct review (and remained so for a century). The circuit courts were given a limited APPELLATE JURISDICTION over the district courts, and the Supreme Court was authorized to review civil cases decided by the circuit courts involving more than $2,000.

Finally, in its famous section 25, the act—consistent with the Framers' intention to assure the supremacy of federal law—gave the Supreme Court power to review final state court judgments rejecting claims of right or immunity under federal law. (State court judgments upholding claims of right under federal law were not made reviewable until 1914.) Supreme Court review of state judgments involving questions of federal law has been a feature of our judicial FEDERALISM ever since 1789, and has served as a profoundly significant instrument for consolidating and protecting national power.

The institutional structure created by the first Judiciary Act proved to be remarkably stable; major structural change did not come until 1891. The Supreme Court has had a continuous existence since 1789, with changes only in the number of Justices. So also have the district courts (though their number has of course undergone major change). Even the circuit courts—architecturally the weakest feature of the system—survived for more than a century.

As to the jurisdiction of the federal courts, changes were incremental in the pre-Civil War period, with the state courts acting as the primary enforcers of the still rudimentary corpus of national law. But the Civil War brought a sea change: Congress was no longer prepared to depend on the state judiciaries to enforce rights guaranteed by the new FOURTEENTH AMENDMENT and by the Reconstruction legislation. By the HABEAS CORPUS ACT of 1867 and the various CIVIL RIGHTS ACTS, Congress extended the lower federal courts' jurisdiction to include claims against state officials for invasion of federal constitutional and statutory rights. These extensions were in turn overtaken by the JUDICIARY ACT OF 1875, giving the federal courts a general jurisdiction to adjudicate civil cases arising under federal law, subject only to a minimum amount-in-controversy. These expansions,

supplemented by subsequent numerous specific extensions of federal trial jurisdiction over various sorts of actions involving national law, signaled the transformation of the federal courts from narrow forums designed to resolve maritime and certain interstate disputes into catholic tribunals playing a principal role in enforcing the growing body of national rights, privileges, and immunities.

The growth of the federal judicial business in the post-Civil War era placed an ever-growing pressure on the federal judicial system. The Supreme Court was especially burdened by the duties of circuit riding and by an increasing caseload. By 1890 the Court had a backlog of 1800 cases; in the same year, 54,194 cases were pending in the lower federal courts. Congress responded to the crisis in the CIRCUIT COURTS OF APPEALS ACT (Evarts Act) of 1891, which fixed the outline of the contemporary federal judicial system. The act established a system of intermediate appellate courts called Circuit Courts of Appeals (not to be confused with the old circuit courts, which were finally abolished in 1911), one for each of (the then) nine circuits and staffed with its own judges. Although a narrow category of district court decisions continued (and continue) to be reviewed directly by the Supreme Court, the Evarts Act created the standard modern practice: appeals went normally from the district courts to the new courts of appeals; the judgments of the latter were in turn reviewable by the Supreme Court.

The second major and seminal innovation of the Evarts Act related to appellate review in the Supreme Court: the act introduced the principle of review at the Court's own discretion (by writ of CERTIORARI) of judgments in the lower courts. This principle was in turn greatly expanded in the so-called Judges' Bill of 1925, which sharply reduced the availability of Supreme Court review as of right of decisions of state and federal courts and substituted for it discretionary review on certiorari—the method of review that, to this day, dominates the Court's docket.

Changes in the structure of the federal judicial system have been few and minor since 1925, although both the statutory jurisdiction and the business of the courts have undergone major transformations. In essence the system remains a three-tier system, with the district courts serving as the trial courts, the courts of appeals as the appellate tribunals of first instance, and the Supreme Court as the court of final review (having also the power to review state court decisions involving issues of federal law). The picture is completed by the existence of special federal tribunals empowered to decide particular categories of cases, and by numerous federal administrative tribunals; the decisions of all of these are typically subject to review in the regular federal courts.

The most important component of the contemporary statutory jurisdiction of the UNITED STATES DISTRICT COURTS encompasses diversity cases involving more than $10,000, criminal prosecutions and civil actions brought by the United States, a large range of actions against the United States and its agencies and officials, federal HABEAS CORPUS, and—most significant—all civil cases in which a plaintiff sues on a claim arising under the Constitution and laws of the United States. The latter, all-encompassing rubric includes not only cases brought pursuant to the hundreds of federal statutes specifying a right to sue but also the numerous cases where that right is a judge-created ("implied") right to enforce a federal statutory or—(of profound significance)—constitutional provision not itself explicitly containing a right of action. In addition, the statutes allow certain diversity and federal question cases brought in the state courts to be removed for trial to a federal district court. Finally, the district courts exercise a significant jurisdiction to review the work of many federal administrative agencies and to review and supervise the work of the system of bankruptcy courts. The jurisdiction of the district courts is occasionally specified as exclusive of the state courts (for example, admiralty, COPYRIGHT, and PATENT); most of their civil jurisdiction is, however, concurrent with that of the state courts.

The country is, in the mid-1980s, divided into ninety-seven districts (including the DISTRICT OF COLUMBIA and Puerto Rico). Each state has at least one district; districts have never encompassed more than one state. The district courts are staffed by 576 active district judges—almost three times the 1950 figure (182 new district judgeships were created between 1978 and 1984 alone). The growth in number of judges has, nevertheless, failed to keep pace with the explosive increase in the caseload that has occurred since the 1960s. In 1940 about 70,000 criminal and civil (nonbankruptcy) cases were filed in the federal courts; in 1960, about 80,000; by 1980, the figure was almost 200,000, and in 1984 it exceeded 275,000. (The compound annual rate of increase in the federal district court case load was under one percent between 1934 and 1960; it has been five percent since 1960.) The increase is due primarily and naturally to the vast growth in the total corpus of federal (constitutional, statutory, common, and administrative) law applied in turn to a growing country with an expansive and mobile economy. It has also been fed, however, in the past twenty-five years by congressional and court-

initiated changes in substantive and remedial rules that have made the federal courts into powerful litigation-attracting engines for the creation and expansion of rights and the redistribution of entitlements and powers in our society. Thus open-ended constitutional and statutory formulas have been used to fuel aggressive judicial review of the validity of federal and state legislative and administrative action and to create an expansive system of remedies against federal and state government (including affirmative claims on the resources of these governments). JUSTICIABILITY requirements (such as STANDING) that previously narrowed the scope of jurisdiction over public law actions have been significantly eroded. And federal court litigation has become increasingly attractive to plaintiffs as a result of provisions for attorneys' fees, the elimination (or inflation-caused erosion) of amount-in-controversy requirements, and the increasing use of CLASS ACTIONS.

These developments are reflected in the changing content of the federal district courts' workload. There were 6,000 suits against the United States in 1960, and almost 30,000 in 1983. There were only 300 CIVIL RIGHTS cases in 1960, almost 20,000 in 1983; 2,100 prisoner postconviction cases in 1960, more than 30,000 in 1983; 500 social security law cases in 1960, more than 20,000 in 1983. In general, about thirty-five to forty percent of the mid-1980s district court civil caseload involve the United States or its officials as a plaintiff or defendant; sixty to sixty-five percent of the civil caseload is "private" (including, however, litigation against state and local governments and officials). Diversity cases have contributed about twenty percent of the caseload since the 1970s. The number of criminal prosecutions has, historically, fluctuated widely in response to special federal programs (peaking during PROHIBITION); since the mid-1970s the criminal caseload has been quite stable and in the mid-1980s contributed about fifteen to twenty percent of the total.

In response to the explosive caseload Congress has acted to allow the district courts to rely substantially on the work of so-called federal magistrates—officials appointed by district judges with wide powers (subject to review by the district judge) to issue warrants, conduct preliminary hearings, try minor criminal offenses, supervise civil discovery, rule on preliminary motions and prisoner petitions, and (with the consent of the parties) even to hear and enter judgment generally in civil cases. The conferring of additional powers on magistrates has evoked controversy as well as some (so far unsuccessful) constitutional attacks.

The UNITED STATES COURTS OF APPEALS (as they

are now called) have jurisdiction to review all final (and some interlocutory) decisions of the district courts. Pursuant to special statutory provisions they also review some cases coming directly from federal administrative agencies (this being an especially significant component of the business of the Court of Appeals for the District of Columbia Circuit). About fifteen percent of their cases are criminal cases, and another fifteen percent are federal and state prisoner postconviction and civil rights cases; only fourteen percent of their docket consists of diversity cases.

The caseload of the courts of appeals has increased dramatically in the last twenty-five years and is, in the mid-1980s, commonly described as constituting a crisis. In the forty years before 1960 that caseload hovered between 1,500 and the peak of 3,700 reached in 1960. In 1970 the figure was almost 11,500, and in 1980 it was over 21,000. From 1980 to 1983 the caseload jumped again to 29,580. From 1960 to 1983 there was an increase of almost 800 percent in the number of appeals from the district courts; the compound annual rate of increase for all cases from 1960 to 1983 was 9.4 percent (compared to 0.5 percent in the preceding twenty-five years).

To manage this workload there exist (in the mid-1980s) twelve courts of appeals assigned to geographical circuits (eleven in the states and one for the District of Columbia) and an additional one (described below) for certain special categories of subject matter. The number of judges in each circuit ranges from six (First) to twenty-eight (Ninth). There are 156 authorized circuit judgeships; in 1960 there were sixty-eight (and as recently as 1978 only ninety-seven). Cases are typically heard by panels of three judges; a few cases of special importance are in turn reheard by the court sitting EN BANC. The increase in number of judges has by no means kept pace with the expansion of the caseload since 1960. As a result, there have been substantial changes in the procedures of these courts: opportunities for oral argument (and even for briefing) have been sharply curtailed and an increasing proportion of cases is disposed of summarily, without opinion. Central staff attorneys (as well as a growing army of conventional law clerks) assist the judges.

From the beginning of our national history Congress has perceived a need to create special tribunals for the adjudication of cases falling outside the traditional areas of federal court jurisdiction. Military tribunals have, from the outset, administered a special body of law through special procedures. The administration of justice in the TERRITORIES in transition toward statehood was perceived as requiring special temporary federal tribunals that would become state courts

upon statehood; the District of Columbia and the territories and dependencies of the United States also require a full panoply of special federal courts to administer local law. Beginning in 1855, with the establishment of a rudimentary Court of Claims, Congress has created a series of special tribunals to adjudicate money claims against the United States. And, particularly with the advent in this century of the modern administrative state, Congress has created numerous administrative agencies and tribunals whose business includes adjudication.

Unlike the ordinary federal courts, the institutional hallmark of most of these tribunals has been specialization. Further, the transitory nature of some of these tribunals, the perceived need to allow some of them to function inexpensively with expeditious or informal procedures, and (in the case of the administrative agencies) the equally strongly perceived need to endow them with a range of policymaking functions in addition to adjudicative functions, has typically led Congress to create them not as tribunals constituted under Article III (with lifetime judges performing an exclusively judicial function) but as special LEGISLATIVE COURTS or administrative tribunals. Their judges typically serve temporary terms and are removable for misfeasance without IMPEACHMENT. The constitutional authority for such tribunals has been much discussed and litigated; Congress's authority to constitute them has virtually always been upheld.

The most important specialized tribunals in the current federal judicial system are: the local courts of the District of Columbia, Puerto Rico, and the territories and dependencies; the system of military courts; the system of bankruptcy courts; the TAX COURT and the CLAIMS COURT, adjudicating certain tax refund claims and certain damage actions against the federal government; the Court of International Trade, adjudicating certain customs disputes; and a large and variegated array of administrative tribunals and agencies. The work of all of these tribunals is typically subject to review, through various forms of proceedings, in the regular federal courts.

In addition, in 1982 Congress created a thirteenth court of appeals, the UNITED STATES COURT OF APPEALS FOR THE FEDERAL CIRCUIT. This is a regular Article III court, whose jurisdiction is not territorial but is defined in terms of subject matter, including appeals from the Claims Court and the Court of International Trade and many patent and trademark cases.

Continuously since 1789 the Supreme Court has been the single institution with nationwide authority to supervise the inferior federal courts and to give voice to a uniform national law. The Court's size has varied from five to ten Justices; since 1869 it has consisted of a Chief Justice and eight associate Justices. The Supreme Court acts *en banc,* not in panels, though individual Justices have the conventional authority to issue stays and take emergency action. The Court acts by majority, but in this century the practice has been to grant a certiorari petition (setting the case for plenary review) if four Justices are in favor.

The caseload explosion in the lower federal courts has imposed major burdens on the Court. The Court disposed of over 4,000 cases in its 1983 term (compared to about 3,300 in 1970, 1,900 in 1960, and 1,200 in 1950). The task is possible because only a small number of cases (usually about 150) are decided on the merits by full opinion after plenary briefing and oral argument. Another 100 to 150 cases are decided on the merits by MEMORANDUM ORDER. The remaining dispositions consist of summary denials of petitions for certiorari (or other writs); there were almost 3,900 of these in 1983–1984. In 1960 there were just under 2,000 new cases docketed in the Court; in 1970, about 3,400; in 1983, about 4,200. The increase in cases docketed means more and more resources devoted to "screening" cases for decision and less to the hearing and disposition of cases on the merits. Thus the time devoted to oral argument has shrunk steadily in this century and now almost never exceeds one hour per case. The length of briefs is limited; and an ever-growing battery of law CLERKS assists in legal research and in the drafting of opinions.

The content of the Court's work reflects the scope and content of the national law. In the 1983 term the Court's decisions by full opinion included three cases within the original jurisdiction; ninety-six civil cases coming from the lower federal courts (of which forty-six involved the federal government, twenty-eight involved state and local governments, and twenty-two were private cases); sixteen federal habeas corpus cases; and thirty-two cases from the state courts (eighteen civil and fourteen criminal). Diversity cases are rarely reviewed. The Court is, increasingly, a constitutional court; about half of its cases tend to involve a constitutional question as the (or a) principal issue. The United States (as party or AMICUS CURIAE) participates in over half of the cases that the Court decides on the merits.

Although the federal judicial system has grown substantially in its 200 years, the federal courts continue to constitute only a small—though disproportionately powerful—component of the American judicial system. (Fewer than three percent of the country's judges are federal Article III judges; the biggest states have judicial systems larger than the federal system.)

The relations between state and federal courts are multifarious and exceedingly complex. Except where Congress has specified that federal court jurisdiction is exclusive, state courts of general jurisdiction exercise a normal competence to adjudicate cases involving issues of federal law (particularly in that many such issues arise by way of defense in civil and criminal cases arising under state law). Their decisions of these cases are subject to Supreme Court review, usually on certiorari; but that Court's jurisdiction in such a case is limited to the federal question in the case and may not be exercised at all if the judgment rests on a valid and dispositive state-law ground. State court judgments on issues of federal law (unless reversed by the Supreme Court) have normal RES JUDICATA effect.

The federal district courts, in turn, adjudicate many questions of state law, not only in diversity cases but also in cases arising under federal law where state law governs one or more issues. No provision for review by the state courts of the correctness of federal court decisions on issues of state law has ever existed; but in a narrow class of cases federal courts will abstain from exercising an otherwise proper federal jurisdiction in order to allow a state law issue to be determined in the state courts. (See ABSTENTION DOCTRINE.) Under the decision in ERIE RAILROAD V. TOMPKINS (1938), on issues of state law (including issues of state common law) state court precedents are accepted as authoritative by the federal courts.

Special problems are presented by the politically sensitive role of the federal courts in controlling the legality of the actions of state and local governments and their officials. Although the ELEVENTH AMENDMENT bars the federal courts from asserting jurisdiction over actions against a state as such, a wide range of remedies against state and local governments and their officials exist in the federal courts. Federal courts routinely review the constitutional validity of state criminal convictions through the writ of habeas corpus. Since the adoption of the Civil Rights Act of 1871, they have exercised jurisdiction to grant INJUNCTIONS and DAMAGES against state and local officials (and, more recently, against local governmental entities as such) for conduct under color of state law—including conduct by officials asserting official power even where the conduct is prohibited by state law—that infringes on the ever-growing corpus of federal constitutional and statutory rules governing STATE ACTION. Federal courts may enjoin state officials from enforcing unconstitutional state statutes and administrative schemes; moreover, the courts' injunctive remedial powers are frequently exercised to assume broad managerial supervision over state agencies and bureaucracies (for example, schools, mental hospitals, prisons). And the ever-burgeoning array of federal conditions and restrictions that accompany federal economic and social programs available to the states are, as a matter of routine, enforceable in the federal courts.

The political sensitivities aroused by the federal courts' jurisdiction to control the validity of state and local government action has led to some statutory and judge-made restrictions on the exercise of this jurisdiction. For over half a century federal court actions to enjoin the enforcement of state statutes on constitutional grounds had to be litigated before THREE-JUDGE COURTS and were subject to direct review by APPEAL to the Supreme Court. (The institution of the three-judge district court was virtually abolished in 1976.) During the New Deal, statutory restrictions were placed on the jurisdiction of the federal courts to interfere with state tax statutes and public utility rate orders. Statutory and judge-made rules restrict the power of the federal courts to enjoin or interfere with pending state court proceedings; and state prisoners who fail to exhaust state court remedies or fail to comply with state procedural rules do not have access to federal habeas corpus.

The federal judicial system appears to operate on one-hundred-year cycles. The structure created in 1789 became increasingly unwieldy after the Civil War and was—after some twenty years of pressure for reform—finally transformed by the Evarts Act of 1891. That act created a stable system which has, in turn, come under increasing pressure from the caseload explosion that began in the 1960s. Relief could come in the form of diminutions in the district courts' original jurisdiction (such as a long-discussed abolition of or reduction in the diversity jurisdiction); but the need for architectural revision has also become increasingly clear in the 1970s and 1980s.

Structural problems center on the appellate tiers. Further substantial increases in the number of circuit judges is an uncertain remedy. Some circuits are already unwieldy and are finding it increasingly difficult to maintain stability and uniformity in the intracircuit law. Increasing the number of circuits would increase intercircuit instability and disuniformity and place further pressure on the finite appellate capacity of our "one Supreme Court"—the latter constituting the obvious structural bottleneck in the system.

More generally, a judicial system administering an enormous and dynamic corpus of national law and adjudicating a rising caseload (approaching 300,000 cases a year) cannot operate forever on an appellate capacity that is limited to some 150–200 judicial opinions with nationwide authority. There is rising concern, too, about the quality of federal justice as the growing caseload leads to an increasing bureaucratization of the federal judicial process, with the judges reduced to an oversight capacity in managing a growing array of magistrates, central staff, and law clerks.

Since the 1970s, two methods of increasing the system's capacity to provide authoritative and uniform judicial pronouncements on issues of national law have been discussed. One consists of greater subject-matter specialization at the appellate level, with special courts of appeals having nationwide authority to deal with specified subjects of federal litigation (for instance, tax cases, administrative appeals); such courts would remove pressure from the regional courts of appeals and the Supreme Court. The alternative (or additional) possibility is to create an additional appellate "tier": a national court of appeals with power to render decisions of nationwide authority, receiving its business by assignment from the Supreme Court or by transfer from the regional courts of appeals. In addition, if the number of certiorari petitions continues to mount, the Supreme Court will eventually have to make some adjustments in its screening procedures (perhaps dealing with these petitions in panels).

Behind these structural problems lie more fundamental questions about the enormous power that the federal courts have come to exercise over the political, economic, and social policies of the nation. Throughout our history intense controversy has surrounded the question whether (and to what extent) a small corps of appointed life-tenured officials should exercise wide-ranging powers to supervise and invalidate the actions of the political branches of federal, state, and local governments. From time to time these debates have threatened to affect the independence of the federal judicial system. Thus, in the 1930s, facing wholesale invalidations of the New Deal program by a "conservative" Supreme Court, President FRANKLIN D. ROOSEVELT proposed to "pack" the Court with additional judges; his plan was widely perceived to be contrary to the spirit of the Constitution and was defeated in Congress. (Shortly thereafter a Court with a new membership and a new judicial philosophy in effect accomplished Roosevelt's purposes.)

In the second half of the twentieth century retaliatory proposals have mostly consisted of attempts to strip a "liberal" Supreme Court of appellate jurisdiction in certain categories of constitutional litigation (for example, REAPPORTIONMENT or abortion), leaving the state courts to be the final arbiters of federal law in these areas. Intense controversy surrounds the question whether Congress has constitutional power to divest the Supreme Court of appellate jurisdiction over specific categories of constitutional litigation. (The one explicit Supreme Court pronouncement on the question, the celebrated EX PARTE MCCARDLE [1869], in sweeping language upheld this power pursuant to the explicit provision of Article III providing that the Court's appellate jurisdiction is subject to "such Exceptions" and "such Regulations" as "the Congress shall make.") Even if Congress has jurisdiction-stripping power, however, its exercise—much like the exercise of the power to "pack" the Court— would be widely perceived as anticonstitutional in spirit. In fact, no such legislation has come near to achieving acceptance, attesting to the vast reservoir of ideological and political strength that the ideal of an independent federal judiciary continues to possess.

The more important and authentic debate that continues to rage as the federal court system enters its third century relates to the proper role of an independent federal judiciary in a nation that is democratic but also committed to the ideal of fidelity to law. The federal courts have come to exercise a power over the political, economic, and social life of this nation that no other independent judicial system in the history of mankind has possessed. Whether that power is wholly benign—or whether it should and can be reduced—is one of the great questions to which the twenty-first century will have to attend.

PAUL M. BATOR

Bibliography

AMERICAN LAW INSTITUTE 1969 Study of the Division of Jurisdiction Between State and Federal Courts. Washington D.C.: American Law Institute.
BATOR, PAUL M.; MISHKIN, PAUL J.; SHAPIRO, DAVID L.; and WECHSLER, HERBERT 1973 The Federal Courts and the Federal System, 2nd ed., with 1981 Supplement. Mineola, N.Y.: Foundation Press.
CARRINGTON, PAUL D.; MEADOR, DANIEL J.; AND ROSENBERG, MAURICE 1976 Justice on Appeal. St. Paul, Minn.: West Publishing Co.
DIRECTOR OF THE ADMINISTRATIVE OFFICE OF THE UNITED STATES COURTS [annually] Annual Reports. Washington, D.C.: United States Government Printing Office.
FRANKFURTER, FELIX and LANDIS, JAMES M. 1928 The Business of the Supreme Court: A Study in the Federal Judicial System. New York: Macmillan.
FRIENDLY, HENRY J. 1973 Federal Jurisdiction: A General View. New York: Columbia University Press.
POSNER, RICHARD A. 1985 The Federal Courts: Crisis and Reform. Cambridge, Mass.: Harvard University Press.
WRIGHT, CHARLES ALAN 1983 The Law of Federal Courts. St. Paul, Minn.: West Publishing Co.

JUDICIARY ACT OF 1789
1 Stat. 73 (1789)

Article III of the Constitution constitutes an authorizing charter for a system of national courts to exercise the JUDICIAL POWER OF THE UNITED STATES, but is not self-executing, needing legislation to bring it to life. Accordingly, the First Congress, in its twentieth enactment, turned to the creation of a JUDICIAL SYSTEM for the new nation. Its work—the First Judiciary Act, approved September 24, 1789—has ever since been celebrated as "a great law." The statute, obeying a constitutional command, constituted a SUPREME COURT. It created the office of Attorney General of the United States. It devised a judicial organization that was destined to survive for a century. And, by providing for Supreme Court review of state court judgments involving issues of federal law, it created a profoundly significant instrument for consolidating and protecting national power.

But it is the decision of the First Congress to take up the constitutional option to establish a system of federal courts "inferior" to the Supreme Court that has been characterized as the act's "transcendent achievement." The Constitution does not require the creation of inferior courts. Nevertheless, the decision to do so came swiftly, actuated by the unanimously shared view that an effective maritime commerce— trading lifeblood for the thirteen states—needed a dependable nationwide body of maritime law, and by a consensus that the most reliable method to assure its development would be to entrust it to a distinctive body of national courts. (Far more controversy surrounded the view, also finding expression in the act, that national courts were needed to assure out-of-state litigants protection against parochial prejudices.)

The act thus created a system of federal courts of original (trial) jurisdiction, establishing a tradition that has survived without interruption to this day. On the other hand, the act gave these courts the authority to adjudicate only a small fraction of the CASES AND CONTROVERSIES encompassed by the federal judicial power, attesting to the clear contemporaneous understanding of the Constitution that it is for Congress to determine which, if any, of the cases, within the federal judicial power should be adjudicated in the first instance in a federal tribunal.

The first section of the act provided for a Supreme Court, consisting of a Chief Justice and five associates. Below this, the act created a curious bifurcated system. The country was divided into districts generally coterminous with state boundaries (Massachusetts and Virginia each had two districts), each with a district court manned by a district judge. In addition, the act divided the country into three circuits, in each of which another trial court, called a CIRCUIT COURT— manned not by its own judges but by two Supreme Court Justices and a district judge—was to sit twice a year in each district within the circuit. These circuit courts, in addition, received a limited APPELLATE JURISDICTION to review district court decisions. The system of circuit courts set up in 1789, with its requirement that Supreme Court Justices sit on circuit as trial judges, persisted for more than a century; it proved to be the weakest architectural feature of the first Judiciary Act.

The act exploited only a fraction of the constitutional potential for original federal court jurisdiction. Significantly, the constitutional grant of federal judicial power over cases arising under the Constitution and laws of the United States (FEDERAL QUESTION JURISDICTION) was largely unused and remained so until 1875. (A notable exception was section 14, the All Writs Act, which, among other matters, authorized Supreme Court Justices and district judges to "grant writs of HABEAS CORPUS" to inquire into the legality of federal detentions.) The act made important use, however, of the power to locate litigation affecting out-of-staters in the new national courts. Thus, the circuit courts were given CONCURRENT JURISDICTION with the state courts over civil cases involving more than $500 "between a citizen of the State where the suit is brought, and a citizen of another State," as well as over civil cases involving more than $500 in which an ALIEN was a party.

The most important grant of jurisdiction to the new district courts gave them "exclusive original cognizance of all civil causes of ADMIRALTY AND MARITIME JURISDICTION," subject to a savings clause preserving COMMON LAW remedies.

The litigation interests of the national government were given narrow recognition in the First Judiciary Act. The circuit courts were given power to adjudicate civil cases involving more than $500 in which the United States were "plaintiffs or petitioners" (suits against the United States were not contemplated); the district courts had power to adjudicate suits at common law involving $100 brought by the United States. The act gave the district courts exclusive original cognizance over certain seizures, penalties, and forfei-

tures. And, finally, Congress provided for the then tiny criminal business of the national government by giving the circuit courts "exclusive cognizance of all crimes and offenses cognizable under the authority of the United States," subject to a concurrent jurisdiction in the district courts to try certain minor criminal offenses.

The circuit courts were given the authority to review final decisions of the district courts in civil and admiralty cases involving more than $50 or $300, respectively. In addition, the first Judiciary Act originated the device, in continuous use ever since, of providing for pretrial removal of certain cases from state to federal court (for example, removal in civil cases to a circuit court by alien defendants and by out-of-staters sued in the plaintiff's home-state court).

The framers of the first Judiciary Act, notwithstanding the later established DOCTRINE that the ORIGINAL JURISDICTION of the Supreme Court does not depend on legislative grant, specified in section 13 what this original jurisdiction was to be; the listing nearly (but not completely) exhausted the constitutional grant, encompassing controversies between states, between a state and a citizen of another state, and suits involving foreign diplomats. Setting another lasting precedent, the act designated only a portion of the original jurisdiction of the Supreme Court as exclusive jurisdiction. In his opinion for the Court in MARBURY V. MADISON (1803), Chief Justice JOHN MARSHALL read section B to give the Supreme Court original jurisdiction over certain cases that Article III had not expressly placed within the Court's original jurisdiction. Accordingly, the Court held this narrow provision of the 1789 act unconstitutional.

Not all lower federal court decisions were made reviewable. For instance, no provision at all was made for review of federal criminal cases (which remained, in the large, unreviewable for a century). The act authorized the Supreme Court to review final judgments in civil cases decided by the circuit courts if the matter in dispute exceeded $2,000.

In its celebrated section 25, Congress asserted the constitutional authority—sustained in MARTIN V. HUNTER'S LESSEE (1816) and COHENS V. VIRGINIA (1821)—to give the Supreme Court authority to review certain final judgments or decisions in the "highest" state court in which a decision "could be had" (language that survives to this day). Significantly, this authority did not encompass all cases involving issues of federal law: review was limited to cases where a state court had *rejected* a claim of right or immunity under federal law. (This limitation eventually proved to create an unacceptable institutional gap and was eliminated by the Judiciary Act of 1914.) A seminal feature of section 25 was its specification that Supreme Court review is limited to the question of federal law in the case.

The first Judiciary Act originated a fundamental structural feature of our legal topography in its section 34, called the Rules of Decision Act, providing (in language that still survives) that, except where federal law otherwise requires, the laws of the several states shall be regarded as "rules of decision" in trials at common law in the federal courts "in cases where they apply." Interpretations of this delphic provision—including the reversal from SWIFT V. TYSON (1842) to ERIE RAILROAD V. TOMPKINS (1938)—have had a significant impact on our judicial FEDERALISM. In addition, the act contained elaborate boilerplate with respect to many matters no longer of current interest, (for example, the exact days for court sessions, quorums, clerks, forms of oaths, bail).

The first Judiciary Act, passed by a Congress many of whose members had participated in the framing of the Constitution, has had a lasting effect, not only on the shape of the federal judicial system but on our thought about the constitutional and structural premises on which that system is based. Created by great statesmen, it set on foot an enterprise that 200 years later still bears its imprint.

PAUL M. BATOR

Bibliography
FRANKFURTER, FELIX and LANDIS, JAMES M. 1928 The Business of the Supreme Court: A Study of the Federal Judicial System. New York: Macmillan.
GOEBEL, JULIUS 1971 History of the Supreme Court of the United States: Antecedents and Beginnings to 1801. Pages 457–508. New York: Macmillan.
WARREN, CHARLES 1923 New Light on the History of the Federal Judiciary Act of 1789. Harvard Law Review 37:49–132.

JUDICIARY ACT OF 1801
2 Stat. 89 (1801)

This maligned congressional enactment was the final achievement of the Federalists and one of their most constructive, but the Federalists so enmeshed it in partisanship that the first important action of THOMAS JEFFERSON's administration was the repeal of the act. It created resident circuit judgeships and enormously expanded federal JURISDICTION. The JUDICIARY ACT OF 1789 had created circuit courts consisting of district court judges and Supreme Court Justices. From the outset the Justices complained about the arduous duty of riding circuit and the necessity of deciding in their appellate capacity the same cases they had decided on circuit. Congress had done nothing to separate the Justices from the circuit courts, despite presidential recommendations. The Republican victories in 1800 spurred judicial reform that was "worth an election to the [Federalist] party," said a Federalist leader. A lame-duck Congress belatedly passed a much needed bill that created six circuit courts staffed by sixteen circuit judges. More important, the bill extended the JURISDICTION OF THE FEDERAL COURTS to include virtually the entire JUDICIAL POWER OF THE UNITED STATES authorized by Article III, including a general grant of FEDERAL QUESTION JURISDICTION—something which Congress did not grant again until 1875. But the bill also reduced the size of the Supreme Court to five when the next vacancy occurred, to prevent Jefferson from making an appointment. Also, President JOHN ADAMS at the last hour appointed sixteen Federalists to the new circuit judgeships. Enraged Republicans determined to pass the JUDICIARY ACTS OF 1802.

LEONARD W. LEVY

Bibliography
TURNER, KATHRYN 1965 Federalist Policy and the Judiciary Act of 1801. William and Mary Quarterly 22:3–32.

JUDICIARY ACT OF 1837

See: Circuit Courts

JUDICIARY ACT OF 1869

See: Circuit Courts

JUDICIARY ACT OF 1875
18 Stat. 470 (1875)

For three-quarters of a century after the abortive JUDICIARY ACT OF 1801, federal courts lacked any general FEDERAL QUESTION JURISDICTION, that is, JURISDICTION over cases arising under federal law. The 1875 act, adopted on the same day as the CIVIL RIGHTS ACT OF 1875, was one of Congress's last pieces of nationalizing legislation during the era of Reconstruction; its primary purpose was to provide a federal judicial forum for the assertion of newly created federal rights. Using the language of Article III of the Constitution, Congress gave the CIRCUIT COURTS jurisdiction over cases "arising under the Constitution or laws of the United States" or under national treaties, provided that the matter in dispute exceeded $500. The act also authorized the REMOVAL OF CASES from state to federal courts by either plaintiffs or defendants, when those cases could have been brought originally in the federal courts.

In part, the 1875 Judiciary Act's sponsors justified this widening of federal jurisdiction as a response to a commerce that had become national in scope. In particular, they sought to relieve railroads from the need to contend with unfriendly state courts in cases involving foreclosure, receivership, taxation, and even injuries to person and property—an objective which Populists came to criticize. In the *Pacific Railroad Removal Cases* (1885) the Supreme Court read the new jurisdictional grant so expansively that in 1887 Congress increased the jurisdictional amount, eliminated removal by plaintiffs, and insulated from APPEAL federal court orders remanding removed cases to the state courts.

The chief long-term significance of the 1875 act was its establishment of a generalized federal question jurisdiction—the jurisdiction that is seen today as the federal courts' indispensable function. In FELIX FRANKFURTER's words, in 1875 the lower federal courts "ceased to be restricted tribunals of fair dealing between citizens of different states and became the primary and powerful reliances for vindicating every right given by the Constitution, the laws, and treaties of the United States."

                                        KENNETH L. KARST

Bibliography

CHADBOURN, JAMES H. and LEVIN, LEO 1942 Original Jurisdiction of Federal Questions. *University of Pennsylvania Law Review* 90:639–674.
FRANKFURTER, FELIX and LANDIS, JAMES M. 1928 *The Business of the Supreme Court.* Pages 64–69. New York: Macmillan.

JUDICIARY ACT OF 1891

See: Circuit Courts of Appeals Act

JUDICIARY ACT OF 1911

See: Judicial Code

JUDICIARY ACT OF 1925
43 Stat. 936 (1925)

The Supreme Court's desire to reduce the burden of postwar litigation reaching its docket, combined with Chief Justice WILLIAM HOWARD TAFT's aggressive program of reform, resulted in the Judiciary Act of 1925. As litigation increased, efforts to expand the Court's discretionary control over its JURISDICTION—begun in the CIRCUIT COURTS OF APPEALS ACT of 1891—gained favor. Taft took the administrative functions of the Chief Justiceship seriously and sponsored a three-man committee of justices charged with formulating a detailed plan to regulate the Court's workload. The eventual proposal, framed mainly by Justice WILLIS VAN DEVANTER, entailed what Professor FELIX FRANKFURTER would later describe as a "drastic transfer of existing Supreme Court business to the circuit courts of appeal." This draft bill was submitted to Congress in 1922. The patchwork appearance of existing national legislation regulating the federal judiciary had prompted confusion and delay, and Taft, testifying in favor of the bill, applauded its "revision and restatement—a bringing together in a harmonious whole" of the earlier "wilderness of statutes." After three years of inaction, Congress finally passed the "Judges' Bill" in early 1925.

The new act reorganized the Court's APPELLATE JURISDICTION, allowing it to center its energies on constitutionally or nationally significant issues. Henceforth, cases would reach the Court from three avenues. Some district court decisions would go directly to the Supreme Court, but most would be shunted to the circuit courts of appeals. Among those exceptional cases that could be directly appealed because of their national importance were those arising under INTERSTATE COMMERCE or antitrust statutes, suits to enjoin enforcement of either ICC orders or state laws, and appeals by the federal government in criminal cases. Review of circuit courts of appeals' decisions was made largely discretionary; unless the Court chose to examine such a case by means of a WRIT OF CERTIORARI, most circuit decisions would be final. This provision thus superseded some of the reforms enacted in the 1891 legislation. Only two kinds of cases might be appealed directly from state courts: where a state law had been sustained against federal constitutional attack or where the state court had voided a federal law or treaty. Although the act left some problems unsolved, it successfully abated the flood of cases inundating the Court.

                                        DAVID GORDON

Bibliography
FRANKFURTER, FELIX and LANDIS, JAMES M. 1927 *The Business of the Supreme Court.* New York: Macmillan.

JUDICIARY ACTS OF 1802
2 Stat. 132, 2 Stat. 156 (1802)

Gloating Federalists declared that the JUDICIARY ACT OF 1801 was as valuable for their party as an election victory. The appointment of only Federalists to the new circuit judgeships, the attempt by a new circuit court to get a Jeffersonian editor indicted for SEDITIOUS LIBEL, and the issuance in 1801 of the show cause order in MARBURY V. MADISON (1803) convinced President THOMAS JEFFERSON's administration that the Federalists meant to continue party warfare against them from the bench. Republicans also opposed the expanded JURISDICTION OF THE FEDERAL COURTS; they wanted litigants to remain primarily dependent on state courts and the United States as dependent as possible on the states for the execution of its laws. The upshot was the repeal of even the constructive reforms of 1801.

Federalists in Congress argued that repeal would subvert the independence of the judiciary and was unconstitutional because the circuit judges had tenure during good behavior. The Republicans answered that the Constitution empowered Congress to establish and therefore to abolish inferior federal courts. The debate on the repealer triggered a prolonged congressional discussion on national JUDICIAL REVIEW. Federalists supported the power of the Supreme Court to hold acts of Congress unconstitutional, while Republicans assaulted judicial review as an undemocratic judicial usurpation, a violation of SEPARATION OF POWERS, and a subversion of LIMITED GOVERNMENT. The only proper check on the popularly elected and politically responsible branches of the national government, Republicans argued, was the outcome of elections. Chief Justice JOHN MARSHALL's opinion in *Marbury* was the Federalist reply from the bench.

Apprehensive about the possibility that the Supreme Court might declare the repealer unconstitutional, Congress passed another judiciary act which abolished the August term of the Court. By fixing one term a year, to be held in February, Congress managed to postpone the next meeting of the Court for fourteen months, allowing a cooling-off period, during which time the Justices could resume their circuit duties. They did, and in STUART V. LAIRD (1803) they sustained the power of Congress to assign them to circuit work. The Judiciary Act of 1802 also increased the number of circuits from three to six. Until the Reconstruction period, the federal judicial system remained basically unchanged after 1802.

LEONARD W. LEVY

Bibliography
ELLIS, RICHARD E. 1971 *The Jeffersonian Crisis: Courts and Politics in the Young Republic.* Pages 4–60. New York: Oxford University Press.

JUDICIARY REFORM ACT
50 Stat. 751 (1937)

This act, a remnant of President FRANKLIN D. ROOSEVELT's court-packing proposal, provided that "whenever the constitutionality of any Act of Congress affecting the public interest is drawn in question in any court of the United States . . . the court shall permit the United States to intervene and become a party." The act further provided for direct APPEAL to the Supreme Court when a lower court held a congressional act unconstitutional in a case to which the United States or a federal officer was a party. Moreover, such appeals were to be expedited on the Court's calendar.

The act also forbade the issuance by any district court of an INJUNCTION suspending enforcement of an act of Congress upon constitutional grounds, unless approved by a specifically convened THREE-JUDGE COURT. (A single judge might grant temporary injunctive relief to prevent "irreparable loss" to a petitioner.) The three-judge court's grant or denial of an injunction was directly appealable to the Supreme Court. The remainder of the act amended the JUDICIAL CODE to provide a replacement when a district court judge was unable to perform his work. The constitutionality of the act was never challenged; although the three-judge court requirement was largely repealed in 1976, other sections are still good law.

DAVID GORDON

JUILLIARD v. GREENMAN

See: Legal Tender Cases

JULIAN, GEORGE
(1817–1899)

An Indiana abolitionist, lawyer, and congressman (1849–1851; 1861–1871), George Washington Julian was an early advocate of emancipation under the government's WAR POWERS. In 1862 he guided the HOMESTEAD ACT through Congress. Julian advocated confiscation of rebel lands and black suffrage. In 1867 he was a member of the committee of seven which drew up ARTICLES OF IMPEACHMENT against President ANDREW JOHNSON. In 1868 he introduced a constitutional amendment that would have granted women's suffrage. After 1871 Julian became a liberal Republican and then a radical Democrat. He published much, including his political memoirs (1884) and a biography of his father-in-law, Congressman Joshua R. Giddings (1892).

PAUL FINKELMAN

Bibliography

JULIAN, GEORGE W. 1884 *Political Reflections, 1840–1872*. Chicago: Jansen, McClurg & Co.

JUREK v. TEXAS

See: Capital Punishment Cases, 1976

JURISDICTION

Jurisdiction is a magical and protean term. In American law it refers to the power of legislatures, the competence of courts to deal with certain types of cases, the allocation of cases between state and federal courts, the power of both state and federal courts over defendants who have only peripheral attachments to the locale of the court, and the territory in which a unit of government exercises its power. Not surprisingly the word shifts its meanings as it moves among these quite different tasks.

The term's confusing spread of meanings has its roots in the English medieval experience. What modern observers would think of as political power accompanied the grant of property; the landlord was lord of more than land; he exercised powers of justice over the people who tilled that soil. Yet that jurisdiction also had limits: above it stood the powers of the monarch, who at least in theory had the power and responsibility to see that the lords rendered justice. Thus the word emerged from the Middle Ages carrying several meanings: the power to make law, the power to adjudicate cases, and, loosely, the territory within which that power was exercised.

We use all three senses today. We speak, for example, of legislative jurisdiction, meaning legislative power, generally allocated by state and federal constitutions. Thus the earliest opinion of the Supreme Court applying the limits of SUBSTANTIVE DUE PROCESS to state economic regulation, in ALLEGEYER V. LOUISIANA (1897), said that the state had exceeded its territorial jurisdiction. Territorial considerations aside, any decision holding a law unconstitutional can be described as a holding that the legislative body has transgressed the limits of its jurisdiction—its lawful authority. The courts have employed this rhetoric especially in defining a state's jurisdiction to tax.

We use the extended, territorial sense of the term when we write of a fugitive's having fled a jurisdiction, or when lawyers ask about which jurisdiction's law applies. Article IV, section 3, of the Constitution uses the term in this sense when it prohibits creation of a new state within the jurisdiction of an existing state without the latter's consent.

The most distinctively legal, though not exclusively constitutional, sense of the term refers to the authority of a court to decide a matter or to issue an order—its subject matter jurisdiction. Some state courts are courts of so-called general jurisdiction, competent to decide all cases within the ordinary bounds of the law. Other state courts are courts of limited jurisdiction, empowered only to decide specified types of cases or to grant only specified forms of relief. A municipal court, for example, may have jurisdiction to award damages only up to a limited dollar amount and may have no jurisdiction at all to grant an INJUNCTION.

In constitutional law jurisdiction has two special meanings, both involving civil cases. One flows from the limitation of the subject matter jurisdiction of the federal constitutional courts in Article III of the Constitution; the other grows from the due process clauses of the Fifth and FOURTEENTH AMENDMENTS.

Fundamental to the constitutional scheme is the proposition that each branch of the federal government must share powers and observe limits not only in regard to the other two branches of government but also in regard to the states. Article III and many statutes thus limit the subject matter jurisdiction of the federal courts to certain types of cases; that article, for example, ordinarily would prohibit a federal court from deciding a case between two citizens of the same state in which no question of federal or maritime law was involved. Because the limitations of Article III describe a fundamental division of authority between state and federal governments, the federal courts have been scrupulous, some would say zealous, not to overstep those subject matter boundaries. Thus even though no party to a lawsuit evinces the least concern about it, a federal court has an independent duty to investigate the basis for its subject matter jurisdiction and to dismiss the suit if jurisdiction is lacking. Such dismissals, like the jurisdictional rules that require them, protect the interests of the state court systems, to which the litigation must go if the federal courts cannot hear it.

The Constitution also limits the powers of the federal government and the states over individual citizens. State courts, for example, must observe a limitation that flows from the Fourteenth Amendment's due process clause. Since *Pennoyer v. Neff* (1878) the Supreme Court has insisted that, regardless of the kind of case involved, the defendant have some connection with the state in which the suit occurs. Over the past century the Court has remolded the basis and expanded the range of personal jurisdiction—changes that, some have suggested, have come in response to an increasingly mobile population and an economy increasingly national in scope. The Court has sometimes based the requirement of personal jurisdiction on the state's lack of power over persons not within its borders—thus harking back to the territorial sense of the term; more recently it has tended to speak less of territorial power and more of unfair inconvenience to a defendant forced to litigate in a distant forum. Whether it has grounded the requirements in FEDERALISM or in fairness to the defendant, however, the Court has insisted that such connections exist in order for a judgment of a court to be entitled to FULL FAITH AND CREDIT.

Whether similar constitutional restrictions on personal jurisdiction apply to federal courts is a more obscure matter. Because the federal government is sovereign throughout the United States, notions of geographical territoriality play no role, and only the inconvenience to the defendant would be at issue in such a case. In a number of instances involving the national economy, such as federal securities law cases, Congress has provided for nationwide personal jurisdiction in the federal courts, and such grants of power have been upheld, presumably because any harm to the defendant is outweighed by the need for a nationally available system of courts supervising the national economy. The outer limits of congressional power have not been tested, for in most cases either venue statutes (controlling the districts in which civil suits may be brought) or the FEDERAL RULES OF CIVIL PROCEDURE limit federal courts to essentially the same reach of personal jurisdiction that a state court would have.

Unlike subject matter jurisdiction, personal jurisdiction can be waived by those entitled to its protection: the Supreme Court has repeatedly held that either by prior agreement or by the simple failure to raise the issue at an early stage of litigation defendants may lose their opportunity to challenge the court's power to decide the case. COLLATERAL ATTACK on a judgment on the ground that the court lacked personal jurisdiction is available only to a defendant who did not appear in the original suit.

Article III's limits on the subject matter jurisdiction of federal courts allocate cases as between state and federal courts; the due process limitations in personal jurisdiction allocate cases between a court, either state or federal, in a particular place and courts in other places more convenient to the defendant. Though both doctrines in their more technical aspects are quintessential lawyer's law, their roots lie in the Constitution's allocations of governmental power and in a tradition of individualism. The same origins underlie the idea of jurisdiction as the limitations on the power of various branches of government. Ultimately all the uses of "jurisdiction" derive from the medieval Western tradition that distinguished between power and justice, making the ability to dispense the latter a function of allocations of the former.

STEPHEN C. YEAZELL

Bibliography

BATOR, PAUL M.; MISHKIN, PAUL J.; SHAPIRO, DAVID L.; and WECHSLER, HERBERT 1973 *Hart and Wechsler's The Federal Courts and the Federal System.* Mineoloa, N.Y.: Foundation Press.

HAZARD, GEOFFREY C. 1965 A General Theory of State-Court Jurisdiction. *Supreme Court Review* 1965:241–289.

MEHREN, ARTHUR T. von, and TRAUTMAN, DONALD 1966 Jurisdiction to Adjudicate: A Suggested Analysis. *Harvard Law Review* 79:1121–1179.

JURISDICTION AND REMOVAL ACT

See: Judiciary Act of 1875

JURISDICTION TO TAX

Prior to the adoption of the FOURTEENTH AMENDMENT, the Supreme Court derived from principles "inhering in the very nature of constitutional government" the rule that states do not have jurisdiction to impose taxes upon persons, things, or activities outside their borders. In modern times, such limits on the legislative jurisdiction of states are derived from the DUE PROCESS clause.

The jurisdictional limitations have been applied in

a variety of settings. A state may not impose a property tax on real or tangible personal property physically located in another state, even though the owner of the property is domiciled and present in the taxing state. However, where movable instrumentalities of commerce—railroad rolling stock, ships, trucks, airplanes—are involved, a state is not limited to taxing those instrumentalities actually in the state on tax day. Instead, the state may use a formula to compute the average presence of such instrumentalities within the state. Such apportionment formulas have been upheld so long as they fairly allocate values to the taxing state.

Property taxes imposed on intangibles—such as stocks and bonds—are not subject to similar limitations. The Court initially permitted the state of domicile of the owner to tax the total value of such intangibles, reasoning that intangible property is often held secretly and might otherwise escape taxation entirely. During the 1920s and 1930s the Court attempted to derive rules that would prevent the multiple taxation of intangibles, but eventually it came to hold that any state within which some interest in an intangible exists can tax. For example, if stocks are held in a trust, the state of domicile of the trustee, the state of domicile of the beneficiary, and the state where the certificates are located may each impose a tax on the total value.

Domicile of the taxpayer is an adequate jurisdictional basis for taxing net income from property and activities outside the state. The only constitutional limitation is the COMMERCE CLAUSE. Nondomiciliary states may also tax the income arising from property and activities within their borders subject to two limitations. A 1959 federal statute (section 381, Title 18, United States Code) provides that a state may not impose a net INCOME TAX if the taxpayer does no more within the state than solicit orders to be delivered from without the state by common carrier. Formulas used to apportion income must not have the effect of reaching out and taxing values beyond the state.

The long-standing rule that states may not levy sales taxes when the seller is in another state and does no more than solicit orders in the taxing state is justified in jurisdictional terms. The buyer's state cannot impose the tax because to do so would be to project its powers beyond its boundaries. A use tax, resting on the purchaser within the state, however, is within the jurisdiction of the buyer's state. But in order to collect use taxes effectively, the buyer's state must be able to compel the seller to collect and remit the tax. The Supreme Court holds that such a duty of collection can be imposed only when there is some

definite link, some minimum connection (such as ownership of property or the presence of solicitors or other employees) between the seller and the state.

Often jurisdictional and commerce problems overlap. For example, if a state seeks to tax income of an interstate business attributable to activities outside the state, the tax can be invalidated either as an assertion of jurisdiction over out-of-state activities or as disadvantaging INTERSTATE COMMERCE because more than one state taxes the same income.

EDWARD L. BARRETT, JR.

Bibliography

HELLERSTEIN, JEROME R.   1968   Recent Developments in State Tax Apportionment and the Circumscription of Unitary Business. *National Tax Journal* 21:487–503.
NOTE   1975   Developments in the Law: Federal Limitations on State Taxation of Interstate Business. *Harvard Law Review* 75:953–1036.

JURY

See: Blue Ribbon Jury; Grand Jury; Petit Jury; Trial by Jury

JURY DISCRIMINATION

Jury discrimination was first recognized as a constitutional problem shortly after the Civil War, when certain southern and border states excluded blacks from jury service. The Supreme Court had little difficulty in holding such blatant RACIAL DISCRIMINATION invalid as a denial of the EQUAL PROTECTION OF THE LAWS guaranteed by the recently adopted FOURTEENTH AMENDMENT. But, beyond such obvious improprieties, what should the principle of nondiscrimination forbid? Some kinds of "discrimination" in the selection of the jury are not bad but good: for example, those incompetent to serve ought to be excused from service, whether their incompetence arises from mental or physical defect, from demonstrably bad character, or from bias. No one has seriously argued that American jury service ought to be determined wholly by lot, as it was among the citizens of Athens. In addition, it has been the uniform policy of American jurisdictions to excuse from service some who are competent, but whose service would work a hardship on them or others: doctors, ministers, and parents who care for small children have been exempted from service on such grounds.

The history of the constitutional law regulating jury

composition has been a story of expanding and compulsory democratization. In our early national history property and voting qualifications were common, and women were systematically excluded or exempted from jury service. At COMMON LAW, indeed, special juries were sometimes employed: a jury of merchants to decide certain kinds of mercantile questions, for example, or in the trial of an ALIEN, a jury half of which spoke his language. Even in the early and middle decades of this century, the Supreme Court upheld against constitutional attack a BLUE RIBBON JURY system, by which jurors were selected supposedly for intelligence and character in a way that resulted in the vast overrepresentation of professional and business classes, in *Fay v. New York* (1947); a highly discretionary and easily abused "key man" system for selecting potential jurors by consultation with community leaders, in SWAIN V. ALABAMA (1965); and the voluntary exemption of women from jury service, in *Hoyt v. Florida* (1961). At present, however, a federal statute requires that the federal jury be drawn from a pool that represents a "fair cross section of the community," and a similar constitutional standard has been imposed by the Supreme Court on the states as well, in TAYLOR V. LOUISIANA (1975).

There are normally three stages in the selection of an American jury at which improper discrimination may occur: the establishment of the master list of all persons eligible for jury service within the JURISDICTION of a particular court (this is called the jury roll); the selection of the panel of potential jurors (called the venire) who will be asked to appear at the courthouse; and the selection from that panel of those who will actually serve on a jury in a particular case or set of cases. The question of discrimination can arise in both civil and criminal cases, but the courts have paid far more attention to the criminal jury. Two distinct provisions of the Constitution of the United States bear upon jury selection: the equal protection clause of the Fourteenth Amendment and the SIXTH AMENDMENT.

In STRAUDER V. WEST VIRGINIA (1879) and NEAL V. DELAWARE (1880) the Court held that the equal protection clause forbade a state to try a black defendant by a jury from which members of his race had been affirmatively excluded, either by statute or by administrative practice. A federal statute passed shortly after the Civil War made such discrimination a crime.

In *Hernandez v. Texas* (1954), dealing with the exclusion of Mexican-Americans, the Supreme Court extended the *Strauder* ruling to other ethnic groups. On the other hand, the Court has repeatedly said that the Constitution does not entitle a defendant to a jury that consists in whole or in part of members of his race, or of any other particular composition. The idea of the jury affirmed in these cases is not that it is a microcosm of society at large, but that it is an institution of justice for which participants may properly be required to be qualified. The equal protection clause does not guarantee a particular mix but protects only against improper exclusions.

What exclusions, beyond racial ones, are improper? In *Hernandez* the Court said that where any group in a community is systematically discriminated against it will need the protection of the Constitution, and added: "Whether such a group exists within a community is a question of fact. When the existence of a distinct class is demonstrated, and it is further shown that the laws, as written or as applied, single out that class for different treatment not based upon some reasonable classification, the guarantees of the Constitution have been violated." But what is a reasonable classification? This question is complicated by the fact that the law has traditionally imposed qualifications for jury service which may, or may not, have differential impact on racial or other protected groups. The Court has accordingly upheld, against equal protection attack, qualifications for jury service that are extremely vague and easily susceptible to abuse—"generally reputed to be honest and intelligent . . . esteemed in the community for their integrity, good character, and good judgment." The burden is on the defendant to show that such qualifications have in fact been abused. Generally speaking, racially disproportionate impact alone is not enough to invalidate a classification under the equal protection clause: actual intent to discriminate must be proved, by direct or circumstantial evidence, as the Court held in WASHINGTON V. DAVIS (1976). But in jury discrimination, proof of a substantial disproportionality in racial (or sexual) balance between the jury pool and the community at large constitutes a prima facie case of intentional discrimination which the government must rebut. (The Sixth Amendment is more protective than the equal protection clause, in those cases to which it applies, for it has no intent requirement, and the Court held in *Duren v. Missouri* (1979) that it not only prohibits discrimination but affirmatively requires that the pool from which the jury is drawn contain a "fair cross section" of the relevant community.)

Who may object to an improper exclusion? In *Peters v. Kiff* (1972), the Supreme Court held that any defendant is entitled to object to improper exclusions from the panel from which his jury is selected, whether or not he is a member of the excluded race. In addition, the Court held in *Carter v. Jury Commission of Greene County* (1976) that members of the excluded race who wish to serve on juries are entitled to bring independent proceedings to attack their exclusion, for they are deprived of equal protection with respect to an important right of CITIZENSHIP.

A separate source of constitutional restrictions on jury discrimination is the Sixth Amendment's guarantee of an "impartial jury" in criminal cases. DUNCAN v. LOUISIANA (1968) held that this provision, which originally applied only to the federal government, was "incorporated" within the Fourteenth Amendment's due process clause, and thus was applicable to the states as well. (See INCORPORATION DOCTRINE.) In *Taylor v. Louisiana* the Court held that the concept of the jury as a "fair cross section of the community" was at the core of the Sixth Amendment and thus applicable to the states. Thus exclusions will be tested not merely under the equal protection clause, which focuses on improper exclusions, but by the affirmative "cross section" principle. The latter principle conceives of the jury not as a group of citizens who are qualified for a task and chosen in a manner free from INVIDIOUS DISCRIMINATION, but as a body fairly chosen from a group that represents the community of which it is a part.

But what does "fairly chosen" mean? The federal statute requires that the jury roll reflect a fair cross section of the community, and that the venire be drawn at random from the roll; this scheme meets any standard of fairness. The courts might impose similar standards on the states. But there remains the crucial stage at which the particular jury panel is selected from the venire, and none of the rulings cited above speak to this matter. This selection is made just before trial in a process in which lawyers and the judge cooperate. Certain jurors are excused "for cause," that is, because there are good reasons why they should not sit in the particular case: admitted bias, acquaintance with one of the parties, and so on. In addition, the parties are allowed a limited number of discretioniary, or "peremptory," challenges to other potential jurors. What happens if the prosecution should exercise its peremptory challenges to keep blacks or women off the jury? If that can be done with impunity, the insistence upon fairness at the other stages of jury selection becomes an empty ritual; but how can a discriminatory exercise of peremptory challenges be established? To require the prosecutor to accept any juror of a particular race or class would be unfair to the state, and upset the balance of the

selection process. The Supreme Court held in *Swain v. Alabama* that the use of peremptory challenges against potential minority jurors is not always unconstitutional, but that systematic racial discrimination is impermissible under the equal protection clause. In *Batson v. Kentucky* (1986) the Court partially overruled *Swain*, holding that a prosecutor cannot constitutionally use peremptory challenges to exclude potential jurors solely on account of their race. If the circumstances raise an inference of such a use of peremptory challenges, the burden shifts to the state to provide "a neutral explanation" for the exclusions.

The effect of the antidiscrimination holdings has also been undercut by the Supreme Court's decision in APODACA V. OREGON (1972) that the states are not required to insist upon unanimous verdicts. (See JURY UNANIMITY.) Even if some members of a discriminated-against class make it to the jury, *Apodaca* means that their views can be disregarded by the majority. On the other hand, the proposition that jurors of the defendant's race or sex will be especially likely to vote for him is an assumption more easily made than proved, and arguably demeaning both to the jurors and to the class to which they belong. And even minority jurors who are outvoted will have a chance to have their views considered. The true basis of the fair cross-section requirement is assurance of the kind of diversity of view and experience that will most advance the kind of collective decision making that, as Harry Kalven and Hans Zeisel show, represents the jury at its best.

As for the distinct institution known as the GRAND JURY, which sits before trial to decide whether the evidence of a particular defendant's guilt is sufficient to justify his INDICTMENT, racial discrimination in its selection is also a violation of the equal protection clause. The indicted individual is entitled to the dismissal of his indictment, as the Court held in *Carter v. Texas* (1900), even though in some sense the defect may be thought to be cured by a properly composed trial jury. The Court has not applied the affirmative "fair cross section" requirements to the state grand jury, nor indeed, as the Court held in HURTADO V. CALIFORNIA (1884), are the states required to employ the institution of the grand jury at all. Discrimination in the selection of state grand juries remains regulated by the equal protection clause, which forbids only intentional discrimination. The federal statute does apply the "fair cross section" requirement to federal grand juries as well as trial juries.

The continued existence of both the grand jury and the trial jury appears to rest on two assumptions.

First, judicial decisions, especially in criminal cases, are assumed to be more just when they are not left to professionals but are also influenced by the views of ordinary people. Second, jury service—again, especially in the criminal process—is seen as popular participation in government. Our constitutional protections against discriminatory selection of jurors are aimed at promoting the ends of justice and the ideal of citizenship.

JAMES BOYD WHITE

Bibliography

JUDICIAL CONFERENCE OF THE UNITED STATES 1961 The Jury System in the Federal Courts. *Federal Rules Decisions* 26:411–504.

KALVEN, HARRY and ZEISEL, HANS 1966 *The American Jury.* Boston: Little, Brown.

LARUE, L. H. 1976 A Jury of One's Peers. *Washington & Lee Law Review* 33:841–876.

JURY SIZE

Traditionally, in the United States, a criminal trial jury—the PETIT JURY—has been composed of twelve persons. Early Supreme Court opinions assumed that in federal criminal cases juries of that size were required by the Constitution. In PATTON V. UNITED STATES (1930) the Court ruled that during the course of a federal trial a criminal defendant could, with the consent of the prosecutor and judge, waive the participation of one or two jurors and agree to have the verdict rendered by less than twelve.

In DUNCAN V. LOUISIANA (1968) the Supreme Court held that under the FOURTEENTH AMENDMENT a person accused of a serious crime in a state court is guaranteed the right to TRIAL BY JURY according to the same standards applied under the Sixth Amendment in the federal courts. Later, in BALDWIN V. NEW YORK (1970), the Court held that a serious, nonpetty crime for purposes of the jury trial guarantee is one where imprisonment for more than six months is authorized. In the wake of *Duncan,* the Court in WILLIAMS V. FLORIDA (1970) decided that trial of a serious crime by a jury of six persons did not violate the constitutional right to trial by jury. Eight years later, the Court in BALLEW V. GEORGIA (1978) ruled that six was the constitutional minimum—that a jury of five persons did not meet the constitutional standard. In *Colgrove v. Battin* (1973) the Court had also ruled that a six-person jury in a civil case in the federal courts did not violate the SEVENTH AMENDMENT right to jury trial.

In early England, the number of jurors on a petit jury came to be firmly fixed at twelve some time in the fourteenth century. The reasons for choosing the number twelve for the jury at common law are shrouded in obscurity; the same number was also in wide use in other countries of Europe from early times. Some writers ascribe this number to mystical and religious considerations, for example, the twelve tribes and the twelve apostles. At the time of the adoption of the Constitution and the BILL OF RIGHTS, the idea of the twelve-person jury was entrenched in the English COMMON LAW system and practice of the colonial society.

In *Williams,* the Court rejected the idea that the history of the drafting of the Sixth Amendment jury trial provision enshrined the twelve-person jury in the Constitution. Instead, the Court adopted a functional approach, relating jury size to the purposes of jury trial. The goals of the jury system were seen as interposing the common-sense judgment of laypersons, permitting community participation in the decision-making process, and making the group large enough to promote group deliberation and obtain a fair cross-section of the community. With respect to these various goals, the court majority found "little reason to think" that there is a significant difference between six and twelve, citing in support "the few experiments" and asserting that neither currently available evidence nor theory suggested contrary conclusions.

The interval between *Williams* and *Ballew* saw the publication of a significant body of SOCIAL SCIENCE RESEARCH examining the effects of changes in jury size. In *Ballew,* although the Court was unanimous on the jury size issue, only two Justices relied on these social science studies in concluding that five-person juries did not adequately fulfill the functions of jury trial outlined in *Williams.* Three Justices had "reservations as to the wisdom—as well as the necessity—of . . . heavy reliance on numerology derived from statistical studies." The same three Justices suggested that the Constitution does not require every feature of the jury to be the same in both federal and state courts, implying that a different, presumably higher, minimum size standard might be applied in the federal courts.

The studies done since *Williams,* through experiment, use of statistical analysis, and theorizing, have inquired whether the size of the jury affects: the likelihood of representation on a jury of ethnic and racial minorities and minority viewpoints that might influence results or the incidence of hung juries; the propensity of juries to reach compromise verdicts; the consistency of verdicts; the likelihood that verdicts reflect community sentiment; and the overall quality of group decision making. A few researchers have also studied the cost savings that might be achieved by reductions in jury size.

In the main, the social scientists have criticized the Court's conclusion in *Williams,* and have argued that decreasing jury size has undesirable effects. Some of these studies have been subjected to methodological criticism, such as the objections to their reliance on small group research. Definitive research on the subject remains to be done. On the issue of the jury's representative character, however, social science has already contributed fairly definitive conclusions. Although it is not possible for a single jury to be representative of the community, six-person juries are less likely than twelve-person juries to contain individuals from minority groups or those who have minority viewpoints. Richard Lempert has suggested that "there may be a positive value in minimizing the number of situations in which minority group members are judged by groups lacking minority representation. . . ."

In other constitutional contexts, judges often rely on intuition and common sense to reach judgments on functional issues, or they take into account constitutional values that transcend a functional approach. The jury size issue, however, involves specific numbers, and intuition and other constitutional values do not provide an adequate basis for drawing the required fine distinctions. One who is not persuaded by the social science studies is therefore relegated to the type of statement made by Justice Powell in *Ballew,* defending the line between five and six: "[A] line has to be drawn somewhere." Under such an approach, the constitutional line could as easily have been drawn between twelve and eleven, and with more historical justification.

Because of the Court's reluctance to overrule recent precedents and because of uncertainty whether social science research can ever demonstrate a sufficient basis for drawing a different line, it seems probable that, for a long time to come, six will remain the constitutional minimum for a criminal jury in the state courts under the Fourteenth Amendment. (Whether the Court will some day adopt Justice Powell's view and apply a different minimum size standard for juries in federal criminal trials is problematic.) Perhaps in some future century when legal historians try to deduce the reasons for choosing six as the constitutionally significant number, they, like their predecessors,

may speculate about the possible mystical value of the number. In the end, they are likely to conclude that its origins, like those of the number twelve, are shrouded in obscurity.

NORMAN ABRAMS

Bibliography
LEMPERT, RICHARD 1975 Uncovering "Nondiscernible Differences: Empirical Research and the Jury Size Cases. *Michigan Law Review* 73:644–708.

JURY TRIAL

See: Trial by Jury

JURY UNANIMITY

The requirement that a jury in a criminal case reach a unanimous decision became generally established in England during the fourteenth century—about the same time that juries came to be composed of twelve persons. Unanimity began to be generally required for jury verdicts in the American colonies in the eighteenth century. The unanimity requirement as commonly applied means that all the members of the jury must agree upon the verdict—whether for conviction or acquittal. If any of the jurors fail to agree, the jury is "hung"—that is, unable to reach a verdict. Under well-established DOCTRINE, after a hung jury the defendant may be retried.

In a series of cases dating back to the end of the nineteenth century, the Supreme Court has assumed that under the Sixth Amendment the verdict of a criminal jury in the federal courts must be unanimous. This assumption has not been tested, however, for there is no provision for less than unanimous criminal verdicts in the federal courts. The decision in DUNCAN V. LOUISIANA (1968) opened the way for the Court to consider the constitutionality of efforts made by many states to change elements in the COMMON LAW jury system. *Duncan* ruled that the FOURTEENTH AMENDMENT protected the right to TRIAL BY JURY in state courts according to the same standards applied under the Sixth Amendment.

To understand the Court's subsequent decisions regarding jury unanimity, it is necessary also to consider its related decisions on JURY SIZE. The Court in WILLIAMS V. FLORIDA (1970) upheld the use of six-person juries for serious criminal cases. The question whether state criminal juries must reach unanimous verdicts was presented for the first time in 1972 in two companion cases, APODACA V. OREGON and JOHNSON V. LOUISIANA. In *Apodaca,* the constitutionality of 10–2 verdicts was sustained under the Sixth and Fourteenth Amendments. In *Johnson,* 9–3 verdicts were upheld under the Fourteenth Amendment alone. In *Apodaca,* a state case, five Justices (one concurring Justice and four dissenters) also expressed the view that the Sixth Amendment required unanimity in federal criminal trials.

In BALLEW V. GEORGIA (1978) the Court rendered its second size-of-jury decision, holding five-person juries to be unconstitutional. Thus, by the time the Court considered the issue in BURCH V. LOUISIANA (1979), it had upheld six-person juries, sustained the constitutionality of 10–2 and 9–3 majority verdicts, and held five-person juries to be unconstitutional. In *Burch,* the Court held that conviction by a 5–1 vote of a six-person jury violated the constitutional right to trial by jury.

The Court has not in modern times decided whether the SEVENTH AMENDMENT requires unanimity in federal civil trials. It can be argued that it so held in two early cases, *American Publishing Company v. Fisher* (1897) and *Springville v. Thomas* (1897), but the Court's nonunanimous verdict decisions in state criminal cases and its decision in *Colgrove v. Battin* (1973) that six-person juries are constitutional in federal civil trials, arguably have undermined those early decisions.

In addressing the unanimity issue in *Apodaca* and *Johnson,* the Court relied heavily on the analysis used in the first size-of-jury case, *Williams v. Florida,* and applied the same functional approach relating the size of the jury to the purposes of a jury trial. From a functional perspective, the unanimity issue has much in common with but is not identical to the jury size question. For example, both involve concerns that juries represent a cross-section of the community and that minority viewpoints be represented. In connection with jury size, the concern is that if the jury is too small, it will not reflect minority views. Where unanimity is departed from, the concern is that minority viewpoints represented on the jury will simply be disregarded and outvoted. A majority of the Court in *Apodaca* rejected this latter claim on the grounds that there was no reason to believe that majority jurors will fail to weigh the evidence and consider rational arguments offered by the minority. The dissenters argued that jury reliability was diminished in a nonunanimous system because there is less pressure to debate and deliberate. Professor Hans Zeisel has made

a similar point: "[T]he abandonment of the unanimity rule is but another way of reducing the size of the jury. But it is reduction with a vengeance, for a majority verdict requirement is far more effective in nullifying the potency of minority viewpoints than is the outright reduction of a jury to a size equivalent to the majority that is allowed to agree on a verdict. Minority viewpoints fare better on a jury of ten that must be unanimous than on a jury of twelve where ten members must agree on a verdict" (1971, p. 722).

The less than unanimous verdict also poses a question not raised in the jury size cases. A majority of the Court in *Johnson* held that nonunanimous verdicts are not inconsistent with proof beyond a REASONABLE DOUBT and therefore do not violate DUE PROCESS. The fact that some members of the jury are not convinced of guilt does not itself establish reasonable doubt, a concept that apparently applies only to the standard of proof that each individual juror subjectively must apply, not a concept applicable to the jury as a group.

Are criminal defendants as well protected from conviction under a nonunanimous verdict system as under a unanimity requirement? The majority in *Apodoca* and *Johnson* conceded that juries would be hung somewhat less frequently under a nonunanimous system but also relied on SOCIAL SCIENCE RESEARCH for the proposition that "the probability that an acquittal minority will hang the jury is about as great as that a guilty minority will hang it." Data in the same study, however, persuaded some of the dissenters that the prosecution would gain "a substantially more favorable conviction ratio" under a nonunanimous system.

By the time *Burch* was decided in 1979, the Court, following the pattern suggested in the 1978 jury size case of *Ballew,* appears to have abandoned any attempt to rely on social science to support its conclusions regarding required jury attributes. In holding 5–1 verdicts unconstitutional, the Court concluded that "having already departed from the strict historical requirements of jury trial, it is inevitable that lines must be drawn somewhere" and relied upon "much the same reasons that led [us] in *Ballew* to decide that use of a five-member jury threatened the fairness of the proceeding. . . ."

The constitutionality of other numerical combinations—for example, 8–4 or 7–5 verdicts or the various possible majorities on juries of seven to eleven members—remains in doubt. In *Burch,* the Court expressly reserved opinion on the constitutionality of nonunanimous verdicts by juries of more than six. Only Justice HARRY A. BLACKMUN, concurring in *Apodaca,* commented that a 7–5 verdict standard would afford him "great difficulty."

The Court's decisions in the nonunanimous verdict cases have been designed to leave room for the states to experiment with different majority verdict systems. But the uncertainty produced by these decisions may discourage experimentation. If the states do introduce additional variations, the notions that "lines must be drawn somewhere" and that at some point "the fairness of the proceeding" is threatened hardly provide an adequate basis for selecting among the numerous lines that may be presented. If the Court is unwilling to rely upon social science research to back up its functional approach, it may find itself without a calculus for resolving constitutional issues in which specific numbers count.

NORMAN ABRAMS

Bibliography

ZEISEL, HANS 1971 And Then There Were None: The Diminution of the Federal Jury. *University of Chicago Law Review* 38:710–724.

JUS DARE

(Latin: "To give the law.") This is the traditional function of the legislature in a constitutional government with SEPARATION OF POWERS and is contrasted with JUS DICERE, the function of courts. A court may be said to have invaded the realm of *jus dare* when it engages in JUDICIAL POLICYMAKING.

DENNIS J. MAHONEY

JUS DICERE

(Latin: "To say [what] the law [is].") This is the traditional function of courts, and it is usually understood as a limitation upon their power (*jus dicere, et non jus dare*). "It is emphatically the province of the judicial department to say what the law is"—Chief Justice JOHN MARSHALL in MARBURY V. MADISON (1803).

DENNIS J. MAHONEY

JUST COMPENSATION

The just compensation clause of the Fifth Amendment demands that a private property owner be made whole financially when property is taken by the federal government for PUBLIC USE. The same requirement is made applicable to the states by the DUE PROCESS clause of the FOURTEENTH AMENDMENT. The requisite compensation is the monetary equivalent of the property taken, putting the owner in as good a position pecuniarily as before the taking, as the Supreme Court held in *Monongahela Navigation Co. v. United States* (1893). Compensation for losses peculiar to the owner, such as loss of investment or business profits, litigation expenses, and relocation costs, is not constitutionally required, but often is made payable by statute.

In recognition of the somewhat elusive nature of the "monetary equivalent" standard, a variety of working rules have been developed to aid the courts. The most important of these rules is the concept of fair market value. Under this concept, the owner is entitled to receive, as just compensation, the price for the property interest taken that would be agreed upon, as of the time of the taking, by a willing and informed seller and a willing and informed buyer, considering the highest and best use for which the property was available and suitable.

The market value test, however, is not an inflexible one, and other methods of estimating value have been held appropriate when reference to actual market data is impossible because there is no actual market for the property, or when the market value test would result in manifest injustice by diverging to an impermissible degree from the full indemnity principle of the Fifth Amendment.

If the property taken is only a part of a single parcel, just compensation includes payment to the owner for any diminution in value of the remainder resulting from the planned use of the part taken, but the value of benefits to the remainder may be offset against the value of the "take." These results, which ordinarily can be measured by the difference in value of the property before and after the taking, can theoretically, although seldom in fact, result in a zero award. Many states, deeming it unfair to deduct enhancements to the remainder, reject the "before and after" test and award the full value of the part taken plus any net consequential damages realized by the remainder after offsetting any special benefits thereto. That either approach is constitutionally permissible was affirmed in *Bauman v. Ross* (1897).

ARVO VAN ALSTYNE

Bibliography

ORGEL, LESTER 1953 *Valuation under the Law of Eminent Domain*, Vol. 1. Charlottesville, Va.: Michie Co.

JUSTICE DEPARTMENT

See: Attorney General and Justice Department

JUSTICIABILITY

Federal judges do not establish legal norms at will or on demand, but only when deciding cases that are justiciable, that is, appropriate for federal court decision. What makes a case justiciable is thus itself an important threshold question, because it determines whether a federal court will exercise its power to formulate and apply substantive law, rather than leaving the issues in the case to be resolved by political or other means. Hence, when the Supreme Court fashions the criteria of justiciability for itself and the lower federal courts, it effectively defines the nature and scope of the JUDICIAL POWER OF THE UNITED STATES—the power to make decisions in accordance with law.

Most justiciability issues arise when litigants who are primarily motivated to vindicate public rights seek to contest the validity of government behavior, especially on constitutional grounds. Such public interest suits are usually designed not so much to redress traditional personal grievances as to vindicate fundamental principles. Commonly the plaintiffs seek DECLARATORY JUDGMENTS or INJUNCTIONS to prevent government officials from carrying on objectionable practices that affect a wide segment of the population. These actions often test and illustrate the degree to which federal judges, particularly Supreme Court Justices, view their power of constitutional oversight as warranted only by the necessity to resolve traditional legal disputes or, instead, by a broader judicial mission to ensure government observance of the Constitution.

In demarcating the federal judicial function, the law of justiciability comprises a complex of subtle doctrines, including STANDING, RIPENESS, MOOTNESS, ADVISORY OPINIONS, and POLITICAL QUESTIONS, among others. The Supreme Court has derived that law from two sources: Article III, which limits federal judicial power to the decision of CASES AND CONTROVERSIES, and nonconstitutional "prudential" rules of the Court's own creation. Both Article III and the rules of prudence incorporate notions of the attributes or qualities of litigation that make the legal issues presented appropriate for judicial determination. The difference between the two is that if Congress wants to have the federal courts entertain public actions, it may override the Court's prudential barriers, but not the constitutional limits of "case" and "controversy."

Three primary, and often mutually reinforcing, conceptions of appropriateness shape the many manifestations of justiciability. One concerns judicial capability. It centers on making federal court adjudication competent, informed, necessary, and efficacious. In this conception, a judicial decision is proper only when adversely affected parties litigate live issues of current personal consequence in a lawsuit whose format assures adversary argument and judicial capacity to devise meaningful remedies. The second conception of appropriateness concerns fairness. It promotes judicial solicitude for parties and interests not represented in the lawsuit, whose rights might be compromised unfairly by a substantive decision rendered without their participation. The third conception concerns the proper institutional and political role in our democracy of the appointed, electorally unaccountable federal judiciary. It cautions federal courts to be sure of the need for imposing restraints, especially constitutional restraints, on other, particularly more representative, government officials.

Whether the policies underlying justiciability doctrine are (or should be) applied in a principled, consistent fashion, depending on the form and characteristics of litigation alone, as the Supreme Court professes, or whether the Court does (or should) manipulate them for pragmatic reasons, is a subject of major controversy among the Court's commentators. Inevitably, the Court has discretion to adjust the degree to which these imprecise and flexible policies must be satisfied in particular cases, given individual variations in the configuration of lawsuits and the inherently relative nature of judgments about judicial capability, litigant need, and the propriety of JUDICIAL ACTIVISM AND RESTRAINT. Assessments of the information and circumstances needed for intelligent, effective adjudication will vary with the levels of generality at which issues are posed and with judicial willingness to act under conditions of uncertainty. Appraisals frequently diverge concerning hardship to, and representation of, present and absent parties who will be affected by rendering or withholding decision. Perhaps most dramatically, Justices differ in their evaluations of the relative importance of judicial control of government behavior and the freedom of politically accountable officials to formulate policy without judicial interference.

In view of the latitude and variation in the Court's self-conscious definition of federal judicial power, it is not surprising that justiciability is a sophisticated, controversial, and difficult field, or that many decisions provoke the skepticism that justiciability DOCTRINE has been manipulated to avoid decision of some issues and advance the decision of others. The Court certainly considers (and is willing to articulate) the degree of concrete focus and clarity with which issues are presented, and how pressing is the need for judicial protection of the litigants. The Court may also consider (but almost certainly will not articulate) a number of the following factors: how substantial, difficult, and controversial the issues are; whether a decision would likely legitimate government action or hold it unconstitutional; how important the Court believes the principle it would announce is and whether the principle could be expected to command public and government acceptance; the possibility of nonjudicial resolution; whether a decision would contribute to or cut off public debate; the expected general public reaction to a decision; the Justices' own constitutional priorities; and a host of other practical considerations that may implicate the Court's capacity to establish and enforce important constitutional principles.

Such judgments appear to have influenced a number of notable justiciability rulings in diverse ways. For example, in *Poe v. Ullman* (1961) the Court held a declaratory judgment challenge to Connecticut's contraception ban nonjusticiable because the statute was not being enforced, but later held the ban unconstitutional in the context of a criminal prosecution. By contrast, in a declaratory judgment challenge to an unenforced prohibition on teaching evolution, the Court, in EPPERSON V. ARKANSAS (1968), held the case justiciable and the prohibition unconstitutional without awaiting a prosecution. Similarly, the Court twice dismissed a seemingly justiciable appeal challenging Virginia's ban on MISCEGENATION, as applied to an annulment proceeding, within a few years of declaring public school segregation unconstitutional in 1954, but in 1967, following the CIVIL RIGHTS advances of the early 1960s, held the law unconstitutional on appeal of a criminal conviction. Moreover, although the Court has deferred decision in some cases where it ultimately held state statutes unconstitutional, it also occasionally appears to have lowered justiciability barriers and rushed to uphold the constitutionality of important federal legislation (the Tennessee Valley Authority and nuclear liability limitation statutes) or to invalidate it when Congress wanted constitutional assistance with ongoing legislative reform (the FEDERAL ELECTION CAMPAIGN ACT).

Perhaps the Court is inclined to insist on a greater showing of justiciability where it expects to hold governmental action unconstitutional than where it expects to uphold the action, in part because of a substantive presumption of the constitutionality of government conduct. Yet any generalization about the relations between justiciability and the Court's substantive views is hazardous, given the many factors and subtle judgments that may be weighed in any given case. What seems certain is that decisions on questions of justiciability will always be influenced by visions of the judicial role and will be difficult to comprehend without understanding those visions.

JONATHAN D. VARAT

Bibliography

BICKEL, ALEXANDER M. 1962 *The Least Dangerous Branch: The Supreme Court at the Bar of Politics.* Chap. 4. Indianapolis: Bobbs-Merrill.

GUNTHER, GERALD 1964 The Subtle Vices of the "Passive Virtues": A Comment on Principle and Expediency in Judicial Review. *Columbia Law Review* 64:1–25.

VARAT, JONATHAN D. 1980 Variable Justiciability and the *Duke Power* Case. *Texas Law Review* 58:273–327.

WRIGHT, CHARLES A.; MILLER, ARTHUR R.; and COOPER, EDWARD H. 1984 *Federal Practice and Procedure.* Vol. 13:278–293. St. Paul, Minn.: West Publishing Co.

JUVENILE PROCEEDINGS

In a juvenile proceeding, a state court is asked to decide whether and how to intervene in the life of a child who may need supervision or protection. These proceedings often take place in a juvenile or family court and usually have two distinct phases: a "jurisdictional" stage, at which the judge must decide whether there are grounds for intervention; and a "dispositional" phase, in which the judge decides how to intervene. Juvenile court statutes typically provide for JURISDICTION in three types of cases: the delinquency case, where a young person is found to have violated a criminal law; the case where the child's conduct is not criminal, but the child is found to be beyond parental control, or in need of supervision because of improper or protocriminal conduct, such as truancy, or running away; and the dependency case, where by reason of parental neglect or abuse the child is in need of protection. Once jurisdiction is established, the court typically has broad discretionary authority in the "dispositional phase" of juvenile proceedings to intervene into the child's life through supervision, or out-of-home placement in foster care or a residential institution.

At COMMON LAW, there were neither special courts nor separate proceedings for minors accused of violating the law. "Infancy" provided a defense, somewhat akin to insanity, in a case where because of immaturity a child lacked the capacity to form the requisite criminal intent. Presumptions made it impossible to find the requisite intent in children under seven, and difficult to find it in those between seven and fourteen. Youths over fourteen were presumed capable. Except for this possible defense, a child could be arrested, indicted, tried, and convicted just like an adult. Minors were regularly charged with crimes, tried like adults, and jailed and imprisoned with adult offenders.

In the nineteenth century, reformers began questioning the appropriateness of treating youthful and adult offenders alike. A revolution began in 1899, when Illinois established the first juvenile court. Hailed as a more humane and effective way of helping children in trouble get back on the track to good citizenship, the Illinois court became a model; by 1925 nearly every state had adopted LEGISLATION providing for some sort of juvenile proceedings. For these new juvenile proceedings, the implicit model of authority was not the traditional criminal trial with adversarial procedures but the family itself, with the state as *parens patriae*.

The philosophy of the early juvenile court emphasized four tenets. The first was rehabilitation, rather than deterrence or punishment. The state's goal was to save the wayward child through appropriate treatment. The second was individualization: justice for children was to be personalized. The court's primary goal was to determine whether a child needed help, and then to prescribe on an individualized basis the appropriate treatment. The third was separation: children were to be kept away from adult criminals who might physically brutalize minors or teach them criminal habits. Finally, juvenile procedure emphasized procedural informality. Although the adversarial determination of facts might be appropriate for a criminal trial where the purpose was punishment, legalistic formalities were thought to be counterproductive in a juvenile proceeding where the purpose was rehabilitation.

Before 1967, because of the philosophy of the juvenile court and its traditions of procedural informality, juvenile proceedings typically offered none of the safeguards afforded adults in criminal trials. Juvenile court practices were virtually unaffected by the recent decisions of the Supreme Court interpreting DUE PROCESS to impose increasingly high procedural standards imposed on state criminal proceedings. Except in a few states, a young person accused of delinquency would not be assigned counsel, had no broad RIGHT AGAINST SELF-INCRIMINATION, was judged by a preponderance of the evidence standard (not proof beyond a REASONABLE DOUBT), had no right to TRIAL BY JURY, and often faced HEARSAY evidence.

The Supreme Court had hinted that due process might demand more. *Haley v. Ohio* (1948) held that a confession given by a fifteen-year-old boy and used in a criminal trial was involuntary. Justice WILLIAM O. DOUGLAS wrote that "[n]either man nor child can

be allowed to stand condemned by methods that flout constitutional requirements of due process of law." More pointed doubts about the procedural informality of juvenile proceedings were expressed in *Kent v. United States* (1966). The Court's holding could be read narrowly: the District of Columbia must use fair procedures to transfer minors from juvenile to adult courts. But in Justice ABE FORTAS's opinion the landmark ruling that was to come the next year was foreshadowed in two respects: first, in the suggestion that the *parens patriae* doctrine of the juvenile court is not "an invitation to procedural arbitrariness"; and second, in the expression of the fear that notwithstanding the paternalistic philosophy of juvenile proceedings, the child may in fact receive "the worst of both worlds: that he gets neither the protections accorded to adults, nor the solicitous care and regenerative treatment postulated for children."

The constitutional watershed came in IN RE GAULT (1967), which held that due process required the states to apply various procedural safeguards to the guilt (or jurisdictional) phase of delinquency proceedings. The Court found that fifteen-year-old Gerald Gault, who had been committed for up to six years at an Arizona Industrial School for making an obscene telephone call, had been deprived of his constitutional rights to adequate written NOTICE of the charges, notice of his RIGHT TO COUNSEL, including assigned counsel, and of his right to confront and cross-examine witnesses; and advice of his privilege against self-incrimination. In a broad opinion rejecting the claim that *parens patriae* and the rehabilitative ideal justified procedural informality, Fortas declared that "unbridled discretion, however benevolently motivated, is frequently a poor substitute for principle and procedure." Although the holdings of *Gault* were expressly limited to the guilt phase of delinquency proceedings, *Gault* broadly declared a principle that children have constitutional rights of their own: "Whatever may be their precise impact, neither the FOURTEENTH AMENDMENT nor the BILL OF RIGHTS is for adults alone."

During the years following *Gault*, the Supreme Court decided several cases that expanded the constitutional rights of children in delinquency proceedings. IN RE WINSHIP (1970) held that the "beyond a reasonable doubt" standard of proof was constitutionally mandated in the adjudicatory stage of delinquency proceedings. *Breed v. Jones* (1975) held that the protections of the DOUBLE JEOPARDY clause were applicable to minors. The juvenile in *Breed* had been put in jeopardy by the original adjudicatory hearing where jurisdiction was established, and the Court found that the juvenile's subsequent criminal trial for the same offense constituted double jeopardy. But in *Swisher v. Brady* (1978) the Court held that the double jeopardy clause did not prohibit Maryland officials from taking exceptions to a SPECIAL MASTER's nondelinquency findings.

Despite the decisions in *Gault, Breed,* and *Winship,* the Court's decision in McKEIVER V. PENNSYLVANIA (1971) reflects the Court's continued commitment to a separate system of justice for children and adults. In *McKeiver* the Court held that jury trials are not constitutionally required in delinquency proceedings. The Court reasoned that because a jury is not "a necessary component of accurate factfinding," denying a juvenile a jury trial would not violate the FUNDAMENTAL FAIRNESS component of the due process clause. In addition, the Court pointed out that "the jury trial, if required as a matter of constitutional precept, will remake the juvenile proceeding into a fully adversary process and will put an effective end to what has been the idealistic prospect of an intimate, informal protective proceeding."

Since *Gault,* juvenile proceedings involving noncriminal misbehavior, or juveniles thought to be beyond parental control, have been questioned on both procedural and substantive grounds. What does *Gault* imply about appropriate procedural safeguards? To what extent may a state restrain the liberty of a minor on the basis of acts that if committed by adults would not be criminal? The Supreme Court has not yet ruled on the due process requirements applicable to these proceedings, and most states do not provide the procedural safeguards now applicable in delinquency proceedings. In addition to voicing procedural concerns, critics have also criticized as vague and overly broad the language defining these "status offenses": running away from home, sexual promiscuity, truancy, and the like. With few exceptions, however, appellate courts have upheld the constitutional validity of these statutes against such attacks. The Supreme Court, which has written no opinion dealing with such proceedings, has sent mixed signals in summary opinions.

Today every state has juvenile proceedings that allow a court, typically a juvenile or family court, to assume jurisdiction over a neglected or abused child and remove the child from the parents' care. Although not protected by explicit language in the Constitution, the interest of parents in their children's upbringing plainly carries great constitutional weight. Beginning with MEYER V. NEBRASKA (1923), the Supreme Court has recognized the constitutional right of parents to direct the rearing of their children. The parents' claim to authority, however, is not absolute. Since the early

nineteenth century, the *parens patriae* power has been held sufficient to empower courts of equity to remove a child requiring protection from parental custody and to appoint a suitable person as guardian.

Statutes authorizing state intervention have been criticized on substantive and procedural grounds. Vague substantive standards of abuse and neglect often leave judges to base their determinations on their own subjective values. As the Supreme Court noted in *Santosky v. Kramer* (1982), the Court has not precisely determined what forms of parental conduct justify state intrusion.

The Court has, however, decided several cases with respect to the procedural requirements where parental rights are terminated on grounds of abuse or neglect. In *Stanley v. Illinois* (1972) the Court relied on the doctrine of IRREBUTTABLE PRESUMPTIONS to hold that it is a denial of DUE PROCESS for unwed fathers to be disqualified from custody of their children without individualized hearings on their fitness. In *Santosky* the Court decided that the "fair preponderance of the evidence" standard, applied in New York parental rights termination proceedings, violated due process: "Before a State may sever completely and irrevocably the rights of parents in their natural child, due process requires that the State support its allegations by at least clear and convincing evidence." In LASSITER V. DEPARTMENT OF SOCIAL SERVICES (1981), however, the Court held that due process does not require assignment of counsel in every case involving the termination of parental rights. Although most jurisdictions do provide counsel for parents in such cases, few provide separate counsel for the children.

Gault has forced revolutionary changes in delinquency proceedings, but the requirements imposed in other sorts of juvenile proceedings have been modest. In the twenty years since that landmark, Supreme Court decisions have extended to young people accused of crime those procedural safeguards essential to an accurate determination of their guilt. To that extent, the Constitution no longer permits the procedural informality that characterized juvenile proceedings for over half a century. *Gault* and its progeny have substantially narrowed but not obliterated the differences between the adult criminal justice process and the juvenile justice process for delinquents. *McKeiver* underlines the conclusion that the Constitution does not require identical procedures for delinquents and adults. The Court has never held that equal protection requires the legal system to treat all those accused of crime the same, whether adults or minors.

Outside the guilt phase of delinquency proceedings, the Court has shown substantial caution, notwithstanding the potentially expansive announcement in *Gault* that children have rights, and that juvenile proceedings will be judged by their performance, not their promise. A number of factors probably underlie this caution. For one thing, the protective and rehabilitative aspirations of the juvenile court have never been rejected by the Court. As *McKeiver* suggests, the traditions of the juvenile court and the values of informality, flexibility, and protection still may carry some weight in constitutional adjudication. More fundamentally, decisions affecting children are special in two important respects that must affect constitutional analysis. First, defining constitutional rights in juvenile proceedings implicates defining parental rights, particularly in cases involving noncriminal misbehavior where the state may be reinforcing parental prerogatives, and in abuse and neglect proceedings, where the state directly challenges parental adequacy. Second, by reason of immaturity, young people may be more susceptible to coercion, and less able to make informed and responsible decisions. Whether considering the VOLUNTARINESS of a confession, the "knowing" WAIVER OF CONSTITUTIONAL RIGHTS, or the need for supervision and control, it would be foolish for the courts to conclude that age is irrelevant.

ROBERT H. MNOOKIN

(SEE ALSO: *Children's Rights; Schall v. Martin.*)

Bibliography

FLICKER, BARBARA 1982 *Standards for Juvenile Justice: A Summary and Analysis.* Juvenile Justice Standards Project. Cambridge, Mass.: Ballinger Publications.

FOX, SANFORD J. 1970 Juvenile Justice Reform: An Historical Perspective. *Stanford Law Review* 22:1187–1239.

MACK, JULIAN W. 1925 The Chancery Procedure in the Juvenile Court. Pages 310–319 in Jane Addams, ed., *The Child, the Clinic, and the Court.* New York: New Republic, Inc., and the Wieboldt Foundation.

PLATT, ANTHONY M. 1977 *The Child Savers: The Invention of Delinquency.* Chicago: University of Chicago Press.

PRESIDENT'S COMMISSION ON LAW ENFORCEMENT AND ADMINISTRATION OF JUSTICE 1967 *Task Force Report: Juvenile Delinquency and Youth Crime.* Washington, D.C.: Government Printing Office.

STAPLETON, W. VAUGHAN and TEITELBAUM, LEE E. 1972 *In Defense of Youth: A Study of the Role of Counsel in American Juvenile Courts.* New York: Russell Sage Foundation.

J. W. HAMPTON, JR. & CO. v. UNITED STATES

See: *Hampton & Co. v. United States*

KAHRIGER, UNITED STATES v.

See: *United States v. Marchetti*

KALVEN, HARRY, JR.
(1914–1974)

Commencing the lectures that became his book, *The Negro and the First Amendment* (1965), Harry Kalven remarked that constitutional law was his hobby. He considered himself a torts teacher who had become interested in some constitutional subjects, and certainly his writings on the constitutional law of DEFAMATION and invasions of PRIVACY show deep understanding of the underlying private law. But Kalven was no constitutional amateur; his work on the jury system and on the FIRST AMENDMENT placed him in the first rank of scholars in both fields.

A long collaboration with Hans Zeisel culminated in the publication of *The American Jury* (1966), a work still hailed for its pathbreaking combination of traditional legal analysis and imaginative empirical study. His essays on defamation and OBSCENITY set patterns of thought that can be seen in scores of later scholarly works, and his article on "the PUBLIC FORUM" probably influenced the course of Supreme Court decisions more than any other single work of its era. (See also: TWO-LEVEL THEORY.)

An effervescent man, Kalven was much beloved by a generation of his students at the University of Chicago Law School, some of whom are numbered today among our leading constitutional scholars. His legacy to them, and to all of us through his scholarship, was a passion for applying careful, particularized analysis—in short, the lawyer's craft—to the ends of justice.

KENNETH L. KARST

Bibliography

In Memoriam: Harry Kalven, Jr. 1975 *The University of Chicago Law Review* 43:1–149. (Includes a complete bibliography of Kalven's writings.)

KANSAS-NEBRASKA ACT
10 Stat 277 (1854)

The Kansas-Nebraska Act declared the MISSOURI COMPROMISE of 1820 void and in its place enacted the policy of "POPULAR SOVEREIGNTY," thereby potentially opening all American territories to SLAVERY.

Democrats had extolled the finality of the COMPROMISE OF 1850 as a permanent resolution of the slavery controversy. Its constitutional elements included the stringent Fugitive Slave Act of 1850; the organization of New Mexico and Utah Territories without a prohibition of slavery; abolition of the slave trade in the DISTRICT OF COLUMBIA; and the "Clayton Compromise," which made all questions arising in the TERRITORIAL COURTS involving blacks' personal freedom or title to slaves directly appealable to the Supreme Court of the United States. The Illinois Democrat STEPHEN A. DOUGLAS, chairman of the Senate Committee on the Territories, disrupted this settlement in 1854, however, by introducing a bill to organize the remainder of the LOUISANA PURCHASE territory in order to facilitate construction of a transcontinental railroad that would have Chicago as its midcontinent terminus.

Douglas's original bill contained minor concessions to slavery, including reenactment of the Clayton Compromise provisions for Kansas Territory. But dissatisfied proslavery senators wrested further concessions. These included the declaration that the Missouri Compromise of 1820 (which prohibited slavery in the Louisiana Purchase territory north of latitude 36°30′, except Missouri) had been superseded by the Compromise of 1850 and was void. The Kansas-Nebraska Bill enacted the principle of popular sovereignty, declaring that "all questions pertaining to SLAVERY IN THE TERRITORIES . . . are to be left to the decision of the people residing therein." It included a vague suggestion that the federal Constitution might in some unspecified way inhibit the power of a territorial legislature to exclude slaves. The bill explicitly endorsed "nonintervention," a code word for an indefinite congeries of proslavery constitutional principles that hinted at an absence of power in any government to inhibit the intrusion of slavery into the territories prior to statehood.

The Kansas-Nebraska Act, together with the Compromise of 1850, surrounded the free states and the free territory of Minnesota with a cordon of territories open to slavery, thus threatening to make the Great Plains a vast proslavery chasm between the free states of the northeast and the free states and territories of the Pacific coast. The Whig party distintegrated, and its place in the North was taken by the new Republican party, which combined Whig economic objectives (free homesteads, federal aid to INTERNAL IMPROVEMENTS) with elements of the Free Soil platform of 1848. These Free Soil principles included the idea that Congress could not establish or permit slavery in a territory and that it could not constitutionally support slavery anywhere outside the extant slave states. Thus the proslavery concessions of 1854 paradoxically resulted in no immediate practical gain for slavery but rather in a widespread dissemination of antislavery constitutional beliefs.

Kansas Territory, organized by the Act, became a theater of struggle for sectional advantage between proslavery Missourians and free-state settlers. The ensuing violence disrupted the Democratic party, especially after President JAMES BUCHANAN tried to force the proslavery LECOMPTON CONSTITUTION on the free-soil majority of Kansas settlers. The Kansas-Ne-

braska Act thus contributed substantially to the disruption of the Union.

WILLIAM M. WIECEK

Bibliography

Russel, Robert R. 1963 *The Issues in the Congressional Struggle over the Kansas-Nebraska Bill, 1854. Journal of Southern History* 29:187–210.

KASSEL v. CONSOLIDATED FREIGHTWAYS CORPORATION

See: *Raymond Motor Transportation v. Rice*

KASTIGAR v. UNITED STATES
406 U.S. 441 (1972)

Until this case the rule was that the Fifth Amendment requires a grant of transactional immunity to displace a claim of the RIGHT AGAINST SELF-INCRIMINATION. Title II of the ORGANIZED CRIME CONTROL ACT of 1970 fixed a single comprehensive standard applicable to grants of immunity in all federal judicial, GRAND JURY, administrative, and legislative proceedings. The new law provided that when a witness is required to testify over his claim of the Fifth Amendment right, "no testimony or other information compelled under the order (or any information directly or indirectly derived from such testimony or other information) may be used against the witness in any criminal cases," except in a prosecution for perjury or failure to comply. The statute thus provided for use immunity, permitting a prosecution based on EVIDENCE not derived from the testimony forced by a grant of immunity. (See IMMUNITY GRANT.)

Kastigar was cited for contempt after he persisted in his refusal to testify concerning unnecessary dental services affecting the draft status of persons seeking to evade the draft. His refusal to testify raised the question whether the grant of use immunity was sufficient to displace the Fifth Amendment right.

A seven-member Supreme Court, voting 5–2, sustained the constitutionality of use immunity. Justice LEWIS F. POWELL declared: "We hold that such immunity from use and derivative use is coextensive with the scope of the privilege against self-incrimination, and therefore is sufficient to compel testimony over a claim of the privilege. . . . Transactional immunity, which accords full immunity from prosecution for the offense to which the compelled testimony relates, affords the witness considerably broader protection than does the Fifth Amendment privilege. The privilege has never been construed to mean that one who invokes it cannot subsequently be prosecuted." Powell dismissed COUNSELMAN V. HITCHCOCK (1892) and its progeny, which established the transactional immunity standard, as OBITER DICTA and therefore not binding. Powell reasoned that a witness who had use immunity against his compelled testimony is in substantially the same position as if he had invoked the Fifth Amendment in the absence of a grant of immunity.

But one who relies on his constitutional right to silence gives the state no possible way to use his testimony, however indirectly, against him, and he has not remotely, from the standpoint of the law, criminally implicated himself. Use immunity permits compulsion without removing the implication of criminality. On the other hand, the values of the Fifth Amendment are not infringed if the state prosecutes on evidence not related to the compelled testimony, and the state has the burden of proving that the prosecution relies on evidence from sources independent of the compelled testimony. The trouble is, as Justice THURGOOD MARSHALL pointed out in dissent, that only the prosecuting authorities know, if even they can know, the chains of information by which evidence was gathered. In any case, use immunity compels a person to be a witness against himself criminally.

LEONARD W. LEVY

Bibliography

LEVY, LEONARD W. 1974 *Against the Law: The Nixon Court and Criminal Justice.* Pages 173–187. New York: Harper & Row.

KATZ v. UNITED STATES
389 U.S. 347 (1967)

Katz ended one era of constitutional protection for FOURTH AMENDMENT rights and began another. In OLMSTEAD V. UNITED STATES (1928) the Supreme Court had virtually exempted from the Fourth Amendment's ban on UNREASONABLE SEARCHES and seizures any search that did not involve a physical intrusion on property and a seizure of tangible things. Although eroded by subsequent decisions, and superseded by a federal statute where wiretapping was required, *Olmstead*'s physical intrusion requirement inhibited constitutional control of aural and visual surveillance for forty years, until *Katz* was decided.

Federal agents, believing that Katz was using a pay telephone to transmit gambling information, attached a listening and recording device to the outside of the phone booth without trying to meet Fourth Amendment requirements. With the information obtained from the device, the police were able to convict Katz, but the Supreme Court overturned the conviction. The Court ruled that Katz was entitled to Fourth Amendment protection for his conversations and that a physical intrusion into an area occupied by Katz was not necessary to bring the amendment into play. "The Fourth Amendment protects people, not places," wrote Justice POTTER STEWART for a virtually unanimous Court (only Justice HUGO L. BLACK dissented). Justice JOHN MARSHALL HARLAN, concurring, developed a test for determining what interests are protected, which has come to be the accepted standard: "first that a person have exhibited an actual (subjective) expectation of privacy and second, that the expectation be one that society is prepared to recognize as 'reasonable.'"

The Court also set out some of the requirements for lawful ELECTRONIC EAVESDROPPING, supplementing those in BERGER V. NEW YORK (1967), many of which were incorporated in Title III of the OMNIBUS CRIME CONTROL AND SAFE STREETS ACT of 1968.

HERMAN SCHWARTZ

KATZENBACH v. MCCLUNG

See: *Heart of Atlanta Motel v. United States*

KATZENBACH v. MORGAN
384 U.S. 641 (1966)

This decision upheld the constitutionality of section 4(e) of the VOTING RIGHTS ACT OF 1965. Section 4(e) provided that no person who had successfully completed sixth grade in a school in which the language of instruction was other than English should be denied the right to vote in any election because of his inability to read or write English. In *Lassiter v. Northampton County Board of Elections* (1959) a unanimous Supreme Court had rejected a black citizen's attack on North Carolina's LITERACY TEST for voting. In *Morgan* the Court, in an opinion by Justice WILLIAM J. BRENNAN and over the dissents of Justices JOHN MARSHALL HARLAN and POTTER STEWART, rejected New York State's argument that in enforcing section 5 of the FOURTEENTH AMENDMENT Congress may prohibit enforcement of state law only if courts determine that the state law violates the FOURTEENTH AMENDMENT.

In light of *Lassiter*, it seemed unlikely that New York's literacy requirement would be judicially found to violate the Constitution. Instead, the Court found Section 4(e) appropriate legislation to enforce the Fourteenth Amendment by assuring the franchise to those who migrated to New York from PUERTO RICO after completing sixth grade, whether or not that right to vote had been unconstitutionally infringed. The *Morgan* view that the Fourteenth Amendment confers discretion upon Congress to act both remedially and prophylactically to protect Fourteenth Amendment rights makes the case a centerpiece for analysis of how far Congress may go to protect or restrict Fourteenth Amendment rights.

THEODORE EISENBERG

KEATING-OWEN CHILD LABOR ACT
39 Stat. 675 (1916)

This law marked the federal government's first attempt to regulate the use of child labor, culminating a decade-long effort by organized labor, social reformers and workers, publicists, and progressive politicians. The act prohibited the shipment in interstate or foreign commerce of any commodity produced in a mine or factory that employed children under the ages of sixteen and fourteen respectively.

Congressional debates over child labor legislation centered on the scope of national power. Opponents of the measure insisted that it involved a regulation of PRODUCTION, not commerce, and hence violated the TENTH AMENDMENT and the controlling precedent of UNITED STATES V. E. C. KNIGHT (1895). Although that decision had been distinguished in other cases involving NATIONAL POLICE POWER uses of the COMMERCE CLAUSE, such as the regulation of adulterated foods, STATES RIGHTS' oriented southern congressmen insisted that the national government could only prohibit harmful items from INTERSTATE COMMERCE. Goods made by children, they insisted, were not harmful in and of themselves. Supporters of a child labor law countered that congressional power over interstate commerce was plenary except for Fifth Amendment limitations. They also maintained that congressional action was imperative because state regulations had proven ineffective.

Supporters of the bill mobilized a broad array of interested groups, coordinated by the highly effective National Child Labor Committee. In addition, some traditionally conservative northern manufacturers lobbied for national action to counter the competitive advantage of new southern industries that operated under ineffectual state laws against child labor. A House committee report reflected this concern, noting that only national power could maintain a national marketplace and prevent unfair competition among the states. Finally, in the summer of 1916, independent progressives convinced a hitherto reluctant President WOODROW WILSON that his support was necessary to insure progressive backing in the forthcoming presidential election. Wilson decisively intervened with southern senators who had prevented passage for nearly six months, and the bill became law on September 1, 1916.

The Keating-Owen Act proved short-lived, for in less than two years the Supreme Court invalidated it in HAMMER V. DAGENHART (1918). A 5–4 majority held that the act regulated production, not interstate commerce, and violated the Tenth Amendment. The *Knight* precedent was reconfirmed, and the Court distinguished its approval of police power regulations of the flow of lottery tickets, adulterated foods, prostitutes, and liquor on the grounds that child labor products were not injurious.

Congress followed the Court's action with a new law based on the taxing power, but it, too, was voided. An effort to secure a child labor amendment to the Constitution languished in the 1920s and 1930s, but finally, in 1938, the FAIR LABOR STANDARDS ACT revived the essential elements of Keating-Owen. The Court sustained the new law in UNITED STATES V. DARBY (1941), expressly overruling *Hammer v. Dagenhart*.

STANLEY I. KUTLER

Bibliography

WOOD, STEPHEN 1968 *Constitutional Politics in the Progressive Era: Child Labor and the Law.* Chicago: University of Chicago Press.

KELLY, ALFRED H.
(1907–1976)

Alfred Hinsey Kelly taught constitutional history for many years at Wayne State University. With his colleague Winfred A. Harbison he wrote *The American Constitution: Its Origins and Development* (1948; 6th ed., with Herman Belz, 1982), now widely regarded as the best single-volume constitutional history ever written. In 1953 Kelly researched the background of the FOURTEENTH AMENDMENT for the NAACP LE-

GAL DEFENSE FUND's brief in BROWN V. BOARD OF EDUCATION (1954), concentrating on establishing the views of the framers of the amendment. He and Fund attorneys THURGOOD MARSHALL and William R. Ming prepared the final version of the historical sections of the brief submitted to the Court; in this brief and in later articles on the Amendment, Kelly distinguished "between the narrow scope of the CIVIL RIGHTS ACT OF 1866 and the much broader purposes of the Fourteenth Amendment itself" and emphasized the "broad equalitarian objectives" advocated by Representatives JOHN A. BINGHAM, THADDEUS STEVENS, and other members of Congress in the debates on the amendment. Kelly also provided inside accounts of the *Brown* litigation in his essay in *Quarrels That Shaped the Constitution* (John Garraty, ed., 1962) and in interviews with Richard Kluger for the latter's *Simple Justice* (1976).

RICHARD B. BERNSTEIN

KEMMLER, IN RE
136 U.S. 436 (1890)
MCELVAINE v. BRUSH
142 U.S. 155 (1891)
O'NEIL v. VERMONT
144 U.S. 155 (1892)

These cases dealt with the meaning of the ban on CRUEL AND UNUSUAL PUNISHMENT and with the INCORPORATION DOCTRINE of the FOURTEENTH AMENDMENT. Kemmler was sentenced to die in the electric chair, then recently invented. He argued that infliction of death by that device would violate the Fourteenth Amendment, because its PRIVILEGES AND IMMUNITIES clause or its DUE PROCESS clause meant that no state could inflict a cruel execution. The Court unanimously ruled that a cruel execution would be one involving torture or lingering death, "something inhuman and barbarous," but that the electric chair was a "humane" form of execution. The Court also held that no clause of the Fourteenth Amendment banned punishments not deemed cruel by state courts. Unlike Kemmler, McElvaine explicitly argued that the Fourteenth Amendment incorporated the Eighth Amendment's ban on cruel punishments; he also argued that solitary confinement of a convict sentenced to death was cruel. Unanimously the Court met and rejected both contentions. In O'Neil's case, however, Justices STEPHEN J. FIELD, DAVID J.

BREWER, and JOHN MARSHALL HARLAN in DISSENTING OPINIONS declared that the Fourteenth Amendment applied Eighth Amendment rights and all "fundamental" rights to the states.

LEONARD W. LEVY

KENNEDY, JOHN F.
(1917–1963)

John Fitzgerald Kennedy entered the White House in 1961 as the heir to the liberal, Democratic party tradition of WOODROW WILSON, FRANKLIN D. ROOSEVELT, and HARRY S. TRUMAN. Youthful, vigorous, and blessed with extraordinary rhetorical powers, Kennedy saw himself as an activist chief executive and pledged to "get the country moving again," especially with respect to economic growth and international competition with the Soviet Union. But during his one thousand days in office, Kennedy's performance often lagged behind his promises.

His appointments to the Supreme Court were unexceptional. To the first vacancy, created by the retirement of CHARLES WHITTAKER, he named deputy attorney general BYRON R. WHITE, a former All-American football player, Rhodes Scholar, and campaign adviser. White's intellect and productivity exceeded those of his predecessor; he often aligned himself with the conservative faction on the WARREN COURT. To replace Justice FELIX FRANKFURTER and to fill the chair once occupied by OLIVER WENDELL HOLMES and BENJAMIN N. CARDOZO, Kennedy named ARTHUR GOLDBERG, a hard-working, conscientious labor lawyer, who usually voted with the liberals on the Warren Court but was blessed with neither intellectual brilliance nor a dashing prose style.

Kennedy's appointments to the lower federal courts were often dreadful, especially in the southern circuits, where "senatorial courtesy" gave great influence to segregationist Democratic senators. The result was Kennedy's appointment of a number of federal district judges who were openly segregationist and, in some instances, openly racist. On the other hand, Kennedy did place THURGOOD MARSHALL on the circuit court in New York; the Department of Justice, under the prodding of Attorney General ROBERT F. KENNEDY, began to intervene to protect CIVIL RIGHTS workers in the South; and Solicitor General Archibald Cox became a forceful and articulate spokesman for racial justice.

The struggle of black Americans to batter down the walls of segregation and win access to the voting booths of the deep South was the great domestic constitutional issue of the Kennedy years. The administration's response to this crisis blended pragmatism and expediency with idealism and occasional moral outrage. While forcing the South to accept the token integration of higher education, the administration did not push hard for similar results in the primary and secondary grades. The official violence inflicted upon civil rights activists during the Birmingham, Alabama, demonstrations led Kennedy to propose to Congress legislation which became, after his death, the landmark CIVIL RIGHTS ACT OF 1964. Many students of the Kennedy presidency regard his televised address in support of this legislation as his finest hour. On the other hand, the Kennedy brothers were not enthusiastic supporters of the 1963 March on Washington, and under pressure from FBI Director J. EDGAR HOOVER they endorsed the electronic surveillance of civil rights leader MARTIN LUTHER KING, JR.

If civil rights received growing constitutional protection from the Kennedy administration, CIVIL LIBERTIES often suffered at the hands of a regime that espoused vigorous presidential leadership and believed that the ends usually justified the means. Outraged that the nation's leading steel producers had raised prices in defiance of an informal agreement with labor and the White House, Kennedy threatened the offending corporations with tax audits, securities law investigations, and cancellation of defense contracts. Robert Kennedy's unremitting war against organized crime figures skirted the boundary of assorted illegalities, including WARRANTLESS SEARCHES and ELECTRONIC EAVESDROPPING. By waging a clandestine war against Fidel Castro's communist regime in Cuba, the Kennedy brothers also displayed a cavalier attitude about the RULE OF LAW. Operation Mongoose, directed by the attorney general, involved acts of sabotage and terrorism against the Cuban regime, most of them in violation of the neutrality laws.

Although their motives were sometimes the highest, John Kennedy and his closest advisers often fostered a disrespect for legal norms and an inflated conception of executive power that would haunt the nation during the decade after his assassination in 1963.

MICHAEL E. PARRISH

Bibliography

NAVASKY, VICTOR 1977 *Kennedy Justice.* New York: Atheneum.
PARMET, HERBERT S. 1983 *JFK: The Presidency of John F. Kennedy.* New York: Dial Press.

KENNEDY, ROBERT F.
(1925–1968)

After brief service in the Department of Justice, Robert F. Kennedy joined the Permanent Subcommittee on Investigations of the United States Senate (then headed by JOSEPH McCARTHY) in 1953 as assistant counsel. When John McClellan became chairman in 1955 he appointed Kennedy chief counsel. In 1957 Kennedy became chief counsel of McClellan's Senate Rackets Committee and achieved national fame during the committee's investigations of teamsters' union leaders David Beck and James Hoffa.

Kennedy was appointed attorney general in 1961 by his brother, President JOHN F. KENNEDY. In this post he distinguished himself by vigorous enforcement of CIVIL RIGHTS—desegregating schools and interstate transportation facilities—and by finally securing the conviction of Hoffa on jury-tampering charges. (See HOFFA V. UNITED STATES, 1966.) As the President's closest adviser he exerted more influence on FOREIGN AFFAIRS than most attorneys general, heading the "executive committee" of the National Security Council during the Cuban missile crisis of 1962.

As a United States senator from New York (1965–1968), Kennedy voted for the GULF OF TONKIN RESOLUTION but later opposed President LYNDON B. JOHNSON's conduct of the VIETNAM WAR. He was assassinated by a Palestinian nationalist while campaigning for the Democratic presidential nomination in 1968.

DENNIS J. MAHONEY

Bibliography

LASKY, VICTOR 1968 *Robert F. Kennedy: The Man and the Myth.* New York: Trident.

KENT, JAMES
(1763–1847)

James Kent, a New York jurist, influenced American constitutional jurisprudence through both his writings and his judicial opinions. Largely because of his *Commentaries on American Law,* Kent was as important a legal figure as any in nineteenth-century America. The *Commentaries* went through fourteen editions by 1900 and innumerable popular abridgments. After publication of the fifth edition, editors came and went, but they wrought their changes mostly in the notes, leaving Kent's work intact. For approximately three-quarters of a century Kent was for many lawyers, throughout the country, their primary legal authority.

Originally a two-volume set when it appeared in 1826, the *Commentaries* were quickly expanded to four. Ostensibly the book was commenced after Kent's mandatory retirement from the bench on reaching age sixty in 1823. Yet, it is possible to see the work in process through Kent's carefully crafted opinions beginning with his appointment to the New York Supreme Court in 1798, and continuing while he was the state's chancellor, 1814–1823. And it is scarcely stretching matters to consider the writing of the *Commentaries* a lifelong process.

Kent's twenty-five years of judicial opinions were imbued with the federalism of the late eighteenth century. At the heart of Kent's jurisprudence was an independent judiciary whose role was to maintain society's moral order. Because of a quirk in New York's 1777 constitution, Kent participated in the veto process as a member of the Council of Revision, which considered all bills passed by the legislature. This process meant that New York judges would have little reason to exercise JUDICIAL REVIEW when a statute's constitutionality was questioned in a case. Having approved the steamboat monopoly bill on several occasions while sitting on the council, for example, New York judges would be unlikely to declare the law contrary to the federal constitution when such a challenge was made in *Livingston v. Van Ingen* (1812) and GIBBONS V. OGDEN (1819, 1820).

The moral order that Kent and his brethren sought to maintain covered many facets of life, including freedom of expression. There was no room in Kent's order of things for BLASPHEMY—"it tends to corrupt the morals of the people, and to destroy good order," he wrote in *People v. Ruggles* (1811)—but a Federalist printer was afforded the defense of truth to the COMMON LAW charge of criminal libel against THOMAS JEFFERSON in PEOPLE V. CROSWELL (1804). The New York Supreme Court was evenly divided in *Croswell*, so that Kent's opinion, based on ALEXANDER HAMILTON's argument, did not become law in itself. A year later the legislature made truth a defense in libel suits, provided the alleged libelous matter "was published with good motives and for justifiable ends." Kent and his colleagues were careful, moreover, in their interpretation of the law, subsequently inserted in the state constitution of 1821, to protect officeholders, setting the groundwork for *Root v. King* (1829), which kept a bridle on attacks on New York public officials until NEW YORK TIMES V. SULLIVAN (1964).

Kent made another major contribution to constitutional law in *Livingston v. Van Ingen* (1812), by elaborately enunciating the doctrine of concurrent commerce powers. The Livingston-Fulton steamboat monopoly symbolized New York's encouragement of commercial enterprise. Under the statute creating the

monopoly, any competitor was required to get a license in order to run a steamboat on New York waters. In his opinion for the state's court of last resort, Kent legitimized the monopoly in a decision that reversed Chancellor JOHN LANSING's refusal to grant the monopoly an INJUNCTION against unlicensed competition. Of particular constitutional moment was the argument that the monopoly violated the federal Constitution's COMMERCE CLAUSE. In rejecting this argument, Kent asserted that in the absence of actual conflict between state and national laws, states retained the powers to regulate commerce. Seven years later in *Ogden v. Gibbons* (1819), Kent found no such conflict between the monopoly and the federal coasting act of 1793. In the United States Supreme Court, however, that served as the basis for JOHN MARSHALL's invalidation of the monopoly in GIBBONS V. OGDEN (1824). Kent's doctrine of concurrent commerce powers persisted, though, largely through the efforts of his former law clerk and judicial colleague, SMITH THOMPSON, and for a time it won the support of the TANEY COURT.

Kent was also responsible for first enunciating what would become the Cherokee doctrine. Speaking for the New York court in *Goodell v. Jackson* (1823), Kent fully developed the paternalistic notion that American Indian peoples, though subject, were sovereign nations, a theme adopted by Thompson in his *Cherokee Nation v. Georgia* dissent (1831), which in turn was adopted by Marshall for the Supreme Court in *Worcester v. Georgia* (1832). (See CHEROKEE INDIAN CASES.)

Important as Kent's occasional constitutional opinions may have been, his major contribution to constitutional development remains the *Commentaries*. There is apparent irony in this accomplishment because Kent did not emphasize constitutional law; instead, he salted that subject into the great body of American law between the law of nations and the construction of wills. Kent succeeded in putting constitutional law in its proper perspective compared to other important aspects of the law. In addition, Kent admirably digested the great Marshall opinions so as, in the opinion of THOMAS REED POWELL, to make them decidedly more palatable than they were in the original. Needless to say, the *Commentaries* continued to vote Federalist.

DONALD ROPER

Bibliography

BAUER, ELIZABETH KELLEY 1952 *Commentaries on the Constitution 1790–1860.* New York: Columbia University Press.

HORTON, JOHN T. 1939 *James Kent: A Study in Conservatism 1763–1847.* New York: Appleton-Century Co.

KENT v. DULLES
357 U.S. 116 (1958)

This decision severely limited the State Department's discretionary passport policies. During the Cold War era, the department routinely denied passports to those who refused to sign a noncommunist affidavit. The Supreme Court held that the department lacked statutory authority for this policy and went on to remark in OBITER DICTUM that the RIGHT TO TRAVEL, which it traced back to MAGNA CARTA, was protected by the DUE PROCESS clause of the FIFTH AMENDMENT.

STANLEY I. KUTLER

KENTUCKY RESOLUTIONS

See: Virginia and Kentucky Resolutions

KER v. CALIFORNIA
374 U.S. 23 (1963)

In *Ker* the Supreme Court clarified the constitutional standards governing the states in SEARCH AND SEIZURE cases. MAPP V. OHIO (1961), in applying the federal EXCLUSIONARY RULE against the states, had left undetermined whether they would retain some latitude to fashion their own search rules. The Court answered this question in *Ker,* holding that the protection against state searches granted by the FOURTEENTH AMENDMENT is coextensive with that of the FOURTH AMENDMENT against federal searches. Only Justice JOHN MARSHALL HARLAN disagreed. The Court's single-standard position, he feared, might lead to dilution of federal search safeguards because the Court would be reluctant to fetter the states with standards beyond their reach.

JACOB W. LANDYNSKI

KEYES v. SCHOOL DISTRICT NO. 1
413 U.S. 189 (1973)

Keyes, the Denver school DESEGREGATION case, was the first such case to reach the Supreme Court from a district outside the South. The case gave the Court an opportunity to decide whether the fact of separation of the races in a city's schools was sufficient to

justify desegregation remedies, even in the absence of any history of state law commanding SEGREGATION or any deliberate segregative action by the school board. The Court found it unnecessary to decide this question. Deliberate segregative actions of the board in one substantial part of the city, the Court said, raised a presumption of de jure segregation affecting the whole district; absent a showing that the district's parts were truly unrelated, a districtwide remedy would be approved on the basis of SWANN V. CHARLOTTE-MECKLENBURG BOARD OF EDUCATION (1971). The Court thus affirmed a busing order affecting twelve percent of the district's pupils. Justice WILLIAM J. BRENNAN wrote for a Court that was no longer unanimous.

Justice LEWIS F. POWELL, in a separate opinion that was more dissent than concurrence, argued that the time had come to scrap the DE FACTO/DE JURE distinction. In his view, *Swann* effectively required a school board to provide a remedy not only for segregation deliberately brought about by its own action or by state law but also for residential segregation—a fact of urban life throughout the country. "Segregative intent" was an illusory concept, he said. Once the fact of racial separation is shown, a board should have the duty to take appropriate steps to minimize school segregation. Massive busing, however, was not an appropriate remedy in his opinion, chiefly because of its costs to the values of the neighborhood school. Justice WILLIAM O. DOUGLAS, concurring, also thought that the de facto/de jure distinction made no sense but thought busing an appropriate remedy. Chief Justice WARREN E. BURGER concurred in the result, Justice WILLIAM H. REHNQUIST dissented, and Justice BYRON R. WHITE did not participate.

KENNETH L. KARST

(SEE ALSO: *School Busing; Columbus Board of Education v. Penick, 1979.*)

KEYISHIAN v. BOARD OF REGENTS
385 U.S. 589 (1967)

ADLER V. BOARD OF EDUCATION (1952) was one of the cases in which the Supreme Court upheld a wide range of regulations barring "subversives" from government employment. *Keyishian* overruled *Adler* and was the culmination of a series of later decisions restricting LOYALTY-SECURITY PROGRAMS, typically by invoking the VAGUENESS and OVERBREADTH doctrines. *Keyishian* struck down some parts of a complex New York law limiting employment in public teaching; the law's use of the term "seditious" was unconstitutionally vague. Other parts of the law were invalid because they prohibited *mere* knowing membership in the Communist party without the specific intent required by ELFBRANDT V. RUSSELL (1966). *Keyishian* confirmed the Court's previous decisions rejecting the doctrine that public employment is a privilege to which government may attach whatever conditions it pleases.

MARTIN SHAPIRO

KIDD v. PEARSON
128 U.S. 1 (1888)

A unanimous Court distinguished manufacturing and all forms of PRODUCTION from INTERSTATE COMMERCE, holding that a state act prohibiting the manufacture of intoxicants did not conflict with the national power to regulate interstate commerce and that the manufacture of a product for export to other states did not make it an article of interstate commerce.

LEONARD W. LEVY

KILBOURN v. THOMPSON
103 U.S. 168 (1881)

Until this case Congress believed that its power of conducting investigations was unlimited and that its judicial authority to punish contumacious witnesses for contempt was unquestionable. After this case both the investigatory and CONTEMPT POWERS of Congress were distinctly limited and subject to JUDICIAL REVIEW. Not until MCGRAIN V. DAUGHERTY (1927) did the Court firmly establish the constitutional basis for oversight and investigatory powers. The decision in *Kilbourn* was so negative in character that the legitimate area of LEGISLATIVE INVESTIGATIONS seemed murky.

Kilbourn developed out of the House's investigation, by a select committee, into the activities of a bankrupt banking firm that owed money to the United States. The committee subpoenaed Kilbourn's records, which he refused to produce, and interrogated him, but he refused to answer on the ground that the questions concerned private matters. The House cited him for contempt and jailed him. He in turn sued for false arrest, and on a writ of HABEAS CORPUS he obtained a review of his case before the Supreme Court.

Unanimously, in an opinion by Justice SAMUEL F. MILLER, the Court held that neither house of Congress can punish a witness for contumacy unless his testimony is required on a matter concerning which "the House has jurisdiction to inquire," and, Miller added, neither house has "the general power of making inquiry into the private affairs of the citizen." The subject of this inquiry, Miller said, was judicial in nature, not legislative, and a case was pending in a lower federal court. The investigation was fruitless also because "it could result in no valid legislation" on the subject of the inquiry. Thus, the courts hold final power to decide what constitutes a contempt of Congress, and Congress cannot compel a witness to testify in an investigation that cannot assist remedial legislation.

LEONARD W. LEVY

KING, MARTIN LUTHER, JR.
(1929–1968)

Martin Luther King, Jr., preeminent leader of the black freedom movement of the 1950s and 1960s, repeatedly challenged America to live up to the egalitarian principles set forth in the three Reconstruction era amendments. "If we are wrong, the Constitution of the United States is wrong," King told his Alabama colleagues in an unpublished speech on December 5, 1955, the day that Montgomery's black citizens began a year-long campaign against discriminatory seating practices on city buses. Victory in that struggle catapulted King to national prominence as an exponent of nonviolent protest against racial oppression, and throughout the twelve remaining years of his life King pursued and expanded his challenge to injustice and exploitation internationally as well as domestically.

Pointing out in his 1964 book, *Why We Can't Wait,* that the United States was "a society where the supreme law of the land, the Constitution, is rendered inoperative in vast areas of the nation" because of explicit RACIAL DISCRIMINATION, King described the CIVIL RIGHTS struggle as a resumption "of that noble journey toward the goals reflected in the PREAMBLE to the Constitution, the Constitution itself, the BILL OF RIGHTS and the THIRTEENTH, FOURTEENTH, and FIFTEENTH AMENDMENTS." Protest campaigns in segregationist strongholds such as Birmingham and Selma, Alabama, stimulated national support for landmark legislative achievements such as the CIVIL RIGHTS ACT OF 1964 and the VOTING RIGHTS ACT of 1965, and produced an all-but-complete victory over de jure segregation by the middle of that decade.

Recognizing that other evils more subtle than segregation also tangibly afflicted the daily lives of millions of black people, King broadened his attack to include all forms of poverty and economic injustice, saying that the movement had to go beyond civil rights to human rights. That progression, coupled with King's outspoken condemnations of America's militaristic foreign policy, particularly its participation in the VIETNAM WAR, led King to advocate basic changes in American society reaching far beyond his previous attacks on racial discrimination.

Identified as a prominent advocate of CIVIL DISOBEDIENCE against immoral segregation statutes even before his influential 1963 "Letter from Birmingham Jail," King defended his position by reference to the long tradition of NATURAL RIGHTS thinking. In his early years of civil rights activism King said that peaceful, willing violation of such statutes forced courts to void unconstitutional provisions, but toward the end of his life King expanded his argument, contending that the weightier moral demands of social justice sometimes required that nondiscriminatory laws also be violated. If any laws blocked the oppressed from confronting the nation with moral issues of human rights and economic justice, then such laws rightfully could be breached. Although King until 1966 had believed that depicting the brutalities of racism best attracted national support for civil rights, in his final years King repeatedly suggested that protesters might have to coerce concessions from unwilling federal officials by obstructing the orderly functioning of society until the desired policy changes were made.

King's challenge to American racism helped to close the gap between constitutional principles and discriminatory practices; his broader struggle against other forms of human injustice left a legacy that will stimulate future generations for years to come.

DAVID J. GARROW

Bibliography
GARROW, DAVID J. 1986 *Bearing the Cross: Martin Luther King, Jr., and the Southern Christian Leadership Conference, 1955–1968.* New York: William Morrow.
KING, MARTIN LUTHER, JR. 1964 *Why We Can't Wait.* New York: New American Library.

KING, RUFUS
(1755–1827)

Rufus King, a Harvard-educated lawyer who had been an officer in the Revolutionary War, represented Massachusetts in the Congress of the Confederation from 1784 to 1787. He was a principal author of the NORTHWEST ORDINANCE, and wrote its provisions prohibiting SLAVERY and protecting the OBLIGATION OF CONTRACTS against legislative impairment.

Although he originally opposed either calling a convention or radically altering the ARTICLES OF CONFEDERATION, he represented Massachusetts at the CONSTITUTIONAL CONVENTION OF 1787. King soon became a spokesman for those who favored a strong national government and for the interests of the large northern states. Very early in the debates he advocated consolidation rather than confederation: although he recognized that it was impossible to annihilate the states, he thought they should be stripped of much of their power. He argued against equal representation of the states in the Senate, and he favored popular election of the President. King proposed the CONTRACT CLAUSE, and, although it was voted down in the Committee of the Whole, he saw that it was inserted into the Constitution by the Committee on Style, of which he was a member. In opposition to GOUVERNEUR MORRIS, he supported the admission of new states on terms of equality with the old. King was also one of the first to recognize publicly that the politically important division of the country was not between large and small states, but between North and South.

Almost immediately after attending the Massachusetts ratifying convention, he moved to New York and was elected one of its original United States senators. King served in the Senate from 1789 to 1796, and was a leading spokesman for ALEXANDER HAMILTON (his political patron) and the Federalist administration.

King returned to the Senate in 1813. Although an opponent of the War of 1812, he refused to attend the HARTFORD CONVENTION, denounced New England's threat of SECESSION, and supported the government financially. Serving in the Senate until 1825, King participated in the debates over the MISSOURI COMPROMISE. Although not an abolitionist, King opposed the extension of SLAVERY, and he contended that it was within the power of Congress to make permanent abolition of slavery a condition of Missouri's admission as a state. He insisted upon constitutional guarantees of the rights of black Missourians.

In his public career, King was the Federalist candidate for vice-president (1804, 1808) and President (1816), and was twice minister to Great Britain (1796–1803, 1825–1826).

DENNIS J. MAHONEY

KINGSLEY BOOKS, INC. v. BROWN
354 U.S. 436 (1957)

Kingsley authorized broad civil remedies to control the merchandising of OBSCENITY. The Supreme Court upheld a New York statute permitting state officials to obtain INJUNCTIONS against the sale of allegedly obscene materials before a judicial determination that the materials were obscene and, after trial, to seize and destroy any material found to be obscene. Rejecting assertions that the statutory scheme was an unconstitutional PRIOR RESTRAINT, the majority concluded that the scheme in actual application did not differ from the criminal remedies sanctioned in *Alberts v. California* (1957), decided the same day. (See ROTH V. UNITED STATES, 1957.)

The dissenters argued that numerous procedural defects rendered the statute unconstitutional. The seizure and destruction of the obscene books were tantamount to "book burning," according to Chief Justice EARL WARREN, for books were judged outside the context of their use. Justices WILLIAM O. DOUGLAS and HUGO L. BLACK, jointly dissenting, argued that an injunction before trial was censorship. They also would have required a finding of obscenity for each publication of the condemned work rather than regulating speech like "diseased cattle and impure butter." Justice WILLIAM J. BRENNAN contended that the statute was vastly defective for permitting a judge, rather than a jury, to determine a work's obscenity.

KIM MCLANE WARDLAW

KINGSLEY INTERNATIONAL PICTURES CORP. v. REGENTS
360 U.S. 684 (1959)

In *Kingsley International Pictures Corp. v. Regents* the state of New York had refused to issue a license for the motion picture *Lady Chatterley's Lover* because it "alluringly portrays adultery as proper behavior." There was no claim that the film constituted an INCITEMENT TO UNLAWFUL CONDUCT. Without deciding whether all licensing schemes for motion pictures were unconstitutional the Supreme Court held that the refusal to grant this license violated the FIRST AMENDMENT. The Court reaffirmed that motion pictures were within the scope of the First Amendment and proclaimed that the amendment's "basic guarantee" is "the freedom to advocate ideas," including the idea that adultery may in some cases be justified.

STEVEN SHIFFRIN

KINSELLA v. KRUEGER

See: *Reid v. Covert*

KIRBY v. ILLINOIS
406 U.S. 682 (1972)

In an effort to eviscerate UNITED STATES V. WADE (1967) without overruling it, a plurality of the Supreme Court held that the RIGHT TO COUNSEL does not apply to pretrial identification procedures that occur before INDICTMENT or other indicia of formal criminal charges. The case involved the most suggestive confrontation imaginable: a one-to-one presentation of the person upon whom police had found a robbery victim's credit cards. Yet the Court held that because this confrontation occurred before Kirby had been formally charged, it was not a "critical stage" of the proceedings requiring counsel to preserve a future right to a FAIR TRIAL.

The distinction between pre- and postindictment identification procedures is dubious for two reasons. First, the vast majority of LINEUPS occur while cases are under investigation, and thus before indictment. Second, all the dangers of irreparable mistaken identification and the inability of counsel to reconstruct the pretrial confrontation—which had been the foundation of *Wade*—apply whether the identification occurs before or after formal charging. The plurality's startling misreading of precedent was highlighted when Justice BYRON R. WHITE, who dissented in *Wade*, dissented in *Kirby* also, saying that *Wade* compelled the opposite result.

Kirby leaves untouched the possible DUE PROCESS objections to an unfair pretrial confrontation. Proof of unfairness would require suppression of testimony about the pretrial procedure as well as the in-court identification by a witness whose perceptions were possibly tainted. A due process objection may be made whether the pretrial confrontation has occurred before or after formal charging. Of course, it is much more difficult for the accused to show that a confrontation was fundamentally unfair than to prove that it was done without counsel.

BARBARA ALLEN BABCOCK

KIRSCHBAUM v. WALLING
316 U.S. 517 (1942)

After UNITED STATES V. DARBY (1941) the Court decided many cases on the coverage of the FAIR LABOR STANDARDS ACT, which benefited employees "engaged in commerce or in the PRODUCTION of goods for commerce." Congress by no means had made the statute coextensive with the limits of its power over INTERSTATE COMMERCE, but every time the Court ruled that the statute covered certain employees, it brought their activities within the scope of the COMMERCE CLAUSE. The leading case is *Kirschbaum,* which extended statutory coverage—and thus the commerce power—to employees who were at least one step away from production. On the theory that service and maintenance employees kept a building safe and habitable, the Court held that a landlord who rented space to a firm that manufactured goods destined for interstate commerce had to pay his janitors and elevator operators the minima fixed by the statute. In *Borden Milk Co. v. Barella* (1945), the Court upheld application of the statute to service employees in a building occupied by the executive offices of a company that carried on its interstate manufacturing elsewhere. In *Martino v. Michigan Window Cleaning Co.* (1946), the employees who benefited from the statute—window cleaners employed by a company to service an industrial building—were two steps removed from production for commerce. Similarly, in *D. A. Schulte v. Gangi* (1946), the Court extended the statute and the commerce power to the maintenance people employed by a building owner who rented space to a firm that worked on intrastate goods and returned them to a contractor who subsequently shipped some of them across state lines. Employees sometimes did lose, but the Court's interpretations in these cases showed that the commerce power virtually authorized Congress to regulate any business, however remote its economic connection with interstate commerce.

LEONARD W. LEVY

KLOPFER v. NORTH CAROLINA
386 U.S. 213 (1967)

Prior to the Supreme Court's decision in *Klopfer,* only defendants in federal courts enjoyed the Sixth Amendment right to a SPEEDY TRIAL. Consequently, legislation in many states permitted prosecutors to postpone bringing pending cases to trial indefinitely. Declaring such state laws unconstitutional, the Court, in an opinion by Chief Justice EARL WARREN, held that the right to a speedy trial is a FUNDAMENTAL RIGHT incorporated by the DUE PROCESS CLAUSE of the FOUR-

TEENTH AMENDMENT and thus fully applicable in state trials.

WENDY E. LEVY

(SEE ALSO: *Incorporation Doctrine.*)

KNIGHT COMPANY, E. C., UNITED STATES v.
156 U.S. 1 (1895)

The issue in the Supreme Court's first interpretation of the SHERMAN ANTITRUST ACT hung on the lawfulness of the Sugar Trust's acquisition of its competitors, and the decision nearly eviscerated the act. An 8–1 Court used the doctrine of DUAL FEDERALISM in dismissing a government suit to dissolve the trust.

When the American Sugar Refining Company (the Sugar Trust) acquired four Philadelphia refineries in 1892 it controlled ninety-eight percent of domestic sugar manufacturing. Attorney General RICHARD OLNEY, who inherited the case from his predecessor, believed that the Sherman Act was founded on a false economic theory; he believed that free competition had been "thoroughly discredited" and that the act should have regulated trusts as a natural development, not prohibited them. There is, however, little evidence of deliberate carelessness in Olney's preparation of the case. Although the MAJORITY OPINION commented upon a lack of EVIDENCE to demonstrate a restraint of trade, the government never believed that such a showing was necessary. Prior decisions had clearly held sales to be a part of commerce; the majority would admit as much here, and a lower court conceded that the trust had sought control of both refining and sales. Clever defense strategy successfully shifted the Court's attention from restraint of INTERSTATE COMMERCE to a consideration whether the commerce power extended to manufacturing.

Chief Justice MELVILLE W. FULLER's opinion for the Court endorsed the defendants' argument. By repeating that manufacturing was separable from commerce, the Court made a formally plausible distinction based solely on precedent. (See KIDD V. PEARSON, 1888.) Although the Sugar Trust had monopolized manufacturing, the Court found no Sherman Act violation because the acquisition of the Philadelphia refineries involved INTRASTATE COMMERCE. Although manufacturing "involves in a certain sense the control of its disposition . . . this is a secondary and not the primary sense." The trust did not lead to control of interstate commerce and so "affects it only incidentally and indirectly." This direct/indirect effects test of the reach of federal regulation had been mentioned in earlier cases (see EFFECTS ON COMMERCE) and was here employed to reach unrealistic ends: "Contracts, combinations, or conspiracies to control domestic enterprise in manufacture, agriculture, mining, PRODUCTION in all its forms, or to raise or lower prices or wages, might unquestionably tend to restrain external as well as domestic trade, but the restraint would be an indirect result, however inevitable and whatever its extent, and such result would not necessarily determine the object of the contract, combination or conspiracy."

Justice JOHN MARSHALL HARLAN, dissenting, posed the basic question: "What, in a legal sense, is a restraint of trade?" The trust was in business to sell as well as manufacture sugar, and most of its sales obviously constituted interstate commerce. Relying on GIBBONS V. OGDEN (1824), Harlan posited a broad view of the commerce power. Any obstruction of commerce among the states was an impairment of that commerce and must be treated as such. The majority's construction of the Sherman Act left the public "at the mercy of combinations." The Sugar Trust's inevitable purpose of preventing free competition doomed it as a restraint of trade. "The general government is not placed by the Constitution in such a condition of helplessness that it must fold its arms and remain inactive while capital combines . . . to destroy competition." Harlan correctly believed that the issue should not have been the contracts of acquisition but rather the trust's control over commerce in sugar.

By excluding manufacturing monopolies from the scope of the antitrust act, the decision in *Knight* cleared the way for the greatest merger and consolidation movement in American history. Chief among the industries taking advantage of the opportunities given them by the Supreme Court were manufacturing and the railroads. Such massive combines as United States Steel Corporation, American Can Company, International Harvester, and Standard Oil of New Jersey can trace their origins to this period. From 1879 to 1897 fewer than a dozen important combinations had been formed, with a total capital of around one billion dollars. Before the century ended, nearly two hundred more combinations formed, with a total capital exceeding three billion dollars. Of some 318 CORPORATIONS in business in 1904, nearly seventy-five percent had been formed after 1897.

The Court's opinion also seriously injured the concept of national supremacy; Fuller's distinction between production and commerce lasted until 1937. In the meantime, the Court had created what ED-WARD S. CORWIN called a "twilight zone" in which national regulation of corporations was uncertain and haphazard. Although the Court would apply the Sherman Act to railroads within two years (see UNITED STATES V. TRANS-MISSOURI FREIGHT ASSOCIATION, 1897), not until the reinterpretation in NORTHERN SECURITIES CO. V. UNITED STATES (1904) would the Sherman Act become an effective tool against big business.

DAVID GORDON

Bibliography

EICHNER, ALFRED S. 1969 *Emergence of Oligopoly: Sugar Refining as a Case Study.* Westport, Conn.: Greenwood Press.

KNOX, PHILANDER C.
(1853–1921)

Although Philander Chase Knox, a Pittsburgh corporation lawyer, had helped create the United States Steel Corporation, he became an active antitrust prosecutor as THEODORE ROOSEVELT's ATTORNEY GENERAL (1901–1904). Knox initiated the efficient and meticulous prosecution in NORTHERN SECURITIES CO. V. UNITED STATES (1904) and successfully argued that case before the Supreme Court. He also began victorious cases against the Salt Trust, the Coal Trust, and the Beef Trust, the latter culminating in the STREAM OF COMMERCE doctrine in SWIFT & COMPANY V. UNITED STATES (1905). Knox's actions helped revive the SHERMAN ANTITRUST ACT and insured a prominent political career after his resignation in 1904. He served as WILLIAM HOWARD TAFT's secretary of state (1909–1913) and later, in the Senate, played a major role in railroad rate legislation. An "irreconcilable" over the League of Nations, Knox believed it imposed unconstitutional obligations under the TREATY POWER.

DAVID GORDON

KNOX v. LEE

See: Legal Tender Cases

KOLENDER v. LAWSON
461 U.S. 352 (1983)

The facts of this case, not revealed by the official report, enhanced its interest. Lawson was a law-abiding black man of unorthodox attire and grooming who suffered frequent police harassment when he walked in white neighborhoods. A 7–2 Supreme Court held VOID FOR VAGUENESS a California statute obligating persons who "wander" the streets to provide credible and reliable identification and to explain their business to the police. The majority reasoned that the statute vested excessive discretion in the police to decide whether to stop and interrogate a suspect or leave him alone in the absence of PROBABLE CAUSE to arrest him. The Court also suggested that the statute compromised the constitutional right to freedom of movement.

LEONARD W. LEVY

KONIGSBERG v. STATE BAR
353 U.S. 252 (1957)
366 U.S. 36 (1961)

In *Konigsberg* I the Supreme Court held that refusal to answer questions about political associations was constitutionally insufficient to justify a state bar association finding of failure to demonstrate good moral character, and consequent denial of bar admission. In *Konigsberg* II the Court upheld a second denial of admission based on the ground that refusal to answer obstructed full investigation of the applicant's qualifications.

MARTIN SHAPIRO

KOREAN WAR

In June 1950 North Korea attacked South Korea; within a week President HARRY S. TRUMAN committed American air, sea, and ground forces to South Korea's defense. The resulting three-year involvement lasted into the administration of DWIGHT D. EISENHOWER and became the largest undeclared war in American history prior to the Vietnam involvement.

The initial rush of events created enduring confusion about the constitutional basis for the American intervention. On June 25, the day following the attack, the United States obtained a United Nations Security Council resolution ordering North Korean withdrawal. Two days later, with fighting continuing, the Security Council requested U.N. members to assist in repelling the aggression. That day, without congressional approval, President Truman publicly ordered American air and naval support for the South Koreans, and throughout his remaining tenure in office he persistently called the conflict a United Nations POLICE

ACTION. The key American decisions had actually preceded the U.N. request, however, and critics, led by Senator Robert A. Taft, convincingly demonstrated that pertinent provisions of the UNITED NATIONS CHARTER (having status as treaty law in the United States) and the United Nations Participation Act gave no constitutional authority to the American President. The necessary agreements for United States peacekeeping forces had never been concluded with the Security Council.

Careful defenders of Truman's actions, especially Secretary of State Dean Acheson, argued that Truman's authority derived from his duty as COMMANDER-IN-CHIEF to protect American interests. One such interest was the preservation of the United Nations as an instrument for peace; another was the security of American forces in the Pacific area. The defenders relied, too, on presidential control of FOREIGN AFFAIRS and on the alleged precedent of eighty-five prior instances of presidential use of military forces without a DECLARATION OF WAR. Not surprisingly, critics also found these sources insufficient, strongly disagreeing about the meaning of Congress's power "to declare war" and about the legal relevance of past episodes of unilateral presidential action. Truman nonetheless followed Acheson's advice and explicitly refused to request formal authorization from Congress.

The war had other constitutional dimensions, as well. In April 1951, after serious policy disagreements, Truman dismissed his outspoken Korean and Far Eastern commander, General of the Army Douglas MacArthur, thereby reaffirming the principle of civilian control over the military. (See CIVIL-MILITARY RELATIONS). Later, in April 1952, when a strike threatened military production for Korea, the President seized American steel mills, an action subsequently held unconstitutional in YOUNGSTOWN SHEET AND TUBE CO. v. SAWYER (1952), a decision that arguably narrowed future presidential prerogatives. The Korean engagement also intensified clashes over the FIRST AMENDMENT by contributing to the anticommunist sentiment tapped by Senator Joseph R. McCarthy. Similarly, the war provided context and impulse for the partially successful congressional effort, in the "Great Debate" of 1951, to restrict additional presidential commitment of troops to Europe. Finally, the war figured rhetorically in calls for limiting the TREATY POWER and EXECUTIVE AGREEMENTS through the BRICKER AMENDMENT.

By the time of the Korean armistice on July 27, 1953, American casualties numbered 142,000, including 33,600 deaths. The war thus stands squarely as de facto precedent for presidential war-making of substantial magnitude, and more so because American courts, in typical fashion, refrained from ruling on its constitutional base. Ironically, memories of the domestic debates over Korea helped generate later efforts, such as the Gulf of Tonkin Resolution (1964), to obtain prior congressional endorsement of foreign military ventures.

CHARLES A. LOFGREN

Bibliography

LOFGREN, CHARLES A. 1969 Mr. Truman's War: A Debate and Its Aftermath. *Review of Politics* 31:223–241.
MURPHY, PAUL L. 1972 *The Constitution in Crisis Times, 1918–1969.* New York: Harper & Row.

KOREMATSU v. UNITED STATES

See: Japanese American Cases

KOVACS v. COOPER
336 U.S. 77 (1949)

After earlier suggesting that a ban on SOUND TRUCKS would be invalid, the Supreme Court held that "loud and raucous" loudspeakers could be prohibited as a reasonable regulation of time, place, and manner of speech. The opinion by Justice STANLEY REED noted interests in residential tranquillity, and it is cited as a PRIVACY decision. Justice FELIX FRANKFURTER, concurring, delivered a major attack on the PREFERRED FREEDOM doctrine.

MARTIN SHAPIRO

KRAMER v. UNION FREE SCHOOL DISTRICT NO. 15
395 U.S. 621 (1969)

New York limited school district VOTING RIGHTS to residents who owned (or leased) real property or were parents (or guardians) of public school children. Following HARPER V. VIRGINIA BOARD OF ELECTIONS

(1966), the Supreme Court held, 6–3, that this restriction denied the EQUAL PROTECTION OF THE LAWS to an adult resident living in his parents' home.

Chief Justice EARL WARREN wrote for the Court. A RATIONAL BASIS for the voting limitation was not enough; it must be justified as necessary to promote a COMPELLING STATE INTEREST. Assuming that New York could limit voting to persons especially interested in school affairs, this law's classification was insufficiently tailored to that purpose; an uninterested, non-taxpaying renter could vote, but Kramer, a taxpayer interested in school matters, could not.

The *Harper* dissenters also dissented here, speaking through Justice POTTER STEWART. The Constitution conferred no right to vote, and no racial classification was involved. Thus there was no reason to heighten judicial scrutiny, and there was a rational basis for limiting the vote to probably-interested persons.

On the same day, in *Cipriano v. Houma,* the Court unanimously invalidated a Louisiana law allowing only property taxpayers to vote on a revenue bond issue.

KENNETH L. KARST

KU KLUX KLAN ACT

See: Force Acts of 1870, 1871

KUNZ v. NEW YORK
340 U.S. 290 (1951)

In a case involving a street-corner preacher whose sermons vigorously denounced other religions, the Supreme Court struck down an ordinance requiring a permit to hold religious meetings in public places. Chief Justice FRED M. VINSON, for an 8–1 majority, wrote that "New York cannot vest restraining control over the right to speak on religious subjects in an administrative official where there are no appropriate standards to guide his action." The ordinance was "clearly invalid as a PRIOR RESTRAINT on the exercise of FIRST AMENDMENT rights."

DENNIS J. MAHONEY

LABOR AND THE ANTITRUST LAWS

Problems relating to the application of antitrust law to labor result from a basic incompatibility between two public policies: the first, embodied in the SHERMAN ACT of 1890, prohibits efforts by anyone to monopolize or restrain competition in the product market; the second, embodied in the NORRIS-LAGUARDIA ACT of 1932 and the WAGNER ACT of 1935, permits workers to combine into unions in order to bargain collectively with employers. COLLECTIVE BARGAINING necessarily assumes, however, the elimination of competition between employees in dealings with their employers; hence the unions' need to achieve a monopoly of the labor market. The ultimate goal of every union is to remove wages, hours, and working conditions as factors in the competition between employers.

The hotly debated question whether Congress intended to include unions within the coverage of the Sherman Act was resolved by the Supreme Court in LOEWE V. LAWLOR (1908), which held a union liable for violation of the Act. Efforts to reverse this result in the CLAYTON ACT of 1914, which declared that the "labor of a human being is not a commodity or article of commerce," and which forbade federal courts from granting INJUNCTIONS against specified kinds of peaceful conduct in labor disputes, were frustrated by extremely narrow constructions of the statutory language by the Supreme Court.

United States v. Hutcheson (1941), which held that the Sherman Act does not reach acts by a union in its own self-interest that do not involve combination with nonlabor groups, marked the beginning of a new period of virtual immunity for unions under the antitrust laws. And in *Allen Bradley v. Local 3, International Brotherhood of Electrical Workers* (1945) the Court, while holding that a conspiracy between the union and electrical parts manufacturers and contractors to monopolize the industry in New York City violated the Sherman Act, declared that if the union had achieved the same result through parallel but separate agreements with each employer, the arrangement would not have been illegal. Thus, Norris-LaGuardia's comprehensive prohibition against the issuance by federal courts of injunctions in labor disputes, the Wagner Act's authorization of the granting by the National Labor Relations Board of "official patents of monopoly" through its certification procedures, and the rise of industry-wide bargaining combined to create a doctrine of "licit monopoly" of the labor market by unions, while the Sherman Act continued to prevent similar domination of the product market by business enterprises.

By the mid-1960s, however, the pendulum had begun to swing back. In *United Mine Workers v. Pennington* (1965) a badly divided Supreme Court held that a union's conspiracy with large mine operators to drive small operators out of the market by establishing wage scales that the latter could not afford to pay violated the antitrust laws. Ten years later, in *Connell Construction Company v. Plumbers & Steamfitters Local 100* (1975), the Supreme Court distinguished union activity that eliminates competition over wages and working conditions—immune under the antitrust laws, even though it affects price competition among employers, because such restriction is the inevitable consequence of collective bargaining—from union activity restricting competition in the product market—unprotected because (in this case) its effect was to drive all nonunion employers, including the more efficient ones, out of the market, whether or not they met union standards for wages and working conditions. The Court's 5–4 decision also held that even though the union's conduct violated the secondary boycott and "hot cargo" provisions of the TAFT-HARTLEY ACT of 1947, for which express penalties are prescribed in that statute, the union was not shielded from additional liability under the Sherman Act.

The critics of the Court's decisions in *Pennington* and *Connell* point out that in both cases the issues involved were mandatory subjects of bargaining under the labor laws. They contend that the legislative history of those laws makes clear that Congress intended to provide specific and exclusive remedies for violations of their substantive provisions (e.g., illegal "secondary boycotts" and "hot cargo" clauses) and rejected the proposed revival of remedies such as injunctions at the request of private parties, as well as punitive damages, which are available under the antitrust laws.

Unquestionably, judicial application of the antitrust laws to labor not only has seriously hampered union efforts to impose uniform wages, hours, and working conditions in the labor market but also has created considerable confusion in the administration of laws governing labor–management relations. It is also true, however, that unrestricted union efforts to monopolize labor markets adversely affect product markets in respect of the cost and availability of products. The question is whether antitrust laws are the proper mechanism for striking a proper balance between the right of workers to organize and to bargain collectively and the right of employers and the general public to be free of union coercive practices that raise prices, restrict output, or otherwise control the product to the detriment of consumers.

Inasmuch as unions derive their coercive powers from industry-wide and market-wide organizations, it is often proposed that they should be precluded from organizing more than one employer in an industry, and that collusion between separate unions should be proscribed. This proposal for "fragmented bargaining" probably is not politically feasible; moreover, it would have its least effect in oligopolistic industries, where, presumably, it is needed the most, and would

have its greatest impact in atomized industries, where it is needed the least. Finally, fragmented bargaining would so weaken union organizations as to undermine completely the national labor policy favoring collective bargaining.

It appears that no satisfactory way has been found to reconcile free-market competitive policies with those permitting workers to combine and to engage in peaceful concerted activities for their mutual aid and protection. The preferable way to establish the necessarily shifting equilibrium between them would seem to be through legislation dealing with specific problems rather than through the application by the judiciary of antitrust laws designed primarily for other purposes.

BENJAMIN AARON

Bibliography
HILDEBRAND, GEORGE H. 1962 *Public Policy and Collective Bargaining.* Pages 152–187. New York: Harper & Row.
MELTZER, BERNARD D. 1965 Labor Unions, Collective Bargaining, and the Antitrust Laws. *University of Chicago Law Review* 32:659–734.
ST. ANTOINE, THEODORE J. 1976 *Connell:* Antitrust Law at the Expense of Labor Law. *Virginia Law Review* 62:603–631.

LABOR AND THE CONSTITUTION

An important aspect of constitutional law has been the connection between individual rights and state or national power to regulate economic affairs. The constitutional treatment of employment is a paradigmatic example: what is the status of the relationship between employer and employee? What power does government have to change it? Of course, the answers to these questions depend on whether they are asked about the pre- or post-New Deal era.

Before the mid-1930s, labor legislation was subjected to searching JUDICIAL REVIEW by a Supreme Court committed to a laissez-faire treatment of economic issues under the DUE PROCESS clauses and a limited conception of federal authority under the COMMERCE CLAUSE. Since the New Deal, constitutional questions involving labor have been dominated by issues of expression and association, and the classification of labor activity as "economic" or "political."

The constitutional treatment of employment prior to the New Deal is best understood against the background of the COMMON LAW, a law dominated by concepts of FREEDOM OF CONTRACT and employment at will. The employer had the right to discharge an employee at any time, and the employee had supposedly equivalent right to quit at any time.

At an early stage, concerted actions by workers to affect contractual relations sometimes were treated as criminal conspiracies. Thus, in the *Philadelphia Cordwainers' Case* (1806), a strike for higher wages by a group of shoemakers was held to be illegal. "A combination of workmen to raise their wages may be considered in a twofold view: one is to benefit themselves, the other is to injure those who do not join their society. The rule of law condemns both."

Later in the nineteenth century, the courts recognized the right of workers to join together. *Commonwealth v. Hunt* (1842) is the landmark. Chief Justice LEMUEL SHAW, for the Supreme Judicial Court of Massachusetts, held that, for a combination of workers to constitute a CRIMINAL CONSPIRACY, the state must prove that the workers had specific criminal objectives or used specific criminal methods. Thereafter, the common law treatment of labor focused on the limits of legitimate labor activity—whether combinations of workers had illegal purposes or used illegal methods.

But many courts at common law continued to take a restrictive view of legal labor activity. In *Vegelahn v. Gunter* (1869), for example, the Massachusetts Court found that strikers had used "intimidation" to interfere with the contractual relationship of the employer and strikebreakers. The "coercive" methods ranged from threats of personal injury to simple "persuasion and social pressure." Similarly, in *Plant v. Woods* (1900), the same court found that a threat by strikers that the employer could "expect trouble in his business" indicated that the strike was "only the preliminary skirmish" in violent industrial warfare; the workers had given "the signal, and in doing so must be held to avail themselves of the degree of fear and dread which the knowledge of such consequences will cause in the minds of those . . . against whom the strike is directed." Thus, in measuring "illegal" objectives and methods, common law courts often assumed that even a low level of labor activity constituted a "signal" that was inherently coercive.

This common law view of the permissible limits of labor activity was read into the Constitution by the Supreme Court in the late nineteenth century, as it interpreted SUBSTANTIVE DUE PROCESS and elaborated a restrictive conception of the federal commerce power.

The Supreme Court constitutionalized the common law of employment by placing "freedom of contract" within the liberty protected by the Fifth and FOURTEENTH AMENDMENTS. Many important cases

concerned legislation designed to regulate the labor market as to hours, wages, and working conditions. This type of legislation—such as the wages and hours law in the leading case of LOCHNER V. NEW YORK (1905)—was invalidated if, in the Court's view, it unreasonably interfered with the contractual freedom of employer and employee. Even when such legislation was upheld, as in MULLER V. OREGON (1908), the Court made a detailed inquiry into the substantive reasonableness of the law.

Notions of freedom of contract were also applied to the activities of labor unions. In 1898, in the aftermath of a violent Pullman strike, Congress passed the ERDMAN ACT, outlawing YELLOW DOG CONTRACTS—contracts by which employees agreed not to join labor unions. In ADAIR V. UNITED STATES (1908) the Supreme Court held that the act violated the due process clause of the Fifth Amendment: "the employer and the employee have equality of right, and any legislation that disturbs that equality is an arbitrary interference with the liberty of contract which no government can legally justify in a free land. . . ." The Court struck down a similar state statute in COPPAGE V. KANSAS (1915), and, in the 1917 case of HITCHMAN COAL V. MITCHELL, relied on the constitutional protection of yellow dog contracts in holding that federal courts could prevent unions from organizing at plants they knew to be covered by such contracts. And in TRUAX V. CORRIGAN (1921) the Court held that an Arizona statute forbidding INJUNCTIONS against PICKETING was unconstitutional, since it protected an activity (picketing) that wrongfully interfered with employers' property rights, in violation of due process.

The Supreme Court narrowly interpreted the commerce power at the beginning of the New Deal, striking down measures such as "Hot Oil" Codes, the AGRICULTURAL ADJUSTMENT ACT, and the NATIONAL INDUSTRIAL RECOVERY ACT. This development was nothing new. Although there had been swings in doctrine, the Court had generally viewed congressional power under the commerce clause with suspicion in the area of employment relations. In HAMMER V. DAGENHART (1918), for example, the Court struck down an act banning commerce in goods produced by child labor, and twenty years later, in CARTER V. CARTER COAL CO. (1936), it struck down an act regulating hours and wages in the coal industry.

The constitutional treatment of employment was changed radically by the watershed events of the New Deal. This period saw the Supreme Court reject its earlier laissez-faire interpretations of due process and its narrow vision of federal commerce power.

During the New Deal the Court abandoned its view

of freedom of contract in employment relations. In WEST COAST HOTEL V. PARRISH (1937) the Court sustained a state minimum wage law for women, holding that contractual freedom could be limited by a reasonable exercise of STATE POLICE POWERS: "Even if the wisdom of the policy be regarded as debatable and its effect uncertain, still the legislature is entitled to its judgment."

National Labor Relations Board v. Jones & Laughlin Steel Corp. (1937) upheld the WAGNER NATIONAL LABOR RELATIONS ACT (NLRA), which entitled workers to organize and required employers to bargain with their employees' chosen representatives. The Court found that the act did not invade freedom of contract: an employer was not compelled to make any agreement, but only to bargain with the employees' representatives in recognition of the "fundamental right" of workers to organize. The Court distinguished the "yellow dog" contract cases on the grounds that the NLRA did not interfere with an employer's right to discharge employees, but only prohibited coercion of employees in the guise of discharge. Despite this disclaimer, it is clear that the Court was departing radically from the rule of its prior cases: the employer was prohibited from discharging employees for union activities, and was required to bargain in good faith with its employees' unions. (See WAGNER ACT CASES.) This new treatment of labor activity was reinforced the same year in *Senn v. Tile Layers Union,* in which the Court upheld a state law permitting peaceful picketing in conjunction with a labor dispute; although the Court distinguished cases such as *Truax,* the picketing involved was neither more peaceful nor less coercive than in prior cases.

The new approach to due process was exemplified by Justice FELIX FRANKFURTER, writing for the Court in *Osborn v. Ozlin* (1940), in an opinion reminiscent of Justice OLIVER WENDELL HOLMES'S classic dissent in *Lochner:* "It is immaterial that state action may run counter to the economic wisdom either of Adam Smith or of J. Maynard Keynes, or may be ultimately mischievous even from the point of view of avowed state policy. Our inquiry must be much narrower. It is whether [the state] has taken hold of a matter within her power, or has reached beyond her borders to regulate a subject which was none of her concern. . . ."

In the 1937 *Jones & Laughlin* case, the Court upheld the NLRA under the commerce clause. The act regulated industrial strife, which had a "close and substantial relation" to commerce, and which was therefore within Congress's "plenary" power to regulate commerce.

The Court also upheld the NATIONAL POLICE POWER in the field of employment relations. UNITED STATES V. DARBY (1941) sustained the constitutionality of the FAIR LABOR STANDARDS ACT, which prohibited the interstate shipment of goods not meeting wage and hour requirements. Overruling the *Hammer* and *Carter Coal* cases, the Court confined its inquiry to the question whether the activity regulated had substantial EFFECTS ON COMMERCE. "The motive and purpose of a regulation of interstate commerce are matters for the legislative judgment upon which the Constitution places no restriction and over which the courts are given no control. . . ."

In sum, the New Deal saw the Supreme Court abandon its protection of the common law of employment in the name of the Constitution. The Court dropped its laissez-faire reading of due process and its restrictive interpretation of the commerce power. Employers are no longer apt to be successful if they claim that their constitutional rights to liberty or property are invaded by ECONOMIC REGULATION, or by state protection of union activity. They have little chance should they claim that congressional regulation of employment exceeds the commerce power.

While the Court has never explicitly revived the due process protection for freedom of contrast or similar economic rights in the context of labor relations, it has continued to see a residuum of inherent employer economic freedom that has a quasi-constitutional dimension manifested in statutory interpretation. This residuum has emerged around the issues of the right of an employer to subcontract work formerly done by its employees, or to close down all or part of its operations. Two questions have presented themselves: whether the employer may be required to bargain with its employees' union about such a decision, and whether such a decision would constitute discriminatory discharge of employees if motivated by antiunion animus.

The NLRA requires an employer to bargain over wages, hours, and working conditions; as to subjects not affecting these areas, an employer may act unilaterally. In *Fibreboard Paper Products v. NLRB* (1964) the Supreme Court held that an employer is required to bargain over a decision to subcontract work, where such subcontracting would simply replace employees with nonemployees doing the same work, and where the employer's motive is to cut costs by reducing the work force. Justice POTTER STEWART, in a concurring opinion, argued that an employer could not be compelled to bargain over managerial decisions "which lie at the core of entrepreneurial control," "those management decisions which are fundamental to the basic direction of a corporate enterprise. . . ."

The Court adopted Justice Stewart's position in *First National Maintenance v. NLRB* (1981), holding that the employer may unilaterally "shut down part of its business purely for economic reasons. . . ." The Court, as if this were a constitutional holding, read Congress's intent narrowly to avoid interference with entrepreneurial freedom: "Congress had no expectation that the elected union representative would become an equal partner in the running of the business enterprise. . . . Management must be free from the restraints of the bargaining process to the extent essential for the running of a profitable business."

The NLRA also prohibits an employer from discharging employees in retaliation for union activities. In *Textile Workers Union v. Darlington Manufacturing Co.* (1965) the Court held that it was not a discriminatory discharge for an employer to close his entire operation and discharge his entire work force, even if motivated by antiunion animus, because the employer would derive no "future benefit" from such a decision. As for a partial shutdown, this would constitute a discriminatory discharge only if it served to discourage union activity in the remainder of the employer's enterprise. Again, the Court construed congressional intent narrowly, as if it were avoiding a constitutional issue: the proposition that a single businessman cannot choose to go out of business if he wants to would represent such a startling innovation that it should not be entertained without the clearest manifestation of legislative intent or unequivocal judicial precedent so construing the Labor Relations Act. These cases were decided on statutory grounds, but they have clear constitutional emanations. The decisions are couched in terms of an inherent, absolute economic liberty untouched by regulatory statutes that look in a contrary direction.

For four decades after the New Deal, no congressional enactment was declared to have exceeded the limits of the commerce power. Congress was allowed virtually unlimited discretion. The consensus was that, as the Supreme Court stated in WICKARD V. FILBURN (1942), "effective restraints on its exercise must proceed from political rather than judicial processes"—anything Congress passed was within the commerce power.

In 1976, in NATIONAL LEAGUE OF CITIES V. USERY, however, the Court invalidated the application of the Fair Labor Standards Act to public employees, holding that the TENTH AMENDMENT prevents Congress from exercising its commerce power with respect to "functions essential to [the] separate and independent existence" of states and their subdivisions. Nevertheless, it does not seem likely in the labor field that

Congress will lose much power to regulate by further restriction of the commerce power or the rebirth of economic due process. Indeed, early in 1985 in GARCIA V. SAN ANTONIO METROPOLITAN TRANSIT AUTHORITY, the Court explicitly overruled *National League of Cities.*

With the proposition established during the New Deal that government support of organized labor does not threaten the constitutional freedom of employers, the fundamental issues shifted to problems of association and expression. These problems arise in the framework of a constitutional jurisprudence which generally distinguishes sharply, for purposes of legislative authority and judicial review, between issues of economic regulation (narrow judicial review) and of the regulation of political activity (substantial review).

In this jurisprudence a key question becomes the classification of activity as "economic" or "political." With a few early exceptions, labor activity generally has been viewed, by both Congress and the Supreme Court, as economic. The "proper" role of unions has been confined to "economic" issues surrounding the collective bargaining process, with the consequence that labor's rights of expression are narrower than those attaching to organizations classified as political, and that Congress has a broader power to regulate association and expression in the labor context.

Prior to the New Deal, the right to organize a union was constitutionally unprotected. Since the New Deal, however, it has become well established (for example, in NAACP V. ALABAMA, 1958) that the protection of the FIRST AMENDMENT encompasses a right of association. But in the labor context it has not been necessary for the Supreme Court explicitly to find that the right to join a union is protected by FREEDOM OF ASSEMBLY AND ASSOCIATION. The right is protected by statute, most prominently Section 7 of the National Labor Relations Act: "Employees shall have the right to self-organization, to form, join, or assist labor organizations, to bargain collectively through representatives of their own choosing, and to engage in other concerted activities for the purpose of collective bargaining or other mutual aid or protection. . . ."

What the Supreme Court has held is that peaceful organizing activities are constitutionally protected. In HAGUE V. CONGRESS OF INDUSTRIAL ORGANIZATIONS (1939) the Court held that FREEDOM OF SPEECH and assembly attached to the dissemination of information regarding the NLRA, as well as peaceful assembly "for the discussion of the Act, and of the opportunities and advantages offered by it. . . ." And in *Thomas v. Collins* (1945) the Court held that freedom of speech and assembly were violated by a statute requiring union organizers to register prior to engaging in any organizing activities, including giving speeches to groups of workers. Although the Court characterized the union activity as economic, it rejected the proposition that "the First Amendment's safeguards are wholly inapplicable to business or economic activity." The case was therefore treated under the First Amendment's requirement that a restriction on speech or assembly be justified by clear public interest, threatened not doubtfully or remotely but by CLEAR AND PRESENT DANGER.

Most lower courts have interpreted the *Hague* and *Thomas* cases to establish a constitutional right to join a labor union. Thus, despite being clearly classified as economic activity, joining a union is protected by the First Amendment. However, the classification of labor activity as economic has consequences for the constitutional treatment of strikes and picketing.

The THIRTEENTH AMENDMENT, prohibiting involuntary servitude, probably protects the right of an individual employee to withhold his or her services. The constitutional status of strikes, however, is unclear. One reason for this is that strikes are "concerted activity" protected by the NLRA; it is therefore usually possible to decide strike questions without facing the constitutional question. However, extensive regulation and limitation of the right to strike has been permitted ever since the New Deal; it thus seems that, at most, the right has a low level of constitutional protection.

Legal limitations on strikes have been based on both their objectives and their methods. Prior to the NLRA, strikes were treated under the "illegal objectives" test of the common law; work stoppages with purposes held by courts to be illegal were prohibited. And today, strikes with certain objectives are unprotected under Section 7 of the NLRA. Thus, for example, a strike loses its protection if its purpose is to compel the employer to commit an unfair labor practice or violate other laws.

Section 7 also withholds protection from strikes that use illegal methods. For example, in *NLRB v. Fansteel Metallurgical Corp.* (1939) the Supreme Court declared unprotected a sitdown strike involving TRESPASS, destruction of property, and violation of state court injunctions. In *Mastro Plastics v. NLRB* (1956) the strike violated the NLRA's requirement of NOTICE to the employer; in *Local 174 v. Lucas Flour* (1962) the strike violated a "no-strike" clause in the union's contract with the employer.

Prior to the New Deal, labor picketing was readily enjoined, either because the ends sought were disapproved or because it was assumed to be intrinsically coercive. The Supreme Court turned this law around in the leading case of THORNHILL V. ALABAMA (1940). That case held unconstitutional a state statute banning all picketing near a business where the purpose of the picketing was to hinder the business. The Court adopted the "clear and present danger" test, treating labor activity as political activity: "The freedom of speech and of the press guaranteed by the constitution embraces at least the liberty to discuss publicly and truthfully all matters of public concern without previous restraint or fear of subsequent punishment. . . . In the circumstances of our times the dissemination of information concerning the facts of a labor dispute must be regarded as within that area of free discussion that is guaranteed by the Constitution." The Court explicitly rejected the assumption that all labor picketing is inherently coercive; it also stated that some "coercion" is permitted by the First Amendment: "Every expression of opinion on matters that are important has the potentiality of inducing action in the interests of one rather than another group in society. But the Group in power at any moment may not impose penal sanctions on peaceful and truthful discussions of matters of public interest merely on showing that others might thereby be persuaded to take action inconsistent with their interests." The Court thus treated labor picketing as full-fledged political activity.

But the Court quickly retreated from this position. Since *Thornhill*, it has become well accepted that labor picketing may be regulated, without violating freedom of speech and assembly, if the picketing is found to be illegal in method or objective.

While violence is an easy case, the Court has—to some extent—returned implicitly to the old assumption that labor picketing is an inherently coercive "signal." This means that picketing can be extensively regulated. Justice WILLIAM O. DOUGLAS, concurring in *Bakery Drivers v. Wohl* (1942), put it this way: "Picketing by an organized group is more than free speech, since it involves patrol of a particular locality and since the very presence of a picket line may induce action of one kind or another, quite irrespective of the nature of the ideas which are being disseminated."

The Court has also, as with other types of labor activity, maintained an "illegal objectives" limitation on picketing. The limitation has been most visible in two areas. The first is picketing with an objective to compel violation of state law or policy. This limitation was first articulated in *Carpenters' & Joiners Union v. Ritter's Cafe* (1942), where the Court held that the First Amendment did not protect picketing that urged an employer to act contrary to a state antitrust statute. By 1950, in *Hughes v. Superior Court,* the Court found a sufficient basis for prohibition in a purpose to violate a state "policy" announced by its courts.

The second visible category of picketing for an improper purpose is picketing for an object outlawed by the NLRA as "union unfair labor practices." For instance, the act explicitly prohibits some types of picketing designed to persuade an employer to recognize and bargain with the picketing union. But it is the secondary boycott that is the union unfair labor practice that is constitutionally most troublesome.

The act forbids a union to "threaten, coerce, or restrain" any person—usually a business—with the object of "forcing or requiring" that person to stop dealing with an employer with whom the union has a labor dispute.

The Supreme Court has recognized the potential conflict between such a prohibition and the First Amendment. In the *Tree Fruits* case, *NLRB v. Fruit & Vegetable Packers* (1964), the Court announced that it would construe the statute narrowly to avoid this constitutional difficulty: "Congress has consistently refused to prohibit peaceful picketing except where used as a means to achieve specific ends which experience has shown are undesirable." The Court therefore distinguished between picketing that attempted to persuade persons not to deal with the secondary employer (which was prohibited), and picketing attempting to persuade people not to buy products made by the primary employer (which was outside the act's prohibition). The Court thus permitted secondary picketing that was narrowly confined to the labor dispute with the primary employer. Subsequently, it limited even this narrow protection. In *Safeco NLRB v. Retail Store Employees Union* (1980), the Court held that the NLRA prohibits picketing confined to the primary employer's products, if those products constitute most of the secondary employer's business. In such a situation, boycotting the struck product is the same as boycotting the secondary employer.

Comparisons of the constitutional treatment of picketing with the treatment of other uses of the PUBLIC FORUM show that labor picketing is treated under standards different from other, similar activities. Consider two cases decided in 1982 by the Supreme Court, both decided without dissent. The cases had one thing in common: each involved a BOYCOTT and picketing by a group. The first, *Longshoremen's Asso-*

ciation v. Allied International, Inc., was a suit for damages arising out of the refusal of the Longshoremen's Union to unload cargo shipped from the Soviet Union, in protest against the Russian invasion of Afghanistan. The boycott was entirely peaceful, it was totally effective, and it was unanimously held to be illegal. The boycott violated the labor statute, and that statute, as applied to this situation, did not infringe anyone's First Amendment rights.

Two months later the Court handed down its opinion in *NAACP v. Claiborne Hardware.* That case involved a suit for damages brought by white merchants in Claiborne County, Mississippi. Their businesses had been disrupted by a boycott, organized by the NAACP in protest against the failure of public officials in the county to desegregate public schools and facilities, hire black policemen, select blacks for jury duty, and end verbal abuse of blacks by law enforcement officers. The boycott, which was held by the Mississippi courts to violate state law, was executed in a less than peaceful, if considerably effective fashion. And it was—in most respects—found by the Supreme Court to be protected by the First Amendment.

Although there are a number of nice legal distinctions that might be noted between these cases and although it may be that the NAACP could not have survived if the Mississippi courts had been affirmed, one is forced to conclude that the two decisions are deeply inconsistent with one another. Of course, there is considerable inconsistency in our decisional law. The trouble here is that the inconsistency grows out of stereotypical thinking. Although labor unions ordinarily are organizations dedicated to economic activity and although economic activity is subject to substantial governmental regulation, sometimes unions engage in political action. The NAACP is often, but perhaps not always, a political action organization and political activity is rightly subject to substantial government protection.

The distinction between economic and political activity is difficult to maintain. At the margin it is difficult to designate conduct as economic and not political, or as political and not economic. But maintenance of the distinction is necessary unless we are prepared either to reduce substantially our political freedom or to reestablish substantive judicial review of economic regulation. (See COMMERCIAL SPEECH.)

Nor is the difficulty of sustaining the distinction in these cases really the problem. All legal distinctions, after all, give actors and decision makers trouble at the margin. The real problem is that even as it is wrong to stereotype individuals, so too is it wrong to stereotype the organizations through which individuals seek to achieve their economic and political goals. In deciding what is protected and what may be regulated, legislatures and courts should look at the organizations' specific conduct, not their general characteristics.

Employer speech—communications by employers with their employees during union organization campaigns—is given significantly lower protection than is the political speech often said to be at the core of the First Amendment. During the early post-New Deal period, the National Labor Relations Board viewed any antiunion speeches or literature from the employer as "interference, restraint or coercion," in violation of the NLRA. This position was rejected in *NLRB v. Virginia Electric & Power Co.* (1941). The Supreme Court held that the act could not, within the First Amendment, prohibit employer speech unless it could be demonstrated, from a total course of conduct, that the speech was coercive. This view was codified in 1947, when the NLRA was amended to provide that speech may be used as evidence of an unfair labor practice only if it contains a "threat of reprisal or force or promise of benefit." In *NLRB v. Gissel Packing* (1969), the Supreme Court made clear that employer speech is entitled to some First Amendment protection, and that the 1947 amendment to the NLRA simply "implements the First Amendment. . . ."

But the actual treatment of employer speech in union organization campaigns makes clear the low level of First Amendment protection that speech enjoys. The NLRB announced as long ago as 1948 that it would regulate union certification elections under a "laboratory conditions" standard: "it is the Board's function to provide a laboratory in which an experiment may be conducted, under conditions as nearly ideal as possible, to determine the uninhibited desires of the employees." This approach has entailed extensive restriction and regulation of employer speech, on several grounds. For example, implied threats of harm to employees for unionization have been held to be illegal except where the consequences are beyond the employer's control and are based on demonstrable probabilities. And under NLRB rulings racial appeals are prohibited unless the party making the appeal proves "that it was truthful and germane. . . ."

As with employee speech and association, this framework differs significantly from mainstream First Amendment doctrine. First, this framework suffers from a vagueness problem; the NLRB and the courts regulate, on an ad hoc basis, speech that in the political arena could be regulated, if at all, only under narrow and precise statutes. Second, with respect to employer threats, labor law turns the First Amendment on its head: an employer may not threaten to close its operation if a union wins an election despite the fact that it would be legal for the employer to close. Thus, the employer is prohibited from advocating or predicting *legal* activity.

Finally, employer speech that appeals to racial prejudice is severely restricted, even though the First Amendment protects such speech in the political arena. Indeed, Nazis may march down the streets in a predominantly Jewish community, but an employer may not state that a union advocates "race-mixing."

The rights of PUBLIC EMPLOYEES, and the relationships of such employees to their employers, raise constitutional questions different from those in private employment. Initially one might think that the major reason for treating public employees differently is that the public employer is a governmental body, and thus that STATE ACTION is involved. This distinction, however, is far less important than the differing economic and political relationships between the union and employer in the two sectors. These differences were summarized by the Supreme Court in ABOOD V. DETROIT BOARD OF EDUCATION (1977):

A public employer, unlike his private counterpart, is not guided by the profit motive and constrained by the normal operation of the market. Municipal services are typically not priced, and where they are they tend to be regarded as in some sense "essential" and therefore are often price-inelastic. . . . The government officials making decisions as the public "employer" are less likely to act as a cohesive unit than are managers in private industry, in part because different levels of public authority . . . are involved, and in part because each official may respond to a distinctive political constituency. . . . Finally, decisionmaking by a public employer is above all a political process. The officials who represent the public employer are ultimately responsible to the electorate. . . . Through exercise of their political influence as part of the electorate, the employees have the opportunity to affect the decisions of government representatives who sit on the other side of the bargaining table. . . . [P]ermitting public employees to unionize . . . gives the employees more influence in the decision making process than is possessed by employees similarly organized in the private sector.

These differences have justified differences in the constitutional treatment of the rights of public employees to join unions and to strike.

As with private employees, the Supreme Court has never explicitly held that public employees have a constitutional right to join a labor union. The Court has, however, found that public employees do not sacrifice their freedoms of association and expression by accepting positions with government. In KEYISHIAN V. BOARD OF REGENTS (1967), for example, the Court specifically rejected the premise that "public employment . . . may be conditioned upon the surrender of constitutional rights which could not be abridged by direct government action." Based on this principle and on the implicit constitutional protection of private union membership under the right of association, the prevailing authority in the lower courts is that public employees have a constitutional right to join a labor union. This right, however, appears to be subject to greater restriction than is the similar right of private employees. Some state courts have held that certain employees, such as police officers or fire-fighters, may be prohibited from joining unions on the grounds that membership in a union would be inconsistent with the performance of their important governmental functions.

The authority is virtually unanimous that public employees do not have a constitutional right to strike. Nor does the statutory protection of strikes by private employees raise a serious question of equal protection. The test here is whether the distinction between public and private employment is rational; it plainly is.

The other side of the expression and association issue is whether employees—in the private or public sector—have the right not to associate. In other words, does the Constitution permit employees to be compelled to support a union against their wishes and beliefs? In this area the economic view of labor activity is prominent: compulsion has been permitted, but only for the economic purposes of COLLECTIVE BARGAINING.

The issue has arisen primarily with regard to agreements between unions and employers to require all employees to pay dues or "agency shop fees" to the union. Most labor statutes, including the NLRA, explicitly permit unions and employers to agree to these requirements. The Supreme Court has found such statutes to be consistent with the First Amendment. In *Railway Employees Department v. Hanson* (1956) and *Machinists v. Street* (1961) the Supreme Court upheld the relevant provision of the Railway Labor Act. In the *Abood* case, the Court upheld a similar state statute that applied to public employees. The Court reasoned that the "free rider" problem (employees who would benefit from, but not pay for, representation) was sufficient justification for Congress and states to permit these agreements.

The courts have, however, consistently emphasized the constitutional limits of this doctrine: dues collected under compulsion may be used only for collective bargaining, and not for political or ideological ends. In both *Street* and *Abood*, the Supreme Court held that, were statutes to permit political use of these funds, the statutes would violate the employees' freedom of association.

Over the years major labor issues have presented themselves as important constitutional problems. *Lochner v. New York* (1905), for example—a case involving labor legislation—is perhaps the best known substantive due process decision of the pre-New Deal period. And the downfall of that doctrine in the economic area can be observed in Court decisions upholding labor legislation; so too can the expansion of federal power under the commerce clause. Moreover, labor issues have influenced the development of the constitutional rights of speech and association.

In the future, the Supreme Court is apt to render fewer constitutional decisions involving labor. Regulation dominates the field and its constitutionality is seldom in doubt. But it can be predicted with considerable confidence that statutory interpretation of labor statutes will reflect any changes in constitutional law that may occur.

HARRY H. WELLINGTON

Bibliography

COX, ARCHIBALD; BOK, DEREK; and GORMAN, ROBERT 1981 *Labor Law: Cases and Materials*, 9th ed. Mineola, N.Y.: Foundation Press.
GETMAN, JULIUS and BLACKBURN, JOHN 1983 *Labor Relations: Law, Practice, and Policy*, 2nd ed. Mineola N.Y.: Foundation Press.
GORMAN, ROBERT 1976 *Basic Text on Labor Law: Unionization and Collective Bargaining.* St. Paul, Minn.: West Publishing Co.
GREGORY, CHARLES and KATZ, HAROLD 1979 *Labor and the Law*, 3rd ed. New York: W. W. Norton.
SUMMERS, CLYDE, WELLINGTON, HARRY, and HYDE, ALAN 1982 *Cases and Materials on Labor Law*, 2nd ed. Mineola, N.Y.: Foundation Press.
WELLINGTON, HARRY 1968 *Labor and the Legal Process.* New Haven, Conn.: Yale University Press.
WELLINGTON, HARRY and WINTER, RALPH 1971 *The Unions and the Cities.* Washington, D.C.: Brookings Institution.

LABOR BOARD CASES

See: Wagner Act Cases

LA FOLLETTE, ROBERT M.
(1855–1925)

Robert Marion La Follette was one of the few giants in the history of the United States Senate, ranking with HENRY CLAY and DANIEL WEBSTER. Born in a Wisconsin log cabin, he was graduated from his state's university in Madison, began his legal practice there, and spent three undistinguished terms (1885–1891) in Congress. During the farmer-labor unrest of the 1890s, La Follette grew considerably more liberal, and in 1901 he entered the governor's mansion with a reform program later called the "Wisconsin idea." It became the basis of the Progressive movement. La Follette, always a Republican, advocated the direct PRIMARY ELECTION as a method of nominating candidates, MINIMUM WAGE AND MAXIMUM HOURS laws, trade unionism, the popular REFERENDUM, strict regulation of the rates and services of railroads and public utilities by government commissions of experts, and radical tax reforms. His success as governor led to his election in 1905 as a United States senator.

During his twenty-year career as a senator he rivaled THEODORE ROOSEVELT and WOODROW WILSON as an influence for political liberalism. The leader of the Senate's Republican insurgents, he exerted special efforts on behalf of increasing the powers of the Interstate Commerce Commission, energetic enforcement of ANTITRUST LAW, a federal income tax law, direct election of senators, and women's suffrage. After the Supreme Court decided STANDARD OIL COMPANY V. UNITED STATES (1911), La Follette denounced the RULE OF REASON and judicial usurpation of the legislative function. Unlike most Republicans he supported the appointment to the Supreme Court of LOUIS D. BRANDEIS; the two men were close friends, thought alike on most matters of political economy, and had collaborated in framing many reform measures. They differed on foreign policy. La Follette opposed American entry into World War I and the League of Nations. Although unpopular for a while during the war, because of pro-German and pacifist sympathies, La Follette emerged from the war as the undisputed leader of American liberalism.

He excoriated illiberal decisions of the Supreme Court. When the Court held unconstitutional congressional measures against child labor and construed antitrust laws to cover trade union activities, La Follette began a national campaign to curb the Court. Because he opposed JUDICIAL REVIEW over Congress, he proposed a constitutional amendment that would have authorized Congress to overcome a judicial veto in the same way as it did a presidential veto, by reenacting the statute by a two-thirds majority.

In 1924, at the peak of his career, La Follette refused to support CALVIN COOLIDGE and formed the Independent Progressive party, which nominated him and BURTON K. WHEELER, a Democrat. The party had only a presidential ticket, no local, state, or other federal candidates. It supported La Follette's Court-curbing amendment and would have restricted judicial invalidation of congressional acts to the Supreme Court only; in addition, it would have fixed a ten-year tenure for federal judges. The Progressives also denounced the Ku Klux Klan, then at the height of its popularity, and the Communist party. They also favored collective bargaining by labor through union representatives of their choice, antimonopoly measures, the restoration of competition, and extensive government ECONOMIC REGULATION. La Follette drew one vote out of every six, compared to the one in twelve received by the Populists in 1892, but carried only his own state.

When "Fighting Bob" died in 1925, his casket was placed in the rotunda of the Capitol, a rare honor, and the nation remembered him, in the words of his own epitaph, as one who "stood to the end for the ideals of American democracy."

LEONARD W. LEVY

Bibliography

LA FOLLETTE, BELLE CASE and LA FOLLETTE, FOLA 1953 Robert M. La Follette. 2 Vols. New York: Macmillan.

LAIRD v. TATUM
408 U.S. 1 (1972)

Protesters against American involvement in the VIETNAM WAR sued to stop Army intelligence surveillance which they claimed had a CHILLING EFFECT on the exercise of their FIRST AMENDMENT rights. Chief Justice WARREN E. BURGER's opinion for the Court, in a 5–4 decision, held that the case lacked RIPENESS because the protesters had presented no "claim of specific present objective . . . or . . . future harm" but only the fear that "the army may at some future date misuse the information in some way" that would harm them.

MARTIN SHAPIRO

LAKE COUNTRY ESTATES, INC. v. TAHOE REGIONAL PLANNING AGENCY
440 U.S. 391 (1979)

Landowners claimed that an appointed bi-state agency regulating development had, through over-regulation, unconstitutionally destroyed the economic value of their property. The Supreme Court, over Justice THURGOOD MARSHALL's dissent, extended TENNEY V. BRANDHOVE (1951) to acts of unelected officials and found members of the planning agency to be absolutely immune from suit under SECTION 1983, TITLE 42, UNITED STATES CODE for their legislation-like acts. The Court also found the agency not to be protected by the ELEVENTH AMENDMENT immunity available to states.

THEODORE EISENBERG

LALLI v. LALLI
439 U.S. 259 (1978)

In *Lalli* a fragmented Supreme Court brought further confusion to the body of EQUAL PROTECTION doctrine governing classifications based on ILLEGITIMACY. A 5–4 majority upheld a New York law that allowed an illegitimate child to inherit from his or her father only if a court, during the father's lifetime and no later than two years after the child's birth, had declared the father's paternity. Justice LEWIS F. POWELL, who had written the MAJORITY OPINION in TRIMBLE V. GORDON (1977), wrote for a plurality of three Justices. Powell distinguished *Trimble* as a case in which even a judicial order declaring paternity would not have allowed inheritance; only the marriage of the child's parents would suffice. In *Lalli* the state could properly insist on the "evidentiary" requirement of a judicial order to establish paternity. The other six Justices all thought *Lalli* and *Trimble* indistinguishable: the four *Lalli* dissenters, plus two who joined the majority in upholding the law. The latter two Justices voted in accordance with their *Trimble* dissents.

The precedential force of *Trimble* may be uncertain, but at least seven Justices (the *Lalli* plurality and dissenters) all agreed that the STANDARD OF REVIEW for testing classifications based on illegitimacy was more rigorous than the RATIONAL BASIS test. Such classifications, said the plurality, would be invalid unless they were "substantially related to permissible state interests."

The state's interest in *Lalli* was the achievement of finality in the settlement of decedents' estates. The court order requirement provided sure proof of paternity. The artificiality of the requirement, however, was illustrated dramatically by the facts of *Lalli* itself, as Justice BYRON R. WHITE, for the dissenters, made clear. The decedent had often acknowledged his children openly; he had even executed a notarized document referring to one of them as "my son" and consenting to his marriage. Paternity had been proved clearly; what was missing was the formality of a court order. Such a judicial proceeding, of course, is least likely in the case in which the father and his illegitimate child are closest, and the father's acknowledgment of paternity has been most clearly established by nonjudicial means. The New York estate planners who wrote the law contrived its inertia to lean against the children of informal unions. *Lalli* is thus reminiscent of an earlier legal order designed to assure a man that his wealth and status would attach to a woman only when he chose to formalize their union and would pass only to the children of such a union.

KENNETH L. KARST

(SEE ALSO: *Freedom of Intimate Association.*)

LAMAR, JOSEPH R.
(1857–1916)

Joseph Rucker Lamar, "an old-fashioned southern gentleman," served on the Supreme Court from 1911 until his death in 1916. As a Justice, Lamar approved the received doctrines of the time such as FREEDOM OF CONTRACT and AFFECTATION WITH A PUBLIC INTEREST. Lamar had been a leading Georgia attorney and had served as a state legislator and member of the Georgia Supreme Court (1903–1905) before his appointment to the Court. He was the fourth of President WILLIAM HOWARD TAFT's appointees and replaced EDWARD D. WHITE, whom Taft had promoted from Associate to Chief Justice.

Lamar joined a Court that included Justices OLIVER WENDELL HOLMES and JOHN MARSHALL HARLAN, leaning to the progressive side. Lamar usually voted with the majority of the Court; he wrote only eight dissents in four years, and one writer counted agreement in 150 of 154 cases sustaining exercise of STATE POLICE POWER and in 71 of 74 cases striking down such legislation. Lamar's apparent conciliation should not be taken to indicate disinterested acquiescence. In UNITED STATES V. GRIMAUD (1911) Lamar substantially strengthened the force of administrative rulings. *Grimaud* placed the law squarely behind such rulings;

Lamar denied that administrative decisions constituted legislative DELEGATIONS OF POWER, and he upheld Congress's right to punish violations as criminal acts if it chose. Although he sometimes supported CIVIL RIGHTS, his most famous opinion came in a labor case: GOMPERS V. BUCK'S STOVE AND RANGE COMPANY (1911). Writing for a unanimous Court, Lamar declared that a secondary boycott constituted an illegal conspiracy in restraint of trade which could be forbidden by INJUNCTION. He rejected the union's claim of FREEDOM OF SPEECH.

Lamar served on the WHITE COURT, a Court that increasingly favored propertied interests. His lack of imagination and creativity were likely seen as virtues by his contemporaries, characteristics of a man well-fitted for the Court.

DAVID GORDON

Bibliography

DINNERSTEIN, LEONARD 1969 Joseph R. Lamar. Pages 1973–1997 in Leon Friedman and Fred L. Israel, eds., *The Justices of the United States Supreme Court, 1789–1969.* New York: Chelsea House.

LAMAR, L. Q. C.
(1825–1893)

Lucius Quintus Cincinnatus Lamar, draftsman of the Mississippi Ordinance of Secession, celebrated eulogist of CHARLES SUMNER, and "Great Pacificator" during the electoral crisis of 1877, was appointed to the Supreme Court by GROVER CLEVELAND in 1888. He was the first Democrat to be appointed in a quarter-century and the first ex-Confederate to serve on the Court. Lamar was sixty-two years old when he received his commission, the second oldest new Justice in the Court's history. But he had been the South's most prominent apostle of sectional reconciliation for more than a decade and the President was primarily interested in the nomination's symbolic dimensions.

Judging exhilarated Lamar, and he was among the Court's most productive members until debilitated by ill health in the spring of 1892. Construction of the public land laws was his specialty, reflecting his experience as Cleveland's reform-minded secretary of the interior. He was also valuable at the conference table. "His was the most suggestive mind that I ever knew," Chief Justice MELVILLE W. FULLER reported, "and not one of us but has drawn from his inexhaustible store." Lamar was equally impressed by his brethren, calling them "the smartest old fellows I ever saw." In 1893, when reminiscing about a long career of public service as Confederate diplomat, congressman,

senator, and cabinet official, he described his judicial experience as "the most impressive incident in my entire intellectual and moral life."

STRICT CONSTRUCTION and traditional canons of interpretation characterized his work in constitutional law. Lamar had no sympathy for the newly fashioned concept of SUBSTANTIVE DUE PROCESS, and he concurred with Justice JOSEPH P. BRADLEY's strident dissent in CHICAGO, MILWAUKEE & ST. PAUL RY. CO. V. MINNESOTA (1890), maintaining that the REASONABLENESS of price regulations was a legislative, not a judicial, question. He also resisted extension of the SWIFT V. TYSON (1842) "general jurisprudence" doctrine to industrial accident cases. Only in the well-trodden COMMERCE CLAUSE field did Lamar consistently vote to restrict the autonomy of the states. And though he was quick to strike down tax laws and police regulations that burdened interstate transactions, Lamar remained obsessed with the necessity of setting limits to Congress's commerce power. In KIDD V. PEARSON (1888), his most influential opinion, Lamar not only formulated the mischievous distinction between commerce and manufacturing but also stated its rationale. "If it be held that the term [commerce] includes the regulation of all such manufactures as are intended to be the subject of commercial transactions in the future," he explained, "it is impossible to deny that it would also include all productive industries that contemplate the same thing. The result would be that Congress would be invested, to the exclusion of the States, with the power to regulate, not only manufacture, but also agriculture, horticulture, stock raising, domestic fisheries, mining—in short, every branch of human industry." For a former Confederate whose cherished doctrine of state SOVEREIGNTY already had been extinguished, such a state of affairs was at once imaginable and unthinkable.

CHARLES W. McCURDY

Bibliography

MAYES, EDWARD 1896 *Lucus Q. C. Lamar, His Life, Times, and Speeches.* Nashville, Tenn.: Publishing House of the Methodist Episcopal Church South.

MURPHY, JAMS B. 1973 *L. Q. C. Lamar, Pragmatic Patriot.* Baton Rouge: Louisiana State University Press.

LAMONT v. POSTMASTER GENERAL OF THE UNITED STATES
381 U.S. 301 (1965)

A 1962 act of Congress required the postmaster general to detain all unsealed mail of foreign origin determined to be "communist political propaganda," and to notify the addressee that the mail would be delivered only if he requested it by returning an official reply card. The Supreme Court, 8–0, held the act unconstitutional as an abridgment of the addressee's FIRST AMENDMENT rights. Justice WILLIAM O. DOUGLAS, for the Court, declared that the act sought to control the flow of ideas and was at war with the wide-open discussion of ideas protected by the amendment.

LEONARD W. LEVY

(SEE ALSO: *Listeners' Rights.*)

LANDIS, JAMES M.
(1899–1964)

James McCauley Landis was a gifted lawyer, professor and dean at Harvard Law School, and writer, whose outstanding contribution to American law was his theoretical analysis and practical championing of REGULATORY COMMISSIONS. He was a student of FELIX FRANKFURTER and co-authored *The Business of the Supreme Court* (1928) with him. Landis chaired both the Securities and Exchange Commission (1934–1937) and the Civil Aeronautics Board (1946–1947), served on the Federal Trade Commission (1933–1934), and wrote *The Administrative Process* (1938), a sympathetic analysis of regulatory commissions. The book discussed the limits on agencies imposed by Congress and the checks on them afforded by JUDICIAL REVIEW, and Landis downplayed the likelihood of administrative abuses of power, arguing that the true danger lay in lethargic enforcement of congressional policy. The efficiency with which these commissions could focus on economic problems by merging executive, legislative, and judicial powers impressed Landis, who saw administrative action as a practical means to achieve realistic ends.

DAVID GORDON

Bibliography
RITCHIE, DONALD A. 1980 *James M. Landis, Dean of the Regulators.* Cambridge, Mass.: Harvard University Press.

LAND ORDINANCE OF 1784

See: Ordinance of 1784

LANDRUM-GRIFFIN ACT
73 Stat. 519 (1959)

Known as the Labor Management Reporting and Disclosure Act, Landrum-Griffin brought internal administration of labor unions within the realm of federal regulation and guaranteed union members certain basic rights. Its goal was union self-regulation and voluntary democratization.

Passage of the measure resulted from a growing national concern influenced by a Senate committee's findings of union leaders' corruption and autocratic behavior. Relying on Congress's constitutional authority to insure the free flow of INTERSTATE COMMERCE, the act restricted secondary BOYCOTTS; strictly controlled union elections; required strict reporting of the unions' financial transactions; outlawed extortion PICKETING; authorized state JURISDICTION over labor disputes not handled by the National Labor Relations Board; and modified union security provisions for certain national unions. In setting forth a Bill of Rights of Members of Labor Organizations, the act reversed the courts' tendency to allow union governance by self-established rules.

The act also made it a criminal offense for a Communist party member to serve as an officer or employee of a labor union until five years after termination of party membership. In UNITED STATES V. BROWN (1965) the Supreme Court ruled this section unconstitutional as a BILL OF ATTAINDER.

PAUL L. MURPHY

Bibliography
MCLAUGHLIN, DORIS and SCHOOMAKER, ANITA 1979 *The Landrum-Griffin Act and Union Democracy.* Ann Arbor: University of Michigan Press.

LAND USE AND THE CONSTITUTION

See: Zoning

LANE v. WILSON

See: Literacy Test

LANGDON, JOHN
(1741–1819)

John Langdon, a financier and businessman who risked his large personal fortune in support of the Revolution, had, by 1787, already served in the Continental Congress and as a colonel in the Revolutionary War; he had also supervised shipbuilding for the navy and had been president of New Hampshire.

As chairman of New Hampshire's delegation to the CONSTITUTIONAL CONVENTION OF 1787, Langdon personally paid the delegation's expenses. He spoke often at the Convention and served on three committees. He favored such nationalist measures as a congressional veto over state legislation and a prohibition of state taxes on exports. He advocated prohibiting Congress, as well as the states, from emitting BILLS OF CREDIT.

After signing the Constitution, Langdon returned home to become leader of the proratification forces in the state convention. He was elected to the United States Senate and became its first president *pro tempore;* and he served seven more years as governor of New Hampshire.

DENNIS J. MAHONEY

Bibliography

ROSSITER, CLINTON 1966 *1787: The Grand Convention.* New York: Macmillan.

LANSING, JOHN, JR.
(1754–1829?)

Mayor John Lansing of Albany was one of three delegates from New York to the CONSTITUTIONAL CONVENTION OF 1787. A former member of Congress and an ally of Governor George Clinton, Lansing was chosen to represent the antinationalist sentiment of the state's political leadership. Lansing was a coauthor of the PATERSON PLAN and a spokesman for the faction that opposed creating a strong national government. He and fellow New York delegate ROBERT YATES withdrew on July 10 charging that the convention was exceeding its congressional mandate to propose amendments to the ARTICLES OF CONFEDERATION.

In the New York debate over RATIFICATION OF THE CONSTITUTION Lansing was one of the anti-Federalist leaders. He was a delegate to the state ratifying convention where he urged defeat of the new Constitution and summoning of a new federal convention. After a proratification majority was assured, Lansing urged conditional ratification and then ratification reserving the right to secede. The long series of proposed amendments—including a BILL OF RIGHTS—that accompanied New York's instrument of ratification was largely Lansing's work.

After 1788 Lansing held state judicial office—serving as Chief Justice and Chancellor—but he never held any federal office except presidential elector.

DENNIS J. MAHONEY

Bibliography

ROSSITER, CLINTON 1966 *1787: The Grand Convention.* New York: Macmillan.

LANZA, UNITED STATES v.
260 U.S. 377 (1922)

There is no DOUBLE JEOPARDY when both state and federal governments outlaw an offense and each prosecutes an individual for the same act. The United States indicted Lanza for violating the VOLSTEAD ACT after the state of Washington had already prosecuted him under a state statute enforcing PROHIBITION. A unanimous Supreme Court, dismissing Lanza's double jeopardy claim, declared that the double jeopardy forbidden by the Fifth Amendment was a second trial for the same offense in the same JURISDICTION. The Court concluded: "It follows that an act denounced as a crime by both national and state sovereignties is an offense against the peace and dignity of both, and may be punished by each." *Lanza* is still good law.

DAVID GORDON

LARKIN v. GRENDEL'S DEN, INCORPORATED
459 U.S. 116 (1982)

Dissenting alone, Justice WILLIAM H. REHNQUIST observed that "silly cases" like this one, as well as great or hard cases, make bad law. Chief Justice WARREN E. BURGER for the Court aimed its "heavy FIRST AMENDMENT artillery," in Rehnquist's phrase, at a statute that banned the sale of alcoholic beverages within 500 feet of a school or church, should either object to the presence of a neighboring tavern. Originally, Massachusetts had absolutely banned such taverns but found that the objective of the STATE POLICE POWER, promoting neighborhood peace, could be fulfilled by the less drastic method of allowing schools and churches to take the initiative of registering objections. In this case a church objected to a tavern located ten feet away. Burger held that vesting the church with the state's veto power breached the prohibition against an ESTABLISHMENT OF RELIGION, on the grounds that the church's involvement vitiated the secular purposes of the statute, advanced the cause of religion, and excessively entangled state and church. Rehnquist argued that a sensible statute had not breached the wall of SEPARATION OF CHURCH AND STATE.

LEONARD W. LEVY

LARSON v. DOMESTIC AND FOREIGN COMMERCE CORPORATION
337 U.S. 682 (1949)

This is a leading decision concerning the SOVEREIGN IMMUNITY of the United States. Plaintiff sued the head of the War Assets Administration (WAA), alleging that the Administrator had sold certain surplus coal to plaintiff, had refused to deliver the coal, and had entered into a contract to sell the coal to others. Because plaintiff sought injunctive relief against WAA officials, ordering them not to sell the coal or to deliver it to anyone other than plaintiff, and because the suit concerned property of the United States, the Supreme Court found the suit to be one against the United States and, therefore, to be barred by sovereign immunity. The Court distinguished *Larson* from suits against officers for acts beyond their statutory powers and from suits seeking to enjoin allegedly unconstitutional behavior, both of which the Court stated would not constitute suits against the sovereign, even if the plaintiff alleges the officer acted unconstitutionally or beyond his statutory powers, "if the relief requested cannot be granted merely by ordering the cessation of the conduct complained of but will require affirmative action by the sovereign or the disposition of unquestionably sovereign property." In cases involving suits against state officials, part of this passage apparently was contradicted by EDELMAN V. JORDAN (1974) and MILLIKEN V. BRADLEY (1977). In each of these cases the Court found that litigation to require a state to pay the costs of future compliance with the Constitution did not constitute a suit against the sovereign. The precise holding in *Larson* became an important and debated issue in PENNHURST STATE SCHOOL AND HOSPITAL V. HALDERMAN (1984), where the Court relied in part on *Larson* to hold that actions in federal court against state officials, alleging violations of state law, are prohibited by the ELEVENTH AMENDMENT.

THEODORE EISENBERG

LARSON v. VALENTE
456 U.S. 228 (1982)

Minnesota required charitable organizations to register and make disclosure when they solicited contributions. Religious organizations were exempted if more than half their contributions came from members. Members of the Unification Church sued in federal court to challenge the law's constitutionality. The Supreme Court, 5–4, held the law invalid.

Justice WILLIAM J. BRENNAN, for the Court, said that the law effectively granted denominational preferences, favoring well-established churches and disfavoring newer churches or churches that preferred public solicitation. This discrimination took the case out of the purpose-effects-entanglement test of LEMON V. KURTZMAN (1971) for ESTABLISHMENT OF RELIGION. Instead, Brennan invoked a searching form of STRICT SCRUTINY, which the state here failed to pass. The state's purported interests in preventing abuse in solicitation were not supported in the record. In any case, Brennan said, the Minnesota law failed *Lemon*'s "entanglement" test by risking the politicizing of religion; one Minnesota legislator had remarked, "I'm not sure why we're so hot to regulate the Moonies [Unification Church] anyway."

The four dissenters thought the plaintiffs lacked STANDING to challenge the law. Two of them also dissented on the merits of the case, arguing that the law did not constitute an intentional discrimination among religions.

KENNETH L. KARST

LASKI, HAROLD J.
(1893–1950)

British political scientist and Socialist party leader Harold Joseph Laski influenced American constitutional thought both through his public writings and through his friendship with leading American jurists and political leaders. Laski studied political science at Oxford University under Ernest Barker, and from 1916 to 1920 was an instructor in government at Harvard University. While teaching at Harvard he met, and began a twenty-year correspondence with, Justice OLIVER WENDELL HOLMES, and he established an even longer-lasting friendship with Professor (later Justice) FELIX FRANKFURTER. He also numbered among his friends and correspondents President FRANKLIN D. ROOSEVELT and Justice BENJAMIN N. CARDOZO.

From 1920 until his death in 1950 Laski taught at the London School of Economics and Political Science. He continued to correspond with his American friends and frequently visited the United States. He affected American jurisprudence mainly by influencing those whose general approach to legal and constitutional problems is called LEGAL REALISM.

Although in his early books, written in America, he had embraced a pluralist doctrine of politics, Laski had by 1931 adopted the Marxist theory of history as class struggle, and thereafter he attempted to formulate a non-Soviet Marxist political theory. He never lost interest in American politics, and his last book was *The American Democracy,* a Marxist account of American history and institutions.

DENNIS J. MAHONEY

Bibliography

DEANE, HERBERT A. 1954 *The Political Ideas of Harold Laski.* Ph.D. dissertation, Columbia University.
HOWE, MARK DEWOLFE 1953 *The Holmes-Laski Correspondence.* 2 Vols. Cambridge, Mass.: Harvard University Press.

LASSITER v. DEPARTMENT OF SOCIAL SERVICES

See: Right to Counsel

LAU v. NICHOLS
414 U.S. 563 (1974)

San Francisco failed to provide non-English-speaking students of Chinese ancestry with an adequate education. The Supreme Court, without dissent, found such an effect to violate Title VI of the CIVIL RIGHTS ACT OF 1964 even absent any intent to discriminate against the students. *Lau*'s employment of an "effects" test under Title VI may not have survived REGENTS OF THE UNIVERSITY OF CALIFORNIA V. BAKKE (1978), a question that divided the Court in *Guardians Association v. Civil Service Commission* (1983). Congress later expressed approval of *Lau* in enacting legislation to assist non-English-speaking students.

THEODORE EISENBERG

LAW ENFORCEMENT AND FEDERAL–STATE RELATIONS

This country has long been committed to the notion that primary responsibility for law enforcement should reside in state and local governments. Over the past century, however, changes in the federal criminal system have affected the traditional balance among federal, state, and local responsibilities for law enforcement. We may be slowly moving in the direction of a national police force.

The Supreme Court has affirmed the constitutionality of an expanded federal legislative authority in the realm of criminal enforcement. Congress has enacted numerous statutes under this expanded federal authority. As a result, the federal criminal code has begun to look more and more like a state criminal code in its substantive content and even in its jurisdictional reach and form.

Over the long term, the balance among the several law enforcement JURISDICTIONS will be determined not only by the breadth of the law on the books but also by its implementation in practice. The type and magnitude of police resources available to the federal government and the attitudes of the electorate and decision makers in key governmental institutions are likely to determine whether a broad federal criminal authority will supplant state and local responsibilities. Here, too, some changes have begun.

The traditional allocation of law enforcement responsibilities assigns to local governments the basic policing of crimes such as homicide, theft, robbery, rape, burglary, muggings, and the like. Local police have responsibility for patrol, for immediate response to reports of crime, and for investigations. A huge number of local officers presently performs those functions nationwide, particularly in metropolitan areas. The idea of a "national police force" directed from Washington, D.C. taking over these functions seems far-reaching. But one can imagine substantial shifts in the traditional division between federal and local responsibilities that would be accompanied by growth of a significantly larger corps of federal police that might fairly be called a national police force.

The jurisdictional reach of the federal criminal code has expanded in many ways over the past century. Most federal criminal legislation not aimed at protecting direct federal interests, such as federal funds or property, has been constitutionally based in Congress's enumerated powers—for example, the POSTAL POWER, the TAXING AND SPENDING POWER, and the power to regulate commerce among the states. (See NATIONAL POLICE POWER.)

Use of the postal and taxing powers as a basis for federal criminal jurisdiction has not changed much over the years. The use of the mails was relied upon early in the mail fraud statute enacted in 1872. A comprehensive registration-tax scheme was utilized in the original major antinarcotics legislation, the HARRISON ACT of 1914. The COMMERCE CLAUSE which began its criminal law history as a fairly narrow jurisdictional base—requiring transportation or travel across a state line—in modern times has been expanded. In a number of statutes, federal jurisdiction is now based on the use of the facilities of commerce such as interstate telephone calls, telegrams, and any kind of interstate movement of persons or goods.

The EFFECT ON COMMERCE formula, originally developed in the economic regulation sphere, has also broadened the bases for federal criminal jurisdiction. The nexus with commerce required under that formula is not very substantial. And the "effect on commerce" formula itself has been extended to situations where the criminal activity merely takes place on the premises of a business whose operations affect commerce. Furthermore, in PEREZ V. UNITED STATES (1971) the Court accepted congressional findings that a type of criminal conduct was part of a class of activities affecting commerce, and held that that type of conduct could be made a federal crime without any showing of an effect upon commerce in the individual case. Although in most cases similar to *Perez* proof of an effect upon commerce probably can be shown, *Perez* represents the furthest expansion of the reach of federal criminal jurisdiction under the commerce power.

The necessity to rely upon enumerated powers led Congress to enact crimes in forms differing markedly from the usual state penal code. Often, otherwise innocuous conduct that provided the basis for federal jurisdiction became the central element of the offense. Congress made criminal the transportation in commerce of lottery tickets, or obscene literature, or women for immoral purposes; depositing a letter in the mails to execute a fraudulent scheme; or affecting commerce by robbery or extortion.

The odd form of these crimes has produced concerns peculiar to federal criminal law. The prosecution of federal crimes often overemphasizes the jurisdiction element. The Supreme Court in four decades has, in five mail fraud cases, faced the question whether mailing was done for purposes of the fraudulent scheme; during the same period, the Court has not once considered the sometimes perplexing question of what constitutes fraudulant conduct under the statute.

The jurisdictional reach of federal criminal statutes has also developed in an odd checkerboard pattern. For example, originally, federal law made it a crime to use the mails to defraud but not the telegraph or telephone. Many such inconsistencies have been eliminated, but some still remain.

The *Perez* decision may also have far-reaching effects on the form of federal crimes. The case is usually cited for its effect in expanding the jurisdictional reach of federal criminal laws. However, the more impor-tant impact of the case may be that Congress can now, if it is so minded, draft a criminal code in a form substantially identical to a state penal code. Under such a code, the federal prosecutor would not have to prove the jurisdictional element in a crime belonging to a commerce-related class of activity; the proof would resemble the evidence offered in comparable state prosecutions.

Congress has not yet fully taken up the *Perez* invitation. In addition to the consumer credit statute enacted in 1964, the most significant statutes using this drafting approach are the illegal gambling business statute and the Comprehensive Drug Abuse Prevention and Control Act, both enacted in 1970. Federal drug crimes, which were historically based on the taxing power, are now based on the commerce power and defined in traditional criminal law terms.

Many traditional crimes have long been subject to punishment under the federal criminal code where a direct federal interest is involved, when the offense occurs on federal property or in a location for which the federal government has a special responsibility, or when federal funds are involved or persons are injured. Thus murder, manslaughter, and rape are federal crimes when committed "within the special maritime and territorial jurisdiction of the United States." And where criminal conduct on federal lands is not punishable by any specific federal enactment but would be a crime under state law, federal law incorporates state law and makes the conduct punishable.

However, traditional crimes have also been made federal offenses where no direct federal interest is involved. Legislation of this type is usually justified on the ground that the crimes involved are often committed by criminal groups organized and operating in more than one state, thus calling for nationwide investigation and prosecution. Such offenses are broadly defined, however, and do not limit federal prosecution to instances where the conduct involved can conveniently only be investigated and prosecuted by federal authorities.

There is today hardly a major crime category treated in state penal codes that is not also a federal crime, even in the absence of a direct federal interest. Ignoring for the moment the jurisdictional limits, examples of such crimes include: prostitution (MANN ACT, 1910); various forms of theft involving stolen motor vehicles, other stolen property, and theft from interstate shipments (Dyer Act, 1919); bank robbery (1934); robbery (Anti-Racketeering Act, 1934); extortion (Anti-Racketeering Act, 1934); kidnaping (1932);

threats (1934); arson (Travel Act, 1961); bribery (Travel Act, 1961); rioting (1968); sexual exploitation of children (1978); and murder (Racketeer Influenced and Corrupt Organizations Act, RICO, 1970).

In several instances, state crimes have played a more direct role in the federal criminal code. In three important pieces of complex criminal legislation—the Travel Act of 1961, the gambling business statute of 1970, and the RICO statute of 1970—Congress adopted the legislative technique of making the commission of certain crimes in violation of state law a federal crime under specified circumstances. In these instances, federal law did not simply cover the same ground as the state crime; it became identical to it.

The effect of these changes in jurisdictional reach, form, and substantive coverage has been to move the federal criminal code closer to the form and content of the fifty state penal codes with which it overlaps. Certain benefits have resulted from these changes. Many anomalies and inconsistencies in federal crime coverage have been eliminated. It is now also easier for the federal government, in a limited fashion, directly to supplement state and local efforts to combat ordinary crime.

These changes also have their costs. The old emphasis on jurisdiction and the checkerboard pattern of coverage have served as a constant reminder of the limited role of the federal government in protecting local communities against ordinary crime. As these elements in the code are eliminated, it becomes easier to think in terms of an expanded federal role.

The balance of responsibility necessarily will continue to remain with the states as long as federal law enforcement resources remain small in comparison to state and local forces, and federal prosecutions remain a small percentage of the total prosecutorial caseload of the country. Overall, there are about fifty major federal criminal enforcement agencies with approximately 50,000 field personnel. Most of these have specialized duties and limited jurisdiction. Approximately 35,000 federal felony prosecutions are initiated annually by about 2,000 federal prosecutors. This federal picture should be contrasted with that at the state and local levels where approximately 19,000 police agencies employ about 500,000 sworn officers, and in excess of 700,000 prosecutions are begun each year by more than 20,000 state and local prosecutors.

A dramatic increase in the number of federal law enforcement personnel or their combination in a single agency would have to occur in order to create the conditions for a major shift of law enforcement responsibilities to the federal realm. However, such a shift could also conceivably occur through a shift of military personnel into domestic law enforcement, or by the development of federal control over state and local agencies.

The growth of existing federal law enforcement agencies has been significant although not dramatic. In the past thirty years, the Federal Bureau of Investigation, the largest federal law enforcement agency and the one with the most general criminal enforcement authority, has grown from 3,000 to 8,000 agents; the Secret Service has expanded from 300 to 1,500; and the Customs Service, from 150 to 600 agents. The Drug Enforcement Administration (DEA) has grown tenfold from 200 to 2,000 agents.

The 1970s and 1980s have seen moves toward consolidation of separate agencies. The Bureau of Narcotics, originally located in the Treasury Department, was shifted to the Department of Justice, and later became the DEA. Recently the FBI, which had never before had any significant investigative responsibility for drug matters, moved strongly into that field and began working closely with DEA. DEA personnel may eventually be absorbed into the FBI, a move that would increase the personnel of that agency by more than one-fifth.

Even if agencies continue to grow and merge, a dramatic shift of law enforcement responsibility from state and local governments to the federal government seems unlikely in the foreseeable future. The creation of a single, really large corps of federal enforcement personnel would require considerable expansion of either the rate of growth or the practice of combining agencies.

Resources for a national police operation might also conceivably become available through increased use of the military to enforce domestic law. There is a strong tradition, founded in part in the same concerns as the commitment to local responsibility for law enforcement, against the involvement of the military in law enforcement. In the context of military surveillance activities directed against civilians, Justice WILLIAM O. DOUGLAS once suggested that "turning the military loose on civilians even if sanctioned by act of Congress . . . would raise serious and profound constitutional questions." A statutory prohibition against the use of the military to enforce domestic law, the POSSE COMITATUS ACT, was enacted in 1878. The act makes it a crime to use the military forces "to execute the laws" except as expressly authorized by Congress or the Constitution.

The Supreme Court has not yet authoritatively interpretated the Posse Comitatus Act. Existing lower court interpretations permit some limited involvement of the military in domestic law enforcement.

Several different constructions of the act were advanced in a series of decisions growing out of the occupation of Wounded Knee, South Dakota, by American Indian Movement members, for example, that the act is violated only by direct active use of federal troops in domestic law enforcement. Specific statutory exceptions also allow the domestic use of the military to enforce the laws, in cases of civil disorder, threats to federal property, and protection of federal parks, foreign dignitaries, and certain federal officials.

Increased federal efforts to combat drug smuggling have strained the Posse Comitatus Act. The desire to use navy ships and air force planes against smugglers led to enactment in 1982 of a statute that made further inroads on the act. Though limited, the new law is important because it is the first statutory modification of the Posse Comitatus Act for ordinary law enforcement purposes in the more than 100 years since its enactment. This is an area where special care should be taken; by a single stroke, Congress can effect a major change in the traditional law enforcement balance.

In the decades of the 1970s and 1980s there has been increasing federal involvement with state and local law enforcement. The Law Enforcement Assistance Administration, established in 1968 and terminated in the late 1970s, involved a massive FEDERAL GRANT-IN-AID program to state and local governments for law enforcement purposes. The potential of this technique for giving the federal government control over local law enforcement policy decisions has not been fully realized.

Formal arrangements of cooperation between federal and state and local agencies are also increasing. Fourteen federal organized crime strike forces and twelve special drug task forces involving cooperating teams of federal, state, and local law enforcement agents have been established in major cities throughout the country. Policymaking committees composed of federal, state, and local law enforcement officials also meet.

The picture presented is one of increasingly close cooperation and interdependence of law enforcement agencies at the federal, state, and local levels. The existing programs do not yet, however, add up to the establishment of a basis for federal control.

As long as there is a national consensus that the primary responsibility for law enforcement should remain at the local level there is no serious likelihood that Congress would authorize the resources to create a national police force to enforce what is becoming a true national criminal code. Any assessment of trends in the national consensus on an issue of this nature is, of course, difficult to make. One can only point to certain factors which serve as general indicators.

The focus and rhetoric of national discourse on the role of federal criminal law enforcement have changed somewhat in recent years. Crime has increasingly become a source of public concern and a standard topic of national political discussion. Correspondingly, the federal government's public pronouncements have assumed increasingly larger responsibilities for federal law enforcement. The federal emphasis in the 1950s and 1960s focused on organized crime and political corruption. In the 1970s the emphasis shifted to white-collar crime. In the 1980s the federal government has added to its emphasized responsibilities a massive attack on drugs and violence.

In the 1960s, the ATTORNEY GENERAL of the United States never spoke of the federal government's role in law enforcement without at least paying lip service to the principle that primary responsibility rests at the local level. In the 1980s the attorney general in his major addresses generally speaks of working closely with state and local law enforcement officials and the development of a national strategy.

Any serious moves toward substantial enlargement of federal law enforcement responsibilities might be opposed by state and local governments. As matters stand, these authorities typically welcome increasing federal assistance and involvement, because the crime problem is too big for local officials to handle alone. Of course, this condition augurs continued growth of the federal arm. One wonders when that growth will begin to be seen as a threat.

Congress itself continues to recite the local responsibility credo even while it expands the scope of the federal code. Although the Supreme Court has not imposed significant constitutional restraints on the reach of federal penal legislation, it has adopted a restrictive maxim of interpretation: unless Congress expresses itself unambiguously it will be presumed not to have intended to change the traditional state–federal balance in law enforcement. If the prospect of a national police force loomed on the horizon, would the Court resurrect significant constitutional limits?

Perceiving the prospect of a national police force simply in the continued expansion of the federal criminal code would be foolish. That growth, however, creates one of the conditions that would enable a national police force to function. And the very existence of an enlarged code may generate some pressure to enforce it actively. Nothing can happen, of course, unless the national consensus breaks down. There, too, some signals could mean that the "impossible" is at least possible. The development of a national police force is not imminent, but there are enough portents to suggest that we should keep in mind words uttered by Justice FELIX FRANKFURTER in YOUNGSTOWN SHEET & TUBE CO. V. SAWYER (1952), a case involving assertion of national executive power: "The accretion of dangerous power does not come in a day. It does come, however slowly, from the generative force of unchecked disregard of the restrictions that fence in even the most disinterested assertion of authority."

NORMAN ABRAMS

Bibliography

ABRAMS, NORMAN 1986 Federal Criminal Law and Its Enforcement. St. Paul, Minn.: West Publishing Co.

——— 1970 Report on Jurisdiction. Pages 33–66 in National Commission on Reform of Federal Criminal Laws: Working Papers, vol. 1. Washington, D.C.: The Commission.

SCHWARTZ, LOUIS B. 1948 Federal Criminal Jurisdiction and Prosecutors' Discretion. Law and Contemporary Problems 13:64–87.

STERN, ROBERT L. 1973 The Commerce Clause Revisited: The Federalization of Intrastate Crime. Arizona Law Review 15:271–285.

LAW OF THE LAND

The phrase "law of the land" has two connotations of constitutional dimension. In general usage it refers to a HIGHER LAW than that of COMMON LAW declaration or legislative enactment. As a result of the SUPREMACY CLAUSE, the Constitution is such a higher law; it is the "supreme law of the land." In the exercise of JUDICIAL REVIEW, the SUPREME COURT claims the office of ultimate interpreter of the Constitution. It has thus become commonplace to think of decisions of the Court as the law of the land.

A second connotation has a specialized meaning that reaches far back into English history and leaves its indelible mark on American constitutional law. In 1215, the barons of England forced King John to sign MAGNA CARTA, pledging his observance of obligations owed to them in return for their fealty to him. Among the provisions was one that declared (in translation from the Latin): "No freeman shall be taken or imprisoned or dispossessed or outlawed or banished, or in any way destroyed, nor will we go upon him, nor send upon him, except by the judgment of his peers, or by the law of the land." Magna Carta was necessar-

ily a feudal document, but this provision was so worded that it retained meaning long after feudalism gave way to the modern constitutional state.

The term "law of the land" consequently continued in English usage, representing that body of FUNDAMENTAL LAW to which appeal was made against any oppression by the sovereign, whether procedural or substantive. By 1354 there had appeared an alternate formulation, "due process of law." In his Second Institute of the Laws of England (1642), Sir EDWARD COKE asserted that "law of the land" and "due process of law" possessed interchangeable meanings; nevertheless, the older version was not thereby supplanted. The PETITION OF RIGHT (1628) played no favorites with the two terms, demanding "that freemen be imprisoned or detained only by the law of the land, or by due process of law and not by the king's special command, without any charge."

In the politically creative period after Independence, American statesmen preferred "law of the land" to "due process," apparently because of its historic association with Magna Carta. All eight of the early state CONSTITUTIONS incorporating the guarantee in full or partial form employed the term "law of the land"; and the same was true of the NORTHWEST ORDINANCE (1787). The first appearance of "due process of law" in American organic law occurred in the Fifth Amendment to the United States Constitution (1791). But that switch of usage did not displace "law of the land." Throughout the nineteenth century state constitutions and state courts spoke in one voice or the other, or even both. As of 1903 a listing by THOMAS M. COOLEY of state constitutions incorporating the legacy from Magna Carta showed "law of the land" outrunning "due process of law." The trend subsequently has been to the latter phrase; yet a 1980 count found eleven states still expressing the guarantee as "law of the land."

The Glorious Revolution of 1688, embodying the political theory that parliamentary enactment was the practical equivalent of the "law of the land," presented a dilemma in interpretation when the versions of the guarantee were introduced into American thought and incorporated into most American constitutions. Legislative supremacy was unacceptable in the New World; the American view was that when sovereignty changed hands the English concept of limitations upon the crown now applied to the legislative as well as the executive branch. It followed that to construe the guarantee as forbidding deprivation of life, liberty, or property except by legislative enactment would be to render its protection meaningless.

The puzzlement of American judges is understandable; only in the latter part of the nineteenth century had the concept been fully disentangled from the related concepts of regularized legislative process and SEPARATION OF POWERS.

The guarantee inherited from Magna Carta is unusual among constitutional limitations. On its face it is not absolute but conditional. The government may not act against persons except by the law of the land or by due process. The thrust is arguably procedural, suggesting original intent may have been to guarantee the protection of a trial. But it can carry substantive meanings as well; those meanings emerged early and had fully developed in England by the late seventeenth century.

Although the wording and position of the state constitutional guarantees varied—some using "law of the land," others "due process of law"; some appending the guarantee to a list of procedural rights, others making it a separate provision—the variation made little difference in judicial response at the procedural level. Not so, however, with respect to substantive content. Where, as in the constitutions of the Carolinas, Illinois, Maryland, and Tennessee, the wording was close to a literal translation of Magna Carta, the guarantee was extended to VESTED RIGHTS, independently of the criminal provisions of the procedural connotation. On the other hand, Connecticut and Rhode Island courts sustained PROHIBITION laws in the 1850s, holding that the phrase "due process of law" in their state constitutions was so enmeshed with entitlements of the criminally accused as to preclude inclusion of substantive right. A third series of cases, from Massachusetts, New Hampshire, New York, and Pennsylvania, read substantive content into the guarantee despite close interrelation with procedural protections. WYNEHAMER V. NEW YORK (1856) requires special consideration. In that case the state's highest court invalidated a prohibition law, insofar as it destroyed property rights in existing liquor stocks, resting its decision on separate constitutional guarantees of both "due process" and "law of the land." Contrary to the opinion of some scholars, *Wynehamer* was not overruled by *Metropolitan Board v. Barrie* (1866); the former case applied to a law with retroactive application, the latter to one that was purely prospective.

The Fifth Amendment associates "due process" with other constitutional guarantees clearly procedural in character, and separates the guarantee of due process from the RIGHT AGAINST SELF-INCRIMINATION only by a comma. Yet in major decisions, DRED SCOTT V. SANDFORD (1857), *Hepburn v. Griswold*

(1870), and ADAIR V. UNITED STATES (1908), the Supreme Court found substantive content in the clause.

In the FOURTEENTH AMENDMENT, due process is not linked to criminal procedure protections, but resembles those state constitutional provisions that had been held in state courts to have substantive content. However, the Supreme Court has disregarded the distinction between the two due process clauses in the federal Constitution. The Court has been abetted by numerous COMMENTATORS ON THE CONSTITUTION who, intent on denying the substantive element in due process, have ignored or misinterpreted the history of state constitutional guarantees of "due process" and "law of the land." The freedom from procedural connotation of Fourteenth Amendment due process made easier the path of substantive content from dissent in the SLAUGHTERHOUSE CASES (1873), to reception in CHICAGO, MILWAUKEE & ST. PAUL RAILWAY COMPANY V. MINNESOTA (1890), to full embrace in LOCHNER V. NEW YORK (1905). The Court's acceptance of the INCORPORATION DOCTRINE, with consequent reading into the Fourteenth Amendment of the various procedural protections enumerated in the BILL OF RIGHTS, largely equates the content of the two due process clauses. This development has written the final chapter in the reinterpretation of "law of the land."

FRANK R. STRONG

Bibliography

HOWARD, A. E. DICK 1968 *The Road from Runnymede: Magna Carta and Constitutionalism in America.* Charlottesville: University Press of Virginia.

REMBAR, CHARLES 1980 *The Law of the Land: The Evolution of Our Legal System.* New York: Simon and Schuster.

LEARY v. UNITED STATES
395 U.S. 6 (1969)

Timothy Leary, a celebrated 1960s connoisseur of mind-altering substances, was found in possession of marijuana and convicted of (1) failure to pay the federal marijuana tax; and (2) transportation and concealment of marijuana, knowing it had been illegally imported into the country. A unanimous Supreme Court held both convictions unconstitutional. Paying the tax would have incriminated Leary under state law; his omission to pay was justified by his RIGHT AGAINST SELF-INCRIMINATION. His other conviction had rested on a statutory presumption that a person in possession of marijuana knew it had been illegally imported. This presumption was irrational; much marijuana was grown in the United States. The presumption thus violated PROCEDURAL DUE PROCESS.

KENNETH L. KARST

LEAST RESTRICTIVE MEANS TEST

When the Supreme Court, in reviewing the constitutionality of legislation, uses the permissive RATIONAL BASIS standard, it demands only that a law be a rational means for achieving a legitimate governmental purpose. When the STANDARD OF REVIEW is more exacting, however, the Court looks more closely at the legislative choice of means, insisting on more than some minimal showing of rationality. In a SEX DISCRIMINATION case, for example, the legislation must be "substantially related" to achieving some important governmental purpose; when STRICT SCRUTINY is the appropriate standard of review, the law must be "necessary" to achieving a COMPELLING STATE INTEREST. However such a heightened standard of review may be phrased, it aims at providing as much protection for constitutional values and interests as may be consistent with the accomplishment of legislative goals. One commonly used formulation of this aim is the Court's insistence that legislation be the "least restrictive means" for attaining the ends the legislature seeks—that is, least restrictive on such constitutionally protected interests as the FREEDOM OF SPEECH, or equality, or the free flow of INTERSTATE COMMERCE.

Some commentators have urged the Supreme Court to use a similar analysis in testing the reasonableness of legislative means even under the "rational basis" standard of review, as in cases involving challenges to ECONOMIC REGULATION. Thus far, however, the Court has employed "least restrictive means" reasoning only when it has consciously used a more demanding standard of review. Thus, in DEAN MILK COMPANY V. MADISON (1951), the Court struck down an ordinance specifying that milk sold in the city as "pasteurized" be pasteurized at an approved plant within five miles of the city center. The Court emphasized that "reasonable nondiscriminatory alternatives" were available to serve the city's health interests. (See STATE REGULATION OF COMMERCE.) And in *Shelton v. Tucker* (1960) the Court invalidated a law requiring every Arkansas teacher to file an annual affidavit listing every organization to which he or she had belonged or made contributions within five years. The Court agreed that Arkansas had a strong interest

in teacher fitness, but said the legislature's sweeping intrusion into associational privacy "must be viewed in the light of less drastic means for achieving the same basic purpose." A narrower inquiry, presumably, would serve that purpose.

Both decisions illustrate how the "least restrictive means" formula can help a court avoid casting aspersions on legislative motive. (See LEGISLATION; LEGISLATIVE INTENT.) Madison's ordinance might have been designed to capture the pasteurization business; Arkansas undoubtedly was seeking to expose and dismiss teachers who were members of the NAACP. In neither case did the Supreme Court openly question the legitimacy of the legislative purpose; taking the government's statement of objective at face value, it said, in effect, "There are ways you could have accomplished that without intruding on constitutionally protected ground." One excellent reason for heightening the standard of review—and thus for insisting on "least restrictive means"—is the suspicion that legislators have acted for questionable purposes. (See SUSPECT CLASSIFICATION.)

KENNETH L. KARST

Bibliography
NOTE 1969 Less Drastic Means and the First Amendment. *Yale Law Journal* 78:464–474.

LECOMPTON CONSTITUTION

In June 1857 less than thirty percent of registered voters in Kansas Territory elected a CONSTITUTIONAL CONVENTION dominated by proslavery delegates. Meeting in Lecompton, the convention drew up a constitution preparatory for statehood that guaranteed the rights of owners of slaves in the territory, excluded free blacks, and submitted to a REFERENDUM the question whether the constitution should be accepted with or without a clause prohibiting the importation of slaves into Kansas (rather than a referendum on the constitution as a whole). Viewing this as a travesty of his principle of territorial SOVEREIGNTY, Illinois Senator STEPHEN A. DOUGLAS broke with the administration of JAMES BUCHANAN, which was pressuring Congress to accept the Lecompton constitution, and led the struggle against it. In three referenda on the constitution, Kansas voted first to accept the constitution with slavery (6,226 to 569, with free-state voters abstaining), then to reject the constitution entirely (10,226 to 166 with proslavery voters abstaining), then finally to reject it entirely again (11,300 to 1,788).

The struggle over the Lecompton constitution left Kansas a territory until 1861, dissipated the influence of the Buchanan administration, drove Douglas into opposition, and destroyed the capacity of the Democratic party to serve as a unifying transsectional force.

WILLIAM M. WIECEK

Bibliography

JOHANNSEN, ROBERT W. 1973 *Stephen A. Douglas.* New York: Oxford University Press.

LEE, RICHARD HENRY
(1732–1794)

Educated in England, Richard Henry Lee practiced law in his native Virginia and became a justice of the peace in 1757. The next year he was elected to the House of Burgesses where his first speech was in favor of a measure to check the spread of SLAVERY. Lee was a leader of opposition to parliamentary taxation of the colonies and wrote the protest of the House of Burgesses against the Sugar Act (1764). When the royal governor dissolved the House of Burgesses in 1774, Lee introduced a resolution, adopted by the rump of the house, calling for a continental congress. As a delegate to the FIRST CONTINENTAL CONGRESS Lee proposed formation of committees of correspondence (a plan he originated with PATRICK HENRY and THOMAS JEFFERSON) and adoption of the continental ASSOCIATION. In June 1776 Lee made the original motions in the Continental Congress for a DECLARATION OF INDEPENDENCE, confederation, and seeking of foreign alliances. He later advocated Virginia's cession of western territorial claims in order to facilitate ratification of the ARTICLES OF CONFEDERATION; and, in 1784, he was elected President of the United States in Congress Assembled.

Lee was chosen as a delegate to the CONSTITUTIONAL CONVENTION OF 1787 but declined appointment, citing conflict with his responsibilities as a member of Congress. When the new Constitution was submitted to Congress, Lee opposed it on the ground that the convention had exceeded its mandate. Seeing that he could not block the proposal, he attempted, but failed, to have Congress add a BILL OF RIGHTS (drafted by GEORGE MASON).

Lee was a leading opponent of RATIFICATION OF THE CONSTITUTION. His seventeen "Letters from the Federal Farmer," widely printed in newspapers, were among the most influential of the various anti-Federalist writings. In the letters Lee presented a wide-ranging critique of the new Constitution: it was consolida-tionist, not federal, and would rob the states of their SOVEREIGNTY; it was aristocratic, or even monarchical, in tendency, not republican; the coexistence of state and federal courts would lead inevitably to conflict; the JUDICIAL POWER OF THE UNITED STATES was so broadly drawn as to permit foreigners and citizens of other states to sue a state in federal court; and, most important, there was no bill of rights. Lee argued and voted against ratification in the Virginia convention of 1788.

Lee was one of Virginia's original United States senators (1789–1792). He was chairman of the committee that drafted the JUDICIARY ACT OF 1789 and floor leader in the Senate for the Bill of Rights. Later in his senatorial career he became a supporter of the Federalist party and the economic program of ALEXANDER HAMILTON. A fervent opponent of slavery, Lee himself held about three dozen slaves.

DENNIS J. MAHONEY

LEE, UNITED STATES v.
455 U.S. 252 (1982)

Members of the Amish religion object, on religious grounds, to paying taxes or receiving benefits under the SOCIAL SECURITY ACT. An Amish employer of Amish workers claimed a constitutional right to refuse to pay Social Security taxes. The Supreme Court unanimously rejected that claim. Chief Justice WARREN E. BURGER, for the Court, accepted STRICT SCRUTINY as the appropriate STANDARD OF REVIEW in cases involving RELIGIOUS LIBERTY, but concluded that the government had established that mandatory participation was necessary to achieving the "overriding governmental interest" in maintaining the Social Security system. In a concurring opinion, Justice JOHN PAUL STEVENS argued against the strict scrutiny standard, saying that claimants of special religious exemptions from laws of general applicability must demonstrate "unique" reasons for being exempted—a standard that would be nearly impossible to meet.

KENNETH L. KARST

LEGAL POSITIVISM

See: Philosophy and the Constitution

LEGAL REALISM

Legal realism was the most significant movement that emerged within American jurisprudence during the 1920s and 1930s. Numerous factors conditioned this development, including pragmatism, SOCIOLOGICAL JURISPRUDENCE, and certain ideas of Justice OLIVER WENDELL HOLMES. The legal realists were not, however, an organized or highly unified group of thinkers. Their concepts had diverse sources, their work branched out in many directions, and their responses to particular issues often varied. The substantial differences between Judge JEROME N. FRANK and Karl N. Llewellyn illustrate these tendencies. Even so, these men and the other realists shared a number of distinctive attitudes and ideas.

The term "legal realism" signifies the basic thrust of the movement, which was to uncover and to explain legal realities. This effort reflects the allegation that some of the most cherished beliefs of lawyers are myths or fictions. The major purpose of the realists' provocative criticisms of these beliefs was not, however, to undermine the American legal system. Rather, it was to facilitate development of an accurate understanding of the nature, interpretation, operation, and effects of law. The realists insisted that achievement of this goal was essential for intelligent reform of legal rules, doctrines, and practices.

This outlook contributed to the realists' intense dissatisfaction with prevailing modes of legal education and scholarship. Both were under the spell of the case method pioneered by Christopher Columbus Langdell, the influential dean of the Harvard Law School from 1870 to 1895. He conceived of legal science as a small number of fundamental principles derived from study of relatively few cases. This conception was anathema to the realists, most of whom taught at leading American law schools. Their objective was to reform and to supplement, however, rather than to discard, the case method. The changes they advocated included focus on the *behavior* of judges and other officials, on their actual *decisions* rather than broad precepts. This emphasis was essential for the understanding of "real" instead of mere "paper" rules. The realists also urged the broadening of legal education to embrace not only the law on the books but also its administration and social impact. The development of this approach required a much closer integration of law and the social sciences than was traditional.

Some of these ideas were an outgrowth of major themes of ROSCOE POUND'S sociological jurisprudence. Still, the realists tended to develop criticisms of legal orthodoxies more radical than Pound's. This tendency is apparent from both the fact-skepticism of Judge Frank and the rule-skepticism of virtually all of the realists. The first of these doctrines stresses the difficulty of predicting findings of fact by judges or jurors, while the second emphasizes the limitations of legal rules. Rule-skepticism takes various forms, one of which is the conception of law as the past or future decisions of judges or other officials. Legal rules are descriptive or predictive rather than prescriptive generalizations about their behavior. This idea stems from Justice Holmes's predictive conception of law, which is one reason for the large shadow he cast over the realist movement.

Rule-skepticism also signifies distrust of the assumption that traditional legal rules or principles are the most influential determinant of judicial decisions. Numerous considerations explain this distrust, the degree of which varied among the realists. The most important factors were: a conviction of the possibility of widely different interpretations of established legal rules and principles; a belief in the existence of competing precedents, each of which could justify conflicting decisions in most cases; an awareness of the ambiguity inherent in legal language; a perception of the rapidity of socioeconomic change; and a study of the teachings of modern psychology. This last factor also influenced the realists' critique of judicial opinions. They attacked the syllogistic reasoning of judges on the ground that it failed to explain their choice of premises, which was all-important. This failure meant that opinions were often misleading rationalizations of decisions, the real reasons for which were unstated.

Rule-skepticism is the basis of some of the most important ideas of the legal realists. Their rejection of the conventional belief that judges do or should interpret rather than make law is a significant example. That belief is untenable because judicial legislation is unavoidable. Judges frequently must choose between competing decisions or interpretations, each of which is consistent with at least some precedents, rules, or principles. Although these generalizations limit judicial freedom, judges retain a substantial amount of room to maneuver.

This analysis underlies the realists' pragmatic approach to the evaluation of law, which emphasizes its practical results or effects. Rule-skepticism also influenced their de-emphasis of legal doctrine for the purpose of explaining and predicting judicial decisions. Instead, the realists stressed the importance of such factors as the personality, attitudes, or policies of judges. A similar emphasis characterized the behavioral jurisprudence developed largely by political scientists after World War II.

Although most of the realists did not specialize in constitutional law, their ideas facilitate understanding of the decisions of the Supreme Court. The Justices frequently must choose between conflicting interpretations of the Constitution, each of which has some legal basis. Their choices depend most basically upon their values, which may vary among Justices and may change over time. These variations help to explain disagreements among the Justices as well as changes in constitutional doctrine. Realism was also a formative influence on the legal philosophy of Justice WILLIAM O. DOUGLAS.

Despite the influence of the realists on American legal thought, the reaction to their ideas has not been uniform. In fact, large numbers of lawyers expressed varying degrees of dissatisfaction with the realist movement from its inception. If some of the concepts of the realists are unsatisfactory, others are enduring contributions to the study of law and the judicial process. Legal realism therefore warrants close scrutiny by students of constitutional law and judicial behavior.

WILFRID E. RUMBLE

Bibliography

FRANK, JEROME 1949 *Law and the Modern Mind.* New York: Coward-McCann.

LLEWELLYN, KARL N. 1962 *Jurisprudence: Realism in Theory and Practice.* Chicago: University of Chicago Press.

RUMBLE, WILFRID E. 1968 *American Legal Realism: Skepticism, Reform, and the Judicial Process.* Ithaca, N.Y.: Cornell University Press.

TWINING, WILLIAM 1973 *Karl Llewellyn and the Realist Movement.* London: Weidenfeld & Nicolson.

LEGAL TENDER CASES

The Legal Tender Cases include the decisions in *Hepburn v. Griswold* (1870), invalidating Civil War legislation authorizing paper money, and *Knox v. Lee* (1871) and *Parker v. Davis* (1871), sustaining postwar legal tender legislation. The various decisions reflect important developments in the nation's economic history, as well as in the Supreme Court's history, concerning the judicial role in questions of political economy, the nature and scope of judicial power, and the relation of politics to judicial opinions.

The greenback legislation of 1862 was designed to facilitate the financing of the Civil War, authorizing payments in demand notes, redeemable not in gold or silver but in interest-bearing twenty-year bonds. The notes were made "lawful money and a legal tender in payment of all debts, public and private, within the United States." The Treasury issued over $400 million in paper money during the war. After 1865, as inflation grew and greenbacks depreciated, creditors demanded payment in specie or at least in paper money equivalent to the rising premium on specie.

Secretary of the Treasury SALMON P. CHASE presided over the government's wartime greenback program. His outward support for paper money only masked his deep-seated hostility. In March 1864, he composed an epigram reflecting his true feelings: "When public exigencies require, Coin must become paper. When public exigencies allow, Paper must become coin." Six years later, as Chief Justice, he invalidated his previous policy.

Chase's role in the first legal tender case provoked intense partisan wrangling, both on and off the bench, and raised questions of the Chief Justice's behavior as the Court's administrative leader. The legal tender controversy had become entangled in partisan politics, as Republicans defended their greenback policy and the opposition Democrats attacked it as unconstitutional and improper. The Justices lined up on the same political grounds. (Chase and the Republicans by then were mutually alienated and the Chief Justice already was courting the Democrats in hopes of winning their presidential nomination.) In numerous state cases, judges similarly voted along party lines.

Chase apparently was determined to project the Court into the political maelstrom of monetary policy. But he did so with a precarious majority. Following the arguments in *Hepburn v. Griswold* in 1869, Republican Justices DAVID DAVIS, SAMUEL F. MILLER, and NOAH SWAYNE unhesitatingly endorsed the greenback policy. Chase, joined by Democrats NATHAN CLIFFORD, STEPHEN J. FIELD, ROBERT C. GRIER, and SAMUEL NELSON voted to invalidate the 1862 law. Grier by then was so senile that his colleagues persuaded him to resign. Chase, however, included his vote in the majority.

Meanwhile, Congress had authorized increasing the number of Justices to nine, giving President ULYSSES S. GRANT two new appointments, including Grier's replacement. On February 7, 1870, he nominated WILLIAM STRONG, who as a member of the Pennsylvania Supreme Court had supported the legal tender legislation, and JOSEPH P. BRADLEY, a railroad lawyer whose clients clearly favored the paper money scheme. On that same day, Chase defiantly announced the decision holding the law unconstitutional. The resulting charge of "court packing" against Grant and the Republicans misses the point: Presidents always seek judges who will support their political goals. In this case, Chase and his allies must bear the responsibility for the Court's embarrassment when it reversed itself a year later.

Chase's opinion invoked some of JOHN MARSHALL's best aphorisms. The Court, he insisted, must declare what the law is and not enforce any law inconsistent with the Constitution. To a point, Chase followed Marshall's MCCULLOCH V. MARYLAND (1819) discussions of IMPLIED POWERS, the NECESSARY AND PROPER clause, and the validity of laws consistent with the "letter and spirit of the Constitution." But where Marshall had appealed to the "spirit" of the Constitution to justify a BROAD CONSTRUCTION of congressional powers, Chase turned the notion on its head, construed those powers narrowly, and used the spirit to discover a limitation nowhere mentioned in the Constitution.

The Constitution, Chase maintained, was designed to establish justice, and a fundamental principle of justice was that preexisting private contracts should not be impaired by governmental action. The CONTRACT CLAUSE of the Constitution, however, applied to STATE ACTION; it said nothing regarding the federal government. But, Chase argued that the Constitution's Framers "intended that the spirit" of the contract clause would apply against all legislative bodies. His reliance on the Fifth Amendment was similarly strained. He found that the prohibition of contracts requiring specie payment in effect deprived people of their property without DUE PROCESS OF LAW; indeed, he maintained that the property was "taken" for a PUBLIC USE without the required JUST COMPENSATION.

Justice Miller's dissent pleaded for judicial restraint. He rebuked Chase's "abstract and intangible" arguments about the "spirit" of the Constitution. Following Marshall's broad reading of the necessary and proper clause, Miller suggested that "the degree of that necessity is for the legislature and not for the court to determine."

Partisan reactions to the decision were predictable. But the focused concerns for the result obscured the majority's far-reaching notions of judicial authority. Chase's bold assertions of judicial superintendence provoked virtually no negative reaction. The political and public acceptance of that doctrine gave a new legitimacy to judicial power. The nation had come a great distance from the protests against judicial excesses following DRED SCOTT V. SANDFORD (1857); indeed, Chase's opinion signaled a new chapter in judicial activism.

Significantly, the newly appointed Justice Strong, and not Miller, spoke for the majority in *Knox v. Lee* (1871) when the Court reversed itself. Strong largely followed Miller's interpretation of Congress's power and the necessity of congressional control over currency policy. But he responded only indirectly to Chase's presumptions of judicial power, contending that judges must assume the constitutionality of congressional acts and rely on congressional determination of what was "necessary and proper." He failed to rebuke Chase's reliance on the "spirit" of the Constitution. Finally, anticipating criticism for the dramatic reversal, Strong chided Chase for having forced the earlier decision when the Court was so divided and on the verge of receiving new appointees. The Chief Justice, joined by Nelson, Clifford, and Field dissented, with the latter two offering additional, separate opinions. The dissenting remarks largely reiterated the majority views of *Hepburn v. Griswold.*

Thirteen years later, in *Juilliard v. Greenman,* the Court, with only Field dissenting, sustained the peacetime use of greenbacks. Justice HORACE GRAY not only used the occasion to reaffirm the constitutionality of greenbacks but flatly declared that the policy involved "a POLITICAL QUESTION, to be determined by Congress when the question of exigency arises, and not a judicial question, to be afterwards passed upon by the Court." A half century later, Chief Justice CHARLES EVANS HUGHES invoked *Juilliard* as the Court, in the GOLD CLAUSE CASES (1935), narrowly acquiesced in President FRANKLIN D. ROOSEVELT's decision to abandon the gold standard. What had begun as one of the most politically conscious and aggrandizing decisions by the Supreme Court ended in self-abnegation and deference to the political branches of the government.

STANLEY I. KUTLER

Bibliography

DAM, KENNETH W. 1982 The Legal Tender Cases. *The Supreme Court Review* 1982:367–412.
FAIRMAN, CHARLES 1971 *Reconstruction and Reunion, 1864–1888,* Vol. XVI of the Oliver Wendell Holmes Devise *History of the Supreme Court of the United States.* New York: Macmillan.
KUTLER, STANLEY I. 1968 *Judicial Power and Reconstruction Politics.* Chicago: University of Chicago Press.

LEGISLATION

In addition to the separation of powers, there are at least two intersections of the Constitution and the legislative process. One concerns the obligation and capacity of legislatures to assess the constitutionality of their proposed enactments. The other concerns the federal judiciary's role in inducing legislatures to meet their constitutional obligations. Within this context there are issues common to state and congressional lawmaking.

The American constitutional scheme obligates legislatures to assess the constitutionality of proposed enactments and to enact only legislation they deem constitutionally permissible. Although this proposition may seem obvious, it has often been contradicted by respectable lawmakers, who assert that legislatures should engage in policymaking without regard to the Constitution and leave constitutional questions exclusively to the courts. Therefore the reasons that legislatures are obligated, no less than courts, to determine the constitutionality of proposed enactments deserve explanation.

If, as Chief Justice JOHN MARSHALL asserted in MARBURY V. MADISON (1803), the Constitution is a law paramount to ordinary legislation, then to assert that legislatures need not consult the Constitution is the equivalent of asserting that individuals need not consult the law before acting. To be sure, people sometimes act in disregard of the law, subject only to the risk of sanctions if they are caught and a court holds their actions to be unlawful. But it would be perverse to conclude from this observation that we are not obligated to obey the law.

The structure and text of the Constitution certainly imply that legislatures must initially determine the legality of their enactments. For example, how would Congress know whether it had the authority to enact a bill without consulting Article I and the other provisions that delegate limited powers to the national government? Indeed, some provisions of the Constitution are explicitly addressed to legislators. Article I, section 9, provides, "No bill of attainder or ex post facto law shall be passed." The FIRST AMENDMENT says, "Congress shall make no law," and the FOURTEENTH AMENDMENT's prohibitions begin with the words, "No state shall make or enforce any law. . . ." Article VI binds legislators and officials "by Oath or Affirmation to support this Constitution. . . ." Although this command does not entail that all constitutional questions are open to all institutions at all times, it does imply that a legislator must vote only for legislation that he or she believes is authorized by the Constitution. If history matters, the obligation of legislatures to interpret the Constitution was affirmed and acted on by various of the Framers and by early legislators and Presidents—some of whom, indeed, expressed this duty or prerogative even in the face of contrary judicial interpretations.

The existence of JUDICIAL REVIEW is sometimes thought to relieve legislatures of the obligations to determine the constitutionality of their enactments. But Chief Justice Marshall's classic justifications for judicial review in *Marbury* do not necessarily imply a privileged judicial function. As Herbert Wechsler wrote: "Federal courts, including the Supreme Court, do not pass on constitutional questions because there is a special function vested in them to enforce the Constitution or police the other agencies of government. They do so rather for the reason that they must decide a litigated issue that is otherwise within their jurisdiction and in doing so they must give effect to the supreme law of the land. That is, at least, what *Marbury v. Madison* was all about." (Wechsler, 1965, p. 1006.) Other arguments for judicial review have accorded the judiciary a special role, and in COOPER V. AARON (1958) the modern Court claimed that it was "supreme in the exposition of the law of the Constitution." But the Court has never implied that JUDICIAL SUPREMACY implies judicial exclusively, or that its privileged position relieves other institutions of the responsibility for making constitutional judgments.

Indeed, some constitutional issues—so-called POLITICAL QUESTIONS—may be committed to the legislative and executive branches to the exclusion of the judiciary. For example, it is widely assumed that the Senate's judgment in an IMPEACHMENT proceeding is not reviewable by the courts even though the decision may involve controverted constitutional questions, and even though the Senate's role in cases of impeachment is more judicial than legislative. In such cases, at least, if the legislature does not consider the constitutional questions, no one will.

If legislatures are obligated to consider constitutional questions, what deference, if any, should they accord prior judicial interpretations of the Constitution? In what might be called the judicial supremacy view, a legislature is in essentially the same position as a state or lower federal court: it must treat the Supreme Court's rulings as authoritative and binding. This was the view expressed by the Court in *Cooper v. Aaron*. Quoting Marshall's assertion in *Marbury* that "[i]t is emphatically the province and the duty of the judicial department to say what the law is," the Justices continued: "This decision declared the basic principle that the federal judiciary is supreme in the exposition of the law of the Constitution, and that principle has ever since been respected by this Court and the Country as a permanent and indispensable feature of our constitutional system."

The polar view is that legislators and other officials may, or must, apply the Constitution according to their best lights. This position was asserted by THOMAS JEFFERSON, ANDREW JACKSON, and ABRAHAM LIN-

COLN, among others. In vetoing the bill to recharter the Bank of the United States in 1832, Jackson wrote:

It is maintained by advocates of the bank that its constitutionality in all its features ought to be considered settled by the decision of the Supreme Court [in McCULLOCH V. MARYLAND (1819)]. To this conclusion I can not assent. . . . The Congress, the Executive, and the Court must each for itself be guided by its own opinion of the Constitution. Each public officer who takes an oath to support the Constitution swears that he will support it as he understands it, and not as it is understood by others. It is as much the duty of the House of Representatives, of the Senate, and of the President to decide upon the constitutionality of any bill or resolution which may be presented to them for passage or approval as it is of the supreme judges when it may be brought before them for judicial decision. The opinion of the judges has no more authority over Congress than the opinion of Congress has over the judges, and on that point the President is independent of both. The authority of the Supreme Court must not, therefore, be permitted to control the Congress or the Executive when acting in their legislative capacities, but to have only such influence as the force of their reasoning may deserve.

The issues presented by these opposed positions are of more than theoretical or historical interest. They have surfaced in recent years in debates over Congress's authority under section 5 of the Fourteenth Amendment to interpret or apply the amendment differently from the Court, and over Congress's power to limit the JURISDICTION OF FEDERAL COURTS over particular issues. For present purposes, I will assume that Congress, as well as state legislatures, must operate within the constitutional doctrines exposited by the United States Supreme Court. What does this obligation entail?

The dimensions of legislative responsibility and some of the difficulties in meeting it are illustrated by considering a bill introduced in the 89th Congress to punish the destruction of draft cards. The bill was enacted in 1965, seemingly in response to public DRAFT CARD BURNING to protest the VIETNAM WAR. It was challenged on First Amendment grounds and upheld by the Court in UNITED STATES V. O'BRIEN (1968).

The governing constitutional standard (as the Court later recapitulated it in O'Brien) was that "a governmental regulation is sufficiently justified . . . if it furthers an important or substantial governmental interest; if the governmental interest is unrelated to the suppression of free expression; and if the incidental restriction on alleged First Amendment freedoms is not greater than is essential to the furtherance of that interest."

Because this area of judicial doctrine was already well developed in 1965, legislators considering the draft card destruction law did not have to engage in much independent constitutional interpretation. They were, however, required to apply existing doctrine to the situation that faced them.

First, a legislator had to determine that his or her reasons for supporting the bill were "unrelated to the suppression of free expression." This obligation meant that he could not vote for the bill if his dominant, or causative, reason for favoring it was to suppress antiwar protests (rather than, say, to facilitate the administration of the selective service). The obligation demanded only introspection, a modicum of self-awareness, and the courage or will to follow the law.

It is worth pausing for a moment to ask why the Constitution should be concerned with a legislator's motivation in voting for a measure rather than simply with the legislation itself. The answer begins with the observation that the First Amendment is designed to protect citizens' freedom to protest against government policies. The Amendment does not, however, forbid all laws that inhibit protests to any extent. For example, the Congress surely may prohibit burning anything, including draft cards, if the activity poses a fire hazard to property that Congress has the power to protect. Thus, legislators have discretion to compromise constitutional values in the pursuit of other legitimate ends of government. However, as the Court's reference to "important or substantial" interests suggests, the First Amendment demands that a legislator treat a law's inhibition of expression as a cost, indeed a cost that should not be lightly imposed. But a legislator who votes for the bill in order to suppress protest, treats the inhibition as a benefit, not a cost. He has confused the credits and debits column on the constitutional balance sheet, for he seeks to bring about the very result that the First Amendment seeks to avert.

The second factual determination—actually a mixture of law, fact, and judgment—stems from the requirement that the law further an "important or substantial governmental interest." In O'Brien the Court was required to speculate about the nature and importance of the interests furthered by the draft card law. As happens frequently in matters concerning the national defense, the Court gave Congress the benefit of the doubt. But, of course, the legislators know what ends they intend a law to serve. Judgments about the importance of those ends, and how well a proposed law will actually accomplish them, are among the core responsibilities of legislators—who do not owe themselves any benefit of the doubt. It would be ironic, to say the least, if the Court deferred to Congress's judgments in these matters when Congress had not actually considered the issues carefully and in good faith.

The preceding paragraphs have not distinguished between the responsibilities of "legislators" and the "legislature." How, in fact, is responsibility for constitutional decision making allocated within the lawmaking process?

The answer seems easiest with respect to motivation. Granting that not even psychoanalysis can always reveal our deepest motivations, a conscientious legislator usually knows why he or she supports or opposes a law. (A contrary position would call into doubt the very foundations of the legislative process.) The Constitution demands that legislators assure themselves that illicit motivations, such as suppressing expression or disadvantaging racial minorities, play no role in their decisions to support the legislation. A legislator who "personally" does not care to pursue an illicit end but who supports a measure to satisfy her constituents' or colleagues' desires for those ends must be taken to have incorporated their ends as her own.

However intimately legislators know their own minds, they often lack the expertise and time to assimilate the complex factual and legal information bearing on the constitutionality of a proposed law. In the ordinary run of cases, these issues must be addressed and resolved through institutional mechanisms. A number of such mechanisms exist and are actually employed.

Federal legislation is typically drafted by lawyers and other specialists—either in an executive agency or department or in a congressional committee—who are familiar with any potential constitutional issues presented by the legislation. The committee to which a bill is referred can call upon its own legal staff or on the American Law Division of the Congressional Research Service of the Library of Congress for assistance with constitutional questions. Individual legislators can also seek advice from the research service and from their own staffs, and constitutional issues may be raised in debates on the floor of the House and Senate. Before signing a bill, the President can consult with the Office of Legal Counsel or seek an opinion from the attorney general. Although most state legislators cannot avail themselves of such rich resources, all have analogous methods for assessing the constitutionality of proposed legislation.

It is sometimes said that legislators have too little time and too much political interest to take constitutional issues seriously. Surely, however, this remark cannot justify legislative inattention to questions of constitutionality—unless one believes that legislators should be held to a lower standard of law-abidingness than individuals or enterprises, who may also lack the time or inclination to follow the law. To the extent that the observation is accurate, it is a source of concern to anyone committed to constitutional democracy.

The principal deterrent against unconstitutional legislative action is the threat of judicial invalidation of a law on the ground of its substantive unconstitutionality. From time to time, courts have also engaged in what might be called "procedural review" of legislative decisions—review that focuses on the process by which the law was enacted.

Procedural review encompasses two different inquiries. One is whether the legislators acted out of unconstitutional motives; the other is whether the legislators adequately considered the factual and legal bases for the law. Chief Justice Marshall alluded to both inquiries in *McCulloch v. Maryland* (1819). With respect to unconstitutional motivation, he wrote: "Should Congress, . . . under the pretext of executing its powers, pass laws for the accomplishment of objectives not entrusted to the government, it would become the painful duty of this tribunal . . . to say that such an act was not the law of the land." And he invoked the Executive's and Congress's attention to the underlying constitutional issues as a basis for judicial deference to their decision:

The bill for incorporating the [first] bank of the United States did not steal upon an unsuspecting legislature, and pass unobserved. Its principle was completely understood and was opposed with equal zeal and ability. After being resisted, first in the fair and open field of debate, and afterwards in the executive cabinet, with as much persevering talent as any measure has ever experienced, and being supported by arguments which convinced minds as pure and as intelligent as this country can boast, it became law. . . . It would require no ordinary share of intrepidity to assert that a measure adopted under these circumstances was a bold and plain usurpation, to which the constitution gives no countenance.

Judicial inquiry into legislative motivation has had a checkered career. The Court in HAMMER V. DAGENHART (1918) and BAILEY V. DREXEL FURNITURE COMPANY (1922) relied on Marshall's "pretext" statement to strike down federal child labor legislation, and the Court in LOCHNER V. NEW YORK (1905) expressed doubt whether the maximum hours law had been adopted for permissible motives.

Inquiries into legislative motivation declined with the judicial modesty of the late 1930s, but it reappeared with the WARREN COURT's resurgence of activism. The Court in ABINGTON SCHOOL DISTRICT

v. SCHEMPP (1963) articulated this standard for assessing establishment of religion claims: "[W]hat are the purpose and primary effect of the enactment? If either is the advancement or inhibition of religion then the enactment exceeds the scope of legislative power as circumscribed by the Constitution." EPPERSON V. ARKANSAS (1968) applied the "purpose" aspect of this test to strike down a law forbidding the teaching of evolutionary theory. GOMILLION V. LIGHTFOOT (1960) struck down the Alabama legislature's redrawing of the boundaries of Tuskegee on the ground that it was designed to exclude black citizens from the city limits. And GRIFFIN V. PRINCE EDWARD COUNTY SCHOOL BOARD (1964) held that the county could not constitutionally close its public schools with the motive of avoiding integration.

In contrast to these decisions, *United States v. O'Brien* (1968) refused to consider the defendant's contention that Congress enacted the draft-card destruction law in order to suppress antiwar protest rather than for any legitimate administrative purposes. And PALMER V. THOMPSON (1971) dismissed the plaintiff's claim that Jackson, Mississippi, had closed its swimming pools in order to avoid integrating them. Writing for the Court in *Palmer,* Justice HUGO L. BLACK emphasized that it was extremely difficult to determine an official's motivation and especially difficult "to determine the 'sole' or 'dominant' motivation behind the choices of a group of legislators." Black also remarked that "there is an element of futility in a judicial attempt to invalidate a law because of the bad motives of its supporters. If a law is struck down for this reason, rather than because of its facial contents or effect, it would presumably be valid as soon as the legislature . . . repassed it for different reasons."

More recently, the Court has repudiated the broadest implications of *O'Brien* and *Palmer*. In ARLINGTON HEIGHTS V. METROPOLITAN HOUSING DEVELOPMENT CORPORATION (1977) Justice LEWIS F. POWELL noted the importance of "[p]roof of racially discriminatory intent or purpose" to claims under the EQUAL PROTECTION clause. The Court held that the complainant was entitled—indeed, required—to prove that the town's refusal to rezone an area to permit multiple-family housing was discriminatorily motivated. The relevent standard was not whether the decision was solely or even dominantly motivated by racial considerations. Rather, proof that racial motivation played any part in the decision shifts to the decision maker "the burden of establishing that the same decision would have resulted even had the impermissible purpose not been considered." In *Mt. Healthy*

City Board of Education v. Doyle (1977) the Court applied a similar standard in reviewing an employee's claim that he had been discharged for exercising First Amendment rights.

The current doctrine is correct. Legislative motives are not always obscure; nor does judicial review usually require inquiring into and aggregating the motives of individual legislators. As Justice Powell noted in *Arlington Heights,* the bizarrely shaped boundaries of Tuskeegee in *Gomillion* revealed "a clear pattern, unexplainable on grounds other than race." Sometimes, as in the school- and pool-closing cases, the historical background and sequence of actions leading up to the contested event may reveal invidious purposes. Placing a substantial burden on the complainant and permitting the respondent to show that the decision was in fact overdetermined by legitimate purposes amply protect against judicial invalidation of legislative policies that were based on legitimate considerations.

Indeed, this objective might be better achieved simply by invalidating a law where unconstitutional motives played any substantial role and permitting the legislature to consider the measure anew. Justice Black's concern to the contrary, such a course is not inevitably futile. Although a legislature may disguise its motivation and reenact the law for illicit reasons, it may also choose to reenact the law for entirely legitimate reasons—or the legislature may have lost whatever interest motivated it to act in the first instance. The Alabama legislature did not attempt to gerrymander Tuskeegee again, nor did Prince Edward County try to close its schools again for a "better" reason.

Judicial inquiry into unconstitutional motivation is sometimes said to be especially intrusive because it requires the judiciary to concern itself directly with the legislative process. In an important sense, however, any form of procedural review is less intrusive than substantive review. The Court leaves to the legislature its assigned task of weighing the costs and benefits of proposed legislation, and requires only that the legislature not count a constitutionally illicit objective as a benefit.

When a law is challenged on the ground that it does not further any valid interests, or does not further them sufficiently, the Supreme Court typically does not ask what ends the legislature actually sought to achieve, but hypothesizes possible objectives and asks whether the law can be upheld in terms of them. For example, in *United States v. O'Brien,* lacking any information about what legitimate objectives Congress actually sought to achieve through the draft card destruction law, the Court upheld the law on the basis of several administrative objectives that the Justices thought the law might serve.

In a widely cited 1972 article Gerald Gunther urged that the Court should be "less willing to supply justifying rationale by exercising its imagination. . . . [It] should assess the means in terms of legislative purposes that have substantial basis in actuality, not mere conjecture." Gunther asserted that a court need not delve into "actual legislative motivation" but can rely on legislative materials such as debates and reports or on a "state court's or attorney general office's description of purpose."

The Court has sometimes taken this approach. For example, in GRISWOLD V. CONNECTICUT (1965) the Court held that the state's anticontraceptive law was not justified as a means of deterring illicit sexual intercourse—the only purpose urged by the state attorney general. The Court did not consider whether the law might be upheld on the more plausible (though constitutionally problematic) ground that the Connecticut legislature believed that contraception was immoral. Whatever the justification for this judicial strategy, it is not likely to identify the legislature's actual purposes: state courts and attorneys general have no privileged access to actual legislative purposes but must rely on the same public materials available to the Supreme Court.

In recent years some Justices, and occasionally a majority of the Court, have limited the objectives that can be considered in support of a challenged regulation to the decision maker's (supposed) actual objectives. This course is easiest for a court to follow when statutory limitations on an agency's mandate foreclose it from pursuing a broad range of objectives. For example, HAMPTON V. MOW SUN WONG (1976) invalidated a United States Civil Service regulation barring resident ALIENS from federal civil service jobs. Writing for the Court, Justice JOHN PAUL STEVENS assumed that Congress or the President might constitutionally have adopted such a requirement for reasons of foreign policy, but held that the commission's jurisdiction was limited to adopting regulations to "promote the efficiency of the federal service." Similarly, in REGENTS OF THE UNIVERSITY OF CALIFORNIA V. BAKKE (1978), Justice Powell refused to consider whether the university's preferential admissions policy was justified as a remedy for past discrimination, holding that the regents were empowered only to pursue educational objectives.

The Supreme Court has sometimes relied on legislative history to refuse to uphold legislation on the basis of objectives that were not intended. For example, in *Weinberger v. Wiesenfeld* (1975), in assessing the constitutionality of the "mother's insurance benefit" provision of the SOCIAL SECURITY ACT, Justice WILLIAM J. BRENNAN wrote for the Court that "the mere recitation of a benign, compensatory purpose is not an automatic shield which protects against an inquiry into the actual purposes underlying a statutory scheme." Although the provision might have been designed to compensate for past economic discrimination against women, the legislative history belied this purpose and the Court refused to uphold the law on a false basis.

Legislative history is often sparse or nonexistent, however. A complex legislative scheme may make a myriad of classifications; the chances are slight that legislative materials will illuminate the classification challenged in any particular case; and the absence of legislative history does not mean that the legislators did not intend to pursue a particular objective. Partly because of these complexities, judicial efforts to limit the purposes on the basis of which laws can be justified have not followed a consistent pattern. The current state of the law is captured in *Kassell v. Consolidated Freightways Corporation* (1981), which struck down a state's highway regulation prohibiting double trailers as an undue burden on INTERSTATE COMMERCE. In a concurring opinion, Justice Brennan wrote that he would give no deference to the state's arguments based on safety because the law was not actually designed to promote safety but to protect local industries. Justice WILLIAM H. REHNQUIST, dissenting, asserted that there was "no authority for the proposition that possible legislative purposes suggested by a state's lawyers should not be considered in COMMERCE CLAUSE cases." The plurality avoided the issue by rejecting the state's safety claims on the merits.

In *McCulloch* Marshall implied that the BANK OF THE UNITED STATES ACT was entitled to special deference because of the attention paid to the constitutional issues within the executive and legislative branches. Because of the difficulty of such an inquiry, however, and perhaps because of its perceived impropriety, the court has seldom conditioned deference on the extent to which the legislature actually considered the factual and legal issues bearing on the constitutional questions at stake. In *Textile Workers Union v. Lincoln Mills* (1957) the Court gave a strained interpretation to a federal statute in order to avoid a difficult constitutional question of federal jurisdiction, to which Congress had apparently paid no attention. In a separate opinion, Justice FELIX FRANKFURTER noted that "this Court cannot do what a President sometimes does in returning a bill to Congress. We cannot return this provision to Congress and respectfully request that body to assume the responsibility placed upon it by the Constitution."

In an article on the *Lincoln Mills* case, ALEXANDER M. BICKEL and Harry Wellington responded that the Court could properly perform such a "remanding function" and that it had sometimes done so, albeit surreptitiously. KENT V. DULLES (1958) is often cited as an example. Rather than decide whether the secretary of state could constitutionally refuse to issue passports to members of the Communist party, the Court held that Congress had not delegated the secretary this authority, thus in effect returning the matter to Congress. More recently, Justice Stevens, dissenting in FULLILOVE V. KLUTZNICK (1980), explicitly urged such a "remand." *Fullilove* upheld a congressional provision requiring that ten percent of the federal funds allocated to public work projects be used to procure services from minority contractors. Justice Stevens's dissent started from the premise that the Constitution disfavors all racial classifications. Noting that the challenged provision was scarcely discussed in committee or on the floor of the Congress, he wrote:

Although it is traditional for judges to accord the same presumption of regularity to the legislative process no matter how obvious it may be that a busy Congress has acted precipitately, I see no reason why the character of their procedures may not be considered relevant to the decision whether the legislative product has [violated the Constitution]. A holding that the classification was not adequately preceded by a consideration of less drastic alternatives or adequately explained by a statement of legislative purpose would be far less intrusive than a final decision [of unconstitutionality]. . . . [T]here can be no separation-of-powers objection to a more tentative holding of unconstitutionality based on a failure to follow procedures that guarantee the kind of deliberation that a fundamental constitutional decision of this kind obviously merits.

"Procedural" judicial review, which takes account of the legislature's consideration of relevant constitutional issues, has two objectives. First, it may foster legislative attention to the Constitution in the first instance. Second, it prevents constitutional concerns from falling between two stools—which happens when a court blindly defers to a judgment that the legislature did not in fact make.

Procedural review seems appropriate where a legislature evidently has ignored issues of law or fact that bear on the constitutionality of an enactment. It is questionable whether a general practice of procedural review would prove workable, however. Among other things, a court will have difficulty in assessing the adequacy of constitutional deliberation from external indicia. Justice Powell, concurring in *Fullilove,*

thus responded to the argument that the legislation was not adequately supported by factual findings or debate:

The creation of national rules for the governance of our society simply does not entail the same concept of record-making that is appropriate to a judicial or administrative proceeding. Congress has no responsibility to confine its vision to the facts and evidence adduced by particular parties. One appropriate source [of facts] is the information and expertise that Congress acquires in the consideration and enactment of earlier legislation. After Congress has legislated repeatedly in an area of national concern, its Members gain experience that may reduce the need for fresh hearings or prolonged debate when Congress again considers action in that area.

In addition to the specific powers and limitations found in the Constitution, the Court has interpreted the DUE PROCESS and equal protection clauses to impose general requirements of "rationality" on the outcome of the legislative process. As stated in *F. S. Royster Guano Company v. Virginia* (1920), the equal protection STANDARD OF REVIEW requires that "the classification must be reasonable, not arbitrary, and must rest upon some ground of difference having a fair and substantial relation to the object of the legislation. . . ." The modern Court has usually articulated an even less demanding RATIONAL BASIS requirement: the law, and any classifications it makes, must plausibly promote some permissible ends to some extent.

The rationality standards may provide a minimal judicial safeguard against laws whose only purpose is constitutionally illicit, without requiring a direct inquiry into legislative motivation. But they may also impose a broader requirement on the legislative process. They may imply what Frank Michelman has described as a "public interest" rather than a "public choice" model of the legislative process.

The public interest model is premised on the possibility of shared public values or ends. "[T]he legislature is regarded as the forum for identifying or defining, and acting towards those ends. The process is one of mutual search through joint deliberation, relying on the use of reason supposed to have persuasive force" (Michelman, 1977, p. 149). The public choice model regards "all substantive values and ends . . . as strictly private. . . . There is no public or general social interest, there are only concatenations of particular interests or private preferences. There is no reason, only strategy. . . . There are no good legislators, only shrewd ones; no statesmen; only messengers" (ibid., p. 148).

The constitutional implications of the two models

can be illustrated by the city ordinance challenged in RAILWAY EXPRESS AGENCY V. NEW YORK (1949). The ordinance prohibited advertisements on the side of vehicles but exempted business delivery vehicles advertising their own business. The most obvious beneficiaries of the exemption were the city's newspapers.

If the Court had adopted a "public choice" model, it would have been pointless to subject the New York ordinance to a rationality requirement: the exemption would be permissible even if its only rationale were to "buy off" the newspapers to get the ordinance enacted or, indeed, to favor the newspapers over other advertisers. Under a "public interest" model, however, the Court would at least ask whether the exemption was related to some extrinsic purpose—and this it did. Justice WILLIAM O. DOUGLAS wrote for the Court that the "local authorities may well have concluded that those who advertise their own wares on their trucks do not present the same traffic problem in view of the nature or extent of the advertising which they use." In a concurring opinion, Justice ROBERT H. JACKSON pointed to "a real difference between doing in self-interest and doing for hire."

Thus, the Court seems nominally to adhere to a public interest model. But the weakness of the rationality standards, and the Court's generosity in imagining possible rationales for classifications (exemplified by *Railway Express Agency* itself), suggest some judicial ambivalence about the extent to which this model should be treated as a constitutional norm. There is some academic controversy about both the norm itself and its judicial enforceability.

JAMES BRADLEY THAYER asserted in his 1901 biography of John Marshall that judicial review implies a distrust of legislatures and that the legislatures "are growing accustomed to this distrust, and more and more readily incline to justify it, and to shed the consideration of constitutional restraints, . . . turning that subject over to the courts; and what is worse, they insensibly fall into a habit of assuming that whatever they can constitutionally do they may do. . . . The tendency of a common and easy resort to this great function is to dwarf the political capacity of the people, and to deaden its sense of moral responsibility." Assessing Thayer's argument is practically impossible, but it seems at least as plausible that the practice of judicial review is a necessary reminder to legislators that their actions are constrained by fundamental public law and not only by their constituents' interests or even their own moral principles.

Thayer's argument nonetheless underscores the point that the Constitution speaks directly to legislatures. In a properly functioning constitutional system, judicial review should be just that—the review of the legislature's considered judgment that the challenged act is constitutionally permissible. Whether this position is "realistic" is another matter. Surely, however, one cannot expect legislators to take their constitutional responsibilities seriously if they and the citizenry at large assume that they have none.

PAUL BREST

Bibliography

BENNETT, ROBERT 1979 "Mere" Rationality in Constitutional Law: Judicial Review and Democratic Theory. *California Law Review* 67:1049–1103.

BICKEL, ALEXANDER and WELLINGTON, HARRY 1957 Legislative Purpose and the Judicial Function: The Lincoln Mills Case. *Harvard Law Review* 71:1–39.

BREST, PAUL 1971 An Approach to the Problem of Unconstitutional Legislative Motive. *Supreme Court Review* 1971:95–146.

ELY, JOHN H. 1970 Legislative and Administrative Motivation in Constitutional Law. *Yale Law Journal* 79:1205–1341.

GUNTHER, GERALD 1982 In Search of Evolving Doctrine on a Changing Court: A Model for a Newer Equal Protection. *Harvard Law Review* 86:1–48.

LINDE, HANS 1976 Due Process of Lawmaking. *Nebraska Law Review* 55:197–255.

MICHELMAN, FRANK 1977 Political Markets and Community Self-Determination: Competing Judicial Models of Local Government Legitimacy. *Indiana Law Journal* 53:145–206.

MORGAN, DONALD G. 1966 *Congress and the Constitution: A Study in Responsibility.* Cambridge, Mass.: Belknap Press.

THAYER, JAMES BRADLEY 1901 *John Marshall.* Boston: Houghton Mifflin.

WECHSLER, HERBERT 1965 The Courts and the Constitution. *Columbia Law Review* 65:1001–1014.

LEGISLATIVE CONTEMPT POWER

Anglo-American legislative bodies have exercised the power to punish nonmembers for contempt of their dignity and proceedings since the time when the High Court of Parliament exercised undifferentiated legislative and judicial power. There is no explicit constitutional warrant for the exercise of the power by Congress, but Congress has exercised it, nonetheless, at least since 1795. There were several instances in the nineteenth century of summary judgments being rendered against nonmembers for such acts of contempt as publishing abusive language about Congress or attempting to bribe its members. In *Anderson v. Dunn* (1821) the Supreme Court held that the power to punish contempts—at least of the latter sort—was inherent in "a deliberate assembly, clothed with the majesty of the people." In KILBOURNE V. THOMPSON (1881), however, the Supreme Court held that Congress did not possess COMMON LAW power to punish as contempt Kilbourne's failure to produce documents subpoenaed by an investigatory committee for a nonlegislative purpose.

Congress defined the statutory offense of contempt of Congress in 1857; this offense was triable before the house against which the contempt was committed, and a contemnor, once convicted, might be confined in the Capitol for the duration of the congressional session. Contempt of Congress remains a statutory offense, but it is no longer prosecuted at the bar of the house. Because bribery of members of Congress is now punishable as a separate offense, the most common contemporary form of contempt of Congress is refusal to testify at or to provide evidence for LEGISLATIVE INVESTIGATIONS. The presiding officer of the offended house (ordinarily only if directed by a vote of the full house) certifies the circumstances of the contempt to the United States attorney in the district where the contempt was committed; the federal attorney may then prosecute the contemnor in federal court.

DENNIS J. MAHONEY

Bibliography
GOLDFARB, RONALD L. 1963 *The Contempt Power.* New York: Columbia University Press.

LEGISLATIVE COURT

The term "legislative court" was coined by Chief Justice JOHN MARSHALL to describe the status of courts created by Congress to serve United States TERRITORIES lying outside the boundaries of any state. Congress had not given the judges of the territorial courts the life tenure and salary guarantees that Article III of the Constitution required for judges of CONSTITUTIONAL COURTS, and Marshall needed to explain the anomaly of federal courts outside the contemplation of Article III. In AMERICAN INSURANCE CO. V. CANTER (1828) he concluded that Congress, in exercising its power to govern the territories, could establish courts that did not fit Article III's specifications. Today this concept of legislative courts embraces all courts created by Congress and staffed by judges who do

not enjoy constitutional protection of their tenure and salaries. Examples include territorial courts, consular courts, the Tax Court of the United States, the Bankruptcy Court, the Court of Military Appeals, and the courts of local jurisdiction operating in the DISTRICT OF COLUMBIA and the Commonwealth of PUERTO RICO.

Just as a legislative court's judges fall outside Article III's guarantees of independence, so it is capable of handling business outside that Article's definition of "the JUDICIAL POWER OF THE UNITED STATES"—something a constitutional court cannot constitutionally do. A legislative court, for example, can be assigned JURISDICTION to give ADVISORY OPINIONS to the President or Congress. Yet, despite Marshall's OBITER DICTUM in the *Canter* opinion that a legislative court is "incapable of receiving" jurisdiction lying within the judicial power, it is clear today that such courts, like administrative agencies, can constitutionally be assigned the initial decision of a great many cases within Article III's definition of that power. (See NORTHERN PIPELINE CONSTRUCTION CO. V. MARATHON PIPE LINE CO., 1982.) Their decisions on such Article III matters are reviewable by constitutional courts, including the Supreme Court, when Congress so provides.

With some difficulty, the Supreme Court has resolved controversies over the status of several courts. The federal courts formerly serving the District of Columbia were held protected by Article III's guarantees of life tenure and salary protection. In this sense, they were constitutional courts. However, the Court also held that the same courts could constitutionally be given work falling outside Article III's specification of CASES AND CONTROVERSIES within the judicial power. In 1970, Congress replaced these "hybrid" courts with a dual court system: the constitutional courts operate under Article III's strictures and the legislative courts handle the local judicial business of the District. In *Palmore v. United States* (1973) the Supreme Court upheld the local courts' power to try local crimes (established by congressional statute), despite their judges' lack of life tenure and salary guarantees.

Similarly, in *Glidden Co. v. Zdanok* (1962), the Court staggered to the ruling—based on two inconsistent opinions, pieced together to make a majority for the result—that the old Court of Claims (see CLAIMS COURT; UNITED STATES COURT OF APPEALS FOR THE FEDERAL CIRCUIT) and the COURT OF CUSTOMS AND PATENT APPEALS were constitutional courts, not legislative courts.

In essence a legislative court is merely an administrative agency with an elegant name. While Congress surely has the power to transfer portions of the business of the federal judiciary to legislative courts, a wholesale transfer of that business would work a fundamental change in the status of our independent judiciary and would seem vulnerable to constitutional attack.

KENNETH L. KARST

Bibliography

NOTE 1962 Legislative and Constitutional Courts: What Lurks Ahead for Bifurcation. *Yale Law Journal* 71:979–1012.

LEGISLATIVE FACTS

The growth of American constitutional doctrine has been influenced, from the beginning, by the traditions of the Anglo-American COMMON LAW. Judges make constitutional law, as they make other kinds of law, partly on the basis of factual premises. Sometimes these premises are merely assumed, but sometimes they are developed with the aid of counsel. However they may be determined, the facts on which a court's lawmaking is premised are called "legislative facts." In modern usage they are sometimes contrasted with "adjudicative facts," the facts of the particular case before the court.

Not all constitutional questions concern the validity of legislation. In the 1970s and 1980s, for example, the Supreme Court went through a period of reappraisal of the EXCLUSIONARY RULE, which excludes from a criminal case some types of EVIDENCE obtained in violation of the Constitution. One factual issue repeatedly raised during this reconsideration was whether the rule actually served to deter police misconduct. In considering that question, the Court was not second-guessing the judgment of a legislature. Yet the question was properly regarded as one of legislative fact; its resolution would provide one of the premises for the Court's constitutional lawmaking.

More frequently, however, the courts consider issues of legislative fact in reviewing the constitutionality of legislation. In many cases, particularly when the laws under review are acts of Congress, the legislature itself has already given consideration to the same fact questions. Congress sometimes writes its own factual findings into the text of a law, explicitly declaring the actual basis for the legislation. In such cases the courts typically defer to the congressional versions of reality. Similar legislative findings are only infre-

quently written into the enactments of state and local legislative bodies, but even there the practice has recently increased. It seems unlikely, however, that judges, especially federal judges, will pay the same degree of deference to those legislative findings.

The courts' treatment of issues of legislative fact is thus seen as a function of the STANDARD OF REVIEW used to test a law's validity. When a court uses the most permissive form of the RATIONAL BASIS standard, it asks only whether the legislature could rationally conclude that the law under review was an appropriate means for achieving a legitimate legislative objective. The BRANDEIS BRIEF was invented for use in just such cases, presenting evidence to show that a legislature's factual premises were not irrational. When the standard of review is heightened—for example, when the courts invoke the rhetoric of STRICT SCRUTINY—arguments addressed to questions of legislative fact can be expected to come from both the challengers and the defenders of legislation. A court's fact-finding task in such a case is apt to be more complicated; the complication is implicit in any standard of review more demanding than the "rational basis" standard, any real interest-balancing by the courts. Arguments about the proper judicial approach to the factual premises for legislation are, in fact, arguments about the proper role of the judiciary in the governmental system. (See JUDICIAL REVIEW; JUDICIAL ACTIVISM AND JUDICIAL RESTRAINT.)

The technique of the Brandeis brief was invented for the occasion of the Supreme Court's consideration of MULLER V. OREGON (1908), upholding a law regulating women's working hours, and has been in fairly frequent use ever since. Increasingly, however, counsel have sought to present evidence on issues of legislative fact to trial courts. An early example was SOUTHERN PACIFIC CO. V. ARIZONA (1945), in which the Supreme Court struck down a law limiting the length of railroad trains. For five and a half months the trial judge heard evidence filling some 3,000 pages in the record; he made findings of legislative fact covering 148 printed pages. Justice HUGO L. BLACK, dissenting, complained that this procedure made the judiciary into a "super-legislature," but courts cannot escape from this kind of factual inquiry unless they adopt Justice Black's permissive views and abandon most constitutional limits on STATE REGULATION OF COMMERCE.

Nor are such trials of legislative fact limited to issues lying within the competence of people like safety engineers. When the California school finance case, SERRANO V. PRIEST (1972), was remanded for trial, the court took six months of expert testimony centered on a single question: Does differential spending on education produce differences in educational quality? (The court's unsurprising answer: Yes.)

As the *Serrano* and *Southern Pacific* cases show, proving legislative facts at trial is considerably more costly than filing a Brandeis brief. It permits cross-examination, however, and sharpens the focus for evidentiary offerings. Even when appellate review seems certain, the trial court's sorting and evaluation of a complex record can aid the appellate court greatly. Expert testimony, the staple of such a trial, typically rests on the sort of opinion and hearsay about which nonexperts ordinarily would not be permitted to testify. Legislative facts, of course, are tried to the judge and not to a jury; furthermore, questions of legislative fact, by definition, touch a great many "cases" not in court that will be "decided" by the precedent made in the court's constitutional ruling. Just as a constitutional case is an especially appropriate occasion for hearing the views of an AMICUS CURIAE, the widest latitude should be allowed to the parties (and to an amicus) to present evidence broadly relevant to the lawmaking issues before the court.

Ultimately there is no assurance that counsel's efforts to educate a court about the factual setting for constitutional lawmaking will improve the lawmaking itself. Yet our courts, with the Supreme Court's encouragement, continue to invite counsel to make these efforts. One of America's traditional faiths, which judges share with the rest of us, is a belief in the value of education.

KENNETH L. KARST

Bibliography

FREUND, PAUL A. 1951 *On Understanding the Supreme Court.* Boston: Little, Brown.
KARST, KENNETH L. 1960 Legislative Facts in Constitutional Litigation. *Supreme Court Review* 1960:75–112.

LEGISLATIVE IMMUNITY

The SPEECH OR DEBATE CLAUSE immunizes federal legislators from civil or criminal actions based on legislative acts. In TENNEY V. BRANDHOVE (1951) the Supreme Court, relying on the COMMON LAW immunity of legislators and the speech or debate clause, held legislators to be immune from federal civil suits based on legislative acts. This legislative immunity, however, does not preclude evidence of legislative acts in criminal prosecutions for corruption.

In what may be an expansion of common law legislative immunity, LAKE COUNTRY ESTATES, INC. V.

TAHOE REGIONAL PLANNING AGENCY (1979) held that the appointed members of a bistate agency enjoyed legislative immunity from suits for constitutional violations. The Court also suggested that state legislative immunity does not depend on the existence of the speech or debate clause. *Lake Country Estates'* extension of absolute legislative immunity to un-elected officials may enable many public bodies or officials that promulgate rules of general application to rely on legislative immunity. For example, in *Supreme Court of Virginia v. Consumers Union of the United States* (1980) the Court concluded that state supreme court justices enjoyed legislative immunity from damages actions based on their promulgation of unconstitutional rules of conduct for the state bar.

THEODORE EISENBERG

Bibliography

EISENBERG, THEODORE 1982 Section 1983: Doctrinal Foundations and an Empirical Study. *Cornell Law Review* 67:492–505.

LEGISLATIVE INTENT

Legislative intent is a construct that courts use to discern the meaning of legislative action, usually in the form of LEGISLATION. The concept is employed in many fields of law—including constitutional law—in the interpretation and application of statutes. In constitutional law, courts also use the concept in determining the purposes or goals of a legislature when they are relevant to deciding the constitutionality of the legislation.

In searching for legislative intent, courts appear to assume that legislation is aimed, in an instrumentally rational fashion, at achieving certain objectives or goals. Sometimes these objectives or goals are stated in rather discrete terms. In HINES V. DAVIDOWITZ (1941), for example, the Supreme Court decided that in passing a law requiring ALIENS to register with federal authorities, Congress had the objective of barring enforcement of state laws that required aliens to register with state officials. At other times, legislative intent is cast in more general terms. Thus in RAILWAY EXPRESS AGENCY V. NEW YORK (1949), the Supreme Court decided that the legislative goal in banning advertisements from some motor vehicles was the promotion of traffic safety.

There has been controversy about reference to legislative intent as a method of giving meaning to legislation, much as there has been controversy about reference to the Framers' intent as a means of giving meaning to the provisions of the Constitution itself. Two lines of criticism have developed, one rooted in doubt about the intelligibility of the concept of legislative intent, the other grounded in skepticism about the legitimacy of the political theory that an appeal to legislative intent presupposes.

Those who question the intelligibility of attempting to ascertain the intent of a legislature argue that it is impossible to ascribe an intent to a multi-member body. First, they point out the difficulty of ascertaining the individual intents of all the legislators and, second, they argue that even if the individual intents could be ascertained, there is no theoretically sound way to combine them to produce a coherent intent of the group.

Those who question the legitimacy of an appeal to legislative intent argue that as a matter of political theory, courts should not be bound by beliefs or wishes of legislators that were not written into the text of the statute but rather only the printed words of the legislation. OLIVER WENDELL HOLMES, for example, urged that courts should ask not what the legislature intended but rather only what the statute means. Instead of looking for evidence of legislative intent, courts should, according to Holmes, consult dictionaries and evidence of contemporary usage to construct the most acceptable interpretation of the statute's meaning.

More recent scholarly criticism has also questioned the validity of the assumption about legislative behavior that legislative intent presupposes. According to these critics, legislatures are merely market arenas in which private interests trade with each other through their legislators to further their own particular advantages. A search for a legislative intent beyond the immediate effects that the statute accomplishes is, according to his view, nonsensical and perhaps politically illegitimate as well.

Legislative intent has remained an important concept in constitutional law in spite of these criticisms. First, courts have developed various methods of dealing with the practical difficulties of constructing a legislative intent. Thus the difficulties associated with discovering the intent of each legislator and of aggregating these individual intents into a group intent have been addressed through the use of presumptions and, in some cases, outright fictions. Often, particularly in the case of state legislation, there is no evidence of legislative intent beyond the words of the statute, but the courts nevertheless generally say they are seeking legislative intention when they are deciding what the legislation means.

The courts indulge in similar assumptions when ad-ditional evidence does exist. For example, courts generally credit statements in committee reports as evidence of legislative purpose, even though there may be little reason to believe that many legislators read the report or agreed with it. Similarly, the speeches of proponents during floor debates (or even in public discourse outside the legislative arena) are also treated as evidence of legislative intent, even though few legislators may have been present during the floor debate (or heard the nonlegislative remarks). Some have argued that the legislative draftsmen or proponents are the "agents" of the legislature and therefore that their intent is the relevant legislative intent. Others urge that silent legislators who vote for the enactment share the intent of those who do speak in favor of the legislation. Another view is that legislatures in effect delegate to identifiable subgroups, such as committees, the task of setting legislative goals in the areas of the subgroups' specialties. Thus the intent of the legislature with respect to a transportation law would be assumed to be the same as the intent of the legislative committee on transportation. Whatever the rationale, courts have created a concept of legislative intent that does not purport to be a true measurement of the intents of the individual legislators. In effect, courts have personified legislatures and sought to ascribe to them an intent as if the legislature were a single person, one who sometimes speaks with several, often conflicting voices about what he wants to accomplish.

The more fundamental questions of political theory which challenge the legitimacy of looking to legislative intent have not been systematically addressed, at least by the courts. Courts have, by and large, assumed that if legislative intent can be constructed, it is relevant and even controlling in the interpretation of legislative action, at least where the terms of the statute are perceived to provide leeway for interpretation.

Legislative intent may have remained important for several reasons. First, the concept is used widely outside of constitutional law for statutory interpretation. Legislatures have learned what courts will consider in searching for legislative intent, and they have adjusted their processes in some measure to provide the appropriate signals to the courts—thus encouraging continued judicial reliance on legislative intent.

Second, adherence to legislative intent may be grounded in judicial support of what the judges believe to be a political ideal. Although courts may recognize that trading among private interests does occur, they may believe that our society nevertheless aspires to a model of legislation that is an instrumentally rational pursuit of objectives that further the public interest.

Finally, courts have evolved several STANDARDS OF REVIEW in constitutional law that make the legislature's goals or objectives relevant to the constitutionality of the legislation. These standards, such as the RATIONAL BASIS test, LEAST RESTRICTIVE MEANS analysis, and the tests for federal PREEMPTION of state regulatory authority, have no doubt helped insure that the search for legislative intent remains a significant part of constitutional adjudication.

Legislative intent is thus important in several areas of constitutional adjudication. Three examples are illustrative. First, courts look to legislative intent to determine whether a legislature gave an administrative official power to take the challenged action. In KENT v. DULLES (1958), for example, the secretary of state denied a passport because the applicant failed to state whether or not he was or had been a communist. The Supreme Court held that Congress had not intended to give the secretary of state the power to deny passports on those grounds. Similarly, courts have ruled on numerous occasions—Hines is an example—that a state statute cannot be enforced because Congress, by enacting legislation on the same subject matter, "intended" to preempt the field from state regulation.

Second, courts often look to legislative intent because the constitutionality of the challenged legislative action depends on the legislature's purpose. Thus legislation mandating that only single-family residences may be built in a certain zone is constitutional if the purposes of the law are to reduce traffic, limit demand on municipal resources, and provide a suburban atmosphere. It will be unconstitutional, however, if the legislative purpose is to exclude minorities from the municipality, as the Supreme Court suggested in ARLINGTON HEIGHTS V. METROPOLITAN HOUSING DEVELOPMENT CORPORATION (1977).

Third, legislative intent is relevant in those areas of constitutional decision making in which courts purportedly scrutinize the "fit" between legislative means and ends. In EQUAL PROTECTION law, for example, legislative classification that disadvantages one person vis-à-vis another is said to be constitutional only if the classification is rationally related to a legitimate legislative goal. While courts tend to hypothesize rather freely about what the legislature could have intended to achieve with the classification, evidence of legislative intent is clearly relevant. More important, when circumstances call for more rigorous scrutiny—as when the classification is based on sex or race—the courts are less willing to speculate about

the legislature's possible purposes, and they search for concrete evidence of legislative intent.

The meaning of legislation—what the legislature sought to accomplish—is often important in constitutional law. Even though theoretical and practical problems are attendant on the concept of legislative intent, courts use the concept in ascribing meaning to legislation in the numerous doctrinal areas in which the courts themselves have made that meaning relevant.

SCOTT H. BICE

Bibliography

DICKERSON, REED 1975 Statutory Interpretation: A Peek into the Mind and Will of a Legislature. *Indiana Law Journal* 50:206–237.
MACCALLUM, GERALD C., JR. 1966 Legislative Intent. *Yale Law Journal* 75:754–787.
RADIN, MAX 1930 Statutory Interpretation. *Harvard Law Review* 43:863–885.

LEGISLATIVE INVESTIGATION

Although congressional power to conduct investigations and punish recalcitrant witnesses is nowhere mentioned in the United States Constitution, the inherent investigative power of legislatures was well established, both in the British Parliament and in the American colonial legislatures, more than a century before the Constitution was adopted. Mention of such power in the early state constitutions was generally regarded as unnecessary, but the Massachusetts and Maryland constitutions both gave explicit authorization; the latter, adopted in 1776, empowered the House of Delegates to ". . . inquire on the oath of witnesses, into all complaints, grievances, and offenses, as the grand inquest of this state," and to ". . . call for all public or official papers and records, and send for persons, whom they may judge necessary in the course of inquiries concerning affairs relating to the public interest."

The basic theory of the power was and is that a legislative house needs it in order to obtain information, so that its law-making and other functions may be discharged on an enlightened rather than a benighted basis. Under the Constitution, the power was first exercised by the House of Representatives in 1792, when it appointed a select committee to inquire into the defeat by the Indians suffered the previous year by federal forces commanded by General Arthur St. Clair. The House empowered the committee "to call for such persons, papers and records as may be necessary to assist in their inquiries." After examining the British precedents, President GEORGE WASHINGTON and his cabinet agreed that the House "was an inquest and therefore might institute inquiries" and "call for papers generally," and that although the executive ought to refuse to release documents "the disclosure of which would endanger the public," in the matter at hand "there was not a paper which might not be properly produced," and therefore the committee's requests should be granted.

For nearly a century thereafter, investigations were conducted frequently and without encountering serious challenge, in Congress and the state legislatures alike. They covered a wide range of subjects, and their history is in large part the history of American politics. Among the most interesting state investigations were those conducted in 1855 by the Massachusetts legislature and the New York City Council, under the leadership of the "Know-Nothing" party, in which Irish Roman Catholicism was the target. Inquiries by the New York City Council into alleged Irish domination of the police force were challenged in the New York Court of Common Pleas, and Judge Charles Patrick Daly's opinion in *Briggs v. McKellar* (1855) was the first to hold that, unlike in Britain, in the United States the legislative investigative power is limited by the Constitution.

Fifteen years later, a congressional investigation was for the first time successfully challenged on constitutional grounds, in KILBOURN V. THOMPSON (1881). The House of Representatives had authorized a select committee to investigate the bankruptcy of the Jay Cooke banking firm (which was a depository of federal funds), and when the witness Kilbourn refused to answer questions, the House cited him for contempt and imprisoned him. After his release on HABEAS CORPUS, Kilbourn sued the House sergeant-at-arms for damages from false imprisonment. In an opinion by Justice SAMUEL F. MILLER, the Supreme Court sustained his claim on the grounds of constitutional SEPARATION OF POWERS, declaring that the Jay Cooke bankruptcy presented no legislative grounds for inquiry and that "the investigation . . . could only be properly and successfully made by a court of justice." The Court has never since invalidated a legislative inquiry on that particular basis, and it is probable that today, under comparable circumstances, a sufficient legislative purpose would be found. But the Court's ruling, that Congress's investigative and contempt powers are subject to JUDICIAL REVIEW and must conform to constitutional limitations, has not since been seriously questioned.

Exclusively until 1857, and commonly until 1935,

Congress enforced its investigative power against recalcitrant witnesses by its own contempt proceedings: a congressional citation for contempt, and its execution through arrest and confinement of the witness by the sergeant-at-arms. (See LEGISLATIVE CONTEMPT POWER.) Judicial review of the contempt was usually obtained by habeas corpus. But the system was cumbersome, and effective only when Congress was in session. To remedy these shortcomings, Congress in 1857 enacted a statute making it a federal offense to refuse to produce documents demanded, or to answer questions put, by a duly authorized congressional investigatory committee. For some years both the contempt and the statutory criminal procedures were used, but since 1935 the contempt procedure has fallen into disuse. Challenges to congressional investigative authority are currently dealt with by INDICTMENT and trial under the criminal statute, now found in section 192, Title 2, United States Code, the constitutionality of which was upheld by the Supreme Court in *In re Chapman* (1897).

The tone of Justice Miller's opinion in the *Kilbourn* case raised doubts about the scope and even the existence of the congressional contempt power, which were repeatedly voiced during the early years of the twentieth century, when Congress conducted investigations damaging to powerful business and financial institutions. In 1912 the House Committee on Banking and Currency launched what became known as the "Money Trust Investigation," in which practically all the leading financiers of the time—J. P. Morgan the elder, George F. Baker, James J. Hill, and others—were called to answer charges of undue concentration of control of railroads and heavy industries in the hands of a few New York bankers. In 1924, Senate committees probed allegations of corruption and maladministration in the Justice, Interior, and Navy departments.

The legality and propriety of these inquiries aroused vigorous public debate. The famous jurist JOHN HENRY WIGMORE wrote of a "debauch of investigations" which raised a "stench" and caused the Senate to fall "in popular esteem to the level of professional searchers of the municipal dunghills," while then Professor FELIX FRANKFURTER accused the critics of seeking to "divert attention and shackle the future," and argued that the investigative power should be left "untrammeled." The doubters and critics were encouraged when a federal district judge, relying on the *Kilbourn* case, quashed a Senate contempt citation against Attorney General Harry M. Daugherty's brother, but the investigative and contempt powers were vindicated when the Supreme

Court reversed that decision and ruled in McGRAIN v. DAUGHERTY (1927) that the investigation was proper as an aid to legislation, and that Mally Daugherty could be required to testify on pain of imprisonment. Consequently, there were no serious or successful legal challenges to the many congressional investigations born of the Great Depression and the "New Deal" period of President FRANKLIN D. ROOSEVELT's administration. (See CONSTITUTIONAL HISTORY, 1933–1945.)

Until this time the main subjects of legislative investigations had been the civil and military operations of the executive branch, industrial and financial problems, and the operation of social forces such as the labor movement. Except for state investigations in the middle years of the nineteenth century directed at Masons and Roman Catholics, ideological matters had not been much involved.

The Russian Revolution of 1917, the spread of communist doctrine, and the Nazi seizure of dictatorial power in Germany soon emerged as major subjects of congressional concern. There were short-lived congressional investigations of communist propaganda in 1919 and 1930, and of Nazi propaganda in 1934. With the establishment of the HOUSE COMMITTEE OF UN-AMERICAN ACTIVITIES in May 1938, SUBVERSIVE ACTIVITIES emerged as the most publicized subject of congressional investigation.

During World War II, in which the United States and the Soviet Union were allies, there was a lull in these inquiries, but the "Iron Curtain" and "Cold War" revived them, and by 1947 they were again front-page news. Soon, names of prosecutors and witnesses—for example, MARTIN DIES, RICHARD M. NIXON, Alger Hiss, Whittaker Chambers, JOSEPH R. McCARTHY, and Patrick McCarran—became household words. The Senate authorized two bodies to join in the hunt for subversion: the Judiciary Committee's Subcommittee on Internal Security headed by Senator McCarran, and the Government Operations Committee's Subcommittee on Investigations under Senator McCarthy, respectively established in 1946 and 1950.

The principal activity of these agencies was summoning individuals to testify about the communist connections of themselves or others, and their proceedings contributed mightily to a period of public recrimination and bitter controversy that lasted for more than a decade. It was also a period of frequent criminal litigation involving congressional investigative power, as numerous witnesses were indicted for refusing to answer such questions. Some witnesses invoked the Fifth Amendment RIGHT AGAINST SELF-INCRIMINATION, and the Supreme Court, in three cases decided in 1955, was unanimously of the opinion that the right is available to witnesses before legislative committees, though three of the Justices thought that the witnesses had not clearly invoked it. Writing for the majority, Chief Justice EARL WARREN confirmed the congressional investigative power and stated further (*Quinn v. United States*):

But the power to investigate, broad as it may be, is also subject to recognized limitations. It cannot be used to inquire into private affairs unrelated to a valid legislative purpose. Nor does it extend to an area in which Congress is forbidden to legislate. Similarly, the power to investigate must not be confused with any of the powers of law enforcement; these powers are assigned under our Constitution to the Executive and Judiciary. Still further limitations on the power to investigate are found in the specific individual guarantees of the BILL OF RIGHTS, such as the Fifth Amendment's privilege against self-incrimination which is in issue here.

Other witnesses, however, invoked the FIRST AMENDMENT's guarantee of FREEDOM OF SPEECH as justification for their refusal to answer, and in 1956 and 1957 two such cases, SWEEZY V. NEW HAMPSHIRE and WATKINS V. UNITED STATES, the first involving a congressional and the second a state investigation, reached the Court. With only Justice TOM C. CLARK dissenting, the Court held that, as a general proposition, First Amendment rights are enjoyed by witnesses in legislative investigations.

But did the First Amendment protect these witnesses from the obligation to answer questions about individual connections with communism? The Court did not meet that issue and based its reversal of both convictions on nonconstitutional grounds. Watkins had not been told that the questions put to him were (as the federal statute requires) "pertinent to the question under inquiry," while in Sweezy's case it was not shown that the state legislature had authorized the investigative agency to ask the questions he declined to answer.

Three years later, however, by a 5–4 vote, the Court held that the First Amendment did not bar requiring a witness to answer questions regarding his own or others' communist connections. (See BARENBLATT V. UNITED STATES; UPHAUS V. WYMAN, 1959.) In his opinion for the Court in the former case, Justice JOHN MARSHALL HARLAN undertook a "balancing . . . of the private and public interests at stake," and concluded that since the Communist party was not "an ordinary political party" and sought overthrow of the government "by force and violence," Congress had "the right to identify a witness as a member of the Communist Party." (See BALANCING TESTS.)

The authority of these two cases was somewhat tarnished in 1963 after Justice ARTHUR J. GOLDBERG had replaced Justice Frankfurter, who had been in the five-member majority. A Florida court authorized a state investigatory committee to require a local branch of the NAACP to produce its membership lists so that the committee could determine whether certain individuals suspected of communist connections were members of the NAACP. Once again the Court divided 5–4, and Justice Goldberg, writing for the majority in GIBSON v. FLORIDA LEGISLATIVE COMMITTEE, ruled that, in the absence of any prior showing of connection between the NAACP and communist activities, such required disclosure was barred by the First Amendment. Three years later, in another New Hampshire investigations case, *DeGregory v. New Hampshire Attorney General,* the Court ruled, 6–3, that the state's interest was "too remote and conjectural" to justify compelling a witness in 1964 to testify about communist activities in 1957.

Since then there have been no Supreme Court and no important state or lower federal court decisions on the constitutional aspects of legislative investigative power. The *Barenblatt* case has not been overruled, and it is perhaps noteworthy that both the *Gibson* and *DeGregory* cases involved state rather than congressional investigations. The attitudes of the Justices who have joined the Court since 1966 remain untested.

It may be surmised, for the future, that if a plausible relation between a legislative inquiry and a valid legislative purpose can be shown, and there are no procedural flaws or manifestations of gross abuse, the Court will be reluctant to deny, on constitutional grounds, the power of a legislative investigating committee to require witnesses to answer questions or produce records.

A different situation might well obtain if a congressional investigating committee should seek to enforce the production of government documents involving NATIONAL SECURITY or for some other reason inappropriate for public disclosure. Presidents have on numerous occasions exercised the right first asserted by George Washington in 1792, to withhold documents "the disclosure of which would endanger the public" or otherwise contravene the public interest. (See EXECUTIVE PRIVILEGE.) Congressional committee efforts to force the production of records of judicial conferences, or other confidential court papers, might likewise encounter constitutional objections based on the separation of powers. Up to the present time, these issues have not confronted the Supreme Court, and the political wisdom of avoiding such confrontations is manifest.

TELFORD TAYLOR

Bibliography

CARR, ROBERT K. 1952 *The House Committee on Un-American Activities.* Ithaca, N.Y.: Cornell University Press.

GOODMAN, WALTER 1968 *The Committee.* New York: Farrar, Straus & Giroux.

LANDIS, JAMES M. 1926 Constitutional Limits on the Congressional Power of Investigation. *Harvard Law Review* 40:153–226.

OGDEN, AUGUST RAYMOND 1945 *The Dies Committee.* Washington, D.C.: Catholic University of America Press.

POTTS, CHARLES S. 1926 Power of Legislative Bodies to Punish for Contempt. *University of Pennsylvania Law Review* 74:691–780.

TAYLOR, TELFORD 1955 *Grand Inquest: The Story of Congressional Investigations.* New York: Simon & Schuster.

LEGISLATIVE JURISDICTION

See: Jurisdiction

LEGISLATIVE POWER

"Legislative power" is a distinctly modern conception which presupposes a modern understanding of "law." In medieval Europe the authority of laws was variously attributed to God, nature, or custom; human authorities "found" or "declared" or enforced the law but were not thought to create it. Consequently, medieval jurists did not distinguish "legislative" from "judicial" powers. Through the end of the sixteenth century, the English Parliament (like its continental counterparts) was primarily regarded as a court, an ultimate court of APPEAL for individuals as well as communities. It was at most an incidental consideration whether Parliament was "representative" because law was not a matter of will but of knowledge.

The modern conception traces the authority of law precisely to the will of the lawmakers. It is this assumption of a pure power to make or unmake the laws that allows for our artificially clear distinction between "legislative" (that is lawmaking) and "judicial" or "executive" (law-applying) powers. In acknowledging law as the creation of particular human wills, the modern view liberates government from encrusted tradition, from folklore and superstition, above all from manipulation by legalistic conjurings. At the same time, however, this view of law opens the chilling prospect of an unlimited coercive power, since the power to create the laws seems, by its very nature, superior to the constraints of law. This sort of reasoning, powerfully advanced by theorists of SOVEREIGNTY in the seventeenth century, was treated by WILLIAM BLACKSTONE in the next century as virtually self-evident: for any court to declare invalid an act of Parliament, he observed, "were to set the judicial power above that of the legislature, which would be subversive of all government."

The Framers of the American Constitution were nonetheless intent on curbing legislative power. Historians have noted that by the standards of their European contemporaries the constitutional perspective of the American Framers was somewhat archaic, most notably in the Framers' acceptance of a HIGHER LAW limitation on legislative power and in their indifference to questions about sovereignty or ultimate authority. But in the decisive respect, the concerns and accomplishments of the Framers reflected their quite modern recognition that no laws are simply given, that the scope of legislative assertion is vast and, as THE FEDERALIST conceded, "the legislative authority necessarily predominates." Thus they set out the legislative powers in the first and longest article of the Constitution, suggesting the primacy of these powers in the governmental scheme and implicitly identifying the reach of the federal government with the reach of its legislative powers. At the same time, the language of Article I emphasizes the open-endedness of legislative power precisely by its focus on the powers rather than the duties, objectives, or obligations of the legislative branch.

Perhaps the most important checks on legislative power in the Constitution are those that seem merely procedural or institutional. In the first place, the Constitution sets up a formidable institutional gauntlet for legislative proposals, requiring that they obtain majorities in each house of Congress and then secure approval from the President (or extraordinary majorities in Congress). The Constitution also seeks to assure some independent authority for the executive branch and the judiciary by removing the selection and tenure of these officers from immediate congressional control. Ultimately, almost all executive and judicial action depends on prior statutory authority and funding from Congress. And it is impossible to say with confidence when a legislative enactment (apart from an actual BILL OF ATTAINDER—imposing criminal sanctions on particular individuals) would be so specific and peremptory as to infringe the essential law-applying authority of the executive or the judiciary. But in practice the institutional reality of the SEPARATION OF POWERS usually does preserve a protective screen of independent judgment between the legislative will and the force of law as applied.

Direct limitations on legislative power in the Constitution are perhaps the most dramatic legacy of the Framers' distrust of legislative power, but they are probably not the most efficacious or important. From the outset, Congress has been emboldened to exercise powers beyond those specifically enumerated in Article I, either by construing implied powers or appealing to the requisites of national SOVEREIGNTY. The Supreme Court sought to give some force to these limitations in the early decades of this century in order to prevent Congress from preempting the legislative authority of the states. But these efforts were repudiated by the Court after the 1930s and the repudiation of judicially enforceable limits has been explicitly reconfirmed in the current era. Even the limitations imposed by the BILL OF RIGHTS on behalf of individual liberty have very rarely been construed by the Supreme Court in ways that threatened federal legislation.

As it has expanded, however, federal legislative power has also been dispersed in striking ways. In recent decades, the federal courts, invoking vague or general constitutional clauses, have assumed the power to impose elaborate requirements on states and localities in a more or less openly legislative (law-creating) manner. Meanwhile, since the 1930s, Congress has delegated more and more legislative power to federal administrative agencies. Though Congress retains the ultimate power to block what courts and agencies do, its passivity may or may not be properly construed as acquiescence. Thus the dispersal of legislative powers seems to threaten the central promise in the modern conception of law—that there is always an identifiable human authority to hold responsible for the law.

JEREMY RABKIN

Bibliography

CORWIN, EDWARD S. 1955 *The "Higher Law" Background of American Constitutional Law.* Ithaca, N.Y.: Cornell University Press.

FISHER, LOUIS 1985 *Constitutional Conflicts between Congress and the President.* Princeton, N.J.: Princeton University Press.

LEGISLATIVE VETO

The legislative veto emerged in the 1930s as an effort to reconcile two conflicting needs. Executive officials sought greater discretionary authority, while Congress wanted to retain control over delegated authority without having to adopt new legislation for that purpose. The resulting accommodation permitted administrators to submit proposals that would become law unless Congress acted to disapprove by simple resolution (a one-house veto) or concurrent resolution (a two-house veto). Evolving forms of the legislative veto came to include requirements of congressional approval as well as opportunities for disapproval; Congress even vested some of the controls in its committees.

Although the legislative veto acquired a reputation as a congressional usurpation of executive power, initially the device favored the President. In 1932 Congress authorized President HERBERT C. HOOVER to reorganize the executive branch. His plans would become law within sixty days unless either house disapproved. The President did not have to secure the support of both houses, as would have been necessary through the regular legislative process. Instead, the burden was placed on Congress to veto his initiatives. Furthermore, to prevent presidential proposals from being buried in committee, filibustered, or changed by Congress, the law limited each opportunity for legislative veto by rules for discharging committees, restricting congressional debate, and prohibiting committee or floor amendments.

The executive branch began to view the legislative veto apprehensively when Congress attached it to statutes governing such important subjects as lend lease, IMMIGRATION, public works, energy, IMPOUNDMENT, federal salaries, foreign trade, and the WAR POWERS. As part of the congressional reassertion after the VIETNAM WAR and WATERGATE, legislative vetoes proliferated in the 1970s. By the late 1970s, Congress seemed on the verge of subjecting every federal regulation to some form of legislative veto.

The lower federal courts upheld some legislative vetoes and invalidated others, but carefully restricted their opinions to the particular statutes challenged. In 1982, however, the UNITED STATES COURT OF APPEALS for the District of Columbia Circuit struck down three laws on such broad grounds as to cast a shadow of illegality over every type of legislative veto. The Supreme Court adopted this comprehensive approach in IMMIGRATION AND NATURALIZATION SERVICE V. CHADHA (1983), invalidating the Immigration

and Nationality Act's authorization for either house of Congress to set aside the attorney general's decision to suspend the DEPORTATION of an alien.

Chief Justice WARREN E. BURGER, joined by five Justices, wrote the OPINION OF THE COURT. The one-house legislative veto in *Chadha* was unconstitutional because it violated both the principle of BICAMERALISM and the presentment clause of the Constitution, which requires every bill, resolution, or vote to which the concurrence of the Senate and House is necessary (except a vote of adjournment) to be presented to the President. Whenever congressional action has the "purpose and effect of altering the legal rights, duties and relations of persons" outside the legislative branch, the Court said, Congress must act through both houses in a bill presented to the President.

Justice LEWIS F. POWELL concurred in the judgment on a narrower ground. Justice BYRON R. WHITE delivered a lengthy dissent, generally supporting the constitutionality of the legislative veto. Justice WILLIAM H. REHNQUIST also dissented, but only on the question of SEVERABILITY. He said that if the Court declared the legislative veto invalid, it should also strike down the attorney general's authority to suspend deportations.

The majority's opinion raises numerous questions. First, in holding the legislative veto severable from the attorney general's authority, the Court ignored clear evidence of a quid pro quo between Congress and the President. If severability could be discerned in this legislative history, presumably it can be found in nearly every statute establishing a legislative veto. This reasoning gives the executive branch a temporary one-sided advantage from an accommodation meant to balance executive and legislative interests.

Second, the Court asserted that the legislative veto's efficiency or convenience would not save it "if it is contrary to the Constitution. Convenience and efficiency are not the primary objectives—or the hallmarks—of democratic government. . . ." Although the legislative veto might be a "convenient shortcut" and an "appealing compromise," the Court said, it is "crystal clear from the records of the Convention, contemporaneous writings and debates, that the Framers ranked other values higher than efficiency." Here the Court played loose with history, for efficiency was indeed an important consideration for the Framers. The decade prior to the CONSTITUTIONAL CONVENTION saw an anxious and persistent search for a form of government that would perform more efficiently than the ARTICLES OF CONFEDERATION.

Third, the Court characterized the presentment

clause as a means of giving the President the power of self-defense against an encroaching Congress. The President's veto would check "oppressive, improvident, or ill-considered measures." This argument is misleading in suggesting that the legislative veto, by evading the President's veto, threatened the independence of the executive branch. In fact, the legislative veto was directed only against measures submitted by the President. Congress could not amend his proposals, but must vote yes or no. A legislative veto, if exercised, simply reestablished the status quo. For example, if either house defeated a reorganization plan the structure of government would remain as before. The President did not need his veto for purposes of "self-defense."

Fourth, the Court said that the Framers had unmistakably expressed their "determination that legislation by the national Congress be a step-by-step, deliberate and deliberative process." But both houses of Congress regularly use "shortcut" methods that pose no problems under *Chadha:* suspending the rules, asking for unanimous consent, placing legislative riders on appropriations bills, and even passing bills that have never been sent to committee.

The Court's theory of government contradicts practices developed over a period of decades by the political branches. Neither administrators nor members of Congress want the static model proffered by the Court. The conditions that spawned the legislative veto over a half-century ago have not disappeared. Executive officials still want substantial latitude in administering delegated authority; legislators still want to maintain control without having to pass new legislation. Surely the executive and legislative branches will develop substitutes to serve as the functional equivalent of the legislative veto. Forms will change; the substance will not.

Instead of a one-house veto over executive reorganization, Congress is likely to require a joint resolution of approval. This device, which satisfies the tests of bicameralism and presentment, requires the President to obtain the support of both Houses within a specified number of days. If one house withholds its support, the effect is a one-house veto.

Internal House and Senate rules offer another option. Congress can require that funds be appropriated only after an authorizing committee has passed a resolution of approval. Although this procedure amounts to a committee veto, the Justice Department may acquiesce, accepting Congress's distinction between authorization and appropriation and reasoning that Congress can control its own internal processes.

Congress can also attach a rider to an appropriations bill to prevent an agency from implementing a proposed action. Because a President will rarely veto an appropriations bill (and probably will never do so because of an objectionable rider), the practical effect of this device is that of a two-house veto. Indeed, House-Senate comity will often produce the effect of a one-house veto.

Statutes can require that selected committees be notified before agency implementation of certain programs. Notification raises no constitutional issue, for it falls within the report-and-wait category already sanctioned by court rulings. But "notification" can become a code word for prior committee approval. Only in unusual circumstances would an agency defy the wishes of its oversight committees.

After *Chadha,* Congress will continue to use informal and nonstatutory methods to control the executive branch. Congress allows agencies to shift funds within an appropriation account provided they obtain committee approval for major changes. Agencies comply because they want to retain this administrative flexibility. Because these "gentlemen's agreements" are not placed in statutes, they are unaffected by *Chadha.* They are not legal in effect. They are, however, in effect legal.

Last, Congress has continued to authorize legislative vetoes in statutes adopted after *Chadha.* Although these provisions are unconstitutional under the Court's decision, agencies are likely to abide by them rather than alienate powerful support committees on Capitol Hill. When the practical needs of executive officials and legislators coincide, they nearly always prevail over formalistic notions of SEPARATION OF POWERS.

LOUIS FISHER

Bibliography

BOLTON, JOHN R. and ABRAMS, KEVIN G. 1984 The Judicial and Congressional Response to the Invalidation of the Legislative Veto. *Journal of Law and Politics* 1:299–355.
STRAUSS, PETER L. 1983 Was There a Baby in the Bathwater? A Comment on the Supreme Court's Legislative Veto Decision. *Duke Law Journal* 1983:789–819.
SYLVESTER, KATHLEEN 1984 After Chadha, A Legal Void. *National Law Journal,* April 23, 1984, pp. 1, 8, 10.

LEHMAN v. SHAKER HEIGHTS

See: Captive Audience

LEISY v. HARDIN
135 U.S. 100 (1890)

Chief Justice MELVILLE W. FULLER, speaking for a six-member majority, ruled that because Congress possesses an EXCLUSIVE POWER under the COMMERCE CLAUSE to regulate interstate transportation, no state may enact a liquor PROHIBITION statute that bars the sale in that state of liquors imported from other states and sold in their original packages. That Congress had not exercised its commerce power was equivalent to a declaration that commerce shall be free. Any DOCTRINE to the contrary, deriving from the LICENSE CASES (1847), said Fuller, was "overthrown." Congress might, however, specifically authorize a state to ban interstate liquors; the Court sustained such an act of Congress in *In re Rahrer* (1891).

LEONARD W. LEVY

LELAND, JOHN
(1754–1841)

A native of Massachusetts and a Baptist minister, John Leland preached in Virginia from 1776 to 1791, becoming a leader in the Baptists' struggle against the Anglican church establishment there and helping to bring about its dismantlement. At first he opposed the federal Constitution on the grounds that it lacked a BILL OF RIGHTS and safeguards against tax-supported clergy; but he later switched his stand —possibly converted by JAMES MADISON personally—and swung Virginia's Baptists behind ratification.

Leland held that state attempts to foster religion only corrupted religion. A defender of both civil and RELIGIOUS LIBERTY, he supported religious rights for all, repudiating the notion of a Christian commonwealth. He opposed attempts to halt Sunday mail delivery, and by denying that government had power to pass sabbath laws, proclaim public days of prayer, or pay chaplains, he assumed a more radical stance on church and state than did most contemporary evangelicals.

THOMAS CURRY

Bibliography

BUTTERFIELD, L. H.   1952   Elder John Leland, Jeffersonian Itinerant. *American Antiquarian Society Proceedings* 62:155–242.

LEMON v. KURTZMAN
403 U.S. 602 (1971) (I)
411 U.S. 192 (1973) (II)

This case involved one of the school aid statutes produced by state legislatures in the wake of BOARD OF EDUCATION V. ALLEN (1968). *Lemon* I stands for three cases joined for decision by the Court. Lemon challenged the constitutionality of a Pennsylvania statute that authorized the Superintendent of Public Instruction to reimburse nonpublic schools for teachers' salaries, textbooks, and instructional materials in secular subjects. *Erley v. DiCenso* and *Robinson v. DiCenso* (1971) challenged a Rhode Island statute that made available direct payments to teachers in nonpublic schools in amounts of up to fifteen percent of their regular salaries.

Both statutes were unconstitutional, Chief Justice WARREN BURGER concluded, and he set forth a three-fold test which continues to be invoked in ESTABLISHMENT OF RELIGION cases: any program aiding a church-related institution must have an adequate secular purpose; it must have a primary effect that neither advances nor inhibits religion; and government must not be excessively entangled with religious institutions in the administration of the program. The Pennsylvania and Rhode Island schemes provided GOVERNMENT AID TO RELIGIOUS INSTITUTIONS. Burger argued that in order to see that these dollars were not used for religious instruction, the states would have to monitor compliance in ways involving excessive entanglement.

Lemon v. Kurtzman returned to the Court (*Lemon* II) two years later on the question of whether the Pennsylvania schools could retain the monies that had been paid out in the period between the implementation of law and the decision of the Supreme Court invalidating it in *Lemon* I. In a PLURALITY OPINION for himself and Justices HARRY BLACKMUN, Lewis F. Powell, and WILLIAM H. REHNQUIST, Chief Justice Burger held that they could. An unconstitutional statute, he suggested, is not absolutely void but is a practical reality upon which people are entitled to rely until authoritatively informed otherwise. Justice BYRON R. WHITE concurred. Justice WILLIAM O. DOUGLAS, joined by Justices WILLIAM J. BRENNAN and POTTER STEWART, dissented. Douglas argued that there was "clear warning to those who proposed such subsidies" that they were treading on unconstitutional ground. "No consideration of EQUITY," Douglas suggested, should allow them "to profit from their unconstitutional venture."

RICHARD E. MORGAN

LEON, UNITED STATES v.

See: Good Faith Exception

LETTERS OF MARQUE AND REPRISAL

Letters of marque and reprisal are commissions that governments of belligerent powers grant to private shipowners (called "privateers") authorizing them to seize the vessels and property of enemy subjects on the high seas. During the Revolutionary War both the states and the Continental Congress issued letters of marque; but the Constitution grants Congress the power to issue them and denies it to the states. Although not a signatory to the Declaration of Paris (1856), which condemned privateering as contrary to the law of nations, the United States has issued no letters of marque since that time.

DENNIS J. MAHONEY

LEVER FOOD AND DRUG CONTROL ACT
40 Stat. 276 (1917)

The administration proposed this legislation to Congress, arguing that "the existence of a STATE OF WAR" made it "essential to the national security and defense" for the federal government to control the supply and pricing of food and fuel. By subjecting those industries AFFECTED WITH A PUBLIC INTEREST to federal regulation, Congress effectively delegated control of significant sectors of the economy to the President. Section 4, the heart of the act, outlawed the destruction, waste, hoarding, or price-fixing of commodities. Further sections, in an exceptionally broad DELEGATION OF POWER, authorized the President to regulate the food industry and to seize and operate "any factory, packing house, oil pipe line, mine, or other plant" engaged in commodity production.

In *United States v. L. Cohen Grocery Company* (1921), a unanimous Supreme Court struck down section 4 for failing to set adequate standards for prices. The criminal provisions unconstitutionally delegated

"legislative power to courts and juries" and deprived "the citizen of the right to be informed of the nature and cause of the accusation against him," violating the Fifth and Sixth Amendments. Although the Court struck down particular provisions for VAGUENESS, it did not reach the issue of the government's authority to regulate prices under the WAR POWERS, and the Lever Act would later serve as a model for other regulatory legislation.

DAVID GORDON

LEVY v. LOUISIANA
391 U.S. 68 (1968)
GLONA v. AMERICAN GUARANTEE & LIABILITY INSURANCE CO.
391 U.S. 73 (1968)

In these decisions the Supreme Court began to subject legislative classifications based on ILLEGITIMACY of parentage to heightened judicial scrutiny. Both cases arose out of Louisiana's statute allowing an action for damages on behalf of the survivors of a decedent against a person who wrongfully caused the decedent's death. *Levy* invalidated, 6–3, a provision denying an illegitimate child the right to recover damages for the death of a parent, and *Glona* invalidated, 6–3, a corresponding provision disallowing a parent's recovery of damages for the death of an illegitimate child.

The two opinions for the Court, by Justice WILLIAM O. DOUGLAS, were very brief. Douglas purported to accept the RATIONAL BASIS STANDARD OF REVIEW. The rights asserted, however, involved "the intimate, familial relationship between a child and his own mother." And illegitimacy bore no relation to the nature of the harm inflicted in either case. The accident of a child's illegitimate birth did not justify denying his rights, and if the state sought to punish the mother of an illegitimate child for her "sin," denying her wrongful death damages was an irrational means for doing so.

It is plain that in these cases the Court was employing a standard of review considerably more demanding than its "rational basis" language suggested. Justice JOHN MARSHALL HARLAN, for the dissenters, took note of this heightened scrutiny, and opposed it. Any definition of the plaintiff class in a wrongful death statute must be artificial; a biological definition would attune the law neither to degrees of love nor to degrees of economic dependence between decedents and survivors. It was not irrational for Louisiana to "simplify" its wrongful death proceedings by using formal marriage as the key to defining the plaintiff class.

Left unspoken by both Douglas and Harlan was the time-dishonored use of the law of illegitimacy in many southern states as a covert form of RACIAL DISCRIMINATION in controlling the transmission of wealth from white fathers to their racially diverse offspring.

KENNETH L. KARST

LIBEL AND THE FIRST AMENDMENT

A central historical question about the FIRST AMENDMENT is to what extent it embodied the received eighteenth-century legal traditions of English law and governmental practice as they were reshaped and renewed in the colonial, revolutionary, and formative periods in America. Or was the amendment a break from these traditions? This issue can be stated either as a question of the intent of the Framers and ratifiers or as a matter of the normative impact of an authoritative text, elaborated in our century within an institutional matrix of JUDICIAL REVIEW radically different from that of the eighteenth century on either side of the Atlantic. However the question be stated, the historical problem is in essence whether the First Amendment is to be regarded as expressing a principle of continuity with the received legal tradition or as constituting a declaration of independence from English law, thereby projecting the American law of freedom of expression on a path of autonomous development.

The general view emphasizes continuity, both as a matter of the original understanding of the Framers of the First Amendment and as a matter of the amendment's later—much later—doctrinal elaborations. Indeed, we conventionally measure continuity or discontinuity by reference to the basic conceptual dichotomy of the English legal tradition, as formulated by WILLIAM BLACKSTONE, the oracle of the COMMON LAW for the framing generation:

where blasphemous, immoral, treasonable, schismatical, seditious, or scandalous libels are punished by the English law . . . the liberty of the press, properly understood, is by no means infringed or violated. The *liberty of the press* is indeed essential to the nature of a free state, but this consists in laying no previous restraints upon publications, and not in freedom from censure for criminal matter when published. Every freeman has an undoubted right to lay what sentiments he pleases before the public: to forbid this is to destroy the freedom of the press: but if he publishes what is improper, mischievous, or illegal, he must take the consequences of his own temerity [*Commentaries on the Laws of England*, 1765, Bk. 4, chap. II, pp. 151–52].

The issue whether the First Amendment embraced or departed from the English legal tradition with respect to subsequent punishment tends to be fixed on the treatment of SEDITIOUS LIBEL. The historical argument for the law of seditious libel has been that government ought to have power to punish its most abusive or subversive critics because criticism of government contains the seeds of a variety of evils—disobedience to government, public disorder, even violence—and that no government can subsist if people have the right to criticize it or to call its agents corrupt or incompetent. This is seen in the work of Leonard W. Levy, ZECHARIAH CHAFEE, and others who have lately examined the First Amendment's historical foundations by looking at seditious libel as the exclusive focus for probing the question of continuity and discontinuity with respect to subsequent punishments. Having narrowed the issue to seditious libel, the scholarly tradition put the question of continuity and discontinuity in all-or-nothing terms: Does the First Amendment as a matter of original understanding, or as a matter of latter doctrinal connotation, repudiate or embrace the concept of seditious libel?

When a question about the relationship of a controversial legal tradition to a broadly phrased constitutional text is put in such terms, the answers are likely to fall out along dialectical lines. So it has been with the rejection-or-reception issue concerning seditious libel. The heated debate on the question by the Federalists and Republicans in connection with the passage of the ALIEN AND SEDITION ACTS of 1798 has been echoed through our history. In modern scholarship, the dialectic begins in 1919 when Zechariah Chafee, troubled deeply by the World War I ESPIONAGE ACT prosecutions, wrote in the *Harvard Law Review* that the Framers of the First Amendment "intended to wipe out the common law of SEDITION, and to make further prosecutions for criticism of the government, without any incitement to law-breaking, forever impossible in the United States of America." Six months later, and plainly in emulation, Justice OLIVER WENDELL HOLMES added the weight of his and LOUIS D. BRANDEIS's authority to the Chafee thesis, when he declared in his great dissent in the *Abrams* case: "I wholly disagree with the argument . . . that the first Amendment left the common law as to seditious libel in force. History seems to me against the notion." But the Chafee position never won the broad adherence that most modern scholars seem to think it had. In the World War I free speech cases before the Supreme court, John Lord O'Brien, who briefed the cases for the Justice Department, stated as the official view of the government that seditious libel prosecutions were not rendered invalid by the First Amendment, either as a matter of original intent or as correctly understood in 1919. And others, including EDWARD S. CORWIN, dissented from the Chafee position. Indeed, Chafee himself seems to have changed his tune by 1949, at least on the issue of the Framers' original intent: "The truth is, I think, that the framers had no very clear idea as to what they meant by 'the freedom of speech or the press.' " The dialectic about seditious libel and the First Amendment entered a new phase with the publication of Leonard W. Levy's seminal work, *Legacy of Suppression,* in 1960. This book argued that with respect to the general conceptions of FREEDOM OF THE PRESS prevalent at the time of the framing and ratification of the First Amendment, there was no solid evidence of a consensus to move away from a purely Blackstonian conception of freedom, that is, a conception limited to protecting only against previous restraints. In particular, Levy found considerable evidence that supported the continuing validity of seditious libel prosecutions, and no clear evidence that any lawyer, pamphleteer, philosopher, or statesman repudiated the concept of seditious libel. There was, Levy recognized, a growing sense of the necessity of the defense of truth, although far from a clear consensus even on that. And there was also a growing insistence on the independent power of the jury in a seditious libel prosecution to determine the issue of truth and the question of the seditious quality of any publication, as well as the other factual issues in the case.

Levy's account of the relationship of the First Amendment as a formal constitutional limitation on the power of Congress and his overall conception of intellectual and legal history respecting freedom of expression has from the beginning been confused by the problem of FEDERALISM. At the same time that he has insisted that the conception of freedom of the press guarded against abridgment by the First Amendment does not invalidate seditious libel, he has described the amendment as denying any power whatever by Congress to legislate with respect to the press, except to protect COPYRIGHT. Thus, he concluded that Congress had no power to pass the Sedition Act of 1798, but on federalism grounds, not because the Sedition Act violated any understandings about press freedom embodied in the First Amendment. The states and the federal courts remained empowered to try seditious libel prosecutions.

But Levy's interpretation of the "Congress shall make no law" language in the First Amendment has taken a distant backseat, in his own writing and in that of others, to his overriding emphasis that "the freedom of speech or of the press" was not understood to repudiate the concept of seditious libel. In other words, the First Amendment was understood to embody a Blackstonian conception of freedom of expression as a matter of original intent.

In NEW YORK TIMES CO. V. SULLIVAN (1964) the Supreme Court gave an authoritative modern answer to the question whether prosecution of seditious libel would survive the First Amendment. An advertisement in March 1960, placed by supporters of MARTIN LUTHER KING, JR., in the *New York Times;* recited the repressive activities of Alabama police with several minor inaccuracies and exaggerations. An Alabama jury awarded a local official $500,000 damages against the *New York Times.* The Supreme Court reacted with sweeping changes in the constitutional status of defamation law. Libel would no longer be viewed as a category of expression beneath First Amendment protection. Instead, the Court found that the political repudiation of the Sedition Act of 1798 had revealed the "central meaning" of the First Amendment: a right to criticize government and public officials. As the Court put it, "[A] rule compelling the critic of official conduct to guarantee the truth of all his factual assertions . . . leads to . . . 'self-censorship.' " The Alabama act, "because of the restraint it imposed upon criticism of government and public officials, was inconsistent with the First Amendment.

In place of actual falsity as a basis for liability, the Court imposed a new standard to govern defamation actions brought by public officials. Now, a public official could recover damages for a defamatory falsehood relating to his official conduct only upon a showing "that the statement was made with 'actual malice'— that is, with knowledge that it was false or with reckless disregard of whether it was false or not."

Sullivan effected important changes in constitutional law and practice. Defamation law previously had been left to the states, subject to gradual common law evolution in state courts not often exposed to First Amendment issues. *Sullivan* federalized this diversity of local rules into a single national body of doctrine overseen by a Court peculiarly sensitive to First Amendment problems. Furthermore, the intangibility of defamation law had left wide discretion in trial court juries; *Sullivan* imposed independent appellate court review of the facts in defamation actions as a First Amendment guarantee. And, in place of the

LICENSE CASES

complexity of overlapping liabilities, offsetting privileges, and jurisdictional diversity, *Sullivan* instituted a simple national rule that put a stringent burden of proof on plaintiffs.

Decisions following *Sullivan* extended the "actual malice" limitation on the law of defamation beyond the case of criticism of high public officials. The rule was expanded to apply to PUBLIC FIGURES in *Curtis Publishing Co. v. Butts* and *Associated Press v. Walker* (1967). A plurality of the Court even stretched the rule to cover private figures, if the matter was "a subject of public or general interest," in *Rosenbloom v. Metromedia, Inc.* (1971). But the Court retreated from *Rosenbloom* three years later in GERTZ V. ROBERT WELCH, INC. (1974). *Gertz* held that a private person may recover without meeting the actual malice standard. Because private figures have only limited access to the media to correct misstatements of others, and because they have not assumed the risk of injury due to defamatory falsehoods against them, the Court found the interests of private figures to weigh more heavily than those of public figures. The states were left free to establish an appropriate standard of liability, provided they do not impose liability without fault. Moreover, the states were forbidden from awarding presumed or punitive DAMAGES absent a showing of actual malice. More recently, in DUN & BRADSTREET, INC. V. GREENMOSS BUILDERS, INC. (1985), the Court retreated still further, permitting recovery of presumed and punitive damages by a private plaintiff without a showing of actual malice, because the defamatory statements did not involve a matter of public concern.

The defamation decisions beginning with *New York Times Co. v. Sullivan* have had the twofold effect of highlighting the core purpose of the First Amendment and constitutionalizing the law of defamation. By invalidating the law of seditious libel, the Court recognized that criticism of government is the type of speech most deserving of First Amendment protection. By establishing minimum standards of liability and limitations on damages for public figures and some private plaintiffs, the Court federalized the law of defamation.

BENNO C. SCHMIDT, JR.

Bibliography

KALVEN, HARRY JR. 1964 The New York Times Case: A Note on "The Central Meaning of the First Amendment." *Supreme Court Review* 1964:191.
LEVY, LEONARD W. 1984 *Emergence of a Free Press.* New York: Oxford University Press.
——— 1960 *Legacy of Suppression: Freedom of Speech and Press in Early American History.* Cambridge, Mass.: Harvard University Press.

LIBERTY OF CONTRACT

See: Freedom of Contract

LICENSE CASES
5 Howard 504 (1847)

In three related cases decided the same day, the Court sustained the constitutionality of temperance statutes of states that had restricted the sale of liquor and required all dealers to be licensed. Although the Justices unanimously concurred in the disposition of the cases, six men wrote nine opinions, and there was no opinion for the Court because a majority could not agree on the reasoning. At one extreme Justice JOHN MCLEAN took the position that the DORMANT POWERS of Congress under the COMMERCE CLAUSE utterly excluded the exercise of CONCURRENT POWERS by the states; but McLean found that the statutes were not regulations of commerce but reasonable exercises of the POLICE POWER. At the other extreme Justice PETER DANIEL supported an exaggerated view of concurrent state commerce powers.

Chief Justice ROGER B. TANEY's view was the least doctrinaire. He observed that two of the three *License Cases* dealt with the retail sale of liquor that was no longer in the original package and therefore raised no INTERSTATE COMMERCE issue. (See ORIGINAL PACKAGE DOCTRINE.) The third case, however, involved liquor imported in the original package from another state and sold in that unbroken package. Thus the business affected by the state's license law was in interstate commerce. Taney therefore confronted the question "whether the grant of power to Congress is of itself a prohibition to the States, and renders all State laws on the subject null and void." His answer to the question, unlike Chief Justice JOHN MARSHALL's, was that unless a state act came into conflict with a law of Congress, the state could constitutionally exercise a concurrent commerce power. On the other hand, he muddled his position by arguing that such a power was no more than the police power of the state, which he defined, promiscuously, as "nothing more or less than the powers of government inherent in every sovereignty to the extent of its dominions." His refusal to distinguish the police power from the commerce power and other powers left his opinion doctrinally murky, and like the opinions by the other Justices it failed to provide a usable test. At least two state judges, JAMES KENT and LEMUEL SHAW, avoided the Supreme Court's quest for a system of definitional categories by suggesting that if Congress did not brush away state legislation, it should be sustained in the absence of an actual or operational conflict with national legislation.

LEONARD W. LEVY

LIEBER, FRANCIS

See: Commentators on the Constitution

LILBURNE, JOHN
(1614–1657)

John Lilburne, whose entire career was a precedent for freedom, was the catalytic agent in the history of the RIGHT AGAINST SELF-INCRIMINATION. Primarily because of him, that right became a respected, established rule of the COMMON LAW. An agitator with an incurably inflamed sense of injustice, Lilburne was called Freeborn John, because of his incessant demands on behalf of the rights of every freeborn Englishman. No one in England could silence or out-talk him, no one was a greater pamphleteer, and no one was more principled in his devotion to political liberty, the rights of the criminally accused, and the freedoms of conscience and press. Making CIVIL DISOBEDIENCE a way of life, Lilburne successively defied king, parliament, and protectorate.

He first focused the attention of England on the injustice of forcing anyone to answer incriminating questions during his 1637 trial. After his release from prison in 1641, he joined the parliamentary cause, rose to a high military position, and became close to Oliver Cromwell; but he resigned his commission to be free to oppose the government. Four times he stood trial for his life, and he spent much of his last twenty years in jail, from which he smuggled out a torrent of tracts. He advocated a special CONSTITUTIONAL CONVENTION to write a constitution for England embodying the reforms proposed by the Levellers, the faction of constitutional democrats that he led.

When Parliament itself arrested and interrogated him, Lilburne became the first hostile witness in a LEGISLATIVE INVESTIGATION to claim a right not to answer questions against or concerning himself. He

successfully made the same claim, under his view of MAGNA CARTA and the PETITION OF RIGHT, before a common law court in 1649, when tried for TREASON. He appealed to the jury above the heads of the judges and convinced the jury to decide on the injustice of the laws used to persecute political prisoners. Twice he persuaded juries to acquit him. In his trials and writings he educated England on the relation of liberty to fair play and DUE PROCESS OF LAW. At his last trial he won the unprecedented right to secure a copy of the INDICTMENT against him and to be represented by counsel in a capital case. Cromwell finally imprisoned him without trial, and Lilburne died in jail.

LEONARD W. LEVY

Bibliography

LEVY, LEONARD W. 1968 *Origins of the Fifth Amendment.* Pages 271–312. New York: Oxford University Press.

LIMITED GOVERNMENT

The idea of limited government is closely associated with political thinkers, mostly of medieval and modern periods, who placed special emphasis on preventing abuses of government. Some spoke of limitations connected with divine law and natural law; others spoke of a SOCIAL COMPACT establishing government for the sake of protecting property and other individual rights. Limited government was also a corollary of the more affirmative approach of ancient philosophers, who taught that ruling bodies could best maintain themselves by respecting social customs, moderating their policies, honoring the contributions of each social class in distributing governmental offices, and fostering self-restraint, patriotism, and other attitudes conducive to the general welfare.

In American constitutional thought limited government is often synonymous with CONSTITUTIONALISM itself. It has three more specific connotations resulting from the three principal ways in which the government can be said to be constitutionally limited: in a jurisdictional sense, limited in the objectives it may pursue; in a procedural sense, limited in the ways it may decide policy questions and adjudicate disputes involving individuals; and limited by the requirement that its policies be compatible with individual rights.

The first sense of limited government refers to the ENUMERATION OF POWERS through which the Constitution outlines the jurisdictional concerns of the national government. This method of limitation has failed. The enumeration of powers is now a dead letter as a result of the nationalizing tendencies of American economic and social life, which the Supreme Court has accommodated through its interpretations of the TENTH AMENDMENT, the COMMERCE CLAUSE, the NECESSARY AND PROPER CLAUSE, the GENERAL WELFARE CLAUSE, and the Civil War Amendments.

As for the second, or procedural, mode of limitation (structural limitations on policy formation and due process limitations on adjudication), some contemporary constitutionalists regard it as the only philosophically acceptable variety. These theorists tend to follow a value-neutral conception of constitutional democracy which is both at odds with citizen presuppositions about the goals of politics and supported by no compelling historical or philosophic argument. Respect for procedural ideas like SEPARATION OF POWERS, representative government, and DUE PROCESS is indeed central to American constitutionalism, but not because that tradition is indifferent to different ways of life and the ends of government. A traditional respect for procedure is rather an aspect of the Enlightenment commitment to liberal toleration or reasoning in human affairs, as opposed especially to precipitous decision and government in the name of divine authority. The value-neutral variety of proceduralism is inconsistent with this tradition because it denies the possibility of rationally defending the practices, conditions, and attitudes conducive to reasoning itself.

Americans typically associate limited government first and foremost with constitutional rights and JUDICIAL REVIEW. "By a limited constitution," wrote ALEXANDER HAMILTON in THE FEDERALIST #78, "I understand one which contains certain specified exceptions to the legislative authority; such, for instance, as that it shall pass no BILLS OF ATTAINDER, no EX POST FACTO laws, and the like. Limitations of this kind can be preserved in practice no other way than through the medium of courts of justice, whose duty it must be to declare all acts contrary to the manifest tenor of the Constitution void."

Yet courts are also agencies of government, and groups throughout American history have opposed judicial protection of some rights as the least majoritarian and therefore least legitimate subordination of other rights. Some theorists believe society has a way of arriving at pragmatic adjustments of conflicting views (lax enforcement of laws against CONTRACEPTION and abortion, for example) that cannot be reconciled at the level of moral principle. They regard judicial intervention in behalf of those persons who brook

no compromise as divisive to the point of undermining everyone's right to live in a peaceful society. Many citizens seem profoundly bitter over their loss of freedom to live and raise their children in communities that exclude sexually suggestive entertainment, political deviants, and others, including members of other races and religions. Their criticism of the judiciary's protection of rights suggests a community oriented understanding of rights, for they themselves want the right to be members of communities that use official power to exclude some kinds of people as equals or to exclude them altogether. This community-oriented conception is highly visible in the demands of some religious groups for organized prayer in public schools despite offense to others.

But a community orientation of sorts is also implicit in demands for public recognition of the RIGHTS OF PRIVACY like those involving property, sexual freedom, and conscience. In effect, persons who demand these rights seek the right to live in communities that honor the rights demanded. Rights to property, for example, are hardly secure if the general public is unwilling to exercise the restraint and undertake the sacrifices that honoring such rights entails. It is therefore not surprising that defenders of property should treat "free enterprise" as an article of the community's gospel and special identity. For if any rights are genuine exemptions from LEGISLATIVE POWER, their enjoyment must not be left to prudential calculation. And if the government has no authority to invade them, those rights must at once be grounded in higher authority and be essential to the nation's identity in a way that it would make no sense to violate them for the sake of saving the nation. The religious right wing of American politics has a point in contending that "secular humanism" is itself something of a religious imposition on fundamentalists, who are thereby forced to live among what they regard as evil practices. Maxims of liberal toleration are no answer to these people because liberals themselves cannot tolerate being governed by thoroughly dedicated fundamentalists—those who would live every aspect of their lives as they think they should, even if that should mean employing coercive government against those who would stop them. Religiously committed folk can be excused for believing that liberalism tolerates illiberalism only by degrading it to a form of play-acting to be confined to churches, the home, or wherever one goes for respite from the serious world of education, work, and government. Defending liberalism thus requires an argument (eventually a persuasive one) that liberalism is a better way of life—that, wherever feasible, it is better for human beings to have a liberal outlook and live in secular communities that tolerate illiberal speech only, not action.

Deepening ideological divisions in American life indicate that constitutional rights can place real limits on government only where public morality favors honoring rights. Hamilton said as much in *The Federalist* #84 where he criticized naïve reliance on BILLS OF RIGHTS to protect the rights themselves. "[W]hatever fine declarations may be inserted in any constitution," he said, the security of rights "must altogether depend on public opinion, and on the general spirit of the people and of the government." It follows that governments that would honor rights effectively should work for the social and economic conditions and attitudes that are favorable to honoring rights. If rights are to remain effective limits on government, the ends of government will have to include the virtue of its citizens. Limited government in a modern sense will have to converge toward limited government in an ancient sense.

SOTIRIOS A. BARBER

(SEE ALSO: *Checks and Balances; Unwritten Constitution.*)

Bibliography

BARBER, SOTIRIOS A. 1984 *On What the Constitution Means.* Baltimore: Johns Hopkins University Press.

BERNS, WALTER 1982 Judicial Review and the Rights and Laws of Nature. *Supreme Court Review* 1982:49–83.

CORWIN, EDWARD S. 1928 The "Higher Law" Background of American Constitutional Law. *Harvard Law Review* 42:149–365.

DWORKIN, RONALD 1981 The Forum of Principle. *New York University Law Review* 56:469–518.

PURCELL, EDWARD A., JR. 1973 *The Crisis of Democratic Theory.* Lexington: University Press of Kentucky.

LINCOLN, ABRAHAM
(1809–1865)

Abraham Lincoln of Illinois served as President of the United States during the nation's greatest crisis, the Civil War. He had previously represented Illinois in the House of Representatives for a single term (1847–1849), during which he introduced the SPOT RESOLUTIONS, implicitly critical of President JAMES K. POLK's administration of the Mexican War, and supported the WILMOT PROVISO, which would have banned slavery from the territory acquired in that war. Lincoln rose to national prominence opposing the policies of Senator STEPHEN A. DOUGLAS, especially Douglas's KANSAS-NEBRASKA ACT, which ex-

tended SLAVERY IN THE TERRITORIES on a local-option basis. In 1856 he joined the fledgling Republican party. Lincoln opposed Douglas's reelection to the Senate in 1858, and the two candidates toured the state together, publicly debating the issues of slavery, POPULAR SOVEREIGNTY, and CONSTITUTIONALISM. During the LINCOLN-DOUGLAS DEBATES, Lincoln severely criticized Chief Justice ROGER B. TANEY's decision in DRED SCOTT V. SANDFORD (1857) as a betrayal of the principles embodied in the DECLARATION OF INDEPENDENCE.

Lincoln's election to the presidency in 1860 triggered the long-impending SECESSION of several slaveholding southern states. Lincoln's presidency was devoted to saving the Union, which meant, in his mind, the rededication of the nation to the principles of the Declaration of Independence, and especially to the proposition that all men are created equal. This work of saving the Union, tragically cut short by an assassin's bullet, was Lincoln's great contribution to American constitutionalism.

In the Lincoln Memorial, directly behind the statue of the Great Emancipator, these words are inscribed:

> In this temple
> as in the hearts of the people
> for whom he saved the Union
> the memory of Abraham Lincoln
> is enshrined forever.

Lincoln did indeed save the Union. But the Union Lincoln saved was older than the Constitution; the Constitution was intended to form a "more perfect Union." When Lincoln began the Gettysburg Address with the magisterial "Fourscore and seven years ago . . ." he intended his listeners to understand that the birth date of the nation was 1776, not 1787, and that the principles of "government of the people, by the people, for the people" were those of the Declaration of Independence. The Constitution was intended to implement those principles more perfectly than had been done by the ARTICLES OF CONFEDERATION. Lincoln at Gettysburg also intended his listeners—and the world—to know that there would be "a new birth of freedom" that would be accomplished by the EMANCIPATION PROCLAMATION, followed, as he intended that it would be, by the THIRTEENTH AMENDMENT. (We may be confident that, had he lived, Lincoln would also have given his support to the FOURTEENTH and FIFTEENTH AMENDMENTS, as part of that same "new birth.")

To understand the Constitution as Abraham Lincoln did must mean, primarily and essentially, to understand the Constitution as an expression of the principles of the Declaration. To do this is to separate the interpretation of the Constitution from all forms of legal positivism, historicism, and moral relativism, that is to say, from all those forms of interpretation that are dominant today in the law schools, universities, and courts of the nation. For, contrary to Lincoln's expectations, his words at Gettysburg have been greatly noted and long remembered: it is their meaning that has been forgotten.

Lincoln did indeed save the Union. At the time of his inauguration, March 4, 1861, seven states had already seceded and joined together to form an independent government called the Confederate States of America. JAMES BUCHANAN, the outgoing President, had been confronted with the SOUTH CAROLINA ORDINANCE OF SECESSION on December 20, 1860, six weeks after Lincoln's election, and more than ten weeks before his inauguration. Buchanan declared secession to be unconstitutional, but coupled his denunciation of secession with a much harsher denunciation of abolitionism. He denied, moreover, that he as President could take any lawful action against secession. Whatever action the federal government ought to take, he lamely concluded, must originate in laws enacted by Congress. But Buchanan had nothing to suggest to Congress, and Congress, at this juncture—the representatives of eight slave states remaining on March 4, 1861—was as divided as the nation itself. No congressional majority could have been formed then for decisive action against the rebellion. Lincoln waited until Congress had gone home, and cannily maneuvered the South Carolinians into firing those shots against Fort Sumter that electrified the North and consolidated public opinion behind his leadership. He then issued his call for 75,000 troops, and set on foot those measures that eventually resulted in the forcible subjugation of the rebellion.

Lincoln insisted that the Constitution ought not to be construed in such a way as to deny to the government any power necessary for carrying out the Constitution's commands. The Constitution required the President to take an oath "to preserve, protect, and defend the Constitution," and made it the duty of the President to "take care that the laws be faithfully executed." Lincoln held it to be absurd to suppose that it was unlawful for him to do those things that were indispensably necessary to preserve the Constitution by enforcing the execution of the laws. Even an action that might otherwise be unlawful, he said, might become lawful, by becoming thus indispensable. Lincoln never conceded that any of his wartime actions were unconstitutional. But supposing that one of them had been so, he asked, ". . . are all the laws

but one to go unexecuted, and the Government itself go to pieces, lest that one be violated?"

Lincoln saved the Union. He prevented the United States from being divided into two or more separate confederacies. It was entirely likely that the North American continent would have been "Balkanized" had the initial secession succeeded. Like the Balkan states, the petty American powers would have formed alliances with greater powers, and North America would have become a cockpit of world conflict. All the evils that the more perfect Union was designed to prevent, those particularly described in the first ten numbers of THE FEDERALIST—large standing armies, heavy taxation, the restriction of individual liberties characteristic of an armed camp—would have come to pass. Civil and religious liberty, the supreme ends of republican government, would, with the failure of the American experiment, "perish from the earth." The "central idea of secession," Lincoln held, "is the essence of anarchy." A constitutional majority, checked and limited, and able to change easily with deliberate changes in public opinion and sentiment, "is the only true sovereign of a free people." To reject majority rule is to turn necessarily either to anarchy or to despotism.

The Lincoln Memorial says that Lincoln saved the Union for "the people." At the outset of the war Lincoln said, "This is essentially a people's contest." Today, when the foulest despotisms call themselves "people's republics," it requires a conscious effort to restore to our minds the intrinsic connection in Lincoln's mind between the cause of the people and fidelity to individual liberty under the rule of law in a constitutional regime. "Our adversaries," Lincoln said, at the outset of the war, "have adopted some declarations of independence, in which, unlike the good old one, penned by THOMAS JEFFERSON, they omit the words 'all men are created equal.' Why? They have adopted a temporary national constitution, in the preamble of which they omit, 'We the People,' and substitute 'We, the deputies of the sovereign and independent States.' Why? Why this deliberate pressing out of view the rights of men and the authority of the people?" Here is the core constitutional question of the Civil War. Lincoln was elected on a platform that called for the recognition of STATES' RIGHTS, "and especially the right of each State to order and control its own domestic institutions according to its own judgment exclusively." Such rights, the Republican platform asserted, and Lincoln repeated in his inaugural, were "essential to that balance of power on which the perfection and endurance of our political fabric depend." For Lincoln, however, the rights of the states were themselves the political expression of the rights of the people, which in turn were the political expression of the rights of men. The proposition that embodied the rights of men was that to which—as he said at Gettysburg—the nation was dedicated at its conception. The Civil War was a result of the fact that the idea of states' rights, and of popular sovereignty, had become divorced, in the public mind of the Confederacy, from the original doctrine of equality in the Declaration of Independence.

The question posed by the Civil War, Lincoln said, was addressed to "the whole family of man." That Lincoln conceived of mankind as in some sense a "family" was of course but another expression of his belief in human equality. Lincoln's question was essentially the same as that addressed by ALEXANDER HAMILTON in *The Federalist* #1: "whether societies of men are really capable or not of establishing good government from reflection and choice, or whether they are forever destined to depend for their political constitutions upon accident and force." The election of Abraham Lincoln was a deliberate decision of the American people, in accordance with the canons of reflection and choice embodied in the Constitution. It remained to be seen therefore whether, in Lincoln's words, "discontented individuals, too few in numbers to control administration according to organic law [can arbitrarily] break up their government, and thus practically put an end to free government upon the earth." But because the leaders of the rebellion "knew their people possessed as much of moral sense, as much devotion to law and order . . . as any other civilized and patriotic people," it was necessary for them to invent "an ingenious sophism which, if conceded, was followed by perfectly logical steps . . . to the complete destruction of the Union. The sophism itself is, that any State of the Union may, consistently with the national Constitution . . . withdraw from the Union without the consent of the Union or of any other State."

The secessionists claimed that membership in the Union resulted from the acts by which the states had ratified the Constitution and that they might therefore withdraw by the same procedure. The Constitution itself, according to this theory, had no higher authority than the will of the people of the several states, acting in their constituent capacity.

In contradiction of this position, Lincoln presented a historical argument, that the Union was older than the states, that the rights of the states were only rights within the Union, and never rights outside of it or independent of it. Although the Declaration of Independence speaks, in its next to last sentence, of all

those "Acts and Things which Independent States may of right do," none of them were ever done by any of the United States independently of each other. This argument, however, is not as conclusive as that other argument, independent of history, which follows from that "abstract truth applicable to all men and all times," to which, at Gettysburg, Lincoln said the nation had been dedicated. This argument Lincoln had been developing throughout his mature life, and is the ground of his constitutionalism, as indeed it is of all his moral and political thought. According to Lincoln, the Civil War was a "people's contest" because the rights of the states, and of the United States, were the rights of the people, either severally or generally. But what are the rights of the people? They are the rights with which the Creator has equally endowed all men—all human beings. These are the unalienable rights, among which are the rights to life, to liberty, and to the pursuit of happiness. Since all men have these rights equally, no man can rule another rightfully except with that other man's consent. Nothing better illuminates the division within the American mind that brought about the Civil War than this passage from a speech in reply to Douglas in 1854: "Judge Douglas," said Lincoln, "frequently, with bitter irony and sarcasm, paraphrases our argument by saying: 'The white people of Nebraska are good enough to govern themselves, *but they are not good enough to govern a few miserable negroes!!*' Well, I doubt not that the people of Nebraska are, and will continue to be as good as the average of people elsewhere. I do not say the contrary. What I do say is, that no man is good enough to govern another man, *without that other's consent.* I say this is the leading principle—the sheet anchor of American republicanism." Slavery, Lincoln observed, is a violation of this principle, not only because "the Master . . . governs the slave without his consent; but he governs him by a set of rules altogether different from those which he prescribes for himself." Republicanism, for Lincoln, meant that those who live under the law share equally in the making of the law they live under, and that those who make the law live equally under the law that they make. Here in essence is the necessary relationship between equality, consent, majority rule, and the rule of law in Lincoln's thought. Here in essence is what unites the principles of the Declaration with the forms of the Constitution. Here is what enables us to distinguish the principles of the Constitution from the compromises of the Constitution (in particular, the compromises with slavery). Here is the essence of Lincoln's understanding of why the argument against slavery and the argument for free government are distinguishable but inseparable aspects of one and the same argument.

The people are collectively sovereign because the people individually, by their consent, have transferred the exercise of certain of their unalienable rights— but not the rights themselves—to civil society. They have done so, the better "to secure these rights." A just government will act by the majority, under a constitution devised to assure with a reasonable likelihood that the action of the majority will fulfill its purpose, which is the equal protection of the indefeasible and equal rights of all. The majority is the surrogate of the community, which is to say, of each individual. Majority rule is not merely obliged to respect minority rights; in the final analysis it has no higher purpose than to secure the rights of that indefeasible minority, the individual. The sovereignty of the people—or of the states—cannot be exerted morally or lawfully for any purpose inconsistent with the security of those original and unalienable rights. Although Lincoln denied any constitutional right to secede, he did not deny a revolutionary right, which might be exercised justly if "by the mere force of numbers, a majority should deprive a minority of any clearly written constitutional right."

In his inaugural address Lincoln repeated his oft-repeated declaration that he had no purpose, "directly or indirectly, to interfere with slavery where it exists." He had, he said, "no lawful right to do so" and he had "no inclination to do so." This, he held, was implied constitutional law, but he was willing to make it express, by an amendment to the Constitution. Lincoln would not, however, agree to any measures that might have as their consequence the extension of slavery to new lands where it did not already exist. As he wrote to his old friend ALEXANDER H. STEPHENS in 1861, "You think slavery is *right,* and ought to be extended; while we think it is *wrong* and ought to be restricted. That I suppose is the rub. It certainly is the only substantial difference between us." Many complex and elaborate explanations have been made of the causes of the Civil War. Lincoln's is at once the shortest and the most profound.

The South claimed the right to extend slavery on the ground that it was a violation of the fundamental equality of the states to allow the citizens of one state or section to emigrate into a federal TERRITORY with their property, while prohibiting the citizens of any other state or section from emigrating into that same federal territory with their property. Lincoln dealt with this argument in 1854—in his first great antislavery speech—as follows: "Equal justice to the South, it is said, requires us to consent to the extending of slavery to new countries. That is to say, inasmuch as you do not object to my taking my hog to Nebraska, therefore I must not object to you taking your slave. Now, I admit this is perfectly logical, if there is no difference between hogs and negroes."

Southerners had come to deny the essential difference between hogs and Negroes, in part because of the enormous economic stake that they had come to have in slave labor, because of the enormous burgeoning of the cotton economy. This was one cause of the change in their opinion of slavery, from a necessary evil to a positive good. Another may be seen in the following from one of Lincoln's 1859 speeches. Douglas, Lincoln said, had "declared that while in all contests between the negro and the white man, he was for the white man . . . that in all questions between the negro and the crocodile he was for the negro." Lincoln interpreted Douglas's statements as "a sort of proposition in proportion, which may be stated thus: As the negro is to the white man, so is the crocodile to the negro; and as the negro may rightfully treat the crocodile as a beast or reptile, so the white man may rightfully treat the negro as a beast or reptile." Douglas's references to "contests" between negroes and crocodiles, and between negroes and whites, reflected popular ideas of "the survival of the fittest" in the evolutionary process. Lincoln, in commenting on these remarks of Douglas, also went out of his way to deny the necessity of any such "contests." Alexander Stephens, who was inaugurated vice-president of the Confederacy in February 1861, conceded that the United States had been founded upon the proposition "that all men are created equal," and that that proposition had indeed (contrary to what Chief Justice Roger B. Taney had said in *Dred Scott v. Sandford*) included black men as well as white. But, Stephens went on, the Confederacy was "founded [and] its corner stone rests upon . . . the great truth that the negro is not the equal to the white man. That slavery—the subordination to the superior race, is his natural and normal condition." "This our new Government," Stephens added, "is the first in the history of the world, based upon this great physical and moral truth." The doctrine of racial superiority became a vital element in the conviction that slavery was a positive good. Without the conviction and the doctrine there could not have been a belief in the South of a constitutional right to extend slavery. That science, in one or another version of evolution, had established the inequality of the races, became the ground for the rejection of the doctrine that all men are created equal.

In fact, the doctrine of racial inequality involves

the denial that there is any natural right, or that there are any "laws of nature and of nature's God." And this is to deny that constitutionalism and the RULE OF LAW rest upon anything besides blind preference. Justice would then be nothing but the interest of the stronger. Abraham Lincoln's speeches, before and during the Civil War, are the supreme repository for that wisdom that teaches us that we as moral beings ought to live under the rule of law. According to this wisdom, it is also in our interest to do so, because upon our recognition of the humanity of other men depends the recognition of our own humanity. And upon the recognition of our own humanity—by ourselves and by others—depends the possibility of our own happiness as human beings. Surely Lincoln was right in saying that the source of all moral principle— no less than of all political and constitutional right— was the proposition "that all men are created equal."

It is doubtful that the history of the world records another life displaying an integrity of speech and deed equal to that of Abraham Lincoln. With an almost perfect understanding of the theoretical ground of free, constitutional government was united an unflinching courage, and a practical wisdom, in doing what had to be done, lest popular government "perish from the earth." Whether, in the third century of the Constitution, Lincoln's legacy will survive in deed depends upon whether we can recover anything of his character and intelligence. But whether or not this republic lasts, as long as the world lasts Lincoln's speeches and deeds will remain as an emblem and a beacon of humanity to all men everywhere who may be struggling out of the dark valley of despotism and aspiring to the broad, sunlit uplands of freedom.

HARRY V. JAFFA

Bibliography
BELZ, HERMAN 1969 *Reconstructing the Union.* Ithaca, N.Y.: Cornell University Press.
FEHRENBACHER, DON E. 1978 *The Dred Scott Case: Its Significance in American Law and Politics.* New York: Oxford University Press.
———— 1979 *Lincoln and the Constitution.* Pages 121–166 in Cullom Davis, ed., *The Public and Private Lincoln: Contemporary Perspectives.* Carbondale: Southern Illinois University Press.
JAFFA, HARRY V. (1952)1983 *Crisis of the House Divided: An Interpretation of the Lincoln–Douglas Debates.* Chicago: University of Chicago Press.
NEVINS, ALAN 1950 *The Emergence of Lincoln.* 2 Vols. New York: Scribner's.
RANDALL, JAMES G. 1951 *Constitutional Problems under Lincoln,* rev. ed. Urbana: University of Illinois Press.

LINCOLN, LEVI
(1749–1820)

Graduated from Harvard University and trained in law, Levi Lincoln fought as a Minuteman in the American Revolution and subsequently held several offices in the revolutionary government of Massachusetts. In 1780 he was a delegate to the convention that drafted the state constitution. After the Revolution he became a leader of the Massachusetts bar as well as a member of the legislature.

In 1781, Lincoln successfully argued in *Quock Walker's Case* (CALDWELL V. JENNISON) that the passage in the MASSACHUSETTS CONSTITUTION declaring that "all men are born free and equal" prohibited any legal recognition of slavery in the state. The decision effectively abolished slavery in Massachusetts.

Having early become a leader of the Republican party, Lincoln served from 1801 to 1805 as attorney general of the United States in the first administration of THOMAS JEFFERSON. In 1811 he declined, on the ground of failing eyesight, President JAMES MADISON'S offer of appointment as an associate Justice of the Supreme Court.

DENNIS J. MAHONEY

LINCOLN-DOUGLAS DEBATES
(1858)

STEPHEN A. DOUGLAS, running for reelection to the United States Senate, agreed to debate his Republican challenger, ABRAHAM LINCOLN, at seven joint appearances in rural Illinois during the summer of 1858. The resulting discourse, promptly reprinted in full in newspapers, produced a classic survey of alternatives for the future of slavery and black people in the American constitutional system.

Douglas defended the concept of territorial SOVEREIGNTY: let the people of the territories, rather than Congress, decide the future of slavery there. He stated that he "cared not whether slavery be voted up or voted down" and accused Lincoln of advocating racial equality. Lincoln emphasized the incompatibility of Douglas's position with the decision in DRED SCOTT V. SANDFORD (1857), in which Chief Justice ROGER B. TANEY had stated that a territorial legislature lacked power to exclude slavery. Douglas responded with the "FREEPORT DOCTRINE": a territorial legislature could exclude slavery simply by not enacting legislation supporting it. Lincoln hinted at a conspiracy involving Taney, Douglas, and the Pierce and BUCHANAN administrations to force slavery into the free states, an allegation Douglas indignantly denied by reasserting the power of each state to fully control its domestic policy.

WILLIAM M. WIECEK

Bibliography

JAFFA, HARRY V. 1959 *Crisis of the House Divided: An Interpretation of the Lincoln–Douglas Debates.* Garden City, N.Y.: Doubleday.

LINCOLN'S PLAN OF RECONSTRUCTION
(1863)

By 1863, President ABRAHAM LINCOLN adopted policies that affected Reconstruction in some of the seceded states. He appointed military governors in Louisiana, Tennessee, and North Carolina and recognized the provisional government of Virginia. The EMANCIPATION PROCLAMATION took effect on January 1, 1863.

Lincoln issued his Proclamation of Amnesty and Reconstruction on December 8, 1863. In it, he offered AMNESTY to all participants in the rebellion, except high-ranking military and civilian officers. He announced his intention to appoint a military governor in each occupied state and to require each occupied state to accept all extant and future policy concerning slavery and emancipation. But otherwise Lincoln's policy was conservative. It assumed preservation of the states' boundaries, constitutions, and laws (except those relating to slavery) and required neither black suffrage nor confiscation. Lincoln proposed to recreate an enfranchised citizenry in each state by requiring all persons to take an oath of future loyalty and support of the laws. When ten percent of a state's 1860 voters had taken the oath, they could reorganize the state's government.

The President's authority to recreate loyal state governments derived from several provisions of Article II, including his powers as COMMANDER-IN-CHIEF, his PARDONING POWER, and his duty to see to the faithful execution of the laws. But, as with his earlier actions in calling for volunteers and suspending HABEAS CORPUS, Lincoln had to make the most of a document that had not contemplated SECESSION, civil war, or Reconstruction.

Though Arkansas and Louisiana complied with Lincoln's terms, Congress refused to seat their representatives. Lincoln and Congress clashed over the more stringent congressional plan of Reconstruction embodied in the WADE-DAVIS BILL of 1864. President

ANDREW JOHNSON later pursued Reconstruction policies similar to Lincoln's.

WILLIAM M. WIECEK

Bibliography

BELZ, HERMAN 1969 *Reconstructing the Union: Theory and Policy During the Civil War.* Ithaca, N.Y.: Cornell University Press.

LINEUP

In opinions whose subtext is unease about eyewitness identification procedures and testimony, the Supreme Court ruled in 1967 that a suspect is entitled to the presence of counsel at a lineup in order to preserve a FAIR TRIAL at which the witnesses can be meaningfully cross-examined. The opinions were delivered in the cases of UNITED STATES V. WADE and *Gilbert v. California.*

If a lineup is conducted without counsel, testimony about the lineup identification is automatically excluded. The question then becomes whether the witness who attended the illegally conducted lineup should be allowed to identify the witness at trial. This question centers on whether the witness could have made the in-court identification without having attended the lineup at which counsel was not present: whether, in other words, the witness had an independent source for the identification.

The lineup cases have generated much litigation and writing, both of a practical and a scholarly sort, about the role of counsel. The Court seemed to envision the attorney as a passive observer who would use what he saw to reconstruct for the fact-finder any unfairness in the lineup procedure. But a lawyer's skills are not necessary for observing, and reconstruction on cross-examination creates the risk that through the knowledge he displays in asking questions a lawyer may become a witness in his own case. Perhaps recognizing that having counsel at lineups was an interim measure and perceiving the analytical difficulties, the Court suggested that other techniques, such as photographing or videotaping lineups, could obviate the need for counsel.

The RIGHT TO COUNSEL at lineups was greatly undercut in *Kirby v. Illinois* (1972), in which the Court held that the right begins only "at or after the initiation of adversary criminal proceedings—whether by way of formal charge, preliminary hearing, INDICT-

MENT, INFORMATION, or arraignment." Because most lineups are part of the investigative stage of a case and occur before any of the indices of a formal charge, *Kirby* necessarily implied that a lawyer or some other observer was not, in fact, generally required.

Untouched by *Kirby*, however, is the argument, made in *Stovall v. Denno* (1967), that identification procedures may be so "unnecessarily suggestive and conducive to irreparable mistaken identification" as to violate DUE PROCESS OF LAW. An example of a due process violation would be showing a crime victim only the suspect dressed in clothes like those of the perpetrator when there was time to arrange a proper lineup. Once such a due process violation is proven, the issue shifts to whether it tainted the in-court identification: whether there was "a very substantial likelihood of irreparable mistaken identification." This decision mirrors that of a court in deciding whether a victim can make an in-court identification after attending a lineup where counsel was not present.

The effect of the lineup decisions has been to focus attention on all of the procedures used in pretrial CONFRONTATION of witnesses and suspects and thus to improve the fairness of these previously unobserved, but critically important, occasions.

BARBARA ALLEN BABCOCK

Bibliography

LEVY, LEONARD W. 1974 *Against the Law.* Pages 242–258. New York: Harper & Row.

LINMARK ASSOCIATES v. WILLINGBORO
431 U.S. 85 (1977)

Without dissent, the BURGER COURT invalidated a local ordinance prohibiting real estate "For Sale" and "Sold" signs. The ordinance sought to reduce the flight by white homeowners from racially integrated neighborhoods. Although a ban upon all signs for aesthetic purposes might survive a constitutional test, wrote Justice THURGOOD MARSHALL, this ordinance violated the FIRST AMENDMENT because the township had selected a particular message for prohibitions.

MICHAEL E. PARRISH

LISTENERS' RIGHTS

The constitutional commitment to FREEDOM OF SPEECH is in part based on the simple idea that people have a right to say what they want to say without government interference. That is, freedom of speech protects the speaker. Yet the FIRST AMENDMENT themes of self-expression and speaker liberty have been recognized only sporadically in Supreme Court opinions. The more prevalent themes in First Amendment jurisprudence have been audience-oriented, albeit implicitly.

One classic justification of freedom of speech has been based on optimistic assessments about the capacity of the marketplace of ideas to distinguish between the false and the true. The emphasis of this justification is not that speakers have a right to say what they want to say, but that speakers must be free to speak so that the society can find truth, that is, so that listeners can hear and evaluate what is said. Listeners' rights are also strongly implicated by the notion that freedom of speech reflects a commitment to democratic self-government. If citizens are to decide how to respond to public issues, they must hear what others have to say. The listeners' rights emphasis of the self-government perspective is best illustrated by ALEXANDER MEIKLEJOHN's observation, approvingly cited by the Supreme Court in COLUMBIA BROADCASTING SYSTEM V. DEMOCRATIC NATIONAL COMMITTEE (1981): "What is essential is not that everyone shall speak, but that everything worth saying shall be said."

For many years, listeners' rights were protected with nary a listener before the Court. In routine cases, the aggrieved speaker invoked the rights of the listeners. In *Thomas v. Collins* (1945), for example, the Court invalidated an attempted prior restraint at the behest of the speaker, in part because of the rights of others "to hear what he had to say."

Ultimately, listeners were permitted to invoke their own rights without any speakers before the Court. In VIRGINIA STATE BOARD OF PHARMACY V. VIRGINIA CITIZENS CONSUMER COUNCIL, for example, consumers challenged a statute that prohibited pharmacists from advertising the prices of prescription drugs. No pharmacist was before the Court, only potential members of the audience for drug price advertising. The Court recognized the rights of "listener" plaintiffs to sue on their own behalf, observing that the First Amendment gives protection "to the communication, to its source and its recipients both."

LAMONT V. POSTMASTER GENERAL (1965) stands for an even broader principle. There the Court struck down a statute directing the postmaster general not to deliver certain "communist political propaganda" unless the addressee, upon notification, requested its delivery. The Court found this to be "an unconstitutional abridgment of the addressee's rights." Many of the potential senders of this "propaganda" were aliens outside the country who had no First Amendment rights of their own. The Court made this distinction explicit in *Kleindeist v. Mandel* (1972). Thus recipients of messages have a First Amendment right to hear that does not depend upon corresponding rights in the speaker. Such rights may extend to situations where the speaker is unwilling to speak; they are then usually referred to as the RIGHT TO KNOW. On the other hand, an unwilling recipient of a message may have a right not to hear, deriving from notions such as a right of privacy.

STEVEN SHIFFRIN

Bibliography

BeVier, Lillian 1980 An Informed Public, an Informing Press: The Search for a Constitutional Principle. *Stanford Law Review* 68:482–517.

Emerson, Thomas I. 1976 Legal Foundations of the Right to Know. *Washington University Law Quarterly* 1976:1–24.

LITERACY TEST

Many states used to require voters to be literate in English. The main constitutional problems raised by this practice arose from the use of literacy tests in southern and border states as a form of RACIAL DISCRIMINATION aimed at denying black citizens their VOTING RIGHTS in violation of the FIFTEENTH AMENDMENT. A typical law conditioned voter registration on the ability to read and write a provision of the state constitution selected by the registrar, to the registrar's "satisfaction." (An Alabama registrar once wrote this explanation for rejecting a black applicant: "Error in spilling.") Some laws also required the applicant to "interpret" or "explain" the constitutional provision, offering even greater opportunities for discriminatory application.

In *Davis v. Schnell* (1949) the Supreme Court summarily affirmed a lower court decision invalidating a requirement that a voter "understand and explain" an article of the United States Constitution; the registrar's discretion was so great that the test was an obvious "device to make racial discrimination easy." However, in LASSITER V. NORTHAMPTON COUNTY BOARD OF ELECTIONS (1959) the Court unanimously upheld a bare literacy requirement, in the absence of any showing of discriminatory application. This distinction had been suggested by the Court as early as WILLIAMS V. MISSISSIPPI (1898).

Meanwhile, the Court had fought two minor voting rights skirmishes with Oklahoma. That state had required voters to pass a literacy test, but excepted any voter whose ancestors had been registered to vote in 1866. Because of this GRANDFATHER CLAUSE, only black registrants were required to take literacy tests; the Court readily invalidated this law in GUINN V. UNITED STATES (1915). After the decision, Oklahoma adopted a law requiring all new voters to register within a twelve-day period; because virtually all the new voters were black, this onerous procedure fell before the Fifteenth Amendment, which "nullifies sophisticated as well as simple-minded modes of discrimination," in *Lane v. Wilson* (1939).

The death blow to voter literacy tests was delivered not by the Court but by Congress, which approached the question gingerly. The VOTING RIGHTS ACT OF 1965 required certain states and counties to suspend their use of literacy tests for five years. This feature of the law was upheld in SOUTH CAROLINA V. KATZENBACH (1966). In the same year, KATZENBACH V. MORGAN (1966) upheld another feature of the 1965 act requiring states to confer the vote on some citizens who, having been educated in Puerto Rico, were literate in Spanish. In 1970, Congress suspended literacy tests for voting throughout the nation, a provision which the Court upheld in OREGON V. MITCHELL (1970) as a valid exercise of the power to enforce the Fifteenth Amendment. Finally, in 1975, Congress made the ban on literacy tests permanent. In practical terms, literacy tests for voters are a thing of the past, and the Supreme Court is unlikely to confront the *Lassiter* issue again.

KENNETH L. KARST

Bibliography

Leibowitz, Arnold H. 1969 English Literacy: Legal Sanction for Discrimination. *Notre Dame Lawyer* 45:7–67.

LITIGATION STRATEGY

Litigation strategy in constitutional cases is shaped by a single animating principle—a desire to increase the likelihood that a black-robed bureaucrat called a judge will act on behalf of a politically vulnerable applicant to alter or set aside the act of a popularly accountable official. Although the degree of tension that exists between democratic political theory and constitutional litigation varies widely depending on the nature of the case and the attributes of the forum—a police brutality case litigated before an elected state judge poses no threat to democratic decision making; an EQUAL PROTECTION challenge to an act of Congress argued before an appointed, life-tenured, federal judge poses a more direct conflict—constitutional cases generally involve persons who are unable to secure redress through more conventional appeals to the political process. Litigation strategy in constitutional cases is designed to increase the potential that a judicial forum will rule in favor of such politically disfavored plaintiffs.

Sustained constitutional litigation in the United States has involved many sets of litigants, including abolitionists versus slaveholders in the period prior to the Civil War; radical reconstructionists versus southern revisionists in the period immediately following the Civil War; business CORPORATIONS versus populist reformers during the first third of the twentieth century; and civil libertarians versus majoritarians during the modern era. Although the political goals of the participants have varied widely, the strategic choices of the contestants have remained remarkably stable, involving five areas: choice of forum; selection of parties; articulation of theories of recovery; choice of tactics; and articulation of antidemocratic apologia.

Choice of forum is the most important strategic decision for a constitutional litigator. In choosing a forum, a constitutional litigator must choose between state and federal court; between a judge and jury; and sometimes between one judge and another. The outcome of many, if not most, constitutional cases turns as much on the wisdom of those strategic choices as on the intrinsic merits of the cases.

Because a constitutional plaintiff is generally seeking to trump a decision that enjoys the imprimatur of democratic decision making, the institutional capacity of the forum to render sustained anti- (or, at least, counter-) majoritarian doctrine is critical to the success of any constitutional litigation campaign. Judges who are themselves elected by the political majority or who are otherwise closely tied to the political process are least likely to enunciate sustained countermajoritarian doctrine. Judges who enjoy maximum political insulation are, on the other hand, in a position to ignore the short-term political consequences of their unpopular decisions. It would, for example, have been impossible for elected judges to have effectively enforced the fugitive slave clause in the pre-Civil War North on behalf of southern slaveholders, or the equal protection clause in the post-World War II South on behalf of black schoolchildren seeking an integrated education.

The search for an insulated judge in constitutional cases has generally led politically vulnerable plaintiffs—whether slaveholders, business corporations, or CIVIL RIGHTS activists—to seek a federal judicial forum, for federal judges are appointed and enjoy life

tenure. Much of the procedural infighting that characterizes constitutional litigation revolves around attempts by plaintiffs to force claims into insulated federal forums and by defendants to deflect them to more politically accountable state courts.

The search for an insulated forum has led many constitutional litigators to view juries with suspicion. Not surprisingly, a principal litigation strategy of the abolitionist bar was to choreograph disputes about alleged fugitive slaves before free state juries in the hope that juries would decline to enforce the Fugitive Slave Act. (See FUGITIVE SLAVERY.) Modern civil rights lawyers have experienced analogous difficulty in persuading juries to return verdicts in favor of unpalatable plaintiffs whose rights may have been violated by a popularly responsible official.

Finally, the choice of forum involves a decision about the identity of the judge or, in less polite terms, judge-shopping. The identity of the judge in a constitutional case is extremely important for two reasons, one obvious and one less well understood. The obvious reason for judge-shopping involves the judge's politics. Because constitutional cases often turn on a clash of values and because the urgency with which a judge views a constitutional case may well depend on his or her view of the relative importance of the conflicting values, the same case may be decided differently by equally competent judges with differing value systems.

The less obvious reason why judge-shopping is important in constitutional cases involves the judge's technical competence. Victory for the plaintiff in constitutional cases depends upon persuading a judge that constitutional doctrine requires the overturning of a presumptively valid decision by another government official. Unless a judge is equipped to understand and evaluate complex argumentation about the meaning of ambiguous textual provisions and judicial PRECEDENT, it will be impossible to persuade the judge that doctrinal factors compel a decision for the plaintiff. Because the inertial advantage in constitutional cases almost always favors government defendants—failure to persuade the judge to act results in perpetuation of the challenged status quo—the inability of a judge to grapple with complex argumentation generally works to the disadvantage of a constitutional plaintiff.

In addition to care in selecting a forum, constitutional litigators expend a good deal of energy on the choice of a plaintiff, seeking to project the most sympathetic and appealing fact pattern. Because the judge's view of the equities may play a substantial role in the outcome of a constitutional case, the capacity of a constitutional plaintiff to evoke sympathy can be crucial. Constitutional lawyers have learned, moreover, that courts respond most favorably to fact patterns that emerge naturally from the interrelationship between a constitutional plaintiff and the government, but balk at being asked to decide artificially constructed TEST CASES.

A difficult decision constitutional litigators face in selecting a plaintiff is whether to bring the case as an individual action involving only named individuals or as a CLASS ACTION on behalf of all similarly situated persons. Militating in favor of class action status is its increased impact. A single class action can provide relief to thousands of people. Class actions, however, have drawbacks. Against the prospect of increased impact must be weighed the risk of loss, for members of a losing class are generally bound by the loss. Moreover, class actions can act as red flags to judges who would be sensitive to the claims of an individual plaintiff but who are reluctant to become involved in litigation seeking institutional change.

The selection of a defendant in a constitutional case also requires careful thought. Most important, the defendant must be capable of providing adequate relief. If injunctive relief is sought, the defendant must be sufficiently senior in the bureaucratic hierarchy to be able to promulgate and implement the changes sought by the action. At the same time, of course, the defendant must be sufficiently involved in the factual dispute giving rise to the lawsuit to justify naming him as an adverse party. If DAMAGES are sought, the defendant must have a sufficiently "deep pocket" to pay the judgment. A damage award against a judgment-proof defendant is hardly worth the effort.

One method of dealing with both the need for a high-ranking defendant and the quest for financial solvency is the naming of an entity-defendant such as the City of New York or the United States in addition to the individual defendants. The extremely complicated interplay between rules limiting the extent to which government entities can be sued in constitutional cases and plaintiffs' interest in suing government entities poses one of the serious tactical dilemmas in constitutional litigation.

A final—and less empirically verifiable—concern in selecting a defendant flows from what may be called the "Redneck-Mandarin dichotomy," which seeks to match a defendant and a judge from different educational and social backgrounds in the hope that the judge will be less constrained in exercising vigorous review powers. Although such an assumption is highly speculative, many constitutional litigators believe, for example, that they perceive a difference between many judges' willingness to exercise vigorous review of the actions of low-ranking police officers and the same judges' willingness to review the decisions of police commissioners.

Given the difficulty of overcoming the inertial advantage enjoyed by the government in constitutional cases, strategic considerations often play a role in the articulation of plaintiff's theory of recovery. It is often advisable to proceed by incremental stages and to develop alternatives to the primary constitutional theory. Thus, for example, litigation aimed at the OVERRULING of the SEPARATE BUT EQUAL DOCTRINE enunciated by PLESSY V. FERGUSON (1896) proceeded by carefully calibrated constitutional steps designed to develop sufficient momentum to make the final decision in BROWN V. BOARD OF EDUCATION (1954) possible. It is, however, extremely difficult to execute a sustained litigation campaign over time, for the factors of chance and changing tides of legal analysis are difficult to predict. On the other hand, asking for too much too soon in the absence of a carefully laid doctrinal foundation places an intolerable degree of pressure on even a sympathetic judge.

In an effort to lessen the tension between constitutional litigation and democratic political theory, litigators often seek to articulate a process-based alternative to their principal substantive theory. Thus, litigators attacking FIRST AMENDMENT violations often invite the court to seize upon a narrower, process-based claim such as VAGUENESS or OVERBREADTH as the basis for invalidating a statute, rather than confront the substantive question of the legislature's power to enact it at all. Similarly, constitutional litigators often seek to link their constitutional theories with nonconstitutional claims, such as a claim based on a statute or a COMMON LAW tort. Posing alternative theories of recovery provides a judge with a less dramatic means of protecting a constitutional value while providing effective relief to the plaintiff. Of course, many such alternative theories of recovery are subject to modification by the legislature, but the short-term result is often indistinguishable from success of the constitutional claim.

Although much litigation strategy depends on a perception of the degree to which constitutional law is shaped by value judgments, constitutional lawyers also recognize the extent to which constitutional litigation shapes community values. The process of bringing a constitutional lawsuit is educational as well as remedial. It seeks to expose the judge to a set of facts and a legal reality that would ordinarily be far from his or her consciousness. It seeks to inform the public of the existence of a social problem that, even if not ultimately amenable to constitutional resolution, requires increased public attention. Viewed as a part of the process by which the interests of the politically powerless can be protected in a democracy, constitutional litigation provides a mechanism not only for classic remedial action but for a sharpening of the underlying social issues for ultimate political resolution. Thus, for example, although under current legal standards it is difficult to establish a violation of the constitutional right of a minority community to receive equal municipal services (discriminatory purpose, not merely disparate effect, must be proven), constitutional litigation provides a forum for the dramatization of unequal treatment as a first step to a political resolution. Similarly, although only the most optimistic believed that courts would actually stop the VIETNAM WAR because it was supposedly carried on in violation of Article 1, section 8, of the Constitution, the repeated presentation of the issue both shaped public perception of the war and helped pave the way for the passage of the War Powers Resolution which attempted to deal with the legal issue of undeclared war.

Two major constraints limit the use of constitutional litigation as an educational vehicle. First is the ethical obligation to refrain from presenting frivolous or inappropriate claims to a court. Judicial attention is a scarce national resource which must be rationed, and lawyers must be prudent in presenting claims that cannot win. In the absence of a good faith belief in the legal—as opposed to the moral—soundness of a claim, it should not be presented to a court. Moreover, even if a claim is sufficiently substantial to satisfy ethical considerations, tactical considerations often argue against presenting a weak claim for adjudication. Losing a constitutional case risks the enunciation of dangerous precedent and acts to legitimate the challenged activity. Thus, although constitutional litigation plays an educational as well as a remedial role, its educational role should be a by-product of a bona fide attempt to secure a legal remedy.

A significant dilemma in planning and executing litigation strategy in constitutional cases is posed by the potential for conflict between the best interest of a plaintiff and the furtherance of the cause that precipitated the case into court. For example, a plaintiff who has gone to court to vindicate a principle and who poses a powerful TEST CASE may be confronted with a settlement offer which, while advantageous to the plaintiff, leaves the legal issue unresolved. Constitutional lawyers, while recognizing this conflict, generally resolve it in favor of the plaintiff and recommend acceptance to their clients, who then make the final decision. Despite the recognition that the inter-

est of the client in a constitutional case should predominate over the advancement of the cause, a disturbing tendency exists on the part of both bench and bar to use a constitutional plaintiff as a convenient vehicle to trigger the enunciation of norms that may benefit society as a whole but which do little for the parties before the Court. William Marbury never did get his commission. (See MARBURY V. MADISON.)

Once a constitutional case is underway, three recurring tactical issues arise. Should immediate relief be sought, usually in the form of a preliminary INJUNCTION? Should the case be pursued as an abstract issue of law or should substantial resources be expended in developing the facts? And how broad a remedy should be sought? It is impossible to formulate even a general rule governing these three issues, except that attorneys with weak cases rarely seek preliminary injunctions and that issues of law should not be presented to a potentially hostile court in the absence of clearly established fact, given that a judge's freedom of action is greatest in determining the facts on an ambiguous record.

A parallel tactical issue defendants in a constitutional case face is whether to move to dismiss—and, thus, to assume the truth of the facts alleged in the complaint for the purposes of the motion—or to force plaintiffs to prove their facts by going to trial. Surprisingly, most defendants, in an effort to save time and resources, attempt dismissal motions, which require courts to rule on the theoretical validity of plaintiff's case without requiring plaintiff to establish the facts. Much constitutional law has been made in denying motions to dismiss and thus creating important legal precedents in cases where plaintiffs might have experienced difficulty in proving their allegations.

Finally, in presenting a constitutional case to a judge, a constitutional litigator will often seek to place it within one of three categories posing the least tension with democratic political theory in order to free the judge to exercise vigorous review. If the case involves a member of a DISCRETE AND INSULAR MINORITY, constitutional litigators will stress the inability of unpopular or disadvantaged minority groups to protect themselves within the traditional political process, thus invoking the special responsibility of courts to act as a bulwark against majoritarian overreaching. If the case involves significant political values, constitutional litigators will stress the responsibility of courts to guarantee the proper functioning of the democratic process. It is not antidemocratic, they argue, for a court to prevent the majority from refusing to permit the democratic process to function properly. If the case involves a "fundamental" value, like marriage or REPRODUCTIVE AUTONOMY, constitutional litigators will argue that the importance of such values warrants increased judicial protection. This third category involves the most controversial exercises of judicial power, because the selection of "fundamental" values appears subjective.

Ultimately, litigation strategy in constitutional cases, even at its most sophisticated, can exert only a relatively weak influence on the outcome. The adjudication of issues that impinge on deeply held values and in many other systems would be relegated solely to the political process is an inherently unpredictable phenomenon. No other area of law fits Tolstoy's vision of history so well as the claim of constitutional lawyers to be able to influence the ocean on which they most often bob like corks.

BURT NEUBORNE

Bibliography

COVER, ROBERT M. 1975 *Justice Accused: Anti-Slavery and the Judicial Process.* New Haven, Conn.: Yale University Press.

GREENBERG, JACK 1977 *Judicial Process and Social Change: Constitutional Litigation.* St. Paul, Minn.: West Publishing Co.

KLUGER, RICHARD 1975 *Simple Justice.* New York: Knopf.

NEUBORNE, BURT 1977 The Myth of Parity. *Harvard Law Review* 90:1105.

LIVINGSTON, HENRY BROCKHOLST
(1757–1823)

There is a modest puzzle regarding Henry Brockholst Livingston's more than sixteen years on the Supreme Court (1806–1823): why was he comparatively silent? Livingston, a New York Jeffersonian, was among the best qualified appointees ever named to the Court. Before his appointment to the New York Supreme Court in 1802, he was at the top of the legal profession, ranked as an equal of his frequent sparring mate, ALEXANDER HAMILTON. Livingston's opinions during his five years on the New York court demonstrated legal erudition, style, and wit. Some of his opinions are still required reading for law students. The New York reports indicate that Livingston had a constant urge to express his thoughts, and he was not only an extremely active dissenter but also constantly rendered SERIATIM OPINIONS. In his four years of New York judicial tenure, Livingston dissented twenty times, concurred on fourteen occasions, and delivered twenty-four seriatim opinions. Those statistics only begin to indicate the battle on the New York court, largely between Livingston and JAMES KENT, both of whom were first-rate jurists. The business of the New York court involved many significant matters but few constitutional questions. Livingston's dissent in *Hitchcock v. Aicken* (1803) argued that the FULL FAITH AND CREDIT clause should be interpreted broadly; ultimately, the MARSHALL COURT, including Livingston, agreed with this reasoning in *Mills v. Duryee* (1813).

In contrast to his active role on the New York court, Livingston was scarcely noticeable on the Marshall Court. In fifteen TERMS he dissented but three times and delivered only five CONCURRING OPINIONS. The fact that he had not shrunk from confronting some of the ablest judges in the country when on the New York court precludes any notion that he was overwhelmed by JOHN MARSHALL and associates. The difference in Livingston's roles on the state court and the Supreme Court is important largely for what it explains about the Marshall Court's constitutional jurisprudence. By the time of Livingston's appointment, Marshall's practice of having one Justice deliver a single opinion for the Court was settled. The Justices, moreover, willingly stifled their differences, save on questions of great moment, usually constitutional. Within this practice, the Justices' common values, regardless of party affiliation, normally made compromise possible. There are indications that Livingston initially had difficulty in adjusting to the ways of the Marshall Court. In the first few cases he heard, Livingston seemed particularly active in questioning counsel, as if he might have wished to dissent, but did not. Apparently, Livingston's policy preferences blended well with the Marshall Court's general mercantile orientation. While on the New York bench Livingston had served as a precursor for nineteenth-century instrumentalist judges who shaped the law to promote commercial development. In this respect, Livingston resembled a fellow Jeffersonian on the Court, WILLIAM JOHNSON. Because of the commercial atmosphere of his home community of Charleston, South Carolina, Johnson, like Livingston, had good reason for thinking as his brethren did on commercial questions. Johnson was even more nationalistic than Marshall. Unlike Johnson, however, THOMAS JEFFERSON apparently did not attempt to goad Livingston into expressing his differences as he had done while a state judge. Another reason that Livingston did not join Johnson and make plural the "first dissenter" may have been that Livingston got along with the rest of the Court much better than Johnson did. When

Livingston died, JOSEPH STORY's rich eulogy to him indicated how fondly he was remembered. Finally, Livingston was a ready adherent to precedent, as he had demonstrated on the New York bench. When a question was settled, Livingston was unlikely to challenge its resolutions, even obliquely. In short, Livingston was a good team player, and our constitutional jurisprudence may be poorer for it. A clear example of the consequences of Livingston's proclivity for compromise is seen in STURGES V. CROWNINSHIELD (1819), in which the Court invalidated a New York insolvent law of 1811 because it had been applied retroactively. On circuit, Livingston had emphatically sustained the same law in *Adams v. Storey* (1817); yet he proceeded to compromise in *Sturges.* It seems likely that Marshall did not wish to say in his opinion that the states had CONCURRENT POWER to pass bankruptcy or insolvency laws, but he did—probably in response to Livingston's urging. Livingston's main role on the Marshall Court and in the development of constitutional jurisprudence was that of a compromiser. His opinions, with few exceptions, are forgettable.

DONALD ROPER

Bibliography

DUNNE, GERALD T. 1969 Brockholst Livingston. In Leon Friedman and Fred L. Israel, eds., *The Justices of the United States Supreme Court.* New York: Chelsea House.
HASKINS, GEORGE LEE, and JOHNSON, HERBERT A. 1981 *Foundations of Power: John Marshall, 1801–1815,* volume II of Freund, Paul A., general editor, *The Oliver Wendell Holmes Devise History of the Supreme Court of the United States.* New York: Macmillan.

LIVINGSTON, ROBERT R., JR.
(1746–1813)

The son of a New York judge, Robert R. Livingston, Jr., was a member of the committees that drafted the DECLARATION OF INDEPENDENCE (which he regarded as premature and did not sign) and the ARTICLES OF CONFEDERATION. With JOHN JAY and GOUVERNEUR MORRIS he drafted the New York constitution of 1777. From 1777 to 1801 he was chancellor of New York. In 1788 he was chairman of the New York state convention where he vigorously supported RATIFICATION OF THE CONSTITUTION. He was later minister to France (1801–1804) and, with JAMES MONROE, negotiated the LOUISIANA PURCHASE TREATY. Livingston became a partner of inventor Robert Ful-

ton and secured a New York steamboat monopoly not broken until GIBBONS V. OGDEN (1824).

DENNIS J. MAHONEY

LIVINGSTON, WILLIAM
(1723–1790)

Governor William Livingston, poet, lawyer, and Revolutionary general, signed the Constitution as a New Jersey delegate to the CONSTITUTIONAL CONVENTION OF 1787. Unable to attend regularly, Livingston was not active in the debates; but he was influential in securing New Jersey's early and unanimous ratification. He was the father of Justice BROCKHOLST LIVINGSTON and the guardian of young ALEXANDER HAMILTON.

DENNIS J. MAHONEY

LOAN ASSOCIATION v. TOPEKA
20 Wall. (87 U.S.) 655 (1875)

The Supreme Court has frequently resorted to HIGHER LAW doctrine to buttress an opinion, but only twice in its history, in TERRETT V. TAYLOR (1815) and in this case, has it relied exclusively on the higher law as the ground for decision. An 8–1 Court, in an opinion by Justice SAMUEL F. MILLER, held unconstitutional a Kansas statute that authorized the city of Topeka to issue public bonds, payable by taxes, for the benefit of a private company that built iron bridges. In the absence of some usable clause of the Constitution, Miller relied on judicially implied limitations on government power "which grow out of the essential nature of all free governments" and protect individual rights "without which the SOCIAL COMPACT could not exist." Topeka and the state legislature had believed that attracting a bridge company promoted public prosperity as did a railroad or a public utility, but because the Court saw only an improper exercise of the tax power "to aid private enterprise and build up private fortunes," it called the statute "a robbery" of the public. Taxation, the Could held, can be exercised only for a public use or public purpose. Justice NATHAN CLIFFORD, the sole dissenter, believed that JUDICIAL REVIEW should be exercised only when the Constitution imposed a prohibition either express or necessarily implied, but not when the Court believed that a legislature had violated "natural justice" or "a general latent spirit" supposedly underlying the Constitution.

LEONARD W. LEVY

LOCHNER v. NEW YORK
198 U.S. 45 (1905)

Lochner v. New York, a landmark decision of 1905, has been discredited by the evolution of constitutional law. Justice RUFUS W. PECKHAM, writing for a 5–4 majority of the Supreme Court, invalidated a New York state statute forbidding employment in bakeries for more than sixty hours a week or ten hours a day. The rationale for the Court's opinion was that the statute interfered with the FREEDOM OF CONTRACT and thus the FOURTEENTH AMENDMENT's right to liberty afforded both the employer and the employee. The Court stated that under the statute, viewed as a labor law, the state had no reasonable ground for interfering with liberty by determining the hours of labor. Seen as a health law, the statute affected only the bakers and not the public. Accordingly, the Court concluded that the law was neither necessary nor appropriate to accomplish its health objective. Moreover, the Court was of the view that if the law were upheld for the bakers, laws designed to protect other workers would also have to be upheld. In either case, said the Court, the statute was an illegal interference with the right to contract.

Justice OLIVER WENDELL HOLMES, in an important and historic dissent, concluded that the legislature had the power to enact a law that interfered with full freedom to contract and that the personal biases of judges could not justify declaring a statute unconstitutional. Said Justice Holmes: "The constitution is not intended to embody a particular economic theory," an obvious reference to the laissez-faire view then widely accepted. Holmes's view was that a law interfered with the Fourteenth Amendment's guarantee of liberty only if "a rational and fair man necessarily would admit that the statute proposed would infringe fundamental principles of our people and our law." The dissent's view was that the statute, viewed either as a health or a labor law, did not violate these principles.

Justice JOHN MARSHALL HARLAN also dissented, arguing with Justice Holmes that the wisdom of the statute or of a particular economic theory is judicially irrelevant. Citing studies that showed the hazards of bakery work, Harlan noted that legislatures in many states had enacted legislation dealing with the number of hours in a work day. Said Justice Harlan: "[I]t is enough for the determination of this case, and it is enough for this Court, to know that the question is one about which there is room for debate and for at least honest difference of opinion." If there are

"weighty substantial" reasons for enacting a law it ought "to be the end of [the] case, for the State is not amenable to the judiciary, in respect of its legislative enactments, unless such enactments are plainly, palpably, beyond all question, inconsistent with the Constitution of the United States."

The Court implicitly overruled the *Lochner* result in BUNTING V. OREGON (1917), but for three decades the decision influenced the Court as it scrutinized carefully and often struck down economic regulations as violations of SUBSTANTIVE DUE PROCESS. It was not until the mid-1930s, in the wake of the Court-packing furor and especially the Court's approval of the constitutionality of the National Labor Relations Act in *National Labor Relations Board v. Jones & Laughlin Steel Corporation* (1937), that judicial intervention in economic legislation declined. Although *Lochner* is now discredited, its focus upon substantive due process and FUNDAMENTAL RIGHTS has emerged in cases dealing with both contraception and abortion, namely GRISWOLD V. CONNECTICUT (1965) and ROE V. WADE (1973).

WILLIAM B. GOULD

LOCKE, JOHN
(1631–1704)

John Locke, the English philosopher of enlightenment, formulated the basic doctrines that influenced the American Framers of 1787. While his famous *Second Treatise*, "Of Civil Government" (1688), alludes to various traditional ways to limit governments, it sets forth an effectual new way, later called liberal CONSTITUTIONALISM. That comprised a sphere of individual liberty, fenced by a right to property, and fixed government, constituted by a majority's consent. Constitutional or civil government is to be representative, responsible, and limited, with powers separated as well as effective, and it is to be kept to its FUNDAMENTAL LAW by a perpetual threat of popular rebellion.

The first of Locke's *Two Treatises of Government* rebutted Robert Filmer's contention that monarchy exists by divine right, derived from the fatherly authority of Adam and of God. Locke thrust at paternalism, which he regarded as the natural foundation of uncivil government and of inhumane civilization in general. Mankind has inclined unthinkingly to obey fathers, who grew to be patriarchs of families and chiefs of tribes, and finally to be oppressive kings and nobles upheld by wealth, power, and the servile flatteries of traditional faiths. The *Letter concerning Toleration* (1689) espoused freedom of conscience and SEPARATION OF CHURCH AND STATE. Locke tried to remove religion from the magistrate's armory and to remake churches into voluntary associations keeping watch on government and on one another. The *Letter* counsels public toleration of religion, but as a thing merely private, and only of civil religions willing to tolerate other faiths and to obey the civil powers. In other writings Locke advocated a reasonable Christianity and a worldly and private education, and he explained human understanding prosaically, as reliably derived from sense impressions rather than from intuitions or divinations.

The first chapters of the *Second Treatise* set forth the famous doctrine of individualism: human beings are naturally free, equal, and occupied with securing themselves, not naturally subordinate to a superior or oriented to something noble or true above themselves. They are not subject to fathers or mothers so soon as they can "shift for themselves," or to husbands or wives if they no longer consent to be spouses, or to some gentleman or lord in his vineyard or estate. On the contrary, they have a natural right to acquire the means of life, to obtain the fruits of their own labor. Locke devised a private right of unlimited acquisition which implicitly indicts any leisured class, authorizes opportunity for the "industrious and rational," and provides powerful incentives for work, invention, and production. Locke was the philosophic father of capitalism, his plan whereby freedom of enterprise produces economic growth and the means of collective security. The profits of entrepreneurs, which Locke defended as incentives, occasioned the later attacks on capitalism as unjust and LIMITED GOVERNMENT as callously narrow.

The central chapters of the *Second Treatise* are Locke's prescription for public powers that will serve the people instead of exploiting them. He insisted upon powerful institutions, what THE FEDERALIST was to call effective or energetic government. A condition without government, Locke eventually maintained, is "very unsafe, very insecure," and people are "driven" to establish a LEGISLATIVE POWER to define laws, judges to apply them, and an executive to enforce them. Despite this agreement with the authoritarian Thomas Hobbes, Locke insisted that raising a state is easy compared to domesticating it. For domesticated or civil government the key is constitutionalism—government according to a man-made fundamental law agreeable to a majority. In particular, the supreme power, which Locke defines as a lawmaking power, is to be set up with a majority's consent (immediate or eventual, express or tacit). This supreme legislative power, however, is also and primarily to be shaped by Locke's enlightened prescriptions for a legislative limited, conditional, and rather democratic. Every actual legislature has by right only this legislative power, the natural CONSTITUTION behind any written constitution, and a consenting majority is to be supposed an enlightened majority. The legislature must aim to preserve individual rights, to govern by declared laws, not to impose TAXATION WITHOUT REPRESENTATION, and not to delegate its powers. Also, a legislature must be broadly representative of "populous" places filled with "wealth and inhabitants." Locke required an assembly of "deputies" of the people, while cautiously but pervasively impugning an aristocratic senate or house.

Locke provided for an executive power that is (unlike a monarch) subordinate to law and yet (like a monarch) able to act beyond law when public necessities require. The executive enforces law, unites the nation's forces for FOREIGN AFFAIRS (Locke's "federative" power), includes the judiciary, and remains, unlike the legislature, permanently on duty. For purposes of lawmaking Locke subordinated the executive to the legislature and attacked executives (such as the British king) who shared in lawmaking. Locke's argument led discreetly toward government by a responsible ministry, a dependence on a popular legislature that was rejected when the American Founders devised the Presidency, and a constitutional monarchy, which is only a "head of the republic," "a badge or emblem" representing the people. Still, executive power is extended by political necessity. In extraordinary situations, such as civil war, executive "prerogative" may extend to actions without authorization of law or even in violation of fundamental law, as when ABRAHAM LINCOLN in 1861 raised troops and monies before Congress had assembled. *Salus populi suprema lex est* is the Two Treatises' motto: the people's benefit is the supreme law. Locke repeated this maxim, which shows the limits of constitutional law, as he urged a king to reapportion an oligarchic house into a representative legislature.

The *Second Treatise* ends by insisting on an extraconstitutional RIGHT OF REVOLUTION, to secure a constitutional order against tyranny and also to help bring about popular constitutionalism. While executive prerogative may extend to reform, it is not to include a "godlike" prince with "a distinct and separate interest," a despot who violates the fiduciary "trust" of office, a conqueror, a usurper, a tyrannical king, or a clique of the rich. Such excesses make power revert to the people, who may set up anew their legislature.

Locke repeatedly called this doctrine new. Each of the last six chapters ends by holding up to governors and peoples the new right of popular rebellion. In effect, Locke justified rebellion against every regime not a constitutional republic, and justified "revolution" of traditional beliefs inimical to individualism and popular government, that is, of almost all traditional beliefs.

The American Framers accepted Locke's broad framework of NATURAL RIGHTS and civil government, while varying details of the Constitution in accord with the cautious versions of MONTESQUIEU and his followers, David Hume and Sir WILLIAM BLACKSTONE. Fearing a political zealotry that might rival the old religious wars, Montesquieu, in his *Spirit of the Laws* (1748), abstained from Locke's fiery language of natural and popular liberty. His modified Lockeanism would allow forms and structures to vary with circumstance, make the judiciary a third separate power, and allow a senate of the successful and wealthy. Montesquieu also sought to introduce humane civilization less by rebellion and more by the spread of commerce and by changes in the private law of contract and inheritance.

ROBERT K. FAULKNER

Bibliography

HARTZ, LOUIS 1955 *The Liberal Tradition in America.* New York: Harcourt, Brace.
STRAUSS, LEO 1953 *Natural Right and History.* Chicago: University of Chicago Press.
VILE, M. J. C. 1967 *Constitutionalism and the Separation of Powers.* Oxford: Clarendon Press.

LODGE, HENRY CABOT
(1850–1924)

A Harvard-trained lawyer who also earned the Ph.D. degree in history, Henry Cabot Lodge was elected three times to the House of Representatives and six times to the United States Senate from Massachusetts. He was a close friend of President THEODORE ROOSEVELT and a national leader of the Republican party.

During his second term in Congress Lodge introduced a bill that would have provided for federal supervision of elections in order to protect the VOTING RIGHTS of black citizens in southern states. But he was wary of such Progressive innovations as women's suffrage and the DIRECT ELECTION of senators. He advocated the constant expansion of the United States through the annexation of Hawaii and other island TERRITORIES, and he supported the Spanish-American War because it promised to lead to annexation of the Philippine Islands. During Roosevelt's administration Lodge was a leading congressional supporter of the Panama Canal project.

In 1918, Lodge used his position as chairman of the Senate Foreign Relations Committee to lead the fight against the Treaty of Versailles. He based his opposition to the League of Nations, a key element of the treaty, on the unconstitutionality of commiting American military forces to combat without the express consent of Congress.

Lodge was known during his lifetime as "the scholar in politics." His vision of an American constitutionalism that was both conservative and nationalistic was presented, in part, in his biographies of GEORGE WASHINGTON, ALEXANDER HAMILTON, and DANIEL WEBSTER.

DENNIS J. MAHONEY

Bibliography

GARRATY, JOHN A. 1965 *Henry Cabot Lodge: A Biography.* New York: Knopf.

LOEWE v. LAWLOR
208 U.S. 274 (1908)

This case fits a pattern of antilabor decisions that supported INJUNCTIONS against trade unions and struck down maximum hours acts, minimum wage acts, and acts prohibiting YELLOW DOG CONTRACTS. In *Loewe*, the Court, while crippling secondary boycotts, held that unions were subject to the antitrust laws and therefore were civilly liable for triple damages to compensate for injuries inflicted by their restraints on INTERSTATE COMMERCE.

Loewe originated in an attempt by the United Hatters Union, AFL, to organize a manufacturer of hats in Danbury, Connecticut. Most hat firms in the country were unionized. The few nonunion firms sweated their workers and were able to undersell unionized competitors, threatening their survival as well as the jobs of their unionized labor. Loewe's firm refused to negotiate a union contract and defeated a strike. The union retaliated with a secondary boycott, a refusal by the national membership of the AFL to buy Loewe's hats or patronize retailers who sold them. Loewe sued the union under the SHERMAN ANTITRUST ACT after the boycott resulted in a substantial loss of orders. The union demurred to the charges, admitting that it had engaged in the boycott but alleging that it had not violated the antitrust law, because that law did not cover the activities of trade unions and because the boycott in this case was not a conspiracy in restraint of commerce among the states. Invoking the DOCTRINE of the Sugar Trust Case (UNITED STATES V. E. C. KNIGHT CO., 1895) that manufacturing is a purely local activity, the union claimed that neither it nor the manufacturer engaged in interstate commerce. Although Loewe's hats, once manufactured, were shipped to purchasing retailers in twenty-one states, the union argued that it did not interfere with the actual transportation across state lines and that any restraint on interstate commerce resulting from the boycott was, according to the Sugar Trust Case, remote and indirect.

Overruling a lower federal court decision in favor of the union, the Supreme Court, in a unanimous opinion by Chief Justice MELVILLE W. FULLER, for the first time held that the Sherman Act applied to union activities; that a secondary boycott conducted across state lines is a conspiracy in restraint of interstate commerce; and that even if the restraint were remote and indirect, the Sherman Act applied because it covered "every" combination in the form of a trust "or otherwise" in restraint of interstate commerce. In 1911, however, the Court embraced the RULE OF REASON, enabling it subsequently to find that corporations, not unions, might engage in reasonable restraints; that is, the act did not prohibit all restraints except by unions. In *Loewe*, however, the Court construed the act broadly, even to the point of using the STREAM OF COMMERCE DOCTRINE to show the scope of the commerce power. There is no evidence, however, that Congress, when adopting the Sherman Act, intended to cover union activities.

The case presents the phenomenon of a labor union being held within the terms of an antitrust act and contrasting opinions of the Court. In the Sugar Trust Case the Court held a ninety-eight percent monopoly not to violate the act because manufacturing is local and any effect upon or relationship with interstate commerce is necessarily indirect; here, though, a small hatmakers' union came within the act because its boycott was interstate, despite its having done nothing to control the price or transportation of the product of a manufacturer. Moreover, the decision in this case came one week after the decision in ADAIR V. UNITED STATES (1908), where the Court declared that there is "no connection between interstate commerce and membership in a labor organization," as it struck down an act of Congress prohibiting the use of yellow-dog contracts by railroads against railroad workers engaged in interstate commerce. If *Adair* correctly invalidated the attempt by Congress to protect railroad workers under the commerce power, then a week later the Court should have decided that

Congress under the same commerce power cannot, via the Sherman Act, reach an admittedly indirect relationship between a hatters' union and interstate commerce. Both the legislative history of the antitrust law and the Sugar Trust and *Adair* precedents opposed the decision in the Danbury Hatters' Case. Following the Court's decision, a triple-damages suit against the union in the lower federal court resulted in a fine of $252,000. The Danbury Hatters went unorganized, hatmakers everywhere suffered, and unionization everywhere was thwarted to an inestimable extent by the threat of Sherman Act suits. *Loewe* is one of the major cases on the subject of LABOR AND THE CONSTITUTION.

LEONARD W. LEVY

Bibliography
LIEBERMAN, ELIAS 1960 *Unions Before the Bar.* Pages 56–70. New York: Harper & Row.

LONG HAUL–SHORT HAUL DISCRIMINATION

Long haul–short haul discrimination was one of the most notorious abuses practiced by railroads in the late nineteenth and early twentieth centuries. The practice involved charging a higher rate for a short haul that was included within a longer haul over the same line. Although Congress outlawed this discriminatory practice in Section 4 of the INTERSTATE COMMERCE ACT (1887), the Supreme Court effectively nullified that section in *ICC v. Alabama Midland Railway Company* (1897). The Court rested its decision on the commission's power to grant exemptions if the long and short hauls did not occur "under substantially similar circumstances and conditions." Sufficient differences existed between hauls to justify departures from Section 4's prohibition. In 1910 Congress revived the prohibition by reenacting the long haul–short haul clause minus the "similar circumstances" clause. Carriers were now forbidden to charge higher rates for shorter (included) hauls *regardless* of different conditions, although the commission was still authorized to make exceptions. A unanimous Supreme Court sustained this provision to *United States v. Atchison, Topeka, & Santa Fe Railway Co.* (1914).

DAVID GORDON

Bibliography
SHARFMAN, ISAIAH L. 1931–1937 *The Interstate Commerce Commission.* 4 Vols. New York: Commonwealth Fund.

*LONGSHOREMEN'S ASSOCIATION
v. ALLIED INTERNATIONAL*

See: Labor and the Constitution

LOOSE CONSTRUCTION

See: Broad Construction

LOPEZ v. UNITED STATES
373 U.S. 427 (1963)

The Supreme Court held that a government agent may surreptitiously record a conversation with a criminal suspect and use the recording to corroborate his testimony. Lopez, a tavern keeper, offered a bribe to a federal tax agent who thereupon recorded the conversation. The Court refused to exclude the recording. Because the agent was on the premises with Lopez's consent, there was no TRESPASS and therefore no violation of the FOURTH AMENDMENT. Because the agent could testify to the conversation, he could use the recording to corroborate his testimony.

HERMAN SCHWARTZ

LORETTO v. TELEPROMPTER MANHATTAN CATV CORP.
458 U.S. 419 (1982)

The Supreme Court in the modern era has used an interest balancing analysis to determine whether government regulation amounts to a TAKING OF PROPERTY for which JUST COMPENSATION must be paid. Here a New York law required landlords to allow cable television companies to install equipment on the landlords' property in order to serve tenants. The Supreme Court, 6–3, held that this governmental authorization of a "permanent physical occupation" of property was, of itself, a "taking"; in such a case no interest balancing need be done.

KENNETH L. KARST

LOTTERY CASE

See: *Champion v. Ames*

LOUISIANA PURCHASE TREATY
(1803)

The Louisiana Purchase Treaty (April 30, 1803) provided for the cession of the French province of Louisiana to the United States for approximately $11,250,000. France had reacquired Louisiana from Spain as part of Napoleon's plan to reestablish a French empire in the New World. The United States had tolerated weak Spanish control at the mouth of the Mississippi, especially since the Pinckney Treaty of 1795 gave Americans the right to navigate the river and use the port of New Orleans; but Louisiana in the hands of Napoleonic France threatened the security, commerce, and growth of the country. President THOMAS JEFFERSON sought a diplomatic resolution, hoping to obtain from France at least the continuation of Spanish guarantees and, at best, the cession of New Orleans together with the Floridas, if France possessed them. In a surprising about-face, however, Napoleon renounced the whole of Louisiana.

The acquisition of Louisiana—some 828,000 square miles, virtually doubling the land area of the United States—challenged the government in several ways. First, the boundaries were obscure. Was Texas included? Or West Florida? Jefferson made pretensions to both. Article III of the treaty said that the inhabitants should be incorporated in the Union and enjoy all the rights of citizens of the United States. Unfortunately, the Constitution Jefferson and his party were pledged to construe strictly made no provision for acquiring foreign territory, much less admitting that territory and its people into the Union. The treaty, Jefferson declared, was "an act beyond the Constitution" and ought to be sanctioned retroactively by amendment. He drafted a 375-word amendment. When congressmen objected that Louisiana might be lost because of constitutional scruples, Jefferson acquiesced in silent expansion of the TREATY POWER even as he reiterated his belief that it made the Constitution "a blank paper by construction." (The Supreme Court, in AMERICAN INSURANCE COMPANY V. CANTER, 1828, later upheld the authority to acquire and govern territory under the treaty and WAR POWERS.) The Senate ratified the treaty on October 20, 1803. Two months later the American flag was raised at New Orleans.

Government of the territory also raised constitutional difficulties. The Enabling Act, in October, vested the President and his agents with full powers, civil and military. Querulous Federalists said it made Jefferson "as despotic as the Grand Turk." The Louisiana Government Act six months later created the Orleans Territory in populous lower Louisiana, extended to it many federal laws, and vested authority in a strong governor and weak legislative council, both appointed by the President. In the view of the President and Congress the rights of self-government, for which Creole Louisianans were unprepared, should be introduced gradually as the territory became "Americanized" in its population, habits, and institutions. The Louisianans demanded immediate statehood. Although this was denied, Congress in March 1805 introduced the second stage of territorial government, including a representative assembly, more or less on the plan of the NORTHWEST ORDINANCE. Five years later the statehood commitment of the treaty was met. The American theory of an expanding union of equal self-governing states thus survived its severest test.

MERRILL D. PETERSON

(SEE ALSO: *Theories of the Union.*)

Bibliography

BROWN, EVERETT S. 1920 *The Constitutional History of the Louisiana Purchase, 1803–1812.* Berkeley: University of California Press.

LOUISVILLE JOINT STOCK LAND BANK v. RADFORD
295 U.S. 555 (1935)

During the Great Depression of the 1930s foreclosure or default on payments threatened to extinguish the small, independent farmer who owned his own property. Congress, exercising its BANKRUPTCY POWER, came to his rescue by passing the FRAZIER-LEMKE (Farm Mortgage) ACT of 1934. The act provided that bankrupt farmers might require a federal bankruptcy court to stay farm mortgage payments for a period of five years, during which time the debtor retained possession of his property and paid his creditor a reasonable rental sum fixed by the court, and at the end of the five years the debtor could buy the property at its appraised value. Because the act operated retroactively it took away rights of the mortgagee, but the CONTRACT CLAUSE limits only the states, not Congress. In the face of that clause the Court had sustained a similar state act in HOME BUILDING & LOAN ASS'N V. BLAISDELL (1934). Nevertheless Justice LOUIS D. BRANDEIS, for a unanimous Court, ruled the act of Congress void. He distinguished *Blaisdell* as less drastic: the statute there had stayed proceed-

ings for two, not five, years. In effect Brandeis read the contract clause into the Fifth Amendment's DUE PROCESS clause, holding that the bankruptcy power of Congress must be exercised subject to SUBSTANTIVE DUE PROCESS. The statute deprived persons of property without due process by not allowing the mortgagee to retain a lien on mortgaged property. The oddest feature of this strained opinion is that it did not mention due process; Brandeis referred only to the clause that prohibited the taking of private property for a public purpose without just compensation, though the government took nothing and sought by the statute to preserve private property. The Court retreated from its position in WRIGHT V. VINTON BRANCH BANK (1937).

LEONARD W. LEVY

LOUISVILLE, NEW ORLEANS & TEXAS PACIFIC RAILWAY v. MISSISSIPPI
133 U.S. 587 (1890)

A 7–2 Supreme Court held here that a state might lawfully require railroads to provide "equal but separate accommodations" without burdening INTERSTATE COMMERCE. The majority distinguished HALL V. DeCUIR (1878) because the Louisiana Supreme Court had held in that case that the state act prohibiting SEGREGATION unlawfully regulated interstate commerce. Here, the Mississippi Supreme Court had said that the Mississippi statute applied solely to INTRASTATE COMMERCE. Moreover, this case did not involve a refusal of accommodations (as in *DeCuir*), so no question of "personal rights" arose. Justice JOHN MARSHALL HARLAN, dissenting, relied on *DeCuir*.

DAVID GORDON

LOVELL v. CITY OF GRIFFIN
303 U.S. 444 (1938)

A municipal ordinance prohibited the distribution of circulars or any other literature within Griffin without a permit from the city manager. Chief Justice CHARLES EVANS HUGHES, for a unanimous Court, held the Griffin ordinance unconstitutional. The ordinance provided no standards to guide the city manager's decision. To vest an official with absolute discretion to issue or deny a permit was an unconstitutional prior restraint that violated the FIRST AMENDMENT. Because the ordinance was INVALID ON ITS FACE, Lovell was entitled to distribute her literature without seeking a permit, and to challenge the ordinance's validity when she was charged with its violation.

RICHARD E. MORGAN

LOVETT, UNITED STATES v.
328 U.S. 303 (1946)

In an opinion by Justice HUGO L. BLACK the Court declared unconstitutional a rider to an appropriation act of 1943 which provided that no salary or other compensation could be paid after November 1943 to three specified employees of the executive branch who had been branded as "subversives" by the HOUSE COMMITTEE ON UN-AMERICAN ACTIVITIES. Congress, Black wrote, had passed a BILL OF ATTAINDER, prohibited by Article I, section 9.

Justices FELIX FRANKFURTER and STANLEY F. REED rejected Black's bill of attainder analysis; but both agreed that the employees were entitled to recover money for the value of services rendered to the government, even after Congress had refused to disburse money to pay their salaries.

MICHAEL E. PARRISH

LOVING v. VIRGINIA
388 U.S. 1 (1967)

For more than a decade following its decision in BROWN v. BOARD OF EDUCATION (1954) the Supreme Court avoided direct confrontation with the constitutionality of MISCEGENATION laws. In *Loving*, the Court faced the issue squarely and held invalid a Virginia law forbidding any interracial marriage including a white partner. The decision is a major precedent in the area of RACIAL DISCRIMINATION as well as the foundation of the modern "freedom to marry." (See MARRIAGE AND THE CONSTITUTION.)

A black woman and a white man, Virginia residents, went to the DISTRICT OF COLUMBIA to be married, and returned to live in Virginia. They were convicted of violating the Racial Integrity Act and given one-year prison sentences, suspended on condition that they leave Virginia. The Virginia appellate courts modified the sentences but upheld the constitutionality of the law. The Supreme Court unanimously re-versed; Chief Justice EARL WARREN wrote for the Court.

Citing the SUSPECT CLASSIFICATION language of *Korematsu v. United States* (1944) (see JAPANESE AMERICAN CASES), Warren said that a "heavy burden of justification" must be carried by a state seeking to sustain any racial classification. The fact that the law punished both the white and black partners to a marriage did not relieve the state of that burden. The law's announced goal of "racial integrity" was promoted only selectively. A white was prohibited from marrying any nonwhite except the descendants of Pocahantas; a black and an Asian, for example, could lawfully marry. The law's obvious goal was the maintenance of white supremacy; it had no legitimate purpose independent of racial discrimination and thus violated the EQUAL PROTECTION clause. PACE V. ALABAMA (1883) was assumed to be overruled.

The Court's opinion also rested on an alternative ground: the statute violated SUBSTANTIVE DUE PROCESS, by interfering with "the freedom to marry." Quoting from the STERILIZATION case, SKINNER V. OKLAHOMA (1942), Chief Justice Warren called marriage "one of the 'basic civil rights of man,' fundamental to our very existence and survival." (See ZABLOCKI V. REDHAIL, 1978; FREEDOM OF INTIMATE ASSOCIATION.)

Justice POTTER STEWART, concurring, merely repeated his earlier statement in *McLaughlin v. Florida* (1964) that a state could never make an act's criminality depend on the race of the actor.

KENNETH L. KARST

LOYALTY OATH

A mild form of loyalty oath is embedded in the Constitution itself. The President must swear (or affirm): "that I will faithfully execute the office of President of the United States, and will to the best of my ability, preserve, protect and defend the constitution of the United States." And Article VI, in conjunction with the supremacy clause, requires that members of Congress, state legislators, and "all executive and judicial officers, both of the United States and of the several states, shall be bound by oath or affirmation, to support this constitution." These are usually called affirmative oaths, in contrast to negative oaths in which oath-takers are required to abjure certain beliefs, words, or acts. In their most searching form, negative oaths probe the past as well as the future.

In Article VI, the constitutional oath of support is immediately followed by the proscription of any religious test for holding office. Loyalty oaths, called test oaths, were rife in an age of warring faiths defended by princes. They tested orthodoxy of belief and thus loyalty to the sovereign. Henry VIII launched Anglo-American constitutional practice on a sea of oaths, whose chief purpose was to root out followers of the pope of Rome. The Stuart kings exacted oaths from the first settlers, and the settlers in turn invoked them against each other. When George Calvert, the Roman Catholic first Lord Baltimore, attempted to settle in Virginia, he was confronted with an oath that he could not take. He perforce made the hard voyage back to England; his successors got their own grant to what became Maryland and promptly imposed an oath pledging fidelity to themselves.

Wary though they became of oaths with a religious content, those who made our Revolution, as well as those who resisted it, routinely exacted political loyalty oaths from military and civilians under their control. When one occupying force displaced the other, it could become a matter of life and liberty to have one's name on the wrong roster. At the same time, there was room for claims of duress and duplicity. BENJAMIN FRANKLIN expressed with his usual pithiness what was doubtless a shared cynicism when he wrote in 1776: "I have never regarded oaths otherwise than as the last recourse of liars."

One might have thought that the Framers, with revolutionary excesses fresh in their memories, meant the constitutional oaths to be exclusive of any others; but when the Civil War came, loyalty oaths again became ubiquitous. In the Confederacy, oaths were linked to the passes routinely required for any travel. Of more gravity, taking an oath was often for captives and hostile civilians the only alternative to rotting in prison or starving. The multiplicity of oaths and the pressure to yield to them resulted in their becoming unreliable indicia of loyalty. Union authorities were impelled to create a bureaucracy to interrogate oath-takers, thus anticipating modern LOYALTY-SECURITY PROGRAMS.

President ABRAHAM LINCOLN favored relatively mild oaths pledging only future loyalty. The sterner Congress fashioned the "ironclad" test oath that required denials of past conduct that secessionists could not possibly make. Those oaths barred even repentant rebels from government and the professions. The Supreme Court plausibly characterized such oaths as legislative punishment, and declared them BILLS OF ATTAINDER, in the TEST OATH CASES (1867).

Little was heard of loyalty oaths in World War I. After that war, many states singled out teachers for loyalty oaths; but they were only affirmative oaths on the constitutional model, repugnant chiefly because of the mistrust implicit in demanding them.

The waves of anticommunist sentiment that subsided only during the World War II alliance with Russia led to a new proliferation of oaths that penalized membership in subversive organizations (sometimes specifying the Communist party) and advocacy or support of violent overthrow of governments.

All this came to a boil in the tormented Cold War-McCarthy era, when oaths old and new, state and federal, were combined with loyalty-security programs to purge communist influences from public employment and licensed occupations.

When oath cases came before the Court in the 1950s, it first sustained the constitutionality of elaborate oaths, requiring only that communist affiliations must be with knowledge of illegal ends (WIEMAN V. UPDEGRAFF, 1952), and suggesting that an employee must have an opportunity for an explanatory hearing (*Nostrand v. Little*, 1960). But in the 1960s, when the tide of public opinion turned against the excesses of the 1950s, the Court turned too. In half a dozen cases, of which the climactic one was KEYISHIAN V. BOARD OF REGENTS (1967), the Court found oaths that were barely distinguishable from those it had upheld in the 1950s to be void for vagueness or overbreadth. The majority opinions paraded an alarming catalog of possible dilemmas that teachers in particular could not escape and overwhelmed the expostulations of dissenters that the Court had created a "whimsical straw man" who was "not only grim but Grimm." For good measure, the Court, in UNITED STATES V. BROWN (1965), unsheathed the bill of attainder weapon of 1867 to strike down an oath that would exclude a former communist from any office in a labor union.

Such successes against negative oaths emboldened teachers and other public servants who resented having essentially affirmative oaths directed at them. But variants of the Article VI oath to support the Constitution were uniformly upheld. The capstone case was *Cole v. Richardson* (1972). There the Court, while reaffirming in generous FIRST AMENDMENT terms the 1960s cases, found no fault in an obligation first to support and defend the constitutions of the United States and the Commonwealth of Massachusetts and, second, to oppose their violent overthrow. The second clause, Chief Justice WARREN E. BURGER wrote, "does not expand the obligation of the first; it simply makes clear the application of the first clause to a particular issue. Such repetition, whether for emphasis or cadence, seems to be the wont of authors of oaths." He added in a footnote that "The time may come when the value of oaths in routine public employment will be thought not 'worth the candle' for all the division of opinion they engender." Justice THURGOOD MARSHALL, arguing in partial dissent that the second clause should be repudiated, reflected the persisting division between willing and unwilling oath-takers when he wrote, understatedly, that "Loyalty oaths do not have a very pleasant history in this country."

The fear that hellfire would follow a false oath must have faded since the seventeenth century. Nowadays public exposure, and a perjury prosecution, are the serious sanctions. Compulsory oath-taking is welcome to some, a matter of indifference to others, an offense to conscience for a few. A notable instance of a loyalty oath that hit the wrong targets occurred at the University of California in 1949–1952. When the university regents, after prolonged and wounding controversy, insisted on their power to impose a noncommunist oath, twenty-six members of the faculty refused to take it and were ejected. They won a pyrrhic victory in the California Supreme Court, which held that the regents' oath had been supplanted by an oath required of all state employees, but that the statewide oath somehow did not contravene a state constitutional prohibition of any test oath beyond the constitutional oath of support. Some of the nonsigners in time returned; one became president of the university and so did the historian of the episode, who called it "a futile interlude."

RALPH S. BROWN

Bibliography

GARDNER, DAVID P. 1967 *The California Oath Controversy.* Berkeley and Los Angeles: University of California Press.

HYMAN, HAROLD M. 1959 *To Try Men's Souls: Loyalty Tests in American History.* Berkeley and Los Angeles: University of California Press.

SAGER, ALAN M. 1972 The Impact of Supreme Court Loyalty Oath Decisions. *American University Law Review* 22:39–78.

LOYALTY-SECURITY PROGRAMS

This hyphenated phrase refers chiefly to the measures that were taken under Presidents HARRY S. TRUMAN and DWIGHT D. EISENHOWER to exclude from public employment, and from defense industries, persons who were believed to pose risks to national security. Because the gravest threat to security was believed to flow from world communism, loyalty and security programs were designed almost entirely to counter communist influence and penetration.

In earlier periods of tension attendant upon wars, LOYALTY OATHS were the preferred device for separating the loyal from the disloyal. If oaths were taken seriously, they were self-enforcing. But when necessity or duplicity led to bales of unreliable oaths, the authorities responded by empowering officials to go behind the oaths with investigations and to make their own judgments. Such procedures, usually under military control and untrammeled by judicial control, were widespread during the Civil War and Reconstruction.

World War I was distinguished by the overzealous prying of the American Protective League and other amateurs who were given extraordinary aid and comfort by the Department of Justice. In World War II the military departments, both determined to avoid the excesses of the crusade against the Kaiser, effectively centralized loyalty screening. They emerged with a minimum of criticism. After the war, the Soviet Union abruptly came to be viewed as enemy rather than ally. The insecurities of the postwar world aroused mistrust and anxiety. President Truman, aiming to forestall harsher congressional action, launched a new kind of program with his EXECUTIVE ORDER 9835 of March 21, 1947.

The Truman loyalty program covered all civilian employees. The Department of Defense had its own program for the armed services. Defense and the Atomic Energy Commission had programs for employees of defense contractors. The Coast Guard screened maritime workers. A few states developed systematic programs of their own. Many millions thus became subject to proceedings that sought to establish whether, in the language of E.O. 9835, there were "reasonable grounds" for a belief that they were disloyal (softened in 1951 to require only a finding of "reasonable doubt" as to loyalty). In 1953 President Eisenhower's Executive Order 10450 replaced the Truman program. It required employment to be "clearly consistent with the interests of the national security." That standard remains in effect.

All of these programs worked from personal histories supplied by the employee (or applicant) backed up by investigative reports. If "derogatory information" led to a tentative adverse judgment, that was usually the end for an applicant's chances of employment. But an incumbent could have the benefit of formal charges, a hearing, and review. The trouble was that the investigations ranged widely into associations, opinions, and flimsy appraisals. The sources of none of these were accessible to the employee. He could only guess who his detractors were.

These programs were only one array in the frantic

mobilization against subversion. They were flanked by oaths and affidavits and questionnaires. To falsify any of these was a criminal offense. In order to establish what associations were forbidden, the 1947 executive order systematized the secret preparation and open use of the ATTORNEY GENERAL'S LIST of Subversive Organizations. Long before and for some years after the heyday of Senator JOSEPH R. MCCARTHY (1950–1954), congressional investigating committees took as their specialty the exposure of groups and individuals with communist ties. Their disclosures encouraged blacklists in private employment, notoriously in films and broadcasting. Senator McCarthy took the lead in stigmatizing the "Fifth-Amendment Communist"—a witness who invoked the RIGHT AGAINST SELF-INCRIMINATION. Senator Patrick A. McCarran initiated the idea that naming names was the only true badge of repentance for those who said they were no longer communists. A mass of legislation sought to expose and condemn the Communist party and its affiliates, while the Department of Justice jailed its leaders for sedition.

All of these measures raised intertwining constitutional problems, so those of loyalty-security programs are not easily isolated. However, two strands can be picked out. First, there were demands for fair process, notably to confront the source of accusations. Second, there were claims for First Amendment rights, set against the supposed necessities of national security. However, the courts often trimmed the reach of the programs without deciding such issues. They would invoke their usual preference for avoiding constitutional collisions, and simply find that executive or legislative authority was lacking.

The position that DUE PROCESS OF LAW was wanting in the rules and administration of employment tests first had to surmount the proposition that employment was not a right but only a privilege that could be summarily withheld. First Amendment claims also encountered this barrier, curtly expressed in Justice OLIVER WENDELL HOLMES'S now battered epigram: "The petitioner may have a constitutional right to talk politics, but he has no constitutional right to be a policeman." After some early hesitation, this dismissive argument was itself dismissed, notably by Justice TOM C. CLARK, who was usually a steadfast supporter of security measures. In an oath case, WIEMAN V. UPDEGRAFF (1952), he wrote for the Court: "We need not pause to consider whether an abstract right to public employment exists. It is sufficient to say that constitutional protection does extend to the public servant whose exclusion . . . is patently arbitrary or discriminatory."

What process is then due? The government perennially opposes the right of confrontation by invoking the need to protect confidential informants. The court came close to requiring a trial-type hearing, with confrontation and cross-examination, in the industrial security case of *Greene v. McElroy* (1959). But it used the avoidance technique. It said that there would have to be, at the threshold, explicit authorization from the President or Congress to conceal sources, and that it could not find such authorization. The decision had little effect. The statute authorizing security removals of government employees still requires only that charges "be stated as specifically as security considerations permit." It is doubtful that, in a time of perceived crisis, and in sensitive employment, the Constitution would be read to compel confrontation.

The Court worked its way to a firmer position on narrowing grounds for removal. It found that First Amendment rights to freedom of association were impaired by a flat proscription of employing communists in a "defense facility." In UNITED STATES V. ROBEL (1967) the employee, a shipyard worker, was an avowed Communist party member. A majority of the Court, declaring that "the statute quite literally establishes guilt by association alone," held that some less restrictive means would have to be employed to guard against disruption or sabotage. If *Robel* and like cases are followed where charges of disloyalty are brought, and where the accusation stems from political associations, the government may be unable to remove an employee except for conduct that would support a criminal prosecution.

This does not mean an end to the reliance on prying and gossiping that made loyalty-security programs disreputable. In satisfying itself of the reliability of applicants for employment, the government (or a private employer) can still probe for flaws of character, so long as standards for expulsion do not invade areas protected by the First Amendment or by ANTIDISCRIMINATION LEGISLATION. Investigators may even demand answers to questions, for example, on communist connections, that come close to protected zones, as long as the ultimate standards are correct, and the questions are helpful in seeing that the standards are satisfied. This seems to be the upshot of a tortuous line of cases involving admission to the practice of law.

From these unavoidable clashes between individual rights and security claims, a remarkable course of events has followed. Once the fevers of the 1950s had subsided, loyalty-security programs simply shrank to very modest levels. It is noteworthy that the VIETNAM WAR did not check the decline. Yet the KOREAN

WAR, which broke out in 1950, undoubtedly deepened the fears of that era.

The contraction has been helped along by the courts. Congress and the executive have perhaps done more to limit the scale at which the federal programs have been operating (the last dismissal on loyalty grounds was in 1968). The PRIVACY ACT of 1974 and similar statutes greatly restricted the flow of official information about misbehavior. President RICHARD M. NIXON abolished the Attorney General's List in the same year. Nudged by lower court decisions, the Civil Service Commission first stopped asking applicants for nonsensitive positions about subversive associations, and then in 1977 scrapped the questions for sensitive jobs too. Appropriations for investigative staff both in the Federal Bureau of Investigation and in the Defense Department have declined.

Do recent developments represent a slackening of our defenses? A revulsion against the excesses of McCarthyism? Because the prime mover in all the loyalty-security programs was hostility to communism, the programs may revive if our relations with the Soviet Union worsen. If the programs do revive, it seems unlikely that the courts will check recurrence of past excesses.

RALPH S. BROWN

Bibliography

BROWN, RALPH S. 1958 *Loyalty and Security: Employment Tests in the United States.* New Haven, Conn.: Yale University Press.

CAUTE, DAVID 1978 *The Great Fear: The Anti-Communist Purge under Truman and Eisenhower.* New York: Simon & Schuster.

DEVELOPMENTS IN THE LAW 1972 The National Security Interest and Civil Liberties. *Harvard Law Review* 85:1130–1326.

LEWY, GUENTER 1983 *The Federal Loyalty-Security Program: The Need for Reform.* Washington and London: American Enterprise Institute.

LUCAS v. 44TH GENERAL ASSEMBLY OF COLORADO

See: *Reynolds v. Sims*

LURTON, HORACE H.
(1844–1914)

President WILLIAM HOWARD TAFT's nomination of his close friend and former colleague, Horace Lurton, to replace Justice RUFUS PECKHAM in December 1909

engendered some skepticism. A Confederate veteran of the Civil War, Lurton was sixty-six and a pronounced conservative. He was, however, known as a patient and gentle man who sought compromise, and his experience clearly fitted him for the office. Lurton had sat on the Tennessee Supreme Court and the Sixth Circuit Court of Appeals (with Taft and WILLIAM R. DAY) and had also taught constitutional law and served as dean of the Law School at Vanderbilt University.

Lurton did not write many majority opinions during his tenure on the Supreme Court. He was usually among a silent majority voting in favor of government authority to sustain, for example, the NATIONAL POLICE POWER (*e.g.,* HOKE V. UNITED STATES, 1913) and the SHERMAN ANTITRUST ACT (STANDARD OIL COMPANY V. UNITED STATES, 1911); he dissented without opinion in HOUSTON, EAST & WEST TEXAS RAILWAY CO. V. UNITED STATES (1914). Most of his opinions dealt with procedural technicalities or the intricacies of employer liability laws.

One of the more frequent, though hardly regular, dissenters, Lurton was often in a minority with Justice OLIVER WENDELL HOLMES. Lurton's particular regard for precedent prompted extensive research to uncover those cases that would justify apparently inconsistent stances.

Shortly after his fourth term of court, in June 1914, Lurton died. His belief in law as the cement of society had led him to oppose JUDICIAL ACTIVISM, particularly when "a valid law, under the Constitution, is to be interpreted or modified so as to accomplish . . . [what a court] shall deem to the public advantage." Despite Lurton's prior experience, his career as a Justice provided little evidence of distinguished achievement.

DAVID GORDON

Bibliography

WATTS, JAMES F., JR. 1969 Horace H. Lurton. In Leon Friedman and Fred L. Israel, eds., *The Justices of the United States Supreme Court, 1789–1969.* New York: Chelsea House.

LUTHER v. BORDEN
7 Howard (48 U.S.) 1 (1849)

In *Luther v. Borden,* a case arising from the aftermath of the Dorr Rebellion (1842), Chief Justice ROGER B. TANEY enunciated the DOCTRINE of POLITICAL QUESTIONS and provided the first judicial exposition of the clause of the Constitution guaranteeing REPUBLI-

CAN FORMS OF GOVERNMENT (Article IV, section 4).

Though Rhode Island was in the forefront of the Industrial Revolution, its constitutional system, derived from the royal charter of 1663 (which was retained with slight modifications as the state's organic act after the Revolution), was an archaic and peculiar blend of democratic and regressive features. Malapportionment and disfranchisement grew intolerably severe as the industrial cities and mill villages filled with propertyless native and immigrant workers. (Perhaps as many as ninety percent of the adult males of Providence were voteless in 1840.) Reform efforts through the 1820s and 1830s were unsuccessful. In 1841–1842, suffragist reformers adopted more radical tactics derived from the theory of the DECLARATION OF INDEPENDENCE, asserting that the people had a right to reform or replace their government, outside the forms of law if need be. They therefore drafted a new state constitution (the "People's Constitution") and submitted it to ratification by a vote open to all adult white male citizens of the state. The regular government, meanwhile, also submitted a revised constitution (the "Freeholders' Constitution") to ratification, but only by those entitled to vote under the Charter. The people's Constitution was ratified, the Freeholders' rejected. Reform leaders then organized elections for a new state government, in which Thomas Wilson Dorr was elected governor. The two governments organized, each claiming exclusive legitimacy. The Freeholders' government declared martial law and, with the tacit support of President John Tyler, used state militia to suppress the Dorrites in an almost bloodless confrontation. It then submitted another revised constitution, ratified in late 1842, that alleviated the problems arising under the Charter.

Dorrites dissatisfied with this outcome created a TEST CASE from an incident of militia harassment and requested the Supreme Court to determine that the Freeholders' government and the subsequent 1842 constitution were illegitimate, on the grounds that the Freeholders' government was not republican and that the people of the state had a right to replace it, without legal sanction if necessary. Taney, for a unanimous Court (Justice LEVI WOODBURY dissenting in part on a martial law point), declined to issue any such ruling. After noting the insuperable practical difficulties of declaring the previous seven years of Rhode Island's government illegitimate, Taney stated that "the courts uniformly held that the inquiry proposed to be made belonged to the political power and not to the judicial." He went on to explain that Dorrite contentions "turned upon political rights and political questions, upon which the court has been

urged to express an opinion. We decline doing so." Taney thus amplified a distinction, earlier suggested by Chief Justice JOHN MARSHALL, between judicial questions (which a court can resolve), and political ones, which can be resolved only by the political branches of government (executive and legislative).

Taney further held that the GUARANTEE CLAUSE committed the question of the legitimacy of a state government to Congress for resolution, and that Congress's decision was binding on the courts, a point later reiterated by Chief Justice SALMON P. CHASE in cases involving the legitimacy of congressional Reconstruction policies. Taney concluded his opinion with an empty concession to the political theory of the Dorrites: "No one, we believe, has ever doubted the proposition that, according to the institutions of this country, the SOVEREIGNTY in every State resides in the people of the State, and that they may alter and change their form of government at their pleasure. But whether they have changed it or not," Taney repeated, "is a question to be settled by the political power," not the courts.

Though the political question doctrine thereby created has never been explained by a definitive rationale, it has proved useful in enabling the courts to avoid involvement in controversies that are not justiciable, that is, not suitable for resolution by judges. (See BAKER V. CARR, 1962.)

WILLIAM M. WIECEK

LYNCH v. DONNELLY
465 U.S. 668 (1984)

The Supreme Court significantly lowered the wall of SEPARATION OF CHURCH AND STATE by sanctioning an official display of a sacred Christian symbol. Pawtucket, Rhode Island, included a crèche, or nativity scene, in its annual Christmas exhibit in the center of the city's shopping district. The case raised the question whether Pawtucket's crèche violated the Constitution's prohibition of ESTABLISHMENT OF RELIGION.

Chief Justice WARREN BURGER for a 5–4 Court ruled that despite the religious nature of the crèche, Pawtucket had a secular purpose in displaying it, as evinced by the fact that it was part of a Christmas exhibit that proclaimed "Season's Greetings" and included Santa Claus, his reindeer, a Christmas tree, and figures of carolers, a clown, an elephant, and a teddy bear. That the FIRST AMENDMENT, Burger argued, did not mandate complete separation is shown by our national motto, paid chaplains, presidential proclamations invoking God, the pledge of allegiance, and religious art in publicly supported museums.

Justice WILLIAM BRENNAN, dissenting, construed Burger's majority opinion narrowly, observing that the question was still open on the constitutionality of a public display on public property of a crèche alone or of the display of some other sacred symbol, such as a crucifixion scene. Brennan repudiated the supposed secular character of the crèche; he argued that "[f]or Christians the essential message of the nativity is that God became incarnate in the person of Christ." The majority's insensitivity toward the feelings of non-Christians disturbed Brennan.

A spokesman for the National Council of Churches complained that the Court had put Christ "on the same level as Santa Claus and Rudolph the Red-Nosed Reindeer." Clearly, the Court had a topsy-turvy understanding of what constitutes an establishment of religion, because in LARKIN V. GRENDEL'S DEN (1982) it saw a forbidden establishment in a STATE POLICE POWER measure aimed at keeping boisterous patrons of a tavern from disturbing a church, yet here saw no establishment in a state-sponsored crèche.

LEONARD W. LEVY

MACDONALD, UNITED STATES v.
456 U.S. 1 (1982)

Chief Justice WARREN E. BURGER for a 6–3 Supreme Court reaffirmed that the protection of the SPEEDY TRIAL provision of the Sixth Amendment does not extend to the period before a defendant is officially accused of the crime and ceases once charges are dismissed. Thus, the period between dismissal of military charges and indictment later in a civil court could not be considered in determining whether delay violated the right to a speedy trial. Dissenters disagreed with the majority's reasoning that the interests served by the right to a speedy trial stood in no jeopardy before accusation or after dismissal of charges.

LEONARD W. LEVY

MACON, NATHANIEL
(1757–1837)

Nathaniel Macon, a North Carolina planter, opposed RATIFICATION OF THE CONSTITUTION because he thought the new government too powerful. Joining THOMAS JEFFERSON's Republican party, Macon was elected to Congress in 1791; with his party he opposed ALEXANDER HAMILTON's economic policies and the ALIEN AND SEDITION ACTS. As speaker (1801–1807), Macon, with his deputy, JOHN RANDOLPH, firmly guided the House of Representatives along administration lines. Although he briefly broke with Jefferson (1807–1809), he supported the unpopular EMBARGO

ACTS. In the House (1791–1815) and later in the Senate (1815–1826), Macon was a spokesman for STATES' RIGHTS, STRICT CONSTRUCTION, and individual liberty.

DENNIS J. MAHONEY

MADDEN v. KENTUCKY
309 U.S. 83 (1940)

A Kentucky statute taxing bank deposits outside the state at a rate five times higher than the tax on intrastate deposits was assailed as breaching several clauses of section one of the FOURTEENTH AMENDMENT. By a 7–2 vote the Supreme Court, speaking through Justice STANLEY F. REED, declared that the states have broad discretion in their tax policies. Reed dismissed the arguments against the statute based on the EQUAL PROTECTION and DUE PROCESS clauses as insubstantial, but the decision in COLGATE V. HARVEY (1935) supported the argument based on the PRIVILEGES AND IMMUNITIES clause. On reconsideration the Court found that lending or depositing money is not a privilege of national CITIZENSHIP and therefore overruled *Colgate*.

LEONARD W. LEVY

MADISON, JAMES
(1751–1836)

James Madison, "the father of the Constitution," matured with the American Revolution. Educated at a boarding school and at patriotic Princeton, he returned to the family plantation in Virginia at age twenty-one, two years before the infamous Coercive Acts. As Orange County mobilized behind the recommendations of the CONTINENTAL CONGRESS, he joined his father on the committee of safety, practiced with a rifle, and drilled with the local militia company. As he wrote much later, in a sketch of an autobiography, "he was under very early and strong impressions in favor of liberty both civil and religious."

Civil and religious liberty were intimately linked in Madison's career and thinking. His early revolutionary ardor is the necessary starting point for understanding his distinctive role among the Founders. The young man first involved himself in local politics, in 1774, to raise his voice against the persecution of dissenters in neighboring Virginia counties. When feeble health compelled him to abandon thoughts of active military service, the gratitude of Baptist neighbors may have helped him win election to the state convention of 1776, which framed one of the earliest, most widely imitated revolutionary constitutions. (See VIRGINIA CONSTITUTION AND DECLARATION OF RIGHTS.) It seems appropriate that Madison's first major office should have been in this convention, his first important act to prepare amendatory language that significantly broadened the definition of freedom of conscience in the Virginia Declaration of Rights. The American Revolution, as he understood it, was a grand experiment, of world-historical significance, in the creation and vindication of governments that would combine majority control with individual freedom, popular self-government with security for the private rights of all. Through more than forty years of active public service, he was at the center of the country's search for a structure and practice of government that would secure both sorts of freedom. His conviction that democracy and individual liberty are mutually dependent—and, increasingly, that neither would survive disintegration of the continental Union—guided his distinctive contributions to the writing and interpretation of the Constitution.

Defeated in his bid for reelection to the state assembly—he refused to offer the customary treats to voters—the promising young Madison was soon selected by the legislature as a member of the Council of State. Two years later, in December 1779, the legislature chose him as a delegate to Congress. Here he gradually acquired a national reputation. He was instrumental in the management of Virginia's western cession, which prepared the way for ratification of the ARTICLES OF CONFEDERATION and creation of a national domain. He introduced the compromise that resulted in the congressional recommendations of April 18,

1783, calling on the states to approve an amendment to the Articles granting Congress power to impose a five percent duty on foreign imports, to complete their western cessions, and to levy other taxes sufficient to provide for the continental debt. He learned that the confederation government's dependence on the states for revenues and for enforcement of its acts and treaties rendered it unable to perform its duties and endangered its very existence.

Reentering Virginia's legislature when his term in Congress ended, Madison became increasingly convinced that liberty in individual states depended on the Union that protected them from foreign intervention and from the wars and rivalries that had fractured Europe and condemned its peoples to oppressive taxes, swollen military forces, and the rule of executive tyrants. In 1786, as he prepared for the Annapolis Convention, Northerners and Southerners clashed bitterly in Congress over the negotiation of a commercial treaty with Spain. When Madison and other delegates decided to propose the meeting of a general convention to revise the Articles of Confederation, they acted in a context of profound, immediate concern for the survival of the Union.

By 1786, however, Madison no longer hoped that a revision of the Articles might reinvigorate the general government, nor was he worried solely by the peril of disunion. In all the states popular assemblies struggled to protect their citizens from economic troubles. Although Virginia managed to avoid the worst abuses, Madison thought continentally. Correspondents warned him of a growing disillusionment with popular misgovernment, particularly in New England, where SHAYS' REBELLION erupted in the winter of 1786. Virginia's own immunity from popular commotions or majority misrule appeared to him in doubt. He had not been able to achieve revision of the revolutionary constitution and had often suffered agonizing losses when he urged support for federal measures or important state reforms. In 1785, in his opinion, only the presence of a multitude of disagreeing sects had blocked the passage of a bill providing tax support for teachers of the Christian religion, which would have been a major blow to freedom of conscience and an egregious violation of the constitution. Personally disgusted by the changeability, injustices, and lack of foresight of even Virginia's laws, Madison feared that the revulsion with democracy, confined thus far to only a tiny (though an influential) few, could spread in time through growing numbers of the people. The crisis of confederation government, as he conceived it, was compounded by a crisis of republican convictions. Either could reverse the Revolution. Neither could be overcome by minor alterations of the Articles of Confederation. To save the Revolution, he wrote to EDMUND PENDLETON, constitutional reform must both "perpetuate the union and redeem the honor of the republican name."

No one played a more important part than Madison in bringing on the CONSTITUTIONAL CONVENTION OF 1787, turning its attention to a sweeping transformation of the federal system, or achieving national approval of its work. Returning from Annapolis, he won Virginia's quick consent to a general convention, wrote the resolutions signaling the Old Dominion's serious commitment to the project, and helped persuade GEORGE WASHINGTON to lead a delegation whose distinguished quality encouraged other states to call upon their best. Reeligible at last, he rushed from Richmond to New York, reentered the Confederation Congress, and worked successfully for measures that significantly improved the prospects for a full, successful meeting. He researched the histories and structures of other ancient and modern confederations and somehow found the time to write a formal memorandum on the "Vices of the Political System of the United States," in which he argued that the mortal ills of the confederation government and the concurrent crisis in the states alike demanded the abandonment of the Articles of Confederation and the creation of a carefully constructed national republic. In Madison's vision, the republic would rise directly from the people; would possess effective, full, and independent powers over matters of general concern; and would incorporate so many different economic interests and religious sects that majorities would seldom form "on any other principles than those of justice and the general good." Urging other members of Virginia's delegation to arrive in Philadelphia in time to frame some general propositions with which the meeting might begin, he reached the city himself the best prepared of all who gathered for the Constitutional Convention.

Madison made several distinctive contributions to the writing of the Constitution. He was primarily responsible for the VIRGINIA PLAN: the resolutions that initiated the Convention's thorough reconstruction of the federal system and served throughout the summer as the outline for reform. In the early weeks of the deliberations, he persuasively explained why no reform could prove effective if it left the general government dependent on the states. Together with JAMES WILSON, he led the delegates who insisted on proportional representation, popular ratification of the fundamental charter, and a careful balance of authority between a democratic House of Representatives and

branches more resistant to ill-considered popular demands. He also urged his fellows not to limit their attention to the weaknesses of the confederation, but to come to terms as well with the vices of democratic government in the states. Constitutional reform, he argued, must also overcome the crisis of republican convictions, both by placing limitations on the states and by creating a greater republic free from the structural errors of the local constitutions. With the latter plea particularly, he opened members' minds to a complete rethinking of the problems of democracy and to the possibility that liberty and popular control might both be safest in a large republic. Although the finished Constitution differed in a number of significant respects from his original proposals, Madison was, by general agreement of historians and his colleagues, the most important of the Framers.

All of which was only part of his enormous contribution to the Constitution's great success. Before departing for Virginia, where he led the Federalists to victory in a close and capably contested state convention, Madison reassumed his seat in the Confederation Congress, helped provide some central guidance for the ratification struggle, and joined with ALEXANDER HAMILTON to write the most important explanation and defense of the completed Constitution. His numbers of THE FEDERALIST, perhaps the greatest classic in the history of American political writing, rationalized the compromises made in the Convention, rendered the document intelligible in terms of democratic theory, and thus contributed as surely to the shaping of the Constitution as the work of the preceding summer. Since early in the nineteenth century, these essays have been recognized as an essential source for understanding the intentions of the Framers, and Madison's essential theme—that the Convention's work was perfectly consistent with the principles of the Revolution, a genuinely democratic remedy for the diseases most destructive to democracy—was still but the beginning of his effort to interpret and insure the triumph of the finished plan.

The reconstructed federal government initiated operations in April 1789. Madison immediately assumed the leading role in the first Congress, which was responsible for filling in the outline of the Constitution as well as for the national legislation it had been created to permit. He drafted parts of Washington's inaugural address, prepared the House of Representatives' reply, and helped defeat proposals to address the President as "highness"—important contributions to the early effort to define the protocol between the branches and to set a democratic tone for the infant regime. He initiated the deliberations that resulted in the first federal tariff and assured a steady source of independent federal revenues. He seized the lead again in the creation of executive departments, successfully insisting that the concept of responsibility required a presidential power to remove executive officials without the consent of Congress. Finally, he took upon himself the principal responsibility for preparing the constitutional amendments that became the BILL OF RIGHTS.

Early in the contest over RATIFICATION OF THE CONSTITUTION, Madison had denied the need for such amendments. He argued that the federal government had not been granted any powers that might threaten the liberties protected in the declarations of the states, and he warned that any effort to prepare a federal bill might actually endanger rights it was intended to preserve: an inadvertent error or omission could become the basis for a claim of positive authority to act. This very train of reasoning, however, suggests why he was open to a change of mind and offers some important clues to understanding his political and constitutional position in the years after 1789.

Throughout the course of constitutional reform, Madison had insisted no less strongly on the need for an effective central government than on a governmental structure that would guarantee the continuing responsibility of rulers to the ruled, along with a considerable residual autonomy for the people in their several states. Even as he worried over the excesses of majorities, he reminded correspondents of the perils posed by rulers who escaped a due dependence on the people; and even as he warned the Constitutional Convention not to leave the general government dependent on the states, he recognized the danger of excessive concentration of authority in federal hands. His contributions to *The Federalist* describe the new regime as neither wholly national nor purely federal in nature, but as a novel, complicated mixture under which concurrent state and central governments, each possessed of only limited authority, would each perform the duties for which they were best equipped and would both resist disturbance of a federal equilibrium that offered new protection for the people. During the ratification contest, Madison was forced to promise that amendments would be added once the Constitution was approved. He realized how useful this could be in reconciling skeptics to the system. But he was also predisposed to be receptive when THOMAS JEFFERSON insisted that a bill of rights would be a valuable, additional security for the liberties and powers that the states and people had intended to reserve.

Among the most consistent themes of Madison's career was his profound respect for FUNDAMENTAL LAW. Written constitutions, in his view, were solemn compacts which created governments and granted them the only powers they legitimately possessed. Rulers guilty of transcending them, he had written in his 1785 MEMORIAL AND REMONSTRANCE against religious assessments, were "Tyrants," those who submitted "slaves." And usurpations of this sort, he added, ought to be resisted on their first appearance, as they had been early in the Revolution, before they could be strengthened by repeated exercise and "entangle the question in precedents." This scrupulous regard for fundamental charters encouraged Madison to change his mind about a bill of rights and shaped his conduct throughout the rest of his career.

Early in Washington's administration, Madison became alarmed about the sectional inequities and other consequences of Hamilton's political economy. He broke with Hamilton entirely when the secretary of the treasury proposed the creation of a national bank, protesting that the Constitution granted Congress no explicit power to charter such a corporation and that a doctrine of IMPLIED POWERS, justifying federal measures by a BROAD CONSTRUCTION of the general clauses, could completely change the character and spirit of a limited, federal system. During the 1790s, as Madison and Jefferson concluded that Hamilton and his supporters were deliberately attempting to subvert the Revolution—to concentrate all power in the general government and most of that in its executive departments—their insistence on a strict construction of the Constitution and a compact theory of its origins became an organizing theme of the Democratic-Republican opposition. Madison's Virginia Resolutions of 1798, part of a larger effort to arouse the states against the ALIEN AND SEDITION ACTS, which the Republicans regarded as a flagrant violation of the FIRST AMENDMENT, identified a Hamiltonian construction of the Constitution as a central feature of a Federalist conspiracy to sweep away all limitations on the exercise of federal power. Madison's great Report of 1800, explaining and defending the resolutions of 1798 against objections from other states, still stands as a striking landmark in the evolution of a modern, literalist interpretation of the First Amendment. In opposition to prevailing understandings that FREEDOM OF THE PRESS afforded guarantees against PRIOR RESTRAINT AND CENSORSHIP, but did not protect a publisher or author from criminal responsibility for statements tending to bring the government or its officers into disrepute, Madison insisted that the federal government was "destitute" of all authority whatever to interfere with the free development and circulation of opinion. In passages with major implications for the future, he denied that a FEDERAL COMMON LAW OF CRIMES had ever operated and suggested that the essence of elective governments was inconsistent with even STATE ACTION to restrain "that right of freely examining public characters and measures and of free communication of the people thereon, which has ever been justly deemed the only effectual guardian of every other right."

In its constitutional dimensions, the Jeffersonian "Revolution of 1800" was intended by its leaders to restore the threatened federal balance and return the general government to the role and limits originally intended by the people. As Jefferson's secretary of state, principal lieutenant, and eventual successor, Madison continued to believe that governmental actions should "conform to the constitution as understood by the Convention that produced and recommended it, and particularly by the state conventions that *adopted* it." He conceded that there were occasions that might justify or even command departures from the letter of the Constitution. He defended the LOUISIANA PURCHASE on these grounds, suggesting that a power to acquire new TERRITORIES was inherent in the concept of a sovereign nation. As President, he acted on the basis of implied executive authority in ordering the occupation of West Florida. He even came to recommend rechartering a national bank, maintaining that repeated acts of every part of government, repeatedly approved of by the nation, had overruled his earlier opinion of the institution's unconstitutionality. In his final days in office, nevertheless, he vetoed a bill providing federal support for INTERNAL IMPROVEMENTS. Although he favored federal action, he insisted on a constitutional amendment in advance. He still believed, as he had written in his "Letters of Helvidius" in 1793, that "a people who are so happy as to possess the inestimable blessing of a free and defined constitution cannot be too watchful against the introduction nor too critical in tracing the consequences of new principles and new constructions that may remove the landmarks of power."

Madison's regard for fundamental law is not to be confused with a minimalist conception of the constitutional scope of federal powers. He recommended the creation of a national university, although the Constitution delegated no explicit power to erect one. He believed that the Constitution granted Congress plenary authority over commerce, not merely ample power to impose a protective tariff but power even

to require a temporary end to foreign trade as in the complete embargo or the various non-intercourse experiments preceding the War of 1812. He was as willing to defend the powers plainly granted to the federal government—over state militias, for example— as he was to guard the liberties protected by the Bill of Rights. Nevertheless, his leadership as President was characterized by deep respect for both the letter and the spirit of the federal compact. If he was diffident in leading Congress into proper preparations for a war, his serious regard for legislative independence was as much at fault as personality or circumstances. If he forbore perhaps too much in the face of flagrantly seditious opposition to the war, this forbearance was not for want of an imaginable alternative. ABRAHAM LINCOLN claimed the powers needed for a greater crisis. Madison deliberately attempted to conduct the War of 1812 at minimal expense to the republican and federal nature of the country. It was at once his weakness and his glory.

The father of the Constitution outlived all the other signers, becoming in his final years a rather troubled, though revered, authority on the creation and construction of the federal charter. The source of his discomfort was his own insistence that the Constitution was a compact among the sovereign peoples of the several states, who remained the only power competent to alter it or to deliver a definitive decision on its meaning. The great Virginian repeatedly denied that this interpretation justified the developing southern doctrine of state INTERPOSITION and NULLIFICATION. He had, in fact, warned Jefferson in 1798 against confusing the constituent authority of the peoples of the states with the powers of an individual state government. Yet neither was he willing to permit the federal courts a power of interpretation that would make the general government the final or exclusive judge in its own cause (or even to concede the courts the power to override the constitutional opinions of the executive and legislative branches). Trapped between his love of Union and his fear of grasping power, he was never able, never willing, to identify an agency or a procedure that, in case of a collision of conflicting understandings of the Constitution, could prevent a revolutionary recourse to the sovereign people. But, then, James Madison was Revolution's child. Admitting that the best constructed government could not secure a nation's liberty if it were not supported by a proper public spirit, he trusted to the end that mutual conciliation and restraint would prove sufficient to preserve the Union he had done so much to shape.

LANCE BANNING

Bibliography

BANNING, LANCE 1984 "The Hamiltonian Madison: A Reconsideration." *Virginia Magazine of History and Biography* 92:3–28.

BRANT, IRVING 1941–1961 *James Madison.* 6 Vols. Indianapolis: Bobbs-Merrill.

KETCHAM, RALPH 1971 *James Madison: A Biography.* New York: Macmillan.

MCCOY, DREW R. 1980 *The Elusive Republic: Political Economy in Jeffersonian America.* Chapel Hill: University of North Carolina Press.

WOOD, GORDON S. 1969 *The Creation of the American Republic, 1776–1789.* Chapel Hill: University of North Carolina Press.

MADISON'S "MEMORIAL AND REMONSTRANCE"
(1785)

This remonstrance is the best evidence of what JAMES MADISON, the framer of the FIRST AMENDMENT, meant by an ESTABLISHMENT OF RELIGION. In 1784 the Virginia legislature had proposed a bill that benefited "Teachers of the Christian Religion" by assessing a small tax on property owners. Each taxpayer could designate the Christian church of his choice as the recipient of his tax money; the bill allowed non-church members to earmark their taxes for the support of local schools, and it upheld the "liberal principle" that all Christian sects and denominations were equal under the law, none preferred over others. The bill did not speak of the "established religion" of the state as had an aborted bill of 1779, and it purported to be based on only secular considerations, the promotion of the public peace and morality rather than Christ's kingdom on earth. Madison denounced the bill as an establishment of religion, no less dangerous to RELIGIOUS LIBERTY than the proposal of 1779 and differing "only in degree" from the Inquisition.

In an elaborate argument of fifteen parts, Madison advocated a complete SEPARATION OF CHURCH AND STATE as the only guarantee of the equal right of every citizen to the free exercise of religion, including the freedom of those "whose minds have not yet yielded to the evidence which has convinced us." He regarded the right to support religion as an "unalienable" individual right to be exercised only on a voluntary basis. Religion, he contended, must be exempt from the power of society, the legislature, and the magistrate. In his trenchant assault on establishments including the one proposed by this mild bill—"it is proper to take alarm at the first experiment on our liberties"—

and in his eloquent defense of separation, Madison stressed the point that separation benefited not only personal freedom but also the free state and even religion itself. His remonstrance, which circulated throughout Virginia in the summer of 1785, actually redirected public opinion, resulting in the election of legislators who opposed the bill, which had previously passed a second reading. Madison then introduced THOMAS JEFFERSON's proposal which was enacted into law as the VIRGINIA STATUTE OF RELIGIOUS FREEDOM.

LEONARD W. LEVY

Bibliography

BRANT, IRVING 1948 *James Madison, Nationalist 1780–1787.* Pages 343–355. Indianapolis: Bobbs-Merrill.

MADISON'S *NOTES OF THE DEBATES*

In the oral arguments in OGDEN V. SAUNDERS (1824), a lawyer wondered what the intentions were of those who framed the Constitution when they included the CONTRACT CLAUSE. "Unhappily for this country and for the general interest of political science," he added, "the history of the Convention of 1787 which framed the Constitution of the United States is lost to the world." It was not lost, but no one who was not an intimate of JAMES MADISON knew that. Incredibly, JOHN MARSHALL wrote his great opinions on constitutional law and JOSEPH STORY wrote his *Commentaries on the Constitution* (1833) without knowing that Madison had in his possession his elaborate manuscript record of the CONSTITUTIONAL CONVENTION.

The Father of the Constitution not only wielded the greatest influence on its formation at the Convention, where he delivered over 200 speeches, but he also kept a record of the debates for nearly four months, a task that he later said "almost killed" him. He sat front and center in a "favorable position for hearing all that passed," and daily he composed a transcript from detailed notes kept of each session. Yet the memory that he had performed the task faded from the minds of participants.

In Madison's will of 1835, leaving his papers to his wife, he wrote that given the interest the Constitution "has inspired among friends of free Government, it was not an unreasonable inference that a report of the proceedings and discussions . . . will be particularly gratifying to the people of the United States, and to all who take an interest in the progress of political science and the course of true liberty." Why he failed to publish those records during his lifetime, indeed, why he kept them a secret, is inexplicable.

Madison worked on his manuscript intermittently for many years, revising and expanding as additional information became available. For example, he incorporated material from the official *Journal, Acts and Proceedings of the Convention* (1819) and even from ROBERT YATES's *Secret Proceedings and Debates* (1821), an Anti-Federalist work that contained useful details through July 5, 1787, including versions of Madison's own speeches. Madison's revisions of his original manuscript revealed his objective of making the record as full and accurate as possible.

After his death in 1836, Dolley Madison offered his papers to the United States. In 1837 Congress agreed on a price of $30,000, and in 1840, fifty-three years after the Convention, Madison's *Notes of the Debates* was published for the first of many times. It remains our most important source by far of what happened at the Constitutional Convention.

LEONARD W. LEVY

Bibliography

MADISON, JAMES 1977 *The Papers of James Madison*, Robert A. Rutland, ed., vol. 10. Chicago: University of Chicago Press.

WARREN, CHARLES 1928 *The Making of the Constitution*. Boston: Little, Brown.

MAGNA CARTA
(1215)

Magna Carta (Latin, great charter), one of the enduring symbols of LIMITED GOVERNMENT and of the RULE OF LAW, was forced upon an unwilling King John by rebellious barons in June of 1215. Since his accession in 1199, John had made enemies at every quarter. The barons resisted heavy taxation exacted to support the king's expensive and unsuccessful wars with the French. Lesser folk complained that royal officials requisitioned, often without payment, food, timber, horses, and carts. Justice in the courts became more sporadic. Quarreling with Pope Innocent III over the election of a new archbishop of Canterbury, John seized church properties, yielding only when the pope threatened to release the English people from their allegiance to the Crown.

By spring of 1215, the barons' discontent had ripened to the point that they formally renounced their allegiance after the king refused their demands that he confirm their liberties by a charter. Under severe pressure, John agreed to meet the barons at Runnymede. There the barons presented a list of demands, the Articles of the Barons, which were then reduced to the form of a charter—the document that later generations came to call Magna Carta.

The charter to which John agreed is an intensely practical document. Rather than being a philosophical tract redolent with lofty generalities, the charter was drafted to provide concrete remedies for specific abuses. Moreover, although the barons were rebelling against the abuse of royal power, they were not seeking to remake the fabric of feudal society. They sought instead to restore customary limits on the power of the Crown, distinguishing between rule according to law and rule by the imposition of arbitrary will.

The barons' interests were essentially selfish. They did not see themselves as disinterested advocates for the common good of the realm. Nevertheless, because the abuses of John's reign touched so many elements of English society, his opponents' demands had implications far beyond the barons' own interests. For example, the charter begins with the declaration that the liberties therein guaranteed run to "all the free men of our kingdom."

Many of Magna Carta's provisions concern feudal relationships having no counterpart in modern times. Certain of the charter's decrees, however, raise issues as vital now as then. Indeed, some of its provisions anticipate rights now embedded in American constitutional law. Among the more relevant are the following:

Chapter 39 declares, "No freed man shall be taken, imprisoned, disseised, outlawed, banished, or in any way destroyed, nor will We proceed against or prosecute him, except by the lawful judgment of his peers and by the LAW OF THE LAND." One should not read this language too broadly; for instance, "judgment of his peers" did not mean, as many have supposed, TRIAL BY JURY. But the requirement of proceedings according to the "law of the land" was significant in the development generally of the rule of law and more specifically of the concept of DUE PROCESS OF LAW. Indeed, "due process of law" and "law of the land" became interchangeable.

Chapter 40 states, "To no one will We sell, to none will We deny or delay, right or justice." Like chapter 39, this provision aimed at curbing abuses in the administration of justice. Several chapters (28, 29, 30, 31) relate to abuses in royal officials' requisitioning of private property and thus are the remote ancestor of the requirement of JUST COMPENSATION in the Fifth Amendment to the United States Constitution. Other chapters (20, 21, 22) require that fines be "according to the measure" of the offense and that fines not be so heavy as to jeopardize one's ability to make a living—reflecting the principle that the criminal law ought not to be administered in a vindictive or unduly oppressive way. Still other provisions deal with the liberties and free customs of cities and towns, with the free flow of commerce, and with church and state—all of these subjects being continuing concerns of American constitutional law.

Beginning with Henry III (who at age nine succeeded John in 1216), king after king reaffirmed Magna Carta. By the end of the fourteenth century, Magna Carta (which had been placed on the statute books in 1297) had established itself as more than a venerable statute; by then it was a FUNDAMENTAL LAW. In 1368, for example—over 400 years before MARBURY V. MADISON (1803)—a statute of Edward III commanded that Magna Carta "be holden and kept in all Points; and if there be any Statute made to the contrary, it shall be holden for none." Here one sees an early germ of the principle contained in the SUPREMACY CLAUSE of the United States Constitution.

The political turmoil of seventeenth-century England saw such parliamentarians as Sir EDWARD COKE and such pamphleteers as JOHN LILBURNE ("Freeborn John") invoking Magna Carta against the pretensions of the Stuart kings. By the end of that century, climaxed by the Glorious Revolution, three new "liberty documents" had been brought into being to stand alongside Magna Carta as assuring the liberties of the subject—the PETITION OF RIGHT (1628), the HABEAS CORPUS ACT (1679), and the BILL OF RIGHTS (1689).

Magna Carta was early carried to the New World. In 1646, some discontented freemen in the Massachusetts colony complained that the laws and liberties they were entitled to as Englishmen were not being enforced. The colony's magistrates responded by drawing up the famous "parallels" of Massachusetts— one column entitled "Magna Charta," the other "fundamentalls of the Massachusetts," the purpose being to argue that the rights assured by Magna Carta and the common law were indeed not denied to the people of Massachusetts. When WILLIAM PENN founded Pennsylvania, he drew upon Magna Carta in drafting the new colony's Frame of Government and, in 1687, was responsible for the first publication in America of Magna Carta.

In the decade between the STAMP ACT (1765) and the outbreak of hostilities with the mother country, Magna Carta became part of the fabric of colonial arguments against British policies. In the petition by the Stamp Act Congress to the king, the Congress declared that both the colonists' right to tax themselves and the right of trial by jury (a right the Crown had circumvented by giving ADMIRALTY courts JURISDICTION to try cases under the Stamp Act) were "confirmed by the Great Charter of English Liberty."

During the period leading up to revolution, the colonists' arguments, in tracts and resolutions, were essentially eclectic. Appeals to the British Constitution, including Magna Carta, were intertwined with arguments that the colonists' entitlement to such rights as taxation only with their consent were based also on the colonial charters and on natural law. As SAMUEL ADAMS put it, Magna Carta itself was a declaration of Britons' "original, inherent, indefeasible NATURAL RIGHTS."

Independence accomplished, the Americans turned to the work of building their own constitutional governments, both state and ultimately federal. The new constitutions reveal both the legacy of British institutions, including Magna Carta, and their perceived limitations. By and large, the contributions of Magna Carta and the other British "liberty" documents are most evident in American bills of rights. Virtually every state constitution has a due process clause, some using the phrase "due process," others using Magna Carta's formulation of "law of the land." For example, the debt owed Magna Carta's chapter 39 is obvious in North Carolina's Declaration of Rights, framed in 1776, "That no freeman ought to be taken, imprisoned, or disseized of his freehold, liberties, or privileges, or outlawed, or exiled, or in any manner destroyed, or deprived of his life, liberty, or property, but by the law of the land."

From the outset, however, American constitutional draftsmen understood their handiwork to go beyond Magna Carta. In North Carolina's ratifying convention (1789), JAMES IREDELL (later to serve on the Supreme Court) called Magna Carta "no constitution" but simply a legislative act, "every article of which the legislature may at any time alter." What Britain lacked, he concluded, the new American constitution supplied.

Throughout the nineteenth century, American courts, both state and federal, commonly invoked Magna Carta in shaping constitutional rights. Thus Magna Carta was relied on in cases involving (to give but a few examples) excessive court costs, open courts and certain remedies, notice and hearing, general application of the laws, and BILLS OF ATTAINDER. Gradually, as a corpus of indigenous American law developed, reliance upon Magna Carta became more and more attenuated, indeed largely rhetorical. By the twentieth century, Magna Carta had long since been irrevocably embedded into the fabric of American CONSTITUTIONALISM, both by contributing specific concepts such as due process of law and by being the ultimate symbol of constitutional government under a rule of law.

A. E. DICK HOWARD

Bibliography

HOWARD, A. E. DICK 1968 *The Road from Runnymede: Magna Carta and Constitutionalism in America.* Charlottesville: University Press of Virginia.

MAHAN v. HOWELL
410 U.S. 315 (1973)

The ideal REAPPORTIONMENT, following REYNOLDS V. SIMS (1964), would establish state legislative districts of equal populations. The question remained: How much deviation from pure mathematical equality would be tolerated? In *Mahan,* the Supreme Court approved, 6–3, a deviation of sixteen percent in the districting of Virginia's lower house, justified by the state's "policy of maintaining the integrity of district lines."

In congressional districting, no such deviation from equality is tolerated (*White v. Weiser,* 1973). However, state legislative districting may include DE MINIMIS departures from equality (up to around ten percent) without any justification (*White v. Regester,* 1973).

KENNETH L. KARST

MAHER v. ROE
432 U.S. 464 (1977)

The Supreme Court here sustained, 6–3, a Connecticut law limiting state medicaid assistance for abortions in the first trimester of pregnancy to "medically necessary" abortions (including "psychiatric necessity"), but providing such aid for childbirth. Justice LEWIS F. POWELL, for the Court, rejected both the claim that the law violated the right of PRIVACY recognized in ROE V. WADE (1973) and the claim that the state's WEALTH DISCRIMINATION violated the EQUAL PROTECTION clause.

There was to be "no retreat from *Roe,*" but Connecticut had placed "no obstacles . . . in the pregnant woman's path to an abortion." An indigent woman suffered no disadvantage from the state's funding of childbirth; she might still have an abortion if she could find the wherewithal; Connecticut had not created her indigency. Nor did the scheme deny equal protec-

tion. There was no SUSPECT CLASSIFICATION requiring STRICT SCRUTINY of the law; neither had the state invaded any FUNDAMENTAL INTEREST by discriminating against the exercise of a constitutional right. The law satisfied the RATIONAL BASIS standard, for it was rationally related to promoting the state's interest in protecting potential life—an interest recognized in *Roe* itself.

Two companion decisions, *Poelker v. Doe* and *Beal v. Doe,* upheld a city's refusal to provide hospital services for an indigent woman's nontherapeutic abortion, and read the SOCIAL SECURITY ACT not to require a state to aid nontherapeutic abortions in order to receive federal medicaid grants.

Justices WILLIAM J. BRENNAN, THURGOOD MARSHALL, and HARRY BLACKMUN all filed opinions dissenting in the three cases. They emphasized the "coercive" effect on poor women of the state's financial preference for childbirth, and the particularly harsh effect of adding unwanted children to poor households.

Even before *Roe,* wealthy women could have abortions by traveling to other states or abroad. *Roe* brought abortion within the means of middleclass women. The *Maher* majority Justices declined to extend the effective right to have an abortion beyond the boundaries of their own socioeconomic environment.

KENNETH L. KARST

(SEE ALSO: *Abortion and the Constitution; Harris v. McRae, 1980; Reproductive Autonomy.*)

MAJORITY OPINION

See: Opinion of the Court

MALLORY v. UNITED STATES

See: McNabb-Mallory Rule

MALLOY v. HOGAN
378 U.S. 1 (1964)

This is one of a series of cases in which the WARREN COURT nationalized the rights of the criminally accused by incorporating provisions of the Fourth through the Eighth Amendments into the FOURTEENTH AMENDMENT. (See INCORPORATION DOCTRINE.) In *Malloy* it was the RIGHT AGAINST SELF-IN-

CRIMINATION. Malloy, a convicted felon on probation, was ordered to testify in a judicial inquiry into gambling activities. He refused to answer any questions concerning the crime for which he had been convicted, and he was held in contempt. Connecticut's highest court, relying on TWINING V. NEW JERSEY (1908) and ADAMSON V. CALIFORNIA (1947), ruled that Malloy's invocation of the Fifth Amendment right had no constitutional basis in the state and that the Fourteenth Amendment did not extend the right to a state proceeding.

The Supreme Court reversed on the ground that the "same standards must determine whether an accused's silence in either a federal or a state proceeding is justified." Had the inquiry been a federal one, said Justice WILLIAM J. BRENNAN for a 5–4 majority, Malloy would have been entitled to refuse to answer because his disclosures might have furnished a link in a chain of evidence to connect him to a new crime for which he might be prosecuted. The Court held that "the Fifth Amendment exception from compulsory self-incrimination is also protected by the Fourteenth against abridgment by the States." *Twining* and *Adamson*, which had held to the contrary, were overruled, although the specific holding in *Adamson* relating to comments on the accused's failure to testify was not overruled until GRIFFIN V. CALIFORNIA (1965). Thus, *Malloy* stands for the DOCTRINE that the Fourteenth Amendment protects against state abridgment the same right that the Fifth protects against federal abridgment. Justices BYRON R. WHITE and POTTER STEWART did not expressly dissent from this doctrine; they contended, rather, that Malloy's reliance on his right to silence was groundless on the basis of the facts. Justices JOHN MARSHALL HARLAN and TOM C. CLARK opposed the incorporation of the Fifth Amendment right into the Fourteenth.

LEONARD W. LEVY

MANDAMUS, WRIT OF

(Latin: "We command.") A writ of mandamus is a judicial order to a lower court or to any agency or officer of any department of government, commanding the performance of a nondiscretionary act as a duty of office for the purpose of enforcing or recognizing an individual right or privilege. (See MARBURY V. MADISON, 1803.)

LEONARD W. LEVY

MANN ACT
36 Stat. 825 (1910)

Congress sought to suppress prostitution in the so-called White Slave Act under the commerce power. Anyone transporting or aiding the transportation of a woman in INTERSTATE or FOREIGN COMMERCE "for the purpose of prostitution or debauchery, or for any other immoral purpose, or with the intent and purpose to induce, entice, or compel such woman or girl" to such immoral acts was guilty of a FELONY. Persuasion to cross state lines for these purposes "whether with or without her consent" was likewise a felony. Another section doubled the already stiff penalties (five years imprisonment or $5,000) in cases involving women under eighteen years of age. The act also authorized the Commissioner-General of Immigration to "receive and centralize information concerning the procuration of alien women and girls" for such purposes and required brothel-keepers to file statements regarding alien employees, exempting the keepers from prosecution for "truthful statements."

In HOKE V. UNITED STATES (1913) the Supreme Court sustained congressional power to enact the law under the COMMERCE CLAUSE, relying squarely on CHAMPION V. AMES (1903): "Congress, as an incident to [the commerce power] may adopt not only means necessary but convenient to its exercise, and the means may have the quality of police regulations."

DAVID GORDON

MANN-ELKINS ACT
36 Stat. 539 (1910)

The ELKINS ACT of 1903 and the HEPBURN ACT of 1906, as well as the decisions they prompted, had reinvigorated the Interstate Commerce Commission (ICC) after disastrous Supreme Court decisions such as INTERSTATE COMMERCE COMMISSION V. CINCINNATI, NEW ORLEANS & TEXAS PACIFIC RAILWAY CO. (1897). The Mann-Elkins Act granted the ICC, for the first time, the power to set original rates; it also authorized the commission to suspend applications for proposed rate increases until it had ascertained their reasonableness. Despite the statute's vesting the commission with such powers, determinations of reasonableness would still be subject to the extraordinarily flexible guidelines of the FAIR RETURN rule laid down in SMYTH V. AMES (1898). The act placed the ICC firmly in control by shifting the BURDEN OF

PROOF on the question of reasonableness from the commission to the carriers. In addition, the act revived a prohibition against LONG HAUL–SHORT HAUL DISCRIMINATION, except where specifically allowed by the commission. The act also brought telephone, telegraph, and cable lines under ICC JURISDICTION. A unanimous Supreme Court sustained many of the act's provisions in *United States v. Atchinson, Topeka & Santa Fe Railroad* (1914).

DAVID GORDON

MANSFIELD, LORD

See: Murray, William

MAPP v. OHIO
367 U.S. 643 (1961)

Mapp v. Ohio brought to a close an abrasive constitutional debate within the Supreme Court on the question whether the EXCLUSIONARY RULE, constitutionally required in federal trials since 1914, was also required in state criminal cases. *Mapp* imposed the rule on the states.

WOLF V. COLORADO (1949) had applied to the states the FOURTH AMENDMENT's prohibition against UNREASONABLE SEARCHES, but it had not required state courts to exclude from trial evidence so obtained. *Mapp*'s extension of *Wolf* was based on two considerations. First, in *Wolf* the Court had been persuaded by the rejection of the exclusionary rule by most state courts; by 1961, however, a narrow majority of the states had independently adopted the rule. Second, the *Wolf* majority was convinced that other remedies, such as suits in tort against offending officers, could serve equally in deterring unlawful searches; time, however, had shown that such remedies were useless. "Nothing can destroy a government more quickly than its failure to observe its own laws," wrote Justice TOM C. CLARK for the Court, "or worse, its disregard of the charter of its own existence."

In *Mapp v. Ohio* the Court asserted emphatically that the exclusionary rule was "an essential part" of the Fourth Amendment and hence a fit subject for imposition on the states despite "passing references" in earlier cases to its being a nonconstitutional rule of evidence. Yet, in some hazy phrasing, the opinion also suggested that the Fifth Amendment's RIGHT AGAINST SELF-INCRIMINATION was the exclusionary

rule's constitutional backbone. Equally confusing was the Court's characterization of the rule as "the most important constitutional privilege" (that is, personal right) guaranteed by the Fourth Amendment while at the same time pointing to the rule's deterrent effect as justification for its imposition. More recently, the Court has settled on deterrence as the crucial consideration, and thus has refused to apply the rule in situations, such as GRAND JURY proceedings in CALANDRA V. UNITED STATES (1974), where in the Court's view the deterrent effect is minimal.

Three dissenters, in an opinion by Justice JOHN MARSHALL HARLAN, expressed "considerable doubt" that the federal exclusionary rule of WEEKS V. UNITED STATES (1914) was constitutionally based and argued that, in any event, considerations of FEDERALISM should allow the states to devise their own remedies for unlawful searches.

(Unlike the well-entrenched federal exclusionary rule, which has gone well-nigh unchallenged on the Court from the beginning, controversy concerning the rule for the states has continued unabated, both on and off the Court, since *Mapp* was decided.)

JACOB W. LANDYNSKI

MARBURY v. MADISON
1 Cranch 137 (1803)

Marbury has transcended its origins in the party battles between Federalists and Republicans, achieving mythic status as the foremost precedent for JUDICIAL REVIEW. For the first time the Court held unconstitutional an act of Congress, establishing, if only for posterity, the doctrine that the Supreme Court has the final word among the coordinate branches of the national government in determining what is law under the Constitution. By 1803 no one doubted that an unconstitutional act of government was null and void, but who was to judge? What *Marbury* settled, doctrinally if not in reality, was the Court's ultimate authority over Congress and the President. Actually, the historic reputation of the case is all out of proportion to the merits of Chief Justice JOHN MARSHALL's unanimous opinion for the Court. On the issue of judicial review, which made the case live, he said nothing new, and his claim for the power of the Court occasioned little contemporary comment. The significance of the case in its time derived from its political context and from the fact that the Court appeared successfully to interfere with the executive branch. Marshall's most remarkable accomplishment, in retrospect, was his massing of the Court behind a poorly reasoned opinion that section 13 of the JUDICIARY ACT OF 1789 was unconstitutional. Though the Court's legal craftsmanship was not evident, its judicial politics—egregious partisanship and calculated expediency—was exceptionally adroit, leaving no target for Republican retaliation beyond frustrated rhetoric.

Republican hostility to the United States courts, which were Federalist to the last man as well as Federalist in doctrine and interests, had mounted increasingly and passed the threshold of tolerance when the Justices on circuit enforced the Sedition Act. (See ALIEN AND SEDITION ACTS.) Then the lame-duck Federalist administration passed the JUDICIARY ACT OF 1801 and, a week before THOMAS JEFFERSON's inauguration, passed the companion act for the appointment of forty-two justices of the peace for the DISTRICT OF COLUMBIA, prompting the new President to believe that "the Federalists have retired into the Judiciary as a stronghold . . . and from that battery all the works of republicanism are to be beaten down and erased." The new Circuit Court for the District of Columbia sought in vain to obtain the conviction of the editor of the administration's organ in the capital for the common law crime of SEDITIOUS LIBEL. The temperate response of the new administration was remarkable. Instead of increasing the size of the courts, especially the Supreme Court, and packing them with Republican appointees, the administration simply repealed the Judiciary Act of 1801. (See JUDICIARY ACTS OF 1802.) On taking office Jefferson also ordered that the commissions for the forty-two justices of the peace for the district be withheld, though he reappointed twenty-five, all political enemies originally appointed by President JOHN ADAMS.

Marbury v. Madison arose from the refusal of the administration to deliver the commissions of four of these appointees, including one William Marbury. The Senate had confirmed the appointments and Adams had signed their commissions, which Marshall, the outgoing secretary of state, had affixed with the great seal of the United States. But in the rush of the "midnight appointments" on the evening of March 3, the last day of the outgoing administration, Marshall had neglected to deliver the commissions. Marbury and three others sought from the Supreme Court, in a case of ORIGINAL JURISDICTION, a WRIT OF MANDAMUS compelling JAMES MADISON, the new secretary of state, to issue their commissions. In December 1801 the Court issued an order commanding Madison to show cause why the writ should not be issued.

A congressman reflected the Republican viewpoint when saying that the show-cause order was "a bold stroke against the Executive," and JOHN BRECKINRIDGE, the majority leader of the Senate, thought the order "the most daring attack which the annals of Federalism have yet exhibited." When the debate began on the repeal bill, Federalists defended the show-cause order, the independence of the judiciary, and the duty of the Supreme Court to hold void any unconstitutional acts of Congress. A Republican paper declared that the "mandamus business" had first appeared to be only a contest between the judiciary and the executive but now seemed a political act by the Court to deter repeal of the 1801 legislation. In retaliation the Republicans passed the repealer and altered the terms of the Court so that it would lose its June 1802 session and not again meet until February 1803, fourteen months after the show-cause order. The Republicans hoped, as proved to be the case, that the Justices would comply with the repealer and return to circuit duty, thereby averting a showdown and a constitutional crisis, which the administration preferred to avoid.

By the time the Court met in February 1803 to hear arguments in *Marbury*, which had become a political sensation, talk of IMPEACHMENT was in the air. A few days before the Court's term, Federalists in Congress moved that the Senate should produce for Marbury's benefit records of his confirmation, provoking Senator James Jackson to declare that the Senate would not interfere in the case and become "a party to an accusation which may end in an impeachment, of which the Senate were the constitutional Judges." By no coincidence, a week before the Court met, Jefferson instructed the House to impeach a U.S. District Court judge in New Hampshire, and already Federalists knew of the plan to impeach Justice SAMUEL CHASE. Jefferson's desire to replace John Marshall with SPENCER ROANE was also public knowledge. Right before Marshall delivered the Court's opinion in *Marbury*, the Washington correspondent of a Republican paper wrote: "The attempt of the Supreme Court . . . by a mandamus, to control the Executive functions, is a new experiment. It seems to be no less than a commencement of war. . . . The Court must be defeated and retreat from the attack; or march on, till they incur an impeachment and removal from office."

Marshall and his Court appeared to confront unattractive alternatives. To have issued the writ, which was the expected judgment, would have been like the papal bull against the moon; Madison would have defied it, exposing the Court's impotence, and the

Republicans might have a pretext for retaliation based on the Court's breach of the principle of SEPARATION OF POWERS. To have withheld the writ would have violated the Federalist principle that the Republican administration was accountable under the law. ALEXANDER HAMILTON's newspaper reported the Court's opinion in a story headed "Constitution Violated by President," informing its readers that the new President by his first act had trampled on the charter of the peoples' liberties by unprincipled, even criminal, conduct against personal rights. Yet the Court did not issue the writ; the victorious party was Madison. But Marshall exhibited him and the President to the nation as if they were arbitrary Stuart tyrants, and then, affecting judicial humility, Marshall in obedience to the Constitution found that the Court could not obey an act of Congress that sought to aggrandize judicial powers in cases of original jurisdiction, contrary to Article III of the Constitution.

The Court was treading warily. The statute in question was not a Republican measure, not, for example, the repealer of the Judiciary Act of 1801. Indeed, shortly after *Marbury*, the Court sustained the repealer in STUART V. LAIRD (1803) against arguments that it was unconstitutional. In that case the Court ruled that the practice of the Justices in sitting as circuit judges derived from the Judiciary Act of 1789, and therefore derived "from a contemporary interpretation of the most forcible nature," as well as from customary acquiescence. Ironically, another provision of the same statute, section 13, was at issue in *Marbury*, not that the bench and bar realized it until Marshall delivered his opinion. The offending section, passed by a Federalist Congress after being drafted by OLIVER ELLSWORTH, one of the Constitution's Framers and Marshall's predecessor, had been the subject of previous litigation before the Court without anyone having thought it was unconstitutional. Section 13 simply authorized the Court to issue writs of *mandamus* "in cases warranted by the principles and usages of law," and that clause appeared in the context of a reference to the Court's APPELLATE JURISDICTION.

Marshall's entire argument hinged on the point that section 13 unconstitutionally extended the Court's original jurisdiction beyond the two categories of cases, specified in Article III, in which the Court was to have such jurisdiction. But for those two categories of cases, involving foreign diplomats or a state as a litigant, the Court has appellate jurisdiction. In quoting Article III, Marshall omitted the clause that directly follows as part of the same sentence: the Court has appellate jurisdiction "with such exceptions, and under such regulations as the Congress shall make." That might mean that Congress can detract from the Court's appellate jurisdiction or add to its original jurisdiction. The specification of two categories of cases in which the Court has original jurisdiction was surely intended as an irreducible minimum, but Marshall read it, by the narrowest construction, to mean a negation of congressional powers.

In any event, section 13 did not add to the Court's original jurisdiction. In effect it authorized the Court to issue writs of *mandamus* in the two categories of cases of original jurisdiction and in all appellate cases. The authority to issue such writs did not extend or add to the Court's jurisdiction; the writ of *mandamus* is merely a remedial device by which courts implement their existing jurisdiction. Marshall misinterpreted the statute and Article III, as well as the nature of the writ, in order to find that the statute conflicted with Article III. Had the Court employed the reasoning of *Stuart v. Laird* or the rule that the Court should hold a statute void only in a clear case, giving every presumption of validity in doubtful cases, Marshall could not have reached his conclusion that section 13 was unconstitutional. That conclusion allowed him to decide that the Court was powerless to issue the writ because Marbury had sued for it in a case of original jurisdiction.

Marshall could have said, simply, this is a case of original jurisdiction but it does not fall within either of the two categories of original jurisdiction specified in Article III; therefore we cannot decide: writ denied, case dismissed. Section 13 need never have entered the opinion, although, alternatively, Marshall could have declared: section 13 authorizes this Court to issue such writs only in cases warranted by the principles and usages of law; we have no jurisdiction here because we are not hearing the case in our appellate capacity and it is not one of the two categories in which we possess original jurisdiction: writ denied, case dismissed. Even if Marshall had to find that the statute augmented the Court's original jurisdiction, the ambiguity of the clause in Article III, which he neglected to quote, justified sustaining the statute.

Holding section 13 unconstitutional enabled Marshall to refuse an extension of the Court's powers and award the judgment to Madison, thus denying the administration a pretext for vengeance. Marshall also used the case to answer Republican arguments that the Court did not and should not have the power to declare an act of Congress unconstitutional, though he carefully chose an inoffensive section of a Federalist statute that pertained merely to writs of mandamus. That he gave his doctrine of judicial review the support of only abstract logic, without reference to history or precedents, was characteristic, as was the fact that his doctrine swept way beyond the statute that provoked it.

If Marshall had merely wanted a safe platform from which to espouse and exercise judicial review, he would have begun his opinion with the problems that section 13 posed for the Court; but he reached the question of constitutionality and of judicial review at the tail-end of his opinion. Although he concluded that the Court had to discharge the show-cause order, because it lacked jurisdiction, he first and most irregularly passed judgment on the merits of the case. Everything said on the merits was OBITER DICTA and should not have been said at all, given the judgment. Most of the opinion dealt with Marbury's unquestionable right to his commission and the correctness of the remedy he had sought by way of a writ of mandamus. In his elaborate discourse on those matters, Marshall assailed the President and his cabinet officer for their lawlessness. Before telling Marbury that he had initiated his case in the wrong court, Marshall engaged in what EDWARD S. CORWIN called "a deliberate partisan *coup.*" Then Marshall followed with a "judicial *coup d'état,*" in the words of ALBERT J. BEVERIDGE, on the constitutional issue that neither party had argued.

The partisan *coup* by which Marshall denounced the executive branch, not the grand declaration of the doctrine of judicial review for which the case is remembered, was the focus of contemporary excitement. Only the passages on judicial review survive. Cases on the REMOVAL POWER of the President, especially concerning inferior appointees, cast doubt on the validity of the dicta by which Marshall lectured the executive branch on its responsibilities under the law. Moreover, by statute and by judicial practice the Supreme Court exercises the authority to issue writs of mandamus in all appellate cases and in the two categories of cases of original jurisdiction. Over the passage of time *Marbury* came to stand for the monumental principle, so distinctive and dominant a feature of our constitutional system, that the Court may bind the coordinate branches of the national government to its rulings on what is the supreme LAW OF THE LAND. That principle stands out from *Marbury* like the grin on the Cheshire cat; all else, which preoccupied national attention in 1803, disappeared in our constitutional law. So too might have disappeared national judicial review if the impeachment of Chase had succeeded.

Marshall himself was prepared to submit to review of Supreme Court opinions by Congress. He was so shaken by the impeachment of Chase and by the thought that he himself might be the next victim in the event of Chase's conviction, that he wrote to Chase on January 23, 1804: "I think the modern doctrine of impeachment should yield to an appellate jurisdiction in the legislature. A reversal of those legal opinions deemed unsound by the legislature would certainly better comport with the mildness of our character than a removal of the judge who has rendered them unknowing of his fault." The acquittal of Chase meant that the Court could remain independent, that Marshall had no need to announce publicly his desperate plan for congressional review of the Court, and that *Marbury* remained as a precedent. Considering that the Court did not again hold unconstitutional an act of Congress until 1857, when it decided DRED SCOTT V. SANDFORD, sixty-eight years would have passed since 1789 without such a holding, and but for *Marbury,* after so long a period of congressional omnipotence, national judicial review might never have been established.

LEONARD W. LEVY

Bibliography
BEVERIDGE, ALBERT J.   1916–1919   *The Life of John Marshall,* 4 vols. Vol. III:50–178. Boston: Houghton Mifflin.
CORWIN, EDWARD S.   1914   *The Doctrine of Judicial Review.* Pages 1–78. Princeton, N.J.: Princeton University Press.
HAINES, CHARLES GROVE   1944   *The Role of the Supreme Court in American Government and Politics, 1789–1835.* Pages 223–258. Berkeley: University of California Press.
VAN ALSTYNE, WILLIAM W.   1969   A Critical Guide to Marbury v. Madison. *Duke Law Journal* 1969:1–47.
WARREN, CHARLES   1923   *The Supreme Court in United States History,* 3 vols. Vol. I:200–268. Boston: Little, Brown.

MARCHETTI v. UNITED STATES
390 U.S. 39 (1968)
GROSSO v. UNITED STATES
390 U.S. 62 (1968)
HAYNES v. UNITED STATES
390 U.S. 85 (1968)
UNITED STATES v. UNITED STATES COIN & CURRENCY
401 U.S. 715 (1971)

In *Marchetti* and *Grosso* the Supreme Court, in opinions by Justice JOHN MARSHALL HARLAN from which only Chief Justice EARL WARREN dissented, held that the RIGHT AGAINST SELF-INCRIMINATION constituted an ironclad defense against a criminal prosecution for failure to register as a gambler pursuant to federal gambling statutes or to pay federal occupational and EXCISE TAXES on gambling. The Court overruled *United States v. Kahriger* (1953) and *Lewis v. United States* (1955), which had held that the Fifth Amendment right could not be asserted by professional gamblers because the federal gambling laws did not compel self-incrimination. In those earlier cases the Court reasoned that the right was inapplicable to prospective acts: a gambler had the initial choice of deciding whether to continue gambling at the price of surrendering his right against self-incrimination, or cease gambling and thereby avoid the need to register and pay the taxes. In 1968 the Court found its earlier reasoning "no longer persuasive."

Justice Harlan explained how the statutes worked. A gambler had an obligation to register annually with the Internal Revenue Service as one engaged in the business of accepting wagers. He paid a $50 occupational tax plus an excise tax of ten percent on the gross amount of all bets. He had to keep daily records of all bets and reveal those records to IRS inspectors. The issue posed by such congressional requirements was not whether the United States may tax gambling, for the unlawfulness of an activity did not preclude its taxation. The issue, rather, was whether the registration, record-keeping, and tax provisions whipsawed gamblers into confessing criminal activities. Federal and state laws made gambling illegal, and the IRS made available to law enforcement agencies the identities of those who complied with the gambling statutes. Gamblers therefore confronted substantial hazards of self-incrimination. On pain of punishment for not complying, they had to provide prosecutors with evidence of their guilt.

Marchetti was convicted of failing to register and pay the occupational tax, Grosso for failing to pay that tax and the excises. Reversing their convictions, the Court distinguished their cases from those in which a criminal had failed to file income tax returns for fear of self-incrimination and another in which the government had required record keeping from persons not engaged in an inherently suspect activity. The mere filing of a tax return, required of all, or the failure to keep routine business records did not identify anyone as a suspect of a crime. In *Haynes*, the Court ruled that a person possessing a sawed-off shotgun is suspect and therefore cannot be compelled to register his weapon, under the National Firearms Act, because of the hazard of self-incrimination. In *United States Coin & Currency* a 5–4 Court applied the *Marchetti* reasoning to a forfeiture proceeding involving property used to violate federal gambling laws.

LEONARD W. LEVY

MARKETPLACE OF IDEAS

The "marketplace of ideas" argument in FIRST AMENDMENT jurisprudence was first enunciated in Justice OLIVER WENDELL HOLMES's dissenting opinion in ABRAMS V. UNITED STATES (1919):

But when men have realized that time has upset many fighting faiths, they may come to believe even more than they believe the very foundations of their own conduct that the ultimate good desired is better reached by free trade in ideas—that the best test of truth is the power of thought to get itself accepted in the competition of the market, and that truth is the only ground upon which their wishes safely can be carried out. That at any rate is the theory of our Constitution. It is an experiment, as all life is an experiment. . . . While that experiment is part of our system I think that we should be eternally vigilant against attempts to check the expression of opinions that we loathe and believe to be fraught with death, unless they so imminently threaten immediate interference with the lawful and pressing purpose of the law that an immediate check is required to save the country.

Holmes's stirring words recall similar but distinct passages from John Milton and John Stuart Mill. Extravagant as Holmes's passage is, it is in significant respects more careful than the implications of Milton's rhetorical question: "[W]ho ever knew truth put to the worse, in a free and open encounter?" Holmes did not claim that truth always or even usually emerges in the marketplace of ideas. Holmes's claim was more confined—that the best test of truth is the competition of the marketplace.

On the other hand, Milton spoke of a free and open encounter; Holmes spoke of the competition of the marketplace. A recurrent problem in First Amendment cases is that these two notions are not the same. Those who seek access to the broadcast media, as in RED LION BROADCASTING V. FCC (1969), or to powerful newspapers, as in MIAMI HERALD PUBLISHING CO. V. TORNILLO (1974), argue that the competition of the marketplace is not free and open. They urge that truth cannot emerge in the market if the gatekeepers do not let it in. A more general criticism of the Holmes position is that the claim that the marketplace is the best test of truth cannot itself be tested without an independent test of truth, yet the argument by its terms denies any superior test of truth that is independent of the marketplace.

These criticisms aside, the question arises whether the marketplace argument overvalues truth. Holmes's view that the expression of opinion should be free until an immediate check is needed to "save the country" has never been adopted by the Supreme Court. Advocacy of illegal action, for example, may be restricted when it is directed to and likely to incite or produce imminent lawless action, whether or not the country itself is endangered. Indeed, if the marketplace argument extends to facts as well as opinions, it is clear that showings far more pedestrian than Holmes's proposed requirements are sufficient to justify repression. The expression of factual beliefs can be restricted in order to protect reputation or privacy, and, in the commercial sphere, to further any substantial government interest.

Nonetheless, the marketplace argument has been a powerful theme in First Amendment law. For example, some defamatory facts and all defamatory opinion are protected in order to guarantee the breathing space we need for robust, uninhibited, and wide-open debate. Ironically, however, the marketplace argument serves to restrict speech as well as to protect it. "Under our Constitution," said the Court in GERTZ V. ROBERT WELCH, INC. (1974), "there is no such thing as a false idea," yet obscenity is divorced from speech protection because it is thought to be unnecessary for the expression of any idea. At bottom, First Amendment methodology is grounded in a paradox. Government must be restrained from imposing its views of truth. But government itself determines when this principle has been abandoned.

STEVEN SHIFFRIN

Bibliography

SCHAUER, FREDERICK 1978 Language, Truth and the First Amendment: An Essay in Memory of Harry Canter. *Virginia Law Review* 64:263, 268–272.

MARRIAGE AND THE CONSTITUTION

Although the constitutional "right to marry" was not securely confirmed by the Supreme Court until its decision in ZABLOCKI V. REDHAIL (1978), the Court had spoken of the freedom to marry as a FOURTEENTH AMENDMENT "liberty" as early as MEYER V. NEBRASKA (1923). Two WARREN COURT decisions had also laid the foundations for SUBSTANTIVE DUE PROCESS protections of marriage. GRISWOLD V. CONNECTICUT (1965) had recognized a RIGHT OF PRIVACY for the marital relationship, and LOVING V. VIRGINIA (1967) had struck down a MISCEGENATION law not only as an unconstitutional RACIAL DISCRIMINATION but also as a due process violation. The *Loving* opinion was explicit enough in speaking of the "freedom to marry," but doubt lingered that the Court meant to carry the principle beyond the racial context of the decision.

Zablocki ended the doubt. The Court held invalid, on equal protection grounds, a law forbidding a resident to marry without a judge's approval when he or she had court-ordered child support obligations. The judge could not approve the marriage unless support payments were kept current and the children were unlikely to become public charges. Some concurring Justices thought the law defective on due process grounds. *Zablocki*'s importance turns not on this doctrinal distinction but on its explicit recognition of marriage as a FUNDAMENTAL INTEREST, requiring STRICT SCRUTINY by the courts of direct and substantial governmental interference.

Just two months earlier, however, in *Califano v. Jobst* (1977), the Court had upheld a portion of the SOCIAL SECURITY ACT terminating disability benefits for a disabled dependent child of a wage earner when the child married a person not entitled to benefits under the act, even though that person was also disabled. Much of the discussion in *Zablocki*'s several opinions was devoted to *Jobst*. The majority distinguished *Jobst* as lacking the "directness and substantiality of the interference with the freedom to marry" present in *Zablocki*. The message was clear: interferences with marriage would demand justification in proportion to their degrees of severity. In *Zablocki* as in *Jobst* a money cost was attached to marriage; in *Zablocki* that cost would be prohibitive in most cases covered by the law.

This version of judicial interest-balancing seems likely to uphold such state restrictions on marriage as blood tests, reasonable age requirements, and insistence on a mentally retarded person's ability to understand the nature of the marriage relationship, even when those restrictions are strictly scrutinized. On principle, the state's power to prohibit POLYGAMY or to deny homosexual couples marriage or some comparable status seems more vulnerable to attack. It would be unrealistic, however, to expect an extension of the constitutional right to marry to homosexuals in the near future. (See SEXUAL PREFERENCE AND THE CONSTITUTION.) And recognition of a constitutional right to multiple marriage is a poor bet even for the distant future.

The extension of constitutional protection to other intimate relationships more closely resembling traditional marriage is already at hand. *Griswold*'s "privacy" protections have been effectively extended to the unmarried in EISENSTADT V. BAIRD (1972) and CAREY V. POPULATION SERVICES INTERNATIONAL (1977). Some states continue to recognize common law marriage, and others have concluded that support obligations may attach to the partners to some informal unions, once the unions end. As the number of unmarried couples living together increases, and as the incidents of unwed union come to resemble those of traditional marriage, formal marriage itself is more clearly seen in its expressive aspects, as a statement of commitment. In these circumstances it makes good sense to think of the right to marry as, in part, a FIRST AMENDMENT right.

KENNETH L. KARST

(SEE ALSO: *Freedom of Intimate Association.*)

Bibliography

KARST, KENNETH L.   1980   The Freedom of Intimate Association. *Yale Law Journal* 89:624–692.
NOTE   1980   Developments in the Law: The Constitution and the Family. *Harvard Law Review* 93:1156–1383, 1248–1296.

MARSH v. ALABAMA
326 U.S. 501 (1946)

When a person sought to distribute religious literature on the streets of a company town, the Supreme Court, 5–3, upheld her FIRST AMENDMENT claim against the owner's private property claims. Stressing the traditional role of free speech in town shopping districts open to the general public, Justice HUGO L. BLACK for the Court noted that, aside from private ownership, this town functioned exactly as did other towns which were constitutionally forbidden to ban leafleting. *Marsh* served as the basis for the later attempt, aborted in HUDGENS V. NLRB (1976), to extend First Amendment rights to users of privately owned SHOPPING CENTERS.

MARTIN SHAPIRO

MARSH v. CHAMBERS
463 U.S. 783 (1983)

A 6–3 Supreme Court sustained the constitutionality of legislative chaplaincies as not violating the SEPARATION OF CHURCH AND STATE mandated by the FIRST AMENDMENT. Chief Justice WARREN E. BURGER for

the Court abandoned the three-part test of LEMON V. KURTZMAN (1971) previously used in cases involving the establishment clause and grounded his opinion wholly upon historical custom. Prayers by tax-supported legislative chaplains, traceable to the FIRST CONTINENTAL CONGRESS and the very Congress that framed the BILL OF RIGHTS, had become "part of the fabric of our society." Justice JOHN PAUL STEVENS, dissenting, asserted that Nebraska's practice of having the same Presbyterian minister as the official chaplain for sixteen years preferred one denomination over others. Justices WILLIAM J. BRENNAN and THURGOOD MARSHALL, dissenting, attacked legislative chaplains generally as a form of religious worship sponsored by government to promote and advance religion and entangling the government with religion, contrary to the values implicit in the establishment clause—privacy in religious matters, government neutrality, freedom of conscience, autonomy of religious life, and withdrawal of religion from the political arena.

LEONARD W. LEVY

MARSHALL, JOHN
(1755–1835)

John Marshall, the third CHIEF JUSTICE of the Supreme Court (1801–1835), is still popularly known as the "Great Chief Justice" and the "Expounder of the Constitution." He was raised in the simple circumstances of backwoods Virginia, but his mother was pious and well educated and his father was a leader of his county and a friend of GEORGE WASHINGTON. Even though Marshall had little formal education, his extraordinary powers of mind, coupled with equity and good humor, made him a natural leader as a young soldier of the Revolution, as a member of the Richmond bar (then outstanding in the country), and as a general of the Virginia militia. He became nationally prominent as a diplomat, having outwitted the wily Charles Talleyrand while negotiating with France's Directory (1797–1798), and as a legislator, having supported Washington's FEDERALISM first in the Virginia Assembly (1782–1791, 1795–1797) and then in the House of Representatives (1799–1800). In June 1800 President JOHN ADAMS named Marshall to replace the Hamiltonian John Pickering as secretary of state, and in January 1801, after the strife-ridden Federalists' epochal defeat, appointed him Chief Justice when JOHN JAY, the first Chief Justice, declined to preside again over "a system so defective."

From its inception Marshall had defended the Constitution. His experience in Washington's ragtag army had made him a national patriot while rousing his disgust with the palsied Confederation. At the crucial Virginia ratifying convention (June 1788) he replied in three important speeches to the fears of PATRICK HENRY and other Anti-Federalists. The proposed Constitution, he argued, was not undemocratic, but a plan for a "well-regulated democracy." It set forth in particular the great powers of taxing and warring needed by any sound government. The state governments would retain all powers not given up expressly or implicitly; they were independently derived from the people. A mix of dependence upon the people and independence and virtue in the judges would prevent federal overreaching. If a law were not "warranted by any of the powers enumerated," Marshall remarked prophetically, the judges would declare it "void" as infringing "the Constitution they are to guard." Two other nonjudicial interpretations of the Constitution are notable. In 1799 Marshall wrote a report of the Virginia Federalists defending the constitutionality of the ill-famed Sedition Act of 1798 (a law he nevertheless had opposed as divisive in the explosive political atmosphere surrounding the French Revolution). If the NECESSARY AND PROPER CLAUSE authorizes punishment of actual resistance to law, he argued, it also authorizes punishment of "calumnious" speech, which is criminal under the COMMON LAW and prepares resistance. A speech to Congress in 1800, once famous in collections of American rhetoric, defended the President's power required by JAY'S TREATY to extradite a British subject charged with murder on a British ship. Because the criminal and the location were foreign, Marshall argued, the question was not a case in law or equity for United States courts; although a treaty is a law, it is a "political law," the execution of which lies with the President, not the courts. The judiciary has no political power whatever; the President is "the sole organ of the nation in its external relations."

As Chief Justice, Marshall raised the office and the Supreme Court to stature and power previously lacking. After having two Chief Justices in eleven years, the Court had Marshall for thirty-four, the longest tenure of any Chief Justice before or since. Individual opinions SERIATIM largely ceased, and dissents were discouraged. The Court came to speak with one voice. Usually the voice was Marshall's. He delivered the OPINION OF THE COURT in every case in which he participated during the decisive first five years, three-quarters of the opinions during the next seven years, and almost all the great constitutional opinions

throughout his tenure. Marshall's captivating and equable temper helped unite a diverse group of justices, many appointed by Republican Presidents bent on reversing the Court's declarations of federal power and restrictions of state power. In the face of triumphant Jeffersonian Republicans, suspicious of an unelected judiciary stocked with Federalists, Marshall was wary and astute. His Court never erred as the JAY COURT did in CHISHOLM V. GEORGIA (1793), which had provoked the ELEVENTH AMENDMENT as a corrective. Nor did he cast antidemocratic contentions in the teeth of the Jeffersonians or their Jacksonian successors, thus to provoke (as had Justice SAMUEL CHASE) IMPEACHMENT proceedings. Marshall's judicial opinions encouraged grave respect for law, treated the Constitution as sacred and its Founding Fathers as sainted men, and fashioned a protective and compelling shield of purpose, principle, and reasoning.

His crucial judicial accomplishment was MARBURY V. MADISON (1803), which laid down the essentials of the American RULE OF LAW. Judges are to oversee executive and legislature alike, keeping the political departments faithful to applicable statutes, to the written Constitution, and to "general principles" of law protecting individual rights and delimiting the functions of each department. A series of important decisions secured individual rights, especially the right to acquire property by contract, against state and general governments. UNITED STATES V. BURR (1807) expounded a narrow constitutional definition of TREASON and made prosecution difficult. STURGES V. CROWNINSHIELD (1819) set strict standards for voiding debts by bankruptcy. FLETCHER V. PECK (1810) and DARTMOUTH COLLEGE V. WOODWARD (1819) enforced as judicially protected contracts a state's sale of land and a state's grant of a corporate charter. Finally, several of Marshall's most famous opinions elaborated great powers for the national government and protected them from state encroachment. MCCULLOCH V. MARYLAND (1819) sustained Congress's authority to charter a bank and in general to employ broad discretion as to necessary and proper means for carrying out national functions. GIBBONS V. OGDEN (1824), the steamboat case, interpreted congressional power under the COMMERCE CLAUSE to protect a national market, a right of exchange free from state-supported monopoly. COHENS V. VIRGINIA (1821) eloquently defended Supreme Court review of state court decisions involving FEDERAL QUESTIONS.

The presupposition of Marshall's CONSTITUTIONAL-

ISM was that the Constitution is FUNDAMENTAL LAW, not merely a fundamental plan, written to impose limits, not just to raise powers, and designed to be permanent, not to evolve or to be fundamentally revised. Interpretation is to follow the words and purposes of the various provisions; amendment is for subordinate changes that will allow "immortality" to the Framers' primary work. Marshall called a written constitution America's "greatest improvement on political institutions." It renders permanent the institutions raised by popular consent, which is the only basis of rightful government. Besides, the American nation was fortunate in its founding: it benefited from a remarkable plan, from a fortunate ratification in the face of jealousy and suspicion in states and people, and from the extraordinary firmness of the first President. Washington had settled the new federal institutions and conciliated public opinion, despite the "infinite difficulty" of ratification and a crescendo of attacks upon his administration as monarchic, aristocratic, and anglophile. So Marshall argued in the penetrating (if somewhat wooden) *Life of George Washington*, a biography he condensed into a schoolbook to impress on his countrymen the character and political principles of "the greatest man in the world."

Marshall understood the Constitution to establish a government, not a league such as that created by the ARTICLES OF CONFEDERATION. The new government possessed sovereign powers of two sorts, legal (the judicial power) and political (legislative and executive). The special function of judges is to apply the law to individuals. It is a power extensive although not, Marshall consistently said, political or policy-oriented. Judicial JURISDICTION extends as far as does the law: common law, statute law, Constitution, treaties, and the law of nations (which Marshall influenced by several luminous opinions). In applying the law to individuals, courts are to care for individual rights, the very object of government in general. By "nature" or by "definition," courts are "those tribunals which are established for the security of property and to decide on human rights." Such rights are contained either in explicit constitutional provisions and amendments, or in "unwritten or common law," which the Constitution presupposes as the substratum of our law (and which Marshall thought was spelled out in traditional law books, such as Sir WILLIAM BLACKSTONE's *Commentaries on the Laws of England*). In short, courts are to construe all law in the light of the rights of person and property that are the object of law— as well as in the light of the constitutional authority of the other branches.

Marshall was fond of contrasting the Americans' "rational liberty," which afforded "solid safety and real security," with revolutionary France's "visionary" civic liberty, which had led to a despotism "borrowing the garb and usurping the name of freedom." While trying AARON BURR, Marshall repeatedly noted the "tenderness" of American law for the rights of the accused. His *Life of Washington* mixes praise of FREEDOM OF SPEECH and of conscience with attacks on religious persecution. Yet Marshall also said that morals and free institutions need to be "cherished" by public opinion; he would not suppose that a free MARKETPLACE OF IDEAS insures progress in public enlightenment. He did suppose that a rather free economic marketplace would lead to progress in national wealth. Marshall defended property rights in the sense of rights of contract or vested rights, rights that vest under contract and originate in a right to the fruits of one's labor and enterprise. By protecting industrious acquisitions the judiciary fosters the dynamic economy of free enterprise. Rational liberty is prudent liberty, which breeds power as well as wealth: the "legitimate greatness" of a "widespreading, rising empire," extending from "the Ste. Croix to the Gulph of Mexico, from the Atlantic to the Pacific." By directly securing the rights of property, courts indirectly secure the "vast republic."

While courts are "the mere instruments of the law, and can will nothing," or at most possess a legal discretion governed by unwritten principles of individual rights, the executive and legislature enjoy broad political discretion for the safety and interrelation of all. President and Congress are indeed subordinate to the Constitution of ENUMERATED POWERS and explicit restrictions. Marshall did not follow ALEXANDER HAMILTON, and would not have followed some later Supreme Courts, in inferring a plenary legislative power. His arguments, however, take aim at enemies on the other flank, at Jeffersonian strict constructionists who allowed only powers explicit in the Constitution or necessarily deduced from explicit powers. A constitution of government is not a "legal code," Marshall replied, and its enumerated powers are vested fully and encompass the full panoply of appropriate means. In *McCulloch*, Marshall set forth the core of the American doctrine of SOVEREIGNTY: the need for great governmental powers to confront inevitable crises. Maryland had placed a prohibitive tax on a branch of the national bank, and its counsel denied federal authority to charter a bank (a power not explicit in the Constitution). Ours is a constitution, Marshall replied, "intended to endure for ages to come, and, consequently, to be adapted to the various *crises* of human affairs." Armies must be marched and taxes raised throughout the land. "Is that construction of the Constitution to be preferred which would render these operations difficult, hazardous, and expensive?" In a similar spirit Marshall defended an executive vigorous in war and FOREIGN AFFAIRS and able to overawe faction and rebellion at home. He struck down, as violating Congress's power to regulate commerce among the states, state acts imposing import taxes or reserving monopolistic privileges. The arguments are typical. Great powers are granted for great objects. A narrow interpretation would defeat the object: the words must be otherwise construed. Thus a nation is raised. Individual enterprise, a national flow of trade, and the bonds of mutual interest breach barriers of state, section, and custom. The machinery of government is geared for great efforts of direction and coercion. The national sovereign, limited in its tasks, supreme in all means needed for their accomplishment, rises over the once independent state sovereignties. Marshall acknowledged the states' independent powers as well as the complexities of federalism: America was "for many purposes an entire nation, and for others several distinct and independent sovereignties." He tried above all to protect the federal government's superior powers from what the Framers had most feared, the encroachments of the states, more strongly entrenched in the people's affections.

Like virtually all of the Framers, Marshall was devoted to popular government. Yet SHAYS' REBELLION of western Massachusetts farmers (1786–1787) had made him wonder whether "man is incapable of governing himself." He thought the new Constitution a republican remedy for the flaws of republican government, and for some time he thought constitutional restraints might suffice to rein the people to sound government. Marshall's republicanism encompassed both representative government and balanced government. The people are to grant their sovereignty to institutions for exercise by their representatives. A more substantial, virtuous, and enlightened Senate and President would balance the more popular House of Representatives, the dangerous house in a popular republic. Marshall came to be troubled by a decline in the quality of American leaders, from the great statesmen of the Revolution and founding, notably Washington, to the "superficial showy acquirements" of "party politicians." He came to be deeply disheartened by the tumultuous growth of democratic control, inspired by THOMAS JEFFERSON and consummated by ANDREW JACKSON. A "torrent of public opinion," inflamed by the French Revolution, aroused the old

debtor and STATES' RIGHTS party during Washington's administration. It led to democratic societies, set up to watch the government, and then to a legislature that conveyed popular demands without much filtering. Marshall had anticipated that Jefferson would ally himself with the House of Representatives, and become leader of the party dominating the whole legislature, thus increasing his own power while weakening the office of President and the fundamentals of balanced government. During Jackson's terms (1828–1836), with the presidency transformed from a check on the majority to the tribune of the majority, Marshall favored reduction of its power, a tenure limited to one term, and even selection of the President by lot from among the senators. He called his early republicanism "wild and enthusiastic democracy," and came to doubt that the constitutional Union could endure in the face of resurgent sectionalism and populism.

The eventual dissolution of political balances made crucial Marshall's decisive accomplishment as he and Jefferson began their terms of office: the confirmation of the judiciary as interpreter and enforcer of the fundamental law. Although Marshall's opinion in *Marbury* denied that courts can exercise political power, it gave courts power to circumscribe the forbidden sphere, to determine the powers of legislatures and executives. Marshall's argument for this unprecedented judicial authority recalled "certain principles . . . long and well established." In deciding cases judges must declare what the law is. The Constitution is the supreme law. Judges must apply the Constitution in preference to statute when the two conflict—else the Constitution is not permanent but "alterable when the legislature shall please to alter it." The argument established the Supreme Court as enforcer of the constitutional government central to America's constitutional democracy. Marshall pointed to the horrors of "legislative omnipotence," only inconspicuously bestowing on courts a ruling potency as the voice of the Constitution. Marshall's opinion, the object of intense scrutiny ever since, was faithful to the CONSTITUTIONAL CONVENTION's supposition that there will be some JUDICIAL REVIEW of statutes and to its suspicion of democratic legislatures. It did not confront certain difficulties, notably those of a Supreme Court (like the TANEY COURT in DRED SCOTT V. SANDFORD, 1857) whose decisions violate the principles of the Constitution. Marshall's judicial reasonings were his attempt to keep judges, and his country, from violating the Constitution that preserves those principles.

ROBERT K. FAULKNER

Bibliography

BEVERIDGE, ALBERT J. 1916–1919 *The Life of John Marshall.* 4 Vols. Boston: Houghton Mifflin.

CORWIN, EDWARD S. 1919 *John Marshall and the Constitution.* New Haven, Conn.: Yale University Press.

FAULKNER, ROBERT K. 1968 *The Jurisprudence of John Marshall.* Princeton, N.J.: Princeton University Press.

HOLMES, OLIVER WENDELL 1952 John Marshall. Pages 266–271 in *Collected Legal Papers.* New York: Peter Smith.

WHITE, G. EDWARD 1976 *The American Judicial Tradition.* Pages 7–34. New York: Oxford University Press.

ZIEGLER, BENJAMIN MUNN 1939 *The International Law of John Marshall.* Chapel Hill: University of North Carolina Press.

MARSHALL, THURGOOD
(1908–   )

Thurgood Marshall, the first black Justice of the Supreme Court, was born in Baltimore in 1908. After graduation from Lincoln University in Pennsylvania, Marshall attended Howard University Law School. Graduating first in his class in 1933, Marshall became one of CHARLES H. HOUSTON's protégés. He began practice in Baltimore, where he helped revitalize the local branch of the National Association for the Advancement of Colored People (NAACP). Houston, who had become special counsel to the NAACP in New York, was developing a program of litigation designed to attack segregated education in the South; Marshall joined the NAACP staff as Houston's assistant in 1936.

Of all the Justices who have served on the Supreme Court, Marshall has the strongest claim to having contributed as much to the development of the Constitution as a lawyer as he has done as a judge. At the start of his career, race relations law centered on the SEPARATE BUT EQUAL DOCTRINE. In his initial years at the NAACP, Marshall brought a number of lawsuits challenging unequal salaries paid to black and white teachers in the South. After Marshall succeeded Houston as special counsel in 1938, he became both a litigator and a coordinator of litigation, most of it challenging segregated education. He also successfully argued a number of cases involving RACIAL DISCRIMINATION in the administration of criminal justice before the Supreme Court. When social and political changes during World War II led to increased black militancy and support for the NAACP, Marshall was able to expand the NAACP's legal staff by hiring an extremely talented group of young, mostly black lawyers. Although he continued to conduct some litigation, Mar-

shall gradually assumed the roles of appellate advocate and overall strategist. Relying on his staff to generate helpful legal theories, he selected the theory most likely to accomplish the NAACP's goals. This process culminated in the five lawsuits decided by the Supreme Court as BROWN V. BOARD OF EDUCATION (1954). Marshall had used his staff to develop these cases and the legal theory that segregation was unconstitutional no matter how equal were the physical facilities. After the Supreme Court held that segregation was unconstitutional and that it should be eliminated "with ALL DELIBERATE SPEED," Marshall and the NAACP staff devoted much of their attention to overcoming the impediments that southern states began to place in the way of DESEGREGATION. These impediments included school closures and investigations and harassment of the NAACP and its lawyers.

Marshall left the NAACP in 1961, having been nominated by President JOHN F. KENNEDY to a position on the UNITED STATES COURT OF APPEALS for the Second Circuit. His confirmation to that position was delayed by southern opposition for over eleven months. During Marshall's four years on the Second Circuit, he wrote an important opinion holding that the DOUBLE JEOPARDY clause applied to the states, anticipating by four years the position that the Supreme Court would adopt in BENTON V. MARYLAND (1969), a decision written by Justice Marshall. He also urged in dissent an expansive interpretation of statutes allowing persons charged with crimes in state courts to remove those cases to federal court. (See CIVIL RIGHTS REMOVAL.) Marshall was nominated as solicitor general by President LYNDON B. JOHNSON in 1965. He served as solicitor general for two years, during which he supervised the disposition of criminal cases imperiled by illegal WIRETAPPING. Johnson appointed him in 1967 to succeed Justice TOM C. CLARK on the Supreme Court.

Justice Marshall's contributions to constitutional development have been shaped by the fact that for most of his tenure his views were among the most liberal on a centrist or conservative Court. As he had at the NAACP, and as have most recent Justices, Marshall relied heavily on his staff to present his views forcefully and systematically in his opinions.

For a few years after Marshall's appointment to the Court, he was part of the liberal bloc of the WARREN COURT. Despite the tradition that newly appointed Justices are not assigned important majority opinions, Justice Marshall wrote several important free speech opinions during his first two years on the Court. In STANLEY V. GEORGIA (1969), he held that a state could not punish a person merely for possessing obscene materials in his home; the only justification for such punishment, guaranteeing a citizenry that did not think impure thoughts, was barred by the FIRST AMENDMENT. AMALGAMATED FOOD EMPLOYEES UNION V. LOGAN VALLEY PLAZA (1968) recognized the contemporary importance of privately owned SHOPPING CENTERS as places of public resort, holding that centers must be made available, over their owners' objections, to those who wish to picket or pass out leaflets on subjects of public interest. PICKERING V. BOARD OF EDUCATION (1968) established the right of public employees to complain about the way in which their superiors were discharging their responsibilities to the public.

With the appointment of four Justices by President RICHARD M. NIXON, Justice Marshall rapidly found himself in dissent on major civil liberties issues. *Stanley* was limited by *United States v. Reidel* (1971) to private possession and not extended to what might have seemed its logical corollary, acquisition of obscene material for private use. *Logan Valley Plaza* was overruled in HUDGENS V. NATIONAL LABOR RELATIONS BOARD (1976), and *Pickering* was limited by a relatively narrow definition of complaints relating to public duties in *Connick v. Myers* (1983). Marshall became part of a small liberal bloc that could prevail only by attracting more conservative members, who could be kept in the coalition by allowing them to write the majority opinions. In the series of death penalty cases, for example, Justice Marshall stated his conclusion that capital punishment was unconstitutional in all circumstances, but when a majority for a narrower position could be found to overturn the imposition of the death penalty in a particular case, he joined that majority.

Thus, after 1970, Marshall rarely wrote important opinions for the Court regarding FREEDOM OF SPEECH, CRIMINAL PROCEDURE, or EQUAL PROTECTION. Two of his opinions in cases about the PREEMPTION of state law by federal regulations, *Jones v. Rath Packing Co.* (1977) and *Douglas v. Seacoast Products* (1977), seem likely to endure as statements of general principle. More often he was assigned to write opinions in which a nearly unanimous Court adopted a "conservative" position. For example, in *Gillette v. United States* (1971), Justice Marshall's opinion for the Court rejected statutory and constitutional claims to exemption from the military draft by men whose religious beliefs led them to oppose participation in some but not all wars. Undoubtedly because of his race and because of his desire to see a majority support positions helpful to blacks, Marshall rarely wrote important opinions in cases directly implicating matters of race, although he did write two significant dissents, one defending AFFIRMATIVE ACTION in REGENTS OF THE UNIVERSITY OF CALIFORNIA V. BAKKE (1978), and another emphasizing blacks' lack of access to political power in MOBILE V. BOLDEN (1980). But Justice Marshall's major contributions have come in areas where the experience of race has historically shaped the context in which apparently nonracial issues arise.

Marshall occasionally received the assignment in important civil liberties cases. His opinion in POLICE DEPARTMENT OF CHICAGO V. MOSLEY (1972) crystallized the equality theme in the law of freedom of speech. There he emphasized the importance for free expression of the rule that governments may not regulate one type of speech because of its content, in a setting where speech with a different content would not be regulated: "[G]overnment may not grant the use of a forum to people whose views it finds acceptable, but deny use to those wishing to express less favored or more controversial views. . . . Selective exclusions . . . may not be based on content alone, and may not be justified by reference to content alone." Unless it were prohibited, discrimination based on content would allow governments, which ought to be controlled by the electorate, to determine what the electorate would hear. Although the *Mosley* principle is probably stated too broadly, because differential regulation of categories of speech such as OBSCENITY or COMMERCIAL SPEECH is allowed, still it serves as a central starting point for analysis, from which departures must be justified.

His opinion in *Memorial Hospital v. Maricopa County* (1974) synthesized a line of cases regarding the circumstances in which a state might deny benefits such as nonemergency medical care for INDIGENTS to those who had recently come to the state. If the benefit was so important that its denial could be characterized as a penalty for exercising the RIGHT TO TRAVEL, it was unconstitutional.

Because of the relatively rapid shift in the Court's composition, most of Justice Marshall's major contributions to the constitutional development have come through dissents. Several major dissenting opinions by Justice Marshall have helped shape the law of equal protection. The opinions criticize a rigid approach in which classifications based on race and a few other categories are to be given STRICT SCRUTINY while all other classifications must be "merely rational." Marshall, in dissents in DANDRIDGE V. WILLIAMS (1970) and SAN ANTONIO INDEPENDENT SCHOOL DISTRICT V. RODRIGUEZ (1973), offered a more flexible approach. He argued that the courts should examine legislation that affects different groups differently by taking into account the nature of the group—the degree to which it has been discriminated against in the past, the actual access to political power it has today—and the importance of the interests affected. Under this "sliding scale" approach, a statute differentially affecting access to WELFARE BENEFITS might be unconstitutional while one with the same effects on access to public recreational facilities might be permitted. A majority of the Court has not explicitly adopted the "sliding scale" approach, but Justice Marshall's sustained criticisms of the rigid alternative have produced a substantial, though not entirely acknowledged, acceptance of a more nuanced approach to equal protection problems.

As *Logan Valley Plaza* showed, Justice Marshall has urged, usually in dissent, an expansive definition of those actors whose decisions are subject to constitutional control. In JACKSON V. METROPOLITAN EDISON Co. (1974) the majority found that the decision of a heavily regulated utility to terminate service for nonpayment was not "state action" under any of the several strands of that DOCTRINE. Justice Marshall's dissent argued that state involvement was significant when looked at as a whole and, more important, pointed out that on the majority's analysis the utility could, without constitutional problems, terminate service to blacks. On the assumption, confirmed in later cases, that the result is incorrect, Justice Marshall's argument effectively demonstrated that the "state action" doctrine is actually a doctrine about the merits of the challenged decision: if it is a decision that the Justices believe should not be controlled by the Constitution, there is no "state action," whereas if it is a decision that the Justices believe should be controlled by the Constitution, there is state action.

Finally, after joining the seminal opinion in GOLDBERG V. KELLY (1968), which held that the Constitution defined the procedures under which public benefits, the "new property" of the welfare state, could be taken away, Justice Marshall dissented in later cases where the Court substantially narrowed the scope of *Goldberg*. His position, in cases such as BOARD OF REGENTS V. ROTH (1972), has been that everyone must be presumed to be entitled to those benefits, and that the presumption can be overcome only after constitutionality-defined procedures have been followed.

In most of the areas of law to which Justice Marshall's opinions have made significant contributions the linked strands of race and poverty appear. Discrimination by nominally private actors and suppression of speech on racial issues have played an important part in the black experience. Similarly, wealth and poverty as grounds for allocating public resources are classifications closely linked to race. Justice Marshall's desire to adopt a more flexible approach to equal protection law stems from his awareness that only such an approach would allow the courts to address difficulties that the ordinary routines of society cause for the poor. For example, his dissent in *United States v. Kras* (1973) objected to the imposition of a fifty dollar filing fee on those who sought discharges of their debts in bankruptcy. But it would be misleading to conclude that Thurgood Marshall's most important role in constitutional development was what he did as a Justice of the Supreme Court. Rather it was what he did as a lawyer for the NAACP before and after the decision in *Brown v. Board of Education*.

MARK V. TUSHNET

Bibliography
KLUGER, RICHARD 1976 *Simple Justice*. New York: Knopf.

MARSHALL v. BARLOW'S, INC.
436 U.S. 307 (1978)

In *Marshall* the Supreme Court held unconstitutional a congressional enactment authorizing Occupational Safety and Health Administration inspectors to conduct WARRANTLESS SEARCHES of employment facilities to monitor compliance with regulations. PROBABLE CAUSE for a warrant can, however, be satisfied on a lesser showing than that required in a search for criminal EVIDENCE.

JACOB W. LANDYNSKI

MARSHALL COURT
(1801–1835)

In 1801 the Supreme Court existed on the fringe of American awareness. Its prestige was slight, and it was more ignored than respected. On January 20, 1801, the day President JOHN ADAMS nominated JOHN MARSHALL for the chief justiceship, the commissioners of the DISTRICT OF COLUMBIA informed Congress that the Court had no place to hold its February term. The Senate consented to the use of one of its committee rooms, and Marshall took his seat on February 4 in a small basement chamber. At the close of 1809, Benjamin Latrobe, the architect, reported that the basement had been redesigned to enlarge the courtroom and provide an office for the clerk and a library room for the Justices. In 1811, however, Latrobe reported that the Court "had been obliged to hold their sittings in a tavern," because Congress had appropriated no money for "fitting up and furnishing the Court-room. . . ." After the British burned the Capitol in 1814 Congress again neglected to provide for the Court. It held its 1815 term in a private home, and for several years after met in temporary Capitol quarters that were "little better than a dungeon." The Court moved into permanent quarters in 1819. In 1824 a New York correspondent described the Court's Capitol chamber: "In the first place, it is like going down cellar to reach it. The room is on the basement story in an obscure part of the north wing. . . . A stranger might traverse the dark avenues of the Capitol for a week, without finding the remote corner in which Justice is administered to the American Republic." He added that the courtroom was hardly large enough for a police court.

The Supreme Court, however, no longer lacked dignity or respect. It had become a force that commanded recognition. In 1819 a widely read weekly described it as so awesome that some regarded it with reverence. That year THOMAS JEFFERSON complained that the Court had made the Constitution a "thing of wax," which it shaped as it pleased, and in 1824 he declared that the danger he most feared was the Court's "consolidation of our government." Throughout the 1820s Congress debated bills to curb the Court, which, said a senator, the people blindly adored—a "self-destroying idolatry." ALEXIS DE TOCQUEVILLE, writing in 1831, said: "The peace, the prosperity, and the very existence of the Union are vested in the hands of the seven Federal judges. Without them, the Constitution would be a dead letter. . . ." Hardly a political question arose, he wrote, that did not become a judicial question.

Chief Justice Marshall was not solely responsible for the radical change in the Court's status and influence, but he made the difference. He bequeathed to the people of the United States what it was not in the political power of the Framers of the Constitution to give. Had the Framers been free agents, they would have proposed a national government that was unquestionably dominant over the states and possessed a formidable array of powers breathtaking in flexibility and scope. Marshall in more than a figurative sense was the supreme Framer, emancipated from a local constituency, boldly using his judicial position as an exalted platform from which to educate the nation to the true meaning, his meaning, of the Constitution. He wrote as if words of grandeur and power and union could make dreams come true. By

the force of his convictions he tried to will a nation into being.

He reshaped the still malleable Constitution, giving clarification to its ambiguities and content to its omissions that would allow it to endure for "ages to come" and would make the government of the Union supreme in the federal system. Marshall is the only judge in our history whose distinction as a great nationalist statesman derives wholly from his judicial career. Justice OLIVER WENDELL HOLMES once remarked, "If American law were to be represented by a single figure, sceptic and worshipper alike would agree without dispute that the figure could be one alone, and that one, John Marshall." That the Court had remained so weak after a decade of men of such high caliber as JOHN JAY, OLIVER ELLSWORTH, JAMES WILSON, JAMES IREDELL, WILLIAM PATERSON, and SAMUEL CHASE demonstrates not their weakness but Marshall's achievement in making the Court an equal branch of the national government.

Until 1807 he cast but one of six votes, and after 1807, when Congress added another Justice, but one of seven. One Justice, one vote has always been the rule of the Court, and the powers of anyone who is Chief Justice depend more on the person than the office. From 1812, BUSHROD WASHINGTON and Marshall were the only surviving Federalists, surrounded by five Justices appointed by Presidents Thomas Jefferson and JAMES MADISON; yet Marshall dominated the Court in a way that no one has ever since. During Marshall's thirty-five-year tenure, the Court delivered 1,106 opinions in all fields of law, and he wrote 519; he dissented only eight times. He wrote forty of the Court's sixty-four opinions in the field of constitutional law, dissenting only once in a constitutional case. Of the twenty-four constitutional opinions for the Court that he did not write, only two were important: MARTIN V. HUNTER'S LESSEE (1816), a case in which he did not sit, and OGDEN V. SAUNDERS (1827), the case in which he dissented. He virtually monopolized the constitutional cases for himself and won the support of his associates, even though they were members of the opposing political party.

Marshall's long tenure coincided with the formative period of our constitutional law. He was in the right place at the right time, filling, as Holmes said, "a strategic place in the campaign of history." But it took the right man to make the most of the opportunity. Marshall had the character, intellect, and passion for his job that his predecessors lacked. He had a profound sense of mission comparable to a religious "calling." Convinced that he knew what the Constitution should mean and what it was meant to achieve, he determined to give its purposes enduring expression and make them prevail. The Court was, for him, a judicial pulpit and political platform from which to address the nation, to compete, if possible, with the executive and legislative in shaping public opinion.

Marshall met few of the abstract criteria for a "great" judge. A great judge should possess intellectual rectitude and brilliance. Marshall was a fierce and crafty partisan who manipulated facts and law. A great judge should have a self-conscious awareness of his biases and a determination to be as detached as human fallibility will allow. In Marshall the judicial temperament flickered weakly; unable to muzzle his deepest convictions, he sought to impose them on the nation, sure that he was right. He intoxicated himself with the belief that truth, history, and the Constitution dictated his opinions, which merely declared the law rather than made the law. A great judge should have confidence in majority rule, tempered by his commitment to personal freedom and fairness. Marshall did not think men capable of self-government and inclined to favor financial and industrial capitalism over most other interests. A great judge should have a superior technical proficiency, modified by a sense of justice and ethical behavior beyond suspicion. Marshall's judicial ethics were not unquestionable. He should have disqualified himself in MARBURY V. MADISON (1803) because of his negligent complicity. He overlooked colossal corruption in FLETCHER V. PECK (1810) to decide a land title case by a doctrine that promoted his personal interests. He wrote the opinion in McCULLOCH V. MARYLAND (1819) before hearing the case. Marshall's "juridical learning," as Justice JOSEPH STORY, his reverent admirer and closest colleague, conceded, "was not equal to that of the great masters in the profession. . . ." He was, said Story, first, last, and always, "a Federalist of the good old school," and in the maintenance of its principles "he was ready at all times to stand forth a determined advocate and supporter." He was, in short, a Federalist activist who used the Constitution to legitimate predetermined results. A great judge should have a vision of national and moral greatness, combined with respect for the federal system. Marshall had that—and an instinct for statecraft and superb literary skills. These qualities, as well as his activism, his partisanship, and his sense of mission, contributed to his inordinate influence.

So too did his qualities of leadership and his personal traits. He was generous, gentle, warm, charming, considerate, congenial, and open. At a time when members of the Court lived together in a common boarding house during their short terms in Washington, his charismatic personality enabled him to preside over a judicial family, inspire loyalty, and convert his brethren to his views. He had a cast-iron will, an astounding capacity for hard work (witness the number of opinions he wrote for the Court), and formidable powers of persuasion. He thought audaciously in terms of broad and basic principles that he expressed axiomatically as absolutes. His arguments were masterful intellectual performances, assuming that his premises were valid. Inexorably and with developing momentum he moved from an unquestioned premise to a foregone conclusion. Jefferson once said that he never admitted anything when conversing with Marshall. "So sure as you admit any position to be good, no matter how remote from the conclusion he seeks to establish, you are gone." Marshall's sophistry, according to Jefferson, was so great, "you must never give him an affirmative answer or you will be forced to grant his conclusion. Why, if he were to ask me if it were daylight or not, I'd reply, 'Sir, I don't know. I can't tell.' " Marshall could also be imperious. He sometimes gave as the OPINION OF THE COURT a position that had not mustered a majority. According to one anecdote, Marshall is supposed to have said to Story, the greatest legal scholar in our history, "That, Story, is the law. You find the precedents."

The lengthy tenure of the members of the Marshall Court also accounts for its achievements. On the pre-Marshall Court, the Justices served briefly; five quit in a decade. The Marshall Court lasted—BROCKHOLST LIVINGSTON seventeen years, THOMAS TODD nineteen, GABRIEL DUVALL twenty-four, WILLIAM JOHNSON thirty, Bushrod Washington thirty-one, and Marshall outlasted them all. Story served twenty-four years with Marshall and ten more after his death; SMITH THOMPSON served fifteen years with Marshall and eight years after. This continuity in personnel contributed to a consistent point of view in constitutional doctrine—a view that was, substantially, Marshall's. From 1812, when the average age of the Court's members was only forty-three, through 1823—twelve successive terms—the Court had the same membership, the longest period in its history without a change, and during that period the Marshall Court decided its most important cases except for *Marbury*.

Marshall also sought to strengthen the Court by inaugurating the practice of one Justice's giving the opinion of the Court. Previously the Justices had delivered their opinions SERIATIM, each writing an opinion in each case in the style of the English courts. That practice forced each Justice to take the trouble of understanding each case, of forming his opinion on it, and showing publicly the reasons that led to his judgment. Such were Jefferson's arguments for seriatim opinions; and Marshall understood that one official opinion augmented the Court's strength by giving the appearance of unity and harmony. Marshall realized that even if each Justice reached similar conclusions, the lines of argument and explanation of doctrine might vary with style and thought of every individual, creating uncertainty and impairing confidence in the Court as an institution. He doubtless also understood that by massing his Court behind one authoritative opinion and by assigning so many opinions to himself, his own influence as well as the Court's would be enhanced. Jefferson's first appointee, Justice Johnson, sought to buck the practice for a while. He had been surprised, he later informed Jefferson, to discover the Chief Justice "delivering all the opinions in cases in which he sat, even in some instances when contrary to his own judgment and vote." When Johnson remonstrated in vain, Marshall lectured him on the "indecency" of judges' "cutting at each other," and Johnson soon learned to acquiesce "or become such a cypher in our consultations as to effect no good at all." Story, too, learned to swallow his convictions to enhance the "authority of the Court." His "usual practice," said Story, was "to submit in silence" to opinions with which he disagreed. Even Marshall himself observed in an 1827 case, by which time he was losing control of his Court, that his usual policy when differing from majority was "to acquiesce silently in its opinion."

Like other trailblazing activist judges, Marshall squeezed a case for all it was worth, intensifying its influence. For Marshall a constitutional case was a medium for explaining his philosophy of the supreme and FUNDAMENTAL LAW, an occasion for sharing his vision of national greatness, a link between capitalism and CONSTITUTIONALISM, and an opportunity for a basic treatise. Justice Johnson protested in 1818, "We are constituted to decide causes, and not to discuss themes, or digest systems." He preferred, he said, to decide no more in any case "than what the case itself necessarily requires." Ordinary Justices decide only the immediate question on narrow grounds; but Marshall, confronted by some trivial question—whether a justice of the peace had a right to his commission or whether peddlers of lottery tickets could be fined—would knife to the roots of the controversy, discover that it involved some great constitutional principle, and explain it in the broadest possible way, making the case seem as if the life of the Union or the supremacy of the Constitution were at stake. His audacity in generalizing was impressive; his strategy was to take the highest ground and make unnerving use of OBITER DICTA; and then, as a matter of tactics, almost unnoticeably decide on narrow grounds. *Marbury* is remembered for Marshall's exposition of JUDICIAL REVIEW, not for his judicial humility in declining JURISDICTION and refusing to issue the WRIT OF MANDAMUS. COHENS V. VIRGINIA (1821) is remembered for Marshall's soaring explication of the supremacy of the JUDICIAL POWER OF THE UNITED STATES, not for the decision in favor of Virginia's power to fine unlicensed lottery ticket peddlers. GIBBONS V. OGDEN (1824) is remembered for its sweeping discourse on the COMMERCE CLAUSE of the Constitution, not for the decision that the state act conflicted with an obscure act of Congress.

Marshall's first major opinion, in *Marbury*, displayed his political cunning, suppleness in interpretation, doctrinal boldness, instinct for judicial survival, and ability to maneuver a case beyond the questions on its face. Having issued the show cause order to Madison, the Court seemingly was in an impossible position once Jefferson's supporters called that order a judicial interference with the executive branch. To decide for Marbury would provoke a crisis that the Court could not survive: Madison would ignore the Court, which had no way to enforce its decision, and the Court's enemies would have a pretext for IMPEACHMENT. To decide against Marbury would appear to endorse the illegal acts of the executive branch and concede that the Court was helpless. Either course of action promised judicial humiliation and loss of independence. Marshall therefore found a way to make a tactical retreat while winning a great strategic victory for judicial power. After upbraiding the executive branch for violating Marbury's rights, Marshall concluded that the Court had no JURISDICTION in the case, because a provision of an act of Congress conflicted with Article III. He held that provision unconstitutional by, first, giving it a sweeping construction its text did not bear and, second, by comparing it to his very narrow construction of Article III. Thus he reached and decided the great question, not argued by counsel, whether the Court had the power to declare unconstitutional an act of Congress. By so doing he answered from the bench his critics in Congress who, now that they were in power, had renounced judicial review during the debate on the repeal of the JUDICIARY ACT OF 1801. Characteristically Marshall relied on no precedents, not even on the authority of THE FEDERALIST #78. Significantly, he chose a safe act of Congress to void—section 13 of the JUDICIARY ACT OF 1789, which concerned not the province of the Congress or the President but of the Supreme Court, its authority to issue writs of mandamus in cases of ORIGINAL JURISDICTION. But Marshall's exposition of judicial review was, characteristically, broader than the holding on section 13. Jefferson, having been given no stick with which to beat Marshall, privately fumed: "Nothing in the Constitution has given them a right to decide for the Executive, more than to the Executive to decide for them," he wrote in a letter. "The opinion which gives to the judges the right to decide what laws are constitutional, and what not, not only for themselves in their own sphere of action, but also for the Legislature and Executive also, in their spheres, would make the judiciary a despotic branch."

The Court did not dare to declare unconstitutional any other act of Congress which remained hostile to it throughout Marshall's tenure. STUART V. LAIRD (1803), decided shortly after Marbury, upheld the repeal of the Judiciary Act of 1801. (See JUDICIARY ACTS OF 1802.) A contrary decision would have been institutionally suicidal for the Court. Marshall's opinion in Marbury was daring enough; in effect he courageously announced the Court's independence of the other branches of the government. But he was risking retaliation. Shortly before the arguments in Marbury, Jefferson instructed his political allies in the House to start IMPEACHMENT proceedings against JOHN PICKERING, a federal district judge; the exquisite timing was a warning to the Supreme Court. Even earlier, Jeffersonian leaders in both houses of Congress openly spoke of impeaching the Justices. The threats were not idle. Two months after Marbury was decided, Justice Chase on circuit attacked the administration in a charge to a GRAND JURY, and the House prepared to impeach him. Senator WILLIAM GILES of Virginia, the majority leader, told Senator JOHN QUINCY ADAMS that not only Chase "but all the other Judges of the Supreme Court," except William Johnson, "must be impeached and removed." Giles thought that holding an act of Congress unconstitutional was ground for impeachment. "Impeachment was not a criminal prosecution," according to Giles, who was Jefferson's spokesman in the Senate. "And a removal by impeachment was nothing more than a declaration by Congress to this effect: you hold dangerous opinions, and if you are suffered to carry them into effect, you will work the destruction of the Union. We want your offices for the purposes of giving them to men who will fill them better."

Intimidated by Chase's impending impeachment,

Marshall, believing himself to be next in line, wrote to Chase that "impeachment should yield to an APPELLATE JURISDICTION in the legislature. A reversal of those legal opinions deemed unsound by the legislature would certainly better comport with the mildness of our character than a removal of the Judge who has rendered them unknowing of his fault." Less than a year after his Marbury opinion the fear of impeachment led an anguished Marshall to repudiate his reasoning and favor Congress as the final interpreter of the Constitution. Fortunately the greatest crisis in the Court's history eased when the Senate on March 1, 1805, failed to convict Chase on any of the eight articles of impeachment. Marshall and his Court were safe from an effort, never again repeated, to politicize the Court by making it subservient to Congress through impeachment.

The Court demonstrated its independence even when impeachment hung over it. In Little v. Barreme (1804) Marshall for the Court held that President Adams had not been authorized by Congress to order an American naval commander to seize a ship sailing from a French port. Justice Johnson on circuit vividly showed his independence of the President who had appointed him. To enforce the EMBARGO ACTS, Jefferson had authorized port officers to refuse clearance of ships with "suspicious" cargoes. In 1808 Johnson, on circuit in Charleston, ordered the clearance of a ship and denounced the President for having exceeded the power delegated by the Embargo Acts. Jefferson could not dismiss as partisan politics Johnson's rebuke that he had acted as if he were above the law. Justice Brockholst Livingston, another Jefferson appointee, also had occasion in 1808 to show his independence of the President. Jefferson supported a federal prosecution for TREASON against individuals who had opposed the embargo with violence. Livingston, who presided at the trial, expressed "astonishment" that the government would resort to a theory of "constructive treason" in place of the Constitution's definition of treason as levying war against the United States and he warned against a "precedent so dangerous." The jury speedily acquitted. After the tongue-lashing from his own appointees, Jefferson won an unexpected victory in the federal courts in the case of the brig William (1808). Federal district judge John Davis in Massachusetts sustained the constitutionality of the Embargo Acts on commerce clause grounds. Davis, a lifelong Federalist, showed how simplistic was Jefferson's raving about judicial politics.

The evidence for the Court's nonpartisanship seems plentiful. For example, Justice Story, Madison's appointee, spoke for an independent Court in Gelston *v. Hoyt* (1818), a suit for damages against government officials whose defense was that they had acted under President Madison's orders. Story, finding no congressional authority for these orders, "refused an extension of prerogative" power and added, "It is certainly against the general theory of our institutions to create discretionary powers by implication. . . ."

On the other hand, the Court supported the theory of IMPLIED POWERS in *McCulloch v. Maryland* (1819), which was the occasion of Marshall's most eloquent nationalist opinion. *McCulloch* had its antecedent in *United States v. Fisher* (1804), when the Court initially used BROAD CONSTRUCTION to sustain an act of Congress that gave to the government first claim against certain insolvent debtors. Enunciating the DOCTRINE of implied powers drawn from the NECESSARY AND PROPER CLAUSE, Marshall declared that Congress could employ any useful means to carry out its ENUMERATED POWER to pay national debts. That the prior claim of the government interfered with state claims was an inevitable result, Marshall observed, of the supremacy of national laws. Although a precursor of *McCulloch, Fisher* attracted no opposition because it did not thwart any major state interests.

When the Court did confront such interests for the first time, in UNITED STATES V. JUDGE PETERS (1809), Marshall's stirring nationalist passage, aimed at states that annulled judgments of the federal courts, triggered Pennsylvania's glorification of state sovereignty and denunciation of the "unconstitutional exercise of powers in the United States Courts." The state called out its militia to prevent execution of federal judgments and recommended a constitutional amendment to establish an "impartial tribunal" to resolve conflicts between "the general and state governments." State resistance collapsed only after President Madison backed the Supreme Court. Significantly, eleven state legislatures, including Virginia's, censured Pennsylvania's doctrines and endorsed the Supreme Court as the constitutionally established tribunal to decide state disputes with the federal courts.

The *Judge Peters* episode revealed that without executive support the Court could not enforce its mandate against a hostile state, which would deny that the Court was the final arbiter under the Constitution if the state's interests were thwarted. The episode also revealed that if other states had no immediate stake in the outcome of a case, they would neither advance doctrines of state sovereignty nor repudiate the Court's supreme appellate powers. When Virginia's high court ruled that the appellate jurisdiction of the Supreme Court did not extend to court judg-

ments and that section 25 of the Judiciary Act of 1789 was unconstitutional, the Marshall Court, dominated by Republicans, countered by sustaining the crucial statute in *Martin v. Hunter's Lessee* (1816). Pennsylvania and other states did not unite behind Virginia when it proposed the constitutional amendment initiated earlier by Pennsylvania, because *Martin* involved land titles of no interest to other states. The fact that the states were not consistently doctrinaire and became aggressive only when Court decisions adversely affected them enabled the Court to prevail in the long run. A state with a grievance typically stood alone. But for the incapacity or unwillingess of the Court's state enemies to act together in their proposals to cripple it, the great nationalist decisions of the Marshall Court would have been as impotent as the one in *Worcester v. Georgia* (1832). *Worcester* majestically upheld the supreme law against the state's despoliation of the Cherokees, but President ANDREW JACKSON supported Georgia, which flouted the Court. Even Georgia, however, condemned the SOUTH CAROLINA ORDINANCE OF NULLIFICATION, and several state legislatures resolved that the Supreme Court was the constitutional tribunal to settle controversies between the United States and the states.

The Court made many unpopular decisions that held state acts unconstitutional. *Fletcher v. Peck*, which involved the infamous Yazoo land frauds, was the first case in which the Justices voided a state act for conflict with the Constitution itself. *Martin v. Hunter's Lessee*, which involved the title to the choice Fairfax estates in Virginia, was only the first of a line of decisions that unloosed shrill attacks on the Court's jurisdiction to decide cases on a WRIT OF ERROR to state courts. In *McCulloch* the Court supported the "monster monopoly," the Bank of the United States chartered by Congress, and held unconstitutional a state tax on its Baltimore branch. In *Cohens* the Court again championed its supreme appellate powers under section 25 of the Judiciary Act of 1789 and circumvented the ELEVENTH AMENDMENT. In STURGES V. CROWNINSHIELD (1819) the Court nullified a state bankruptcy statute that aided victims of an economic panic. In GREEN V. BIDDLE (1821) the Court used the CONTRACT CLAUSE when voiding Kentucky acts that supported valuable land claims. In OSBORN V. BANK OF THE UNITED STATES (1824) it voided an Ohio act that defied *McCulloch* and raised the question whether the Constitution had provided for a tribunal capable of protecting those who executed the laws of the Union from hostile state action.

When national supremacy had not yet been established and claims of state sovereignty bottomed state statutes and state judicial decisions that the Court overthrew, state assaults on the Court were inevitable, imperiling it and the Union it defended. Virginia, the most prestigious state, led the assault which Jefferson encouraged and SPENCER ROANE directed. Kentucky's legislature at one point considered military force to prevent execution of the *Green* decision. State attacks were vitriolic and intense, but they were also sporadic and not united. Ten state legislatures adopted resolutions against the Marshall Court, seven of them denouncing section 25 of the 1789 Act, which was the jurisdictional foundation for the Court's power of judicial review over the states. In 1821, 1822, 1824, and 1831 bills were introduced in Congress to repeal section 25. The assault on the Court was sharpest in the Senate, whose members were chosen by the state legislatures. Some bills to curb the Court proposed a constitutional amendment to limit the tenure of the Justices. One bill would have required seriatim opinions. Others proposed that no case involving a state or a constitutional question could be decided except unanimously; others accepted a 5–2 vote. One bill proposed that the Senate should have appellate powers over the Court's decisions.

Throughout the 1820s the attempts to curb the Court created a continuing constitutional crisis that climaxed in 1831, when Marshall despondently predicted the repeal of section 25 and the dissolution of the Union. In 1831, however, the House, after a great debate, defeated a repeal bill by a vote of 138–51; Southerners cast forty-five of the votes against the Court. What saved the Court was the inability of its opponents to mass behind a single course of action; many who opposed section 25 favored a less drastic measure. The Court had stalwart defenders, of course, including Senators DANIEL WEBSTER and JAMES BUCHANAN. Most important, it had won popular approbation. Although the Court had enemies in local centers of power, Americans thrilled to Marshall's paeans to the Constitution and the Union and he taught them to identify the Court with the Constitution and the Union.

A perceptible shift in the decisions toward greater tolerance for state action also helped dampen the fires under the Court in Marshall's later years. The coalition that Marshall had forged began to dissolve with the appointments of Justices Smith Thompson, JOHN MCLEAN, and HENRY BALDWIN. BROWN V. MARYLAND (1827), MARTIN V. MOTT (1827), AMERICAN INSURANCE COMPANY V. CANTER (1828), WESTON V. Charleston (1829), CRAIG V. MISSOURI (1830), and the CHEROKEE INDIAN CASES (1832) continued the lines of doctrine laid down by the earlier Marshall Court. But the impact of new appointments was felt in the decisions of *Ogden v. Saunders* (1827), WILLSON V. BLACKBIRD CREEK MARSH COMPANY (1829) and PROVIDENCE BANK V. BILLINGS (1830). In Marshall's last decade on the Court, six decisions supported nationalist claims against seventeen for state claims. During the same decade there were ten decisions against claims based on VESTED RIGHTS and only one sustaining such a claim. The shift in constitutional direction may also be inferred from the inability of the Marshall Court, because of dissension and illness, to resolve CHARLES RIVER BRIDGE V. WARREN BRIDGE, MAYOR OF NEW YORK V. MILN, and BRISCOE V. BANK OF KENTUCKY, all finally decided in 1837 under Marshall's successor against the late Chief Justice's wishes. Before his last decade the only important influence on the Court resulting from the fact that Republicans had a voting majority was the repudiation of a FEDERAL COMMON LAW OF CRIMES.

What was the legacy of the Marshall Court? It established the Court as a strong institution, an equal and coordinate branch of the national government, independent of the political branches. It established itself as the authoritative interpreter of the supreme law of the land. It declared its rightful authority to hold even acts of Congress and the President unconstitutional. It maintained continuing judicial review over the states to support the supremacy of national law. In so doing, the Court sustained the constitutionality of the act of Congress chartering the Bank of the United States, laying down the definitive exposition of the doctrine of implied powers. The Court also expounded the commerce clause in *Gibbons v. Ogden* (1824), with a breadth and vigor that provided the basis for national regulation of the economy generations later. Finally, the Court made the contract clause of the Constitution into a bulwark protecting both vested rights and risk capital. *Fletcher* supported the sanctity of public land grants to private parties, encouraging capital investment and speculation in land values. NEW JERSEY V. WILSON (1812) laid down the doctrine that a state grant of tax immunity constituted a contract within the protection of the Constitution, preventing subsequent state taxation for the life of the grant. DARTMOUTH COLLEGE V. WOODWARD (1819) protected private colleges and spurred the development of state universities; it also provided the constitutional props for the expansion of the private corporation by holding that a charter of incorporation is entitled to protection of the contract clause. The Marshall Court often relied on nationalist doctrines to prevent state measures that sought to regulate or thwart corporate development. Just as national supremacy, judicial review, and the Court's appellate jurisdiction were often interlocked, so too the interests of capitalism, nationalism, and judicial review were allied. Time has hardly withered the influence and achievements of the Marshall Court.

LEONARD W. LEVY

Bibliography

BAKER, LEONARD 1974 *John Marshall.* New York: Macmillan.

BEVERIDGE, ALBERT J. 1919 *The Life of John Marshall.* Vols. 3 and 4. Boston: Houghton Mifflin.

CORWIN, EDWARD S. 1919 *John Marshall and the Constitution: A Chronicle of the Supreme Court.* New Haven: Yale University Press.

HAINES, CHARLES G. 1944 *The Role of the Supreme Court in American Government and Politics, 1789–1835.* Berkeley: University of California Press.

HASKINS, GEORGE LEE and JOHNSON, HERBERT Q. 1981 *Foundations of Power: John Marshall, 1801–1815.* Volume 2 of the *Oliver Wendell Holmes Devise History of the Supreme Court of the United States.* New York: Macmillan.

KONEFSKY, SAMUEL J. 1964 *John Marshall and Alexander Hamilton.* New York: Macmillan.

MORGAN, DONALD G. 1954 *Justice William Johnson: The First Great Dissenter.* Columbia: University of South Carolina Press.

WARREN, CHARLES 1923 *The Supreme Court in United States History,* 3 vols. Boston: Little, Brown.

MARSHALL PLAN

At the Harvard University commencement exercises on June 5, 1947, Secretary of State George C. Marshall proposed that the United States undertake a vast program of postwar economic aid to assist the countries of Europe to rebuild from World War II. Neither Secretary Marshall nor President HARRY S. TRUMAN offered any constitutional authority for such a program, although some members of Congress, led by Senator ROBERT A. TAFT of Ohio, contended that the expenditure could not be justified under either the FOREIGN AFFAIRS power or the TAXING AND SPENDING POWER. Acting on the initiative of the United States, sixteen European nations formed the Organization of European Economic Cooperation (OEEC) which in turn issued a report setting forth Europe's collective needs and resources. The Soviet Union and other East European countries were invited to participate, but de-

clined. Thereafter, on April 3, 1948, following the Soviet-sponsored coup in Czechoslovakia, which turned the tide of congressional opinion and caused the Marshall Plan expenditures to be justified as a national defense measure, the United States Congress passed the Economic Cooperation Act, to be administered by the Economic Cooperation Administration. Within four years and after the expenditure of $12–$13 billion in American loans and grants-in-aid, Europe made tremendous strides toward economic recovery. Coupled with increased military security (evidenced primarily in the signing of the NORTH ATLANTIC TREATY in 1949 and formation of the North Atlantic Alliance), this extensive economic recovery helped quell fears of Soviet expansion into Western Europe. The Marshall Plan and the OEEC resulting from it also created a precedent for further economic integration among the participating states of Western Europe.

BURNS H. WESTON

Bibliography

PRICE, HARRY BAYARD 1955 *The Marshall Plan and Its Meaning.* Ithaca, N.Y.: Cornell University Press.

MARTIAL LAW

See: Civil–Military Relations and the Constitution

MARTIN, LUTHER
(1748–1826)

Luther Martin represented Maryland in the Continental Congress and signed the DECLARATION OF INDEPENDENCE. He was attorney general of Maryland from 1778 to 1805 and one of the early leaders of the American bar. Martin also represented Maryland at the CONSTITUTIONAL CONVENTION OF 1787, where he was a leader of the small-state faction. Although he favored the Convention's purpose, he consistently advocated positions that would have prevented the establishment of a strong central government. Fearing tyranny, he endorsed a one-term presidency and opposed JAMES MADISON's plan to allow a congressional veto of state or local laws.

The question of congressional REPRESENTATION seemed to him one of the most vexing problems. He favored a unicameral legislature and spoke fervently against proportionate representation at the House of Representatives, both in the Convention and afterward. His opposition in Philadelphia helped produce the deadlock that nearly wrecked the convention, but he served on the committee that framed the GREAT COMPROMISE and supported its recommendation. Martin favored JUDICIAL REVIEW but opposed authorizing Congress to create federal courts on the ground that state courts would suffice; they were bound by federal law and their decisions could be appealed to the Supreme Court. Martin also thought that the clause prohibiting interference with the OBLIGATION OF CONTRACTS was unwise; he warned of the inevitability of "great public calamities and distress" when such intervention would become essential—an argument vindicated in HOME BUILDING & LOAN V. BLAISDELL (1934). As the summer progressed, Martin grew increasingly restive. He opposed allowing suspension of the writ of HABEAS CORPUS and he strongly favored granting Congress power to tax or completely prohibit the slave trade. An opponent of slavery, he labeled its recognition in the Constitution "absurd and disgraceful to the last degree." Martin also concluded that later changes rendered the SUPREMACY CLAUSE, which he originally had proposed, "worse than useless." For these reasons, and because the Constitution contained no BILL OF RIGHTS, he opposed its ratification. In his influential tract of 1788 against RATIFICATION OF THE CONSTITUTION, a major anti-Federalist statement, Martin presented the fullest argument of the time in favor of equal representation of the states in Congress. Despite his opposition to the Constitution, Martin later switched his party allegiance and became known as the "Federalist bulldog."

A brilliant lawyer despite his later alcoholism, Martin appeared frequently in the Supreme Court and in state trials; he defended his old friend Justice SAMUEL CHASE at the latter's IMPEACHMENT trial in 1804 and represented AARON BURR against a TREASON charge three years later, winning both cases. (See EX PARTE BOLLMAN AND SWARTWOUT, 1807.) Among dozens of Court appearances, his most famous cases were FLETCHER V. PECK (1810) and MCCULLOCH V. MARYLAND (1819). In *McCulloch*, he eloquently defended Maryland's right to tax the federally chartered Bank of the United States, arguing for the application of the Tenth Amendment. Shortly after losing *McCulloch*, Martin suffered a severe stroke. After living as a penniless derelict for some time, he was eventually taken in by Burr. He died in 1826.

DAVID GORDON

Bibliography

CLARKSON, PAUL S. and JETT, R. SAMUEL 1970 *Luther Martin of Maryland.* Baltimore: Johns Hopkins University Press.

MARTIN v. HUNTER'S LESSEE
1 Wheaton 304 (1816)

Appomattox ultimately settled the issue that bottomed this case: were the states or was the nation supreme? As a matter of law, the opinion of the Supreme Court supplied the definitive answer, but law cannot settle a conflict between competing governments unless they agree to abide by the decision of a tribunal they recognize as having JURISDICTION to decide. Whether such a tribunal existed was the very issue in this case; more precisely the question was whether the Supreme Court's APPELLATE JURISDICTION extended to the state courts. In 1810 Virginia had supported the Court against state sovereignty advocates. Pennsylvania's legislature had resolved that "no provision is made in the Constitution for determining disputes between the general and state governments by an impartial tribunal." To that Virginia replied that the Constitution provides such a tribunal, "the Supreme Court, more eminently qualified . . . to decide the disputes aforesaid in an enlightened and impartial manner, than any other tribunal which could be erected." (See UNITED STATES V. JUDGE PETERS, 1809.) The events connected with the *Martin* case persuaded Virginia to reverse its position. The highest court of the state, the Virginia Court of Appeals, defied the Supreme Court, subverted the JUDICIAL POWER OF THE UNITED STATES as defined by Article III of the Constitution, circumvented the SUPREMACY CLAUSE (Article VI), and held unconstitutional a major act of Congress—all for the purpose of repudiating JUDICIAL REVIEW, or the Supreme Court's appellate jurisdiction over state courts and power to declare state acts void.

The *Martin* case arose out of a complicated and protracted legal struggle over land titles. Lord Fairfax died in 1781, bequeathing valuable tracts of his property in Virginia's Northern Neck to his nephew, Denny Martin, a British subject residing in England. During the Revolution Virginia had confiscated Loyalist estates and by an act of 1779, which prohibited alien enemies from holding land, declared the escheat, or reversion to the state, of estates then owned by British subjects. That act of 1779 did not apply to the estates of Lord Fairfax, who had been a Virginia citizen. The Treaty of Peace with Great Britain in 1783, calling for the restitution of all confiscated estates and prohibiting further confiscations, strengthened Martin's claim under the will of his uncle. In 1785, however, Virginia had extended its escheat law of 1779 to the Northern Neck, and four years later had granted some of those lands to one David Hunter. JAY'S TREATY of 1794, which protected the American property of British subjects, also buttressed Martin's claims. By then a Virginia district court, which included Judge ST. GEORGE TUCKER, decided in Martin's favor; Hunter appealed to the state's high court. JOHN MARSHALL, who had represented Martin, and James Marshall, his brother, joined a syndicate that arranged to purchase the Northern Neck lands. In 1796 the state legislature offered a compromise, which the Marshall syndicate accepted: the Fairfax devisees relinquished claim to the undeveloped lands of the Northern Neck in return for the state's recognition of their claim to Fairfax's manor lands. The Marshall syndicate accepted the compromise, thereby seeming to secure Hunter's claim, yet thereafter completed their purchase. In 1806, Martin's heir conveyed the lands to the syndicate, and in 1808 he appealed to the Court of Appeals, which decided in favor of Hunter two years later.

The Martin-Marshall interests, relying on the Treaty of 1783 and Jay's Treaty, took the case to the Supreme Court on a WRIT OF ERROR under section 25 of the JUDICIARY ACT OF 1789. That section provided in part that the nation's highest tribunal on writ of error might reexamine and reverse or affirm the final judgment of a state court if the state court sustained a state statute against a claim that the statute was repugnant to the Constitution, treaties, or laws of the United States, or if the state court decided against any title or right claimed under the treaties or federal authority. Chief Justice Marshall took no part in the case, and two other Justices were absent. Justice JOSEPH STORY, for a three-member majority and against the dissenting vote of Justice WILLIAM JOHNSON, reversed the judgment of the Virginia Court of Appeals, holding that federal treaties confirmed Martin's title. In the course of his opinion Story sapped the Virginia statutes escheating the lands of alien enemies and ignored the "compromise" of 1796. The mandate of the Supreme Court to the state Court of Appeals concluded: "You therefore are hereby commanded that such proceedings be had in said cause, as according to right and justice, and the laws of the United States, and agreeable to said judgment and instructions of said Supreme Court . . ." (*Fairfax's Devisee v. Hunter's Lessee*, 1813).

The state court that received this mandate consisted of eminent and proud men who regarded the Supreme Court as a rival; the man who dominated the state court was SPENCER ROANE, whose opinion Story had reversed. Roane, the son-in-law of PATRICK HENRY, was not just a judge; he was a state political

boss, an implacable enemy of John Marshall, and the man whom THOMAS JEFFERSON would have appointed Chief Justice, given the chance. To Roane and his brethren, Story's opinion was more than an insulting encroachment on their judicial prerogatives. It raised the specter of national consolidation, provoking the need to rally around the STATES' RIGHTS principles of the VIRGINIA AND KENTUCKY RESOLUTIONS. Roane consulted with Jefferson and JAMES MONROE, and he called before his court the leading members of the state bar, who spoke for six days. Munford, the Virginia court reporter, observed: "The question whether this mandate should be obeyed excited all that attention from the Bench and Bar which its great importance truly merited." The reporter added that the court had its opinions ready for delivery shortly after the arguments. That was in April 1814, when the Republican political organization of Virginia dared not say anything that would encourage or countenance the states' rights doctrines of Federalist New England, which opposed the War of 1812 and thwarted national policies. Not until December 1815, when the crisis had passed and secessionism in the North had dissipated, did the Virginia Court of Appeals release its opinions.

Each of four state judges wrote opinions, agreeing that the Constitution had established a federal system in which SOVEREIGNTY was divided between the national and state governments, neither of which could control the other or any of its organs. To allow the United States or any of its departments to operate directly on the states or any of their departments would subvert the independence of the states, allow the creature to judge its creators, and destroy the idea of a national government of limited powers. Although conflicts between the states and the United States were inevitable, the Constitution "has provided no umpire" and did not authorize Congress to bestow on the Supreme Court a power to pass final judgment on the extent of the powers of the United States or of its own appellate jurisdiction. Nothing in the Constitution denied the power of a state court to pass finally upon the validity of state legislation. The states could hold the United States to the terms of the compact only if the state courts had the power to determine finally the constitutionality of acts of Congress. Section 25 of the Judiciary Act was unconstitutional because it vested appellate powers in the Supreme Court in a case where the highest court of a state has authoritatively construed state acts. In sum, the position of the Court of Appeals was that the Supreme Court cannot reverse a state court on a matter of state or even federal law, but a state court can hold unconstitutional an act of the United States. Thus, Roane, with Jefferson's approval, located in the state courts the ultimate authority to judge the extent of the powers of the national government; in 1798 Jefferson had centered that ultimate authority in the state legislatures. At the conclusion of their opinions, the Virginia judges entered their judgment:

> The court is unanimously of opinion, that the appellate power of the Supreme Court of the United States does not extend to this court, under a sound construction of the constitution of the United States; that so much of the 25th section of the act of Congress to establish the judicial courts of the United States, as extends the appellate jurisdiction of the Supreme Court to this court, is not in pursuance of the constitution of the United States; that the writ of error, in this cause, was improvidently allowed, under the authority of that act; that the proceedings thereon in the Supreme Court were *Coram non judice* [before a court without jurisdiction], in relation to this court, and that obedience to its mandate be declined by the court.

When the case returned a second time to the Supreme Court on writ of error, Marshall again absented himself and Story again wrote the opinion. The *Martin* Court, consisting of five Republicans and one Federalist, was unanimous, though Johnson concurred separately. Story's forty-page opinion on behalf of federal judicial review is a masterpiece, far superior to Marshall's performance in MARBURY V. MADISON (1803) on behalf of national judicial review. In its cadenced prose, magisterial tone, nationalist doctrine, incisive logic, and driving repetitiveness, Story's opinion foreshadowed Marshall's later and magnificent efforts in MCCULLOCH V. MARYLAND (1819), COHENS V. VIRGINIA (1821), and GIBBONS V. OGDEN (1824), suggesting that they owe as much to Story as he to Marshall's undoubted influence on him. Because the Constitution, as Roane pointed out, had neither expressly empowered Congress to extend the Court's appellate jurisdiction to the state courts nor expressly vested the Court itself with such jurisdiction, Story had to justify BROAD CONSTRUCTION. The Constitution, he observed, was ordained not by the sovereign states but by the people of the United States, who could subordinate state powers to those of the nation. Not all national powers were expressly given. The Constitution "unavoidably deals in general language," Story explained, because it was intended "to endure through a long lapse of ages, the events of which were locked up in the inscrutable purpose of Providence." The framers of the Constitution, unable to foresee "what new changes and modifications of power might be indispensable" to achieve its purposes, expressed its powers in "general terms, leaving to the legislature,

from time to time, to adopt its own means to effectuate legitimate objects. . . ." From such sweeping premises on the flexibility and expansiveness of national powers, Story could sustain section 25. He found authority for its enactment in Articles III and VI.

Article III, which defined the judicial power of the United States, contemplates that the Supreme Court shall be primarily an appellate court, whose appellate jurisdiction "shall" extend to specified CASES AND CONTROVERSIES. "Shall" is mandatory or imperative: the Court *must* exercise its appellate jurisdiction in *all* cases, in law and EQUITY, "arising under the Constitution, the Laws of the United States, and Treaties made. . . ." It is, therefore, the case, not the court from which it comes, that gives the Supreme Court its appellate jurisdiction, and because cases involving the Constitution, federal laws, and treaties may arise in state courts, the Supreme Court must exercise appellate jurisdiction in those cases. Contrary to Roane, that appellate jurisdiction did not exist only when the case came from a lower federal court. The Constitution required the establishment of a Supreme Court but merely authorized Congress to exercise a discretionary power in establishing lower federal courts. If Congress chose not to establish them, the Court's mandatory appellate jurisdiction could be exercised over only the state courts. The establishment of the lower federal courts meant that the appellate jurisdiction of the Supreme Court extended concurrently to both state and federal courts.

Article VI, the supremacy clause, made the Constitution itself, laws in pursuance to it, and federal treaties the supreme law of the land, binding on state courts. The decision of a state court on a matter involving the supreme law cannot be final, because the judicial power of the United States extends specifically to all such cases. To enforce the supremacy clause, the Supreme Court must have appellate jurisdiction over state court decisions involving the supreme law. That a case involving the supreme law might arise in the state courts is obvious. Story gave the example of a contract case in which a party relied on the provision in Article I, section 10, barring state impairments of the OBLIGATIONS OF A CONTRACT, and also the example of a criminal prosecution in which the defendant relied on the provision against EX POST FACTO laws. The Constitution, he pointed out, was in fact designed to operate on the states "in their corporate capacities." It is "crowded" with provisions that "restrain or annul the sovereignty of the States," making the Court's exercise of appellate power over state acts unconstitutional no more in derogation of state sovereignty than those provisions or the principle of national supremacy. Not only would the federal system survive the exercise of federal judicial review; it could not function without such review. The law must be uniform "upon all subjects within the purview of the Constitution. Judges . . . in different States, might differently interpret a statute, or a treaty of the United States, or even the Constitution itself: If there were no revising authority to control these jarring and discordant judgments, and harmonize them into uniformity, the laws, the treaties and the Constitution of the United States would be different in different states," and might never have the same interpretation and efficacy in any two states.

Story's opinion is the linchpin of the federal system and of judicial nationalism. It remains the greatest argument for federal judicial review, though it by no means concluded the controversy. Virginia's hostility was so intense that a case was contrived in 1821 to allow the Supreme Court to restate the principles of *Martin*. (See COHENS V. VIRGINIA, 1821.) As a matter of fact, though, federal judicial review and the constitutionality of section 25 remained bitterly contested topics to the eve of the Civil War.

LEONARD W. LEVY

Bibliography

BEVERIDGE, ALBERT J. 1916–1919 *The Life of John Marshall*, 4 vols. Vol. IV:145–167. Boston: Houghton Mifflin.

CROSSKEY, WILLIAM WINSLOW 1953 *Politics and the Constitution*, 2 vols. Pages 785–817. Chicago: University of Chicago Press.

HAINES, CHARLES GROVE 1944 *The Role of the Supreme Court in American Government and Politics, 1789–1835.* Pages 340–351. Berkeley: University of California Press.

MARTIN v. MOTT
12 Wheaton 19 (1827)

Mott, having avoided militia duty during the War of 1812, was fined by a court-martial. The Constitution authorized Congress to call forth the militia, and President JAMES MADISON, under congressional authority, had called upon the state militias for military service. Several states, which opposed the war, obstructed compliance, arguing that the national government had no authority to determine when the state militias could be called or to subject them to federal governance. Mott relied on such arguments. The Court unanimously held, in an opinion by Justice JOSEPH STORY, that the President, with congressional authorization, had exclusive power to decide when and under what exigencies the militia might be called to duty, and that his decision not only binds the states but places their militias under the control of officers appointed by the President.

LEONARD W. LEVY

MARYLAND TOLERATION ACT
(April 2, 1649)

This landmark in the protection of liberty of conscience was the most liberal in colonial America at the time of its passage by the Maryland Assembly under the title, "An Act Concerning Religion," and it was far more liberal than Parliament's TOLERATION ACT of forty years later. Until 1776 only the Rhode Island Charter of 1663 and Pennsylvania's "Great Law" of 1682 guaranteed fuller RELIGIOUS LIBERTY.

Maryland's statute, framed by its Roman Catholic proprietor, Lord Baltimore (Cecil Calvert), was the first public act to use the phrase "the free exercise" of religion, later embodied in the FIRST AMENDMENT. More noteworthy still, the act symbolized the extraordinary fact that for most of the seventeenth century in Maryland, Roman Catholics and various Protestant sects openly worshiped as they chose and lived in peace, though not in amity. The act applied to all those who professed belief in Jesus Christ, except antitrinitarians, and guaranteed them immunity from being troubled in any way because of their religion and "the free exercise thereof." In other provisions more characteristic of the time, the act fixed the death penalty for blasphemers against God, Christ, or the Trinity, and it imposed lesser penalties for profaning the sabbath or for reproaching the Virgin Mary or the apostles. Another clause anticipated GROUP LIBEL laws by penalizing the reproachful use of any name or term such as heretic, puritan, popish priest, anabaptist, separatist, or antinomian.

At a time when intolerance was the law in Europe and most of America, Maryland established no church and tolerated all Trinitarian Christians, until Protestants, who had managed to suspend the toleration act between 1654 and 1658, gained political control of the colony in 1689.

LEONARD W. LEVY

Bibliography

HANLEY, THOMAS O'BRIEN 1959 *Their Rights and Liberties: The Beginnings of Religious and Political Freedom in Maryland.* Westminister, Md.: Newman Press.

MASON, GEORGE
(1725–1792)

An influential Virginia leader of the Revolutionary period, George Mason served only a single term (1759–1760) in the colony's House of Burgesses. Family responsibilities and a dislike for routine legislative work kept him at his estate in Fairfax County, where he was active in local public affairs. He was a member and treasurer of the Ohio Company (1752–1773), the Virginia enterprise to explore and settle the Northwest Territory. Mason opposed parliamentary taxation of the colonies and, as justice of the peace, connived at evasion of the Stamp Act. His Fairfax Resolves of 1774 were introduced by his friend and neighbor GEORGE WASHINGTON in the House of Burgesses and prefigured the Declaration and Resolves of the FIRST CONTINENTAL CONGRESS. In 1775 Mason succeeded Washington as a member of Virginia's provisional legislature and was elected to the Committee of Safety, the de facto executive. At the Virginia convention of 1776, Mason wrote the VIRGINIA DECLARATION OF RIGHTS and a major part of the constitution. At the same convention he was appointed, along with GEORGE WYTHE, EDMUND PENDLETON, and THOMAS JEFFERSON, to a committee to revise the state's laws; and, although he resigned from the committee, many of his drafts were included in the final product. Throughout the Revolution he remained active in military and western affairs, and he was the author of an early plan for ceding the Northwest Territory to Congress and organizing its government.

Mason was at the meeting at Mount Vernon in 1785 that set in train the movement toward a constitutional convention; and he was elected to, but did not attend, the Annapolis Convention. He was a delegate to the CONSTITUTIONAL CONVENTION OF 1787 where he was one of the five most frequent speakers. He made his mark at the convention as a spokesman for republican nationalism. He favored a president elected directly by the people for a single seven-year term and assisted by a council. He opposed any mention of slavery in the Constitution as degrading to the document. He was a member of the committee that proposed the GREAT COMPROMISE but bitterly opposed the later compromise which gave twenty years' protection to the slave trade. Most decisively he desired to see a BILL OF RIGHTS included in the new constitution: "The laws of the United States are to be paramount to state bills of rights," he warned, and a constitutional guarantee of rights "would give great quiet to the people." The motion to draft a bill of rights was defeated, and Mason, who had been active in framing the new Constitution, accordingly refused to sign it. He sent his proposed bill of rights to RICHARD HENRY LEE who tried, but failed, to have Congress add it before transmitting the Constitution to the states.

Mason opposed RATIFICATION OF THE CONSTITUTION in the Virginia convention of 1788 because of its supposed antirepublican tendencies, its compromise with slavery, and its want of a bill of rights. When the convention voted to ratify the Constitution it appended a declaration of rights that closely followed Mason's declaration of 1776.

Mason thereafter retired from public life. He declined appointment as a United States senator in 1790. Shortly before his death he told Thomas Jefferson that the machinations of ALEXANDER HAMILTON in favor of urban monied interests were bearing out Mason's predictions about the Constitution.

Throughout his public career Mason adhered to principle even in apparent contradiction to his self-interest. Although he held some 300 slaves he abominated slavery as an institution and favored a plan of gradual compensated emancipation preceded by education. Although he was an active Anglican layman, he favored measures to end the ESTABLISHMENT OF RELIGION in Virginia.

DENNIS J. MAHONEY

Bibliography

ROWLAND, KATE MASON 1892 *The Life of George Mason, Including His Speeches, Public Papers, and Correspondence.* New York: Putnam's.

RUTLAND, ROBERT ALLEN 1961 *George Mason, Reluctant Statesman.* Williamsburg, Va.: Colonial Williamsburg, distributed by Holt, Rinehart & Winston, New York.

MASSACHUSETTS v. LAIRD
400 U.S. 886 (1970)

In 1969, the legislature of Massachusetts attempted to nullify the VIETNAM WAR. It passed an act declaring the war unconstitutional, exempting Massachusetts citizens from service in the war, and directing the state attorney general to seek a Supreme Court ruling on the constitutionality of the war. Accordingly, the attorney general filed suit in the state's name against the secretary of defense, Melvin Laird, requesting an order prohibiting the secretary from sending any Massachusetts citizen to Vietnam. As the suit was between a state and a citizen of another state, it would have come within the ORIGINAL JURISDICTION of the Supreme Court. The Court, however, voted 6–3 to deny leave to file the complaint. Justice WILLIAM O. DOUGLAS, who passionately desired an opportunity to rule on the constitutionality of the war, filed an unusual fourteen-page dissent from the denial memorandum.

DENNIS J. MAHONEY

MASSACHUSETTS v. MELLON

See: *Frothingham v. Mellon*

MASSACHUSETTS BAY, COLONIAL CHARTERS OF
(1629, 1691)

In 1629 King Charles I granted a royal charter to Puritan leaders of the New England Company, incorporating them as the Massachusetts Bay Colony. In the same year Puritan leaders received authorization to migrate to New England and take the charter with them. As a result the Puritans controlled Massachusetts and sought to create a godly commonwealth. The charter authorized the freemen of the company to meet in a General Court or legislature, and to choose a governor, a deputy governor, and assistants, seven of whom could function as the General Court. The charter vested power in these men to govern Massachusetts Bay in every respect and guaranteed that all inhabitants "shall have and enjoy all liberties and immunities of free and natural subjects . . . as if they . . . were born within the realm of England." The Puritans, who governed themselves, enjoyed the rights of Englishmen, and put an ocean between themselves and England, became obstinately independent.

Massachusetts admitted only church members to freemanship, but the little oligarchy in control refused to allow the freemen a right to participate in governing, a violation of the charter. In 1634 the freemen, on seeing the charter for themselves, demanded full participation in government. From then on, the freemen in the towns chose two deputies from each town as members of the General Court, making it a representative body. Conflict between the freemen and the assistants led to an agreement that without a majority vote of each no law should be passed; that soon led to BICAMERALISM. In the 1640s the battle of the freemen for their charter rights led to the MASSACHUSETTS BODY OF LIBERTIES and to the MASSACHUSETTS GENERAL LAWS AND LIBERTIES, which, with the charter, became the basis of FUNDAMENTAL LAW in the colony, the functional equivalent of a written CONSTITUTION.

In the succeeding decades Massachusetts proved to be aloof from English concerns and refractory in many ways, even claiming that its charter made it independent of Parliament. Relations deteriorated after the Restoration and finally, in 1684, England vacated the charter of 1629. In 1686 James II appointed his own governor of the new Dominion of New England, which combined the New England colonies, New York, and New Jersey. The king's governor ruled without a representative legislature and sought to insinuate the Church of England into Puritan New England. News of the overthrow of James II led to a parallel Glorious Revolution in New England—and elsewhere in America. Each of the colonies that had been absorbed within the dominion resumed its prior governmental practices.

In 1691 King William III, advised by people who had experienced the independence of Massachusetts, officially restored self-government to Massachusetts on royal terms. The charter of 1691 turned Massachusetts from comparative autonomy to a royal colony. The king appointed its governor and his deputy, and the governor could veto legislation—a model for a strong executive in later American history. The General Court consisted of two houses, the lower one elected by the people of the towns who sent two deputies each to the General Court; these elected representatives chose the governor's council, which also served as the upper house. The freemanship of church members disappeared under the new charter, which replaced the religious test with a property qualification on the right to vote. The General Court was empowered to legislate, to create a judicial system, and to elect the upper house—subject to the governor's veto. The government established by the second charter recognized a clear SEPARATION OF POWERS between the three branches. The charter also embodied the principle of liberty of conscience for "all Christians (Except Papists)" and, like the first charter, also guaranteed the rights of Englishmen.

LEONARD W. LEVY

Bibliography

OSGOOD, HERBERT L. (1904)1957 *The American Colonies in the Seventeenth Century.* 3 Vols. Gloucester, Mass.: Peter Smith.

MASSACHUSETTS BOARD OF RETIREMENT v. MURGIA
427 U.S. 307 (1976)

In *Murgia* the Supreme Court, asked to subject AGE DISCRIMINATION to heightened judicial scrutiny, declined the invitation, 7–1. In a per curiam opinion the Court upheld a state law limiting membership in the uniformed state police to persons under the age of fifty, irrespective of an older person's ability to pass physical or other tests of qualification. There was not a murmur in the Court's opinion about IRREBUTTABLE PRESUMPTIONS, nor was age a SUSPECT CLASSIFICATION; although the aged were not free from discrimination, they had not experienced "purposeful unequal treatment" or disabilities imposed "on the basis of stereotyped characteristics not truly indicative of their abilities." With that breathtaking inaccuracy behind it, the Court applied the most permissive form of RATIONAL BASIS review, noted that physical ability generally declines with age, and concluded that because the mandatory retirement rule was not "wholly unrelated" to the objective of maintaining a physically fit police force, the law was valid. Justice THURGOOD MARSHALL, in lone dissent, repeated his long-standing argument that the Court should abandon its "two-tier" system of STANDARDS OF REVIEW in favor of a system that matched the level of judicial scrutiny in EQUAL PROTECTION cases to the interests at stake in each case.

KENNETH L. KARST

MASSACHUSETTS BODY OF LIBERTIES
(1641)

The Massachusetts Body of Liberties, which resulted from popular demand that the fundamental law of the colony be written, was primarily a set of constitutional safeguards protecting personal freedom and the procedures of DUE PROCESS. By 1634 the colonists were demanding publication of the colony's laws as a curb on the magistrates' discretionary powers. The magistrates opposed publication as a restraint of their lawful powers; they believed that law should develop in Massachusetts Bay as had the COMMON LAW in England, over time and by custom. More to the point, publication would invite direct comparison with En-

glish law and one provision of the charter forbade establishment of any laws repugnant to those of England.

For the remainder of the decade a number of attempts were made to formulate a document that would satisfy these demands. One plan, drawn up by the Reverend John Cotton, may have been rejected because of its biblical severity or its failure to be sufficiently comprehensive. In 1638, the Reverend Nathaniel Ward, a barrister active at Lincoln's Inn before his emigration, submitted a proposal that was eventually sent to the towns for their consideration and revision early in 1641. Despite years of inaction and obstruction by the magistrates the General Court finally adopted this draft that autumn.

The first "liberty," paraphrasing the thirty-ninth article of MAGNA CARTA, specified conformity to the traditional rights of Englishmen, as exemplified in Magna Carta and the common law, and to "the word of God." The Body of Liberties was undeniably a product of the Puritan colony: a large portion outlined ecclesiastical rights and responsibilities. One section, drawn from Cotton's code, listed twelve capital crimes and cross-referenced each one to the appropriate biblical verse.

Over forty liberties were devoted to "Juditiall Proceedings" and their adjunct rights. In addition to defining a few lesser offenses, the Body of Liberties provided extensive guarantees for each step in legal proceedings. The use of summonses was regulated and a right to BAIL was assured. Written pleadings were permitted in court and, unlike English practice, cases would not be abated for minor technical errors. Parties were granted the right to TRIAL BY JURY and to challenge any of the jurors. Other liberties protected rights now taken for granted. Among these were provisions for a SPEEDY TRIAL, a limited privilege against self-incrimination, as well as prohibitions of DOUBLE JEOPARDY and "inhumane barbarous and cruel" punishments. (See CRUEL AND UNUSUAL PUNISHMENT.) The Body of Liberties also guaranteed FREEDOM OF SPEECH in courts and public assemblies and freedom of movement. Other sections covered the "Liberties of Women," children's rights, and those of servants.

Despite these and other innovations the deputies were dissatisfied with the document. They found it overly broad and poorly defined and insisted upon specified penalties—the Body of Liberties provided them only for capital crimes—and precise limits to magisterial power. Eventually, widespread discontent resulted in the passage in 1648 of the extensively de-

tailed MASSACHUSETTS GENERAL LAWS AND LIBER-
TIES.

DAVID GORDON

Bibliography
HASKINS, GEORGE L. 1960 *Law and Authority in Early Massachusetts.* New York: Macmillan.

MASSACHUSETTS CIRCULAR LETTER
(February 11, 1768)

This document reveals the American conception of a CONSTITUTION as a supreme FUNDAMENTAL LAW limiting government by definite restraints upon power. SAMUEL ADAMS drafted the document, which the Massachusetts House of Representatives adopted and sent to the assemblies of other colonies to secure their assent to the contention that the TOWNSHEND ACTS of 1767 and all other taxes levied by Parliament on America were unconstitutional. The right to private property, Adams wrote, is an unalterable natural and constitutional right "engrafted into the British Constitution, as a fundamental law. . . ." Parliament had violated that right by TAXATION WITHOUT REPRESENTATION. Although Parliament was the supreme legislature in the empire, it could act lawfully only within the sphere of its legitimate powers. Echoing the Swiss jurist EMERICH DE VATTEL, who distinguished a constitution from ordinary statutory law, Adams declared that in all free states the constitution is fixed, and "as the supreme Legislative derives its Power and Authority from the Constitution, it cannot overleap the bounds of it, without destroying its own foundation. . . ." The constitution, Adams stated, "ascertains and limits" both SOVEREIGNTY and allegiance.

London censured the "Seditious Paper" of Massachusetts and declared that Massachusetts had subverted "the true principles of the constitution." To the British, as Sir WILLIAM BLACKSTONE contended in his *Commentaries,* Parliament could not act unconstitutionally; it knew no practical limits. To the Americans, an unconstitutional act was one that exceeded governmental authority. "Unconstitutional" did not mean impolitic or inexpedient, as it meant in Britain; it meant a lawless government act that need not be obeyed. The Massachusetts Circular Letter thus fortified the emergence of a new conception of constitutional law.

LEONARD W. LEVY

Bibliography
MILLER, JOHN C. 1943 *Origins of the American Revolution.* Pages 257–264. Boston: Little, Brown.

MASSACHUSETTS CONSTITUTION
(October 25, 1780)

The "Constitution or Form of Government for the Commonwealth of Massachusetts" is the classic American state CONSTITUTION and the oldest surviving written constitution in the United States (or the world), distinguished in addition by the fact that it was framed by the world's first CONSTITUTIONAL CONVENTION. But for two states which merely modified their COLONIAL CHARTERS, all the original thirteen states except Massachusetts had adopted their first constitutions by 1778 and in every case the body that enacted ordinary legislation framed the constitution and promulgated it. The Massachusetts legislature also framed a constitution but resorted to the novel step of submitting it to the voters for approval, and they rejected it. Then, in accordance with a proposal first advanced in the CONCORD TOWN RESOLUTIONS of 1776, a special constitutional convention elected for the sole purpose of drawing up a document of FUNDAMENTAL LAW performed the task and sent it out for ratification, article by article. Universal manhood suffrage prevailed in the vote for delegates to the convention and for popular ratification. Massachusetts, following democratic procedures for institutionalizing the SOCIAL COMPACT THEORY of government to devise a frame of government and a supreme law, provided the model that subsequently became common throughout the United States. The Massachusetts constitution of 1780, with amendments, still continues as the constitution of that commonwealth.

JOHN ADAMS, the principal framer of the constitution, once proudly wrote, "I made a Constitution for Massachusetts, which finally made the Constitution of the United States." His exaggeration was pardonable, because no other state constitution so much influenced the framing of the national Constitution. Some earlier state constitutions had referred to the principle of SEPARATION OF POWERS but had made their legislatures dominant, even domineering. Massachusetts not only provided the fullest statement of the principle but also put it into practice. Its judges, appointed by the governor, were to hold office "during GOOD BEHAVIOR" with undiminishable salaries. Its governor was the model for the presidency of the United States. He was to be elected by the voters, rather than by the legislature as in other states, and be a strong executive. He appointed the members of his own council or cabinet and, indeed, appointed all judicial officers down to local magistrates and registers of probate as well as sheriffs, coroners, and the state attorney general. He was "commander-in-chief of the army and navy"; he had the PARDONING POWER; and he alone among the first governors of the thirteen states had a sole VETO POWER over legislation, which could be overridden only by a two-thirds vote of both houses. The state senate and house of representatives were also precursors of the national bicameral system. No original state constitution had a better system of CHECKS AND BALANCES than Massachusetts's.

Its constitution was divided into three parts: a preamble, a declaration of rights, and a frame of government. The preamble, on the general purposes of the state, explicitly embodied the social compact theory of the origin of the body politic. The declaration of rights, although containing little not found in constitutions previously framed by other states, was the most comprehensive compendium of its kind, and it phrased the rights which it guaranteed in language most influential in framing the BILL OF RIGHTS of the Constitution of the United States. The injunction against "UNREASONABLE SEARCHES and seizures" in the FOURTH AMENDMENT derives from the Massachusetts Declaration of Rights, and the injunction "shall not" instead of the pallid "ought not" ("liberty of the press ought not be restrained") was also a Massachusetts innovation. The one grave deficiency of the Massachusetts document was its creation of a multiple ESTABLISHMENT OF RELIGION that was inconsistent with its guarantee of RELIGIOUS LIBERTY.

LEONARD W. LEVY

Bibliography
ADAMS, WILLI PAUL 1980 *The First American Constitutions.* Chapel Hill: University of North Carolina Press.
PETERS, RONALD M., JR. 1978 *The Massachusetts Constitution of 1780: A Social Compact.* Amherst: University of Massachusetts Press.

MASSACHUSETTS GENERAL LAWS AND LIBERTIES

In 1646, the General Court of Massachusetts Bay appointed a committee to "correct and compose in good order all the liberties, lawes, and orders extant with us." The committee's work, publication of which was delayed until 1648, was far more comprehensive than the earlier MASSACHUSETTS BODY OF LIBERTIES. The framing of the General Laws and Liberties capped

a movement for codification that had grown because the Body of Liberties had failed to curb the magistrates' discretion. Frequent legislation compounded popular confusion over the state of the law, but even so, the General Laws did not include all the laws in force.

The new code incorporated eighty-six of the one hundred items in the Body of Liberties and covered subjects from business regulations to property laws. It generally followed English practice. Plaintiffs could easily attach land, the law guaranteed a SPEEDY TRIAL, and juries could return "special" verdicts—practices foreign to English proceedings. Also unlike English practice, forms of action were relatively unimportant; substance took precedence in Massachusetts. Like contemporary English statutory abridgments and practice manuals, the General Laws were listed alphabetically to encourage reference and use. They were revised in 1660 and 1672 and served as the prototype for other colonies' legal codes.

DAVID GORDON

MASSACHUSETTS RESOLUTIONS

See: Embargo Acts

MASSES PUBLISHING COMPANY v. PATTEN
244 Fed. 535 (1917)

Judge LEARNED HAND's *Masses* opinion was one of the first federal opinions dealing with free speech. It remains influential even though Hand was reversed by the court of appeals and many years later himself abandoned his initial position. A postmaster had refused to accept the revolutionary monthly *The Masses* for mailing, citing the ESPIONAGE ACT. Hand, sitting in a federal district court, interpreted the act not to apply to the magazine. He noted that any broad criticism of a government or its policies might hinder the war effort. Nevertheless, to suppress such criticism "would contradict the normal assumption of democratic government." Hand advanced a criminal incitement test. He conceded that words can be "the triggers of action" and, if they counseled violation of law, were not constitutionally protected. If, however, the words did not criminally incite and if the words stopped short "of urging upon others that it is their duty or their interest to resist the law . . . one should not be held to have attempted to cause its violation."

Hand's concentration on the advocacy content of

the speech itself is thought by some to be more speech-protective than the CLEAR AND PRESENT DANGER rule's emphasis on the surrounding circumstances.

MARTIN SHAPIRO

MASSIAH v. UNITED STATES
377 U.S. 201 (1964)

After a defendant had been indicted and released on BAIL, a bugged co-defendant who had turned police informer, engaged him in an incriminating conversation. The Supreme Court held that the Sixth Amendment prohibits deliberate elicitation of information from an indicted person in the absence of his counsel and ruled that defendant's incriminating statements were inadmissible at trial.

BARBARA ALLEN BABCOCK

MASTER, SPECIAL

See: Special Master

MATHEWS v. ELDRIDGE
424 U.S. 319 (1976)

GOLDBERG V. KELLY (1970) established a PROCEDURAL DUE PROCESS right to an evidentiary hearing prior to the termination of state WELFARE BENEFITS. Eldridge, whose Social Security disability benefits had been terminated without a prior hearing, could be pardoned for thinking that *Goldberg* controlled his case. In the event, a 6–2 Supreme Court explained how that view was mistaken, and established its basic test for determining whether a particular procedure satisfied the demands of DUE PROCESS.

The government conceded that the disability benefit was the sort of statutory "entitlement" that constituted a "property" interest protected by the due process guarantee. The government nonetheless argued that a *prior* hearing was not required; rather, due process was satisfied by a posttermination hearing at which the beneficiary might review the evidence, submit evidence of his own, and make arguments for reconsideration. Under the existing procedures, a beneficiary who prevailed in such a posttermination hearing was entitled to full retroactive relief. A majority of the Court agreed with the government's argument.

In a passage often quoted in later opinions, the Court set out the factors relevant to determining "the specific dictates of due process," once a "liberty" or "property" interest is impaired: "First, the private interest that will be affected by the official action; second, the risk of an erroneous deprivation of such interest through the procedures used, and the probable value, if any, of additional or substitute procedural safeguards; and finally, the Government's interest, including the function involved and the fiscal and administrative burdens that the additional or substitute procedural requirement would entail." Here, eligibility for disability benefits was not based on need, the standard for welfare eligibility in *Goldberg*. The Court assumed that a delayed payment would harm the typical disability beneficiary less than the typical welfare recipient. The medical question of disability, in contrast with the "need" question in a welfare case, was more focused and less susceptible to erroneous decision. The costs of pretermination hearings would be great. In short, the Court balanced its factors on the government's side.

The *Eldridge* due process calculus implies a strong presumption of constitutionality of whatever procedures a legislative body or government agency may choose to provide persons deprived of liberty or property. This presumption grows naturally out of the Court's limited choice of factors to be balanced, emphasizing material costs and benefits and ignoring the role of procedural fairness in maintaining each individual's sense of being a respected, participating citizen.

KENNETH L. KARST

MATTHEWS, STANLEY
(1824–1889)

Stanley Matthews's political connections and his legal work for railroads led to his Supreme Court nomination in 1881; these same activities also nearly prevented him from taking a place on the bench. Like his predecessor, NOAH SWAYNE, Matthews had been an Ohio antislavery Democrat and a Democratic appointee as a United States attorney. By 1860, however, he had switched to the Republican party. After Civil War military service, he became an important leader of the Cincinnati bar. Before the Ohio Supreme Court, Matthews represented the Cincinnati Board of Education and supported its authority to abolish religious instruction in the public schools. His eloquent argument defended SEPARATION OF CHURCH AND STATE as the best way to insure RELIGIOUS LIBERTY.

Matthews served as one of RUTHERFORD B.

HAYES's lawyers during the contested electoral battle in 1877. Near the end of his administration, Hayes nominated Matthews to succeed Swayne, but because of internal Republican patronage feuds, as well as questions about Matthews's railroad connections, the Senate took no action. President JAMES A. GARFIELD, under pressure from Hayes's allies and prominent business interests, resubmitted the nomination. After a long, bitter fight, the Senate confirmed Matthews by a one-vote majority.

Matthews clearly served railroad interests when he joined the Court's decision in WABASH, ST. LOUIS & PACIFIC RAILROAD CO. V. ILLINOIS (1886), substantially weakening the state regulatory doctrine of *Munn v. Illinois* (1877). Similarly, he concurred in the nearly unanimous decision in the CIVIL RIGHTS CASES (1883), which capped a legal and political counterassault against racial equality.

The *Wabash* case, while limiting state regulation, decisively stimulated federal ECONOMIC REGULATION under the COMMERCE CLAUSE. Matthews relied on an expansive conception of national power in BOWMAN V. CHICAGO AND NORTHWESTERN RAILWAY CO. (1888), ruling invalid a state's prohibition of liquor shipments from other states. However desirable the state's regulation, Matthews said, it infringed on Congress's EXCLUSIVE POWER. In *Poindexter v. Greenhow* (1885) Matthews relied on the CONTRACT CLAUSE when he held that states could not lawfully repudiate their debts.

Matthews's most important cases involved the interpretation of the FOURTEENTH AMENDMENT. In HURTADO V. CALIFORNIA (1884) he held for the Court that even in a capital case an accusation by INFORMATION rather than INDICTMENT by a GRAND JURY did not deny DUE PROCESS OF LAW contrary to the FOURTEENTH AMENDMENT. The *Hurtado* ruling stood for nearly a half century as a barrier to any tendency toward nationalizing CIVIL RIGHTS and CIVIL LIBERTIES. Yet in YICK WO V. HOPKINS (1886) Matthews spoke for the Court on one of those rare occasions when it advanced civil rights. Holding unconstitutional the discriminatory application of a San Francisco ordinance requiring licensing of wooden laundries, used to destroy Chinese businesses, Matthews described the Fourteenth Amendment in libertarian terms that usually were reserved for corporate cases. Indeed, he cast the plight of the Chinese in language that any good entrepreneur could understand: "For, the very idea that one man may be compelled to hold his life, or the means of living, or any material right essential to the enjoyment of life, at the mere will of another, seems to be intolerable in any country

where freedom prevails, as being the essence of slavery itself."

Matthews spoke for the Court in one of the Mormon antipolygamy cases, sustaining congressional action and invoking the prevailing norms of the family and marriage. He also voted to strike down the Ku Klux Klan laws in UNITED STATES V. HARRIS (1883); he agreed with the majority that AMERICAN INDIANS were not citizens in *Elk v. Wilkins* (1884); and he concurred that state MISCEGENATION laws were constitutional in PACE V. ALABAMA (1883).

Matthews epitomized the nation's retreat from the reforming zeal of Reconstruction. The controversy surrounding Matthews's appointment eventually subsided, and he carried out his duties until his death in early 1889.

STANLEY I. KUTLER

Bibliography

FILLER, LOUIS 1969 Stanley Matthews. In Leon Friedman and Fred L. Israel, eds., *The Justices of the Supreme Court*, Vol. 2:1351–1378. New York: Chelsea House.

MAGRATH, C. PETER 1963 *Morrison R. Waite: The Triumph of Character*. New York: Macmillan.

MAXIMUM HOURS AND MINIMUM WAGES LEGISLATION

Regulation of the employment relationship was an important aspect of the movement toward state intervention in economic affairs, which began in the late 1800s. The transition from small individual to large corporate employers and the development of a factory system with a numerous wage-earning class resulted in pervasive exploitation of employees. The principal method of alleviating the economic injustice was statutory regulation of employment conditions. The spectrum of protective legislation was wide, including factory safety, child labor, workers' compensation, and the hours and wages of employment. In these early days the laws were state laws.

The protracted constitutional contest over hours and wage legislation was one aspect of the larger theme of SUBSTANTIVE DUE PROCESS, a concept developed by the Supreme Court at the turn of the century. Liberty included FREEDOM OF CONTRACT, which included the employment contract, of which hours and wages were the main components. The Court held that laws regulating hours and wages violated the guarantee of DUE PROCESS OF LAW if the purpose of the law was invalid or if the means were not reasonably related to a valid purpose.

Hours legislation began in the 1870s. Reformers perceived the duration of the workday as related to the employees' health and safety, protection of which was a valid legislative purpose. In its first opinion on the subject, HOLDEN V. HARDY (1898), the Court sustained a law limiting the hours of men working in mines to eight a day. The hazardous nature of the work justified the limitation as a valid health and safety measure. In MULLER V. OREGON (1908) an hours limitation for women was sustained on the theory that the "weaker sex" required special protection.

Beyond these two exceptional situations the Court at first prohibited hours regulation. The prototype case was LOCHNER V. NEW YORK (1905). A 5–4 Court invalidated a law restricting the work of bakery employees to ten hours a day and sixty hours a week. Despite massive documentation, the Court refused to recognize that the baking industry posed any special health danger to which hours of work were reasonably related. More broadly, the Court concluded that the law was not truly a health law, but a "purely labor law" to regulate hours, an impermissible objective.

This strict view yielded to persistent pressures. In BUNTING V. OREGON (1917) hours regulation of adult males in factories was sustained as a valid health measure, a result clearly inconsistent with *Lochner*, which was not even mentioned in the opinion. Thereafter the validity of hours regulation was not seriously questioned.

Massachusetts passed the first minimum wage statute in 1912 and within ten years there were fifteen such state laws. Proponents urged that health was impaired by wages below a subsistence level. The Court was at first unpersuaded, and, in ADKINS V. CHILDREN'S HOSPITAL (1923), it invalidated a District of Columbia minimum wage law for women. Wages were the "heart of the contract" and, unlike hours, had no relation to health. Contrary to hours regulation, women were entitled to no special wage protection. The minimum wage was invalid also because it bore no relation to the value of the service rendered. But a law curing this deficiency was invalidated in MOREHEAD V. NEW YORK EX REL. TIPALDO (1936).

One principal justification for protective legislation was that the inequality of economic power between employers and employees made true freedom of contract illusory. This argument was expressly rejected by the Court, which candidly declared in COPPAGE V. KANSAS (1915) that it was "impossible to uphold freedom of contract and the right of private property without at the same time recognizing as legitimate those inequalities of fortune that are the necessary result of the exercise of those rights." Social Darwinism was thus enshrined in the Constitution.

In 1937, that year of constitutional revolution, minimum wage legislation became constitutional by a 5–4 vote. WEST COAST HOTEL CO. V. PARRISH upheld a minimum wage for women. *Adkins* was overruled. The Court purported surprise at the employer's reliance on liberty of contract. Not only was the health/subsistence rationale accepted but, more broadly, it was now accepted as a valid legislative purpose to prevent "exploitation of a class of workers who are in unequal position with respect to bargaining power."

Federal regulation of hours and wages was first exercised in limited contexts. An eight-hour day for railroad workers was upheld under the COMMERCE CLAUSE in WILSON V. NEW (1917). Congress has long regulated both wages and hours of work performed by employees of contractors with the federal government. Examples are the Davis-Bacon Act, which regulates wages for work on public buildings and other public works, and the Walsh-Healey Public Contracts Act, which regulates both wages and hours for work on supply contracts. The constitutionality of both statutes is unquestioned under the TAXING AND SPENDING POWER.

Finally, in the FAIR LABOR STANDARDS ACT of 1938, Congress legislated for private employment generally, superseding most state laws. The act required the payment of a minimum wage and overtime for all hours over forty a week to all employees engaged in commerce or the production of goods for commerce. The main purpose was not health but to bolster the economy. The FLSA was sustained under the commerce power in UNITED STATES V. DARBY (1941). A substantive due process argument was rejected without analysis. It was "no longer open to question" that neither Fifth nor FOURTEENTH AMENDMENT due process limited the fixing of minimum wages or maximum hours, and it made no difference that the regulations applied to both men and women.

That has been the view of the matter ever since. In other contexts the Court repudiated the *Lochner* substantive due process approach to protective legislation. What was once a burning issue now appears to be a closed chapter in constitutional law. The scope of the STATE POLICE POWER was underscored in striking fashion by the upholding in *Day-Brite Lighting, Inc. v. Missouri* (1952) of a law that required employers to give employees four hours off from work in order to vote—with full pay.

WILLIAM P. MURPHY

Bibliography

DE VYVER, FRANK T. 1939 Regulation of Wages and Hours Prior to 1938. *Law and Contemporary Problems* 6:323–332.

DODD, E. MERRICK 1943 From Maximum Wages to Minimum Wages: Six Centuries of Regulation of Employment Contracts. *Columbia Law Review* 43:643–687.

MAXWELL v. DOW
176 U.S. 581 (1900)

This case was decided at a time when the Court was subjecting the FOURTEENTH AMENDMENT to an accordionlike motion, expanding SUBSTANTIVE DUE PROCESS to protect the rights of property and contracting PROCEDURAL DUE PROCESS for persons accused of crime. After HURTADO V. CALIFORNIA (1884), when the Court held that the concept of due process did not guarantee INDICTMENT by GRAND JURY, persons accused of crime resorted to the INCORPORATION DOCTRINE, claiming that the Fourteenth Amendment, through either its due process clause or its PRIVILEGES AND IMMUNITIES clause, incorporated provisions of the BILL OF RIGHTS, thus extending to the states the same trial standards. Utah accused Maxwell by an INFORMATION, rather than an indictment, and tried him by a jury of eight rather than twelve. The Fifth and SIXTH AMENDMENTS would have made such procedures unconstitutional in federal courts. Maxwell argued that the Fourteenth Amendment guaranteed the federal standards in state proceedings. Justice JOHN MARSHALL HARLAN, dissenting, adopted Maxwell's arguments. Justice RUFUS PECKHAM, for the remainder of the Court, held that neither the due process nor the privileges and immunities clause of the Fourteenth Amendment embodied Fifth or Sixth Amendment rights. Peckham also ruled that TRIAL BY JURY "has never been affirmed to be a necessary requisite of due process of law" and that an eight-member jury was constitutional. In 1968 DUNCAN V. LOUISIANA, overruling *Maxwell*, held trial by jury to be a fundamental right of due process of law for persons accused of crime, but under today's constitutional law, the JURY SIZE need not be twelve members in a state proceeding.

LEONARD W. LEVY

MAYFLOWER COMPACT

See: Social Compact Theory

MAYOR OF NEW YORK v. MILN
11 Peters 102 (1837)

This was the first case decided by the TANEY COURT involving a COMMERCE CLAUSE issue, and the Supreme Court finessed that issue. Justice JOSEPH STORY, dissenting alone, said that he took consolation in knowing that the late Chief Justice (JOHN MARSHALL) concurred in his view that the city of New York had unconstitutionally regulated FOREIGN COMMERCE, a subject exclusively belonging to Congress. The city required incoming ship captains to supply vital statistics on every immigrant they brought to harbor. The city argued that passengers were not commerce, but if they were, the voyage having ceased, no foreign commerce was involved; the requirement of the information on passengers was an exercise of the POLICE POWER, a precautionary measure against paupers, vagabonds, convicts, and pestilence.

By a vote of 6–1, in an opinion by Justice PHILIP BARBOUR, the Court sustained the regulation as a valid exercise of the police power. Barbour disavowed giving any opinion on the question whether the states shared CONCURRENT POWERS over foreign commerce. Justice SMITH THOMPSON, concurring separately, agreed with Story that the facts showed a regulation of foreign commerce, but he believed that in the absence of congressional legislation, the states retained a CONCURRENT POWER. The early and simplistic victory for the police power in this case solved little, because the Court did not face the question of the scope of the police powers when they affected SUBJECTS OF COMMERCE.

LEONARD W. LEVY

MAYSVILLE ROAD BILL
(1830)

President ANDREW JACKSON's veto of the Maysville Road Bill challenged the INTERNAL IMPROVEMENTS component of HENRY CLAY's AMERICAN SYSTEM on constitutional and policy grounds and enhanced the role of the President in the legislative process.

In 1816, President JAMES MADISON vetoed the "Bonus Bill," which would have provided federal support for internal improvements such as the Cumberland Road, on the ground that the Constitution did not authorize expenditure of federal funds for anything except the powers explicitly enumerated in it. The Maysville Road Bill would have funded completion of a twenty-mile spur of the National Road entirely within the state of Kentucky. Jackson defended his veto on the ground that the Maysville Road was wholly intrastate and therefore outside the power of the federal government. Jackson also vetoed the bill in order to promote economy in the national government. He thus asserted a presidential prerogative in legislative policy, as well as a quasi-constitutional position, associated with the Democratic Party for the next thirty years, of hostility to expenditure of federal funds for internal improvements.

WILLIAM M. WIECEK

(SEE ALSO: *Veto Power.*)

MCCARDLE, EX PARTE
7 Wallace (74 U.S.) 506 (1869)

In *Ex Parte McCardle*, Chief Justice SALMON P. CHASE, for the Supreme Court, validated congressional withdrawal of the Court's jurisdiction over appeals in HABEAS CORPUS proceedings under an 1867 statute but reasserted the Court's appellate authority in all other habeas cases.

A federal circuit court remanded William McCardle, a Mississippi editor hostile to Republican Reconstruction policies, to military custody. When he appealed to the Supreme Court, Democrats predicted that the Justices would use his case as a vehicle to hold unconstitutional the trial of civilians by military commissions in southern states undergoing Reconstruction. Democrats inferred from the earlier decision of EX PARTE MILLIGAN (1866) that a majority of the Court believed that military commissions could not constitutionally try civilians accused of crimes where courts were functioning in peacetime. Alarmed congressional Republicans, seeing this essential machinery of Reconstruction threatened, enacted a narrow statute in 1868 that revoked Supreme Court appellate authority in habeas cases under the HABEAS CORPUS ACT OF 1867.

In the *McCardle* opinion, Chief Justice Chase acknowledged the validity of this repeal under the "exceptions clause" of Article III, section 2, but pointedly reminded the bar that the 1868 repealer "does not affect the JURISDICTION which was previously exercised." In *Ex Parte Yerger* (1869), the Court promptly affirmed this OBITER DICTUM, accepting a *habeas* appeal under section 14 of the JUDICIARY ACT OF 1789 and rebuking Congress for the 1868 repealer. *McCardle* is therefore historically significant as evidence not of judicial submission to political threats during Reconstruction but rather of the Court's uninterrupted determination to preserve its role in questions of CIVIL LIBERTIES.

McCardle remains important in the modern debate on congressional power to curtail the Supreme Court's APPELLATE JURISDICTION over cases raising controversial issues such as SCHOOL BUSING, school prayer, and abortion. Some constitutional scholars have argued that Congress cannot erode the substance of the JUDICIAL POWER OF THE UNITED STATES vested in the Supreme Court by Article III, section 1, through jurisdictional nibbling at the Court's appellate authority, but the extent to which Congress can affect substantive rights by jurisdictional excisions remains controverted.

WILLIAM M. WIECEK

(SEE ALSO: *Judicial System.*)

MCCARRAN ACT

See: Internal Security Act

MCCARRAN-WALTER ACT

See: Immigration

MCCARTHY, JOSEPH R.

See: McCarthyism

MCCARTHYISM

On February 9, 1950, Senator Joseph R. McCarthy of Wisconsin claimed that 205 communists were presently "working and shaping the policy of the State Department." Although McCarthy produced no documentation for this preposterous charge, he quickly emerged as the nation's dominant Cold War politician—the yardstick by which citizens measured patriotic or scurrilous behavior. McCarthy's popularity was not difficult to explain. Americans were frightened by Soviet aggression in Europe. The years since World War II had brought a series of shocks—the Hiss trial, the fall of China, the KOREAN WAR—which fueled the Red Scare and kept it alive.

President HARRY S. TRUMAN played a role as well. In trying to defuse the "Communist issue," he established a federal LOYALTY-SECURITY PROGRAM with few procedural safeguards. The program relied on nameless informants; it penalized personal beliefs and associations, not just OVERT ACTS; and it accelerated the Red hunt by conceding the possibility that a serious security problem existed inside the government and elsewhere. Before long, state and local officials were competing to see who could crack down hardest on domestic subversion. Indiana forced professional wrestlers to sign a LOYALTY OATH. Tennessee ordered the death penalty for those seeking to overthrow the *state* government. Congress, not to be outdone, passed the INTERNAL SECURITY ACT of 1950 over Truman's veto, requiring registration of "Communist action groups," whose members could then be placed in internment camps during "national emergencies."

Despite his personal commitment to CIVIL LIBERTIES, President Truman appointed four Supreme Court Justices who opposed the libertarian philosophy of WILLIAM O. DOUGLAS and HUGO L. BLACK. As a result, JUDICIAL REVIEW was all but abandoned in cases involving the rights of alleged subversives. The Court upheld loyalty oaths as a condition of public employment, limited the use of the Fifth Amendment by witnesses before congressional committees, and affirmed the dismissal of a government worker on the unsworn testimony of unnamed informants. As ROBERT G. MCCLOSKEY noted, the Court "became so tolerant of governmental restriction on freedom of expression as to suggest it [had] abdicated the field."

By the mid-1950s, the Red Scare had begun to subside. The death of Joseph Stalin, the Korean armistice, and the Senate's censure of Senator McCarthy all contributed to the easing of Cold War fears. There were many signs of this, though none was more dramatic than the Supreme Court's return to libertarian values under Chief Justice EARL WARREN. In *Slochower v. Board of Higher Education* (1956) the Court overturned the discharge of a college teacher who had invoked the Fifth Amendment before a congressional committee. In *Sweezy v. New Hampshire* (1956) it reversed the conviction of a Marxist professor who had refused, on FIRST AMENDMENT grounds, to answer questions about his political associations. In WATKINS V. UNITED STATES (1957) it held that Congress had "no general authority to expose the private affairs of individuals without justification. . . ." "No inquiry is an end in itself," wrote Warren. "It must be related to and in furtherance of a legitimate [legislative] task of Congress."

The reaction in Congress was predictable. A South Carolina representative called the WARREN COURT "a greater threat to this union than the entire confines of Soviet Russia." Bills were introduced to limit the Court's JURISDICTION in national security cases, and

legislators both state and federal demanded Warren's IMPEACHMENT. Although this uproar probably caused some judicial retreat in the late 1950s, the Supreme Court played an important role in blunting the worst excesses of the McCarthy era.

DAVID M. OSHINSKY

Bibliography

OSHINSKY, DAVID M. 1983 *A Conspiracy So Immense: The World of Joe McCarthy.* New York: Free Press.

MCCLOSKEY, ROBERT G.
(1916–1969)

Robert G. McCloskey earned his Ph.D. at Harvard University, and he taught American government at Harvard from 1948 to 1969. He was by training a political scientist and by scholarly instinct a historian concerned with contemporary events; the modern Supreme Court created a challenge that filled the major portion of his intellectual life. The philosophy of judicial self-restraint in the light of the Court's limited competence and resources appealed to McCloskey at least in part because it struck a chord in his own character. He distrusted the flamboyant, preferring cautious interpretation. By nature judicious, he was suspicious of a Court that too precipitously proclaimed eternal verities. He wrote *American Conservatism in the Age of Enterprise* (1951), *The American Supreme Court* (1961), and *The Modern Supreme Court* (published posthumously in 1972), and he edited the papers of Justice JAMES WILSON.

MARTIN SHAPIRO

MCCOLLUM v. BOARD OF EDUCATION
333 U.S. 203 (1948)

During the late 1940s and 1950s "RELEASED TIME programs" were popular around the country. Public school boards and administrators cooperated with churches and synagogues to provide religious education for students according to their parents' choices. Under the arrangement in Champaign-Urbana, Illinois, students whose parents had so requested were excused from their classes to attend classes given by religious educators in the school buildings. Nonparticipating pupils were not excused from their regular classes.

McCollum, whose child Terry attended the public

schools, challenged the Illinois practice on the grounds that it violated the establishment clause of the FIRST AMENDMENT. The case was the first church–state controversy to reach the Court since EVERSON V. BOARD OF EDUCATION the year before, and Justice HUGO L. BLACK again delivered the opinion of the Court.

Referring to the theory of strict separation announced as OBITER DICTUM in his *Everson* opinion, Black held that the Illinois arrangement fell squarely within the First Amendment's ban. He stressed particularly the utilization of tax-supported facilities to aid religious teaching.

Justice FELIX FRANKFURTER concurred in an opinion in which Justices ROBERT JACKSON, WILEY B. RUTLEDGE, and HAROLD H. BURTON joined. These four had dissented from *Everson*'s approval of state aid to the transportation of children to religious schools.

Justice Jackson also concurred separately, rejecting the sweeping separationism of the Black opinion. Pointing out that there was little real cost to the taxpayers in the Illinois program, he agreed that the Court should end "formal and explicit instruction" such as that in the Champaign schools, but cautioned against inviting ceaseless petitions to the Court to purge school curricula of materials that any group might regard as religious.

Justice STANLEY F. REED, the lone dissenter, had concurred in the result in *Everson*. Here he argued that the majority was giving "establishment" too broad a meaning; unconstitutional "aid" to religion embraced only purposeful assistance directly to a church, not cooperative relationships between government and religious institutions.

McCollum seemed to represent a deepening Supreme Court commitment to the theory of strict SEPARATION OF CHURCH AND STATE, but it was significantly limited by another released-time case, ZORACH V. CLAUSEN (1952).

RICHARD E. MORGAN

MCCRAY v. UNITED STATES
195 U.S. 27 (1904)

Together with CHAMPION V. AMES (1903), the decision in *McCray* played a seminal role in the expansion of a NATIONAL POLICE POWER. Responding to lobby pressure, Congress in 1902 passed a clearly discriminatory EXCISE TAX on oleomargarine colored yellow to resemble butter. Relying on its power to regulate INTERSTATE COMMERCE, Congress sought to force yel-

low oleo off the market by taxing it at a rate forty times greater than naturally colored oleo. The act was attacked as an encroachment on STATE POLICE POWERS, a TAKING OF PROPERTY without DUE PROCESS, and a violation of the fundamental principles inherent in the Constitution.

Justice EDWARD D. WHITE, for a 6–3 Court, refused to inquire into Congress's intent and sustained the tax. He argued that the Court could not examine the wisdom of a particular act and, reiterating an OBITER DICTUM from *Champion*, said the remedy for "unwise or unjust" acts ". . . lies not in the abuse by the judicial authority of its functions, but in the people, upon whom . . . reliance must be placed for the correction of abuses." The Court pointedly dismissed WILLIAM GUTHRIE's argument that the validity of a tax ought to be determined by its natural and reasonable effect, regardless of pretext, though it would adopt his reasoning in BAILEY V. DREXEL (1922). The act's purpose—to suppress the sale of yellow oleo rather than to raise revenue—was immaterial. White concluded a judicial abdication of power in this case (although the Court would reassert it in *Bailey*) by stating that the Court could not help but sustain a congressional act even if that body "abused its lawful authority by levying a tax which was unwise or oppressive, or the result of the enforcement of which might be to indirectly affect subjects not within the powers delegated to Congress."

Chief Justice MELVILLE W. FULLER and Justices HENRY B. BROWN and RUFUS PECKHAM dissented without opinion.

DAVID GORDON

MCCULLOCH v. MARYLAND
4 Wheat. 316 (1819)

Speaking for a unanimous Supreme Court, Chief Justice JOHN MARSHALL delivered an opinion upon which posterity has heaped lavish encomiums. JAMES BRADLEY THAYER thought "there is nothing so fine as the opinion in McCulloch v. Maryland." ALBERT BEVERIDGE placed it "among the very first of the greatest judicial utterances of all time," while William Draper Lewis described it as "perhaps the most celebrated judicial utterance in the annals of the English speaking world." Such estimates spring from the fact that Marshall's vision of nationalism in time became a reality, to some extent because of his vision. Beveridge was not quite wrong in saying that the *McCulloch* opinion "so decisively influenced the growth of the Nation that, by many, it is considered as only second in importance to the Constitution itself." On the other hand, Marshall the judicial statesman engaged in a judicial coup, as his panegyrical biographer understood. To appreciate Marshall's achievement in *McCulloch* and the intense opposition that his opinion engendered in its time, one must also bear in mind that however orthodox his assumptions and doctrines are in the twentieth century, they were in their time unorthodox. With good reason Beveridge spoke of Marshall's "sublime audacity," the "extreme radicalism" of his constitutional theories, and the fact that he "rewrote the fundamental law of the Nation," a proposition to which Beveridge added that it would be more accurate to state that he made of the written instrument "a living thing, capable of growth, capable of keeping pace with the advancement of the American people and ministering to their changing necessities."

The hysterical denunciations of the *McCulloch* opinion by the aged and crabbed THOMAS JEFFERSON, by the frenetically embittered SPENCER ROANE, and by that caustic apostle of localism, JOHN TAYLOR, may justly be discounted, but not the judgment of the cool and prudent "Father of the Constitution," JAMES MADISON. On receiving Roane's "Hampden" essays assaulting *McCulloch*, Madison ignored the threat of state nullification and the repudiation of JUDICIAL REVIEW, but he agreed with Roane that the Court's opinion tended, in Madison's words, "to convert a limited into an unlimited Government." Madison deplored Marshall's "latitude in expounding the Constitution which seems to break down the landmarks intended by a specification of the Powers of Congress, and to substitute for a definite connection between means and ends, a Legislative discretion as to the former to which no practical limit can be assigned." Few if any of the friends of the Constitution, declared Madison, anticipated "a rule of construction . . . as broad & as pliant as what has occurred," and he added that the Constitution would probably not have been ratified if the powers that Marshall claimed for the national government had been known in 1788–1789. Madison's opinion suggests how far Marshall and the Court had departed from the intentions of the Framers and makes understandable the onslaught that *McCulloch* provoked. Although much of that onslaught was a genuine concern for the prostration of STATES' RIGHTS before a consolidating nationalism, Taylor hit the nail on the head for the older generation of Jeffersonians when he wrote that *McCulloch* reared "a monied interest."

The case, after all, was decided in the midst of a depression popularly thought to have been caused by the Bank of the United States, a private corporation chartered by Congress; and *McCulloch* was a decision in favor of the hated bank and against the power of a state to tax its branch operations. The constitutionality of the power of Congress to charter a bank had been ably debated in Congress and in Washington's cabinet in 1791, when ALEXANDER HAMILTON proposed the bank bill. Constitutional debate mirrored party politics, and the Federalists had the votes. The Court never passed judgment on the constitutionality of the original BANK OF THE UNITED STATES ACT, though it had a belated opportunity. In 1809 a case came before the Court that was remarkably similar to *McCulloch:* state officials, acting under a state statute taxing the branches of the bank, forcibly carried away from its vaults money to pay the state tax. In *Bank of the United States v. Deveaux* (1809), Marshall for the Court, deftly avoiding the questions that he confronted in *McCulloch*, found that the parties lacked the DIVERSITY OF CITIZENSHIP that would authorize JURISDICTION. With the bank's twenty-year charter nearing expiration, a decision in favor of the bank's constitutionality might look like pro-Federalist politics by the Court, embroiling it in a dispute with President Madison, who was on record as opposing the bank's constitutionality, and with Congress, which supported Madison's policies.

The United States fought the War of 1812 without the bank to help manage its finances, and the results were disastrous. The war generated a new wave of nationalism and a change of opinion in Madison's party. In 1816 President Madison signed into law a bill chartering a second Bank of the United States, passed by Congress with the support of young nationalists like HENRY CLAY and JOHN C. CALHOUN and opposed by a Federalist remnant led by young DANIEL WEBSTER. The political world was turned upside down. The bank's tight credit policies contributed to a depression, provoking many states to retaliate against "the monster monopoly." Two states prohibited the bank from operating within their jurisdictions; six others taxed the operations of the bank's branches within their jurisdictions. The constitutionality of Maryland's tax was the issue in *McCulloch*, as well as the constitutionality of the act of Congress incorporating the bank.

Six of the greatest lawyers of the nation, including Webster, WILLIAM PINKNEY, and LUTHER MARTIN, argued the case over a period of nine days, and only three days later Marshall delivered his thirty-six-page opinion for a unanimous Court. He had written much of it in advance, thus prejudging the case, but in a sense his career was a preparation for the case. As

Roane conceded, Marshall was "a man of profound legal attainments" writing "upon a subject which has employed his thoughts, his tongue, and his pen, as a politican, and an historian for more than thirty years." And he had behind him all five Jeffersonian-Republican members of the Court.

Arguing that Congress had no authority to incorporate a bank, counsel for Maryland claimed that the Constitution had originated with the states, which alone were truly sovereign, and that the national government's powers must be exercised in subordination to the states. Marshall grandiloquently turned these propositions around. When Beveridge said that Marshall the solider wrote *McCulloch* and that his opinion echoed "the blast of the bugle of Valley Forge" (where Marshall served), he had a point. Figuratively, Old Glory and the bald eagle rise up from the opinion— to anyone stirred by a nationalist sentiment. The Constitution, declared Marshall, had been submitted to conventions of the people, from whom it derives its authority. The government formed by the Constitution proceeded "directly from the people" and in the words of the PREAMBLE was "ordained and established" in their name, and it binds the states. Marshall drove home that theme repeatedly. "The government of the Union . . . is, emphatically, and truly, a government of the people. In form and in substance it emanates from them. Its powers are granted by them, and are to be exercised directly on them, and for their benefit." A bit later Marshall declared that the government of the Union though limited in its powers "is supreme within its sphere of action. . . . It is the government of all; its powers are delegated by all; it represents all, and acts for all." And it necessarily restricts its subordinate members, because the Constitution and federal laws constitute the supreme law of the land. Reading this later, ABRAHAM LINCOLN transmuted it into "a government of the people, by the people, for the people."

Marshall's opinion is a state paper, like the DECLARATION OF INDEPENDENCE, the Constitution itself, or the Gettysburg Address, the sort of document that puts itself beyond analysis or criticism. But there were constitutional issues to be resolved, and Marshall had not yet touched them. Madison agreed with Roane that "the occasion did not call for the general and abstract doctrine interwoven with the decision of the particular case," but *McCulloch* has survived and moved generations of Americans precisely because Marshall saw that the "general and abstract" were embedded in the issues, and he made it seem that the life of the nation was at stake on their resolution in the grandest way.

Disposing affirmatively of the question whether Congress could charter a bank was a foregone conclusion, flowing naturally from unquestioned premises. Though the power of establishing corporations is not among the ENUMERATED POWERS, seeing the Constitution "whole," as Marshall saw it, led him to the doctrine of IMPLIED POWERS. The Constitution ought not have the "prolixity of a legal code"; rather, it marked only "great outlines," with the result that implied powers could be "deduced." Levying and collecting taxes, borrowing money, regulating commerce, supporting armies, and conducting war are among the major enumerated powers; in addition, the Constitution vests in Congress the power to pass all laws "necessary and proper" to carry into execution the powers enumerated. These powers implied the means necessary to execute them. A banking corporation was a means of effectuating designated ends. The word "necessary" did not mean indispensably necessary; it did not refer to a means without which the power granted would be nugatory, its object unattainable. "Necessary" means "useful," "needful," "conducive to," thus allowing Congress a latitude of choice in attaining its legitimate ends. The Constitution's Framers knew the difference between "necessary" and "absolutely necessary," a phrase they used in Article I, section 10, clause 2. They inserted the NECESSARY AND PROPER CLAUSE in a Constitution "intended to endure for ages to come, and, consequently, to be adapted to the various crises of human affairs." They intended Congress to have "ample means" for carrying its express powers into effect. The "narrow construction" advocated by Maryland would abridge, even "annihilate," Congress's discretion in selecting its means. Thus, the test for determining the constitutionality of an act of Congress was: "Let the end be legitimate, let it be within the scope of the Constitution, and all means which are appropriate, which are plainly adapted to that end, which are not prohibited, but consist with the letter and spirit of the Constitution, are constitutional." That formula yielded the conclusion that the act incorporating the bank was valid.

Such was the BROAD CONSTRUCTION that "deduced" implied powers, shocking even Madison. The Court, he thought, had relinquished control over Congress. He might have added, as John Taylor did, that Marshall neglected to explain how and why a private bank chartered by Congress was necessary, even in a loose sense, to execute the enumerated powers. In *Construction Construed* (1820) Taylor gave five chapters to *McCulloch,* exhibiting the consequences of Marshall's reasoning. Congress might legislate on local agriculture and manufactures, because they were necessary to war. Roads were still more necessary than banks for collecting taxes. And:

Taverns are very necessary or convenient for the offices of the army.. . . But horses are undoubtedly more necessary for the conveyance of the mail and for war, than roads, which may be as convenient to assailants as defenders; and therefore the principle of implied power of legislation will certainly invest Congress with a legislative power over horses. In short, this mode of construction completely establishes the position, that Congress may pass any internal law whatsoever in relation to things, because there is nothing with which war, commerce and taxation may not be closely or remotely connected.

All of which supported Taylor's contention that Marshall's doctrine of implied powers would destroy the states and lead to a government of unlimited powers, because "as ends may be made to beget means, so means may be made to beget ends, until the co-habitation shall rear a progeny of unconstitutional bastards, which were not begotten by the people."

Marshall's reasoning with respect to the second question in the case incited less hostility, though not by much. Assuming Congress could charter the bank, could a state tax its branch? Marshall treated the bank as a branch or "instrument" of the United States itself, and relying on the SUPREMACY CLAUSE (Article VI), he concluded that if the states could tax one instrument to any degree, they could tax every other instrument as well—the mails, the mint, even the judicial process. The result would cripple the government, "prostrating it at the foot of the States." Again, he was deducing from general principles in order to defeat the argument that nothing in the Constitution prohibits state taxes on congressionally chartered instruments. Congress's power to create, Marshall reasoned, implied a power to preserve. A state power to tax was a power to destroy, incompatible with the national power to create and preserve. Where such repugnancy exists, the national power, which is supreme, must control. "The question is, in truth, a question of supremacy," with the result that the Court necessarily found the state act unconstitutional.

That was Marshall's *McCulloch* opinion. Roane and Taylor publicly excoriated it, and Jefferson spurred them on, telling Roane, who rejected even federal judicial review, "I go further than you do." The Virginia legislature repudiated implied powers and recommended an amendment to the Constitution "creating a tribunal for the decision of all questions, in which the powers and authorities of the general government and those of the States, where they are in conflict, shall be decided." Marshall was so upset

by the public criticism that he was driven for the first and only time to reply in a series of newspaper articles. Still, Ohio allied itself with Virginia and literally defied, even nullified, the decision in *McCulloch*. (See OSBORN V. BANK OF THE UNITED STATES, 1824; COHENS V. VIRGINIA, 1821.) Pennsylvania, Indiana, Illinois, and Tennessee also conducted a guerrilla war against the Court, and Congress seriously debated measures to curb its powers. Fortunately the common enemies of the Court shared no common policies. *McCulloch* prevailed in the long run, providing, together with GIBBONS V. OGDEN (1824), the constitutional wherewithal to meet unpredictable crises even to our time. *McCulloch* had unforeseen life-giving powers. Marshall, Beveridge's "supreme conservative," laid the constitutional foundations for the New Deal and the Welfare State.

LEONARD W. LEVY

Bibliography

BEVERIDGE, ALBERT J.   1916–1919   *The Life of John Marshall,* 4 vols. Vol. IV: 283–339. Boston: Houghton Mifflin.
HAINES, CHARLES GROVE   1944   *The Role of the Supreme Court in American Government and Politics, 1789–1835* Pages 351–368. Berkeley: University of California Press.
WARREN, CHARLES   1923   *The Supreme Court in United States History,* 3 vols. Vol. I:499–540. Boston: Little, Brown.

MCELVAINE v. BRUSH

See: *In Re Kemmler*

MCGOWAN v. MARYLAND

See: Sunday Closing Laws

MCGRAIN v. DAUGHERTY
273 U.S. 135 (1927)

In KILBOURN V. THOMPSON (1881) the Supreme Court had held that because Article I of the Constitution assigned Congress no power beyond the lawmaking power, Congress might constitutionally investigate "the private affairs of individuals" only for the purpose of gathering information to write new legislation. *McGrain* restated this requirement of legislative purpose, but rejected, 8–0, a challenge to the contempt conviction of the brother of Harry M. Daugherty who had failed to appear before a Senate committee investigating the failure of former Attorney General Daugherty to prosecute the malefactors in the Teapot Dome scandal.

In reality the investigation was not aimed at developing new legislation but at exposing malfeasance in the executive branch, a task that might have been deemed constitutionally appropriate for Congress if it were not for the simplistic *Kilbourn* theory. The gap between theory and reality was bridged by the creation of a presumption that congressional investigations had a legislative purpose, a presumption that was not to be overcome simply by showing that an investigation also had a purpose of public exposure.

The *McGrain* technique of requiring a legislative purpose for a congressional investigation, and then invoking a presumption of legislative purpose even when exposure was clearly a principal motive, had important consequences in post-World War II cases where anticommunist investigating committees were seeking to punish leftist speakers by public exposure precisely because the FIRST AMENDMENT prohibited Congress from passing legislation punishing such speech. The Court invoked the presumption of legislative purpose both to blind itself to the actual "exposure for exposure's sake" being conducted and to establish a congressional interest in lawmaking that outweighed whatever incidental infringement on speech the Court was willing to see.

MARTIN SHAPIRO

(SEE ALSO: *Legislative Investigations.*)

MCHENRY, JAMES
(1753–1816)

Irish-born physician James McHenry was a Maryland delegate to the CONSTITUTIONAL CONVENTION OF 1787 and a signer of the Constitution. Absent for most of June and July, he participated little in debate; but, when present, he took detailed notes which are a valuable record of the deliberations. He was later secretary of war (1796–1800).

DENNIS J. MAHONEY

MCILWAIN, CHARLES H.
(1871–1968)

Charles Howard McIlwain, a lawyer and political scientist, taught at Princeton and Harvard Universities. His major fields of interest were political theory and British constitutional history. His *The American Revolution: A Constitutional Interpretation* won the Pulitizer Prize in 1923. In that book he showed that the revolution was "the outcome of a collision between two mutually incompatible interpretations of the British constitution." His *Constitutionalism: Ancient and Modern* (1940, revised 1947) argued that the essence of CONSTITUTIONALISM was the balance between governmental power and the JURISDICTION of an independent judiciary and traced the roots of American constitutionalism through English history to classical Rome.

DENNIS J. MAHONEY

MCKEIVER v. PENNSYLVANIA
403 U.S. 528 (1971)

Although IN RE GAULT (1967) extended some basic procedural rights to juvenile offenders, young people continued to be tried in most states before judges who exercised great discretion, supposedly to protect juveniles. McKeiver, a juvenile defendant, faced possible incarceration for five years and requested TRIAL BY JURY, which the state denied. By a 6–3 vote, the Supreme Court decided that DUE PROCESS OF LAW does not guarantee trial by jury to juvenile offenders. Justice HARRY BLACKMUN for a plurality of four wrote an opinion based on the unrealistic premise that the juvenile system is fundamentally sound and enlightened, but he did not explain how it assured fundamental fairness. Justice JOHN MARSHALL HARLAN found Blackmun's opinion romantic but concurred nevertheless because he still opposed DUNCAN v. LOUISIANA (1968), which extended trial by jury to the states. Justice WILLIAM J. BRENNAN concurred because he thought, mistakenly, that publicity served as a check on juvenile court judges. Justices WILLIAM O. DOUGLAS, HUGO L. BLACK, and THURGOOD MARSHALL dissented. *McKeiver* short-circuited expectations that the Court would require essentially all the rights of the criminally accused for juveniles who commit adult crimes and face the prospect of serious punishment.

LEONARD W. LEVY

MCKENNA, JOSEPH
(1843–1926)

Few Justices sat longer upon the Supreme Court than Joseph McKenna, the son of an Irish immigrant baker, who served for twenty-seven years from 1898 until

1925 under three Chief Justices. During McKenna's tenure, the nation's political system grappled with the problems generated by industrialization, urbanization, and rising class conflict. The same problems followed many of the issues that came before the Court, whose decisions lacked consistency and predictability.

When President WILLIAM MCKINLEY named McKenna, his old House of Representatives colleague, to the seat vacated by Justice STEPHEN J. FIELD, he recognized not distinction at the bar or on the bench but loyal service. McKenna had been a four-term representative from California, a member of the Ninth Circuit Court of Appeals, and attorney general of the United States. In these roles McKenna had earned a justified reputation for devotion to the Republican party, the protective tariff, and the interests of his chief patron, the railroad mogul Leland Stanford. Even as a member of the circuit court, McKenna had written several opinions protecting Stanford's powerful Southern Pacific company from the unfriendly behavior of local and state officials who sought to regulate the carrier's rates and terminal facilities.

As a member of the Supreme Court during the high tide of the Progressive Era, however, McKenna supported the efforts of THEODORE ROOSEVELT's and WILLIAM HOWARD TAFT's administrations to bring the country's major railroads under a larger measure of administrative control through the Interstate Commerce Commission (ICC). Times had changed. By the turn of the century, even the railroads desired a degree of federal regulation that would protect them from conflicting state laws and the debilitating rate wars which drained away profits. McKenna wrote opinions for the Court that confirmed the new relationship between the carriers and the federal government by upholding the ICC's statutory powers with respect to fact-gathering and rate-making.

McKenna also became a robust supporter of congressional efforts to regulate other aspects of the nation's economic and social life under authority of the COMMERCE CLAUSE. He joined Justice JOHN M. HARLAN's crucial opinion in CHAMPION V. AMES (1903), which laid the foundation for a NATIONAL POLICE POWER by giving Congress the authority to exclude from the channels of INTERSTATE COMMERCE supposedly harmful goods such as lottery tickets. McKenna later applied this principle in his own opinions, which sustained the PURE FOOD AND DRUG ACT and also the Mann Act, banning the transportation of women in interstate commerce for immoral purposes.

To his great credit, McKenna was able to accept the extension of the national power doctrine to child labor in the famous case of HAMMER V. DAGENHART (1918), even while others who had endorsed the earlier decisions turned their backs upon logic and history. Nor did he join the majority in the case of ADAIR V. UNITED STATES (1908), where six Justices overturned Congress's attempt to ban YELLOW DOG CONTRACTS on the nation's railroads. McKenna's dissent placed the authority of Congress to regulate commerce above the contractual freedom of corporate management.

A stout nationalist and a moderate Republican who remained capable of accepting many progressive reforms, McKenna nonetheless displayed a checkered record with regard to state and federal efforts to assist the working class and organized labor. He refused, for example, to permit the state of Kansas to outlaw yellow dog contracts in all private industry, although he endorsed Congress's effort to do so on the interstate railroads. He cast his vote with RUFUS PECKHAM in LOCHNER V. NEW YORK (1905) and with GEORGE H. SUTHERLAND in ADKINS V. CHILDREN'S HOSPITAL (1923), when the majority struck down MAXIMUM HOURS AND MINIMUM WAGE LEGISLATION on the grounds of FREEDOM OF CONTRACT. Yet McKenna spurned that conservative shibboleth in MULLER V. OREGON (1908), WILSON V. NEW (1917), and BUNTING V. OREGON (1917). On the other hand, not many opinions could match in reactionary tone McKenna's dissent in the *Arizona Employers' Liability Cases* (1919), where he argued that liability without fault violated the DUE PROCESS clause of the FOURTEENTH AMENDMENT.

Like most of his brethren on the WHITE COURT, McKenna gave the green light to federal and state efforts to stamp out dissent during World War I. He voted to uphold the convictions of Charles Schenck and Eugene V. Debs as well as those of Jacob Abrams and Joseph Gilbert, although the latter two cases provoked sharp dissents from OLIVER WENDELL HOLMES and LOUIS D. BRANDEIS. If sometimes contractual freedom had to give way before the power of Congress, McKenna believed, so, too, did the liberty to protest against the government in time of war.

MICHAEL E. PARRISH

Bibliography

MCDEVITT, BROTHER MATTHEW 1946 *Joseph McKenna: Associate Justice of the United States.* Washington, D.C.: Catholic University Press.

SEMONCHE, JOHN E. 1978 *Charting the Future: The Supreme Court Responds to a Changing Society, 1890–1920.* Westport, Conn.: Greenwood Press.

MCKINLEY, JOHN
(1780–1852)

Like several other Jacksonian Justices on the TANEY COURT, John McKinley was a product of the Southwest. Born in Virginia, he went with his family to Kentucky where he learned law and began practice. In 1818 he moved to Huntsville, Alabama, then a frontier town, where he practiced law and pursued a diversified political career—first as a supporter of HENRY CLAY and then, when Clay's fortunes waned in Alabama, of ANDREW JACKSON. This timely shift got him a Senate seat in 1826. He served there until 1830, when he lost reelection. He then returned to the Alabama legislature, and in 1832 he went to the United States House of Representatives where he served for one term. After another term in the state legislature in 1836, he was elected by that body to the Senate but chose instead to accept an appointment to the Supreme Court from MARTIN VAN BUREN in 1837.

McKinley's legislative career lacked distinction, but the policy preferences he revealed were those that would guide his work on the Court: in addition to unswerving loyalty to Jackson and Van Buren, he was a strict states' rights man, though he never argued out his case philosophically or constitutionally. In good Jacksonian fashion he was suspicious of monopolies and hated the second Bank of the United States. He also had a strong preference for land laws that favored small settlers and a firm belief that SLAVERY was a state problem and that property in slaves was entitled to legal protection.

McKinley's fifteen years on the Supreme Court (1837–1852) were unproductive and frustrating, both for him and for those who worked with him. In general, states' rights ideas guided his judicial behavior, but he never spoke for the Court in any important cases. He took his duties seriously, as Chief Justice ROGER B. TANEY pointed out in his brief eulogy, and was decent and fairminded to the best of his ability. But during his entire tenure, which was interrupted by illness and frequent absences, he wrote only about twenty opinions for the Court, all routine.

Perhaps his most notorious opinion came in BANK OF AUGUSTA V. EARLE (1839) where, both on circuit and in a lone dissent at Washington, he held that a CORPORATION chartered in one state (a bank in the *Earle* case) could not do business within the boundaries of another state without the latter's express consent. McKinley's position was consistent with a deep concern for state SOVEREIGNTY, but it was, as Justice JOSEPH STORY observed in dismay, totally unrealistic in an age when interstate corporate business was increasingly the norm. McKinley dissented twenty-three times but none of his dissents attracted support and none pioneered new law. Many were unwritten, evidence of the Justice's increasing isolation from the ongoing operations of the Court.

McKinley was also isolated on his own circuit, although Supreme Court Justices, as senior circuit judges, ordinarily dominated the district judges with whom they sat. Not so on the Fifth Circuit where district judges Philip K. Lawrence and, to a lesser extent, Theodore H. McCaleb held the upper hand. There is evidence also that leading members of the circuit bar held the Justice in disrepute. Part of the problem was the 10,000 miles of annual travel (which left McKinley little time to study cases) and the large number of cases (2,700 at each of the two terms in 1839 by his reckoning). His circuit also included Louisiana, where the civil law received from France and the COMMON LAW formed a mixture that was well-nigh incomprehensible to all save lawyers who grew up with it. The main difficulty on circuit as on the full Court, however, was McKinley himself. His talents were simply too modest for the duties of his office. Even his eulogizers found nothing about his legal ability to praise, and all evidence points to the correctness of CARL B. SWISHER's assessment: that John McKinley, of all the Justices on the Taney Court, was the least distinguished.

R. KENT NEWMYER

Bibliography

GATELL, FRANK O. 1969 John McKinley. In Leon Friedman and Fred L. Israel (eds.), *The Justices of the United States Supreme Court 1789–1969*, Vol. 1, pages 769–792. New York: Chelsea House.

Proceedings in Relation to the Death of the Late Judge McKinley 1852 14 Howard iii–v.

MCKINLEY, WILLIAM
(1843–1901)

William McKinley, an Ohio Republican who was President of the United States from 1897 to 1901, spent most of his term in office preoccupied with foreign affairs. An imperialist, he advocated the annexation of Hawaii and, after successfully prosecuting a war against Spain, acquired the Philippines and PUERTO RICO for the United States. McKinley continued the domestic policies of his predecessor, GROVER CLEVELAND, but unlike most Chief Executives in the late nineteenth century, McKinley saw the presidency as a powerful office. He frequently relied on expert and academic commissions to offer him advice on specific problems.

McKinley's lack of interest in enforcing the SHERMAN ANTITRUST ACT paralleled BENJAMIN HARRISON's, but McKinley's failure to enforce the law vigorously is more significant because he held office during the second greatest merger movement in American history. His three attorneys general—one of whom, JOSEPH MCKENNA, would be his sole appointment to the Supreme Court—initiated only three cases under the act. The most important antitrust cases decided during McKinley's tenure, UNITED STATES V. TRANS-MISSOURI FREIGHT ASSOCIATION (1897) and *Addyston Pipe & Steel Co. v. United States* (1899), had been started under prior administrations.

DAVID GORDON

Bibliography

GOULD, LEWIS L. 1980 *The Presidency of William McKinley.* Lawrence: Regents Press of Kansas.

MCLAUGHLIN, ANDREW C.
(1861–1947)

A protégé of THOMAS COOLEY at the University of Michigan, Andrew Cunningham McLaughlin took over his course in American constitutional history and later taught that subject at the University of Chicago for thirty years. In his 1914 presidential address before the American Historical Association, McLaughlin criticized CHARLES BEARD's monolithic emphasis on economic factors. McLaughlin also rejected the tone of exaltation that imbued the work of JOHN FISKE and others on the CONSTITUTIONAL CONVENTION OF 1787. In his first major book, *Confederation and Constitution* (1905), McLaughlin emphasized the constructive aspects of the ARTICLES OF CONFEDERATION and of the Confederation period. He construed the Articles as the product of a war against centralism and as the world's first written CONSTITUTION to establish a federal system, whose origins he traced to the British Empire. His other important works, distinguished for their judicious interpretations, were *Courts, Constitutions, and Parties* (1912), *Foundations of American Constitutionalism* (1932), and *Constitutional History of the United States* (1935), which won a Pulitzer Prize.

LEONARD W. LEVY

MCLAUGHLIN v. FLORIDA

See: Miscegenation

MCLAURIN v. OKLAHOMA STATES REGENTS

See: *Sweatt v. Painter*

MCLEAN, JOHN
(1785–1861)

John McLean's appointment to the Supreme Court on March 6, 1829, was ANDREW JACKSON's first and the first from the old Northwest and Ohio, where McLean had grown to manhood. He studied law with Arthur St. Clair, Jr., was admitted to the bar in 1807, and maintained an active full-time practice in Lebanon, Ohio, until his 1812 election to Congress, where he served two terms. As a National Republican, he favored a protective tariff and a national bank. From 1816 to 1822 he served as judge of the Ohio Supreme Court where he gained a respect for the COMMON LAW and developed a penchant for bending it "to the diversity of our circumstances," as he put it in one case. While serving on that court, McLean assiduously cultivated political favor, first with JAMES MONROE and JOHN QUINCY ADAMS, and, when the latter began to falter, with Jackson. His efforts paid off, first in 1822 with an appointment as Commissioner of the General Land Office, then in 1823 as Postmaster General, where his brilliant administrative abilities won him a national reputation. Adams reappointed him to head the Post Office Department, and Jackson was willing to do the same but nominated him to the Supreme Court when McLean indicated an unwillingness to make political removals.

McLean served as Associate Justice from 1829 to 1861, during a period of rapid transition in American law. At the outset the new Justice inclined toward Jacksonian STATES' RIGHTS dogma, as in his dissent from CONTRACT CLAUSE orthodoxy in CRAIG V. MISSOURI (1830). More revealing yet was his practical-minded opinion for the majority in BRISCOE V. BANK OF THE COMMONWEALTH OF KENTUCKY (1837), which held that the notes of the Commonwealth Bank were not BILLS OF CREDIT prohibited by Article I, section 10, even though the state owned the bank and the notes circulated as legal tender.

Despite his result-oriented approach in such cases as *Briscoe* and MAYOR OF NEW YORK V. MILN (1837) (where he supported STATE POLICE POWER regulations against the charge that they were regulations of INTERSTATE COMMERCE), McLean was not a Jacksonian judge. Indeed, he moved steadily toward a conservative nationalism similar to that of Justice JOSEPH STORY, who became his closest friend on the Court. That McLean was solidly conservative on property rights and CORPORATION questions is clear from his majority opinion in behalf of contractual sanctity in PIQUA BRANCH BANK V. KNOOP (1854). His nationalism was apparent in the CHEROKEE INDIAN CASES (*Worcester v. Georgia*) in 1832 (where he joined JOHN MARSHALL against Georgia and Jackson), and in *Holmes v. Jennison* in 1840 (where he concurred in ROGER B. TANEY's dissent which asserted the supremacy of the federal government in the area of foreign policy). His "high-toned FEDERALISM" in COMMERCE CLAUSE cases can be seen in the LICENSE CASES (1847) and PASSENGER CASES (1849) and in his majority opinion in *Pennsylvania v. Wheeling and Belmont Bridge Company* (1852) which struck down a Virginia law authorizing a bridge that obstructed commerce over a navigable river. His dissent in COOLEY V. BOARD OF WARDENS OF PHILADELPHIA (1851) reaffirmed the theory of his friend Story that the power to regulate foreign and interstate commerce belonged exclusively to Congress.

McLean disliked slavery and his opinions often revealed his free-soil sentiments; but he regularly conceded the legality of the institution. Thus his separate opinion in PRIGG V. PENNSYLVANIA (1842) upheld the right of northern states to protect free Negroes from unlawful rendition, but it also affirmed the power of Congress to require the states to return fugitives. Equivocation was unavoidable, too, in GROVES V. SLAUGHTER (1841) where in a separate opinion McLean argued that slavery was a local institution under state control and that the power of Congress to regulate interstate commerce did not prevent a state from regulating the importation of slaves. Free states presumably could prohibit slaves from being brought into their jurisdiction and liberate slaves once they arrived, but slave states could also regulate imports and exports of slaves for sale. On circuit McLean also ruled against freedom when he thought the law obliged him to do so.

McLean's proslavery decisions, which were condemned in the free-soil press, increasingly ran counter to his presidential plans which, to the distress of some of his colleagues, he relentlessly pursued from the bench. In DRED SCOTT V. SANDFORD (1857) his political ambition, now focused on the Republican party, influenced his judicial behavior. In a separate dissent, he argued that Congress had the power to prohibit slavery in the TERRITORIES, that Negroes could be citizens, and that Dred Scott was free by virtue of his residence in a free state and a free territory.

McLean has been unfairly blamed for the Court's wide-ranging, politically explosive decision—a burden we now know should fall most heavily on Taney and JAMES M. WAYNE. But there is no doubt that McLean's determination to dissent gave Taney and Wayne a good excuse to confront the whole problem of SLAVERY IN THE TERRITORIES.

McLean was not a legal scholar, he pioneered no new DOCTRINE, and he did not greatly refine the process of constitutional adjustment to new circumstances that was the hallmark of the TANEY COURT. Greatness, however, is not only rare but relative, and on a Court burdened with mediocrity McLean looked good. His opinions were generally solid and persuasive (as in the great copyright case of *Wheaton v. Peters* in 1834) and he assuredly carried more than his share of the Court's heavy work load (with nearly 250 majority opinions and numerous dissents). He was one of the few Justices of the period who went to the considerable trouble of publishing his circuit opinions (in six volumes) and whose circuit opinions were worth publishing. It is true that his political ambition contributed to the politicization of the judicial process. Still, he cherished the Court as an institution and worked diligently through it to preserve the Union under the Constitution.

R. KENT NEWMYER

Bibliography

GATELL, FRANK O. 1969 John McLean. In Leon Friedman and Fred L. Israel (eds.), *The Justices of the United States Supreme Court, 1789–1969*, Vol. 1, pages 535–567. New York: Chelsea House.

WEISENBURGER, FRANCIS P. 1937 *The Life of John McLean: A Politician on the United States Supreme Court.* Columbus: Ohio State University Press.

MCNABB v. UNITED STATES

See: McNabb-Mallory Rule

MCNABB-MALLORY RULE

Partly in response to the problem posed by the VOLUNTARINESS test, the Supreme Court made an unexpected departure from that test in *McNabb v. United States* (1943) and *Mallory v. United States* (1957). Under the "McNabb-Mallory Rule," a confession obtained by law enforcement officers during a period of unnecessary delay in bringing an arrested person before a magistrate for arraignment was inadmissible in federal prosecutions. The rule was based not on constitutional grounds but on the Court's supervisory authority over the administration of criminal justice in the federal courts. The rule created more problems than it attempted to solve, and in 1968, Congress abolished it.

In *McNabb*, five brothers were arrested for murder and held in barren detention cells for forty-eight hours. Isolated from friends and family, and without the assistance of counsel, they were repeatedly interrogated until confessions were obtained. (See POLICE INTERROGATIONS AND CONFESSIONS.) Only after they confessed were they taken before a magistrate for arraignment. The confessions were admitted into EVIDENCE at trial and the McNabbs were convicted.

The Court, with only Justice STANLEY F. REED dissenting, reversed the convictions on the ground that they were unlawfully obtained during a period of prolonged custodial delay. Federal laws in effect at the time of the Court's decision required officers to take an arrested person "immediately" before a magistrate for arraignment. At arraignment, the magistrate advises the defendant of the charges against him, of his constitutional rights, and sets a preliminary hearing date at which the government must show legal cause for the detention.

Justice FELIX FRANKFURTER devoted much of his opinion for the Court to an analysis of the policies behind the immediate arraignment laws. He concluded that they were intended to protect the rights of arrested persons and to deter the police from secret third-degree interrogation of persons not yet arraigned.

Finding that the officers who arrested the McNabbs had acted in willful disobedience of the laws requiring immediate arraignment, the Court suppressed the confessions. Suppression, Frankfurter explained, would promote the policies behind the laws and ensure the fair and effective administration of the federal criminal justice system by disallowing convictions based on unfair police procedures.

Two years after *McNabb*, Congress adopted Rule 5(a) of the FEDERAL RULES OF CRIMINAL PROCEDURE. The rule required that an arrested person be taken, "without unnecessary delay," before the nearest available commissioner or any other nearby officer empowered to commit persons charged with offenses against the laws of the United States. The rule, by failing to include remedies for its violation, left intact the *McNabb* mandate that confessions obtained during a period of unlawful detention be suppressed. Any

questions regarding the continuing viability of the *McNabb* rule were put to rest by the Court's opinion in *Mallory*.

Mallory was arrested with two other suspects on rape charges. Although the police had sufficient evidence to consider Mallory the prime suspect, he was not arraigned until ten hours after his arrest, during which time he was continually interrogated and finally signed a written confession. At trial, the signed confession was introduced into evidence; Mallory was convicted and received the death sentence.

Frankfurter delivered the opinion of a unanimous Court, which held the confession inadmissible because Mallory had not been arraigned without unnecessary delay as required by Rule 5(a). The Court's interpretation of Rule 5(a) was based on the principles announced earlier in the *McNabb* decision. Delays in arraignment must be prevented in order to prevent abusive and unlawful law enforcement practices aimed at obtaining confessions of guilt from suspects in custody who have not been informed by a judicial officer of the charges against them or of their constitutional rights.

After *Mallory* the law prevailing in the federal courts, commonly referred to as the "McNabb-Mallory Rule," was that any confession made by a suspect under arrest, in violation of Rule 5(a), was inadmissible in evidence. The problem with the McNabb-Mallory Rule was that it operated arbitrarily to exclude from evidence otherwise free and voluntary confessions merely because of delay in arraignment. In other words, the United States Supreme Court had failed to consider the obvious: a delayed arraignment does not imply the involuntariness of a confession.

Criticized as illogical and unrealistic, the McNabb-Mallory Rule was abolished in 1968 when Congress enacted Title II of the OMNIBUS CRIME CONTROL AND SAFE STREETS ACT. The act provides in part that confessions shall not be inadmissible solely because of delay in arraignment, if they are voluntary and made within six hours of arrest or during a delay in arraignment that is reasonable, considering the transportation problems in getting a defendant before a magistrate. Thus, the voluntary nature of the confession is the test of its admissibility, and delay in arraignment is only one factor for the judge to consider.

WENDY E. LEVY

Bibliography

STEPHENS, OTIS H., JR. 1973 *The Supreme Court and Confessions of Guilt.* Pages 63–89. Knoxville: University of Tennessee Press.

MCREYNOLDS, JAMES C.
(1862–1946)

James Clark McReynolds, a Tennessee Democrat, first came to national attention as an antitrust prosecutor during the THEODORE ROOSEVELT and WILLIAM HOWARD TAFT administrations. He was a Tennessee Gold Democrat, friendly with Colonel Edward House, WOODROW WILSON's key adviser. His antitrust reputation led to his appointment as Wilson's attorney general in 1913. Within a year, however, McReynolds found himself at odds with the administration and powerful congressmen. Wilson "kicked McReynolds upstairs" to the Supreme Court in 1914. From then until his retirement in 1941, McReynolds distinguished himself as a consistent and implacable foe of Progressive and New Deal regulatory programs.

McReynold's hostility to trusts largely derived from his ideas of individualism and freedom from arbitrary restraints. Throughout his judicial career he resolutely supported the business community and was instinctively suspicious of governmental regulation. "If real competition is to continue, the right of the individual to exercise reasonable discretion in respect of his own business methods must be preserved," McReynolds wrote in FEDERAL TRADE COMMISSION V. GRATZ (1920). In that case, the Court limited the authority of the FTC, the creation of which had been one of the Wilson administration's primary achievements; McReynolds wrote that the courts, not the commission, would decide the meaning of "unfair method of competition." In *St. Louis and O'Fallon Railroad v. United States* (1929) the Court resolved a longstanding dispute between the Interstate Commerce Commission (ICC) and railroads as to whether original or replacement costs should be considered for valuation and rate purposes. Speaking for a narrow majority, McReynolds overturned ICC policy by ruling that the commission had to base its determination of rates on replacement costs, which were higher.

McReynolds resisted the claims of organized labor. For example, he joined his colleagues in rejecting federal child labor laws and a District of Columbia minimum wage statute. When the Court in 1919 sustained an Arizona law holding employers responsible for on-the-job accidents whether or not they were negligent, McReynolds dissented, caustically arguing that such laws served "to stifle enterprise, produce discontent, strife, idleness and pauperism."

Without exception, McReynolds supported the conviction of political radicals during the "Red Scare" period following World War I. A decade later, when the Court turned against restrictive state measures on speech and press, McReynolds parted company with the majority, dissenting in STROMBERG V. CALIFORNIA (1931) and NEAR V. MINNESOTA (1931). Similarly, McReynolds's ill-concealed contempt for blacks led to dissent from decisions striking down an all-white primary law and ordering a new trial for the Scottsboro defendants. Finally, when the Court, in MISSOURI EX REL. GAINES V. CANADA (1938), began its long process of overturning segregation, McReynolds bitterly assailed the majority opinion.

Some of McReynolds's opinions defending individual rights remain relevant. In MEYER V. NEBRASKA (1923) he spoke for the Court in striking down a state statute prohibiting German language instruction in the public schools; in PIERCE V. SOCIETY OF SISTERS (1925) he ruled against an Oregon statute that had the effect of proscribing parochial school education; and in CARROLL V. UNITED STATES (1925) he vehemently protested against violations of the FOURTH AMENDMENT in enforcing PROHIBITION. In MYERS V. UNITED STATES (1926) he dissented from what he considered to be an almost unlimited approval of presidential power to remove federal officials, a view vindicated nine years later when the Court unanimously rejected President FRANKLIN D. ROOSEVELT's attempt to remove a federal trade commissioner.

The New Deal years provide the sharpest focus for McReynolds's views of constitutional law, both when he joined in majority opinions and later in the bitter dissents that represent his most familiar legacy. McReynolds combined his ideological reaction to the New Deal with a passionate, almost pathological, hatred for Franklin D. Roosevelt. The Justice was scathing in his private remarks and, at times, indiscreet in public. In his courtroom dissent in the GOLD CLAUSE CASES (1935) McReynolds emotionally proclaimed: "This is Nero at his worst. The Constitution is gone!" When the New Deal gained a few early Court victories, McReynolds dissented, as in the gold clause cases, in NEBBIA V. NEW YORK (1934), and in ASHWANDER V. TENNESSEE VALLEY AUTHORITY (1936). As one of the "Four Horsemen," he participated in striking down thirteen New Deal measures between 1934 and 1936. When the Court made its famous shift, beginning in 1937 with WEST COAST HOTEL COMPANY V. PARRISH and the WAGNER ACT CASES, McReynolds joined his fellow conservatives in outraged dissent. As their spokesman in *National Labor Relations Board v. Friedman-Marks Clothing* (1937), he argued that the WAGNER ACT regulated production, not commerce, and thus exceeded the boundaries of congressional power as set in long-standing precedents. Similarly, he considered the SOCIAL SECURITY ACT unconstitutional; he registered a lone dissent against the approval of the securities registration provisions of the PUBLIC UTILITIES HOLDING COMPANY ACT; and, finally, he provided the sole dissent to the Court's recognition in 1940 that labor PICKETING was entitled to protection as an exercise of FREEDOM OF SPEECH.

Few Supreme Court Justices have been more outspoken or more doctrinaire than McReynolds; and few have been so incompatible with colleagues. McReynolds refused to speak to fellow Wilson appointee John H. Clarke, who was too liberal, and to LOUIS D. BRANDEIS and BENJAMIN N. CARDOZO, who were both liberal and Jewish. Even Chief Justice Taft found him "selfish and prejudiced" and difficult to like. He was committed to laissez-faire individualism and racial segregation, and he was unyielding and hostile to any political beliefs he regarded as deviant.

STANLEY I. KUTLER

Bibliography

MASON, ALPHEUS THOMAS 1956 *Harlan Fiske Stone: Pillar of the Law.* New York: Viking.
PASCHAL, JOEL F. 1951 *Mr. Justice Sutherland: A Man Against the State.* Princeton, N.J.: Princeton University Press.

MECHANICAL JURISPRUDENCE

This pejorative epithet was introduced in 1908 by the American jurist ROSCOE POUND. It and similar rubrics—"the jurisprudence of conceptions," "slot machine, phonograph, T-square theories of law"— were widely used to caricature patterns of juristic thought and judicial action that deduced conclusions from unexamined, predetermined conceptions by purely mechanical logical processes, disregarded socioeconomic realities and practical consequences, and understated the degree of judicial lawmaking by attributing a machinelike automatism to the judicial process.

The "sociological jurisprudence" and "legal realism" of Justices OLIVER WENDELL HOLMES, HARLAN FISKE STONE, and BENJAMIN N. CARDOZO were often hailed as correctives for mechanical jurisprudence because they viewed law and logic instrumentally as means to social ends, and they acknowledged judicial lawmaking.

A perennial juristic allurement, mechanical jurisprudence was exemplified by many Supreme Court "economic DUE PROCESS" and COMMERCE CLAUSE decisions between 1895 and 1937. In due process cases

such as LOCHNER V. NEW YORK (1905) and ADKINS V. CHILDREN'S HOSPITAL (1923), the Court invoked the laissez-faire doctrine, FREEDOM OF CONTRACT, which regarded workers and employers as bargaining equals, in holding state and federal legislation unconstitutional. In commerce clause cases such as UNITED STATES V. E. C. KNIGHT CO. (1895) and CARTER V. CARTER COAL CO. (1936), the Court used economically unrealistic distinctions between "commerce" and PRODUCTION, and "direct" and "indirect" EFFECTS ON COMMERCE in invalidating federal legislation. A classic expression of mechanical jurisprudence is the passage of Justice Owen Roberts's opinion in UNITED STATES V. BUTLER (1936) where he said the Court had only to compare the statute with the appropriate constitutional clause to see if they squared.

Such decisions led finally to President FRANKLIN D. ROOSEVELT's 1937 "Court reform" bill, designed, he said, "to save the Constitution from the Court and the Court from itself." But the Court swiftly reversed and reformed itself, abandoning these mechanical constitutional interpretations. Later, in WICKARD V. FILBURN (1942), it reemphasized that its recognition of economic realities had made "the mechanical application of legal formulas no longer feasible."

HOWARD E. DEAN

Bibliography

POUND, ROSCOE 1908 Mechanical Jurisprudence. *Columbia Law Review* 8:605–623.
STERN, ROBERT L. 1951 The Problems of Yesteryear—Commerce and Due Process. *Vanderbilt Law Review* 4:446–468.

MEIKLEJOHN, ALEXANDER
(1872–1964)

Alexander Meiklejohn was a philosopher, president of Amherst College, and director of an experimental college at the University of Wisconsin. After his long academic career he became a CIVIL LIBERTIES publicist. His *Free Speech and Its Relation to Self-Government* (1948) presented the FIRST AMENDMENT as the foundation of political democracy. He advocated that citizens should have the same unlimited FREEDOM OF SPEECH as their representatives. Regarding the CLEAR AND PRESENT DANGER TEST and BALANCING TESTS as annulments of the First Amendment, he criticized OLIVER WENDELL HOLMES and ZECHARIAH CHAFEE as proponents of a stunted interpretation of free speech. In the McCarthy period he defended the right of communists to teach. His essay, "The First Amendment Is An Absolute," written when he was almost ninety, summarized his position, which was not really absolutist. Distinguishing "the freedom of speech" from "speech," he believed that private defamation, OBSCENITY, perjury, false advertising, and solicitation of crime were not constitutionally protected. His ABSOLUTISM seems to have extended to speech concerning all matters of public policy, education, philosophy, arts, literature, and science, but he believed that even protected speech was subject to reasonable regulations of time and place. Meiklejohn was closer to Holmes and Chafee than he admitted.

LEONARD W. LEVY

MEMOIRS v. MASSACHUSETTS
383 U.S. 413 (1966)

Nine years after ROTH V. UNITED STATES, still unable to agree upon a constitutional definition of OBSCENITY, the Supreme Court reversed a state court determination that John Cleland's *Memoirs of a Woman of Pleasure,* commonly known as *Fanny Hill,* was obscene. The three-Justice PLURALITY OPINION, written by Justice WILLIAM J. BRENNAN, held that the constitutional test for obscenity was: "(a) the dominant theme of the material taken as a whole appeals to a prurient interest in sex; (b) the material is patently offensive because it affronts contemporary community standards relating to the description or representation of sexual matters; and (c) the material is utterly without redeeming social value."

Despite an OBITER DICTUM in JACOBELLIS V. OHIO (1964), it was believed—and the Massachusetts courts had held—that *Roth* did not require unqualified worthlessness before a book might be deemed obscene. Justice Brennan twisted the *Roth* reasoning (that obscenity was unprotected because it was utterly worthless) into a constitutional test that was virtually impossible to meet under criminal standards of proof. Thus a finding of obscenity would become rare, even where the requisite prurient interest appeal and offensiveness could be demonstrated.

The Massachusetts courts had tried the book in the abstract; a host of literary experts testified to its social value. The circumstances of the book's production, sale, and publicity were not admitted. Justice Brennan noted that evidence that distributors commercially exploited *Fanny Hill* solely for its prurient appeal could have justified a finding, based on the purveyor's own evaluation, that *Fanny Hill* was utterly without redeeming social importance.

Justices HUGO L. BLACK, WILLIAM O. DOUGLAS, and POTTER J. STEWART concurred in the result, Black and Douglas adhering to their view that obscenity is protected expression. Stewart reiterated his view that the First Amendment protected all but "hardcore pornography."

Justice TOM C. CLARK, dissenting, rejected the importation of the "utterly without redeeming social value" standard into the obscenity test, which he believed would give the "smut artist free rein." Reacting against the continuous flow of pornographic materials to the Supreme Court, he reasserted that the Court should apply a "sufficient evidence" standard of review of lower courts' obscenity decisions.

Justice JOHN MARSHALL HARLAN, dissenting, argued that although the federal government could constitutionally proscribe only hard-core pornography, the states could prohibit material under any criteria rationally related to accepted notions of obscenity.

Justice BYRON R. WHITE, also dissenting, argued that *Roth* counseled examination of the predominant theme of the material, not resort to minor themes of passages of literary worth to redeem obscene works from condemnation.

KIM MCLANE WARDLAW

MEMORANDUM ORDER

Most orders of any court are not accompanied by opinions, but are simply stated in memorandum form. The Supreme Court issues thousands of such memorandum orders each year, granting or denying such requests as applications for review, applications for permission to appear IN FORMA PAUPERIS, applications for permission to file briefs AMICI CURIAE, or PETITIONS FOR REHEARING.

Some memorandum orders effectively decide cases; the denial of a petition for CERTIORARI is one example, and another is the dismissal of an APPEAL "for want of a substantial federal question." Occasionally the Court summarily affirms the decision of a lower court, issuing no opinion but only a memorandum order. The denial of certiorari generally has little force as a PRECEDENT; however, both lower courts and commentators do draw conclusions concerning the Court's view when they see a consistent pattern of refusal to review lower court decisions reaching the same conclusion. The summary affirmance of a decision in a memorandum order does establish a precedent, but the precedent is limited to the points necessarily decided by the lower court, and does not extend to the reasoning in that court's opinion. The practice of deciding major issues through memorandum orders is often criticized on the ground that decisions will not be understood as principled if they are not explained.

KENNETH L. KARST

Bibliography

BROWN, ERNEST J. 1958 The Supreme Court, 1957 Term—Foreword: Process of Law. *Harvard Law Review* 72:77–95.

MEMPHIS v. GREENE
451 U.S. 100 (1981)

Because the City of Memphis blocked a street at the point where a white neighborhood bordered a black neighborhood, residents of the black neighborhood had to drive around the white neighborhood in order to get to and from the city center. Black residents brought a CLASS ACTION against the city, seeking an INJUNCTION to keep the street open. They failed in the federal district court, but the court of appeals held that the closing violated their right to hold and enjoy property, guaranteed by the CIVIL RIGHTS ACT OF 1866.

The Supreme Court, with Justice JOHN PAUL STEVENS writing for a 6–3 majority, rejected the statutory claim, saying the street closing had caused only minor inconvenience, and had not damaged the plaintiff's property values. The question remained whether the THIRTEENTH AMENDMENT, of its own force, forbade anything but slavery itself. The Court did not reach this broad question, saying only that the street closing here was not a BADGE OF SERVITUDE. Justice THURGOOD MARSHALL, for the dissenters, scored the majority for ignoring "the plain and powerful symbolic message of the 'inconvenience' ": to fence out "undesirables."

KENNETH L. KARST

MENTAL ILLNESS AND THE CONSTITUTION

Mental illness has played two apparently different roles in American law generally: as a limitation on state authority to impose ordinary legal standards on individuals and as a basis for increasing state authority over individuals. The paradigmatic limiting use of mental illness is the defense of insanity for conduct that would otherwise be subject to criminal liability.

Its paradigmatic use to increase state authority is in civil commitment of people who, apart from their mental illness, would not be subject to state confinement or control. In both guises, however, the same underlying justification is advanced—that a mentally ill person deserves specially beneficial treatment from the state, either to excuse him from ordinary standards of criminal liability or to protect and treat him under civil commitment laws.

Until the 1960s, constitutional doctrine paid scant attention to any of the legal usages for mental illness. Beginning in that decade, lower federal courts began to scrutinize these uses and to invoke constitutional norms in the service of that scrutiny. The central problem was that the promise of special beneficence for mental illness proved false on close examination. Although insanity was denoted a defense to criminal liability, in practice defendants thus found "not guilty" were automatically confined to state maximum security institutions indistinguishable from prisons (and often with harsher custodial conditions), were provided with virtually no psychiatric treatment, and were typically held for longer terms than if they had been convicted of the offenses charged. Similarly, individuals who were civilly committed, ostensibly for protection and treatment, in fact were regularly confined in brutal state institutions, provided no semblance of psychiatric treatment, subjected to degrading impositions such as numbing, physically harmful drug dosages, strait-jacketed isolation, and confined for long terms.

Confronted with these facts, federal courts found various violations of constitutional rights, all derived essentially from the proposition that DUE PROCESS required the state to justify any deprivation of liberty and, where that justification was based on a promise of beneficent treatment, to fulfill that promise. Thus the District of Columbia Circuit Court held in *Rouse v. Cameron* (1966) that those found not guilty by reason of insanity had a "right to treatment" and not simply custodial confinement, and in *Bolton v. Harris* (1968) that these defendants could not be automatically confined after an insanity acquittal but only if found "mentally ill" and "in need of treatment" according to civil commitment standards. For civilly committed people generally, that court found in *Lake v. Cameron* (1966) a liberty-based presumption against automatic commitment to a secure institution and a consequent right to treatment in the "least restrictive alternative" setting. Other federal courts concluded that civilly committed people generally had a constitutional right to treatment and that civil commitment must rest on proof of "danger to self or others," not simply mental illness as such, and proof moreover that would satisfy the criminal law "beyond REASONABLE DOUBT."

For more than a decade after these rulings, the Supreme Court held back from any definitive holding either to endorse or to reject these doctrinal innovations. During the 1960s, the Court did demonstrate concern for the problem of unfulfilled and even hypocritical state promises of therapeutic benefits as a justification for increased social controls. The most significant context for this Supreme Court concern was not mental illness but rather the juvenile court system, where states sought to justify the absence of criminal law procedural protections by invoking the promise of therapy. In IN RE GAULT (1967) the Court found these promises insufficiently convincing and required extensive recasting of juvenile court procedures.

In 1972 the Supreme Court first addressed the systemic implications of this same problem for state authority generally premised on mental illness. In *Jackson v. Indiana* the Court overturned common state practice regarding criminal defendants found mentally incompetent to stand trial. Traditional doctrine purported to excuse such disabled defendants from standing trial, ostensibly to benefit them; but the practical consequence was that these defendants were treated in the same way and as badly as those found not guilty by insanity. The defendants were given long-term, even lifetime, confinement in harsh facilities without semblance of psychiatric care, even if the offense charged were a petty MISDEMEANOR. The Court ruled in *Jackson* that this disposition violated due process; the conditions of this confinement must provide treatment with reasonable prospect that the defendant will be made competent to stand trial. The practical result of this ruling has been substantially to increase the treatment resources provided to defendants found incompetent for trial. To justify the confinement of defendants who, after a substantial period of confinement, remain disabled for trial purposes, a state must invoke its civil commitment laws.

With this one exception, however, the Supreme Court was hesitant during the 1970s to address the constitutional law issues raised by state invocations of mental illness. The dominant motif of the Court's work during this time can be seen in its resolution in 1979 of the question of the requisite BURDEN OF PROOF in civil commitment proceedings. The Court acknowledged that substantial due process liberty interests were at stake, but nonetheless concluded that the state's beneficent purpose toward the allegedly mentally ill person justified a less stringent burden than the criminal standard of proof; hence in *Addington v. Texas* (1979) the Court required an intermediate standard of "clear and convincing evidence."

This impulse to find some seeming middle ground between fundamentally opposed premises is also apparent in the Court's equivocal approach to the question of a constitutional right to treatment for persons confined to state mental institutions. In O'CONNOR V. DONALDSON (1975) the Court ruled that a state could not commit a person on grounds of mental illness alone but only with an added finding of danger to self or others. The Court refused, however, to decide whether a state was obliged to provide treatment to such a person rather than impose merely custodial confinement. The same issue returned to the Court in *Youngberg v. Romeo* (1982), this time regarding an institutionalized person who was retarded rather than mentally ill. Again the Court avoided a definitive resolution, ruling that the plaintiff was constitutionally entitled to "minimal treatment" that reasonably promised to reduce his aggressive outbursts—as opposed to the harsh behavior controls, such as prolonged shackling, that the state had used. The Court did not, however, reach the broader issue whether the state was obliged to provide treatment with any promise of greater benefits such as ultimate freedom from confinement.

In 1983 the Court departed from its previous pattern of equivocation in these matters. In a 5–4 decision the Court held in *Jones v. United States* that a criminal defendant found not guilty by insanity could be confined to a mental institution without regard to the maximum term for which he might have been sentenced for the offense charged. The Court ruled, moreover, that the insanity acquittal itself justified the defendant's confinement without any necessary invocation of civil commitment standards, thus effectively disapproving the 1968 court of appeals decision in *Bolton*. The Court in effect treated the "criminally insane" as different from either "criminals" or the "insane." This differential treatment can work a marked disadvantage, as the defendant in the *Jones* case found. But, the Court appeared to conclude, the defendant chooses to plead criminal insanity and thus knowingly embraces the risk of his ultimate disadvantage. Indeed, in AKE V. OKLAHOMA (1985) the Court made it easier to invoke the insanity defense by ruling that an indigent defendant is entitled to a court-appointed psychiatrist. The specific context of that case was a capital offense, where the risk of indefinite confinement following an insanity acquittal might seem invariably worthwhile; but the Court did not limit its holding to capital cases.

It is not clear whether the Court's definitive rulings in the context of criminal insanity will be followed by similar resolutions in other aspects of state authority regarding mentally ill people. The Court may have felt a special need to address criminal insanity as such because of the extraordinary public attention resulting from John Hinckley's acquittal for insanity in 1982 on the charge of attempting to assassinate President RONALD REAGAN. Whatever the future directions of judicial rulings, however, the underlying questions regarding the justifications for and scope of state authority in these matters remain difficult.

The dominant theme of the constitutional principle set out by lower courts in the 1960s and 1970s has been that mental illness is relevant to the exercise of state power only where the state promises therapeutic benefit, and that the Constitution requires that this promise be kept. Keeping the promise, however, is easier said than done. Both diagnosis and treatment of mental illness is uncertain. Furthermore, adequate therapy, either in state institutions or in community treatment facilities, will require supervision of complex bureaucracies and large expenditures of funds. Supervision of this process will severely strain both the courts' enforcement capacities and traditional conceptions of judicial authority. Some observers thus conclude that the lower courts were correct in seeing the failure and even hypocrisy of states regarding their therapeutic promises, but these courts merely compounded this error by invoking the Constitution to add new promises that similarly cannot be fulfilled.

If courts cannot and should not attempt to enforce the promise of therapy, what response is proper in the face of egregious state abuses? Some have argued that states should simply be barred from giving mental illness special legal relevance in any circumstances, as a justification either for increasing or withholding state power over individuals. In this view, states could confine people for "dangerousness" only by applying ordinary criminal law standards, and those standards should make no special dispensation for the mentally ill. A few states have essentially abolished the insanity defense and sharply limited the availability of civil commitment. Similarly, some judicial decisions such as *Rogers v. Okin* (1980) have found a constitutional right to *refuse* treatment, notwithstanding that a person has been civilly committed as mentally ill and dangerous. The premise of these decisions is not that the state might fail to keep its therapeutic promise;

it is rather that the promise may be kept with excessive rigor, and that the state may thereby transgress valued boundaries of individual integrity and dignity. Though these lower court decisions do not directly embrace the view that would abolish all state mental illness powers, they share the underlying suspicion of therapeutically justified state impositions, and they apparently prefer modes of social control that do not directly purport to invade mental processes, such as imprisonment for criminal convictions.

This underlying premise is a temptingly plausible response to the sorry history of state abuse of the mentally ill. But the premise fails both as social policy and as constitutional doctrine. The consequences were disastrous for large numbers of people who were removed from state institutions in the 1960s and 1970s, in part as a response to court decisions, and were "dumped" into communities with no facilities to receive them or willingness to respond to their special needs. As constitutional doctrine, the abolitionist doctrine relies on a conception of due process "liberty" that takes insufficient account of the psychological conditions of individual autonomy that lie beneath this prized constitutional right. This conception ignores the ways in which mental illness can distort an individual's capacity to acknowledge his need for help, including state-administered assistance. It may be that state power can never be trusted to provide this help, that this is the lesson of the history of state abuse of mentally ill people in the criminal and civil law context. But this lesson has not yet been clearly written into constitutional doctrine.

ROBERT A. BURT

Bibliography

BROOKS, ALEXANDER D. 1974 *Law, Psychiatry and the Mental Health System,* and 1980 *Supplement.* Boston: Little, Brown.

BURT, ROBERT A. 1979 *Taking Care of Strangers: The Rule of Law in Doctor–Patient Relations.* New York: Free Press.

SCULL, ANDREW 1977 *Decarceration: Community Treatment and the Deviant: A Radical View.* Englewood Cliffs, N.J.: Prentice-Hall.

MENTAL RETARDATION AND THE CONSTITUTION

The Supreme Court first addressed the constitutional status of mentally retarded people in BUCK V. BELL (1927). In an opinion by Justice OLIVER WENDELL

HOLMES, the Court upheld a state statute authorizing compulsory STERILIZATION of "mental defectives." In dismissing the claim that this imposition wrongly discriminated against retarded people and thereby denied them EQUAL PROTECTION under the FOURTEENTH AMENDMENT, Holmes appeared to invoke "minimal scrutiny" (as it was later termed), holding that the legislature might reasonably find retardation both inheritable and socially harmful. It was not until the 1970s that courts took a different, more protective stance toward retarded people. In so doing, they challenged the social attitudes of fear and aversion that lay beneath not only sterilization laws but also the general state policy, dating from the late nineteenth century, of excluding retarded people from community facilities (such as public schools) and consigning them to large, geographically isolated residential institutions.

The modern decisions involved two constitutional approaches. The first approach was to recognize a constitutional "right to treatment" for residents of state institutions. This right was initially formulated in 1971 when a federal district court held that brutal custodial conditions in an Alabama institution must be remedied by intensive educational and treatment programs conducted by new cadres of professionally qualified staff. In *Youngberg v. Romeo* (1982) the Supreme Court effectively endorsed this constitutional holding, deriving as a proposition of SUBSTANTIVE DUE PROCESS that, although the state was not required to offer any services to retarded people, if the state chose to provide residential facilities, then those facilities must meet certain minimal standards.

The second constitutional approach was initially formulated in 1972, when a federal district court overturned a state statute excluding retarded children from public schools on the ground that they were "ineducable." The court appeared to conclude that all retarded people were educable to some degree. This holding was quickly adopted by other federal courts to overturn similar state statutes and, moreover, was endorsed by Congress in the EDUCATION OF ALL HANDICAPPED CHILDREN ACT (1975) requiring education of all children, no matter how severely impaired, as a condition on federal funding of public schools.

These two constitutional approaches of substantive due process and equal protection analysis were blended by a 1977 district court ruling that a state institution for the retarded must be wholly closed and its residents moved to small-scale community homes

on the grounds that the "right to treatment" could not be effectively protected in any large, isolated institutional setting and that, like racial SEGREGATION, separation of retarded people from contact with mentally normal people was INVIDIOUS DISCRIMINATION. A congressional act of 1975 also indicated preference for community over institutional retardation facilities; but the Supreme Court, in PENNHURST STATE SCHOOL v. HALDERMAN (1981) without addressing the initial constitutional ruling, held that Congress had spoken only with "hortatory" rather than mandatory intention.

In 1985 the Supreme Court finally did address the question whether mentally retarded people warranted specially protected constitutional status, but its answer was ambiguous. The specific issue in *Cleburne v. Cleburne Living Center* (1985) was the validity of a local ZONING ordinance that specifically excluded group residences for "feeble-minded" people, even though fraternity and sorority houses, dormitories, and nursing homes for "convalescents or aged" people were explicitly permitted. The Fifth Circuit overturned the ordinance, citing the immutability of retardation, its stigmatized social history (as evidenced by sterilization laws based on spurious scientific findings and by brutalizing, isolated institutional residences), and the political vulnerability of retarded people. Because retardation could be relevant to some state classifications such as school programming or employment eligibility, however, the court found that it was more like gender than like race, a "quasi-suspect" rather than a SUSPECT CLASSIFICATION. Applying intermediate scrutiny, the court found insufficient justification for the zoning exclusion.

The Supreme Court declined to follow this analysis. It concluded that retardation classifications warranted no special judicial scrutiny for several reasons: the legitimate relevance of retardation for some classificatory purposes, the nonjudicial expertise seemingly required to evaluate such purposes, and the political strength of retardation advocates as evidenced by the 1975 congressional acts (notwithstanding that Congress had also acted against race and gender discrimination in recent decades). The Court nonetheless invalidated the zoning ordinance on the ground that it was based merely on "vague, undifferentiated fears" about retarded people. This rationale does not readily fit the conventional conception of "minimal scrutiny" equal protection analysis, given that fears regarding the irrationality and uncontrollability of retarded people have some plausible claim to factuality, even though this claim is unreliably documented and inapplicable to most retarded people.

The Court's invalidation of the zoning ordinance in *Cleburne* must thus rest on an unacknowledged premise, either that minimal scrutiny equal protection analysis (as applied to all state classifications) now requires more clearly demonstrated reasonableness than has heretofore been demanded or that retarded people do warrant some degree of special judicial protection to ensure that differential classifications of them have factual bases beyond "vague, undifferentiated fears."

ROBERT A. BURT

Bibliography

BURT, ROBERT A. 1985 Pennhurst: A Parable. Pages 265–364 in Robert Mnookin, ed., *In the Interest of Children*. New York: W. H. Freeman.

MERE EVIDENCE RULE

A SEARCH WARRANT must identify the place to be searched and the items to be seized. Such items may include fruits or instrumentalities of crime (such as stolen money or burglar's tools) or contraband (such as illegal drugs). In *Gouled v. United States* (1921) the Supreme Court held that search warrants could not issue to seize mere EVIDENCE of crime.

In WARDEN V. HAYDEN (1967), however, the Court held that warrants could issue for mere evidence so long as there was a "nexus" between the evidence and the criminal behavior. ZURCHER V. STANFORD DAILY (1978) illustrates the effect of the rule's abandonment. The Stanford University student newspaper published photographs of a campus disturbance between the police and demonstrators. Because the police observed only two of their assailants, a warrant was obtained for a search of the newspaper's offices. The warrant affidavit did not allege any involvement in the unlawful acts by newspaper staff members. During the search, police examined the paper's photographic labs, files, desks, and waste paper baskets. Since no new evidence was discovered, no items were taken.

One commentator has summarized the "mere evidence rule" after *Zurcher* as follows: *Zurcher* represents a case in which none of the items searched for by the police was a fruit or instrumentality of a crime, or contraband. Under the pre-*Hayden* rule, the warrant used in *Zurcher* could not have been issued. Yet the present broad rule is so well established that the Supreme Court's majority opinion did not even discuss the issue.

CHARLES H. WHITEBREAD

Bibliography

WHITEBREAD, CHARLES H. 1980 *Criminal Procedure*. Mineola, N.Y.: Foundation Press.

METROPOLITAN LIFE INSURANCE CO. v. WARD
470 U.S.   (1985)

This decision departed from a long series of Supreme Court decisions upholding the constitutionality of state taxes against attack under the EQUAL PROTECTION clause. Alabama taxed the gross premiums of insurance companies by imposing a one percent tax on companies organized in Alabama, and a tax of three percent or four percent on companies organized in other states. In an opinion by Justice LEWIS F. POWELL, the Supreme Court held, 5–4, that this discrimination failed even the RATIONAL BASIS test, because its only articulated purpose—to create a tax advantage for domestic economic interests over out-of-state interests—was illegitimate. Congress, in its 1945 act permitting the states to discriminate in favor of local insurance companies, had insulated such laws from attack under the COMMERCE CLAUSE, but had not purported to speak to any issue of equal protection.

In an unusual division of the Court, Justice SANDRA DAY O'CONNOR dissented, joined by Justices WILLIAM J. BRENNAN, THURGOOD MARSHALL, and WILLIAM H. REHNQUIST. Justice O'Connor pointed to previous decisions recognizing the legitimacy of state efforts to promote domestic industry, and made the unanswerable point that Alabama's tax scheme was rationally related to such a purpose. Furthermore, she said, Congress in 1945 understood that it was authorizing laws of this very kind. She also accused the majority of reviving active judicial scrutiny of state ECONOMIC REGULATION. Although the latter prediction seems unlikely to come true, the fear that it expresses is not dispelled by the majority's opinion.

KENNETH L. KARST

Bibliography

COHEN, WILLIAM 1985 Federalism in Equality Clothing: A Comment on Metropolitan Life Insurance Company v. Ward. *Stanford Law Review* 38:1–27.

MEYER v. NEBRASKA
262 U.S. 390 (1923)

Meyer represented an early use of SUBSTANTIVE DUE PROCESS doctrine to defend personal liberties, as distinguished from economic ones. Nebraska, along with other states, had prohibited the teaching of modern foreign languages to grade school children. Meyer, who taught German in a Lutheran school, was convicted under this law. The Supreme Court, 7–2, held the law unconstitutional. Justice JAMES C. MCREYNOLDS wrote for the Court in *Meyer* and in four companion cases from Iowa, Ohio, and Nebraska. Justice OLIVER WENDELL HOLMES, joined by Justice GEORGE SUTHERLAND, dissented in all but the Ohio cases.

McReynolds began with a broad reading of the "liberty" protected by the FOURTEENTH AMENDMENT: "it denotes not merely freedom from bodily restraint, but also the right of the individual to contract, to engage in any of the common occupations of life, to acquire useful knowledge, to marry, establish a home and bring up children, to worship God according to the dictates of his own conscience, and, generally, to enjoy those privileges long recognized at common law as essential to the orderly pursuit of happiness by free men." State regulation of this liberty must be reasonably related to a proper state objective; the legislature's view of reasonableness was "subject to supervision by the courts." The legislative purpose to promote assimilation and "civic development" was readily appreciated, given the hostility toward our adversaries in World War I. However, "no adequate reason" justified interfering with Meyer's liberty to teach or the liberty of parents to employ him during a "time of peace and domestic tranquillity."

Holmes concurred in the Ohio cases, because Ohio had singled out the German language for suppression. But he could not say it was unreasonable for a state to forbid teaching foreign languages to young children as a means of assuring that all citizens might "speak a common tongue." Because "men might reasonably differ" on the question, the laws were not unconstitutional.

Meyer was thus a child of LOCHNER V. NEW YORK (1905), taking *Lochner*'s broad view of the judicial role in protecting liberty. Yet, although substantive due process has lost its former vitality in the field of ECONOMIC REGULATION, *Meyer*'s precedent remains vigorous in the defense of personal liberty. *Meyer* was reaffirmed in GRISWOLD V. CONNECTICUT (1965), LOVING V. VIRGINIA (1967), and ZABLOCKI V. RED-

HAIL (1978), three modern decisions protecting the FREEDOM OF INTIMATE ASSOCIATION.

KENNETH L. KARST

MIAMI HERALD PUBLISHING COMPANY v. TORNILLO
418 U.S. 241 (1974)

It may be argued that FREEDOM OF SPEECH is meaningless unless it includes access to the mass media so that the speech will be heard. Here the Supreme Court unanimously struck down a Florida statute requiring a newspaper to provide a political candidate free space to reply to its attacks on his personal character. Noting that the statute infringed upon "editorial control and judgment," the Court held that "any [governmental] compulsion to publish that which 'reason' tells . . . [the editors] . . . should not be published is unconstitutional."

Tornillo was a major blow to proponents of a right of access. When compared to RED LION BROADCASTING COMPANY V. FEDERAL COMMUNICATIONS COMMISSION (1969), it raises the question whether the FIRST AMENDMENT provides greater protection for the press than for the electronic media. In light of the large number of one-newspaper towns, the scarcity rationale for allowing government to compel access to broadcast channels would seem to apply even more strongly to the print media. Ultimately the distinction may be between the public ownership of the channels and the private ownership of the print media. If so, the Court has not explained or defended this linking of speech rights to property rights.

MARTIN SHAPIRO

MICHAEL M. v. SUPERIOR COURT
450 U.S. 464 (1981)

A boy of 17½ was convicted of rape under a California statute making it a crime for a male to have intercourse with a female under 18; the girl's age was 16½. A fragmented Supreme Court voted 5–4 to uphold the conviction against the contention that the statute's SEX DISCRIMINATION—the same act was criminal for a male but not for a female—denied the EQUAL PROTECTION OF THE LAWS.

There was no opinion for the Court. The majority Justices, however, agreed in accepting the California Supreme Court's justification for the law: prevention of illegitimate teen-age pregnancies. The risk of pregnancy itself, said Justice WILLIAM H. REHNQUIST, served to deter young females from sexual encounters; criminal sanctions on young males only would roughly "equalize" deterrents.

The dissenters argued that California had not demonstrated its law to be a deterrent; thirty-seven states had adopted gender-neutral statutory rape laws, no doubt on the theory that such laws would provide even more deterrent, by doubling the number of persons subject to arrest. When both parties to an act are equally guilty, argued Justice JOHN PAUL STEVENS, to make the male guilty of a FELONY while allowing the female to go free is supported by little more than "traditional attitudes toward male–female relations."

KENNETH L. KARST

MICHELIN TIRE COMPANY v. ADMINISTRATOR OF WAGES
423 U.S. 276 (1976)

Opening the way for increased local revenue, a unanimous Court overruled *Low v. Austin* (1872) and sustained a state property tax on imported goods even though they retained their character as imports. The Court held that the IMPORT-EXPORT CLAUSE did not prohibit such a tax if it were imposed without discrimination on all goods in the state.

DAVID GORDON

(SEE ALSO: *Original Package Doctrine.*)

MICHIGAN v. LONG

See: Adequate State Grounds; Stop and Frisk

MICHIGAN v. SUMMERS
452 U.S. 692 (1981)

A 6–3 Supreme Court held that if the police had a valid warrant to search a home for illegal drugs, they had authority to detain the occupants of the premises during the search. They could therefore lawfully require a suspect to remain in the house, arrest him after finding the contraband, and search his person incident to the arrest. The dissenters argued that the FOURTH AMENDMENT prevented the police from seizing a person without PROBABLE CAUSE in order to

make him available for arrest should probable cause be revealed by the search.

LEONARD W. LEVY

MIDDENDORF v. HENRY
425 U.S. 25 (1976)

A 5–3 Supreme Court ruled that servicemen have no RIGHT TO COUNSEL in summary courts-martial. Justice WILLIAM H. REHNQUIST's majority opinion concluded that such proceedings did not constitute criminal prosecutions within the Sixth Amendment's guarantee, and he also disposed of a Fifth Amendment DUE PROCESS claim as without merit.

DAVID GORDON

MIFFLIN, THOMAS
(1744–1800)

General Thomas Mifflin, a wealthy Philadelphia Quaker, was a member of the Pennsylvania Assembly and of the First and Second Continental Congresses before serving as quartermaster general of the Army (1775–1778). He was elected to Congress in 1782, and in 1783 became President of the United States in Congress Assembled. Mifflin was speaker of the Pennsylvania Assembly in 1787, when he was chosen as chairman of his state's delegation to the CONSTITUTIONAL CONVENTION OF 1787. The records of the convention do not indicate that Mifflin ever spoke in the debates, although he did sign the Constitution. In 1790 he presided over the state CONSTITUTIONAL CONVENTION. He served as governor of Pennsylvania from 1790 to 1799, a period that included the WHISKEY REBELLION.

DENNIS J. MAHONEY

Bibliography
ROSSITER, CLINTON 1966 *1787: The Grand Convention.* New York: Macmillan.

MILITARY JUSTICE

The Constitution, in language taken from the ARTICLES OF CONFEDERATION, empowers Congress to "make Rules for the Government and Regulation of the land and naval Forces." Congress has enacted Articles of War and Articles for the Government of the Navy since 1775, but in 1950 the two systems were fused in the Uniform Code of Military Justice (UCMJ).

Criminal justice under the UCMJ resembles that in civilian courts more than it differs. As in most states, the type of trial court depends on the gravity of the offense. Petty offenses are dealt with by nonjudicial punishment or summary court-martial; more serious offenses may be tried before a special or general court-martial. The types of court-martial differ in number of members and in the maximum punishment they may impose. The rules of EVIDENCE are about the same as in the federal courts; and a defendant tried by a special or general court-martial enjoys the RIGHT TO COUNSEL at government expense. The Supreme Court held in *Middendorf v. Henry* (1976) that the right to free counsel does not apply in summary courts-martial, which more closely resemble administrative hearings than criminal trials.

The major difference between military and civilian criminal justice is the absence of a jury. The members of the court are appointed by the convening authority, who can, theoretically, "pack the court." However, the accused can avoid the possibility of command influence by electing trial by a military judge sitting alone, who is responsible only to the Judge Advocate General of his service. When the military judge sits with members of a court-martial his role is like that of a civilian judge, except that the members determine the sentence if the accused is convicted. There is an elaborate system of review but, except in a limited class of cases, APPEAL to the Court of Military Appeals (three civilian judges appointed by the President) is not by right.

The UCMJ does not provide for review by any civilian court: findings and sentences of courts-martial, as affirmed under the code, are "final and conclusive" and "binding upon all . . . courts . . . of the United States." The Supreme Court has always held that, absent provision by Congress, there can be no direct appeal from the decisions of military tribunals. The federal courts have, however, developed several techniques of collateral review—notably HABEAS CORPUS, MANDAMUS, and suits for back pay in the COURT OF CLAIMS—which effectively ensure that military courts are subject to constitutional supervision.

The federal courts had long collaterally reviewed court-martial convictions to ensure that there was JURISDICTION over person, offense, and sentence. The Supreme Court after World War II imposed new limits on court-martial jurisdiction over person and offense. In the UCMJ, courts-martial were granted jurisdiction over many categories of civilians, including honorably discharged servicemen and civilians accompanying the armed forces outside the United States. In a series of decisions, including UNITED STATES EX REL. TOTH V. QUARLES (1955) and REID V. COVERT (1956), the Supreme Court held that a court-martial could not constitutionally try any civilian in peacetime. There are still some gray areas, such as jurisdiction over retired regulars and certain reservists.

Thereafter the Court held that a court-martial could not constitutionally try a member of the armed forces for an offense that had no "service connection"; the leading case, *O'Callahan v. Parker* (1969), involved the attempted rape of a civilian by a soldier off-post, on leave, and out of uniform. Despite a subsequent decision in which the Court suggested a dozen factors to be considered in determining whether a crime was "service-connected," there are still many doubtful cases, particularly those involving off-post use or possession of drugs. The Court of Military Appeals and the inferior federal courts have made two exceptions to the requirement of service connection. Considering that *O'Callahan* was based on the loss of TRIAL BY JURY, they have permitted courts-martial to try offenses regardless of service connection committed outside the jurisdiction of American civilian courts or punishable by not more than six months' confinement, so that the accused would not in any case be constitutionally entitled to a jury.

Until after World War II the BILL OF RIGHTS had no application to courts-martial: if jurisdiction existed over person, offense, and sentence, federal courts would not consider allegations of even the grossest unfairness. Chief Justice SALMON P. CHASE, concurring in EX PARTE MILLIGAN (1866), declared that "the power of Congress, in the government of the land and naval forces, is not affected by the fifth or any other amendment." Historical evidence concerning the framers of the Bill of Rights justifies Chase's dictum: President JAMES MADISON, for example, approved the conviction of General William Hull in 1814, although the court-martial had denied Hull's request for the assistance of counsel.

The Supreme Court has never set aside a court-martial conviction for denial of constitutional DUE PROCESS, but it would almost certainly do so if confronted with a clear case of such denial. No such case has yet reached the Court because the protections of the Bill of Rights (except trial by jury and the right to BAIL) are embodied in the UCMJ. A coerced confession, for example, would violate not only the Fifth Amendment but also the UCMJ and thus constitute a denial of "military due process." In addition the Court of Military Appeals has consistently construed the UCMJ in such a way as to avoid conflict with the Supreme Court's construction of the Constitution. Military exigency may, however, justify some relaxation of civilian standards. Military rulings on constitutional issues must conform to Supreme Court standards, absent a showing that special military conditions require a different rule. Thus PARKER V. LEVY (1974) held that the "general articles" which prohibit "conduct unbecoming an officer and a gentleman" and "disorders and neglects to the prejudice of good order and discipline" are not unconstitutionally vague or overbroad.

JOSEPH W. BISHOP, JR.

Bibliography

BISHOP, JOSEPH W., JR. 1974 *Justice under Fire: A Study of Military Law.* Chaps. 2, 3, 4. New York: Charterhouse.
WIENER, FREDERICK BERNAYS 1958 Courts-Martial and the Bill of Rights: The Original Practice. *Harvard Law Review* 72:1–49, 266–304.

MILITARY RECONSTRUCTION ACTS
14 Stat. 428 (1867)
15 Stat. 2 (1867)
15 Stat. 14 (1867)

The first Military Reconstruction Act established procedures for the resumption of self-government and normalized constitutional status for ten states of the former Confederacy. Though it preserved extant governments intact for the time being, it authorized military peacekeeping and required adoption of new state constitutions. It also mandated black suffrage.

By February 1867, congressional Republicans realized that the FOURTEENTH AMENDMENT, even if ratified, constituted an insufficient program of Reconstruction. They were unwilling to accept the forfeited-rights theory of southern state status propounded by Rep. THADDEUS STEVENS, or to sanction indefinite military governance. However, the intransigence of President ANDREW JOHNSON and the Machiavellian politics of congressional Democrats, who both demanded immediate and unconditional restoration of white rule in the South, convinced the Republicans that federal supervision of the process of recreating state governments was essential if the freedmen and Republican war objectives were not to be abandoned.

The first Military Reconstruction Act divided the ex-Confederate states (Tennessee excepted) into five military districts each under the command of a regular brigadier general, who was charged with peacekeep-

ing responsibilities. He was empowered to use either ordinary civilian officials or military commissions to accomplish this objective. Though the commissions were authorized to overrule civilian authorities if necessary, the act did not replace the state governments previously created under presidential authority. Rather, under the first and subsequent Military Reconstruction Acts (1867–1868), the commanding general was required to call for the election of delegates to CONSTITUTIONAL CONVENTIONS. In these elections, blacks were entitled to vote, and whites disfranchised by the Fourteenth Amendment were excluded. The new state constitution had to enfranchise blacks. When it was ratified by a majority of eligible voters, elections were to be held under it for new state governmental officials. Only then would the existing governments cede authority. The new legislature had to ratify the Fourteenth Amendment and present its state constitution to Congress. Congress would then complete the process by admitting the state's congressional delegation to their seats.

President Johnson vetoed the first measure, asserting several grounds for its unconstitutionality. First, it imposed an "absolute domination of military rulers" whose "mere will is to take the place of all law," subjecting the southern people to "abject slavery." Second, Congress lacked power to impose governments on the southern states, particularly because those states remained part of the Union. Third, the act would deny individual liberties, including the requirements of TRIAL BY JURY, warrants, DUE PROCESS, and HABEAS CORPUS. Johnson also opposed the measure because the requirements of black suffrage would "Africanize the southern part of our territory," and, finally, because the anomalous status of the ten states which had been denied representation in Congress since 1865 cast a cloud over legislation affecting them. Congress immediately overrode the veto.

Under the procedure specified by the Military Reconstruction Acts, all southern states were reorganized and readmitted between 1868 and 1870. The military presence remained for nearly another decade, however, because of turbulence caused by antiblack and anti-Unionist terrorism. The Republican governments established under congressional Reconstruction were overthrown by "Conservative" or "Redeemer" white-supremacist Democratic regimes by 1877, when the process of Reconstruction was effectively terminated.

WILLIAM M. WIECEK

(SEE ALSO: *Constitutional History, 1865–1877.*)

MILLER, SAMUEL F.
(1816–1890)

Samuel Freeman Miller was a towering figure on the Supreme Court from his appointment by ABRAHAM LINCOLN in 1862 until his death in 1890. He sat with four Chief Justices, participated in more than 5,000 decisions of the Court, and was its spokesman in ninety-five cases involving construction of the Constitution. No previous member of the Court had written as many constitutional opinions. Miller's contemporaries regarded him as one of the half-dozen great Justices in American history, a remarkable achievement for a self-educated lawyer who had never held public office, either in his native Kentucky or in adopted Iowa, prior to his appointment to the Court. Justice HORACE GRAY claimed that if his legal training had been less "unsystematic and deficient," Miller would have been "second only to [JOHN] MARSHALL."

Miller looked and acted the part of a great magistrate. He was tall and massive; he had a warm, unaffected disposition and was said to be "as ready to talk to a hod-carrier as to a cardinal." His instinct for what he often called "the main points, the controlling questions," his impatience with antique learning and philosophical abstraction, and his unrivaled reputation for industry, integrity, and independence all enhanced his stature. Candor and intellectual self-reliance pervaded his opinions, and he often stated quite bluntly his assumption that law and practical good sense were of one piece: "This is the honest and fair view of the subject, and we think it conflicts with no rule of law" (Pettigrew v. United States, 1878); "if this is not DUE PROCESS OF LAW it ought to be" (Davidson v. New Orleans, 1878); "this is just and sound policy" (Iron Silver Mining Co. v. Campbell, 1890).

Statecraft rather than formal jurisprudence was Miller's forte, and he emerged as the Court's balance-wheel soon after coming to the bench. His career ultimately spanned three tumultuous decades in which the Justices constantly quarreled, often rancorously, about the scope of federal and state powers and the Court's role in protecting private rights against the alleged usurpations of both. Scores of cases involved highly charged political issues. Yet Miller always remained detached. He never permitted differences of opinion to affect personal relations with his brethren; he met counsels of heat and passion with chilly distaste. Miller's capacity for detachment was, in part, a matter of personality. But it was also a function of his modest view of the Court's role in the American system of government. He resisted doctrinal formulations that curtailed the discretion of other lawmakers, spoke self-consciously about "my conservative habit of deciding no more than is necessary in any case," and often succeeded in accommodating warring factions of more doctrinaire colleagues by narrowing the issue before the Court. As early as 1870, Chief Justice SALMON P. CHASE said he was "beyond question, the dominant personality upon the bench."

The first principles of Miller's constitutional understanding were derived from HENRY CLAY and the Whig party. Although he abandoned the Whigs for the Republican party in 1854, Miller never ceased to regard Clay as the quintessential American statesman or to reaffirm the Kentucky sage's belief in a BROAD CONSTRUCTION of national powers, the primacy of the legislative department in shaping public policy, and the duty of government at all levels to encourage material growth. Miller's adherence to the first two principles was especially apparent in his work on the CHASE COURT. In EX PARTE MILLIGAN (1866), he joined the minority of four, concurring, who suggested that Congress might constitutionally have established martial rule in Indiana. And in Tyler v. Defrees (1870), a confiscation case, Miller flatly rejected the doctrine "long inculcated, that the Federal Government, however strong in a conflict with a foreign foe, lies manacled by the Constitution and helpless at the feet of a domestic enemy." Early in 1868, when the movement to impeach President ANDREW JOHNSON gathered momentum and the Court initially established jurisdiction in EX PARTE MCCARDLE, Miller conceded privately that "in the threatened collision between the Legislative branch of the government and the Executive and judicial branches I see consequences from which the cause of free government may never recover in my day." He added, however, that "the worst feature I now see is the passion which governs the hour in all parties and persons who have a controlling influence." In contrast, Miller not only counseled caution and delay while Congress proceeded to divest the Court of jurisdiction over McCardle but also dissented in TEXAS V. WHITE (1869). He regarded the status of states still undergoing military reconstruction as a POLITICAL QUESTION which only Congress could decide. Hepburn v. Griswold (1870), the first of the LEGAL TENDER CASES, evoked his most celebrated defense of congressional authority. There Miller sharply criticized the majority's reliance on the "spirit" of the Constitution, which, he insisted, "substitutes . . . an undefined code of ethics for the Constitution, and a court of justice for the National Legislature. . . . Where there is a choice of means, the selection is for Congress, not the Court."

Miller was not always such a positivist in rejecting considerations arising from the spirit of the Constitution. In the SLAUGHTERHOUSE CASES (1873), which came up during fierce public debate over the Enforcement and Klu Klux Klan Acts, Miller intervened decisively to preserve "the main features" of the federal system. Although the powers of Congress were not directly at issue, his opinion for the Court undercut every FOURTEENTH AMENDMENT theory that had been advanced in other cases to justify federal jurisdiction over perpetrators of racially motivated private violence. The Fourteenth Amendment's PRIVILEGES AND IMMUNITIES clause, Miller explained for a majority of five, protected only the handful of rights that necessarily grew out of "the relationship between the citizen and the national government." The really fundamental privileges and immunities of CITIZENSHIP, including the rights to protection by the government, to own property, and to contract, still remained what they had been since 1789—rights of state citizenship. To bring all CIVIL RIGHTS under the umbrella of national citizenship, Miller concluded, would be "so great a departure from the structure and spirit of our institutions" and would so "fetter and degrade the State governments by subjecting them to the control of Congress" that it should not be permitted "in the absence of language which expresses such purpose too clearly to admit of doubt."

Over the succeeding seventeen years, Miller's voting record in civil rights cases remained consistent with the views he expounded in 1873. He joined the majority in UNITED STATES V. CRUIKSHANK (1876) and the CIVIL RIGHTS CASES (1883), both of which severely reduced the range of "appropriate legislation" Congress was authorized to enact; he voted to invalidate the Ku Klux Klan Act altogether in UNITED STATES V. HARRIS (1883). In EX PARTE YARBROUGH (1884), an important Enforcement Act case, Miller consolidated his formal approach to protecting civil rights in a federal system. Speaking for a unanimous Court, he sustained federal jurisdiction over persons who violently interfered with the exercise of VOTING RIGHTS in a federal election. Congress's authority to reach private action in *Yarbrough*, he explained, flowed not from the FIFTEENTH AMENDMENT but from both its power to regulate the time, place, and manner of federal elections and its duty "to provide, in an election held under its authority, for security of life and limbs to the voter." By emphasizing the national ramifications of private action in *Yarbrough*, Miller managed to distinguish *Cruikshank* in much the same way that he had distinguished between rights of national citizenship and rights of state citi-

zenship in the *Slaughterhouse Cases*. Both formulations were designed to set principled limits to the exercise of Congress's affirmative powers to protect civil rights.

The impulse to preserve "the main features" of the federal system also shaped Miller's work in cases involving governmental interventions in economic life. He was certainly not immune to the laissez-faire ethos of the late nineteenth century, and his opinion for the Court in LOAN ASSOCIATION V. TOPEKA (1875) has long been regarded as one of the most significant expressions of natural law constitutionalism in American history and as an important building block in the growth of SUBSTANTIVE DUE PROCESS. There he held that a contract for $100,000 in municipal bonds, issued to lure a manufacturing firm to Topeka, was unenforceable. The people's tax dollars, he proclaimed, could not "be used for purposes of private interest instead of public use." Yet Miller resisted the urge, spearheaded by Justice STEPHEN J. FIELD, to link the "public use" principle with the Fourteenth Amendment and the concept of "general jurisprudence" in order to limit the exercise of all the states' inherent powers—police, taxation, and eminent domain.

The sweeping doctrines advanced by Field and other doctrinaire advocates of laissez-faire conflicted with three working principles of Miller's constitutional understanding, each of which militated against dramatic enlargement of federal judicial power at the expense of the states. The first was his Whiggish predisposition to allow state governments ample room to channel economic activity and develop resources for the general good. A broad construction of the Fourteenth Amendment, he asserted in the *Slaughterhouse Cases*, "would constitute this Court a perpetual censor upon all legislation of the States" and generate state inaction, even in the face of clear public interests, for fear of endless litigation. Miller also believed that it was not the function of federal courts to sit in judgment on state courts expounding state law. He repeatedly invoked this second working principle in the long line of cases that began with GELPCKE V. DUBUQUE (1864). There the Court insisted that municipal bonds issued to subsidize railroad construction were unquestionably for a "public use" despite recent state court decisions to the contrary. The *Gelpcke* majority defended federal judicial intervention on the ground that municipal bonds were a species of commercial paper and therefore the question of bondholder rights "belong[ed] to the domain of general jurisprudence." Miller dissented. In his view, extension of the principle of SWIFT V. TYSON (1842) to the construction of state statute law was an unconscionable act of federal usurpation, and he accurately predicted that it would spawn a generation of conflict between federal courts and recalcitrant state and local officials.

The apparent inconsistency between Miller's opinion in *Loan Association v. Topeka* and his stance in the *Slaughterhouse Cases* and in the *Gelpcke* line of municipal-bond cases is readily explained. All of them did raise similar conceptual issues; each hinged, in part, on the application of the "public use" principle to governmental aid of private enterprise in the form of either monopoly grants or cash subsidies. But for Miller, if not for his colleagues, the controlling factor in *Loan Association v. Topeka* was that it had been tried under the DIVERSITY JURISDICTION of a federal court, and pertinent state law had not yet been framed on the subject. As a result, Miller later explained in *Davidson v. New Orleans* (1878), the Court had been free to invoke "principles of general constitutional law" which the Kansas court was equally free to adopt or reject in subsequent cases involving similar circumstances. The concepts of substantive due process and "general jurisprudence," on the other hand, failed to maintain the ample autonomy for state governments which Miller regarded as an indispensable component of the American polity.

Miller ultimately failed to stave off the luxuriation of substantive due process, just as he had failed to curb the majority's impulse to invoke *Swift* in the municipal-bond cases. "It is in vain to contend with judges who have been at the bar the advocates for forty years of rail road companies, and all the forms of associated capital," he told his brother-in-law late in 1875. "I am losing interest in these matters. I will do my duty but will fight no more." Yet Miller's views did make a difference, particularly in the conference room. What remained influential was Miller's third working principle of constitutional interpretation. He recommended resistance to Field's syllogistic reasoning and quest for immutable principles; he suggested, instead, that once the Court had determined to protect private rights against state interference, it was best to decide cases on the narrowest possible grounds, to employ open-ended doctrinal formulas amenable to subsequent alteration, and to elaborate the meaning of due process through what he called a "gradual process of inclusion and exclusion." Thus Miller described local aid of manufactures as "robbery" in *Loan Association v. Topeka*, but he added that "it may not be easy to draw the line in all cases so as to decide what is a public use in this sense and what is not." He also endorsed the notoriously vague

doctrine of "business AFFECTED WITH A PUBLIC INTEREST" in *Munn v. Illinois* (1877). And in CHICAGO, MILWAUKEE & ST. PAUL RY. V. MINNESOTA (1890), when the Court finally invalidated a state law on due process grounds, Miller concurred "with some hesitation" but filed an opinion cautioning his colleagues against the adoption of a rigid formula, such as "fair value," to determine whether rate-making authorities had acted "arbitrarily and without regard to justice and right."

Miller's immediate successors disregarded the advice, but during the 1930s interest revived in his conception of the judicial function, particularly among FELIX FRANKFURTER's circle at the Harvard Law School. Frankfurter, who called Miller "the most powerful member of his Court," insisted in 1938 that judging was not at all like architecture. Rather than framing doctrinal structures with clean lines and the appearance of permanence, Frankfurter explained, "the Justices are cartographers who give temporary location but do not ultimately define the evershifting boundaries between state and national power, between freedom and authority." Miller could not have described his own views with greater clarity or force.

CHARLES W. MCCURDY

Bibliography

FAIRMAN, CHARLES 1938 *Mr. Justice Miller and the Supreme Court, 1862–1890.* Cambridge, Mass.: Harvard University Press.

FRANKFURTER, FELIX (1938)1961 *Mr. Justice Holmes and the Supreme Court.* Cambridge, Mass.: Harvard University Press.

GILLETTE, WILLIAM 1969 Samuel Miller. Pages 1011–1024 in Leon Friedman and Fred Israel, eds., *The Justices of the Supreme Court, 1789–1965.* New York: Chelsea House.

MILLER v. CALIFORNIA
413 U.S. 15 (1973)
PARIS ADULT THEATRE I v. SLATON
413 U.S. 49 (1973)

For the first time since ROTH V. UNITED STATES (1957), a Supreme Court majority agreed on a definition of OBSCENITY. The Court had adopted the practice of summarily reversing obscenity convictions when at least five Justices, even if not agreeing on the appropriate test, found the material protected. The states were without real guidelines; and the requirements of JACOBELLIS V. OHIO (1964) that each

Justice review the material at issue had transformed the Court into an ultimate board of censorship review.

To escape from this "intractable" problem, the *Miller Court* reexamined obscenity standards. Chief Justice WARREN E. BURGER's majority opinion, reaffirming *Roth,* articulated specific safeguards to ensure that state obscenity regulations did not encroach upon protected speech. The Court announced that a work could constitutionally be held to be obscene when an affirmative answer was appropriate for each of three questions:

(a) whether "the average person applying contemporary community standards" would find that the work, taken as a whole, appeals to the prurient interest . . .;
(b) whether the work depicts or describes, in a patently offensive way, sexual conduct specifically defined by the applicable state law; and
(c) whether the work, taken as a whole, lacks serious literary, artistic, political or scientific value.

Three aspects of the *Miller* formula are noteworthy. First, the work need not be measured against a single national standard, but may be judged by state community standards. Second, state obscenity regulations must be confined to works that depict or describe sexual conduct. Moreover, the states must specifically define the nature of that sexual conduct to provide due NOTICE to potential offenders. Third, the Court rejected the "utterly without redeeming social value" standard of MEMOIRS v. MASSACHUSETTS (1966). To merit FIRST AMENDMENT protection, the work, viewed as a whole, must have serious social value. A token political or social comment will not redeem an otherwise obscene work; nor will a brief erotic passage condemn a serious work.

In a COMPANION CASE, *Paris Adult Theater I,* the Court held that regulations concerning the public exhibition of obscenity, even in "adult" theaters excluding minors, were permissible if the *Miller* standards were met. The prohibition on privacy grounds against prosecuting possession of obscene material in one's home, recognized in STANLEY v. GEORGIA (1969), does not limit the state's power to regulate commerce in obscenity, even among consenting adults.

Justice WILLIAM J. BRENNAN, joined by Justices POTTER J. STEWART and THURGOOD MARSHALL, dissented in both cases. Abandoning the views he expressed in *Roth* and *Memoirs,* Brennan concluded that the impossibility of definition rendered the outright suppression of obscenity irreconcilable with the First Amendment and the FOURTEENTH AMENDMENT. The Court's inability to distinguish protected speech from unprotected speech created intolerable

fair notice problems and chilled protected speech. Furthermore, "institutional stress" had resulted from the necessary case-by-case Supreme Court review. Instead of attempting to define obscenity, Brennan would balance the state regulatory interest against the law's potential danger to free expression. He recognized the protection of juveniles or unconsenting adults as a state interest justifying the suppression of obscenity. Justice WILLIAM O. DOUGLAS, separately dissenting, also denounced the vague guidelines that sent persons to jail for violating standards they could not understand, construe, or apply.

The Court's attempt to articulate specific obscenity standards was successful to the extent it reduced the number of cases on the Supreme Court docket. Nevertheless, as Justice Brennan noted, and the history of obscenity decisions confirms, any obscenity definition is inherently vague. The Court thus remains the ultimate board of censorship review.

KIM MCLANE WARDLAW

Bibliography

LOCKHARD, WILLIAM B. 1975 Escape from the Chill of Uncertainty: Explicit Sex and the First Amendment. *Georgia Law Review* 9:533–587.

MILLETT v. PEOPLE OF ILLINOIS
117 Illinois 294 (1886)

This was the first case in which a court held a regulatory statute unconstitutional on the ground that it violated the doctrine of FREEDOM OF CONTRACT. Illinois required coalmine owners to install scales for the weighing of coal in order to determine the wages of miners. Millett, an owner, contracted with his miners, in violation of the statute, to pay by the boxload rather than by weight. The state supreme court, overturning his conviction, unanimously declared that the statute deprived him of DUE PROCESS substantively construed. Miners, the court said, could contract as they pleased in regard to the value of their labor, and owners had the same freedom of contract. The court summarily dismissed the contention that the regulation was a valid exercise of the POLICE POWER on the ground that the legislature had not protected the miners' safety or the property of others. A few months later the Pennsylvania high court, in *Godcharles v. Wigeman* (1886), held unconstitutional a state act that prohibited owners of mines or factories from paying workers in kind rather than in money wages. Such cases were forerunners of LOCHNER v. NEW YORK (1905) and its progeny.

LEONARD W. LEVY

MILLIGAN, EX PARTE
4 Wallace 2 (1866)

In 1861, Chief Justice ROGER B. TANEY contrived a possibility of executive–judicial, civil–military clashes (*Ex parte Merryman*); in 1863 the Supreme Court averted similar confrontations (EX PARTE VALLANDIGHAM; PRIZE CASES). But in 1866–1867, the CHASE COURT, in the TEST OATH and *Ex parte Milligan* decisions, overcame its restraint.

In 1864, an Army court sentenced Lambden (spelling various) Milligan, a militantly antiwar, Negrophobe Indianan, to death for overtly disloyal activities. President ANDREW JOHNSON commuted the sentence to life imprisonment. Milligan's lawyer, employing the 1863 HABEAS CORPUS ACT, in 1865 appealed to the federal circuit court in Indiana for release. The judges, including Justice DAVID DAVIS, divided on whether a civil court had JURISDICTION over a military tribunal and on the legitimacy of military trials of civilians. This division let the petition go to the Supreme Court. There, in 1866, Attorney General HENRY STANBERY denied that any civil court had jurisdiction; special counsel BENJAMIN F. BUTLER insisted on the nation's right to use military justice in critical areas.

Milligan's lawyers included JAMES A. GARFIELD, JEREMIAH BLACK, and DAVID DUDLEY FIELD. Milligan, they argued, if indictable, was triable in civil courts for TREASON. Alternatively, they insisted that the Army court had failed to obey the 1863 Habeas Corpus Act's requirement to report on civilian prisoners. Further, they asserted that the Constitution's barriers against the use of military power in a state not in rebellion were fixed and unmodifiable, though Congress, they admitted, had authority to use military justice in the South.

All the Justices concurred about the military court's dereliction in not reporting Milligan's arrest. For the Court's bare majority, Justice Davis held that neither President nor Congress could establish military courts to try civilians in noninvaded areas, and, implicitly, that the final decision as to what areas were critical was the Court's. Martial law must never exist where civil courts operated, he stressed, although both had co-existed since the war started. SALMON P. CHASE, speaking also for Justices SAMUEL MILLER, NOAH SWAYNE, and JAMES WAYNE, disagreed. Congress could extend military authority in Indiana under the WAR POWERS without lessening BILL OF RIGHTS protections, Chase asserted. The option was Congress's, not the Court's.

The majority view in *Milligan* was at once seized upon by supporters of President Johnson, the white South, and the Democratic party, though even Justice Davis stressed that he referred not at all to the South. Until military reconstruction clarified matters, the duties of the Army, acting under President Johnson's orders and the FREEDMEN'S BUREAU statute, were complicated greatly by misuses of the *Milligan* decision in the southern state courts, complications increased by the Test Oath decisions. Taken together, the *Milligan* and the Test Oath decisions greatly limited the capacity of both the nation and the states to provide more decent, color-blind justice in either civil or military courts (including those of the Freedmen's Bureau), and to exclude from leadership in politics and the professions persons who had sparked SECESSION and war.

In subsequent decades, legal writers THOMAS COOLEY and ZECHARIAH CHAFEE reconstructed *Milligan* into a basic defense of individual liberty and of civilian primacy over the military. Both men were flaying dragons perceived by Victorian Social Darwinists and by critics of World War I witch-hunts. Milligan was never a merely theoretical threat. Neither the civil police and courts of Indiana nor the federal government, except for the Army, evidenced capacity to deal with him. In light of existing alternatives, the Army's decision to try Milligan (not its failure to report its decision and verdict) is defensible.

Republican criticism of the *Milligan* decision never threatened the Court. Instead, from 1863 through 1875, the Congress increased the Court's habeas corpus jurisdiction as well as that in admiralty, bankruptcy, and claims. The *Milligan* decision, paradoxically, became a major step in the Court's successful effort to regain the prestige that it had squandered in DRED SCOTT v. SANDFORD (1857), and that Taney had risked dissipating altogether in *Merryman*.

HAROLD M. HYMAN

Bibliography

GAMBIONE, JOSEPH G.   1970   *Ex Parte Milligan:* The Restoration of Judicial Prestige? *Civil War History* 16:246–259.

KUTLER, STANLEY I.   1968   *Judicial Power and Reconstruction Politics.* Chaps. 6–8. Chicago: University of Chicago Press.

MILLIKEN v. BRADLEY
418 U.S. 717 (1974)
433 U.S. 267 (1977)

The DESEGREGATION of public schools in many large cities poses a problem: the cities are running out of white pupils, as white families move to the suburbs. In the early 1970s, some federal district judges began to insist on desegregation plans embracing not only city districts but also surrounding suburban districts. In the first such case to reach the Supreme Court, the Justices divided 4–4, thus affirming without opinion the DECISION of the court of appeals, which had reversed the district court's order for metropolitan relief. The case had come from Richmond, Virginia; Justice LEWIS F. POWELL, the former president of the Richmond school board, had disqualified himself.

Milliken, the Detroit school desegregation case, came to the Court the next year. Justice Powell participated, and a 5–4 Court held that interdistrict remedies were inappropriate absent some showing of a constitutional violation by the suburban district as well as the city district. Chief Justice WARREN E. BURGER wrote for the majority, joined by the other three appointees of President RICHARD M. NIXON and by Justice POTTER STEWART. Justices THURGOOD MARSHALL, BYRON R. WHITE, and WILLIAM O. DOUGLAS all wrote dissenting opinions, and Justice WILLIAM J. BRENNAN also dissented.

This decision was the first major setback for school desegregation plaintiffs, but it did not entirely foreclose metropolitan relief. Justice Stewart, who joined the majority opinion, concurred separately as well, saying he would be prepared to accept metropolitan relief not only where a suburban district had committed a constitutional violation, but also where state officials had engaged in racially discriminatory conduct such as racial gerrymandering of district lines or discriminatory application of housing or ZONING laws.

When the Detroit case returned to the Court three years later, it added a weapon to the arsenal of desegregation remedies. As part of a desegregation decree, the district court ordered the establishment of remedial education programs; the Supreme Court unanimously affirmed, with the Chief Justice again writing for the Court. The remedy must not exceed the constitutional violation, he wrote, but here, unlike the situation in *Milliken I*, the remedy was "tailored to cure the condition that offend[ed] the Constitution."

KENNETH L. KARST

MINERSVILLE SCHOOL DISTRICT v. GOBITIS

See: Flag Salute Cases

MINIMUM WAGES

See: Maximum Hours and Minimum Wages Legislation

MINISTERIAL ACT

A ministerial act is one an official performs as a matter of legal duty, without any personal discretion and without judging the merits. For example, in MARBURY V. MADISON (1803), Chief Justice JOHN MARSHALL described delivery of an appointee's commission as a ministerial act of the secretary of state.

DENNIS J. MAHONEY

MINNESOTA v. BARBER
136 U.S. 313 (1890)

The Supreme Court unanimously held unconstitutional as a violation of the COMMERCE CLAUSE a Minnesota statute that prohibited the sale for human consumption of meat slaughtered in another state and not inspected in Minnesota. The statute, the Court declared, forced citizens to buy only Minnesota meat, denying them the benefits of competition in INTERSTATE COMMERCE.

LEONARD W. LEVY

MINNESOTA RATE CASES
230 U.S. 352 (1913)

In these cases a unanimous Supreme Court reaffirmed state power to regulate INTRASTATE COMMERCE even if it should indirectly affect INTERSTATE COMMERCE. Justice CHARLES EVANS HUGHES stressed the supremacy of federal authority but, reaching back to COOLEY V. BOARD OF WARDENS OF PHILADELPHIA (1852), held that states could regulate interstate commerce when Congress had not yet chosen to act.

The cases before the Court represented extensive litigation throughout the country. The Railroad & Warehouse Commission of Minnesota and the state legislature had issued orders fixing maximum rail rates within the state. Although the rates they set were purely intrastate, both sides agreed that interstate rates would be affected. The cases arose as STOCK-HOLDERS' SUITS to prevent the application of the prescribed rates to interstate operators. (See EX PARTE YOUNG, 1908.) On the principal question whether the orders fixed rates that interfered with interstate commerce, Hughes agreed that if the rates imposed a direct burden on commerce, they must fall. He then began a lengthy exposition of the nature of commercial regulation in the federal system, concluding that "it is competent for a state to govern its internal commerce . . . although interstate commerce may incidentally or indirectly be involved." Unless and until Congress acted, state action might well be legal even if touching interstate commerce. Only Congress could judge the necessity for action and, having decided to, it could intervene "at its discretion for the complete and effective government" of even local conduct affecting interstate commerce. The Minnesota actions were, therefore, within the state's power but would be superseded if Congress acted. The Court thus broadly upheld state ratemaking authority; it also implicitly affirmed federal power over intrastate railroad activity affecting interstate commerce, a significant step it would take explicitly the following year in HOUSTON, EAST & WEST TEXAS RAILWAY COMPANY v. UNITED STATES (1914).

DAVID GORDON

MINOR v. HAPPERSETT
21 Wallace 162 (1875)

MORRISON R. WAITE delivered the unanimous opinion of the Supreme Court holding that a woman, though a citizen of the United States and of the state in which she resides, had no right to vote as a privilege of national CITIZENSHIP protected by the PRIVILEGES AND IMMUNITIES clause of the FOURTEENTH AMENDMENT. The laws of her state allowed only men to vote, and the amendment did not change that by making any new voters.

LEONARD W. LEVY

MINTON, SHERMAN
(1890–1965)

Born in Indiana in 1890, Sherman Minton attended Indiana University and Yale Law School. After military service during World War I, several years in private practice, and brief service as attorney for an Indi-

ana state agency, Minton was elected to the United States Senate in 1934. A fervent advocate of President FRANKLIN D. ROOSEVELT's "New Deal," Minton supported measures expanding the federal government's role in ECONOMIC REGULATION powers despite his concern that the Supreme Court might declare such measures unconstitutional. As the Court repeatedly struck down New Deal legislation, Minton proposed that the votes of at least seven Justices be necessary to invalidate an act of Congress; in 1937, Minton worked vigorously for the enactment of Roosevelt's Court reorganization plan. After Minton was defeated for reelection in 1940, he served briefly as one of Roosevelt's special assistants. In the spring of 1941 Roosevelt appointed Minton to the Seventh Circuit Court of Appeals. In 1949 President HARRY S. TRUMAN appointed Minton to the Supreme Court to fill the vacancy created by the death of Justice WILEY B. RUTLEDGE; this appointment was as much a product of Truman's close friendship with Minton as of Truman's desire to appoint Justices with prior judicial experience. Ill health forced Minton's retirement in 1956.

Minton believed that the Supreme Court could not impose libertarian standards upon a government and a people that did not favor them. Minton's commitment to judicial restraint and his resistance to what he perceived as JUDICIAL POLICYMAKING followed directly from his frustration as a senator with the Court's opposition to New Deal legislation and his participation in efforts to curb the Court's powers.

Minton disappointed liberals who had hoped that he would work as vigorously for judicial protection of individual liberties as for the legitimation of governmental economic regulation. He consistently voted to uphold statutes and other governmental programs intended to protect the national security, rejecting challenges asserting violation of individual liberties. In CRIMINAL PROCEDURE cases, Minton tended to uphold convictions. For example, in UNITED STATES V. RABINOWITZ (1950) Minton held for the Court that the FOURTH AMENDMENT permits WARRANTLESS SEARCHES and seizures, so long as they are reasonable. Where litigants sought review of state criminal decisions, Minton was reluctant to disturb state procedures or court decisions absent a showing of significant unfairness affecting the verdict. Minton was ready to invalidate STATE ACTION discriminating against minorities, but he was disinclined to find state action. He emphasized the literal meaning of congressional statutes, rarely resorting to external aids or evidence of legislative intent; in the absence of express statutory language, federal regulation did not preempt concurrent state regulation.

Minton stressed the importance of the Court's collegial atmosphere. He disliked personal disputes among the Justices and did his best to reduce their intensity or to dissipate them altogether. Minton viewed the task of writing opinions for the Court as the preparation of functional instruments of collective policy. He rarely wrote concurrences or dissents, for he believed that separate opinions tended to vitiate the authority of majority opinions and to sow discord among the Justices. After his retirement in 1956, Minton minimized the significance of his tenure on the Court; he believed that his most important judicial act was his vote in BROWN V. BOARD OF EDUCATION (1954) to strike down SEGREGATION of public schools.

RICHARD B. BERNSTEIN

Bibliography

WALLACE, HARRY L. 1959–1960 Mr. Justice Minton: Hoosier Justice on the Supreme Court. *Indiana Law Journal* 34:145–205, 383–424.

MIRANDA v. ARIZONA
384 U.S. 436 (1966)

Miranda is the best known as well as the most controversial and maligned self-incrimination decision in the history of the Supreme Court. Some of the harshest criticism came from the dissenters in that case. Justice BYRON R. WHITE, for example, declared that the rule of the case, which required elaborate warnings and offer of counsel before the RIGHT AGAINST SELF-INCRIMINATION could be effectively waived, would return killers, rapists, and other criminals to the streets and have a corrosive effect on the prevention of crime. The facts of *Miranda*, one of four cases decided together, explain the alarm of the four dissenters and of the many critics of the WARREN COURT. The majority of five, led by Chief Justice EARL WARREN, reversed the kidnap-and-rape conviction of Ernesto Miranda, who had been picked out of a LINEUP by his victim, had been interrogated without mistreatment for a couple of hours, and had signed a confession that purported to have been voluntarily made with full knowledge of his rights, although no one had advised him that he did not need to answer incriminating questions or that he could have counsel present. The Court reversed because his confession had been procured in violation of his rights, yet had been admitted in EVIDENCE. Warren conceded that the Court could not know what had happened in the interrogation room and "might not find the . . . state-

ments to have been involuntary in traditional terms." Justice JOHN MARSHALL HARLAN, dissenting, professed to be "astonished" at the decision. Yet the Court did little more than require that the states follow what was already substantially FBI procedure with respect to the rights of a suspect during a custodial interrogation.

The doctrinal significance of the case is that the Fifth Amendment's self-incrimination clause became the basis for evaluating the admissibility of confessions. The Court thus abandoned the traditional DUE PROCESS analysis that it had used in state cases since BROWN V. MISSISSIPPI (1936) to determine whether a confession was voluntary under all the circumstances. (See POLICE INTERROGATIONS AND CONFESSIONS.) Moreover, the Court shifted to the Fifth Amendment from the Sixth Amendment analysis of ESCOBEDO V. ILLINOIS (1964), when discussing the RIGHT TO COUNSEL as a means of protecting against involuntary confessions. *Miranda* stands for the proposition that the Fifth Amendment vests a right in the individual to remain silent unless he chooses to speak in the "unfettered exercise of his own will." The opinion of the Court lays down a code of procedures that must be respected by law enforcement officers to secure that right to silence whenever they take a person into custody or deprive him of his freedom in any significant way.

In each of the four *Miranda* cases, the suspect was not effectively notified of his constitutional rights and was questioned incommunicado in a "police-dominated" atmosphere; each suspect confessed, and his confession was introduced in evidence against him at his trial. The Court majority demonstrated a deep distrust for police procedures employed in stationhouse interrogation, aimed at producing confessions. The *Miranda* cases showed, according to Warren, a secret "interrogation environment," created to subject the suspect to the will of his examiners. Intimidation, even if only psychological, could undermine the will and dignity of the suspect, compelling him to incriminate himself. Therefore, the inherently compulsive character of in-custody interrogation had to be offset by procedural safeguards to insure obedience to the right of silence. Until legislatures produced other procedures at least as effective, the Court would require that at the outset of interrogation a person be clearly informed that he has the right to remain silent, that any statement he makes may be used as evidence against him, that he has the right to the presence of an attorney, and that if he cannot afford an attorney, one will be appointed to represent him.

These rules respecting mandatory warnings, Warren declared, are "an absolute prerequisite to interrogation." The presence of a lawyer, he reasoned, would reduce coercion, effectually preserve the right of silence for one unwilling to incriminate himself, and produce an accurate statement if the suspect chooses to speak. Should he indicate at any time before or during interrogation that he wishes to remain silent or have an attorney present, the interrogation must cease. Government assumes a heavy burden, Warren added, to demonstrate in court that a defendant knowingly and intelligently waived his right to silence or to a lawyer. "The warnings required and the waiver necessary in accordance with our opinion today are prerequisites," he emphasized, "to the admissibility of any statement made by a defendant."

Warren insisted that the new rules would not deter effective law enforcement. The experience of the FBI attested to that, and its practices, which accorded with the Court's rules, could be "readily emulated by state and local law enforcement agencies." The Constitution, Warren admitted, "does not require any specific code of procedures" for safeguarding the Fifth Amendment right; the Court would accept any equivalent set of safeguards.

Justice TOM C. CLARK, dissenting, observed that the FBI had not been warning suspects that counsel may be present during custodial interrogation, though FBI practice immediately altered to conform to Warren's opinion. Clark, like Harlan, whose dissent was joined by Justices POTTER STEWART and Byron White, would have preferred "the more pliable dictates" of the conventional due process analysis that took all the circumstances of a case into account. Harlan also believed that the right against self-incrimination should not be extended to the police station and should not be the basis for determining whether a confession is involuntary. White wrote a separate dissent, which Harlan and Stewart joined, flaying the majority for an opinion that had no historical, precedential, or textual basis. White also heatedly condemned the majority for weakening law enforcement and for prescribing rules that were rigid, but still left many questions unanswered. (See MIRANDA RULES.)

LEONARD W. LEVY

Bibliography

KAMISAR, YALE 1980 *Police Interrogations and Confessions.* Pages 41–76. Ann Arbor: University of Michigan Press.

WHITEBREAD, CHARLES H. 1980 *Criminal Procedure.* Pages 292–310. Mineola, N.Y.: Foundation Press.

MIRANDA RULES

In MIRANDA V. ARIZONA (1966) the Supreme Court held that a person subject to custodial POLICE INTERROGATION must be warned that any statement he makes can be used against him, that he has a right to remain silent, and that he has a right to the presence of an attorney and that one will be appointed for him if he is indigent. A defendant may waive these rights. A WAIVER must be voluntary and intelligent. In the absence of a fully effective alternative, these warnings must be given and a valid waiver taken as the constitutional prerequisite to the admissibility of any product of custodial police interrogation.

The *Miranda* opinion left unresolved numerous issues. For example: When is a person in custody? What constitutes interrogation? What are the standards for measuring the validity of a purported waiver of the *Miranda* rights? May voluntary statements that are inadmissible for failure to comply with *Miranda* be introduced to impeach the credibility of a defendant's trial testimony? How is the burden of proving VOLUNTARINESS and compliance with the *Miranda* requirements allocated?

Post-*Miranda* cases have lessened considerably the constraints the decision had imposed upon law enforcement officials. For example, the police are required to give a suspect the *Miranda* warnings only if the suspect is in custody at the time of interrogation. In OROZCO V. TEXAS (1969) the Court held that a person is in custody any time that he is not free to leave whether in his own home, a hospital, a police car, or the stationhouse. ESTELLE V. SMITH (1981) held that when an indicted defendant, who has not put his mental state in issue, is compelled to undergo a court-ordered psychiatric examination, he is in custody and is entitled to the *Miranda* warnings prior to the evaluation by a mental health professional. However, most courts have held that a suspect is not in custody when in an open, natural environment. Examples include STOP AND FRISK situations, traffic arrests, accident investigations, or searches at international borders.

The second prerequisite to requiring the *Miranda* warnings is that the suspect be the subject of interrogation. The *Miranda* opinion defined interrogation as "questioning initiated by law enforcement officers." In RHODE ISLAND V. INNES (1980), the Court elaborated, stating that "interrogation" meant "express questioning or its functional equivalent" including "any words or actions on the part of the police . . . reasonably likely to elicit an incriminating response from the subject." By contrast, a statement freely and voluntarily made without any interrogation is admissible as a "threshold confession" or "spontaneous statement." If, for example, a person walks into a police station and states that he has killed someone, the police are not required to stop the person wishing to speak and give that person the warnings.

If both custody and interrogation are present, the police must give the warnings or take a valid waiver before proceeding. The police may not presume that a suspect knows of the *Miranda* rights. The form of the warnings may vary, however, so long as the words used give a clear, understandable warning of all the rights, taking into account the circumstances and the characteristics of the suspect.

In OREGON V. ELSTAD (1985) the Supreme Court held that an invalid confession obtained without the suspect being informed of his *Miranda* rights would not invalidate a later confession made after the suspect was informed of his rights, so long as the confession was obtained without coercion. However, in NEW YORK V. QUARLES (1984) the Court established a "public safety" exception, stating that if reasonable concern for public safety is present, a police officer need not recite the *Miranda* warnings before questioning a suspect in custody.

The accused, after receiving the warnings, may voluntarily waive any of his *Miranda* rights. The government must demonstrate voluntariness under all the circumstances. A signed waiver form is strong, but not conclusive, evidence of voluntariness. An effective waiver need not be written, however, and it may be implied from the accused's conduct.

Once the suspect terminates the interrogation or requests counsel, he may not be reinterviewed without being provided access to the requested attorney even if the suspect is given a second set of *Miranda* warnings. In EDWARDS V. ARIZONA (1981) the Court held that once an accused requests counsel, questioning must cease until counsel is present or until the accused "initiates further communication, exchanges or conversation with the police." In *Smith v. Illinois* (1984), the Court followed this precedent by holding that, once the accused has requested an attorney, no further questions or responses may be used to cast doubt on the request.

By contrast, in *Fare v. Michael C.* (1979) the Court held that a juvenile's request for a probation officer during questioning does not have the same constitutional effect as a request for a lawyer. The Court based its distinction on the fact that a lawyer's principal responsibility is to defend his client, while a probation officer has a duty to report and prosecute misconduct by a juvenile. In addition, probation officers are not necessarily qualified to provide legal assistance. Consequently, a juvenile's request for his probation officer is not a per se invocation of the *Miranda* RIGHT TO COUNSEL.

The issue of voluntariness arises in nonwaiver contexts as well. The Court has held that voluntary confessions obtained in violation of the *Miranda* rules, though not admissible in the State's case-in-chief as evidence of guilt, may be admitted to impeach a testifying defendant's credibility. In the leading case, HARRIS V. NEW YORK (1971), the defendant denied in court that he had sold heroin to an undercover agent. During cross-examination, Harris was asked whether he had made certain statements following his arrest that were inconsistent with his in-court testimony. Even though the prosecution conceded that the statements were obtained in violation of *Miranda,* the Supreme Court upheld the trial judge's ruling that the statements could be considered by the jury in evaluating the defendant's credibility.

When the defendant's statements are truly involuntary, they may not be admitted into evidence for any purpose. *Mincey v. Arizona* (1978) is illustrative, holding that the defendant's statements were inadmissible because they were obtained while the defendant was hospitalized and barely able to speak.

Whether the issue arises in the waiver or in the impeachment context, the burden of proving voluntariness under all the circumstances rests on the government. *Miranda* described it as a "heavy burden," a term which a number of courts have interpreted as requiring proof beyond a REASONABLE DOUBT. The Supreme Court, however, stopped this trend by holding, in *Lego v. Twomey* (1972), that proof by a preponderance of the evidence will suffice in federal court, though the states may impose a higher burden in state proceedings.

CHARLES H. WHITEBREAD

Bibliography

WHITEBREAD, CHARLES H. 1980 *Criminal Procedure.* Mineola, N.Y.: Foundation Press.

MISCEGENATION

The fear of racial mixture migrated to the New World with the earliest colonists. In 1609, planters headed for Virginia were reminded by a preacher of the injunction that "Abrams posteritie keepe to themselves." Of course, they did no such thing. From the beginning, there was a shortage of women; white men freely interbred with both Indian and black women, even before the great waves of slave importation. During the era of slavery, interracial sex cut across all strata of the white male population, from the poorest indentured servants to the wealthiest planters. THOMAS JEFFERSON was merely the most celebrated of the latter. Mulattoes were, in fact, deliberately bred for the slave market. Miscegenation laws, forbidding an interracial couple to marry or live together, were not designed to prevent interracial sex but to prevent the transmission of wealth and status from white fathers to their interracial offspring. Laws governing ILLEGITIMACY served a similar purpose, particularly in southern states. To this day, a majority of "blacks" in the United States are of interracial descent.

The adoption of the FOURTEENTH AMENDMENT offered an obvious opportunity for the Supreme Court to hold miscegenation laws unconstitutional on EQUAL PROTECTION grounds. When the occasion arose in PACE V. ALABAMA (1883), however, the Court unanimously upheld such a law, saying that it applied equally to punish both white and black partners to an intimate relationship. The constitutional validity of miscegenation laws went largely unquestioned until the great mid-twentieth-century rediscovery of racial equality as the Fourteenth Amendment's central meaning. Following BROWN V. BOARD OF EDUCATION (1954), it was only a matter of time before the miscegenation issue would reach the Supreme Court. As it happened, the period of time was short. In *Naim v. Naim* (1955–1956) the Court fudged, dismissing an appeal in a jurisdictional evasion that Herbert Wechsler properly scored as "wholly without basis in the law." Unquestionably, the Court adopted this avoidance technique because of the political storm that had greeted the *Brown* decision. Playing on the white South's fear of race mixture was a standard scare tactic of politicians favoring SEGREGATION. Recognizing this fear, the NAACP, in planning its assault on segregated higher education, had deliberately chosen as its plaintiff in MCLAURIN V. OKLAHOMA STATE REGENTS (1950) a sixty-eight-year-old graduate student. The *Brown* opinion itself had been carefully limited to the context of education, and the *Naim* evasion was cut from the same political cloth.

For a decade, the Court was spared the inevitable confrontation. In *Mclaughlin v. Florida* (1964), it invalidated a law forbidding unmarried cohabitation by an interracial couple. Assuming for argument the validity of the state's law forbidding interracial marriage, the Court nonetheless held that the cohabitation law

denied equal protection. The reasoning of *Pace v. Alabama,* the Court said, had not withstood analysis in more recent decisions. Finally, in LOVING V. VIRGINIA (1967), the Court put an end to the whole ugly pretense about "racial purity," holding invalid a law forbidding interracial marriage. Equal protection and SUBSTANTIVE DUE PROCESS grounds served as alternative basis for the decision. *Loving* thus stands not only for a principle of racial equality but also for a broad "freedom to marry." (See FREEDOM OF INTIMATE ASSOCIATION.) The principle of equality is often liberty's cutting edge.

KENNETH L. KARST

Bibliography

FRAZIER, E. FRANKLIN 1939 (rev. ed. 1966). *The Negro Family in the United States.* Chap. IV. Chicago: University of Chicago Press.
MYRDAL, GUNNAR 1944 *An American Dilemma: The Negro Problem and Modern Democracy.* Chap. 5. New York: Harper & Brothers.

MISDEMEANOR

A misdemeanor is one of a class of offenses considered less heinous, and punished less severely, than FELONIES. Generally, misdemeanors are punishable by fine or by incarceration in facilities other than penitentiaries for terms of up to one year. Federal law and most state statutes classify all crimes other than felonies as misdemeanors. Two standards have traditionally been used to distinguish felonies from misdemeanors: the place of imprisonment (a penitentiary as opposed to a jail); and the length of imprisonment (more than one year for felonies, a lesser term for misdemeanors).

The Supreme Court has held that criminal defendants charged with misdemeanors are entitled to certain guarantees of the BILL OF RIGHTS. In ARGERSINGER V. HAMLIN (1972), an indigent defendant was convicted of carrying a concealed weapon, a misdemeanor offense, and sentenced to ninety days in jail. An attorney was not appointed to represent the defendant even though he did not waive this right. The Supreme Court ruled that the RIGHT TO COUNSEL was applicable to misdemeanors where the defendant received a jail term. In *Scott v. Illinois* (1979), however, the Supreme Court declined to find a right to counsel at trial where loss of liberty is merely a possibility and does not, in fact, occur.

The Supreme Court also held, in BALDWIN V. NEW YORK (1970), that the Sixth Amendment requires that defendants accused of serious crimes be afforded the right to TRIAL BY JURY. This right applies to misdemeanors where imprisonment for more than six months is authorized. (See INFORMATION.)

CHARLES H. WHITEBREAD

Bibliography

LaFAVE, W. and SCOTT, A. 1972 *Criminal Law.* St. Paul, Minn.: West Publishing Co.

MISHKIN v. NEW YORK

See: *Memoirs v. Massachusetts*

MISSISSIPPI v. JOHNSON
4 Wallace (71 U.S.) 475 (1867)
GEORGIA v. STANTON
6 Wallace (73 U.S.) 50 (1868)

In these cases, the Supreme Court refused to enjoin President ANDREW JOHNSON and Secretary of War EDWIN M. STANTON from enforcing the MILITARY RECONSTRUCTION ACTS. The Justices unanimously refused to act in the Mississippi case, holding that legislatively mandated executive duties were not enjoinable. Georgia subsequently argued that the military laws threatened its corporate sovereignty, but Justice SAMUEL NELSON found this a POLITICAL QUESTION unfit for judicial scrutiny. Nelson hinted, however, that the Court might favorably consider an action based on property rights. Shortly afterward, in an unreported case (*Mississippi v. Stanton*, 1868), the Justices evenly divided on that question. Consequently, the judiciary never ruled on the constitutionality of military reconstruction; yet these decisions involved an important recognition of SEPARATION OF POWERS and the limits of JUDICIAL POWER.

STANLEY I. KUTLER

MISSISSIPPI UNIVERSITY FOR WOMEN v. HOGAN
458 U.S. 718 (1982)

Joe Hogan, a male registered nurse, was rejected by a state university's all-female school of nursing. A 5–4 Supreme Court held that Hogan's exclusion violated his right to EQUAL PROTECTION OF THE LAWS. For the majority, Justice SANDRA DAY O'CONNOR rejected the argument that, by excluding males, the university was compensating for discrimination against women. Rather, the all-female policy "tends to perpetuate the stereotyped view of nursing as an exclusively woman's job." The university thus failed the test set by CRAIG V. BOREN (1976) for SEX DISCRIMINATION cases. The dissenters, making a case for diversity of types of higher education, emphasized that Hogan could attend a coeducational state nursing school elsewhere in Mississippi.

KENNETH L. KARST

MISSOURI v. HOLLAND
252 U.S. 416 (1920)

MISSOURI V. HOLLAND confirmed the status of treaties as supreme law. Although becoming "perhaps the most famous and most discussed case in the constitutional law of foreign relations" it arose from a narrower Progressive Era desire to prevent indiscriminate killing of migratory birds, which key states had proved unable or unwilling to end by themselves. Congress first legislated hunting restrictions in March 1913, but lower federal courts invalidated them on TENTH AMENDMENT grounds as exceeding the federal government's commerce power, intruding on STATE POLICE POWERS, and usurping the states' well-established position in American law as trustees for their citizens of wild animals. The federal government feared the outcome of a final test of the 1913 act sufficiently to delay Supreme Court action. Instead, responding to suggestions from Elihu Root and others, the Wilson administration concluded the Migratory Bird Treaty of 1916 with Great Britain (acting on behalf of Canada). This committed both nations to restrict hunting of the birds, and in the United States President WOODROW WILSON signed implementing legislation in July 1918.

Several lower courts, including one that had ruled against the 1913 legislation, quickly upheld the 1918 act. In one of these cases the state of Missouri had sought to enjoin federal game warden Ray P. Holland from enforcing the new law. Appealing to the Supreme Court, Missouri argued that because, in the absence of a treaty, the legislation would be clearly invalid on Tenth Amendment grounds, it must fall even with a treaty base, for otherwise constitutional limitations would become a nullity. The Supreme Court upheld the 1918 legislation in a 7–2 vote (but with no written dissent filed).

Echoing the government's defense of the challenged act, the core of Justice OLIVER WENDELL HOLMES's opinion for the Court was a standard federal supremacy argument. Whether or not the 1913 legislation had been invalid, the 1918 act implemented a treaty; because the Constitution explicitly delegated the TREATY POWER to the federal government and gave status as supreme law to treaties made "under the authority of the United States," Tenth Amendment objections had no force.

Less restrained, even cryptic, was Holmes's language, which provided a basis for years of controversy. After questioning whether the requirement that treaties be made under the authority of the United States meant more than observance of the Constitution's prescribed forms for treaty-making, Holmes defended an organic, expansive conception of the Constitution. Its words had "called into life a being the development of which could not have been foreseen completely by the most gifted of its begetters." The Migratory Bird Case needed consideration "in light of our whole experience." The question finally became whether the treaty was "forbidden by some invisible radiation from the general terms of the 10th Amendment." Holmes thereby camouflaged his admissions that treaties must involve matters of national interest and must not contravene specific constitutional prohibitions.

In the 1920s and early 1930s, when the Court often adhered to the doctrine of DUAL FEDERALISM, MISSOURI V. HOLLAND arguably offered constitutional grounds for otherwise suspect federal legislation if appropriate treaties were concluded. (Proponents of child labor regulation toyed with the approach.) Fears about its potential in this respect lingered into the 1950s, when the case was a frequent target for backers of the BRICKER AMENDMENT. Yet after 1937 the Supreme Court routinely accepted broader interpretations of TAXING AND SPENDING POWERS, the COMMERCE CLAUSE, and the FOURTEENTH AMENDMENT, so in practice the case's importance diminished.

CHARLES A. LOFGREN

Bibliography

HENKIN, LOUIS 1972 *Foreign Affairs and the Constitution.* Mineola, N.Y.: Foundation Press.
LOFGREN, CHARLES A. 1975 *Missouri v. Holland* in Historical Perspective. *Supreme Court Review* 1975:77–122.

MISSOURI COMPROMISE
(1820)

The Missouri Compromise provided a simple constitutional and geographical expedient for resolving a crisis of the Union growing out of slavery's expansion into the western TERRITORIES. Because the compromise formed the basis of a balance of the free and slave states in the Union for a generation, its abrogation in the 1850s destabilized the constitutional system and intensified the disruption of the Union.

In 1819, Representative James Tallmadge of New York offered an amendment to the Missouri statehood enabling bill that would prohibit the further introduction of slavery into Missouri and would free all children born to slaves after the state's admission, but hold them in servitude until age 25. Free-state congressmen supported congressional power thus to restrict the admission of Missouri by arguments derived from four constitutional sources: the new states clause of Article IV, section 3, giving Congress discretionary authority to admit new states into the Union; the territories clause of the same article and section, empowering Congress to make "Regulations respecting the Territory" of the nation; the slave trade clause of Article I, section 9, permitting congress to control the "Migration" of persons; and the GUARANTEE CLAUSE of Article IV, section 4, which required all states to have a REPUBLICAN FORM OF GOVERNMENT. Supporters of the Tallmadge amendment, citing the DECLARATION OF INDEPENDENCE, argued that slavery was incompatible with republican government.

Opponents of the Tallmadge amendment rejected all these arguments, insisting particularly that the logical implications of the republicanism argument would subvert slavery in the states where it already existed. The first Missouri crisis was resolved by a package of statutes that admitted Missouri without the Tallmadge restriction, admitted Maine as a free state, and prohibited the introduction of slavery into the remainder of the Louisiana Purchase territory north of Missouri's southern boundary. This compromise was subsequently supplemented by an informal process of admitting paired free and slave states, thus preserving a balance between the sections in the Senate.

On the eve of its statehood Missouri precipitated the second crisis by adopting provisions in its new constitution that would have prohibited the abolition of slavery without the consent of slaveholders and that required the state legislature to prohibit the ingress of free blacks. Constitutional arguments over the second controversy turned on the PRIVILEGES AND IMMUNITIES clause of Article IV, section 2, which introduced the question of the constitutional status of free black people. This issue went unresolved because the compromise that settled the second crisis simply provided that nothing Missouri might do in legislative compliance with the constitutional mandate should be construed to deny any citizen a privilege or immunity to which he was entitled, a toothless provision that Missouri flouted in 1847 by excluding free blacks.

THOMAS JEFFERSON warned at the time that "a geographical line, coinciding with a marked principle, moral and political, once conceived and held up to the angry passions of men, will never be obliterated." His somber prediction was fulfilled in the 1850s. The WILMOT PROVISO of 1846, which would have prohibited the introduction of slavery into territories acquired as a result of the Mexican War, inaugurated a period of controversy that terminated in the destruction of the Union in 1860. Democrats and southern political leaders in 1848 began to insist that the first Missouri restriction was unconstitutional and to demand its repeal. Repeal was accomplished by the KANSAS-NEBRASKA ACT of 1854; and Chief Justice ROGER B. TANEY gratuitously held that the Missouri Compromise had been unconstitutional all along in his opinion in DRED SCOTT V. SANDFORD (1857). Yet during Secession Winter, Senator JOHN J. CRITTENDEN resurrected the Missouri Compromise as the centerpiece of his compromise proposals, which recommended extrapolating the Missouri line all the way to the Pacific. But by 1860 sectional developments had made the constitutional settlement of 1820 obsolete.

WILLIAM M. WIECEK

Bibliography

MOORE, GLOVER 1953 *The Missouri Controversy, 1819–1821.* Lexington: University of Kentucky Press.

MISSOURI ex rel. GAINES v. CANADA
305 U.S. 337 (1938)

This was the first decision establishing minimum content for equality within the SEPARATE BUT EQUAL DOCTRINE. Missouri law excluded blacks from the state university; Gaines, a black applicant, was thus rejected by the university's law school. Missouri's separate university for blacks had no law school, and so the state offered to pay his tuition at a law school in a neighboring state. Represented by NAACP lawyers, Gaines sought a WRIT OF MANDAMUS to compel his admission to the state university law school. The state courts denied relief, and the Supreme Court reversed, 6–2.

Chief Justice CHARLES EVANS HUGHES, for the majority, said, "The admissibility of laws separating the races in the enjoyment of privileges afforded by the State rests wholly upon the equality of the privileges which the laws give to the separated groups within the State." The case was thus a doctrinal milestone on the road to BROWN V. BOARD OF EDUCATION (1954). Henceforth the Court would demand real equality in a segregated system of education. Because the education of blacks in the southern and border states had emphasized separateness and deemphasized equality—even equality of physical facilities and school spending—it would have been enormously expensive for the states to satisfy the test of *Gaines* by providing parallel educational systems. *Brown*'s question—whether segregation itself imposed an unconstitutional inequality—was a natural extension of the inquiry launched in *Gaines*.

KENNETH L. KARST

MISSOURI PACIFIC RAILROAD v. HUMES
115 U.S. 512 (1885)

A CORPORATION, invoking the FOURTEENTH AMENDMENT, employed SUBSTANTIVE DUE PROCESS against a state statute, but the Supreme Court, led by Justice STEPHEN J. FIELD, unanimously construed due process in an exclusively procedural sense. A statute might seriously depreciate the value of property, Field declared, but "if no rule of justice is violated in the provisions for the enforcement of such a statute," it could not be said to deprive a person of property without due process. The case was a replay of *Davidson v. New Orleans* (1878), which Field quoted. In 1886, the Court began to abandon the *Davidson-Humes* view of due process. (See STONE V. FARMERS' LOAN & TRUST CO.)

LEONARD W. LEVY

MITCHUM v. FOSTER
407 U.S. 225 (1972)

The federal anti-INJUNCTION statute prohibits a federal court from granting an injunction to stay state court proceedings "except as expressly authorized by Act of Congress, or where necessary in aid of its JURISDICTION, or to protect or effectuate its judgments." In *Mitchum*, relying on the "basic alteration" in our federal system wrought by the Reconstruction-era legislation, the Supreme Court decided that SECTION 1983, TITLE 42, UNITED STATES CODE (originally part of the Civil Rights Act of 1871), constituted an exception to the prohibition despite the absence of an express reference in section 1983 to the anti-injunction statute. Recent scholarship, which implicitly supports *Mitchum*, suggests that the original 1793 version of the anti-injunction statute sought merely to prohibit individual Supreme Court Justices from enjoining state proceedings and was not intended to be a comprehensive ban on federal injunctions against state proceedings. The Court's prior decision in YOUNGER V. HARRIS (1971) limits *Mitchum*'s practical importance. *Younger*, which relied on nonstatutory grounds, severely restricted federal courts' discretion to enjoin pending state proceedings.

THEODORE EISENBERG

MOBILE v. BOLDEN
446 U.S. 55 (1980)

A fragmented Supreme Court majority upheld, 6–3, Mobile's at-large system for electing city commissioners, although the system diluted the voting strength of black voters by submerging them in a white majority. The plurality found that purposeful RACIAL DISCRIMINATION had not been demonstrated. (See WASHINGTON V. DAVIS, 1976; ROGERS V. LODGE, 1982.) In 1982 Congress amended the VOTING RIGHTS ACT OF 1965 to permit reliance on racially discriminatory "results" to show a violation of the act's prohibitions.

KENNETH L. KARST

MONELL v. DEPARTMENT OF SOCIAL SERVICES
436 U.S. 658 (1978)

In 1961, MONROE V. PAPE had held municipalities effectively immune from suit under SECTION 1983, TITLE 42, UNITED STATES CODE. *Monell* reinterpreted the legislative history relied upon in *Monroe* to conclude that municipalities may be sued under section 1983 but are liable only for acts constituting official policy. Not every violation of federal rights by municipal employees gives rise to an action against the municipality.

THEODORE EISENBERG

MONETARY POWER

The monetary power of Congress flows from one express constitutional grant and a melange of others, cemented by the NECESSARY AND PROPER CLAUSE.

The enumerated power deals with coin and has never been significant in American constitutional law. Congress's more important powers over the money supply—to charter banks and endow them with the right to issue circulating notes, to emit BILLS OF CREDIT, and to make government paper a legal tender—are only implied. From the administration of GEORGE WASHINGTON to the age of FRANKLIN D. ROOSEVELT, few questions were debated with more intensity than the nature and scope of Congress's IMPLIED POWERS over the currency. At no point, however, did the Supreme Court offer sustained resistance to the extension of Congress's authority. In MCCULLOCH V. MARYLAND (1819), the lodestar case on the monetary power, the MARSHALL COURT upheld incorporation of a bank as an appropriate means for executing "the great powers, to lay and collect taxes; to borrow money; to regulate commerce; to declare and conduct a war; and to raise and support armies and navies." The HUGHES COURT invoked the same undifferentiated list of enumerated powers, reinforced by the necessary and proper clause, in the GOLD CLAUSE CASES (1935), where the last potential limitation on Congress's monetary power was swept away.

Two factors account for the Court's acquiescence. The ambiguous legacy of the CONSTITUTIONAL CONVENTION OF 1787 was especially important. Monetary questions loomed large in the political history of the Confederation era, and some of the Founders, perhaps a majority, wanted to constitutionalize a settlement. They acted decisively to curtail state power. Article I, section 10, provides that "no state shall . . . coin money; emit bills of credit; [or] make anything but gold and silver coin a tender in payment of debts." But the Founders were more circumspect when dealing with the scope of national power. JAMES MADISON's motion to vest Congress with a general power "to grant charters of incorporation" was not adopted because, as RUFUS KING explained, the bank question might divide the states "into parties" and impede ratification. JAMES WILSON suggested that the power to incorporate a bank was implied anyway; but GEORGE MASON, the only other delegate to speak on the matter, disagreed.

Conflicting conceptions of implied powers also materialized without being resolved in the much longer debate on Congress's authority to augment the money supply with government paper. The original draft of the Constitution, as reported to the convention by the Committee of Detail, empowered Congress "to borrow money and emit bills on the credit of the United States." When this section was reached in debate, GOUVERNEUR MORRIS moved to strike out the emission clause; the motion was ultimately carried by a vote of nine states to two. Yet there was no meeting of minds on the implications of Morris's motion before the roll call. Wilson, Mason, and virtually everyone else who spoke assumed that striking out the emission power was equivalent to prohibiting congressional exercise of such a power. Morris said that "the monied interest will oppose the plan of government if paper emissions be not prohibited." But NATHANIEL GORHAM remarked that he was for "striking out, without inserting any prohibition." And that was precisely what happened. Gorham neither mentioned the concept of implied powers nor flatly stated that eliminating the power to emit was by no means equivalent to prohibiting it. His remarks nonetheless suggest that at least some of the Founders assumed, despite Morris's protestations to the contrary, that to vote for his motion was to leave the paper money question to be settled as problems arose.

The sequence of federal legislation on banking and the currency was the second factor that shaped the growth of Congress's monetary power in constitutional law. Once the Constitution had been ratified, Congress was required to assert implied powers either to incorporate a bank or to issue paper money. Sanctioned exercise of one power could be expected to provide at least a modicum of constitutional authority for assertion of the other. Yet the Founders' distrust of government paper was so intense that it was possible for a skillful statesman to obscure the close constitutional relationship between the powers to incorporate banks and emit paper money by treating the former as a conservative policy alternative to the latter. ALEXANDER HAMILTON was such a statesman.

In his Report on the National Bank (1790) Hamilton stressed the "material differences between a paper currency, issued by the mere authority of Government, and one issued by a Bank, Payable in coin." The proposed national bank, he said, would serve as a financial arm of the government and a ready lender to the Treasury; its capital stock, consisting primarily of public securities, would be monetized in the form of bank notes redeemable in specie, thereby multiplying the nation's active capital and stimulating trade. Paper money, in contrast, was just too "seducing and dangerous an expedient," for "there is almost a moral certainty of its becoming mischievous." Much of the constitutional theory he mustered later to justify Congress's power to incorporate a bank was equally applicable to its power to issue paper money. But it is unlikely that the congressmen who approved the BANK OF THE UNITED STATES ACT or President Washington, who signed the bill despite forceful constitu-

tional arguments against it by THOMAS JEFFERSON and others, would have sanctioned Hamilton's BROAD CONSTRUCTION of the government's implied powers in order to facilitate emissions of paper money. In view of JOHN MARSHALL's language regarding the sanctity of contracts in OGDEN V. SAUNDERS (1827), it is equally significant the *McCulloch* involved national bank notes rather than depreciated government paper.

Between 1812 and 1815 there occurred another series of events with implications almost as great as *McCulloch* for the development of Congress's monetary power. The First Bank's charter expired in 1811; its successor was not created until 1816. When the War of 1812 began, then, the government had to finance its operations without the aid of a national banking system. On four separate occasions Congress followed President Madison's recommendation and authorized the emission of Treasury notes, fundable into government bonds and receivable for all duties and taxes owed to the government. Every piece of paper issued in 1812, 1813, and 1814 had a large denomination, carried a fixed term, and bore interest. But the 1815 issue was of bearer notes without interest, in denominations from three, five, and ten dollars upward, receivable in payments to the United States without time limit. Debate in Congress suggests that the notes were fully expected to circulate as currency. Nobody objected to them on constitutional grounds and all were retired soon after the war. Nevertheless, the 1815 Treasury notes provided what John Jay Knox later called "a fatal precedent."

Knox's was a shrewd observation. The Madison administration's Treasury notes were indistinguishable from the bills of credit which Gouverneur Morris and others thought they had prohibited at the Constitutional Convention. In defense of his motion to strike the emission clause, Morris had emphasized that "a responsible minister" could meet emergencies without resort to bills of credit. The remaining power "to borrow money," he had explained, would enable the Treasury to issue "notes"—a term which he understood to mean interest-bearing, fixed-term paper in contradistinction to "bills" which he defined as interest-free paper issued by the government in payment of its obligations. The Treasury notes emitted by the Madison administration were clearly of the latter variety. Moreover, the receivability of those notes for all public debts undermined Madison's own constitutional understanding of 1787. He had suggested that the Convention ought to retain the emission power while expressly prohibiting the power to make government paper a legal tender.

As he noted in his journal, however, Madison had "acquiesce[d]" in the Convention's decision once he "became satisfied that striking out the words would not disable the Government from the use of public notes as far as they could be safe and proper; and would only cut off the pretext for a paper currency and particularly for making the bills a tender either for public or private debts." At Philadelphia, moreover, only Madison had emphasized the legal tender question. And as the bullionists on the Court learned during the post-Civil War LEGAL TENDER CASES, it was extremely difficult to deny Congress the legal tender power once its power to emit bills of credit had been conceded and *McCulloch* had established its discretion in the choice of appropriate means.

Yet the distrust of money-supply decisions made by legislation retained such great vitality during the nineteenth century that an attempt was made to proscribe irredeemable government paper on constitutional grounds. It came in *Hepburn v. Griswold* (1870). Speaking for a 4–3 majority, Chief Justice SALMON P. CHASE declared that the legal tender legislation he had recommended during his tenure as ABRAHAM LINCOLN's secretary of the treasury was invalid insofar as it impaired the value of preexisting private debts. Chase began by reiterating Marshall's *McCulloch* commentary on implied powers and "the painful duty of this tribunal" with regard to laws inconsistent with the "letter and spirit" of the Constitution. He admitted that Congress had an "undisputed power" to emit bills of credit; in VEAZIE BANK V. FENNO (1869) he had said that Congress might even levy prohibitive taxes on the notes of state-chartered banks in order "to provide a currency for the whole country." But the legal tender power was distinguishable. It was not necessary, though perhaps convenient, for Congress to impart legal tender qualities to its paper in order to guarantee circulation. And legislation that impaired contracts was not only contrary to the "spirit" of the Constitution as Marshall and others had understood it but also deprived creditors of property without DUE PROCESS or JUST COMPENSATION.

The narrow construction of Congress's authority expounded in *Hepburn* did not endure. SAMUEL MILLER, dissenting along with NOAH SWAYNE and DAVID DAVIS, had claimed that the majority's reliance on the "spirit" of the Constitution substituted "an undefined code of ethics for the Constitution." In their view, *McCulloch* had established that "where there is a choice of means, the selection is for Congress, not the Court." WILLIAM STRONG and JOSEPH BRADLEY, whom ULYSSES S. GRANT nominated to the Court on the very day *Hepburn* was decided, agreed with the *Hepburn* dissenters and voted to overrule Chase's previous majority in *Knox v. Lee* (1871). Bradley stated in a concurring opinion that once the power to emit bills of credit had been conceded, "the incidental power of giving such bills the quality of legal tender follows almost as a matter of course." Strong's opinion for the Court responded forcefully to the "TAKING" claims advanced in *Hepburn*. An 1834 act passed pursuant to Congress's power "to coin money and regulate the value thereof," he pointed out, had established a new regulation of the weight and value of gold coins. Creditors had sustained consequential injuries as a result, for antecedent debts had become "solvable with six per cent less gold than was required to pay them before." But it had never been imagined that Congress had taken property without due process of law. Congress's implied monetary powers, Strong concluded, were as plenary as its enumerated monetary power: "Contracts must be understood as made in reference to the possible exercise of the rightful authority of the government, and no obligation of contract can extend to the defeat of legitimate governmental authority."

Two other Chase Court decisions, *Bronson v. Rodes* (1869) and *Trebilock v. Wilson* (1872), reflected the law's continuing favor for freedom in private contract despite Strong's sweeping language regarding the plenary nature of Congress's monetary power. There the Court held that agreements specifically requiring payment in gold and silver coin could not be satisfied by tenders of irredeemable government paper. Coin was still a legal tender under federal law, the Court explained; because the Legal Tender Acts did not expressly prohibit parties from drafting contracts requiring payment in specie, it remained "the appropriate function of courts . . . to enforce contracts according to the lawful intent and understanding of the parties." Creditors found *Bronson* and *Trebilock* particularly reassuring in the Populist era. Although the Civil War greenbacks became redeemable at par in 1879, apprehensions of currency devaluation by "free coinage" of silver prompted virtually all draftsmen of long-term debt obligations to specify repayment in gold coin of a given weight and fineness. But the monetary crisis of 1933 led not only to another, apparently final abandonment of the gold standard and a substantial depreciation of the currency but also to a joint resolution of Congress that proclaimed gold clauses in private contracts to be "against public policy" and void. Eight years later, EDWARD S. CORWIN remarked that "no such drastic legislation from the point of view of property rights had ever before been enacted by the Congress."

The Court nonetheless sustained the resolution by a 5–4 margin in the GOLD CLAUSE CASES (1935). In *Bronson* and *Trebilock*, Chief Justice CHARLES EVANS HUGHES explained for the majority, the Court had mandated the enforcement of contracts containing gold clauses at a time when Congress had not prohibited such agreements. Now Congress had acted; "parties cannot remove theirs transactions from the reach of dominant constitutional power by making contracts about them." JAMES MCREYNOLDS filed a discursive dissent in which he claimed, among other things, that the Constitution "is gone." In one respect his argument had some merit. Many of the Founders, perhaps a majority, had assumed that adoption of Gouverneur Morris's motion to strike the power to emit bills of credit precluded all government paper designed to circulate as money. Yet contracts were enforceable in government paper and only government paper after 1933. From another perspective, however, McReynolds's claim was simply perverse. The constitutional text does not forbid Congress to issue paper money, and American constitutional law not only sets limitations on what government does but also legitimizes government's authority to act affirmatively in the face of changing public interests. It was no accident that when Marshall emphasized the importance of remembering that "it is a *constitution* we are expounding," he did so in the leading case involving Congress's monetary power.

CHARLES W. MCCURDY

Bibliography

CORWIN, EDWARD S. 1941 *Constitutional Revolution, Ltd.* Claremont, Calif.: Claremont Colleges.

DAM, KENNETH W. 1982 The Legal Tender Cases. *Supreme Court Review* 1981:367–412.

HURST, JAMES WILLARD 1973 *A Legal History of Money in the United States, 1774–1970.* Lincoln: University of Nebraska Press.

KNOX, JOHN JAY 1882 *United States Notes: A History of the Various Uses of Paper Money by the Government of the United States.* New York: Scribner's.

MONROE, JAMES
(1758–1831)

James Monroe was the last veteran of the American Revolution to serve as President of the United States. He had abandoned his studies at the College of William and Mary to join the army, and he rose to the rank of lieutenant colonel. He later read law under THOMAS JEFFERSON and, in 1782, was elected to the legislature of his native Virginia. From 1783 to 1786 he represented Virginia in Congress, where one of his chief concerns was the unsuccessful attempt to amend the ARTICLES OF CONFEDERATION to provide for a stronger central government. A committee chaired by Monroe drafted an amendment that would have given Congress the power to regulate commerce, but no action was taken on the amendment.

Notwithstanding his views on the Confederation, Monroe opposed RATIFICATION OF THE CONSTITUTION, primarily because it created too strong a central government and vested too much power in the President. He publicly professed to see in the proposed system a tendency toward monarchy and aristocracy, and he privately complained that the South would be outvoted on sectional issues.

From 1790 to 1794, Monroe represented Virginia in the United States Senate. There he was a leader of the Republican party and an opponent of the programs of ALEXANDER HAMILTON and especially of the BANK OF THE UNITED STATES ACT. He left the Senate in 1794 to become ambassador to France. He served as governor of Virginia (1799–1802), then held diplomatic posts abroad for the Jefferson administration, including an assignment as one of the negotiators of the LOUISIANA PURCHASE TREATY. He was again elected governor in 1811 but resigned to become secretary of state under President JAMES MADISON. During the War of 1812 he also acted as secretary of war.

Monroe's presidency (1817–1825) was notable for the rhetoric of constitutional literalism and STRICT CONSTRUCTION. He opposed congressional schemes for federally funded INTERNAL IMPROVEMENTS (such as highways and canals) on the grounds that there was no constitutional authority for them; but he suggested a constitutional amendment to confer such authority. In 1820, despite reservations about the constitutionality of its conditions on admission of a state, Monroe approved the MISSOURI COMPROMISE limiting expansion of SLAVERY IN THE TERRITORIES. And in 1823, on the advice of Secretary of State JOHN QUINCY ADAMS, he asserted presidential control over FOREIGN AFFAIRS by proclaiming the MONROE DOCTRINE. During his administration, the opportunity for peaceful westward development was assured by the negotiation of treaties fixing the borders of the United States with Canada and with the Spanish and Russian possessions in North America.

The most pressing constitutional question of his time was the place of slavery in the American republic. Himself a slaveholder, Monroe favored gradual, compensated emancipation followed by settlement of ex-slaves in Africa. To that end he was a founding member of the American Colonization Society; and the capital of Liberia, the African state settled through the society's efforts, was named in his honor.

Monroe's last active role in public affairs was as president of the Virginia CONSTITUTIONAL CONVENTION of 1829.

DENNIS J. MAHONEY

Bibliography
AMMON, HARRY 1971 *James Monroe: The Quest for National Identity.* New York: McGraw-Hill.

MONROE v. PAPE
365 U.S. 167 (1961)

This case, a fountainhead of modern CIVIL RIGHTS doctrine, arose out of an unconstitutional search conducted by Chicago police officers. The victim sought damages in an action brought under SECTION 1983, TITLE 42, UNITED STATES CODE, which authorizes suits for deprivations, under COLOR OF LAW, of rights, privileges, or immunities secured by the Constitution and laws of the United States. *Monroe* settled that section 1983 protects all FOURTEENTH AMENDMENT rights and not merely those narrowly defined rights that the SLAUGHTERHOUSE CASES (1873) found to be protected by the Fourteenth Amendment's PRIVILEGES AND IMMUNITIES clause. Early litigation under section 1983 had suggested possible links between the scope of the privileges and immunities clause and the rights protected by section 1983. *Monroe* also confirmed earlier holdings in federal civil rights cases that the phrase "under color of" law in section 1983 includes official acts not authorized by state law. *Monroe*'s third holding, that cities could not be made defendants in section 1983 cases, was overruled in MONELL V. DEPARTMENT OF SOCIAL SERVICES (1978).

THEODORE EISENBERG

MONROE DOCTRINE
2 Richardson, *Messages and Papers of the Presidents* 207 (1823)

The United States, the first true revolutionary nation, became, in 1823, the guardian of the emerging revolutionary states of the New World. The American constitutional ideal of republican, LIMITED GOVERNMENT, founded on NATURAL RIGHTS and SOCIAL COMPACT, stood in opposition to the constitutional system of Europe, based on hereditary privilege. The countries of the Western Hemisphere, becoming independent in the early nineteenth century, would, in rejecting the European system, seem naturally to embrace the American ideal.

JOHN QUINCY ADAMS, secretary of state to President JAMES MONROE, perceived the threat to the Americas from the reactionary Concert of Europe and the Holy Alliance. Adams formulated, and Monroe announced, a policy of resistance to any attempt to restore European hegemony in the Americas. Although Adams counseled use of diplomatic channels, Monroe, on the advice of Secretary of War JOHN C. CALHOUN, announced the doctrine in his 1823 State of the Union Message.

The proclamation of the Monroe Doctrine was a significant assertion of executive power in FOREIGN AFFAIRS. Although Monroe's address repeatedly stressed America's neutrality in European wars and in the colonial revolutions against Spain, his declaration that "we should consider any attempt on their part to extend their system to any portion of this hemisphere as dangerous to our peace and safety" was a clear warning that American interests would be vindicated by force, if necessary. The President, therefore, committed the country to potential military action outside its borders and announced the fact to Congress rather than asking for congressional authorization.

The Constitution, of course, makes no provision for so sweeping an assertion of executive authority over foreign affairs or so general a commitment of American power abroad. Yet the Monroe Doctrine swiftly became part of the UNWRITTEN CONSTITUTION, the accretion of customs and precedents that fill the constitutional lacunae.

DENNIS J. MAHONEY

Bibliography
PERKINS, DEXTER 1955 *A History of the Monroe Doctrine.* Boston: Little, Brown.

MONTESQUIEU
(1689–1755)

The political philosophy of Charles de Secondat, Baron de la Brede et de Montesquieu, was an important influence on American constitutional thought. The leading republican theorist of the generation immediately preceding the American Revolution, he was referred to more frequently by the delegates to the CONSTITUTIONAL CONVENTION OF 1787 than any other theoretical writer. JAMES MADISON (in THE

FEDERALIST #43) called him "the oracle . . . who is always consulted and cited." In the debates on the RATIFICATION OF THE CONSTITUTION the authority of Montesquieu was invoked by partisans ranging from LUTHER MARTIN to ALEXANDER HAMILTON.

Montesquieu's most important work was *The Spirit of the Laws* (1748). The book seems obscure and difficult to most readers, at least partly because the author tried to combine a philosophic inquiry, intended for a few readers only, with practical political advice meant for a much wider audience. In Montesquieu's practical teaching, based on observation, philosophic reflection, and first-hand experience, the American founders found the apparent resolution of two key problems of American politics: how to reconcile popular government with a vast extent of territory and how to reconcile energetic government with the security of liberty.

Montesquieu was the first political philosopher to treat FEDERALISM at any length. He believed, with the classical theorists, that republican government was possible only in small societies, for there alone could be found the virtue and public-spiritedness necessary if people are to govern themselves. But small republics are in constant danger from larger, despotic neighbors. The solution was the federal republic: "a convention by which several bodies politic consent to become citizens of a larger state . . . a society of societies who form a new one, which can enlarge itself through new associates who join."

But a large republic, even a federal republic, is liable to destruction through internal strife. Sectional and religious differences divide the people and make republican virtue impossible. For this, too, Montesquieu had an answer: "Commerce cures destructive prejudices; and it is almost a general rule that wherever there is commerce there are gentle ways of life." Commerce tends to make people peaceful and tolerant, and it makes them aware of their interdependence for security and comfort.

Montesquieu's greatest influence on American CONSTITUTIONALISM is seen in the twin doctrines of SEPARATION OF POWERS and CHECKS AND BALANCES. Montesquieu adopted the idea of separation of powers from JOHN LOCKE, but he fundamentally modified it by defining the three branches of government as legislative, executive, and judicial. Although Montesquieu introduced separation of powers in a famous chapter "On the Constitution of England," that chapter actually comprises not a description of the English government but rather a presentation of the conditions necessary for liberty and safety. Checks and balances, according to Montesquieu, are modifications of separation of powers necessary to keep any one branch of government from becoming despotic and to promote harmony of action.

DENNIS J. MAHONEY

Bibliography

ALLEN, WILLIAM BARCLAY 1972 Montesquieu: The Federalist-Anti-Federalist Debate. Unpublished Ph.D. dissertation, Claremont Graduate School.
PANGLE, THOMAS L. 1973 *Montesquieu's Philosophy of Liberalism.* Chicago: University of Chicago Press.

MOODY, WILLIAM H.
(1853–1917)

After studying law in the offices of novelist-lawyer Richard Henry Dana, William Henry Moody of Massachusetts first came to national attention as a special prosecutor in the Fall River ax-murder case of Lizzie Borden (1892). In 1895 he went to Congress where he served as a Republican until President THEODORE ROOSEVELT appointed him secretary of the navy in 1902. When PHILANDER C. KNOX left the administration for the Senate in 1904, Moody replaced him as attorney general. Philosophically comfortable with the President, Moody spent much of his tenure directing the prosecution of the Beef Trust. Although Knox had begun the case, Moody successfully argued SWIFT & COMPANY V. UNITED STATES (1905) before the Supreme Court, helping to lay the basis for the STREAM OF COMMERCE doctrine. As attorney general, Moody directed active participation by the Department of Justice in many facets of national ECONOMIC REGULATION, from antitrust proceedings to railroad regulation under the ELKINS ACT.

Roosevelt rewarded Moody's service and his commitment to a strong national government by appointing him to succeed Justice HENRY B. BROWN on the Supreme Court in 1906. Although Moody's service on the Court formally lasted until 1910, he was rarely present the last two years. Moody took part in relatively few cases during his tenure, but his opinions fulfilled Roosevelt's expectations and reflected Moody's moderate Progressivism. As a Justice, Moody continued his support of regulatory legislation, often voting with the Court to extend or strengthen federal authority. Moody joined the majority in LOEWE V. LAWLOR (1908), holding that the SHERMAN ANTITRUST ACT covered labor boycotts, and he wrote for the dissenters in the first EMPLOYERS' LIABILITY CASES (1908), asserting that Congress had power to regulate employer–employee relations in INTERSTATE COMMERCE issues. Although that dissent typified Moody's willingness to expand the reach of federal powers, he also supported exercises of STATE POLICE POWER when they worked no interference with federal powers. An adherent of judicial self-restraint, Moody opposed judicial legislation and he silently concurred in MULLER V. OREGON (1908), in which the BRANDEIS BRIEF offered convincing EVIDENCE to the Court of the benefits of maximum hours legislation. In TWINING V. NEW JERSEY (1908), perhaps his best-known opinion, Moody, for the Court, declared that the RIGHT AGAINST SELF-INCRIMINATION was not an "essential element" of DUE PROCESS OF LAW incorporated in the FOURTEENTH AMENDMENT and applicable to the states. If the people of the state were dissatisfied with the law, he declared, recourse "is in their own hands."

Stricken with acute rheumatism, Moody retired in 1910 and died, a semi-invalid, seven years later.

DAVID GORDON

MOORE, ALFRED
(1755–1810)

A staunch Federalist in an Anti-Federalist state, Alfred Moore served as North Carolina's attorney general from 1782 to 1791 and was prominent in securing RATIFICATION OF THE CONSTITUTION there. He defended the state Confiscation Act in BAYARD V. SINGLETON (1787), opposing JUDICIAL REVIEW. President JOHN ADAMS appointed him to the Supreme Court in 1799 but he resigned in 1804 because of ill health. During his tenure Moore wrote only one opinion, in *Bas v. Tingy* (1800), a prize case. Moore's unexceptional opinion, together with those of the other Justices, lent support to congressional legislation dealing with the quasi-war with France.

DAVID GORDON

MOORE v. CITY OF EAST CLEVELAND
431 U.S. 494 (1977)

Although it produced no OPINION OF THE COURT, *Moore* is a major modern Supreme Court precedent confirming the Constitution's protection of the family. A 5–4 Court held invalid a city ordinance limiting occupancy of certain residences to single families and defining "family" in a way that excluded a family composed of Inez Moore, her son, and two grandsons who were not brothers but cousins. Justice LEWIS F. POWELL, for a plurality of four Justices, concluded that "such an intrusive regulation of the family" required careful scrutiny of the regulation's justification. The city's asserted justifications—avoiding overcrowding, traffic and parking problems, and burdens on its schools—were served only marginally by the ordinance. The plurality thus concluded that the ordinance denied Mrs. Moore liberty without DUE PROCESS OF LAW.

Justice JOHN PAUL STEVENS, concurring, characterized the ordinance as a TAKING OF PROPERTY without due process or compensation. Chief Justice WARREN E. BURGER, dissenting, would have required Moore to exhaust her state administrative remedies before suing in federal court. Three other Justices dissented on the merits, rejecting both due process and EQUAL PROTECTION attacks on the ordinance and more generally opposing heightened judicial scrutiny of legislation merely on the basis of its effect on a family like the Moores.

The plurality opinion has become a standard citation for the reemergence of SUBSTANTIVE DUE PROCESS, and more specifically for a constitutional right of an extended—but traditional—family to choose its own living arrangements. In a wider perspective the decision can be seen as part of the growth of a FREEDOM OF INTIMATE ASSOCIATION. The decision was not, however, a blow against covert RACIAL DISCRIMINATION. East Cleveland was a predominantly black city, with a black commission and city manager. The ordinance, like ordinances in many white communities, was designed to maintain middle-class nuclear family arrangements. In this perspective, the plurality opinion is seen to collide with *Village of Belle Terre v. Boraas* (1974), which had upheld an ordinance excluding "unrelated" groups from single-family residences. Justice Powell's distinction of *Belle Terre* amounted to this: families are different. But he offered no definition of "family" apart from a generalized bow to "a larger conception of the family," including an extended family of blood relatives, for which he found support in "the accumulated wisdom of civilization." Of such stuff is substantive due process made.

KENNETH L. KARST

Bibliography
BURT, ROBERT A. 1979 The Constitution of the Family. *Supreme Court Review* 1979:329, 388–391.

MOORE v. DEMPSEY
261 U.S. 86 (1923)

Moore was a landmark for two of the twentieth century's most important constitutional developments: the emergence of the DUE PROCESS clause of the FOURTEENTH AMENDMENT as a limitation on state CRIMINAL PROCEDURE, and the assumption by the federal judiciary of a major responsibility for supervising the fairness of state criminal processes, through HABEAS CORPUS proceedings.

For all its importance, the case began as a squalid episode of racist ferocity. Returning from World War I, a black Army veteran sought to organize black tenant farmers of Phillips County, Arkansas, into a farmers' union. In October 1919—a year disfigured by racial violence in both North and South—these farmers held a meeting in a rural church to plan efforts to obtain fair accountings from their white landlords. At this remove in time it requires effort to understand that such a meeting, in such a place, for such a purpose, was seen as revolutionary. A sheriff's deputy fired at the church; blacks who were armed fired back, killing the deputy and wounding his companion. Hundreds of new deputies were sworn; they and hundreds of troops arrested most of the county's black farmers, killing resisters. Responsible estimates of the black dead ranged from twenty-five to 200.

About 120 blacks were indicted for various crimes, including the murder of the deputy. The trial juries, like the grand jury that had issued the INDICTMENTS, were all white. Twelve men were convicted of murder and sentenced to death; dozens of others were sentenced to long prison terms. The twelve sentenced to death filed APPEALS in two groups of six each. One group, after multiple appeals, was released in 1923 by order of the Arkansas Supreme Court, for excessive delay in their retrial. The convictions of the remaining six, however, were affirmed by the state supreme court, and the U.S. Supreme Court denied certiorari. They unsuccessfully sought habeas corpus in the state courts, and again the Supreme Court declined to review the case.

By now the NAACP had mounted a national fund-raising drive to support the six petitioners. Their execution, set for September 1921, was postponed by the filing of a habeas corpus petition in the federal district court. That court dismissed the writ. On direct appeal, the Supreme Court reversed, 7–2, with an opinion by Justice OLIVER WENDELL HOLMES. (The opinion refers, apparently erroneously, only to the five petitioners who were tried together; the petition of the

sixth was consolidated for hearing and decision.)

On REMAND to the district court, counsel for the six petitioners struck a deal; the habeas corpus petition would be dismissed and the sentence commuted to twelve years' imprisonment, making the men eligible for immediate parole. In 1925 the governor of Arkansas granted an "indefinite furlough," releasing them along with the others convicted following the Phillips County "insurrection."

The federal habeas corpus petition in *Moore* alleged that counsel appointed to represent the five defendants tried together did not consult with his clients before the trial; requested neither delay nor change of VENUE nor separate trials; challenged not a single juryman; and called no defense witnesses. The trial took forty-five minutes, and the jury "deliberated" less than five minutes. A lynch mob had been dissuaded from carrying out its purpose by a local committee, appointed by the governor to combat the "insurrection," who assured the mob that justice would be done swiftly. Two black witnesses swore they had been whipped and tortured into testifying as the prosecution wished. Holmes summarized the petition: "no juryman could have voted for an acquittal and continued to live in Phillips county, and if any prisoner, by any chance, had been acquitted by a jury, he could not have escaped the mob."

The Supreme Court held that these facts, if proved, justified two conclusions: the state had violated PROCEDURAL DUE PROCESS, and the federal district court should grant the writ of habeas corpus. Today both conclusions seem obvious. In 1923, however, the Supreme Court had not yet begun to impose significant federal constitutional limitations on the fairness of state criminal proceedings. *Moore* lighted the path that would lead, in less than half a century, to an expansion of the liberty protected by the due process clause, applying virtually the entire BILL OF RIGHTS to the states. (See INCORPORATION DOCTRINE.)

Moore's other conclusion, concerning the reach of federal habeas corpus, also broke new ground. In FRANK V. MANGUM (1915), a case involving strikingly similar facts, the Court had rejected a claim to federal habeas corpus relief on the ground that the state courts had provided a full "corrective process" for litigating the accused's federal constitutional claims. Only in the absence of such a corrective process, the Court had held, could a federal habeas corpus court intervene. *Moore* did not explicitly overrule *Frank*, but it did look in a different direction. Justice Holmes, in his characteristically laconic way, said only that if "the whole proceeding is a mask," with all participants in the state trial swept to their conclusion by a mob, and if the state courts fail to correct the wrong, "perfection in the [state's] machinery for correction" could not prevent the federal court from securing the accused's constitutional rights. The right claimed in *Moore*, of course, goes to the essence of due process of law; when the basic fairness of a state criminal trial is challenged, the fact that the state courts have already had a chance to look into the matter seems a weak justification for barring federal habeas corpus.

From *Moore* through FAY V. NOIA (1963), the Supreme Court steadily widened access to federal habeas corpus for persons challenging constitutionality of state convictions. STONE V. POWELL (1976) and WAINWRIGHT V. SYKES (1977) marked the BURGER COURT's reversal of the direction of doctrinal change. Indeed, *Stone* revived the doctrine of *Frank v. Mangum* in cases involving claims based on the FOURTH AMENDMENT's guarantee against UNREASONABLE SEARCHES and seizures. Yet, despite these limitations, *Moore*'s legacy, even in the field of federal habeas corpus, remains vital to a system of national constitutional standards of fairness for persons accused of crime.

KENNETH L. KARST

Bibliography

BATOR, PAUL M.　1963　Finality in Criminal Law and Federal Habeas Corpus for State Prisoners. *Harvard Law Review* 76:441, 483–493.

WATERMAN, J. S. and OVERTON, E. E.　1933　The Aftermath of Moore v. Dempsey. *St. Louis Law Review* (now *Washington University Law Review*) 18:117–126.

MOOSE LODGE #107 v. IRVIS
407 U.S. 163 (1972)

Irvis, a black, was refused service at a Harrisburg, Pennsylvania, branch of the Moose Lodge, a fraternal organization whose fraternity knew bounds. Irvis sued under federal CIVIL RIGHTS laws for an INJUNCTION requiring the Pennsylvania liquor board to revoke the lodge's license so long as it continued to discriminate on the basis of race. The Supreme Court held, 6–3, in an opinion by Justice WILLIAM H. REHNQUIST, that Irvis was not entitled to the relief he sought. The state's licensing was not, of itself, sufficient to satisfy the STATE ACTION limitation of the FOURTEENTH AMENDMENT, and the Constitution offered no protection against RACIAL DISCRIMINATION by a private club.

In the majority's view, nothing in the case approached the "symbiotic relationship" between the state and private racial discrimination shown in BURTON V. WILMINGTON PARKING AUTHORITY (1961). Although Pennsylvania liquor licensees were subjected to a number of state regulations, that supervision did not "encourage" racial discrimination. Furthermore, because many liquor licenses had been issued in the area, the lodge's license fell short of creating a state-supported monopoly. Thus the state had not implicated itself in the lodge's discriminatory policies.

Justices WILLIAM O. DOUGLAS and WILLIAM J. BRENNAN wrote separate DISSENTING OPINIONS, each joined by Justice THURGOOD MARSHALL. The dissenters emphasized the degree of monopoly power of clubs licensed to sell liquor and the state's detailed regulation of licensees.

KENNETH L. KARST

MOOTNESS

Article III's CASE OR CONTROVERSY restriction precludes federal courts from declaring law except in the context of litigation by parties with a personal stake in a live dispute that judicial decision can affect. They may not resolve moot questions—questions whose resolution can no longer affect the litigants' dispute because events after the commencement of litigation have obviated the need for judicial intervention. However live the issues once were, however much the parties (and the public) may desire a declaration of law, and however far the litigation may have progressed when the mooting events occur, Article III requires dismissal of the lawsuit. Common examples include a criminal defendant's death during appeal of a jail sentence, enactment of a new statute superseding one whose enforcement the plaintiff seeks to enjoin, or full satisfaction of a party's litigation demands.

Other cases exhibit less certainty that the substantive issues raised no longer need judicial action to forestall anticipated harm. In these cases, mootness questions are more troublesome. They inevitably introduce discretion to exercise or withhold judgment, discretion potentially influenced by the substantive issues' public importance. Thus, in DeFUNIS V. ODEGAARD (1974) a divided Supreme Court refused to decide the constitutionality of a race-conscious AFFIRMATIVE ACTION program for law school admissions when it appeared fairly certain that the challenger, who had only become a student through lower court victories, would be graduated irrespective of the lawsuit's outcome.

Several DOCTRINES reveal mootness to be a matter of degree. First, when changed circumstances moot the main dispute, but adjudication could produce collateral consequences, the issue is not moot, as when a prisoner's sentence expires before his appeal is decided, but the conviction might subject him to other civil or criminal penalties. Second, cases where defendants voluntarily agree to refrain from challenged behavior are not moot absent proof that they are unlikely to resume the behavior. This rule protects plaintiffs by preventing defendants from manipulating the mootness doctrine to avoid adverse decisions. Third, issues are not moot, despite passage of the immediate problem, when they are "capable of repetition, yet evading review," that is, when they arise sporadically, do not persist long enough to be reviewed before ceasing each time, and are reasonably likely to threaten the challengers again. Suits challenging ELECTION rules, where the immediate election passes before judicial resolution but the rules probably would affect the challengers in subsequent elections, or litigation challenging an abortion restriction that necessarily can apply to a woman only during the term of pregnancy are important instances where an unbending application of the mootness doctrine might deny judicial protection to persons periodically subject to harm. Finally, the Court generously allows a CLASS ACTION to continue, despite developments eliminating any need to protect the party bringing the lawsuit on behalf of the class, if the case is not moot as to other members of the class.

These refinements give federal courts some flexibility either to reach issues of their choice without pressing necessity to protect the parties or to decline to rule by insisting on a higher degree of probability that the threat of harm continues. Like other JUSTICIABILITY doctrines, mootness is not only a constitutional doctrine itself but a somewhat pliable tool of constitutional governance.

JONATHAN D. VARAT

Bibliography

NOTE 1974 The Mootness Doctrine in the Supreme Court. *Harvard Law Review* 88:373.

MOREHEAD v. NEW YORK ex rel. TIPALDO
298 U.S. 587 (1936)

In June 1936 the Supreme Court ended its term with an opinion so startling that even the Republican party repudiated it at the party's national convention. The Republican plank read: "We support the adoption of State laws to abolish sweatshops and child labor and to protect women and children with respect to MAXIMUM HOURS, MINIMUM WAGES and working conditions. We believe that this can be done within the Constitution as it now stands." "This" was precisely what the Court had ruled could not be done. It had defended STATES' RIGHTS as it struck down national legislation, and in NEBBIA V. NEW YORK (1934) it had declared, "So far as the requirement of DUE PROCESS of law is concerned, a state is free to adopt whatever economic policy may reasonably be deemed to promote public welfare. . . ." Just two weeks before the *Tipaldo* decision, the Court had announced, in CARTER V. CARTER COAL COMPANY (1936), as it had in the SCHECHTER POULTRY CORP. V. UNITED STATES (1935), that the regulation of labor was a local matter reserved by the TENTH AMENDMENT to the states, and specifically the Court had referred to the fixing of wages as a state function. Thus the resolution of *Tipaldo* came as a surprise. The Court used the FREEDOM OF CONTRACT doctrine, derived from SUBSTANTIVE DUE PROCESS, to hold that the states lack power to enact minimum wage laws. The precedent that controlled the case, the Court ruled, was ADKINS V. CHILDREN'S HOSPITAL (1923).

Although *Adkins* had seemed to block minimum wage legislation, the Court grounded that decision on the statute's failure to stipulate that prescribed wages should not exceed the value of labor services. New York had carefully framed a minimum wage law for women and children that embodied the Court's *Adkins* standard: the state labor commission was empowered to fix wages "fairly and reasonably commensurate with the value of the service or class of service rendered." By a 5–4 vote the Court held the state act unconstitutional. Justice PIERCE BUTLER, speaking for the majority, declared, "Forcing the payment of wages at a reasonable value does not make applicable the principle and ruling of the Adkins Case." The right to make contracts for wages in return for work "is part of the liberty protected by the due process clause," Butler said, and the state was powerless to interfere with such contracts. Women were entitled to no special consideration. Any measure that deprived employers and women employees the freedom to agree on wages, "leaving employers and men employees free to do so, is necessarily arbitrary."

Chief Justice CHARLES EVANS HUGHES dissented on ground that the statute was a reasonable exercise of the POLICE POWER, and he distinguished this case from *Adkins* because the *Tipaldo* statute laid down an appropriate standard for fixing wages. Justices HARLAN FISKE STONE, LOUIS D. BRANDEIS, and BENJAMIN N. CARDOZO concurred in Hughes's opinion but in a separate dissent by Stone they went much further. Stone accused the majority of having decided on the basis of their "personal economic predilections." He repudiated the freedom of contract DOCTRINE, adding: "There is grim irony in speaking of the freedom of contract of those who, because of their economic necessities, give their services for less than is needful to keep body and soul together." Following the reasoning of Justice OLIVER WENDELL HOLMES, dissenting in *Adkins,* Stone declared that it made no difference what wage standard the statute fixed, because employers were not compelled to hire anyone and could fire employees who did not earn their wages. Stone would have followed the principle of *Nebbia,* which the majority ignored, and he would have overruled *Adkins.* A year later, after President FRANKLIN D. ROOSEVELT proposed packing the Court, it overruled *Adkins* and *Tipaldo* in WEST COAST HOTEL V. PARRISH (1937).

LEONARD W. LEVY

Bibliography
LEONARD, CHARLES A.   1971   *A Search for a Judicial Philosophy: Mr. Justice Roberts and the Constitutional Revolution of 1937.* Pages 88–93. Port Washington, N.Y.: Kennikat Press.

MORGAN v. VIRGINIA
328 U.S. 373 (1946)

This was the first transportation SEGREGATION case brought to the Supreme Court by the NAACP; counsel for the appellant were THURGOOD MARSHALL and WILLIAM H. HASTIE. A Virginia law required racial segregation of passengers on buses. A black woman, riding from Virginia to Maryland, refused to move to a rear seat; she was convicted of a MISDEMEANOR and fined $10. Eighteen states forbade such segregation of passengers, and ten states required it. In 1878 the Supreme Court had invalidated a state law forbidding racial segregation on an interstate carrier as an undue burden on INTERSTATE COMMERCE in HALL V. DECUIR. The NAACP lawyers rested on the *Hall* precedent, and did not argue that the Virginia law violated the FOURTEENTH AMENDMENT.

In an opinion by Justice STANLEY F. REED, the Supreme Court held, 7–1, that the law unduly burdened interstate commerce. Although the usual analysis of a STATE REGULATION OF COMMERCE involves a balance of burdens on commerce against competing state interests such as health or safety, the Court avoided any discussion of a state interest in segregation, saying only that a uniform national rule of passenger seating was required for interstate carriers, if any rule was to be adopted. Justice HAROLD BURTON dissented.

KENNETH L. KARST

MORMON CHURCH v. UNITED STATES

See: *Church of Jesus Christ of Latter-Day Saints v. United States*

MORRILL ACT
12 Stat. 503 (1862)

The Morrill Land Grant College Act provided a basis for state support of public universities and thereby profoundly influenced the course of American higher education.

Under the Land Ordinance of 1785, section 16 of every township was sold and the proceeds used to create a "school fund." In the late 1850s, Vermont Republican Justin Morrill promoted the "Illinois Idea," which would have authorized further land grants to create an "industrial college" in each state. But southern Democrats objected on constitutional grounds, seeing in Morrill's bill a threat to STATES' RIGHTS. In 1862, with these opponents withdrawn from Congress, the Land Grant College Act was passed. It provided that 30,000 acres of public lands be assigned to each state for each of its senators and representatives (or land scrip in an equivalent amount issued to states lacking available public lands). The proceeds of the land sales were to be invested to support a college "to teach such branches of learning as are related to agriculture and the mechanic arts," as well as "military tactics," "in order to promote the liberal and practical education of the industrial classes." The American land-grant colleges are the result of this policy.

WILLIAM M. WIECEK

MORRIS, GOUVERNEUR
(1752–1816)

A lawyer and businessman descended from a wealthy, landed family, Gouverneur Morris was elected to New York's first provincial congress in 1775. The next year, he was a member of the committee that drafted the state's first CONSTITUTION and wrote the message to New York's delegates to the Continental Congress instructing them to vote for the DECLARATION OF INDEPENDENCE. He was himself sent to the Continental Congress in 1778 and was a signer of the ARTICLES OF CONFEDERATION. In 1780 he moved to Philadelphia and served as assistant superintendent of finance under ROBERT MORRIS. In this last capacity, he drafted a report to Congress that contained the first official proposal for a national currency: a decimal coinage based on the Spanish dollar.

Gouverneur Morris was elected to Pennsylvania's delegation to the CONSTITUTIONAL CONVENTION OF 1787. In the debates of the Convention he spoke more frequently than any other delegate. He was an advocate of strong national government, but also of aristocratic privilege. His view of humankind was extraordinarily cynical, and, distrusting any higher motives, he desired to institutionalize private interests as a guarantee of liberty. Although, like Robert Morris, he proposed a senate chosen for life from men of great wealth, the proposal arose partly out of fear that otherwise the rich would corrupt the democratic elements of the regime. He favored a provision to allow Congress to veto state laws and wanted to unite the executive and judiciary in a council of revision to veto national legislation. He favored direct election of the President and congressional representation proportional to taxation; he opposed any constitutional protection of slavery or the slave trade. He was against giving Congress the power to admit new states on terms of equality, and throughout his life he advocated governing the western territories as provinces while retaining power in the East.

Morris was elected to the Committee on Style, along with WILLIAM SAMUEL JOHNSON (its chairman), JAMES MADISON, JAMES WILSON, and RUFUS KING. The committee entrusted Morris with the duty of preparing its report, and so Morris became the principal author of the actual words of the Constitution. He also devised the formula for signing the document—the signatures bearing witness to the unanimous consent of the states—and drafted the letter by which the Convention transmitted its work to Congress.

ALEXANDER HAMILTON asked Morris to collaborate in writing THE FEDERALIST, but Morris declined. He served as a senator from New York from 1800 to 1803, supporting the JUDICIARY ACT OF 1801 and advocating the annexation—by force if necessary—of Louisiana. His public career also included a brief term as minister to France and the founding chairmanship of the Erie Canal Commission.

Morris opposed the War of 1812 as sectional and ill-conceived. The former champion of strong national government became an advocate of STATES' RIGHTS; he even counseled SECESSION of New York and New England from the Union. Morris was disappointed when the HARTFORD CONVENTION resolutions failed to embody that step.

DENNIS J. MAHONEY

Bibliography

MINTZ, MAX M. 1970 *Gouverneur Morris and the American Revolution.* Norman: University of Oklahoma Press.
ROOSEVELT, THEODORE 1888 *Gouverneur Morris.* (American Statesman Series.) Boston: Houghton Mifflin.

MORRIS, ROBERT
(1734–1806)

The English-born merchant and patriot Robert Morris was an early supporter of colonial rights, opposing the Stamp Act and signing the Non-Importation Agreement in 1765. As a member of the Second Continental Congress (1776–1788), Morris voted against the DECLARATION OF INDEPENDENCE because it was premature; but he later signed the Declaration as well as the ARTICLES OF CONFEDERATION. He earned the nickname "Financier of the Revolution" because of his role in raising money to support the Army. In 1781, Congress chose him to be superintendent of finance. While serving in that capacity he organized the Bank of North America, chartered by Congress as a device for borrowing money to pay the costs of the new government. In 1783, he resigned the "insupportable situation" of superintendent of finance, giving as his reason that "to increase our debts while the prospect of paying them diminishes does not consist with my ideas of integrity."

He was a member of the Pennsylvania delegation to the CONSTITUTIONAL CONVENTION OF 1787. There he nominated GEORGE WASHINGTON to be presiding officer, but otherwise, despite his reputation in Pennsylvania politics as a speaker who "bears down all before him," he remained silent throughout the debates. He was a strong nationalist, and desired a Senate comprising men of great and established property appointed for life. Morris signed the Constitution, and, in a letter, recommended it as "the subject of infinite investigation, disputation, and declamation," but still the work not of angels or devils but of "plain, honest men."

Morris and his friends supported the Constitution not least because it promised economic stability, security of contracts, and relief from the harassment of the Bank of North America by the state governments. But Morris's support for ratification seems only to have increased the fervor of some anti-Federalists.

Morris would have been a leading candidate to become the first secretary of the treasury, but he did not want the post. Instead, in 1789, he was elected to the United States Senate, where he became a leader of the Federalist faction and a key ally of ALEXANDER

HAMILTON in the matter of the assumption of state debts.

Morris retired from public life in 1795, and devoted his time to the management of his financial affairs, including his speculation in western lands. That speculation brought him, in 1797, to financial ruin and to three and one-half years in debtors' prison.

DENNIS J. MAHONEY

MORROW, WILLIAM W.
(1843–1929)

William W. Morrow served nearly thirty-two years on the federal bench. President BENJAMIN HARRISON in 1892 appointed him to the Northern District of California; President WILLIAM MCKINLEY in 1897 elevated him to the Ninth Circuit Court of Appeals, where he served until retirement in 1923.

His most influential opinion came in *In Re Wong Kim Ark* (1897). Morrow relied on history and precedent in the Ninth Circuit to define a COMMON LAW basis for CITIZENSHIP. He held that under the first section of the FOURTEENTH AMENDMENT a child whose parents were subjects of the emperor of China but domiciled in the United States at the time of the child's birth derived his citizenship from the place of birth rather than the father's citizenship. Morrow's opinion, which the Supreme Court affirmed in UNITED STATES v. WONG KIM ARK (1898), confirmed the claims of thousands of Chinese to American citizenship.

Morrow's opinion in *United States v. Wheeler et al.* (1912) revealed his profound suspicion of federal authority. Arizona officials had refused to prosecute the perpetrators of the Bisbee deportations, in which private citizens had forcibly removed over 200 members of the Industrial Workers of the World from Arizona to New Mexico. The United States sought to prosecute the leaders of the deportation under the conspiracy section of the FORCE ACT OF 1870. Morrow, however, rejected federal intervention. He held that the Fourteenth Amendment applied only to those rights explicitly provided for by Congress and which had not been historically entrusted to the states. Morrow reasoned that the acts of private individuals did not constitute STATE ACTION under the amendment, that the 1870 act applied only to the rights of freedmen, and that Congress had not passed any statute making kidnapping a federal crime. Morrow refused to allow the federal government to intervene, no matter how just the cause, in an area traditionally left to the STATE POLICE POWER.

Morrow's conservative jurisprudence paralleled his Republican politics. Through three decades of service on the Ninth Circuit he provided leadership to a court committed, like himself, to precedent and DUAL FEDERALISM.

KERMIT L. HALL

Bibliography

JURY, JOHN G. 1921 William W. Morrow. *California Law Review* 10:1–7.

MUELLER v. ALLEN
463 U.S. 388 (1983)

In this major case on the SEPARATION OF CHURCH AND STATE, the Supreme Court altered constitutional law on the issue of state aid to parents of parochial school children. The precedents had established that a state may not aid parochial schools by direct grants or indirectly by financial aids to the parents of the children; whether those aids took the form of tax credits or reimbursements of tuition expenses did not matter. In this case the state act allowed taxpayers to deduct expenses for tuition, books, and transportation of their children to school, no matter what school, public or private, secular or sectarian.

Justice WILLIAM H. REHNQUIST for a 5–4 Court ruled that the plan satisfied all three parts of the purpose, effect, and no-entanglement test of LEMON V. KURTZMAN (1971). That all taxpaying parents benefited from the act made the difference between this case and the precedents, even though parents of public school children could not take advantage of the major tax deduction. Rehnquist declared that the state had not aided religion generally or any particular denomination and had not excessively entangled the state with religion even though government officials had to disallow tax deductions for instructional materials and books that were used to teach religion. According to the dissenters, however, the statute had not restricted the parochial schools to books approved for public school use, with the result that the state necessarily became enmeshed in religious matters when administering the tax deductions. The dissenters also rejected the majority point that the availability of the tax deduction to all parents distinguished this case from the precedents. The parents of public school children simply were unable to claim the large deduction for tuition. Consequently the program had the effect of advancing the religious mission of the private sectarian schools.

LEONARD W. LEVY

MUGLER v. KANSAS
123 U.S. 623 (1887)

In *Mugler* the Supreme Court took a significant step toward the acceptance of SUBSTANTIVE DUE PROCESS, announcing it would henceforth examine the reasonableness involved in an exercise of STATE POLICE POWER. A Kansas statute prohibited the manufacture or sale of intoxicating liquor; the state arrested Mugler for making and selling malt liquor and also closed a brewery for being a public nuisance.

Justice JOHN MARSHALL HARLAN addressed the issue: did the Kansas statute violate the FOURTEENTH AMENDMENT guarantee of DUE PROCESS OF LAW? He declared that such a prohibition "does not necessarily infringe" any of those rights. Although an individual might have an abstract right to make liquor for his own purposes, as Mugler contended, that right could be conditioned on its effect on others' rights. The question became who would determine the effects of personal use on the community? Harlan found that power lodged squarely in the legislature which, to protect the public health and morals, might exercise its police power. But, bowing to JOSEPH CHOATE's argument, he admitted that such power was limited. Harlan asserted that the courts would not be bound "by mere forms [or] . . . pretenses." They had a "solemn duty—to look at the substance of things"; absent a "real or substantial relation" of the act to its objects, the legislation must fall as a "palpable invasion of rights secured by the FUNDAMENTAL LAW." The Kansas statute easily passed this test, however, and Harlan denied any interference or impairment of property rights. Harlan likewise dismissed the contention that the closing of a brewery amounted to a TAKING OF PROPERTY without JUST COMPENSATION, thereby depriving its owners of due process. Justice STEPHEN J. FIELD dissented in part, urging the Court to adopt substantive due process.

DAVID GORDON

(SEE ALSO: *Allgeyer v. Louisiana*, 1897.)

MULLER v. OREGON
208 U.S. 412 (1908)

Despite the Supreme Court's previous rejection of a maximum hour law for bakers in LOCHNER V. NEW YORK (1905), here the Justices unanimously sustained an Oregon statute limiting women to ten hours' labor in "any mechanical establishment, or factory, or laundry." The sole issue was the law's constitutionality as it affected female labor in a laundry. Lawyers for Muller contended that the law violated FREEDOM OF CONTRACT, that it was class legislation, and that it had no reasonable connection with the public health, safety, or welfare. The state countered with LOUIS D. BRANDEIS's famous brief elaborately detailing similar state and foreign laws, as well as foreign and domestic experts' reports on the harmful physical, economic, and social effects of long working hours for women.

Justice DAVID BREWER, speaking for the Court, based his opinion on the proposition that physical and social differences between the sexes justified a different rule respecting labor contracts, thereby allowing him to distinguish *Lochner*. Although the Constitution imposed unchanging limitations on legislative action, Brewer acknowledged that the FOURTEENTH AMENDMENT's liberty of contract doctrine was not absolute. He invoked HOLDEN V. HARDY (1898), sustaining an eight-hour day for Utah miners, and portions of *Lochner* that similarly approved some exceptional regulations. Brewer declared that although the legislation and opinions cited in the BRANDEIS BRIEF were not "authorities," the Court would "take judicial cognizance of all matters of general knowledge."

The accepted wisdom that women were unequal and inferior to men animated Brewer's opinion. Women's physical structure and their maternal functions, he said, put them at a disadvantage. Long hours of labor, furthermore, threatened women's potential for producing "vigorous" children; as such their physical well-being was a proper object of interest "in order to preserve the strength and vigor of the race." Beyond Brewer's concerns for the "future well-being of the race," he contended that the long historical record of women's dependence upon men demonstrated a persistent reality that women lacked "the self-reliance which enables one to assert full rights." Legislation such as the Oregon maximum hour law, Brewer concluded, was necessary to protect women from the "greed" and "passion" of men and therefore validly and properly could "compensate for some of the burdens" imposed upon women.

Taken out of context, Brewer's remarks obviously reflected paternalistic and sexist notions. Yet they also reflected prevailing sentiments, which he invoked to justify an exception to his normally restrictive views of legislative power. The same arguments were advanced by those who sought an opening wedge for ameliorating some of the excesses of modern industrialism.

Although the *Muller* decision did not overrule *Lochner,* it reinforced a growing line of precedents to counter *Lochner. Muller* eventually led to BUNTING V. OREGON (1917), approving maximum hour laws for both sexes, a decision that Chief Justice WILLIAM HOWARD TAFT believed in 1923 had tacitly overruled *Lochner*—mistakenly, as it turned out, for the Court invoked *Lochner* to strike down a minimum wage law in ADKINS V. CHILDREN'S HOSPITAL (1923).

STANLEY I. KUTLER

(SEE ALSO: *Sex Discrimination.*)

Bibliography

MASON, ALPHEUS T.   1946   *Brandeis: A Free Man's Life.* New York: Viking Press.

MULTIMEMBER DISTRICT

A multimember district (MMD) is a political district with more than one representative. European countries with proportional REPRESENTATION divide multiple representatives proportionally by party vote, normally producing many small, doctrinaire parties and volatile, schismatic governments. In United States MMDs, at-large, winner-take-all elections have been the rule, notably with ELECTORAL COLLEGE delegations. Winner-take-all puts more than proportional value on shiftable votes. Scholars believe that it has helped produce the American pattern of stable, center-seeking, two-party coalitions attentive to minorities who can form part of a winning coalition.

A ten-member, winner-take-all MMD offers less demographic variety—and less direct claim on any particular representative—than ten single-member districts; so MMDs have often been attacked for depersonalizing representation and submerging minorities. On the other hand, voters in MMDs have a mathematical advantage over voters in single-member districts (SMDs) because a $\frac{1}{10}$ vote for ten representatives has more chance of affecting the overall election outcome than a full vote for one representative. Moreover, MMD representatives, who answer to one large constituency rather than to ten small ones, are thought more likely to vote as a bloc than SMD representatives. Hence, an MMD voter may have less access to his representative than does an SMD voter, but he also may have more power over electoral and legislative outcomes.

MMDs share with GERRYMANDERS the "standards problem": the incommensurability of the various ways in which dilution or concentration of a group can enhance or diminish the group's power for different purposes. Short of ordering proportional representation, there is no way to equalize a group's (or a group member's) effective power. Accordingly, the Supreme Court has been cautious in intervening against MMDs, as it has against gerrymanders. In *Delaware v. New York* (1966) it was unmoved by Delaware's argument that New York voters, with sixty-four delegates to the Electoral College, has 2.3 times as much chance to affect the election outcome as Delaware voters, with only three delegates.

Likewise, with the exceptions of judicially created MMDs and legislatively created ones drawn with the proven intent of submerging minorities, the Court has been tolerant of MMDs, even where their effect has been to submerge minorities. In *Whitcomb v. Chavis* (1971) and MOBILE V. BOLDEN (1980) the Court held that submerging a minority is not per se a violation of the FOURTEENTH or FIFTEENTH AMENDMENT. Purposeful discrimination must also be shown, as in *White v. Regester* (1973) and ROGERS V. LODGE (1982), where the plaintiffs demonstrated intentional discrimination against minority groups. Congressional critics (of the *Mobile* case) in 1982 succeeded in amending the VOTING RIGHTS ACT of 1965 to make racially disproportionate election results one "circumstance" relevant to the determination of a violation of the act. The amendment added a proviso that racially proportional representation is not required, but it left to the courts the task of giving meaning to its calculatedly uncertain operative language.

WARD E. Y. ELLIOTT

Bibliography

BANZHAF, JOHN E.   1966   Multi-Member Electoral Districts—Do They Violate the "One Man, One Vote" Principle? *Yale Law Journal* 75:1309–1338.

ELLIOTT, WARD E. Y.   1975   *The Rise of Guardian Democracy: The Supreme Court's Role in Voting Rights Disputes, 1845–1969.* Cambridge, Mass.: Harvard University Press.

MUNDT-NIXON BILL
(1948–1949)

Karl Mundt of South Dakota and RICHARD M. NIXON of California, members of the HOUSE COMMITTEE ON UN-AMERICAN ACTIVITIES, sponsored the first anticommunist bill of the Cold War era. They contended that a house-cleaning of the executive department and a full exposure of past derelictions regarding communists would come only from a body in no way corrupted by ties to the administration. The measure (HR 5852) contained antisedition provisions but also reflected the view that the constitutional way to fight communists was by forcing them out into the open. The bill thus would have required the Communist party and "front" organizations to register with the Department of Justice and supply names of officers and members. It would also require that publications of these organizations, when sent through the mails, be labeled "published in compliance with the laws of the United States, governing the activities of agents of foreign principals."

The measure passed the House by a large margin but failed in the Senate after becoming a controversial factor in the presidential campaign of 1948. The bill was denounced by the Republican candidate, Thomas E. Dewey, and numerous respected national publications as a form of unwarranted thought control.

PAUL L. MURPHY

(SEE ALSO: *Subversive Activities and the Constitution.*)

Bibliography

COHEN, MURRAY and FUCHS, ROBERT F. 1948 Communism's Challenge and the Constitution. *Cornell Law Quarterly* 34:182–219, 352–375.

MUNICIPAL BANKRUPTCY ACT
48 Stat. 798 (1934)

This legislation, amending the Bankruptcy Act of 1898, declared "a national emergency caused by increasing financial difficulties of many local governmental units." Hearings on the bill disclosed that over 2,000 municipalities in all forty-eight states were in default—including such cities as Detroit and Miami—to an estimated total of nearly three billion dollars. The act conferred ORIGINAL JURISDICTION on federal bankruptcy courts in proceedings for the relief of "any municipality or other political subdivision of any State." Such taxing districts were thus enabled to file petitions asserting their inability to meet their debts. The act required submission of a "plan of readjustment" to accommodate a municipality's debts. The courts could enforce a plan that was "fair [and] equitable" and was approved by either two-thirds or three-quarters of the creditors, depending on the nature of the district. Section 80(k) stated that "nothing contained in this chapter shall be construed to limit or impair the power of any State to control . . . any political subdivision" and required state approval of these bankruptcy petitions.

A 5–4 Supreme Court invalidated this act in ASHTON V. CAMERON COUNTY WATER DISTRICT (1936), but the Court sustained a substantially similar act in *United States v. Bekins* (1938).

DAVID GORDON

Bibliography

JACKSON, ROBERT H. 1941 *The Struggle for Judicial Supremacy.* New York: Knopf.

MUNICIPAL IMMUNITY

Although precise practice varied among the states, two distinctions shaped municipalities' COMMON LAW liability. First, cities were immune from harms resulting from the exercise of governmental functions, such as fire protection, but they were not immune for harms attending proprietary functions, such as running a business. This sovereignlike immunity drew upon cities' legal connection to sovereign states, but it was independent of the ELEVENTH AMENDMENT immunity which states enjoy from suit in federal court. Since *Lincoln County v. Luning* (1890), cities and counties have not been viewed as part of the state for Eleventh Amendment purposes. Second, courts distinguished between discretionary functions, for which cities were immune, and ministerial activities, for which cities were not immune. As long as municipal liability was largely a branch of common law liability, courts articulated no significant distinctions between the treatment of federal claims against cities and claims brought under state law.

MONROE V. PAPE (1961), which reinvigorated SECTION 1983, TITLE 42, UNITED STATES CODE, and transformed the liability of state and local officials for violations of federal law into a question of federal statutory interpretation, laid the groundwork for greater municipal liability for violations of federal rights. But *Monroe* also retarded this development by interpreting section 1983 not to authorize suits against municipalities for violations of federal law. Indeed, the Court suggested that Congress doubted its constitutional authority to do so.

Between 1961 and 1978 litigants employed, with mixed success, various techniques to exploit *Monroe*'s federalization of official liability law, while at the same time avoiding *Monroe*'s holding that section 1983 did not authorize suits against cities. While these techniques were still developing, MONELL V. DEPARTMENT OF SOCIAL SERVICES (1978) drastically changed the law of municipal liability. *Monell* reinterpreted the legislative history relied on in *Monroe*, concluded that Congress had meant to subject cities to suit for violations of federal law, and overruled *Monroe*'s limitation on suits against cities. But *Monell* also held that Congress had not intended cities to be liable merely because they had employed an individual wrongdoer. Under *Monell,* cities are liable for violation of federal law only if the violation is "by its lawmakers or by those whose edicts or acts may fairly be said to represent official policy."

The question whether an alleged violation of federal law may be characterized as official policy became even more critical when, in OWEN V. CITY OF INDEPENDENCE (1980), the Court held that cities may not rely on the good faith defense available to individual officials as part of the law of EXECUTIVE IMMUNITY. *Owen* also severed the final links between municipalities' common law immunities and their modern amenability to suit under federal law. The Court rejected reliance by cities on sovereign-based immunities; a higher sovereign, the United States, had in section 1983 commanded municipal liability. The immunity for discretionary acts fell because "a municipality has no 'discretion' to violate the Federal Constitution." Cities achieved a modest victory when, in *City of Newport v. Fact Concerts, Inc.* (1981), the Court reaffirmed their traditional immunity from punitive damages claims.

THEODORE EISENBERG

Bibliography
SCHNAPPER, ERIC   1979   Civil Rights Litigation After *Monell. Columbia Law Review* 79:213–266.

MUNN v. ILLINOIS

See: Granger Cases

MURDOCK v. PENNSYLVANIA
319 U.S. 105 (1943)

A city ordinance required anyone offering goods for sale or engaged in solicitation (as opposed to sale from fixed premises) to obtain a license and pay a fee. Jehovah's Witnesses charged with violating the ordinance challenged it as a violation of the free exercise clause of the FIRST AMENDMENT.

Justice WILLIAM O. DOUGLAS, delivering the OPINION OF THE COURT, held that although the Witnesses offered literature for sale, their activity was "as evangelical as the revival meeting," occupying the same high estate under the First Amendment as worship in churches and preaching from pulpits. On the same day the Court vacated the judgment in *Jones v. Opelika* (1942), where the Court had previously upheld such an ordinance against a similar challenge.

Justice STANLEY F. REED dissented, arguing that JONES V. OPELIKA had been correctly decided. Justices OWEN ROBERTS, FELIX FRANKFURTER, and ROBERT H. JACKSON joined Reed's dissent. Justice Frankfurter also dissented separately, arguing that persons are not constitutionally "exempt from taxation merely because they may be engaged in religious activities or because such activities may constitute the exercise of a constitutional right."

Murdock represented a step away from the traditional doctrine of REYNOLDS V. UNITED STATES (1879) which had held that otherwise valid secular regulations could be enforced against nonconforming behavior even if that behavior were religiously motivated. (See RELIGIOUS LIBERTY.)

RICHARD E. MORGAN

MURPHY, FRANK
(1890–1949)

President FRANKLIN D. ROOSEVELT appointed Frank Murphy to the Supreme Court in 1940. Murphy, who had been mayor of Detroit and governor of Michigan, was ATTORNEY GENERAL at the time of his appointment as a Justice. As attorney general he created the Civil Rights Section (now division) of the Department of Justice and supported a vigorous antitrust program. As spokesman for the Supreme Court in constitutional matters, Murphy made modest but significant contributions. But as author of CONCURRING and DISSENTING OPINIONS in constitutional areas of individual freedom, Murphy voiced some of the more eloquent and impassioned defenses of human liberty in the Court's history.

Murphy's tenure on the Court spanned the decade of the 1940s. That period witnessed the consolidation of the federal and state power to deal with pressing economic and social problems. Murphy eagerly joined in this judicial retreat from the philosophy of LOCHNER V. NEW YORK (1905). Murphy's contribution to the de-Lochnerization of constitutional law was highlighted by his opinions for the Court in *North American Co. v. Securities & Exchange Commission* (1946) and *American Power & Light Co. v. Securities & Exchange Commission* (1946). Those decisions validated the "death sentence" clauses of the PUBLIC UTILITY HOLDING COMPANY ACT OF 1935, the last major piece of New Deal legislation to be challenged. In language reminiscent of JOHN MARSHALL's language in GIBBONS V. OGDEN (1824), Murphy declared that the COMMERCE CLAUSE is "an affirmative power commensurate with the national needs." It gives Congress authority "to undertake to solve national problems directly and realistically, giving due recognition to the scope of state power," as well as to other constitutional provisions.

His first assignment to write a Court opinion produced a historic chapter in the development of FREEDOM OF SPEECH. In THORNHILL V. ALABAMA (1940) the Court held an Alabama antipicketing statute unconstitutional on its face. Murphy wrote that information concerning labor disputes is "within the area of free discussion . . . guaranteed by the Constitution." Such speech can be abridged only if there is a CLEAR AND PRESENT DANGER that substantive evils may arise before the merits of the discussion can be tested in the market of public opinion. The Court, though later permitting certain "time, place, and manner" restrictions on picketing, has never repudiated the *Thornhill* doctrine.

Another landmark free speech opinion written by Murphy was CHAPLINSKY V. NEW HAMPSHIRE (1942). Although controversial, the decision proved to be an influential forerunner of the Court's doctrinal notion that certain kinds of speech are of such slight social value as not to deserve full FIRST AMENDMENT protection. Such speech, said Murphy, includes "the lewd and obscene, the profane, the libelous, and the insulting or 'FIGHTING' WORDS—those which by their very utterance inflict injury or tend to incite an immediate BREACH OF THE PEACE."

Murphy also made a provocative contribution to the once raging judicial battle over whether the FOURTEENTH AMENDMENT totally or only selectively incorporates the BILL OF RIGHTS. While agreeing with Justice HUGO L. BLACK's total INCORPORATION DOCTRINE, Murphy in a dissent in ADAMSON V. CALIFORNIA (1947) proposed an "incorporation-plus" approach. A state proceeding, he wrote, may be so wanting in DUE PROCESS as to warrant constitutional condemnation "despite the absence of a specific provision in the Bill of Rights." Murphy's suggestion has proved functionally similar to the Court's final choice of the "selective incorporation approach."

Murphy was seldom assigned to write majority opinions in other constitutional areas. Among the few that he did write were the short-lived Fourth Amendment opinion in TRUPIANO V. UNITED STATES (1948) and the influential FULL FAITH AND CREDIT opinion in *Industrial Commission v. McCartin* (1947). Thus

most of his deeply held views on the constitutional rights of individuals had to find expression in concurring and dissenting opinions. Through these he developed his judicial philosophy and expressed his ardent opposition to restricting the constitutional rights of racial and religious minorities, the economically disadvantaged, and those accused of crime.

The most durable and the most highly praised of all these individualized opinions is his dissent from what Murphy called "this legalization of racism" in KOREMATSU V. UNITED STATES (1944). The Court there upheld the wartime relocation of all persons of Japanese ancestry residing on the West Coast. Murphy dissected the military report upon which the relocation was based, and found the report filled with discredited and questionable racial and sociological factors beyond the realm of expert military judgment. To Murphy, the relocation was nothing more than racial discrimination that was "utterly revolting among a free people who have embraced the principles set forth in the Constitution of the United States." This dissent has been described by commentators as a classic in Supreme Court literature, and as one that "should be engraved in stone."

In *Falbo v. United States* (1944), Justice Murphy wrote that the law "knows no finer hour than when it cuts through formal concepts and transitory emotions to protect unpopular citizens against discrimination and persecution." His instinctive empathy for the constitutional rights of the oppressed and the unpopular constitutes Murphy's lasting contribution to the development of constitutional law.

EUGENE GRESSMAN

Bibliography

FINE, SIDNEY 1984 *Frank Murphy: The Washington Years.* Ann Arbor: University of Michigan Press.
HOWARD, J. WOODFORD 1968 *Mr. Justice Murphy.* Princeton, N.J.: Princeton University Press.

MURPHY v. FLORIDA
421 U.S. 794 (1975)

Jack "Murph the Surf" Murphy appealed a Florida robbery conviction. He claimed that he was denied a FAIR TRIAL because the jurors learned about his previous robbery and murder convictions, and about the circumstances of the instant case, from newspaper reports. The Supreme Court, 8–1, sustained his conviction.

Speaking through Justice THURGOOD MARSHALL, the Court held that juror exposure to information concerning the accused does not presumptively deny DUE PROCESS OF LAW. Since the VOIR DIRE did not discover juror hostility and there was no inflamed community sentiment, the totality of circumstances did not show inherent or actual prejudice.

DENNIS J. MAHONEY

(SEE ALSO: *Free Press/Fair Trial.*)

MURPHY v. FORD
390 F. Supp. 1372 (1975)

On September 8, 1974, President GERALD R. FORD granted to his predecessor, RICHARD M. NIXON, a "full, free and absolute pardon . . . for all offenses" that he might have committed while President. A Michigan lawyer brought suit in federal District Court for a DECLARATORY JUDGMENT invalidating the pardon. The District Court judge dismissed the suit, holding that the PARDONING POWER is unlimited, except in cases of IMPEACHMENT, and may as properly be exercised before criminal proceedings begin as after conviction. Citing THE FEDERALIST, the judge argued that the intention of the Framers in establishing the pardoning power was to provide for just such instances.

DENNIS J. MAHONEY

(SEE ALSO: *Articles of Impeachment [Nixon]; Watergate and the Constitution.*)

MURPHY v. WATERFRONT COMMISSION OF N.Y. HARBOR

See: Two Sovereignties Rule

MURRAY, WILLIAM
(Lord Mansfield)
(1705–1793)

The leading Tory constitutionalist of the eighteenth century, William Murray was appointed a judge after a career as a barrister and parliamentarian and service as attorney general. As Baron (later Earl) Mansfield, he was Lord Chief Justice of the Court of King's Bench from 1756 until 1788. He was active in the debates of the House of Lords and served for fifteen years in the cabinet. He opposed repeal of the Stamp Act in 1766, arguing that since the colonists were virtually represented in Parliament their complaints of TAXA-TION WITHOUT REPRESENTATION were without merit. Mansfield was a firm advocate of coercion in dealing with America, and he was the author of the Quebec Act of 1775.

In the WILKES CASES of 1763–1770 he held GENERAL WARRANTS illegal. He was tolerant of religious deviance and disapproved of prosecution of either Roman Catholic recusants or Protestant dissenters. In SOMERSET'S CASE (1772) he freed an escaped slave who had been recaptured in England, ruling that slavery was too odious to be supported by COMMON LAW. In SEDITIOUS LIBEL cases he allowed the jury to decide only the fact of publication, reserving the question of law—whether the published words were libelous—to be decided by the judge.

DENNIS J. MAHONEY

MURRAY'S LESSEE v. HOBOKEN LAND & IMPROVEMENT COMPANY
18 Howard 272 (1856)

This case raised the question whether an act of Congress provided DUE PROCESS OF LAW in the proceedings it laid down for exacting payments due to the treasury by collectors of the customs. For the first time the Supreme Court expounded the meaning of due process of law, which limited all branches of government. The Court interpreted due process exclusively in terms of PROCEDURAL DUE PROCESS. The settled usages and modes of proceedings in English law, "before the emigration of our ancestors," that were not unsuited to the civil and political conditions of America constituted due process.

LEONARD W. LEVY

MUSKRAT v. UNITED STATES
219 U.S. 346 (1911)

In one of a series of TEST CASES, the Court here refused to hear the suits involved because the parties failed to meet the constitutional requirement of CASES OR CONTROVERSIES (Article III, section 2). Congress had authorized certain INDIANS to sue the United States in the COURT OF CLAIMS and directed the ATTORNEY GENERAL to defend. The object was to determine the validity of certain congressional acts regarding Indian lands. The Court dismissed the suits, denying that Congress had the authority to create a case and designate parties to it.

DAVID GORDON

(SEE ALSO: *Ashwander v. Tennessee Valley Authority*, 1936; *Collusive Suit.*)

MYERS v. UNITED STATES
272 U.S. 52 (1926)

An 1876 statute authorized presidential appointment and removal of postmasters with the ADVICE AND CONSENT of the Senate. (See APPOINTING AND REMOVAL POWER.) President WOODROW WILSON appointed Myers with Senate consent but later removed him without consulting that body. Myers filed suit in the COURT OF CLAIMS and appealed that court's adverse decision to the Supreme Court.

Chief Justice, and former President, WILLIAM HOWARD TAFT, in a broad construction of Article II, found the statute unconstitutional. For a 6–3 majority he insisted upon the necessity for the nation's chief executive officer to be able to remove subordinates freely: "To hold otherwise would make it impossible for the President . . . to take care that the laws be faithfully executed."

Justices OLIVER WENDELL HOLMES, JAMES C. McREYNOLDS, and LOUIS D. BRANDEIS dissented. Brandeis declared that implying an unrestricted power of removal from the power of appointment "involved an unnecessary and indefensible limitation upon the constitutional power of Congress." History and present state practice demonstrated "a decided tendency to limit" the executive's removal power, and he also cited the DOCTRINES of CHECKS AND BALANCES and the SEPARATION OF POWERS.

The Court limited the doctrinal reach of *Myers* in HUMPHREY'S EXECUTOR V. UNITED STATES (1935).

DAVID GORDON

NAACP v. ALABAMA
357 U.S. 449 (1958)

In this decision the Supreme Court first recognized a FREEDOM OF ASSOCIATION guaranteed by the FIRST AMENDMENT. Alabama, charging that the NAACP had failed to qualify as an out-of-state CORPORATION, had sought an INJUNCTION preventing the association from doing business in the state. In that proceeding, the state obtained an order that the NAACP produce a large number of its records. The association substantially complied, but refused to produce its membership lists. The trial court ruled the NAACP in contempt and fined it $100,000. The state supreme court denied review, and the U.S. Supreme Court unanimously reversed.

Justice JOHN MARSHALL HARLAN wrote for the Court. First, the NAACP had STANDING to assert its members' claims; to rule otherwise would be to require an individual member to forfeit his or her political privacy in the act of claiming it. On the constitutional merits, Harlan wrote: "Effective advocacy . . . is undeniably enhanced by group association"; thus "state action which may have the effect of curtailing the freedom to associate is subject to the closest scrutiny." The privacy of association may be a necessary protection for the freedom to associate "where a group espouses dissident beliefs." Here, disclosure of NAACP membership in Alabama during a time of vigorous civil rights activity had been shown to result in members' being fired from their jobs, physically threatened, and otherwise harassed. Only a COMPEL-LING STATE INTEREST could justify this invasion of political privacy. That compelling interest was not shown here. The names of the NAACP's rank-and-file members had no substantial bearing on the state's interest in assuring compliance with its corporation law.

This same technique—solemnly accepting the state's account of its purposes, ignoring possible improper motives, and concluding that those state interests were not "compelling"—was employed in other cases involving efforts by southern states to force disclosures of NAACP membership such as *Bates v. Little Rock* (1960) and *Shelton v. Tucker* (1960).

KENNETH L. KARST

(SEE ALSO: *Gibson v. Florida Legislative Investigation Commission, 1963.*)

NAACP v. BUTTON
371 U.S. 415 (1962)

The Supreme Court held that Virginia statutes forbidding one person to advise another that his legal rights had been violated and to refer him to a particular attorney were unconstitutional as applied to activities of the NAACP and its legal defense fund. The furtherance of litigation designed to challenge the constitutionality of RACIAL DISCRIMINATION was a mode of expression and association protected by the FIRST and FOURTEENTH AMENDMENTS. The Court acknowledged that INTEREST GROUP LITIGATION, aimed at changing constitutional law through TEST CASES, was not only professional legal activity subject to state regulation but also constitutionally protected political activity.

MARTIN SHAPIRO

(SEE ALSO: *NAACP Legal Defense & Educational Fund.*)

NAACP v. CLAIBORNE HARDWARE COMPANY

See: Labor and the Constitution

NAACP LEGAL DEFENSE & EDUCATIONAL FUND

The NAACP Legal Defense & Educational Fund, Inc., was founded in 1939 by board members of the National Association for the Advancement of Colored People to conduct the legal program of the association through a corporation qualified to receive tax deductible contributions. The association was not tax exempt, because it lobbied. Board members of the association served on the board of the Fund; the Fund's director and some of its lawyers also were employees of the association.

In 1957 the Internal Revenue Service (IRS) objected to the interlocking staff and board because it enabled an organization not tax exempt to influence one entitled to tax exemption. The IRS required termination of the interlocking arrangement. Thereafter the Fund and the association were no longer formally linked, and the Fund functioned entirely independently with its own board, staff, budget, and policies. The Fund has since represented individuals and organizations with no relationship to the association at all as well as members and branches of the association.

In 1984 the Fund's staff consisted of twenty-four lawyers, with offices in New York and Washington, D.C., and several hundred cooperating lawyers across the United States. Its budget was $6.7 million. It has served as a model for the public interest law movement generally, including other legal defense funds, such as those dealing with discrimination against Hispanics, Asians, women, the handicapped, homosexuals, and the aged, as well as public interest firms representing environmental, consumer, migrant worker, and other groups.

The Fund's director-counsel was THURGOOD MARSHALL, who served until 1961 and was succeeded by Jack Greenberg, who directed the organization until 1984, when he was succeeded by Julius L. Chambers.

The Fund has been involved in most of the leading cases dealing with racial discrimination in the United States, including BROWN V. BOARD OF EDUCATION (1954), which held unconstitutional racial SEGREGATION in public education, the principle of which was ultimately extended to all other governmental activities. *Brown* was the culmination of a planned litigation effort which built upon earlier Fund cases involving RACIAL DISCRIMINATION in graduate and professional schools. In the 1960s, the Fund provided representation in most of the cases generated by the CIVIL RIGHTS movement, including representation of MARTIN LUTHER KING, JR. Thereafter, following passage of the Civil Rights Acts of the mid-1960s, the Fund brought most of the leading cases enforcing those laws. The Fund has represented civil rights claimants in more than 2,000 cases dealing with education, employment, VOTING RIGHTS, housing, PRISONERS' RIGHTS, CAPITAL PUNISHMENT, health care, and other areas of the law.

JACK GREENBERG

Bibliography
RABIN, ROBERT L.   1976   Lawyers for Social Change: Perspectives on Public Interest Law. *Stanford Law Journal* 28:207–261.

NARCOTICS REGULATION

See: Drug Regulation

NARDONE v. UNITED STATES
302 U.S. 379 (1937)

After the Supreme Court largely exempted ELECTRONIC EAVESDROPPING from constitutional control in OLMSTEAD V. UNITED STATES (1928), protection against WIRETAPPING was sought legislatively. In 1934, Congress passed the COMMUNICATIONS ACT, section 605 of which provided that "no person" could intercept and divulge radio and wire communications. In *Nardone v. United States* the Supreme Court ruled that section 605 extended to federal agents; later the Court applied it also to state officers in *Benanti v. United States* (1957). The Justice Department construed section 605 very narrowly, however, and it was rarely invoked. It has been largely superseded by Title III of the OMNIBUS CRIME CONTROL AND SAFE STREETS ACT (1968).

HERMAN SCHWARTZ

NASHVILLE CONVENTION RESOLUTIONS
(1850)

Fearing that Congress might enact the WILMOT PROVISO, abolish the slave trade in the DISTRICT OF COLUMBIA, or adopt other antislavery measures, southern separatists called for a convention of slave states to meet at Nashville in June 1850. The convention adopted resolutions asserting that: the TERRITORIES were the joint property of the people of all the states; Congress could not discriminate among owners of different kinds of property in the territories, and hence could not exclude slaves; and the federal government must protect all forms of property, including slaves, in the territories. However, the moderates who dominated the convention added that if the free states refused to recognize these principles, the slave states would accept a division of the territories by extending the MISSOURI COMPROMISE line to the Pacific, an extraordinary concession on the central constitutional issue that disgusted the radicals. A poorly attended adjourned session of the convention, dominated by radicals, met in November 1850, denounced the COMPROMISE OF 1850, advocated SECESSION, but proposed no immediate program. The resolutions of the Nashville Convention are thus significant principally as an indication of the slave states' inability to unite on a secessionist platform.

WILLIAM M. WIECEK

(SEE ALSO: *Slavery and the Constitution.*)

Bibliography
POTTER, DAVID M. 1976 *The Impending Crisis, 1848–1861.* New York: Harper & Row.

NATIONAL ASSOCIATION FOR THE ADVANCEMENT OF COLORED PEOPLE

See: NAACP Legal Defense & Educational Fund

NATIONAL EMERGENCIES ACT

See: Emergency Powers

NATIONAL ENVIRONMENTAL POLICY ACT

See: Environmental Regulation

NATIONAL INDUSTRIAL RECOVERY ACT
48 Stat. 195 (1933)

The National Industrial Recovery Act (NIRA) was the best-known and, perhaps, in President FRANKLIN D. ROOSEVELT's words, "the most important and far-reaching legislation ever enacted" by the New Deal Congress. The act was designed to curb unemployment, stimulate business recovery, and end the competitive wars of the Great Depression. By May 1935, over 750 codes covering some twenty-three million people had been created under the NIRA's authority. Even before Roosevelt's inauguration, his "brain trust" had begun to plan a recovery bill. Introduced May 17, 1933, the bill raised questions of constitutionality. Congress passed it, however, and Roosevelt signed it into law on June 16.

The act declared a national emergency and justified congressional action under the COMMERCE CLAUSE and the GENERAL WELFARE CLAUSE. Section 2 established the National Recovery Administration (NRA) to supervise the NIRA, limiting its operation to two years. The heart of the act, section 3, provided for the framing of "codes of fair competition" by private businessmen and trade associations. After meeting certain requirements and obtaining presidential approval, these codes became "standards of fair competition" with the full force of federal law, regulating industrywide prices, wages, and practices. Such an extraordinary DELEGATION OF POWER was unprecedented: it allowed private citizens to draft codes to rule industry and provided, at best, minimal policy guidelines and standards. Violations of the codes "in any transaction in or affecting INTERSTATE or FOREIGN COMMERCE [were] deemed an unfair method of competition in commerce within the meaning of the FEDERAL TRADE COMMISSION ACT." Upon complaint or failure of an industry to formulate a code, the President could establish a compulsory code. Section 7 prescribed three mandatory provisions for every code: availability of COLLECTIVE BARGAINING, employee freedom from coercion to join or refrain from joining a union, and compliance with regulated MAXIMUM HOURS AND MINIMUM WAGES. The various clauses of this section constituted the broadest regulation of wages and hours in American history to that date. The NRA also incorporated in its "blanket code" a provision outlawing child labor in industries without specific codes. Although the NIRA prohibited monopolies and monopolistic practices, it exempted code-covered industries from the antitrust laws. Title II of the NIRA established a Public Works Administration to stimulate construction and, by spending its $3.3 billion budget, to increase purchasing power.

Serious questions of the act's constitutionality eventually reached the Supreme Court, however, and in SCHECHTER POULTRY CORP. V. UNITED STATES (1935) a unanimous Court voided the NIRA for unconstitutionally delegating power to the President and exceeding the limits of the commerce power. Despite this decision and PANAMA REFINING COMPANY V. RYAN (1935), invalidating other provisions, Congress gradually replaced the act with new and more effective legislation. Although historians debate whether the NRA impeded or encouraged recovery and reform, the lessons of this experiment in economic planning provided valuable experience for drafting later legislation such as the WAGNER (NATIONAL LABOR RELATIONS) and FAIR LABOR STANDARDS ACTS.

DAVID GORDON

Bibliography

LYON, LEVERETT S. ET AL. 1935 *The National Recovery Administration: An Analysis and Appraisal.* Washington, D.C.: Brookings Institution.
ROOS, CHARLES F. 1937 *NRA Economic Planning.* Bloomington: Indiana University Press.

NATIONAL LABOR RELATIONS ACTS

See: Taft-Hartley Act; Wagner Act

NATIONAL LEAGUE OF CITIES v. USERY
426 U.S. 833 (1976)

This case proved that obituaries for DUAL FEDERALISM were premature. It arose after Congress amended the FAIR LABOR STANDARDS ACT (FLSA), in 1974, to extend wages-and-hours coverage to nearly all public employees. Several states, cities, and intergovernmental organizations sought to enjoin enforcement of the new provisions. Admitting that the employees in question would come within the federal commerce power if they worked in the private sector, the plaintiffs argued that congressional regulation of employment conditions for state and municipal workers violated "the established constitutional DOCTRINE of INTERGOVERNMENTAL IMMUNITY." A three-judge district court disagreed, ruling that under MARYLAND V. WIRTZ (1968), which had upheld the application of

WAGES AND HOURS REGULATIONS to public schools and hospitals, an employee's public status was irrelevant to the scope of congressional authority. On APPEAL, the Supreme Court reversed the lower court, 5–4, holding that the FLSA amendments could not constitutionally be applied to public employees performing "traditional governmental functions."

Writing for the Court, Justice WILLIAM H. REHNQUIST initially confronted the sweep of the COMMERCE CLAUSE recognized in GIBBONS V. OGDEN (1824). The grant of congressional power was plenary, he conceded, but did not override "affirmative limitations" on Congress. The TENTH AMENDMENT provided the most explicit source for such a limitation, for in FRY V. UNITED STATES (1975) the Court had offered the dictum that the amendment "expressly declared the constitutional policy that Congress may not exercise power in a fashion that impairs the States' integrity or their ability to function effectively in a federal system." Yet Rehnquist emphasized a less explicit limitation—the overall federal structure. Within it, states perform essential governmental functions, and state decisions about these functions, which include fire protection and law enforcement, must be free from federal interference. Wages and hours legislation constituted a forbidden infringement, because it "operate[s] directly to displace the States' freedom to structure integral operations in areas of traditional governmental functions. . . ." Indeed, he expressly held the Court had wrongly decided *Wirtz*.

But the meaning of *National League of Cities* as precedent is not clear. Justice HARRY A. BLACKMUN qualified his crucial fifth vote with a concurrence that interpreted the Court as "adopt[ing] a balancing approach." For him, the decision did not preclude regulation of states in areas, such as environmental protection, where the federal interest was demonstrably greater. And the Court itself expressly left open the power of Congress to regulate even traditional state functions by employing the TAXING AND SPENDING POWER or by enforcing the FOURTEENTH AMENDMENT. (See FITZPATRICK V. BITZER, 1976.)

In dissent, Justice WILLIAM J. BRENNAN charged that the decision contained "an ominous portent of destruction of our constitutional structure" and delivered a "catastrophic body blow" to the commerce power. In his view, Rehnquist had misread earlier case law and had abandoned the plain meanings of the commerce and SUPREMACY CLAUSES. Moreover, Rehnquist's "essential function test" was "conceptually unworkable," for it failed to clarify the distinction between essential and other state activities.

The Court's opinion did lack a reasoned test for

determining the essential functions of states *"qua states."* It also ran counter to forty years of judicial acceptance of broad congressional power under the commerce clause. Accordingly, *National League of Cities* led to further litigation over state immunity from federal regulation and injected the Supreme Court into issues long dormant. In GARCIA V. SAN ANTONIO METROPOLITAN TRANSIT AUTHORITY (1985) a different 5–4 majority flatly overruled *National League of Cities,* but the dissenters promised that disinterment of the 1976 decision awaited only one more vote.

CHARLES A. LOFGREN

Bibliography

BARBER, SOTIRIOS A. 1976 *National League of Cities v. Usery:* New Meaning for the Tenth Amendment? *Supreme Court Review* 1976:161–182.

LOFGREN, CHARLES A. 1980 The Origins of the Tenth Amendment: History, Sovereignty, and the Problem of Constitutional Intention. Pages 331–357 in Ronald K. L. Collins (ed.), *Constitutional Government in America.* Durham, N.C.: Carolina Academic Press.

NAGEL, ROBERT F. 1981 Federalism as a Fundamental Value: *National League of Cities* in Perspective. *Supreme Court Review* 1981:81–109.

NATIONAL POLICE POWER

The "national police power" is not, strictly speaking, a constitutional power of Congress. Rather, it is a phrase describing the power of Congress, acting under the enumerated powers, to enact "police legislation." The term "police legislation" includes criminal law as well as health, morals, safety, antidiscrimination, and environmental statutes.

Under our federal system, national police power regulation has always been controversial. Police matters are historically state or local concerns, and yet some problems seem to call for a national solution. The recurring issues, therefore, are whether Congress should address a problem that has historically been attacked at the state or local level and whether the courts can articulate any principled limits on congressional power to do so.

The Constitution provides a number of sources of power for national police legislation. The most important are the congressional powers to regulate commerce, to tax, and to spend. However, several other powers should not be overlooked. The postal power makes possible laws to protect consumers from fraudulent or obscene materials transmitted through the mails, subject to significant First Amendment limita-

tions. The enabling clauses of the THIRTEENTH and FOURTEENTH AMENDMENTS open the way for a variety of antidiscrimination laws. (See JONES V. ALFRED H. MAYER CO. [1968], racial discrimination in housing; UNITED STATES V. GUEST [1966], violence against minorities in the use of public facilities.)

Because such local activities as manufacturing or gambling are not themselves interstate commerce, they are not, without more, subject to federal commerce clause regulation. However, constitutional developments during the twentieth century have marked out two techniques which, alone or in combination, permit virtually unlimited regulation of local activity under the aegis of the COMMERCE CLAUSE: prohibition of INTERSTATE COMMERCE and linking a local activity to an "effect" on interstate commerce.

A few early statutes prohibited particular forms of interstate commerce (such as transportation of diseased cattle or use of unsafe locomotives) because they physically endangered the stream of commerce. In 1895, however, Congress took a further critical step by prohibiting the interstate transportation of lottery tickets. Transportation of the tickets harmed nobody; Congress was obviously concerned that the use of the tickets in the receiving state was harmful to public morals. Thus the prohibition on transportation really was a technique to assist the states in stamping out national (or international) lotteries. Under traditional assumptions, of course, the regulation of gambling or of consumer fraud was a state responsibility, but individual state regulation of lotteries had proved ineffectual.

In CHAMPION V. AMES (1903), often referred to as "The Lottery Case," the Supreme Court upheld the federal statute by a 5–4 vote. The majority believed that the shipment of articles in interstate commerce that were harmful to the public safety or morals was a "misuse" of commerce, the prohibition of which lay well within the commerce power. This rationale paved the way for many later statutes which treated various goods or persons as "outlaws" of commerce and thus prohibited their shipment. For example, the courts upheld regulation or prohibition of interstate transportation of adulterated food, prostitutes, obscene literature, and stolen cars upon the authority of *Champion.* In addition, the Court upheld statutes banning the interstate shipment of items (such as liquor or goods produced by convict labor) that violated the laws of the receiving state.

In addition to permitting regulation of interstate transportation of goods, *Champion* provided authority for regulation of the use of the goods after they arrived. Finally, although most of the commerce-prohibition cases involved regulation of purely commercial activity, the Court in *Caminetti v. United States* (1917) found no constitutional objection to punishing a man for transporting a woman to whom he was not married across the state lines for immoral, but wholly noncommercial, purposes. (See HOKE V. UNITED STATES, 1913.)

The usefulness of the commerce-prohibiting technique suffered a temporary but sharp reverse after Congress decided to use it for the purpose of abolishing child labor. In HAMMER V. DAGENHART (1918) the Supreme Court held that Congress could not prohibit the transportation in interstate commerce of goods made by children, because the goods were lawfully produced in the state of origin and harmless both to interstate commerce and to users in the receiving state. The government tried to show that the law was necessary to achieve fair interstate competition, because states allowing child labor had an unfair advantage over those prohibiting it. The Court said that Congress had no power to equalize comparative advantages or disadvantages among the states.

Justices OLIVER WENDELL HOLMES'S dissent in *Hammer* seemingly demolished the majority opinion and ultimately became the law when UNITED STATES V. DARBY overruled *Hammer* in 1941. *Darby* made clear that Congress could prohibit the interstate shipment of harmless goods manufactured by workers whose wages or working hours violated the FAIR LABOR STANDARDS ACT. The Court in *Darby* accepted the theory, rejected by the *Hammer* majority, that Congress could use the commerce-prohibiting technique to improve labor conditions in the state of origin and to achieve fair competition among states. After *Darby*, therefore, there was no longer any obstacle to the achievement of police goals by the prohibition of interstate commerce in people or goods, absent the violation of some other constitutional norm.

In the landmark commerce clause case of GIBBONS V. OGDEN (1824) Chief Justice JOHN MARSHALL seemingly established that a local activity could be regulated by Congress under the commerce clause if the activity "affected" other states. Nevertheless there arose a confusing body of case law on the extent to which local affairs could be regulated because of their effect on interstate commerce. On the one hand, for example, the Shreveport case, HOUSTON, EAST AND WEST TEXAS RAILWAY V. UNITED STATES (1914), allowed the Interstate Commerce Commission to regulate intrastate railroad rates because low rates for intrastate hauls and high rates for interstate hauls unfairly discriminated against interstate commerce. On the other hand, early antitrust cases, including

UNITED STATES V. E. C. KNIGHT CO. (1895), cast doubt on Congress's power to regulate monopolies in manufacturing because manufacturing was considered local; the Court evidently assumed that granting regulatory power to the national government would prevent the states from regulating the activity.

In several cases during the 1930s, narrow majorities of the Supreme Court invalidated New Deal legislation that sought to regulate local activity affecting interstate commerce (such as labor relations in coal mining in CARTER V. CARTER COAL CO., 1936). By the late 1930s, however, these cases had been disapproved. By the time of WICKARD V. FILBURN (1942) there was no longer any doubt that Congress had power to regulate purely local and individually trivial activities which (when cumulated) substantially affected interstate commerce. In that case the Court ruled that Congress could regulate home consumption of wheat because of its aggregate effect on an interstate market.

Thus the "affecting commerce" rationale was available when Congress turned to national police legislation. The Fair Labor Standards Act not only prohibited interstate transportation of goods manufactured by persons whose wages or hours violated the act; it also directly prohibited the production of such goods for interstate commerce. *United States v. Darby* upheld the manufacturing prohibition on two distinct theories. The Court held that manufacturing could be prohibited (even if transportation had not been prohibited) because production of goods under substandard labor conditions was a form of unfair competition that substantially affected interstate commerce. In addition, the Court upheld the manufacturing ban as a necessary and proper incident of Congress's power to prohibit interstate transportation of the goods. This latter theory opened the way for Congress to ban virtually any local activity if it also bans interstate transportation of the persons who conduct the activity or the goods produced by it.

Congress has frequently resorted to the "affecting commerce" rationale when it pursues fundamentally noneconomic objectives. The Court has generously upheld federal statutes upon determining that Congress has "rationally" concluded that a local activity substantially affected commerce. For example, the Court upheld in KATZENBACH V. MCCLUNG (1964) a federal prohibition on racial discrimination, as applied to a restaurant that had purchased food from a local seller who had purchased it in interstate commerce. The Court's tenuous theory was that Congress could rationally conclude that discrimination in such restaurants decreased interstate sales of food.

(See HEART OF ATLANTA V. UNITED STATES, 1964.)

The "affecting commerce" rationale has opened the way for a vast expansion of federal criminal law. In PEREZ V. UNITED STATES (1971) the Court upheld a conviction under the federal loan-sharking statute, even though the defendant had no apparent contact with interstate commerce. In previous cases, such as *Katzenbach v. McClung*, the characteristic used to identify the regulated party had a connection to interstate commerce, but in *Perez*, the characteristic ("loan-sharking") had no such connection. However, the Court deferred to congressional findings that loansharking is used by multistate organized crime rings to raise or launder money to take over legitimate businesses. It then held that because loansharks as a "class" substantially affect interstate commerce, any member of the class can be reached by a federal criminal statute, regardless of the individual's actual interstate connections. Of course, this approach is drastically overinclusive, but it is justifiable because it is difficult to ascertain in a given case whether a particular loanshark has connections to organized crime and thus to interstate commerce. The *Perez* theory that Congress can criminalize an entire class, when some members of that class substantially affect interstate commerce, undergirds several other federal racketeering, gambling, and drug abuse statutes. (See LAW ENFORCEMENT AND FEDERAL–STATE RELATIONS.)

The "prohibiting commerce" and the "affecting commerce" techniques, used separately or together, thus provide the authority for virtually limitless expansion of national police power. Given only slight ingenuity in statute-drafting, a local activity which Congress wishes to regulate or prohibit can be linked somehow to interstate commerce.

Nevertheless, the Court has employed a number of low-visibility judicial techniques to slow the federalization of police power. It has frequently construed narrowly statutes that make unexpected intrusions into local domains, reasoning that Congress should clearly state its intention to expand national police power. Moreover, in construing federal criminal statutes, the Court takes into account its view of an appropriate balance between state and federal law enforcement. These constructional techniques require Congress at least to face and consider the implications of a drastic extension of federal power. Similarly, the Court may hold that an ambiguous criminal statute fails to give fair warning to those affected by it if a broad construction would punish essentially local activity.

In considering congressional police power under the commerce clause, the most important open question is whether a majority of the Supreme Court will hold that a "trivial" effect on interstate commerce is an insufficient foundation. A number of Justices have written that questions of degree are important to them and that the cumulative effect on commerce of the class of regulated activities must be "substantial." In several cases involving federal stripmining legislation, for example, including HODEL V. VIRGINIA SURFACE MINING AND RECLAMATION ASSOCIATION and *Hodel v. Indiana* (1981), the court unanimously upheld statutes which regulated stripmining on steep slopes and on farmland against claims that land use control is a uniquely local function. The Court found that Congress had acted rationally in identifying the environmental effects of stripmining as substantial burdens on interstate commerce and that the means chosen by Congress were rational. Two Justices wrote separately to emphasize that their concurrence was based on the substantiality of the effect. In the past, other Justices have expressed similar reservations. If a majority of the Supreme Court were actually to assess the substantiality of the effect on commerce of the class of regulated activities before upholding a statute, it would be much less clear than it seems today that the Constitution imposes no effective limit on the national police power under the commerce clause.

By using its power to tax an activity, Congress can discourage, regulate, or prohibit the activity. Consequently, a power intended to furnish Congress with the means for raising revenue can be effectively employed for police purposes. Occasional taxpayers have contended that a so-called tax is really regulatory in purpose and effect, and consequently not a tax at all. In early cases, such as UNITED STATES V. DOREMUS (1919), the Court upheld tax statutes with patently obvious regulatory goals, taking the tax label at face value. The court turned a blind eye to the fact that the tax would destroy the taxed business, that it produced little or no revenue, or that its administrative provisions were inappropriate for tax collection.

However, when Congress sought to prohibit child labor by taxing income from the sale of products made by children, the Court rebelled. In BAILEY V. DREXEL FURNITURE CO. (1922) it concluded that the tax was actually a regulatory measure, for it provided for a tax of ten percent on annual net income if the taxpayer knowingly used child labor on even a single occasion. Thus, said the Court, Congress had used the taxing power as a pretext for an attempt to regulate manufacturing—something it had previously held beyond Congress's power.

Ultimately, the court abandoned any effort to distinguish taxation from regulation. In upholding the federal gambling tax, which obviously was intended to stamp out illegal gambling rather than to raise revenue, the Court noted that a federal tax is valid even though it may destroy the taxed activity, raises little revenue, and contains enforcement provisions more appropriate to a criminal statute than a tax provision. In *United States v. Kahriger* (1953), decided over a strong dissent by Justice FELIX FRANKFURTER, the Court held that unless the tax law contains penalty or administrative provisions "extraneous to any tax need," it is valid.

The Court later limited its *Kahriger* precedent. MARCHETTI V. UNITED STATES (1968) held that the registration requirement for gamblers entailed coerced self-incrimination, in violation of the Fifth Amendment. Nevertheless, unless a tax runs afoul of a specific provision of the Bill of Rights, it seems unlikely that the Court will ever again seek to patrol the troubled border between taxation and regulation. There is little need for the distinction, now that virtually any activity it seeks to regulate through taxation could be easily reached through the commerce power.

Through its power to spend for the general welfare, Congress can enlist state or private cooperation in achieving an endless list of regulatory goals. All it needs to do is place conditions on offers of federal money. If the offer is sufficiently generous, the recipients are virtually certain to accept the conditions.

In the 1930s the Supreme Court made a doomed attempt to limit the traditional practice of regulation through conditional grants. It held that a federal program of payments to farmers, upon condition that they contractually agree to limit their acreage, was an invalid attempt to regulate agriculture and thus an incursion into a matter left to the states. In UNITED STATES V. BUTLER (1936) it declared that Congress could not purchase submission to a regulation that it could not impose directly.

The *Butler* prohibition on conditional spending lasted only a year. The SOCIAL SECURITY ACT contained a joint federal-state taxing and spending program to pay unemployment compensation. To induce the states to participate, Congress imposed a payroll tax on employers. However, a taxpayer received a credit of ninety percent of the federal tax if its state levied a payroll tax and adopted a system for distributing benefits that complied with the federal statute. As a practical matter, this credit, which had the effect of a federal expenditure, required states to participate in the program. Nevertheless, the court upheld that statute in STEWARD MACHINE COMPANY V. DAVIS (1937), approving the concept of "cooperative federal-

ism" and declaring that no state was coerced into adopting an unemployment compensation system. However, the Court indicated that it might have some doubts if the federal law imposed conditions that were unreasonable or unrelated in subject matter to legitimate national objectives or entailed surrender by states of quasi-sovereign powers.

Since *Steward Machine,* the Court has consistently upheld conditional spending programs in the few cases that have raised the issue. For example, in *Oklahoma v. Civil Service Commission* (1947) it sustained a system of conditional highway construction grants to states. A recipient state had to consent to a provision in the HATCH ACT precluding administration by any person involved in political campaigns. Because the state was free to reject federal funding, no coercion was involved.

Conditional federal grants have been used to achieve a wide variety of federal police objectives, particularly in the areas of environmental protection, affirmative action, education, and health services. However, in PENNHURST STATE SCHOOL V. HALDERMAN (1981) the Court sounded a warning. If a state is to be bound by a condition on its receipt of federal funds, the condition must be unambiguously stated in the statute. Otherwise, a state's acceptance might not have been knowing and voluntary. Like the requirement that Congress make a clear statement that it intends a criminal statute to reach an essentially local activity, the clear statement rule of *Pennhurst* requires Congress to focus on the issue of federalism when it adopts a conditional spending program.

Congress has ample power to achieve national police power objectives. The commerce clause, the postal, taxing, and spending power, and the enabling clauses of the Thirteenth and Fourteenth Amendments furnish authority for almost any conceivable expansion of national regulatory jurisdiction. However, the Court has suggested (sometimes in OBITER DICTUM) potential limitations on these powers which might someday be invoked to constrain an extension of federal authority.

Much more important than any judicially imposed limits are the political constraints on the national police power. Various structural elements of the national government assure sympathetic treatment for arguments based on federalism; for example, states opposing federal intrusion are protected by the fact that each state has two senators (regardless of population). Among other factors, state legislative control over House districting and the state-oriented organization of national political parties also assure respectful treatment for state or local contentions that extension of federal regulation is unnecessary. Similarly, the selection of the President by the Electoral College emphasizes the importance of states. The powerful representation of states at the national level, the tradition that police regulation is performed at the state level, and the inertia of Congress all work together to assure that intrusions by the national government into matters of state concern are likely to occur only when a broad national consensus emerges that centralization is necessary.

MICHAEL ASIMOW

Bibliography
CUSHMAN, ROBERT E. 1919 National Police Power under the Commerce Clause of the Constitution. *Minnesota Law Review* 3:289–319, 381–412, 452–483.
——— 1920 National Police Power under the Postal Power of the Constitution. *Minnesota Law Review* 4:402–440.
KADEN, LEWIS B. 1979 Politics, Money and State Sovereignty: The Judicial Role. *Columbia Law Review* 79:847–897.
STERN, ROBERT L. 1973 The Commerce Clause Revisited: Federalization of Intrastate Crime. *Arizona Law Review* 15:271–285.
WECHSLER, HERBERT 1954 The Political Safeguards of Federalism: The Role of the States in the Composition and Selection of the National Government. *Columbia Law Review* 54:543–560.

NATIONAL PROHIBITION CASES

See: Amending Process; Eighteenth Amendment

NATIONAL SECURITY ACT
69 Stat. 495 (1947)

This act embodies the most comprehensive reorganization ever undertaken of the means by which the WAR POWERS are to be exercised. The act unified the command of the armed forces, officially organized the Joint Chiefs of Staff, created the Air Force department, and established the office of secretary of defense. The separate army and navy establishments recognized in the Constitution, together with the air force, became a single, permanent "National Military Establishment."

Furthermore, the act erected, within the executive branch, the National Security Council. The original intention of Congress seems to have been to constrict the President's freedom of action in defense and FOREIGN AFFAIRS by prescribing the persons to be consulted and the manner of consultation in national security decision making. In fact, however, strong and politically skillful Presidents have used the council to strengthen their own positions, as, for example, President JOHN F. KENNEDY did during the Cuban missile crisis of 1962.

Under the National Security Council the act created the Central Intelligence Agency (CIA), with a broad charter to conduct foreign intelligence-gathering activities, as well as to process and disseminate intelligence gathered by other agencies. The act specifically prohibited domestic intelligence activities on the part of the CIA.

DENNIS J. MAHONEY

NATIONAL SECURITY AND THE FOURTH AMENDMENT

The right to individual privacy and the preservation of national security have jarred against each other for centuries. "National security cases . . . often reflect a convergence of First and FOURTH AMENDMENT values not present in cases of 'ordinary' crime," wrote Justice LEWIS F. POWELL for a unanimous Supreme Court in UNITED STATES V. UNITED STATES DISTRICT COURT (1972). The early English cases, such as the WILKES CASES (1763–1770), establishing the right to keep the government out of a home unless it has PROBABLE CAUSE and a judicially approved warrant to enter, arose from successful challenges by political dissidents to searches by royal officers hunting for seditious writings. Preventing such infringements on both personal security and free expression was the main purpose of the Fourth Amendment. Today, Presidents claim inherent executive power to break into homes, to make physical SEARCHES AND SEIZURES, to open mail, and to video-tape, WIRETAP, and bug—again in order to protect national security.

Where the surveillance is directed against national security threats by *domestic* groups or individuals, the Supreme Court has held that the President has no inherent executive power, and a warrant must first be obtained. The government's needs will not be presumed to outweigh the threats such a power poses for the rights of free speech and personal security; rather, a search against domestic threats must be approved in advance by a neutral magistrate. The Court did suggest that Congress could authorize less stringent procedures for domestic intelligence gathering than for crime detection, but so far Congress has not done so.

Foreign national security issues have been treated very differently. Courts have generally accepted the claim of inherent presidential power to use electronic surveillance, video-tapes, and physical entries against both foreigners and Americans in order to obtain foreign intelligence, without obtaining prior judicial approval. The power is justified on several grounds: the need for stealth, speed, and secrecy to counter foreign threats; the executive's superior experience and knowledge of FOREIGN AFFAIRS and the judiciary's relative lack of competence in such matters; and the executive's primacy in foreign affairs in the constitutional scheme. This power is limited to intelligence gathering, so that when the investigation becomes a criminal investigation and the warrantless interception is made for the purpose of gathering evidence for a prosecution, the requirements of Title III of the OMNIBUS CRIME CONTROL AND SAFE STREETS ACT must be satisfied. This inherent intelligence gathering power, moreover, can be exercised only by the President or the attorney general; a lower-level official cannot authorize intelligence-gathering break-ins or wiretaps on his own, without judicial approval.

In 1976, a Senate committee issued a massive documentation of the many abuses of Fourth Amendment rights perpetrated by executive officers and the intelligence agencies from the 1930s through the 1970s. The Central Intelligence Agency, for example, admitted wiretapping people it considered "left-wingers" both in this country and abroad in a project it called "Operation Chaos," even though the agency had no authority to operate domestically. It was trying to find links between antiwar groups and foreign powers, which were never found. The military eavesdropped on radio messages in the late 1960s and early 1970s in connection with civil disorders, with full knowledge that such eavesdropping was illegal. In 1969, President RICHARD M. NIXON authorized taps on four journalists and thirteen government employees, allegedly to discover who was leaking foreign affairs information; these taps were kept in operation for over two years even though it quickly became clear that nothing pertinent to the leaks was being learned.

In reaction to these revelations and to the Watergate abuses, Congress in 1978 banned electronic surveillance for foreign national security purposes within the United States, without prior judicial approval. Under the Foreign Intelligence Surveillance Act (FISA) the executive branch no longer has inherent power to tap and bug for foreign intelligence-gathering purposes. With the approval of the attorney general, a federal official may apply to a specially selected court (composed of regular federal judges) which sits in se-

cret. The court must issue a warrant if it finds probable cause to believe, first, that the target is a foreign power or agent, and, second, that certain procedures to minimize the interception have been set up; an American who, on behalf of a foreign power, engages in clandestine intelligence gathering that may involve criminal activity, may be considered a foreign agent, though not for activities protected by the FIRST AMENDMENT. Other control procedures are also established, though they are less stringent than those for electronic surveillance for crime detection under Title III. The FISA applies to foreign intelligence gathering by any type of electronic, mechanical, or other surveillance device, but not to physical break-ins, mail openings, and the like—these remain subject to the more traditional claims of inherent presidential power.

Although the FISA was held constitutional by a federal district court, there is still no definitive Supreme Court ruling on the existence of inherent executive power to break into homes for foreign national security purposes or to eavesdrop on Americans without a warrant.

HERMAN SCHWARTZ

Bibliography
CARR, JAMES G. 1977 (1981 supp.) *The Law of Electronic Surveillance.* New York: Clark Boardman.
SCHWARTZ, HERMAN 1977 *Taps, Bugs, and Fooling the People.* New York: Field Foundation.
UNITED STATES, CONGRESS, SENATE SELECT COMMITTEE TO STUDY GOVERNMENTAL OPERATIONS WITH RESPECT TO INTELLIGENCE ACTIVITIES 1976 *III Final Report.* 94th Congress, 2d session.

NATURAL GAS REGULATION

See: Economic Regulation

NATURALIZATION

Naturalization was defined by the Supreme Court in BOYD V. NEBRASKA EX REL. THAYER (1892) as "the act of adopting a foreigner, and clothing him with the privileges of a native citizen." Congress, under Article I, section 8, of the Constitution, has complete discretion to determine what classes of ALIENS are eligible for naturalization; an individual may claim naturalization as a right only upon compliance with the terms that Congress imposes. Exercising this discretion in the Immigration and Nationality Act of 1952, Congress denied eligibility to those persons who advocate the violent overthrow of the government and limited it to those who have resided in the United States for at least five years, are of "good moral character," and take an oath in open court to support and defend the Constitution, to bear true faith and allegiance to the same, and to bear arms or perform noncombative service in behalf of the United States.

Any naturalized citizen who is proved to have taken the oath of citizenship with mental reservations or to have concealed acts or affiliations that, under the law, would disqualify him for naturalization, is subject, upon these facts being conclusively shown in a proper proceeding, to cancellation of his certificate of naturalization. While this action remedies a fraud on the naturalization court that the United States would otherwise be powerless to correct, it subjects a naturalized citizen to possible loss of CITIZENSHIP from which native-born citizens are spared and thus arguably calls into question Justice WILLIAM O. DOUGLAS's announcement in *Schneider v. Rusk* (1964) that "the rights of citizenship of the native-born and of the naturalized person are of the same dignity and are co-extensive."

Although naturalization normally is accomplished through individual application and official response on the basis of general congressional rules, naturalization can also be extended to members of a group, without consideration of their individual fitness. Such collective naturalization can be authorized by Congress, as in cases of naturalization of all residents of an annexed TERRITORY or of a territory made a state, or by a treaty.

RALPH A. ROSSUM

Bibliography
GORDON, CHARLES and ROSENFIELD, HARRY N. 1984 *Immigration Law and Procedure*, Vol. 3, chaps. 14–18. New York: Matthew Bender.
HERTZ, MICHAEL T. 1976 Limits to the Naturalization Power. *Georgetown Law Journal* 64:1007–1045.

NATURAL LAW

See: Higher Law; Natural Rights

NATURAL RIGHTS AND THE CONSTITUTION

The Constitution as it came from the Philadelphia convention contained no bill of rights. Indeed, the word right (or rights) appears only once in it, and

there only in the context of Congress's power to promote the progress of science and useful arts "by securing for limited Times to Authors and Inventors the exclusive Right to their respective Writings and Discoveries" (Article 1, section 8). In the view of the Anti-Federalists, the Constitution should have begun with a statement of general principles, or of "admirable maxims," as PATRICK HENRY said in the Virginia ratifying debates, such as the statement in the VIRGINIA DECLARATION OF RIGHTS of 1776: "That all men are by nature equally free and independent, and have certain inherent rights, of which, when they enter a state of society, they cannot by any compact deprive or divest their posterity; namely, the enjoyment of life and liberty, with the means of acquiring and possessing property, and pursuing and obtaining happiness and safety." In short, a bill of rights ought to be affixed to the Constitution containing a statement of natural rights.

The Federalists disagreed. They conceded that the Constitution might properly contain a statement of *civil* rights, and they were instrumental in the adoption of the first ten amendments which we know as the BILL OF RIGHTS, but they were opposed to a general statement of first principles in the text of the Constitution. However true, such a statement, by reminding citizens of the right to abolish government, might serve to undermine government, even a government established on those principles. And, as Publius insisted, the Constitution was based on those principles: "the Constitution is itself, in every rational sense, and to every useful purpose, A BILL OF RIGHTS" (THE FEDERALIST #84). It is a bill of natural rights, not because it contains a compendium of those rights but because it is an expression of the natural right of everyone to govern himself and to specify the terms according to which he agrees to give up his natural freedom by submitting to the rules of civil government. The Constitution emanates from us, "THE PEOPLE of the United States," and here in its first sentence, said Publius, "is a better recognition of popular rights than volumes of those aphorisms which make the principal figure in several of our State bills of rights and which would sound much better in a treatise of ethics than in a constitution of government." Natural rights point or lead to government, a government with the power to secure rights, and only secondarily to limitations on governmental power.

This is not to deny the revolutionary character of natural rights, or perhaps more precisely, of the natural rights teaching. The United States began in a revolution accompanied by an appeal to the natural and unalienable rights of life, liberty, and the pursuit of happiness. But these words of the DECLARATION OF INDEPENDENCE are followed immediately by the statement that "to secure these rights, Governments are instituted among Men." Natural rights point or lead to government in the same way that the Declaration of Independence points or leads to the Constitution: the rights, which are possessed by all men equally by nature (or in the state of nature), require a well-governed civil society for their security.

The link between the state of nature and civil society, or between natural rights and government, is supplied by the laws of nature. The laws of nature in this (modern) sense must be distinguished from the natural law as understood in the Christian tradition, for example. According to Christian teaching, the natural law consists of commands and prohibitions derived from the inclinations (or the natural ordering of the passions and desires), and is enforced, ultimately, by the sanction of divine punishment. According to Hobbes and Locke, however—the principal authors in the school of natural rights—the laws of nature are merely deductions from the rights of nature and ultimately from the right of self-preservation. Because everyone has a natural right to do whatever is necessary to preserve his own life, the state of nature comes to be indistinguishable from the state of war where, in Hobbes's familiar phrase, life is solitary, poor, nasty, brutish, and short; even in Locke's more benign version, and for the same reason, the state of nature is characterized by many unendurable "inconveniences." In short, in the natural condition of man the enjoyment of natural rights is uncertain and human life itself becomes insufferable. What is required for self-preservation is peace, and, as rational beings, men can come to understand "the fundamental law of nature" which is, as Hobbes formulates it, "to seek peace, and follow it." From this is derived the second law of nature, that men enter in a contract with one another according to which they surrender their natural rights to an absolute sovereign who is instituted by the contract and who, from that time forward, represents their rights. More briefly stated, each person must consent to be governed, which he does by laying down his natural right to govern himself. In Locke's version, political society is formed when everyone "has quitted his natural power"—a power he holds as of natural right—and "resigned it up into the hands of the community." In the same way, Americans of 1776 were guided by "the Laws of Nature and of Nature's God" when they declared their independence and constituted themselves as a new political community. Commanding nothing—for these are not laws in the proper sense of commands that must be obeyed—the laws of nature point to government as the way to secure rights, a government that derives its "just powers from the consent of the governed." (See SOCIAL COMPACT THEORY.)

It is important to understand that in the natural rights teaching neither civil society nor government exists by nature. By nature everyone is sovereign with respect to himself. Civil society is an artificial person to which this real person, acting in concert with others, surrenders his natural and sovereign powers, and upon this agreement civil society becomes the sovereign with respect to those who consented to the surrender. It is civil society, in the exercise of this sovereign power, that institutes and empowers government. So it was that "we [became] the People of the United States" in 1776 and, in 1787–1788, that we ordained and established "this CONSTITUTION for the United States of America." The Constitution is the product of the "will" of the sovereign people of the United States (The Federalist #78).

The power exercised by this people is almost unlimited. Acting through its majority, the people is free to determine the form of government (for, as the Declaration of Independence indicates, any one of several forms of government—democratic, republican, or even monarchical—may serve to secure rights) as well as the organization of that government and the powers given and withheld from it. It will make these decisions in the light of its purpose, which is to secure the rights of the persons authorizing it. This is why the doctrine of natural rights, if only secondarily, leads or points to limitations on government; and this is why the people of the United States decided to withhold some powers and, guided by the new "science of politics" (The Federalist #9), sought to limit power by means of a number of institutional arrangements.

Among the powers withheld was the power to coerce religious opinion. Government can have authority over natural rights, said THOMAS JEFFERSON, "only as we have submitted [that authority] to them, [and] the rights of conscience we never submitted, we could not submit."

Among the institutional arrangements was the SEPARATION OF POWERS, and the scheme of representation made possible by extending "the sphere of society so as to take in a greater variety of parties and interests thus making it less probable that a majority of the whole will have a common motive to invade the rights of other citizens" (The Federalist #10). First among these rights, according to Locke, is the property right, for, differing somewhat from Hobbes in this respect, Locke understood the natural right of self-preservation primarily as the right to acquire property. Publius had this in mind when he said that "the first object of government . . . [is] the protection of different and unequal faculties of acquiring property" (*The Federalist* #10). The large (commercial) republic is a means of securing this natural right as well as the natural right of conscience, for, within its spacious boundaries, there will be room for a "multiplicity of [religious] sects" as well as a "multiplicity of [economic] interests" (*The Federalist* #51).

Just as a "respect to the opinions of mankind" required Americans to announce the formation of a people that was assuming its "separate and equal station . . . among the powers of the earth," so a jealous concern for their natural rights required this people to *write* a Constitution in which they not only empowered government but, in various complex ways, limited it.

WALTER BERNS

Bibliography

JAFFA, HARRY V. 1975 *The Conditions of Freedom: Essays in Political Philosophy.* Pages 149–160. Baltimore: Johns Hopkins University Press.

STORING, HERBERT J. 1978 The Constitution and the Bill of Rights. Pages 32–48 in M. Judd Harmon, ed., *Essays on the Constitution of the United States.* Port Washington, N.Y.: Kennikat.

STRAUSS, LEO 1953 *Natural Right and History.* Introduction and chap. 5. Chicago: University of Chicago Press.

NAVIGABLE WATERS

See: Subjects of Commerce

NEAGLE, IN RE

See: Sawyer, Lorenzo

NEAL v. DELAWARE
103 U.S. 370 (1881)

Justice JOHN MARSHALL HARLAN, for a majority of 7–2, laid down an important principle in JURY DISCRIMINATION cases: the fact that no black person had ever been summoned as a juror in the courts of a state presents "a *prima facie* case of denial, by the officers charged with the selection of grand and petit jurors, of that equality of protection" secured by the

FOURTEENTH AMENDMENT. *Neal* differed from VIRGINIA V. RIVES (1880), here reaffirmed, because the prisoner in *Rives* had merely alleged the exclusion of blacks, which the state denied, while here the state conceded the exclusion. The state chief justice explained that "the great body of black men residing in this State are utterly unqualified by want of intelligence, experience or moral integrity, to sit on juries." Harlan called that a "violent presumption." *Neal* did nothing to prevent the elimination of blacks from juries in the South, because in the absence of a state confession of constitutional error, blacks had the burden of proving deliberate and systematic exclusion of their race. (See NORRIS V. ALABAMA, 1935.)

LEONARD W. LEVY

NEAR v. MINNESOTA
283 U.S. 697 (1931)

Although GITLOW V. NEW YORK (1925) had accepted for the sake of argument that the FIRST AMENDMENT's FREEDOM OF SPEECH guarantees were applicable to the states through the DUE PROCESS clause of the FOURTEENTH AMENDMENT, *Near* was the first decision firmly adopting the INCORPORATION DOCTRINE and striking down a state law in its totality on free speech grounds. Together with STROMBERG V. CALIFORNIA (1931), decided in the same year and also with a 5–4 majority opinion by Chief Justice CHARLES EVANS HUGHES, *Near* announced a new level of Supreme Court concern for freedom of speech.

A Minnesota statute authorizing injunctions against a "malicious, scandalous and defamatory newspaper, magazine or other periodical" had been applied against a paper that had accused public officials of neglect of duty, illicit relations with gangsters, and graft. Arguing that hostility to PRIOR RESTRAINT AND CENSORSHIP are the very core of the First Amendment, the Court struck down the statute. Yet *Near*, the classic precedent against prior restraints, is also the doctrinal starting point for most defenses of prior restraint. The Court commented in OBITER DICTUM that "the protection even as to previous restraint is not absolutely unlimited," and listed as exceptions wartime obstruction of recruitment and publication of military secrets, OBSCENITY, INCITEMENTS to riot or forcible overthrow of the government, and words that "may have all the effect of force."

In emphasizing the special First Amendment solicitude for criticisms of public officials, whether true or false, *Near* was an important way station between

Gitlow's implicit acceptance of the constitutional survival in the United States of the English COMMON LAW concept of SEDITIOUS LIBEL and the rejection of that concept in NEW YORK TIMES V. SULLIVAN (1964).

MARTIN SHAPIRO

NEBBIA v. NEW YORK
291 U.S. 502 (1934)

Both the desperate economic conditions in the American dairy industry and the legal responses to the dairy crisis, during the depression years 1929–1933, exemplified the dilemmas that the Great Depression posed for American law. Vast, unmarketable surpluses of fluid milk and other dairy products, widespread mortgage foreclosures in dairy centers of rural America, and wild swings in dairy prices and consumption, all spelled extreme distress for the industry and its marketing institutions.

Among the states that responded with new legislation was New York, whose dairy industry constituted about half the value of its farm income and served the great urban concentration of population in the city of New York and its metropolitan area. In framing a program to deal with the crisis, New York's lawmakers knew they were forced to walk through a constitutional minefield. Despite provisions of the 1933 federal AGRICULTURAL ADJUSTMENT ACT intended to give the states some latitude in control of dairy commerce involving interstate milksheds, federal district courts around the country had struck down state laws seeking to control interstate movements of fluid milk or the terms on which it could be marketed. In addition, even laws seeking to regulate only in-state production and distribution were challenged as invalid under the AFFECTED WITH A PUBLIC INTEREST rule; indeed, in numerous previous decisions the Supreme Court had in obiter dicta listed dairies among the enterprises that clearly were "ordinary" or "purely private" businesses, not affected with a public interest and therefore not subject to price regulation. In NEW STATE ICE CO. V. LIEBMANN (1932), for example, the Court had denied the legislature of Oklahoma authority to regulate ice manufacturing and selling on the ground that it was "a business as essentially private in its nature as the business of the grocer, the dairyman, the butcher, the baker, the shoemaker, or the tailor."

Mindful of this background, the New York legislature conducted a lengthy investigation of the fluid milk industry and its travails. In addition to making a record, thereby, as to the condition of the farmers and distribution system, the price collapse and its consequences, and the extensive effects of the crisis on the state's economy, when the legislature drafted a new Milk Control Law in March 1933, it explicitly denominated it as emergency legislation and provided for its termination one year following. By this maneuver, the legislators hoped to slip the knot of "affected with a public interest" and give the Milk Control Law safe harbor in the EMERGENCY POWERS and POLICE POWER area in the event that courts proved unimpressed with the statute's assertion that the milk industry was "a business affecting the public health and interest."

Like similar legislation enacted in New Jersey, Illinois, and other dairy states, the New York law included power to fix prices in the virtually plenary grant of authority to the milk control agency that was established. The board was also empowered to license producers, establish maximum retail prices and the spread between prices paid producers and charged consumers, and regulate interstate fluid milk entrants to the New York market.

The price-fixing provision came before the bench in an appeal from the conviction of a storekeeper for selling milk at retail below the price established by the new milk control agency. When the New York Court of Appeals affirmed the conviction, the case was carried to the Supreme Court. Counsel contended that price control violated the "affected with a public interest" standard, subjecting Nebbia to improper regulation in violation of his FOURTEENTH AMENDMENT right to DUE PROCESS.

By a 5–4 vote, the Court upheld the New York law. Justice OWEN J. ROBERTS's opinion did not rest on the narrow grounds that the milk control program was of an emergency nature; instead, it addressed in broadest possible terms the nature of the police power and the constitutional limitations upon which states might exercise it. The long history of the "affected with a public interest" doctrine came to an end with *Nebbia*, the majority opinion going back to Chief Justice MORRISON R. WAITE's language in *Munn v. Illinois* (1877). (See GRANGER CASES.) Waite had used the phrase "affected with a public interest" as the equivalent of "subject to the exercise of the police power," the Court now declared: "It is clear that there is no closed class or category of businesses affected with a public interest, and the function of courts in the application of the Fifth and Fourteenth Amendments is to determine in each case whether circumstances vindicate the challenged regulation as a reasonable exertion of governmental authority or condemn it as arbitrary or discriminatory." By repudiating the doctrine of affection with a public interest, which was based on SUBSTANTIVE DUE PROCESS OF LAW, the Court weakened the due process clause as a bastion of property rights. The due process clause, Roberts observed, made no mention of sales, prices, business, contracts, or other incidents of property. Nothing, he added, was sacred about the prices one might charge. The state, Roberts declared, "may regulate a business in any of its aspects, including the prices to be charged for the products or commodities it sells." The crux of this opinion, which prefigured a transformation in constitutional law, was this statement: "So far as the requirement of due process is concerned . . . a state is free to adopt whatever economic policy may reasonably be deemed to promote public welfare, and to enforce that policy by legislation adapted to its purpose. The courts are without authority either to declare such policy, or, when it is declared by the legislature, to override it."

Handed down not long after HOME BUILDING & LOAN ASSOCIATION V. BLAISDELL (1934), a decision that did extensive damage to once sacrosanct CONTRACT CLAUSE doctrine, the *Nebbia* decision was anathema to property-minded conservatives who saw the juridical scaffolding for VESTED RIGHTS as collapsing in the early New Deal years, even before the Court fight and the wholesale reversal of doctrine that came after 1935. Indeed, *Nebbia* may be read as present-day constitutional law.

HARRY N. SCHEIBER

Bibliography

GOLDSMITH, IRVING B. and WINKS, GORDON W. 1938 Price Fixing: From *Nebbia* to *Guffey.* Pages 531–553 in Douglas B. Maggs, ed., *Selected Essays on Constitutional Law.* Chicago: Association of American Law Schools.

NEBRASKA PRESS ASSOCIATION v. STUART
427 U.S. 539 (1976)

In *Nebraska Press Association v. Stuart* the Court addressed for the first time the constitutionality of a prior restraint on pretrial publicity about a criminal case. Noting the historic conflict between the FIRST and Sixth AMENDMENTS, the Court refused to give either priority, recognizing that the accused's right to an unbiased jury must be balanced with the interests in a free press. At issue was a narrowly tailored GAG ORDER in a sensational murder case restraining the press from publishing or broadcasting accounts of the accused's confessions or admissions or "strongly implicative" facts until the jury was impaneled.

Applying the standard of DENNIS V. UNITED STATES (1951) and inquiring whether "the gravity of the 'evil,' discounted by its improbability justified such invasion of free speech as is necessary to avoid the danger," the Court struck down the gag order. To determine whether the record supported the extraordinary measure of a prior restraint on publication, the Court considered the nature and extent of pretrial news coverage, the likelihood that other measures would mitigate the effects of unrestrained pretrial publicity, and the effectiveness of a restraining order to prevent the threatened danger, and, further, analyzed the order's terms and the problems of managing and enforcing it. The gag order was critically flawed because it prohibited publication of information gained from other clearly protected sources.

Justice WILLIAM J. BRENNAN, joined by Justices POTTER J. STEWART and THURGOOD MARSHALL, concurring, argued that a prior restraint on the press is an unconstitutionally impermissible method for enforcing the Sixth Amendment. Refusing to view the First and Sixth Amendments as in irreconcilable conflict, he noted that there were numerous less restrictive means by which a fair trial could be ensured. Justice BYRON R. WHITE doubted whether prior restraints were ever justifiable, but did not believe it wise so to announce in the first case raising that question. Justice LEWIS F. POWELL emphasized the heavy burden resting on a party seeking to justify a prior restraint.

KIM MCLANE WARDLAW

(SEE ALSO: *Free Press/Fair Trial; Prior Restraint and Censorship.*)

NECESSARY AND PROPER CLAUSE

The enumeration of powers in Article I, section 8, gives Congress the power to do such specific things as "regulate commerce . . . among the several States" and "raise and support Armies." At the end of the list is the power "to make all Laws which shall be necessary and proper for carrying into execution the foregoing Powers, and all other Powers vested by this Constitution in the Government of the United States, or in any Department or Officer thereof." The Anti-Federalists called this the "elastic clause" or the "sweeping power." They predicted it would centralize all governmental power in the national government. JAMES MADISON denied this charge in THE FEDERALIST #23. He observed that the clause spoke of power to execute only those powers that were specified elsewhere in the document, and that the power vested by the clause would have been implicit in the grant of other powers even without the clause. (See IMPLIED POWERS.) The clause, therefore, did not conflict with the principle of enumerated national powers, Madison argued. Events have vindicated Anti-Federalist fears.

THOMAS JEFFERSON and ALEXANDER HAMILTON took opposing positions on the meaning of the word "necessary" in the clause during their debate in 1791 on the constitutionality of the first BANK OF THE UNITED STATES ACT. Hamilton argued that the nation needed a BROAD CONSTRUCTION of congressional powers so that the government could employ a wide variety of means useful to the discharge of its responsibilities. Jefferson countered that a broad construction would enable Congress to encroach upon the reserved powers of the states whenever its measures might serve as means to ends within its enumerated powers. To safeguard STATES' RIGHTS, such encroachments should be permitted only when "absolutely necessary," said Jefferson—only, that is, when failure to encroach would nullify the grant of federal power. Hamilton's view prevailed first with President GEORGE WASHINGTON in 1791 and later in the Supreme Court, when JOHN MARSHALL's opinion in MCCULLOCH V. MARYLAND upheld the second national bank in 1819.

Marshall construed national powers in terms of a few authorized national ends. Most important, he understood the COMMERCE POWER and related powers as authorizing the pursuit of national prosperity and the various military and diplomatic powers as authorizing the pursuit of national security. This ends-oriented conception of national powers was the view of *The Federalist* #41, which also gave greatest emphasis to the goals of national prosperity and security. When Marshall held in *McCulloch* that Congress could pursue its authorized ends without regard for the reserved powers of the states, he was saying, in effect, that Congress could do what it wanted to relative to state powers so long as it gave the right reasons. Marshall suggested a hierarchy of constitutional values, with state powers subordinated to Congress's version of national prosperity and security. The opinion thus brought virtually all state powers within Congress's potential control, because, with changing conditions, Congress might consider any social practice (education, for example) as an instrument of the nation's prosperity and security.

But to suggest that Congress can act for the right reasons is not to say that Congress can disregard states' rights at will. Marshall's theory of the necessary and proper clause was still consistent with the idea of enumerated powers because it presupposed a limited number of nationally authorized ends. Marshall thus stated that the judiciary would be prepared to invalidate pretextual uses of national power to reach ends reserved to the states. In the twentieth century, the Supreme Court refused to give effect to Marshall's commitment to invalidate pretextual uses of congressional power, thus fulfilling the Anti-Federalist prediction of what the clause eventually would be.

The Court first upheld pretextual uses of power as means to eliminating state bank notes in VEAZIE BANK V. FENNO (1869) and margarine colored to resemble butter in MCRAY V. UNITED STATES (1904). These acts were aimed at what Congress considered the nation's economic health. They were therefore valid under Marshall's theory of the commerce power. But, in the meanwhile, the Court had moved away from Marshall's conception to a limited view of the nation's commerce as those things that crossed state lines. Pretexts were necessary unless the Court chose to abandon this artificial view; instead of correcting the mistake which necessitated pretexts, the Court established precedents for them. Later the Court upheld enactments that obviously were not aimed at the national goals implicit in Congress's enumerated powers. The Court thus upheld the TAXING POWER as a weapon against drug abuse in UNITED STATES V. DOREMUS (1919) and the commerce power as a means of combating gambling, illicit sex, and other practices usually said to be reserved to the STATE POLICE POWER, as in HOKE V. UNITED STATES (1913). These decisions turned Marshall's theory of the necessary and proper clause on its head. Where Marshall had upheld incursions into state powers as means to nationally authorized ends, the Court was now upholding national powers as means to state ends. As a result the NATIONAL POLICE POWER can today be used to reach an indefinite variety of purposes, and the necessary and proper clause authorizes almost anything that might be useful for addressing what Congress views as a national problem.

Limits on national power do remain in the BILL OF RIGHTS, in other sources of individual rights such as the Civil War amendments, and in principles derived from the Constitution's institutional arrangements. Because the states do constitute a part of those arrangements, the Court still says it will protect various state rights to participate in federal government action, such as the right to equal representation in the Senate. But such states' rights limitations on national power are of little contemporary significance. For the most part, the necessary and proper clause has been construed in a way that has destroyed the notion that the enumeration of powers limits the national government.

SOTIRIOS A. BARBER

Bibliography

BERNS, WALTER 1961 The Meaning of the Tenth Amendment. Pages 126–148 in Robert A. Goldwin, ed., *A Nation of States.* Chicago: Rand McNally.

GUNTHER, GERALD, ED. 1969 *John Marshall's Defense of McCulloch v. Maryland.* Stanford, Calif.: Stanford University Press.

NELSON, SAMUEL
(1792–1873)

On March 5, 1845, Samuel Nelson became a Justice of the Supreme Court and judge of the Second Circuit. President JOHN TYLER nominated the New York Democrat in the belief that his record of moderation compiled over twenty-one years in the New York courts, including thirteen as associate and then chief justice of the state supreme court, would resolve eighteen months of wrangling between the chief executive and the Senate over the high court vacancy. Unanimous Senate confirmation made Nelson the Court's thirty-first justice.

Nelson's most significant contribution to constitutional development involved the admiralty clause in Article III, section 2, of the Constitution. That clause specified that the federal courts should exclusively exercise the ADMIRALTY AND MARITIME JURISDICTION. He interpreted the clause to extend federal JURISDICTION while retaining for the states an area of constitutional responsibility. Nelson first suggested the position, later adopted by the full Court in PROPELLER GENESEE CHIEF V. FITZHUGH (1851), that where INTERSTATE COMMERCE was involved the admiralty clause extended federal jurisdiction to inland rivers and lakes (*New Jersey Steam Navigation Co. v. Merchant's Bank,* 1848). He carefully rooted this expansion in an 1845 act that established admiralty jurisdiction in "certain cases, upon the lakes and navigable waters connecting with" the oceans. Nelson left to state courts responsibility for vessels that operated on lakes and rivers exclusively within the same state. This interpretation rested on two constitutional themes that pervaded his other opinions: congressional domination of matters of law as opposed to constitutional principles, and belief in a scheme of dual SOVEREIGNTY.

Even in this single instance of doctrinal leadership Nelson lost the initiative. New members of the Court and the quickening tempo of commercial life in the western United States rendered his emphasis on dual sovereignty obsolete. Almost always eager for accommodation, he acquiesced. In 1869 he spoke for the Court in holding that from the time of *Genesee Chief* federal admiralty jurisdiction on the lakes and rivers stemmed from the JUDICIARY ACT OF 1789 rather than from the act of 1845 (*The Eagle v. Frazer,* 1869). Through this about-face, Nelson acknowledged that litigants could use federal district courts in admiralty cases arising in INTRASTATE COMMERCE.

The concept of dual sovereignty also informed his attitude toward the COMMERCE CLAUSE. In the LICENSE CASES (1847) and PASSENGER CASES (1849) he concurred with Chief Justice ROGER B. TANEY's opinions sustaining STATE POLICE POWER, and in the 1849 cases he was the only Justice not to write a separate opinion. When Congress acted under the commerce clause, Nelson supported national power. Speaking for the Court in *Pennsylvania v. Wheeling and Belmont Bridge Co.* (1856), his most important commerce clause opinion, he confirmed Congress's power to deal with navigation and interstate commerce on inland rivers.

Nelson's constitutional jurisprudence also stressed JUDICIAL SELF-RESTRAINT and SEPARATION OF POWERS. He voted only once with a majority to strike down a federal law in *Hepburn v. Griswold* (1870). He deferred to presidential management of FOREIGN AFFAIRS, but dissented in the PRIZE CASES (1863) because he thought President ABRAHAM LINCOLN had infringed on Congress's war-making powers.

Nelson believed that federal JUDICIAL POWER should protect slaveholders, but that the Court should exercise it benignly. Acting on this belief, he persuaded the Court in 1856 to rehear DRED SCOTT V. SANDFORD (1857). In his draft opinion for the Court, he argued that the laws of Missouri made Scott a slave and that the Court could ignore the questions of the legal status of slaves and the constitutionality of the MISSOURI COMPROMISE. This position raised the hackles of Justices JOHN MCLEAN and BENJAMIN R. CURTIS, and Chief Justice Taney took from Nelson responsibility for preparing the Court's opinion. Nelson, believing that the Chief Justice's decision to reach major issues was unwise, submitted his draft opinion for the Court as his own, even retaining the pronoun "we" in the printed version.

Nelson continued in the post-Civil War era as a

hardworking jurist and able legal technician. He agreed in February 1871 to serve on the *Alabama* Claims Commission. His appointment by a Republican president underscored as much his reputation as an impartial jurist as it did his knowledge of admiralty, maritime, and prize law.

Nelson resigned from the Court on November 28, 1872. Often described as a doughface (a Northerner who took a southern view on slavery), Nelson is better understood as a political moderate concerned about the fate of the Union, disposed to antislavery rather than proslavery views, and committed to the position that the judicial role should emphasize discretion, restraint, and deference to legislative leadership. In view of his twenty-six years on the Court, he contributed surprisingly little to constitutional jurisprudence.

KERMIT L. HALL

Bibliography

GATELL, FRANK OTTO 1969 Samuel Nelson. Pages 817–839 in Leon Friedman and Fred L. Israel, eds., *The Justices of the United States Supreme Court 1789–1969: Their Lives and Major Opinions.* New York: Chelsea House.

NEW HAMPSHIRE SUPREME COURT v. PIPER
470 U.S. (1985)

In *Piper* the Supreme Court followed *United Building and Construction Trades Council v. Camden* (1984) and applied a two-step analysis for applying the PRIVILEGES AND IMMUNITIES clause of Article IV. The Court held, 8–1, that New Hampshire's rule limiting the practice of law to New Hampshire citizens violated the clause. First, the clause was properly invoked; doing business in the state is a privilege that is "fundamental" to the preservation of interstate harmony. Second, the state had not sufficiently justified its exclusion of Piper, who lived in Vermont, 400 yards from the New Hampshire border, and intended to maintain a law office in New Hampshire.

KENNETH L. KARST

NEW JERSEY v. T.L.O.
469 U.S. (1985)

In *New Jersey v. T.L.O.* a unanimous Supreme Court held that the FOURTH AMENDMENT's prohibition against unreasonable SEARCHES AND SEIZURES applies to searches of students conducted by public school officials. A majority of the Court (6–3) also held that school officials need not obtain a SEARCH WARRANT before searching a student under their authority and that their searches can be justified by a lower standard than probable cause to believe that the subject of the search has violated or is violating the law. Instead, the legality of the search depends on the reasonableness of the search under all the circumstances.

According to Justice BYRON R. WHITE's majority opinion, determining reasonableness requires a twofold inquiry: first, whether the search was justified at its inception, and, second, whether the search as actually conducted was reasonably related in its scope to the circumstances that initially justified it. Ordinarily, the search is justified at its inception if there are reasonable grounds for suspecting that the search will produce EVIDENCE that the student has violated or is violating either the law or the school rules. The search is permissible in scope if the measures adopted are reasonably related to the objectives of the search and are not excessively intrusive in light of the age and sex of the student and the nature of the infraction.

PATRICK DUTTON

Bibliography

DUTTON, PATRICK 1985 School Searches: Recent Applications of the United States and California Constitutions. *Journal of Juvenile Law* 9:106–128.

NEW JERSEY v. WILSON
7 Cranch 164 (1812)

This case was the vehicle by which the Supreme Court made a breathtaking expansion of the CONTRACT CLAUSE. In the colonial period New Jersey had granted certain lands to an Indian tribe in exchange for a waiver by the Indians of their claim to any other lands. The grant provided that the new lands would be exempt from taxation in perpetuity. In 1801, over forty years later, the Indians left the state after selling their lands with state permission. The legislation repealed the tax exemption statute and assessed the new owners, who challenged the constitutionality of the repeal act.

A unanimous Supreme Court, overruling the state court, held that the grant of a tax immunity was a contract protected by the contract clause. By some species of metaphysics the Court reasoned that the tax immunity attached to the land, not to the Indians, and therefore the new holders of the land were tax exempt. Chief Justice JOHN MARSHALL's opinion, voiding the state tax, gave a retroactive operation to the contract clause; the grant of tax immunity predated the clause by many years. More important, Marshall ignored the implications of his DOCTRINE that such a grant was a contract. According to this decision, a state, by an act of its legislature, may contract away its sovereign power of taxation and prevent a successive legislature from asserting that power. The doctrine of VESTED RIGHTS, here converted into a doctrine of tax immunity, handicapped the revenue capabilities of the states, raising grave questions about the policy of the opinion. As a matter of political or constitutional theory, the Court's assumption that an attribute of SOVEREIGNTY can be surrendered by a legislative grant to private parties or to their property was, at the least, dubious. Although Marshall restricted the states, he allowed them to cede tax powers by contract rather than thwart the exercise of those powers on rights vested by contract.

The growth of CORPORATIONS revealed the significance of the new doctrine of tax immunity. States and municipalities, eager to promote the establishment of banks, factories, turnpikes, railroads, and utilities, often granted corporations tax immunity or other tax advantages as an inducement to engage in such enterprises, and the corporations often secured their special privileges by corrupt methods. This case permitted the granting of tax preferences and constitutionally sanctioned political corruption and the reckless development of economic resources. But permission is not compulsion; the legislatures, not the judiciary, granted the contracts. The Court simply extended the contract clause beyond the intentions of its framers to protect vested rights and promote business needs.

LEONARD W. LEVY

NEW JERSEY COLONIAL CHARTERS

New Jersey received its first charter from its proprietors, John Berkeley and George Carteret, in 1664. The charter established representative institutions of government, contained a clause on RELIGIOUS LIBERTY similar to that in the RHODE ISLAND CHARTER of 1663, and guaranteed that only the general assembly could impose taxes. In 1676 Berkeley sold his share of New Jersey to Quakers, leaving Carteret proprietor of East New Jersey. In 1677 the Quaker proprietors issued a "Charter or Fundamental Laws, of West New Jersey," the work, probably, of WILLIAM PENN. The

charter included clauses on liberty of conscience, TRIAL BY JURY, and several protections for the criminally accused; the charter is memorable, however, because it functioned as a written CONSTITUTION of FUNDAMENTAL LAW. It began with the provision that the "COMMON LAW or fundamental rights" of the colony should be "the foundation of the government, which is not to be altered by the Legislative authority . . . constituted according to these fundamentals. . . ." The legislature was enjoined to maintain the fundamentals and to make no laws contradicting or varying from them.

In 1682 a Quaker group headed by Penn gained control of East New Jersey and in the following year issued "The Fundamental Constitutions" for that province. The charter of 1683, which was modeled on the Pennsylvania Frame of Government of 1682 (see PENNSYLVANIA COLONIAL CHARTERS), recognized CONSCIENTIOUS OBJECTION, banned any ESTABLISHMENT OF RELIGION, paraphrased chapter 39 of MAGNA CARTA, and included a variety of provisions that resembled a bill of rights, far more numerous than in the English BILL OF RIGHTS of 1689. Although New Jersey became a royal colony in 1702, the seventeenth-century Quaker charters are significant evidence of the grip which CONSTITUTIONALISM had upon influential colonial thinkers.

LEONARD W. LEVY

Bibliography
ANDREWS, CHARLES MCLEAN 1936 *The Colonial Period of American History.* Vol. 3:138–180. New Haven, Conn.: Yale University Press.

NEW JERSEY PLAN

The adoption of the VIRGINIA PLAN by the CONSTITUTIONAL CONVENTION OF 1787 frightened state sovereignty supporters and nationalists from small states. A bicameral Congress apportioned on the basis of population would have enabled the great states to dominate the new government. On June 15, 1787, WILLIAM PATERSON of New Jersey introduced a substitute plan that retained the "purely federal" (confederated) character of the ARTICLES OF CONFEDERATION. Under the Article a unicameral Congress in which each state had one vote preserved the principle of state equality.

As CHARLES PINCKNEY observed, if New Jersey had an equal vote, she would "dismiss her scruples, and concur in the national system." The New Jersey plan, though merely amending the Articles, was a small states' nationalist plan, not a state sovereignty plan. It recommended a Congress with powers to regulate commerce and to raise revenue from import and stamp duties, and it would have authorized requisitions from the states enforceable by a national executive empowered to use the military against states defying national laws and treaties. The plan recommended a national judiciary with broad JURISDICTION, extending to cases arising out of the regulation of commerce and the collection of the revenue. The nucleus of the SUPREMACY CLAUSE, making national law the supreme law of the states, was also part of the plan. It was a warning to large-state nationalists that they would have to compromise on the issue of REPRESENTATION. The Committee of the Whole defeated the plan 7–3, with one state divided. The Convention was thereafter stymied until the GREAT COMPROMISE was adopted. (See CONSTITUTIONAL HISTORY, 1776–1789.)

LEONARD W. LEVY

Bibliography

BRANT, IRVING 1950 *James Madison: Father of the Constitution, 1787–1800.* Pages 46–54. Indianapolis: Bobbs-Merrill.

NEW ORLEANS v. DUKES
427 U.S. 297 (1976)

Only once since 1937 has the Supreme Court struck down a state ECONOMIC REGULATION as a denial of the EQUAL PROTECTION OF THE LAWS. That case was *Morey v. Doud* (1957). In *Dukes*, the Court unanimously overruled *Morey*; a per curiam opinion reaffirmed the appropriateness of the RATIONAL BASIS standard of review in testing economic regulations against the demands of both equal protection and SUBSTANTIVE DUE PROCESS.

Dukes involved a New Orleans ordinance prohibiting the sale of food from pushcarts in the French Quarter, but exempting vendors who had been selling from pushcarts for eight years. This GRANDFATHER CLAUSE, said the Court, was rationally related to the city's legitimate interest in preserving the area's distinctive character while accommodating substantial reliance interests of long-term businesses.

KENNETH L. KARST

NEWSMAN'S PRIVILEGE

See: Reporter's Privilege

NEW STATE ICE COMPANY v. LIEBMANN
285 U.S. 262 (1932)

An Oklahoma law required ice dealers to obtain a license before entering the market because their business was AFFECTED WITH A PUBLIC INTEREST. A 6–2 majority could find no exceptional circumstances such as monopoly or emergency—that is, no public interest in regulation—justifying the restriction and so struck down the law as a violation of DUE PROCESS. Echoing Justice OLIVER WENDELL HOLMES's dissent in TYSON & BROTHER V. BANTON (1927), Justice LOUIS D. BRANDEIS, with Justice HARLAN FISKE STONE concurring, insisted that the assessment of local conditions and requirements was a legislative concern. Seeking to justify a state's right to experiment with social and economic legislation, Brandeis wrote: ". . . we must be ever on our guard, lest we erect our prejudices into legal principles."

DAVID GORDON

(SEE ALSO: *Ribnik v. McBride, 1928; Nebbia v. New York, 1934.*)

NEW YORK v. BELTON

See: Automobile Searches

NEW YORK v. FERBER
458 U.S. 747 (1982)

This decision demonstrated the BURGER COURT's willingness to add to the list of categories of speech excluded from the FIRST AMENDMENT's protectioh. New York, like the federal government and most of the states, prohibits the distribution of material depicting sexual performances by children under age 16, whether or not the material constitutes OBSCENITY. After a New York City bookseller sold two such films to an undercover police officer, he was convicted under this law. The Supreme Court unanimously affirmed his conviction.

Justice BYRON R. WHITE, for the Court, denied that state power in this regulatory area was confined to the suppression of obscene material. The state's interest in protecting children against abuse was compelling; to prevent the production of such materials, it was necessary to forbid their distribution. Child PORNOGRAPHY—the visual depiction of sexual conduct by children below a specified age—was "a category of material outside the protection of the First Amendment."

The Court also rejected the argument that the law was overbroad, thus abandoning a distinction announced in BROADRICK V. OKLAHOMA (1973) to govern OVERBREADTH challenges. Henceforth the overbreadth doctrine would apply only in cases of "substantial overbreadth," whether or not the state sought to regulate the content of speech.

KENNETH L. KARST

NEW YORK v. MILN

See: *Mayor of New York v. Miln*

NEW YORK v. QUARLES
467 U.S. 649 (1984)

Justice WILLIAM REHNQUIST, for a 5–4 Supreme Court, announced a public safety exception to the MIRANDA RULES. In a situation where concern for the public safety must supersede adherence to MIRANDA V. ARIZONA (1966), the prosecution may use in EVIDENCE incriminating statements made during a custodial interrogation before the suspect receives notice of his constitutional rights. Here, the Court reinstated a conviction based on the evidence of a gun and information concerning its whereabouts. Dissenters disagreed on whether the case showed a threat to the public safety, but produced no principled argument against the exception to *Miranda*.

LEONARD W. LEVY

NEW YORK v. UNITED STATES

See: *Graves v. New York*

NEW YORK CENTRAL RAILROAD COMPANY v. WHITE
243 U.S. 188 (1917)

The New York Workmen's Compensation Act of 1914 made employers liable to compensate injured workers in certain cases without regard to fault. The statute thereby departed from time-honored COMMON LAW rules of liability, particularly the fellow-servant doctrine and contributory negligence. The act established a graduated scale of compensation based on the loss of earning power, prior wages, and the character and duration of the disability suffered. Death benefits would be paid according to the survivors' needs.

Here, a night watchman was injured while guarding tools and materials used in the construction of a new station and tracks designed for INTERSTATE COMMERCE. A 9–0 Supreme Court held that the watchman was not in interstate commerce within the meaning of the first EMPLOYERS' LIABILITY ACT. Justice MAHLON PITNEY, for the Court, declared that his work "bore no direct relation to interstate transportation." Pitney rejected claims that the New York act violated the FOURTEENTH AMENDMENT's prohibition against a TAKING OF PROPERTY without DUE PROCESS OF LAW and deprived both parties of the FREEDOM OF CONTRACT. "It needs no argument to show that such a rule [fellow-servant] is subject to modification or abrogation by a state upon proper occasion." Because "the public has a direct interest in this as affecting the common welfare," the Court sustained the act as a reasonable exercise of the STATE POLICE POWER. Pitney also rejected the argument that the exclusion of certain workers from the statute's coverage was an arbitrary classification in violation of the EQUAL PROTECTION clause of the Fourteenth Amendment. He concluded that the classification was reasonable in view of the "inherent risks" associated with the various occupations.

DAVID GORDON

NEW YORK CHARTER OF LIBERTIES AND PRIVILEGES
(October 30, 1683)

The first enactment of the first general assembly in New York was a statute but had the characteristics of a charter or CONSTITUTION of FUNDAMENTAL LAW. Its purpose was to establish a government "that Justice and Right may be Equally done to all persons . . . ," an early forerunner of the principle of EQUAL PROTECTION OF THE LAWS. After describing the organs of government and empowering every freeholder to vote for representatives, the statute paraphrased chapter 39 of MAGNA CARTA and provided that no taxes should be imposed but by the general assembly. Then followed protections of the rights of the criminally accused, including a right to INDICTMENT by GRAND JURY in criminal cases. Another provision of the document, after protecting RELIGIOUS LIBERTY, created a multiple ESTABLISHMENT OF RELIGION. It allowed the towns on Long Island to elect Christian ministers of their choice, to be supported by town rates, and declared that "all" the other Christian churches in the province were "priviledged Churches . . . Established" by law. Elsewhere in Christendom, an established church meant a church of a single denomination preferred over all others.

The Privy Council disallowed the statute in 1686. In 1691, after James II was overthrown, the general assembly substantially reenacted it but again it was disallowed, probably because it curbed the royal prerogative. Although the statute never became law, it is early evidence of the high regard that colonists had for Magna Carta, written guarantees of their liberties, and the principle that there should be no TAXATION WITHOUT REPRESENTATION.

LEONARD W. LEVY

Bibliography

ANDREWS, CHARLES MCLEAN 1936 *The Colonial Period of American History.* Vol. 3:114–121. New Haven, Conn.: Yale University Press.

NEW YORK TIMES CO. v. SULLIVAN
376 U.S. 254 (1964)

MARTIN LUTHER KING, JR., was arrested in Alabama in 1960 on a perjury charge. In New York a group of entertainers and civil rights activists formed a committee to help finance King's defense. They placed a full-page advertisement in the *New York Times* appealing for contributions. The ad charged that King's arrest was part of a campaign to destroy King's leadership of the movement to integrate public facilities and encourage blacks in the South to vote. It asserted that "Southern violators" in Montgomery had expelled King's student followers from college, ringed the campus with armed police, padlocked the dining hall to starve them into submission, bombed King's home, assaulted his person, and arrested him seven times for speeding, loitering, and other dubious offenses.

L. B. Sullivan, a city commissioner of Montgomery, filed a libel action in state court against the *Times* and four black Alabama ministers whose names had appeared as endorsers of the ad. He claimed that because his duties included supervision of the Montgomery police, the allegations against the police defamed him personally.

Under the common law as it existed in Alabama and most other states, the *Times* had little chance of winning. Whether the statements referred to Sullivan was a fact issue; if the jury found that readers would identify him, it was immaterial that the ad did not name him. Because the statements reflected adversely on Sullivan's professional reputation they were "libelous per se"; that meant he need not prove that he actually had been harmed. The defense of truth was not available because the ad contained factual errors (for example, police had not "ringed the campus," though they had been deployed nearby; King had been arrested four times, not seven). A few states recognized a privilege for good faith errors in criticism of public officials, but Alabama was among the majority that did not.

The jury awarded Sullivan $500,000. In the Alabama Supreme Court, the *Times* argued such a judgment was inconsistent with FREEDOM OF THE PRESS, but that court merely repeated what the United States Supreme Court had often said: "The First Amendment of the United States Constitution does not protect libelous publications."

When the case reached the Supreme Court in 1964, it was one of eleven libel claims, totaling $5,600,000, pending against the *Times* in Alabama. It was obvious that libel suits were being used to discourage the press from supporting the CIVIL RIGHTS movement in the South. The *Times* urged the Court to equate these uses of libel law with the discredited doctrine of SEDITIOUS LIBEL and to hold that criticism of public officials could never be actionable.

Only three Justices were willing to go that far. The majority adopted a more limited rule, holding that public officials could recover for defamatory falsehoods about their official conduct or fitness for office only if they could prove that the defendant had published with "actual malice." This was defined as "knowledge that [the statement] was false or with reckless disregard of whether it was false or not." The Court further held that this element had to be established by "clear and convincing proof," and that, unlike most factual issues, it was subject to independent review by appellate courts. The Court then reviewed Sullivan's evidence and determined that it did not meet the new standard.

The decision was an important breakthrough, not only for the press and the civil rights movement but also in FIRST AMENDMENT theory. Until then, vast areas of expression, including libel and commercial speech, had been categorically excluded from First Amendment protection. Also, the decision finally repudiated the darkest blot on freedom of expression in the history of the United States, the Sedition Act of 1798.

Over the next few years, the Court went out of its way to make the new rule effective. It defined "reckless disregard" narrowly (*St. Amant v. Thompson,* 1967). It extended the *Sullivan* rule to lesser public officials (*Rosenblatt v. Baer,* 1966), to candidates for public office (*Monitor Patriot Co. v. Roy,* 1971), to PUBLIC FIGURES (*Associated Press v. Walker,* 1967), and to criminal libel (*Garrison v. Louisiana,* 1964). After 1971 the Court retreated somewhat, declining to extend the *Sullivan* rule to private plaintiffs and permitting a de facto narrowing of the public figure category.

From its birth the rule has been criticized, by public officials and celebrities who believe it makes recovery too difficult, and by the news media, which argue that the rule still exposes them to long and expensive litigation, even though ultimately they usually win. The Court, however, has shown no inclination to revise the rule. In *Bose Corp. v. Consumers Union* (1984), the Court was invited to dilute it by abandoning independent appellate review of findings of "actual malice." The Court refused, holding such review essential "to preserve the precious liberties established and ordained by the Constitution."

DAVID A. ANDERSON

Bibliography

KALVEN, HARRY, JR. 1964 The New York Times Case: A Note on "The Central Meaning of the First Amendment." *Supreme Court Review* 1964:191–221.

PIERCE, SAMUEL R., JR. 1965 The Anatomy of an Historic Decision: *New York Times Co. v. Sullivan. North Carolina Law Review* 43:315–363.

NEW YORK TIMES CO. v. UNITED STATES
403 U.S. 713 (1971)

New York Times Co. v. United States, more commonly known as the Pentagon Papers case, is one of the landmarks of contemporary prior restraint doctrine. Only NEAR V. MINNESOTA (1931) rivals it as a case of central importance in establishing the FIRST AMENDMENT's particular and extreme aversion to any form of official restriction applied prior to the act of speaking or the act of publication.

The dramatic facts of the case served to keep it before the public eye even as it was being litigated and decided. On June 12, 1971, the *New York Times* commenced publication of selected portions of a 1968 forty-seven-volume classified Defense Department study entitled "History of United States Decision Making Process on Vietnam Policy" and a 1965 classified Defense Department study entitled "The Command and Control Study of the Tonkin Gulf Incident Done by the Defense Department's Weapons Systems Evaluation Group in 1965." Collectively these documents came to be known as the Pentagon Papers. Within a few days other major newspapers, including the *Washington Post,* the *Los Angeles Times,* the *Detroit Free Press,* the *Philadelphia Inquirer,* and the *Miami Herald* also commenced publication of the Pentagon Papers. The papers had been provided to the *New York Times* by Daniel Ellsberg, a former Defense Department official and former government consultant. Ellsberg had no official authority to take the Pentagon Papers; his turning over the papers to the *New York Times* was similarly unauthorized.

When the newspapers commenced publication, the United States was still engaged in fighting the VIETNAM WAR. Claiming that the publication of the Pentagon Papers jeopardized national security, the government sought an INJUNCTION against any further publication of the papers, including publication of scheduled installments yet to appear. In the United States District Court for the Southern District of New York, Judge Murray Gurfein issued a temporary restraining order against the *New York Times,* but then denied the government's request for a preliminary injunction against publication, finding that, in light of the extremely high hurdle necessary to justify a prior restraint against a newspaper, "the publication of these historical documents would [not] seriously breach the national security." (See PRIOR RESTRAINT AND CENSORSHIP.) The United States immediately appealed, and the Court of Appeals for the Second Circuit, on June 23, 1971, remanded the case for further consideration in light of documents filed by the United States indicating that publication might pose "grave and immediate danger to the security of the United States." The Second Circuit continued to enforce the stay it had previously issued, in effect keeping the *Times* under the restraint of the temporary restraining order. On the same day, however, the United States Court of Appeals for the District of Columbia Circuit, in a case involving the *Washington Post's* publication of the Pentagon Papers, affirmed a decision of the district court refusing to enjoin further publication. On June 24, the *New York Times* filed a petition for a WRIT OF CERTIORARI and motion for expedited consideration in the Supreme Court, and on the same day the United States asked that Court for a stay of the District of Columbia circuit's ruling in the *Washington Post* case. The two cases were consolidated and accelerated, with briefs filed on June

26, oral argument the same day, and a decision of the Supreme Court on June 30, only seventeen days after the first publication of the papers in the *New York Times.*

In a brief PER CURIAM opinion, the Supreme Court affirmed the District of Columbia Circuit, reversed the Second Circuit, and vacated the restraints. Noting the "heavy presumption" against prior restraints, and the consequent "heavy burden of . . . justification" necessary to support a prior restraint, the Court found that the United States had not met that especially heavy burden.

The Court's per curiam opinion was accompanied by a number of important separate opinions by individual Justices. Justices HUGO L. BLACK and WILLIAM O. DOUGLAS made it clear that in their view prior restraints were never permissible. Justice WILLIAM J. BRENNAN would not go this far, but found it noteworthy that "never before has the United States sought to enjoin a newspaper from publishing information in its possession." For him "only governmental allegation and proof that publication must inevitably, directly, and immediately cause the occurrence of an evil kindred to imperiling the safety of a transport already at sea [citing *Near v. Minnesota*] can support even the issuance of an interim restraining order." In agreeing that the restraint was improper, Justice THURGOOD MARSHALL emphasized the absence of statutory authorization for governmental action to enjoin a newspaper. And Justice JOHN MARSHALL HARLAN, joined by Chief Justice WARREN E. BURGER and Justice HARRY A. BLACKMUN, dissented. The dissenters were disturbed by the alacrity of the proceedings, and in addition thought that the executive's "constitutional primacy in the field of FOREIGN AFFAIRS" justified a restraint at least long enough to allow the executive to present its complete case for the necessity of restriction. The most doctrinally illuminating opinions, however, were those of Justices POTTER J. STEWART and BYRON R. WHITE. For them only the specific nature of the restriction rendered it constitutionally impermissible. Had the case involved criminal or civil sanctions imposed after publication—subsequent punishment rather than prior restraint—they indicated that the First Amendment would not have stood in the way.

As highlighted by the opinions of Justices Stewart and White, therefore, the *Pentagon Papers* case presents the problem of prior restraint in purest form. The judges had the disputed materials in front of them, and thus there was no question of a restraint on materials not before a court, or not yet published.

And the evaluation of the likely effect of the materials was made by the judiciary, rather than by a censorship board, other administrative agency, or police officer. Under these circumstances, why might a prior restraint be unconstitutional when a subsequent punishment for publishing the same materials would be upheld? What justifies a constitutional standard higher for injunctions than for criminal sanctions? It cannot be that prior restraints in fact "prevent" more things from being published, for the deterrent effect of a criminal sanction is likely to inhibit publication at least as much as an injunction. Someone who is willing knowingly to violate the criminal law, in order to publish out of conscience, may also be willing to violate an injunction. Is the special aversion against prior restraint, visible in the Pentagon Papers case, based on principle, or is it little more than an anachronism inherited from John Milton and WILLIAM BLACKSTONE, and transferred from a milieu in which prior restraint was synonymous with unreviewable determinations of an administrative censorship board?

The result in the Pentagon Papers case was not inconsistent with prior cases. The case did, however, present more clearly the puzzling nature of the virtually absolute prohibition against prior restraints under circumstances in which subsequent punishment of the very same material would have been permissible. Yet the case is also significant for reasons that transcend the doctrine of prior restraint. When confronted with a constitutional objection to a governmental policy, a court typically must evaluate the justification for the policy, and assess the likelihood of some consequences that the policy is designed to prevent. When that consequence and the governmental attempt to forestall it relates to war, national security, or national defense, judicial deference to governmental assertions of likely consequences has traditionally been greatest, even if the putative restriction implicates activities otherwise protected by the Constitution. When national security has been invoked, constitutional protection has often been more illusory than real. At every level in the Pentagon Papers case the courts conducted their own independent assessments of the likely dangers to national security and to troops overseas. The Supreme Court's decision was at least partly a function of the Justices' unwillingness to accept governmental incantation of the phrase "national security" as dispositive. Certainly executive determinations concerning the effect of publications on national security still receive greater deference than do other executive predictions about the effect of publications. But the Pentagon Papers case stands for the proposition that even when national security is claimed the courts will scrutinize for themselves the necessity of restriction. The decision, therefore, speaks not only to prior restraint but also, and more pervasively, to the courts' willingness to protect constitutional rights even against wartime governmental restrictions imposed in the name of national security.

FREDERICK SCHAUER

Bibliography

HENKIN, LOUIS 1971 The Right to Know and the Duty to Withhold: The Case of the Pentagon Papers. *University of Pennsylvania Law Review* 120:271–280.
JUNGER, PETER 1971 Down Memory Lane: The Case of the Pentagon Papers. *Case Western Reserve Law Review* 23:3–75.
KALVEN, HARRY, JR. 1971 Foreword: Even When a Nation Is at War. *Harvard Law Review* 85:3–36.

NIEMOTKO v. MARYLAND
340 U.S. 268 (1951)

The VINSON COURT here unanimously reversed the convictions of two Jehovah's Witnesses who had been charged with disorderly conduct for attempting to hold religious services in a city park without a permit. Local officials had refused to issue the permit, citing ordinances or administrative standards that governed the procedure, but such permits had been routinely approved for other religious and patriotic groups. The city's refusal to issue a permit to the Jehovah's Witnesses under these circumstances, the Court held, was both an unconstitutional prior restraint on speech and a denial of EQUAL PROTECTION.

MICHAEL E. PARRISH

NINETEENTH AMENDMENT

Ratification of the women's suffrage amendment in 1920 marked the culmination of a struggle spanning three quarters of a century. Under the leadership of organizations including the National Woman's Suffrage Association and the National Women's Party, over 2 million women participated in some 900 campaigns before state and federal legislators, party officials, and referendum voters. By the time the amendment was adopted, a majority of the states had already given some recognition to women's VOTING RIGHTS.

Political agitation for enfranchisement began in 1848, at the first women's rights convention in Seneca Falls, New York. In its Declaration of Sentiments, the convention included suffrage as one of the "inalienable rights" to which women were entitled. As the century progressed, the vote assumed increasing importance, both as a symbolic affirmation of women's equality and as a means to address a vast array of sex-based discrimination in employment, education, domestic law, and related areas. Once the Supreme Court ruled in MINOR V. HAPPERSETT (1875) that suffrage was not one of the PRIVILEGES AND IMMUNITIES guaranteed by the FOURTEENTH AMENDMENT to women as citizens, the necessity for a state or federal constitutional amendment became apparent.

The struggle for women's rights was a response to various forces. Urbanization, industrialization, declining birth rates, and expanding educational and employment opportunities tended to diminish women's role in the private domestic sphere while encouraging their participation in the public sphere. So too, women's involvement, first with abolitionism and later with other progressive causes, generated political commitments and experiences that fueled demands for equal rights.

Those demands provoked opposition from various quarters. The liquor industry feared that enfranchisement would pave the way for PROHIBITION, while conservative political and religious leaders, as well as women homemakers, painted suffrage as an invitation to socialism, anarchism, free love, and domestic discord. Partly in response to those claims, many leading suffragists became increasingly conservative in their arguments and increasingly unwilling to address other causes and consequences of women's inequality. That strategy met with partial success. As they narrowed their social agenda, women's rights organizations expanded their political appeal. The growing strength of the suffrage movement, together with women's efforts in World War I, finally helped prompt the United States to join the slowly increasing number of Western nations that had granted enfranchisement.

Yet to many leading women's rights activists, the American victory proved scarcely less demoralizing than defeat. The focus on enfranchisement had to some extent deflected attention from other issues of critical importance for women, such as poverty, working conditions, birth control, health care, and domestic relations. Without a unifying social agenda beyond the ballot, the postsuffrage feminist movement foundered, splintered, and for the next half century, largely dissolved. During that period, women did not vote as a block on women's issues, support women candidates, or, with few exceptions, agitate for women's rights. Despite their numerical strength and access to the ballot, women remained subject to a vast range of discrimination in employment, education, WELFARE BENEFITS, credit standards, family law, and related areas. Although the Nineteenth Amendment itself was urged as a ground for qualifying women to serve on juries, most courts rejected this argument except where jury service was tied to voter status.

Yet however limited its immediate affects, the Nineteenth Amendment marked a significant advance toward equal rights. Enfranchisement was a necessary if not sufficient condition for women to exercise significant political leverage. Moreover, the skills, experience, and self-esteem that women gained during the suffrage campaign helped lay the foundation for a more egalitarian social order.

DEBORAH L. RHODE

Bibliography
CATT, CARRIE CHAPMAN and SHULER, NETTIE ROGERS 1970 *Woman Suffrage and Politics.* New York: Americana Library Edition.
STANTON, ELIZABETH CADY; ANTHONY, SUSAN B., GAGE, MATILDA JOSLYN; and HARPER, IDA H., eds. 1881–1922 *History of Woman Suffrage.* New York: Fowler & Wells.

NINTH AMENDMENT

Largely ignored throughout most of our history, the Ninth Amendment has emerged in the past twenty years as a possible source for the protection of individual rights not specifically enumerated in the Constitution's text. Although no Supreme Court decision has yet been based squarely on an interpretation of the Ninth Amendment, it has been mentioned in several leading cases in which the Court enlarged the scope of individual rights. Lawyers, scholars, and judges are understandably intrigued by a provision that, on the basis of language, seems ideally suited to provide a constitutional home for newly found rights: "The enumeration of certain rights in the Constitution shall not be construed to deny or disparage others retained by the people."

The historical origins of the Ninth Amendment lay in JAMES MADISON'S concern that the inclusion of specified rights in the BILL OF RIGHTS might leave other rights unprotected. He recognized, moreover, that the inherent limitations of language could thwart the intent of the authors of the Bill of Rights to provide a permanent charter of personal freedom. These concerns, which led Madison originally to question the wisdom of a Bill of Rights, caused him to propose, in the First Congress, a resolution incorporating the present language of the Ninth Amendment. It was adopted with little debate.

It is not surprising that the Ninth Amendment lay dormant throughout most of our history. The holding in BARRON V. BALTIMORE (1833) that the Fifth Amendment was not applicable to the states limited the scope of the Ninth Amendment also: all provisions of the Bill of Rights restricted the United States only. Moreover, the federal government, being one of limited powers, did not move into those areas of activity that would trigger claims of infringement of rights not specified in the Constitution. Challenges to federal actions were more likely to take the form that the President or Congress lacked power under the Constitution rather than that the actions abridged an individual right. Even the specific guarantees of the Bill of Rights spawned only a trickle of litigation until well into the twentieth century.

The states, of course, had broad POLICE POWERS to legislate in the areas of welfare, health, education, morality, and business. Until the latter part of the nineteenth century, however, the Supreme Court's review of state legislation served primarily to assure that states did not unduly burden or tax interstate businesses. Court decisions in these areas were not based on individual rights but rather on a judicially created doctrine that Congress's power to regulate INTERSTATE COMMERCE carried with it a prohibition against state laws that were viewed by the Court as unreasonably burdensome or discriminatory as applied to interstate businesses. The post-Civil War Amendments provided the textual basis for challenges to state law as violating individual rights.

The Supreme Court, however, moved quickly to limit the scope of the THIRTEENTH AMENDMENT and FOURTEENTH AMENDMENT. In the famous SLAUGHTERHOUSE CASES (1873) the Court virtually eliminated the PRIVILEGES AND IMMUNITIES clause of the Fourteenth Amendment as a protection for individual rights by limiting the clause to such rights as interstate travel, petitioning the federal government for redress of grievances, protection while abroad, or the privilege of HABEAS CORPUS. The EQUAL PROTECTION and DUE PROCESS clauses were also narrowly interpreted so as to preclude broad challenges to state regulatory statutes, as was the Thirteenth Amendment in *Slaughterhouse* and the CIVIL RIGHTS CASES (1883).

Despite the *Slaughterhouse Cases,* those seeking constitutional support for the protection of property rights against ECONOMIC REGULATION looked elsewhere in the Fourteenth Amendment, and ultimately found a home in the due process clause. Toward the end of the nineteenth century the Court expanded the meaning of "liberty" and "property" to include the right to enter into business relationships. Hundreds of state laws were invalidated under this expanded concept of SUBSTANTIVE DUE PROCESS. This view of the Fourteenth Amendment, together with narrow interpretations of Congress's power under the COMMERCE CLAUSE and the TAXING AND SPENDING POWER, led to the New Deal constitutional crisis of the 1930s. In the spring of 1937 a narrow Court majority shifted ground, broadening Congress's enumerated powers and limiting the due process clause to its present scope, namely, that state regulatory laws should bear a reasonable relationship to a valid legislative purpose. Throughout this long constitutional journey the Ninth Amendment was an unused instrument, because those who challenged state laws relied primarily on the Fourteenth Amendment's due process clause whose scope had been so broadened that there was no need to develop a theory of unenumerated rights.

As the Court in the 1930s and 1940s finally rejected the claim that the Constitution contained rights that protected business against government regulation, the enumerated rights in the Bill of Rights were gradually being incorporated into the meaning of the words "liberty" and "property" of the Fourteenth Amendment's due process clause. By the end of the 1960s, substantive rights guaranteed by the FIRST AMENDMENT, and most of the procedural rights of the Fourth, Fifth, Sixth, and Eighth Amendments were made binding on the states. In this legal development the Ninth Amendment was inconsequential, because the Court employed the judicial technique of incorporating into the due process clause rights enumerated in the Bill of Rights. There was little need to develop the concept of "unenumerated" rights, so long as the due process clause of the Fourteenth Amendment provided the vehicle for making the Bill of Rights binding on the states.

Thus, during the early 1960s, as the process of incorporating the Bill of Rights into the Fourteenth Amendment was moving forward, the Supreme Court maintained a consensus developed as early as UNITED STATES V. CAROLENE PRODUCTS CO. (1938). On matters of economic and social legislation (the type of law that gave rise to the substantive due process controversies of the pre-New Deal era) the Supreme Court would have a limited role to play. Legislation (either state or federal) would be assumed to be valid unless arbitrary or unreasonable, or unless shown to violate a specific provision of the Constitution. Laws

reflecting prejudice against certain minorities, or laws infringing personal liberties of the kind enumerated in the Bill of Rights, or other specific provisions of the Constitution, would be subject to a more demanding form of judicial scrutiny.

The Court remained divided on the meaning of specific constitutional guarantees, but these divisions resulted from differences over the meaning of enumerated rights, rather than from differences over whether newly identified, unenumerated, rights should be read into the Constitution. In this constitutional world, an amendment that spoke of unenumerated rights had little to offer as a defense of personal rights. However, a Connecticut law that prohibited the use of contraceptives jolted this consensus and led to the emergence of the Ninth Amendment as a possible vehicle for the protection of rights not specifically guaranteed in other provisions of the Constitution. After two decades of not enforcing its statute, and after thwarting attempts to overturn it in the Supreme Court, Connecticut prosecuted a doctor who was giving contraceptive advice to a married couple in a BIRTH CONTROL clinic. He was charged with "aiding and abetting" a violation of the law prohibiting the use of contraceptives.

The case, GRISWOLD V. CONNECTICUT (1965), presented a difficult problem for a Court majority wedded to the notion that only arbitrary, or capricious, or invidiously discriminatory laws, or those that violated a specific constitutional right, could be invalidated. All of the Justices agreed that the Connecticut statute was foolish, but the Court was obviously troubled as to why it was unconstitutional for a state to decide that it wished to discourage extramarital sexual relations and that the ready availability of contraceptives, including contraceptives for married persons, increased the likelihood of extramarital sex by eliminating the fear of pregnancy. Connecticut claimed that in order to achieve the objective of deterring sex outside of marriage the state could prohibit the use of all contraceptives, thus making them less available. If no specific constitutional right had been violated, why could not Connecticut make its own mistakes, leaving it to the people, through their elected representatives, to correct them?

The Supreme Court's answer, in an opinion by Justice WILLIAM O. DOUGLAS, was to create a right of marital privacy which was found in "penumbras, formed by emanations" from other guarantees found in enumerated rights, specifically those in the First, Third, Fourth, and Fifth Amendments. The Ninth Amendment was also mentioned, but the constitutional approach of the majority was to expand existing rights in order to create a new right of marital privacy which the Connecticut law was held to contravene.

Three Justices (Chief Justice EARL WARREN and Justices ARTHUR GOLDBERG and WILLIAM J. BRENNAN), in an opinion by Goldberg, relied specifically on the Ninth Amendment as an additional basis for striking down the law. Justice Goldberg's standard for defining rights "retained by the people" seemed to strike a widely criticized note of open-ended substantive due process. He referred to FUNDAMENTAL RIGHTS and to the "traditions" and "conscience of our people" in order to determine whether a right was to be regarded as "fundamental." It is not surprising that this language prompted a vigorous dissent from Justice HUGO L. BLACK, who regarded the majority and concurring Justices as having engaged in the same unprincipled personal jurisprudence as the conservative Justices who had written the concept of FREEDOM OF CONTRACT into the Constitution in the early part of the twentieth century.

Viewed in isolation, the *Griswold* case might have been regarded merely as involving a slight broadening of enumerated rights to encompass the basic right to decide whether or not to conceive a child. Whether the Court reached this result by finding the new right lurking in "penumbras" formed by "emanations" from existing rights, or by discovering new "unenumerated" rights, was probably of no great concern, because the Connecticut statute was so unreasonable, even in the context of the state's asserted objective of promoting moral behavior, that the law should have been declared invalid under a REASONABLENESS standard. But strong movements were developing in the country during the 1960s and 1970s. Women were moving rapidly toward equality of opportunity to participate in American life. Attitudes about private sexual behavior, marriage, cohabitation, and family relationships were all changing toward an increased respect for individual choice.

In the 1970s the Court responded by recognizing some of these new attitudes and enshrining them in constitutionally protected rights. In EISENSTADT V. BAIRD (1972), for example, the principles of *Griswold* were extended to include the right of an unmarried person to the acquisition and use of contraceptives. The culmination of this trend was ROE V. WADE (1973), where the Court recognized constitutional protection of a woman's right to procure an abortion, particularly during the first twenty-six weeks of pregnancy. *Roe v. Wade*, in turn, generated renewed debate among constitutional scholars over the proper role of the Court in intervening to overturn the legislative decisions of democratically elected legislatures. In this debate the Ninth Amendment started to assume new significance because it provided a possible textual basis for an expanded jurisprudence of individual liberty.

The Ninth Amendment was mentioned in *Roe v. Wade*, but only as one of a number of constitutional provisions to support the Court's conclusion that "liberty" encompassed a woman's child-bearing decision. Justice Douglas, who had written the majority opinion in *Griswold*, based his concurrence in *Roe v. Wade* primarily on the Ninth Amendment and suggested a broad range of personal autonomy rights such as "control over development and expression of one's intellect, interest, tastes, and personality," "freedom of choice in the basic decisions of one's life respecting marriage, divorce, procreation, contraception, and the education and upbringing of children," "freedom to care for one's health and person, freedom from bodily restraint or compulsion, freedom to walk, stroll, or loaf."

After *Roe v. Wade* (perhaps relying on Justice Douglas's expansive concurrence) some litigants sought to use the Ninth Amendment as a basis for expanding personal autonomy rights beyond the scope of sexual privacy. Many lower courts appeared receptive to such claims as the right, under the Ninth Amendment, to control one's personal grooming and appearance and the right to be protected from disclosing personal information. However, in *Kelley v. Johnson* (1976) the Supreme Court upheld a regulation limiting the length of a police officer's hair. Personal autonomy issues continue to be litigated, but the Ninth Amendment is rarely involved as a basis for decision.

Because interest in the Ninth Amendment started with cases involving sexual privacy, it is not surprising that the amendment continues to be used to attack state antisodomy laws. Apart from a summary affirmance in 1976 of a district court opinion, the Court has not specifically addressed the issue of the rights of homosexuals. In 1985 the Court of Appeals for the Fourth Circuit upheld a Ninth Amendment claim that right of private consensual sexual behavior was beyond the reach of state regulation. But even if the Supreme Court should sustain the decision of the Circuit Court the Supreme Court's preferred rationale is likely to be substantive due process, that is, enlarging the definition of "sexual privacy" as part of the "liberty" protected by the Fourteenth Amendment.

One could well conclude that the Ninth Amendment should be allowed to return to the oblivion it experienced prior to the *Griswold* case. Persistent references to the Ninth Amendment by lower court judges, however, and even by Supreme Court Justices (for example, Chief Justice WARREN E. BURGER in RICHMOND NEWSPAPERS, INC. v. VIRGINIA, 1980) suggest that the amendment could serve as an analytical tool for the appraisal of new claims of constitutional rights. If it is to serve as something more than a superfluous additional citation, the Ninth Amendment must offer the promise of the development of a more coherent body of law than has thus far emerged as the Court has recognized new claims of unenumerated constitutional rights.

At present the Court deals with such rights primarily through the technique employed in *Griswold* and its progeny. The Court usually tries to base its decisions on one or more specific constitutional provisions, and then expands those provisions to include new rights. Typical was the *Richmond Newspaper* case, where the Court held that the public had a right of access to criminal trials. Chief Justice Burger's plurality opinion was based on principles said to derive from the First Amendment, even though the amendment itself specifically guarantees, for these purposes, only the rights of speech, press, and assembly. The Chief Justice made specific reference to rights that were not "enumerated" in the Constitution and pointed out that James Madison's concern with the danger of protecting only enumerated rights led to the adoption of the Ninth Amendment.

Despite his reference to the Ninth Amendment, the Chief Justice's approach in *Richmond Newspapers* would appear to be similar to earlier cases, including *Griswold*, where new rights were recognized because they were analogous to existing rights. Freedom of association is a judicially recognized derivation of the First Amendment protection for freedom of expression, and the requirement of proof beyond a REASONABLE DOUBT is derived from the enumerated guarantee of due process. Recognizing the right of marital privacy or the right to terminate a pregnancy may involve a greater leap from the enumerated rights in the First, Fourth, and Fifth Amendments, but the technique of deriving the rights from enumerated rights did not start with *Griswold* or *Roe v. Wade*. Once the leap is made, the further development of the right becomes merely a matter of interpretation of the newly perceived rights.

An alternate approach to the development of unenumerated rights would look instead to the open-ended clauses of the Constitution such as the PRIVILEGES AND IMMUNITIES clauses in Article IV and the Fourteenth Amendment, or the due process clause—or even no clause at all. Some Justices have viewed the developments since *Griswold* as a revival of open-ended substantive due process. This view has characterized the approach of Justices FELIX FRANKFURTER and JOHN MARSHALL HARLAN to the incorporation of procedural rights into the Fourteenth Amendment. They would have relied on the meaning of "liberty" rather than on the lifting of a "right" from the Bill of Rights and transferring the right to the Fourteenth Amendment (the approach of Justice Brennan and ultimately a majority of the Court).

If the Ninth Amendment is to serve as a meaningful vehicle for the protection of unenumerated rights, it should, at the least, have something more to offer than the expansion of enumerated rights exemplified by *Roe v. Wade* and *Richmond Newspapers* or the open-ended substantive due process approach of Justices Frankfurter, Harlan, and Stewart. The Ninth Amendment offers two potential contributions: historical justification and constitutional standard. The historical justification, articulated by Justice Goldberg in *Griswold* and by Chief Justice Burger in *Richmond Newspapers*, provides a powerful support for the argument that "unenumerated rights" have a place in the Constitution.

The same history also suggests a constitutional standard: a range of rights protected by the entire text of the Constitution. To leave the Ninth Amendment open-ended, with no obligation on the part of judges to link unenumerated rights to enumerated rights, would render the amendment indistinguishable from the nontextually based substantive due process. Moreover, confining "retained" rights to those analogous to enumerated rights would be consistent with Madison's conception of the Ninth Amendment. He was not seeking to create new rights. He was concerned that the enumeration of the rights in the Bill of Rights could not possibly take into account similar but undefined rights that could not be fully delineated in a constitutional text. The Ninth Amendment was the original "safety net" to compensate for the imperfection of language and the inability to provide for changing circumstances. Such an approach leaves room for a gradual expansion of rights, but requires some grounding for each newly recognized right in the constitutional text. A text-based standard is one that requires far less justification, in terms of democratic political theory, than a frankly noninterpretivist standard.

Does the Ninth Amendment, as so limited, add an additional dimension to the technique employed in

Griswold or *Richmond Newspapers?* If rights "retained" under the Ninth Amendment are those analogous to rights found elsewhere in the Constitution, how does this approach differ from the approach of Justice Douglas in *Griswold,* which found rights in the "penumbras" formed by "emanations" from existing rights?

One obvious response is that the Ninth Amendment is itself a textual, historically valid justification for this approach to the enforcement of enumerated rights. It thus has a "leg-up" in the quest for legitimacy of judicial intervention. Moreover, Ninth Amendment analysis should derive from the entire text of the Constitution and not merely from other rights. Thus, as Justice Brennan noted in *Zobel v. Williams* (1982), the RIGHT TO TRAVEL can be discerned as a necessary consequence of nationhood as embodied in several constitutional provisions. Similarly, protection of VOTING RIGHTS can be derived from constitutional provisions that contemplate broad voter participation. The Ninth Amendment has never defined absolute rights. Rather, jurisprudence based on the Ninth Amendment will require placing on the balancing scales those individual unenumerated rights that might otherwise be ignored but that are sufficiently analogous to enumerated rights, or to our governmental structure, as to require constitutional protection.

NORMAN REDLICH

Bibliography

BLACK, CHARLES 1981 *Decision According to Law.* New York: Norton.

DUNBAR, L. 1956 James Madison and the Ninth Amendment. *Virginia Law Review* 42:627–643.

ELY, J. H. 1980 *Democracy and Distrust: A Theory of Judicial Review.* Cambridge, Mass.: Harvard University Press.

LAYCOCK, DOUGLAS 1981 Taking Constitutions Seriously: A Theory of Judicial Review by John Hart Ely. *Texas Law Review* 59:343–394.

PATTERSON, B. 1955 *The Forgotten Ninth Amendment* 27; *The Constitution of the United States of America: Analysis and Interpretations,* S. Doc. No. 92–82, 92d Cong.

REDLICH, N. 1961 Are There Certain Rights . . . Retained by the People? *NYU Law Review* 37:787, 802–808.

RHOADES, LYMAN AND PATULA, RODNEY R. 1973 The Ninth Amendment: A Survey of Theory and Practice in the Federal Courts Since *Griswold v. Connecticut. Denver Law Journal* 50:153–176.

VAN ALSTYNE, WILLIAM 1981 Slouching Toward Bethlehem with the Ninth Amendment. *Yale Law Journal* 91:207–216.

NIX v. WILLIAMS
104 S. Ct. 2501 (1984)

A 7–2 Supreme Court held that although an accused's incriminating statements could not be admitted as EVIDENCE because police had interrogated him in violation of his RIGHT TO COUNSEL, physical evidence discovered on the basis of his incriminating statements could be introduced against him if the prosecution, by a preponderance of proof, could show that such evidence would inevitably have been discovered even in the absence of accused's statements. The case produced an "inevitable discovery" exception to the EXCLUSIONARY RULE: any FRUIT OF THE POISONOUS TREE may be used as evidence if it would have been inevitably or ultimately discovered, just as if it had been discovered on the basis of independent or uncontaminated leads. (See BREWER V. WILLIAMS, 1977.)

LEONARD W. LEVY

NIXON, RICHARD M.
(1913–)

Richard Milhous Nixon, the thirty-seventh President of the United States, was born in Yorba Linda, California. An alumnus of Whittier College and Duke University Law School, he practiced law in Whittier, California, from 1937 to 1942. After a brief stint in the enforcement of wartime price controls, he entered the Navy and served with it in the South Pacific. Upon his release from duty he was elected to the House of Representatives from the Twelfth District of California. Shortly he gained national prominence as a member of the HOUSE COMMITTEE ON UN-AMERICAN ACTIVITIES, and he played a decisive role in generating the perjury case against Alger Hiss. Nixon was elected to the Senate from his home state in 1950, gaining new notoriety in denouncing the Democrats for having "lost" China to communism. In 1952 he was elected vice-president as the running mate of DWIGHT D. EISENHOWER. Nixon had riveted national attention—once again—with an impassioned defense on radio and television of his acceptance of money from a political "slush" fund. As vice-president he drew international notice through his "kitchen debate" with Soviet Premier Nikita Khrushchev. Nixon was nominated for President by his party in 1960, but lost to the Democrats' JOHN F. KENNEDY in a close election. Two years later Nixon ran for governor of California and lost. He reentered the private practice of law, this time in New York City. Maintaining and broadening his political contacts, he was again nominated for the presidency by the Republicans in 1968. His campaign theme was a pledge to heal the divisions in the nation that the Vietnam War had created and to bring the hostilities to an honorable conclusion. He won a plurality of the popular vote over the Democrats' HUBERT H. HUMPHREY and George C. Wallace, candidate of the American Independence Party.

As President, Nixon took advantage of the dramatic expansion of the office that had been taking place since the time of FRANKLIN D. ROOSEVELT, recognizing that the public had grown accustomed to regarding the Chief Executive as the undisputed architect of national policies. But Nixon stretched his authority with less restraint than his predecessors, undertaking steps violative of the law and of the Constitution itself. A full explanation for his actions may never be forthcoming. Possibly he felt keenly that his party's inability to capture or control Congress would continue to frustrate his desire to dismantle many New Deal and Great Society programs. He may also have been guided by inner compulsions of ambition and feelings of inadequacy he never articulated. Nixon, at any rate, interpreted by his own lights the constitutional prerogatives of his office, including an assumed right to ignore or modify the letter and intent of laws.

Nixon, for example, did not consider himself obligated to respect the law of 1972 requiring that EXECUTIVE AGREEMENTS arrived at with foreign governments be reported to Congress within sixty days, cavalierly submitting them late. Moreover, he sometimes negotiated them at a lower diplomatic level and labeled them "arrangements." Under Nixon's stewardship, executive agreements were entered into on major matters and formal treaties almost invariably on minor matters—a reversal of the traditional relationship between the two forms of diplomatic undertakings.

Although a few Presidents had sometimes impounded funds appropriated by Congress, the step was generally taken in conformity with congressional intent or under the President's authority as COMMANDER-IN-CHIEF. Nixon broke fresh ground in his assertion of a constitutional power to decline to spend appropriated funds. For him IMPOUNDMENT was a legitimate tool of the President to alter policy set by Congress—and he employed it on a scale hitherto unknown. While some of the funds he refused to release came out of military, space, and public works appropriations, vast amounts also came out of social and environmental programs. By 1973 Nixon's impoundments totaled about $18 billion, between seventeen and twenty percent of the funds he could claim to control. Nixon and his aides maintained that he was following patterns established by previous Presidents. The evidence is, however, that his predecessors did not aim to contravene the will of Congress, but merely postpone immediate expenditure. Nixon, on the other hand, used impoundment to terminate or curtail programs. He defended his actions on the ground that the executive power of the President included a constitutional right to be the people's defender against Congress's inability to hold down nondefense spending.

Nixon's boldness had the effect of giving the executive an item veto of appropriation bills—a remedy long sought by Presidents, and provided for in the CONFEDERATE CONSTITUTION, but consistently withheld from Presidents since first requested by President ULYSSES S. GRANT in 1873. Whatever the merit of the device, Nixon's insistence on exercising it in defiance of Congress was a usurpation of power.

Although WIRETAPPING without formal authorization had long been employed occasionally by Presidents, Nixon was the first Chief Executive who systematically resorted to its use. His practice of it grew out of a determination to keep under wraps the "secret" B-52 raids over Cambodia in 1969. Nixon was apparently fashioning a new conception of his office, metamorphosing it into a "plebiscitary presidency"—one in which the Chief Executive would assume widened power under the Constitution, relying on a reshaped Supreme Court to validate his actions. Nixon's expressed concern was that leaks of information about the "secret war" were putting national security in jeopardy. He ordered the tapping of telephones of members of the National Security Council staff and of several newspaper reporters. The taps were conducted without court order and in patent violation of Title III of the OMNIBUS CRIME CONTROL AND SAFE STREETS ACT of 1968. By countenancing not only illegal wiretapping but, shortly, burglary (in the case of Daniel Ellsberg, who revealed the so-called Pentagon Papers), the hiring of *agents provacateurs* (to conduct "dirty tricks" in election campaigns), and the subverting of the Internal Revenue Service (to punish "enemies"), Nixon was substituting his personal sanction for established law.

In assuming this prerogative, Nixon believed he was exercising what he regarded as INHERENT POWER to maintain national and domestic security. This claim of "inherent power," sometimes also set forth by previous Presidents, has never been recognized as valid by the courts. In UNITED STATES V. UNITED STATES DISTRICT COURT (1972) the Supreme Court by an 8–0 vote ruled unconstitutional the Nixon administration's practice of engaging in domestic electronic surveillance without a judicial warrant.

Nixon's assertion of an EXECUTIVE PRIVILEGE to reject a SUBPOENA became the issue in the case of UNITED STATES V. NIXON (1974). The suit revolved around Nixon's refusal to surrender tapes containing information relevant to the prosecution of some of his close aides for offenses that included obstruction of justice by "covering up" the administration's involvement in the Watergate break-in. In its unanimous decision requiring the President to turn over the tapes, the Supreme Court recognized that a President is entitled to confidentiality of communication— needful for "protection of the public interest in candid, objective, and even blunt or harsh opinion in presidential decisionmaking." But, the Court concluded, "when the ground for asserting privilege as to subpoenaed material sought for use in a criminal trial is based only on the generalized interest in confidentiality, it cannot prevail over the fundamental demands of DUE PROCESS OF LAW in the fair administration of criminal justice. The generalized assertion of privilege must yield to the demonstrated, specific need for EVIDENCE in a pending criminal trial."

Nixon toyed with the idea of disobeying the decision, but decided to comply, surrendering the tapes covered in the decision. Indeed, he published their contents, thus providing the House Judiciary Committee with the "smoking gun"—the now famous words in which the President counseled inducing the Central Intelligence Agency to limit the FBI's investigation of the Watergate burglary.

Nixon's use of the POCKET VETO was also remarkable. As intended by the Framers of the Constitution it may be used at the end of a session of Congress when a President who does not sign a bill cannot return it to Congress because it stands adjourned. Nixon unhesitatingly used pocket vetoes when Congress was merely in brief recess. In *Kennedy v. Simpson* (1973) a district court overturned as misused Nixon's pocket veto of the Family Practice of Medicine Bill, which had been opposed by only three members of Congress.

Nixon's transgressions of the law and the Constitution contributed to the passage of two major pieces of legislation. One was the CONGRESSIONAL BUDGET AND IMPOUNDMENT CONTROL ACT of 1974, which detailed the arrangements under which Congress may monitor the deferral by a President of appropriated funds. The second law, responding to the deployment of troops in Asia, first by President LYNDON B. JOHNSON and then by Nixon, was the War Powers Resolution of 1973, severely restricting the ability of a President to use military force outside the United States without congressional authorization. Nixon and all succeeding Presidents have denounced this law as an unconstitutional abridgment of the power of the President to direct the armed forces.

Nixon made two nominations to the Supreme Court that failed of confirmation. In 1969 he submitted the name of Judge Clement F. Haynsworth of South Carolina, a designation that met implacable opposition from CIVIL RIGHTS groups and labor unions. Early the following year Nixon sent forward the name of Judge G. Harrold Carswell of the Fifth Circuit Court of Appeals in Florida. Denounced as a racist in many quarters, although he had renounced his older views on race, Carswell was also opposed as lacking the superior qualifications required for a seat on the highest court.

In addition to placing HARRY A. BLACKMUN of Minnesota, LEWIS F. POWELL, Jr., of Virginia, and WILLIAM H. REHNQUIST of Arizona on the Supreme Court, Nixon also appointed the fourteenth Chief Justice, Judge WARREN E. BURGER of the District of Columbia Court of Appeals, whose conservative speeches and advocacy of judicial restraint appealed to the President. Nixon had been especially impressed by an address that Burger delivered in 1967 on the subject of "law and order," from which Nixon had borrowed during the 1968 campaign for the Presidency. He was mindful, too, of the support Burger had given him during his critical time in the 1952 campaign.

Nixon was the first Chief Executive to resign the Presidency—a consequence of the Watergate affair that convulsed the nation from 1972 to 1974. The reasons for the burglary—carried out by Nixon's political aides at the headquarters of the Democratic party—have never been adduced. From the start of the investigation the administration tried to cover up its connection to the crime. In the long drawnout effort to get at the truth, the focus of the quest became the President himself: what did he know and when did he know it? The evidence lay in the recordings of conversations in his office that Nixon was revealed to have been making for years. The President turned over the critical tapes just as the House of Representatives seemed on the verge of voting to impeach him. He surrendered his office on August 9, 1974. The following month, his successor, GERALD R. FORD, issued the former President a "full, free, and absolute" pardon for any crimes he may have committed.

HENRY F. GRAFF

Bibliography

KURLAND, PHILIP B. 1978 *Watergate and the Constitution.* Chicago: University of Chicago Press.
NATHAN, RICHARD P. 1973 *The Plot That Failed: Nixon and the Administrative Presidency.* New York: Wiley.
NIXON, RICHARD M. 1978 *R.N.: The Memoirs of Richard Nixon.* New York: Grosset & Dunlap.
SCHLESINGER, ARTHUR M., JR. 1973 *The Imperial Presidency.* Boston: Little, Brown.
WHITE, THEODORE H. 1975 *Breach of Faith: The Fall of Richard Nixon.* New York: Atheneum.

NIXON, UNITED STATES v.
418 U.S. 683 (1974)

This litigation unfolded contemporaneously with congressional investigation of the Watergate affair and with proceedings in the House of Representatives for the IMPEACHMENT of President RICHARD M. NIXON. (See WATERGATE AND THE CONSTITUTION.) A federal GRAND JURY had indicted seven defendants, including Nixon's former attorney general and closest White House aides, charging several offenses, including conspiracy to obstruct justice by "covering up" the circumstances of a burglary of Democratic party offices in Washington. The grand jury named Nixon as an unindicted co-conspirator. A special prosecutor had been appointed to handle this prosecution. To obtain evidence, the special prosecutor asked Judge John Sirica to issue a SUBPOENA ordering Nixon to produce electronic tapes and papers relating to sixty-four White House conversations among persons named as conspirators, including Nixon himself.

Judge Sirica issued the subpoena in mid-April 1974; on May 1, Nixon's counsel moved to quash the subpoena and to expunge the grand jury's naming of the President as a co-conspirator. Sirica denied both motions and ordered Nixon to produce the subpoenaed items. When Nixon appealed, the special prosecutor asked the Supreme Court to hear the case, bypassing the court of appeals. The Court granted that motion and advanced argument to July 8. On July 24 the Court upheld the subpoena, 8–0, including the votes of three Nixon appointees. Justice WILLIAM H. REHNQUIST, formerly a Justice Department official under the indicted ex-attorney general, had disqualified him-

self. A week following the decision, before Nixon had complied with it, the House Judiciary Committee recommended his impeachment. When Nixon turned over the tapes on August 5, they included a conversation that even his strongest supporters called a "smoking gun." On August 9 the President resigned.

A year earlier a White House press officer had said Nixon would obey a "definitive" decision of the Supreme Court about the tapes. At ORAL ARGUMENT in the Supreme Court, however, Nixon's counsel, pressed to say that the President had "submitted himself" to the Court's decision, evaded any forthright promise of compliance. Even after the Court's decision, the press reported, Nixon and his aides debated for some hours whether he should comply with the subpoena. Some have reported that the Court's unanimity was an important factor influencing that decision.

The Court itself seems to have been impressed with the need for unanimity; its bland opinion, formally attributed to Chief Justice WARREN E. BURGER, bore the external marks of a document hurriedly negotiated—as investigative reporters have said it was. The Court brushed aside objections to its JURISDICTION, such as the FINAL JUDGMENT RULE. Nixon also argued that the courts had no jurisdiction over an "intrabranch" dispute between the President and his subordinate, the special prosecutor. Responding, the Court emphasized the "uniqueness" of the conflict, but apart from that comment its argument bordered on incoherence. After gratuitously remarking that the executive branch had exclusive discretionary control over federal criminal prosecutions, the Court reversed field, discovering a guarantee of independence for the special prosecutor in the regulation that appointed him and promised not to remove him absent a consensus among certain congressional leaders. Both the Court's propositions were dubious. (See APPOINTING AND REMOVAL POWER.) Yet the Court marched on to some heroic constitutional issues concerning relations between the executive and judicial branches.

Both sides had appealed to the abstraction of SEPARATION OF POWERS. Nixon argued first that the judiciary lacked power "to compel the President in the exercise of his discretion," and second that the President enjoyed an EXECUTIVE PRIVILEGE to keep confidential his conversations with his advisers. The first argument blurred two separate issues: the President's immunity from judicial process and the POLITICAL QUESTION issue of his discretion to control disclosure of his conversations. This latter claim of absolute executive privilege overlapped his second main argument.

That argument began with an absolute privilege claim, but if that claim failed the President sought to persuade the Court to recognize a wide scope for a qualified privilege.

The special prosecutor, opposing both presidential immunity and the claim of absolute privilege, assumed the existence of a qualified privilege. That privilege was lost, he argued, when there was substantial reason to believe that the participants in a presidential conversation had been planning a crime.

The Court's opinion, like Nixon's argument, blurred the boundaries of separate issues in the case. The decision to uphold the subpoena, however, implicitly rejected the claim of presidential immunity, and the Court expressly rejected the claim of absolute privilege. A qualified privilege did exist, the Court said—by way of assumption, not demonstration—but the privilege was defeated when the specific confidential information sought was shown to be relevant, admissible evidence for a pending federal prosecution. The Court thus disposed of the case without mentioning Nixon's own possible complicity in crime; it dismissed the question whether the President could constitutionally be named as a co-conspirator.

Today some form of a qualified executive privilege is assumed to exist, but the scope of the privilege remains largely undefined. *Nixon*'s most important contribution to our constitutional law, however, lay elsewhere: in its reaffirmation that even the highest officer of government is not beyond the reach of the law and the courts. Nixon's brief had included this remark, designed to reassure: "it must be stressed we do not suggest the President has the attributes of a king. *Inter alia*, a king rules by inheritance and for life." The *Nixon* decision reminded us that there are also other differences.

KENNETH L. KARST

Bibliography
SYMPOSIUM 1974 United States v. Nixon. *UCLA Law Review* 22:1–140.

WOODWARD, BOB and ARMSTRONG, SCOTT 1979 *The Brethren: Inside the Supreme Court.* Pages 285–347. New York: Simon & Schuster.

NIXON v. ADMINISTRATOR OF GENERAL SERVICES
433 U.S. 425 (1977)

Ex-president RICHARD M. NIXON sued to prevent implementation of the Presidential Recordings and Materials Preservation Act. In upholding the constitutionality of the act, the Supreme Court rejected Nixon's contentions that it violated SEPARATION OF POWERS and EXECUTIVE PRIVILEGE, abridged Nixon's RIGHT OF PRIVACY and FREEDOM OF ASSOCIATION, and constituted a BILL OF ATTAINDER.

DENNIS J. MAHONEY

NIXON v. CONDON
286 U.S. 73 (1932)

After the decision in NIXON V. HERNDON (1927), Texas amended its statute, giving a political party's state executive committee the power to set voting qualifications for the party's PRIMARY ELECTIONS. The Democratic party's committee limited primary voting to whites. Nixon, a black, again was denied a primary ballot and again sued election officials for DAMAGES. The Supreme Court reversed a dismissal of the action, holding, 5–4, that the committee's conduct was STATE ACTION in violation of the FOURTEENTH AMENDMENT. The line of "Texas primary cases" continued with GROVEY V. TOWNSEND (1935).

KENNETH L. KARST

NIXON v. FITZGERALD
457 U.S. 731 (1982)
HARLOW v. FITZGERALD
457 U.S. 800 (1982)

In these cases the Supreme Court significantly expanded the scope of EXECUTIVE IMMUNITY in actions for DAMAGES brought by persons injured by official action. Fitzgerald sued former President RICHARD M. NIXON and two of his aides, alleging that he had been dismissed from an Air Force job in retaliation for revealing to a congressional committee a two billion dollar cost overrun for a transport aircraft.

In *Nixon* the Court held, 5–4, that the President is absolutely immune from civil damages—not merely for the performance of particular functions but for all acts within the "outer perimeter" of his official duties. Justice LEWIS F. POWELL, for the majority, rested his decision not on the text of the Constitution but on "the constitutional tradition of the SEPARATION OF POWERS." Unlike other executive officers, who have only a qualified immunity from damages actions, the President occupies a unique place in the government. He must be able to act without fear of intrusive inquiries into his motives. The dissenters agreed that some of the President's functions should be clothed in absolute immunity, but argued that a qualified immunity from suit was sufficient in most cases to protect presidential independence.

In *Harlow* the Court, 8–1, rejected the aides' claim of absolute immunity, but broadened the scope of qualified executive immunity. Under previous decisions, this immunity was lost when the official negligently violated "clearly established" rights or acted with malicious intention to deprive constitutional rights or to cause harm. The Court here eliminated the "malicious intention" test for losing the immunity. A great many actions for damages against executive officials are based on claims of right that are not "clearly established." *Harlow* forbids damages in such a case even though the official acts with malice.

KENNETH L. KARST

NIXON v. HERNDON
273 U.S. 536 (1927)

This decision was the first in a series of "Texas primary cases." Texas law disqualified blacks from voting in Democratic party PRIMARY ELECTIONS. Nixon, refused a ballot under this law, sued election officers for damages under the federal CIVIL RIGHTS laws, asserting a denial of EQUAL PROTECTION OF THE LAWS under the FOURTEENTH AMENDMENT and a denial of the right to vote on account of race, in violation of the FIFTEENTH AMENDMENT. (See VOTING RIGHTS.) The Supreme Court reversed a dismissal of the action, holding for Nixon on his equal protection claim and not discussing the Fifteenth Amendment. The next case in the series was NIXON V. CONDON (1932).

KENNETH L. KARST

NLRB v. FRIEDMAN-HARRY MARKS CLOTHING CO.

See: Wagner Act Cases

NLRB v. FRUEHAUF TRAILER COMPANY

See: Wagner Act Cases

NLRB v. JONES & LAUGHLIN STEEL CORP.

See: Wagner Act Cases

NO-KNOCK ENTRY

Police are not allowed to enter a house to search or make an ARREST unless they have procured a warrant based on PROBABLE CAUSE, according to PAYTON V. NEW YORK (1980) and *Vale v. Louisiana* (1970). If police cannot get a warrant because of EXIGENT CIRCUMSTANCES, they may act on probable cause alone. In either case, the Supreme Court has not articulated specific rules for no-knock entries. At COMMON LAW, police could not make a forcible entry unless admittance was refused after they announced their authority and purpose, and the FEDERAL CODE OF CRIMINAL PROCEDURE prescribes the same requirements. But the Court has not made this rule into a formal FOURTH AMENDMENT requirement. Rather, the Court emphasizes that entries must always be reasonable, and forcible entries must be based on exigent circumstances. A few states authorize by statute the issuance of no-knock warrants, but any blanket sanctioning of such entries probably would be held to violate the Fourth Amendment.

CATHERINE HANCOCK

Bibliography
LAFAVE, WAYNE R. 1978 *Search and Seizure: A Treatise on the Fourth Amendment.* Vol. 2:122–140. St. Paul, Minn.: West Publishing Co.

NOLO CONTENDERE

(Latin: "I do not choose to contest [it].") This statement, variously defined as plea and not a plea, indicates that the defendant will not fight a charge against him. Of the same immediate effect as a guilty plea, it admits the facts charged but cannot be used as a confession of guilt in any other proceeding. Acceptance by a court is discretionary.

DAVID GORDON

NONINTERPRETIVISM

See: Constitutional Interpretation

NONTESTIMONIAL COMPULSION

See: Testimonial Compulsion

NORMAN v. BALTIMORE & OHIO RAILROAD COMPANY

See: Gold Clause Cases

NORRIS, GEORGE W.
(1861–1944)

George William Norris, a progressive Republican from Nebraska, served in the House of Representatives from 1903 to 1913. He led the revolt against Speaker Joseph Cannon that, in 1910, broke the power of the speaker to control virtually all legislation in the house. As a United States senator (1913–1943) Norris was the author of the TWENTIETH AMENDMENT, which ended the "lame duck" sessions of Congress, and co-author of the NORRIS-LaGuardia Act (1932), which outlawed YELLOW DOG CONTRACTS and restricted use of federal court INJUNCTIONS against labor strikes, and of the TENNESSEE VALLEY AUTHORITY ACT (1933). Norris supported most of President FRANKLIN D. ROOSEVELT's "New Deal" and criticized Supreme Court decisions that held such legislation unconstitutional. Although he favored a constitutional amendment to restrict national JUDICIAL REVIEW, he opposed Roosevelt's plan to pack the Court with pro-administration justices.

DENNIS J. MAHONEY

Bibliography

LOWITT, RICHARD 1963–1978 *George W. Norris.* 3 Vols. Syracuse, N.Y.: Syracuse University Press; Urbana, Ill.: University of Illinois Press.

NORRIS v. ALABAMA
294 U.S. 587 (1935)

Clarence Norris, one of the Scottsboro boys (see POWELL V. ALABAMA, 1932), on retrial moved to quash the INDICTMENT and trial venire (pool of potential jurors) on the ground that qualified black citizens were systematically excluded from jury service solely on the basis of race. On denial of his motion by the trial judge, Norris was retried and again found guilty. The state supreme court affirmed the JUDGMENT of the trial court that no JURY DISCRIMINATION existed. The Supreme Court, voting 8–0, reversed the judgment after reviewing the evidence for itself for the first time in such a case. The evidence showed that for a generation or more no black person had been called for jury service in the county and that a substantial number of black persons qualified under state law. In an opinion by Chief Justice CHARLES EVANS HUGHES, the Court ruled that the evidence of black exclusion made a *prima facie* case of denial of the EQUAL PROTECTION guaranteed by the FOURTEENTH AMENDMENT. *Norris* began a line of cases that led to the virtual extinction of RACIAL DISCRIMINATION in the composition of juries.

LEONARD W. LEVY

NORRIS-LAGUARDIA ACT
47 Stat. 70 (1932)

Reeling from a string of adverse court decisions, labor saw the Norris-LaGuardia Act of 1932 as Congress's long overdue remedy for Supreme Court antipathy. A panel of experts, including Professor FELIX FRANKFURTER, helped to draft a bill to end the abuse of labor INJUNCTIONS, and, as eventually passed by large majorities in Congress, the act greatly diminished the use of federal injunctions in labor disputes. The act recognized the need for COLLECTIVE BARGAINING and encouraged union formation, ending years of misinterpretation of the spirit, if not the letter, of the CLAYTON ACT. One of the key provisions of the new act (section 4) outlawed the issuance of federal injunctions against those who "whether acting singly or in concert" might strike, aid, or publicize strikes, join unions, or assemble peacefully. YELLOW DOG CONTRACTS, sustained in HITCHMAN COAL & COKE COMPANY V. MITCHELL (1917), were also rendered unenforceable (section 3). In DUPLEX PRINTING PRESS COMPANY V. DEERING (1921) the Court had unjustifiably declared that the Clayton Act provision covering labor disputes applied only to related parties, employer and employee, not to those engaged in a secondary boycott. Section 13 rewrote that practice by redefining "labor dispute" so that the parties need no longer be in "proximate relation" to each other. Although the act divested federal courts of injunctive power, it provided exceptions where illegal acts or injury were likely. Moreover, the employers had to make "every reasonable effort" to negotiate a settlement before seeking an injunction (section 8).

The act's explicitly stated purpose was to foster labor's right to organize and act without federal judicial interference. The act created no new substantive rights but enlarged the area in which labor could operate. The act's procedures would be upheld in *Lauf v. E. G. Shinner & Company* (1938) and its substance upheld in *New Negro Alliance v. Sanitary Grocery Company* (1938).

DAVID GORDON

NORTH ATLANTIC TREATY
63 Stat. 2241 (1949)

Following World War II, the Soviet Union rapidly expanded its influence in Eastern and Central Europe. Fearing a further "Communist offensive," the West, led initially by Belgium, Canada, France, Luxembourg, the Netherlands, the United Kingdom, and the United States, negotiated the North Atlantic Treaty which, it was hoped, would deter Soviet expansionism. The treaty was signed by twelve countries on April 4, 1949, and presently lists a total of sixteen countries among its signatories. The primary objectives of the treaty are as stated in its preamble: "to promote stability and well-being in the North Atlantic area" and "to unite . . . for collective defense and for the preservation of peace and security." The treaty stipulates that "an armed attack against one or more of the [State] Parties in Europe or North America shall be considered an attack against them all" and that, in the event of such an attack, each State Party shall take "such action as it deems necessary, including the use of armed force, to restore and maintain the security of the North Atlantic area." Some commentators have suggested that this language may effect an unconstitutional delegation of United States authority to declare war. The argument is of minimal concern, however, inasmuch as Article 11 of the treaty provides that all of the treaty's provisions shall be "carried out by the Parties in accordance with their respective constitutional processes." The discretionary language of Article 5 ("such action as it deems necessary") reinforces this conclusion.

BURNS H. WESTON

(SEE ALSO: *Status of Forces Agreements; Treaty Power.*)

Bibliography

FOX, WILLIAM T. and SCHILLING, WARNER R., EDS. 1973 *European Security and the Atlantic System.* New York: Columbia University Press.
SAULLE, MARIA RITA 1979 *NATO and Its Activities.* Dobbs Ferry, N.Y.: Oceana Publications.

NORTHERN PIPELINE CONSTRUCTION COMPANY v. MARATHON PIPE LINE COMPANY
458 U.S. 50 (1982)

If Congress were to make a wholesale transfer of JURISDICTION over matters within the JUDICIAL POWER OF THE UNITED STATES to administrative agencies or LEGISLATIVE COURTS, the result would be a serious risk of undermining the independence of the judiciary. Then, under what circumstances can Congress make any such transfer? The question blurs constitutional doctrine with practical statecraft. In *Marathon* the Supreme Court had an opportunity to illuminate this subject, which has long seemed impervious to light.

In the BANKRUPTCY ACT (1978) Congress created a category of bankruptcy judges, who would hold office not during good behavior (as do judges of CONSTITUTIONAL COURTS) but for fourteen-year terms. The act authorized the bankruptcy judges to decide not only matters peculiar to bankruptcy, such as the marshaling and distribution of assets and the discharge of bankrupts from certain liabilities, but also "related" matters, including actions on behalf of bankrupts against other persons, based on state law. The Supreme Court, 6–3, held that the grant of jurisdiction over the "related" matters exceeded the limits of Article III.

Four Justices concluded that federal jurisdiction over matters not involving "public rights"—dealings between the national government and others, or subject to that government's regulation—must be vested in constitutional courts, with certain limited exceptions. Three Justices espoused balancing Article III's concerns for judicial independence against other practical needs of administering the governmental system. Neither view commanded a majority of the Court, and the doctrinal murk deepened.

KENNETH L. KARST

(SEE ALSO: *Thomas v. Union Carbide Agricultural Products Company,* 1985.)

NORTHERN SECURITIES CO. v. UNITED STATES
193 U.S. 197 (1904)

A bare majority of the Supreme Court, in a broad construction of congressional power under the COMMERCE CLAUSE, upheld the constitutionality of the SHERMAN ANTITRUST ACT as applied to holding companies. The Court thus extended the scope of the Sherman Act to companies not directly engaged in such commerce which nevertheless controlled INTERSTATE COMMERCE.

The formation in 1901 of the Northern Securities Company, a holding company comprising both the Hill-Morgan and the Harriman interests, united parallel competing lines. In March 1902, the government filed an EQUITY suit to dissolve the company. The question was clear: was a holding company, whose subsidiaries' operations were its only connection with interstate commerce, exempt from the Sherman Act? The Court split 5–4 but without a majority opinion.

Justice JOHN MARSHALL HARLAN, for the plurality, followed UNITED STATES V. TRANS-MISSOURI FREIGHT ASSOCIATION (1897) and other cases, arguing that the Sherman Act established competition as a test for interstate commerce. Harlan declared that a combination need not be directly in commerce to restrain it: intent to restrain or potential for restraint was all that was needed, and here potential restraint could be found in the reduction of competition resulting from the holding company's formation. Harlan refused to interpret the statute using the RULE OF REASON. He also broadly construed the commerce clause, curtly dismissing defense allegations that the INJUNCTION violated state sovereignty and the TENTH AMENDMENT. Justice DAVID J. BREWER concurred only in Harlan's result. Abandoning his earlier opinions, Brewer now embraced the rule of reason but concluded that even under that rule the Northern Securities Company clearly constituted an unlawful restraint of trade.

Justices EDWARD D. WHITE and OLIVER WENDELL HOLMES each wrote dissents. The former followed the definition of interstate commerce in UNITED STATES V. E. C. KNIGHT COMPANY (1895), stressing that stock ownership did not place the defendants within the scope of the Sherman Act. Holmes's first written dissent on the Supreme Court emphasized a COMMON LAW reading of the statute. He believed that the holding company device was neither a combination nor a contract in restraint of trade. Holmes asserted that this case so nearly resembled *Knight* as to require no deviation from that opinion.

Counted by THEODORE ROOSEVELT "one of the greatest achievements of my administration because it emphasized the fact that the most powerful men in this country were held to accountability before the law," this decision's importance lay both in Harlan's insistence on the supremacy of federal law and in the reinvigoration of a law that business had hoped the Court rendered ineffectual in *Knight*.

DAVID GORDON

Bibliography
APPEL, R. W., JR. 1975 The Case of the Monopolistic Railroadman. In John A. Garraty, ed., *Quarrels That Have Shaped the Constitution.* New York: Harper & Row.

NORTHWESTERN FERTILIZER CO. v. HYDE PARK
97 U.S. 659 (1878)

In 1867 the Illinois legislature chartered the company for a term of fifty years to manufacture fertilizer, from dead animals, outside the city limits of Chicago. The nearby village of Hyde Park regarded the company's factory as an unendurable nuisance, injurious to the public health. Immediately before the legislature chartered the company it empowered the village to abate public nuisances excepting the company. The village passed an ordinance prohibiting the existence of any company engaged in any offensive or unwholesome business within a distance of one mile. The ordinance put the fertilizer company out of business. It invoked its chartered rights against the ordinance, which it claimed violated the CONTRACT CLAUSE.

On the basis of past decisions the Court should have accepted the company's argument, holding that the village had no authority to abate its factory. By a vote of 7–1, however, the Supreme Court ruled that the village had validly exercised its police power to protect the public health. Justice NOAH SWAYNE for the Court declared that the company's charter must be construed narrowly and held that it provided no exemption from liability or nuisances. Swayne quoted from the decision earlier that term in BOSTON BEER CO. V. MASSACHUSETTS in which the Court announced the DOCTRINE of INALIENABLE POLICE POWER. Both cases had the result of weakening the contract clause's traditional protection of chartered rights.

LEONARD W. LEVY

NORTHWEST ORDINANCE
(1787)

This congressional enactment, which applied to the territory northwest of the Ohio River, was the most significant accomplishment of the United States under the ARTICLES OF CONFEDERATION. In effect the ordinance provided for self-government under constitutional law in the TERRITORIES, thus "solving" a colonial problem by avoiding it. The pattern for government, which subsequently was extended to other western territories, allowed for growth from a system of congressional government to statehood and admission to the Union "on an equal footing with the original States, in all respects whatever. . . ." As soon as a district reached a population of 5,000 males of voting age, each one possessing a fifty-acre freehold was entitled to vote for representatives to a general assembly. The assembly had authority to elect a delegate to Congress with the right to debate but not to vote. When the population reached 60,000, the territory could apply for admission as a state, on condition that it had a REPUBLICAN FORM OF GOVERNMENT and a state constitution. Ohio, Illinois, Indiana, Michigan, and Wisconsin were formed out of the Northwest Territory; this ordinance established a model for territorial governance and the admission of other states in the American West.

The ordinance was the first federal document to contain a bill of rights. To extend "the fundamental principles of civil and RELIGIOUS LIBERTY," Congress provided articles that were to have constitutional status, remaining "forever . . . unalterable" except by common consent. These articles guaranteed that the inhabitants of a territory should always be entitled to the writ of HABEAS CORPUS, TRIAL BY JURY, representative government, and judicial proceedings "according to the course of the COMMON LAW" (in effect, a provision for DUE PROCESS OF LAW.) As an extra safeguard the articles encapsulated a provision from MAGNA CARTA by insuring that no person should be deprived of liberty or property "but by the judgment of his peers, or the LAW OF THE LAND." In addition, the articles protected the right to BAIL except in capital cases, enjoined that all fines should be "moderate," and prohibited CRUEL OR UNUSUAL PUNISHMENT. Another article that provided a federal precedent for a similar provision in the BILL OF RIGHTS of the Constitution of the United States dealt with EMINENT DOMAIN: no person's property could be taken except in a public exigency, when he must be fully compensated for its value. The CONTRACT CLAUSE of the Constitution also originated in this ordinance: one article declared that no law should ever be made or have force that in any manner interfered with or affected existing private contracts made in good faith and without fraud. Other articles encouraged "schools and the means of education" and protected Indian lands and liberties. One provision of the ordinance had the effect of reducing sex discrimination in land ownership and preventing the introduction of the law of primogeniture; it ordained that the property of anyone dying intestate (without a will) should be distributed in equal parts to all children or next of kin. The ordinance also protected the religious sentiments and modes of worship of all orderly persons, without exception, and in a precedent-making clause declared, "There shall be neither slavery nor involuntary servitude" in the Northwest Territory or states formed from it. The ordinance, which was probably drafted in the main by RUFUS KING and NATHAN DANE, remains one of the most constructive and influential legislative acts in American history.

LEONARD W. LEVY

Bibliography
PHILBRICK, FRANCIS S.   1965   *The Rise of the New West, 1754–1830.* Pages 120–133. New York: Harper & Row.

NORTZ v. UNITED STATES

See: Gold Clause Cases

NOTICE

When unsure what is right, American society often falls back on a process in which people on all sides of a disputed question have their say before a decision is rendered. Moreover, even if one cannot participate in a governmental decision, our notions of the state require that one know in advance the standards by which officials will judge us. To have one's say or to conform one's behavior to a standard one must know of the proceeding or the standard. Because such knowledge is so essential to this scheme of things, the Constitution at numerous points requires that those affected by governmental actions receive notice.

Clauses as diverse and specific as the requirement that Congress publish a journal and the prohibitions against EX POST FACTO laws and BILLS OF ATTAINDER, as well as the more general requirements of the DUE PROCESS clauses require notice in various circumstances. Because of its generality the due process clause has generated most of the litigation about constitutionally required notice. In PROCEDURAL DUE PROCESS cases courts have struggled to distinguish two situations: those in which persons need have only the *opportunity* of finding out about contemplated government actions, and situations in which they must receive more individualized attention. The maxim that ignorance of the law is no excuse expresses the proposition that the legislature need not tell each of us that it has passed some law. We rely instead on the hope that our legislators represent us and on the opportunity we have to adjust our behavior after the law takes effect. The Supreme Court has, however, required that laws defining criminal acts be sufficiently specific to enable persons who *do* look at them to tell what acts are prohibited.

As the focus of government attention narrows from all citizens (the subject of statutes) to more specific contexts, the Constitution requires more elaborate and specific forms of notice, notice that is often linked with a subsequent hearing. Thus the Court has not required the Colorado legislature to notify all the citizens of Denver before altering their property assessments, but it has required notice (and a hearing) for individual property owners on a block to be assessed on the basis of frontage feet. Similarly with administrative or judicial adjudication: persons whose property or liberty stands in jeopardy must receive notice of the threatened governmental action.

Even in such individual adjudication, however, due process requires only that parties who will be bound by official decisions receive the best notice practicable given the circumstances. For example, in a suit to approve the trustee's stewardship of a common trust fund with more than a hundred beneficiaries, the Court required individual notice only to those beneficiaries who could easily be located; members of the group thus notified shared an interest with the unnotified and would represent them, the Court said in *Mullane v. Central Hanover Bank & Trust* (1950).

Once it has notified them with appropriate specificity, government requires much of its citizens; until such notice, however, it can require little.

STEPHEN C. YEAZELL

Bibliography

TRIBE, LAURENCE H. 1978 *American Constitutional Law.* Chap. 10. Mineola, N.Y.: Foundation Press.

NOXIOUS PRODUCTS DOCTRINE

The first step in development of a NATIONAL POLICE POWER was the "noxious products doctrine," which Justice JOHN MARSHALL HARLAN propounded in CHAMPION V. AMES (1903). According to this doctrine, Congress has the power to prohibit INTERSTATE COMMERCE in any item that is so injurious to the public—in this case, lottery tickets—as to pollute the commerce of which it is a part. In HAMMER V. DAGENHART (1918), the doctrine became a limitation on the commerce power: because the products of child labor were not inherently more harmful than those of adult labor, Congress lacked power to forbid their interstate transportation. The doctrine was abandoned after UNITED STATES V. DARBY LUMBER (1941).

DENNIS J. MAHONEY

NULLIFICATION

THOMAS JEFFERSON first suggested the doctrine of nullification in the second Kentucky Resolutions (1799), where he asserted that the sovereign states are the only proper judges of whether the federal government has violated the Constitution and "that a nullification . . . [by] those sovereignties, of all unauthorized acts . . . is the rightful remedy." (See VIRGINIA AND KENTUCKY RESOLUTIONS.) In the 1820s, South Carolinians Robert J. Turnbull and Whitemarsh Seabrook laid the doctrinal foundations of an expanded nullification argument by denouncing the expansion of federal authority. In *Consolidation* (1824), THOMAS COOPER argued that the states remained independent sovereigns, having given only limited and express powers to Congress.

JOHN C. CALHOUN systematized and refined the Carolinians' constitutional arguments. He maintained that the people of the separate states never relinquished their SOVEREIGNTY, and that sovereignty was indivisible. In ratifying the Constitution, the states created a government of limited, specified, and delegated authority. Calhoun used the legal doctrine of agency to explain the federal relationship: "The States . . . formed the compact, acting as sovereign and independent communities. The General Government is but [their] creature . . . a government emanating from a compact between sovereigns . . . of the character of a joint commission . . . having, beyond its proper sphere, no more power than if it did not exist." ("Address on the Relation of the States and the Federal Government," 1831.) When the federal government (the agent) exceeded its authority, the states (the principals), in the exercise of their sovereign power, could "interpose" their authority by nullifying the federal statute or action, which would be void in the nullifying states. If three-fourths of the other states adopted a constitutional amendment empowering the federal government to perform the nullified act, the state then had the choice of acquiescing or of withdrawing from the compact (the federal Constitution) by SECESSION. But Calhoun emphasized that nullification was a peaceable alternative, not a preliminary step, to secession.

Calhoun's theory found application in a dispute, ostensibly over protective tariffs, that produced the Nullification Crisis of 1832. For a decade, Carolinians had declared that their objections to specific federal programs such as INTERNAL IMPROVEMENTS or the national bank were merely specific parts of a larger objection to federal intrusion into the states' internal autonomy. The antitariff struggle was, in James Henry

Hammond's metaphor, a "battle at the outposts" to prevent an assault on the real "citadel," slavery. When the Tariff of 1832 failed to meet Carolinian demands for an abrogation of the 1828 Tariff of Abominations, a South Carolina convention adopted an ordinance nullifying it and prohibiting its enforcement in the state.

President ANDREW JACKSON reacted forcefully. In his "Proclamation to the People of South Carolina" (1832), he denounced the theory of secession, insisting that the federal government was a true government to which the states had surrendered a part of their sovereignty. (See JACKSON'S PROCLAMATION.) "Disunion by armed force is treason," he warned. Congress enacted the FORCE ACT (1833), which provided for alternative means of collecting the tariff in South Carolina and enhanced the president's power to use militia and regular forces to suppress resistance to federal authority. Congress also began a downward revision of the tariff. With the crisis over the tariff assuaged, the South Carolina legislature denounced Jackson's "Proclamation" and a subsequent convention made the empty gesture of nullifying the Force Act.

In 1837, Calhoun offered six congressional resolutions that would have opened all federal TERRITORIES to slavery. Congress adopted four of these, including one declaring that the federal government was only a "common agent" of the states and possessed only "delegated" powers. But antislavery agitation in the North increased, and many Northerners endorsed the WILMOT PROVISO (1846), which would have excluded slavery from the territories acquired as a result of the Mexican War. To meet this threat, other southern radicals, including Robert Barnwell Rhett, Edmund Ruffin, and William Lowndes Yancey, turned to secession, which subsumed nullification.

Though the Union victory in the Civil War left the doctrines of state sovereignty, INTERPOSITION, nullification, and secession all defunct, southern political leaders briefly and ineffectually exhumed interposition theories during efforts in the late 1950s to thwart desegregation in southern universities and schools.

WILLIAM M. WIECEK

Bibliography
CURRENT, RICHARD W. N. 1963 *John C. Calhoun.* New York: Washington Square Press.
FREEHLING, WILLIAM W. 1965 *Prelude to Civil War: The Nullification Controversy in South Carolina, 1816–1836.* New York: Harper & Row.

NULLIFICATION CONTROVERSY

See: Constitutional History, 1829–1848

OBITER DICTUM

(Latin: "Said in passing.") In an opinion, a judge may make observations or incidental remarks. Because these comments are unnecessary to the DECISION, they are not a part of the HOLDING and thus do not bind the court in later cases. Such statements are often referred to by the plural, dicta.

DAVID GORDON

OBLIGATION OF CONTRACTS

The CONSTITUTIONAL CONVENTION OF 1787, engaged as it was in producing a frame of national government, provided in the Constitution for only a very few restrictions on the LEGISLATIVE POWER of the STATES. Among these was the proscription of any state law impairing the obligation of contracts; that the delegates omitted to include a similar prohibition as to Congress is attributable entirely to the fact that they did not contemplate the existence of national contract law. The phrase "obligation of contracts" did not exist as a term of art, but originated in the Constitution; its meaning is not as obvious as it may seem.

The moral obligation of contracts derives from the voluntary agreement of parties who promise to perform certain duties in exchange for some valuable consideration. In the NATURAL RIGHTS political philosophy of the Framers of the Constitution, the obligation to obey the law itself derives from a SOCIAL COM-PACT, in which the individual obliges himself to obey in exchange for the state's guarantee of security for his life, liberty, and property. The moral obligation of contracts, of course, cannot be impaired by state law.

But contracts are also legally binding under the COMMON LAW (as modified from time to time by statute). One of the things that induces men to enter into contracts is the knowledge that the state, by its courts and officers, stands ready to enforce the contractual duties undertaken by the parties. This knowledge is especially important when, as in contracts for lending money, one party will have already performed his side of the bargain while the promise of the other party remains "executory," that is, to be performed in the future. The CONTRACT CLAUSE of the Constitution was intended to prevent state law from undermining the enforceability at law of obligations voluntarily entered into.

The Framers of the Constitution well knew the temptation to repudiate obligations improvidently undertaken. SHAYS' REBELLION, which had just been suppressed in Massachusetts, had been directed against judicial enforcement of farm mortgage loans. The CONTINENTAL CONGRESS, sitting at the same time as the Convention, recognized the same danger and wrote into the NORTHWEST ORDINANCE a provision that "no law ought ever to be made or have force in the said territory, that shall, in any manner whatever, interfere with or affect private contracts, or engagements, *bona fide*, and without fraud previously formed."

The history of the constitutional guarantee against impairment of contracts has been the story of slow, but steady, erosion. Much of the erosion has been effected by limiting the extent of the legal obligation or by discovering remedies that purport to leave the obligation intact while depriving the obligee of the benefit of his bargain. In STURGES V. CROWNINSHIELD (1819) Chief Justice JOHN MARSHALL defined the obligation of a contract as "the law which binds the parties to perform their agreement." Subsequently, in OGDEN V. SAUNDERS (1827), over Marshall's vigorous dissent, the majority held that the "law" in Marshall's definition was the municipal law of contracts in force where and when the contract was entered into, which local law became part of the contract regardless of any contrary intent of the parties to it. The legislature (or courts) may alter the law of contracts so long as the alteration is prospective in effect. Even after *Ogden v. Saunders,* however, the Supreme Court continued to read the contract clause as proscribing retroactive state legislation affecting contracts.

In times of economic distress, when the number of debtors exceeds the number of creditors, the majority tends to use the political process to shield itself from the consequences of improvident engagements. When the economic hardship is prolonged, even constitutional barriers may be unable to withstand the pressure for relief. Under such pressure, courts have held debtors' relief legislation constitutional by distinguishing the obligation of the contract from the remedies available when the contract is breached. Thus, for example, in HOME BUILDING AND LOAN COMPANY V. BLAISDELL (1933) the HUGHES COURT held that a state law extending the contractual time for repayment of mortgage loans and precluding creditors from exercising their contractual right to sell the mortgaged property to satisfy the debt did not impair the obligation of the loan contract (because the debtor still owed the money) but merely altered the remedy. This sophistical holding permitted the form of the constitutional guarantee to endure even as its substance drained away.

In recent years the Court has partially repudiated the rationale of *Blaisdell* and has revived the contract clause as a check on state ECONOMIC REGULATION. In UNITED STATES TRUST CO. V. NEW JERSEY (1977) as regards public contracts, and in ALLIED STRUCTURAL STEEL CO. V. SPANNAUS (1978) as regards private contracts, the Court subjected statutes that apparently impaired the obligation of contracts to a higher STANDARD OF REVIEW than is commonly applied to economic legislation.

DENNIS J. MAHONEY

Bibliography

FRIED, CHARLES 1981 *Contract as Promise: A Theory of Contractual Obligation.* Cambridge, Mass.: Harvard University Press.

O'BRIEN, UNITED STATES v.
391 U.S. 367 (1968)

The *O'Brien* opinion is today widely cited in briefs and judicial opinions defending governmental action against claims of violation of the FREEDOM OF SPEECH. In 1965 Congress amended the SELECTIVE SERVICE ACT to make it a crime to destroy or mutilate a draft registration card. The amendment's legislative history made clear that it was aimed at antiwar protest, but the Supreme Court nonetheless upheld, 8–1, the conviction of a protester for DRAFT CARD BURNING, rejecting his FIRST AMENDMENT claims.

Writing for the Court, Chief Justice EARL WARREN assumed that SYMBOLIC SPEECH of this kind was entitled to First Amendment protection. However, he announced a doctrinal formula now dear to the hearts of government attorneys, a formula that seemed to apply generally to all First Amendment cases: "[W]e think it clear that a government regulation is sufficiently justified if it is within the constitutional power of the Government; if it furthers an important or substantial governmental interest; if the governmental interest is unrelated to the suppression of free expression; and if the incidental restriction on alleged First Amendment freedoms is no greater than is essential to the furtherance of that interest."

This very case seemed appropriate for application of the formula to overturn the protesters' conviction, but it was not to be. Here, Warren said, the power of the federal government to "conscript manpower" was clear; further, he placed great importance on the government's interests in keeping draft cards intact. As for the purpose to suppress expression, the Chief Justice took away what he had just given to First Amendment challengers: the Court should not inquire, he said, into possible improper congressional motivations for an otherwise valid law. (See LEGISLATION.) Finally, he said, the government's interests could not be served by any less restrictive means.

It is hard to avoid the conclusion that the Justices, embattled on political fronts ranging from SEGREGATION to school prayers, thought it prudent not to add to the Court's difficulties a confrontation with Congress and the President over the VIETNAM WAR. Justice WILLIAM O. DOUGLAS, however, dissented alone on the ground that the Court should consider the constitutionality of military CONSCRIPTION in the absence of a DECLARATION OF WAR by Congress.

KENNETH L. KARST

Bibliography

ELY, JOHN HART 1975 Flag Desecration: A Case Study in the Roles of Categorization and Balancing in First Amendment Analysis. *Harvard Law Review* 88:1482–1508.

NIMMER, MELVILLE B. 1973 The Meaning of Symbolic Speech under the First Amendment. *UCLA Law Review* 21:29–62.

O'BRIEN v. BROWN
409 U.S. 1 (1972)

This decision involved challenges to the unseating of delegates to the Democratic National Convention. The Supreme Court refused to decide the case and stayed the lower court's decision, since the full convention had not met on the question and little time was available to decide delicate, "essentially political" issues. Three Justices dissented.

WARD E. Y. ELLIOTT

OBSCENITY

Obscenity laws embarrass ALEXIS DE TOCQUEVILLE's claim that there is "hardly a political question in the United States which does not sooner or later turn into a judicial one." It is not merely that the obscenity question became a serious judicial issue rather much later than sooner. It is that the richness of the questions involved have been lost in their translation to the judicial forum.

Obscenity laws implicate great questions of political theory including the characteristics of human nature, the relationship between law and morals, and the appropriate role of the state in a democratic society. But these questions were barely addressed when the Court first seriously considered a constitutional challenge to obscenity laws in the 1957 cases of ROTH V. UNITED STATES and *Alberts v. California*.

The briefs presented the Court with profoundly different visions of FIRST AMENDMENT law. Roth argued that no speech including obscenity could be prohibited without meeting the CLEAR AND PRESENT DANGER test, that a danger of lustful thoughts was not the type of evil with which a legislature could be legitimately concerned, and that no danger of antisocial conduct had been shown. On the other hand,

the government urged the Court to adopt a balancing test that prominently featured a consideration of the value of the speech involved. The government tendered an illustrative hierarchy of nineteen speech categories with political, religious, economic, and scientific speech at the top; entertainment, music, and humor in the middle; and libel, obscenity, profanity, and commercial PORNOGRAPHY at the bottom. The government's position was that the strength of public interest needed to justify speech regulation diminished as one moved down the hierarchy and increased as one moved up.

In response to these opposing contentions, the Court took a middle course. Relying on cases like BEAUHARNAIS V. ILLINOIS (1952), the Court seemed to embrace what HARRY KALVEN, JR., later called the TWO-LEVEL THEORY of the First Amendment. Under this theory, some speech is beneath the protection of the First Amendment; only that speech within the amendment's protection is measured by the clear and present danger test. Thus some speech is at the bottom of a two-level hierarchy, and the *Roth* Court sought to explain why obscenity deserved basement-level nonprotection.

History, tradition, and consensus were the staple of the Court's argument. Justice WILLIAM J. BRENNAN explained that all "ideas having even the slightest redeeming social importance" deserve full First Amendment protection. But, he said, "implicit in the history of the First Amendment is the rejection of obscenity as utterly without redeeming social importance." Then he pointed to the consensus of fifty nations, forty-eight states, and twenty obscenity laws passed by the Congress from 1842 to 1956. Finally, relying on an OBITER DICTUM from CHAPLINSKY V. NEW HAMPSHIRE (1942), the Court explained that obscene utterances "are of such slight social value as a step to truth that any benefit that may be derived from them is clearly outweighed by the social interest in order and morality."

From the perspective of liberal, conservative, or feminist values, the Court's reliance on the *Chaplinsky* quotation amounts to a cryptic resolution of fundamental political questions. Liberals would advance several objections. Some would suggest that the Court underestimates the contribution to truth made by sexually oriented material. David Richards, for example, has suggested that

pornography can be seen as the unique medium of a vision of sexuality . . . a view of sensual delight in the erotic celebration of the body, a concept of easy freedom without consequences, a fantasy of timelessly repetitive indulgence. In opposition to the Victorian view that narrowly defines proper sexual function in a rigid way that is analogous to ideas of excremental regularity and moderation, pornography builds a model of plastic variety and joyful excess in sexuality. In opposition to the sorrowing Catholic dismissal of sexuality as an unfortunate and spiritually superficial concomitant of propagation, pornography affords the alternative idea of the independent status of sexuality as a profound and shattering ecstasy [1974, p. 81].

Even some liberals might find these characterizations overwrought as applied to Samuel Roth's publications, such as *Wild Passion* and *Wanton by Night*. Nonetheless, many of them would argue that even if such publications have no merit in the MARKETPLACE OF IDEAS, individuals should be able to decide for themselves what they want to read. Many would argue along with John Stuart Mill that "[T]he only purpose for which power can be rightfully exercised over any member of a civilized community, against his will, is to prevent harm to others." Such a principle is thought to advance the moral nature of humanity, for what distinguishes human beings from animals is the capacity to make autonomous moral judgments. From this perspective, the *Roth* opinion misunderstands the necessity for individual moral judgments and diminishes liberty in the name of order without a proper showing of harm.

Conservatives typically agree that humans are distinguished from animals by their capacity to make rational moral judgments. They believe, however, that liberals overestimate human rational capacity and underestimate the importance of the state in promoting a virtuous citizenry. Moreover, they insist that liberals do not sufficiently appreciate the morally corrosive effects of obscenity. From their perspective, obscenity emphasizes the base animality of our nature, reduces the spirituality of humanity to mere bodily functions, and debases civilization by transforming the private into the public. As Irving Kristol put it, "When sex is a public spectacle, a human relationship has been debased into a mere animal connection."

Feminists typically make no objection to erotic material and make no sharp separation between reason and passion. Their principal objection is to the kind of sexually oriented material that encourages male sexual excitement in the domination of women. From their perspective, a multibillion dollar industry promotes antifemale propaganda encouraging males to get, as Susan Brownmiller put it, a "sense of power from viewing females as anonymous, panting playthings, adult toys, dehumanized objects to be used, abused, broken and discarded." From the feminist

perspective, the *Roth* opinion's reference to the interests in order and morality obscures the interest in equality for women. From the conservative perspective, the opinion is underdeveloped. From the liberal perspective, it is wrong-headed.

Liberals gained some post-*Roth* hope from the Court's treatment of the obscenity question in STANLEY V. GEORGIA (1969). In *Stanley* the Court held that the possession of obscenity in the home could not be made a criminal offense without violating the First Amendment. More interesting than the holding, which has since been confined to its facts, was the Court's rationale. The Court insisted that "our whole constitutional heritage rebels at the thought of giving government the power to control men's minds." It denied the state any power "to control the moral content of a person's thoughts." It suggested that the only interests justifying obscenity laws were that obscene material might fall into the hands of children or that it might "intrude upon the sensibilities or privacy of the general public."

Many commentators thought that *Stanley* would be extended to protect obscene material where precautions had been taken to avoid exposure to children or nonconsenting adults. Indeed such precautions were taken by many theaters, but the Supreme Court (the composition of which had changed significantly since *Stanley*) reaffirmed *Roth* and expanded on its rationale in *Paris Adult Theatre I v. Slaton* (1973).

The Court professed to "hold that there are legislative interests at stake in stemming the tide of commercialized obscenity, even assuming it is feasible to enforce effective safeguards against exposure to the juvenile and the passerby. These include the interest of the public in the quality of life and the total community environment, the tone of commerce in the great city centers, and, possibly, the public safety itself." The Court did not suggest that the link between obscenity and sex crimes was anything other than arguable. It did insist that the "States have the power to make a morally neutral judgment that public exhibition of obscene material, or commerce in such material, has a tendency to injure the community as a whole . . . or to jeopardize, in Chief Justice Earl Warren's words, the State's 'right . . . to maintain a decent society.'"

Several puzzles remain after the Court's explanation is dissected. First, "arguable" connections to crime do not ordinarily suffice to justify restrictions of First Amendment liberties. A merely arguable connection to crime supports restriction only if the speech involved is for some other reason outside First

Amendment protection. Second, as the Court was later to recognize in YOUNG V. AMERICAN MINI THEATRES, INC. (1976), the reference to quality of life, the tone of commerce in the central cities, and the environment have force with respect to all sexually oriented bookstores and theaters whether or not they display obscene films or sell obscene books. The Court in MILLER V. CALIFORNIA (1973) limited the definition of obscenity to that material which the "average person, applying contemporary community standards" would find that "taken as a whole appeals to the prurient interest" and "depicts and describes, in a patently offensive way, sexual conduct specifically defined by the applicable state law"; and which, "taken as a whole, lacks serious literary, artistic, political, or scientific value." No one has suggested that these restrictions on the definition bear any relationship to the tone of commerce in the cities.

Moreover, if the intrusive character of public display were the issue, mail order sales of obscene material should pass muster under the First Amendment; yet there is no indication that the Court is prepared to protect such traffic. As interpreted in the *Paris Adult Theatre* opinion, *Stanley v. Georgia* appears to protect only those obscene books and films created and enjoyed in the home; the right to use in the home amounts to no more than that. There is no right to receive obscene material—even in plain brown wrappers.

Perhaps least convincing is the Court's attempt to harmonize its *Paris Adult Theatre* holding with liberal thought. It claims to have no quarrel with the court's insistence in *Stanley* that the state is without power "to control the moral content of a person's thoughts." Because obscene material by the Court's definition lacks any serious literary, artistic, political, or scientific value, control of it is said to be "distinct from a control of reason and the intellect." But this is doubletalk. The power to decide what has serious artistic value is the power to make moral decisions. To decide that material addressing "reason" or the "intellect" is all that is important to human beings is ultimately to make a moral decision about human beings. Implicit in the latter idea, of course, is the belief that the enjoyment of erotic material for its own sake is unworthy of protection. But the view is much more general. The Court supposes that human beings have a rational side and an emotional side, that the emotional side needs to be subordinated and controlled, and that such suppression or control is vital to the moral life. That is why the Court believes that the contribution of obscenity to truth is outweighed by the state's inter-

est in morality. The Court's insistence on the right to maintain a decent society is in fact an insistence on the state's interest in the control of the "moral content of a person's thoughts."

Finally, it is simply dazzling for the Court to suggest that the states are engaged in a "morally neutral" judgment when they decide that obscene material jeopardizes the right to maintain a decent society. When states decide that "a sensitive key relationship of human existence, central to family life, community welfare, and the development of human personality can be debased and distorted by commercial exploitation of sex," they operate as moral guardians, not as moral neutrals. Nonetheless, the Courts' bows to liberal theory in *Paris Adult Theatre* are revealing, and so are the guarded compromises of the obscenity test adopted in *Miller v. California*. The bows and compromises reflect, as do the opinions of the four dissenting Justices in *Paris Adult Theatre*, that America is profoundly divided on the relationship of law to morality and on the meaning of free speech. Since *Paris Adult Theatre* and *Miller*, and despite those decisions, the quantity of erotic material has continued to grow. At the same time, feminist opposition to pornography has ripened into a powerful political movement. The Supreme Court's decisions have neither stemmed the tide of commercial pornography nor resolved the divisions of American society on the issue. These political questions will continue to be judicial questions.

STEVEN SHIFFRIN

Bibliography
CLOR, HARRY M. 1969 *Obscenity and Public Morality*. Chicago: University of Chicago Press.
KALVEN, HARRY, JR. 1960 The Metaphysics of the Law of Obscenity. *Supreme Court Review* 1960:1–45.
LEDERER, LAURA, ed. 1980 *Take Back the Night: Women on Pornography*. New York: Bantam Books.
RICHARDS, DAVID A. J. 1974 Free Speech and Obscenity Law: Toward a Moral Theory of the First Amendment. *University of Pennsylvania Law Review* 123:45–99.

O'CONNOR, SANDRA DAY
(1930–   )

Sandra Day O'Connor, the first woman Justice to serve on the Supreme Court, was appointed by President RONALD REAGAN in 1981. She had served previously as the nation's first woman senate majority leader in her home state of Arizona and as a member of the Arizona Court of Appeals. In announcing her nomination the President extolled her as someone who would be a rigid adherent of constitutional principles, taking an exacting view of the SEPARATION OF POWERS as a limitation on JUDICIAL ACTIVISM, and respecting the role of FEDERALISM in the constitutional scheme. Although there is little doubt that one motivation in appointing O'Connor was to deprive the Democrats of the opportunity of appointing the first woman Justice, the President's expectations have, by and large, not been disappointed.

For O'Connor constitutional jurisprudence means, above all, an adherence to enduring constitutional principles, recognizing that, while the application of these principles may change, the principles themselves are rooted in the constitutional text and in the precepts that animate the Constitution. In her dissent in *Akron v. Akron Center for Reproductive Health* (1983), O'Connor complained that the majority's decision rested "neither [on] sound constitutional theory nor [on] our need to decide cases based on the application of neutral principles." It is not entirely clear yet whether the Justice mistakenly identifies constitutional principles with "neutral principles." Her opinions generally indicate an awareness that the Constitution is not neutral with respect to its ends and purposes. She has refused to accept the prevailing view that the Constitution is merely a procedural instrument that is informed by no purposes or principles beyond the procedures themselves.

In CRIMINAL PROCEDURE cases O'Connor has adhered to the principle she enunciated in KOLENDER V. LAWSON (1983): "Our Constitution is designed to maximize individual freedoms within a framework of ORDERED LIBERTY. Statutory limitations on those freedoms are examined for substantive authority and content as well as for definiteness or certainty of expression." The Justice has used this rationale to resist unwarranted attempts to expand criminal DUE PROCESS rights beyond those clearly prescribed or fairly implied by the Constitution. For example, in OREGON V. ELSTAD (1985) O'Connor refused to extend the FRUIT OF THE POISONOUS TREE doctrine either to uncoerced inculpatory statements made after police violation of the MIRANDA RULES, or as in NEW YORK V. QUARLES (1984), to nontestimentary EVIDENCE produced as a result of a *Miranda* violation. In the latter case O'Connor concluded that Justice WILLIAM H. REHNQUIST's majority opinion had created "a fine-spun new DOCTRINE on public safety exigencies incident to custodial interrogation, complete with the hair-splitting distinctions that currently plague our FOURTH AMENDMENT jurisprudence." Moreover, dissenting in *Taylor v. Alabama* (1982), O'Connor would

not have allowed an illegal ARREST to taint a confession that followed appropriate *Miranda* warnings; nor in *South Dakota v. Neville* (1983) would she allow the claim that the refusal to take a blood-alcohol test is protected by the RIGHT AGAINST SELF-INCRIMINATION.

O'Connor has been no less resolute in her efforts to protect the constitutional role of the states in the federal system. In her dissent in GARCIA V. SAN ANTONIO METROPOLITAN TRANSIT AUTHORITY (1985) she remarked that the principle of "state autonomy . . . requires the Court to enforce affirmative limits on federal regulation of the states." The majority opinion, she continued, created the "real risk that Congress will gradually erase the diffusion of power between state and nation on which the Framers based their faith in the efficiency and vitality of our Republic." O'Connor has also staunchly supported the "exhaustion" doctrine of federal HABEAS CORPUS review as a means "to protect the state courts' role in the enforcement of federal law and prevent disruption of state judicial proceedings." The rule that all federal claims must first be exhausted in state court proceedings is, as she wrote in *Engle v. Isaac* (1982), a recognition that "the State possesses primary authority for defining and enforcing the criminal law." She continued that "[f]ederal intrusions into State criminal trials frustrate both the States' sovereign power to punish offenders and their good-faith attempts to honor constitutional rights." And in HAWAII HOUSING AUTHORITY V. MIDKIFF (1984) O'Connor made clear that the Court would accord the utmost deference to state legislatures in matters of "social legislation."

O'Connor was less deferential, however, in the instance where a state maintained a women-only nursing school. Writing for the majority in MISSISSIPPI UNIVERSITY FOR WOMEN V. HOGAN (1982), O'Connor stated that in "limited circumstances a gender-based classification favoring one sex can be justified if it intentionally and directly assists members of the sex that is disproportionately burdened." Here, the SEX DISCRIMINATION actually harmed the intended beneficiaries by perpetuating "stereotyped" and "archaic" notions about the role of women in society.

O'Connor has urged the Court to reexamine some important issues connected with the ESTABLISHMENT OF RELIGION clause of the FIRST AMENDMENT. Concurring in WALLACE V. JAFFREE (1985), O'Connor agreed that an Alabama law providing for a moment of silence was unconstitutional because it sought to sanction and promote prayer in public schools. She dissented, however, from the Court's decision in AGUILAR V. FELTON (1985) striking down the use of federal funds to provide remedial education by public school teachers for parochial school students. While agreeing in LYNCH V. DONNELLY (1983) that every governmental policy touching upon religion must have a secular purpose, O'Connor suggested that the entanglement test propounded in LEMON V. KURTZMAN (1971) should be reexamined.

In the area of EQUAL PROTECTION rights, O'Connor has taken the firm stance that rights belong to individuals. In *Ford Motor Company v. Equal Employment Opportunity Commission* (1982), and in her concurring opinion in FIREFIGHTERS LOCAL #1784 V. STOTTS (1984), O'Connor argued that remedies must be limited to those who can demonstrate actual injury and must be fashioned in a way that protects the settled expectations of innocent parties. She thus adheres to the original intention of the framers of the FOURTEENTH AMENDMENT and of the CIVIL RIGHTS ACT OF 1964, reaffirming the principle that lies at the heart of constitutional jurisprudence—that rights belong to individuals and not to the racial or gender group of which they are members. Employing narrowly construed and analytical opinions, O'Connor has begun to build a solid base for the Court's return to a jurisprudence that looks to the articulation of the Constitution's enduring principles.

EDWARD J. ERLER

Bibliography

CORDRAY, RICHARD A. and VRADLIS, JAMES T. 1985 The Emerging Jurisprudence of Justice O'Connor. *University of Chicago Law Review* 52:389–459.

O'CONNOR, SANDRA DAY 1981 Trends in the Relationships between the Federal and State Courts from the Perspective of a State Court Judge. *William and Mary Law Review* 22:801–815.

O'CONNOR v. DONALDSON
422 U.S. 563 (1975)

Donaldson was initially billed as the case that would decide whether a mental patient held in custody had a constitutional "right to treatment." Ultimately the Court did not decide that issue, but it did make some important pronouncements on the relation between MENTAL ILLNESS AND THE CONSTITUTION.

Kenneth Donaldson was committed to a state hospital at the request of his father; the committing judge found that he suffered from "paranoid schizophrenia." Although the commitment order specified "care, maintenance, and treatment," for almost fifteen years Donaldson received nothing but "milieu therapy"—

the hospital superintendent's imaginative name for involuntary confinement. Donaldson finally sued the superintendent and others for damages under SECTION 1983, TITLE 42, UNITED STATES CODE, claiming they had intentionally denied his constitutional rights. The federal district judge instructed the jury that Donaldson's rights had been denied if the defendants had confined him against his will, knowing that he was neither dangerous nor receiving treatment. The jury awarded damages, and the court of appeals affirmed, specifically endorsing the district court's theory of a mental patient's constitutional right to treatment.

The Supreme Court unanimously held that Donaldson had stated a valid claim, but remanded the case for reconsideration of the hospital superintendent's assertion of EXECUTIVE IMMUNITY. Justice POTTER STEWART, for the Court, said that a finding of mental illness alone could not justify a state's confining a person indefinitely "in simple custodial confinement." The Court did not reach the larger question of a "right to treatment"; it disclaimed any need to decide whether persons dangerous to themselves or others had a right to be treated during their involuntary confinement by the state, or whether a nondangerous person could be confined for purposes of treatment. But when the state lacked any of the usual grounds for confinement of the mentally ill—the safety of the person confined or others, or treatment for illness—involuntary confinement was a denial of liberty without DUE PROCESS OF LAW. Confinement was not justified, for example, in order to provide the mentally ill with superior living standards, or to shield the public from unpleasantness. To support the latter point, the Court cited FIRST AMENDMENT decisions including COHEN V. CALIFORNIA (1971). Chief Justice WARREN E. BURGER concurred in the Court's opinion, but wrote separately to express his opposition to any constitutional "right to treatment."

KENNETH L. KARST

OFFICE OF MANAGEMENT AND BUDGET

The rapid growth of the federal government in the twentieth century has created the need for an institution to coordinate both fiscal and substantive policy. In 1921, Congress empowered the President to prepare and submit a BUDGET for the government. Previously, the government had had no central budgeting function: the various agencies had made funding requests directly to the appropriations committees in Congress. The President exercises the budgeting function through the Office of Management and Budget (OMB). Although OMB controls the requests that Congress receives, Congress is free to appropriate any amount that it considers appropriate.

The budgeting function accords the President an important opportunity to set the agenda for congressional deliberations over appropriations. Notwithstanding the modern presence of a budget process within Congress itself, Congress finds itself responding initially to the President's views of the best resource allocation for the government. And, of course, Congress is aware that its departure from the President's recommended budget may result in the presidential veto of an appropriations bill. In consequence, through OMB the President exercises great influence on actual appropriations. Moreover, appropriations usually confer discretion concerning the amounts to be spent and the precise uses to be made of the funds. The President supervises the agencies' actual spending through OMB.

OMB also exercises limited control over the substantive policies that the agencies follow. The Supreme Court, in MYERS v. UNITED STATES (1926), recognized presidential power to "supervise and guide" the executive agencies in their exercise of power that Congress has delegated to them. This does not extend to the independent regulatory commissions because, in HUMPHREY'S EXECUTOR v. UNITED STATES (1935), the Supreme Court declared those commissions to be independent of the President except for the constitutional power to appoint their members, and except for powers over them that Congress explicitly grants the President, such as budget review.

Policy supervision therefore concentrates on the executive agencies. In part because of doubts about the extent of the President's power to dictate policy even when it is formed in the executive agencies, OMB has usually limited its supervision to requiring agencies to comply with procedural directives imposed by Presidential EXECUTIVE ORDERS. These directives are thought to be less intrusive than outright commands setting substantive policy. Several Presidents have directed the agencies to prepare analyses of the costs and benefits of their regulations, and to submit them to OMB for review and comment. In view of the size of the executive establishment and the complexity of the issues it considers, this kind of procedural supervision and occasional ad hoc consultation on major policy decisions is the most that the relatively small bureaucracy that serves the President in OMB can hope to accomplish.

HAROLD H. BRUFF

Bibliography

MILLS, GREGORY B. and PALMER, JOHN L., eds. 1984 *Federal Budget Policy in the 1980s.* Washington D.C.: The Urban Institute Press.

OFFICIAL IMMUNITY

See: Executive Immunity; Judicial Immunity; Legislative Immunity; Municipal Immunity; Sovereign Immunity

OGDEN v. SAUNDERS
12 Wheaton 213 (1827)

Ogden established the doctrine that a state bankruptcy act operating on contracts made after the passage of the act does not violate the OBLIGATION OF A CONTRACT. The majority reasoned that the obligation of a contract, deriving from positive law, is the creature of state laws applicable to contracts. A contract made after the enactment of a bankruptcy statute is, therefore, subject to its provisions; in effect the statute enters into and becomes part of all contracts subsequently made, limiting their obligation but not impairing it.

For a minority of three, Chief Justice JOHN MARSHALL dissented, losing control of his Court in a constitutional case for the first and only time during his long tenure. He would have voided all state bankruptcy acts that affected the obligation of contracts even prospectively. Grounding his position in the immutable HIGHER LAW principles of morality and natural justice, he maintained that the right of contract is an inalienable right not subject to positive law. The parties to a contract, not society or government, create its obligation. Marshall believed that the majority's interpretation of the CONTRACT CLAUSE would render its constitutional prohibition on the states "inanimate, inoperative, and unmeaning." Had his opinion prevailed, contractual rights of property vested by contract would have been placed beyond government regulation, making the contract clause the instrument of protecting property that the Court later fashioned out of the DUE PROCESS clause substantively construed. Until then, despite Marshall's fears, the contract clause remained the principal bastion for the

DOCTRINE of VESTED RIGHTS. This case, however, ended the Court's doctrinal expansion of that clause. *Ogden* prevented constitutional law from confronting the nation with a choice between unregulated capitalism and socialism.

LEONARD W. LEVY

OHIO LIFE INSURANCE AND TRUST CO. v. DE BOLT

See: *Piqua Branch Bank v. Knoop*

OKANOGAN INDIANS v. UNITED STATES

See: Pocket Veto Case

OLIVER, IN RE
333 U.S. 257 (1948)

Since 1917 Michigan had maintained a unique GRAND JURY system, allowing a single judge to be a grand jury with all its inquisitorial powers as well as retain his judicial power to punish for contempt any witness whose testimony he believed to be false or evasive. In the course of a secret grand jury proceeding, a judge summarily sentenced Oliver for contempt. The Supreme Court held the Michigan procedure a violation of SIXTH AMENDMENT rights—denial of PUBLIC TRIAL and of an opportunity to defend himself—without DUE PROCESS OF LAW, contrary to the FOURTEENTH AMENDMENT. Justice HUGO L. BLACK spoke for a 7–2 majority.

LEONARD W. LEVY

OLIVER v. UNITED STATES
466 U.S. 170 (1984)

A 6–3 Supreme Court, speaking through Justice LEWIS F. POWELL, reinvigorated the sixty-year-old "open fields" DOCTRINE, according to which the FOURTH AMENDMENT, whose language protects "persons, houses, papers, and effects," does not extend to open fields. No one doubts that the police, or public, may view land from a plane. The question in *Oliver* was whether the police could ignore "No Trespassing" signs and make a warrantless investigation of fenced-

in backlands used to grow marijuana, seize EVIDENCE, and introduce it in court despite a TRESPASS on private property. Powell declared that no one could reasonably have a constitutionally protected expectation of privacy in an open field, well away from the curtilage or land immediately surrounding a house (and therefore part of the area to which the Fourth Amendment's protection extends). The dissenters objected that the language of the amendment does not expressly include many areas which the Court has ruled to be within its protection, such as telephone booths, offices, curtilages, and other places which one may reasonably expect to be secure against warrantless police intrusion.

LEONARD W. LEVY

OLMSTEAD v. UNITED STATES
277 U.S. 438 (1928)

Federal agents installed WIRETAPS in the basement of a building where Roy Olmstead, a suspected bootlegger, had his office and in streets near his home. None of Olmstead's property was trespassed upon. A sharply divided Supreme Court admitted the wiretap EVIDENCE in an opinion that virtually exempted ELECTRONIC EAVESDROPPING from constitutional controls for forty years. The dissents by Justices OLIVER WENDELL HOLMES and LOUIS D. BRANDEIS are classic statements of the government's obligation to obey the law.

Olmstead argued that because the prosecution's evidence came entirely from the wiretaps, it could not be used against him; wiretapping, he claimed, was a SEARCH AND SEIZURE under the FOURTH AMENDMENT, and because the amendment's warrant and other requirements had not been met, the wiretap evidence was illegally obtained. He also claimed that use of the wiretap evidence violated his RIGHT AGAINST SELF-INCRIMINATION under the Fifth Amendment; further, that because the agents had violated a state statute prohibiting wiretapping, the evidence was inadmissible, apart from the Fourth and Fifth Amendments.

Chief Justice WILLIAM HOWARD TAFT, writing for a five-Justice majority, rejected all Olmstead's contentions. The self-incrimination claim was dismissed first: the defendants had not been compelled to talk over the telephone but had done so voluntarily. This aspect of *Olmstead* has survived to be applied in cases such as HOFFA V. UNITED STATES (1966). As to the Fourth

Amendment claims: first, the Court ruled that the amendment was violated only if officials trespassed onto the property of the person overheard, and no such trespass had taken place—the agents had tapped Olmstead's telephones without going onto his property. Second, the Court limited Fourth Amendment protection to "material things," not intangibles like conversations. Third, the Court seemed to deny any protection for the voice if projected outside the house. As to the claim that the agents' violation of the state statute required excluding the evidence, the Chief Justice found no authority for such exclusion.

Justice Holmes wrote a short dissent, condemning the agents' conduct as "dirty business." Justice Brandeis wrote the main dissent in which he disagreed with the majority's reading of the precedents, its very narrow view of the Fourth Amendment, and its willingness to countenance criminal activity by the government. For him, the Fourth Amendment was designed to protect individual privacy, and he warned that the "progress of science in furnishing the Government with means of espionage" called for a flexible reading of the amendment to "protect the right of personal security." He stressed that because a tap reaches all who use the telephone, including all those who either call the target or are called, "WRITS OF ASSISTANCE or GENERAL WARRANTS are but puny instruments of tyranny and oppression when compared with wiretapping." Responding to the argument that law enforcement justified both a narrow reading of the amendment and indifference to the agents' violation of state law, he wrote: "Experience should teach us to be most on our guard to protect liberty when the Government's purposes are beneficent. . . . The greatest dangers to liberty lurk in insidious encroachment by men of zeal, well-meaning but without understanding. . . . Our Government is the potent, the omnipresent teacher. For good or for ill, it teaches the whole people by its example."

Although the decision was harshly criticized, it endured. In *Goldman v. United States* (1942), *Olmstead* was read to allow police to place a microphone against the outside of a wall, because no trespass onto the property was involved. Wiretapping itself remained outside constitutional controls, though section 605 of the COMMUNICATIONS ACT of 1934 was construed by the Supreme Court in NARDONE V. UNITED STATES (1937) to bar unauthorized interception and divulgence of telephone messages.

In 1954, however, *Olmstead* began to be undermined. In IRVINE V. CALIFORNIA (1954), the Court indicated that intangible conversations were protected by the Fourth Amendment. The Court found

a trespass when the physical penetration was only a few inches into a party wall as in SILVERMAN V. UNITED STATES (1961) or by a thumbtack as in *Clinton v. Virginia* (1964). Finally, in KATZ V. UNITED STATES (1967), the Supreme Court overruled *Olmstead*, holding that a trespass was unnecessary for a violation of the Fourth Amendment and that the amendment protects intangibles, including conversations.

HERMAN SCHWARTZ

Bibliography
MURPHY, WALTER F. 1966 *Wiretapping on Trial: A Case Study in the Judicial Process.* New York: Random House.

OLNEY, RICHARD
(1835–1917)

In 1893 President GROVER CLEVELAND offered the post of ATTORNEY GENERAL to Richard Olney. A Massachusetts Democrat and highly successful railroad lawyer, Olney sought the advice of his major clients. All agreed he should accept the office and one even continued him on the payroll after he took the post, a conflict of interest that reflected the biases Olney allowed to influence his actions in office.

Olney was one of a few lawyers in the country who had litigated the recently passed SHERMAN ANTITRUST ACT; he had successfully defended the Whiskey Trust, and he believed that section 2 of the act was "void because of vagueness, indefiniteness, and ambiguity." While Olney served as attorney general, the Department of Justice initiated no new antitrust suits against business combinations.

Olney is most often remembered for his weak presentation of the government case in UNITED STATES V. E. C. KNIGHT & COMPANY (1895). Although the prosecution had been begun under President BENJAMIN HARRISON, Olney was responsible for choosing *Knight* to test the Sherman Act's constitutionality. Even as attorney general he specifically rejected the belief that "the aim and effect of this statute are to prohibit and prevent" trusts, and he contended that "literal interpretation" of the act was "out of the question" because of the act's overbroad terms. His ineffective prosecution contributed to a government loss, crippling enforcement of the Sherman Act for nearly a decade. Olney saw *Knight* as a vindication of his personal views and as an excuse to ignore the law; although he ought to have chosen a stronger case, the federal judges who so narrowly construed the act must share responsibility for the outcome.

Olney's antipathy to the Sherman Act ran deep.

He was determined to break the Pullman strike in 1894, and although he had to rely on the Sherman Act to secure lower court INJUNCTIONS, he abandoned that successful tack in the Supreme Court. He convinced a unanimous Court in IN RE DEBS (1895) to rely instead upon the inherent power of the executive branch to protect the national interest in the flow of INTERSTATE COMMERCE.

Olney also argued POLLOCK V. FARMERS' LOAN & TRUST COMPANY (1895) before the Supreme Court, although his actions resulted in insufficient time for government preparation and may have cost the government its case. The Court struck down the tax, a decision Olney considered "a great blow to the power of the Federal government . . . a national misfortune."

DAVID GORDON

Bibliography

EGGERT, GERALD 1974 *Richard Olney: Evolution of a Statesman.* University Park: Pennsylvania State University Press.

OLSEN v. NEBRASKA EX REL. REFERENCE & BOND ASSOCIATION
313 U.S. 236 (1941)

Sustaining a Nebraska statute regulating fees charged by private employment agencies, the Supreme Court specifically reversed RIBNIK V. MCBRIDE (1928). Justice WILLIAM O. DOUGLAS reiterated earlier dissents of Justices OLIVER WENDELL HOLMES (see TYSON & BROTHER V. BANTON, 1927) and LOUIS D. BRANDEIS (see NEW STATE ICE COMPANY V. LIEBMANN, 1932), declaring that the need and appropriateness of legislation concerning the public interest ought to be left to state legislatures.

DAVID GORDON

OMNIBUS ACT
15 Stat. 73 (1868)

The Omnibus Act readmitted six of the Confederate states to full congressional representation and terminated military governance in them.

After the process of restoration mandated by the MILITARY RECONSTRUCTION ACTS was largely completed, Congress readmitted Arkansas in June 1868 and, three days later, by the Omnibus Act readmitted

Alabama, Florida, Georgia, Louisiana, North Carolina, and South Carolina. The Omnibus Act declared that each of the six states had complied with the conditions specified in the Military Reconstruction Acts, required each to ratify the FOURTEENTH AMENDMENT, and imposed the "fundamental condition" that the state constitutional provisions for black suffrage be inviolate. All the congressmen and senators of these states were seated by late July 1868.

Georgia's full readmission was delayed for two years, however, because the state legislature excluded all black members and admitted several whites disfranchised by the Fourteenth Amendment or the Military Reconstruction Acts. Congress by special legislation forced a rescission of these actions, and Georgia once again underwent military supervision until its readmission. Virginia, Mississippi, and Texas were also readmitted in 1870, thus bringing the formal process of Reconstruction to a close.

WILLIAM M. WIECEK

OMNIBUS CRIME CONTROL AND SAFE STREETS ACT
92 Stat. 3795 (1968)

The most extensive anticrime legislation in the nation's history, this measure reflected the public's fear of rising crime and its demand for federal protection. Congress enacted a massive and restrictive piece of legislation, called by its critics an invasion of basic CIVIL LIBERTIES. Particularly distasteful to President LYNDON B. JOHNSON, who signed it with reluctance, were titles permitting broad use of WIRETAPPING in federal and state cases, and a section seeking to overturn controversial Supreme Court rulings on the rights of defendants.

The act authorized law enforcement grants to aid local police departments in planning, training, and research and a block grant procedure whereby funds were given to the states to be allocated to their communities under a statewide plan. It channeled funds to improve techniques for combating organized crime and for preventing and controlling riots. The most controversial provision of the act purported to overturn Supreme Court decisions in *Mallory v. United States* (1957), MIRANDA V. ARIZONA (1966), and UNITED STATES V. WADE (1967), authorizing greater freedom in POLICE INTERROGATION of suspects accused of crimes against the United States, and in the use of LINEUPS to identify criminals.

The measure specified permissive new conditions

under which confessions could be introduced in federal courts. The trial judge was to determine the issue of voluntariness, out of the hearing of the jury, basing that determination on such criteria as time lapse between arrest and arraignment, whether the defendant knew the nature of the charged offense, when the defendant was advised of or knew of the right to remain silent and the RIGHT TO COUNSEL, and whether the defendant was without assistance of counsel when questioned and giving the confession.

The act's provisions on ELECTRONIC EAVESDROPPING permitted warrant-approved wiretapping and bugging in investigations of a wide variety of specified crimes, and authorized police to intercept communications for forty-eight hours without a warrant in an "emergency" where organized crime or NATIONAL SECURITY was involved. Further, it authorized any law officer or any other person obtaining information in conformity with such a process to disclose or use it as appropriate. The law forbade the interstate shipment to individuals of pistols and revolvers, and over-the-counter purchase of handguns by individuals who did not live in the dealer's state. But it specifically exempted rifles and shotguns from these controls.

Passed overwhelmingly a few hours after the assassination of ROBERT F. KENNEDY, the act still drew the opposition of liberals troubled by its criminal law sections and concerned that its permissive wiretap section did not contain proper constitutional safeguards. Constitutional issues aside, the act failed to achieve its objectives.

PAUL L. MURPHY

Bibliography

NATIONAL COMMISSION ON THE CAUSES AND PREVENTION OF VIOLENCE 1970 *Law and Order Reconsidered.* Washington, D.C.: Government Printing Office.

O'NEIL v. VERMONT

See: *In Re Kemmler*

ONE PERSON, ONE VOTE

The National Municipal League popularized the slogan "one man, one vote" from the 1920s to the 1960s to promote REAPPORTIONMENT to equalize political districts. Reapportionment had lagged far behind urban growth, leaving the largest urban districts by 1960 with only half the legislative representatives per capita of the smallest rural ones.

Urban spokesmen claimed that "malapportionment" produced stagnant "barnyard governments" indifferent to urban concerns and needs. They demanded one person, one vote to stop urban blight and revitalize state governments. These conjectural claims did not win reapportionment from legislators reluctant to tamper with their own districts, nor from voters, who repeatedly defeated reapportionment INITIATIVES. But they did persuade political and legal writers and study commissions, who called for courts or commissions to order reapportionment where legislators and voters would not.

The Supreme Court declined this invitation in COLEGROVE V. GREEN (1946) but accepted one person, one vote in REYNOLDS V. SIMS (1964) as the "fundamental principle" of the Constitution. Political scientists, black rights groups, the *New York Times,* and the DWIGHT D. EISENHOWER and JOHN F. KENNEDY administrations had endorsed that principle.

Some critics thought that the Court had confused individual suffrage with group REPRESENTATION, misconstrued the FOURTEENTH AMENDMENT, and ignored the "standards problem" of equalizing group representation, because gerrymandering could still deny equal weight to votes. Others saw little evidence of revitalization or greater equality in substance to match the greater equality in form, and they believed that by overriding legislative and popular majorities, the Court seemed to have devalued the very representative institutions to which it granted equal access in form.

The WARREN COURT's adoption of one person, one vote was a remarkable political success, affecting more people than school DESEGREGATION or criminal justice cases, with less help from Congress and less damaging backlash. But its practical contributions to equal representation and vital government remain a matter of dispute.

WARD E. Y. ELLIOTT

Bibliography

ELLIOTT, WARD E. Y. 1975 *The Rise of Guardian Democracy: The Supreme Court's Role in Voting Rights Disputes, 1845–1969.* Cambridge, Mass.: Harvard University Press.

ON LEE v. UNITED STATES
343 U.S. 737 (1952)

The Supreme Court held, 5–4, that government informers who deceptively interrogated criminal suspects and simultaneously transmitted the conversations to other government agents via electrical transmitters had not violated the FOURTH AMENDMENT or the antiwiretap provisions of section 605 of the COMMUNICATIONS ACT; the agents who listened might testify to the overheard conversations. Because entry had been consented to—although the consent was obtained deceptively—it was not a TRESPASS, and under OLMSTEAD V. UNITED STATES (1927) the intrusion did not violate the Fourth Amendment. It was also not WIRETAPPING, nor did it become illegal because it might be immoral. The Court reaffirmed *On Lee* in UNITED STATES V. WHITE (1971).

HERMAN SCHWARTZ

OPEN HOUSING LAWS

Many believe housing, the last major area covered by Congress's 1960s CIVIL RIGHTS program, to be the key to at least short-term progress in INTEGRATION. Despite numerous ANTIDISCRIMINATION LAWS, segregated housing patterns threaten much of the civil rights agenda, including integrated public education. Yet until the 1960s the federal government promoted segregated housing. Federal housing agencies, such as the Federal Housing Administration, required racially RESTRICTIVE COVENANTS in federally assisted projects. In Executive Order 11063 (1962), President JOHN F. KENNEDY prohibited housing discrimination in federal public housing and in housing covered by mortgages directly guaranteed by the federal government. Title VI of the CIVIL RIGHTS ACT OF 1964, which outlawed discrimination in programs receiving federal financial assistance, extended the ban to nearly all federally assisted housing.

Title VIII of the CIVIL RIGHTS ACT OF 1968 was the first comprehensive federal open housing law. Title VIII bans discrimination on the basis of race, color, religion, or national origin in the sale, lease, and financing of housing, and in the furnishing of real estate brokerage services. A 1974 amendment extends the ban to discrimination on the basis of sex. Title VIII exempts single-family houses sold or rented by owners and small, owner-occupied boarding houses. Congress's consideration of Title VIII was affected by the assassination of Martin Luther King, Jr. House opponents of the measure had tried to delay its consideration in the hope that intervening national events would sway Congress against it. But during the delay, Dr. King was assassinated and passage of the act followed swiftly.

Courts have construed Title VIII to cover activities other than the direct purchase, sale, or lease of a dwelling. For example, Title VIII prohibits discriminatory refusals to rezone for low-income housing. Most courts find that practices with greater adverse impact on minorities, even if undertaken without discriminatory purposes, impose some burden of justification. This view links Title VIII litigation to a similar line of EMPLOYMENT DISCRIMINATION cases decided under Title VII of the Civil Rights Act of 1964.

To enforce its provisions, Title VIII authorizes the secretary of housing and urban development to seek to conciliate disputes, but the Department of Housing and Urban Development (HUD) initially must defer to state or local housing agencies where state law provides relief substantially equivalent to Title VIII. In *Gladstone, Realtors v. Village of Bellwood* (1979) the Supreme Court held that Title VIII also authorized direct civil actions in federal court without prior resort to HUD or to state authorities. An ATTORNEY GENERAL finding a pattern or practice of housing discrimination is authorized to seek relief in federal court.

Two months after Title VIII's enactment the Supreme Court found Section 1982, Title 42, United States Code, a remnant of section 1 of the CIVIL RIGHTS ACT OF 1866, to be another federal open housing law. Section 1982 grants all citizens the same right "as is enjoyed by white citizens" to purchase and lease real property. In JONES V. ALFRED H. MAYER CO. (1968) the Court construed section 1982 to prohibit a racially motivated refusal to sell a home to a prospective black purchaser. In *Sullivan v. Little Hunting Park, Inc.* (1969) the Court found that violations of section 1982 may be remedied by damages awards or by injunctive relief. There are, therefore, two federal open housing laws, which, in the area of RACIAL DISCRIMINATION, overlap. But section 1982 contains none of Title VIII's exemptions, provides for none of its administrative machinery, and contains no express list of remedies.

THEODORE EISENBERG

Bibliography

BELL, DERRICK A., JR. 1980 *Race, Racism and American Law*, 2nd ed. Boston: Little, Brown.
DORSEN, NORMAN; BENDER, PAUL; NEUBORNE, BURT; and LAW, SYLVIA Emerson, Haber and Dorsen's *Political and Civil Rights in the United States*, 4th ed. II:1063–1149. Boston: Little, Brown.

OPINION OF THE COURT

An appellate court would give little guidance to inferior courts, the legal community, or the general public concerning the law if it merely rendered a DECISION and did not explain the RATIO DECIDENDI, or the grounds for its decision. It is the court's reading of the law and the application of legal principles to the facts that gives a reported case value as PRECEDENT and permits the judicial system to follow the doctrine of STARE DECISIS. By ancient custom, Anglo-American judges, at least at the appellate level, publish opinions along with their decisions.

The general practice of English courts at the time of the American Revolution, and the general practice today in most of the British Commonwealth, is for the members of multijudge courts to deliver their opinions SERIATIM, that is, severally and in sequence. This practice was followed by the United States SUPREME COURT during its early years. However, when JOHN MARSHALL became CHIEF JUSTICE in 1801 he instituted the practice of delivering a single "opinion of the court." The effect of this change was to put the weight of the whole Court behind a particular line of reasoning (usually Marshall's), and so to make that line of reasoning more authoritative. At the time, Marshall's innovation was criticized by many, including President THOMAS JEFFERSON, either because it permitted lazy Justices to evade the responsibility of thinking through the cases on their own or because it fortified the Federalist majority in its conflicts with Republican legislators and state governments.

The opinion of the court is not necessarily unanimous. A majority of the Justices customarily endorses a single opinion, however, and that majority opinion is issued as the opinion of the court, with the Chief Justice—or the senior Justice, if the Chief Justice is not in the majority—assigning responsibility for writing the opinion. A Justice who disagrees with the decision of the case may file a DISSENTING OPINION; a Justice who agrees with the result, but disagrees with the rationale, or desires to supplement the majority opinion, may file a CONCURRING OPINION. When there is no majority opinion, the opinion signed by the largest number of Justices in support of the decisions is called the PLURALITY OPINION, and no opinion of the court is issued. In some important cases in the past, and increasingly during the BURGER COURT years, the number of separate opinions has presented an appearance resembling a return to seriatim opinions.

DENNIS J. MAHONEY

ORAL ARGUMENT

Lawyers argue points of law orally before courts at all levels. The Supreme Court regulates oral argument by court rule. Some cases are decided summarily,

without full briefing and argument, on the papers filed by the parties seeking and opposing Supreme Court review. About 150 cases per TERM are decided with briefs and oral argument. The arguments begin in October, early in the term, and (absent extraordinary circumstances) end in the following April, so that all opinions can be finished by the end of the term.

In the Court's early years oral argument was a leisurely affair; argument in MCCULLOCH V. MARYLAND (1819) lasted nine days. Today, given the increase in the Court's business and increasing doubt that illumination is proportional to talk, argument is normally limited to one-half hour for each side. More time may be allocated to a case that is unusually complicated or important. Permission to argue is only rarely granted to an AMICUS CURIAE, except for the SOLICITOR GENERAL, who is often allowed to argue orally for the United States as amicus curiae.

The Justices have already read the briefs when they hear counsel. Accordingly, oral argument is no longer a place for oratory. Justices interrupt with their questions and even conduct debates with each other through rhetorical questions to counsel. Time limits on argument are strictly enforced; the red light flashes on the lectern, and counsel stops.

Normally within a few days after oral argument the Justices meet in CONFERENCE to discuss groups of cases and vote tentatively on their disposition. The Justices regularly say that oral argument, fresh in their minds, influences their thinking in "close" cases. Whether a case is close, however, is a characterization very likely formed before a Justice hears what counsel have to say.

KENNETH L. KARST

Bibliography
STERN, ROBERT L. and GRESSMAN, EUGENE 1978 *Supreme Court Practice*, 5th ed. Chap. 14. Washington, D.C.: Bureau of National Affairs.

ORDERED LIBERTY

A loosely used term, diversely applied in scholarly literature and judicial opinions, "ordered liberty" suggests that fundamental constitutional rights are not absolute but are determined by a balancing of the public (societal) welfare against individual (personal) rights. In this dialectical perspective, the thesis is "order," its antithesis "liberty"; the synthesis, "ordered liberty," describes a polity that has reconciled the conflicting demands of public order and personal freedom.

Justice BENJAMIN N. CARDOZO's majority opinion for the Court in PALKO V. CONNECTICUT (1937) provided what was probably the first judicial recognition of "ordered liberty." Acknowledging the difficulty of achieving "proper order and coherence," Cardozo identified some constitutionally enumerated rights that were *not* of the essence of a scheme of "ordered liberty," and thus not incorporated in the FOURTEENTH AMENDMENT and applied to the states: "to abolish [these rights] is not to violate a principle of justice so rooted in the traditions and conscience of our people as to be ranked fundamental." On the other hand, rights such as "freedom of thought and speech" were "of the very essence of a scheme of ordered liberty" because they constituted "the matrix, the indispensable condition, of nearly every other form of freedom."

HENRY J. ABRAHAM

Bibliography

ABRAHAM, HENRY J. 1987 *Freedom and the Court: Civil Rights and Liberties in the United States,* 5th ed. New York: Oxford University Press.

ORDINANCE OF 1784

One of the most important constitutional questions of the founding era was that of the status of the western TERRITORIES. In 1783, as a concession to secure ratification of the ARTICLES OF CONFEDERATION, states with claims to western lands ceded them to Congress. In April 1784 Congress adopted an ordinance of government for the ceded territory drafted by THOMAS JEFFERSON. That ordinance, although it never went into effect, embodied the principle that the territories were not to be mere colonies but would become states within the Union. The principle was fulfilled under the NORTHWEST ORDINANCE and the Constitution.

The Ordinance of 1784 created eight "states" in the West and prescribed for them three stages of evolution culminating in full equality with the original thirteen states. But, unlike the Northwest Ordinance, which provided for gradual advance toward self-government by the settlers, the Ordinance of 1784 conferred self-government immediately. Jefferson's proposal to ban SLAVERY from the territories was defeated in Congress by a vote of seven states to six.

Rather than allow squatters to benefit, Congress made the Ordinance effective only when the western lands were officially offered for sale, and that did not happen until after the Ordinance was superseded.

DENNIS J. MAHONEY

OREGON v. BRADSHAW

See: *Edwards v. Arizona*

OREGON v. ELSTAD
470 U.S.   (1985)

The Supreme Court reaffirmed MIRANDA V. ARIZONA (1966) yet made another exception to it. For a 6–3 majority, Justice SANDRA DAY O'CONNOR held that initial failure to comply with the MIRANDA RULES does not taint a second confession made after a suspect has received the required warnings and has waived his rights. In this case the suspect had not blurted out an incriminating statement before police questioned him. They arrested him, with a warrant, at his home and began an interrogation without advising him of his rights. He confessed. They took him to the station and gave him the warnings, but they did not inform him that his prior confession could not be used against him as proof of his guilt. O'Connor, commenting that a contrary decision might "disable the police," ruled that the second confession need not be suppressed because of the illegality of the first. She treated the illegal confession as if it had been voluntarily made. Her focus on the voluntariness of that initial confession suggested that if coercion had then been present, it would have tainted a second confession made after the *Miranda* warnings. The Court, therefore, reaffirmed *Miranda*. Nevertheless, the case taught that the police may ignore *Miranda*, secure a confession, and then give the warnings in the hope of getting an admissible confession once the suspect thinks "the cat is out of the bag." Justice WILLIAM J. BRENNAN savaged the Court's opinion in a dissent that O'Connor claimed had an "apocalyptic tone" and distorted much of what she had said. She denied Brennan's accusation that the majority's opinion had a "crippling" effect on *Miranda*.

LEONARD W. LEVY

OREGON v. HASS

See: Police Interrogation and Confessions

OREGON v. MITCHELL
400 U.S. 112 (1970)

This decision suggested some short-lived constitutional limits on Congress's power to regulate voting. The 1970 amendments to the VOTING RIGHTS ACT

OF 1965 lowered from twenty-one to eighteen the minimum voting age for federal, state, and local elections, suspended LITERACY TESTS throughout the nation, prohibited states from imposing RESIDENCE REQUIREMENTS in presidential elections, and provided for uniform national rules for absentee registration and voting in presidential elections. (See VOTING RIGHTS AMENDMENTS.) The Supreme Court unanimously upheld the suspension of literacy tests and, over Justice JOHN MARSHALL HARLAN's dissent, found the residency and absentee voting provisions valid. Four Justices found the age limit reduction constitutional for all elections and four Justices found it unconstitutional for all elections. Because Justice HUGO L. BLACK found the age limit reduction constitutional only for federal elections, the case's formal HOLDING, though reflecting only Justice Black's view, was to sustain the age reduction only in federal elections. The many separate opinions in *Mitchell* also reviewed the question, first addressed in KATZENBACH V. MORGAN (1966), of Congress's power to interpret and alter the scope of the FOURTEENTH AMENDMENT. In 1971, in response to *Mitchell,* the TWENTY-SIXTH AMENDMENT lowered the voting age to eighteen in all elections.

THEODORE EISENBERG

ORGANIZED CRIME CONTROL ACT
84 Stat. 922 (1970)

Heralded as the most comprehensive federal law ever enacted to combat organized crime, this act was not limited to that use alone. Its provisions applied to a wide range of offenses, on the theory that the involvement of organized crime in a particular criminal act is not always clear. The detection of such involvement was one purpose of the law.

The legislation contained thirteen titles, a number of which aroused sharp criticism on constitutional grounds. One controversial title reinforced and expanded the investigatory power of GRAND JURIES by authorizing special grand juries to return INDICTMENTS and to report to UNITED STATES DISTRICT COURTS concerning criminal misconduct by appointive public officials involving organized criminal activity or concerning organized crime conditions in their areas. An individual named in such a report was entitled to a grand jury hearing, with the right to call witnesses and to file a rebuttal to the report. Another title replaced all previous laws governing witness IM-

MUNITY GRANTS; the title authorized federal legislative, administrative, and judicial bodies to grant witnesses immunity from prosecution using their testimony. The new section thus substituted "use immunity" for the "transaction immunity" that had previously protected such witnesses from prosecution for any events mentioned in or related to their testimony regardless of independent evidence against them.

Other provisions authorized detention of recalcitrant witnesses for CONTEMPT until they complied with court orders to testify, but for no longer than eighteen months, authorized convictions for perjury based on obviously contradictory statements made under oath (no longer requiring proof of the crime by any particular number of witnesses or by any particular type of EVIDENCE), and the use of depositions in criminal cases subject to constitutional guarantees and certification by the ATTORNEY GENERAL that the case involved organized crime. Still other sections limited to five years the period in which government action to obtain evidence could be challenged as illegal and limited the disclosure of government records previously required by ALDERMAN V. UNITED STATES (1969). Finally, the act authorized increased sentences up to twenty-five years for persons convicted of felonies, provided they were found to be dangerous and to be "habitual" offenders, "professional" criminals, or "organized crime figures."

Although the whole measure was denounced by the New York City Bar Association as containing "the seeds of official repression," only the narrowed witness immunity provisions were challenged. In KASTIGAR V. UNITED STATES (1972) the Supreme Court ruled that they did not violate the Fifth Amendment RIGHT AGAINST SELF-INCRIMINATION.

PAUL L. MURPHY

Bibliography
CONGRESSIONAL QUARTERLY 1973 *Congress and the Nation,* vol. 3. Washington, D.C.: Congressional Quarterly.

ORIGINAL JURISDICTION

The original jurisdiction of a court (as distinguished from APPELLATE JURISDICTION) is its power to hear and decide a case from the beginning. In the federal court system, the district courts originally hear the overwhelming majority of cases. Most discussion and litigation concerning the JURISDICTION OF FEDERAL COURTS centers on the district courts' original JURISDICTION. Yet the term "original jurisdiction" is heard most frequently in discussion and litigation concerning the jurisdiction of the Supreme Court.

The Constitution itself establishes the Supreme Court's original jurisdiction. After setting out the types of cases subject to the JUDICIAL POWER OF THE UNITED STATES, Article III distributes the Supreme Court's jurisdiction over them: "In all cases affecting ambassadors, other public ministers and consuls, and those in which a state shall be a party, the Supreme Court shall have original jurisdiction. In all other cases mentioned, the Supreme Court shall have appellate jurisdiction. . . ."

From the beginning, Congress has given the district courts CONCURRENT JURISDICTION over some of the cases within the Supreme Court's original jurisdiction, offering plaintiffs the option of commencing suit in either court. The Supreme Court has given this practice its stamp of constitutional approval. Furthermore, because the Court is hard-pressed by a crowded docket, it has sought ways of shunting cases to other courts. Thus, even when a case does fall within the Court's original jurisdiction, the court has conferred on itself the discretion to deny the plaintiff leave to file an original action. Typically the Court decides only three or four original jurisdiction cases each year, conserving its institutional energies for its main task: guiding the development of federal law by exercising its appellate jurisdiction.

Congress, however, cannot constitutionally diminish the Court's original jurisdiction. Nor can Congress expand that jurisdiction; the dubious reading of Article III in MARBURY V. MADISON (1803) remains firmly entrenched. However, the Supreme Court does entertain some actions that have an "original" look to them, even though Article III does not list them as original jurisdiction cases: HABEAS CORPUS is an example; so are the common law WRITS OF MANDAMUS and PROHIBITION. The Court hears such cases only when they can be characterized as "appellate," calling for Supreme Court supervision of actions by lower courts.

Of the two types of original jurisdiction cases specified in Article III, the state-as-party case has produced all but a tiny handful of the cases originally decided by the Supreme Court. Officers of foreign governments enjoy a broad diplomatic immunity from suit in our courts, and, for motives no doubt similarly diplomatic, they have not brought suits in the Supreme Court. (The "ambassadors" and others mentioned in Article III, of course, are those of foreign governments, not our own.)

The state-as-party cases present obvious problems of SOVEREIGN IMMUNITY. The ELEVENTH AMENDMENT applies to original actions in the Supreme Court; indeed, the amendment was adopted in response to just such a case, CHISHOLM V. GEORGIA (1793). Thus a state can no more be sued by the citizen of another state in the Supreme Court than in a district court. However, when one state sues another, or when the United States or a foreign government sues a state, there is no bar to the Court's jurisdiction.

The spectacle of nine Justices of the Supreme Court jointly presiding over a trial has a certain Hollywood allure, but the Court consistently avoids such proceedings. The SEVENTH AMENDMENT commands TRIAL BY JURY in any common law action, and at first the Supreme Court did hold a few jury trials. The last one, however, took place in the 1790s. Since that time the Court has always managed to identify some feature of an original case that makes it a suit in EQUITY; thus jury trial is inappropriate, and findings of fact can be turned over to a SPECIAL MASTER, whose report is reviewed by the Court only as to questions of law.

The source of the substantive law applied in original actions between states is FEDERAL COMMON LAW, an amalgam of the ANGLO-AMERICAN COMMON LAW, policies derived from congressional statutes, and international law principles. Thus far no state has defied the Supreme Court sufficiently to test the Court's means of enforcing its decrees, but some states have dragged out their compliance for enough years to test the patience of the most saintly Justice.

KENNETH L. KARST

Bibliography

NOTE 1959 The Original Jurisdiction of the United States Supreme Court. *Stanford Law Review* 11:665–719.

ORIGINAL PACKAGE DOCTRINE

In BROWN V. MARYLAND (1827) the Supreme Court had before it a challenge to a state statute requiring all importers of goods from foreign countries to take out a $50 license. Instead of simply holding that such a license tax imposed only on importers from foreign countries violated the constitutional clause prohibiting states from laying "any IMPOSTS or duties on imports or exports," Chief Justice JOHN MARSHALL used the occasion to decide just when goods imported from abroad ceased being imports exempted from taxation by the states. He concluded that no tax could be imposed on the goods or their importer so long as the goods had not been sold and were held in the original packages in which they were imported. He also said the principles laid down "apply equally to importations from a sister state."

The original package DOCTRINE had a long career

as applied to goods imported from abroad. In *Low v. Austin* (1872) the Court held that a state could not collect its uniform property tax on cases of wine which the importer held in their original package on tax day. Much later, in *Hooven & Allison Co. v. Evatt* (1945), the Court applied the doctrine to immunize bales of hemp from state property taxation, so long as the importer held them in their original package— the bales. Along the way, not surprisingly, the Court struggled in many cases with such problems as what constitutes the original package, and when it is broken.

Finally, in MICHELIN TIRE CORP. V. WAGES (1976) the Court upheld the imposition of a nondiscriminatory property tax upon tires imported from abroad and held in their original packages. It discussed at length the decision in *Low v. Austin*, overruled it, and appeared to be saying that only taxes discriminating against FOREIGN COMMERCE will be held invalid. Hence, it appears that the rules governing taxation of imports will now be similar to those applied to taxing such goods from other states, with the original package doctrine playing no part in the decisions.

Marshall's suggestion in *Brown v. Maryland* that the original package doctrine applied to state *taxation* of goods imported from other states was early rejected. In WOODRUFF V. PARHAM (1869) the Court upheld a state sales tax applied to an auctioneer who brought goods from other states and sold them in the taxing state in the original and unbroken packages. The IMPORT-EXPORT CLAUSE was determined to apply only to traffic with foreign nations, not to interstate traffic. The Court indicated its feeling that it would be grossly unfair if a resident of a state could escape from state taxes on all merchandise that he was able to import from another state and keep in its original package.

In 1890, however, the Court held that the original package doctrine applied to invalidate state *regulations* of goods imported from other states until the goods were sold or the package broken. The decision, LEISY V. HARDIN (1890), invalidated a state prohibition law as applied to sales within the state by the importer of kegs and cases of beer. Federal statutes were then enacted permitting states to exclude alcohol even in original packages. But the original package doctrine persisted with reference to other state regulations for nearly half a century. The Court found reasons in many cases to avoid applying the doctrine but did not effectively repudiate it until 1935. In *Baldwin v. G. A. F. Seelig* (1935) the Court, after reviewing the cases applying the original package doctrine said:

"In brief, the test of the original package is not an ultimate principle. . . . It makes a convenient boundary and one sufficiently precise save in exceptional conditions. What is ultimate is the principle that one state in its dealing with another may not place itself in a position of economic isolation. Formulas and catchwords are subordinate to this overmastering requirement."

Today the original package doctrine is of interest only to historians.

EDWARD L. BARRETT, JR.

(SEE ALSO: *State Regulation of Commerce; State Taxation of Commerce.*)

Bibliography

NOWAK, JOHN E.; ROTUNDA, RONALD D.; and YOUNG, NELSON J. 1979 *Handbook on Constitutional Law.* Pages 285–290. St. Paul, Minn.: West Publishing Co.
POWELL, THOMAS R. 1945 State Taxation of Imports: When Does an Import Cease to Be an Import? *Harvard Law Review* 58:858–876.
RIBBLE, F. D. G. *State and National Power over Commerce.* Pages 196–199. New York: Columbia University Press.

OROZCO v. TEXAS
394 U.S. 324 (1969)

In an opinion by Justice HUGO L. BLACK, the Supreme Court held that a conviction based on incriminating admissions obtained by police in the absence of notification of the MIRANDA RULES, even though the prisoner was at home, away from the coercive surroundings of a stationhouse, violated the RIGHT AGAINST SELF-INCRIMINATION.

LEONARD W. LEVY

OSBORN v. BANK OF THE UNITED STATES
9 Wheaton 738 (1824)

On its constitutional merits, *Osborn* was a replay of MCCULLOCH V. MARYLAND (1819). Ohio had sought to drive out the congressionally chartered bank by taxing its branches $50,000 each and by seizing money from its vaults. The bank sued the state auditor in a federal court for recovery of the money. The state argued that the ELEVENTH AMENDMENT barred the court from taking JURISDICTION, but, on APPEAL to the Supreme Court, Chief Justice JOHN MARSHALL concluded that the amendment applied only when the state was named as a party defendant—a position abandoned by the Court in later decisions. (See EX PARTE YOUNG, 1908.) On the principles of *McCulloch*, the auditor was liable for his TRESPASS.

Osborn's lasting doctrinal contribution was its sweeping definition of congressional power under Article III to confer FEDERAL QUESTION JURISDICTION on the federal courts. Marshall's view, which remains good law, was that cases "arising under" the Constitution, or federal laws, or treaties included—for purposes of defining congressional power to confer jurisdiction—any case in which federal law might *potentially* be dispositive. It made no difference that federal law was not implicated in the bank's complaint for trespass; the arguable invalidity of the bank's charter might possibly be raised as a defense to such an action. Although similar words ("arises under") are used in the statutes defining federal question jurisdiction, they have been interpreted more narrowly. *Osborn* thus defines congressional power, not its exercise.

The *Osborn* decision heightened the vehemence of state denunciations of the Court's judicial nationalism and even of its appellate jurisdiction. President ANDREW JACKSON's veto of the bank bill of 1832 probably reflected the prevailing belief—despite *McCulloch* and *Osborn*—that Congress had no constitutional authority to charter a corporation.

LEONARD W. LEVY
KENNETH L. KARST

O'SHEA v. LITTLETON
414 U.S. 488 (1974)

Protesters against RACIAL DISCRIMINATION in Cairo, Illinois, obtained a federal court INJUNCTION against a state judge and magistrate, forbidding continuation of various discriminatory BAIL, sentencing, and jury-fee practices in criminal cases. The Supreme Court reversed, 6–3, on RIPENESS grounds. Although some plaintiffs had previously suffered such discrimination, none were now threatened with prosecution. Thus there was no live CASE OR CONTROVERSY.

Once a prosecution was commenced, YOUNGER V. HARRIS (1971) would forbid a federal injunction. (See ABSTENTION DOCTRINE.) Thus potential plaintiffs in such cases must file their complaints within a narrow time period.

KENNETH L. KARST

OTIS, JAMES, JR.
(1725–1783)

Massachusetts lawyer, Harvard graduate (1743), and ideologue of the American Revolution, James Otis, Jr., became constitutionally significant with PAXTON'S CASE (1761), which concerned the issuance of WRITS OF ASSISTANCE by the Superior Court of Massachusetts. Confronted with the reality that the writs, which empowered customs officers to search all suspected houses, typified many kinds of general SEARCH WARRANTS within British law, Otis resorted to the HIGHER LAW. Using sources from MAGNA CARTA to BONHAM'S CASE (1610), Otis argued not only that incompatibility with natural and COMMON LAW rendered general searches void but also that the court should proclaim that invalidity. Although he did not advocate outright JUDICIAL REVIEW of an act of Parliament by a colonial court, the interpretation of the writs that Otis urged on the court would have had that result.

Although Otis's present fame derives heavily from *Paxton's Case*, he gained little contemporary notice from his performance in it, for his brief was not published until 1773. Rather, the principal constitutional services of the case were that it resulted in Otis's election to the Massachusetts General Court (legislative), thereby giving him a forum for his views and enabling him to assemble and rehearse the constitutional arguments that he later applied to those issues that directly generated the American Revolution.

Limiting the power of Parliament was central to Otis's thought: "To say the Parliament is absolute and arbitrary is a contradiction. The parliament cannot make 2 and 2, 5; Omnipotency cannot do it; the supreme power in a state is JUS DICERE [to announce the law] only;—JUS DARE [to construct the law] strictly speaking belongs only to God. . . . Should an act of Parliament be against any of his natural laws, which are immutably true, their declaration would be contrary to eternal truth, equity and justice, and consequently void." Otis's constitutional significance, however, does not emanate from this belief, which most contemporaries shared, but from the corollaries he extracted from it. Otis first transformed the British constitution into a fixed rather than a flexible barrier to Parliament, which he redefined as a subordinate creature of the constitution rather than one of its components. Of even greater import, Otis characterized the courts as umpires of Parliament's power. "The judges of England," he wrote, "have declared in favor of these sentiments when they expressly declare; that acts of Parliament against natural equity are void. That acts against the fundamental principles of the British Constitution are void." To assert that all earthly power, even that of Parliament, had limits was a ubiquitous platitude; to imply that agencies outside Parliament could calibrate and enforce these limits challenged the axiom of parliamentary supremacy that, for most Englishmen, lay at the foundation of their constitution.

A disembodied and didactic use of sources, ranging from Magna Carta to Hugo Grotius, provided Otis's intellectual ammunition. In *Bonham's Case*, for example, the *Reports* of Sir EDWARD COKE mentioned courts' controlling acts of Parliament and adjudging them void. Coke's meaning, however, was constructive rather than constitutional and involved no judicial effort to subjugate Parliament. The case pitted not the legislature against the courts but two clashing private parties and raised questions of which conflicting laws applied. Coke reasoned that the common law courts, acting with, rather than against, another court in the form of Parliament, should give the laws a reasonable construction that was jointly desired. Otis bloated the case, however, into precedent for constitutional regulation of Parliament under judicial aegis.

Otis repeatedly denied the revolutionary implications of his ideology, stressing that Parliament was the British Empire's supreme but not absolute legislature and could alone rescind its statutes. Despite these denials, however, Otis's assumptions intrinsically approached the threshold of the right to revolution against unconstitutional parliamentary acts.

Having asserted limits to Parliament's authority, Otis enumerated the colonial rights that lay beyond them. As a delegate to the STAMP ACT CONGRESS (1765) and in his *Rights of the British Colonies* (1764), written against the Sugar Act, Otis condemned taxation of the colonists by a Parliament to which they had directly elected no representatives. (See TAXATION WITHOUT REPRESENTATION.) As moderator of the Boston town meetings, he also opposed juryless trials under the TOWNSHEND ACTS of 1767.

Widely regarded as the premier theorist of the radical cause in the 1760s, Otis had great influence on the constitutional ideology of the developing revolution. He edited many of the *Farmer's Letters* (1767) by JOHN DICKINSON, while JOHN ADAMS adapted much of Otis's reasoning in *Paxton's Case* against juryless ADMIRALTY trials in *Sewall v. Hancock* (1768–1769).

WILLIAM CUDDIHY

Bibliography

WATERS, JOHN 1968   *The Otis Family.* Chapel Hill: University of North Carolina Press.

OVERBREADTH

Judges frequently encounter the claim that a law, as drafted or interpreted, should be invalidated as overbroad because its regulatory scope addresses not only behavior that constitutionally may be punished but also constitutionally protected behavior. The normal judicial response is confined to ruling on the law's constitutionality as applied to the litigant's behavior, leaving the validity of its application to other people and situations to subsequent adjudication. Since THORNHILL V. ALABAMA (1940), however, the Supreme Court has made an exception, most frequently in FIRST AMENDMENT cases but applicable to other precious freedoms, when it is convinced that the very existence of an overbroad law may cause knowledgeable people to refrain from freely exercising constitutional liberties because they fear punishment and are unwilling to litigate their rights. In such cases, the aggregate inhibition of guaranteed freedom in the regulated community is thought to justify both holding the overbroad law INVALID ON ITS FACE and allowing one to whom a narrower law could be applied constitutionally to assert the overbreadth claim. Unlike the alternative of narrowing the unconstitutional portions of an overbroad statute case by case, facial invalidation prevents delay in curing the improper deterrence. Moreover, courts most effectively can address the inhibition of those who neither act nor sue by allowing those who do to raise the overbreadth challenge.

Like a VAGUENESS challenge, an overbreadth challenge implicates judicial governance in two controversial ways. First, if successful, the challenge completely prohibits the law's enforcement, even its constitutional applications, until it is narrowed through reenactment or authoritative interpretation. Second, the challenge requires a court to gauge the law's applications to unidentified people in circumstances that must be imagined, often ignoring the facts of the situation before them—a practice of hypothesizing that is at odds with the court's usual application of law to the facts of concrete CASES OR CONTROVERSIES.

Overbreadth differs from vagueness in that the constitutional defect is a law's excessive reach, not its lack of clarity; yet the defects are related. A law that punished "all speech that is not constitutionally protected" would, by definition, not be overbroad, but it would be unduly vague because people would have to speculate about what it outlawed. A law that prohibited "all speaking" would be unconstitutionally overbroad, but it also might be vague. Although clear enough if taken literally, it might be understood that the legislature did not intend the full reach of its broadly drafted law, and the public would have to speculate about what the contours of the intended lesser reach might be. A law that banned "all harmful speech" would be both overbroad and vague on its face. The key connection, however, is the improper inhibiting effect of the broad or vague law.

As with vagueness, the federal courts approach overbreadth challenges to state and federal laws differently. A federal court must interpret a federal law before judging its constitutionality. In doing so, the court may reduce the law's scope, if it can do so consistently with Congress's intent, a course that may minimize constitutional problems of overbreadth. Only state courts may authoritatively determine the reach of state laws, however. Consequently, when the Supreme Court reviews an overbreadth challenge to a state law on appeal from a state court—which review usually occurs because the challenger raised the claim in defense of state court proceedings against him— the Court must accept the state court's determination of the law's scope and apply its own constitutional judgment to the law as so construed. By contrast, if parties threatened with enforcement of a state statute sue in federal court to have the law declared unconstitutionally overbroad before they are prosecuted or sued in state court, the federal court faces the additional complication of determining the overbreadth question without the guidance of any state court interpretation of the law in this case. If past interpretations of the law's terms make its breadth clear, there is no more difficulty than in Supreme Court review of a state court case. But if there is some question whether a state court might have narrowed the state law, especially in light of constitutional doubts about it, the federal court faces the possibility of making its own incorrect interpretation and basing an overbreadth judgment on that unstable premise.

With other constitutional claims involving uncertain state laws, a federal court normally will abstain from deciding the constitutional question until clarification is sought in state court. However, because the prolongation of CHILLING EFFECTS on constitutionally protected conduct is the basis of the vagueness of overbreadth doctrines, the Supreme Court indicated in DOMBROWSKI V. PFISTER (1965) and *Baggett v. Bullitt* (1964) that abstention is generally inappropriate if the problem would take multiple instances of adjudication to cure. *Babbitt v. United Farm Workers* (1979) followed the implicit corollary, requiring abstention where a single state proceeding might have obviated the need to reach difficult constitutional issues. But BROCKETT V. SPOKANE ARCADES, INC. (1985) shunned abstention in a case where state court clarification was feasible in an expeditious single proceeding, but where the litigants objecting to overbreadth were not people to whom the law could be validly applied but people who desired to engage in constitutionally protected speech. In that circumstance, at least where the unconstitutional portion of the statute was readily identifiable and severable from the remainder, the Court chose to strike that portion rather than abstain to see if the state court would remove it by interpretation.

Brockett also expressed a preference for partial over facial invalidation whenever challengers assert that application of a statute to them would be unconstitutional. The Court's ultimate objective is to invalidate only a statute's overbroad features, not the parts that legitimately penalize undesirable behavior. It permits those who are properly subject to regulation to mount facial overbreadth attacks only to provide an opportunity for courts to eliminate the illegitimate deterrent impact on others. Partial invalidation would do such people no good, and those who are illegitimately deterred from speaking may never sue. In order to throw out the tainted bathwater, the baby temporarily must go too, until the statute is reenacted or reinterpreted with its flaws omitted. Where, as in *Brockett,* one asserts his own right to pursue protected activity, however, no special incentive to litigate is needed. The Court can limit a statute's improper reach through partial invalidation and still benefit the challenger. *Brockett*'s assumption that the tainted part of the statute does not spoil the whole also undercuts Henry Monaghan's important argument that allowing the unprotected to argue overbreadth does not depart from normal STANDING rules because they always assert their own right not to be judged under an invalid statute. The part applied to them is valid, and they are granted standing to attack the whole only to protect others from the invalid part. Finally, the claim that a law is invalid in all applications because based on an illegitimate premise has elements of both partial and facial invalidation. As the invalid premise affects the challenger as well as everyone else, there is no need to provide a special incentive to litigate, but because the whole law is defective, total invalidation is appropriate.

The seriousness of striking the whole of a partially invalid law at the urging of one to whom it validly applies, together with doubts about standing and the reliability of constitutional adjudication in the context of imagined applications, renders overbreadth an exceptional and controversial DOCTRINE. The determination of what circumstances are sufficiently compelling to warrant the doctrine's use has varied from time to time and among judges. The WARREN COURT focused mainly on the scope of the laws' coverage, the chilling effect on protected expression, and the ability of the legislature to draw legitimate regulatory boundaries more narrowly. The Court seemed convinced that overbroad laws inhibited freedom substantially, and thus made that inhibition the basis of invalidation, especially when the laws were aimed at dissidents and the risk of deliberate deterrence was high, as in APTHEKER V. SECRETARY OF STATE (1964), *United States v. Robel* (1967), and *Dombrowski v. Pfister* (1965). The BURGER COURT has continued to employ the overbreadth doctrine when deterrence of valued expression seems likely, as in *Lewis v. New Orleans* (1974), which struck down a law penalizing abusive language directed at police, and in SCHAD V. MT. EPHRAIM (1981), which struck down an extremely broad law banning live entertainment.

Justice BYRON R. WHITE has led that Court, however, in curtailing overbreadth adjudication. As all laws occasionally may be applied unconstitutionally, there is always a quantitative dimension of overbreadth. White's majority opinion in BROADRICK V. OKLAHOMA (1973) held that the overbroad portion of a law must be "real and substantial" before it will be invalidated. That standard highlights the magnitude of deterrent impact, which depends as much on the motivations of those regulated as on the reach of the law. *Broadrick* also emphasized the need to compare and offset the ranges of a statute's valid and invalid applications, rather than simply assess the dimensions of the invalid range. This substituted a judgment balancing a statute's legitimate regulation against its illegitimate deterrence of protected conduct for a judgment focused predominantly on the improper inhibition.

Broadrick initially limited the "substantial overbreadth" approach to laws seemingly addressed to conduct, leaving laws explicitly regulating expression, especially those directed at particular viewpoints, to the more generous approach. In *Ferber v. New York* (1982) and *Brockett*, however, substantial overbreadth was extended to pure speech cases as well. That these cases involved laws regulating OBSCENITY might suggest that some Justices find the overbreadth doctrine an improper means to counter deterrence of marginally valued expression. More likely, however, the Court generally is abandoning its focus on the subject of a law's facial coverage in favor of a comparative judgment of the qualitative and quantitative dimensions of a law's legitimate and illegitimate scope, whatever speech or conduct be regulated.

Still, the reality of deterrence and the value of the liberty deterred probably remain major factors in overbreadth judgments, even if more must be considered. For example, the Court's pronouncement in BATES V. STATE BAR OF ARIZONA (1977) that overbreadth analysis generally is inappropriate for profit-motivated advertising rested explicitly on a judgment that advertising is not easily inhibited and implicitly on the historic perception of COMMERCIAL SPEECH as less worthy of protection.

Overbreadth controversies nearly always reflect different sensitivities to the worth of lost expression and of lost regulation of unprotected behavior, or different perceptions of the legitimacy and reliability of judicial nullification of laws that are only partially unconstitutional, or different assessments of how much inhibition is really likely, how easy it would be to redraft a law to avoid overbreadth, and how important broad regulation is to the effective control of harmful behavior. Despite controversy and variations in zeal for application of the overbreadth doctrine, however, its utility in checking repression that too sweepingly inhibits guaranteed liberty should assure its preservation in some form.

JONATHAN D. VARAT

Bibliography

ALEXANDER, LAWRENCE A. 1985 Is There an Overbreadth Doctrine? *San Diego Law Review* 22:541–554.
MONAGHAN, HENRY P. 1981 Overbreadth. *Supreme Court Review* 1981:1–39.
NOTE 1970 The First Amendment Overbreadth Doctrine. *Harvard Law Review* 83:844–927.

OVERRULING

The authority of the Supreme Court to reconsider and overrule its previous decisions is a necessary and accepted part of the Court's power to decide cases. By one estimate, the Supreme Court overruled itself on constitutional issues 159 times through 1976 and in each case departed from the doctrine of STARE DECISIS.

The basic tenet of *stare decisis,* as set forth by WIL-LIAM BLACKSTONE, is that PRECEDENTS must generally be followed unless they are "flatly absurd" or "unjust." The doctrine promotes certainty in the law, judicial efficiency (by obviating the constant reexamination of previously settled questions), and uniformity in the treatment of litigants. The roots of the doctrine, which is fundamental in Anglo-American jurisprudence, have been traced to Roman civil law and the Code of Justinian.

Justices and commentators have disagreed about the proper application of *stare decisis* to constitutional decision making. Justice (later Chief Justice) EDWARD D. WHITE, in his dissenting opinion in POLLOCK V. FARMERS LOAN & TRUST CO. (1895), observed:

The fundamental conception of a judicial body is that of one hedged about by precedents which are binding on the court without regard to the personality of its members. Break down this belief in judicial continuity, and let it be felt that on great constitutional questions this court is to depart from the settled conclusions of its precedessors, and to determine them all according to the mere opinion of those who temporarily fill its bench, and our Constitution will, in my judgment, be bereft of value and become a most dangerous instrument to the rights and liberties of people.

Under this view, *stare decisis* should be applied with full force to constitutional issues.

The more commonly accepted view is that *stare decisis* has a more limited application in CONSTITUTIONAL INTERPRETATION than it does in the interpretation of statutes or in ordinary common law decision making. Although Congress, by a simple majority, can override the Supreme Court's erroneous interpretation of a congressional statute, errors in the interpretation of the Constitution are not easily corrected. The AMENDING PROCESS is by design difficult. In many instances only the Court can correct an erroneous constitutional decision.

Moreover, the Court will on occasion make decisions that later appear to be erroneous. As Chief Justice JOHN MARSHALL remarked in MCCULLOCH V. MARYLAND (1819), the Constitution requires deductions from its "great outlines" when a court decides specific cases. Because the modern Supreme Court generally accepts for review only cases in which principles of broad national importance are in competition, its decisions necessarily involve difficult questions of judgment. In view of the difficulties inherent in amending the Constitution, any errors made by the Court in the interpretation of constitutional principles must be subject to correction by the Court in later decisions.

The classic statement of this view was expressed by Justice LOUIS D. BRANDEIS in his dissenting opinion in *Burnet v. Coronado Oil & Gas Co.* (1932): "[I]n cases involving the Federal Constitution, where correction through legislative action is practically impossible, this Court has often overruled its earlier decisions. The Court bows to the lessons of experience and the force of better reasoning, recognizing that the process of trial and error, so fruitful in the physical sciences, is appropriate also in the judicial function." The Court has relied on Brandeis's reasoning in later decisions, such as EDELMAN V. JORDAN (1974), overruling previous constitutional precedents.

An additional reason for applying *stare decisis* less rigidly to constitutional decisions is that the judge's primary obligation is to the Constitution itself. In the words of Justice FELIX FRANKFURTER, concurring in *Graves v. New York* (1939), "the ultimate touchstone of constitutionality is the Constitution itself and not what we have said about it."

Some critics of *stare decisis* suggest that it has no place whatsoever in constitutional cases. For example, Chief Justice ROGER B. TANEY reasoned in the PASSENGER CASES (1849) that a constitutional question "is always open to discussion" because the judicial authority of the Court should "depend altogether on the force of the reasoning by which it is supported." The more generally accepted view, however, was stated by the Court in *Arizona v. Rumsey* (1984): "Although adherence to precedent is not rigidly required in constitutional cases, any departure from the doctrine of *stare decisis* requires special justification." Consistent with this view, the Supreme Court generally seeks to provide objective justification for the overruling of past precedents, apart from the fact that the Court's personnel may have changed.

One of the most commonly expressed reasons for overruling a previous decision is that it cannot be reconciled with other rulings. This rationale is in a sense consistent with *stare decisis* in that the justification for the overruling decision rests on competing but previously established judicial principles. In GIDEON V. WAINWRIGHT (1963), for example, which overruled BETTS V. BRADY (1942), the Court asserted not only that the rationale of *Betts* was erroneous but also that *Betts* had abruptly departed from well-established prior decisions. *Betts* had held that the DUE PROCESS clause of the FOURTEENTH AMENDMENT does not impose on the states, as the Sixth Amendment imposes on the federal government, the obligation to provide counsel in state criminal proceedings. *Gideon* expressly rejected this holding, thereby ruling that indigent defendants have the right to appointed counsel in such cases. Similarly, in WEST COAST HO-TEL CO. v. PARRISH (1937) the Court concluded that it had no choice but to overrule its earlier decision in ADKINS v. CHILDREN'S HOSPITAL (1923), which had held a minimum wage statute for women unconstitutional under the due process clause. The Court reasoned that *Adkins* was irreconcilable with other decisions permitting the regulation of maximum hours and other working conditions for women.

The Court frequently argues, too, that the lessons of experience require the overruling of a previous decision. In ERIE RAILROAD CO. v. TOMPKINS (1938), for example, the Court reasoned that in nearly one hundred years the doctrine of SWIFT v. TYSON (1842) "had revealed its defects, political and social." And in MAPP v. OHIO (1961) the Court held the EXCLU-SIONARY RULE applicable to the states, saying that the experience of various states had made clear that remedies other than the exclusionary rule could not effectively deter unreasonable searches and seizures. The Court therefore overruled WOLF v. COLORADO (1949), which only two decades earlier had ruled that states were free to devise their own remedies for enforcing SEARCH AND SEIZURE requirements applicable to the states through the due process clause of the Fourteenth Amendment.

The Court also justifies overruling decisions on the basis of changed or unforeseen circumstances. In BROWN v. BOARD OF EDUCATION (1954), for example, the Court referred to the change in status of the public schools in rejecting the application of the SEPARATE BUT EQUAL DOCTRINE of PLESSY v. FERGUSON (1896). And in PROPELLER GENESEE CHIEF v. FITZHUGH (1851), one of the earliest overruling decisions, the Court stressed that when it had erroneously held in *The Thomas Jefferson* (1825) that the ADMIRALTY AND MARITIME JURISDICTION of the federal government was limited "to the ebb and flow of the tide," commerce on the rivers of the West and on the Great Lakes had been in its infancy and "the great national importance of the question . . . could not be foreseen."

Other considerations may also suggest a decision's susceptibility to being overruled. Thus a decision on an issue not fully briefed and argued may be entitled to less precedential weight than one in which the issue received full and deliberate consideration. Or, the fact that an issue was decided by a closely divided Court may suggest a higher probability of error and make later reconsideration more likely. By contrast, as the Court recognized in *Akron v. Akron Center for Reproductive Health* (1983), a carefully considered decision, repeatedly and consistently followed, may

be entitled to more respect than other constitutional holdings under principles of *stare decisis*.

As the Court develops constitutional doctrine, it may limit or distinguish a previous decision, gradually eroding its authority without expressly overruling it. Such a doctrinal evolution may both portend an overruling decision and establish the groundwork for it.

The Court's willingness to reconsider its prior constitutional decisions and in some instances to overrule itself is implicit in the general understanding of the Constitution as a document of broad outlines intended to endure the ages. Yet it has been suggested that the Court risks a loss of confidence as a disinterested interpreter of the Constitution whenever it overrules itself. Because of its antimajoritarian character, the Court must be sensitive to the need for restraint in exercising its power of JUDICIAL REVIEW. If it overrules itself too frequently and without adequate justification, its reputation may suffer. The Constitution's general language, however, leaves wide room for honest differences as to its interpretation and application. An objective and detached overruling opinion, which faithfully seeks to apply constitutional principles on the basis of the constitutional text and history, is on occasion to be expected and need not jeopardize public confidence in the Court.

JAMES R. ASPERGER

Bibliography
BERNHARDT, CHARLOTTE C. 1948 Supreme Court Reversals on Constitutional Issues. *Cornell Law Quarterly* 34:55–70.
BLAUSTEIN, ALBERT P. and FIELD, ANDREW H. 1958 "Overruling" Opinions in the Supreme Court. *Michigan Law Review* 57:151–194.
ISRAEL, JEROLD H. 1963 Gideon v. Wainwright: The "Art" of Overruling. *Supreme Court Review* 1963:211–272.
NOLAND, JON D. 1969 Stare Decisis and the Overruling of Constitutional Decisions in the Warren Years. *Valparaiso University Law Review* 4:101–135.
REED, STANLEY 1938 Stare Decisis and Constitutional Law. *Pennsylvania Bar Association Quarterly* 1938:131–150.

OVERT ACTS TEST

The overt acts test originated in the seventeenth century in suggestive remarks by ROGER WILLIAMS, William Walwyn, and Baruch Spinoza, primarily to promote the cause of RELIGIOUS LIBERTY. To the same end, PHILLIP FURNEAUX, in the next century, developed the test and THOMAS JEFFERSON adopted it.

Such libertarians advocated the test as an alternative to the prevailing BAD TENDENCY TEST, according to which the expression of an opinion was punishable if it tended to stir animosity to the established religion of a state or to the government or its officers or measures. Thus, the preamble to Jefferson's VIRGINIA STATUTE OF RELIGIOUS FREEDOM declared that allowing the civil magistrate to restrain the profession of opinions "on the supposition of their ill tendency . . . at once destroys all religious liberty." The government's rightful purposes, Jefferson continued, were served if its officers did not interfere until "principles break out into overt acts against peace and good order." The overt acts test, therefore, sharply distinguished words from deeds, and, in Furneaux's words, was based on the proposition that the "penal laws should be directed against overt acts only."

When the Sedition Act of 1798 incorporated the principles of ZENGER'S CASE (1735), libertarians who had advocated those principles finally abandoned them as inadequate protections of the FREEDOM OF THE PRESS and embraced the overt acts test. Only a radical minority ever advocated the test in cases of political expression, yet it survived down to the twentieth century. Justices HUGO L. BLACK and WILLIAM O. DOUGLAS found the test admirably suited to their ABSOLUTISM. Dissenting in YATES V. UNITED STATES (1957), Black said, "I believe that the FIRST AMENDMENT forbids Congress to punish people for talking about public affairs, whether or not such discussion incites to action, legal or illegal."

The overt acts test would provide the utmost protection for words and make the principle of FREEDOM OF SPEECH immunize every kind of verbal crime. The test ignores the fact that in some instances words themselves can be crimes (contempt of court, perjury, OBSCENITY, the verbal agreement in a CRIMINAL CONSPIRACY) or can violate laws validly governing the time and place of assemblies, parades, PICKETING, and SOUNDTRUCKS AND AMPLIFIERS. Words can also cause severe injury, constitute INCITEMENT TO UNLAWFUL CONDUCT, or otherwise solicit crime. The overt acts test draws a bright but fake constitutional line between speech and action; an indistinct zone would be more appropriate. Nevertheless, the Supreme Court in BRANDENBURG V. OHIO (1969), a leading free speech case, almost flirted with the overt acts test when it held that a state may not constitutionally "forbid or proscribe advocacy of the use of force or of law violation except where such advocacy is directed to inciting or producing imminent lawless action and is likely to incite or produce such action." The Constitution contains a different overt acts test

in the TREASON clause (Article 3, section 3), which specifies that unless a person accused of treason confesses in open court, two witnesses to the same overt act must prove his guilt. The clause also defines the required overt act as making war against the United States or "adhering to their Enemies, giving them aid and comfort." The treason clause, therefore, prevents the punishment of "constructive" treason, which consists of any words or acts construed by the government or a court to be tantamount to treason. Thus, the overt acts provision of the treason clause helps guarantee CIVIL LIBERTY by preventing the crime of treason from being used expansively to silence opponents of the government.

LEONARD W. LEVY

Bibliography

GREENAWALT, KENT 1980 Speech and Crime. *American Bar Foundation Research Journal* 1980:647–785.

OWEN v. CITY OF INDEPENDENCE
445 U.S. 622 (1980)

In MONELL V. DEPARTMENT OF SOCIAL SERVICES (1978) the Supreme Court held that municipalities may be liable under SECTION 1983, TITLE 42, UNITED STATES CODE, for deprivations of constitutional rights if the deprivation results from official policy. In *Owen*, the Court held that municipalities may not avail themselves of the good-faith defense or qualified immunity enjoyed by individual defendants in section 1983 cases. Thus, a municipality may be liable for unconstitutional acts even if its officials reasonably believe in good faith that their acts are constitutional.

THEODORE EISENBERG

OYAMA v. CALIFORNIA
332 U.S. 633 (1948)

In *Terrace v. Thompson* (1923) the Supreme Court had upheld the power of a state to limit land ownership to U.S. citizens. *Oyama*, together with TAKAHASHI V. FISH AND GAME COMMISSION (1948), both undermined *Terrace* and signaled a changing judicial attitude toward RACIAL DISCRIMINATION.

California's Alien Land Law forbade land ownership by ALIENS ineligible for CITIZENSHIP; under existing federal law, that category was largely limited to persons of Asian ancestry. Invoking its law, California sought to take over title to land held in the name of a young U.S. citizen, on the ground that it was really owned by his father, an alien ineligible for citizenship. The father had paid for the land, and so under the law was presumed its owner. A similar presumption would not apply to ownership of land by citizens of other races. Without purporting to rule on the general validity of the Alien Land Law, the Supreme Court held, 7–2, that the presumption denied the EQUAL PROTECTION OF THE LAWS.

KENNETH L. KARST

P

PACE v. ALABAMA
106 U.S. 583 (1883)

To white supremacists, the miscegenation issue was crucially important. The often unexpressed fear of interracial sex involving white women underlay all sorts of RACIAL DISCRIMINATION. The states punished adultery and fornication much more severely when the parties were of different races than when both were of the same race. *Pace* challenged the constitutionality of Alabama's statute, but the Supreme Court unanimously held that the unequal punishment did not violate the EQUAL PROTECTION clause of the FOURTEENTH AMENDMENT because both the interracial fornicators were subject to the same punishment.

LEONARD W. LEVY

(SEE ALSO: *Loving v. Virginia, 1967.*)

PACIFISTS

See: Conscientious Objection

PACKERS & STOCKYARDS ACT
42 Stat. 159 (1921)

After a Federal Trade Commission investigation damaging to the meat-packing industry in 1919–1920, popular sentiment demanded decisive action. Congress responded with this statute regulating both the packers and the stockyards. As one of its sponsors declared, the statute merely reenacted old principles in order to restore and maintain competition. Indeed, the clause banning "unfair" competition restated section 5 of the FEDERAL TRADE COMMISSION ACT. Other provisions forbade giving "undue or unreasonable advantage" (repeating section 3 of the INTERSTATE COMMERCE ACT) or apportioning items by geographic area (I.C.A., section 5; SHERMAN ANTITRUST ACT, section 1). Violators might be brought before the secretary of agriculture, who could issue CEASE-AND-DESIST ORDERS; APPEALS lay to federal CIRCUIT COURTS. Stockyards subject to the act were required to register and provide "reasonable" services and charges. The secretary could determine new rates and order compliance, although the act provided no standards for his guidance. Perhaps because of a CONSENT DECREE negotiated with the industry in 1920, the Department of Justice was reluctant to prosecute the packers. Their disinclination, and the packers' efforts to avoid the consent decree, materially contributed to the act's passage. In enacting this statute, Congress emphasized public concern over and commitment to strict accountability to the nation's antitrust laws. (See STAFFORD V. WALLACE, 1922.)

DAVID GORDON

Bibliography

GORDON, DAVID 1983 The Beef Trust: Antitrust Law and the Meat Packing Industry, 1902–1922. Ph.D. diss., Claremont Graduate School.

PAINE, THOMAS
(1737–1809)

Thomas Paine, the son of an English Quaker tradesman, became the great propagandist of the American and French revolutions. Before sailing to Philadelphia in 1774, with a letter of recommendation from BENJAMIN FRANKLIN, Paine had been a corsetmaker, a privateer, a tax assessor, a songwriter, and a tobacconist. In Philadelphia, he became editor of the *Pennsylvania Magazine*, crusading for abolition of slavery, proscription of dueling, greater rights for women, and easier availability of divorce.

Paine became the spokesman for the American Revolution when, in January 1776, he published a pamphlet called *Common Sense*. The pamphlet sharply attacked "the constitutional errors of the English form of government," including monarchy and CHECKS AND BALANCES. Paine declared that "the constitution of England is so complex, that the nation may suffer for years together without being able to discover in which part the fault lies." He argued for minimal government: "Society is in every state a blessing, but government even in its best state is but a necessary evil." Paine concluded *Common Sense* with a proposal for a "Continental Charter" of government based on large and equal REPRESENTATION and featuring a presidency rotated among the provincial delegations.

Between 1776 and 1783, Paine published a series of thirteen essays called *The Crisis*, chronicling "the times that try men's souls." Although in *Common Sense* he had denounced the English constitution, by the time he wrote *The Crisis* #7 in 1778, Paine had come to wonder "whether there is any such thing as the English constitution?" *The Crisis* #13, published in 1783, presented an argument for a strong and permanent national union, because "we have no other national SOVEREIGNTY than as the United States."

As the CONSTITUTIONAL CONVENTION OF 1787 met, however, Paine was en route to Europe to promote a scheme for building iron bridges. The outbreak of the French Revolution in 1789 found him in Paris. He became a French citizen and a member of the revolutionary Convention; he was the principal author of the Declaration of the Rights of Man and Citizen. When Edmund Burke denounced the French Revolution, Paine responded with *The Rights of Man*, the nearest thing he ever wrote to a systematic treatise on politics. Not an originator of ideas but a popularizer, Paine grounded his case for the revolution in the concepts of NATURAL RIGHTS and SOCIAL COMPACT. "Every civil right," he wrote, "has for its foundation some natural right pre-existing in the individual, but to the enjoyment of which his individual power is not, in all cases, sufficiently competent."

In 1792 the French revolutionary government fell into the hands of a radical faction; Paine was imprisoned and only narrowly escaped the guillotine. During his year in prison he wrote *The Age of Reason*, an apology for deism and religious rationalism with an anti-Christian tenor.

Paine's release from prison was arranged by the American ambassador, JAMES MONROE. For nearly a decade Paine remained in France as a journalist and political commentator. In 1802 he returned to America where he wrote polemical articles for the newspapers in support of THOMAS JEFFERSON's Republican party until his death in 1809.

DENNIS J. MAHONEY

Bibliography

CANAVAN, FRANCIS 1972 Thomas Paine. Pages 652–658 in Leo Strauss and Joseph Cropsey, eds., *History of Political Philosophy*. Chicago: Rand McNally.

HAWKE, DAVID FREEMAN 1974 *Paine*. New York: Harper & Row.

PALKO v. CONNECTICUT
302 U.S. 319 (1937)

Palko, decided in the sesquicentennial year of the Constitution, highlights the difference between the constitutional law of criminal justice then and now. The *Palko* Court, which was unanimous, included five of the greatest judges in our history—CHARLES EVANS HUGHES, LOUIS D. BRANDEIS, HARLAN FISKE STONE, HUGO L. BLACK, and the Court's spokesman, BENJAMIN N. CARDOZO. In one respect Cardozo's opinion is a historical relic, like HURTADO V. CALIFORNIA (1884), MAXWELL V. DOW (1900), and TWINING V. NEW JERSEY (1908), which he cited as governing precedents. In another respect, *Palko* rationalized the Court's INCORPORATION DOCTRINE of the FOURTEENTH AMENDMENT by which it selected FUNDAMENTAL RIGHTS to be safeguarded against state violation.

Palko was sentenced to life imprisonment after a jury found him guilty of murder in the second degree. The state sought and won a new trial on the ground that its case had been prejudiced by errors of the trial court. Palko objected that a new trial on the same INDICTMENT exposed him to DOUBLE JEOPARDY, but he was overruled. At the second trial the jury's verdict of murder in the first degree resulted in a sentence of death. Had the case been tried in a federal court, the double jeopardy claim would have been good. The question raised by Palko's case was whether a double standard prevailed—one for state courts and the other for federal—or whether the Fifth Amendment's guarantee against double jeopardy applied to the state through the DUE PROCESS clause of the Fourteenth Amendment.

Cardozo declared that Palko's contention was even broader: "Whatever would be a violation of the original BILL OF RIGHTS (Amendments 1 to 8) if done by the federal government is now equally unlawful by force of the Fourteenth Amendment if done by a state." The Court answered, "There is no such general rule," thus rejecting the theory of total incorporation. Nevertheless, said Cardozo, by a "process of absorption"—now referred to as selective incorporation—the Court had extended the due process clause of the Fourteenth Amendment to include FIRST AMENDMENT freedoms and the RIGHT TO COUNSEL in certain cases, yet it had rejected the rights of the criminally accused, excepting representation by counsel for ignorant INDIGENTS in capital prosecutions. The rationalizing principle that gave coherence to the absorption process, Cardozo alleged, depended on a distinction among the various rights. Some were "fundamental" or "of the very essence of a scheme of ORDERED LIBERTY," like FREEDOM OF SPEECH or religion. By contrast, TRIAL BY JURY, indictment by GRAND JURY, and the RIGHT AGAINST SELF-INCRIMINATION were not: justice might be done without them. The right against double jeopardy, the Court ruled summarily, did not rank as fundamental and therefore received no protection against the states from the due process clause of the Fourteenth Amendment. BENTON V. MARYLAND (1969) overruled *Palko*, showing that even "fundamental" value judgments change with time. All that remains of *Palko* is the abstract principle of selective incorporation.

LEONARD W. LEVY

Bibliography
ABRAHAM, HENRY J. 1977 *Freedom and the Court,* 3rd ed. Pages 64–70. New York: Oxford University Press.

PALMER, ALEXANDER M.
(1872–1936)

Appointed attorney general in 1919, Alexander Mitchell Palmer soon faced violence stirred up by the extreme left. After a series of bombings, Palmer campaigned against CIVIL LIBERTIES and unsuccessfully urged adoption of a new SEDITION law. His overreaction to alleged domestic radicals, particularly his "Red Raids" into private homes, mass arrests, and deportations of aliens, earned him widespread censure. Palmer also used the emergency WAR POWERS to attempt an end to the coal strike in 1919, exciting further criticism. These circumstances all contributed to his losing the 1920 Democratic presidential nomination for which he had been a leading contender. He nevertheless remained a party regular and helped write the 1932 party platform.

DAVID GORDON

Bibliography
COBEN, STANLEY (1963) 1972 *A. Mitchell Palmer: Politician.* New York: Da Capo Press.

PALMER v. THOMPSON
402 U.S. 217 (1971)

Under a federal court order to integrate its public recreational facilities, Jackson, Mississippi, closed four of its five public swimming pools and surrendered the city's lease on the fifth pool. In a 5–4 decision, the Supreme Court sustained the closings, stating that a legislative act does not "violate EQUAL PROTECTION solely because of the motivations of the men who voted for it." *Palmer*'s statement that legislative motive is irrelevant was undermined in WASHINGTON V. DAVIS (1976) and ARLINGTON HEIGHTS V. METROPOLITAN HOUSING DEVELOPMENT CORPORATION (1977).

THEODORE EISENBERG

PALMER RAIDS
(1919–1920)

In the aftermath of World War I and the Russian Revolution, waves of European immigration aggravated domestic inflation and unemployment. Labor strikes, often violent, were rampant, and the Communist party was organized.

Under pressure from the press and the public, WOODROW WILSON's attorney general, A. MITCHELL PALMER, conducted a series of raids between autumn 1919 and spring 1920 against the homes and offices of suspected ALIENS and radical leaders. The raids were conducted without ARREST WARRANTS or SEARCH WARRANTS, and those detained were denied the right to HABEAS CORPUS. Several thousand persons were detained, and over 500 alien radicals were deported.

DENNIS J. MAHONEY

PALMORE v. SIDOTI
466 U.S. 429 (1984)

When Linda Palmore was divorced from Anthony Sidoti, a Florida court awarded custody of their daughter to Palmore. Later, Sidoti sought custody on the ground that Palmore, a white woman, had been cohabiting with a black man, whom she shortly married. The state court changed the custody on the sole ground that the mother had "chosen for herself and her child, a life-style unacceptable to her father and to society." The child would, if she remained with her mother, be "more vulnerable to peer pressures" and would suffer from "social stigmatization." The Supreme Court unanimously reversed.

For the Court, Chief Justice WARREN E. BURGER reaffirmed the need for STRICT SCRUTINY of governmental action based on race. Racial prejudice indeed existed, but the potential injury from such private biases was not a constitutionally acceptable basis for the custody change. The decision has symbolic importance, but seems unlikely to make much difference in actual awards of child custody, which can be rested on a variety of grounds in the name of the "best interests of the child" without any explicit consideration of race.

KENNETH L. KARST

PANAMA CANAL TREATIES
33 Stat. 2234 (1903)
TIAS 10030 (1977)

At the turn of the twentieth century the United States emerged as a major power in world politics. Central to that major-power status were America's merchant shipping and the navy that protected it. The disadvantage of being a continental power with shores on two oceans became obvious during the Spanish-American War when redeployment of warships from the Pacific to the Atlantic Ocean, by way of Cape Horn, took two months to complete. The United States government determined to construct a canal across Central America through the Isthmus of Panama. The United States negotiated a treaty with Colombia, in which

the isthmus was located, but that treaty was rejected by the Colombian Senate in August 1903.

In November 1903, with American encouragement, Panama declared its independence from Colombia; two weeks later Panama signed a treaty (sometimes called the Hay-Bunau Treaty) permitting the United States to build the Panama Canal. The United States Senate gave its ADVICE AND CONSENT to ratification of the treaty the following February.

In the treaty the United States undertook to defend both the canal and the Republic of Panama and to make nominal annual payments to Panama from the revenue of the canal. The treaty gave the United States permanent control "as if it were sovereign" over the Panama Canal Zone, a strip of land ten miles wide dividing the republic—which retained nominal sovereignty over the zone—in two. For nearly three-quarters of a century the Canal Zone was governed as an American TERRITORY. When President LYNDON B. JOHNSON made (mostly symbolic) concessions to Panama following civil unrest there in the 1960s, members of Congress accused him of usurping Congress's exclusive power over the territories.

Negotiations between four successive administrations and the Panamanian government, conducted over more than thirteen years, resulted in two pacts signed in 1977, the Panama Canal Treaty and the Panama Canal Neutrality Treaty. Together, these agreements abolished the Canal Zone, returned the zone and the canal to Panamanian SOVEREIGNTY, and provided for the future operation of the waterway under joint, and ultimately under Panamanian, control. The campaign to win the advice and consent of the Senate to the treaties proved to be a major test of the constitutional roles of the executive and the Senate in the exercise of the TREATY POWER. The original Panama Canal Treaty had been approved after an unprecedentedly short debate; the length of the debate over the new treaties was exceeded in the twentieth century only by that over the TREATY OF VERSAILLES.

Ratification of the treaties in 1978, with numerous amendments and "conditions," proved to be only the beginning of a new struggle. The treaties were not self-executing but required implementing legislation; that gave members of the House of Representatives, some of whom objected to the President and the Senate giving away "American territory" without their participation, a chance to affect the terms of the transfer. Over the objections of both President JIMMY CARTER and the Panamanian government, Congress wrote into the implementing legislation provisions authorizing the President to intervene militarily to protect American interests in the former Canal Zone. The episode serves to illustrate the extent of congressional power, under the Constitution, to influence the conduct of FOREIGN AFFAIRS, over which the President is often assumed to have exclusive control.

DENNIS J. MAHONEY

Bibliography

CRABB, CECIL V. and HOLT, PAT M. 1980 The Panama Canal Treaties. *Invitation to Struggle: Congress, the President and Foreign Policy.* Chap. 3. Washington, D.C.: Congressional Quarterly.

PANAMA REFINING CO. v. RYAN
293 U.S. 388 (1935)

In 1933 the price of wholesale gasoline had fallen to two and a half cents a gallon, that of crude oil to ten cents a barrel. The states, unable to cut production and push up prices, clamored for national controls. Congress responded with section 9(c) of the NATIONAL INDUSTRIAL RECOVERY ACT, authorizing the President to prohibit the shipment in INTERSTATE COMMERCE of petroleum produced in excess of quotas set by the states. By a vote of 8–1 the Supreme Court, in an opinion by Chief Justice CHARLES EVANS HUGHES, for the first time in history held an act of Congress unconstitutional because it improperly delegated legislative powers to the President without specifying adequate standards to guide his discretion. Moreover, the act did not require him to explain his orders. Vesting the President with "an uncontrolled legislative power," Hughes said, exceeded the limits of delegation; he did not explain how much delegation is valid and by what standards.

Justice BENJAMIN N. CARDOZO disagreed. He found adequate standards in section 1 of the statute: the elimination of unfair competitive practices and conservation of natural resources. These objectives guided the President's discretion, Cardozo explained. The principle of SEPARATION OF POWERS, which the majority used to underpin its opinion, should not be applied with doctrinaire rigor. Moreover, the statute, Cardozo observed, "was framed in the shadow of a national disaster" which raised unforeseen contingencies that only the President could face from day to day. The standards for his discretion had to be broad, and he need never give reasons for EXECUTIVE ORDERS. Cardozo's opinion notwithstanding, the Court in effect removed the oil industry from effective con-

trols, to its detriment and that of the national economy. This case marked the New Deal's debut before the Court.

LEONARD W. LEVY

(SEE ALSO: *Delegation of Power.*)

PAPACHRISTOU v. JACKSONVILLE

See: Vagrancy Laws

PARDEE, DON ALBERT
(1837–1919)

President JAMES A. GARFIELD on May 3, 1881, appointed Don Albert Pardee judge of the Fifth Circuit Court. From 1891 to his death Pardee presided as senior judge of the Fifth Circuit Court of Appeals.

Pardee's most significant constitutional opinions involved the STATE POLICE POWER and VESTED RIGHTS. In *New Orleans Water-Works Co. v. St. Tammany Water-Works Co.* (1882) the judge held that the Louisiana legislature had exceeded its powers by incorporating a new company to compete with an enterprise that had enjoyed a monopoly over the distribution of the water supply to the city of New Orleans. "Arguments in cases like the one under consideration," Pardee observed, "are generally based on the assumption that the sovereign . . . is absolutely unfettered with regard to . . . all the rights of property. I am not prepared to take this advanced ground." He enjoined the new company from further construction and held that the legislature could not invoke its police power "without compensation of the vested rights of the New Orleans Water-Works Company."

Pardee did accept broader legislative discretion under the police power when moral objectives were involved. In *United States ex rel. Hoover v. Ronan, Sheriff* (1887) he rejected an argument that a Georgia statute violated the DUE PROCESS and EQUAL PROTECTION provisions of the FOURTEENTH AMENDMENT by requiring would-be saloonkeepers in unincorporated towns and cities to obtain signatures from residents in order to secure a retail license. In *Ex Parte Kinnerbrew* (1888), he found on moral benefit grounds that the Georgia local option liquor law was compatible with the federal COMMERCE CLAUSE.

Pardee insisted on the power of the federal judiciary to frame a constitutional jurisprudence that separated the state police power into public and private sector concerns. As a result, reverence for vested property rights and public morality gilded his judicial conservatism.

                                        KERMIT L. HALL

Bibliography
BRYAN, PAUL E. 1964 Don Albert Pardee. *Dictionary of American Biography*, Vol. 14:201–202. New York: Scribner's.

PARDONING POWER

The power of pardon—the power to relieve a person of the legal sanctions imposed for illegal conduct—was reluctantly put in the hands of the President by the CONSTITUTIONAL CONVENTION OF 1787. The reluctance derived from the fact that it was too much akin to the royal prerogative to afford dispensation to favorites from obedience to the law, a prerogative supposedly eliminated by the English BILL OF RIGHTS in 1689. The Framers were concerned lest the power should be used to shelter the treasonous activities of a President and his henchmen. The most persuasive argument on behalf of a presidential pardoning power was its potential use to reconcile warring factions. Because it would, for this purpose, be an effective tool only if it were readily available to strike a deal at any time, and because Congress was not expected to be in session all, or even most, of the time, it properly devolved on the executive.

The power of pardoning for criminal activities is all but plenary. There is the constitutional limitation that pardon may not be used to relieve from impeachment or its sanctions. Otherwise, a pardon can be granted before conviction, indeed before indictment, and it can be conferred absolutely or conditionally, provided that the conditions themselves are not unconstitutional. However, whether a pardon can be conferred over the objection of the grantee is not clear, for acceptance of a pardon is generally thought to be an acknowledgment of commission of a crime.

On the whole, the pardon power has not been used for political ends as was anticipated. The partisan strife of the Old World did not, with rare exceptions, see its counterpart on the American scene. The political nature of the power can be seen in the pardons to the WHISKEY REBELS, to those convicted under the ALIEN AND SEDITION ACTS, and in the AMNESTY—granted by Congress—to the rebels of the Civil War. President GERALD R. FORD's pardon of ex-President RICHARD M. NIXON after the Watergate affair was, perhaps, the most blatant partisan use of the power.

The Supreme Court, in SCHICK V. REED (1974), has legitimated the almost unlimited power of executive pardon. Although the history of the origins as recounted in *Schick* is somewhat suspect, *Schick* remains the definitive statement, unless and until the Court revises it through later opinions.

                                        PHILIP B. KURLAND

Bibliography
CORWIN, EDWARD S. 1957 *The President: Office and Powers 1787–1957*, 4th ed. New York: New York University Press.

PARHAM v. HUGHES

See: Illegitimacy

PARHAM v. J. R.
442 U.S. 584 (1979)

The notion of "voluntary" civil commitment of mental patients takes on a special meaning when the patients are children: under a typical state's law they can be committed by the joint decision of their parents and mental hospital authorities. This case, a CLASS ACTION on behalf of all children detained in Georgia mental hospitals, was brought in order to establish a child's PROCEDURAL DUE PROCESS right to an adversary hearing before being so committed. Although the lower federal court agreed with the plaintiff's theory, the Supreme Court reversed in an opinion by Chief Justice WARREN E. BURGER.

The Court was unanimous in rejecting the broadest due process claim in behalf of the children. There were constitutionally protected "liberty" interests at stake in a commitment, both the freedom from bodily restraint and the freedom from being falsely labeled as mentally ill. However, applying the interest-balancing calculus suggested in MATHEWS V. ELDRIDGE (1976), the Court concluded that a child's due process rights did not extend to an adversary precommitment hearing. The majority concluded that due process required no more than informal "medical" inquiries, once near the time of commitment and periodically thereafter, by a "neutral fact-finder" who would determine whether the standards for commitment were satisfied. There need be no adversary proceeding, but this neutral decision maker should interview the child.

The Court's opinion emphasized the importance of maintaining parents' traditional role in decision making for their children. (See CHILDREN'S RIGHTS.)

Although some parents might abuse their authority, the law had historically "recognized that natural bonds of affection lead parents to act in the best interests of their children." On the surface, *J. R.* is a "family autonomy" decision. Yet, as Robert Burt has shown, the Court's solicitude for parental authority was expressed in the context of parental decisions validated by state officials. Other decisions suggest that the Court's primary deference runs not to parents but to "state-employed behavioral professionals."

Justice WILLIAM J. BRENNAN, for three partially dissenting Justices, agreed that pre-confinement hearings were not constitutionally required in all cases where parents sought to have their children committed, but he argued that due process did require at least one postadmission hearing. The informal inquiries approved by the Court did not meet this standard.

KENNETH L. KARST

(SEE ALSO: *Mental Illness and the Constitution.*)

Bibliography
BURT, ROBERT A. 1979 The Constitution of the Family. *Supreme Court Review* 1979:329–395.

PARIS ADULT THEATRE I v. SLATON

See: *Miller v. California*

PARKER v. BROWN
317 U.S. 341 (1943)

A California statute compelled raisin growers to comply with the orders of a state-sponsored marketing monopoly. Farmers could sell thirty percent of their crop on the open market; the remainder went to the state commission, which controlled the interstate supply and price. This law survived challenge when a unanimous bench followed reasoning laid out earlier by Justice HARLAN FISKE STONE in DISANTO V. PENNSYLVANIA (1927). Here Stone dismissed statutory objections: the SHERMAN ANTITRUST ACT applied only to individual, not state, action; neither did the COMMERCE CLAUSE forbid this state regulation. Most important, Congress, in the AGRICULTURAL MARKETING AGREEMENT ACT, did not preempt this state legislation but reflected a congressional policy to encourage it.

DAVID GORDON

(SEE ALSO: *State Regulation of Commerce.*)

PARKER v. DAVIS

See: Legal Tender Cases

PARKER v. LEVY
417 U.S. 733 (1974)

In a celebrated trial of the VIETNAM WAR era, Captain Howard Levy, an Army physician, was convicted by COURT MARTIAL for violating provisions of the UNIFORM CODE OF MILITARY JUSTICE that penalized willful disobedience of the lawful command of a superior officer, "conduct unbecoming an officer and a gentleman," and conduct "to the prejudice of good order and discipline in the armed forces." The Third Circuit Court of Appeals had held that these provisions were unconstitutionally vague in violation of the DUE PROCESS clause of the Fifth Amendment and overbroad in violation of the FIRST AMENDMENT.

Justice WILLIAM H. REHNQUIST, for the Supreme Court, reversed and upheld Levy's conviction. Rehnquist's opinion rejected the contention that the provisions of the Uniform Code of Military Justice were too vague and overbroad. "The fundamental necessity for obedience, and the consequent necessity for imposition of discipline, may render permissible within the military that which would be constitutionally impermissible outside it," he wrote. Justices WILLIAM O. DOUGLAS, WILLIAM J. BRENNAN, THURGOOD MARSHALL, and POTTER STEWART dissented. The last wrote, "I cannot believe that such meaningless statutes as these can be used to send men to prison under a Constitution that guarantees due process of law."

MICHAEL E. PARRISH

PARLIAMENTARY PRIVILEGE

Parliamentary privilege, a term originating in England, refers to a bundle of rights that Parliament and every American legislature claimed and exercised. Article I of the Constitution safeguards several of these rights, including the right of the House of Representatives to choose its speaker, the right of each house to judge the elections and qualifications of members, the right of the houses to determine their own rules of procedure, and the rights of members to be free from arrest while performing their duties and to enjoy FREEDOM OF SPEECH in carrying out their duties. (See SPEECH OR DEBATE CLAUSE.) In addition, parliamentary privilege included the right, which derived from the judicial authority of Parliament, to punish for contempt.

The power to punish for contempt in both England and America proved to be incompatible with freedom of speech for critics of government, especially of the legislature. In colonial America the most suppressive body was the popularly elected assembly, which in effect enforced the law of SEDITIOUS LIBEL by punishing contempts or breaches of parliamentary privilege. An assembly, needing no GRAND JURY to indict and no PETIT JURY to convict, could summon, interrogate, and fix criminal penalties against anyone who had written, spoken, or printed words tending to impeach the assembly's conduct, question its authority, derogate from its honor, affront its dignity, or defame its members.

The practice of punishing seditious scandals or contempts against the government began in America with the first assembly that met in Virginia and continued well after the adoption of the Constitution. In 1796, for example, the New York Assembly jailed a lawyer for his offensive publications, and in 1800 the United States Senate found a Jeffersonian editor guilty of a "high breach of privileges" because of his seditious libels. As late as 1874 the Texas legislature, having expelled a hostile journalist, ordered his imprisonment for violating its order. The Supreme Court has held that the House of Representatives has the implied power to punish for contempt. Theoretically Congress still retains that power; in practice Congress refers its charges to a federal prosecutor who seeks a grand jury INDICTMENT. (See LEGISLATIVE CONTEMPT POWER.)

LEONARD W. LEVY

Bibliography

CLARKE, MARY PATTERSON (1943)1971 *Parliamentary Privilege in the American Colonies.* New York: Da Capo Press.

WITTKE, CARL (1921)1970 *The History of English Parliamentary Privilege.* New York: Da Capo Press.

PAROCHIAL SCHOOLS

See: Government Aid to Religious Institutions

PARTIES, POLITICAL

See: Political Parties and the Constitution; Political Parties in Constitutional Law

PASSENGER CASES
7 Howard 283 (1849)

Two states imposed a tax on the masters of vessels for each alien passenger they landed in the country. By a 5–4 vote, the Supreme Court held the state acts unconstitutional. Each of the Justices in the majority wrote an opinion, and none spoke for the Court. Three of the four dissenters wrote opinions. The report of the cases takes 290 pages and reflects chaos in judicial interpretation. The Justices squabbled about DORMANT POWERS, EXCLUSIVE POWERS, CONCURRENT POWERS, and the COMMERCE CLAUSE in relation to the POLICE POWER, but they settled nothing doctrinally.

LEONARD W. LEVY

PATENT

Article I grants to Congress the power to "promote the Progress of Science and useful Arts, by securing for limited times to Authors and Inventors the exclusive Right to their respective Writings and Discoveries." This clause confers on the federal government authority to provide for both patents and COPYRIGHTS.

United States patent law derives from the English experience. During Tudor times, English monarchs granted various monopolies (such as ones over salt) to royal favorites. The populace arose against the high prices charged by such monopolies. In 1623, Parliament enacted the germinal Statute of Monopolies. The statute declared monopolies void but as an exception allowed letters patent for fourteen years to the "true and first inventors" of "new manufactures."

In America, some states prior to adoption of the Constitution granted patents to inventors. But in listing the limited and specific powers of the federal legislature, the drafters of the Constitution agreed that patents and copyrights should be among those powers. As JAMES MADISON argued in THE FEDERALIST #43, "the States cannot separately make effectual provision for either." The drafters perceived that the interests of both a unified national economy and a strong system of incentives for invention required that a patent power lie in the federal government.

The constitutional power specifies both the *end* of the patent system (progress of the useful arts) and the *means* for achieving it (secure for a limited time to inventors the exclusive right to their discoveries). The power is only an enablement and does not of its own force create any patent rights. Nevertheless, the first Congress in 1790 enacted a patent statute. An 1836 statute revised the patent laws and created the Patent Office. A 1952 statute restated the patent laws in their current form. An inventor of a new and useful product or process may obtain from the Patent Office a patent granting for a number of years (currently seventeen) the right to exclude others from making, selling, or using the invention defined by the claims in the patent.

Although most questions concerning patentability are defined by statute, the Constitution limits Congress's power to authorize patent monopolies. In *Graham v. John Deere Co. of Kansas City* (1966), the Supreme Court stressed that Congress may not authorize patents that "remove existent knowledge from the public domain." Rejecting a NATURAL RIGHTS theory of patents for inventions, the Court emphasized the utilitarian function of patents: they stimulate innovation and the disclosure of new knowledge. Patents may issue only for inventions that advance the state of technology. This constitutional standard of innovation finds expression in the patent law DOCTRINE of "nonobviousness," which bars a patent for any discovery that would have been obvious at the time of invention to a person with ordinary skill in the pertinent art who had knowledge of all the prior art.

A patent may issue for virtually any type of useful product or process. In *Diamond v. Chakrabarty* (1980), the Supreme Court upheld the potential patentability of a live, genetically altered strain of microorganism.

DONALD S. CHISUM

Bibliography

CHISUM, DONALD S. 1978 *Patents: A Treatise on the Law of Patentability, Validity and Infringement.* New York: Matthew Bender.

MACHLUP, FRITZ 1958 An Economic Review of the Patent System. Study No. 15, Subcommittee on Patents, Trademarks & Copyrights, Judiciary Committee, 85th Congress, 2d Session.

PATERSON, WILLIAM
(1745–1806)

William Paterson played a major role in the framing of the United States Constitution. His stubborn advocacy of state equality influenced the kind of government that was formed. He also was an active member of the United States Supreme Court who served as an important link between the Framers of the Constitution and the Supreme Court of JOHN MARSHALL.

Born in Ireland, Paterson moved to New Jersey at an early age, graduated from the College of New Jersey (Princeton), studied law, and was admitted to the bar in 1768. Supporting the movement for independence, he soon became a prominent member of New Jersey's revolutionary generation and served in its provincial legislature. Paterson drafted the state's first constitution and became its first attorney general. During the 1780s he built up his legal practice by defending the interests of wealthy landowners and creditors. In the political battles of that decade he advocated the supremacy of the peace treaty of 1783 over state laws, opposed the emission of paper money, and supported the movement to create a strong central government.

In 1787 New Jersey selected Paterson as one of its delegates to the CONSTITUTIONAL CONVENTION. Although he favored increasing the power of the national government, Paterson vigorously opposed the proposal of the VIRGINIA PLAN, as drafted by JAMES MADISON and presented by EDMUND RANDOLPH, that REPRESENTATION in both houses of the national legislature be apportioned according to population. Paterson feared this provision would give too much power to the larger states and place smaller states like New Jersey, Connecticut, and Delaware at a disadvantage. As an alternative he proposed the NEW JERSEY PLAN of government. Its principal feature was the continuance of the unicameral legislature of the ARTICLES OF CONFEDERATION in which each state had only one vote. The plan also would have: provided the federal government with the power to levy imposts and regulate trade and collect funds from states that did not comply with federal requisitions; created a Supreme Court with broad powers; and made the laws and treaties of the United States the supreme law of the land, with the state judiciaries bound to obey them despite any contrary state laws. Should a state or individuals within a state refuse to obey the laws of Congress or its treaties, the federal government would have had the right to use force to compel obedience. In other words, the central issue separating the proponents of the New Jersey Plan from those who favored the Virginia Plan was representation, not nationalism. Although the convention rejected Paterson's proposal, the delegates from the small states remained strongly opposed to proportional representation in Congress. In fact, the convention almost foundered on this issue, but it finally resolved the matter by adopting the so-called GREAT COMPROMISE that provided for representation by population in the lower house of a bicameral Congress and equal representation of each state in the upper house. With this matter settled, Paterson threw his complete support behind the new Constitution.

In 1789 the New Jersey legislature elected Paterson to the first United States Senate where, along with OLIVER ELLSWORTH, he helped to write the JUDICIARY ACT OF 1789. This law created a system of lower federal courts, broadly defined their JURISDICTION, created the office of attorney general, and gave the Supreme Court APPELLATE JURISDICTION over the final decisions of state courts in all matters relating to the Constitution and federal laws and treaties. As a senator, Paterson also enthusiastically supported ALEXANDER HAMILTON's proposals to fund the national debt at face value with full interest, and for the federal government to assume all state debts. In November 1790 Paterson resigned his seat in the Senate to become governor of New Jersey. In this capacity he undertook the task of codifying the state's laws, which were published in 1800. He also worked closely with Hamilton in 1791 to form the generally unsuccessful "Society for Establishing Useful Manufactures"; the society created a small industrial city on the banks of the Passaic River, which became known as Paterson.

Early in 1793 President GEORGE WASHINGTON appointed Paterson to the United States Supreme Court. For the next decade he had an active career on the bench participating in almost all the important decisions rendered by the high court. These decisions reveal Paterson to have been, above all else, a firm advocate of the supremacy of the federal over the state governments. In *Penhallow v. Doane's Administrators* (1795) he expounded an extremely nationalist interpretation of the origins and nature of the Union, arguing that even during the 1780s the Continental Congress represented the "supreme will" of the American people. In the important and controversial case of WARE V. HYLTON (1796) Paterson held that the treaty of peace with Great Britain (1783), which guaranteed that no legal obstacles would be placed in the way of the recovery of debts owed by Americans to British creditors, was part of the "supreme law of the land," rendering invalid a Virginia statute (1777) that allowed the sequestration of debts owed to British subjects before the Revolution.

Paterson also believed in a strong and independent judiciary. In 1795 while on circuit in Pennsylvania he delivered an opinion in VAN HORNE'S LESSEE V. DORRANCE that espoused the doctrine of VESTED RIGHTS and the right of the courts to void a statute repugnant to the Constitution. Although the case involved a state law that contradicted a state constitution, Paterson's argument had broader theoretical implications, and his remarks on the subject of JUDICIAL REVIEW are the fullest and most important statements by a Justice of the United States Supreme Court before John Marshall's opinion in MARBURY V. MADISON (1803). In HYLTON V. UNITED STATES (1796) Paterson agreed with the other Justices in upholding the constitutionality of a federal tax on carriages enacted in 1794. Because the key issue was whether the carriage tax was a DIRECT TAX or an excise tax, Paterson's opinion contained a long discussion of the intention of the Framers of the Constitution as to what kinds of taxes required apportionment among the states according to population. Paterson also expounded on the intention of the Framers in *Calder v. Bull* (1798) when he concurred with the rest of the Court in interpreting the provision of Article I, section 10, prohibiting state legislatures from enacting EX POST FACTO laws as extending only to criminal, not civil laws.

Like so many Federalists, Paterson refused to recognize the legitimacy of the Republican opposition during the 1790s. When Congress passed the ALIEN AND SEDITION ACTS, in 1798, he vigorously enforced them. While riding circuit in Vermont he urged a federal grand jury to indict Democratic-Republican Congressman Matthew Lyon for bringing the President and the federal government into disrepute with his various criticisms. "No government," Paterson observed, "can long subsist when offenders of this kind are suffered to spread their poison with impunity." In the trial that followed Paterson continued to pursue Lyon, emphasizing that the tendency of the Congressman's words be made the test of his intent. Paterson also made clear his belief that the Supreme Court alone had the final authority to determine the constitutionality of laws of Congress, a position the Republican defense had denied. After the jury convicted Lyon, Paterson imposed a harsh sentence of four months in jail and a $1,000 fine. In 1800 Paterson also presided over the trial of Anthony Haswell, a Bennington, Vermont, newspaperman who had rallied to Lyon's defense, and following Haswell's conviction sentenced him to two months in prison and fined him $200. Paterson's actions during the crisis of 1798, along with those of SAMUEL CHASE, are among the clearest examples of the partisan nature of the Federalist judiciary during the late 1790s. Many Jeffersonians were incensed by the proceedings, and had the attempt to remove Chase from the Supreme Court proven successful in 1805, they probably would have gone after Paterson next.

When Oliver Ellsworth resigned as Chief Justice

in 1800, most Federalists in the Senate felt the post should go to Paterson. But by then President JOHN ADAMS had openly broken with the Hamiltonian wing of the party, and he appointed John Marshall instead. Paterson accepted this development graciously; in fact, he described the new Chief Justice as "a man of genius" whose "talents have at once the lustre and solidity of gold." When the Jeffersonians took political power in 1801, Paterson backed away from his earlier extremism and supported Marshall's strategy of avoiding direct political confrontations with the Republican majority in Congress. When the JUDICIARY ACT OF 1801 was repealed, some of the more belligerent Federalists, including Justice Chase, wanted the Supreme Court to declare the repeal act unconstitutional. Riding circuit in Virginia, Marshall opposed this strategy, and declared the law constitutional in STUART V. LAIRD. The decision was immediately appealed to the Supreme Court where Marshall would not be allowed to participate in the case because he had already ruled on it in the lower court. In early 1803 Paterson delivered the Supreme Court's decision on the question. Not only did he side with Marshall, he delivered a warning to the more combative Federalists that "the question is at rest and ought not now to be disturbed." Among other things, the decision clearly indicated that the Federalist-dominated Supreme Court was willing to acquiesce in the "Revolution of 1800." It also went a long way toward reducing concerns, at least among moderates in THOMAS JEFFERSON's administration, about the high court's tendency to engage in partisan politics.

In the fall of 1803, Paterson was injured in a carriage accident. He missed the February 1804 term of the Supreme Court; and although he rode circuit the following year, he never fully recovered. He died in 1806.

RICHARD E. ELLIS

Bibliography
GOEBEL, JULIUS, JR. 1971 *History of the Supreme Court of the United States, Vol. I: Antecedents and Beginnings to 1801.* New York: Macmillan.
O'CONNOR, JOHN E. 1979 *William Paterson: Lawyer and Statesman, 1745–1806.* New Brunswick, N.J.: Rutgers University Press.

PATERSON PLAN

See: New Jersey Plan

PATTON v. UNITED STATES
281 U.S. 276 (1930)

In this case a unanimous Supreme Court, speaking through Justice GEORGE SUTHERLAND, held that the constitutional right to a jury in a federal court included exactly twelve members who were to render a unanimous verdict. (See JURY SIZE; JURY UNANIMITY.) Sutherland also declared that a defendant might waive his right to a jury or consent to a jury of less than twelve. Forty years later, in WILLIAMS V. FLORIDA (1970), a case involving a state court, the Court held that fixing the number of required jurors at twelve was a "historical accident" and "cannot be regarded as an indispensable component of the Sixth Amendment."

DAVID GORDON

(SEE ALSO: *Waiver of Constitutional Rights.*)

PAUL v. DAVIS
424 U.S. 693 (1976)

Even before GOLDBERG V. KELLY (1970) the Supreme Court assumed that the guarantee of PROCEDURAL DUE PROCESS attached to state impairments of "liberty" or "property" interests—concepts that bore their own constitutional meanings as well as their traditional COMMON LAW meanings. *Goldberg* and its successors added to those meanings a new category of protected "entitlements" established by statute or other state action. BISHOP V. WOOD (1976) and *Paul v. Davis* turned this development upside down, using the idea of "entitlements" under state law to *confine* the reach of due process.

In *Paul*, police officers circulated a flyer containing the names and photographs of persons described as "active shoplifters." Davis, one of those listed, had been arrested and charged with shoplifting, but the case had not been prosecuted and the charge had been dismissed. He sued a police officer in a federal district court, claiming damages for a violation of his federal constitutional rights. The Supreme Court held, 5–3, that the alleged harm to Davis's reputation did not, of itself, amount to impairment of a "liberty" interest protected by the due process guarantee. For the majority, Justice WILLIAM H. REHNQUIST manhandled precedents that had established reputation as a "core" constitutionally protected interest, asserting that the Court had previously offered protection to reputation only when it was harmed along with some other interest established by state law, such as a right to employment. Justice WILLIAM J. BRENNAN, for the dissenters, showed how disingenuous was this characterization of the precedents.

Probably the majority's main concern was to keep the federal CIVIL RIGHTS laws from becoming a generalized law of torts committed by state officers, with the federal courts as the primary forum. Yet the majority opinion cannot be taken at face value. Unquestionably the notion of "liberty" interests protected by due process still includes a great many interests not defined by state law, such as FIRST AMENDMENT liberties.

KENNETH L. KARST

PAUL v. VIRGINIA
8 Wallace 168 (1869)

In 1866, Virginia prohibited out-of-state insurance companies from doing business without a substantial deposit; domestic companies were not so required. Convicted of violating the 1866 act, Paul filed a WRIT OF ERROR and BENJAMIN R. CURTIS argued his case. Justice STEPHEN J. FIELD, for a unanimous Supreme Court, rejected Paul's Article IV PRIVILEGES AND IMMUNITIES argument, declaring that CITIZENSHIP could apply only to natural persons. Field further asserted that insurance contracts were not articles of commerce and that the issuance of a policy was not a transaction in INTERSTATE COMMERCE. *Paul* was often cited as a limitation on congressional power on the incorrect assumption that congressional and state regulatory power were mutually exclusive. *Paul* remained law until virtually overturned in UNITED STATES V. SOUTH-EASTERN UNDERWRITERS ASSOCIATION (1944), involving congressional power, after which Congress authorized state regulation.

DAVID GORDON

PAXTON'S CASE
Gray, *Mass. Repts.*, 51 469 (1761)

In *Paxton's Case*, the Massachusetts Superior Court considered whether to continue issuing WRITS OF ASSISTANCE, which, by a British statute of 1662, empowered customs officers to search all houses for contraband. Massachusetts opposed these writs; its legislation had repudiated the general SEARCH WARRANTS they resembled in favor of uniformly specific warrants. Other stimulants to the case were frequent

searches under the writs, tense relations with local British customs officers, the belief that customs regulations had been enforced against local merchants with discriminatory rigor, and the thwarted ambitions of the powerful Otis family for appointment to the Superior Court.

The death of King George II terminated existing writs after six months, and local merchants asked the court not to replace them. In the initial hearing Josiah Gridley argued the positions of the customs establishment that the act of 1662 defined writs of assistance as general search warrants and that a local statute had empowered the court to issue them by giving it the same jurisdiction as the one that issued them in England. Oxenbridge Thacher and JAMES OTIS, JR., representing the merchants, inaccurately replied that the local court had not recently exercised the powers of the English tribunal, the Court of Exchequer.

Otis, son of the candidate for a seat on the Superior Court, cited a magazine article to prove that the writs did not currently operate as GENERAL WARRANTS in Britain and had not been so intended by the statute of 1662. Legions of British laws authorized general searches, however, and Otis relied primarily on the HIGHER LAW. Since general searches allegedly violated natural and COMMON LAW, Otis reasoned that writs of assistance were intrinsically void if worded as the statute prescribed and should be judicially construed as specific search warrants.

Otis's use of sources was heavily didactic. He cited Sir EDWARD COKE, whose *Institutes* exaggerated MAGNA CARTA into a prohibition of general search warrants, and he wrongly read into Coke a further requirement that all search warrants be specific. Otis also stretched BONHAM'S CASE (1610) to hold that common law courts could "control" unreasonable Parliamentary legislation and render it void. Only private interests had actually clashed in *Bonham's Case*, not levels of law or government as Otis implied. Although Otis had not advised the court explicitly to disallow a Parliamentary statute, he misused *Bonham's Case* to advocate a judicial construction of the act that would have had the effect of disallowance.

Persuaded by Otis's eloquence, the court delayed its decision, found that the writs used in England were general, and approved their local issuance over Otis's continued objections. The Massachusetts legislature responded by reducing the salaries of the judges and passing a bill, vetoed by the governor, to define the writs as specific warrants. THOMAS HUTCHINSON, whose appointment as Chief Justice had blocked the judicial aspirations of the Otises, later traced his political demise to his courtroom support of writs of assistance. *Paxton's Case* is one of the leading precedents for the FOURTH AMENDMENT and probably inspired the rejection by later Massachusetts courts (1763–1766) of customary search warrants against felons in *Bassett v. Mayhew* and other cases.

WILLIAM CUDDIHY

Bibliography

SMITH, M. H. 1978 *The Writs of Assistance Case.* Berkeley: University of California Press.

PAYTON v. NEW YORK
445 U.S. 573 (1980)

The FOURTH AMENDMENT, which the FOURTEENTH makes applicable to the states, says that the "right of people to be secure in their . . . houses . . . shall not be violated." *Payton* was the first case in which the Supreme Court confronted the issue whether police may enter a private home, without an ARREST WARRANT or consent, to make a FELONY arrest. New York, sustained by its courts, authorized warrantless ARRESTS, by forcible entry if necessary, in any premises, if the police had PROBABLE CAUSE to believe a person had committed a felony. In Payton's case the police seized EVIDENCE in PLAIN VIEW at the time of arrest and used it to convict him.

A 6–3 Supreme Court, in an opinion by Justice JOHN PAUL STEVENS, reversed and held the state statute unconstitutional. Absent EXIGENT CIRCUMSTANCES, "a man's house is his castle" and unlike a public place may not be invaded without a warrant. Stevens found slight guidance in history for his position on the special privacy of the home in the case of a felony arrest, but he insisted that the Fourth Amendment required a magistrate's warrant. Justice BYRON R. WHITE for the dissenters declared that the decision distorted history and severely hampered law enforcement; the amendment required only that a warrantless felony arrest be made on probable cause in daytime. (See STEAGALD V. UNITED STATES, 1981.)

LEONARD W. LEVY

PECKHAM, RUFUS W.
(1838–1909)

Rufus Wheeler Peckham, the last of President GROVER CLEVELAND's four appointees to the Supreme Court, was commissioned in 1896 following eight years of service on the New York Court of Appeals.

His name is linked most often with one of the half dozen most fulsomely denounced Supreme Court decisions in American history. Speaking for a majority of five in LOCHNER V. NEW YORK (1905), Peckham invoked the SUBSTANTIVE DUE PROCESS doctrine of "liberty of contract," which he had established in an incipient form in ALLGEYER V. LOUISIANA (1897), and invalidated a statute regulating the hours worked by bakeshop employees. (See FREEDOM OF CONTRACT.) Peckham's opinion infuriated progressive reformers, evoked one of Justice OLIVER WENDELL HOLMES's most famous dissents, and ultimately contributed a new term to the lexicon of constitutional discourse in America. More than four generations later, "Lochnerism" is habitually used by commentators to describe the horrible consequences of interventionist JUDICIAL REVIEW in defense of doctrinally abstract constitutional rights.

Holmes once remarked that the "major premise" of Peckham's jurisprudence was "God damn it." It was an apt observation. Peckham was outraged by the increasing propensity of state legislatures and the Congress to transcend "the proper functions of government," and he not only conceptualized the judicial function in essentially negative terms but also regarded the Court as an appropriate forum for battling the ominous evils of centralization and socialism. For Peckham, the Court's role in constitutional adjudication was to police the boundaries separating the rights of the individual, the powers of the states, and the authority of the general government in such a way as to keep each within its proper sphere. Otherwise, he warned while still on the New York bench, "in addition to the ordinary competition that exists throughout all industries, a new competition will be introduced, that of competition for the possession of the government."

Peckham had boundless confidence in his capacity to draw objective lines between these mutually limiting spheres. He dissented in CHAMPION V. AMES (1903) on the ground that a federal statute prohibiting interstate distribution of lottery tickets was not a regulation of commerce at all but rather an attempt by Congress to usurp the reserved power of the states to regulate public morals. And in *Lochner* Peckham conceded that state governments might prevent individuals from making certain kinds of contracts, only to conclude that there was no "direct relation" between the hours worked by bakeshop employees and either the public health or the health, safety, and morals of the workers. Peckham, in short, knew a police regulation or an exercise of the commerce power when he saw one. Holmes may have been astonished when Peckham claimed that legitimate governmental interventions were readily distinguishable from those with only a "pretense" of legitimacy. But most Americans were accustomed to the claim. The spate of veto messages issued by President Cleveland were strikingly similar to Peckham's judicial opinions in both substance and style.

Peckham's voting record in cases involving race relations reflected another principal goal of the Cleveland Democracy—"home rule" for the South. The great spokesman for liberty of contract joined the majority in HODGES V. UNITED STATES (1906), which denied federal JURISDICTION over conspiracies to prevent blacks from making or carrying out labor contracts. He also concurred in BEREA COLLEGE V. KENTUCKY (1908), where the Court upheld a statute prohibiting even voluntary interracial education. If Peckham perceived a principled difference between the right of employers and employees to contract in *Lochner* and the right of individuals freely to associate in *Berea College,* he never described it. Yet it appears that Peckham rarely worried about such overarching conceptual problems. He not only managed to keep race relations and employment contract issues in separate analytical compartments but also voted to impose more stringent PUBLIC USE requirements on state governments when they regulated prices under the POLICE POWER than when they exercised the EMINENT DOMAIN power. Peckham stridently criticized the DOCTRINE of *Munn v. Illinois* (1877) throughout his career, arguing that storage rates charged by grain elevator firms were not subject to regulation because the owners had not devoted their property "to any public use, within the meaning of the law." (See GRANGER CASES.) In *Clark v. Nash* (1905), however, he sustained a law that permitted individuals to condemn rights-of-way across their neighbors' land for irrigation and mining purposes. "What is a public use," Peckham declared, "may frequently and largely depend upon the facts surrounding the subject, and . . . the people of a State . . . must in the nature of things be more familiar with such facts" than the federal judiciary.

Peckham wrote 448 opinions during his fourteen years on the Court, more than thirty percent of which were dissents. Very few of his majority opinions have stood the test of time. Modern commentators almost unanimously regard most of the results he reached to be insupportable and his mode of reasoning unfathomable. But it was Peckham himself who best summed up both the implications of his work for American public life and the internal contradictions that hastened its demise. "At times there seems to

be a legal result which takes no account of the obviously practical result," he wrote in *Sauer v. City of New York* (1907). "At times there seems to come an antithesis between legal science and common sense."

CHARLES W. MCCURDY

Bibliography
SKOLNIK, RICHARD 1969 Rufus Peckham. Pages 1685–1703 in Leon Friedman and Fred L. Israel, eds., *The Justices of the United States Supreme Court, 1789–1967.* New York: Chelsea House.

PEIK v. CHICAGO & NORTHWESTERN RAILWAY COMPANY

See: Granger Cases

PELL v. PROCUNIER
417 U.S. 817 (1974)

In a case that helped delineate the boundaries between the traditional FIRST AMENDMENT freedoms and the expanding area of PRISONERS' RIGHTS, several prisoners and professional journalists challenged the constitutionality of a California prison regulation that forbade press interviews with particular inmates. The argument for the prisoners' rights was that this regulation abridged their FREEDOM OF SPEECH; the journalists claimed the rule inhibited their newsgathering capabilities, thus violating the FREEDOM OF PRESS. The Justices voted 6–3 against the inmates and 5–4 against the journalists. Because the prisoners had alternative means of communication (friends or family, for example) the California regulation did not violate their rights. The majority based its rejection of the journalists' position on the purpose of the regulation—to prevent particular individuals from gaining excessive influence through special attention—and the reporters' otherwise free access to prisoners. Furthermore, the regulation did not prohibit the press from publishing what it chose.

DAVID GORDON

PENDENT JURISDICTION

When a federal court has JURISDICTION over a case presenting a FEDERAL QUESTION, the court may also take jurisdiction over closely related claims based on state law. According to *Gibbs v. United Mine Workers of America* (1966), pendent jurisdiction over a state law claim is appropriate when the state and federal claims share "a common nucleus of operative fact." If the federal claim is itself insubstantial, or is dismissed before the case is tried, it will not serve as a basis for getting a state claim heard by the federal court; such a case should be dismissed. The federal court has discretion to decline pendent jurisdiction over a state claim when the state issues are apt to predominate in the case (making it more appropriate for hearing in a state court), or when the combination of federal and state claims is apt to produce jury confusion. (See ANCILLARY JURISDICTION.)

In PENNHURST STATE SCHOOL & HOSPITAL V. HALDERMAN (1984) the Supreme Court drastically curtailed use of pendent jurisdiction in CIVIL RIGHTS cases. The Court held that the ELEVENTH AMENDMENT bars a federal court from entertaining an action—whether for DAMAGES or for INJUNCTION—against a state officer, when the action is based on an alleged violation of state law.

KENNETH L. KARST

Bibliography

WRIGHT, CHARLES ALAN 1983 *The Law of Federal Courts,* 4th ed. Pages 103–109. St. Paul, Minn.: West Publishing Co.

PENDLETON, EDMUND
(1721–1803)

Admitted to the bar in 1745, Edmund Pendleton became a justice of the peace in 1751 and a member of the Virginia House of Burgesses in 1752. He was a leader of the conservative patriot faction in Virginia and opposed PATRICK HENRY on many issues, including colonial reaction to the Stamp Act of 1765. Pendleton opposed the act and, as a justice of the peace, declared it unconstitutional, but he did not approve of Henry's famous resolutions against it. He became a member of the committee of correspondence in 1773 and a delegate to the FIRST CONTINENTAL CONGRESS in 1774. Between 1774 and 1776 he was president of both the Virginia convention (the provisional legislature) and the Committee of Safety (the de facto executive). He presided over the Virginia convention of 1776 which passed the resolution Pendleton had drafted instructing Virginia's delegates to the Continental Congress to seek a DECLARATION OF INDEPENDENCE, adopted the VIRGINIA DECLARATION OF RIGHTS AND CONSTITUTION, and appointed a committee, including Pendleton, GEORGE WYTHE, and THOMAS JEFFERSON, to revise the state's laws. He was elected speaker of the first House of Delegates under the new constitution (1776–1777) and then appointed first presiding judge of the court of chancery (1777–1779). In 1779 he became presiding judge of the court of appeals, the state's highest court, a position he held until his death. In COMMONWEALTH V. CATON (1782), he stated that laws repugnant to the state constitution were void, but he reserved the question of whether his court could so declare them.

Pendleton was unanimously chosen president of the Virginia convention of 1788 at which he argued and voted for the RATIFICATION OF THE CONSTITUTION. He declined President GEORGE WASHINGTON's offer of a federal district judgeship in order to remain on the state court. As an indication of his virtues as a judge, it is said that only one of his judicial decisions was ever reversed, and in that case he reversed himself.

DENNIS J. MAHONEY

PENDLETON ACT
22 Stat. 403 (1883)

A fundamental change in the operation of American government began with the adoption of the Civil Service Act of 1883—known as the Pendleton Act, for its sponsor, Senator George H. Pendleton (Democrat of Ohio). The act created a merit system for selection of non-policymaking employees of the United States government to replace the "spoils" system which rewarded political supporters. Although the immediate stimulus for adoption of the act was the assassination of President JAMES GARFIELD by a disappointed office seeker, a politically independent civil service had been a major goal of reformers for many years.

The act based eligibility for affected federal employment on performance in competitive examinations, and it created a Civil Service Commission to supervise the examinations and handle personnel administration. Initially extending to less than ten percent of federal employees, the competitive civil service now includes over ninety percent. Much of this growth was a result of the Ramspeck Act (Civil Service Act of 1940) which authorized the President to place virtually all federal employment under the system by EXECUTIVE ORDER. The Civil Service Reform Act (1978) abolished the Civil Service Commission but retained the principle of political neutrality established by the Pendleton Act.

DENNIS J. MAHONEY

Bibliography

ROSENBLOOM, DAVID H. 1971 *Federal Service and the Constitution.* Ithaca, N.Y.: Cornell University Press.

PENN, WILLIAM
(1644–1718)

The scion of a wealthy English family, William Penn attended Oxford University, studied law, and managed the family's estates before becoming a Quaker in the mid-1660s. Throughout the rest of his life Penn engaged in Quaker preaching and propaganda. He was imprisoned on at least three occasions for publishing pamphlets about his religious beliefs. His acquittal in 1670 on a charge of unlawful preaching led to BUSHELL'S CASE, which ended the punishment of jurors who decided contrary to a judge's instructions. In the political campaigns of the late 1670s, Penn agitated for RELIGIOUS LIBERTY and frequent parliamentary elections.

Penn's involvement with America began in 1682, when he became a trustee of the colony of West Jersey, which he and eleven others had purchased for settlement by Quakers, and helped to frame its charter. King Charles II granted the proprietary colony of Pennsylvania to Penn in 1681 as settlement of a large debt that the king owed Penn's father; the following year Penn leased the area now known as Delaware and added it to the colony. Penn described his intentions for the colony as a "holy experiment" in religious and political liberty. In 1682, during a two-year sojourn in America, he wrote a Frame of Government (constitution) for the colony, granting the settlers freedom of religion, procedural guarantees in criminal cases, and limited self-government.

In 1697 Penn drafted, and submitted to the Board of Trade, the first proposal for a federal union of the English colonies in North America. His plan would have created a "congress," comprising two representatives from each colony, competent to legislate on any matter related to "the public tranquility and safety."

During a visit to Pennsylvania in 1701 Penn granted the residents a new charter, the Charter of Privileges, creating a unicameral legislature, greatly expanding the scope of colonial self-government, and providing for Delaware's establishment as a separate entity. Shortly thereafter, he returned to England, where he died.

DENNIS J. MAHONEY

(SEE ALSO: *Pennsylvania Colonial Charters.*)

Bibliography

WILDES, HARRY E. 1974 *William Penn.* New York: Macmillan.

PENN CENTRAL TRANSPORTATION CO. v. NEW YORK CITY
438 U.S. 104 (1978)

Some governmental regulations of the use of property are severe enough to be called TAKINGS OF PROPERTY, for which JUST COMPENSATION must be made under the explicit terms of the Fifth Amendment (governing federal government action) or interpretations of the FOURTEENTH AMENDMENT'S DUE PROCESS clause (governing state action). This decision illustrates how difficult it is to persuade the Supreme Court that a regulation constitutes a "taking."

A New York City ordinance required city approval before a designated landmark's exterior could be altered. The owner of Grand Central Terminal sought to build a tall office building on top of the terminal, and was refused permission on aesthetic grounds. The Supreme Court held, 6–3, that this regulation did not constitute a "taking."

Justice WILLIAM J. BRENNAN, for the majority, conceded that the taking/regulation distinction had defied clear formulation, producing a series of "ad hoc factual inquiries." This regulation, however, was analogous to ZONING under a comprehensive plan; over 400 landmarks had been designated. Further, the owner's loss was reduced by transferring its air-space development rights to other property in the city.

For the dissenters, Justice WILLIAM H. REHNQUIST argued that the law's severely destructive impact on property values was not justified by either of the usual "exceptions": the banning of "noxious uses," or the imposition of widely shared burdens to secure "an average reciprocity of advantage" (as in the case of zoning). Penn Central had suffered a huge loss of value, not offset by benefits under the landmark law.

KENNETH L. KARST

PENNHURST STATE SCHOOL & HOSPITAL v. HALDERMAN
451 U.S. 1 (1981)
457 U.S. 1131 (1984)

Pennhurst worked major changes in the interpretation of the ELEVENTH AMENDMENT and in the PENDENT JURISDICTION of federal courts over claims based on state law. These changes remove one important weapon from the arsenal of CIVIL RIGHTS plaintiffs.

Terri Lee Halderman, a resident of Pennhurst, a state institution for the mentally retarded, commenced a CLASS ACTION in federal district court against Pennhurst and a number of state and local officials. She alleged that squalor, abuse of residents, and other conditions at Pennhurst violated the federal DEVELOPMENTALLY DISABLED ASSISTANCE AND BILL OF RIGHTS ACT of 1975, the DUE PROCESS clause of the FOURTEENTH AMENDMENT, and Pennsylvania's statute governing mental retardation. After a long trial, the district court agreed with her on all counts, and held that mentally retarded people in the state's care had a due process right to live in "the least restrictive setting" that would serve their needs. The court's INJUNCTION ordered the defendants to close Pennhurst and place its residents in "suitable living arrangements." The court of appeals affirmed, but rested decision only on the federal statute. The Supreme Court reversed, instructing the lower courts to consider whether the district court's order was justified on the basis of the Constitution or state law. On REMAND, the court of appeals avoided the constitutional issue, holding that state law required reaffirmance of the "least restrictive setting" ruling. When the case returned to the Supreme Court, the Court held, 5–4, that the Eleventh Amendment barred the district court's injunction. (The case was then settled, with the state agreeing to close Pennhurst and to move its residents to their home communities, or to other institutions if they were aged or ill.)

Justice LEWIS F. POWELL's OPINION OF THE COURT announced that the doctrine of SOVEREIGN IMMUNITY is a constitutional principle, based on the Eleventh Amendment, which gives a state immunity from suit in a federal court by an individual plaintiff. In Powell's novel reading, EX PARTE YOUNG (1908) stands for a narrow exception to this immunity, allowing a suit in federal court for an injunction against a state officer only when the plaintiff's claim is based on a violation of the federal Constitution. (Perhaps violations of federal statutes will fit within this category, because of the operation of the SUPREMACY CLAUSE.) Suits in federal court against state officers—even suits for injunctive relief—are thus barred by the Eleventh Amendment when they are based on claimed violations of state law.

Prior to Pennhurst an action in federal court founded on FEDERAL QUESTION JURISDICTION could include a claim for relief on state law grounds, when both the federal and state claims arose out of the same facts. However, Powell said, this doctrine of pendent jurisdiction rests only on concerns for efficiency and convenience, concerns that must give way to the force of the Eleventh Amendment.

For the dissenters, Justice JOHN PAUL STEVENS decried the Court's overruling of some two dozen precedents, and defended the long-established understanding of Ex parte Young: that when a state officer's conduct is illegal (under either federal or state law), the officer is "stripped" of the cloak of the sovereign's immunity. Here it was perverse to clothe Pennsylvania's officers with the state's Eleventh Amendment immunity when they were acting in violation of their sovereign's commands as embodied in state law. Justice WILLIAM J. BRENNAN, dissenting separately, argued that the amendment does not bar a suit by a citizen against the citizen's own state.

The Pennhurst majority opinion is vulnerable to criticism for its historical analysis of the Eleventh Amendment, for its casual dismissal of the importance of the federal courts' pendent jurisdiction, and for its choice to confer immunity on wrongdoing officials in the name of the sovereignty of the very state that had made the officials' conduct illegal. These criticisms seem minor, however, in the light of another one that is far more grave. The majority, in denying private citizens a vital judicial remedy against official lawlessness, weakened the rule of law.

KENNETH L. KARST

Bibliography

SHAPIRO, DAVID L. 1984 Wrong Turns: The Eleventh Amendment and the Pennhurst Case. Harvard Law Review 98:61–85.

PENNSYLVANIA v. NELSON
350 U.S. 497 (1956)

The Supreme Court banned outright state prosecutions for SEDITION against the United States by ruling, in Pennsylvania v. Nelson, that Congress had already preempted that field of SOVEREIGNTY. The decision had the effect of limiting the states to punishing sedition against state or local, but not federal, government.

Steve Nelson, an avowed communist, had been convicted for violating Pennsylvania's stringent sedition law by his words and actions concerning the federal government; he was sentenced to serve twenty years in prison and pay large fines. The state supreme court reversed, holding the state law had been superseded by the Smith Act. The Supreme Court upheld and extended this ruling. Chief Justice EARL WARREN used three criteria or a three-part criterion in ruling that there was no longer room for state action in this field. The scheme of federal regulation, he maintained, which included the Smith Act, the INTERNAL SECURITY ACT of 1950, and the COMMUNIST CONTROL ACT of 1954, was "so pervasive" as to leave no room for state regulation. Further, these federal statutes demonstrated a federal interest "so dominant" as to preclude state action on the same subject; and for the state to enforce its federal law presented a "serious danger of conflict" with the administration of the federal program. Three Justices dissented, arguing that Congress had not intended to preempt the internal security field.

Following the decision all pending proceedings under the state sedition laws were dismissed or abandoned. Congress considered a measure to set aside the decision but failed to enact it.

PAUL L. MURPHY

PENNSYLVANIA COLONIAL CHARTERS
(April 25, 1682; October 28, 1701)

WILLIAM PENN, the proprietor of Pennsylvania, was a Quaker, a humanitarian, a champion of RELIGIOUS LIBERTY, and a stalwart advocate of CIVIL LIBERTIES. His two charters for his colony gave it representative institutions of government and bills of rights far in advance of the times. The 1682 Frame of Government called itself a "charter of liberties" that had the character of FUNDAMENTAL LAW. Any act of government that "infringed" on the designated liberties, said the Frame, "shall be held of no force or effect." Inhabitants possessing one hundred acres of land "at one penny an acre" were declared "freemen" capable of electing or being elected representatives, including members of the upper house—an innovation. The Frame separated church and state and guaranteed religious liberty by its provision that all persons professing God should be free to worship as they pleased and not be compelled to frequent or maintain any worship or ministry. FAIR TRIAL, which Penn and the Quakers had been denied in England, was here protected. At a time when defendants could not testify on their own behalf, the Frame allowed all persons to plead their own cases. Trial by a twelve-member jury of the VICINAGE, whose judgment was to be "final" (see BUSHELL'S CASE, 1670) and INDICTMENT by GRAND JURY in capital cases were guaranteed. The

RIGHT TO BAIL was recognized and excessive fines were banned.

The 1701 Charter of Privileges, which replaced the Frame and remained the basis of government in Pennsylvania until 1776, also had the character of a CONSTITUTION to which ordinary legislation must conform or be of no effect. Its provisions for the "Enjoyment of Civil Liberties" and for religious liberty, and its ban against an ESTABLISHMENT OF RELIGION extended to all inhabitants "for ever." Among their innovations was a guarantee that "all criminals shall have the same Privileges of Witnesses and Council [sic] as their Prosecutors," the source of the comparable clauses in the SIXTH AMENDMENT. England did not allow counsel to all defendants until 1836. Pennsylvania's colonial charters had a marked influence on the development of the concept of a bill of rights in America.

LEONARD W. LEVY

Bibliography

PERRY, RICHARD L., ed. 1959 Sources of Our Liberties. Pages 204–221, 251–260. New York: American Bar Foundation.

PENNSYLVANIA CONSTITUTION OF 1776
(August 16, 1776)

Pennsylvania's short-lived first CONSTITUTION, superseded in 1790, is notable because it was the most unorthodox and democratic of the constitutions of the original states. Although the extralegal "convention" that framed the document exercised full powers of government and remained in session as the legislature, the constitution was FUNDAMENTAL LAW. Its preamble, stressing NATURAL RIGHTS theory, declared that it was "for ever" unalterable; its declaration of rights was made part of the constitution and inviolable; and its frame of government created a legislature without the power "to add to, alter, abolish, or infringe" any part of the constitution.

The declaration of rights was superior to the more famous VIRGINIA DECLARATION OF RIGHTS, Pennsylvania's model. Pennsylvania omitted the right to BAIL and the ban against excessive fines and CRUEL AND UNUSUAL PUNISHMENTS but added FREEDOM OF SPEECH, assembly, and petition; separated church and state; recognized the right of CONSCIENTIOUS OBJECTION; protected the RIGHT TO COUNSEL in all criminal cases; and provided for the right to bear arms and the RIGHT TO TRAVEL or emigrate—all constitutional "firsts" in the United States. To create a political democracy controlled by the people, the frame of government established a powerful unicameral legislature, with no upper house to check the lower and no governor to veto its legislation. The legislature's proceedings had to be made public and its doors were to be open to the public. In effect all males of voting age could vote, because the constitution enfranchised all taxpayers (all men had to pay a POLL TAX) and their sons, and anyone who could vote was eligible to hold office. Proportional representation, based on the number of taxable inhabitants, governed the apportionment of the legislature.

In place of a governor the constitution established a council, elected by the people, representing each county, with a president or chairman. The council had weak executive powers but for the power to make appointments, including all judges. The constitution instituted few checks and did recognize SEPARATION OF POWERS. Its strangest institution was the council of censors, a popularly elected body that met for one year in every seven and was charged with the responsibility of seeing that the constitution was preserved inviolate; it could review the performance of all public officers, order IMPEACHMENTS, recommend repeal of legislation, and call a convention to revise the constitution. That council met only once and was so politically divided that it did nothing. But the VERMONT CONSTITUTION OF 1777, based on Pennsylvania's, copied the council of censors and kept it until 1869. The Pennsylvania Constitution of 1790 followed the MASSACHUSETTS CONSTITUTION OF 1780.

LEONARD W. LEVY

Bibliography

SELSON, J. PAUL (1936)1971 *The Pennsylvania Constitution of 1776.* New York: Da Capo Press.

PENSACOLA TELEGRAPH CO. v. WESTERN UNION TELEGRAPH CO.
96 U.S. 1 (1878)

This case is significant because the Supreme Court, following GIBBONS V. OGDEN (1824), declared that the congressional power to regulate INTERSTATE COMMERCE extends to newly invented instrumentalities of commerce, here the telegraph. In 1866 Congress had prohibited the states from granting telegraph monopolies. Florida, seeking to control telegraphic transmission within its JURISDICTION, conferred exclusive rights on the Pensacola company. A 7–2 Court, speaking through Chief Justice MORRISON R. WAITE, held the state act unconstitutional for conflict with the act of Congress. Accordingly, the company had no valid chartered right to exclude competitors.

LEONARD W. LEVY

PENUMBRA THEORY

Writing for the Supreme Court in GRISWOLD V. CONNECTICUT (1965), Justice WILLIAM O. DOUGLAS commented that "specific guarantees in the BILL OF RIGHTS have penumbras, formed by emanations from those guarantees that help give them life and substance." The occasion for this shadowy suggestion was the Court's decision holding unconstitutional the application to a BIRTH CONTROL clinic of a state law forbidding the use of contraceptive devices, even by the married couples whom the clinic had aided. Although nothing in the Constitution specifically forbade such a law, Justice Douglas rested decision on a RIGHT OF PRIVACY founded in this "penumbra" theory. A number of constitutional guarantees created "zones of privacy." One such zone included the "right of association contained in the FIRST AMENDMENT." Other protections of privacy were afforded by the THIRD AMENDMENT'S limitations on the quartering of troops, the FOURTH AMENDMENT'S protections against unreasonable SEARCHES AND SEIZURES, and the Fifth Amendment's RIGHT AGAINST SELF-INCRIMINATION. "The present case, then, concerns a relationship lying within the zone of privacy created by several fundamental constitutional guarantees."

This "penumbra" theory, which has had no generative power of its own, is best understood as a last-ditch effort by Justice Douglas to avoid a confrontation with Justice HUGO L. BLACK over a doctrinal issue dear to Black's heart. In his famous dissent in ADAMSON V. CALIFORNIA (1947), Black had derided "the natural-law–due-process formula" that allowed judges, with no warrant in the constitutional text, "to trespass, all too freely, on the legislative domain of the States as well as the Federal Government." Douglas had joined Black's *Adamson* dissent, and perhaps hoped that his *Griswold* opinion, by maintaining a formal tie to the specifics of the Bill of Rights, might persuade Black to come along. Black, of course, would have none of it: "I get nowhere in this case by talk about a constitutional 'right of privacy' as an emanation from one or more constitutional provisions. I like my privacy as well as the next one, but I am nevertheless compelled to admit that government has a right to invade it unless prohibited by some specific constitutional provision."

The Court subsequently relocated its new right of privacy in the liberty protected by the DUE PROCESS clause of the FOURTEENTH AMENDMENT, and no further "penumbras" have been seen in the land. Nonetheless, the *Griswold* decision has been an unusually influential precedent, not only for the Supreme Court's abortion decisions but also for the development of a generalized FREEDOM OF INTIMATE ASSOCIATION. Not every penumbra darkens the road ahead.

KENNETH L. KARST

Bibliography

KAUPER, PAUL G. 1965 Penumbras, Peripheries, Emanations, Things Fundamental and Things Forgotten: The Griswold Case. *Michigan Law Review* 64:235–282.

PEONAGE

Peonage is a system of debt bondage, in which a laborer is bound to personal service in order to work off an obligation to pay money. The system originated in the newly independent countries of Spanish America early in the nineteenth century, and in Hawaii and the Philippines later, as a substitute for various institutions used in the colonial era to marshal a labor force. In some of these countries the system continues to exist. In its classic form, peonage involves a trivial advance of money to a worker, in exchange for a contractual obligation to work for a term, or until the debt is repaid. From then on, the laborer is bound by law to serve the employer, and efforts to quit are met with the force of the state: arrest, imprisonment, return to the employer's service.

Peonage was also part of a larger system of involuntary servitude that emerged in the American South after the Civil War. As such, though whites have sometimes been its victims, peonage has served as a substitute for black slavery. After the slave states were forced by emancipation to shift from a labor regime based on status and force to one of free labor based on contract and choice, peonage emerged as a system that hid the wolf of involuntary servitude in the sheep's clothing of contract.

Peonage as a customary system for coerced black labor had its origin in the contract-enforcement sections of the BLACK CODES (1865–1875) and other labor-related statutes of the era. These provided both civil and criminal penalties for breach of labor contracts, punished VAGRANCY, prohibited enticement of laborers from their jobs, and hampered or penalized agents inducing the emigration of laborers. Southern states also permitted the leasing of convict labor and adopted a criminal-surety system, whereby a person convicted of a MISDEMEANOR would have his fine and costs paid by a prospective employer and then be obliged to work for the surety. Though the Black Codes were soon repealed, the FREEDMEN'S BUREAU at the same time emphasized labor contracts as the nexus of the employer–employee relationship for former slaves, and this later encouraged the use of contracts as a device for forcing black labor.

In 1867, when Congress enacted the Peonage Act to abolish peonage in New Mexico Territory, it also made it applicable to "any other Territory or State of the United States." The act made it a FELONY to hold a person in a condition of peonage, or to arrest a person for that purpose. It voided statutes and "usages" enforcing the "voluntary or involuntary service or labor of any persons as peons in liquidation of a debt or obligation, or otherwise."

United States District Judge Thomas G. Jones began the legal struggle against peonage in a vigorous GRAND JURY charge, reported as *The Peonage Cases* (1903), defining peonage broadly as "the exercise of dominion over their persons and liberties by the master, or employer, or creditors, to compel the discharge of the obligation, by service or labor, against the will of the person performing the service." In *Clyatt v. United States* (1905), the Supreme Court upheld the use of the Peonage Act for the prosecution of a peonmaster. Brushing aside both STATE ACTION and DUAL SOVEREIGNTY arguments, Justice DAVID J. BREWER found authorization for direct federal power over peonage in the enforcement clause (section 2) of the THIRTEENTH AMENDMENT. But he also held that debt was the "basal fact" of peonage, thus limiting federal action to cases where an actual debt could be shown.

After publication of the "Report on Peonage" (1908) by the United States Department of Justice, prompted by discovery of occasional instances of white peonage (usually of immigrants), the Supreme Court, in BAILEY V. ALABAMA (1911), used the Peonage Act to strike down Alabama contract-enforcement statutes that permitted quitting to be *prima facie* evidence of an intent to defraud the employer. The Court held that the Peonage Act voids "all legislation which seeks to compel the service or labor by making it a crime to refuse or fail to perform it." In *United States v. Reynolds* (1914), the Court invalidated Alabama criminal-surety statutes, describing the plight of a black peon caught in them as being "chained to an everturning wheel of servitude." But peonage has proved to be a remarkably tenacious form of servitude for blacks in the rural South, highlighted by the 1921 massacre of eleven black peons by their Georgia master, and by the establishment of peonage under federal and state auspices in refugee camps after the 1927 Mississippi River flood.

While physical force or threat of prosecution plainly constitute peonage, other forms of compulsion present interpretive problems. Thus subterfuges as well as outright violations of the Peonage Act persist into the present, despite the invalidation or repeal of the state labor-contract statutes that provided the original basis of peonage. The threat of deportation has proved an effective means of keeping alien migrant workers in a condition of involuntary or underpaid labor, and lower federal courts have divided as to whether this constitutes peonage.

WILLIAM M. WIECEK

Bibliography

COHEN, WILLIAM 1976 Negro Involuntary Servitude in the South, 1865–1940: A Preliminary Analysis. *Journal of Southern History* 42:31–60.

DANIEL, PETE 1972 *The Shadow of Slavery: Peonage in the South, 1901–1969.* Urbana: University of Illinois Press.

NOVAK, DANIEL A. 1978 *The Wheel of Servitude: Black Forced Labor After Slavery.* Lexington: University Press of Kentucky.

PEOPLE v. CROSWELL
3 Johnson's Cases (N.Y.) 336 (1804)

The state of New York, run by Jeffersonians, indicted Harry Croswell, a Federalist editor, for the crime of SEDITIOUS LIBEL, because he wrote that President THOMAS JEFFERSON had paid a scurrilous journalist to defame GEORGE WASHINGTON. Croswell was convicted at a trial presided over by the Jeffersonian chief justice of the state, Morgan Lewis, who embraced the position of the prosecution in ZENGER'S CASE (1735). Lewis ruled that truth was not a defense against a charge of seditious libel and that the jury's sole task was to decide whether the defendant had published the statements charged, leaving the court to decide their criminality as a matter of law.

ALEXANDER HAMILTON, representing Croswell on his appeal to the state's highest court, advocated the protections of the Sedition Act of 1798: truth as a defense and determination by the jury of the criminality of the publication. FREEDOM OF THE PRESS, declared Hamilton, was "the right to publish, with impunity, truth, with good motives for justifiable ends, though reflecting on government, the magistracy, or individuals." Spenser Ambrose, the Jeffersonian prosecutor, defended the remote BAD TENDENCY TEST. By the time the court decided the case, Ambrose had become a member of it. Had he been eligible to vote, the court would have supported the suppressive views of Lewis and Ambrose. As it was, the court split 2–2. Judge BROCKHOLST LIVINGSTON joined Lewis, while Judge SMITH THOMPSON joined the opinion of JAMES KENT, a Federalist who adopted Hamilton's argument.

In 1805 the state legislature enacted a bill allowing the jury to decide the criminality of a publication and permitted truth as a defense if published "with good motives for justifiable ends." On the whole that was the standard that prevailed in the United States until NEW YORK TIMES V. SULLIVAN (1964).

LEONARD W. LEVY

PER CURIAM

(Latin: "By the court.") A *per curiam* opinion represents the views of the court and summarily disposes of the issue before the court by applying settled law. (See RES JUDICATA). Generally the opinion is short and it is always unsigned, although dissents will occasionally be filed.

DAVID GORDON

PEREZ v. BROWNELL

See: *Trop v. Dulles*

PEREZ v. UNITED STATES
402 U.S. 146 (1971)

In sustaining a conviction for the federal crime of "loan-sharking," the Supreme Court upheld Title II of the CONSUMER CREDIT PROTECTION ACT as valid under the COMMERCE CLAUSE. For an 8–1 Court, Justice WILLIAM O. DOUGLAS rehearsed a congressional committee's finding that extortionate credit practices were linked to organized, interstate crime and vitally affected INTERSTATE COMMERCE. He rejected petitioner's contention that the crime of loan-sharking was necessarily local in nature. Justice POTTER STEWART, in dissent, argued that there had been no showing of interstate movement or effect in Perez's case, and worried that Congress might preempt the whole field of criminal law.

DENNIS J. MAHONEY

PERRY v. UNITED STATES

See: Gold Clause Cases

PERRY EDUCATION ASSOCIATION v. PERRY LOCAL EDUCATORS' ASSOCIATION
460 U.S. 37 (1983)

Perry provided the leading modern opinion setting guidelines governing FIRST AMENDMENT claims of access to the PUBLIC FORUM. A school district's collective bargaining agreement with a union (PEA) provided that PEA, but no other union, would have access to the interschool mails and to teacher mailboxes. A rival union (PLEA) sued in federal district court, challenging the constitutionality of its exclusion from the school mails. The district court denied relief, but the court of appeals held that the exclusion violated the EQUAL PROTECTION clause and the First Amendment. The Supreme Court reversed, 5–4, rejecting both claims.

Justice BYRON R. WHITE wrote for the Court, setting out a three-category analysis that set the pattern for later "public forum" cases such as CORNELIUS V. NAACP LEGAL DEFENSE AND EDUCATIONAL FUND, INC. (1985). First, the streets and parks are "traditional" public forums, in which government cannot constitutionally forbid all communicative activity. Any exclusion of a speaker from such a traditional public forum based on the content of the speaker's message must be necessary to serve a COMPELLING STATE INTEREST. Content-neutral regulations of the "time, place, and manner" of expression in such places may be enforced when they are narrowly tailored to serve significant state interests and they leave open "ample alternative channels" of communication.

Second, the state may open up other kinds of public property for use by the public for expressive activity. The state may close such a "designated" public forum, but so long as it remains open it must be made available to all speakers, under the same constitutional guidelines that govern traditional public forums.

Third, communicative uses of public property that is neither a traditional nor a designated public forum may be restricted to those forms of communication that serve the governmental operation to which the property is devoted. The only constitutional limits on such restrictions on speech are that they be reasonable, and that they not be imposed in order to suppress a particular point of view. The *Perry* case, said Justice White, fit this third category: the school mail system was neither a traditional public forum nor designated for public communicative use; rather it could be limited to school-related communications, including those from PEA, the teachers' elected bargaining agent. Such a limitation did not exclude PLEA because of its point of view.

Justice WILLIAM J. BRENNAN, for the four dissenters, argued that the exclusion of PLEA was "viewpoint discrimination," and thus that the case did not turn on the characterization of the school mails as a public forum.

The *Perry* formula capped a process of doctrinal development focused on what HARRY KALVEN, JR., named "the concept of the public forum." In its origin, the concept expanded the First Amendment's protections of speech. *Perry* marks the success of a campaign, highlighted by Justice WILLIAM H. REHNQUIST's opinion in *United States Postal Service v. Greenburgh Civic Association* (1981), to convert the public forum concept into a preliminary hurdle for would-be speakers to clear before they can establish their claims to the FREEDOM OF SPEECH on government property or in government-managed systems of communication.

KENNETH L. KARST

PERSON

The Constitution contains dozens of references to "persons" but nowhere defines the term. When the Framers of the original document identified persons who might hold federal office or be counted in determining a state's representation in Congress or the ELECTORAL COLLEGE, they used "persons" in its everyday sense—even when they provided that slaves should be counted as "three fifths of all other Persons." Focusing on the allocation of governmental powers, they had little occasion to ponder the philosopher's question: what does it mean to be a person? It was the addition to the Constitution of a body of constitutional rights against the government—first in the BILL OF RIGHTS and later in the FOURTEENTH AMENDMENT—that gave the philosopher's question constitutional significance.

In court, that question is never raised in wholesale terms but always in the context of particular issues. The Fourteenth Amendment's DUE PROCESS and EQUAL PROTECTION clauses, for example, offer their protections to "any person." Should those protections extend to a corporation? To a fetus? A philosopher, asked to say whether a corporation or a fetus more closely resembles some ideal model of a person, might be forgiven for failing to predict the Supreme Court's conclusions in *Santa Clara County v. Southern Pacific Railroad* (1886) and ROE V. WADE (1973) that corporations were included but fetuses were not. The Court, like many another human institution, defines its terms with substantive purposes in mind.

The notion that a corporation might be a "person" for some constitutional purposes had been suggested early in the nineteenth century. The point was not explicitly argued to the Supreme Court, however, until *San Mateo County v. Southern Pacific Railroad* (1882). In that case former Senator ROSCOE CONKLING, representing the railroad, made use of the journal of the joint congressional committee that had drafted the Fourteenth Amendment, a committee on which he had served. Conkling strongly intimated that the committee had used the word "person" for the specific purpose of including corporations. The case was dismissed for MOOTNESS, but in the *Santa Clara* case Chief Justice MORRISON R. WAITE interrupted ORAL ARGUMENT to say that the Court had concluded that the equal protection clause, in referring to a "person," extended its benefit to a corporation—a ruling that has since been followed consistently in both equal protection and due process decisions. Much of the later development of SUBSTANTIVE DUE PROCESS as a guarantee of FREEDOM OF CONTRACT and a protection against ECONOMIC REGULATION thus rested on a proposition of law whose basis was never articulated in an opinion of the Supreme Court.

To be a person, for constitutional purposes, is to be capable of holding constitutional rights. Our system of rights is premised on the idea that a right either "belongs" to someone—some person—or does not exist. The DOCTRINES of STANDING and mootness, as they govern our federal courts, reflect this assumption. We are accustomed to speak of "individual rights." Yet any claim to any right is an appeal to principle—and a principle is an abstraction that governs a great many "cases" not in court. Every claim of "individual" right, in other words, is a claim on behalf of a group composed of all those who fit the claim's underlying principle. Only a person can claim a constitutional right, but every such claim is made by a person as an occupant of a role: a homeowner whose house has been searched by the police, a would-be soapbox orator, a natural father disqualified from having custody of his child.

Although corporations—or even whole states—are capable of asserting constitutional claims, and although every "individual" constitutional right is capable of being generalized to extend to a group, nonetheless there remains an important sense in which we hold constitutional rights as persons. Today's constitutional law recognizes a body of substantive rights founded on the essentials of being a person. Here the philosopher's question must be asked; some model of what it means to be a person is implicit in such developments as the emergence of a RIGHT OF PRIVACY or a FREEDOM OF INTIMATE ASSOCIATION.

These rights of "personhood" (to use the Supreme Court's expression in *Roe v. Wade*) attach to natural persons. They rest on the assumption, usually not articulated, that although each human being is unique, we all share certain elements of our common humanity. The assumption is that each of us is conscious of a continuing identity; has some conception of his or her own good; is capable of forming and changing purposes; has a sense of justice—is, in short a "moral person" and not just a biological organism. Of course, the biological person has received its own constitutional protections: the FOURTH AMENDMENT'S guarantee against unreasonable searches and seizures runs in part to our "persons"; a woman's right to have an abortion is based on her right to control the use of her body. It is the moral person, however, who is the focus of the newer rights of "personhood."

The principal doctrinal foundation for these rights has been a renascent SUBSTANTIVE DUE PROCESS. Yet similar values form the substantive core of the Fourteenth Amendment's guarantee of the equal protection of the laws. That guarantee originated as part of the nation's response to slavery and to efforts in the postabolition South to create a system of serfdom to substitute for slavery. In law, of course, a slave was not a person; an item of property could claim no rights. Yet the original Constitution's two provisions recognizing slavery referred not to "slaves" but to "persons"—as if the draftsmen, resigned to the necessity of their unholy bargain with the southern states, nonetheless could not bring themselves to deny their common humanity with the men and women held as slaves. Seventy years later, in DRED SCOTT V. SANDFORD (1857), Chief Justice ROGER B. TANEY expressed quite another view of the Framers' understanding. At the nation's founding, Taney said, blacks had been considered "an inferior class of beings," incapable of CITIZENSHIP. The modern revival of the Fourteenth Amendment's principle of equal citizenship serves, above all, to protect the claim of each of us to be treated by the society as a person—one who has rights as a respected, responsible, participating member of our community.

                                    KENNETH L. KARST

Bibliography

GRAHAM, HOWARD JAY 1938 The "Conspiracy Theory" of the Fourteenth Amendment. *Yale Law Journal* 47:371–403; 48:171–194.

HORWITZ, MORTON J. 1985–1986 *Santa Clara* Revisited: The Development of Corporate Theory. *West Virginia Law Review* 88:173–224.

NOONAN, JOHN T., JR. 1976 *Persons and Masks of the Law: Cardozo, Holmes, Jefferson, and Wythe as Makers of the Masks.* New York: Farrar, Straus & Giroux.

TRIBE, LAURENCE H. 1978 *American Constitutional Law.* Chap. 15. Mineola, N.Y.: Foundation Press.

VINING, JOSEPH 1978 *Legal Identity: The Coming of Age of Public Law.* New Haven, Conn.: Yale University Press.

PERSONAL LIBERTY LAWS

Between 1826 and 1858, all the free states east of Illinois enacted "personal liberty laws" providing one or more procedural remedies to persons seized as fugitive slaves. These included the writs of HABEAS CORPUS and personal replevin. Some personal liberty laws also provided jury trial to alleged fugitives; prohibited kidnaping or enticement of black persons out of state; imposed more stringent state procedures for recaptions; or provided the services of state's attorneys to alleged fugitives. The Vermont Freedom Act of 1858 declared every slave who came into the state free.

In PRIGG V. PENNSYLVANIA (1842), Justice JOSEPH STORY held that state statutes interfering with recaptures under the 1793 Fugitive Slave Act were unconstitutional. But in an OBITER DICTUM unique to him, Story stated that state officials need not participate in a recapture under federal authority. This spurred enactment of statutes prohibiting state officials such as judges and sheriffs from participating in fugitive recaptures and prohibiting the use of state facilities such as jails to slave-catchers trying to hold runaways. Proslavery spokesmen tirelessly denounced the personal liberty laws. In his last annual message, President JAMES BUCHANAN blamed the crisis of 1860 on them. South Carolina cited the laws as justification for its SECESSION.

                                  WILLIAM M. WIECEK

Bibliography

MORRIS, THOMAS D. 1974 *Free Men All: The Personal Liberty Laws of the North, 1780–1861.* Baltimore: Johns Hopkins University Press.

PERSONNEL ADMINISTRATOR OF MASSACHUSETTS v. FEENEY
442 U.S. 256 (1979)

In selecting applicants for state civil service positions, Massachusetts preferred all qualifying veterans of the armed forces over any qualifying nonveterans. Because fewer than two percent of Massachusetts veterans were women, the preference severely restricted women's public employment opportunities. A nonveteran woman applicant challenged the preference as a denial of the EQUAL PROTECTION OF THE LAWS; the Supreme Court, 7–2, upheld the preference's constitutionality.

The Court, speaking through Justice POTTER STEWART, followed WASHINGTON V. DAVIS (1976) and held that SEX DISCRIMINATION, like RACIAL DISCRIMINATION, is to be found only in purposeful official conduct. A discriminatory impact, of itself, is thus insufficient to establish the sex discrimination that demands the judicial scrutiny set out in CRAIG V. BOREN (1976). Here the veterans preference disadvantaged nonveteran men as well as women; there was no basis for assuming that the preference was "a pretext for preferring men over women." Rather it was aimed at rewarding the sacrifices of military service and easing the transition from military to civilian life.

Justice THURGOOD MARSHALL dissented, joined by Justice WILLIAM J. BRENNAN: legislators act for a variety of reasons; the question is whether an improper purpose was one motivating factor in the governmental action. Here the discriminatory impact of the law was not merely foreseeable but inevitable. The result was to relegate female civil servants to jobs traditionally filled by women. Other less discriminatory means were available for rewarding veterans (bonuses, for example); the state's choice of this preference strongly suggested intentional gender discrimination. A similar "foreseeability" argument was persuasive to a majority of the Court four weeks later, in the context of school segregation. (See COLUMBUS BOARD OF EDUCATION V. PENICK, 1979.)

                                    KENNETH L. KARST

PETERS, RICHARD
(1744–1828)

President GEORGE WASHINGTON on April 11, 1792, commissioned Richard Peters judge of the United States District Court for Pennsylvania, a position he filled until his death. His duties included presiding with a Supreme Court Justice over the federal CIRCUIT COURT in the state.

Peters contributed significantly to the development of a distinctly American ADMIRALTY AND MARITIME LAW, including features borrowed from civil and COMMON LAW precedents. In cases like *Warder v. La-Belle Creole* (1792), he was among the first American judges to advance a risk-reward calculus intended to facilitate the expansion of commerce.

His constitutional opinions touched the civil and criminal JURISDICTIONS of the lower federal courts and the law of TREASON. Peters in 1792 joined his fellow circuit court judges in HAYBURN'S CASE in refusing to determine the qualifications of Revolutionary War pensioners under a congressional act. This task, the judges concluded, fell outside the JUDICIAL POWER OF THE UNITED STATES. Peters, however, had a broad view of federal judicial power. In *United States v. Worrall* (1798) he urged recognition of a FEDERAL COMMON LAW OF CRIMES, a position subsequently rejected by the Supreme Court.

Peters's nationalism also shaped his views of treason and the supremacy of the federal courts. In *United States v. John Fries* (1800) he charged the jury that "levying war against the United States" included armed opposition to the collection of taxes. (See FRIES' REBELLION.) During the famous *Olmstead* controversy in Pennsylvania, Peters ordered the governor and the General Assembly to pay a judgment outstanding against the state in the federal court. Peters withheld issuing compulsory process for fear of an armed clash, but Chief Justice JOHN MARSHALL in UNITED STATES V. JUDGE PETERS (1809) vindicated the judge's nationalism.

Peters's Federalist political principles flowed into his jurisprudence. He was a "Republican Schoolmaster," who exploited the lower federal bench to promote commercial development, federal judicial independence, and national authority.

KERMIT L. HALL

Bibliography

PRESSER, STEPHEN B. 1978 A Tale of Two Judges: Richard Peters, Samuel Chase, and the Broken Promise of Federalist Jurisprudence. *Northwestern University Law Review* 73:26–111.

PETITION FOR REDRESS OF GRIEVANCES

See: Freedom of Petition

PETITION OF RIGHT
(June 7, 1628)

This statute is among the foremost documents in Anglo-American constitutional history. The Petition of Right protected the liberty of the subject and contributed to the development of the RULE OF LAW and the concept of FUNDAMENTAL LAW. The Framers of the Constitution regarded the act of 1628 as part of their COMMON LAW inheritance establishing rights against government. In its time, however, the statute limited only the royal prerogative or executive authority.

In 1626 Charles I, exercising his prerogative, had exacted a "forced loan" from his subjects. The poor paid it by having to quarter soldiers in their homes and having to serve in the army or face trial by a military tribunal. Five knights refused to make a contribution of money to the crown on the grounds that it was an unconstitutional tax; they were imprisoned by order of the king's council. When they sought a writ of HABEAS CORPUS, the Court of King's Bench, in *Darnel's Case* (1627), ruled that because the return to the writ showed the prisoners to be held on executive authority, no specific cause of imprisonment had to be stated.

The forced loan and the resolution of *Darnel's Case* caused a furor. After the House of Commons adopted resolutions against arbitrary taxation and arbitrary imprisonment, Sir EDWARD COKE introduced a bill to bind the king. The House of Lords sought to "save" the SOVEREIGNTY of the king by allowing a denial of habeas corpus for reasons of state. Coke, opposing such an amendment to the bill, argued that it would weaken MAGNA CARTA, and he warned: "Take heed what we yield unto: Magna Charta [sic] is such a fellow that he will have no 'sovereign.'" The Lords finally agreed and the king assented.

The Petition of Right reconfirmed Magna Carta's provision that no freeman could be imprisoned but by lawful judgment of his peers or "by the LAW OF THE LAND." The Petition also reconfirmed a 1354 reenactment of the great charter which first used the phrase "by DUE PROCESS OF LAW" instead of "by the law of the land." By condemning the military trial of civilians, the Petition invigorated due process and limited martial law. One section of the Petition provided that no one should be compelled to make any loan to the crown or pay any tax "without common consent by act of parliament." Americans later relied on this provision in their argument against TAXATION WITHOUT REPRESENTATION. Other sections of the act of 1628 provided that no one should be imprisoned or be forced to incriminate himself by having to answer for refusing an exaction not authorized by Parliament. Condemnation of imprisonment without cause or merely on executive authority strengthened the writ of habeas corpus. (See HABEAS CORPUS ACT OF 1679; BILL OF RIGHTS [ENGLISH].) The THIRD AMENDMENT of the Constitution derives in part from the Petition of Right.

LEONARD W. LEVY

Bibliography

RELF, FRANCIS H. 1917 *The Petition of Right.* Minneapolis: University of Minnesota Press.

PETIT JURY

The petit jury is the trial jury, as distinguished from the GRAND JURY. The petit jury decides questions of fact in cases at law, and renders the verdict, formally declaring its findings. Traditionally, in Anglo-American law, the jury decided by unanimous vote of twelve members, but this is not constitutionally required.

DENNIS J. MAHONEY

(SEE ALSO: *Jury Discrimination; Jury Size; Jury Unanimity; Trial by Jury.*)

PHELPS, EDWARD J.
(1822–1900)

Edward John Phelps was a Vermont Democrat who, in frequent appearances before the Supreme Court, championed the rights of private property. An outstanding orator—he was frequently likened to DANIEL WEBSTER or WILLIAM EVARTS—Phelps served as president of the American Bar Association (1880–1881) and as Kent Professor of Law at Yale (1881–1900). He declared that America's problems stemmed from "a vicious and altogether unnecessary enlargement of the electorate"; this attitude explained his belief that the Constitution was too hallowed to be "hawked about the country, debated in the newspapers . . . [and] elucidated by pot-house politicians, and dung-hill editors."

DAVID GORDON

PHILADELPHIA v. NEW JERSEY
437 U.S. 617 (1978)

In a 7–2 decision, the Supreme Court invalidated a New Jersey environmental protection law that prohibited the importation of solid waste originating or collected out of state. Justice POTTER STEWART, writing for the majority, concluded that the law unduly burdened INTERSTATE COMMERCE. The worthlessness of the regulated commodity did not exclude it from the operation of the COMMERCE CLAUSE; nor was the law permissible because its goals were environmental rather than economic. New Jersey could not require other states to bear the whole burden of conservation of its landfill sites. (See ENVIRONMENTAL REGULATION AND THE CONSTITUTION.)

DENNIS J. MAHONEY

PHILADELPHIA & READING RAILROAD CO. v. PENNSYLVANIA
(State Freight Tax Case)
15 Wallace 232 (1873)

Pennsylvania imposed a tonnage tax on all freight transported within the state, including freight shipped out of and into the state. The transportation of freight for exchange or sale, said Justice WILLIAM STRONG for a 7–2 Supreme Court, is commerce, and a clear tax on such commerce among states is an unconstitutional burden on INTERSTATE COMMERCE that might injure commercial intercourse in the country. Strong added that the transportation of persons or merchandise through a state or from one to another is a subject of national importance requiring, under the rule of COOLEY v. BOARD OF WARDENS (1852), uniform and exclusive regulation by Congress. This still is an important case on STATE TAXATION OF COMMERCE.

LEONARD W. LEVY

PHILOSOPHY AND THE CONSTITUTION

The Constitution is one of the great achievements of political philosophy; and it may be the only political achievement of philosophy in our society. The Framers of the Constitution and the leading participants in the debates on RATIFICATION shared a culture more thoroughly than did any later American political elite. They shared a knowledge (often distorted, but shared nevertheless) of ancient philosophy and history, of English COMMON LAW, of recent English political theory, and of the European Enlightenment. They were the American branch of the Enlightenment, and salient among their membership credentials was their belief that reasoned thought about politics could guide them to ideal political institutions for a free people. They argued passionately about the nature of SOVEREIGNTY, of political REPRESENTATION, of republicanism, of CONSTITUTIONALISM; and major decisions in the ferment of institution-building that culminated in 1787 were influenced, if never wholly determined, by such arguments. The final form of the new federal Constitution embodied radically new views about the location of sovereignty—now located "in the people" in a stronger sense than any philosopher except Jean-Jacques Rousseau would have recognized—and about the function of the SEPARATION OF POWERS and BICAMERALISM.

Philosophy has never again played the role it played at the founding of the Republic, except perhaps in inspiring some ABOLITIONIST CONSTITUTIONAL THEORY. To be sure, "philosophy" in a loose sense has always influenced politicians and judges, who are part of society. The Supreme Court in the late nineteenth and early twentieth centuries expressed in its decisions a laissez-faire "philosophy" compounded of Darwinism, a version of NATURAL RIGHTS theory, and conservative economic beliefs. When the Court abandoned that "philosophy," they adopted another, more progressivist and pragmatic, and more attuned to, though at most only loosely connected with, the renascent empiricism among academic philosophers. Occasionally, the Court has adverted to specific philosophical doctrines, from JOHN MARSHALL in FLETCHER V. PECK (1810) to GEORGE H. SUTHERLAND in UNITED STATES V. CURTISS-WRIGHT EXPORT CORP. (1936) (on the necessary existence of sovereign power). Individual Justices like OLIVER WENDELL HOLMES may have been influenced by philosophical reading and by contact with professional philosophers. But, on the whole, while "philosophy" has had an influence, philosophy has had little—except to the extent that the "philosophy" of the present is always shaped in part by the philosophy of the past. (The decreased influence of philosophy has not lessened the relevance of philosophical issues.)

There are a number of reasons for the decreased influence of philosophy. In the open society the Framers helped to create, their style of argument, dependent on a relatively homogeneous and classically educated elite, could not maintain its political importance. Also, political philosophy itself became less unified. Widely divergent views were united under the umbrella of the Enlightenment by common opposition to entrenched privilege and hieratic religion. Once common enemies were vanquished, philosophical comrades parted company.

Another reason for the decreased influence of philosophy is that philosophy admits of no binding authorities, while law does, and does essentially. The Framers were creating a new political system. No one since then, except to some extent the Reconstruction Congresses, has had that luxury. Later contributors to our constitutional development have always had to interpret, and to attempt to maintain at least the appearance of continuity with, what has gone before.

Curiously, while recent philosophical thinking has had little discernible influence on constitutional law, the reverse is not true. The decisions of the WARREN COURT and the public discussion they generated certainly contributed, probably significantly, to the revival of interest among American philosophers in social and political questions, a revival that became apparent in the CIVIL RIGHTS era of the 1950s and 1960s and that is still in full flower.

Whatever the influence or lack of it of philosophy on constitutional law, philosophical discussion among academic constitutional lawyers may have reached greater intensity in the 1980s than at any time since the 1780s. Constitutional law, like law in general, raises deep and perplexing philosophical questions. The questions that arise most immediately are questions of political philosophy, and of these the one that has generated most discussion is what is known as the "antimajoritarian difficulty": how can it be appropriate for the enormously consequential power of JUDICIAL REVIEW to be vested ultimately in nine individuals who are not chosen by the people and who are not politically accountable to anyone at all? The problem is especially vexing when the Court, in the space of three decades, has outlawed SEGREGATION, forbidden religious activity in the public schools, required REAPPORTIONMENT of the state legislatures and local government, created a constitutional code of CRIMINAL PROCEDURE, established a right to abortion, and found in the EQUAL PROTECTION clause a command that government shall not engage in SEX DISCRIMINATION.

There are three principal types of answer to the question how a democratic society can countenance such judicial power. The first answer, and the natural answer for any lawyer, is the claim that the Supreme Court has this power because the Constitution says it does. But the Constitution does not say that, at least not explicitly. The power of judicial review is nowhere explicitly granted. Now, in a sense, the lawyer's answer is still right. The Constitution as it has been interpreted from 1803 to the present does create the power of judicial review. The propriety of some form of judicial review is disputed by no one. Even so, it is noteworthy that at the very foundation of American constitutional law we encounter the problem of CONSTITUTIONAL INTERPRETATION.

Given a document, and given agreement that its commands are to be put into practice by legal institutions, how do we decide what it commands? How do we decide what it means? Neither the words alone nor anything we know about the writers' intentions is likely to answer straightforwardly all the questions time will bring forth. For that matter, is it the document we are primarily concerned to interpret, or the political and doctrinal tradition proceeding from the document that we are concerned to interpret and to continue? And how are interpretation and continuation related?

It is important to distinguish between the document and the tradition and to ask how our commitments to each are interrelated. For example, we are firmly committed, by our allegiance to the tradition, to certain DOCTRINES, such as the effective application of the BILL OF RIGHTS to the states and of the equal protection clause to the federal government, which can be deduced from the document only by extremely generous canons of interpretation. Some argue that if we are committed to these doctrines, then we must accept and continue to apply those generous canons. But that conclusion does not follow at all. Law, like any tradition, can sanctify mistakes.

The problem of interpretation does not arise only at the stage of justifying judicial review. It arises also at every application of judicial review. What is the Court to do with this power? The lawyerly answer, and again clearly the right answer in some sense, is that the Court should enforce the Constitution. But once more, how do we decide what the Constitution means?

The lawyerly exponent of judicial review also invites, by appealing to the Constitution, the most fundamental question: why do we care about the document or the tradition at all? It may be that to ask this question is to go beyond the domain of the lawyer as lawyer; but lawyers and judges are people, and every person who bears allegiance to the document or the tradition must face this question. Note, however: even though all lawyers and judges must face this question of political philosophy in deciding whether to carry out their roles, it does not follow that they must also appeal to substantive political philosophy in the course of carrying out their roles. Whether they must do that, and whether they could avoid doing that if they tried, are further issues.

The difficulties with the lawyerly justification and exposition of judicial review have prompted two other main theories of judicial review. In one theory, judicial review is justified by the need to protect individual rights against infringement by majoritarian government. Exponents of this theory have drawn heavily on a neo-Kantian strain of contemporary American political philosophy in attempting to elucidate individual rights and the limits of the majority's legitimate power. In the other theory, judicial review does not purport to limit but merely to purify the democratic process. Judicial intervention is necessary to protect political speech and participation and to prevent distortion of the process by majority prejudice, but all in the name of more perfect majoritarianism.

Opposed as they are on the significance of individual rights, these two theories share an ambivalent relationship to the Constitution and the interpretive tradition. Whence comes the notion that individual autonomy should be protected, or that majoritarian democracy should be purified but not otherwise limited? Is it just that the Constitution says so? The Constitution says neither of these things explicitly; and it says both too much and too little to make either of these views a completely satisfactory reading of the document as a whole.

On the other hand, if someone claims to read the Constitution as protecting individuality (or purified majoritarianism) because of the independent moral weight of those values, why does the historical document come into it at all? Is not every appeal to the Constitution by a proponent of independently grounded values of autonomy or purified majoritarianism in some sense mere manipulation of other people's allegiance to the Constitution for itself?

We see that the questions raised by the lawyerly approach to judicial review are not so easily avoided. Still, the competing approaches we have noted alert us to dimensions of the problem not previously apparent. First, if the justification for judicial review is to promote general values such as autonomy or purified majoritarianism, that may help us decide how specific bits of the Constitution should be interpreted. Second, the tradition may refer to certain goals—justice, autonomy, democracy—which the tradition itself views as having a value and grounding outside and independent of the tradition. If the tradition commands allegiance both to its own specific content and to external values, it contains within itself the seeds of possible contradiction. What does faithfulness to the tradition then require?

As of the 1980s, the newest philosophical interest of academic constitutional lawyers is in hermeneutics. Whether there are answers here, and whether any such answers will influence the course of constitutional law, remains to be seen. Hermeneutics may bring new insight into the various meanings of the idea of operating in a tradition. Barring some remarkable feat of philosophical bootstrapping, hermeneutics will not answer the most fundamental philosophical question about constitutional law: why care about the tradition at all? And there is a final irony. Because the political community is made up of individuals who must confront this fundamental question, the community must confront it also, even though from another perspective it is by shared allegiance to the tradition that the community is defined.

DONALD H. REGAN

Bibliography

DWORKIN, RONALD (1977)1978 *Taking Rights Seriously.* Cambridge, Mass.: Harvard University Press.
ELY, JOHN H. 1980 *Democracy and Distrust: A Theory of Judicial Review.* Cambridge, Mass.: Harvard University Press.
LAYCOCK, DOUGLAS 1981 Taking Constitutions Seriously: A Theory of Judicial Review. *Texas Law Review* 59:343–394.
TRIBE, LAURENCE H. 1978 *American Constitutional Law.* Mineola, N.Y.: Foundation Press.
WOOD, GORDON S. 1969 *The Creation of the American Republic, 1776–1787.* Chapel Hill: University of North Carolina Press for the Institute of Early American History and Culture at Williamsburg, Va.

PICKERING, JOHN
(1738?–1805)

In March 1803 the House of Representatives impeached John Pickering, federal district judge for New Hampshire, of habitual drunkenness, uttering blasphemy and profanity from the bench, and making decisions contrary to law. During his Senate trial Pickering introduced a defense of insanity; but the Senate, in a partisan vote, found him "guilty as charged" and removed him from office. The vote was a warning to other Federalist judges that Congress did not need to convict them of a specific crime in order to remove them. (See IMPEACHMENT.)

DENNIS J. MAHONEY

PICKETING

Picketing typically consists of one or more persons patrolling or stationed at a particular site, carrying or wearing large signs with a clearly visible message addressed to individuals or groups approaching the site. Some form of confrontation between the pickets and their intended addressees appears an essential ingredient of picketing. Congress and the National Labor Relations Board have distinguished between picketing and handbilling, however, and merely passing out leaflets without carrying a placard does not usually constitute picketing. What stamps picketing as different from more conventional forms of communication, for constitutional and other legal purposes, ordinarily seems to be the combination of a sign big enough to be seen easily and a confrontation between picketer and viewer.

Constitutional determinations concerning picketing have usually involved LABOR unions that are advertising a dispute with employers and appealing to the public or fellow employees for support. The assistance sought might be a refusal by customers to patronize the picketed business or a refusal by workers to perform services or make deliveries there. In addition, picketing has often been a weapon of CIVIL RIGHTS demonstrators, political and religious activists, environmentalists, and other interest groups.

The leading Supreme Court decision upholding picketing as an exercise of FREEDOM OF SPEECH protected by the FIRST AMENDMENT is THORNHILL V. ALABAMA (1940). In striking down a state antipicketing statute, Justice FRANK MURPHY declared that an abridgment of the right to publicize through picketing or similar activity "can be justified only where the clear danger of substantive evils arises under circumstances affording no opportunity to test the merits of ideas by competition for acceptance in the market of public opinion." Despite this sweeping language, the actual holding in *Thornhill* was narrow. The Alabama courts were prepared to apply a criminal statute to prohibit a single individual from patrolling peacefully in front of an employer's establishment carrying a sign stating truthfully that the employer did not employ union labor.

Following *Thornhill* two principal themes have dominated the Supreme Court's analysis of the constitutional status of picketing. One is the "unlawful objectives" test and the other is the concept of picketing as "speech plus." Under the first approach, as illustrated by GIBONEY V. EMPIRE STORAGE & ICE CO. (1949), even peaceful picketing may be proscribed if its "sole, unlawful immediate objective" is the violation of a valid public policy or statutory mandate. Picketing is treated like any other type of communication, oral or written, which may also be forbidden if it produces a CLEAR AND PRESENT DANGER of, or a direct INCITEMENT to, substantive evils that government is entitled to prevent. A message delivered by pickets, however, might constitute a clearer and more present danger than the same message in a newspaper advertisement, for picketing physically confronts the addressee at the very moment of decision.

A conceptual weakness of the "unlawful objectives" test is that it can sustain almost any restriction on picketing by too loose a characterization of the pickets' purpose as illegal. In *Teamsters Local 695 v. Vogt, Inc.* (1957), a 5–3 Supreme Court upheld a state court INJUNCTION against peaceful organizational picketing on the ground that its purpose was to coerce the employer to force its employees to join the union. Even so, in *Amalgamated Food Employees Union v. Logan Valley Plaza* (1968) Justice THURGOOD MARSHALL could sum up the prior DOCTRINE by declaring that the cases in which picketing bans had been approved "involved picketing that was found either to have been directed at an illegal end . . . or to have been directed to coercing a decision by an employer which, although in itself legal, could validly be required by the State to be left to the employer's free choice."

Picketing as "speech plus" refers to two elements that arguably distinguish it from pure speech. First, it involves physical activity, usually the patrolling of a particular location. It is therefore subject to TRESPASS laws, and to other laws governing the time, place, and manner of expression, such as laws limiting sound levels, regulating parades, or forbidding the obstruction of public ways. Furthermore, picketing enmeshed with violence or threats of violence may be enjoined or prosecuted as assault and battery. Second, picketing may serve as a "signal" for action, especially by organized groups like labor unions, without regard to the ideas being disseminated. Some scholars have challenged the "pure speech/speech plus" dichotomy, contending that all speech, oral or written, has certain physical attributes, and can evoke stock responses from a preconditioned audience.

A further strand of Supreme Court free speech analysis is the notion that government may not engage in "content control." Thus, in POLICE DEPARTMENT OF CHICAGO V. MOSLEY (1972) the Court invalidated a city ordinance that forbade all picketing next to any school while it was in session, but exempted "peaceful picketing of any school involved in a labor dispute." That constituted "an impermissible distinction between labor and other peaceful picketing." The "no content control" doctrine obviously must be qualified by the "unlawful objectives" test.

In 1980 the Supreme Court extended the "unlawful objectives" test so far as to strip it of any practical limitations. A 6–3 majority held in *NLRB v. Retail Employees Local 1001* (*Safeco*) that picketing asking customers not to buy a nonunion product being distributed by a second party was an unlawful BOYCOTT of the distributor. Six Justices considered the prohibition justified constitutionally by Congress's purpose of blocking the "coercing" or "embroiling" of neutrals in another party's labor dispute. In *Safeco*, for the first time ever, the Supreme Court clearly sustained a ban on peaceful and orderly picketing addressed to, and calling for seemingly lawful responses by, individual consumers acting on their own.

Safeco might be explained on the basis that labor picketing is only "economic speech," like commercial advertising, and thus subject to lesser constitutional safeguards than political or ideological speech. Although such a distinction would contradict both established precedent and the traditional recognition of picketing as the working person's standard means of communication, at least it would preserve full-fledged free speech protections for picketing to promote political and ideological causes.

THEODORE J. ST. ANTOINE

Bibliography

COX, ARCHIBALD 1951 Strikes, Picketing and the Constitution. *Vanderbilt Law Review* 4:574–602.
GREGORY, CHARLES O., and KATZ, HAROLD A. (1946) 1979 *Labor and the Law.* New York: Norton.
JONES, EDGAR A., JR. 1956 Free Speech: Pickets on the Grass, Alas!—Amidst Confusion, a Consistent Principle. *Southern California Law Review* 29:137–181.

PIERCE, FRANKLIN
(1804–1869)

A New Hampshire attorney and politician, Pierce was nominated as a compromise presidential candidate by the Democrats in 1852. Pierce was a supporter of the COMPROMISE OF 1850 and a long-time opponent of abolitionists and antislavery Democrats. In 1854 he supported the KANSAS-NEBRASKA ACT, which led to a mini-civil war in "bleeding Kansas." Pierce's role in the passage of this act and his generally pro-southern positions undermined most of his other legislative proposals and his popularity in the North. During the Civil War Pierce's shrill attacks on ABRAHAM LINCOLN's administration made Pierce appear to be a full-fledged Copperhead.

PAUL FINKELMAN

Bibliography

NICHOLS, ROY F. 1931 *Franklin Pierce: Young Hickory of the Granite State.* Philadelphia: University of Pennsylvania Press.

PIERCE, WILLIAM
(1740?–1789)

William Pierce, a veteran of the Revolutionary War and a member of Congress, was a delegate from Georgia to the CONSTITUTIONAL CONVENTION OF 1787. He spoke only infrequently, and he left the Convention on July 1, under pressure of private business difficulties. Pierce did not sign the Constitution but wrote to ST. GEORGE TUCKER: "I approve of its principles and would have signed it with all my heart, had I been present."

Pierce kept fairly detailed notes of the debates while he was present. The notes were published in 1828 and include brief character sketches of each of the delegates.

DENNIS J. MAHONEY

PIERCE v. SOCIETY OF SISTERS
268 U.S. 510 (1925)

Pierce provided a doctrinal link between the SUBSTANTIVE DUE PROCESS of the era of LOCHNER v. NEW YORK (1905) and that of our own time. The Supreme Court unanimously invalidated an Oregon law requiring children to attend public schools. A church school and a military school, threatened with closure, sued to enjoin the law's enforcement. Although the law threatened injury to the schools, their challenge to it was based not on their own constitutional rights but on the rights of their pupils and the children's parents. By allowing the schools to make this challenge, the Court made a major exception to the usual rule denying a litigant's STANDING to assert the constitutional rights of others. Here there was a close relationship between the schools and their patrons, and failure to allow the schools to assert the patrons' rights might cause injury to the schools that no one would contest in court. Parents, fearing prosecution and unwilling to bear the expense of suit, might simply send their children to public schools.

In an opinion by Justice JAMES C. MCREYNOLDS, the Court held that the law unconstitutionally invaded the parents' liberty, guaranteed by the FOURTEENTH AMENDMENT's due process clause, to direct their children's education and upbringing. The decision rested squarely on the notion that important personal liberties could be seriously restricted by the state only upon a showing of great public need. Although *Pierce* thus traced its lineage to earlier decisions protecting economic liberty, it provided support for a later genera-

tion of decisions protecting marriage and family relationships against state intrusion. (See FREEDOM OF INTIMATE ASSOCIATION.)

Pierce is also cited regularly as a RELIGIOUS LIBERTY precedent, defending the right of parents to choose religious education for their children. (See WISCONSIN V. YODER, 1971.)

KENNETH L. KARST

PIERSON v. RAY
386 U.S. 547 (1967)

Pierson is an important case involving individual immunities from suits under SECTION 1983, TITLE 42, UNITED STATES CODE. Clergymen who violated an unlawful "whites only" waiting room policy in a Jackson, Mississippi, bus terminal were arrested and convicted. They brought an action under section 1983 against the arresting police officers and a state judge for depriving the clergymen of their constitutional rights. The Supreme Court both reaffirmed what it asserted to be the absolute immunity of judges from suit at COMMON LAW and refused to interpret section 1983 to abolish that traditional immunity. Although the police officer defendants were not granted absolute immunity, the Court did grant them a defense if the otherwise unconstitutional arrests were made in good faith and with PROBABLE CAUSE.

THEODORE EISENBERG

PINCKNEY, CHARLES
(1757–1824)

Charles Pinckney, a wealthy and ambitious young lawyer from South Carolina, was one of the most active members of the CONSTITUTIONAL CONVENTION OF 1787. A supporter of strong national government, Pinckney had already proposed in Congress several amendments to strengthen the government under the ARTICLES OF CONFEDERATION. He had unsuccessfully urged Congress to call a convention to amend the Articles.

Selected as a delegate to the Federal Convention, Pinckney drafted a comprehensive plan for revising the articles which he introduced immediately after EDMUND RANDOLPH proposed the VIRGINIA PLAN. The PINCKNEY PLAN was never debated in the Convention or the Committee of the Whole, although the Committee of Detail may have drawn some ideas or phrases from it.

Pinckney was one of the most frequent speakers in the debates, but the Constitution, as written, reflected his influence only in minor points and details. In a speech before signing, Pinckney announced that he would support the Constitution despite "the contemptible weakness and dependence of the Executive."

In his later career, Pinckney was a delegate to the South Carolina ratifying convention and to the state CONSTITUTIONAL CONVENTION of 1790, three times governor, a member of the legislature and of both houses of Congress, and minister of the United States to Spain.

DENNIS J. MAHONEY

PINCKNEY, CHARLES COTESWORTH
(1746–1825)

A British-educated, slaveholding lawyer, General Charles Cotesworth Pinckney represented South Carolina at the CONSTITUTIONAL CONVENTION OF 1787 and signed the Constitution. In the convention he worked for a strong national government and for protection of the slaveholding interests. As a leading spokesman for RATIFICATION in South Carolina, he defended the compromises on SLAVERY and argued that a BILL OF RIGHTS was unnecessary.

In 1791, Pinckney declined President GEORGE WASHINGTON's offer of a seat on the Supreme Court. The chief leader of the southern Federalists, Pinckney was nominated for vice-president in 1800, and for President in both 1804 and 1808.

DENNIS J. MAHONEY

Bibliography

ZAHNISER, MARVIN R. 1967 *Charles Cotesworth Pinckney, Founding Father.* Chapel Hill: University of North Carolina Press.

PINCKNEY PLAN
(1787)

The brash young South Carolinian CHARLES PINCKNEY arrived at the CONSTITUTIONAL CONVENTION OF 1787 bearing his own comprehensive draft of a new CONSTITUTION based on proposals he had made to amend the ARTICLES OF CONFEDERATION during his three years in Congress. He presented it to the convention immediately after EDMUND RANDOLPH presented the VIRGINIA PLAN. The Pinckney Plan was never debated, but it was referred to the Committee on Detail which may have drawn some ideas or phrases from it.

There was no copy of the Pinckney Plan among the papers of the convention. Pinckney himself later published what he claimed was his plan, but this was actually a fabrication closely resembling the finished Constitution. On the basis of this (fraudulent) published version and Pinckney's own extravagant claims about his influence, many historians and popular writers have attributed more significance to the Pinckney Plan and its author than either actually had.

In the twentieth century, historians J. Franklin Jameson and ANDREW C. MCLAUGHLIN reconstructed the details of the original Pinckney Plan. The proposal was certainly quite nationalistic, with no state role in the election of either house of Congress, an unconditional congressional veto over state laws, and a very powerful national executive.

DENNIS J. MAHONEY

Bibliography

MCLAUGHLIN, ANDREW C. 1904 The Pinckney Plan. *American Historical Review* 9:135–147.

PINK, UNITED STATES v.
315 U.S. 203 (1942)

In *Pink*, the Supreme Court reaffirmed a DOCTRINE articulated five years earlier in UNITED STATES V. BELMONT (1937): that the President has exclusive constitutional authority to recognize foreign governments and to take all steps necessary to effect such recognition. In *Belmont*, the Court recognized the federal government's STANDING to sue to enforce an EXECUTIVE AGREEMENT known as the "Litvinov Agreement." As part of the process of recognition of the Soviet Union by the United States in 1933, this agreement assigned to the United States nationalized Russian assets located within the United States.

In *Pink*, the Court was again confronted with the controversial Litvinov Assignment. In this case, while recognizing the federal government's rights under the Litvinov Assignment as required by *Belmont*, the New York courts rejected the government's claims of ownership of the assets in question, contending that to enforce the assignment would violate New York public policy against the confiscation of private property. The Supreme Court reversed, 5–2, emphasizing that an executive agreement, like a TREATY, is part of the "supreme law of the land" that no state may frustrate without interfering unconstitutionally with the federal government's exclusive competence in respect of FOREIGN AFFAIRS. In so doing, the Court reasserted the supremacy of an executive agreement over all inconsistent state law or policy.

BURNS H. WESTON

Bibliography

CARDOZO, MICHAEL H. 1962 The Authority in Internal Law of International Treaties: The Pink Case. *Syracuse Law Review* 13:544–553.

FORKOSCH, MORRIS D. 1975 The Constitution and International Relations. *California Western International Law Journal* 5:219, 246–249.

HENKIN, LOUIS 1972 *Foreign Affairs and the Constitution.* Mineola, N.Y.: Foundation Press.

LEARY, M. A. 1979 International Executive Agreements: A Guide to the Legal Issues and Research Sources. *Law Library Journal* 72:1–11.

PINKNEY, WILLIAM
(1764–1822)

William Pinkney studied law under SAMUEL CHASE and subsequently practiced in Baltimore. Although he opposed the RATIFICATION OF THE CONSTITUTION in the Maryland convention of 1788, he later became one of the nation's foremost constitutional lawyers. He held public office continuously from 1788 until his death, serving in the state legislature, in both houses of Congress, as a diplomat in important foreign capitals, and as ATTORNEY GENERAL of the United States under President JAMES MADISON. Although as a young man he favored gradual compensated emancipation in Maryland, Pinkney was a vigorous spokesman for the slave states in the Senate debates over the MISSOURI COMPROMISE (1820).

Between political and diplomatic assignments Pinkney conducted what was probably the most lucrative legal practice in the United States, arguing seventy-two cases before the Supreme Court. He was counsel for the New Hampshire state appointed board of trustees in DARTMOUTH COLLEGE V. WOODWARD (1819), unsuccessfully arguing that the college was a public CORPORATION whose charter could be altered by the state. In MCCULLOCH V. MARYLAND (1819), however, he won the day, contending for the constitutionality of a congressionally chartered bank and against the power of the state to tax it. And in COHENS V. VIR-GINIA (1821) he successfully argued for the Supreme Court APPELLATE JURISDICTION over state criminal cases.

As an advocate, Pinkney won the praise of both judges and opposing counsel. Chief Justice JOHN MARSHALL called him "the greatest man I ever saw in a court of justice" and Marshall's successor, ROGER B. TANEY, said that in thirty years, "I have seen none to equal Pinkney." His enduring significance in American constitutional history derives from his incisive and original arguments in cases of first impression.

PAUL FINKELMAN

Bibliography

PINKNEY, REV. WILLIAM 1853 *The Life of William Pinkney.* New York: D. Appleton & Co.

PIQUA BRANCH OF THE STATE BANK OF OHIO v. KNOOP
16 Howard 369 (1854)

In NEW JERSEY V. WILSON (1812) the Supreme Court had held that a state grant of a tax immunity was a contract within the protection of the CONTRACT CLAUSE. In this case Ohio chartered a bank with the proviso that six percent of its net profits would be taxed in lieu of other taxation. The states competed with each other to entice private business to settle within their borders on the supposition that the more banks, railroads, and factories a state had, the greater would be its prosperity. Special privileges to CORPORATIONS were common, and they often wrote their own charters. Ohio, gripped by an anticorporate movement, reneged by passing an act to tax banks at the same rate as other properties. The bank refused to pay the new tax on the ground that its charter was a contract the obligation of which had been impaired by the tax. (See OBLIGATION OF CONTRACTS.) By a vote of 6–3 the Supreme Court invalidated the tax. To the contention that the power to tax was an inalienable attribute of SOVEREIGNTY, which could not be contracted away, the Court replied that the making of a public contract is an exercise of sovereignty. To the argument that one legislature, by granting a charter of tax immunity, could not bind its successors, the Court replied that the contract clause made the charter binding. In effect the Court cautioned the states to govern wisely, because the Court would not shield them from their imprudence if it took the form of contracts. Corporations throughout the country profited enormously.

LEONARD W. LEVY

PITNEY, MAHLON
(1858–1924)

Mahlon Pitney was the last of President WILLIAM HOWARD TAFT's appointments to the Supreme Court. Organized labor and some progressives vigorously protested the nomination because of Pitney's antilabor opinions as a New Jersey state judge, but his views paralleled Taft's. During Pitney's decade on the bench (1912–1922), he made prophets of his critics, as his opinions reflected a consistent hostility to the claims of organized labor. Nevertheless, Taft, as Chief Justice, derided Pitney as a "weak" member of his Court.

In COPPAGE V. KANSAS (1915) Pitney concluded that a Kansas statute prohibiting YELLOW DOG CONTRACTS violated FREEDOM OF CONTRACT. The opinion largely followed doctrine laid down in LOCHNER V. NEW YORK (1905), and reinforced in ADAIR V. UNITED STATES (1908), when the Court nullified an 1898 congressional law prohibiting railroads from imposing yellow dog contracts. In *Coppage*, Pitney attacked the state law as a restraint on a worker's right to contract, a right he saw as essential to the laborer as to the capitalist, "for the vast majority of persons who have no other honest way to begin to acquire property, save by working for money." Rejecting the statute's avowed intent of enabling workers to organize and bargain collectively, Pitney held that its primary effect was to interfere with "the normal and essentially innocent exercise of personal liberty or of property rights."

Two years later, Pitney wrote the Supreme Court's opinion favoring labor INJUNCTION and again sustained the validity of yellow dog contracts. In HITCHMAN COAL AND COKE CO. V. MITCHELL (1917) he upheld an injunction forbidding the United Mine Workers from seeking to organize workers who had previously agreed not to join a union. Every miner who had affiliated with the union "was guilty of a breach of contract," he said; furthermore, Pitney found that the union knowingly had violated the employer's "legal and constitutional right to run its mine 'non-union.'" Pitney's implacable defense of yellow dog contracts and injunctions galvanized labor's growing antagonism to the federal judiciary and its demands for congressional relief. Eventually, in 1932, the NORRIS-LAGUARDIA ACT forbade federal courts to enforce yellow dog contracts or issue labor injunctions, thus severely limiting the effects of Pitney's COPPAGE and HITCHMAN opinions.

In DUPLEX PRINTING CO. V. DEERING (1921) Pitney reinforced the judicial ban on secondary BOYCOTTS, thus frustrating organized labor's understanding that the CLAYTON ACT (1914) had legalized such practices. Pitney followed an earlier decision against secondary boycotts (LOEWE V. LAWLOR, 1908) and argued that a sympathetic strike supporting a secondary boycott could not be deemed "peaceful and lawful persuasion as allowed in the Clayton Act." Although Pitney regularly invoked judicial doctrines that inhibited labor's right to organize, he occasionally defied prediction. In *Mountain Timber Co. v. Washington* (1917) Pitney led a 5–4 majority that sustained a state WORKERS' COMPENSATION law requiring all employers to contribute to a general state fund, regardless of whether their employees had been injured. He found that the statute did not deprive employers of their property without DUE PROCESS OF LAW, and furthermore, it had a reasonable relationship to the GENERAL WELFARE. Four years later, in TRUAX V. CORRIGAN (1921), he joined OLIVER WENDELL HOLMES, LOUIS D. BRANDEIS, and JOHN H. CLARKE in dissent against Chief Justice Taft's opinion invalidating an Arizona law modeled on the labor provisions of the Clayton Act. In another rare deviation from his norm, Pitney joined the dissenters who favored the dissolution of the United States Steel Corporation.

Typically, judges such as Pitney would presume that regulatory laws such as Kansas's prohibition of yellow dog contracts and the labor provisions of the Clayton Act violated liberty of contract or property rights. Yet Pitney made no such assumption when an individual confronted the criminal process. In the notorious case of FRANK V. MANGUM (1915), for example, Pitney maintained that the state of Georgia had "fairly and justly" done its duty. Pitney also vigorously supported the national government's prosecution of dissenters and radicals following World War I. In *Pierce v. United States* (1920) he sustained the conviction of socialists who "knowingly" and "recklessly" distributed "highly colored and sensational" and "grossly false" statements about the government's conduct of the war. The *Pierce* decision solidified the Court's shift from Holmes's CLEAR AND PRESENT DANGER interpretation of the FIRST AMENDMENT to the less speech-protective BAD TENDENCY TEST.

Pitney approved the Court's invalidation of the child labor laws; he dissented from the majority's approval of widening the authority of the Interstate Commerce Commission; and he dissented from Justice CHARLES EVANS HUGHES's expansive reading of the COMMERCE CLAUSE in the "Shreveport Case," HOUSTON, EAST AND WEST TEXAS RAILWAY COMPANY V. UNITED STATES (1914). In short, Pitney's judicial career faithfully reflected the conservative reaction to much of the political and legal thrust of the Progressive movement.

STANLEY I. KUTLER

Bibliography

LEVITAN, DAVID M. 1954 Mahlon Pitney—Labor Judge. *Virginia Law Review* 40:733–770.

PITT, WILLIAM
(Lord Chatham)
(1708–1778)

William Pitt the elder was one of Britain's greatest statesmen and one of freedom's staunchest friends. He led Britain from near defeat in the Seven Years War to victory and worldwide empire.

In the WILKES CASES debates (1763–1770) Pitt denounced GENERAL WARRANTS as illegal and subversive of liberty and opposed any surrender of PARLIAMENTARY PRIVILEGE. During the 1766 debate over repeal of the Stamp Act, Pitt insisted that "the distinction between legislation and taxation is essentially necessary to liberty," and that while Britain was "sovereign and supreme, in every circumstance of government and legislation whatsoever," Parliament had no right to tax those not represented therein. "There is," he declared, "a plain distinction between taxes levied for purposes of raising a revenue, and duties imposed for the regulation of trade." Later that year, as earl of Chatham, Pitt was again called to head the government. During his administration (but while he was incapacitated by illness) his chancellor of the exchequer procured passage of the TOWNSHEND ACTS.

In the 1770s Chatham urged conciliation with the American colonies, but he opposed any measure tending toward dissolution of the empire. His final speech, delivered in 1778, was against a motion to withdraw British troops and recognize American independence.

DENNIS J. MAHONEY

PLAIN VIEW DOCTRINE

The FOURTH AMENDMENT protects persons and their effects against unreasonable SEARCHES AND SEIZURES. However, articles exposed to the plain view of others are subject to a warrantless seizure on PROBABLE CAUSE, for no search is involved and hence no invasion of privacy results. (Plain view differs from abandonment. Exposure of an article to plain view may result from carelessness; abandonment signifies a deliberate relinquishment of the right of ownership. In either case, there is no constitutionally protected interest in the privacy of the article.)

Three conditions must be met for a plain view seizure to be constitutional, according to the decision in COOLIDGE V. NEW HAMPSHIRE (1971). First, the officer who sees the article must have a legal right to be where he is. Second, discovery of the article by the police must be "inadvertent," not a result of prior information that would have enabled the police to obtain a warrant beforehand. (This requirement is relaxed in a SEARCH INCIDENT TO ARREST, where a seizure made within the limited scope of the authorized search is lawful even if the finding of the evidence was anticipated.) Finally, the incriminating nature of the evidence must be "immediately apparent," so that no additional intrusion on privacy is necessary in order to establish that fact. (The term "immediately apparent" was modified in *Brown v. Texas* (1983) to mean probable cause; certainty is not required.)

An emergency "hot pursuit" of a suspect into private premises, as in WARDEN V. HAYDEN (1967), provides the widest latitude for a plain view seizure; the search for the suspect and his weapons is permitted to extend throughout the entire place until he is apprehended. Barring emergencies, however, a plain view of the interior of a house, obtained through a window or open door, does not permit a warrantless entry of premises any more than does testimony of the senses (say, the odor of marijuana) that criminal activity is afoot. In searches of buildings, therefore, the plain view serves to authorize a seizure only when a lawful search is already in progress when the view is obtained. A different standard applies to automobiles: a plain view of evidence in an automobile on the road not only permits seizure of the evidence but also may provide probable cause for a WARRANTLESS SEARCH of the entire vehicle. Since *Brown,* even a closed container may be seized under the plain view doctrine if the contents can be reliably inferred from its outside appearance—for example, a tied balloon of a type commonly used to carry narcotics.

JACOB W. LANDYNSKI

Bibliography

LAFAVE, WAYNE R. 1978 *Search and Seizure: A Treatise on the Fourth Amendment.* Vol. 2:589–595, 601–605. St. Paul, Minn.: West Publishing Co.

PLANNED PARENTHOOD v. ASHCROFT

See: Reproductive Autonomy

PLANNED PARENTHOOD OF CENTRAL MISSOURI v. DANFORTH
428 U.S. 52 (1976)

Following ROE V. WADE (1973), Missouri adopted a comprehensive law regulating abortion. Planned Parenthood, which operated an abortion clinic, and two eminent physicians sued in federal district court challenging the constitutionality of most of the law's provisions. On appeal, the Supreme Court unanimously upheld three of the state's requirements and by divided vote invalidated four others. Justice HARRY A. BLACKMUN wrote for the Court.

The Court sustained the law's definition of "viability" of a fetus: "when the life of the unborn child may be continued indefinitely outside the womb by natural or artificial life-supportive systems." The state's failure to set a specific time period survived a challenge for VAGUENESS; the Court assumed that the physician retained the power to determine viability. The Court also upheld a requirement of written certification by a woman of her "informed" consent to an abortion, and certain record-keeping requirements.

The Court invalidated, 6–3, a requirement of consent to an abortion by the husband of the pregnant woman, and invalidated, 5–4, a parental consent requirement for unmarried women under age eighteen. Recognizing the husband's strong interest in the abortion decision, the Court concluded that when spouses disagreed, only one of them could prevail; that one must be the woman. As for parental consent, the opinion offered no broad charter of CHILDREN'S RIGHTS but concluded that a "mature" minor's right to have an abortion must prevail over a parent's contrary decision (*H. L. v. Matheson*, 1981). The state had little hope of restoring a family structure already "fractured" by such a conflict.

The Court invalidated, 6–3, a prohibition on saline amniocentesis as an abortion technique. The procedure was used in more than two-thirds of all abortions following the first trimester of pregnancy; its prohibition would undermine *Roe*. Finally, the state had required a physician performing an abortion to use professional skill and care to preserve the life and health of a fetus. The requirement was held invalid, 6–3, because it was not limited to the time following the stage of fetal viability.

The question of the doctor's role in determining viability and preserving fetal life returned to the Court in *Colautti v. Franklin* (1979). There the Court invalidated, 6–3, on vagueness grounds, a Pennsylvania law requiring a doctor to exercise care to protect a fetus when there was "sufficient reason to believe that the fetus may be viable." As in *Roe* and *Danforth*, the Court paid considerable deference to physicians, leaving undefined their control over their patients' constitutional rights.

KENNETH L. KARST

(SEE ALSO: *Abortion and the Constitution; Reproductive Autonomy.*)

Bibliography

COHEN, LESLIE ANN 1980 Fetal Viability and Individual Autonomy: Resolving Medical and Legal Standards for Abortion. *UCLA Law Review* 27:1340–1364.

PLEA BARGAINING

The overwhelming majority of convictions in American criminal courts occur when the accused pleads guilty to a charge; few defendants receive a full judicial trial. "Plea bargaining" describes a variety of incentives and pressures that produce this result and that are commonly encountered in American criminal courts. Some plea bargaining is explicit: defendants are led by the prosecutor or the judge to plead guilty in return for the promise of some concession or in fear of harsh treatment meted out to those who insist on a trial. The reward for defendants may be release on bail before trial, the dropping or reduction of charges, or the lightening of punishment imposed after conviction. Some defendants may plead guilty out of a sense of contrition, but more probably acquiesce in conviction because they expect more lenient treatment if they do not insist on their right to trial.

Overt negotiation to induce a defendant to plead guilty is often not necessary. The incentive structure is built into the culture of the courthouse and into the substantive criminal code itself. Those accused of crime learn the culture from cellmates, friends, and lawyers. Under most modern American penal codes, the same criminal conduct typically permits the defendant to be charged with one or more of several distinct offenses, each carrying different levels of potential punishment. Some of the potential sentences are severe: not just CAPITAL PUNISHMENT but punishment for common offenses by prison terms that may exceed the length of a person's vigorous adulthood. It would be practically impossible and morally unthinkable to apply such severe sanctions in a substantial portion of the cases.

The system is thus dominated at every level by official discretion; police, prosecutors, judges, and correctional officials are expected to extend leniency to most offenders lest the system become brutal and the courthouses overloaded. The guilty plea thus provides incentives for the state as well as the defendant. The courts are prepared to try only about ten percent of the cases potentially before them, and prosecutors value convictions obtained without the effort and expense of trial.

The relationship of this system of official discretion, including plea bargaining, with constitutional norms is strained, to say the least. Enforcement of criminal laws in America is predominantly the responsibility of over 3,000 distinct and varying local systems for the administration of criminal justice. The system generally gives a central role to professional police and prosecutorial organizations rather than to the active supervising magistracy that the Fourth, Fifth, and Sixth Amendments apparently contemplated for federal prosecutions.

The dominance of plea bargaining and the discretionary power to bring and dismiss charges tend to reduce the likelihood of direct confrontation between constitutional doctrine and everyday law enforcement practice. Officials are motivated to settle cases in which the lawfulness of their behavior appears likely to be challenged. Moreover, the dominance of discretion permits some rationalization of enforcement policies, better managerial control of scarce resources, and reduction of the uncertainties of trial for both officials and defendants. The system also permits the public at large to avoid facing the contradictions inherent in the penal policies embodied in the criminal codes of most states.

The guilty plea system potentially conflicts with constitutional norms in three principal ways. First, the system is in some tension with DUE PROCESS standards. In America the guilty plea wholly substitutes for a judicial trial. In Europe, the judge typically must conduct an independent investigation of guilt, whether or not the accused confesses. Even before the modern constitutional revolution in criminal justice, the Supreme Court recognized the dangers inherent in convictions based solely upon guilty pleas, insisting in such cases that convictions be based on knowing and voluntary WAIVER OF RIGHTS. In a series of decisions between 1960 and 1970 the Court spelled out this requirement in specific terms: an admission of guilt in open court by an accused who is adequately counseled and informed by a neutral judge of his rights and of the possible consequences of waiving them by pleading guilty. This formula requires only a rather formalistic colloquy between defendant and judge in open court to ascertain the accused's knowledge and VOLUNTARINESS of the plea. It also pre-cludes active participation by the judge in the negotiations that induce the plea, through promises of leniency or threats of severity. It is also understood that bargains, once struck, must be observed by the government. Beyond these requirements due process is satisfied so long as the bargaining is fair according to the standards of commercial bargaining. Thus a defendant may be held to his plea despite his insistence that he is innocent. Troubling issues arise when an accused pleads guilty, despite his belief in his own innocence, because he recognizes the long odds against acquittal and the high risk of a more severe penalty after conviction at trial. Although the Court has held such pleas to be voluntary and to satisfy due process standards, doubts continue regarding the voluntariness of many such pleas.

A second cluster of constitutional concerns about the guilty plea system centers on the question of equal treatment for all similarly situated defendants. The guarantees of due process and EQUAL PROTECTION somewhat limit the arbitrary and disparate imposition of punishment. Yet the plea bargaining system grants to some defendants concessions that are unlikely to be extended to all. Indeed, if the concessions were equally available, they would lose much of their force in persuading defendants to plead guilty. Moreover, the process of negotiation operates outside the formal protections of the criminal process, within an area of official discretion that is seldom subjected to independent scrutiny. Opportunities abound for arbitrary discrimination.

The third and most pressing set of constitutional concerns about plea bargaining has received the least satisfactory treatment by the Supreme Court. When a defendant pleads guilty, he waives a host of constitutionally protected rights, including TRIAL BY JURY or by a judge, the RIGHT AGAINST SELF-INCRIMINATION, the right to CONFRONTATION and cross-examination of witnesses, and the right to challenge evidence against him. Government officials encourage the waiver of these rights by promising reduced punishment, and by threatening greater punishment for those who insist on their constitutionally guaranteed rights. This process appears to be an UNCONSTITUTIONAL CONDITION on the exercise of rights.

Despite these constitutional concerns, and despite widespread public dissatisfaction, plea bargaining seems to be a permanent feature of the American system of criminal justice. If the Supreme Court has thus far acquiesced in the system's constitutionality, perhaps the Court is not yet persuaded that a satisfactory alternative has been demonstrated.

ARTHUR ROSETT

Bibliography

ROSETT, ARTHUR I. and CRESSY, DONALD 1976 *Justice by Consent: Plea Bargains in the American Courthouse.* Philadelphia: Lippincott.
SCHULHOFER, STEPHEN J. 1984 Is Plea Bargaining Inevitable? *Harvard Law Review* 97:1037–1107.

PLESSY v. FERGUSON
163 U.S. 537 (1896)

Until BROWN V. BOARD OF EDUCATION (1954), *Plessy* was the constitutional linchpin for the entire structure of Jim Crow in America. Borrowed from LEMUEL SHAW in ROBERTS V. BOSTON (1851), the *Plessy* Court established the SEPARATE BUT EQUAL DOCTRINE: black persons were not denied the EQUAL PROTECTION OF THE LAWS safeguarded by the FOURTEENTH AMENDMENT when they were provided with facilities substantially equal to those available to white persons.

Florida enacted the first Jim Crow transportation law in 1887, and by the end of the century the other states of the old Confederacy had followed suit. Louisiana's act, which was challenged in *Plessy,* required railroad companies carrying passengers in the state to have "equal but separate accommodations" for white and colored persons by designating coaches racially or partitioning them. Black citizens, who denounced the innovation of Jim Crow in Louisiana as "unconstitutional, unamerican, unjust, dangerous and against sound public policy," complained that prejudiced whites would have a "license" to maltreat and humiliate inoffensive blacks. Plessy was a TEST CASE. Homer A. Plessy, an octoroon (one-eighth black), boarded the East Louisiana Railroad in New Orleans bound for Covington in the same state and sat in the white car; he was arrested when he refused to move to the black car. Convicted by the state he appealed on constitutional grounds, invoking the THIRTEENTH and Fourteenth AMENDMENTS. The Court had already decided in LOUISVILLE, NEW ORLEANS & TEXAS PACIFIC RY. V. MISSISSIPPI (1890) that Jim Crow cars in INTRASTATE COMMERCE did not violate the COMMERCE CLAUSE.

Justice JOHN MARSHALL HARLAN was the only dissenter from the opinion by Justice HENRY B. BROWN. That the state act did not infringe the Thirteenth Amendment, declared Brown, "is too clear for argument." The act implied "merely a legal distinction" between the two races and therefore had "no tendency to destroy the legal equality of the two races, or reestablish a state of involuntary servitude." Har-

lan, believing that STATE ACTION could have no regard to the race of citizens when their CIVIL RIGHTS were involved, would have ruled that compulsory racial SEGREGATION violated the Thirteenth Amendment by imposing a BADGE OF SERVITUDE.

The chief issue was whether the state act abridged the Fourteenth Amendment's equal protection clause. One reads Brown's opinion with an enormous sense of the feebleness of words as conveyors of thought, because he conceded that the object of the amendment "was undoubtedly to enforce the absolute equality of the two races before the law," yet he continued the same sentence by adding, "but in the nature of things it could not have been intended to abolish distinctions based on color. . . ." As a matter of historical fact the intention of the amendment was, generally, to abolish legal distinctions based on color. The Court pretended to rest on history without looking at the historical record; it did not claim the necessity of adapting the Constitution to changed conditions, making untenable the defense often heard in more recent years, that the decision fit the times. *Plessy* makes sense only if one understands that the Court believed that segregation was not discriminatory, indeed that it would violate the equal protection clause if it were discriminatory. Brown conceded that a statute implying a legal inferiority in civil society, lessening "the security of the right of the colored race," would be discriminatory, but he insisted that state-imposed segregation did not "necessarily imply the inferiority of either race to the other. . . ." There was abundant evidence to the contrary, none of it understandable to a Court that found fallacious the contention that "the enforced separation of the two races stamps the colored race with a badge of inferiority. If this be so, it is not by reason of anything found in the act, but solely because the colored race chooses to put that construction on it." That segregation stamped blacks with a badge of inferiority was not fallacious. The fallacy was that only they imputed inferiority to segregation. Jim Crow laws were central to white supremacist thought. That blacks were inherently inferior was a conviction being stridently trumpeted by white supremacists from the press, the pulpit, and the platform, as well as from the legislative halls, of the South. The label, "For Colored Only," was a public expression of disparagement amounting to officially sanctioned civil inequality. By the Court's own reasoning, state acts compelling racial segregation were unconstitutional if inferiority was implied or discrimination intended.

The separate but equal doctrine was fatally vulnerable for still other reasons given, ironically, by the

Court in *Plessy*. It sustained the act as a valid exercise of the POLICE POWER yet stated that every exercise of that power "must be reasonable, and extend only to such laws as are enacted in good faith for the promotion of the public good, and not for the annoyance or oppression of a particular class." Jim Crow laws were not only annoying and oppressive to blacks; they were not reasonable or for the public good. The Court asserted that the question of reasonableness must be determined with reference "to the established usages, customs and traditions" of the people of the state. The proper standard of reasonableness ought to have been the equal protection clause of the Constitution, not new customs of the white supremacists of an ex-slave state. Even if the custom of segregation had been old, and it was not, the Court was making strange doctrine when implying that discrimination becomes vested with constitutionality if carried on long enough to become customary. Classifying people by race for the purpose of transportation was unreasonable because the classification was irrelevant to any legitimate purpose.

The only conceivable justification for the reasonableness of the racial classification was that it promoted the public good, which Brown alleged. The effects of segregation were inimical to the public good, because, as Harlan pointed out, it "permits the seeds of race hate to be planted under the sanction of law." It created and perpetuated interracial tensions. Oddly the Court made the public-good argument in the belief that the commingling of the races would threaten the public peace by triggering disorders. In line with that assumption Brown declared that legislation is powerless to eradicate prejudice based on hostile "racial instincts" and that equal rights cannot be gained by "enforced commingling." These contentions seem cynical when announced in an opinion sanctioning inequality by sustaining a statute compelling racial segregation. The argument that prejudice cannot be legislated away overlooked the extent to which prejudice had been legislated into existence and continued by Jim Crow statutes.

Harlan's imperishable dissent repeated the important Thirteenth Amendment argument that he had made in the CIVIL RIGHTS CASES (1883) on badges of servitude. That amendment, he declared, "decreed universal civil freedom in the country." Harlan reminded the Court that in STRAUDER V. WEST VIRGINIA (1880), it had construed the Fourteenth Amendment to mean that "the law in the States shall be the same for the black as for the white" and that the amendment contained "a necessary implication of a positive immunity, or right . . . the right to exemption from unfriendly legislation against them distinctively as colored—exemption from legal discriminations, implying inferiority in civil society, lessening the security of their enjoyment of rights which others enjoy. . . ." To Harlan, segregation was discriminatory per se. The state act was unreasonable because segregation was not germane to a legitimate legislative end. He meant that the Fourteenth Amendment rendered the state powerless to make legal distinctions based on color in respect to public transportation. A railroad, he reminded the Court, was a public highway exercising public functions available on the same basis to all citizens. "Our Constitution," said Harlan, "is color-blind, and neither knows nor tolerates classes among citizens." He thought the majority's decision would prove in time to be as pernicious as DRED SCOTT V. SANDFORD (1857). As for the separate but equal doctrine, he remarked that the "thin disguise" of equality would mislead no one "nor atone for the wrong this day done."

Plessy cleared the constitutional way for legislation that forced the separation of the races in all places of public accommodation. Most of that legislation came after *Plessy*. In the CIVIL RIGHTS CASES, the Court had prevented Congress from abolishing segregation, and in *Plessy* the Court supported the states in compelling it. Not history and not the Fourteenth Amendment dictated the decision; it reflected its time, and its time was racist. As Justice Brown pointed out, even Congress in governing the DISTRICT OF COLUMBIA had required separate schools for the two races. The Court did not invent Jim Crow but adapted the Constitution to it.

LEONARD W. LEVY

Bibliography

KLUGER, RICHARD 1973 *Simple Justice: The History of Brown v. Board of Education and Black America's Struggle for Equality.* Pages 71–83. New York: Knopf.

OBERST, PAUL 1973 The Strange Career of *Plessy v. Ferguson. Arizona Law Review* 15:389–418.

OLSON, OTTO, ed. 1967 *The Thin Disguise: Turning Point in Negro History: Plessy v. Ferguson.* New York: Humanities Press.

WOODWARD, C. VANN 1971 The National Decision Against Equality. Pages 212–233 in Woodward, *American Counterpoint: Slavery and Racism in the North–South Dialogue.* Boston: Little, Brown.

PLURALITY OPINION

In some cases the majority of Justices of the Supreme Court, although agreeing on the DECISION, do not agree on the reasoning behind the decision. In such cases, there is no OPINION OF THE COURT; instead there are two or more opinions purporting to explain the decision. If one opinion is signed by more Justices than any other, it is called the "plurality opinion." A plurality opinion may be cited as precedent in later cases, but, unlike a majority opinion, it is not an authoritative statement of the Court's position on the legal or constitutional issues involved.

DENNIS J. MAHONEY

PLYLER v. DOE
457 U.S. 202 (1982)

Experimenting with ignorance, the Texas legislature authorized local school boards to exclude the children of undocumented ALIENS from the public schools, and cut off state funds to subsidize those children's schooling. The Supreme Court, 5–4, held that this scheme denied the alien children the EQUAL PROTECTION OF THE LAWS. The OPINION OF THE COURT, by Justice WILLIAM J. BRENNAN, contains the potential for important future influence on equal protection DOCTRINE.

The Court was unanimous on one point: the FOURTEENTH AMENDMENT's guarantee of equal protection for all PERSONS extends not only to aliens lawfully admitted for residence but also to undocumented aliens. The question that divided the Court was what that guarantee demanded—an issue that the Court's recent opinions had typically discussed in language about the appropriate STANDARD OF REVIEW. In SAN ANTONIO INDEPENDENT SCHOOL DISTRICT V. RODRIGUEZ (1973) the Court had rejected the claim that EDUCATION was a FUNDAMENTAL INTEREST, and had subjected a state system for financing schools to a deferential RATIONAL BASIS standard. A significant OBITER DICTUM, however, had suggested that a total denial of education to a certain group of children would have to pass the test of STRICT SCRUTINY. (See GRIFFIN V. COUNTY SCHOOL BOARD OF PRINCE EDWARD COUNTY, 1964.) Furthermore, although alienage was, for some purposes, a SUSPECT CLASSIFICATION, the Court had not extended that characterization to laws discriminating against aliens who were not lawfully admitted to the country.

Justice Brennan's analysis blurred the already indistinct lines dividing levels of judicial scrutiny in equal protection cases. He suggested that some form of "intermediate scrutiny" was appropriate, and even hinted at a preference for strict scrutiny. Eventually, though, he came to rest on rhetorical ground that could hold together a five-Justice majority. Because the Texas law imposed a severe penalty on children for their parents' misconduct, it was irrational unless the state could show that it furthered "some substantial goal of the State," and no such showing had been made. In a concurring opinion, Justice LEWIS F. POWELL remarked that heightened scrutiny was proper, on analogy to the Court's decisions about classifications based on ILLEGITIMACY. Justice THURGOOD MARSHALL, also concurring, repeated his argument for recognition of a "sliding scale" of standards of review, and accurately noted that this very decision illustrated that the Court was already employing such a system. No one should be surprised when the Court holds invalid a supremely stupid law that imposes great hardship on a group of innocent people.

Chief Justice WARREN E. BURGER, writing for the four dissenters, agreed that the Texas policy was "senseless." He argued nonetheless that the Court, by undertaking a "policymaking role," was "trespass-[ing] on the assigned function of the political branches." In allocating scarce state resources, Texas could rationally choose to prefer citizens and lawfully admitted aliens over aliens who had entered the country without permission; for the dissenters, that was enough to validate the law.

The *Plyler* opinion was narrow, leaving open the question whether a similar burden of substantial justification would be imposed on a discrimination against undocumented aliens who were adults, or even against innocent children when the discrimination was something less than a total denial of education. Justice Brennan did suggest that judicial scrutiny might properly be heightened in cases of discrimination against aliens—even undocumented aliens—who had established "a permanent attachment to the nation." Although it is unlikely that this view could command a majority of the Court today, the remark may bear fruit in the future.

KENNETH L. KARST

(SEE ALSO: *Immigration.*)

POCKET VETO

If Congress adjourns within ten days after passing a bill, the President can prevent the bill's enactment by merely withholding his signature (Article I, section 7, clause 3, of the Constitution). By means of this extension of the VETO POWER, the President can kill legislation without giving any reason and without the possibility of being overridden.

DENNIS J. MAHONEY

POCKET VETO CASE
Okanogan Indians v. United States
279 U.S. 655 (1929)

A unanimous Supreme Court, speaking through Justice EDWARD SANFORD, held that a bill passed by Congress, but not signed by the President, had died when the 69th Congress adjourned between its first and second sessions. The POCKET VETO may therefore be used during the adjournment between sessions, and not merely at the final adjournment, of a particular Congress.

In *Wright v. United States* (1938) and *Kennedy v. Sampson* (1965) federal courts established that the pocket veto could not be used during intrasession adjournments.

DENNIS J. MAHONEY

POELKER v. DOE

See: *Maher v. Roe*

POINTER v. TEXAS
380 U.S. 400 (1965)

A state court had allowed the introduction in EVIDENCE of the transcript of an absent witness's testimony given at a preliminary hearing when the defendant, unrepresented by counsel, could not effectively cross-examine. The Supreme Court, disallowing an exception to the HEARSAY RULE, held that "the SIXTH AMENDMENT's right of an accused to confront the witnesses against him is a fundamental right and is made obligatory on the State by the FOURTEENTH AMENDMENT." The Court also held that the RIGHT OF CONFRONTATION is governed by the same standards in state and federal courts.

LEONARD W. LEVY

POLICE ACTION

The phrase "police action" is not a term of art, or one having any precise legal significance, but simply an expression or euphemism occasionally employed to describe the use of the armed forces of the United States and other nations to resist what is perceived as a violation of international law, a notable example being American use of the armed forces against the North Korean invasion of South Korea in 1950. (See KOREAN WAR AND THE CONSTITUTION.) President HARRY S. TRUMAN based his decision to use American forces to defend South Korea on the fact that the North Korean aggression constituted a violation of the UNITED NATIONS CHARTER, as declared in a resolution of the Security Council. (The Soviet Union, which of course treated the North Korean invasion as "self-defense," chose to absent itself from that meeting of the Council and thereby lost the opportunity to veto the resolution.) Subsequently, in 1957, Senator John Bricker and other conservative congressmen who were opposed to American intervention in Korea (not because they had any sympathy for communist imperialism but because they were isolationists) attempted to remove such justifications of presidential use of troops by unsuccessfully proposing that the Constitution be amended to require affirmative action by Congress before a treaty obligation could be implemented. (See STATE OF WAR; BRICKER AMENDMENT.)

The phrase has occasionally been employed, although not officially, in other situations in which the United States has used its armed forces without a DECLARATION OF WAR or other explicit sanction by Congress, such as President JOHN F. KENNEDY's 1962 blockade of Cuba. A pejorative variation of it was sometimes employed by opponents of American intervention in VIETNAM, who contended that the United States should not act as an "international policeman" or "international gendarme." Although it would have been appropriate, it seems to have been used by no one to describe President Jimmy Carter's unsuccessful attempt, in April 1980, to mount a military raid to free American hostages in Iran.

The characterization has never been officially or generally applied to a declared war.

JOSEPH W. BISHOP, JR.

Bibliography
SEARS, KENNETH C. 1956 Bricker-Dirksen Amendment. *Hastings Law Journal* 8:1–17.

POLICE DEPARTMENT OF CHICAGO v. MOSLEY
408 U.S. 92 (1972)

Mosley is the leading modern decision linking EQUAL PROTECTION doctrine with the FIRST AMENDMENT. Chicago adopted an ordinance prohibiting PICKETING within 150 feet of a school during school hours, but excepting peaceful labor picketing. Earl Mosley had been picketing on the public sidewalk adjoining a high school, carrying a sign protesting "black discrimination," and after the ordinance was adopted he sought declaratory and injunctive relief, arguing that the ordinance was unconstitutional. The Supreme Court unanimously agreed with him.

Justice THURGOOD MARSHALL, for the Court, concluded that the exemption of labor picketing violated the equal protection clause of the FOURTEENTH AMENDMENT. This conclusion followed the lead of Justice HUGO L. BLACK, concurring in COX v. LOUISIANA (1965). Yet Justice Marshall's opinion speaks chiefly to First Amendment values and primarily cites First Amendment decisions. "[A]bove all else, the First Amendment means that government has no power to restrict expression because of its message, its ideas, its subject matter, or its content." As Chief Justice WARREN E. BURGER noted in a brief concurrence, so broad a statement is not literally true; the Court has upheld regulations of speech content in areas ranging from DEFAMATION to OBSCENITY. Yet *Mosley* properly stakes out a presumption in favor of "equality of status in the field of ideas"—a phrase borrowed from ALEXANDER MEIKLEJOHN.

The *Mosley* opinion makes two main points. First, regulations of message content are presumptively unconstitutional, requiring justification by reference to state interests of compelling importance. Second, "time, place, and manner" regulations that selectively exclude speakers from a PUBLIC FORUM must survive careful judicial scrutiny to ensure that the exclusion is the minimum necessary to further a significant government interest. Together, these statements declare a principle of major importance: the principle of equal liberty of expression.

KENNETH L. KARST

Bibliography
KARST, KENNETH L. 1976 Equality as a Central Principle of the First Amendment. *University of Chicago Law Review* 43:20–68.

POLICE INTERROGATION AND CONFESSIONS

In the police interrogation room, where, until the second third of the century, police practices were unscrutinized and virtually unregulated, constitutional ideals collide with the grim realities of law enforcement. It is not easy to talk about the defendant's right to silence and his RIGHT TO COUNSEL when the defendant has confessed to a heinous crime—for example, the rape and murder of a small child as in BREWER v. WILLIAMS (1977) or the kidnapping, robbery, and murder of a cab driver, by a shotgun blast to the back of the head, as in RHODE ISLAND v. INNIS (1980)—and the confession seems quite credible. Thus, for many years few matters have split the Supreme Court, troubled the legal profession, and agitated the public as much as the confession cases.

Not surprisingly, the most famous confession case of all, MIRANDA v. ARIZONA (1966), is regarded as the high-water mark of the WARREN COURT's "DUE PROCESS revolution." Nor is it surprising that the decision became the prime target of those who attributed an increase of crime to the softness of judges. *Miranda*, which finally applied the RIGHT AGAINST SELF-INCRIMINATION to the informal proceedings in the interrogation room, emerged only after a long struggle, and increasing dissatisfaction, with the test for admitting confessions that preceded it—the "voluntariness" test based on the "totality of circumstances." *Miranda* can be understood only in light of the Court's prior efforts to deal with the intractable confession problem.

Until well into the eighteenth century, doctrines concerning confessions did not affect the admissibility of extrajudicial narrative statements of guilt offered as EVIDENCE, but dealt only with the conditions under which immediate conviction followed a confession as a plea of guilty. It was not until *The King v. Warickshall* (1783) that an English court clearly expressed the notion that confessions might be unworthy of credit because of the circumstances under which they were obtained. In that case the judges declared: "A free and voluntary confession is deserving of the highest credit, because it is presumed to flow from the strongest sense of guilt, and therefore it is admitted as proof of the crime to which it refers; but a confession forced from the mind by the flattery of hope, or by the torture of fear, comes in so questionable a shape when it is to be considered as the evidence of guilt, that no credit ought to be given to it; and therefore it is rejected."

Because a separate rule against coerced confessions emerged in eighteenth-century English cases nearly a century after the right against self-incrimination had become established, JOHN H. WIGMORE, the great master of the law of evidence, concluded that the two rules had no connection. But Leonard W. Levy, the leading student of the origins of the right against self-incrimination, strongly disagrees. He maintains that "[t]he relationship between torture, *compulsory* self-incrimination, and *coerced* confessions was an historical fact as well as a physical and psychological one" and that "in the 16th and 17th centuries, the argument against the three, resulting in the rules that Wigmore said had no connection, overlapped" (Levy 1968, pp. 265, 288–289 n.102).

Levy points out that Baron Geoffrey Gilbert, in his *Law of Evidence,* "written before 1726 though not published until thirty years later, stated that though the best evidence of guilt was a confession, 'this confession must be voluntary and without compulsion; for our Law in this differs from the Civil Law, that it will not force any Man to accuse himself; and in this we do certainly follow the Law of Nature, which commands every Man to endeavor his own Preservation . . .'" (Levy 1968, p. 327). Baron Gilbert's phrasing, "our Law . . . will not force any Man to accuse himself," Levy says, "expressed the traditional English formulation of the right against self-incrimination, or rather against *compulsory* self-incrimination. The element of compulsion or involuntariness was always an essential ingredient of the right and, before the right existed, of protests against incriminating interrogations" (ibid., pp. 327–328).

Although Levy insists that this was a historical blunder, both in the United States and in England the confession rules and the right against self-incrimination were divorced and, with the one notable exception of *Bram v. United States* (1897), went their separate ways—until the two rules were intertwined in MALLOY V. HOGAN (1964) and fused in the famous *Miranda* case (1966). Moreover, for most of its life the voluntariness test was essentially an alternative statement of the rule that a confession was entitled to credit so long as it was free of influence that made it untrustworthy or "probably untrue." Wigmore reflected the law prevailing at the time when in 1940 he pointed out that a confession was not inadmissible because of "any *breach of confidence*" or "any *illegality* in the method of obtaining it," or "because of any connection with the *privilege against self-incrimination.*"

In *Bram v. United States* (1897) the Supreme Court did rely explicitly on the self-incrimination clause of the Fifth Amendment in holding a confession inadmissible. But the Court soon abandoned the *Bram* approach, perhaps stung by the criticism of Wigmore and others that it had misread history, and until the mid-1960s *Bram* amounted only to an early excursion from the prevailing due process–voluntariness test.

The right against self-incrimination was not deemed applicable to the states until 1964, and by that time the Supreme Court had decided more than thirty state confession cases. Moreover, even if the Fifth Amendment right against self-incrimination had been deemed applicable to the states much earlier, the law pertaining to "coerced" or "involuntary" confessions still would have developed without it. For until *Miranda* (1966), the prevailing view was that the suspect in the police interrogation room was not being compelled to be a witness against himself within the meaning of the privilege; he was threatened neither with perjury for testifying falsely nor contempt for refusing to testify at all. Because the police have no legal authority to compel statements, there is no legal obligation to answer, ran the argument, to which a privilege can apply.

So long as police interrogators were not required to advise suspects of their rights nor to permit them to consult with lawyers who would do so, there could be little doubt that many a suspect would assume that the police had a legal right to an answer. Still worse, there could be little doubt that many a suspect would assume, or be led to believe, that there were *extralegal* sanctions for refusing to cooperate. Small wonder that commentators decried the legal reasoning that excluded the privilege against self-incrimination from the stationhouse for so many years as "casuistic," "a quibble," and a triumph of logic over life.

Wigmore long condemned the statement of the confession rule in terms of voluntariness for the reason that "the fundamental question for confessions is whether there is any danger that they may be untrue . . . and that there is nothing in the mere circumstance of compulsion to speak in general . . . which creates any risk of untruth." But only two years after the Supreme Court handed down its first FOURTEENTH AMENDMENT due process cases, BROWN V. MISSISSIPPI (1936), Charles McCormick defended the voluntariness terminology on the ground that it might reflect a recognition that the confession rule not only protects against the danger of untrustworthiness but also protects an interest closely akin to that protected by the right against compulsory self-incrimination. Three decades later, the *Miranda* Court would agree. McCormick also suggested that the entire course of decisions in the confessions field could best be understood as "an application to confessions both of a privilege against evidence illegally obtained . . . and of an overlapping rule of incompetency which excludes the confessions when untrustworthy" (1954, p. 157). In the advanced stages of the voluntariness test, the Court would again make plain its agreement with McCormick.

Thus, in *Spano v. New York* (1959) the Court, speaking through Chief Justice EARL WARREN, pointed out that the ban against involuntary confessions turns not only on their unreliability but also on the notion that "the police must obey the law while enforcing the law; that in the end life and liberty can be as much endangered from illegal methods used to convict those thought to be criminals as from the actual criminals themselves." And the following year, in *Blackburn v. Alabama* (1960), the Court, again speaking through Chief Justice Warren, recognized that "a complex of values underlies the stricture against use by the state of confessions which, by way of convenient shorthand, this Court terms involuntary."

The "untrustworthiness" rationale, the view that the rules governing the admissibility of confessions were merely a system of safeguards against false confessions, could explain the exclusion of the confession in *Brown v. Mississippi* (1936), where the deputy sheriff who had presided over the beatings of the defendants conceded that one had been whipped, "but not too much for a Negro." And the untrustworthiness rationale was also adequate to explain the exclusion of confessions in the cases that immediately followed the *Brown* case such as CHAMBERS V. FLORIDA (1940), *Canty v. Alabama* (1940), *White v. Texas* (1940), and *Ward v. Texas* (1942), for they, too, involved actual or threatened physical violence.

As the crude practices of the early cases became outmoded and cases involving more subtle pressures began to appear, however, it became more difficult to assume that the resulting confessions were untrustworthy. In *Ashcraft v. Tennessee* (1944), for example, although the confession was obtained after some thirty-six hours of almost continuous interrogation, there was good reason to think that the defendant had indeed been involved in the murder. The man whom the defendant named as his wife's killer readily admitted his involvement and accused the defendant of hiring him to do the job. Moreover, after the interrogation had ceased and the defendant had been examined by his family physician, he made what the doctor described as an "entirely voluntary" confession, in the course of which he explained why he wanted his wife killed. Nevertheless, calling the extended questioning "inherently coercive," a 6–3 majority, speaking through Justice HUGO L. BLACK, held that Ashcraft's confession should not have been allowed into evidence. Under the circumstances, the *Ashcraft* case seemed to reflect less concern with the reliability of the confession than disapproval of police methods which appeared to the Court to be dangerous and subject to serious abuse.

Although he dissented in *Ashcraft,* Justice FELIX FRANKFURTER soon became the leading exponent of the "police misconduct" or "police methods" rationale for barring the use of confessions. According to this rationale, in order to condemn and deter abusive, offensive, or otherwise objectionable police interrogation methods, it was necessary to exclude confessions produced by such methods regardless of how relevant and credible they might be, a point underscored in ROGERS V. RICHMOND (1961). After more conventional methods had failed to produce any incriminating statements, a police chief pretended to order petitioner's ailing wife brought down to headquarters for questioning. Petitioner promptly confessed to the murder for which he was later convicted. The trial judge found that the police chief's pretense had "no tendency to produce a confession that was not in accord with the truth" and in his charge to the jury he indicated that the admissibility of the confession should turn on its probable reliability. But the Court, speaking through Justice Frankfurter, held that convictions based on involuntary confessions must fall

not because such confessions are unlikely to be true but because the methods used to extract them offend an underlying principle in the enforcement of our criminal law; that ours is an accusatorial and not an inquisitorial system. . . . Indeed, in many of the cases in which the command of the Due Process Clause has compelled us to reverse state convictions involving the use of confessions obtained by impermissible methods, independent corroborating evidence left little doubt of the truth of what the defendant had confessed. Despite such verification, confessions were found to be the product of constitutionally impermissible methods in their inducement. . . . The attention of the trial judge should have been focused, for purpose of the Federal Constitution, on the question whether the [police behavior] was such as to overbear petitioner's will to resist and bring about confessions not freely self-determined—a question to be answered with complete disregard of whether or not petitioner in fact spoke the truth.

The "voluntariness" test seemed to be at once too wide and too narrow. In the sense of wanting to confess, or doing so in a completely spontaneous manner, as one might confess to rid one's soul of guilt, no confession reviewed by the Court under the "voluntariness" test had been voluntary. On the other hand, in the sense that the situation always presented a choice between two alternatives, all confessions examined by the Court had been voluntary.

As the voluntariness test evolved, it became increasingly clear that terms such as "voluntariness" and "coercion" were not being used as tools of analysis, but as mere conclusions. When a court concluded that the police had resorted to unacceptable interrogation techniques, it called the resulting confession "involuntary" and talked of "overbearing the will." When, on the other hand, a court concluded that the methods the police had employed were permissible, it called the resulting confession "voluntary" and talked of "self-determination." Moreover, such terms as "voluntariness," "coercion," and "overbearing the will" focused directly on neither of the two underlying reasons that led the courts to bar the use of confessions—the offensiveness of police interrogation methods or the risk that these methods had produced an untrue confession.

Another problem with the due process "totality of the circumstances"–voluntariness test was that it was amorphous, elusive, and largely unmanageable. Almost everything was relevant—for example, whether the suspect was advised of his rights; whether he was held incommunicado; the suspect's age, intelligence, education, and prior criminal record; the conditions and duration of his detention—but almost nothing was decisive. Except for direct physical coercion no single factor or combination of them guaranteed exclusion of a confession as involuntary. Because there were so many variables in the voluntariness equation that one determination seldom served as a useful precedent for another, the test offered police interrogators and trial courts little guidance. Trial courts were encouraged to indulge their subjective preferences, and appellate courts were discouraged from active review.

In the thirty years between *Brown* (1936) and *Miranda* (1966) the Court had reviewed about one state confession case per year and two-thirds of these had been death penalty cases. Indeed, the Court's workload had been so great that it had even denied a hearing in most death penalty cases. Not surprisingly, Justice Black remarked in the course of the oral argument in *Miranda*: "If you are going to determine [the admissibility of the confession] each time on the circumstances, [if] this Court will take them one by one, [it] is more than we are capable of doing."

The Supreme Court's dissatisfaction with the elusive "voluntariness" test and its quest for a more concrete and manageable standard led to the decisions in MASSIAH V. UNITED STATES (1964) and ESCOBEDO V. ILLINOIS (1964) and culminated in the 1966 *Miranda* decision.

Massiah grew out of the following facts: After he had been indicted for various federal narcotics violations and retained a lawyer, and while he was out on bail, Massiah was invited by his codefendant, Colson, to discuss the pending case in Colson's car. Massiah assumed that he was talking to a partner in crime, but Colson had become a secret government agent. A radio transmitter had been concealed in Colson's car to enable a nearby federal agent to overhear the Massiah-Colson conversation. As expected, Massiah made incriminating statements.

Despite the fact that Massiah was neither in "custody" nor subjected to "police interrogation," as that term is normally used, the Supreme Court held that his damaging admissions should have been excluded from evidence. The decisive feature of the case was that after adversary criminal proceedings had been initiated against him—and Massiah's RIGHT TO COUNSEL had "attached"—government agents had deliberately elicited statements from him in the absence of counsel.

Massiah was soon overshadowed by *Escobedo*, decided a short five weeks later. When Danny Escobedo had been arrested for murder he had repeatedly but unsuccessfully asked to speak to his lawyer. Instead, the police induced Escobedo to implicate himself in the murder. Although Escobedo had incriminated himself before he had been indicted or adversary criminal proceedings had otherwise commenced against him, a 5–4 majority held that under the circumstances "it would exalt form over substance to make the right to counsel . . . depend on whether at the time of the interrogation, the authorities had secured a formal indictment." At the time the police had questioned him, Escobedo "had become the accused and the purpose of the investigation was to 'get him' to confess his guilt despite his constitutional right not to do so."

Until *Miranda* moved the case off center-stage two years later, the meaning and scope of *Escobedo* was a matter of widespread disagreement. In large part this was due to the accordion-like quality of Justice ARTHUR J. GOLDBERG's majority opinion. At some places the opinion suggested that a suspect's right to counsel was triggered once the investigation ceased to be a general inquiry into an unsolved crime and began to "focus" on him, regardless of whether he was in "custody" or asked for a lawyer. Elsewhere, however, the opinion seemed to limit the holding to its special facts (Escobedo had specifically requested and been denied an opportunity to seek his lawyer's advice, the police had failed to warn him of his right to remain silent, and he was in police custody).

The *Escobedo* dissenters read the majority opinion broadly: "The right to counsel now not only entitles the accused the counsel's advice and aid in preparing for trial but stands as an impenetrable barrier to any interrogation once the accused has become suspect. From that very moment apparently his right to counsel attaches." The dissenters expressed a preference for a self-incrimination approach, rather than a right to counsel approach. The right against self-incrimination, after all, proscribed only compelled statements. "It is incongruous to assume," they argued, "that the provision for counsel in the Sixth Amendment was meant to amend or supersede the self-incrimination provision of the Fifth Amendment, which is now applicable to the States." Two years later, in *Miranda*, the Court would focus on the Fifth Amendment, but it would define "compulsion" within the meaning of the privilege in a way that displeased the four *Escobedo* dissenters (all of whom also dissented in *Miranda*).

Dissenting in *Ashcraft* in 1944, Justice ROBERT H. JACKSON agreed that custody and questioning of a suspect for thirty-six hours is "inherently coercive," but quickly added: "And so is custody and examination for one hour. Arrest itself is inherently coercive and so is detention. . . . But does the Constitution prohibit use of all confessions made after arrest because questioning, while one is deprived of freedom, is 'inherently coercive'?" Both Jackson and Justice Black, who wrote the majority opinion in *Ashcraft*, knew that in 1944 the Court was not ready for an affirmative answer to Jackson's question. But by 1966 the Court had grown ready.

Ernesto Miranda had been arrested for rape and kidnapping, taken to a police station, and placed in an "interrogation room," where he was questioned about the crimes. Two hours later the police emerged from the room with a signed confession. In the 1940s or 1950s Miranda's confession unquestionably would have been admissible under the voluntariness test; his questioning had been mild compared to the objectionable police methods that had rendered a resulting confession involuntary in past cases.

The Supreme Court, however, had become increasingly dissatisfied with the voluntariness test. Miranda's interrogators admitted that neither before nor during the questioning had they advised him of his right to remain silent or his right to consult with an attorney before answering questions or his right to have an attorney present during the interrogation. These failures were to prove fatal for the prosecution.

In *Miranda* a 5–4 majority, speaking through Chief Justice Warren, concluded at last that "all the principles embodied in the privilege [against self-incrimination] apply to informal compulsion exerted by law-enforcement officers during in-custody questioning." Observed the Court:

An individual swept from familiar surroundings into police custody, surrounded by antagonistic forces, and subjected to the persuasions [described in various interrogation manuals, from which the Court quoted at length] cannot be otherwise than under compulsion to speak. As a practical matter, the compulsion to speak in the isolated setting of the police station may well be greater than in courts or other official investigations, where there are often impartial observers to guard against intimidation or trickery. . . . Unless adequate protective devices are employed to dispel the compulsion inherent in custodial surroundings, no statement obtained from the defendant can truly be the product of his free choice.

The adequate protective devices necessary to neutralize the compulsion inherent in the interrogation environment are the now familiar "*Miranda* warnings." Although *Miranda* is grounded primarily in the right against self-incrimination, it also has a right to counsel component designed to protect and to reinforce the right to remain silent. Thus, prior to any questioning a person taken into custody or otherwise deprived of his freedom of action in any significant way must not only be warned that he has a right to remain silent and that "anything said can and will be used against [him]," but must also be told of his right to counsel, either retained or appointed. "[T]he need for counsel to protect the Fifth Amendment privilege," stated the Court, "comprehends not merely a right to consult with counsel prior to any questioning but also to have counsel present during any questioning if the defendant so desires."

A suspect, of course, may waive his rights, provided he does so voluntarily, knowingly, and intelligently. But no valid WAIVER OF CONSTITUTIONAL RIGHTS can be recognized unless specifically made after the warnings have been given. Moreover, "[t]he mere fact that [a person] may have answered some questions or volunteered some statements . . . does not deprive him of the right to refrain from answering any further inquiries until he had consulted with an attorney and thereafter consents to be questioned."

Although a great hue and cry greeted the case, *Miranda* may fairly be viewed as a compromise between the old voluntariness test (a standard so elusive and unmanageable that its safeguards were largely illusory) and extreme proposals (based on an expansive reading of *Escobedo*) that threatened to "kill" confessions.

Miranda allows the police to conduct general on-the-scene questioning even though the person arrested is both uninformed and unaware of his rights. It allows the police to question a person in his home or office, provided they do not restrict the person's freedom to terminate the meeting. (Indeed, the opinion seems to recommend that the police question a suspect in his home or place of business.) Moreover, "custody" alone does not call for the *Miranda* warnings. The Court might have held that the inherent pressures and anxieties produced by arrest and detention are substantial enough to require neutralizing warnings. But it did not. Thus, so long as the police do not question one who has been brought to the station house, *Miranda* leaves them free to hear and act upon volunteered statements, even though the volunteer neither knows nor is advised of his rights. (This point was recognized by dissenting Justice BYRON R. WHITE in *Miranda*.)

Surprisingly, *Miranda* does not strip police interrogation of its characteristic secrecy. To the extent that any lawyer worth his salt will tell a suspect to remain silent it is no less clear that any officer worth his salt will be sorely tempted to get the suspect to do just the opposite. But no stenographic transcript (let alone an electronic recording) of the waiver transaction, or the questioning that follows a waiver, need be made; no disinterested observer (let alone a judicial officer) need be present. There is language in *Miranda* suggesting that the police must make an objective record of the waiver transaction but this language has been largely overlooked or disregarded by the lower courts. And nowhere in the *Miranda* opinion does the court explicitly require the police to make either tape or verbatim stenographic recordings of the crucial events.

On the eve of *Miranda*, there were doubts that law enforcement could survive if the Court were to project defense counsel into the police station. But the *Miranda* Court did so only in a quite limited way. It never took the final step (and, as a practical matter, the most significant one) of requiring that the suspect first consult with a lawyer, or actually have a lawyer present, in order for his waiver of constitutional rights to be considered valid.

Whether suspects are continuing to confess because they do not fully grasp the meaning of the *Miranda* warnings or because the police are mumbling, hedging, or undermining the warnings, or whether the promptings of conscience and the desire "to get it over with" are indeed overriding the impact of the warnings, or whether admissions of guilt are quid pro quos for reduced charges or lighter sentences, it is plain that in-custody suspects are continuing to confess with great frequency. This result would hardly have ensued if *Miranda* had fully projected counsel into the interrogation process, requiring the advice or presence of counsel before a suspect could waive his rights.

Because *Miranda* was the centerpiece of the Warren Court's revolution in CRIMINAL PROCEDURE, and

one of the leading issues of the 1968 presidential campaign, almost everyone expected the BURGER COURT to treat *Miranda* unkindly. And it did, but only for a decade.

The first blow was struck in HARRIS V. NEW YORK (1971), which held that statements preceded by defective *Miranda* warnings, and thus inadmissible to establish the prosecution's initial case, could nevertheless be used to impeach the defendant's credibility if he took the stand. The Court noted, but seemed untroubled, that some comments in the landmark opinion seemed to bar the use of statements obtained in violation of *Miranda* for any purpose.

A second impeachment case, *Oregon v. Hass* (1975), seemed to inflict a deeper wound. In *Hass*, the police advised the suspect of his rights and he asserted them. Nevertheless, the police refused to honor the suspect's request for a lawyer and continued to question him. That such a flagrant violation of *Miranda* should produce evidence that may be used for impeachment purposes is especially troublesome; under these circumstances, unlike those in *Harris*, it is fair to assume that no hope of obtaining evidence usable for the government's case-in-chief operates to induce the police to comply with *Miranda*. *Hass*, then, was a more harmful blow to *Miranda* that was *Harris*.

Even more disturbing than the impeachment cases is their recent extension to permit the use of a defendant's prior silence to impeach his credibility if he chooses to testify at his trial. In JENKINS V. ANDERSON (1980) the Court held that a murder defendant's testimony that he had acted in self-defense could be impeached by showing that he did not go to the authorities and report his involvement in the stabbing. In *Fletcher v. Weir* (1982) the Court held that even a defendant's post-arrest silence—so long as he was not given and need not have been given the *Miranda* warnings—could be used to impeach him if he decided to testify at trial.

Still other blows were struck by *Michigan v. Mosley* (1975) and *Oregon v. Mathiason* (1977). Although language in *Miranda* can be read as establishing a per se rule against any further questioning of one who had asserted his right to silence, *Mosley* held that under certain circumstances, which the case left unclear, if the police cease questioning on the spot, they may try again and succeed at a later interrogation session. *Mathiason*, a formalistic, crabbed reading of *Miranda*, demonstrates that even police station interrogation is not necessarily "custodial." (The suspect had agreed to meet a police officer in the state patrol office and had come to the office alone.)

For supporters of *Miranda,* the most ominous note of all was struck by Justice WILLIAM H. REHNQUIST, speaking for the Court in *Michigan v. Tucker* (1974). The *Tucker* Court viewed the *Miranda* warnings as "not themselves rights protected by the Constitution" but only "prophylactic standards" designed to "safeguard" or to "provide practical reinforcement" for the right against self-incrimination. And it seemed to equate "compulsion" within the meaning of that right with "coercion" or "involuntariness" under the pre-*Miranda* due process test. It seemed to miss the point that much greater pressures were necessary to render a confession "involuntary" under the old test than are needed to make a statement "compelled" under the new. That was one of the principal reasons the old test was abandoned in favor of *Miranda.*

A lumping together of self-incrimination "compulsion" and pre-*Miranda* "involuntariness," which appears to be what the Court did in *Tucker,* seemed to approach a rejection of the central premises of *Miranda.* Moreover, the Supreme Court has no supervisory power over state criminal justice. By stripping *Miranda* of its most apparent constitutional basis without explaining what other bases for it there might be, the Court in the *Tucker* opinion seemed to be preparing the way for the eventual overruling of *Miranda.*

A decade later, in NEW YORK V. QUARLES (1984) and in OREGON V. ELSTAD (1985), a majority of the Court, relying heavily on language in the *Tucker* opinion, again drew a distinction between statements that are actually "coerced" or "compelled" and those that are obtained merely in violation of *Miranda*'s "procedural safeguards" or "prophylactic rules." *Quarles* admitted a statement a handcuffed rape suspect had made when questioned by police about the whereabouts of a gun he had earlier been reported to be carrying. The Court, speaking through Justice Rehnquist, "conclude[d] that the need for answers to questions in a situation posing a threat to the public safety outweighs the need for the prophylactic rule protecting [the] privilege against self-incrimination." *Elstad* held that the failure to give *Miranda* warnings to a suspect who made an incriminating statement when subjected to custodial interrogation in his own home did not bar the use of a subsequent station house confession by the suspect when the second confession was immediately preceded by *Miranda* warnings. The court, speaking through Justice SANDRA DAY O'CONNOR, rejected the argument that a *Miranda* violation "necessarily breeds the same consequences as police infringement of a constitutional right, so that evidence uncovered following an unwarned statement must be suppressed as 'fruit of the poisonous tree.'" Although *Quarles* and *Elstad* can be read very narrowly, and *Tucker,* too, can be limited to its special facts, the Court's language in these cases—language that "deconstitutionalizes" *Miranda*—may prove to be far more significant than the cases' specific holdings.

In light of the *Tucker* majority's undermining of the basis for *Miranda* and against the background of such cases as *Harris, Hass,* and *Mathiason,* a 1980 confession case, *Rhode Island v. Innis,* posed grave dangers for *Miranda.* The defendant had been convicted of heinous crimes: kidnapping, robbery, and murder. He had made incriminating statements while being driven to a nearby police station, only a few minutes after being placed in the police vehicle. Any interrogation that might have occurred in the vehicle was brief and mild—much more so than the direct, persistent police station interrogation in *Miranda* and its companion cases. Two police officers conversing with one another in the front of the car, but in Innis's presence, had expressed concern that because the murder occurred in the vicinity of a school for handicapped children, one of the children might find the missing shotgun and injure himself. At this point, Innis had interrupted the officers and offered to lead them where the shotgun was hidden.

The Court might have taken an approach suggested by earlier dissents and limited *Miranda* to custodial station house interrogation or its equivalent (for example, a five-hour trip in a police vehicle). It did not do so. The Court might have taken a mechanical approach to interrogation and limited it, as some lower courts had, to situations where the police directly address a suspect. Again, it did not do so. It might have limited interrogation to situations where the record establishes (as it did not in *Innis*) that the police intended to elicit an incriminating response, an obviously difficult test to administer. It did not do this either.

Instead, the Court, speaking through Justice POTTER STEWART (one of the *Miranda* dissenters), held that "*Miranda* safeguards come into play whenever a person in custody is subjected to either express questioning or its functional equivalent." The term "interrogation" includes "any words or actions on the part of the police (other than those normally attendant to arrest and custody) that the police should know are reasonably likely to elicit as incriminating response from the suspect." Although the *Innis* case involved police "speech," the Court's definition embraces police tactics that do not. Thus, the Court seems to have repudiated the position taken by a number of lower courts that confronting a suspect with physical evidence or with an accomplice who has already confessed is not interrogation because it does entail verbal conduct on the part of the police.

One may quarrel, as the three dissenters did, with the Court's application of its definition of "interrogation" to the *Innis* facts (the Court concluded that the defendant had not been interrogated). But *Innis* ia a harder case than most because there was "a basis for concluding that the officer's remarks were for some purpose *other* than that of obtaining evidence from the suspect. An objective listener could plausibly conclude that the policeman's remarks . . . were made solely to express their genuine concern about the danger posed by the hidden shotgun" and thus not view their conversation "as a demand for information" (White 1980, pp. 1234–1235).

In any event, considering the various ways in which the *Innis* Court might have given *Miranda* a grudging interpretation, its generous definition of "interrogation" seems much more significant than its questionable application of the definition to the particular facts of the case. In *Innis* the process of qualifying, limiting, and shrinking *Miranda* came to a halt. Indeed, it seems fair to say that in *Miranda*'s hour of peril the *Innis* Court rose to its defense.

If *Innis* encouraged *Miranda*'s defenders, EDWARDS V. ARIZONA (1981) gladdened them even more. For *Edwards* was the first clear-cut victory for *Miranda* in the Burger Court. Sharply distinguishing the *Mosley* case, which had dealt with a suspect's assertion of his right to remain silent, the *Edwards* Court, speaking through Justice White (another of the *Miranda* dissenters), held that when a suspect invokes his right to counsel the police cannot try again. Under these circumstances, a valid waiver of the right to counsel cannot be established by showing "only that [the suspect] responded further to police-initiated custodial interrogation," even though he was again advised of his rights at a second interrogation session. He cannot be questioned anew "until counsel has been made available to him, unless [he] himself initiates further communication, exchanges or conversation with the police." Thus, *Edwards* reinvigorates *Miranda* in an important respect. (But a more recent case, *Oregon v. Bradshaw* (1983), interprets "initiation of further communication" so broadly that it seems to sap *Edwards* of much of its vitality.)

Although *Miranda* maintained the momentum generated by *Escobedo*, it represented a significantly different approach to the confession problem. Although the *Miranda* Court understandably tried to preserve some continuity with the loose, groping *Escobedo* opinion, it has become increasingly clear that, by shifting from a right to counsel base to a self-incrimination base, *Miranda* actually marked a fresh start in describing the circumstances under which Fifth and Sixth Amendment protections attach. *Escobedo* assigned primary significance to the amount of guilt available to the police at the time of questioning; the opinion therefore contains much talk about "focal point" and the "accusatory stage." But *Miranda* attaches primary significance to the conditions surrounding or inherent in the interrogation setting; thus the opinion contains much discussion of the "interrogation environment" or the "police-dominated" atmosphere that "carries its own badge of intimidation."

If the requisite inherent pressures exist, *Miranda* applies whether or not the individual being questioned is a "prime suspect" or has become "the accused." On the other hand, if these pressures are not operating, an individual is not entitled to the *Miranda* warnings—no matter how sharply the police have focused on him or how much they consider him the "prime suspect" or "the accused." In short, *Miranda* did not enlarge *Escobedo* so much as displace it.

The same, however, cannot be said for *Massiah*. Although *Miranda* has dominated the confessions scene ever since it was handed down, *Massiah* has emerged as the other major Warren Court confession doctrine. As strengthened by two Burger Court decisions, *Brewer v. William* (1977) (often called "the Christian burial speech" case) and *United States v. Henry* (1980), the *Massiah* doctrine holds that once "adversary" or "judicial" proceedings have commenced against an individual (by way of INDICTMENT, INFORMATION, or initial appearance before a magistrate), deliberate government efforts to elicit incriminating statements from him, whether done openly by uniformed police officers (as in *Williams*) or surreptitiously by secret government agents (as in *Massiah* and *Henry*) violate the individual's right to counsel.

Williams revivified *Massiah*. Indeed, one might even say that *Williams* disinterred it. For until the decision in *Williams* there was good reason to think that *Massiah* had only been a steppingstone to *Escobedo* and that both cases had been largely displaced by *Miranda*.

But *Massiah* is alive and well. And the policies underlying the *Massiah* doctrine are quite distinct from those underlying *Miranda*. The *Massiah* doctrine represents a pure right to counsel approach. It comes into play regardless of whether a person is in custody or is being subjected to interrogation in the *Miranda* sense. There need not be any compelling influences at work, inherent, informal, or otherwise.

The most recent *Massiah* case, *United States v. Henry* (1980), applied *Massiah* to a situation where the Federal Bureau of Investigation (FBI) had instructed its secret agent, ostensibly a fellow prisoner, not to question the defendant about the crime and there was no showing that he had. Nevertheless, the defendant's incriminating statements were held inadmissible. It sufficed that the government had "intentionally create[d] a situation likely to induce [the defendant] to make incriminating statements without the assistance of counsel." The FBI created such a situation when it instructed its secret agent to be alert to any statements made by the defendant, who was housed in the same cellblock. Even if the agent's claim were accepted that he did not intend to take affirmative steps to obtain incriminating statements, the agent "must have known that such propinquity likely would lead to that result." *Henry* not only reaffirmed the *Massiah* doctrine but significantly expanded it. Thus, the *Massiah* doctrine has emerged as a much more potent force than it ever had been during the Warren Court era.

The Burger Court's generous reading of *Miranda* in *Innis* and *Edwards* and its even more generous reading of *Massiah* in the *Henry* case have reaffirmed the Court's commitment to control police efforts to obtain confessions by constitutional rules that transcend "untrustworthiness' and "voluntariness."

Regardless of its shortcomings and the hopes it never fulfilled (or the fears about the case that proved unfounded), *Miranda* was an understandable and long-overdue effort—and the Court's most ambitious effort ever—to solve the police interrogation–confession problem. At the very least it formally recognized an interrogated suspect's self-incrimination privilege, and a right to counsel for rich and poor alike designed to protect and effectuate that privilege; generated a much greater general awareness of procedural rights; and emphatically reminded the police that they neither create the rules of interrogation nor act free of JUDICIAL REVIEW.

Miranda was an attempt to do in the confessions area what the Warren Court had done elsewhere— take the nation's ideals down from the walls, where they had been kept framed to be pointed at with pride on ceremonial occasions, and live up to them. The degree to which *Miranda* actually succeeded is debatable, but the symbolic quality of the decision

extends far beyond its actual impact upon police interrogation methods.

YALE KAMISAR

Bibliography

BAKER, LIVA 1983 *Miranda: Crime, Law and Politics.* New York: Atheneum.
BERGER, MARK 1980 *Taking the Fifth: The Supreme Court and the Privilege against Self-Incrimination.* Lexington, Mass.: Lexington Books.
GRAHAM, FRED 1970 *The Self-Inflicted Wound.* New York: Macmillan.
KAMISAR, YALE 1980 *Police Interrogation and Confessions: Essays in Law and Policy.* Ann Arbor: University of Michigan Press.
LEVY, LEONARD W. 1968 *Origins of the Fifth Amendment.* New York: Oxford University Press.
MCCORMICK, CHARLES T. 1954 *Evidence.* St. Paul, Minn. West Publishing Co.
STEPHENS, OTIS 1973 *The Supreme Court and Confessions of Guilt.* Knoxville: University of Tennessee Press.
WHITE, WELSH S. 1981 Interrogation without Questions. *Michigan Law Review* 78:1209–1251.
WIGMORE, JOHN HENRY 1940 *Evidence,* 3rd ed. Boston: Little, Brown.

POLICE POWER

The police power is the general power of a government to legislate for the comfort, safety, health, morals, or welfare of the citizenry or the prosperity and good order of the community.

DENNIS J. MAHONEY

(SEE ALSO: *Inalienable Police Power; National Police Power; Reserved Police Power; State Police Power.*)

POLITICAL PARTIES AND THE CONSTITUTION

The United States Constitution is virtually silent on politics. It touches upon elections, but even here the subject is treated in a most gingerly fashion by delegating the power to set the "Times, Places and Manner of holding Elections for Senators and Representatives" to the legislature of each state. Even the qualification for voting in national elections was left to the states, by the provision that whoever was qualified to vote for members of the "most numerous branch of the State Legislature" could also vote for members of the House of Representatives.

The Founders saw peril in politics. The Constitution was an effort to provide a solution to politics. To JAMES MADISON in THE FEDERALIST #10, one of the greatest virtues of the Constitution was that it provided an antidote to the "mischiefs of faction." Because attempting to prevent the emergence of faction would be a cure worse than the disease, the only alternative was to provide a system of FEDERALISM on a continental scale so that no faction or conspiracy among factions could reach majority size, thereby becoming a party. Representative government centered in a legislature became the superior form of government because the "temporary or partial considerations" of factions would be regulated by "passing them through the medium of a chosen body of citizens, whose wisdom . . . will be more consonant to the public good than if pronounced by the people themselves. . . ." GEORGE WASHINGTON in his Farewell Address (the drafting of which was shared by Madison and ALEXANDER HAMILTON) warned of "the danger of parties in the State [founded on] geographical discriminations [and] against the baneful effects of the spirit of party generally."

The Constitution was designed also to solve the political problems inherent in the presidency. In effect, Article II provided for a two-tiered presidential selection: *nomination* by the electors and *election* by the House of Representatives. Under the original Article II the process began with selection of electors in a manner provided by each state legislature. In the first election under the Constitution, in 1788–1789, the electors were chosen by legislature in seven states and by voters in six. Next, electors were to meet in their state capitals, never nationally. There is no ELECTORAL COLLEGE; that term is nowhere to be found in the Constitution or in *The Federalist*. At the prescribed meeting at the state capital each elector had the right and obligation to cast ballots for *two persons*—not two votes, but separate votes for two different people, one not from the same state as the elector. If a candidate received an absolute majority of all electoral votes, he was declared the President; the candidate with the second largest vote became vice-president. If no candidate received an absolute majority, the House of Representatives would choose from the top five names, with each state having one vote, regardless of the population of the state. If two candidates received an absolute majority in a tie vote (as happened between THOMAS JEFFERSON and AARON BURR in 1800), the House would choose between the top two.

This system was virtually designed to produce a *parliamentary* government—a strong executive elected by the lower house of the legislature. During the first two decades of the Republic, the primary functions of the national government were to implement the scheme of government contemplated by the Constitution, and that required one-time-only policies, such as the establishment of the major departments, the establishment of the judiciary, and the exercise of SOVEREIGNTY as a nation-state among nation-states, manifest in various kinds of treaties. Policies had to be adopted to assume all the debts previously incurred by the CONTINENTAL CONGRESS and the national government under the ARTICLES OF CONFEDERATION; laws were also adopted to assume all the debts incurred during the war by the thirteen states. All these policies and many others emanated from the executive branch. Congress looked to President Washington for leadership and accepted Secretary of the Treasury Alexander Hamilton as Washington's representative. Although consensus around Washington was replaced with polarization, even before JOHN ADAMS became President, the Federalists carried the necessary majorities through legislative meetings (caucuses) led mainly by Hamilton. But at the same time, all the power to enact the policies—all the power "expressly delegated" to the national government by Article I, section 8—was lodged in Congress. Inevitably, politics came out as a modified parliamentarism, with a strong executive elected by the lower house.

These arrangements seem to have been intentional on the part of the Framers of the Constitution. Without a national meeting, and with each elector having to cast ballots for two separate persons, it was to be expected that several candidates for President would be identified. The concept of the "favorite son" actually goes back to George Washington himself, and the expectation that there would be a large number of favorite sons is strongly implied by the provision that in the event of no absolute majority the top five names would be submitted to the House. Surely this means that more than five meaningful candidates would normally be produced and that final election in the House would be the norm also. With this modified parliamentary system, the Constitution and politics became synonymous. The politics of the two to three decades of the founding period followed the lines prescribed by the Constitution—or, to put it another way, flowed fairly strictly within channels established by the Constitution.

This original system was transformed within a generation following the founding. At some point during the Jefferson administration, the regime of the founding was replaced by a regime of ordinary government. One-time-only policies were replaced by routine and repeatable policies, such as INTERNAL IMPROVE-MENTS, land grants, personal claims, tariffs, PATENTS, surveys, and other services. This type of national government is precisely what was intended by Article I, section 8. The TENTH AMENDMENT (1791) merely made more explicit what was already unmistakably clear in Article I, that the important powers of governing were to be reserved to the states. What was not intended, however, was that the political solution prevailing during the first generation would come unstuck. Political parties had already emerged despite Washington's warnings, and the discipline of their members virtually destroyed the so-called Electoral College by requiring that each elector be pledged to a presidential candidate "nominated" prior to their selection as electors. Political parties captured the *nominating* phase of presidential selection. For twenty years thereafter the method of nomination was by legislative caucus—derisively called King Caucus. As the two major parties spread their influence to districts where they had voters but no members of Congress, the party leaders had to work out a method of nomination more representative than King Caucus. That solution, the presidential nominating convention, was adopted in 1832 and remained the institution of party government until 1952.

The national party system was by this time no longer working within prescribed constitutional channels but had created some new channels for itself. *More significantly, the party system in the 1820s and 1830s created a realm of politics independent of the Constitution.*

In another sense, however, the Constitution was having the last word. First, Congress had become the central power of the national government. There was no longer any development toward parliamentary government but clearly toward congressional government, as WOODROW WILSON put it in his important text later in the nineteenth century. Second, the nominating convention, in providing the President with a popular base independent of Congress, produced the SEPARATION OF POWERS that many feel the Constitution had intended—a system of coequal branches each with its own separate constituency.

Third, and most important, the functions of the national government had come more into proportion with the intent of Article I, section 8. That is to say, a politics independent of the Constitution came only at the expense of the kinds of functions the national government had been required to perform during the founding decades. In fact, the relationship ought to be put the other way around. The change of functions from the one-time-only policies of the founding to the ordinary policies of the rest of the nineteenth century had been responsible for the political changes, thus confirming a fundamental and well-nigh universal pattern: *every regime tends to create a politics consonant with itself.* Thus, when the regime (the Constitution and its government) of the founding shifted to a regime of policies arising literally under the provisions of Article I, section 8, politics changed accordingly. For more than a century after 1832 the national government was congressional government; the national politics during that epoch was a function of party government; and together, government and politics were consistent with, and reinforced, a strictly *federal* Constitution in which the national government had a highly limited and specialized role in the life of the country.

A third regime emerged out of the New Deal, not from the increased size of the national government but from the addition to that government of significant new functions. The significant departure from tradition arose out of the enactment of a large number of policies that can be understood only as regulatory and redistributive policies. In effect, the national government acquired its own POLICE POWERS and added its own regulatory and redistributive policies to those of the states. These additions—which were validated by the Supreme Court—brought on a third regime.

Congress did more than enact the new policies that gave the national government its new functions and its directly coercive relationship to citizens. Congress also literally created a new form of government by delegating powers to the executive branch. Each of the new regulatory policies adopted by Congress identified broadly the contours of a problem and then delegated to the executive virtually all the discretion necessary to formulate the actual rules to be imposed on citizens. Technically, this is called the DELEGATION OF POWER, and the rationalization was that Congress had indeed passed the law and left to administrative agencies the power only to "fill in the details." But in fact the executive branch filled in more than details. Just as Woodrow Wilson called the national government of the nineteenth century congressional government, we can with no greater distortion entitle the regime following the New Deal as presidential government.

National politics began to change accordingly. Signs of the weakening of party democracy were already fairly clear during the New Deal. President FRANKLIN

D. ROOSEVELT had tried to rebuild the Democratic party into a programmatic kind of presidential party. The most dramatic moment in that effort was the "purge of 1938," an unprecedented effort by a President to defeat or demote the opposition within his own party in order to make it into a modern instrument of program development and enactment. History records that Roosevelt failed, but the meaning of that failure was not lost on the Democrats or Republicans: the President can no longer depend on locally organized opportunistic parties and must develop his own, independent base of popular support. If this support could no longer be found through political parties, the President would have to do it directly, through the media of mass communication. The President's constituency became the public *en masse.*

The presidential conventions of 1952 were the last of the traditional conventions, where parties still controlled the nominations through the control that state party leaders had over the delegates. And if ANDREW JACKSON can be considered the revolutionary who gave birth to the national conventions, DWIGHT D. EISENHOWER was a revolutionary who turned them into vestigial organs. As the 1952 Republican Convention approached, the Eisenhower forces had to confront the fact that ROBERT A. TAFT was ahead. Their only available strategy was to question the credentials of several state delegations whose members, pledged to Taft, had been selected by the traditional method of virtual appointment by state leaders and were pledged to vote slavishly for the candidate designated by the state leadership. Failing to convince the credentials committee, the Eisenhower leaders took their objections to the convention floor in the form of a "fair play" motion. The debate took place over national television—despite Taft's objections—and the Eisenhower motion swayed enough neutral delegations to gain the majority vote and the momentum sufficient to win the nomination. More important than the immediate victory was the long-range result, which was to weaken the foundations of the traditional party system itself. Progressively from that time, delegates came to be treated as factors in their own right, as individuals to be courted rather than as pawns within a state delegation controlled by state party leaders.

Once the delegates became meaningful individuals, the process of selection had to be democratized. Just as the nominating convention once was a means of democratizing the legislative caucus, the primaries became the means of democratizing conventions. But the primaries are as much a reflection as a cause of the decline of party government, including the decline of party control of the presidential selection process. Party government was already seriously undermined before the spread of selection of pledged delegates by primary elections. The transformed convention was, then, a reflection of the broader process of the decline of state and national political parties. The presidential nomination was becoming an open process by which presidential candidates amassed individual delegates, who had little in common with each other or with the candidate to whom they were pledged. The popular base of the presidency became a mass base. It was no longer the outcome of a process by which state party leaders and their delegations formed coalitions around the candidate most likely to win the nomination and election for President.

Serious students of American political parties have been arguing for more than a decade over the political reforms of the 1960s and 1970s associated with the loosening of the national parties and the virtual displacement of the national conventions. Some argue that the decline of political parties and of the convention as the institution of party government was unintentionally caused by the reforms. Others argue that parties had already declined and that the decline of conventions as the real decision-making body was already happening; therefore, the reforms were more a reflection of the decline than a cause of it. Most significant, however, is the emergence of the new regime: a new form of politics consonant with the regime of regulation and redistribution, with its presidential government.

Many of the current disagreements continue because we are still in the midst of the transformation and the ultimate form has not yet fully emerged. Two distinct scenarios or models can be drawn from the prevailing political analyses. One is "dealignment," tending toward mass democracy—that is, a direct relationship between the President and the masses of people unmediated by any representative institution at all, whether party or legislature. The second scenario is an alignment or realignment model anticipating the restoration of the two major parties. Such a development could require the abolition of some reforms instituted in the 1960s and 1970s that radically unhinged certain features of the traditional party system, and adoption of new measures aimed at restoring the power of party bosses in the presidential nominating process.

The resolution is likely to be a fusion of the two models. The entire functioning of the national government has come to rest upon the President; the expectations of all Americans focus there, and the relationship between the President and the people will continue to be direct. This is the essence of mass politics. At the same time, however, there is strong evidence of a resurgence in the headquarters of the national political parties. Yet there is no place for these parties in the direct line of communication between the President and his mass base. Thus, if these parties are to survive and prosper at the national level they will have to find functions other than the traditional ones of intervening between the masses and the President by controlling the nominating process and political campaigns. The creation of such new functions would require the national leadership to organize from the bottom up, district by district, but in fact the national headquarters are organizing from the top down. They are developing their base in the electorate by collecting data for the computerized analysis of categories of voters. These techniques permit efficient mass mailings to solicit voters and, more important, sponsors who will make millions of donations in units of less than $50 apiece. These are not electoral parties in the traditional sense. Nor are they European-style "mass parties" or social democratic parties. They are what, for lack of an established word, can be called "taxation parties," whose main function is to defray the tremendous cost of the capital necessary to maintain the computers, collect the data, analyze the data, write the letters and stuff the envelopes, and design and communicate the spot announcements and other commercial messages on extremely expensive network television.

American national politics has been in a state of transition for a long time. Professional students of elections, polling, and political parties have all been expecting some kind of "realignment" at least since 1964. Major reforms of the parties and of elections have followed each presidential election since that time; their main result has been to prevent forever the outcome of the previous convention and election. Although the Democrats have been the major reformers, mainly because they have been the major losers in national elections, the Republicans have followed them in these reforms almost immediately. The national political process has not yet adjusted effectively to the regime of regulation and redistribution. In other words, although politics ultimately takes some form consonant with the regime, there is no guaranteeing that the adjustments will be successful and stable.

This fact points to the most important contrast between the present regime and the two previous ones:

National politics is flowing through channels increasingly independent of the Constitution; that is, efforts to restore party government have been oblivious to the historic relationship between the Constitution and politics.

This is not to suggest that politics is operating unconstitutionally or outside the spirit of Supreme Court decisions. It means only that efforts to restore the parties, and to reform nominations and elections accordingly, have concentrated on the flow itself rather than on the constitutional structure that ultimately determines the flow. Having recognized the many problems with American politics since the New Deal, reformers have attempted to change the politics. They have persisted in this approach even while recognizing two grievous perils in it. First, because some interests inevitably gain or lose from any political reform, there is always a suspicion that these gains were known and sought in advance. The legitimacy of the system can be badly hurt by the more generalized suspicion that the established electoral process is being manipulated. Second, some reform efforts have come close to violating the FIRST AMENDMENT, and in fact the Supreme Court declared such a violation in BUCKLEY V. VALEO (1976), striking down a law attempting to set limits on the amounts individuals could spend in campaigns. That case is definitely not the end of litigation involving First Amendment rights involved in political reforms. (See POLITICAL PARTIES AND THE SUPREME COURT.)

Politics can be understood as the never-ending process of adjusting to a given structure of government, or regime, by seeking sufficient power and consensus to change the structure or influence its direction. If a change in the conduct of politics is sought, the appropriate route is the exercise of the historic right to change the Constitution and the structure of government. The forms of politics would change accordingly. We have constitutional rights to change our government. As Madison argued in *The Federalist* #10, the attempt to regulate politics is a cure worse than the disease. If there are problems with American national politics—and there appears to be wide agreement on this proposition throughout the political spectrum—then the time may have come to reexamine the structure of government, including the Constitution itself. An extensive revision of the Constitution is neither necessary nor appropriate. The last major constitutional change was triggered by the New Deal, without a single constitutional amendment. Once we recognize that politics is most stable and most respected when it is consonant with constitutional forms, reformers might be convinced to focus at least some of their energies away from political reform and toward constitutional reform.

THEODORE J. LOWI

Bibliography

AGAR, HERBERT 1966 *The Price of Union.* Boston: Houghton Mifflin.

BINCKLEY, WILFRED 1947 *President and Congress.* New York: Knopf.

BURNHAM, WALTER DEAN 1970 *Critical Elections and the Mainsprings of American Politics.* New York: Norton.

CHARLES, JOSEPH 1961 *The Origins of the American Party System.* New York: Harper & Row.

GINSBERG, BENJAMIN 1982 *The Consequences of Consent.* Reading, Mass.: Addison-Wesley.

LOWI, THEODORE J. (1967)1975 Party, Policy and Constitution in America. In William N. Chambers and Walter Dean Burnham, eds., *The American Party System—Stages of Political Development.* New York: Oxford University Press.

POLSBY, NELSON 1983 *Consequences of Party Reform.* New York: Oxford University Press.

SHEFTER, MARTIN 1978 Party Bureaucracy and Political Change. In Louis Maisel and Joseph Cooper, eds., *Political Parties: Development and Decay.* Beverly Hills, Calif.: Sage Publications.

POLITICAL PARTIES IN CONSTITUTIONAL LAW

"No America without democracy, no democracy without politics, no politics without parties. . . ." So begins Clinton Rossiter's commentary on American political parties. Nonetheless, the Supreme Court has said in *Elrod v. Burns* (1976) that "partisan politics bears the imprimatur only of tradition, not the Constitution." Despite the absence of constitutional reference to political parties, the Constitution has had substantial influence in shaping the two-party system and in defining the contested boundary between governmental authority and political party autonomy.

Frank Sorauf has observed that "[t]he major American political parties are in truth three-headed political giants, tripartite systems of interactions. . . . As a political structure they include a party organization, a party in office, and a party in the electorate. . . ." All three branches of political parties are defined, limited, and authorized, at least in part, by constitutional DOCTRINE. All three are shaped in part by specific constitutional arrangements.

Two-party politics, which has persisted throughout the nation's history, began in the struggle between Federalists and Anti-Federalists over the RATIFICATION OF THE CONSTITUTION. Provisions of the Constitution have reinforced the two-party system, especially Article II, section 1, empowering each state to select presidential electors, and the TWELFTH AMENDMENT, requiring an absolute majority of the ELECTORAL COLLEGE or, failing that, of state delegations in the House of Representatives for election of the President. The majority rule tends to compel the coalition of disparate factions into two parties, because only the establishment of broad coalitions offers any prospect of securing the majority necessary for election of the President.

Although no constitutional rule requires that members of the House of Representatives be elected by plurality vote or from single-member districts, these understandings soon took root after ratification of the Constitution. The popular election of the United States senators mandated by the SEVENTEENTH AMENDMENT has the effect of creating single-member districts for the selection of members of that house. These constitutional practices strengthen the two-party system, requiring broad coalitions to secure a majority, the only guarantee of electoral victory under these rules.

The Constitution's provision for a federal structure of government also shapes the party system. Unlike the majority rule's incentive for factions to consolidate into two parties, the federal structure encourages wide dispersion of influence within the party ranks. Because offices and powers at the state and local levels are more accessible and often more important than those in the national government, party organizations in each state and locale grow independent of one another and are largely free from sanctions imposed by any national party organization. This dispersion of party organization is heightened by the mandate of Article I, section 1, and the Twelfth Amendment for state-by-state selection of the electors who choose the President.

States began to regulate political parties in the late eighteenth century, and these regulations became commonplace during the Progressive era. The STATE POLICE POWER was regarded as a sufficient basis for the imposition of governmental authority upon the parties. The state-prescribed Australian ballot, antifusion legislation, and state-operated primaries were introduced at the same time as laws regulating the structure and activities of political parties. All of these were intended to curb political "bosses" and "machines."

By the beginning of World War II, the constitutions of seventeen states and the statutes in virtually all states referred to political parties—conferring rights on them, regulating their activities, or both. State regulatory schemes went beyond prescribing the methods by which parties would select nominees for office and the qualifications of parties for places on the ballot. Many states also regulated the selection and composition of district, county, and state political party committees, the authority and duties of those committees, and the rules for their operation.

Whether the national government has similar authority to regulate political parties has seldom been tested, for Congress has not chosen to enact legislation recognizing party associations or regulating their structure and activities. Any such federal power could, however, be thought to derive from several constitutional sources.

Article IV, section 1, of the Constitution grants Congress a broad power to regulate the time, place, and manner of electing senators and representatives. In UNITED STATES V. CLASSIC (1941) the Supreme Court construed this provision to allow Congress to regulate individual conduct and also to modify those state regulations of federal elections that the Constitution authorizes. The Court has also cited the NECESSARY AND PROPER CLAUSE as an additional source of congressional authority over federal elections, and in EX PARTE YARBROUGH (1884) it declared that Congress has the power, as an attribute of republican government, to pass laws governing federal elections, especially to protect them against fraud, violence, and other practices that undermine their integrity. And, although no constitutional provision explicitly extends the authority of Congress to regulate presidential elections, the Court affirmed this power in *Burroughs v. United States* (1934), OREGON V. MITCHELL (1970), and BUCKLEY V. VALEO (1976).

Congressional power to regulate elections does not necessarily imply power to regulate political parties. But the Supreme Court has taken a major step in that direction by bringing federal PRIMARY ELECTIONS, which are principally a party process for selecting candidates, within the ambit of Article I. In *United States v. Classic* the Justices held that: "Where state law has made the primary an integral part of the procedure of choice, or where in fact the primary effectively controls the choice, the right of the elector to have his ballot counted at the primary is . . . included in the right [to vote in congressional elections] protected by Article I, sec. 2." This right to vote in congressional elections may be protected by Congress under Article I, section 4. Subsequently, the Court has treated *Classic* as recognizing a general congressional power to regulate primary elections for federal offices.

A wholly distinct doctrinal technique for imposing judicial limits upon party affairs, which may extend congressional legislative authority to party activities, grew out of the White Primary Cases. In NIXON V. HERNDON (1927) the Supreme Court held that because the sponsorship of a primary election by a state was STATE ACTION subject to the FOURTEENTH AMENDMENT, the exclusion of black voters from such a primary was unconstitutional. Even when the state authorized the party executive committee to determine party membership, NIXON V. CONDON (1932) held the ensuing primary to constitute state action. State authorization of a ballot position for candidates selected in party-sponsored primaries, without any state-prescribed primary rules or state operation of the primary, was held in SMITH V. ALLWRIGHT (1944) to be state action in violation of the FIFTEENTH AMENDMENT.

Many commentators and judges regard TERRY V. ADAMS (1953)—the last of the White Primary Cases—as extending constitutional limitation to party activities beyond primary elections. In *Terry* the Supreme Court held that the Fifteenth Amendment prohibited a local group, the Jaybird Democratic Association, from excluding blacks from a preprimary straw vote, paid for and operated exclusively by the association, to endorse candidates to run in the statutorily recognized Democratic party primary. The four-member plurality of the *Terry* Court concluded that the Jaybirds were part of the Democratic party. Only three Justices said that the Jaybird straw vote was limited by the Fifteenth Amendment because it was "an integral part, indeed the only effective part, of the electoral process."

Nonetheless, most judicial decisions now treat party organizations as state-affiliated agencies. State laws often closely prescribe the structure, organization, and duties of local, district, and state party units. Hence, the lower federal court cases have held that the EQUAL PROTECTION CLAUSE governs the selection and apportionment of members of local, district, and state party committees and conventions. Several decisions of the Court of Appeals for the District of Columbia have also applied the Fourteenth Amendment to national party conventions, because those conventions are integral parts of the process of selecting the President. But in at least one case that court suggested that the developing law of "state action," as defined by the Supreme Court, had excluded party conventions from the scope of the Fourteenth Amendment.

In defining the scope of the Fourteenth and Fifteenth Amendments, and thus the scope of congressional power to enforce those amendments, several appellate courts have distinguished between parties' candidate selection activities and their management of "internal affairs." Ronald Rotunda has suggested "a functional standard" in which "all integral steps in an election for public office are public functions and therefore state action subject to some judicial scrutiny." The functional distinction, though plausible and attractive, is difficult to apply in practice. Party activists often seek to influence the selection of party candidates, presumably to assure that party nominees reflect the policies of the party organization. Working through party organizations, they endorse candidates in the primary, expend money on their behalf, and mobilize primary voters for them. These activities could easily be construed as part of the selection of candidates; yet it seems unlikely that they fall within the reach of the prohibitions of the Fourteenth and Fifteenth Amendments—and thus the reach of Congress's power to enforce those amendments.

One further source of governmental authority to regulate political parties is the power to attach restrictions to special statuses or benefits accorded to candidates and parties under federal and state laws. Generally, the Supreme Court has rejected legislation that requires the surrender of constitutional rights as a condition for attaining a governmental benefit. (See UNCONSTITUTIONAL CONDITIONS.) Although it recognized in *Buckley v. Valeo* (1976) that political expenditures constitute protected speech under the FIRST AMENDMENT, the Supreme Court nonetheless upheld the PRESIDENTIAL ELECTION CAMPAIGN FUND ACT's limits on political party expenditures for nomination conventions and on candidate spending in presidential nomination and general election campaigns subsidized by federal money. This decision has broad implications for state regulatory authority in the thirteen states that provide public grants to candidates and political parties.

In virtually all states political parties receive automatic access to the ballot if they obtain a certain percentage of votes cast in a prior election. And in every state the ballot carries the party label to identify the candidates nominated by qualified political parties. These state benefits to political parties may justify state regulation of the structure, organization, and operation of political parties. Moreover, these benefits may strengthen claims that party activities constitute state action, thus bringing them within the ambit of both judicial and congressional authority under the Civil War amendments.

Although the Constitution has been interpreted to allow government to extend special recognition to political parties, especially major parties, governmental assistance to parties is circumscribed by constitutional limits. In *Buckley v. Valeo* the Supreme Court

not only held that financial subventions were within congressional authority under the GENERAL WELFARE CLAUSE; it also sustained definitions of eligibility that tended to reinforce the position of the major parties. Full public financing is available only to a party whose presidential candidate in the previous election received at least 25 percent of the popular vote. Some minor parties and candidates are eligible for lesser funding; others are not.

The party, seen as part of the electorate, is recognized by state eligibility requirements for voter participation in primary elections. Connecticut's closed party primary survived the challenge that it abridged independent voters' right to vote and freedom of association. A lower federal court held that the state law validly served "to protect party members from 'intrusion by those with adverse political principles,' and to preserve the integrity of the electoral process," and the Supreme Court affirmed in *Nader v. Schaffer* (1976). The courts have not decided whether political parties' freedom of association protects them from intrusion into the nominating process by persons who are not party members.

State authority to protect the integrity of party membership rolls is limited by the Fourteenth Amendment. A voter's freedom to associate with a party is apparently abridged if state-mandated enrollment rules unduly delay participation in a party primary. In *Kusper v. Pontikes* (1973) the Supreme Court invalidated a law requiring party enrollment twenty-three months in advance of a primary in which the voter wished to participate.

States also have power to protect the integrity of party nominating procedures by limiting independent or third-party candidacies by those who have been affiliated with another party. Hence, in *Storer v. Brown* (1974) the Supreme Court sustained a state law requiring an independent or new-party candidate to disaffiliate from his prior party at least a year in advance of his new party's primary. And in *American Party of Texas v. White* (1974) the Justices upheld a state law prohibiting persons who had voted in a party's most recent primary from signing petitions to qualify another party's candidate or an independent candidate for the ballot. The Court has also intimated that it would sustain "sore loser" statutes which prohibit a candidate who has participated in a party's nominating contest from subsequently qualifying as an independent candidate or opposition party aspirant in the same election. But in the same case, *Anderson v. Celebrezze* (1983), the Court held that states may not protect established parties by setting early filing deadlines that bar independent candidates arising from opposition to the platforms or candidates of major parties, when those become known.

The Constitution has been interpreted to allow preferred ballot access to established parties. Hence, in *Jennes v. Fortson* (1971) the Court sustained a statute giving automatic ballot access to parties that had obtained twenty percent or more of the vote in the prior election, while requiring others to gain ballot placement by obtaining petition signatures equivalent to five percent of those eligible to vote in the prior election. Nonetheless, in *Williams v. Rhodes* (1968) the Court rejected statutory schemes so complex or burdensome as to make it virtually impossible for any but the Democratic and Republican parties to obtain ballot access.

Promotion of political parties through minimal restrictions on the First Amendment right to associate and on the right to vote are justified by a wide array of governmental interests. The Supreme Court has said that states may protect political parties in order to assure "stability of the political system," to avoid confusion or deception, to "avoid frivolous or fraudulent candidacies prompted by short-range political goals, pique, or personal quarrel." Congress, in providing public financing of parties and candidates, can seek to avoid funding hopeless candidacies with large sums of public money or fostering proliferation of splinter parties. In the aggregate these justifications represent a constitutional hospitality toward political parties, at least when legislators grant them special statuses.

Several developments in constitutional doctrine suggest that long-established governmental regulation of political parties may now stand on treacherous ground. The 1950s saw the emergence of an independent First Amendment freedom of association, principally in cases involving dissident or oppressed groups, especially the Communist party. As early as 1952, in *Ray v. Blair*, the Supreme Court sustained a Democratic party requirement that candidates for presidential elector swear to vote for the presidential and vice-presidential candidates selected by the national Democratic party. Such an oath "protects a party from intrusion by those with adverse political principles." But until the 1970s there was little other judicial recognition that the freedom of association might secure rights of major political parties against governmental regulation.

In *Cousins v. Wigoda* (1975) and *Democratic Party v. LaFollette* (1981) the Supreme Court specifically announced that the First Amendment protected national party conventions in their establishment of rules for the selection of delegates, even in the face of contrary state laws or local party practices. In both cases, the Supreme Court announced that "the National Democratic party and its adherents enjoy a constitutionally protected right of political association." Both cases also applied the traditional standard in First Amendment cases; only a COMPELLING STATE INTEREST warranted abridgment of the "rights of association" of the national Democratic party.

In *LaFollette* the Court concluded that Article II, section 1, of the Constitution, which empowers each state to "appoint" presidential electors in the manner directed by the legislature, bears such a "remote and tenuous" connection to "the means by which political party members in a State associate to elect delegates to party nominating conventions . . . as to be wholly without constitutional significance." This conclusion sets aside one possible constitutional basis for state power to regulate party activities in selecting presidential nominees. Together, *Cousins* and *LaFollette* signal judicial reluctance to sweep every stage in the candidate selection process, especially those conducted by the parties themselves, within the scope of governmental regulation.

Indeed, in *Cousins* the Supreme Court specifically declined to "decide" or to "intimate" decisions on several critical issues of governmental authority to regulate parties, thus suggesting that large areas of the law remain open despite the assumption of past practices and of lower court decisions that party affairs are subject to extensive regulation. First, the Court did not decide "whether the decisions of a National Political Party in the area of selection constitute state or governmental action" limited by the Fourteenth and Fifteenth Amendments, and thus subject to congressional regulation. Second, the Justices left open the question "whether national political parties are subject to the principles of the REAPPORTIONMENT decisions, or other constitutional restraints, in their methods of delegate selection or allocation." Third, the Court did not decide "whether or to what extent national political parties and their nominating conventions are regulable by, or only by, Congress."

Although the sweeping associational rights of political parties recognized in *Cousins* and *LaFollette* have sometimes been regarded as limited by the Supreme Court's reference to the special "national interest" in presidential nominating conventions, the Court has relied on those decisions to protect party autonomy below the national level. In *Rivera-Rodriguez v. Popular Democratic Party* (1982) the Court cited *Cousins* and *LaFollette* in holding that a territorial political party, empowered by law to select a replacement for a deceased territorial legislator originally elected on the party ticket, was "entitled to adopt its own procedures to select . . . [a] replacement" and "was not required to include nonmembers in what can be analogized to a party primary election."

These developments suggest that the emerging First Amendment rights of parties may give them broad autonomy to order their affairs. At a minimum, party organizations can make a strong claim to order the selection, structure, and operation of party committees and conventions free from state regulation, even if those committees and conventions participate actively in candidate selection primaries. The federal courts have held that a state law prohibiting party committees from endorsing candidates in primaries violated First Amendment speech and associational rights; they avoided deciding, however, whether party campaign activities such as contributing money were similarly protected in those primary contests. If party assemblies actually select candidates, they may claim autonomy under *Cousins* and *LaFollette*, which held that party rules overrode contrary state laws in prescribing the selection of delegates to national party nominating conventions.

At the farthest reaches, the First Amendment might be construed to allow parties a substantial role in prescribing party membership and qualifying candidates for participation in party primaries established by the states. A state has a legitimate interest in an orderly election process that encourages qualified persons to participate in elections free of fraud, intimidation, and corruption; but its interests do not warrant limitations on the First Amendment associational rights of political parties. Parties may therefore establish voter enrollment and candidate eligibility rules to prevent the intrusion into party primaries of candidates and voters who do not share the party's goals. These party rules would, of course, be subject to the limits that the Supreme Court has already imposed to protect the constitutional rights to vote and associate. Such a theory of party autonomy is consistent with the modern understanding of the First Amendment and with contemporary Supreme Court declarations of party associational rights. It is a theory awaiting full explication and recognition.

DAVID ADAMANY

Bibliography

GEYH, CHARLES 1983 "It's My Party and I'll Cry If I Want To": State Intrusions upon the Associational Freedoms of Political Parties. *Wisconsin Law Review* 1983:211–240.
GOTTLIEB, STEPHEN E. 1982 Rebuilding the Right of Association: The Right to Hold a Convention as a Test Case. *Hofstra Law Review* 11:191–247.
KESTER, JOHN G. 1974 Constitutional Restrictions on Political Parties. *Virginia Law Review* 60:735–784.
NOTE 1978 Equal Representation of Party Members on Political Party Central Committees. *Yale Law Journal* 88:167–185.
ROSSITER, CLINTON L. 1960 *Parties and Politics in America.* Ithaca, N.Y.: Cornell University Press.
ROTUNDA, RONALD D. 1975 Constitutional and Statutory Restrictions on Political Parties in the Wake of *Cousins v. Wigoda. Texas Law Review* 53:935–963.
SORAUF, FRANK J. 1980 *Party Politics in America.* Boston: Little, Brown.

POLITICAL PHILOSOPHY OF THE CONSTITUTION

It is a commonplace that the Constitution provides for a LIMITED GOVERNMENT, one that depends upon a system of CHECKS AND BALANCES. And this in turn is said to reflect a realistic opinion both about the nature of man and about the purposes and risks of government. The general government is limited in that much is left to the states to do, to the extent and in the ways the states choose to act. The very existence of the states and many of the things they do are taken for granted; they do not depend upon the Constitution. Even the states formed pursuant to the Constitution automatically assumed, upon admission to the Union, virtually all of the prerogatives (or STATES' RIGHTS) of the original thirteen, including the status of being largely independent of the other states and in many respects independent of the general government.

The states play vital parts in the periodic choices of United States senators, representatives, and presidential electors. Otherwise, the Constitution, once ratified, depends upon the states for relatively few things in order to permit the general government to function within its appointed sphere. Various restrictions are placed upon the states, primarily with a view to preventing interferences by them with the proper activities of the general government. In addition, the states are obliged by the Constitution to respect various legal determinations in other states. But, by and large, the states are left fairly autonomous, however republican they are required and helped to be under the Constitution. (Although the Civil War and its Reconstruction amendments had effects upon the original constitutional dispensation, these amendments are consistent with, if not the natural culmination of, the initial dedication of the Constitution to liberty and equality.)

The general government is limited in still another critical respect by the SEPARATION OF POWERS, which makes the Constitution seem far less simple than it really is. Virtually everything that may be done by any branch of that government must take account, if it does not require the immediate cooperation, of the other two branches. Thus, Congress can enact laws alone, but it is easier to do so in collaboration with the President; how the judges will understand and how the President will execute these laws must be anticipated. The President alone commands the armed forces, but what those forces consist of and how they are equipped depends on congressional provisions, as does the very declaration of the wars in which such forces may be used. The judges interpret and apply laws, but, apart from the Supreme Court, all courts of the general government depend for their JURISDICTION and for their very existence upon the Congress, and for the execution of their decrees upon the President. Many other such interdependencies are evident.

We can even see in the references to divinity in the DECLARATION OF INDEPENDENCE an oblique anticipation of the qualified separation of powers found in the Constitution itself. There are four references of this kind in the Declaration. The first reference to God, and perhaps the second as well, regarded God as legislator; it is He that orders things, ordaining what is to be. That is, He first comes to sight as lawgiver or lawmaker. Next, God is seen as judge. Finally, He is revealed as executive, as One Who extends protection, enforcing the laws that have been laid down (with a suggestion as well of the dispensing power of the executive). Thus, the authors of the Declaration portrayed even the government of the world in the light of their political principles.

The constitutional dispersal of powers (between state and general governments, among branches of the general government, and between congressional houses with quite different constituencies) testifies to the recognition that those who wield power have to be watched, and perhaps shackled or at least hobbled. This understanding may be seen also in the ways the people discipline themselves, agreeing to proceed in accordance with constitutional forms. Such precautions make sense, however, only if there is indeed a considerable power to be exercised.

Preeminent among the powers of the general government are those that must be exercised countrywide if they are to be used effectively. These include the plenary (but not necessarily exclusive) powers of the general government with respect to commerce "among the several States," taxes, "the common defense," and international relations, all of which are reinforced by the NECESSARY AND PROPER CLAUSE. And so there has been no need for a "living" Constitution to "grow," except perhaps to grow out of the artificial limitations imposed by those periodic misinterpretations of the Constitution that have failed to appreciate the full extent of the powers intended to be vested in the general government.

Here and there the Constitution restricts the exercise of the plenary powers conferred upon the general government—but those restraints tend to be "procedural." "Substantive" restraints upon such powers would be unreasonable should they have to be employed in unpredictable but grave circumstances. The Constitution assumes the prudence of those who wield power. Thus, for example, no matter how the tax power is hedged in, Congress can still so use its discretion here as to ruin the country.

The prudence relied upon is to be directed to the advancement of the goals enumerated in the PREAMBLE. There are elsewhere in the Constitution further indications of what is taken for granted as legitimate ends of government, such as in references to "the Progress of Science and useful Arts," to "public safety," to the control of "disorderly Behaviour," to a "Republican Form of Government," and to "the Law of Nations." And, of course, the Declaration of Independence states in an authoritative manner the enduring ends of American government rooted in the inalienable rights of men.

That the Declaration of Independence is taken for granted is evident even in the way the Constitution is dated: "in the Year of our Lord one thousand seven hundred and Eighty seven and of the Independence of the United States of America the Twelfth." It seems to be taken for granted as well that the prudence relied upon both in the Declaration and in the Constitution is generally to be promoted by free discussion of public issues, however salutary a temporary secrecy may be on occasion. Such discussion is presupposed by the relations of the various branches of government to one another and by what they say to each other. Thus, judges deliberate and set forth their conclusions in published opinions; the President, in exercising his VETO POWER, is to give "his Objections," which objections are to be considered by Congress; the members of Congress are protected in their exercise of freedom of speech as legislators. A continental FREEDOM OF SPEECH and FREEDOM OF THE PRESS were presupposed as well, even before the ratification of the FIRST AMENDMENT, by the repeated indications in the Constitution of 1787 that it is an ultimately sovereign people who establish and continually assess the government.

The SOVEREIGNTY of the people is central to the constitutional system, moderated though the people's control may be by the use of representatives and by indirect selections of various officers of government. Each of the seven articles of the original Constitution, including the judiciary article, testifies to the understanding that the people are ultimately to have their way, however carefully they have disciplined themselves in restricting the manner in which they insist upon having their way. The people are sovereign, and for good reasons: it is a government designed for their happiness; they themselves have ordained it and are to support it. Besides, no one else is obviously better qualified to decide what is in the best interests of the country.

An essential equality among people is indicated in various ways, including in the equal status of the states and in the freedom of citizens to move among the states. Majority rule is taken for granted again and again. No male–female or rich–poor distinction is recognized. The Constitution does not even recognize an intrinsic difference among the races, however much grudging accommodation there may have had to be to existing slavery institutions. And, of course, no government in the United States may grant TITLES OF NOBILITY.

To defer to the genuine sovereignty of the people is to submit, in effect, to that rule of law contemplated by MAGNA CARTA. It is only through law that a people, in their political capacity, can truly speak or be spoken to. Dependence upon the RULE OF LAW points to LEGISLATIVE SUPREMACY, which is indicated again and again in the Constitution, not least in its IMPEACHMENT provisions. It is peculiar, then, that we rely as much as we now do on JUDICIAL REVIEW—that is, on the duty of courts to assess congressional enactments for their constitutionality. Of course, this duty, too, can be put in terms of respect for the rule of law. But it is difficult to find in the text of the Constitution any provision for judicial review or even any indication that it was ever anticipated by the Framers. In fact, the care with which the President's veto (the executive counterpart to judicial review) is established argues against the opinion that judges are intended by the Constitution to examine formally sufficient acts of Congress for their constitutionality, except perhaps whenever the prerogatives of the courts themselves are immediately threatened. What does seem to be anticipated by the Constitution is an even more con-

siderable power for judges than judicial review seems to offer, but one which the appellate courts of the general government have largely surrendered. This is their indirect but nevertheless critical power of supervising the COMMON LAW (and hence the moral sensibilities) of the country, subject to whatever regulations legislatures may choose to provide. In any event, these courts are entitled, perhaps even obliged, to interpret acts of Congress in accordance with the Constitution, proceeding in each case before them on the reasonable assumption (until Congress clearly indicates otherwise) that nothing unconstitutional or unjust is intended.

In the American constitutional system, both the rule of law and an ultimate dependence upon the sovereignty of the people mean that property is to be respected. (And this respect probably implies, considering the evident commercial presuppositions of the Constitution, that economic interests are to be advanced.) Respect for property is the private counterpart to that political deference to the public seen in genuine republican government. The protections of property in the THIRD, FOURTH, Fifth, SEVENTH, and Eighth Amendments draw upon a principle that is already evident in the original Constitution.

Deference to the public, and to republicanism, also takes the form of a concern for "the Blessings of Liberty." That a considerable liberty is taken for granted by the Constitution may be seen in its assurances with respect to HABEAS CORPUS, to BILLS OF ATTAINDER, to the crime of TREASON, to RELIGIOUS TESTS, and to "INDICTMENT, Trial, Judgment and Punishment, according to Law." It may be seen as well in the spirit of liberty which pervades the governmental system, making much of a people's freely choosing what they will have done for them, by whom, and upon what terms.

But however much liberty, property, and equality are to be respected, there is no question under the Constitution but that there should be effective governance, and governance with respect to the most important matters facing the country as a whole. However "limited" the exercise of power may be, primarily because of the different parts played by the three branches of the general government and by the states, great powers do exist for the general government to exercise. In any extended contest, the Constitution assumes that a determined Congress can have its way both with the President and with the courts. The Constitution was itself fashioned by a deliberative body which resembles much more the Congress than it does either the presidency or the judiciary. In the very nature of things, lawmaking (whether entrusted to one hand or to many) is at the heart of sovereignty, providing the necessary mandates for those who either interpret or execute the laws.

Lawmaking may be seen as well in what the people at large in their sovereign capacity have done in "ordain[ing] and establish[ing] this Constitution." Thus, the preeminence of lawmaking may be seen not only in what the CONSTITUTIONAL CONVENTION did in drafting the Constitution but even more in what the people did in the RATIFICATION OF THE CONSTITUTION. The provision of a workable AMENDING PROCESS also presupposes that the people retain their ultimate authority—and that standards exist by which they may examine and modify constitutional arrangements from time to time.

The Framers of the Constitution applied those standards, set forth in the Declaration of Independence, to the needs and opportunities of their day. Such standards were understood to be rooted in nature. The American people considered themselves sanctified by Providence, or at least peculiarly fitted because of their experiences and circumstances, to discern and to follow the guidance of nature. Americans looked to political philosophers and other students of law and government for help in their recourse to nature—and they invoked with confidence writers from Plato and Aristotle to John Locke and Adam Smith. But none of these writers was authoritative; all of them could be exploited, along with the considerable historical record (sacred and profane, ancient and modern) repeatedly drawn upon in debate. The diversity of the many sources casually, if not cavalierly, put to use by the Framers suggests that the astute political thought of eighteenth-century Americans was, in certain respects, distinctive to them. They were eminently practical and yet high-minded constitutionalists who seemed willing to leave many private concerns, and vital personal virtues, to the ministrations of local government and of common-law judges (as well as to church and family), while they entrusted the government of the United States both with the GENERAL WELFARE (including the economy of the country) and with external affairs (including the common defense).

However extensive and even awesome those governmental powers may be, the powers retained by the people to revise whatever is done by government in their name remain even greater. The ultimate sovereignty of the people may be seen not only in the constitutional provision for amendments but also in

that natural RIGHT OF REVOLUTION vigorously relied upon in the Declaration of Independence.

Intrinsic to the political philosophy of the Constitution is the recognition that a bad law may still be constitutional, and hence that the political must be distinguished from the legal (or judicial). This understanding means that in order for the constitutional government empowered by the people (as well as for the all-powerful people themselves) to contribute to the common good in a regular and enduring manner, there must be constant and informed recourse by Americans (citizens and public servants alike) to the instructive dictates of prudence.

GEORGE ANASTAPLO

Bibliography
ALVAREZ, LEO PAUL DE, ED. 1976 *Abraham Lincoln, the Gettysburg Address and American Constitutionalism.* Irving, Texas: University of Dallas Press.
ANASTAPLO, GEORGE 1971 *The Constitutionalist: Notes on the First Amendment.* Dallas, Texas: Southern Methodist University Press.
———— 1965 The Declaration of Independence. *St. Louis University Law Journal* 9:390–415.
———— 1984 Mr. Crosskey, the American Constitution, and the Natures of Things. *Loyola University of Chicago Law Journal* 15:181–260.
———— 1987 *The Constitution of 1787: A Commentary.* Athens, Ohio: Swallow Press/Ohio University Press. (Reprinted from *Loyola University of Chicago Law Journal* [1986] 18:1.)
CROSSKEY, WILLIAM W. 1953 *Politics and the Constitution in the History of the United States.* Chicago: University of Chicago Press.
EIDELBERG, PAUL 1968 *The Philosophy of the American Constitution: A Reinterpretation of the Intentions of the Founding Fathers.* New York: Free Press.
SHARP, MALCOLM P. 1973 Crosskey, Anastaplo and Meiklejohn on the United States Constitution. *University of Chicago Law School Record* 20:3–18.
STORY, JOSEPH 1833 *Commentaries on the Constitution of the United States.* Boston: Hilliard, Gray & Co.

POLITICAL QUESTION

As early as MARBURY V. MADISON (1803) the Supreme Court recognized that decisions on some governmental questions lie entirely within the discretion of the "political" branches of the national government—the President and Congress—and thus outside the proper scope of JUDICIAL REVIEW. Today such questions are called "political questions."

Among the clauses of the federal Constitution held

to involve political questions, the one most frequently cited has been Article IV, section 4, under which the federal government "shall guarantee to every State in this Union a REPUBLICAN FORM OF GOVERNMENT." Federal courts, and particularly the Supreme Court, have argued that as the definition of "republican" is at the heart of the American political system, only the "political branches," which are accountable to the sovereign people, can make that definition. The electorate can ratify or reject the definition by reelecting or defeating their representatives at the next election. The choice of definition, Justice FELIX FRANKFURTER said, dissenting in BAKER V. CARR (1962), entails choosing "among competing theories of political philosophy," which is not a proper judicial function.

Thus the Supreme Court has refused to review political decisions in cases involving two governments, each claiming to be the legitimate one of a state (LUTHER V. BORDEN, 1849); the question whether the post-Civil War Reconstruction governments in southern states were republican (*Georgia v. Stanton* and MISSISSIPPI V. JOHNSON, 1867); the "republican" nature of the INITIATIVE and REFERENDUM (*Pacific Telephone & Telegraph Co. v. Oregon*, 1912; *Hawke v. Smith*, 1920); lack of REAPPORTIONMENT by state legislatures (COLEGROVE V. GREEN, 1946); contested elections (*Taylor & Marshall v. Beckham*, 1900); certain presidential actions (*Mississippi v. Johnson*, 1867); certain cases arising in Indian territory (CHEROKEE INDIAN CASES, 1831–1832); and FOREIGN AFFAIRS (*Foster v. Neilson*, 1829; *Charlton v. Kelly*, 1913).

The Supreme Court has never successfully differentiated those questions proper for judicial interpretation from those that are reserved to the "political" branches. A plurality of the Justices having held in *Colegrove v. Green* (1946) that a state legislature's failure to reapportion itself after the decennial federal census was a political question, for example, the Court in *Baker v. Carr* decided that such inaction raised a question under the equal protection clause of the FOURTEENTH AMENDMENT rather than the guarantee clause, and therefore raised an issue proper for judicial decision. After having handed down a line of cases holding that contested elections were matters in which the final decision could come only from the relevant legislative body, the Court overturned the refusal by the House of Representatives (POWELL V. MCCORMACK, 1969) to seat a member who, in the Court's view, had been excluded unconstitutionally.

The Court has been relatively consistent in holding various foreign relations issues to constitute political questions, because of the necessity for the country to speak with one voice, the inability of courts to develop a body of principles to govern such issues, and what Justice Frankfurter described in *Perez v. Brownell* (1958) as the "constitutional allocation of governmental function" concerning foreign affairs to the President and Congress. Matters such as the existence of a state of war, the relevance of a treaty, the boundaries of the nation, and the credentials of foreign diplomats have been left to congressional and presidential diplomats. But the Court stated in REID V. COVERT (1957) that even the provisions of a treaty or EXECUTIVE AGREEMENT are reviewable if citizens assert violations of their rights. And, in the face of government claims that the travel of Americans abroad raises diplomatic issues fit only for executive discretion, the Court has enunciated the RIGHT TO TRAVEL abroad and has made substantive rulings for and against claims of that right (KENT V. DULLES, 1958; APTHEKER V. SECRETARY OF STATE, 1964; ZEMEL V. RUSK, 1965).

The Supreme Court's variable commitment to the political question doctrine may be explained by reasons that are nondoctrinal. The Court appears to resort to the doctrine when only two substantive judgments are possible, the first being unacceptable to the Court because it would likely go unenforced and the second being equally unacceptable because it would violate a major tenet of American political ideology. In *Colegrove v. Green*, for example, the plurality suggested that the Illinois legislation might ignore a HOLDING that the legislature's refusal to redesign badly malapportioned congressional districts was unconstitutional—and the House of Representatives might take no action. Yet upholding such a malapportionment, which gave some citizens a vote of far greater weight than that of others, would have run contrary to the American belief that all citizens are equal in the electoral process. Similarly, the Court in *Mississippi v. Johnson* had the choice of deciding that the Reconstruction state governments were illegitimate, a ruling that the President and Congress surely would have ignored; or that the governments, which had been imposed by the federal government on citizens denied the right to participate in the election process, were legitimate—which would have offended the basic American idea of SOVEREIGNTY of the people. In both cases the Court invoked the political question doctrine and left decision in the hands of the "political branches."

The very notion of "political branches," however, is untenable. Article III of the Constitution makes the federal judiciary indirectly accountable insofar as it may enable the people's representatives in Congress to strip the courts of JURISDICTION over matters the people believe the courts to have mishandled. Federal judges, too, are liable to IMPEACHMENT—although this resource has never been taken for purely political purposes since the earliest days of the nineteenth century.

Court decisions necessarily affect power. The decision in PLESSY V. FERGUSON (1896) legitimizing SEPARATE BUT EQUAL railroad cars for black and white passengers encouraged southern states to establish racially segregated schools; the holding of BROWN V. BOARD OF EDUCATION (1954) that "separate but equal" schools violated the equal protection clause stripped the states of that power, transferring the power to define SEGREGATION and integration to the federal courts, the Congress, and, in some cases, to the President. The Court's upholding of ECONOMIC REGULATION affecting wages, hours, unionization, social security, job safety, and competition shifted power from employers to state and federal legislatures, executives, and REGULATORY AGENCIES, as well as to unions, and enabled the United States to consolidate a system of welfare capitalism under which privately owned property is systematically regulated by governmental bodies.

The Court nonetheless insists that the judicial branch is apolitical, because its own institutional power depends on the electorate's belief that the Court is above politics. As JAMES MADISON pointed out in THE FEDERALIST #51, the Court possesses neither the power of the purse nor that of the sword. It is entirely dependent for the enforcement of its decisions on the willingness of the population and public officials to carry them out. Were the Court's decisions to be ignored, the Court's prestige would suffer; in a circular fashion, the loss of prestige would increase the possibility that subsequent decisions would go unheeded.

The Court's decisions find ready compliance when the decisions reflect a societal consensus. The difference between the Court's 1946 *Colegrove* decision that malapportionment was a political question and its contrary 1962 *Baker* decision can be linked to the large-scale movement of population to urban areas underrepresented in the legislatures. By 1962 a majority of the nation's population could be expected to concur in a decision that enhanced its political power. Promise of additional support from the President was implicit in the appearance of Attorney General ROBERT F. KENNEDY before the Court to argue as AMICUS CURIAE for reapportionment, for Kennedy was, of course, the brother of President JOHN F. KENNEDY, who owed his office to urban votes.

The political question device derives its legitimacy from the necessity to preserve an independent judiciary in the American political system. The device is justifiable because it enables the judiciary to maintain its independence by withdrawing from no-win situations. In addition, it prevents the courts from usurping the role of the ballot box. The Supreme Court, declaring the presence of a political question, tacitly admits that it cannot find and therefore cannot ratify a social consensus that does not violate basic American beliefs. The Court has no moral right to impose rules upon a country not yet ready for them. The political question doctrine, which permits the Court to restrain itself from precipitating impossible situations that might tear the social fabric, gives the electorate and its representatives time to work out their own rules, which can ultimately be translated into constitutional doctrine through judicial decision. The doctrine of political questions is more than a self-saving mechanism for the Court; it is also an affirmation of a governmental system based on popular sovereignty.

PHILIPPA STRUM

Bibliography

BICKEL, ALEXANDER M. 1962 *The Least Dangerous Branch.* Indianapolis: Bobbs-Merrill.

SCHARPF, FRITZ W. 1966 Judicial Review and the Political Question: A Functional Analysis. *Yale Law Journal* 75:517–546.

STRUM, PHILIPPA 1974 *The Supreme Court and "Political Questions."* University: University of Alabama Press.

POLK, JAMES KNOX
(1795–1849)

The eleventh President's constitutional beliefs blended STRICT CONSTRUCTION, expediency, and continental vision. He returned to a central theme of Jacksonian constitutionalism to harmonize these divergent interests: the President was the tribune of the people, the only nationally elected federal official.

Polk stressed the SEPARATION OF POWERS in order to legitimate the popularly based presidential power he exercised. He recognized that congressional committees had legitimate claims to information held by the executive branch, but he spurned congressional requests that intruded upon areas of constitutional responsibility he believed assigned to the President, most notably FOREIGN AFFAIRS. He rebuffed, in 1848, Senate advice to negotiate a treaty of extradition with Prussia and to secure the purchase rights of the Hudson's Bay Company on the Columbia River. Yet Polk acknowledged that Congress commanded a broad sphere of constitutional responsibility; he vetoed only three legislative acts.

Polk contributed significantly to the constitutional development of the COMMANDER-IN-CHIEF clause. Unlike ABRAHAM LINCOLN, he believed that the clause granted only military leadership to the President. Yet Polk made use of this power to implement his policy of continentalism. He ordered General ZACHARY TAYLOR into disputed territory between the United States and Mexico knowing that such actions were likely to precipitate hostilities. When the Mexicans responded with force, Congress was left to ratify a war rather than to fulfill its constitutional mandate to declare it. Throughout the ensuing conflict Polk established the precedent that a vigorous conception of the commander-in-chief clause meant control over military affairs.

Tough and efficient, Polk was a transitional figure in the constitutional evolution toward the modern presidency. Unlike his twentieth-century counterparts, Polk, with his strict constructionist beliefs, did not think that the right of self-defense or the inherent authority of the commander-in-chief bestowed on him the power to wage war against another country without congressional authorization.

KERMIT L. HALL

Bibliography

McCOY, CHARLES A. 1960 *Polk and the Presidency.* Austin: University of Texas Press.

POLLAK, WALTER H.
(1887–1940)

Walter H. Pollak, an active supporter of CIVIL LIBERTIES, argued a number of important cases before the Supreme Court. He represented the defendant in GITLOW V. NEW YORK (1925) and, although he lost that case, succeeded in convincing the Court that the FOURTEENTH AMENDMENT incorporates the FIRST AMENDMENT guarantees of FREEDOM OF THE PRESS and FREEDOM OF SPEECH against the states. With ZECHARIAH CHAFEE, Pollak served on the Wickersham Committee and investigated "lawlessness in law enforcement." He also took part in WHITNEY V. CALI-

FORNIA (1927) and successfully defended the "Scottsboro boys" in POWELL V. ALABAMA (1932) and NORRIS V. ALABAMA (1935).

DAVID GORDON

POLLOCK v. FARMERS' LOAN & TRUST CO.
157 U.S. 429 and 158 U.S. 601 (1895)

CHARLES EVANS HUGHES called these decisions a "self-inflicted wound" comparable to the decision in DRED SCOTT V. SANDFORD (1857). Here the Supreme Court held unconstitutional an 1894 act of Congress that fixed a flat tax of two percent on all annual incomes over $4,000. Pollock filed a STOCKHOLDER'S SUIT against the trust company to prevent it from complying with the statute which, he claimed, imposed a DIRECT TAX without apportioning it among the states on the basis of population. The trust company, the party of record on the side of the tax, avoided the appearance of collusion by hiring the president of the American Bar Association, JAMES COOLIDGE CARTER; RICHARD OLNEY, attorney general of the United States, was on the same side as AMICUS CURIAE. Theirs was the easy task because history and all the precedents proved that the clause of Article 1, section 9, referring to direct taxes, meant only taxes on people or on land. The Court had so declared in HYLTON V. UNITED STATES (1796) and in several other cases, especially SPRINGER V. UNITED STATES (1881), a direct precedent; the Court there had unanimously sustained an earlier income tax as imposing an indirect tax and therefore not subject to the requirement of apportionment.

Counsel for Pollock, led by JOSEPH H. CHOATE, buttressed a weak case with an impassioned argument intended to provoke judicial fear and reflecting the panic felt by many conservatives. Choate warned that the Court had to choose between "the beginning of socialism and communism" and the preservation of private property, civilization, and the Constitution. He appealed to the Court to substitute its discretion for that of Congress.

Justice HOWELL E. JACKSON not having participated, an eight-member Court decided the case. All agreed that the federal tax on municipal bonds was unconstitutional, because government instrumentalities were exempt from taxation (see INTERGOVERNMENTAL IMMUNITIES). On the question of the validity of the tax on income from personal property, the

Court divided evenly. But on the question of the validity of the tax on income from real estate, the Court voted 6–2 that it was a direct tax unconstitutionally assessed. Nothing favorable can be said about Chief Justice MELVILLE W. FULLER's opinion for the majority. He took for granted the very proposition he should have proved, asserting that a tax on the income from land was indistinguishable from a tax on the land itself. Clearly, however, the income that may derive from rents, timber, oil, minerals, or agriculture is distinguishable from a tax on acreage or on the assessed value of the land itself. Fuller distinguished away the precedents: *Hylton* had decided only that a tax on carriages was not a direct tax, and *Springer* had decided only the narrow point that a tax on a lawyer's fees was not a direct one. Neither case, Fuller declared, dealt with a tax on the income from land, and he made much of the point that such a tax is unique because of the undisputed fact that a tax on the land itself is undoubtedly a direct tax. Justices EDWARD D. WHITE and JOHN MARSHALL HARLAN, dissenting, concluded that history and STARE DECISIS demanded a different ruling, and they warned that when the Court virtually annulled its previous decisions on the basis of the policy preferences of a majority that happened to dominate the bench, the Constitution was in jeopardy.

The tie vote of the Court on all other issues meant that the decision of the CIRCUIT COURT prevailed, leaving in force the taxes on corporate income, wages and salaries, and returns from investments. Accordingly, Choate moved for a rehearing, which was granted, and Justice Jackson attended. The trust company, which was supposed to defend the income tax act, did not retain Carter or replace him, thus leaving Olney to defend it. He took half the time permitted by the Court for his presentation.

The arguments the second time focused on the validity of the tax on the income from personal property, mainly interest and dividends. Fuller, speaking for a bare majority, again read the Court's opinion. Six weeks earlier he had based his position on the uniqueness of a tax on the income from land; now he took the opposite view, reasoning that if a tax on the income from land is a direct tax, so is a tax on the income from personal property. Having found the statute void in significant respects, he reasoned next that the invalidity of some sections contaminated the rest: since the sections were inseparable, all were void because some were.

When Fuller finished his opinion, Harlan began to read his dissent; it sizzled in its language and delivery. He ended a systematic refutation by pounding his desk, shaking his finger in the face of the Chief Justice, and shouting, "On my conscience I regard this decision as a disaster!" (*The Nation* magazine described Harlan as an "agitator" who expounded "the Marx gospel from the bench.") He accused the majority of an unprecedented use of judicial power on behalf of private wealth by striking down a statute whose policy they disliked and by doing it against all law and history. He also pointed out, as did the other dissenters, Justices White, Jackson, and HENRY B. BROWN, that the parts of the statute that were not unconstitutional per se, and might be reenacted if Congress chose, taxed the income of people who earned their money from wages and salaries but who derived no income from land or invested personal property. The decision, said Brown, is "nothing less than a surrender of the taxing power to the moneyed class" making for "a sordid despotism of wealth." It "takes invested wealth," said White, and "reads it into the Constitution as a favored and protected class of property...." It was, said Jackson, "the most disastrous blow ever struck at the constitutional power of congress" and made the tax burden fall "most heavily and oppressively upon those having the least ability" to pay.

Public opinion was opposed to the Court, though it had vigorous supporters especially among the Republican newspapers in the East. The *New York Sun* exclaimed in delight, "Five to Four, the Court Stands Like a Rock." The *New York Herald Tribune* hailed the Court for halting a "communist revolution." The Democratic party, however, recommended an amendment to the Constitution vesting Congress with the power denied by the Court. The SIXTEENTH AMENDMENT was not ratified, though, until 1913, by which time the nation's maldistribution of wealth had intensified. For eighteen years, as EDWARD S. CORWIN wrote, "the veto of the Court held the sun and moon at pause," while the great fortunes went untaxed. The government during that time raised almost all of its revenues from EXCISE TAXES and tariffs, whose burden fell mainly on consumers. In 1913 the average annual income in the United States was $375 per capita.

LEONARD W. LEVY

Bibliography

CORWIN, EDWARD S. 1932 *Court over Constitution.* Pages 177–209. Princeton, N.J.: Princeton University Press.

KING, WILLARD L. 1950 *Melville Weston Fuller.* Pages 193–221. New York: Macmillan.

PAUL, ARNOLD M. 1960 *Conservative Crisis and the Rule of Law: Attitudes of Bar and Bench, 1887–1895.* Pages 159–220. Ithaca, N.Y.: Cornell University Press.

SHIRAS, GEORGE, 3RD and SHIRAS, WINFIELD   1953 *Justice George Shiras Jr. of Pittsburgh.* Pages 160–183. Pittsburgh: University of Pittsburgh Press.

POLLOCK v. WILLIAMS
322 U.S. 4 (1944)

A Florida statute made the failure to perform services according to an agreement (for which an advance had been made) *prima facie* evidence of an intent to defraud. The Supreme Court, in an opinion by Justice ROBERT H. JACKSON, voided the statute, 7–2, as a violation of the THIRTEENTH AMENDMENT and of the Anti-Peonage Act of 1867. At issue before the Court was a HABEAS CORPUS petition for "an illiterate Negro laborer in the toils of law for the want of $5." His failure to perform agreed-upon labor for that advance resulted in a $100 fine, in default of which he was sentenced to sixty days' imprisonment. Jackson held that the Thirteenth Amendment and the Anti-Peonage Act "raised both a shield and a sword against forced labor because of debt."

DAVID GORDON

POLL TAX

A poll tax (CAPITATION TAX, head tax) is typically levied on every adult (or adult male) within the taxing JURISDICTION. An old technique for raising revenue, the tax in its compulsory form raises no important constitutional questions. (Under Article I, section 9, Congress can levy a poll tax only by apportionment to the national census. Congress has not in fact raised revenue this way.)

Serious constitutional issues have been raised in this century by poll taxes whose payment is "voluntary," enforced only by conditioning voter registration on their payment. Early in the nation's history, payment of such taxes came to replace property ownership as a qualification for voting. By the Civil War, however, widespread acceptance of universal suffrage had virtually eliminated the poll tax as a condition on voting.

In a number of southern states, the poll tax returned in the 1890s along with SEGREGATION as a means of maintaining white supremacy. In theory and in early practice, poor whites as well as blacks were kept from voting by this means. Later, however, some registrars learned to use the device mainly for purposes of RACIAL DISCRIMINATION, requiring only black would-be voters to produce their receipts for poll tax payments—in some states for payments going back to the voter's twenty-first year. The poll tax gradually fell from favor as a means of keeping blacks from voting; "good character" requirements and LITERACY TESTS, for example, were more readily adapted to this purpose. By 1940 only seven states retained the poll tax as a voting condition.

In BREEDLOVE V. SUTTLES (1937), a case involving a white applicant for registration, the Supreme Court upheld Georgia's use of the poll tax as a condition on voting. The poll tax remained a CIVIL RIGHTS issue, kept alive in Congress by the regular introduction of bills to abolish its use. Southern committee chairmanships and senatorial filibusters succeeded in sidetracking this legislation. When the TWENTY-FOURTH AMENDMENT was finally submitted to the states in 1962, it forbade the use of poll taxes as a condition on voting only in federal, not state, elections. The Amendment was ratified in 1964.

Two years later, the Supreme Court held, in HARPER V. VIRGINIA BOARD OF ELECTIONS (1966), that conditioning voting in state elections on poll tax payments denied the EQUAL PROTECTION OF THE LAWS. Only four states still retained the device, but its elimination eloquently symbolized the relation between VOTING RIGHTS and the equal CITIZENSHIP of all Americans.

KENNETH L. KARST

Bibliography
MYRDAL, GUNNAR   1944 *An American Dilemma: The Negro Problem and Modern Democracy.* Chaps. 22–23. New York: Harper & Brothers.

POLYGAMY

Because polygamy was one of the early tenets of the Mormon Church, the movement to eradicate plural marriage became bound up with religious persecution. The Supreme Court has consistently held that the FIRST AMENDMENT's protections of RELIGIOUS LIBERTY do not protect the practice of plural marriage. Thus REYNOLDS V. UNITED STATES (1879) upheld a criminal conviction for polygamy in the Territory of Utah, and DAVIS V. BEASON (1880) upheld a conviction for voting in the Territory of Idaho in violation of an oath required of all registrants forswearing belief in polygamy. The corporate charter of the Mormon Church in the Territory of Utah was revoked, and its property forfeited to the government, in CHURCH OF JESUS CHRIST OF LATTER-DAY SAINTS V. UNITED STATES (1890). The church's First Amendment claim was waved away with the statement that belief in polygamy was not a religious tenet but a "pretense" that was "contrary to the spirit of Christianity."

It would be comforting if this judicial record were confined to the nineteenth century, but it was not. In *Cleveland v. United States* (1946), the Court upheld a conviction of Mormons under the MANN ACT for transporting women across state lines for the purpose of "debauchery" that took the form of living with them in polygamous marriage. The Court's opinion, citing the nineteenth-century cases and even quoting the "spirit of Christianity" language with approval, was written by none other than Justice WILLIAM O. DOUGLAS.

More recently, the Court has recognized a constitutional right to marry, and in a number of contexts has afforded protection for a FREEDOM OF INTIMATE ASSOCIATION. (See MARRIAGE AND THE CONSTITUTION.) With or without the ingredient of religious freedom, SUBSTANTIVE DUE PROCESS doctrine seems amply to justify an extension of these rights to plural marriage among competent consenting adults. Yet the force of conventional morality in constitutional adjudication should not be underestimated; the Supreme Court is not just the architect of principle but an institution of government. Polygamy is not on the verge of becoming a constitutional right.

KENNETH L. KARST

Bibliography

LARSON, GUSTAVE O. 1971 *The "Americanization" of Utah for Statehood.* San Marino, Calif.: Huntington Library.

POMEROY, JOHN NORTON

See: Commentators on the Constitution

POPULAR SOVEREIGNTY

"Popular sovereignty" was a solution proposed by some northern Democrats to the problem of slavery's access to the TERRITORIES. As an alternative to the WILMOT PROVISO, Michigan Senator Lewis Cass proposed in 1847 that slavery be left "to the people inhabiting [the territories] to regulate their internal concerns their own way." He later concluded that congressional prohibition of SLAVERY IN THE TERRITORIES was unconstitutional. Popular sovereignty was a radical innovation: never before had residents of the territories been thought to be invested with SOV-

EREIGNTY, let alone a territorial sovereignty implying that the federal government lacked substantive regulatory power over the territories.

Illinois Senator STEPHEN A. DOUGLAS took up popular sovereignty in 1854, recommending that the MISSOURI COMPROMISE be jettisoned in order to get the slavery question out of Congress and leave it to the settlers of the territories. Though adopted in the KANSAS-NEBRASKA ACT, popular sovereignty soon fell into disfavor in both the North and the South. Douglas and other northern Democrats rejected the travesty made of it by President JAMES BUCHANAN in his attempt to force slavery into Kansas, while southern leaders abandoned it in favor of a constitutional program that would have forced slavery into all the territories.

WILLIAM M. WIECEK

Bibliography

JOHANNSEN, ROBERT W. 1973 *Stephen A. Douglas.* New York: Oxford University Press.

POPULAR SOVEREIGNTY
(in Democratic Political Theory)

The Constitution's first words bespeak its derivation from popular authority: "We the people of the United States . . . do ordain and establish this Constitution." The DECLARATION OF INDEPENDENCE expresses the principle of this act: "to secure these rights, governments are instituted among men, deriving their just powers from the consent of the governed." The specific doctrine of popular sovereignty behind these familiar phrases still needs to be clarified and distinguished from related but distinct doctrines.

This doctrine of popular SOVEREIGNTY relates primarily not to the Constitution's operation but to its source of authority and supremacy, ratification, amendment, and possible abolition. When JAMES MADISON wrote in THE FEDERALIST #49 that "the people are the only legitimate fountain of power," he referred to what he had called in *The Federalist* #40 (paraphrasing the Declaration) "the transcendent and precious right of the people to 'abolish or alter their governments.'" Legitimate power derives primarily from the people's original consent to their form of government, not from their continuing role in it. Because popular consent is the "pure, original fountain of all legitimate authority," ALEXANDER HAMILTON, in *The Federalist* #22, presents the RATIFICATION OF THE CONSTITUTION by conventions specially elected by the people, a mode recently pioneered by the states, as crucial to its legitimacy. *The Federalist* both opens and closes remarking that for a whole people so to choose their constitution by voluntary consent, far from being typical, is an unprecedented prodigy.

This American mode of popular consent to the institution of government formalized the notion in JOHN LOCKE's *Second Treatise* of "the Constitution of the Legislative being the original and supreme act of the Society, antecedent to all positive Laws in it, and depending wholly on the People." It provides a peaceful, certain, and solemn alternative to violent and irregular acts but remains ultimately an expression of the right to revolution; Madison almost admits in *The Federalist* #40 that adoption of the Constitution was authorized not under the ARTICLES OF CONFEDERATION but only by popular consent as an exercise of revolutionary right. Such popular sovereignty could always be exercised again not only by regular amendment but by revolution.

For the Founders, legitimate government not only had to derive its powers originally from the consent of the people but also had to gain the consent of their regularly elected representatives to legislate for them and tax them. The revolutionary controversy was fundamentally waged, first, over the American invocation of Locke's position that government "must *not raise Taxes* on the Property of the People, *without the Consent of the People,* given by themselves, or their Deputies," and then over its extension to no legislation without REPRESENTATION.

Such popular sovereignty still is not identical with popular government. The Founders generally regarded the British constitution, for example, with its hereditary king and lords, as a legitimate and even free government because the British (unlike the American) people were represented (albeit imperfectly) in the House of Commons. Republican government, although the form of government best exhibiting the capacity of mankind for self-government, was not the only form compatible with popular consent as the basis of legitimate power. Because Madison correctly believed that the character of the American people makes them unlikely to exercise their sovereign right to replace their republican government with one of another form, this point is relevant less to our domestic than to our foreign policy, which in principle should recognize the right of other sovereign peoples to consent to other forms of government.

Republican government itself differs for the Founders from the populism some later doctrines equate with popular sovereignty. *The Federalist* treats republican government as a species of popular government in that it is administered by officials appointed directly or indirectly by the people and holding office for limited periods or during GOOD BEHAVIOR. It differs from the other species, which they called "democracy" and by which they meant direct democracy, by its reliance on representation. *The Federalist* regards this difference not as an evil necessitated by size (as some Anti-Federalists did) but as a superiority making possible both size, with all its advantages, and government by "men who possess most wisdom to discern, and most virtue to pursue, the common good of the society." (THOMAS JEFFERSON in a letter to JOHN ADAMS called such republican officials "the natural aristocracy.") Republican representatives should refine and enlarge the public views because the reason, not the passion, the cool and deliberate sense, not the temporary errors and delusions, of the public should prevail. The Founders regarded the American republic as embodying the sovereignty of the public reason because it was so constructed as to encourage representatives, especially the Senate, President, and courts, to withstand popular error and passion until popular good sense could respond to argument and events. Their opinion that such an outcome would generally emerge in the few years allowed by the Constitution reveals confidence in both representatives and constituents as well as distrust.

The supremacy of the Constitution and JUDICIAL REVIEW, distinctive features of American CONSTITUTIONALISM, are paradoxical results of this doctrine of popular sovereignty. Hamilton in *The Federalist* #78, like JOHN MARSHALL in MARBURY V. MADISON (1803), based them on the Constitution's being the special act of the sovereign people: "the Constitution ought to be preferred to the statute, the intention of the people to the intention of their agents." The equation of popular sovereignty with the supremacy of the Constitution, let alone with judicial review, may become problematic once the people who ordained and established the Constitution are long dead. Jefferson suggested in a letter to an unpersuaded Madison that all constitutions naturally expire every generation. Madison in reply adduced the danger of faction and the need of even the most rational government for the prejudice that results from stability, but Jefferson continued to believe in the right of each generation to choose its own form of government. The jural argument for constitutional supremacy was stated by Hamilton in *Phocion* #2 (and echoed in *The Federalist* #78): "The constitution is the compact made between the society at large and each individual. The society therefore, cannot without breach of faith and injustice, refuse to any individual, a single advantage which he derives under that compact . . . until the compact is dissolved with the same solemnity and certainty with which it was made." Ultimately the identity of popular sovereignty with constitutional supremacy depends on an enlightened public opinion animated by the spirit of the Constitution.

That the Founders tended not to call the doctrine expounded here "popular sovereignty" reflects their being republicans and constitutionalists rather than populists. Not the people simply but their reason especially as solemnly embodied in their Constitution is sovereign. More fundamentally, since governments are instituted by consent "to secure these rights," their legitimacy depends not only on consent but on the security of individual rights. Debates such as that over "popular sovereignty" between ABRAHAM LINCOLN and STEPHEN DOUGLAS reveal the potential tension between popular consent and equal rights.

NATHAN TARCOV

Bibliography

EPSTEIN, DAVID F. 1984 *The Political Theory of the Federalist.* Chicago: University of Chicago Press.

JAFFA, HARRY V. (1959)1982 *Crisis of the House Divided: An Interpretation of the Issues in the Lincoln-Douglas Debates.* Chicago: University of Chicago Press.

TARCOV, NATHAN 1985 American Constitutionalism and Individual Rights. Pages 101–125 in Robert Goldwin and William Schambra, eds., *How Does the Constitution Secure Rights?* Washington, D.C.: American Enterprise Institute.

PORNOGRAPHY

The Supreme Court's OBSCENITY decisions define the forms of pornography that are protected from censorship by the FIRST AMENDMENT. As a practical matter, this protection is quite broad. Most pornography is also a unique kind of speech: about women, for men. In an era when sexual equality is a social ideal, the constitutional protection of pornography is a vexing political issue. Should pornographic imagery of male dominance and female subordination be repudiated through censorship, or will censorship inevitably destroy our commitment to free speech?

In ROTH V. UNITED STATES (1957) the Court found obscene speech to be unworthy of First Amendment protection because it forms "no essential part of any exposition of ideas." Yet precisely because of pornography's ideational content, some of it was deemed harmful and made criminal. The Court could avoid examining the specific nature of this harm, once it had located obscenity conveniently outside the consti-

tutional pale. But it could not avoid defining obscenity, and thereby identifying the justification for its censorship.

The essential characteristic of "obscene" pornography is its appeal to one's "prurient interest," which is a genteel reference to its capacity to stimulate physical arousal and carnal desire. But such pornography must also be "offensive," and so, to be censored, sex-stimulant speech must be both arousing and disgusting. The meaning of offensiveness depends upon the subjective judgment of the observer, and is best captured by Justice POTTER STEWART's famous aphorism in JACOBELLIS V. OHIO (1964): "I know it when I see it."

Given the limitations of the criminal process, obscenity laws did not make offensive pornography unavailable in the marketplace. As HARRY KALVEN, JR. pointed out, few judges took the evils of obscenity very seriously, although constitutional rhetoric made the law appear to be "solemnly concerned with the sexual fantasies of the adult population." The Court's chief goal was the protection of admired works of art and literature, not the elimination of pornographic magazines at the corner drug store. Sporadic obscenity prosecutions may occur in jurisdictions where the "contemporary community standard" of offensiveness allows convictions under MILLER V. CALIFORNIA (1973). But the constitutional validity of a legal taboo on "hard-core" pornography became largely irrelevant to its suppliers and consumers, even as that material became sexually explicit and more violent in its imagery during the 1970s.

That same decade saw a legal revolution in equality between the sexes, embodied in judicial decisions based on the guarantees of EQUAL PROTECTION and DUE PROCESS. Women won legal rights to control and define their own sexuality, through litigation establishing rights to contraception and abortion, and through legislative reforms easing restrictions on prosecutions for sexual assault. Pornography also became a women's issue, as feminists such as Catharine MacKinnon attacked it as "a form of forced sex, a practice of sexual politics, an institution of gender inequality." Women marched and demonstrated against films and magazines portraying them as beaten, chained, or mutilated objects of sexual pleasure for men. In 1984, their protests took a legal form when MacKinnon and Andrea Dworkin drafted an ordinance adopted by the Indianapolis City Council, outlawing some types of pornography as acts of SEX DISCRIMINATION.

By using the concept of equal protection as a basis to attack pornographic speech, the council set up a dramatic assault upon First Amendment doctrine, making embarrassed enemies out of old constitutional friends. As a strategic matter, however, the council needed a COMPELLING STATE INTEREST to justify censorship of speech that did not fall into the obscenity category. The ordinance defined offensive pornography more broadly than *Miller*'s standards allow, because it went beyond a ban on displays of specific human body parts or sexual acts. Instead, it prohibited the "graphic sexually explicit subordination of women" through their portrayals as, for example, "sexual objects who enjoy pain or humiliation," or "sexual objects for domination, conquest, violation, exploitation, possession or use."

As a philosophical matter, sex discrimination is a good constitutional metaphor for the harms attributed to pornography, namely, the loss of equal CITIZENSHIP status for women through the "bigotry and contempt" promoted by the imagery of subordination. But as a matter of DOCTRINE, the causal link between the social presence of pornography and the harms of discrimination is fatally remote. Free speech gospel dictates that "offensive speech" may be censored only upon proof of imminent, tangible harm to individuals, such as violent insurrection (BRANDENBURG V. OHIO, 1969), a physical assault (COHEN V. CALIFORNIA, 1971), or reckless tortious injury to reputation (NEW YORK TIMES V. SULLIVAN, 1964). The closest historical analogue to the creation of a cause of action for class-wide harm from speech is the criminal GROUP LIBEL statute upheld by a 5–4 Supreme Court in BEAUHARNAIS V. ILLINOIS (1952). But this remedy has been implicitly discredited by *New York Times* and *Brandenburg*, given its CHILLING EFFECT upon uninhibited criticism of political policies and officials.

It came as no surprise when early court decisions struck down Indianapolis-type ordinances as void for vagueness, as an unlawful PRIOR RESTRAINT on speech, and as an unjustified restriction of protected speech as defined by the earlier obscenity decisions. The courts could accept neither the equal protection rationale nor the breadth of the ordinances' scope, as both would permit too great an encroachment upon the freedoms of expression and consumption of art, literature, and political messages. Ironically, it is the potentially endemic quality of the imagery of women's subordination that defeats any attempt to place a broad taboo upon it.

Eva Feder Kittay has posed the question, "How is it that within our society, men can derive a sexual charge out of seeing a woman brutalized?" Her answer to that loaded question is that our conceptions of sexuality are permeated with conceptions of domination, because we have eroticized the relations of power: men eroticize sexual conquering, and women eroticize being possessed. Pornography becomes more than a harmless outlet for erotic fantasies when it makes violence appear to be intrinsically erotic, rather than something that is eroticized. The social harm of such pornography is that it brutalizes our moral imagination, "the source of that imaginative possibility by which we can identify with others and hence form maxims having a universal validity."

The constitutional source for an analysis of brutalizing pornography lies in the richly generative symbols of First Amendment law itself. That law already contains the tolerance for insistence "on observance of the civic culture's norms of social equality," in the words of Kenneth L. Karst. Any acceptable future taboo would be likely to take the form of a ban on public display of a narrowly defined class of pictorial imagery, simply because that would be a traditional, readily enforceable compromise between free speech and equality. Any taboo would be mostly symbolic, but it would matter. Only by limiting the taboo can we avoid descending into the Orwellian hell where censorship is billed as freedom.

CATHERINE HANCOCK

Bibliography

BRYDEN, DAVID 1985 Between Two Constitutions: Feminism and Pornography. *Constitutional Commentary* 2:147–189.

KALVEN, HARRY, JR. 1960 The Metaphysics of Obscenity. *Supreme Court Review* 1960:1–45.

KITTAY, EVA FEDER 1983 Pornography and the Erotics of Domination. Pages 145–174 in Carol C. Gould, ed., *Beyond Domination: New Perspectives on Women and Philosophy*. Totowa, N.J.: Rowman & Allanheld.

MACKINNON, CATHARINE A. 1984 Not a Moral Issue. *Yale Law & Policy Review* 2:321–345.

NOTE 1984 Anti-Pornography Laws and First Amendment Values. *Harvard Law Review* 98:460–481.

POSSE COMITATUS ACT
20 Stat. 145 (1878)

Representative James P. Knott (Democrat of Kentucky) introduced this act as an amendment to the Army Appropriation Act of 1878. It provides that "it shall not be lawful to employ any part of the Army of the United States, as a posse comitatus, or otherwise, for the purpose of executing the laws" except as specifically authorized by Congress. The act has applied to the Air Force since 1947; it has been extended to the Navy and Marine Corps by administrative regulations. Originally enacted as a step in the dismantling of Reconstruction, this provision banned the practice implicitly authorized by the JUDICIARY ACT OF 1789, and used before the Civil War to enforce the FUGITIVE SLAVE ACT, of including military forces in the federal marshal's posse. The act remains on the books (section 1835, Title 18, United States Code) as an expression of the fundamental division between the military and civilian realms: the armed forces are not a LAW ENFORCEMENT agency.

Congress has authorized the use of the armed forces to suppress insurrection, domestic violence, unlawful combination, or conspiracy that obstructs the execution of federal law or impedes the course of justice, or that deprives any class of people of constitutional rights that the state authorities cannot or will not protect. That provision of the FORCE ACT OF 1871 (now section 333, Title 10, United States Code) was invoked by President DWIGHT D. EISENHOWER in 1958 when he used Army units to disperse the mob in Little Rock, Arkansas, that resisted a federal court's school DESEGREGATION order (see COOPER V. AARON), and by President RICHARD M. NIXON, in 1970, when he ordered federal troops to assist in quelling a riot in Detroit, Michigan.

DENNIS J. MAHONEY

POSTAL POWER

Seven words of Article I, section 8, of the Constitution grant the postal power to Congress. Under the power "To Establish Post Offices and Post Roads" liberally construed, Congress has built offices and constructed roads for handling the mails and maintained an extensive nationwide delivery service. Congress has vested in the Postal Service, now in corporate form, monopoly powers over the delivery of letters and extensive, though often untested, POLICE POWERS over the mails.

The postal system in the United States traces its roots to a 1692 crown patent to Thomas Neale by William and Mary, granting a monopoly of the colonial posts, including all profits therefrom. The Post Office was established on July 26, 1775, by the CONTINENTAL CONGRESS to assure effective communications and to eliminate what was viewed as a tax by the British Post Office. The ARTICLES OF CONFEDERATION granted exclusive postal power to Congress, and the Constitution carried forward the congressional power over the mails.

At the time of the CONSTITUTIONAL CONVENTION the activities of the Post Office were widely accepted,

and there was little sentiment for change or elaboration. Indeed, the postal power was virtually undebated, and only one reference to it is to be found in THE FEDERALIST. The breadth of the congressional interpretation of the postal power, therefore, finds neither support nor contradiction in the Constitution or the debates concerning its adoption.

The postal monopoly, contained in the so-called private express statutes, generally makes it unlawful for private carriers to carry letters and packets, unless postage has been paid thereon and canceled. This provision is, in effect, a 100 percent tax on the carrying of letters outside the Postal Service. The monopoly dates from colonial days, and it was and is justified on the economic grounds that it is necessary to retain monopoly power over profitable routes and services so that the Postal Service can provide uniform and inexpensive service nationwide, even along uneconomic and remote routes. The Articles of Confederation specifically granted the monopoly, giving the Congress "sole and exclusive power." The absence of these words in Article I, section 8, leaves the constitutionality of the monopoly unclear, but the few courts that have considered the question have held in its favor. Historically, monopoly had been an integral feature of the British and colonial postal systems, as well as those of many other Western nations.

The extent of the postal power has been the subject of debate in the Congress and of occasional litigation. The earliest questions concerned post roads: did Congress have authority to construct new roads, or only to designate existing state roads as postal routes? The issue had not been discussed by the Framers or, with one exception (New York), at the state conventions. Congress determined that it had power to appropriate funds to construct post roads, but not to construct them directly. The Supreme Court had never decided the question, although Chief Justice JOHN MARSHALL in OBITER DICTUM in MCCULLOCH V. MARYLAND (1819) suggested that the power included construction. In the construction of the first of these roads, the Cumberland Road, Congress and the President adopted a working compromise by seeking the consent of the affected states prior to approval of the bill. Many other post roads were constructed following similar procedures. The Supreme Court ultimately put the question of construction authority to rest in *Kohl v. United States* (1876) by holding that the federal government may condemn land, by analogy to EMINENT DOMAIN, for a post office site.

Postal statutes and regulations grant police powers to the Postal Service, imposing rules designed to protect the public welfare and limiting mailability. Safety regulations (for example, mailability of poisons and explosives) and mechanical rules (size and packaging standard), have not been the subject of serious challenge. The statute imposing fines and imprisonment for mail fraud was held constitutional in *Public Clearing House v. Coyne* (1904) and several later cases. Other statutory determinations of nonmailability have similarly been upheld. *Ex parte Jackson* (1878) upheld a criminal conviction under a federal statute prohibiting mailing of newspapers containing advertisements for lotteries. In the late eighteenth and early nineteenth centuries, relying on *Jackson* and other holdings, Congress greatly expanded the exclusionary power to cover libelous matter, OBSCENITY, and the like, and these provisions remain a part of present law. The Supreme Court has repeatedly upheld the constitutionality of the congressional power to exclude obscene materials from the mails.

From 1872 until 1970, the Post Office was an executive department and the postmaster general had CABINET status. Prompted by heavy economic losses from Post Office operations, problems with postal deliveries, and charges of political inefficiency, Congress in 1970 created the United States Postal Service to take over the functions of the Post Office Department. Removing the operations of the Post Office (including appointment of the postmaster general) from direct political influence and granting to the Post Office a substantial degree of fiscal autonomy were among the major objects of the reorganization. The new Postal System is organized as a public CORPORATION, owned entirely by the federal government, under the management of a board of governors. The board appoints the postmaster general, who is the chief executive officer of the Postal Service, but is no longer a cabinet member. The board and the officers have wide discretion with respect to management, services, and expenditures, subject to congressional oversight. Postal rates, formerly established directly by Congress, are now determined by a presidentially appointed Postal Rate Commission on the basis of recommendations made by the board of governors.

STANLEY SIEGEL

Bibliography

JOHNSTON, JOSEPH F., JR. 1968 The United States Postal Monopoly. *Business Lawyer* 23:379–405.
PAUL, JAMES C. and SCHWARTZ, MURRAY L. 1961 *Federal Censorship: Obscenity in the Mail.* New York: Free Press.
PROJECT: POST OFFICE 1968 *Southern California Law Review* 41:643–727.

ROGERS, LINDSAY 1916 *The Postal Power of Congress.* Baltimore: Johns Hopkins University Press.

POUND, ROSCOE
(1870–1964)

Roscoe Pound was a prominent legal educator, a distinguished philosopher of law, and a prolific writer. His major contribution to American law was his formative role in the development of SOCIOLOGICAL JURISPRUDENCE. He elaborated this instrumentalist approach during the Progressive era, the spirit of which pervaded his writings. His thought had a conservative side to it, however, which became more influential in the latter stages of his life. He expressed this conservatism not only in his eulogies of the COMMON LAW but also in his criticism of the New Deal and the "service state," his indictment of administrative tribunals, and his fulminations against LEGAL REALISM.

Although Pound did not specialize in constitutional law, he promoted better understanding of the realities of the judicial process in this field through his critique of MECHANICAL JURISPRUDENCE, his explanation of the broad scope of judicial discretion and JUDICIAL POLICYMAKING, and his contrast between the "law in the books and the law in action." He was also a trenchant critic of the extreme individualism underlying numerous decisions of the Supreme Court well into the twentieth century.

The quality of Pound's voluminous writings, which spanned almost the entire *corpus juris,* varied substantially. His best scholarship consisted, in the main, of his influential articles on legal thought and reform published from 1905 to 1916. These works included "Liberty of Contract" (1909), which was one of his few publications to focus on constitutional questions. *The Spirit of the Common Law* (1921), *The Formative Era of American Law* (1938), and *The Development of Constitutional Guarantees of Liberty* (1957) are today his most useful books for students of constitutional law and history. His *Jurisprudence* (1959) was the most comprehensive statement of his legal philosophy.

WILFRID E. RUMBLE

Bibliography

WIGDOR, DAVID 1974 *Roscoe Pound.* Westport, Conn.: Greenwood Press.

POVERTY

See: Indigent; Wealth Discrimination

POWELL, LEWIS F.
(1907–   )

Lewis Franklin Powell, Jr., has always eluded conventional portraiture. In broad brush, Powell appears the archetypal conservative: a successful corporate lawyer, a director of eleven major companies, a pillar of Richmond, Virginia's civic and social life. The roll call of legal honors—president of the American Bar Association, the American College of Trial Lawyers, and the American Bar Foundation—does little to dispel the impression.

The portrait, however, needs serious refinement. During Virginia's "massive resistance," when the Byrd organization chose to close public schools rather than accept racial integration, Powell, as chairman of the Richmond Public School Board, fought successfully to keep Richmond's open. As vice-president of the National Legal Aid and Defender Society, he helped persuade the organized bar to support publicly financed legal services for the poor. Jean Camper Cahn, a black leader with whom he worked in that endeavor, found Powell "so curiously shy, so deeply sensitive to the hurt or embarrassment of another, so self-effacing that it is difficult to reconcile the public and private man—the honors and the acclaim with the gentle, courteous, sensitive spirit that one senses in every conversation, no matter how casual. . . ."

The portrait of the private practitioner parallels that of the Supreme Court Justice. The broad picture is again one of orthodox adherence to the canons of restraint. Powell labored diligently to limit the powers of the federal courts. He sought to narrow the STANDING of litigants invoking federal JURISDICTION to instances of actual injury in WARTH V. SELDIN (1975). He dissented when the Court in *Cannon v. University of Chicago* (1979) inferred from federal statutes a private cause of action. He greatly restricted the power of federal judges to review claims of unlawful SEARCH AND SEIZURE raised by state defendants in STONE V. POWELL (1976). And he urged the sharp curtailment of federal equitable remedies such as student BUSING for racial balance, in cases like KEYES V. DENVER SCHOOL DISTRICT #1 (1973).

While working to limit federal judicial power, Powell championed the power of others to operate free of constitutional strictures. Thus prosecutors should enjoy discretion in initiating prosecution, police and GRAND JURIES in pursuing EVIDENCE, trial judges in questioning jurors, welfare workers in terminating assistance, and military officers in conducting training.

The "hands-off" view applied especially to public education. Powell, a former member of the Virginia Board of Education, wrote the Court opinion preserving the rights of states to devise their own systems of public school finance in SAN ANTONIO SCHOOL DISTRICT V. RODRIGUEZ (1973). And the former chairman of the Richmond School Board spoke for the broad discretion of school authorities to administer student suspensions and corporal punishment, dissenting in GOSS V. LOPEZ (1975) and writing for the Court in INGRAHAM V. WRIGHT (1977).

Even so, a corner of the jurist's nature has been reserved for personal circumstances of particular poignancy. An early opinion afforded a black construction worker in Mississippi, father of nine, the opportunity to confront his accusers and establish his innocence in *Chambers v. Mississippi* (1973). Another Powell opinion, in MOORE V. EAST CLEVELAND (1977), voided a municipal housing ordinance that prevented an elderly woman from living with her adult sons and grandchildren. Another, SOLEM V. HELM (1983), held unconstitutional a life sentence without parole imposed by state courts on the perpetrator of seven nonviolent felonies. Even in the sacrosanct area of education, the Justice concurred in PLYLER V. DOE (1982) rather than leave children of illegal aliens "on the streets uneducated."

The cases of compassion are remarkable in one respect. Vindication of the individual claims meant overriding the most cherished of Powell's conservative tenets: the protection of state criminal judgments from meddlesome review on petition for federal writs of HABEAS CORPUS, and the recognition of only those rights tied closely to the constitutional text. Powell, plainly nervous about damaging these principles, narrowed the rulings almost to their actual facts. The cases thus testify both to a strength and a weakness in the jurist, the strength being that of an open mind and heart, the weakness being that of cautious case-by-case adjudication that leaves law bereft of general guidance and sure content.

The dichotomy between the cases of compassion and the towering doctrinal efforts of the school finance case (*Rodriguez*) and the search and seizure case (*Stone*) illustrates the different dimensions of the man himself. Powell, for example, privately deplored the arrogance of the national communications media and the maleficence of the criminal element. But he was, by nature, reserved, considerate, as eager to listen as to talk. Thus, even on subjects of strong feeling, the tempered judgment often triumphed. This quality marked his opinions dealing with the press. In a concurrence more libertarian than the Court opinion he joined in BRANZBURG V. HAYES (1972), Powell urged that "a proper balance" be struck on a "case-by-case basis" between the claims of newsmen to protect the confidentiality of sources and the need of grand juries for information relevant to criminal conduct. In GERTZ V. ROBERT WELSH INC. (1974), perhaps his most important opinion on the FIRST AMENDMENT, Powell balanced a plaintiff's interest in his good reputation against press freedoms, permitting private citizens to recover in libel on a standard less than "knowing or reckless falsehood" but greater than liability without fault. Balancing of individual and societal claims characterized Powell's opinions involving the rights of radical campus organizations, the unconventional use of national symbols, and even many criminal cases, where fact-specific rulings on the admissibility of suspect LINEUPS, for example, began to replace the per se EXCLUSIONARY RULES of the WARREN COURT.

Balancing does not permit confident forecasting of appellate outcomes. Case-by-case weighing of facts and circumstances can constitute a dangerous delegation of the Supreme Court's own authority on constitutional matters to trial judges, police and prosecutors, and potential litigants, all of whom capitalize on the uncertainty of law to work their own wills. But balancing suited Powell's preference for a devolution of authority and, in cases like GERTZ, achieved a thoughtful accommodation of competing interests.

In his most famous opinion, UNIVERSITY OF CALIFORNIA REGENTS V. BAKKE (1978), Powell, the balancer, struck a middle course on the flammable question of benign preferences based on race. The immediate question in *Bakke* was whether the medical school of the University of California at Davis could set aside sixteen of one hundred places in its entering class for preferred minorities. Eight Justices took polar positions. Four argued that Title VI of the CIVIL RIGHTS ACT OF 1964 prohibited any preference based on race. Four others contended that both the act and the constitution permitted the Davis program. Powell, the ninth and deciding Justice, alone sought to accommodate both the American belief in the primacy of the individual and the need to heal a history of oppression based on race.

It has become common to note that the Supreme Court under WARREN E. BURGER did not, as some feared, dismantle the activist legacy of the Warren Court. Many of the influential Justices, Powell, POTTER STEWART, and BYRON R. WHITE among them, were more pragmatic than ideological. Thus the Court trimmed here, expanded there, and approached complex questions cautiously. Powell's opinions exhibit, as much as those of any Justice, this Court's composite frame of mind. Like him, the Court he served has eluded conventional description.

J. HARVIE WILKINSON III

Bibliography

GUNTHER, GERALD 1972 In Search of Judicial Quality in a Changing Court: The Case of Justice Powell. *Stanford Law Review* 24:1001–1035.

HOWARD, A. E. DICK 1972 Mr. Justice Powell and the Emerging Nixon Majority. *Michigan Law Review* 70:445–468.

SYMPOSIUM 1977 [Justice Lewis F. Powell] *University of Richmond Law Review* 11:259–445.

SYMPOSIUM 1982 [Justice Lewis F. Powell] *Virginia Law Review* 68:161–458.

POWELL, THOMAS REED
(1880–1955)

Constitutional lawyer and political scientist Thomas Reed Powell taught for twenty-five years at Harvard Law School. He was a prolific writer of articles on constitutional law and especially on the issues of STATE TAXATION OF COMMERCE and INTERGOVERNMENTAL IMMUNITIES from taxation. His published analyses of constitutional DOCTRINES and Supreme Court decisions frequently influenced the future course of constitutional law, as, for example, in reducing the protection from taxation afforded by the ORIGINAL PACKAGE DOCTRINE. He was also a commentator on the activities of the Supreme Court: he was critical of its anti-New Deal decisions in the 1930s, of the proliferation of separate opinions in the 1940s, and of the prevalence of rhetorical excess over rigorous logic at all times. His last public lectures were published in 1956 as *Vagaries and Varieties in Constitutional Law.*

DENNIS J. MAHONEY

POWELL v. ALABAMA
287 U.S. 45 (1932)

Powell was the famous "Scottsboro boys" case in which "young, ignorant, illiterate blacks were convicted and sentenced to death without the effective appointment of counsel to aid them. The trials were in a hostile community, far from the defendants' homes; the accusation was rape of two white women, a crime "regarded with especial horror in the community."

In an early major use of the DUE PROCESS clause to regulate the administration of criminal justice by the states, the Supreme Court held that the trials were fundamentally unfair. The facts of the case made this portentous holding an easy one: the defendants were tried in one day, the defense was entirely pro forma, and the death sentence was immediately imposed on all seven defendants without regard to individual culpability or circumstance. *Powell* was not a Sixth Amendment RIGHT TO COUNSEL case; three decades would pass before that guarantee was imported into due process in GIDEON V. WAINWRIGHT (1963). But the language of the Court in expounding the importance of counsel to a fair trial was repeatedly quoted as the Sixth Amendment right developed: "[the layman] lacks both the skill and knowledge adequately to prepare his defense, even though he has a perfect one. He requires the guiding hand of counsel at every step in the proceedings against him. Without it, though he be not guilty, he faces the danger of conviction because he does not know how to establish his innocence."

Although *Powell* is usually cited as a case in which defendants had no counsel at all, there was actually a lawyer at their side, but he came late into the case and was unfamiliar with Alabama law. In discussing the failure of due process, the Court referred to the lack of investigation and consultation by this last-minute volunteer. Thus, *Powell* has implications for the developing doctrine of ineffective assistance of counsel.

BARBARA ALLEN BABCOCK

POWELL v. MCCORMACK
395 U.S. 486 (1969)

Adam Clayton Powell, Jr., a flamboyant clergyman of indifferent ethics, for many years represented a New York City district in Congress. In 1967, after Powell won reelection despite a conviction for criminal contempt of court and a record of misappropriation of public funds, the House of Representatives denied him a seat. In a special election, he received eighty-six percent of the votes and again appeared to take his seat. The House then passed a resolution "excluding" Powell.

Powell and thirteen of his constituents then sued Speaker John McCormack and several other officers of the House of Representatives. Powell lost in both the District Court and the Court of Appeals, and his case was not heard by the Supreme Court until after

the Ninetieth Congress had adjourned. Powell had, in the meanwhile, been reelected, and was seated as a member of the Ninety-First Congress.

The Supreme Court, in an 8–1 decision, declined to hold the case moot, finding that Powell's claim for back pay was sufficient for a justiciable controversy. In an opinion by Chief Justice EARL WARREN, the Court proceeded to overturn some long-standing assumptions about the constitutional status of CONGRESSIONAL MEMBERSHIP.

The Court held that the houses of Congress, although they are the judges of the qualifications provided in the Constitution itself (Article I, section 5) may not add to the qualifications provided in the Constitution (Article I, section 2). If a person elected to the House is qualified by age, CITIZENSHIP, and residence, he may not be excluded. Of course, once a member has been seated, he may be expelled by a two-thirds vote for any offense the House believes is "inconsistent with the trust and duty of a member" (*In re Chapman*, 1897). But, in Powell's case the Court held that exclusion was not equivalent to expulsion. (See POLITICAL QUESTIONS.)

DENNIS J. MAHONEY

POWELL v. PENNSYLVANIA

See: Waite Court

PRATT, CHARLES
(Lord Camden)
(1714–1794)

The leading Whig constitutionalist of eighteenth-century England, Charles Pratt was appointed a judge after a career as a barrister and parliamentarian and service as attorney general. Arguing SEDITIOUS LIBEL cases, he had maintained that the jury was competent to decide the questions both of law and of fact. He was Chief Justice of the Court of Common Pleas from 1762 until 1766. In the WILKES CASES he declared GENERAL WARRANTS contrary to the principles of the constitution and held their issuance by secretaries of state illegal. He also discouraged prosecution of Roman Catholic recusants. As Baron (later Earl) Camden, he made his first speech in the House of Lords in 1765 supporting the American position on the Stamp Act. In the debates on the Declaratory Act he called TAXATION WITHOUT REPRESENTATION "sheer robbery" and denounced the fiction of virtual representation. He became Lord Chancellor in 1766 but resigned in 1770 after disagreeing with the cabinet about several matters, including policy toward America. He continued to support the American position in the House of Lords and, with Lord Chatham, favored reconciliation with the colonies. He returned to the cabinet in 1782 and was Lord President of the Council from 1784 until his death.

DENNIS J. MAHONEY

PRAYER, SCHOOL

See: Religion in Public Schools

PREAMBLE

The part of the Constitution that we read first is the part of the original Constitution that was written last. The Preamble, which sets forth the noble purposes for which the Constitution is "ordained and established," was composed by the CONSTITUTIONAL CONVENTION's Committee of Style. The committee sat between September 8 and September 11, 1787, after the Convention had debated and voted on all of the substantive provisions of the Constitution; its mandate was to arrange and harmonize the wording of the resolutions adopted by the delegates during the preceding four months. The task of actually drafting the document fell to GOUVERNEUR MORRIS of New York, and so the authorship of the Preamble must be ascribed to him.

Morris made two major changes in the Preamble as it was reported by the Committee of Detail and referred to the Committee of Style. The earlier version had begun, "We, the people of the states of . . ." and then had listed the thirteen states in order, from north to south; Morris changed this to the now familiar "We, the people of the United States. . . ." And the earlier version had merely stated that the people ordained and established the Constitution; Morris added the list of purposes for which they did so. Each of these changes has been the occasion of some controversy.

The reference to the "people of the United States" was a source of irritation to the Anti-Federalists. PATRICK HENRY, for example, in the Virginia ratifying convention, denounced the use of the phrase as a harbinger of a national despotism. The Convention, he said, should have written instead, "We, the States. . . ." In ANTI-FEDERALIST CONSTITUTIONAL THOUGHT, only the states, as the existing political

units, to which the people had already delegated all the powers of government, could constitute a federal union and redelegate some of their powers to the national government. Reference to the constituent authority of "the people of the United States" seemed to imply consolidation, not confederation.

It is unlikely that Morris, the Committee of Style, or the Convention had any such implication in mind. The Convention had approved a preamble that referred to the people of all thirteen states. The committee had to "harmonize" that with the provision that the Constitution would become effective when it was ratified by any nine states. There would likely be a time, therefore, when there would be nine states in the Union and four outside of it; but no one could predict which would be the nine and which the four. So long as the Constitution would become effective with less than thirteen states in the Union, listing the thirteen states in the Preamble would be misleading and inaccurate. Whichever states did ratify the Constitution would be the "United States," and it would be the people of those "United States" that had ordained the Constitution. Moreover, the Constitution provided for the future admission of additional states, and the people of those states, too, would ordain and establish the Constitution.

But Henry's objection was ill-founded for another reason. The DECLARATION OF INDEPENDENCE had pronounced the Americans "one people" and had given to their political Union the name of the "United States of America." The states and the Union had been born together on July 4, 1776, when a new nation was brought forth upon this continent. The one people certainly possessed the right to alter or abolish their former government and to establish a new government more conducive to their future safety and happiness. "We, the people of the United States," are identical to the "one people" that in the Declaration of Independence dissolved the political bonds that formerly connected us to Great Britain.

The list of purposes for ordaining and establishing the Constitution is perhaps more perplexing. The Convention had never debated or voted on such a list; and yet each delegate must have had some such purposes in mind throughout the deliberations. How else could he have gauged or judged the propriety of the measures upon which he did debate and vote? Morris and the Committee of Style must have thought it fitting to provide this terse apologia for their summer's deliberations; and the delegates apparently agreed, for there is no record of any objection to the Preamble as it was reported by the committee.

The Preamble lists the purposes for which the Constitution was created: to form a more perfect Union, to establish justice, to insure domestic tranquillity, to provide for the common defense, to promote the general welfare, and to secure the blessings of liberty, not only for the founding generation but also for "posterity." It, in effect, declares to a candid world the causes for which the people have chosen to replace the ARTICLES OF CONFEDERATION with a new Constitution. The purposes listed in the Preamble are consistent with what the Declaration of Independence asserts to be the end of all governments instituted among men, namely to secure the equal and inalienable natural rights of all to life, liberty, and the pursuit of happiness.

The Preamble does not purport to create any offices or to confer any powers; as JOSEPH STORY later wrote, "Its true office is to expound the nature and extent and application of the powers actually conferred by the Constitution, and not substantially to create them." Although COMMENTATORS ON THE CONSTITUTION have, over the years, purported to find in the Preamble justification for the exercise of INHERENT POWERS of government, no court has ever held that the Preamble independently grants power to the government or to any of its officers or agencies. In fact, in *Jacobson v. Massachusetts* (1905), the Supreme Court specifically rejected that interpretation.

The Preamble concludes by proclaiming that the people "do ordain and establish this Constitution." EDWARD S. CORWIN correctly pointed to the active voice and present tense of this phrase. The act of constituting a government occurs at a particular moment in time; but the authority of the Constitution depends on the continuous consent of the governed. The people, as Corwin wrote, " 'do ordain and establish,' *not* did ordain and establish." Thus does the Preamble play its role in the preservation of constitutional government. An afterthought of the Constitutional Convention, a rhetorical flourish by the Committee of Style, the Preamble has been memorized by schoolchildren and declaimed by orators and statesmen on public occasions for two centuries. And every time it is recited it calls to mind the purposes of our federal Union and unites the people more firmly to the cause of republican liberty.

DENNIS J. MAHONEY

Bibliography

CORWIN, EDWARD S.   1920   *The Constitution and What It Means Today.* Princeton, N.J.: Princeton University Press.

EIDELBERG, PAUL   1968   *The Political Philosophy of the Constitution.* New York: Free Press.

ROSSITER, CLINTON   1966   *1787: The Grand Convention.* New York: Macmillan.

PRECEDENT

In MARBURY V. MADISON (1803) Chief Justice JOHN MARSHALL rested the legitimacy of JUDICIAL REVIEW of the constitutionality of legislation on the necessity for courts to "state what the law is" in particular cases. The implicit assumption is that the Constitution is law, and that the content of constitutional law is determinate—that it can be known and applied by judges. From the time of the nation's founding, lawyers and judges trained in the processes of the COMMON LAW have assumed that the law of the Constitution is to be found not only in the text of the document and the expectations of the Framers but also in judicial precedent: the opinions of judges on "what the law is," written in the course of deciding earlier cases. (See STARE DECISIS.)

Inevitably, issues that burned brightly for the Framers of the Constitution and of its various amendments have receded from politics into history. The broad language of much of the Constitution's text leaves open a wide range of choices concerning interpretation. As the body of judicial precedent has grown, it has taken on a life of its own; the very term "constitutional law," for most lawyers today, primarily calls to mind the interpretations of the Constitution contained in the Supreme Court's opinions. For a lawyer writing a brief, or a judge writing an opinion, the natural style of argumentation is the common law style, with appeals to one or another "authority" among the competing analogies offered by a large and still growing body of precedent.

The same considerations that support reliance on precedent in common law decisions apply in constitutional adjudications: the need for stability in the law and for evenhanded treatment of litigants. Yet adherence to precedent has also been called the control of the living by the dead. Earlier interpretations of the Constitution, when they seem to have little relevance to the conditions of society and government here and now, do give way. As Chief Justice EARL WARREN wrote in BROWN V. BOARD OF EDUCATION (1954), "In approaching [the problem of school SEGREGATION], we cannot turn the clock back to 1868 when the [FOURTEENTH] AMENDMENT was adopted, or even to 1896 when PLESSY [V. FERGUSON] was written. We must consider public education in the light of its full development and its present place in American life. . . ." Justice OLIVER WENDELL HOLMES put the matter more pungently: "It is revolting to have no better reason for a rule of law than that so it was laid down in the time of Henry IV."

Although the Supreme Court decides only those issues that come to it in the ordinary course of litigation, the Court has a large measure of control over its own doctrinal agenda. The selection of about 150 cases for review each year (out of more than 4,000 cases brought to the Court) is influenced most of all by the Justices' views of the importance of the issues presented. (See CERTIORARI, WRIT OF.) And when the Court does break new doctrinal ground, it invites further litigation to explore the area thus opened. For example, scores of lawsuits were filed all over the country once the Court had established the precedent, in BAKER V. CARR (1962), that the problem of legislative REAPPORTIONMENT was one that the courts could properly address. The Justices see themselves, and are seen by the Court's commentators, as being in the business of developing constitutional DOCTRINE through the system of precedent. The decision of particular litigants' cases today appears to be important mainly as an instrument to those lawmaking ends. The theory of *Marbury v. Madison,* in other words, has been turned upside down.

Lower court judges pay meticulous attention to Supreme Court opinions as their main source of guidance for decision in constitutional cases. Supreme Court Justices themselves, however, give precedent a force that is weaker in constitutional cases than in other areas of the law. In a famous expression of this view, Justice LOUIS D. BRANDEIS, dissenting in *Burnet v. Coronado Oil & Gas Co.* (1932), said, "in cases involving the Federal Constitution, where correction through legislative action is practically impossible, this court has often overruled its earlier decisions. The court bows to the lessons of experience and the force of better reasoning, recognizing that the process of trial and error, so fruitful in the physical sciences, is appropriate also in the judicial function."

Although this sentiment is widely shared, Justices often are prepared to defer to their reading of precedent even when they disagree with the conclusions that produced the earlier decisions. Justice JOHN MARSHALL HARLAN, for example, regularly accepted the authoritative force of WARREN COURT opinions from which he had dissented vigorously. The Court as an institution occasionally takes the same course, making clear that it is following the specific dictates of an earlier decision because of the interest in stability of the law, even though that decision may be out of line with more recent doctrinal developments.

The Supreme Court is regularly criticized, both from within the Court and from the outside, for failing to follow precedent. But a thoroughgoing consistency of decision cannot be expected, given the combination of three characteristics of the Court's decisional process. First, the Court is a collegiate body, with the nine Justices exercising individual judgment on each case. Second, the body of precedent is now enormous, with the result that in most cases decided by the Court there are arguable precedents for several alternative doctrinal approaches, and even for reaching opposing results. Indeed, the system for selecting cases for review guarantees that the court will regularly face hard cases—cases that are difficult because they can plausibly be decided in more than one way. Finally, deference to precedent itself may mean that issues will be decided differently, depending on the order in which they come before the Court. The Court's decision in *In re Griffiths* (1973), that a state cannot constitutionally limit the practice of law to United States citizens, is still a good precedent; yet, if the case had come up in 1983, almost certainly it would have been decided differently. (See ALIENS.)

The result of this process is an increasingly fragmented Supreme Court, with more PLURALITY OPINIONS and more statements by individual Justices of their own separate views in CONCURRING OPINIONS and dissents—thus presenting an even greater range of materials on which Justices can draw in deciding the next case. In these circumstances, it is not surprising that some plurality opinions, such as that in MOORE V. CITY OF EAST CLEVELAND (1977), are regularly cited as if they had a precedent value equal to that of OPINIONS OF THE COURT.

The range of decisional choice offered to a Supreme Court Justice by this process is so wide as to call into the question the idea of principled decision on which the legitimacy of judicial review is commonly assumed to rest. Yet the hard cases that fill the Supreme Court's docket—the very cases that make constitutional law and thus fill the casebooks that law students study—do not typify the functioning of constitutional law. A great many controversies of constitutional dimension never get to court, because the law seems clear, on the basis of precedent; similarly, many cases that do get to court are easily decided in the lower courts. Although we celebrate the memory of our creative Justices—Justices who are remembered for setting precedent, not following it—the body of constitutional law remains remarkably stable. In a stable society it could not be otherwise. As Holmes himself said in another context, "historic continuity with the past is not a duty, it is only a necessity."

KENNETH L. KARST

Bibliography

EASTERBROOK, FRANK H.   1982   Ways of Criticizing the Court. *Harvard Law Review* 95:802–832.

LEVI, EDWARD H.   1949   *An Introduction to Legal Reasoning*. Chicago: University of Chicago Press.

LLEWELLYN, KARL N.   1960   *The Common Law Tradition*. Boston: Little, Brown.

MONAGHAN, HENRY P.   1979   Taking Supreme Court Opinions Seriously. *Maryland Law Review* 39:1–26.

PREEMPTION

The SUPREMACY CLAUSE of the Constitution (Article VI, clause 2) requires that inconsistent state laws yield to valid federal laws. Preemption is the term applied to describe invalidation of state laws by superior federal law.

Strictly speaking, the issue of preemption is not one of constitutional law. The issue is not what Congress has the power to do, but what Congress has done. Where Congress has made an articulate decision whether particular state laws should survive a new scheme of federal regulation, the issue is settled. For example, in enacting minimum federal standards for automobile pollution control equipment in 1967, Congress prohibited states from enforcing more restrictive standards but made an exception for the State of California. There has been no need for litigation to mark the contours of preemption in that context. Insofar as there is a "doctrine" of preemption, it concerns the treatment of preemption by federal laws where Congress has ignored the issue.

Since preemption cases theoretically turn on construction of federal statutes to determine whether Congress intended to preempt state laws, there are limits to generalizations that can be drawn from the decisions. Each case construes a federal statute with a distinct regulatory structure and legislative history. It is particularly difficult to classify the simplest form of preemption cases—those where the claim is made that the terms of federal and state law are flatly inconsistent. Federal law may, for example, give express permission to engage in conduct prohibited by state law. An early famous case of this type was GIBBONS V. OGDEN (1824).

The most complex issues of preemption arise where it is concededly possible to comply with mandates of both state and federal law. The question then arises whether Congress intended to "occupy the field," or whether the challenged state law's enforcement would interfere inordinately with the policies of the federal law. State law may provide additional sanctions for conduct prohibited by federal law. (In *California v. Zook,* 1949, the Court sustained a state law that punished interstate motor transport operating without a federal permit.) State law may impose more stringent regulations than federal law. (In *Napier v. Atlantic Coast Line R.R.,* 1926, the Court held that a state law requiring railroad safety equipment was preempted by a federal law that required less equipment.) Finally, it may be argued that state law is, in some general way, inconsistent with the purposes of federal law. (In *New York Telephone Co. v. New York State Department of Labor,* 1979, the Court sustained state payment of unemployment compensation benefits to strikers as not inconsistent with the policy of free COLLECTIVE BARGAINING under federal labor law.)

The Court has announced general tests for determining whether Congress has "occupied the field." An often-quoted summary of the standards for finding congressional intent to preempt state law is contained in *Rice v. Santa Fe Elevator Corp.* (1947). "The scheme of federal regulation may be so pervasive as to make reasonable the inference that Congress left no room for the States to supplement it. . . . Or the Act of Congress may touch a field in which the federal interest is so dominant that the federal system will be assumed to preclude enforcement of state laws on the same subject. . . . Or the state policy may produce a result inconsistent with the objective of the federal statute." These standards are peculiarly devoid of content, as the Court admitted in the sentence following those just quoted: "It is often a perplexing question whether Congress has precluded state action or by the choice of selective regulatory measures has left the POLICE POWER of the States undisturbed except as the state and federal regulations collide."

The lack of any pattern to the preemption cases can be explained in that each case seeks to ascertain congressional intent in a unique context. Since, however, contentious preemption questions arise precisely because Congress has ignored the existence of related state laws, the "intent of Congress" is a fiction that fails to describe the Court's decision process. The controlling factors in judicial decision are similar to those that would have confronted the intelligent legislator who had grappled with them. The judges' social values, views as to the legislative wisdom of the federal and state laws, and general views of the federal system may be as decisive as technical consideration of how well the federal and state schemes would mesh.

In many cases, there are potential issues of constitutional validity of the challenged state law in addition to the preemption question. Some preemption decisions can be explained as a part of the Court's general practice of avoiding unnecessary constitutional questions. Often, the preemption question is decided, articulately or *sub silentio*, by the same criteria that would have governed the avoided constitutional question. The preemption doctrine may be preferred by the Court because the judicial decision striking down a state law is tentative, and congressional attention is invited to the issue. If Congress does nothing, the issue is avoided. If Congress makes an articulate choice to withdraw the preemption barrier, the inescapable constitutional question benefits from the additional data supplied by congressional decision. A final attraction of the preemption rationale, beyond the tentativeness of a preemption decision, may be that each decision can be truly ad hoc, resting on a fictional finding of congressional intent to preempt that governs only the particular federal statutory scheme before the Court.

WILLIAM COHEN

Bibliography

COHEN, WILLIAM 1982 Congressional Power to Define State Power to Regulate Commerce: Consent and Preemption. Pages 523–547 in Terrance Sandalow and Eric Stein, eds., *Courts and Free Markets: Perspectives from the United States and Europe.* Oxford: Clarendon Press.

CRAMTOM, ROGER 1956 Pennsylvania v. Nelson: A Case Study in Federal Preemption. *University of Chicago Law Review* 26:85–108.

PREFERRED FREEDOMS

Because FIRST AMENDMENT freedoms rank at the top of the hierarchy of constitutional values, any legislation that explicitly limits those freedoms must be denied the usual presumption of constitutionality and be subjected to STRICT SCRUTINY by the judiciary. So went the earliest version of the preferred freedoms doctrine, sometimes called the preferred position or preferred status doctrine. It probably originated in the opinions of Justice OLIVER WENDELL HOLMES, at least implicitly. He believed that a presumption of constitutionality attached to ECONOMIC REGULATION, which needed to meet merely a RATIONAL BASIS test, as he explained dissenting in LOCHNER V. NEW YORK (1905). By contrast, in ABRAMS V. UNITED STATES (1919) he adopted the CLEAR AND PRESENT DANGER test as a constitutional yardstick for legislation such as the ESPIONAGE ACT OF 1917 or state CRIMINAL SYNDICALISM statutes, which limited FREEDOM OF SPEECH.

Justice BENJAMIN N. CARDOZO first suggested a more general hierarchy of constitutional rights in PALKO V. CONNECTICUT (1937), in a major opinion on the INCORPORATION DOCTRINE. He ranked at the top those "fundamental principles of liberty and justice which lie at the base of all our civil and political institutions." He tried to distinguish rights that might be lost without risking the essentials of liberty and justice from rights which he called "the matrix, the indispensable condition, of nearly every other form of freedom." These FUNDAMENTAL RIGHTS came to be regarded as the preferred freedoms. A year later Justice HARLAN F. STONE, in footnote four of his opinion in UNITED STATES V. CAROLENE PRODUCTS (1938), observed that "legislation which restricts the political processes" might "be subjected to more exacting judicial scrutiny" than other legislation. He suggested, too, that the judiciary might accord particularly searching examination of statutes reflecting "prejudice against DISCRETE AND INSULAR MINORITIES."

The First Amendment freedoms initially enjoyed a primacy above all others. Justice WILLIAM O. DOUGLAS for the Court in MURDOCK V. PENNSYLVANIA (1943) expressly stated: "FREEDOM OF THE PRESS, freedom of speech, FREEDOM OF RELIGION are in a preferred position." In the 1940s, despite bitter divisions on the Court over the question whether constitutional rights should be ranked, as well as the question whether the Court should ever deny the presumption of constitutionality, a majority of Justices continued to endorse the doctrine. Justice WILEY B. RUTLEDGE for the Court gave it its fullest exposition in *Thomas v. Collins* (1945). Justice FELIX FRANKFURTER, who led the opposition to the doctrine, called it "mischievous" in KOVACS V. COOPER (1949); he especially disliked the implication that "any law touching communication" might be "infected with presumptive invalidity." Yet even Frankfurter, in his *Kovacs* opinion, acknowledged that "those liberties . . . which history has established as the indispensable conditions of an open as against a closed society come to the Court with a momentum for respect lacking when appeal is made to liberties which derive merely from shifting economic arrangements."

The deaths of Murphy and Rutledge in 1949 and their replacement by TOM C. CLARK and SHERMAN MINTON shifted the balance of judicial power to the Frankfurter viewpoint. Thereafter little was heard about the doctrine. The WARREN COURT vigorously defended not only CIVIL LIBERTIES but CIVIL RIGHTS and the rights of the criminally accused. The expansion of the incorporation doctrine and of the concept of EQUAL PROTECTION OF THE LAWS in the 1960s produced a new spectrum of FUNDAMENTAL INTERESTS demanding special judicial protection. Free speech, press, and religion continued, nevertheless, to be ranked, at least implicitly, as very special in character and possessing a symbolic "firstness," to use EDMOND CAHN's apt term. Although the Court rarely speaks of a preferred freedoms doctrine today, the substance of the doctrine has been absorbed in the concepts of strict scrutiny, fundamental rights, and selective incorporation.

LEONARD W. LEVY

Bibliography
MCKAY, ROBERT B. 1959 The Preference for Freedom. *New York University Law Review* 34:1184–1227.

PRESENTMENT

A presentment is a written accusation of criminal offense prepared, signed, and presented to the prosecutor by the members of a GRAND JURY, acting on their own initiative rather than in response to a bill of INDICTMENT brought before them by the government. By returning a presentment, the grand jury forces the prosecutor to indict. The presentment procedure permits the grand jury to circumvent prosecutorial inertia or recalcitrance to initiate criminal proceedings. The grand jury's presentment power originated long before there were government prosecutors. The presentment is a descendant of the grand jury's original function: to initiate criminal proceedings by accusing those whom the grand jurors knew to have reputedly committed offenses.

CHARLES H. WHITEBREAD

Bibliography
TESLIK, W. RANDOLPH 1975 *Prosecutorial Discretion: The Decision to Charge.* Washington, D.C.: National Criminal Justice Reference Service.

PRESIDENTIAL ELECTION CAMPAIGN FUND ACT

See: Federal Election Campaign Acts

PRESIDENTIAL ORDINANCE-MAKING POWER

As a means of carrying out constitutional and statutory duties, Presidents issue regulations, proclamations, and EXECUTIVE ORDERS. Although this exercise of legislative power by the President appears to contradict the doctrine of SEPARATION OF POWERS, the scope of administrative legislation has remained broad. Rules and regulations, as the Supreme Court noted in *United States v. Eliason* (1842), "must be received as the acts of the executive, and as such, be binding upon all within the sphere of his legal and constitutional authority."

It is established DOCTRINE that "the authority to prescribe rules and regulations is not the power to make laws, for no such power can be delegated by the Congress," as a federal court of appeals declared in *Lincoln Electric Co. v. Commissioner of Internal Revenue* (1951). Nevertheless, vague grants of delegated authority by Congress give administrators substantial discretion to make federal policy. Over a twelve-month period from 1933 to 1934 the National Recovery Administration issued 2,998 orders. This flood of rule-making activity was not collected and published in one place, leaving even executive officials in doubt about applicable regulations.

Legislation in 1935 provided for the custody of federal documents and their publication in a "Federal Register." The Administrative Procedure Act of 1946 established uniform standards for rule-making, including notice to the parties concerned and an opportunity for public participation. Recent Presidents, especially GERALD FORD, JIMMY CARTER, and RONALD REAGAN, have attempted to monitor and control the impact of agency regulations on the private sector.

Proclamations are a second instrument of administrative legislation. Sometimes they are hortatory in character, without legislative effect, such as proclamations for Law Day. Other proclamations have substantive effects, especially when used to regulate international trade on the basis of broad grants of statutory authority. Still other proclamations have been issued solely on the President's constitutional authority, as with pardons and AMNESTIES and ABRAHAM LINCOLN's proclamations in April 1861. When a statute prescribes a specific procedure in an area reserved to Congress and the President follows a different course, proclamations are illegal and void.

From ancient times a proclamation was literally a public notice, whether by trumpet, voice, print, or posting. Yet in 1873 the Supreme Court in *Lapeyre v. United States* declared that a proclamation by the President became a valid instrument of federal law from the moment it was signed and deposited in the office of the secretary of state, even though not published. These early proclamations eventually found their way into the *Statutes at Large*, but not until the Federal Register Act of 1935 did Congress require the prompt publication of all proclamations and executive orders that have general applicability and legal effect.

Executive orders are a third source of ordinance-making power. They draw upon the constitutional power of the President or powers expressly delegated by Congress. Especially bold were the orders of President FRANKLIN D. ROOSEVELT from 1941 to 1943; without any statutory authority he seized plants, mines, and companies. Actions that exceed legal bounds have been struck down by the courts, a major example being the Steel Seizure Case (YOUNGSTOWN SHEET AND TUBE CO. V. SAWYER, 1952). Executive orders cannot supersede a statute or override contradictory congressional expressions.

Congress has used its power of the purse to circumscribe executive orders. After President RICHARD M. NIXON issued executive order 11605 in 1971, rejuvenating the SUBVERSIVE ACTIVITIES CONTROL BOARD, Congress reduced the agency's budget and expressly prohibited it from using any of the funds to implement the President's order. Congress has also prevented the President from using appropriated funds to finance agencies created solely by executive order.

LOUIS FISHER

Bibliography
FLEISHMAN, JOEL L. and AUFSES, ARTHUR H.   1976 Law and Orders: The Problem of Presidential Legislation. *Law and Contemporary Problems* 40:1–45.
HART, JAMES   1925   *The Ordinance Making Powers of the President of the United States.* Baltimore: Johns Hopkins University Press. [Reprinted in 1970 by Da Capo Press.]

PRESIDENTIAL POWERS

The powers of the American presidency are amorphous and enormous. Perhaps they can be defined only by saying that they are made adequate to the problems to which the power is addressed. Although these powers purportedly derive from the specifications of the Constitution itself, in fact their definition is to be found in the behavior of the American Presidents since 1789. During this time the executive branch, largely with the acquiescence of Congress and the encouragement of the Supreme Court, has come to resemble the monolithic authority to be found in governments that have succeeded to the authority of czars and emperors. LIMITED GOVERNMENT is now constitutionally limited only by the first eight Amendments and Article I, section 9, and even then only at the discretion of the Supreme Court.

The reason for the accumulation of power in the presidency is not hard to find. Power goes to the official who can use it. It is easy for the President to be that official because, as Justice ROBERT H. JACKSON wrote in YOUNGSTOWN SHEET & TUBE CO. V. SAWYER (1952):

Executive power has the advantage of concentration in a single head in whose choice the whole Nation has a part, making him the focus of public hopes and expectations. In drama, magnitude and finality his decisions so far overshadow any others that almost alone he fills the public eye and ear. No other personality in public life can begin to compete with him in access to the public mind through modern methods of communications. By his prestige as head of state and his influence upon public opinion he exerts a leverage upon those who are supposed to check and balance his power which often cancels their effectiveness.

The doctrine of SEPARATION OF POWERS, not to be found in terms in the Constitution, has receded to the vanishing point so far as the presidency is concerned. And the principle of CHECKS AND BALANCES, intrinsic in the Constitution as a whole, has also been diminished when it comes to putting restraints on the President.

Essentially there are two conflicting theses on the powers of American Presidents, depending in large part on whether it is believed that the opening words of the Second Article: "The Executive power shall be vested in a President of the United States," is itself a grant of power or, as was the case with Articles I and III, is simply a designation of the office with the powers of that official to be found in the provisions that followed. In sum, the question is whether everything that comes after the first sentence in Article II is a redundancy so far as presidential powers are concerned. A reading of the origins of the article would clearly deflate the concept of a presidency replete with the royal prerogatives that the nation had so roundly condemned in the DECLARATION OF INDEPENDENCE itself.

Even the view taken by THEODORE ROOSEVELT, however, is not so broad as to leave no need for separation of powers. Roosevelt asserted "that the executive power was limited only by specific restrictions and prohibitions appearing in the Constitution or imposed by Congress under its Constitutional powers." Roosevelt's immediate successor in office, WILLIAM HOWARD TAFT, had espoused a different reading: "The true view of the executive function is . . . that the President can exercise no power which cannot be fairly and reasonably traced to some specific grant of power or justly implied and included within such grant as proper and necessary." Taft's was the better reading of the origins of the constitutional provisions, although even he later turned to the Roosevelt reading when he was on the Supreme Court. But Roosevelt's was the better reading of the history of the presidency and a better prediction of what the presidency was to become.

The last important Supreme Court opinion on presidential powers, perhaps because it was one of the few outside the area of CIVIL LIBERTIES that rejected a presidential reach for power beyond his grasp, came in 1952 in the Steel Seizure Case. There the Court was thoroughly divided. The dissenters, led by Chief Justice FRED M. VINSON, read the INHERENT POWERS of the presidency as all but limitless, in keeping with the construction given by most political scientists. Justice HUGO L. BLACK went to the other extreme in his opinion for the Court. For him the chief magistrate had only those powers specifically provided by the terms of the Constitution and those powers properly conferred upon him by Congress. But of all the opinions in *Youngstown*, the one most often looked to by constitutional lawyers, including those sitting on the Court, has been that of Justice Robert H. Jackson, for whom there was no plain rule but rather a sliding scale:

1. When the President acts pursuant to an express or implied authorization of Congress, his authority is at its maximum, for it includes all that he possesses in his own right plus all that Congress can delegate. . . .

2. When the President acts in absence of either a congressional grant or denial of authority, he can only rely upon his own independent powers, but there is a zone of twilight in which he and Congress may have concurrent authority, or in which its distribution is uncertain. Therefore, congressional inertia, indifference or quiescence may sometimes, at least as a practical matter, enable, if not invite, measures of independent presidential responsibility. In this area, any test of power is likely to depend on the imperative of events and contemporary imponderables rather than on abstract theories of law.

3. When the President takes measures incompatible with the express or implied will of Congress, his power is at its lowest ebb, for then he can rely only upon its constitutional powers minus any constitutional powers of Congress over the matter. . . . Presidential claim to a power at once so conclusive and preclusive must be scrutinized with caution, for what is at stake is the equilibrium established by our constitutional system.

Jackson concluded his opinion, saying: "With all its defects, delays and inconveniences, men have discovered no technique for long preserving free government except that the Executive be under the law, and that the law be made by parliamentary deliberations. Such institutions may be destined to pass away.

But it is the duty of the Court to be the last, not first, to give them up."

The concept of the RULE OF LAW continues to diminish as the nation embraces first the description in CLINTON ROSSITER's *Constitutional Dictatorship*, and then that of Arthur Schlesinger in his *Imperial Presidency*. We continue, however, to parse the sentences of the Constitution in order to justify or oppose presidential authority. But there is less reality in this exercise as each day succeeds the next.

The catalogue of presidential powers specifically stated in the Constitution is neither long nor extensive. He is given a conditional power of veto of all legislation, subject to being overridden by a two-thirds vote of each house. The remainder of his powers are specified in Article II, section 7: he is to be COMMANDER-IN-CHIEF of the armed forces, including the militia when in the service of the United States; he may require opinions from his principal cabinet officers; he may grant pardons and reprieves for offenders against the national laws; he may enter into TREATIES with foreign nations with the ADVICE AND CONSENT of two-thirds of the Senate; he is to nominate ambassadors, ministers, and consuls, members of the Supreme Court, and such other officers as are not otherwise provided for by the Constitution, plus such other officers as Congress shall provide; he may fill vacancies while the Senate is not in session; he shall address Congress on the state of the union and recommend the passage of measures he deems necessary and expedient; he may convene Congress and adjourn it when the two houses do not agree on adjournment; he shall receive ambassadors and other public ministers from foreign countries; "he shall take Care that the Laws be faithfully executed"; and he shall commission all officers of the United States. In fact, however, these bare bones of presidential authority have had much meat placed on them by presidential practices, by legislative delegation, and by judicial approval. It can hardly be gainsaid that the authors of the constitutional language would be much surprised were they to return to the scene to see what it is said that they have wrought.

The slivers of presidential power specifically authorized by the Constitution have been bundled like fasces to create huge authority in the President under the banners of FOREIGN AFFAIRS powers; WAR POWERS; fiscal powers; legislative powers and administrative powers. None of these rests exclusively on any specific authority granted by the Constitution but rather on combinations and permutations of them combined with "intrinsic" or "necessary and proper" powers, although the NECESSARY AND PROPER

CLAUSE itself was a grant only to the legislative branch.

Probably the most extensive, and perhaps the most important, of the modern President's powers is to be found in his hegemony over the nation's foreign relations. As Archibald Cox has written: "The United States' assumption of a leading role in world affairs built up the presidency by focussing world attention upon the president. The constitution, combined with necessity, gives the president greater personal authority in foreign affairs than domestic matters. A succession of presidents pushed these powers to, and sometimes beyond, their limits. The personal manner in which they conducted international relations doubtless influenced their style in dealing with domestic matters." But it has been "necessity," not the Constitution, that vested this great personal power in the President. There are only two plausible grounds in the Constitution for great presidential authority in the area of foreign relations. It is he who names and receives ambassadors, which was early construed to mean that he was the sole spokesman of the nation with regard to foreign nations. It is he who is charged with the negotiation of treaties. But both in the appointment of ambassadors and in the making of treaties, the Founders required the collaboration of the Senate: a majority vote of acquiescence in the case of ambassadors and a two-thirds vote of the Senate to validate a treaty.

What the Constitution did not give the President by way of powers in this area, he has been given by Congress or he has taken for himself, and what he has taken for himself has generally been legitimated by Supreme Court decision. Much of relations with foreign nations that was committed to Congress—for example, the power over FOREIGN COMMERCE, the war-making authority—has become irrelevant to the modern Constitution. For the Supreme Court has declared that the powers over foreign affairs that are the President's do not derive from the Constitution but rather are a direct inheritance from the Crown of England. In UNITED STATES V. CURTISS-WRIGHT EXPORT CORP. (1936) the Court said: "As a result of the separation from Great Britain by the colonies acting as a unit, the powers of external SOVEREIGNTY passed from the Crown not to the colonies severally, but to the colonies in their collective and corporate capacity as the United States. . . . Sovereignty is never held in suspense. When, therefore, the external sovereignty of Great Britain in respect to the colonies ceased, it immediately passed to the Union." Not only did this power inhere in the Union; it belonged directly to the President, although where it was before

there was a President is not made clear. But, said the Court, it did not come through the Constitution or the Congress. It is a "very delicate, plenary and exclusive power of the President as the sole organ of the federal government in the field of international relations—a power which does not require as a basis for its exercise an act of Congress." It is somewhat strange, if the foreign relations power never belonged to the states, that the Founders thought it necessary to take it from them in the specific words of Article I, section 10: "No state shall enter into any treaty, alliance, or confederation; grant LETTERS OF MARQUE AND REPRISAL; . . . No state shall, without the consent of Congress . . . keep troops, or ships of war in time of peace, enter into any agreement or compact with another state, or with a foreign power, or engage in war, unless actually invaded. . . ." It is strange, too, that Congress can consent to the exercise of foreign affairs powers by the states, if that power properly belongs exclusively to the President.

The coalescence of this power over foreign relations solely in the President has also had the effect of eliminating specific checks on him by the Senate. The Constitution clearly gives the power to negotiate treaties to the President, but it requires the consent of two-thirds of the Senate to validate a treaty. The requirement of Senate approval has often proved a stumbling block, as it was when the Senate refused to consent to the United States' entry into the League of Nations and when the Senate imposed qualifications on the treaty ceding the Panama Canal Zone back to Panama. But the President and the Supreme Court have found a way out of some of these restraints. An agreement with a foreign nation may be called an EXECUTIVE AGREEMENT rather than a "treaty," and an "executive agreement" does not require Senate approval, according to the decisions in UNITED STATES V. BELMONT (1937) and UNITED STATES V. PINK (1942). There is no guide, however, to say what the province of a treaty may be to distinguish it from that of an executive agreement. The justification for evading presidential responsibility to the Senate is, however, often founded on the ground that effectuation of such agreements usually requires congressional legislation, and a majority of both houses is said to be as good as or better than two-thirds of the Senate in ratifying the presidential action and easier to secure.

It has been argued, but not very cogently, that the foreign affairs powers of the President somehow derive from the Commander-in-Chief Clause of Article II. ALEXANDER HAMILTON's explanation of that provision in THE FEDERALIST #69 as to the limited authority of the commander-in-chief still seems to be the better understanding of it: "It would amount to nothing more than the supreme command and direction of the military and naval forces, as first General and Admiral of the Confederacy."

The foreign affairs powers of the President are as broad as they have become not because of constitutional delegation but because of the exigencies that have caused the Presidents to seize the power to meet the problems. Neither the public nor the Congress has shown much aversion to this presidential usurpation.

Presidential war powers, like presidential foreign affairs powers, rest on practice and precedent rather than on constitutional authorization. Thus, despite the provision of Article 1, section 8, giving Congress the power to declare war, wars have tended to be a consequence of executive action, sometimes confirmed by a congressional DECLARATION OF WAR and sometimes carried on without one. Five times in American history, Congress has declared war: the War of 1812, the Mexican War of 1848, the Spanish American War of 1898, and World Wars I (1917) and II (1941). Each time American military and naval forces had been committed to action before the actual declaration took place. In most instances when military forces have been engaged against foreign powers there has been no declaration of war even when the conflict reached such vast scales as the country's commitments to the KOREAN WAR and VIETNAM WAR. It has been argued that there were de facto declarations in such instances as Korea and Vietnam by congressional silence or appropriations for the military, but that was not what the Founders had in mind. For them war was thought too serious a matter to be left to generals and Presidents.

Congress has come up with a statute attempting to resolve the problem of presidential usurpation of the war power. The WAR POWERS RESOLUTION of 1973 provides that a President can order military action without a declaration of war by Congress, but he must inform Congress within forty-eight hours of doing so. Troops cannot be committed for more than sixty days except when Congress so authorizes, and Congress is empowered to order an immediate withdrawal of American forces by CONCURRENT RESOLUTION not subject to presidential veto. The statute is of dubious constitutional validity, giving presidential powers to Congress and congressional powers to the President. It is not likely to be the subject of a successful court test, for courts cannot act expeditiously enough nor can they effectuate a decree against the will of either of the other branches.

The essential fact is that the Constitution gives to Congress the power to declare war, to raise and support the armed forces, to make rules for the governance of the armed forces, to call up the militia, and to regulate it. It gives to the President the powers of commander-in-chief, which is only an authority to act in command of the military services so that no mere military officer shall be without civilian oversight.

The greater problem with presidential war powers is whether they enhance his authority over domestic civilian affairs. The Court has tended to sustain extraordinarily broad powers for the executive during the course of a war, as in the JAPANESE AMERICAN CASES (1943–1944), allowing relocation of native and foreign-born Japanese from the West Coast into concentration camps. When war has ended, the Court tends to look more dubiously on executive war powers, holding in DUNCAN v. KAHANOMOKU (1946), for example, that it was an abuse of authority to declare martial law in Hawaii on the day after the Japanese bombed Pearl Harbor. So far as civilian activities are concerned, it is said that war does not give the executive any new powers but simply justifies the use of granted powers reserved for emergencies. The fact is that, in contemporary times, Congress has provided the President with more EMERGENCY POWERS than he ever has occasion to use, generally leaving to him the discretion to determine whether an emergency warrants calling such powers into play. The concept of emergency powers, itself nowhere to be found in the Constitution, has long since expanded beyond the realms of war powers to justify presidential action in the economic and social realm as well as in the areas of military combat and foreign affairs. The confiscation of Iranian assets in the United States to ransom American captives from the Iranians in 1980 affords an example of the extension of presidential authority far beyond what the Constitution provided; but in DAMES & MOORE v. REGAN (1981) the flimsiest statutory delegation was held sufficient to justify the President's actions.

The Constitution gave the President no powers over the national fisc. It was very clear at the CONSTITUTIONAL CONVENTION OF 1787 that the authority over national finance—what went into the national purse and what came out of it—belonged to Congress and Congress alone, subject, of course, to the presidential power of veto. Article 1, section 7, commands that the House of Representatives alone shall originate revenue measures. Article 1, section 8, gives to the Congress the "power to lay and collect taxes," "to pay the debts," "to borrow money," "to coin money," and to punish counterfeiting. And Article 1, section 9, clause 7, provides that "no money shall be drawn from the Treasury, but in consequence of appropriations made by law." If any principle of responsible government can be said to have been derived from the Glorious Revolution of 1688 in England and the American Revolution, it is that a popularly elected legislature is the only safe place in which to place the power of the purse.

This is not to deny that at all times in our history the executive branch has played a more or less important role in the creation and effectuation of fiscal policy, from the roles of Secretaries of the Treasury Hamilton and ALBERT GALLATIN and ANDREW JACKSON's war on the BANK OF THE UNITED STATES to contemporary times when it would appear that the executive is dominant and Congress subordinate with regard to all the fiscal powers that the Constitution gave to the Congress. But the role of the executive branch has essentially been defined by the Congress. If the executive power is now so great in fiscal matters, the reason is not that the Constitution has conferred the power on the President but that Congress has done so. Thus, one frustrating restraint on presidential fiscal policy derives from the autonomy over the money supply granted by Congress to the Federal Reserve Board, an agency independent of the President.

The nation has evolved from one in which the national government's principal role was that of the protector of the lives and property of the citizenry against encroachment by foreign governments and other citizens to one in which the government manages the economy, for better or worse, in a state where the government has assumed responsibility for the social welfare as well as the physical protection of the citizenry. And as the progression has gone on, so too has Congress relinquished more and more authority to the President. But the President can be said to have these powers only at the will of Congress and to exercise them only in order to enforce the laws faithfully. Indeed, the DELEGATION OF POWER has gone so far as for Congress to have provided by law that the President may refuse to enforce its legislation by IMPOUNDMENT of appropriated funds, provided notice is given to Congress and Congress acquiesces.

Although Congress now has its own budget-making procedures, the dominant BUDGET, derived from the President's Office of Management and Budget, is submitted to Congress more by way of command than suggestion. The concept of an executive budget derives from the 1920s when Congress first enacted a demand that the President supply one. Since then, however, the Office of Management and Budget has grown from a simple accounting agency into a fiscal ombudsman for the entire government. It is a force second only to that of the President himself within the executive branch and it has not been bashful about exercising its powers. But if the beast is a presidential pet, it is nonetheless a creature of a Congress dedicated to transferring to the President the powers that the Constitution gave to Congress.

In constitutional terms, the President's role in the legislative process was originally to be very small. Most important, of course, was the power to veto the acts passed by Congress. And even here, unlike the power of the Crown to forestall parliamentary will as expressed in legislation, the President was given only a conditional veto, subject to being overridden by two-thirds of each house of Congress. The VETO POWER is, however, fully effective only for a President who prefers a limited role for government. Obviously, his veto cannot create legislation but only prevent it. A forceful President seeking to impose his will by way of persuading Congress to action rather than inaction can, however, use the veto as a bargaining-tool, a threat to cancel what Congress wants unless it gives the President what he wants. Stalemate is a frequent consequence of a profligate use of the veto power.

The President also has the power by constitutional provision to adjourn Congress, when the two houses are unable to agree on adjournment, and to convene Congress. The power to prorogue Parliament was a sore point with the colonists and they had no intention of conferring such authority on any executive of their own.

There was an imitation of the royal prerogative that was to come into existence even though it was not planned by the Founders. The Constitution provides that the President "shall from time to time give the Congress information of the state of the union, and recommend to their consideration such measures as he shall judge necessary and expedient." Like the Queen's message to the opening of Parliament, this device has been used by the executive administration to offer a legislative program to Congress. Indeed, most legislation of importance that comes to enactment in Congress tends to be that which the President has recommended to it or which the President supports by lobbying in Congress. Legislation that does not bear the imprimatur of the President seldom makes its way to enactment, although presidential recommendations are frequently amended in the process of legislative consideration and sometimes are unrecognizable by the time they emerge from both houses. But the influence of the President, utilizing the Office of Management and Budget for details, on the making of the laws is extraordinarily strong. And while there is no provision for presidential budget making in the Constitution, the fact is that the budget that he submits is the foundation on which the congressional budget-making process depends.

In fact, the President indulges in a great deal of lawmaking himself. With the demise of the ban on the delegation of legislative power, which occurred when the Supreme Court was reconstituted by FRANKLIN D. ROOSEVELT, most of the rules governing American society are made by the executive branch. Legislation has tended to take the form of generalized programs whose details are to be filled by agencies of the executive branch. Indeed, some legislation is created by the President even in the absence of authorization for it by the Congress. This takes the form of so-called EXECUTIVE ORDERS theoretically directed to the enforcement of the laws by persons in the executive branch, but usually with the same effect as rules directed to the governed rather than the governors. Very rare indeed is the instance, like the steel seizure case, when the Court has throttled an executive order. Thus, most of the rules governing the lives of Americans are to be sought not in the statutes-at-large but rather in the Federal Register where are to be found the results of the exercise of delegated legislative authority as well as executive orders that do not rest on any actual delegation.

It would seem that the originators of the departments of government thought of them as semiautonomous, with their functions defined by Congress and their secretaries responsible to either the President or the Congress, or both, as prescribed by the legislation creating those offices. The provision for a power in the President to call on the principal officers of government for their opinions would have been redundant if in fact it had been anticipated that all executive officials were directly subordinate to the President. It was probably GEORGE WASHINGTON's organization of his department chiefs into a cabinet rather than the words of the Constitution that made for the hierarchical system headed by the President that has been taken for granted since early in the nineteenth century. The cabinet is not a constitutional body and has no constitutional powers. The powers of the department heads are dependent on legislative rather than constitutional provision, except for their duties to give opinions to the President on demand. Thus by custom and by legislation, and perhaps through the charge of the Constitution to the President faithfully to execute the laws, it has come to

be accepted that the executive branch, for all its multitude of offices, is an entity for which the President is responsible both to Congress through the legislature's oversight function, and to the voting public. Surely this notion of the unitary nature of the executive branch and the exceptions thereto—independent administrative agencies—underlies the judgment of the Supreme Court in MYERS V. UNITED STATES (1926) establishing the right of the President to remove officials at his will. This accepted principle is not contradicted by the obligation of the President or other executive officials to abide by their own regulations, which are created by him or them and which are subject to change by him or them. (See APPOINTMENT AND REMOVAL POWER.)

The whole of the executive branch acts subordinately to the command of the President in the administration of federal laws, so long as they act within the terms of those laws. Their offices confer no right to violate the laws, whether they take the form of constitution, statute, or treaty.

The United States does have in the presidency a "constitutional dictatorship" or a "plebiscitary President." The "benevolent monarch" of contemporary times, however, is still subject to the force of public opinion, sometimes expressed through representatives, sometimes expressed through the print and electronic media, sometimes expressed in the streets, and every four years expressed through the ballot boxes. One-term Presidents may become the rule. Despite all the centralization of authority, however, the greatest power of the presidency in this democracy is not the power of command. It is the power to lead a nation by moral suasion. It takes a great President to do that well, and that is why history records so few great Presidents.

PHILIP B. KURLAND

Bibliography

CORWIN, EDWARD S. 1957 *The President: Office and Powers 1787–1957.* 4th rev. ed. New York: New York University Press.
COX, ARCHIBALD 1976 Watergate and the Constitution of the United States. *University of Toronto Law Journal* 26:125–139.
KOENIG, LOUIS W. 1975 *The Chief Executive.* 3d ed. New York: Harcourt, Brace, Jovanovich.
KURLAND, PHILIP B. 1978 *Watergate and the Constitution.* Chicago: University of Chicago Press.
NEUSTADT, RICHARD E. 1960 *Presidential Power.* New York: John Wiley & Sons.
PIOUS, RICHARD M. 1979 *The American Presidency.* New York: Basic Books.
ROSSITER, CLINTON 1948 *Constitutional Dictatorship.* Princeton, N.J.: Princeton University Press.

SCHLESINGER, ARTHUR M., JR. 1973 *The Imperial Presidency.* Boston: Houghton Mifflin Co.

PRESIDENTIAL SPENDING POWER

The Constitution assigns to Congress the exclusive power to authorize spending. Article I, section 9, prohibits money being drawn from the Treasury "but in Consequence of Appropriations made by law." Nevertheless, the power of the purse is shared with the President because Congress has found it necessary to delegate substantial discretion over the expenditure and allocation of funds.

In his first message to Congress, President THOMAS JEFFERSON recommended that Congress appropriate "specific sums to every specific purpose susceptible of definition." He quickly recognized the impracticability of this principle, later admitting that "too minute a specification has its evil as well as a too general one." Lump-sum appropriations are routinely passed by Congress, especially during emergency periods. The magnitude of these lump sums, frequently in the billions of dollars, overstates the amount of flexibility available to administrators. Their scope of discretion is narrowed by general statutory controls, nonstatutory controls embedded in committee reports and other parts of the legislative history, and agreements and understandings entered into by Congress and the agencies.

The conflicting needs of administrative flexibility and congressional control are often reconciled by "reprogramming" agreements. An agency is given some latitude to shift funds *within* an appropriation account, moving them from one program to another. Legislative controls have gradually tightened. Initially the appropriation committees required regular reporting by the agencies, but reprogrammings over a designated dollar threshold must now be approved by appropriations subcommittees and, in some cases, by authorizing committees that have JURISDICTION over the program. Although these reprogramming procedures are largely nonstatutory and therefore fall short of legally binding requirements, they have become highly formalized and structured. They are incorporated not only in congressional documents but also in agency directives, instructions, and financial management manuals.

Another form of executive spending discretion results from transfer authority. A transfer involves the shifting of funds from one appropriation account to another (in contrast to reprogramming, where funds remain within an account). Moreover, the authority to transfer funds must be explicitly granted by statute. Transfer authority is usually accompanied by limitations, such as allowing a five percent leeway, that help preserve the general budgetary priorities of Congress. When agencies use transfer or reprogramming authority to spend funds on programs that had been previously rejected by Congress, or to enter into long-term financial commitments, Congress responds by adopting additional statutory and nonstatutory restrictions.

Agencies have access to billions of dollars that are hidden from public and congressional view. Confidential and secret funding collides with the requirement of Article I, section 9, of the Constitution: "A regular Statement and Account of the Receipts and Expenditures of all public Money shall be published from time to time." Confidential funds appeared as early as 1790, when Congress appropriated $40,000 to the President to pay for special diplomatic agents. Congress let the President decide the degree to which these expenditures would be made public. Since that time confidential (unvouchered) funds have been made available to many agencies that have domestic as well as foreign responsibilities.

Confidential funding is overt at least in the sense that the amounts are identified in appropriation or authorization bills. Secret funding is covert at every stage, from appropriation straight through to expenditure and auditing. Appropriations, ostensibly for the Defense Department or other agencies, are later siphoned off and allocated to the Central Intelligence Agency and other parts of the intelligence community. Absent congressional authorization, a federal taxpayer lacks STANDING to challenge the constitutionality of confidential or secret funding. The establishment of intelligence committees in the 1970s restored some semblance of congressional control. Legislation for the White House and the General Accounting Office has also tightened legislative control over unvouchered funds. With each increase in the scope of executive spending discretion, Congress participates ever more closely in administrative matters.

LOUIS FISHER

(SEE ALSO: *Impoundment.*)

Bibliography

FISHER, LOUIS 1975 *Presidential Spending Power.* Princeton, N.J.: Princeton University Press.
WILMERDING, LUCIUS, JR. 1943 *The Spending Power: A History of the Efforts of Congress to Control Expenditures.* New Haven, Conn.: Yale University Press.

PRESIDENTIAL SUCCESSION

The framework for electing a President and vice-president every four years is spelled out in the Constitution. As originally adopted, the Constitution was not clear about certain aspects of succession to the Presidency in the event something happened to the elected President. The Framers were content to establish the office of vice-president and to add the general provisions of Article II, section 1, clause 6: "In Case of the Removal of the President from Office, or of his Death, Resignation, or Inability to discharge the Powers and Duties of the said Office, the same shall devolve on the vice-president and the Congress may by Law provide for the Case of Removal, Death, Resignation or Inability, both of the President and Vice-President, declaring what Officer shall then act as President, and such officer shall act accordingly, until the Disability be removed, or a President shall be elected."

The Framers left unanswered questions concerning the status of a vice-president in cases of removal, death, resignation, and inability, the meaning of the term "inability," and the means by which the beginning and ending of an inability should be determined. Because no event occurred to trigger the succession provision, these ambiguities were of no consequence during the first half century of our nation's existence. Although three vice-presidents died in office and another resigned, the presidency and vice-presidency never became vacant at the same time. If that eventuality had come to pass, the president pro tempore of the Senate would have served as President under the provisions of a 1792 statute on presidential succession.

The ambiguities inherent in the succession provision surfaced in 1841 when President William Henry Harrison died in office. Despite protests that he had become only the "acting president," Vice-President JOHN TYLER assumed the office and title of President for the balance of Harrison's term. Tyler's claiming of the presidency, said JOHN QUINCY ADAMS, was "a construction in direct violation both of the grammar and context of the Constitution. . . ."

The precedent established by Tyler was followed twice within the next twenty-five years when Vice-Presidents MILLARD FILLMORE and ANDREW JOHNSON became President upon the deaths in office of Presidents ZACHARY TAYLOR and ABRAHAM LINCOLN. In 1881 the precedent became an obstacle to Vice-President CHESTER A. ARTHUR's acting as President during the eighty days that President JAMES A. GARFIELD hovered between life and death after being shot by an assassin. The view was strongly expressed at the time that if Arthur were to succeed to the presidency, then according to the Tyler precedent he would be President for the remainder of the presidential term regardless of whether Garfield recovered. Arthur made clear that he would not assume presidential responsibility lest he be labeled a usurper.

In the twentieth century the Tyler precedent was followed on the four occasions when Presidents died in office (WILLIAM MCKINLEY, WARREN G. HARDING, FRANKLIN D. ROOSEVELT, and JOHN F. KENNEDY). Once again, however, it became an obstacle to a vice-president's acting as President during the lengthy period WOODROW WILSON lay ill, unable to discharge the powers and duties of office. For the most part, presidential responsibility was assumed by the President's wife, doctor, and secretary.

Between 1955 and 1957 the lack of clarity in the succession provision was highlighted when President DWIGHT D. EISENHOWER sustained a heart attack, an attack of ileitis, and a stroke. Efforts to have Congress address the question were unsuccessful, but important groundwork for reform was established. President Kennedy's assassination in 1963 became the catalyst for implementing that reform. Congress proposed and the states ratified the TWENTY-FIFTH AMENDMENT to the Constitution to resolve the major issues surrounding the subject of presidential succession. The amendment confirmed that the vice-president becomes President for the remainder of the term in the case of death, removal, or resignation. In the case of an inability, the amendment provided that the vice-president serves as acting President only for the duration of the inability. The amendment provided for two methods of establishing the existence of an inability. The President was authorized to declare his own inability and, in such event, its termination. For the case where the President does not or cannot declare his own inability, it empowered the vice-president and a majority of the Cabinet to make the decision. If the President should dispute their determination, Congress decides the issue.

The amendment also established a mechanism for filling a vice-presidential vacancy: presidential nomination and confirmation by a majority of both houses of Congress. The Twenty-Fifth Amendment is supplemented by a statute on presidential succession adopted in 1947 which provided for the Speaker of the House of Representatives to serve as President in the event of a double vacancy in the offices of President and vice-president.

The Twenty-Fifth Amendment served the nation well in the 1970s when both a President and vice-president resigned from office during the same presidential term. Twice vice-presidents were nominated by the President and confirmed by Congress. The first of those vice-presidents, GERALD R. FORD, became President of the United States upon the resignation of RICHARD M. NIXON on August 9, 1974. Ford's succession, as did the eight preceding successions of vice-presidents, took place in a manner that demonstrated the stability and continuity of government in the United States.

JOHN D. FEERICK

Bibliography

BAYH, BIRCH 1968 *One Heartbeat Away.* Indianapolis: Bobbs-Merrill.

FEERICK, JOHN D. 1965 *From Failing Hands.* New York: Fordham University Press.

———— 1976 *The Twenty-Fifth Amendment.* New York: Fordham University Press.

SILVA, RUTH 1951 *Presidential Succession.* Ann Arbor: University of Michigan Press.

PRESUMPTION OF CONSTITUTIONALITY

See: Rational Basis; Standard of Review

PRETRIAL DISCLOSURE

The rules and practices governing pretrial disclosure to the opposing party differ dramatically in criminal and civil litigation. In civil disputes, each side has access to virtually all relevant information possessed by the other. In criminal cases, however, there has been a continuing debate which has focused on how much disclosure the prosecutor, with his superior investigative resources, should be required to make. The argument against wide-ranging disclosure is that it will result in witness intimidation and perjury. The arguments for disclosure are that a criminal trial should not be a "sporting event" in which one side tries to surprise the other, and that disclosure of the prosecution's EVIDENCE would aid the effective assistance of counsel to the accused guaranteed by the Sixth Amendment. (See RIGHT TO COUNSEL.)

Proponents of greater disclosure in criminal cases have made some gains in recent years through the expansion of DISCOVERY statutes. Rule 16 of the FEDERAL RULES OF CRIMINAL PROCEDURE is typical. The rule currently provides that, absent special circumstances, the government must disclose upon request:

the defendant's own statements; his record of prior convictions; and documents, tangible evidence, or reports of examinations of the defendant or scientific tests the government intends to introduce at trial. The most striking difference between this rule and civil practice is that the criminal rule does not give the defense the power either to discover the identity of government witnesses or to compel them to testify under oath prior to trial. Several states provide for disclosure of prosecution witness lists, but Congress in 1974 rejected such a provision in the federal rules on the usual argument that disclosure of the identity of witnesses would possibly subject them to intimidation.

In addition to the slow but steady statutory expansion of pretrial disclosure by the government to the defense, there has been a reciprocal movement to entitle the prosecution to learn more about the defense case before trial. The argument that the policies underlying the Fifth Amendment RIGHT AGAINST SELF-INCRIMINATION shield the defense from any disclosure has largely been unsuccessful. Under the federal and many state rules, the defense can be requested to disclose any tangible evidence or results of physical or mental examinations it intends to introduce at trial, and to give notice of an alibi or insanity defense. The Supreme Court has upheld the constitutionality of compelling defense disclosure, provided that discovery is a two-way street; if the defendant is required to disclose alibi witnesses, for example, the government must also disclose any evidence that refutes the alibi.

Against the background of limited formal discovery rules, prosecutors frequently open files to the defense in an attempt to induce guilty pleas. Sometimes, also, judges exert informal pressure toward open discovery in order to avoid trial delays that might be caused by surprise evidence.

The Supreme Court has repeatedly held that a defendant has no general constitutional right to discovery, but it has required that the prosecution sometimes reveal "favorable" evidence. In *Brady v. Maryland* (1963) the government failed to disclose to a murder defendant that his companion had once admitted to a government agent that he had done the actual killing. The Court held that such a failure to disclose violates DUE PROCESS where the evidence is "material to guilt or punishment," irrespective of the good faith of the prosecution.

The lower courts generally gave an expansive reading to the *Brady* decision, but the Supreme Court curbed this development in *United States v. Agurs* (1976). The *Agurs* Court held that if the defense has not requested favorable evidence, or has made only a general request, a failure to disclose gives the defendant no constitutional right to a new trial unless there is a strong probability that the result of the first trial would not have been different had the favorable evidence been disclosed. Moreover, an appellate court should not grant a new trial so long as the trial judge remains reasonably convinced of the defendant's guilt. The *Agurs* Court also said that the failure to disclose evidence that reveals that the prosecution's case includes perjured testimony or the failure to disclose favorable evidence after it has been specifically requested by the defense, is "rarely excusable." In these two situations, the Constitution requires that the defendant be given a new trial if there is any reasonable possibility that the verdict would have been different had the undisclosed evidence been admitted.

Thus, *Agurs* provided some ammunition to both sides of the debate over criminal discovery: it limited the general due process right but also created a category for all but automatic reversal when the prosecution fails to respond to a defense request for specific information or when the prosecution case includes the knowing use of perjury.

BARBARA ALLEN BABCOCK

Bibliography
BABCOCK, BARBARA 1982 Fair Play: Evidence Favorable to an Accused and Effective Assistance of Counsel. *Stanford Law Review* 34:1133–1182.

PREVENTIVE DETENTION

Preventive detention is the jailing of an accused not to prevent bail-skipping but to protect public safety pending trial. Although pretrial incarceration of criminal defendants has long been condoned when necessary to assure their appearance in court, the constitutional status of preventive detention is far less certain. The Supreme Court has never directly addressed the issue, in part because until quite recently it was rendered largely academic by a federal statutory right to BAIL in noncapital cases and by similar rights granted in most state constitutions. Since 1970, however, District of Columbia courts have been authorized to deny pretrial release in certain cases to suspects charged with "dangerous" crimes, and several states have recently amended their constitutions to allow detention under similar circumstances. Following this activity, Congress in 1984 passed a nationwide program of preventive detention, substantially curtailing the federal statutory right to bail for the first time since the right was enacted in 1789.

The constitutionality of these programs is not altogether free from doubt. To begin with, the Eighth Amendment bars the federal government from requiring "excessive bail." Commentators have waged a spirited debate over whether that prohibition implies that some bail must be set. Many constitutional scholars have argued that the Framers intended to provide an affirmative right to bail to all defendants who do not pose an unacceptable risk of flight, and that without such a right the "excessive bail" clause would be a senseless bar against the government's doing indirectly what it remained free to do directly. Others have contended that the clause is aimed at the courts, not at Congress, and that a restriction on judicial discretion in setting bail is fully consistent with legislative authority to determine the circumstances under which bail should be granted at all.

The Supreme Court's decisions and opinions on the issue have been inconclusive. In *Stack v. Boyle* (1951) the Court held that bail was "excessive" when set higher than necessary to assure the accused's presence at trial. Strictly speaking, the ruling concerned only the level at which bail may be set if it is set, but the Court also hinted that the right to bail in the first place, long accorded by federal statute, might have a constitutional dimension: "Unless this right to bail before trial is preserved, the presumption of innocence, secured only after centuries of struggle, would lose its meaning."

The rule of *Stack v. Boyle* regarding bail amounts has remained undisturbed, despite general recognition that in practice bail is frequently set with a covert eye to whether the defendant seems likely to commit crimes before trial. The Supreme Court quickly backed away, however, from its strong if cryptic endorsement of the "right to bail." In *Carlson v. Landon* (1952) the Court approved the denial of bail, for reasons of public safety, to alien communists held pending deportation hearings. The Eighth Amendment, the Court explained, does not grant "a right to bail in all cases," but only provides "that bail shall not be excessive in those cases where it is proper to grant bail." The Court noted in particular that the amendment "has not prevented Congress from determining the classes of cases in which bail should be allowed."

Despite these seemingly categorical remarks, the effect of *Carlson* on the legacy of *Stack v. Boyle* remains unclear. The *Carlson* decision seems to have been based primarily on the differences between a criminal prosecution against a citizen and a deportation proceeding against an alien; the Court concluded only that "the Eighth Amendment does not require that bail be allowed under the circumstances of these cases."

Whether or not the Eighth Amendment provides a right to bail, preventive detention may raise questions of constitutionality under the DUE PROCESS clauses of the Fifth and FOURTEENTH AMENDMENTS. In *Bell v. Wolfish* (1979) the Supreme Court rejected a related argument, suggested in part by its own opinion in *Stack v. Boyle,* that the "presumption of innocence" limits what the government may do to a criminal defendant before conviction. The Court explained in *Wolfish* that the presumption of innocence is nothing but an evidentiary rule to be applied at trial; "it has no application to a determination of the rights of a pretrial detainee." The due process clauses, however, do apply before the commencement of trial, and *Wolfish* and later decisions have made clear that those clauses, in addition to constraining the permissible forms of detention and setting minimum procedural safeguards, also bar absolutely the "punishment" of an accused before conviction.

In testing for punishment in this context, the Supreme Court has considered, among other things, the government's reasons for imposing a given measure. The highest local court in the District of Columbia concluded in 1981 that incarceration for preventive purposes is nonpunitive and hence may be imposed before trial. The Supreme Court reasoned differently in BROWN V. UNITED STATES (1965), concluding that a preventive rationale should not stop confinement from being punishment for purposes of the BILL OF ATTAINDER clauses, but it has made no similar determination under the due process clauses.

The question whether the Constitution permits pretrial detention for purposes other than assuring a defendant's appearance in court thus remains open. A small part of the question was answered in SCHALL V. MARTIN (1984), where the Court upheld a state program of preventive detention for accused juvenile delinquents, but *Schall* relied heavily on the special prerogatives which the Constitution allows the state with respect to juveniles. Whether unconvicted adults may be jailed to keep them from committing future crimes remains a question to be decided.

The difficulty of the question reflects the strain placed on constitutional norms by the exigencies of the pretrial period. Preventive detention is difficult to reconcile with the ideal of due process, but many people are understandably made uneasy by the thought of defendants "walking the streets" while awaiting trial for serious crimes. A partial solution to the dilemma may be found in the Sixth Amendment's guarantee of a speedy trial: greater fidelity to that provision would alleviate to some extent both the risks associated with pretrial release and the inherent tension between due process and any restraint on the liberty of unconvicted defendants.

ABNER J. MIKVA

Bibliography
VERRILLI, DONALD B., JR. 1982 The Eighth Amendment and the Right to Bail: Historical Perspectives. *Columbia Law Review* 82:328–362.

PRICE, UNITED STATES v.
383 U.S. 787 (1966)

Eighteen defendants implicated in the murder of three CIVIL RIGHTS workers in Mississippi challenged the INDICTMENTS against them under the federal CIVIL RIGHTS ACT OF 1866 and that of 1870. One act applied only to persons conspiring to violate any federally protected right, the other only to persons acting "under COLOR OF LAW" who willfully violated such rights. Previous decisions of the Supreme Court had limited the two statutes. "Under color of law" covered only officers and in effect meant STATE ACTION, thus excluding private persons from prosecution. The language of the conspiracy statute notwithstanding, the Court had previously applied it to protect only the narrow class of rights that Congress could, apart from the FOURTEENTH AMENDMENT, protect against private individuals' interference, thus excluding the bulk of civil rights. Justice ABE FORTAS for a unanimous Court ruled that when private persons act in concert with state officials they all act under color of law, because they willfully participate in the prohibited activity (deprivation of life without DUE PROCESS OF LAW) with the state or its agents. Fortas also ruled that the 1870 act meant what it said: it safeguarded *all* federally protected rights secured by the supreme law of the land. By remanding the cases for trial, the Court made possible the first conviction in a federal prosecution for a civil rights murder in the South since Reconstruction.

LEONARD W. LEVY

PRICE-FIXING

See: Antitrust Law and the Constitution; Economic Regulation

PRIGG v. PENNSYLVANIA
16 Peters 539 (1842)

In 1839 Edward Prigg was convicted of kidnapping for removing an alleged fugitive slave from Pennsylvania without obtaining a warrant from a state judge as required by a Pennsylvania act of 1826. Prigg eventually appealed to the United States Supreme Court. Justice JOSEPH STORY, speaking for the Court, overturned his conviction. Story determined: (1) The federal Fugitive Slave Law of 1793 was constitutional. This was the first Supreme Court decision on that issue. (2) All state laws interfering with the rendition of fugitive slaves were unconstitutional. (3) The Fugitive Slave clause of the United States Constitution (Article IV, section 2, clause 3) was in part self-executing, and a slaveowner or his agent could capture and return a runaway slave under a right of self-help, without relying on any statute or judicial procedure, as long as the capture did not breach the peace. (4) State jurists and officials ought to help enforce the federal act of 1793, but Congress could not compel them to do so. Chief Justice ROGER B. TANEY concurred in Story's decision, but not his reasoning. Taney distorted Story's opinion by erroneously asserting that Story had declared it was illegal for state officials to aid in the rendition of fugitive slaves. In fact, Story encouraged the states to aid in the rendition process, but he believed Congress could not compel state assistance. After the decision many free states enacted PERSONAL LIBERTY LAWS which removed state support for the federal act of 1793. With few federal officials to help masters, the law went unenforced in much of the North. This situation helped lead to the passage of a new and harsher fugitive slave law in 1850.

PAUL FINKELMAN

Bibliography

FINKELMAN, PAUL 1979 *Prigg v. Pennsylvania* and Northern State Courts: Antislavery Use of a Proslavery Decision. *Civil War History* 25:5–35.

PRIMARY ELECTION

The primary election for selecting candidates is a uniquely American innovation. First adopted in Wisconsin in 1905, it has since spread to every other state. Generally it is the required method for selecting major POLITICAL PARTIES' nominees, whose names are automatically placed on the general election ballot, and for narrowing the field in nonpartisan elections.

The Supreme Court has not heard a modern constitutional challenge to state authority to compel political parties to select their candidates at primaries or to define party membership for these purposes. In *Cousins v. Wigoda* (1975), however, the Supreme Court held that Illinois could not require the Democratic National Convention to seat delegates selected in the state's primary; and in *Democratic Party v. La-Follette* (1981) the Court held that Wisconsin's delegates could not be bound by state law to follow candidate preferences expressed by voters in the state's presidential primary. In both cases, the Justices declared that the "party and its adherents enjoy a constitutionally protected right of political association." And in *Democratic Party* the Court said that "the freedom to associate . . . necessarily presupposes the freedom to identify the people who constitute the association, and to limit association to those people only." The Justices recognized state interests in the conduct of primary elections, however, and their decisions specifically addressed attempts to regulate the conduct of national party conventions and delegates. States might be able to limit the privilege of automatic access to the ballot to those parties conforming with state primary laws.

The Supreme Court has upheld state primary laws that protect the interests of political parties. In 1976 it affirmed a lower court judgment upholding a state's closed primary against a challenge that it abridged the right to vote and violated the RIGHT OF PRIVACY in political affiliation and belief. Similarly, the Court upheld, in *Rosario v. Rockefeller* (1973), an extended waiting period for voters wishing to change party registration, thus protecting party primaries from invasion by opposition party adherents and from casual participation by independent voters. But in *Kusper v. Pontikes* (1973), the Court acknowledged a competing interest in voter participation by rejecting a waiting period so long that the voter wishing to change party affiliation was excluded entirely from at least one primary election.

The Supreme Court has concluded that Congress has authority to regulate primary elections to nominate candidates for federal office, including prohibition of fraud, bribery, and other practices that deprive voters of rights, in UNITED STATES V. CLASSIC (1941) and *Burroughs v. United States* (1934), and regulation of political finance practices, in BUCKLEY V. VALEO (1976). Additional authority to regulate primaries is encompassed within the enforcement clauses of the FOURTEENTH and FIFTEENTH AMENDMENTS.

The principal clauses of these amendments also have independent application to primary elections, apart from any regulatory legislation Congress may enact. Once a state has established the primary for nominating candidates, the ONE PERSON-ONE VOTE principle of the apportionment cases applies. RACIAL DISCRIMINATION in primaries has been held unconstitutional, whether these barriers are established by the state, as in NIXON V. HERNDON (1927), or by political parties pursuant to state authorization to define party membership, as in NIXON V. CONDON (1932) and SMITH V. ALLWRIGHT (1944). Racial discrimination has also been held unconstitutional in a primary operated exclusively by a political party following the state's repeal of its primary election system. The most far-reaching application of the Fifteenth Amendment, in TERRY V. ADAMS (1953), prohibited racial discrimination in a "pre-primary" straw vote conducted by an all-white political club, when such "pre-primaries" had regularly proved determinative of elections.

In *Cousins v. Wigoda* the Supreme Court held that state primary laws do not supersede the authority of national party conventions over the selection and seating of delegates, but it did not choose to make a broad decision between competing claims of FREEDOM OF ASSOCIATION of political parties and governmental authority to regulate nomination activities. On one side of this continuing constitutional controversy lie assertions of FIRST AMENDMENT rights of parties to define their own membership, to control the composition and operation of party bodies, and to nominate candidates. On the other side lie assertions of state and congressional authority to regulate elections, of congressional power specifically granted in the enforcement clauses of the Fourteenth and Fifteenth Amendments, and of the independent operation of the principal clauses of those amendments. Notwithstanding the Supreme Court's reluctance to decide this question broadly, the Court's decisions have increasingly recognized the freedom of association of political parties.

DAVID ADAMANY

PRINCE v. MASSACHUSETTS
321 U.S. 158 (1944)

Massachusetts law provided that no boy under twelve or girl under eighteen could engage in street sale of any merchandise. Prince was the guardian of a nine-year-old girl. Both were Jehovah's Witnesses and sold Witness literature. The question was whether the statute impermissibly infringed on the free exercise of religion.

Writing for the Court, Justice WILEY B. RUTLEDGE

balanced the broad powers of the state to protect the health and welfare of minors against the FIRST AMENDMENT claims and held that the state's power prevailed. Justices FRANK MURPHY and ROBERT H. JACKSON dissented.

Prince follows the "secular regulation" approach to RELIGIOUS LIBERTY introduced by UNITED STATES V. REYNOLDS (1879).

RICHARD E. MORGAN

PRIOR INCONSISTENT TESTIMONY

See: Confrontation

PRIOR RESTRAINT AND CENSORSHIP

History has rooted in our constitutional tradition of freedom of expression the strongest aversion to official censorship. We have learned from the English rejection of press licensing and from our own experiences that the psychology of censors tends to drive them to excess, that censors have a stake in finding things to suppress, and that—in systems of wholesale review before publication—doubt tends to produce suppression. American law tolerated motion picture censorship for a time, but only because movies were not thought to be "the press" in FIRST AMENDMENT terms. Censorship of the movies is now virtually dead, smothered by stringent procedural requirements imposed by unsympathetic courts, by the voluntary rating system, and, most of all, by public distaste for the absurdities of censorship in operation.

American law has tolerated requirements of prior official approval of expression in several important areas, however. No one may broadcast without a license, and the government issues licenses without charge to those it believes will serve the "public interest." Licensing is also grudgingly tolerated—because of the desirability of giving notice and of avoiding conflicts or other disruptions of the normal functions of public places—in the regulation of parades, demonstrations, leafleting, and other expressive activities in public places. But the courts have taken pains to eliminate administrative discretion that would allow officials to censor PUBLIC FORUM expression because they do not approve its message.

Notwithstanding these areas where censorship has been permitted, the clearest principle of First Amendment law is that the least tolerable form of official regulation of expression is a requirement of prior official approval for publication. It is easy to see the suffocating tendency of prior restraints where all expression—whether or not ultimately deemed protected by the First Amendment for publication—must be submitted for clearance before it may be disseminated. The harder question of First Amendment theory has been whether advance prohibitions on expression in specific cases should be discredited by our historical aversion to censorship. The question has arisen most frequently in the context of judicial INJUNCTIONS against publication. Even though injunctions do not involve many of the worst vices of wholesale licensing and censorship, the Supreme court has tarred them with the brush of "prior restraint."

The seminal case was NEAR V. MINNESOTA (1931), handed down by a closely divided Court but never questioned since. A state statute provided for injunctions against any "malicious, scandalous, and defamatory newspaper," and a state judge had enjoined a scandal sheet from publishing anything scandalous in the future. The Minnesota scheme did not require advance approval of all publications, but came into play only after a publication had been found scandalous, and then only to prevent further similar publications. Nevertheless, the majority of the Justices concluded that to enjoin future editions under such vague standards in effect put the newspaper under judicial censorship. Chief Justice CHARLES EVANS HUGHES's historic opinion made clear, however, that the First Amendment's bar against prior restraint was not absolute. Various exceptional instances would justify prior restraints, including this pregnant one: "No one would question but that a government might prevent actual obstruction to its recruiting service or the publication of the sailing dates of transports or the number and location of troops."

It was forty years before the scope of the troop ship exception was tested. The *Pentagon Papers* decision of 1971, NEW YORK TIMES CO. V. UNITED STATES, reaffirmed that judicial injunctions are considered prior restraints and are tolerated only in the most compelling circumstances. This principle barred an injunction against publication of a classified history of the government's decisions in the Vietnam war, although—unlike *Near*—the government had sought to enjoin only readily identifiable material, not unidentified similar publications in the future. Ten different opinions discussed the problem of injunctions in national security cases, and the only proposition commanding a majority was the unexplained conclu-

sion that the government had not justified injunctive relief.

The central theme sounded in the opinions of the six majority Justices was reluctance to act in such difficult circumstances without guidance from Congress. Accepting the premise that there was no statutory authority for an injunction, several considerations support the Court's refusal to forge new rules concerning the disclosure of national secrets. First, the Court's tools are inadequate for the task; ad hoc evaluations of executive claims of risk are not easily balanced against the First Amendment's language and judicial interpretation. Second, dissemination of secret information often arises in the context of heated disagreements about the proper direction of national policy. One's assessment of the disclosure's impact on security will depend on one's reaction to the policy. Third, it would be particularly unsatisfactory to build a judge-made system of rules in an area where much litigation must be done *in camera*. Thus, general rules about specific categories of defense-related information cannot be fashioned by courts. The best hope in a nuclear age for accommodating the needs of secrecy and the public's RIGHT TO KNOW lies in the legislative process where, removed from pressures of adjudicting particular cases, general rules can be fashioned. The courts' proper role in this area is to review legislation, not try to devise rules of secrecy case by case.

Chilling this victory for freedom of the press were admonitions, loosely endorsed by four Justices, that the espionage statutes might support criminal sanctions against the *New York Times* and its reporters. No journalists were indicted, but the prosecutions of Daniel Ellsberg and Anthony Russo rested on a view of several statutes that would reach the press by punishing news-gathering activities necessarily incident to publication. Since the dismissal of these cases for reasons irrelevant to these issues, the extent of possible criminal liability for publishing national security secrets remains unclear.

The *Pentagon Papers* case underlines how little the United States has relied on law to control press coverage of national defense and foreign policy matters. For most of our history the press has rarely tested the limits of its rights to publish. Secrets were kept because people in and out of government with access to military and diplomatic secrets shared basic assumptions about national aims. The Vietnam war changed all that. The *Pentagon Papers* dispute marked the passing of an era in which journalists could be counted on to work within understood limits of discretion in handling secret information.

The third major decision striking down a judicial order not to publish involved neither national security nor scandal but the right of a criminal defendant to a fair trial. A state court enjoined publication of an accused's confession and some other incriminating material on the ground that if prospective jurors learned about it they might be incapable of impartiality. In NEBRASKA PRESS ASSOCIATION V. STUART (1976) the Supreme Court decided that the potential prejudice was speculative, and it rejected enjoining publication on speculation. The majority opinion examined the evidence to determine the nature and extent of pretrial publicity, the effectiveness of other measures in mitigating prejudice, and the effectiveness of a prior restraint in reducing the dangers. This opinion determined that the impact of pretrial publicity was necessarily speculative, that alternative measures short of prior restraint had not been considered by the lower courts, and that prior restraint would not significantly reduce the dangers presented.

On one issue of considerable importance, the Court seemed to be in full agreement. The opinions endorsed controls on parties, lawyers, witnesses, and law enforcement personnel as sources of information for journalists. These GAG ORDERS have been controversial among many journalists and publishers who think the First Amendment should guarantee the right to gather news. Although freeing the press from direct control by limiting prior restraint, the Court approved an indirect method of reaching the same result, guaranteeing that the press print no prejudicial publicity, by approving direct controls on sources of prejudicial information. The Court has subsequently held that pretrial motions may be closed to the public and the press with the consent of the prosecutor and the accused but over the objection of the press, in GANNETT CO. V. DePASQUALE (1979). This case involved access to judicial proceedings, not prior restraints on the press, and was decided largely on Sixth Amendment grounds. The Court reached the opposite result with respect to trials in RICHMOND NEWSPAPERS V. VIRGINIA (1980), but acknowledged that the right of access to trials is not absolute.

These decisions and others have firmly established that the First Amendment tolerates virtually no prior restraints. This DOCTRINE is one of the central principles of our law of FREEDOM OF THE PRESS. On the surface, the doctrine concerns only the form of controls on expression. It bars controls prior to publication, even if imposition of criminal or civil liability following publication would be constitutional. But, as with most limitations of form, the prior restraint doctrine has important substantive consequences. Perhaps the most important of these consequences is that the doctrine is presumably an absolute bar to any wholesale system of administrative licensing or censorship of the press, which is the most repellent form of government suppression of expression. Second, the prior restraint doctrine removes most of the opportunities for official control of those types of expression for which general rules of control are difficult to formulate. The message of the prior restraint doctrine is that if you cannot control expression pursuant to general legislative standards, you cannot control it at all—or nearly at all, as the *Pentagon Papers* decision suggests, by suggesting an exception allowing an injunction in a truly compelling case of national security. A third effect of the doctrine is that by transferring questions of control over expression from the judiciary to the legislatures, it provides an enormously beneficial protection for the politically powerful mass media, if not for other elements of society with strong First Amendment interests but weaker influence in the legislative process.

Although the Supreme Court has exceeded its historical warrant in subjecting judicial injunctions to the full burden of our law's traditional aversion to prior restraints, there are sound reasons for viewing all prior controls—not only wholesale licensing and censorship—as dangerous to free expression. Generally it is administratively easier to prevent expression in advance than to punish it after the fact. The inertia of public officials in responding to a *fait accompli*, the chance to look at whether expression has actually caused harm rather than speculate about the matter, public support for the speaker, and the interposition of juries and other procedural safeguards of the usual criminal or civil process all tend to reinforce tolerance when expression can only be dealt with by subsequent punishment. Moreover, all prior restraint systems, including injunctions, tend to divert attention from the central question of whether expression is protected to the subsidiary problem of promoting the effectiveness of the prior restraint system. Once a prior restraint is issued, the authority and prestige of the restraining agent are at stake. If it is disobeyed, the legality of the expression takes a back seat to the enforcement of obedience to the prior restraint process. Moreover, the time it takes a prior restraint process to decide produces a systematic delay of expression. On the other hand, where law must wait to move against expression after it has been published, time is on the side of freedom. All in all, even such prior restraints as judicial injunctions—which are more discriminating than wholesale censorship—tend toward irresponsible administration and an exaggerated assessment of the dangers of free expression.

BENNO C. SCHMIDT, JR.

Bibliography

BLASI, VINCENT 1981 Toward a Theory of Prior Restraint: The Central Linkage. *Minnesota Law Review* 66:11.

EMERSON, THOMAS 1955 The Doctrine of Prior Restraint *Law and Contemporary Problems* 20:648.

SCHMIDT, BENNO C., JR. 1977 Nebraska Press Association: An Expansion of Freedom and Contraction of Theory. *Stanford Law Review* 29:431.

PRISONERS' RIGHTS

Some might think that the very term "prisoners' rights" is an oxymoron, because the essence of being imprisoned is the reduction or elimination of rights. Prisoners have traditionally been deprived of VOTING RIGHTS and, obviously, of the right to travel outside the prison confines, often of the right to communicate freely with the outside world and of the right of conjugal relationships, and, at times, of the right of ACCESS TO COURTS to complain about even those rights that they retain.

There is a tension in constitutional doctrine between the need to enforce discipline in the difficult circumstances of the prison and the necessity of recognizing that in a society of law, even prisoners ought to have remedies for violation of whatever constitutional rights they possess and also to have the right to be immune from arbitrary and capricious actions of the prison hierarchy. This tension has expressed itself in judicial opinions in two major ways: first, the enunciation of a "hands-off doctrine" that precludes JURISDICTION to review complaints of inmates; and second, the determination, either broadly or narrowly, of the nature of the rights that a prisoner might have. In times when the cluster of rights is extremely narrow, the distinction between the first mode of analysis and the second is not great.

As late as 1963 a commentator could write that there is a "conviction held with virtual unanimity by the courts that it is beyond their power to review the internal management of the prison system." Much of this changed, however, when the Supreme Court held in *Wolff v. McDonnell* (1974), as part of its expansion of PROCEDURAL DUE PROCESS to the decision making of many institutions, that "a prisoner is not wholly stripped of constitutional protections when he is imprisoned for crime. There is no iron curtain drawn between the Constitution and the prisons of this country."

Still, the definition of rights for prisoners is almost always husbanded with conditions and recognition of concerns for the difficulties the warden faces. Where the FIRST AMENDMENT is concerned, RELIGIOUS LIBERTY is guaranteed but only to the extent that the opportunities to exercise that freedom must be "reasonable." Similarly, when the right to speak and communicate is concerned, the Court limited it in PELL V. PROCUNIER (1974) to the kind of expression that is "not inconsistent with [their] status as . . . prisoner[s] or with the legitimate penological objectives of the corrections system." In *Lee v. Washington* (1968) the Court implied that even racial SEGREGATION may be tolerated when it is essential to "prison security and discipline." And the Court held in *Hudson v. Palmer* (1984), a departure from previous expansion of privacy rights, that "the FOURTH AMENDMENT had no applicability to a prison cell."

With the wonderful perversity that makes legal development fascinating, the Supreme Court, in the late 1970s, expanded prisoners' rights of access to courts, while almost simultaneously narrowing the grounds for constitutional challenge.

Litigation concerning prisoners' rights is an indicator of concern about individual rights generally. As the Court changes its views of the breadth and definition of such rights, the treatment of alleged institutional wrongs in a correctional setting is like the canary a miner takes along down the shaft. Constitutional litigation during the 1960s and 1970s created massive exposure of the internal workings of correctional institutions and pressure for change. In many instances, wholesale reforms were imposed upon these institutions as a consequence of the litigation. But the canary is weakening. (See INSTITUTIONAL LITIGATION.)

MONROE E. PRICE

Bibliography

NOTE 1963 Beyond the Ken of the Courts: A Critique of Judicial Refusal to Review the Complaints of Convicts. *Yale Law Journal* 72:506.

PRIVACY

See: Right of Privacy

PRIVACY ACT
88 Stat. 1896 (1974)

The Privacy Act was passed in response to public concern about "data banks" maintained by United States government agencies. Often, a person did not know what agencies held files on him or what such files contained. In addition, information provided to one government agency—often under a promise of confidentiality—was passed on to a second agency to be used for a different purpose, and that without the knowledge or consent of the individual concerned.

The act was passed by Congress and signed by President GERALD R. FORD in December 1974. According to its provisions: an individual is to have access to any files concerning him maintained by a government agency (except law-enforcement and national security files); an individual who believes that information about him in a government file is inaccurate or incomplete may seek injunctive relief to correct the file; no agency is to use information provided by an individual for other than the original purpose, or to provide the information to another agency, without the individual's consent; no agency may deny benefits to individuals who refuse to disclose their social security numbers; and no agency may maintain records describing the exercise of rights protected by the FIRST AMENDMENT.

DENNIS J. MAHONEY

Bibliography

O'BRIEN, DAVID M. 1979 *Privacy, Law, and Public Policy.* New York: Praeger.

PRIVACY AND THE FIRST AMENDMENT

William L. Prosser has listed four categories of invasion of privacy: intrusion upon the plaintiff's seclusion or solitude, or into his private affairs; public disclosure of embarrassing private facts about the plaintiff; publicity which places the plaintiff in a false light in the public eye; and appropriation, for the defendant's advantage, of the plaintiff's name or likeness. Absent the communication of information disclosed by the intrusion, the first category of invasion raises no FIRST AMENDMENT issue.

The second category, the public disclosure of embarrassing private facts, clearly does raise a First Amendment issue. When does the FREEDOM OF THE PRESS to report "news" outbalance the individual's RIGHT TO PRIVACY, even if the disclosure is of embarrassing private facts? Thus far, the Supreme Court has only partially answered that question. In COX BROADCASTING CORPORATION V. COHN (1975) the Court held that the state could not impose liability for invasion of privacy by reason of the defendant's television news disclosure of the name of a rape victim. The Court held that the First Amendment immunized the press from such liability where the information disclosed was truthful and had already been publicly disclosed in court records. Subsequent decisions have indicated that such a First Amendment privilege applies as well to the publication of material in at least some official records designated confidential—for example, information about a criminal proceeding involving a juvenile, even though it was obtained from sources other than the public record. But what of intimate private fact disclosures that do not involve criminal proceedings, or other official action? Or suppose the disclosure of private facts is embarrassing to the subject, but does not injure reputation. Which prevails, the plaintiff's right of privacy or the defendant's FREEDOM OF SPEECH? The Supreme Court thus far has been silent on these issues, and the lower courts have offered no satisfactory answers.

The third category, known as "false light" privacy, was the subject of the Supreme Court's decision in *Time, Inc. v. Hill* (1967). Defendant's report in *Life* magazine of plaintiffs' encounter with gangsters was in part false, though not reputation injuring. The Supreme Court held that the defendant was entitled to a First Amendment defense in a false-light privacy action unless the defendant knew the matter reported was false or published with reckless disregard of the truth. The Court acknowledged that this standard was borrowed from the First Amendment defense to DEFAMATION which it had fashioned in NEW YORK TIMES V. SULLIVAN (1964). Where *Sullivan* had involved statements about a public official, *Hill* seemingly extended the First Amendment privilege to statements about "a matter of public interest." The First Amendment defamation defense was later expanded in GERTZ V. ROBERT WELCH, INC. (1974) to apply to reports involving "public figures" as well as "public officials," and to require at least a negligence standard of liability as regards defamation of nonpublic figures. The Supreme Court has not had occasion to reconsider the impact of the First Amendment upon "false light" privacy cases since its decision in *Gertz*.

The fourth category is more generally referred to as the "right of publicity." It differs fundamentally from the other categories in that the injury does not consist of embarrassment and humiliation. It is based rather upon the wrongful appropriation of a person's (usually a celebrity's) name or likeness for commercial purposes. The measure of recovery is based upon the value of the use, not the injury suffered from mental distress. The only Supreme Court decision to consider the impact of the First Amendment upon the right of publicity has been *Zacchini v. Scripps-Howard Broadcasting Co.* (1977). The plaintiff performed a "human cannonball" act at a county fair. The defendant photographed his entire act and broadcast it in a local television news program. Plaintiff sued for infringement of his right of publicity. The Supreme Court held that the defendant was not entitled to a First Amendment defense. The Court regarded this as "the strongest case" for the right of publicity because it involved "the appropriation of the very activity by which the entertainer acquired his reputation in the first place." Even in the usual case, where a celebrity's name or likeness is used in order to sell a product, the lower courts have not found the First Amendment to constitute a defense, and it seems unlikely that the Supreme Court would take a contrary view. On the other hand, where the name or likeness is used as a part of an informational work, such as a biography or a biographical motion picture, in most cases the First Amendment would appear to constitute a valid defense.

MELVILLE B. NIMMER

Bibliography

NIMMER, MELVILLE B. 1968 The Right to Speak from *Times* to *Time:* First Amendment Theory Applied to Libel and Misapplied to Privacy. *California Law Review* 56:935–967.

PROSSER, WILLIAM L. 1971 *Torts,* 4th ed. St. Paul, Minn.: West Publishing Co.

PRIVILEGE, EVIDENTIARY

See: Evidentiary Privileges

PRIVILEGE AGAINST SELF-INCRIMINATION

See: Right Against Self-Incrimination

PRIVILEGED COMMENT

See: Libel and the First Amendment

PRIVILEGE FROM ARREST

That legislators should be free from the threat of arrest except for notorious crimes while attending legislative sessions or en route to or from them has been recognized in English law for at least 1300 years. After the American Revolution that privilege was inserted into several state constitutions and the ARTICLES OF CONFEDERATION.

Because the privilege does not extend to "TREASON, FELONY, or BREACH OF THE PEACE," it amounts in practice to immunity from arrest in civil matters, such as nonpayment of debts. The privilege is less a guarantee of legislative independence from executive abuse than a protection of public business from interference growing out of private disputes.

DENNIS J. MAHONEY

PRIVILEGES AND IMMUNITIES

The Constitution's two privileges and immunities clauses were born of different historical circumstances and inspired by different purposes. Yet they are bound together by more than their textual similarity. Both clauses look to the formation of "a more perfect Union," both sound the theme of equality, and both have raised questions about the role of the federal judiciary in protecting NATURAL RIGHTS.

The original Constitution's Article IV set out several principles to govern relations among the states. The FULL FAITH AND CREDIT CLAUSE established one such principle, and so did the clauses providing for interstate rendition of fugitive felons and fugitive slaves. (See SLAVERY AND THE CONSTITUTION; FUGITIVE SLAVERY; FUGITIVE FROM JUSTICE.) Along with these "interstate comity" provisions was included this guarantee: "The citizens of each state shall be entitled to all privileges and immunities of citizens in the several states." Called "the basis of the Union" by ALEXANDER HAMILTON in THE FEDERALIST #80, the first privileges and immunities clause aimed at preventing a state from subjecting another state's citizens to discriminatory treatment of the kind customarily given to ALIENS. The framers saw the clause as embodying the principles of a much longer provision in the ARTICLES OF CONFEDERATION, which had begun with this statement of objective: "The better to secure and perpetuate mutual friendship and intercourse among the people of the different states in this union. . . ."

From the beginning everyone understood that Article IV's privileges and immunities clause could not mean exactly what it said. A Virginian who came to Boston surely had a right to engage in trade, but just as surely could not expect to be a candidate for governor of Massachusetts. What principle distinguished these two activities? Early in the nineteenth century, Justice BUSHROD WASHINGTON, sitting on circuit in CORFIELD V. CORYELL (1823), read the clause to guarantee equality for out-of-state citizens only as to "those privileges and immunities which are, in their nature, fundamental; which belong, of right, to the citizens of all free governments; and which have, at all times, been enjoyed by the citizens of the several states which comprise this Union. . . ." Washington went on to list "some" of those "fundamental" privileges, in language broadly inclusive of nearly every sort of right imaginable. Not only did a citizen of one state have a right "to pass through, or to reside in any other state for purposes of trade, agriculture, professional pursuits, or otherwise"; he also had the right, said Washington, to "enjoyment of life and liberty, with the right to acquire and possess property of every kind, and to pursue and obtain happiness and safety; subject nevertheless to such restraints as the government may justly prescribe for the general good of the whole." Other rights were listed, such as a right of access to a state's courts and a right to nondiscriminatory taxation. Portentously, the passage ended by mentioning "the elective franchise" as a fundamental right.

No one, not even Washington, thought a state had a constitutional duty to let out-of-staters vote in state elections. The inference arises that in offering his list of "fundamental" privileges and immunities Washington had in mind something beyond a catalogue of rights of interstate equality. That broader objective may have been to make Article IV's privileges and immunities clause into a generalized federal constitutional guarantee of liberty, available to local citizens and out-of-staters alike—with identification and enforcement of "fundamental" liberties in the hands of the federal judiciary.

This "natural rights" vision of the privileges and immunities clause of Article IV has never found favor in the Supreme Court. The Court has not interpreted the clause as a source of substantive rights, apart from the right to some measure of equality in a state's treatment of citizens of other states. The term "citizens" has been consistently limited, in this context, to natural persons who are citizens of the United States, thus excluding both corporations and aliens from the clause's protection. The substantive reach of the clause, too, was narrow in the Court's early interpreta-

tions: the right to pursue a common calling, the right to own and deal with property, the right of access to state courts.

Even in this restrictive interpretation, the interstate equality demanded by the clause overlaps with the antidiscrimination principle that restricts STATE REGULATIONS OF COMMERCE. The same law, in other words, might violate both the implied limitations of the COMMERCE CLAUSE and the privileges and immunities clause of Article IV. Yet the commerce clause has been a more significant guarantee against interstate discrimination. The commerce clause presumptively forbids a state to discriminate against INTERSTATE (or FOREIGN) COMMERCE, even when the persons engaging in that commerce are the state's own citizens. And the commerce clause, unlike the privileges and immunities clause, protects both corporations and aliens from discrimination against their activities in commerce.

A major shift in judicial attitude toward the privileges and immunities clause was signaled by TOOMER V. WITSELL (1948). South Carolina licensed shrimp boats in coastal waters, demanding license fees of $25 per boat from residents and $2,500 from nonresidents. (Since the adoption of the FOURTEENTH AMENDMENT, state residence and state citizenship have been treated as virtually equivalent.) The Supreme Court held this discrimination a violation of both the commerce clause and the privileges and immunities clause, and in its opinion reformulated the latter clause's governing doctrine. Henceforth any state discrimination against citizens of other states would be held invalid unless the state demonstrated a "substantial reason for the discrimination" apart from their out-of-state citizenship. In *Doe v. Bolton* (1973), a companion case to ROE V. WADE (1973), the Court applied the *Toomer* formula to strike down a Georgia law allowing only state residents to obtain abortions in Georgia.

Toomer seemed to have dispatched the "fundamental" privileges limitation in favor of a straightforward requirement of substantial justification for discrimination against out-of-staters. But here as elsewhere in constitutional law the idea of FUNDAMENTAL INTERESTS has had remarkable recuperative power. BALDWIN V. FISH & GAME COMMISSION (1978) revived the doctrine to uphold a Montana law that charged a state resident $9 for an elk hunting license and a nonresident $225. (The nonresident might also use the license to kill one bear and one deer, to shoot game birds, and to fish. The same package of sanguinary privileges would cost a resident $30.) Elk hunting, said the Court, was a sport, not a means to livelihood; equal access for out-of-staters to Montana elk was "not basic to the maintenance of well-being of the Union," and thus not a "fundamental" privilege protected by Article IV against interstate discrimination. Only four weeks later, in HICKLIN V. ORBECK (1978), the Court returned to the *Toomer* approach to invalidate an Alaska law giving preference to state residents in employment in jobs related to construction of the Alaska pipeline. The state had not offered substantial justification for the discrimination, the Court said, and therefore it was invalid. *Baldwin* was not cited.

The cleanest way to resolve the tension between these two decisions would have been to abandon *Baldwin* as a doctrinal sport. Instead, the Supreme Court combined both lines of decision in a new formula. In *United Building & Construction Trades Council v. Mayor and Council of Camden* (1984) and SUPREME COURT OF NEW HAMPSHIRE V. PIPER (1985) the Court established a two-part test for determining the validity of a state law challenged under Article IV's privileges and immunities clause. The first inquiry follows *Baldwin*: the law is limited by the clause only when its discrimination against out-of-staters touches a privilege that is "fundamental" to interstate harmony. The Court made clear in *Piper* that access to a means of livelihood is such a privilege. The second inquiry follows *Toomer* and *Hicklin*: if the privilege in question is "fundamental," the discrimination is invalid unless there is a "substantial" reason for treating out-of-staters differently, and the law's discrimination bears a "substantial relationship" to that objective. The second requirement states an intermediate STANDARD OF REVIEW for judicial scrutiny of both the state's purposes and its discriminatory means.

Special problems have plagued the Supreme Court's efforts to apply the privileges and immunities clause of Article IV to cases in which the discriminating states have acted as purchasers of goods and services, or owners of property, or proprietors of enterprises. In the *Camden* case, the Court refused to recognize a general exemption of such activities from the strictures of the clause; if the activities affected a "fundamental" interest, the clause would be implicated. In the same breath, however, the Court suggested that the state's interests as a market participant might be relevant to the second part of the new two-part inquiry: the question of justification for discriminating against out-of-staters. Justification for some state preferences for local citizens may be found in the citizens' obligations to support local government. *Toomer*'s teaching is that the justification must be substantial.

Thus far the privileges and immunities clause of Article IV has been applied only to state laws discriminating against out-of-staters. Concurring in *Zobel v. Williams* (1982), Justice SANDRA DAY O'CONNOR argued for a broader application of the clause that would place constitutional limits on any state law—even a law discriminating between different groups of the state's own citizens—when the law disadvantages persons who have only recently arrived in the state. Justice O'Connor would have found a violation of the clause in Alaska's law distributing the state's oil revenues to Alaska citizens in proportion to the length of their residence; she argued that the law imposed "disabilities of alienage"—a result the clause was designed to forbid. The majority, holding the law invalid on equal protection grounds, rejected this novel interpretation in favor of the conventional view: the privileges and immunities clause of Article IV is inapplicable to such a case, for the clause speaks only to discrimination against citizens of other states.

A second privileges and immunities clause was added to the Constitution in 1868 as part of the Fourteenth Amendment: "No state shall make or enforce any law which shall abridge the privileges or immunities of citizens of the United States." Justice ROBERT H. JACKSON, concurring in EDWARDS V. CALIFORNIA (1941), said expansively that "[t]his clause was adopted to make United States citizenship the dominant and paramount allegiance among us." The fact is that the amendment's framers did not sharply differentiate the functions of the various clauses of the amendment's first section and did not speak with one voice concerning the purposes of the privileges and immunities clause. Undoubtedly, however, the clause was meant to have some effect as a limitation on the states. The amendment's opening sentence "overruled" DRED SCOTT V. SANDFORD (1857) by conferring United States citizenship and state citizenship on "all persons born or naturalized in the United States and subject to the jurisdiction thereof." The privileges and immunities clause, following immediately in the amendment's text, surely was intended to give some substantive content to the rights of citizenship, and particularly to the equal citizenship of blacks. (See EQUAL PROTECTION OF THE LAWS.) Yet the Supreme Court, in its first encounter with the clause, read it, as Justice STEPHEN J. FIELD aptly said in dissent, to be "a vain and idle enactment, which accomplished nothing." In the SLAUGHTERHOUSE CASES (1873) a 5–4 majority, distinguishing the privileges and immunities of national citizenship from those of state citizenship, confined the former to rights established elsewhere in the Constitution and federal laws and to rights that were already fairly inferable from the relation of a citizen to the national government. (Examples of the latter would be the right to United States protection in other countries, the right to enter public lands, or the right to inform federal authorities of violations of federal law.) The majority described *Corfield*'s list of "fundamental" rights as privileges of state citizenship, subject to Article IV's guarantee of interstate equality but untouched by the new privileges and immunities clause of the Fourteenth Amendment.

The Court feared that a contrary reading of the privileges and immunities clause, coupled with the power of Congress to enforce the Fourteenth Amendment, would not only "constitute this court a perpetual censor upon all legislation of the states" but also "bring within the power of Congress the entire domain of civil rights heretofore belonging exclusively to the states." Such a result, the Court accurately said, would radically restructure the federal union, centralizing power in the national government. No doubt some congressional proponents of the Fourteenth Amendment had hoped for precisely that result. The *Slaughterhouse Cases* dissenters viewed the prospect with equanimity and even sought to revive the natural rights philosophy of *Corfield* in the name of the Fourteenth Amendment. In doctrinal terms, however, they lost the battle decisively. The Court has never given the Fourteenth Amendment's privileges and immunities clause any significant content that is distinctively its own.

Occasional flurries of activity have suggested impending revitalization of the clause. Justice HUGO L. BLACK made the clause a centerpiece in his effort to persuade the Court to recognize the total incorporation of the Bill of Rights into the Fourteenth Amendment. (See INCORPORATION DOCTRINE.) And for a season the clause came to life as a limitation on state taxing power, until MADDEN V. KENTUCKY (1940) overruled COLGATE V. HARVEY (1935). Individual Justices have promoted the clause in concurring opinions, such as that of Justice Jackson in *Edwards v. California* (1941) (right to move freely from state to state) and that of Justice OWEN ROBERTS in HAGUE V. COMMITTEE FOR INDUSTRIAL ORGANIZATION (1939) (right to assemble to discuss national legislation), but these ventures have been largely superseded by the development of other constitutional limitations on the states.

In the modern era, Justice Jackson's *Edwards* argument has borne fruit in the development of a constitutional RIGHT TO TRAVEL. The right is now well established as a limitation on state power, but the right's source in the Constitution remains unspecified. The commerce clause is one obvious candidate, and not just one but both privileges and immunities clauses have also been nominated. (Congressional interferences with the freedom of foreign travel have been tested against the Fifth Amendment's DUE PROCESS clause.) Plainly, the Supreme Court has no need to rely on either privileges and immunities clause as an independent source for the right to travel.

Although the natural rights approach to constitutional adjudication failed to make headway in the name of either of the privileges and immunities clauses, in the field of ECONOMIC REGULATION the views of the *Slaughterhouse Cases* dissenters came to prevail for almost half a century under the banner of SUBSTANTIVE DUE PROCESS. (See FREEDOM OF CONTRACT.) That experiment in JUDICIAL ACTIVISM was closed in the 1930s, but a similar philosophy has informed the revival of substantive due process as a protection of personal freedoms. Some commentators have suggested that the Fourteenth Amendment's privileges and immunities clause may be an apt vessel for these newer constitutional liberties, or even for yet-to-be-discovered affirmative constitutional obligations of government. After a century and more on the constitutional shelf, all the vessel needs is a little polishing.

KENNETH L. KARST

Bibliography

ELY, JOHN HART   1980   *Democracy and Distrust: A Theory of Judicial Review.* Pages 22–30. Cambridge, Mass.: Harvard University Press.

FAIRMAN, CHARLES   1971   *Reconstruction and Reunion, 1864–88, Part One.* Chap. 20. (Volume VI, History of the Supreme Court of the United States.) New York: Macmillan.

KURLAND, PHILIP B.   1972   The Privileges and Immunities Clause: "Its Hour Come Round at Last?" *Washington University Law Quarterly* 1972:405–420.

SIMSON, GARY J.   1979   Discrimination against Nonresidents and the Privileges and Immunities Clause of Article IV. *University of Pennsylvania Law Review* 128:379–401.

VARAT, JONATHAN D.   1981   State "Citizenship" and Interstate Equality. *University of Chicago Law Review* 48:487–572.

PRIVY COUNCIL

The Privy Council together with the monarch constitutes "the Crown," which is, in theory, the executive branch of the British government. Association of the council in the exercise of executive power was a check against the abuse of that power. The council is appointed for life and comprises members of the royal family, ministers and former ministers of state, judges, and distinguished subjects. In practice, the cabinet has become, through an evolutionary process, the executive committee of the Privy Council.

In the seventeenth and eighteenth centuries the Privy Council exercised the royal prerogative of disallowing acts of the colonial legislatures. At the same time the council was the highest court of appeal from the colonial courts (a function now exercised by the judicial committee of the Privy Council). The role of the Privy Council in the political order of the British Empire was thus suggestive of both the VETO POWER and JUDICIAL REVIEW.

Some of the early state constitutions provided for a council to share the executive power or to review acts of the legislature. At the CONSTITUTIONAL CONVENTION OF 1787 various unsuccessful proposals for a plural executive reflected the British notion of the Privy Council as a check against royal tyranny.

DENNIS J. MAHONEY

PRIZE CASES
2 Black (67 U.S.) 635 (1863)

In the *Prize Cases*, a 5–4 majority of the Supreme Court sustained the validity of President ABRAHAM LINCOLN's blockade proclamations of April 1861, refusing to declare unconstitutional his unilateral actions in meeting the Confederacy's military initiatives.

Lincoln proclaimed a blockade of southern ports on April 19 and 27, 1861. Congress authorized him to declare a state of insurrection by the Act of July 13, 1861, thereby, at least in the view of the dissenters, giving formal legislative recognition to the existence of civil war. By the Act of August 6, 1861, Congress retroactively ratified all Lincoln's military actions. The *Prize Cases* involved seizures of vessels bound for Confederate ports prior to July 13, 1861.

For the majority, Justice ROBERT C. GRIER held that a state of civil war existed de facto after the firing on Fort Sumter (April 12, 1861) and that the Supreme Court would take judicial notice of its existence. Though neither Congress nor President can declare war against a state of the Union, Grier conceded, when states waged war against the United States government, the President was "bound to meet it in the shape it presented itself, without waiting for Congress

to baptize it with a name." Whether the insurgents were to be accorded belligerent status, and hence be subject to blockade, was a POLITICAL QUESTION to be decided by the President, whose decision was conclusive on the courts. Grier reproved the dissenters by reminding them that the court should not "cripple the arm of the government and paralyze its power by subtle definitions and ingenious sophisms."

Justice SAMUEL NELSON for the dissenters (Chief Justice ROGER B. TANEY, and Justices JOHN CATRON and NATHAN CLIFFORD) argued that only Congress can declare a war and that consequently the President can neither declare nor recognize it. A civil war's "existence in a material sense . . . has no relevancy or weight when the question is what constitutes war in a legal sense." Lincoln's acts before 13 July 1861 constituted merely his "personal war against those in rebellion." Therefore seizures under the blockade proclamations were illegal.

The *Prize Cases* permitted the federal government the convenient ambiguity of treating the Confederacy as an organized insurgency and as a conventional belligerent. The opinions also had an implicit relevance to other disputed exercises of presidential authority. Defenders of a broad executive power could argue that the majority opinion's reasoning supported the constitutionality of Lincoln's call for volunteers, of his suspension of the writ of HABEAS CORPUS, and perhaps also of the EMANCIPATION PROCLAMATION.

WILLIAM M. WIECEK

PROBABLE CAUSE

The FOURTH AMENDMENT guarantees in part that "The right of the people to be secure in their persons, houses, papers and effects, against UNREASONABLE SEARCHES and seizures shall not be violated, and no warrants shall issue but upon probable cause. . . ." The determination of probable cause necessarily turns on specific facts and often requires the courts and the police to make most difficult decisions. The need for probable cause in American CRIMINAL PROCEDURE arises in three instances: probable cause to ARREST or detain, probable cause to search, and probable cause to prosecute. The first two derive constitutional status directly from the Fourth Amendment and govern the conduct of the police. An inquiry by a judge or GRAND JURY into probable cause for prosecution is not constitutionally required in state cases; however, this check on the exercise of prosecutorial discretion is prescribed by statute or state constitutional mandate in most states and is constitutionally required by the Fifth Amendment in federal cases.

As to arrest and search, the language of the Fourth Amendment does not distinguish between SEARCHES AND SEIZURES of objects, and arrests—"seizures" of the person. While one might assume that the term would have equivalent meanings in both the search and arrest contexts, the differences between arrests of suspects and searches for evidence or contraband require the probable cause standard to be applied to different types of data for the two procedures. Probable cause for a search does not automatically support an arrest, nor does a valid ARREST WARRANT necessarily support a search.

Probable cause in the arrest context was defined by the United States Supreme Court in *Beck v. Ohio* (1964) as turning on "whether at that moment [of arrest] the facts and circumstances within [the officers'] knowledge and of which they [have] reasonably trustworthy information [are] sufficient to warrant a prudent man in believing that the [suspect] had committed or was committing an offense. There are two potential sources of information—personal knowledge and "trustworthy" secondary data. The Supreme Court has clearly established that secondary data—information not within the officer's personal knowledge—can supply sufficient grounds for an arrest. Thus, the police may rely on reports from other cities or states to support valid arrests, as in *Whitely v. Warden* (1971). Credible information supplied by an informant may also be used.

The officer's specific knowledge derived from direct contact with the arrestee is usually the primary support for a finding of probable cause. It is clear such information must be specific. Mere knowledge that, for example, a suspect has been convicted in the past coupled with an unidentified INFORMANT'S TIP alleging current criminal activity has been held to be insufficient.

Even specific EVIDENCE linking an individual to a crime will not justify an arrest if the evidence has been discovered unconstitutionally. An arrest cannot be justified by evidence seized pursuant to the arrest; as the Court said in *Sibron v. New York* (1968): "An incident search may not precede an arrest and serve as part of its justification."

Evidence discovered in an on-street investigative encounter that has not yet reached the level of an arrest may be properly used to create probable cause. For example, if as a result of a STOP-AND-FRISK encounter on the street, authorized by TERRY V. OHIO (1968), an officer feels a weapon, he has probable cause

to arrest for carrying a concealed weapon. Similarly, if in the course of a temporary detention the suspect fails adequately to account for his suspicious actions or if he affirmatively discloses incriminating evidence, probable cause to arrest may be established. The same is true if the suspect runs away. While flight alone does not create probable cause to arrest, it is a significant factor to be considered in the overall assessment.

By contrast, however, as the Court held in *Brown v. Texas* (1979), the mere failure of a suspect to identify himself, without more, does not supply probable cause. Nor may a valid arrest rely on an individual's failure to protect his innocence when found with suspects for whom probable cause exists, as in *United States v. Di Re* (1948).

Di Re also stands for the proposition that mere presence of an individual in the company of others who are properly suspected of criminal activity does not constitute probable cause. Subsequent cases, however, have made clear that there are limits to this principle. The difficulties here have largely come with possessory offenses. On the one hand, the Court in *Johnson v. United States* (1947) held that a tip that opium was being smoked coupled with the smell of opium outside a hotel room did not give rise to probable cause to arrest everyone in the room. Although there was probable cause to believe a crime was being committed, there was insufficient information to determine who was committing it. Yet in KER V. CALIFORNIA (1963) the Court upheld the arrest of a married couple found in their kitchen with a brick of marijuana, even though the tip leading them there had linked only the husband to the contraband. The Court reasoned that the combination of the wife's presence in a small kitchen with obvious contraband, coupled with information that the husband had been using the apartment as a base for his drug activities, gave sufficient grounds for a reasonable belief that they were both in possession of marijuana.

This requirement of linking probable cause specifically to the arrestee was again mentioned by the Court in YBARRA V. ILLINOIS (1979). There the police procured a valid warrant to search a tavern believed to be the center of drug activity. In executing the warrant, the police searched about a dozen of the tavern's patrons, including Ybarra. While the case thus actually dealt with the legitimacy of the search rather than an arrest, the Court stated: "[W]here the standard is probable cause, a search or *seizure of a person* must be supported by probable cause particularized with respect to that person. This requirement cannot be undercut or avoided by simply pointing to the fact that coincidentally there exists probable cause to search or seize another or to search the premises where the person may happen to be." (Emphasis added.) *Ybarra* thus reinforces the requirement that probable cause be particularized to the person arrested; mere presence at a place connected with criminal activity, or in the company of suspected criminals, without more, is inadequate.

Finally, the Court held in *Gerstein v. Pugh* (1975) that whenever a suspect has been arrested without a warrant and with no prior INDICTMENT, he is entitled to a quick judicial check on the police conclusion that there is probable cause to detain him if he will undergo a "significant pretrial restraint on liberty"—more than the mere condition that he return for trial. This hearing, while constitutionally required if these conditions are met, need not be adversary and does not give rise to a RIGHT TO COUNSEL. As with the hearing to obtain an arrest warrant, this proceeding does not even require the accused's presence. The standard of proof is simply whether there is probable cause to believe the suspect has committed a crime.

The search context is the second major area in which the issue of probable cause arises. Most courts hold that probable cause for a search exists when the facts and circumstances in a given situation are sufficient to warrant a man of reasonable caution to believe that seizable objects are located at the place to be searched. (See BRINEGAR V. UNITED STATES, 1949; CARROLL V. UNITED STATES, 1925.)

The probable cause determination is generally based on the information supplied to the magistrate in the application for a search warrant. An application must be sworn to and must allege the place to be searched, the property to be seized, the person having the property if it is to be taken from his control, and the underlying crime. There is no requirement that everything must be set out in the application itself; affidavits may be attached or sworn statements taken before the magistrate. Because applications are usually submitted by police officers who do not have legal training, the language of the application is to be construed in a nontechnical way. Nevertheless, if the application is all that is submitted, and it is expressed in "conclusory" terms only, it will be insufficient to establish probable cause. Sufficient data must be contained in either the application itself or the supporting affidavits to justify the magistrate in issuing the warrant.

Although no blanket assertion can explain all cases involving probable cause for the issuance of search warrants, one useful rule of thumb is that if the affidavit and supporting documents allege facts that can explain to the magistrate the basis for the probable cause determination, a warrant based on such an affidavit is likely to be good. On the other hand, when an affidavit asserts a mere conclusion such as "we have it on good information and do believe there are drugs at the suspect's home," there is no independent basis for the magistrate's determination. A warrant based on such a showing is likely to be invalid.

The hardest issue arises when the affiant police officer is not the source of the information but is relying on an informant. Most of the Supreme Court's decisions concerning the required credibility of informants have arisen in cases involving SEARCH WARRANTS rather than arrest warrants, but the standards for use of informants in both contexts are the same.

The Supreme Court first enunciated the requirements for a valid informant-based warrant in AGUILAR V. TEXAS (1964). According to this test, the affidavit must: (a) set forth sufficient underlying circumstances to demonstrate to a neutral and detached magistrate how the informant reached his/her conclusion; *and* (b) establish the reliability or credibility of the informant. In the subsequent case, SPINELLI V. UNITED STATES (1969), the Supreme Court explained that the absence of a statement detailing the manner in which the informant's data were gathered renders it especially important that "the tip describe the accused's criminal activity in sufficient detail that the magistrate may know that he is relying on something more substantial than a casual rumor . . . or an accusation based merely on an individual's general reputation."

The *Aguilar/Spinelli* test has, however, been rejected by ILLINOIS V. GATES (1983). The Court in *Gates* introduced a totality-of-the-circumstances test, stating that it was not necessary to establish the credibility of the informant as a separate element to a valid search warrant. Instead, reliability and credibility of the informer and his basis of knowledge are considered as intertwining considerations that may illuminate the probable cause issue. In *Gates* the police received an anonymous informant's letter containing details of the defendants' involvement in drug trafficking which were corroborated by police investigations. The Court held that this provided a sufficient basis for a finding of probable cause.

Finally, according to *Henry v. United States* (1959), if the police had probable cause to arrest or search, the fact that the information on which they relied turns out to be false does not invalidate the arrest or search. Sufficient probability is the touchstone of Fourth Amendment reasonableness. (See PRELIMINARY HEARING.)

CHARLES H. WHITEBREAD

Bibliography

LaFave, Wayne R. 1978 *Search and Seizure: A Treatise on the Fourth Amendment.* St. Paul, Minn.: West Publishing Co.

PROCEDURAL DUE PROCESS OF LAW, CIVIL

The Fifth Amendment forbids the United States to "deprive" any person of "life, liberty, or property without DUE PROCESS OF LAW." The FOURTEENTH AMENDMENT imposes an identical prohibition on the states.

Due process is the ancient core of CONSTITUTIONALISM. It is a traditional legal expression of concern for the fate of persons in the presence of organized social power. The question of according due process arises when governments assert themselves adversely to the interests of individuals.

In modern usage "due process" connotes a certain normative ideal for decisions about the exercise of power. Very broadly, it has come to mean decisions that are not arbitrary, but are aligned with publicly accepted aims and values; are not dictatorial, but allow affected persons a suitable part in their making; and are not oppressive, but treat those affected with the respect owed political associates and fellow human beings. It is from the liberal individualist tradition that these abstract due process standards—of reason, voice, and dignity—have drawn their more concrete content. That content includes the definition of proper aims for state activity, the canons of legitimating participation and consent, and the conceptions of human personality that set the threshold of respectful treatment.

The law distinguishes between "substantive" and "procedural" due process. An arbitrary or groundless decision may violate substantive due process regardless of how it came to be made. O'CONNOR V. DONALDSON (1975), for example, held that no antecedent procedure will justify incarceration of a harmless eccentric. Conversely, a peremptory decision may violate procedural due process regardless of purposive justification. Guilt in fact will not justify sudden, final dismissal of a faithless government employee without a hearing, as the Supreme Court stated in ARNETT V. KENNEDY (1974). The due process claim is "procedural" rather than "substantive" when it questions not the state's authority to impose the harm in question by an adequate decision process, but rather the adequacy of the process actually used.

Of course, procedural demands gain much of their power from their perceived contribution to substantive accuracy and enlightenment. Justice FELIX FRANKFURTER stated in JOINT ANTI-FASCIST COMMITTEE V. McGRATH (1951): "No better instrument has been devised for arriving at truth than to give a person in jeopardy of serious loss notice of the case against him and an opportunity to meet it. Nor has a better way been found for generating the feeling, so important to a popular government, that justice has been done."

The focal concern of procedural due process is the set of procedures, epitomized by the judicial trial, whereby governing rules and standards are brought to bear on individuals in specific cases. The doctrine also has some further extension to the formation of the governing rules and standards. Due process can support a claim for direct voice in the formation process, for example, by industry members regarding regulatory standards under consideration by an administrative agency. It can also be the ground of an objection to the nonrepresentative character of the political process in which a standard originates, for example, a restriction on professional entry adopted by a board composed of self-interested professionals. There may also be a due process failure in the way a legal standard is formulated. The standard may be too vague and ill-defined to ensure even-handed application or allow for effective submission of proofs and arguments by someone contesting its application; or, conversely, it may be so narrowly drawn as to represent an arbitrary or vindictive discrimination against a disfavored few. Lawmaking defects of these various kinds are chiefly the concern of doctrines of SEPARATION OF POWERS, unconstitutional delegation, VAGUENESS, and prohibition of BILLS OF ATTAINDER, but they cannot in practice be held entirely separate from procedural due process claims.

In *Joint Anti-Fascist Refugee Committee v. McGrath* Justice Frankfurter invoked a history in which the adversary judicial trial has dominated our law's vision of procedural due process, as the model of a procedure designed to assure reason, voice, and dignity to individuals threatened with harm by the state. Criminal due process shows the fullest development of the adversarial model, just as criminal proceedings tend to maximize the conditions bespeaking the need for adversarial safeguards: charges specifically directed against the accused individual, by highly visible officers acting in the state's name, threatening not only tangible deprivation of liberty or wealth but also public degradation. Some state-initiated proceedings against individuals, such as those brought to establish paternity or terminate parental status, while nominally civil in character, resemble criminal prosecutions in their accusatory and stigmatic implications or in the gravity of their threatened sanctions, leaving little doubt about the need to grant respondents something approaching the full set of due process safeguards. Such safeguards were required by the Court in LASSITER V. DEPARTMENT OF SOCIAL SERVICES (1981). As cases of impending state-imposed harm depart further from the criminal prosecution paradigm, however, they reveal that puzzling issues of political and legal principle are latent in the general ideal of due process. Such cases pose two distinct questions for due process doctrine. First, does the occasion demand any kind of proceeding at all? Assuming an affirmative answer, the second question is, what process is due?

Events that from certain perspectives are describable as deprivations of life, liberty, or property in which the state is implicated—for example, a creditor acting under a legal privilege to repossess consumer goods from an assertedly defaulting debtor—may occur with no provision in the law for any process at all. The most theoretically telling of recent judicial encounters with due process doctrine has been concerned with defining the occasions when some trial-type process is constitutionally required.

Due process further stands for a constitutionally mandated procedural code for the fair conduct of whatever trial-type proceedings are to occur. In this second aspect, due process doctrine is a compendium of answers to such varied questions as: May the hearing be postponed until after the onset of the deprivation (such as a summary suspension of a student from school) or must there be a predeprivation hearing? May the state depart from COMMON LAW rules regarding HEARSAY evidence, allow its judges to interrogate witnesses, use publication rather than personal contact as a means of notifying concerned parties of pending proceedings, or deny parties the assistance of counsel in small claims tribunals?

The answers found in due process doctrine to such questions will bind a government just insofar as it chooses, or is required by the first aspect of the doctrine, to use judicial-type forums or trial-type proceedings to carry out their pursuits. The chief problems posed by such questions are the recurrent ones of JUDICIAL REVIEW and CONSTITUTIONAL INTERPRETATION: from what sources, by what modes of reasoning, shall the answers be drawn, given the breadth and imprecision of constitutional text? Historically, the main methodological alternatives and debates have arisen in the context of criminal prosecutions and been thence carried over to the civil side.

Constitutional claims to trial-type proceedings are most obviously compelling when individuals stand to be harmed by actions of officials performing state functions or wielding state powers. Yet even in such cases the individual interests at stake may be found insufficient to call due process rights into play. On a textual level, the question plainly is whether the affected interest is identifiable as "life, liberty, or property." History, however, discloses contrasting approaches to that question. It was once commonly supposed that any serious imposition on an individual—any "grievous loss"—could qualify as a constitutionally significant deprivation. A chief feature of contemporary due process doctrine is that the potency of a harm as a due process trigger turns not on such an ordinary assessment of its weight or practical severity but rather on a technical, categorical judgment about its legal "nature." In adjudicating what categories of interests legally qualify as "life," "liberty," or "property" for due process analysis, the Court has drawn eclectically on sources both naturalistic and positivistic—on both a HIGHER LAW tradition and on currently enacted law.

This eclecticism, and indeed the entire complex practice of categorically excluding some concededly weighty interests from due process protection, has apparently evolved out of the Court's encounters with modern welfare state activism. Consider the case of a government worker unceremoniously fired, or of a disability pensioner whose monthly payments are cut off. In such cases the underlying due process values of reason, voice, and dignity may seem to call as strongly for a chance to be heard as in cases of revocation of a professional license or dispossession of land or goods. Yet neither a government job nor a disability benefit is "property" in the common speech of our own culture or that of the constitutional Framers; and although their loss might be called a loss of liberty, to speak so broadly would bring within the sweep of procedural due process many cases that evidently do not belong there, for example, denial of admission to a state university.

The Court's response, in cases like GOLDBERG V. KELLY (1970) and BISHOP V. WOOD (1976), has been to say that "property" may, indeed, include all manner of beneficial relations with the state or others, but only insofar as those relations are legal entitlements in the sense that explicit (or positive) law protects against their impairment. Thus a probationary employee lacking contractual term or statutory tenure may be peremptorily dismissed and the mere applicant peremptorily rejected; but the tenured employee has a right to be heard on the question of cause for dismissal, and the disability claimant under a statute containing definite eligibility rules may not be delisted—or even denied initial admission to benefits—without some opportunity to be heard on the issue of eligibility.

The method of equating due process protected "property" with positive legal entitlement—that is, by reference to clearly ordained, subconstitutional law—has several attractive features. It flows easily from the observation in BOARD OF REGENTS V. ROTH (1972) that a chief purpose of "the ancient institution of property" has been to "protect . . . expectations upon which people must rely in their daily lives" against being "arbitrarily undermined." Moreover, the positive-entitlement conception makes a neat fit with the idea that a fair hearing is the nub of due process. Entitlement makes directly clear what the hearing shall be about, for any law framing an entitlement must specify issues available for contest by anyone complaining of deprivation. Finally, entitlement analysis may seem to keep the judiciary clear of imposing on popularly accountable branches of government any political values or ends not accepted by those branches themselves. A judge enforcing due process rights appears to do little more than take seriously the decision of the lawmakers to create the entitlement in the first place.

The Court on some occasions has gone so far as to say that no interest qualifies as due process protected property except insofar as a legal rule safeguards its continued enjoyment. It seems clear that such statements cannot be taken literally. For example, the Court consistently refuses to approve procedures involving state officers in the repossession of goods bought on credit, without affording a prompt hearing to the buyer, no matter how clearly the applicable state law states that the buyer's entitlement to continued possession is to lapse upon the creditor's filing of notice of default (as distinguished from a judicial finding of default). Here it must be the brute reality of the buyer's established possession of the goods that comprises the constitutionally protected property, regardless of the explicit legal rules concerning its protection or duration.

The possession cases illustrate the naturalistic or higher law side of the Court's eclectic method of interest characterization. Protection of established possession against disorderly or unjustified incursion is an ancient fixture in both the rhetoric and the practice of Anglo-American common law and liberty. There are other common liberties similarly, if not all quite so anciently, esteemed: personal mobility and bodily security; liberties of conscience, intellect, and expres-

sion; domestic sanctuary, marital intimacy, and family solidarity; occupational freedom and professional autonomy. Although some of these interests find mention in the Bill of Rights, they mostly lack specific constitutional recognition.

The Court has used the "liberty" branch of the due process guarantee as a warrant for procedural protection for such interests, quite apart from their status as entitlements under positive law—and without overprecious worry about their status at ancestral common law. Regardless of whether the state's law purports, or ever did purport, to make into legal rights a schoolchild's security against corporal punishment (INGRAHAM V. WRIGHT, 1977), a parent's retention of child custody (*Santosky v. Kramer,* 1982), or a parolee's preference for remaining at liberty (*Morrissey v. Brewer,* 1972), those interests have been held protected, by the due process clause itself, against peremptory impairment by STATE ACTION. They are treated as constitutional entitlements regardless of whether they are statutory ones. It is easy to imagine why naturalist as well as positivist elements thus enter into the Court's characterizations. Welfare state activism positively invites forms of reliance and dependence which, however historically novel, evoke the essential purposes of due process; but the activist state is also prone to tread insensitively on old but still vital concerns that courts recognize as traditional freedoms.

The conclusion that an interest jeopardized by government action does qualify as someone's "life, liberty, or property" does not end the due process inquiry, for the question then remains of how much "process" is "due." It has been said that due process entails, at a minimum, "some kind of hearing" for the exposed individual. Precisely what kind depends on a judicial assessment: one which, according to the formulation in MATHEWS V. ELDRIDGE (1976), is supposed to take account of the gravity of the individual interest at stake, the utility of the requested procedures in avoiding factually misinformed or legally erroneous decisions, and the cost of those procedures to the pursuit of legitimate state objectives. The results of such a calculus can range from the heavy procedural armor available to criminal defendants in capital cases to the simple "opportunity to present his side of the story" that, under GOSS V. LOPEZ (1975), is due a student facing a short disciplinary suspension from school.

An important and oft-contested feature of the constitutionally guaranteed process is its timing relative to the deprivation. The Court long stood by the general proposition that (apart from "emergency" situations, such as seizure of contraband) due process meant predeprivation process. The Court continues to insist on some opportunity for in-person hearing prior to "core" deprivations such as dispossession of tangible property. In several cases, such as *Arnett v. Kennedy* and *Mathews v. Eldridge*, involving government jobs and other "benefits," the Court has accepted postponement of a live hearing until after the fall of the axe, when there has been predeprivation notice and opportunity for written protest, as long as there is adequate assurance for reparation in case the deprivation is eventually found unjustified.

Under pressure of the "mass justice" conditions imposed by modern governmental benefit programs involving very large numbers of eligibility decisions, there has been indication in recent cases and commentaries of tolerance for an alternative due process model, one less concerned than the traditional trial-type model with participation values. In this alternative managerial model, the measure of due process is not the quality of the opportunity given affected individuals for a say in the resolution of their own cases but quality control in the production of decisions. The aim is not voice for the individual but accuracy in the aggregate of the resolutions reached over a period of program administration. As advocates of this alternative model recognize, two factors are required to justify the model's use in any given setting: first, the relative dominance of individuals' interests in receiving their entitlements over their dignitary interests in participation; and, second, the value of such a systems management approach in maximizing the receipt of entitlements.

When judges find constitutional protection, under the broad cover of "liberty," for selected interests not specified as rights by constitutional text or other clearly uttered law, and when they determine just what form and quantum of process is "due" in respect of particular kinds of deprivations, they have obviously entered on the work of ranking substantive ends and values. Yet courts doing this kind of due process adjudication have not evinced great worry about usurpation of the lawmaking function. One reason may be that by merely requiring the state to provide some kind of hearing when it acts adversely to some individual's interests, a court does not consider itself ultimately to be preventing lawmakers from reaching whatever substantive results they choose.

However, the judicial act of fashioning procedural requirements, and attaching these to a select set of liberties, is not without substantive force. Procedural requirements can place serious practical obstacles in the way of legislative pursuits. They may be expen-

sive. They may cause a formalization or distancing of some relations that lawmakers could reasonably prefer to leave more informal, close, or open, such as the relations among teachers and students in a school. They may deter valued candor—as from evaluators of candidates for jobs, promotions, university admissions, professional licenses—insofar as due process entitles the subjects of adverse reports to disclosure or CONFRONTATION. Procedural requirements may thus force lawmakers to weigh some programmatic objectives against others that would be jeopardized by pursuing the former within the procedural rules laid down by courts.

Due process protection for interests that are not entitlements established by positive law may have a subtler substantive import. If the jeopardized interest enjoys no specific protection under any law aside from the due process clause itself, there is no obvious focus for the required process. A hearing on the issue of whether the contested deprivation is "without due process" may seem pointless, lacking some legal restriction on the conditions in which the deprivation is authorized. This problem has arisen in a number of cases involving dispossession of public housing tenants, when neither the laws governing the housing programs not the leases issued to tenants purported to restrict in any way the power of administrators to evict tenants at any time, for any reason or no reason.

Courts in this situation may supply the missing substantive entitlement on their own, by finding in the due process guarantee a protection against deprivations not rationally related to the purposes of the governmental activity in question. Thus a court may bar a public housing administrator from evicting a tenant who has been cohabiting with a nonspouse, if the court concludes that excluding the cohabitation is not rationally related to the court's understanding of the purposes of public housing. In such a case, the crossover from procedural to substantive concerns is glaringly evident.

A similar crossover is less evident, but still detectible, when a court responds to the lack of a positive law entitlement by requiring the state itself to enunciate some restrictions of purpose or circumstance on lawful impairment of the protected interest, which can provide a basis for due process hearings when official deprivations impend. For the court must then stand ready to decide whether the state's restrictions measure up to constitutional standards of protectiveness. A statute solemnly declaring that tenants may not be evicted "except as the Administrator shall decide is required for the general good" could not satisfy a court determined to afford procedural due process protection to the tenant's possessory interest viewed as an entitlement.

The alternative possibility, of requiring procedural protection even in the absence of legal restrictions on official discretion, rarely seems to have caught the Supreme Court's attention. Responsible officials, even when legally free to act at will, can always try to explain their decisions to persons adversely affected, and give the latter a chance to respond. Such an interchange will sometimes make a practical difference, by changing the officials' perceptions of the relevant facts or values. But even when it does not it may well serve any or all of the elemental purposes of due process: ensuring a voice in decisions for affected individuals, securing their recognition as persons deserving respect, and promoting consistency of official actions with goals and values that responsible officials are prepared to state and defend publicly.

Why has such a view of procedural due process, as serving process values apart from the aim of ensuring that persons receive the treatment legally due them, failed to gain judicial support? Most obviously, such an approach would cast very widely the due process net. If we see due process as broadly concerned with the quality of interaction between official and citizen, rather than more narrowly with vindication of the citizen's legal rights, then any state-inflicted "grievous loss" will seem to bring into play the constitutional standards of decisional procedure—a perhaps daunting result in light of the ubiquity of the welfare state.

The Court's limited extension of procedural protection beyond positive legal entitlements to possessory interests and a select set of liberties seems to represent its aversion to three unpalatable alternatives: first, deformation of the constitutional due process mandate by restricting its reach to entitlements specifically found in subconstitutional positive law; second, intrusive overextension of the mandate to all cases of palpably harmful state action; and third, free-form judicial choice among substantive values and policy goals. The Court apparently cannot avoid all three dangers fully and simultaneously. It has needed supplementary techniques to make good the avoidance of both trivialization and globalization of the range of the due process mandate, and these techniques have put heavy pressure on both doctrinal shapeliness and judicial self-discipline.

For example, the danger of trivialization constantly lurks in a crucial indeterminacy in the concept of legally defined entitlement as the equivalent of due process protected property. The problem is that of distributing components of a positive legal regime between the categories of substance and procedure. Suppose, as in *Bishop v. Wood,* that police officers are dismissable whenever, but only when, a designated superior has given the employee a written notice of dismissal for malfeasance in the performance of duty. Straightforwardly read, the law means to make the legal condition of dismissability not actual malfeasance but delivered written notice of dismissal. An entitlement-based due process doctrine then would logically require a hearing but only on the bootless issue of delivery of the notice. A judge can logically avoid that result by reading the law to condition dismissability on actual malfeasance, although that reading will make the law unconstitutional if the law includes no adequate provision for hearing on the malfeasance question. Whether such a reading seems unacceptably self-destructive will depend on the primacy of due process values in the reader's constitutional understanding.

Similar puzzles affect questions about whose entitlement is established by a plain statutory restriction on official discretion. A striking example is *O'Bannon v. Town Court Nursing Center* (1980), where a statute provided for financial assistance to needy elderly persons in meeting their costs of residence in officially approved nursing homes, and also set conditions of approval for the homes. Thus it was apparently unlawful for officials either to deny certification to homes meeting the conditions or to deny benefits to eligible residents of certified homes. When officials proposed to decertify a certain home, its residents claimed a due process right to be heard on the issued of the home's certifiability. The Supreme Court concluded that the residents had no constitutional right to such a hearing because their entitlement was just to benefits while residing in a certified home; the entitlement to certification belonged strictly to the nursing home operators.

Given the close practical resemblance of the residents' interests to the strongly protected interests of tenants in uninterrupted possession, a court could reasonably have concluded that they, too, were entitled to certification of their home if in fact it met the legal standards, and therefore they had due process rights to be heard on that issue. The Court's contrary conclusion was obviously influenced by concerns about overextended application of the constitutional due process mandate.

Claims to due process are not confined to situations in which the claimant's legal posture is defensive or the adversaries are government officials. They may arise also where individuals are exposed to the state's judicial power by their involvement in private legal controversies; and even where (the due process claim aside) there impends no legal proceeding at all but just some harm at a fellow citizen's hands.

The defendant in a private civil lawsuit faces possible deprivation, by officers wielding state powers, of wealth through a money judgment or of personal liberty through an injunctive decree. The occasion is obviously one to activate due process concerns, and civil defendants are held entitled to such procedural due process essentials as a fair and orderly hearing before an unbiased judge.

For reasons not quite so obvious, so are civil plaintiffs. A tempting explanation is that having allowed its courts to take charge of a private dispute, the state is obliged to have them do so in a way that satisfies the due process demand for reason, voice, and dignity. Yet this explanation seems incomplete. Some assistance is better than none. The state does not injure or oppress claimants to whom it offers procedurally flawed assistance against violators of the kinds of interests typically at stake in civil cases, unless the state is affirmatively obligated to secure those interests against violations by private as well as governmental agents. Suppose, for example (as the Supreme Court apparently did in TRUAX V. CORRIGAN, 1921) that the state is constitutionally obligated to protect landowners against disturbance by PICKETING. On such a view, a disturbed landowner can cite a refusal of protection as a deprivation of property and demand a hearing on the question of the state's justification for refusal. In other words, the landowner can demand a hearing on whether the picketing is for some special reason legally privileged. The state can meet this demand by letting the landowner sue the picketers for injunctive relief, but only if the procedural conditions of the suit satisfy due process standards of fairness from the plaintiff's point of view.

Thus denial of fair procedure to a civil plaintiff comes within the traditional due process concern about injurious treatment of individuals by the state, just insofar as we see the state's failure to protect the plaintiff's interests against the defendant's encroachments as itself a form of injury. Such is the SOCIAL COMPACT view according to which persons entering political association surrender to the state the use of force, for the safer protection of their several "lives, liberties, and estates." The state's regime of law and order then overrides the natural liberty of self-help, but only by replacing it with the state's obligation to protect.

Some such account seems necessary to complete the explanation of the conceded due process rights of civil plaintiffs. Yet other current law ostensibly rejects this account. United States v. Kras (1973) and Logan v. Zimmerman Brush Co. (1982) together indicate that the state may usually condition a would-be civil plaintiff's ACCESS TO THE COURTS on payment of filing fees, thus effectively excluding whoever cannot pay. Such a doctrine is hard to square with the idea of a state's affirmative duty to protect the litigable interests of its citizens, arising out of the latter's relinquishment of self-help by private force.

When a government sues a citizen in an otherwise ordinary civil dispute, involving property or contract rights or tort claims, the citizen sued will of course have the due process rights normally enjoyed by privately sued civil defendants. The reverse case, of a civil dispute in which the citizen is the one seeking relief for a TRESPASS, breach of contract, or other civil wrong by a governmental defendant, is complicated by the doctrine of SOVEREIGN IMMUNITY. In general, that doctrine means that the governments of the states and the Union may not be sued without the consent of their respective legislatures. If the courts find that such consent has not been given, the citizen alleging deprivation by governmental action will lack recourse in the ordinary courts, a situation presenting an obvious and a serious due process concern. In many such cases, the constitutionally guaranteed right of due process must prevail over sovereign immunity and entitle the victimized citizen to relief in constitutional litigation. That would surely be the result, for example, if government officials sought to imprison someone, or seize privately held land or goods, without ever giving the victim a fair chance to contest the legal and factual basis for such action. The citizen would be able to gain preventive relief or compensation in a CIVIL RIGHTS action based on the due process clause of the Fifth or Fourteenth Amendment.

The question of due process rights is most puzzling when seizures of possessions, or other violations of core interests generally given legal protection, are carried out by private agents with no apparent state complicity—a finance company sending its own forces to repossess an automobile securing an overdue debt, or a repair shop collecting an unpaid bill by retaining and eventually selling the repaired article. People do not usually take such "self-help" actions, or think them prudent, unless the actions are in some sense authorized, if not positively enabled, by state law. Thus lawmakers may authorize and enable a creditor's private repossession of chattel security by exempting such activity from liability for crime (theft) or civil wrong (conversion of goods). Indeed, the law usually goes farther, making it wrongful for the debtor to resist the seizure by force. The law doubtless otherwise contributes to the ability of creditors to make their seizures effective, as by securing the wealth used to pay for the requisite services. The utility of the repair shop's liquidation-by-sale depends on law allowing extinction of the debtor's legal claim to the goods in favor of the person who buys them from the repair shop. In short, self-help creditor remedies are evidently deliberate creations of state law, particular components of the state's total scheme of legally recognized and sanctioned rights and liabilities. In that sense, at least, the self-helping creditor inflicts significant deprivations under cover of the state's power, while affording no opportunity for the deprivee to be heard on the matter.

Even so, the Supreme Court concluded in FLAGG BROTHERS V. BROOKS (1978) that laws authorizing creditor self-help do not in general violate due process. In defense of this result, it might have been urged that the due process requirement is satisfied by the debtor's opportunity to sue later for restorative or compensatory relief in case the creditor's seizure was in fact unjustified. Such a rationale would accord with the holding in *Ingraham v. Wright* that paddling a student without a hearing comports with due process so long as compensatory relief for an unjustified paddling can be obtained later in a lawsuit. Yet courts have not usually explained in this way their tolerance for unilateral, peremptory creditor self-help, apparently seeing the difficulty of reconciling such an account with prevailing due process doctrine for cases of seizure by state officers, which strictly requires the state to provide some kind of judicial supervision, and a hearing for the deprivee as promptly as the case permits.

Courts instead have seen the issue presented by private self-help activities as one of state action, and, as in the *Flagg Brothers* case, have concluded that the due process guarantee has no application to such activities however much they may practically depend on the support of law. The reason for this judicial diffidence, as important as it is simple, is the difficulty of distinguishing in principle between the due process claim raised by the case of the self-helping creditor and that raised by many, if not all, other cases of intentional or foreseeable infliction, by private agents, of civilly actionable harm, that is, of torts, breaches of contract, breaches of trust, and so forth. Often, if not always, it will be possible to show compellingly how the law has contributed directly to the occasion or motive for committing the injurious act or to the injurer's practical power to inflict it, or to the practical defenselessness of the victim. But the idea of a consti-

tutional right to a predeprivation hearing, or even an accelerated postdeprivation hearing, in all cases of ordinary private legal wrongs stretches due process too far. Every ordinary contract dispute cannot be a constitutional case.

Thus courts have been led to conclude that the deprivations of property wrought by private creditor self-help are not violations of due process for the reason that they are not attributable to the state. The position is that due process generally is not concerned with exercises of power by persons not identified with the state or perceived as acting on its behalf, in forms not conventionally understood as distinctive to the state. This position is unfortunately at odds with the premise which apparently underlies recognition of the due process rights of civil plaintiffs—the premise, that is, of an affirmative state duty to protect the persons and possessions of inhabitants against gross violation by private as well as public agents.

The difficulty is of a kind that logically must appear somewhere within any body of constitutional doctrine in which a first aim is that of securing spheres of individual liberty against social coercion, and a first institutional device is that of legal rights, themselves an obvious form of collective force. In the constitutionalist vision there is indissoluble tension between law's aim, personal liberty, and its instrument, state power. In this field of contradictory forces are situated all legal rights, including due process rights. Thus it happens that the same due process claims which from one viewpoint represent the state's liberating engagement to protect each person against incursion by others or by the social aggregate, from another perspective represent the state's oppressive oversight of affairs perhaps better and more properly left to the concerned individuals.

In no setting is the dilemma more evident than in that of the family, which in our culture has most strongly represented the value of social solidarity as opposed to that of individuals severally free to treat at arm's length in civil society. PARHAM V. J. R. (1979), a case in which due process claims were asserted on behalf of a minor child being committed by parents to a mental institution, illustrates the difficulty. The Court there assumed "that a [minor] child has a protectable interest . . . in not being . . . erroneously" committed; said that parents must be generally supposed to act in their children's best interests; said that "the risk of error inherent in the parental decision . . . [is] sufficiently great" that parental discretion cannot be "absolute and unreviewable"; and concluded, not resoundingly, that "some kind of inquiry should be made by a 'neutral fact finder' to determine whether . . . [the child] satisf[ies] the medical standards for admission."

Of the largest questions of current meaning and future role for due process in our civic culture, the Supreme Court's irresolute posture in the *Parham* case is emblematic. If due process is an epitome of libertarian law, it is also—by the same token, Max Weber would advise—an epitome of bureaucratic law. Due process as we know it is a hallmark of a formally rational law designed to liberate as it organizes and orders: to liberate energy and will by the promise of regularity, calculability, and impartiality, and by insistent strong demarcation of the private from the public sphere.

But our due process is a hallmark, too, of hierarchical formal ordering; that is, of ordering by preordained rules emanating from specialized governing authorities (representative or accountable as those authorities may be, of or to the governed). There are always spheres of life in which due process is problematic because those spheres want ordering that is more contextual and less abstract, more responsive and less prefigured, more empathic and less impersonal, more interactive and less distanced, more participatory and less authoritative, than what "due process" has traditionally signified. Conversely, "due process" invokes sensibilities resistant to a general movement toward a more thoroughly democratized polity, in which the personal and the political aspects of life would be much less sharply separated than we have tended to keep them. In any such movement due process would necessarily be transformed—transformed but not discarded, since we are unlikely to forsake the ideals of reason, voice, and dignity, or the conviction that individuals are not just parts of social wholes.

FRANK I. MICHELMAN

Bibliography

BREST, PAUL 1982 State Action and Liberal Theory: A Casenote on *Flagg Brothers v. Brooks. University of Pennsylvania Law Review* 130:1296–1330.

FRIENDLY, HENRY J. 1975 Some Kind of Hearing. *University of Pennsylvania Law Review* 123:1267–1317.

KADISH, SANFORD 1957 Methodology and Criteria in Due Process Adjudication—A Survey and Criticism. *Yale Law Journal* 66:319–363.

MASHAW, JERRY L. 1983 *Bureaucratic Justice: Managing Social Security Disability Claims.* New Haven, Conn.: Yale University Press.

MICHELMAN, FRANK 1977 Formal and Associational Aims in Procedural Due Process. Pages 126–171 in J. Roland Pennock and John Chapman, eds., *Nomos XVIII: Due Process* New York: New York University Press.

MINOW, MARTHA 1985 Beyond State Intervention in the Family: For Baby Jane Doe. *Michigan Journal of Law Reform* 18:933–1014.

MONAGHAN, HENRY 1977 Of "Liberty" and "Property." *Cornell Law Review* 62:405–444.

REICH, CHARLES 1964 The New Property. *Yale Law Journal* 73:733–787.

VAN ALSTYNE, WILLIAM 1977 Cracks in "The New Property": Adjudicative Due Process in the Administrative State. *Cornell Law Review* 62:445–493.

PROCEDURAL DUE PROCESS OF LAW, CRIMINAL

The Barons at Runnymede did better than they knew. When they induced King John in 1215 to announce in MAGNA CARTA that no man should be imprisoned or dispossessed "except by the lawful judgment of his peers and by the LAW OF THE LAND," they laid the basis for a text that was to have greater significance in the development of American constitutional law than any other. In time "judgment of his peers" and "law of the land" came to be rendered alternatively as DUE PROCESS OF LAW and in that form were adopted in the Fifth Amendment to the United States Constitution as a restriction upon the federal government: "No person shall . . . be deprived of life, liberty or property, without due process of law." In 1868, substantially the same language was employed in the FOURTEENTH AMENDMENT as a restriction upon the states. Thus was embedded in the Constitution a phrase whose exegesis was to generate hundreds of decisions, libraries of commentary, and unending controversy, to this day. The Supreme Court has, over the years, used the due process clause to develop a variety of substantive restraints upon the power of government. This article, however, will deal only with the sense of due process closest to its original conception, namely, as the source of restrictions on the procedures through which governmental authority may be exercised over the individual in criminal cases.

In determining the procedures the Constitution requires of the federal government in criminal cases, the due process clause of the Fifth Amendment has been of limited significance. The BILL OF RIGHTS contains a variety of provisions explicitly directed to CRIMINAL PROCEDURE, and these rather than the due process clause have served as the principal vehicles for the development of a constitutional law of criminal procedure. So, for example, the Supreme Court has developed the constitutional law of permissible SEARCH AND SEIZURE through interpretations of the

FOURTH AMENDMENT; the constitutional law with respect to DOUBLE JEOPARDY and the RIGHT AGAINST SELF-INCRIMINATION through interpretations of the Fifth Amendment; the constitutional law with respect to SPEEDY and PUBLIC TRIAL, TRIAL BY JURY, NOTICE, CONFRONTATION of opposing witnesses, and the RIGHT TO COUNSEL through interpretations of the Sixth Amendment; and the constitutional law barring excessive BAIL, fines, and CRUEL AND UNUSUAL PUNISHMENT through interpretations of the Eighth Amendment. On the other hand, in determining the procedures the Constitution requires of state governments the due process clause of the Fourteenth Amendment has played the significant and decisive role.

What due process of law required and by what principles its meaning was to be ascertained were questions that were to preoccupy the Court for generations. They were raised early in MURRAY'S LESSEE V. HOBOKEN LAND & IMPROVEMENT CO. (1856), a civil case involving the meaning of the Fifth Amendment's due process clause: "The Constitution contains no description of those procedures which it was intended to allow or forbid. It does not even declare what principles are to be applied to ascertain whether it be due process. It is manifest that it was not left to the legislative power to enact any process that might be devised. The article is a restraint on the legislative as well as on the executive and judicial powers of government, and cannot be so construed as to leave Congress free to make any process 'due process of law' by its mere will." Nor, as the Court might have added, could the article be so construed as to leave the Court free to determine what is and what is not due process by *its* mere will. The effort of the Court to come to terms with this challenge is the central feature of the constitutional history of due process.

An early effort to state a principle for interpreting due process was the test of whether a procedure was in accord with settled practices in England before the Revolution and not rejected here after settlement. A practice that met this test accorded due process; a practice that did not failed to accord due process. The test served its purpose in some cases, but it soon proved insufficient, for whatever value it had as a fixed determinant of meaning was overbalanced by its inability to reflect changing times and needs and evolving perceptions of what fairness requires. For example, the settled English practice of initiating a prosecution, customarily continued in this country, was INDICTMENT by a GRAND JURY. Did this mean that due process fastened that procedure upon the

states? This was the question at issue in HURTADO V. CALIFORNIA (1884), where the Court faced a California innovation permitting a prosecutor to initiate a prosecution by filing an INFORMATION on his own, after a preliminary hearing before a magistrate on whether there was sufficient cause. The Court upheld the procedure despite its deviance from settled practice because it could find in the new procedure no significant prejudice to the rights of the accused. More decisive than the state of English practice was whether the challenged procedure comported with "those fundamental principles of liberty and justice which lie at the base of all our civil and political institutions." To regard established usage as "essential to due process of law would be to deny every quality of the law but its age, and to render it incapable of progress or improvement." Thus, the Court limited the traditional test: a practice sanctioned by immemorial usage necessarily accorded due process, but one not so sanctioned was not necessarily inconsistent with due process. In time, however, the Court rejected the remaining limb of the test as well. It had been well settled in England that a FELONY defendant had no right to be represented by counsel, and although that had been rejected in the United States Constitution and in the states, the change had not gone so far as to require appointment of counsel for INDIGENT defendants. In POWELL V. ALABAMA (1932) the Court held nevertheless that the failure to appoint counsel for uneducated and indigent defendants in a capital case in circumstances in which they had no real opportunity to present a defense denied due process of law. Of more significance to the Court was its judgment of the "fundamental nature" of the right to be represented by counsel, which in these circumstances was essential to the right to be heard at all.

The test, then, that came to prevail in judging the constitutionality of procedures in state criminal prosecutions was that of fundamental fairness in the circumstances of the particular case. Over the years a variety of formulations were used in an effort to give greater content to the test. Concerning each procedural safeguard that was being asserted, the Court would ask whether it was "of the very essence of a scheme of ORDERED LIBERTY," or whether a "fair and enlightened system of justice would be impossible without it," or whether "liberty and justice" would exist if it were sacrificed, or whether it was among those "immutable principles of justice, acknowledged . . . wherever the good life is a subject of concern." Concerning the procedure applied in the contested prosecution, the Court asked whether it violated a "principle of justice so rooted in the traditions and conscience of our people as to be ranked as fundamental," or whether its use subjected a person to "a hardship so acute and shocking that our polity would not endure it," or whether it offended "those canons of decency and fairness which express the notions of justice of English-speaking peoples even toward those charged with the most heinous offenses," for due process "embodies a system of rights based on moral principles so deeply imbedded in the traditions and feelings of our people as to be deemed fundamental to a civilized society as conceived by our whole history."

Whether any or all of these phrases succeeded in accomplishing anything more than to remit the issue to the intuitive sense of fairness of each Justice; whether, as Justice HUGO L. BLACK asked in ROCHIN V. CALIFORNIA (1952), there could possibly be "avenues of investigation . . . open to discover 'canons' of conduct so universally favored that this Court should write them into the Constitution" were issues that troubled the Justices and commentators alike. These doubts led to the development of an alternative test to determine the meaning of due process; namely, that due process should be taken to mean no more and no less than the specific guarantees of the Bill of Rights. In short, the due process clause of the Fourteenth Amendment "incorporated" as restrictions upon the states the provisions of the first eight amendments originally written as restrictions upon the federal government. The first Justice JOHN MARSHALL HARLAN was the first to advance the argument in several of his dissenting opinions, including *Hurtado* and *O'Neil v. Vermont* (1892). The issue was revived in modern times when Justice Black took up the cudgels in ADAMSON V. CALIFORNIA (1947).

The *Adamson* case involved the constitutionality of California law allowing adverse comment to the jury on a defendant's failure to explain or deny evidence against him. In a federal prosecution this practice would have violated the Fifth Amendment's right against self-incrimination. But, of course, under the settled doctrine this was not determinative. The Court had to find that this particular aspect of the self-incrimination privilege—that which disallowed comment on its exercise—was essential to fundamental fairness to the defendant, and this the majority declined to do. The majority could find nothing in the California practice that denied the defendant a FAIR TRIAL. He was not compelled to testify. True, if he did testify he would open the record to evidence of his prior convictions, but, "When evidence is before a jury that threatens conviction, it does not seem unfair to require him to choose between leaving the adverse evidence unexplained and subjecting himself

to impeachment through disclosure of former crimes." Justice Black dissented, arguing that a violation of the Fifth Amendment right against self-incrimination was necessarily a denial of due process under the Fourteenth Amendment.

Justice Black's arguments in favor of the INCORPORATION DOCTRINE, as first announced in *Adamson* and developed in later opinions, notably in his concurrence in DUNCAN V. LOUISIANA (1968), were grounded in a study of the history of the adoption of the Fourteenth Amendment, which convinced him that it was the intent of the amendment's framers that it should incorporate the Bill of Rights as a restraint upon the states. For Black, the Constitution did not endow the Court with power to expand and contract the meaning of due process to accord with the Court's assessment of what fundamental fairness required at any particular time. The fundamental fairness test was a resort to "natural law," depending "entirely on the particular judge's idea of ethics and morals instead of requiring him to depend on the boundaries fixed by the written words of the Constitution." Such a test was inconsistent with "the great design of a written Constitution." The specific language of the Bill of Rights would confine the power of the Court to read its own predilections into the Constitution.

Moreover, Black believed that the Bill of Rights, more reliably than the fundamental fairness test, would guide the Court to outcomes consistent with the values of a democratic society. In Black's view the judgment of the Framers of the Constitution would serve better than each Justice's personal judgment in determining what fairness required in criminal prosecutions. Indeed, the record of the Court's administration of its fundamental fairness test was for Black the clearest demonstration of his argument. He was speaking hyperbolically when he said in *Rochin* that the traditional test had been used "to nullify the Bill of Rights," but the fact was that in most instances the Court, as in *Adamson*, had used the fairness standard to uphold state convictions that would have been reversible had the specific provisions of the Bill of Rights been applicable.

Black's primary antagonist on this use, as on many others, was Justice FELIX FRANKFURTER, in later years joined by the second Justice JOHN MARSHALL HARLAN. They rejected Black's interpretation of the history of the Fourteenth Amendment's adoption, finding no plausible evidence that it was intended to incorporate the Bill of Rights as a restraint upon the states. But, beyond that, they advanced a very different approach to CONSTITUTIONAL INTERPRETA-

TION. According to Frankfurter and Harlan, the provisions of the first eight amendments were not equally fundamental. Some, like the guarantees of FREEDOM OF SPEECH and religion, stated enduring values and were, therefore, binding on the states through the "independent potency" of the Fourteenth Amendment. Others, such as those protecting the right against self-incrimination and jury trials, "express the restricted views of Eighteenth-Century England regarding the best methods for the ascertainment of facts." Not every procedure that was historically protected by these provisions was necessary for fundamental fairness, though some might be of this character. Still others, such as the requirement of a grand jury indictment and the right to a jury in civil cases where the amount in controversy exceeded twenty dollars, were largely historical relics. The terms of the Bill of Rights, all of them and only them, were, therefore, an unsuitable text for carrying out the commands of fundamental justice embodied in the requirement of due process of law. Changing circumstances would create new and unforeseen problems, casting new light on the question whether a given procedural guarantee was "fundamental." Only an evolving and flexible due process could assure preservation of the procedural requirements of a free society without binding the criminal process unnecessarily to the forms of the past.

Justices Frankfurter and Harlan conceded that the Court had sustained state procedures whose use would have been forbidden under the Bill of Rights. What mattered, however, was that it had done so only after satisfying itself in each case that the defendant had not been denied fundamental fairness. For example, the Fifth Amendment might forbid a federal prosecutor to APPEAL a conviction of a lesser offense than that charged and to prosecute under the original indictment if the appeal succeeds, but, as the Court held in *Palko v. Connecticut* (1937), the requirements of civilized justice would not be compromised by permitting a state to continue a similar prosecution until it achieved a trial free of substantial error. A jury of twelve persons might be required of federal prosecutions by the Sixth Amendment, but, as the Court held in *Maxwell v. Dow* (1900), it did not follow that a person could not receive a fundamentally fair trial in a state court before a jury of fewer members. Where, on the other hand, state practices fatally infected the justice of the convictions—as in *Powell v. Alabama* (1932) where the accused was deprived of a fair opportunity to present a defense, or in BROWN v. MISSISSIPPI (1936), where torture was used to extract a confession, or in MOORE v. DEMPSEY (1923)

where the trial itself was a sham and a pretense—the Court did not hesitate to employ the fundamental fairness standard of due process to strike down the convictions.

In addition, Justices Frankfurter and Harlan emphasized the importance of the Court's avoiding excessive intrusions into the autonomy of the states. The Framers had deliberately chosen to create a federal rather than a wholly centralized system, partly to assure the limitation of power through its dispersal but also to obtain the benefits of autonomy and diversity in state government. Total incorporation of the Bill of Rights into the Fourteenth Amendment would impose a constitutional straitjacket on the states, stifling experimentation by the states in the administration of justice in the name of an unneeded uniformity.

As for the peril of judges' confusing their purely personal preferences with the requirements of the Constitution, Frankfurter and Harlan argued that this risk was inherent in JUDICIAL REVIEW—no less under the incorporation doctrine than under the fundamental fairness test. Giving meaning to particular provisions of the Bill of Rights, whose major provisions were written in open and general terms, would require judicial inquiry equally broad and open. The peril of judgment on the basis of personal preferences, they argued, must be met by judicial deference to the judgment of state governments and by a rigorous search for the fundamentals of fairness required by the nature and commitments of our society.

Though Justice Black lost the debate in *Adamson*, he continued to advance the cause of total incorporation to his final days on the Court. He never succeeded in persuading a majority, but although he lost some battles he won the war. When the dust cleared two decades after *Adamson*, the fundamental fairness standard (though significantly modified) still reigned as the accepted test of due process, but every provision of the Bill of Rights bearing on criminal procedure, with the single exception of the requirement of grand jury indictments, had been held applicable to the states.

This development occurred through the increased use of the strategy of SELECTIVE INCORPORATION, under which selected clauses of the Bill of Rights were held to be binding on the states as such in the view that they were required by fundamental fairness. Consistency with prior decisions was grounded in the view that what the Court had repeatedly rejected was the theory of total incorporation, not the view that some provisions of the Bill of Rights could be binding on the states through the due process clause. As Justice BENJAMIN N. CARDOZO, an early opponent of the total incorporation doctrine, had observed in PALKO V. CONNECTICUT (1937): "In [certain] situations immunities that are valid as against the federal government by force of the specific pledges of particular amendments have been found to be implicit in the concept of ordered liberty and thus, through the Fourteenth Amendment, become valid as against the states." Yet it is important to note that this justification for the new doctrine blurred an important distinction in the traditional view, which was that some *rights* protected by the provisions of the Bill of Rights might prove so central to ordered liberty that they were also binding on the states through the due process clause. This was not to say, however, that certain *provisions* of the Bill of Rights, in their entirety with all their interpretations, were incorporated by the due process clause.

In the decade following *Adamson* the Court was apparently not yet ready to take this leap from the traditional view to the new doctrine of selective incorporation. Instead, the Court developed a number of significant expansions in its conception of what fundamental fairness required that prepared the ground for the flowering of the selective incorporation theory a decade later. An early important instance was WOLF V. COLORADO (1949), in which the Court held, in an opinion by Justice Frankfurter, that "the security of one's privacy against arbitrary intrusion by the police—which is at the core of the Fourth Amendment— . . . is implicit in 'the concept of ordered liberty' " and hence enforceable against the states through the due process clause. Still, the opinion was careful not to say that the Fourth Amendment as such was applicable to the states, and the Court declined to apply the remedy it had developed for enforcing the Fourth Amendment in federal prosecutions—excluding the unlawfully seized evidence. Other cases carried the movement forward. The Court in *Rochin* found that pumping an accused's stomach to obtain incriminating evidence was so "shocking to the conscience" that due process required the conviction to be reversed. Increasingly the Court found the failure to appoint counsel for indigent defendants to violate due process under the "totality of circumstances" rule of BETTS V. BRADY (1942), which required specific prejudice to be identified in the record. The circumstances in which the Court held confessions involuntary and, therefore, barred by due process were extended in *Spano v. New York* (1959) beyond physical coercion to include situations in which the defendant's will had been overborne by more subtle means of influence, such as persistent interrogation and trickery.

In the 1960s, however, the traditional test of fundamental fairness yielded to selective incorporation as the Court's dominant approach in reviewing the constitutionality of state prosecutions. A change of mood had taken place. For a variety of reasons—change in the composition of the Court, the CIVIL RIGHTS movement, the "War against Poverty"—the consensus on the Supreme Court moved toward greater intervention on behalf of criminal defendants, the great majority of whom were poor and members of minority groups. The continued enlargement case by case of the requirements of "fundamental fairness" was one possible alternative. But if, as the Justices apparently increasingly believed, excesses in the states' administration of criminal justice required extensive judicial correction, then something more was needed than the power to intervene in occasional cases of gross injustice. As a consequence the 1960s saw one of the remarkable accomplishments of the Warren Court—the federalization of state criminal procedure through the selective incorporation of the Bill of Rights.

Mapp v. Ohio (1961) marked the beginning. Effective control of state law enforcement required a constitutional remedy for law enforcement excesses. The EXCLUSIONARY RULE, which barred admission of unconstitutionally obtained evidence, had been developed decades earlier as a remedy in federal prosecutions. In *Wolf v. Colorado* the Court had declined to apply the exclusionary rule to the states, saying that a conviction based on reliable physical evidence was not fundamentally unfair just because the police had obtained the evidence by unconstitutional means. In *Mapp* the Court overruled that holding. The Court had, after all, already held in *Wolf* that the Fourth Amendment's RIGHT OF PRIVACY was enforceable against the states. It seemed natural to take the further step of holding that the remedy used to enforce Fourth Amendment privacy rights against federal violations was no less required to enforce "due process" privacy rights against state violations. If Fourth Amendment rights were basic to liberty, so must be the only practical means for their enforcement.

The next major case, GIDEON V. WAINWRIGHT (1963), also had features that made it a relatively easy case for extending selective incorporation. The Court had earlier held in *Betts* that appointment of counsel for indigents, though required by the Sixth Amendment for federal prosecutions, was not necessarily a fundamental right protected by due process. In the special circumstances of some particular prosecution, failure to appoint counsel might constitute a lack of fundamental fairness, but absence of counsel would not necessarily create this level of prejudice in every case. However, the "special circumstances" doctrine was gradually undermined in successive cases as the Court increasingly was able to find those circumstances in cases that were typical. As Justice Harlan observed, "The Court had come to realize . . . that the mere existence of a serious criminal charge constituted in itself special circumstances requiring the services of counsel at trial." Against this background there was little resistance to overruling *Betts* and, in the process, holding that the Sixth Amendment's guarantee of counsel was one of those clauses which fundamental fairness required to be imposed upon the states by the Fourteenth Amendment.

From then on scarcely a TERM of Court in the 1960s went by without the Court's OVERRULING some prior case to hold that an additional provision of the Bill of Rights was necessary to fundamental fairness and was, therefore, incorporated in due process. In 1965, in *Griffin v. California*, the Court overruled *Adamson* and held that the Fifth Amendment right against self-incrimination was protected by due process. The Sixth Amendment right to confrontation of witnesses was held to be incorporated in *Pointer v. Texas* (1965), and the rights to a speedy and public trial and to compulsory process for obtaining witnesses were also held to be incorporated in KLOPFER V. NORTH CAROLINA and *Washington v. Texas* (1967). In DUNCAN V. LOUISIANA (1968), the Court overruled earlier decisions and held that the Sixth Amendment's right to a jury trial was incorporated in due process. In BENTON V. MARYLAND (1969), *Palko* was overruled and the double jeopardy provision was held applicable to the states. The job was done. To all intents and purposes, the contours of due process of law required of the states by the Fourteenth Amendment had come to be defined by the specific guarantees of the Bill of Rights limiting the federal government.

One may fairly ask of this constitutional tour de force how well it was defended in doctrinal analysis. The position favoring total incorporation had a forceful logic: once the initial premise was accepted, it followed that every provision of the Bill of Rights and every interpretation of those provisions developed for federal prosecutions should apply equally to state prosecutions. But how was the theory of selective incorporation to be justified? Did the Court seriously mean that all the rights the Court had previously found in selected provisions of the Bill of Rights—such as the jury trial provision of the Sixth Amendment, the Fifth Amendment's protection against self-incrimination, the Fourth Amendment restraints upon search and seizure (including the right to have even reliable evidence excluded if it were unlawfully obtained)—all were so fundamental that "a fair and enlightened system of justice would be impossible" without them? This conclusion could scarcely stand scrutiny. As the Court had noted in earlier cases holding these guarantees unprotected by due process, a large portion of the democratic world, with claims to a civilized and enlightened system of justice no less strong than ours, offers no such guarantees.

Very little effort was made to address this challenge until Justice BYRON R. WHITE (in a footnote, ironically) did so in his opinion for the Court in *Duncan v. Louisiana* (1968), holding the jury trial guarantee of the Sixth Amendment incorporated by the due process clause. He ascribed the rejection of the earlier holdings to a new interpretation of what fundamental fairness meant. The Court had previously understood it to require those guarantees that a system of justice anywhere at any time would have to accord to be called civilized. In the newer cases, however, the Court proceeded on the view that fairness required those guarantees that are necessary to an "Anglo-American regime of ordered liberty." It is not required, White noted, that a procedural guarantee be "necessarily fundamental to fairness in every criminal system that might be imagined," but that it be fundamental "in the context of the criminal processes maintained by the American states."

Whether this revision of the fundamental fairness test suffices as a basis for selecting particular provisions of the Bill of Rights for incorporation is problematic. If the new test refers to practices that have so long been accorded in American systems of justice that they have come to be regarded as among the distinguishing characteristics of American justice, then "fundamental" becomes equivalent to "traditional," all the provisions of the Bill of Rights are fundamental, and the accepted test of selective incorporation becomes in fact the rejected test of total incorporation. It would appear, however, that something more was meant. Criminal justice systems, like other social institutions, are complex and comprise a variety of elements that function in a delicate ecological relationship. Given the particular functioning of some procedural protection in the American system, it may be that the protection is fundamental to fairness in that system, although it would not be in a system with a different assortment of procedural elements with differing functional relationships. So, in the *Duncan* case, Justice White noted that although it was easy to imagine a fair system that used no juries, in which alternative guarantees and protections would serve the purposes the jury serves in English and American systems, no American jurisdiction had undertaken to construct such a system.

If this latter interpretation of fundamental fairness were taken seriously, the Court would be obliged to undertake in each case a factual examination of the complex functioning of the state's criminal justice system, with particular attention to how the functioning of the system as a whole colors the significance of the practice at issue. But no such inquiry was made in the *Duncan* case. The opinion drew attention to the long-standing concern about overzealous prosecutors and biased judges. But it made no effort to examine such questions as whether the routine availability of appellate review in the state courts and COLLATERAL ATTACK in the federal courts rendered a jury trial less indispensable as a protection against such abuses; or why, if the use of a jury for this purpose made it a requirement of fundamental fairness in the American system, it was not required in all civilized systems; or whether a jury of randomly chosen citizens in fact served as a check against bias rather than as a source of bias. The Court also pointed generally to the traditional acceptance in America of a jury power of nullification in the application of the law. But the Court failed to consider why this power is significant, and why, in other systems, a comparable power of nullification is not seen to be required by fundamental fairness.

The point is not that the Court could not have made a case for the conclusion that fundamental fairness required the jury in the American system of justice, but that it did not try. Nor did the Court do better in the other cases applying the doctrine of selective incorporation. In the end, therefore, there is force in the conclusion that the Court's attempt to shore up the doctrinal case for selective incorporation was an illusory post hoc rationalization.

An additional consideration, strongly pressed by Justice Harlan in his dissenting opinions, lends further support to that conclusion. Even if it be granted that a guarantee to be found in a provision of the Bill of Rights is required by fundamental fairness in an American system of justice, it does not follow that each and every interpretation of that provision developed in federal prosecutions is equally required for fundamental fairness. For example, the Fifth Amendment's privilege against self-incrimination has been held in federal prosecutions to preclude judicial or prosecutorial comment on the failure of the defendant to respond to the evidence against him. The Fifth Amendment's protection against double jeopardy has been interpreted to attach at the time the jury is first sworn. The Sixth Amendment's guarantee of a jury trial in criminal cases had once been held to require a unanimous verdict of the jury. But even if the core

concept of the privilege against self-incrimination, the double jeopardy protection, and the jury trial guarantee were found to be necessary for fundamental fairness, it would scarcely follow that each and every one of these interpretations of the federal guarantees is also necessary. Yet, in sharp contrast to the requirements of the avowed theory of selective incorporation, this is what the Court had held in every instance: a conclusion that a clause of the Bill of Rights is applicable to the states necessarily entails that each and every interpretation of that clause developed in federal prosecutions, regardless of its rationale or significance, becomes fully applicable as well, as Harlan said, "jot-for-jot and case-for-case" and "freighted with [its] entire accompanying body of federal doctrine" (*Duncan v. Louisiana*, 1968; *Malloy v. Hogan*, 1964). This conclusion constitutes further evidence that the Court was not taking seriously the only theory it had advanced to support its doctrine of selective incorporation.

Putting aside the doctrinal warrant of the approach to procedural due process that has come to prevail, what has been its impact on the administration of criminal justice in the states and what is its likely bearing on the future of due process? It is clear that the values of federalism have been heavily overrun. Given the expansive, pervasive, and often highly detailed regulations the Court has imposed on the processes of criminal justice under warrant of the Bill of Rights, one has to conclude that the autonomy of state government has been drastically curtailed.

At the same time, it is almost certainly true that the procedural rights accorded the accused in state courts have been greatly expanded over what they would have been had this federalization not taken place. The expansion of constraints upon the administration of justice during the era of the Warren Court in the 1960s has been one of the notable characteristics of that Court. Few state courts and no state legislatures could have been expected on their own to have achieved anything like a comparable expansion. People will differ over whether the balance between effective law enforcement and the rights of the accused thereby achieved resulted in a preferable system of criminal justice than would have been obtained under the earlier doctrine. Most would agree, however, that the coalescing of the minimum constitutional rights of the accused in both state and federal prosecutions has tended to produce a constitutional jurisprudence more understandable to the citizen who does not typically distinguish between state and federal government in considering the rights of the accused.

On the other hand, the presumed advantage in

using the Bill of Rights to measure what due process requires of the states—that it eliminates the uncertainty and the need for personal, subjective decision-making by judges imposed by the traditional view—has hardly been evident. In deciding what searches are "reasonable" within the Fourth Amendment, how far that Amendment protects a right of privacy against new forms of ELECTRONIC EAVESDROPPING, when noncoercive POLICE INTERROGATION becomes violative of the Fifth Amendment's right against self-incrimination, what punishment, including CAPITAL PUNISHMENT, is "cruel and unusual" within the Eighth Amendment (which the Court in TROP V. DULLES (1958) conceded had to be determined by "the dignity of man" and "evolving standards of decency"), it was readily apparent that the text of the Bill of Rights scarcely spoke for itself and in fact invited no less an assessment and choice among competing values on the basis of the Justice's sense of what justice and fairness required. Fixed meanings have not triumphed over flexible ones, and judicial subjectivity has not been contained. More seriously, insofar as the Court has proceeded on the false assumption that the need for judicial value choosing has been overcome, it has handicapped itself in the task of developing a well-considered method of decision-making that would discipline and make more rational the inevitable process of choosing among competing values.

This concern is particularly pressing because the Court has recognized that due process is still open-ended, that although due process includes the incorporated clauses of the Bill of Rights, those clauses do not exhaust the content of due process. The 1952 decision in *Rochin*, that a state denied due process by using evidence pumped from the accused's stomach against his will, was reaffirmed in SCHMERBER V. CALIFORNIA (1966) under the principle that due process precludes action against an accused that "shocks the conscience" and violates one's "sense of justice," notwithstanding the inapplicability of any other provision of the Bill of Rights. Similar evidence of the vitality of the older tests of due process where the Bill of Rights does not reach are the Court's decisions in IN RE WINSHIP (1970), holding that an essential requirement of due process in criminal cases is proof of guilt beyond a REASONABLE DOUBT, and in the CAPITAL PUNISHMENT CASES OF 1976, finding in due process a requirement of articulated criteria to guide the judge or jury in determining whether to impose capital punishment.

One may conclude that despite the victory of selective incorporation the task of developing a defensible method and set of criteria to govern the determination of those criminal procedures that are constitutionally permissible is very much before the Court. How it could best be met is uncertain. One proposed approach would entail a consideration of a number of issues. In this view the Court would begin by drawing out the implications of the basic values animating constitutional restraints on the criminal process: fairness to the accused, protection of personal dignity, and the reliability of the processes for determining guilt. Next, the Court would determine how gravely the controverted procedure impugned those values and how seriously certain restraints would prejudice the due administration of criminal justice. Finally, the Court would seek ways of rooting the inevitable final choices in ground more secure than the personal judgment of the majority of the Justices on the optimum operation of the system of criminal justice. Another approach, less oriented to consequentialist considerations, would have the Court determine the fundamental legal rights of persons, including the constitutional rights of the accused, in terms of the requirements of a general political theory that best account for the moral principles embedded in the Constitution, laws, and culture of our society. Whatever the answer, the task is a formidable one. Indeed, the effort may ultimately be futile, as those believe who view the Court as indistinguishable from any other political body in the exercise of its power. But to the extent that the Court accepts the claim that its exercise of political power is based on reason and disinterestedness—that is, on law—it can scarcely abandon the goal of writing opinions that give credence to the claim. However one may approve its results, the doctrine of selective incorporation, with its oversimplifications and misperceptions, and its dubious doctrinal underpinnings, has not served that goal well.

SANFORD H. KADISH

Bibliography

ALLEN, FRANCIS A.   1953   Due Process and State Criminal Procedures: Another Look. *Northwestern University Law Review* 48:16–35.

DWORKIN, RONALD M.   1975   Hard Cases. *Harvard Law Review* 88:1057–1109.

FAIRMAN, CHARLES   1949   Does the Fourth Amendment Incorporate the Bill of Rights? The Original Understanding. *Stanford Law Review* 2:5–173.

FRIENDLY, HENRY   1965   The Bill of Rights as a Code of Criminal Procedure. *California Law Review* 53:929–956.

HENKIN, LOUIS   1963   "Selective Incorporation" in the Fourteenth Amendment. *Yale Law Journal* 73:74–88.

KADISH, SANFORD H.   1957   Methodology and Criteria in

Due Process Adjudication—A Survey and Criticism. *Yale Law Journal* 66:319–363.

NOTE 1949 The Adamson Case: A Study in Constitutional Technique. *Yale Law Journal* 58:268–287.

NOWAK, JOHN E. 1979 Foreword: Due Process Methodology in a Post-Incorporation World. *Journal of Criminal Law and Criminology* 70:397–423.

PROCLAMATION OF NEUTRALITY

(1793)

The Proclamation of Neutrality (April 22, 1793) was issued by President GEORGE WASHINGTON upon notification that France and Britain were at war. It pledged the United States to "pursue a course friendly and impartial" toward the belligerents and enjoined observance on all citizens upon pain of prosecution. Neutrality was bound to be difficult because of intense partisan feelings about the war, the privileges and obligations of the French alliance, and British rejection of American claims of neutral rights on the seas.

The importance of the proclamation for the Constitution was twofold. First, as a unilateral declaration by the President it seemed to preempt the power of Congress to decide questions of war and peace. Secretary of State THOMAS JEFFERSON, although he acquiesced in the proclamation, had made this objection in the cabinet, and it was taken up by the Republicans. In a notable series of articles under the signature Pacificus, Secretary of the Treasury ALEXANDER HAMILTON defended the proclamation. His claim of independent executive authority in FOREIGN AFFAIRS was opposed by JAMES MADISON as Helvidius, who compared it to the royal prerogative of the English constitution. (Hamilton's argument prevailed in history, though Madison's antipathy to overriding executive power has not lacked supporters.) Second, as the conduct of neutrality was executive altogether, it afforded the first instance of government by administrative lawmaking. Decisions were made in the cabinet, without statutory authority, with the guidance only of the customary law of nations. Divided and uncomfortable in this work, the cabinet officers submitted twenty-nine questions to the ruling of the Supreme Court. The court declined to rule, however, and thus established the precedent against ADVISORY OPINIONS. Meanwhile, the government's attempt to prosecute violators of the proclamation was defeated by unsympathetic juries. Not until June 1794 did Congress enact a neutrality law, which codified the rules developed in the cabinet during the preceding year.

MERRILL D. PETERSON

Bibliography

THOMAS, CHARLES M. 1931 *American Neutrality in 1793: A Study in Cabinet Government.* New York: Columbia University Press.

PROCUNIER v. MARTINEZ

416 U.S. 396 (1974)

Speaking through Justice LEWIS F. POWELL, the Supreme Court invalidated California prison regulations censoring inmates' correspondence and prohibiting attorney–client interviews conducted by law students and legal paraprofessionals. The censorship provisions had permitted prison officials to ban correspondence in which inmates "unduly complain," "magnify grievances," or expressed "inflammatory political, racial, religious or other views or beliefs." These vague standards, the Court held, violated the FIRST AMENDMENT rights of prisoners and those with whom they corresponded. The prohibition on the use of law students and paralegals was held to be an unjustified restriction on prisoners' ACCESS TO THE COURTS.

MICHAEL E. PARRISH

PRODUCTION

Until the transformation of the constitutional law of ECONOMIC REGULATION, beginning in 1937, "production" described economic activities that the Supreme Court regarded as local or intrastate in character and therefore beyond Congress's power to regulate under the COMMERCE CLAUSE. In 1895 the Court ruled in UNITED STATES V. E. C. KNIGHT CO. that every form of production and matters related to it were stages of economic activity that preceded the buying, selling, and transportation of goods among the states. Manufacturing, mining, agriculture, domestic fisheries, stock raising, and labor had only an "indirect" effect upon commerce, by judicial definition. Because commerce came after production the United States had no constitutional authority to extend the SHERMAN ANTITRUST ACT to monopolies in production, nor could it control the trade practices of poultry dealers, or regulate agricultural production, or fix the MAXIMUM HOURS AND MINIMUM WAGES of miners. In UNITED STATES V. DARBY (1941) the Court sustained the constitutionality of the FAIR LABOR STANDARDS

ACT, which applied to workers engaged in production of goods for sale in INTERSTATE COMMERCE; in the next year the Court in WICKARD V. FILBURN (1942) ended any remaining vestiges of the doctrine that Congress could not regulate production. The Court ruled that, although certain economic activities are local or intrastate, the commerce clause extends Congress's power to them if they affect commerce, making their regulation an appropriate way of governing commerce among the states.

LEONARD W. LEVY

PROFFITT v. FLORIDA

See: Capital Punishment Cases, 1976

PROGRESSIVE CONSTITUTIONAL THOUGHT

During the Progressive era, roughly from 1900 to 1920, the Constitution and the SUPREME COURT came in for considerable criticism on the part of historians, political theorists, statesmen, intellectuals, and journalists. The criticisms involved five issues: the origins of the Constitution's authority; claims that the Constitution, and the system of government it supported, were antiquated and needed to be modified in light of developments in modern science; protests that the Supreme Court functioned as an instrument of business interests; demands that the Constitution be reinterpreted to allow for federal regulation of industry; and similar demands that it become the agency of social reform.

Prior to the Progressive era the Constitution's authority rested on the assumption that it was a neutral document capable of rendering objective judgments based on either transcendent religious principles or secular doctrines like natural law. The first challenge to that assumption came from J. ALLEN SMITH's *The Spirit of American Government* (1907), in which the Constitution was alleged to be a "reactionary" document designed to thwart the democratic principles of the DECLARATION OF INDEPENDENCE by means of CHECKS AND BALANCES and JUDICIAL REVIEW of legislative actions of popular majorities. But the most thorough critique of the Constitution's presumed disinterested authority fell like a blockbuster with the publication of CHARLES A. BEARD's *An Economic Interpretation of the Constitution* (1913). Here readers

discovered that the movement toward RATIFICATION OF THE CONSTITUTION in 1787–1789 was led by merchants, manufacturers, creditors, and land speculators whose primary concern was to protect their own interests from what JAMES MADISON called "overbearing factions." THE FEDERALIST's authors, Beard was aware, hardly concealed the fact that they regarded protection of property as the essence of liberty. But Beard's exposure of the economic motives of the Framers did much to demystify the moral character of the Constitution by disclosing the "interests" behind it.

While the historian Beard tried to unmask the sacred image of the Constitution, political theorists tried to reestablish it on a more scientific foundation. In *The Process of Government* (1908) Arthur Bentley suggested that the scholar must penetrate beyond the formal structure of the Constitution to appreciate the forces and pressures that act upon it through interest group demands. But the dynamic of amoral interest politics was precisely what troubled WOODROW WILSON and other Progressive idealists. First in *Congressional Government* (1884), then in *Constitutional Government in the United States* (1908), and finally in a series of campaign speeches published as *The New Freedom* (1912), Wilson indicted the Constitution for weakening the executive branch of government, allowing interests and power to prevail in the legislature's standing committees, accepting as inevitable factional antagonisms detrimental to the public good, and upholding the letter of the law rather than the life of the state. Criticizing *The Federalist* for bequeathing a static, mechanist concept of government, Wilson wanted a Constitution "accountable to Darwin, not to Newton," a Constitution as "a living organism" capable of growth and adaption, one that would coordinate the branches of government so that liberty could be preserved not on the basis of diversity—Madison's premise—but of unity forged by presidential leadership.

Critical of the Constitution, Progressives also became disillusioned with a Supreme Court as an obstacle in the path of social reform. THEODORE ROOSEVELT exploded in anger when the Court invalidated state LEGISLATION involving child labor, tenement house reform, and other goals of Progressivism. Yet, curiously, Progressives disagreed whether the Court had a right to do so. In *The Supreme Court and the Constitution* (1912), Beard argued that the right of judicial review was the clear intent of *The Federalist*. In *Our Judicial Oligarchy* (1912) Gilbert E. Roe expounded the opposing case, arguing that the courts had usurped authority in reviewing legislative acts. While both authors scorned judges disposed to preserving property rights at the cost of social justice, they continued to differ as to whether the Supreme Court could hold unconstitutional laws void or whether it should defer to the legislative process and exercise what the followers of OLIVER WENDELL HOLMES called "judicial restraint."

Progressives were far more unified in advocating regulation. All the writers associated with the liberal *New Republic*—HERBERT CROLY, Walter Weyl, Walter Lippmann, John Dewey, and LOUIS D. BRANDEIS—wanted to see corporate enterprise subordinated to the public good by means of industrial commissions, surveillance of trusts and monopolies, banking and railroad legislation, and the like. All also agreed that standing in the way of federal regulatory policies was a debilitating Jeffersonian heritage that made private rights anterior to public responsibilities, a destructive individualism that frustrated the ideals of political authority and civic duty. "Only by violating the spirit of the Constitution," Lippmann boldly declared, "have we been able to preserve the letter of it." Many of the Progressives were Hamiltonian nationalists convinced that both the Constitution and the Republic could be preserved from the corruptions of business interests only by augmenting the authority of an efficient and enlightened state. Many were also pragmatists who believed that the Constitution should be interpreted not from within but from without, not in terms of its inherent logic or precedent but in light of its consequences as society experiences the Court's rulings.

Progressives succeeded in realizing a number of reforms through the AMENDING PROCESS, specifically the income tax, women's suffrage, and the DIRECT ELECTION of senators. As with the INITIATIVE, RECALL, and REFERENDUM in state governments, and direct PRIMARY ELECTIONS in national politics, the constitutional amendments aimed to allow people to participate more directly in the decisions affecting their lives. Whereas *The Federalist*'s authors believed that liberty could best be preserved by distancing the people from the immediate operations of government, the Progressives saw no conflict between republican liberty and participatory democracy.

JOHN PATRICK DIGGINS

Bibliography

COMMAGER, HENRY STEELE 1950 *The American Mind: An Interpretation of American Thought and Character Since the 1890s.* New Haven, Conn.: Yale University Press.

ROSTOW, EUGENE V. 1970 The Realist Tradition in Law. Pages 203–218 in Arthur M. Schlesinger, Jr., and Morton White, eds., *Paths of American Thought.* Boston: Beacon Press.

PROHIBITION

A recurring theme in American constitutional history is the attempt of a majority to impose its moral standards on society by legislation. The nineteenth-century temperance movement, along with its close ally, the ABOLITIONIST movement, constituted such a moral majority. That movement sought the legal prohibition of alcoholic beverages.

State and local prohibition statutes were accepted by the Supreme Court in MUGLER V. KANSAS (1887) as valid applications of the STATE POLICE POWER. That such laws deprived citizens of their liberty and property without DUE PROCESS OF LAW had been asserted, before the Civil War, only in the state court case of WYNEHAMER V. NEW YORK (1856).

In the early twentieth century the prohibition movement acquired a new ally in the Progressive movement, and, after nineteen states adopted prohibition laws, agitation shifted to the national level. In 1917 Congress enacted prohibition as a wartime austerity measure. The same year Congress proposed the EIGHTEENTH AMENDMENT, which, when ratified in 1919, raised prohibition to constitutional status. Repeal came fourteen years later with adoption of the TWENTY-FIRST AMENDMENT.

The failure of the "noble experiment" of national prohibition is frequently cited by opponents of other types of majoritarian legislation on moral issues, such as laws against SEGREGATION, handguns, abortion, and drugs.

DENNIS J. MAHONEY

PROHIBITION, WRIT OF

To lawyers as well as others, the term PROHIBITION calls to mind a law forbidding the making, distribution, or possession of intoxicating liquors. In law, however, the term has an ancient COMMON LAW meaning that retains vitality today. The writ of prohibition is an order from a higher court commanding a lower court to stop hearing a matter outside the lower court's JURISDICTION. From the beginning prohibition has been considered an extraordinary writ, one that the higher court may or may not grant, in its discretion. It is not normally to be used as a substitute for an APPEAL or a petition for a WRIT OF CERTIORARI.

A statute dating from the JUDICIARY ACT OF 1789 is interpreted to empower the UNITED STATES COURTS OF APPEALS and the Supreme Court to issue writs of prohibition to lower federal courts. Under this law, the Supreme Court can also issue writs of prohibition to state courts.

KENNETH L. KARST

PROHIBITION OF SLAVE TRADE ACT
2 Stat. 426 (1807)

Colonial legislatures had often tried to restrict the importation of slaves for economic reasons, and THOMAS JEFFERSON's famous deleted passage in the DECLARATION OF INDEPENDENCE denounced the royal disallowance of these bills. After Independence, all the states (except Georgia until 1798) prohibited the importation of slaves from abroad. The CONSTITUTIONAL CONVENTION OF 1787 permitted Congress to legislate against the international trade but at the insistence of the South Carolina delegates prohibited it from exercising that power for twenty years (Article I, section 9). After 1790, the Pennsylvania Abolition Society and the American Convention of Abolition Societies demanded interim legislation against the trade. Their lobbying produced the Act of March 22, 1794, prohibiting Americans from fitting out in American ports for the international trade. But South Carolina shocked the nation's conscience by reopening the trade in 1803.

President Jefferson urged Congress to ban the international trade at the earliest possible moment, and Congress responded with the Act of March 2, 1807, which prohibited the importation of slaves from foreign nations and dependencies, penalized persons engaging in the trade and purchasers from them, and provided for forfeiture of slaving vessels. The Act of May 15, 1820, declared slaving to be piracy, punishable by death. But enforcement of the ban was deliberately half-hearted, and the illegal trade brought in approximately a thousand blacks a year from Africa and the Caribbean. Though some southern spokesman in the late 1850s demanded a reopening of the trade, the CONFEDERATE CONSTITUTION also prohibited it.

WILLIAM M. WIECEK

Bibliography

WIECEK, WILLIAM M. 1977 *The Sources of Antislavery Constitutionalism in America, 1760–1848.* Ithaca, N.Y.: Cornell University Press.

PROPELLER GENESEE CHIEF v. FITZHUGH
12 Howard 443 (1851)

An act of Congress extended the ADMIRALTY AND MARITIME JURISDICTION of the United States Courts in matters of contract and tort arising upon the Great Lakes and connecting navigable rivers. In the case of *The Thomas Jefferson* (1825), the Court had confined federal admiralty and maritime jurisdiction to tide waters. Here, the Supreme Court, by a vote of 8–1, sustained the constitutionality of the act of Congress by ruling that JURISDICTION should not depend on the ebb and flow of the tide as in England but on the fact that the United States has "thousands of miles" of public navigable waters in which there is no tide. The TANEY COURT thus considerably expanded federal jurisdiction.

LEONARD W. LEVY

PROVIDENCE BANK v. BILLINGS
4 Peters 514 (1830)

This case anticipated the DOCTRINE of the CHARLES RIVER BRIDGE CO. V. WARREN BRIDGE CO. (1837) case and limited the doctrine of tax immunity established by NEW JERSEY V. WILSON (1812). The Court here, through Chief Justice JOHN MARSHALL, established the principle that a corporate charter should not be construed to vest more rights than are found in its express provisions. A state taxed a bank for the first time long after chartering it. The bank contended that its charter implied a tax immunity, because a state power to tax the bank could destroy it, contrary to its charter. The Court sustained the tax against the CONTRACT CLAUSE argument, reasoning that the state had made no express contract to relinquish its power to tax and that the relinquishment of that power "is never to be assumed." Chartered privileges "must be expressed . . . or they do not exist."

LEONARD W. LEVY

PRUDENTIAL INSURANCE COMPANY v. BENJAMIN
328 U.S. 408 (1946)

The dissenters in UNITED STATES V. SOUTH-EASTERN UNDERWRITERS (1944) feared that declaring insurance to be INTERSTATE COMMERCE, subject to congressional regulation, would create chaos by rendering state regulation of that industry void. An act of Congress, however, left most such regulation standing and Justice WILEY RUTLEDGE headed a unanimous Court sustaining a state tax that discriminated against interstate commerce. Assuming that such a tax would be invalid in the absence of congressional action, here Congress had decided that uniformity of regulation and taxation was necessary and had authorized even discriminatory state regulation and taxation of the insurance business.

DAVID GORDON

(SEE ALSO: *State Regulation of Commerce.*)

PRUNEYARD SHOPPING CENTER v. ROBINS
447 U.S. 74 (1980)

HUDGENS V. N.L.R.B. (1976) had held that the FIRST AMENDMENT did not compel private owners of SHOPPING CENTERS to permit their property to be used for expressive activity. In *PruneYard,* California's supreme court held that the state constitution required a shopping center owner to permit the collection of signatures on a petition. The Supreme Court unanimously affirmed. Justice WILLIAM H. REHNQUIST, for the Court, concluded that the state law did not work an uncompensated TAKING OF PROPERTY. Nor did it violate the owner's First Amendment rights by compelling it to convey a message. Justice LEWIS F. POWELL, concurring, argued that under other circumstances an owner might have such a First Amendment right.

KENNETH L. KARST

PUBLIC ACCOMMODATIONS

The refusal of hotels, restaurants, theaters, and other public accommodations to serve blacks was not exclusively a southern phenomenon. In the South, however, the practice was an essential part of a system of racial dominance and dependency, long after the THIRTEENTH AMENDMENT abolished slavery and the FOURTEENTH AMENDMENT recognized the CITIZENSHIP of the freed slaves. Aware of the role played by this form of RACIAL DISCRIMINATION in the system of white supremacy, Congress adopted the CIVIL RIGHTS ACT OF 1875, the last major CIVIL RIGHTS act of the Reconstruction era. The law prohibited public accommodations, including railroads along with the types already mentioned, from denying access to any person on account of race. The Supreme Court

held this law unconstitutional, saying that when Congress enforced the Fourteenth Amendment it had no power to reach private action. (See CIVIL RIGHTS CASES, 1883; STATE ACTION.)

Later came the Jim Crow laws—state laws requiring racial SEGREGATION in all manner of public places, including public accommodations. This practice received the Court's blessing in PLESSY V. FERGUSON (1896), a case involving the segregation of seating in railroad cars. (See SEPARATE BUT EQUAL DOCTRINE.) By the end of the nineteenth century, the denial of access for blacks to public accommodations in the South was firmly rooted in both law and custom.

Soon after the Supreme Court decided BROWN V. BOARD OF EDUCATION (1954), the modern civil rights movement turned to the problem of access to public accommodations. The reason for direct action such as freedom rides and SIT-INS was not that seats in the front of the bus arrive at a destination before back seats do, or that black college students yearn to perch on lunch counter stools. Public accommodations became a target for civil rights demonstrators for exactly the same reason that they had been made the vehicles for racial discrimination in the first place: segregation and the refusal of service to blacks were powerful symbols of racial inferiority, highly visible denials of the entitlement of blacks to be treated as persons and citizens. Employment discrimination and housing discrimination might touch material interests of great importance, but no interest is more important than self-respect. The primary target of the civil rights movement was the stigma of caste.

Within a few years after the *Brown* decision, the Supreme Court had held unconstitutional nearly the whole range of Jim Crow laws. Racial segregation practiced by state institutions, or commanded or authorized by state laws, failed the test of the Fourteenth Amendment even before Congress reentered the public accommodations field. In most of the states of the North and West, civil rights laws commanded equal access not only to public accommodations—such laws merely reinforced the common law duties of innkeepers and common carriers—but also to other businesses. In the South, however, private discrimination continued in most hotels, restaurants, and barber shops. The Supreme Court was repeatedly invited to decide whether the Fourteenth Amendment established a right of access to such places, free of racial bias, but the Court repeatedly declined the invitation. (See BELL V. MARYLAND, 1964.)

As part of the CIVIL RIGHTS ACT OF 1964, Congress adopted a comprehensive public accommodations law, forbidding discrimination in the same types of places that had been covered by the 1875 act. (Railroads were forbidden to discriminate by modern interpretations of the INTERSTATE COMMERCE ACT of 1887.) Before the year was out, the Supreme Court had upheld the public accommodations portion of the 1964 act, on the basis of the power of Congress to regulate interstate commerce. (See HEART OF ATLANTA MOTEL V. UNITED STATES, 1964.)

The 1964 act is limited in its coverage, reaching an establishment only if it "affects commerce" or if its discrimination is "supported by STATE ACTION." The act exempts both private clubs and small rooming houses lived in by their proprietors. Now that the Supreme Court has interpreted the CIVIL RIGHTS ACT OF 1866 as a broad guarantee against private racial discrimination in the sale of property and other contracting, and validated the law as a congressional enforcement of the Thirteenth Amendment, at least some of the limitations of the 1964 act have been made irrelevant. For example, a barber shop is covered by the 1964 act if it is located in a covered hotel, but not if it is independent. Under recent interpretations of the 1866 act, any barber shop would violate the law by refusing service on the basis of the customer's race. (See JONES V. ALFRED H. MAYER CO., 1968; RUNYON V. MCCRARY, 1976.)

The substantive core of the Fourteenth Amendment is a principle of equal citizenship. (See EQUAL PROTECTION OF THE LAWS.) Even in the absence of civil rights legislation, that principle demands that the organized community treat each of us, irrespective of race, as a respected, participating member. Racially based denial of access or segregation in places of public accommodations—even those privately owned—is a deliberate denial of the status of equal citizenship, as the sit-in demonstrators knew and helped the rest of us to understand.

KENNETH L. KARST

Bibliography
LEWIS, THOMAS P. 1963 The Sit-in Cases: Great Expectations. *Supreme Court Review* 1963:101–151.
POLLITT, DANIEL H. 1960 Dime Store Demonstrations: Events and Legal Problems of the First Sixty Days. *Duke Law Journal* 1960:315–365.
WOODWARD, C. VANN 1966 *The Strange Career of Jim Crow*, 2d (rev.) ed. New York: Oxford University Press.

PUBLIC EMPLOYEES

The government may regulate public employees more extensively than citizens at large because legitimate employer interests in controlling job-related behavior supplement the government's general constitutional power to control the behavior of private citizens. Government employers constitutionally are less free than private employers to control their employees, however, for the simple reason that the Constitution primarily limits government, not private, power. Eligibility criteria, work rules, and myriad personnel decisions take on constitutional dimensions in public sector employment that are absent from the private sector.

The competing analogies of government as citizen-regulator and government as private employer raise related questions. How much more power may the government exercise over its employees than over citizens at large? What constitutional limits bind public employers that do not bind private employers? The two questions tend to converge because, inevitably, the government affects its employees as regulator and employer simultaneously.

The constitutional issues comprise both substance and process. What substantive freedoms may the government require its employees to forgo as a condition of employment and what are the permissible and impermissible bases for disadvantaging public employees? Procedurally, when, how, and with what opportunity to respond, must government employers inform their employees of the reasons for adverse personnel actions?

The constitutional values at stake clash and mesh in complex ways. Government workers have individual rights to exercise substantive freedoms without improper penalty and to be treated fairly by the government. These often vie with government interests in effective, honest, efficient, and democratic management of the public's business. The government also has interests in employee loyalty and in the confidential execution of public policy. These may war with the value of freedom for dissident employees to bring important information to public attention and to check abuse of government power by other officials. Inevitably, public employees have greater opportunities than ordinary citizens both to impede legitimate government action and to prevent government abuse.

Public employees' own rights and the implication of their activities for public governance make the constitutional balance important and intricate, especially given this century's extensive increase in public employment. The existence of 3 million federal employees and 13 million more state and local government workers makes sacrifices of their constitutional freedoms of considerable consequence, both personal and societal. Yet their numbers create a potent political force able to secure statutory job protection and to fend off arbitrary treatment as a group, diminishing the need for constitutional protection. In addition, the size of the public work force increases legitimate government claims to constitutional flexibility in employee management.

Speaking in broad historical terms, Supreme Court decisions on the constitutional status of public employees reflect varying sensitivity to one or a combination of these competing considerations at different periods. Three major themes are discernible, however. The earliest, simplest, and perhaps most powerful is broad deference to government employment prerogatives. This deference rests on the common understanding that the Constitution creates no constitutional right to government employment. The frequently invoked corollary is that those who want the privilege of government work may be compelled to forgo exercising constitutional rights that the government cannot deny private citizens. Justice OLIVER WENDELL HOLMES, then still a state court judge, succinctly expressed this RIGHT–PRIVILEGE DISTINCTION theme in *McAuliffe v. Mayor of New Bedford* (1892). Holmes rejected a policeman's claim that his discharge for political activity violated his right of free expression, commenting that the officer "may have a constitutional right to talk politics, but he has no constitutional right to be a policeman."

The Supreme Court invoked this theme before and after *McAuliffe.* At very different stages of constitutional development over the past century, the Court has consistently upheld government power to foster a nonpartisan civil service by requiring vast numbers of public employees to refrain from active participation in politics, a cherished right of the citizenry at large. The Court has also upheld government requirements that public employees vow to uphold and defend the federal and state constitutions and not attempt their unlawful overthrow, that they live in the employing JURISDICTION, and that national security employees not publish writings about their work until the intended publication is screened to cull out classified information. In the early 1950s, moreover, the Court tolerated government efforts to disqualify from public jobs people who had advocated the forceful overthrow of the government, or who belonged to groups that did, or who refused to reveal their association with such groups, even in circumstances in which private citizens could not be punished for saying or doing the same things.

The right–privilege distinction remains a powerful influence, but Cold War hysteria and McCarthy-era purges of government employees suspected of subversive beliefs provoked the realization that adverse personnel decisions may involve more than legitimate government interests in employee relations, worker loyalty, bureaucratic neutrality, and government efficiency. The Court began to impose constitutional limits narrowly designed to protect public employees from invidiously selective maltreatment. This second theme protects against improper government motivation, but not against broad impact. Restrictions on the political freedom of numerous public employees are tolerated for the legitimate advantages of having a nonpartisan bureaucracy, but government may not penalize even a few for constitutionally unacceptable reasons, such as dislike of their beliefs. In UNITED STATES V. LOVETT (1946), for example, the Court struck down as a BILL OF ATTAINDER a provision of an appropriations law prohibiting payment of the salaries of three named government employees declared guilty of SUBVERSIVE ACTIVITY not by a court but by a House of Representatives subcommittee. Similarly, WIEMANN V. UPDEGRAFF (1952) took a stand against GUILT BY ASSOCIATION and held that government employment could not be denied for membership in a group advocating unlawful overthrow of the government if the member lacked knowledge of the group's unlawful aim.

With the advent of the WARREN COURT, constitutional protection for public employees expanded with the gradual adoption of a third, more complex approach that perceived several values at risk in government treatment of public employees. Increased solicitude for the employees' personal freedom, heightened awareness that jobs often carry some sense of entitlement, and growing appreciation of the part that government workers play in citizen self-government, intensified objections to blatant instances of ideologically discriminatory treatment. Reports of the death of the right–privilege distinction may have been exaggerated, but its hold weakened considerably. Various methods used to weed out allegedly subversive public employees, especially LOYALTY OATHS and compelled disclosure of an individual's associations, were invalidated on VAGUENESS and OVERBREADTH grounds, because the Court thought those methods of employment disqualification would excessively inhibit freedom of expression and association. Those developments paralleled the Warren Court's general expansion of citizen immunity from regulation affecting individual liberty and culminated in a series of decisions between 1966 and 1968, including ELFBRANDT V. RUSSELL (1966) and KEYISHIAN V. BOARD OF REGENTS (1967), that forbade public employers from requiring their employees as a condition of employment to relinquish the expanded constitutional freedoms they enjoyed as citizens. *Pickering v. Board of Education* (1968) appeared to complete the rejection of Holmes's view in *McAuliffe* by holding that a teacher could not be dismissed for speaking on issues of public concern involving her employer.

After the Warren Court era ended, the broadest implications of the demise of the right–privilege distinction were curtailed when the Court reaffirmed the constitutionality of government efforts to keep the civil service broadly—and neutrally—apolitical. The opposition to narrower but selective disadvantaging based on ideological viewpoint remained, however. The Court has disallowed the firing of public employees for belonging to the wrong political party, except where party affiliation is a legitimate qualification for the particular job. The political patronage practice may distort the political beliefs of public employees, but because it represents discrimination against ideologically disfavored viewpoints, it also elicits the narrower concern for preventing selective arbitrariness. In 1983 the Court drew an uncertain line between a worker grievance and a citizen complaint, allowing dismissal of public employees without constitutional restraint for employee speech on matters of personal interest, but retaining *Pickering*'s FIRST AMENDMENT protection against dismissal for speech as a citizen on matters of public concern. It endorsed neither government's right to impose any conditions on public employment it chooses, nor the employees' personal rights of self-expression. Rather, the Court stressed the government's need for flexibility in employee discipline and the public, not personal, value of employee freedoms.

Protection against employment sanctions imposed for constitutionally unacceptable reasons also underlies the Court's public employees PROCEDURAL DUE PROCESS decisions. Significantly, these protections developed after, not before, the Court established substantive limits on the reasons the government legitimately could invoke to disadvantage its employees. The possibility of intentional government arbitrariness, rather than government indifference to valuable employment opportunities, seems to have prompted the development of procedural protections surrounding the loss of government employment benefits.

The development was part of the procedural due process revolution of the Warren Court. Government benefits that did not have to be granted at all, including employment, could not be taken away once awarded without providing certain constitutionally imposed minimum procedures. Rejecting both extremes, the Court never recognized a right to government work but also denied the government the unre-stricted freedom to withhold it. Nor has the Court required that reasons and a fair process always be provided before an individual loses an employment opportunity. Instead, the Court has let the government decide whether to hold out a job as offering some job protection or security of employment. If the government bestows no entitlement by statute or practice, several rules apply. No reason is needed to discharge or refuse to hire. If defamatory reasons nonetheless are given for an adverse personnel action, the employee must have an opportunity to defend against the charge. In any event, constitutionally illegitimate reasons may not form the public basis of the adverse action. If the government does hold out a job as offering employment security of any sort, moreover, the Court disallows deprivation of the secured position until constitutionally adequate notice, reasons, and other procedures are followed. The government worker may not be deprived of employment prospects either for illegitimate reasons or for legitimate reasons that do not apply to his circumstances.

The constitutional law of public employee regulation inevitably affects the efficiency of government operations, the personal freedoms of the workers, and the public interest in checking government abuse and being apprised of how public policy is being enforced. Accommodating these interests is, and will remain, an important and complex constitutional problem.

JONATHAN D. VARAT

Bibliography

NOTE 1984 Developments in the Law—Public Employment. *Harvard Law Review* 97:1611, 1738–1800.
VAN ALSTYNE, WILLIAM W. 1969 The Constitutional Rights of Public Employees. *UCLA Law Review* 16:751–772.

PUBLIC FIGURE

The concept of a public figure features prominently in modern FIRST AMENDMENT law involving libel suits. NEW YORK TIMES V. SULLIVAN (1964) prevented public officials (officeholders and candidates for office) from recovering damages for defamation without proof of actual malice, that is, proof that the statement was made with the knowledge that it was false or with reckless disregard whether it was or not. In *Curtis Publishing Company v. Butts* (1967) the Supreme Court extended the actual malice rule to public figures, described by the Court as private persons in positions of considerable influence or able to attract attention because they had thrust themselves into public controversies. A public figure commands public interest and therefore has sufficient access to the mass media to be able, like an officeholder, to publicize his response to falsehoods about him. He invites comment and his remarks make news. The Justices unanimously agreed that for the sake of a robust FREEDOM OF THE PRESS, the actual malice rule applies to public figures, but they disagreed in specific cases on the question whether a particular person, such as the former wife of the scion of a famous family is a public figure, the question before the court in *Time Incorporated v. Firestone* (1976). The Court has tended to deny the press's claim that the party suing for damages is a public figure.

LEONARD W. LEVY

PUBLIC FORUM

Laws that regulate the time, place, and manner of speech are not considered inherently problematic under the FIRST AMENDMENT, in contrast to laws that regulate the content of speech. As a general matter, would-be speakers can be denied the use of a particular public space for their expressive activities if other proper uses of that space would be unduly disturbed and if different speakers with different messages also would be denied use of the space.

The "public forum" DOCTRINE represents an important gloss on the general doctrine that accords government fairly wide authority to regulate speech in public places. For spaces that are designated public forums—streets, parks, and sidewalks, for example—the regulatory authority of government is subject to careful scrutiny under the First Amendment. Public forums, unlike other public spaces, cannot be devoted entirely to nonexpressive uses; some accommodation of the claims of would-be speakers must be made. In addition, when the content of the speech is taken into account in governing the use of a public forum, as when political criticism or commercial advertising but not expression of a labor grievance is disallowed on a public sidewalk, an especially strong presumption of invalidity stalks the regulation. Even content-neutral regulations regarding the time and manner of speech in a public forum pass muster under the First Amendment only if they are "narrowly tailored to serve a significant government interest, and leave open ample alternative channels of communication."

The historical derivation of the public forum doctrine can be traced to an oft-quoted OBITER DICTUM by Justice OWEN J. ROBERTS in HAGUE V. CIO (1939):

Wherever the title of streets and parks may rest, they have immemorially been held in trust for the use of the public and, time out of mind, have been used for purposes of assembly, communicating thoughts between citizens, and discussing public questions. The privilege of a citizen of the United States to use the streets and parks for communication of views on national questions may be regulated in the interest of all; it is not absolute, but relative, and must be exercised in subordination to the general comfort and convenience, and in consonance with peace and good order; but it must not, in the guise of regulation, be abridged or denied.

The dictum repudiated the doctrine, endorsed by the Supreme Court forty years earlier, that government's ownership of the land on which streets and parks are situated gave officials the nearly plenary authority of a private landlord to regulate access to those spaces. The phrase "public forum" was first employed as a legal term of art by HARRY KALVEN, JR., in an influential article on the topic of speech in public places. The Supreme Court's most comprehensive discussion of the public forum doctrine is in PERRY EDUCATION ASSOCIATION V. PERRY LOCAL EDUCATORS' ASSOCIATION (1983).

Public streets, parks, state capitol grounds, and sidewalks have been held by the Court to be "quintessential" public forums. Public auditoriums and meeting rooms, state fair grounds, and public school classrooms have also been held to be public forums, although the tenor of judicial opinions suggests that officials may have somewhat more regulatory authority to preserve the special character of such places than may be exercised over open spaces such as streets and parks. The Court has denied public forum status to a jailyard, a military base portions of which were open to the public, residential mailboxes, and an internal communications system used for delivering messages and posting notices within a school district. The most important criterion for deciding whether a space constitutes a public forum is the traditional use of that type of space, not necessarily in the particular locale but rather as a general practice nationwide. Some Justices have contended that the dominant consideration should be whether the use of the space for expressive purposes is basically incompatible with other legitimate uses, but that position has not won acceptance by a majority of the Court.

The public forum doctrine has been criticized, primarily on two counts. First, it is claimed that the analytical device of categorizing public places on the basis of their general characteristics fails to give sufficient weight to considerations peculiar to each particular dispute over the use of public property for expressive purposes. Case-by-case variations in the degree to which expressive and regulatory values are implicated tend, so this criticism goes, to be overshadowed by the characterization of a place in gross as either a public forum or not. Particularly as applied to places that do not qualify as public forums, the categorization approach of the public forum doctrine permits government to regulate speech that may be highly appropriate in the particular circumstances and that may not impose serious burdens on other uses of the public space.

Second, and somewhat in tension with the first criticism, it is sometimes maintained that the public forum doctrine is misleading in that the designation of a place as a public forum or not has little resolving power in actual cases. Thus, the regulation of speech based on its content is highly disfavored, even as applied to places that are not public forums. It is not clear what the public forum doctrine adds to the presumption against regulation based on content. In addition, because a COMPELLING STATE INTEREST can justify the regulation of speech in a public forum and because places that are not public forums typically are devoted to activities that conflict somewhat with the use of such places for expressive purposes, it is not obvious that the public forum designation alters dramatically the balancing of conflicting uses that must take place in all disputes over access to public land.

Probably the most important aspect of the public forum doctrine is the principle that public forums cannot be closed off entirely to marches, DEMONSTRATIONS, rallies, and individual acts of expression. In contrast, uniformly enforced blanket prohibitions on expressive activities in places that are not public forums are permissible as a general matter under the First Amendment. Apart from this issue of blanket prohibitions, the significance of the public forum doctrine lies mainly in the tendency of courts to weigh competing particularistic considerations more favorably to speakers when the situs in dispute is a public forum.

VINCENT BLASI

(SEE ALSO: *City of Los Angeles v. Taxpayers for Vincent*, 1984.)

Bibliography

KALVEN, HARRY, JR. 1965 The Concept of the Public Forum. *Supreme Court Review* 1965:1–32.
STONE, GEOFFREY 1974 Fora Americana: Speech in Public Places. *The Supreme Court Review* 1974:233–280.

PUBLIC PURPOSE DOCTRINE

The DOCTRINE of public purpose has been used, in the course of American constitutional history, as a standard by which courts have determined the legitimacy of state EMINENT DOMAIN and taxation legislation. In different periods the doctrine has been mobilized to advance divergent ideological causes and varying constitutional interpretations.

The first distinct phase in the doctrine's history ran from the early nineteenth century to the 1870s, when it was prominent as a justification for new and often far-reaching uses of eminent domain and taxation. During that period the doctrine was a bulwark of positive government. From the 1870s to the World War I period, the doctrine became something quite different in the hands of conservatives who sought to enshrine laissez-faire policy as constitutional law. Arguments treating the public purpose doctrine as a limitation on government action were often prominent, in the new constitutional view of VESTED RIGHTS, as arguments based on FREEDOM OF CONTRACT. A third phase began in the 1930s, when state and federal courts were confronted with challenges to urban slum clearances and redevelopment projects that involved new uses of both eminent domain and taxation powers. Again the doctrine of public purpose found a prominent place in constitutional law, with legal opinion and judicial rulings seriously divided for a time as to what view of public purpose ought to prevail.

Formulation of a "public purpose" standard as a canon for testing the legitimacy of governmental action first became prominent in American decisions when states began to expand the reach of their transportation policies in the early nineteenth century. Projects such as the great Erie Canal enterprise in New York, and similar public works in other states, required powers of eminent domain for the agencies responsible for construction. When legislatures devolved the eminent domain power upon private chartered corporations that built bridges, roads, canals, and railroads, there was widespread agreement that some constitutional limitation should be formulated to prevent indiscriminate delegation of such high sovereign powers. Legal commentators and judges often invoked the Fifth Amendment's reference to PUBLIC USE as a limitation upon eminent domain TAKINGS OF PROPERTY by state authority; many state constitutions used the same phrase in their takings clauses, and even when no express constitutional limitation referred to public use the state courts read it into their law as a fundamental principle of justice. Was a privately owned turnpike corporation engaged in a "public" activity, however? How was the distinction between "public" activities and those merely "private" to be drawn?

Gradually the phrase "public purpose" assumed

nearly the same standing, as a measure of legitimacy, as "public use." One of the early decisions on turnpikes, for example, acknowledged the uniquely "public" character of such roads. They were, a New York judge declared in 1823, "the most public roads or highways that are known to exist, and in point of law, they are made entirely for public use, and the community has a deep interest in their construction and preservation." A few years later, New York's chancery court upheld the exercise of eminent domain powers by a privately owned railroad corporation. It was legitimate for the state to devolve the power to expropriate, on payment of compensation, the court declared, "not only where the safety but also where the interest or even the expediency of the state is concerned." In WEST RIVER BRIDGE V. DIX (1848), the earliest Supreme Court case during the first sixty years of the Republic's history where the eminent domain power was ruled upon directly, it was a direct taking by a state—not devolution of the power on a corporation— that was challenged; but the opinions in the case left no doubt that states enjoyed wide discretion in deciding what activities should qualify as "public" in use or purpose, hence were eligible to exercise the eminent domain power if vested in them by the legislatures.

A parallel development in legal doctrine reinforced the impact of the foregoing line of decisions. This other development was in riparian law and its relationship, which changed over time, to public law in the states. As the state legislatures enacted a growing body of law regulating interests in streams—fisheries, navigation, shoreline development, damming of waters for millpower—the courts were called upon to rule on the legitimate reach of the regulatory power. The courts derived from English COMMON LAW distinctions between streams owned by the sovereign; streams "private in ownership but public in use" and so subject to broad regulatory control; and streams strictly private in ownership and in use, whose private character immunized owners against loss from regulation or taking without compensation. Repeatedly, lawyers and judges drew the analogy between waterways in public use and the chartered railroad, canal, bridge, and road companies that were private in ownership, yet "public" in purpose and use. The analogy lent additional legitimacy to "public purpose" as a doctrine which supported state action that forced private rights to yield to communal needs. Private companies were given special privileges in promotion of drainage, wharf facilities, supply of water to urban centers, and transportation facilities, as the Ohio Supreme Court declared in 1836, "because the public has an interest in them." Hence it was consistent to force private owners to yield to takings, for purposes of such enterprises, under eminent domain.

Although the doctrine had been used initially to support a large view of eminent domain power, it was soon employed also in support of tax-financed subsidies to private business firms. As enthusiasm for railroad construction swept the country in the middle decades of the nineteenth century, voters in hundreds of local communities and many state legislatures proved willing to extend cash subsidies—money raised through taxation—to private railroads, to guarantee railroad bonds, or to purchase stock in such railroads. Again, "public purpose" proved to be the vehicle for legitimation of such use of public funds. The Michigan high court, for example, in 1852 turned back a challenge to the constitutionality of such tax-supported aid on the ground that railroad corporations were "created for public benefit" and so were distinguishable from "strictly private corporations . . . [in which] private advantage is the ultimate as well as the immediate object of their creation." The landmark state case, widely followed, was *Sharpless v. Philadelphia*, decided by the Pennsylvania court in 1853. Termed in the court's decision "beyond all comparison, the most important cause that has ever been in this Court," the case was decided in favor of the constitutionality of state subsidies. Taxation must be for a public purpose, the court emphasized, and despite private ownership the railroad companies receiving aid represented such a purpose.

The spreading practice of extending public aid to corporations alarmed many jurists, however; and by the late 1860s, opposition to such a broad reading of "public purpose" and "public use" concepts had grown strong. Emblematic of the issue was the policy of Wisconsin, where the legislature by 1874 had authorized public, tax-supported aid to telegraph, steamship, hotel, waterworks, gas, construction, bridge, canal, river improvement, and dry-dock corporations. The constitutions of the newly admitted western states commonly designated as "public purpose" enterprises firms engaged in logging, road building, irrigation and reclamation, railroads, river improvement, and drainage for mining or agriculture. Such enterprises were routinely granted eminent domain power, and many of them received subsidies. In the East and Midwest, several states allowed manufacturing corporations of all kinds to condemn and flood lands for power sites. Such laws were defended as aid to companies with an important public purpose, comparable to the grants of similar eminent domain powers to gristmills in colonial Massachusetts. In a few states—

among them Georgia, New York, Alabama, and Vermont—the courts invalidated such grants of power. In most state tribunals, however, the broad view of "public purpose" continued to prevail.

Indicative of the emerging conservative jurisprudence on the issue were decisions of Judge THOMAS M. COOLEY's Michigan court in 1870 against public aid to railroads and in 1877 against a milldam flooding act. In Cooley's view, set forth more systematically in his treatise, *Constitutional Limitations* (1868), "Everything that may be done under the name of taxation is not necessarily a tax; and it may happen that an oppressive burden imposed by the government, when it comes to be carefully scrutinized, will prove, instead of a tax, to be an unlawful confiscation of property, unwarranted by any principle of constitutional government." Further distinguished authority for the same view came from the Iowa Supreme Court. Chief Justice JOHN F. DILLON—like Cooley, a treatise writer who pressed his concern for vested rights on the legal profession and the courts in the late nineteenth century—wrote an opinion for the Iowa court in 1862 that struck down railroad bond aid as a confiscation of citizens' property without compensation and a violation of DUE PROCESS.

The conservative assault led by Dillon and Cooley soon enlisted the aid of the Supreme Court. In LOAN ASSOCIATION V. TOPEKA (1874) the Court declared unconstitutional a Kansas municipal bond issue in aid of a bridge-manufacturing company. Justice SAMUEL F. MILLER's opinion for the majority denounced the use of tax funds for a "private interest instead of a public use"; and he termed it robbery to exercise the taxing power in this way. It was a sudden and surprising use of the public purpose doctrine to limit state legislative power—in contrast with its earlier use to enlarge state power and legitimate new activities.

The conservative version of public purpose did not carry the day altogether, even as the jurisprudence of vested rights was gaining ascendancy. Thus the Supreme Court repeatedly turned back assaults on state aid to railroads, with a solid majority maintaining that transportation had always been considered a "public purpose" activity and so eligible for eminent domain power and aid with tax funds. *Olcott v. The Supervisors* (1873) upheld the validity of local bonds issued to aid railroads in a Wisconsin municipality, in the face of efforts to repudiate them. In language squarely in the line of doctrine that had come down from JAMES KENT's views on turnpikes half a century earlier, the Court asserted that railroads had a "public highway character. . . . Though the ownership is private, the use is public." Use of tax funds to subsidize manufac-

turing companies suffered a different fate, however, in light of the *Loan Association* decision. Thus Clyde Jacobs calculated that from 1870 to 1910 some forty public purpose cases challenging tax aid to businesses came before the federal courts and state high courts. In thirty-nine of the forty, public aid was found invalid on the ground that it was not for a public purpose. Moreover, numerous state courts interpreted the "public purpose" provisions in state constitutions to forbid subsidies or relief payments to the blind, for example, or to farmers who had suffered from weather or crop failure.

In the Supreme Court, however, a manifest softening of the commitment to public purpose as a limiting doctrine became evident in decisions on the constitutionality of grants of taxing and eminent domain power to special-purpose irrigation districts. The Court ruled in *Fallbrook Irrigation District v. Bradley* (1896) that local geographical and climatic conditions required a considerable legislative discretion as to what constituted public purpose. In other cases that tested the constitutionality of using tax revenues to finance state enterprises such as public utilities and even grain warehouses, the Court moved still further toward allowing legislatures to do so. By the early 1920s public purpose as a national constitutional doctrine was no longer a major support for vested property rights or limitation upon governmental power, even though the Court, beginning with *Fallbrook*, explicitly treated public purpose as a FOURTEENTH AMENDMENT issue.

The Supreme Court also abandoned in 1916 a residual doctrine that had enjoyed considerable judicial respect in many jurisdictions since the 1850s, the doctrine that "public use" (justifying takings by the state) should be interpreted as "use by the public" and not in broad "public purpose" terms. In *Mt. Vernon-Woodberry Company v. Alabama Power Company* (1916), Justice OLIVER WENDELL HOLMES, writing for the Court, declared flatly that "the inadequacy of the use by the general public as a universal test is established."

The deep economic crisis in the 1930s and the social dislocations it generated led to the third distinct phase of the public purpose doctrine's history. The application, throughout the nation, of federal aid to urban slum clearance and housing development produced challenges in both federal and state courts to the constitutionality of using eminent domain and taxation powers for such purposes. Especially where private real-estate and financial interests were given a key role in housing, the public purpose of takings and public expenditures for such programs was questioned. By 1940 such objections had been rejected, and the public programs upheld, in the courts of twenty-eight states. Many of these opinions concluded that where "public welfare" was served the public purpose test was met—a broad concept of legitimacy for eminent domain (and taxation) that found expression also in *United States ex rel. Tennessee Valley Authority v. Welch* (1946), a leading Supreme Court decision validating takings by a federal agency for purposes of regional development. It was for Congress to decide what was a public use, the Court declared; no "departure . . . [from] judicial restraint," with deference to the legislative branch, was warranted.

The language of the *Welch* decision was imported into state and federal courts' review of another wave of urban slum clearance programs in the 1940s and 1950s, following World War II. In this later period, more than mere slum clearance was at issue; the urban programs often embraced comprehensive "urban redevelopment" objectives, typically employed private financial and entrepreneurial interests in the projects, and often involved sweeping condemnation programs that took land and buildings that did not fit the "slum" classification. Rejecting a public purpose challenge to comprehensive redevelopment, in which some of the property taken ended up in the hands of private developers, not government itself, a federal district court in a landmark 1953 ruling, *Schneider v. District of Columbia*, declared: "the term 'public use' has progressed as economic facts have progressed, and so projects such as railroads, public power plants, the operation of mines under some conditions, and, more recently, low-cost housing have been held to be public uses for which private property may be seized. Moreover, . . . the variation in the term from '[public] use' to '[public] purpose' indicates a progression in thought." So long as the taking is necessary to the public purpose that the legislature has determined and defined, the court concluded, eminent domain powers necessary to accomplishment of that purpose must be deemed legitimate.

The valedictory came in *Berman v. Parker* (1954), when the Supreme Court affirmed that public purpose was a concept coterminous with "public welfare," hence embraced objectives across a broad spectrum that included "public safety, public health, morality, peace and quiet, law and order," to list only "some of the more conspicuous examples." Once pursuit of public purpose in these terms was accepted, then eminent domain, taxation, or the STATE POLICE POWER might be used to accomplish the goals set forth. Judicial review under the Fifth and Fourteenth Amendments was not out of the question, at least in some

jurists' views. Justice FELIX FRANKFURTER, for example, in a concurring opinion in *Welch*, wrote: "But the fact that the nature of the subject matter gives the legislative determination nearly immunity from judicial review does not mean that the power to review is wanting." In the subsequent history of taking, however, it was the eminent domain/police power distinction, and not the public purpose doctrine, on which constitutional challenges to regulation would turn. The purposes for which eminent domain or taxation could be used did seem "nearly immune," in light of modern constitutional interpretation of the GENERAL WELFARE CLAUSE.

HARRY N. SCHEIBER

Bibliography
JACOBS, CLYDE E. 1954 *Law Writers and the Courts: The Influence of Thomas M. Cooley, Christopher G. Tiedman, and John F. Dillon upon American Constitutional Law.* Berkeley and Los Angeles: University of California Press.
NICHOLS, PHILIP, JR. 1940 The Meaning of Public Use in the Law of Eminent Domain. *Boston University Law Review* 20:615–624.
SCHEIBER, HARRY N. 1971 The Road to *Munn:* Eminent Domain and the Concept of the Public Purpose in the State Courts. *Perspectives in American History* 5:327–402.
WOODBURY, COLEMAN, ED. 1953 *Urban Redevelopment: Problems and Practices.* Chicago: University of Chicago Press.

PUBLIC TRIAL

"In all criminal prosecutions, the accused shall enjoy the right to a speedy and public trial. . . ." The language of the Sixth Amendment appears to assure that criminal courtrooms in the United States will be open—that there will be no secret trials. But the issue of openness in the process of criminal justice has only recently reached a point of consensus in the Supreme Court after nearly forty years of experimentation with successive constitutional tests.

Conflicting values underlay the debate. One was that of the open society, with the public free to observe and criticize the activities of government, including the courts. The other was fairness to someone accused of a crime: his or her right to a trial uninfluenced by public passion or prejudice. The two values do not usually conflict, but it hardly needs to be said that they may clash in a country that has known mob-dominated courtrooms and lynchings.

The constitutional conflict first surfaced in a series of cases starting with BRIDGES V. CALIFORNIA (1941).

The issue was whether American, like British, judges could punish as a contempt of court any comment on a pending criminal case that had a tendency to interfere with the administration of justice. In *Bridges* two persons had been held in contempt: a labor leader for a telegram criticizing a judicial decision against his union, and a newspaper editor for an editorial admonishing a judge not to grant probation to two convicted union members. By a 5–4 vote the Supreme Court reversed both contempt convictions. The Court's opinion, by Justice HUGO L. BLACK, said the FIRST AMENDMENT barred punishment for such comments unless they presented a CLEAR AND PRESENT DANGER—the test framed by Justice OLIVER WENDELL HOLMES in the early sedition cases such as ABRAMS V. UNITED STATES (1919)—of causing "disorderly and unfair administration of justice." Later decisions made plain that it would be extremely difficult for authorities to meet that test. Justice WILLIAM O. DOUGLAS said in *Craig v. Harney* (1947): "A trial is a public event. What transpires in the courtroom is public property. . . . There is no special perquisite of the judiciary which enables it, as distinguished from other institutions of democratic government, to suppress, edit, or censor events which transpire in proceedings before it."

Nevertheless, concern remained about the possible effect of outside comment on the criminal justice process, especially on the impartiality of jurors. Justice FELIX FRANKFURTER felt so strongly about the matter that he wrote an impassioned opinion in *Maryland v. Baltimore Radio Show* (1950), when the Supreme Court refused to review a state appellate court decision reversing on First Amendment grounds the contempt conviction of a radio broadcaster who had broadcast, before a murder trial, the record of the defendant and alleged evidence of his guilt.

The Supreme Court dealt with the problem of prejudicial press comment on criminal cases another way: by reversing convictions when there was reason to think the jury might have been improperly influenced by the outside comment. The Court first found that prejudicial comment had violated a defendant's constitutional right to fair trial in IRVIN V. DOWD (1961). Justice Frankfurter, still preferring to proceed against the press itself, wrote bitterly in a concurring opinion: "The Court has not yet decided that, while convictions must be reversed and miscarriages of justice result because the minds of jurors or potential jurors were poisoned, the poisoner is constitutionally protected in plying his trade." But the device of contempt to prevent prejudicial comment never found favor with a majority. In *Sheppard v. Maxwell* (1966) the Court

outlined other measures to prevent the prejudicing of juries in notorious cases: delaying or moving the trial, for example, or sequestering the jury once it had been selected.

Then a new prophylactic device was taken up by some trial courts around the country: INJUNCTIONS against press institutions and representatives forbidding reports, before trial, of evidence and other material that might prejudice potential jurors. These gag orders, as the press angrily called them, followed the approach adopted by Britain in the Criminal Justice Act of 1967. That act allowed the press to attend pretrial committal proceedings, thereby assuring scrutiny of the process, but forebade reporting on them until after the trial itself was completed—unless the defendant waived the restriction. But in 1976 the Supreme Court held that the First Amendment stood in the way of this approach, too. In NEBRASKA PRESS ASSOCIATION V. STUART the press had been enjoined from reporting, before trial, the alleged confession and other especially prejudicial matters about the defendant in a gruesome multiple murder case in a small Nebraska town. The Court's opinion, by Chief Justice WARREN E. BURGER, declined to adopt an absolute rule against such restraints. But the decision against them, on the extreme facts of that case, made it most unlikely that gag orders would ever be permissible; and trial courts stopped issuing them.

A last round of the constitutional debate about fair trial and free speech tested still another prophylactic device: closing the courtroom to the public and the press during sensitive phases of pretrial or trial proceedings. In GANNETT V. DEPASQUALE (1979) counsel for the defendants moved to close a pretrial hearing on motions to suppress confessions and other EVIDENCE, arguing that reports of the hearing would prejudice future jurors if the evidence were in fact suppressed. The prosecutor did not object, and the trial judge closed the courtroom. A newspaper then challenged the order. The Supreme Court decided that the "public trial" clause of the Sixth Amendment was for the benefit of the defendant alone, who could waive it, and that outsiders had no STANDING to insist on an open courtroom. The majority put aside First Amendment considerations.

A year later the Court did consider the First Amendment and decided that it limited the closing of courtrooms. In RICHMOND NEWSPAPERS V. VIRGINIA a 7–1 majority found unconstitutional the exclusion of the public (and with it the press) from a criminal trial. There was no opinion of the Court, but various Justices shared the view expressed by Chief Justice Burger that the First Amendment assures the public a "right of access" to criminal trials that can be denied only for strong and articulated reasons. Indications are that the right extends also to civil cases, and to pretrial proceedings as well as trials.

The decision was an extraordinary doctrinal conclusion to the long cycle of constitutional litigation. For the Supreme Court had for the first time said that the First Amendment was not only a shield protecting the right to speak or publish but also a sword helping the public to gain access to information about government institutions. How far that new doctrine would be taken was uncertain. But in American courtrooms, at least, a constitutional presumption favors openness.

ANTHONY LEWIS

Bibliography

LEWIS, ANTHONY 1980 A Public Right to Know about Public Institutions: The First Amendment as Sword. *The Supreme Court Review* 1980:1–25.

SCHMIDT, BENNO C. 1977 Nebraska Press Association: An Expansion of Freedom and Contraction of Theory. *Stanford Law Review* 29:431–476.

PUBLIC USE

The "taking" clause of the Fifth Amendment limits the power of EMINENT DOMAIN by demanding that governmental taking of private property be for a public use. The Supreme Court held in CHICAGO, BURLINGTON & QUINCY RAILROAD CO. v. CHICAGO (1897) that the same requirement applies to the states through the FOURTEENTH AMENDMENT.

Although some early decisions defined the public use standard to include a right of "use by the public," that approach was repudiated by the Court. As early as 1905 in *Clark v. Nash*, the Court held that a state could authorize a private person to condemn an easement for irrigation across a neighbor's land. "What is a public use," said the Court, "may frequently and largely depend upon the facts surrounding the subject." In the arid environment of Utah, the taking of a private irrigation easement could properly be deemed a public use, because it was "absolutely necessary" to agricultural development. On similar grounds, the Court's decision in *Strickley v. Highland Boy Gold Mining Co.* (1906) sustained the statutory authority of a mining company to condemn a private easement for transporting ore to a railroad loading site. These decisions were followed by many others intimating that any use conducive to the public benefit was a public use for which eminent domain could be invoked, including reclamation of swamp lands,

establishment of water and electrical power systems, development of transportation facilities, and creation of public parks.

The broad public benefit test has, in recent years, been assimilated with the RATIONAL BASIS approach invoked by the Supreme Court in reviewing regulations of economic interests under the DUE PROCESS clause. In the leading case, *Berman v. Parker* (1954), the court sustained the use of eminent domain to acquire various separate parcels of private property in blighted areas in furtherance of a community redevelopment project. The fact that the property to be condemned would be resold or leased to private persons for redevelopment purposes did not transgress the public use limitation, for "when the legislature has spoken, the public interest has been declared in terms well-nigh conclusive. In such cases the legislature, not the judiciary, is the main guardian of the public needs to be served. . . . The concept of the public welfare is broad and inclusive."

Under this expansive and deferential approach, eminent domain may be exercised as a means for achieving practically any use or objective within the power of the legislative body.

ARVO VAN ALSTYNE

Bibliography

NICHOLS, PERRY 1983 *The Law of Eminent Domain*, Vol. 2A. New York: Matthew Bender & Co.

PUBLIC UTILITIES REGULATION

See: Economic Regulation

PUBLIC UTILITY HOLDING COMPANY ACT
49 Stat. 803 (1935)

This measure was an important part of the legislative program of President FRANKLIN D. ROOSEVELT. Two leading supporters of the bill were Senators GEORGE NORRIS and HUGO L. BLACK. The act's objective was to disperse ownership and control of the nation's gas and electric utilities, then highly concentrated in pyramids of corporations with holding companies at the top. The act required holding companies to register with the Securities and Exchange Commission and authorized the SEC to limit a company's operations to a single region. A "death sentence" provision authorized dissolution of a company that did not show, within five years, that it was serving an efficient local function.

The great holding companies sought to challenge the constitutionality of the entire act in an early TEST CASE, but government lawyers managed to persuade the Supreme Court to defer the omnibus attack and consider the act's registration requirement separately. The Court upheld that requirement in *Electric Bond & Share Co. v. SEC* (1938). The other provisions of the law came before the Court after Roosevelt had appointed seven Justices. Those provisions were sustained, with broad readings of Congress's power under the COMMERCE CLAUSE, in *North American Co. v. SEC* (1946) and *American Power & Light Co. v. SEC* (1946). By 1952, more than 750 holding companies had been dissolved.

KENNETH L. KARST

Bibliography

FREUND, PAUL A.   1951   *On Understanding the Supreme Court.* Pages 99–110. Boston: Little, Brown.

PUERTO RICO, CONSTITUTIONAL STATUS OF

No clear definition exists of how and to what extent the Commonwealth of Puerto Rico fits within the federal constitutional system. Undoubtedly, the *Puerto Rican Federal Relations Act*, enacted by Congress in 1950 "in the nature of a compact" between Congress and the people of Puerto Rico, and the adoption by Puerto Ricans of their own constitution in 1952 were intended to work a significant change in the previous colonial relationship between the island and the United States. The nature and scope of this change, however, have not been conclusively ascertained by federal courts ruling on the matter.

Puerto Rico, which had become a self-governing overseas province of the Kingdom of Spain under the Royal Decree of 1897, was ceded to the United States in 1898 under the Treaty of Paris which ended the Spanish-American War. It became an unincorporated TERRITORY of the United States, subject to the plenary command of Congress. Under various Supreme Court decisions it is clear that, until 1952, Puerto Rico was a domestic possession of the United States, neither a foreign country nor an integral part of the nation, merely belonging to it. Congressional authority over the island and its people encompassed the entire domain of SOVEREIGNTY, both national and local, and was completely unconstrained by the federal Constitution, except as regards those basic prohibitions

which go "to the very root of the power of Congress to act at all" and "which the Constitution has established in favor of human liberty and are applicable to every condition or status." (See INSULAR CASES.) Wielding its plenary powers, the United States established a military government in Puerto Rico from 1898 to 1900, when a civil regime was installed under the Foraker Act, providing a meager participation of Puerto Ricans in the island's government. In 1917 Congress enacted a second Organic Act (Jones Act) providing a measure of self-government and granting United States CITIZENSHIP collectively to the people of Puerto Rico, while retaining all major elements of sovereignty.

In 1950 a bill to provide for the organization of a constitutional government by the people of Puerto Rico was introduced in Congress. Its provisions were not to be effective until accepted in a REFERENDUM by Puerto Rican voters. After a favorable vote on the new federal act by the island electorate, a CONSTITUTIONAL CONVENTION was held in Puerto Rico and the fundamental law drafted there was adopted by the majority of the islanders in 1952. In transmitting the newly adopted Puerto Rican Constitution to Congress, President HARRY S. TRUMAN recognized that with such approval "full authority and responsibility for local self-government [would] be vested in the people of Puerto Rico." In 1953 the United Nations recognized that Puerto Ricans, exercising the right of self-determination, had achieved a new constitutional status, and had "been invested with attributes of political sovereignty which clearly identify the status of self-government attained by the Puerto Rican people as that of an autonomous political entity."

It is generally accepted by federal courts that after 1952 "Puerto Rico's status changed from that of a mere territory to the unique status of COMMONWEALTH." The Supreme Court itself stated in *Examining Board v. Flores* (1976) that "the purpose of Congress in its 1950 and 1952 legislation was to accord to Puerto Rico the degree of autonomy and independence normally associated with a State of the Union." However, the precise extent of the referred "autonomy" and the constitutional basis for statelike status are very much in doubt. Thus, while the Supreme Court has now accepted that "Puerto Rico is to be deemed sovereign over matters not ruled by the federal Constitution" and that Puerto Rican legislation and court decisions deserve the same regard in federal courts as those of a state, it has also ruled in *Harris v. Rosario* (1980) that Congress under the territorial clause may still "treat Puerto Rico differently from States so long as there is a rational basis for its actions."

Likewise, the Court, after acknowledging that Puerto Rico is subject to federal constitutional requirements regarding FREEDOM OF SPEECH, DUE PROCESS, EQUAL PROTECTION, and reasonable SEARCH AND SEIZURE, has indicated that such guarantees are binding either directly under the BILL OF RIGHTS or indirectly by operation of the FOURTEENTH AMENDMENT, expressly refusing to fix one or the other as the source or basis of their applicability. The Court has yet to write on a clean slate in dealing with the new constitutional status of Puerto Rico.

JAIME B. FUSTER

Bibliography

FUSTER, JAIME B.   1974   Origin of the Doctrine of Territorial Incorporation and Its Implications for the Power of the Commonwealth of Puerto Rico. *University of Puerto Rico Law Review* 43:259–294.

PURE FOOD AND DRUG ACT
34 Stat. 768 (1906)

Typical of the progressive legislation passed after the turn of the century, this act extended the NATIONAL POLICE POWER to regulate the quality of food and drugs in INTERSTATE COMMERCE. A personal crusade by the chief chemist of the Department of Agriculture together with the muckrakers' stomach-churning exposés fanned public opinion. President THEODORE ROOSEVELT's backstage maneuvering also helped secure passage of this federal inspection act on June 30, 1906.

The act outlawed the manufacture of "adulterated or misbranded" food or drugs and prohibited their introduction into interstate or FOREIGN COMMERCE. Congress gave the secretaries of agriculture, treasury, and commerce and labor authority to issue regulations enforcing the act and specifically provided PROCEDURAL DUE PROCESS for violators. The act forbade: misbranding of food; the use of imitations, substitutes, harmful additives, rotten ingredients; and concealment of "damage or inferiority." Drugs were required to meet federal standards of quality, purity, and strength or clearly label their departures from the standards.

The Supreme Court sustained this act in HIPOLITE EGG COMPANY v. UNITED STATES (1911) as a legitimate exercise of congressional power over commerce. Congress substantially tightened and extended it in the FOOD, DRUG, AND COSMETIC ACT of 1938.

DAVID GORDON

QUERN v. JORDAN
440 U.S. 332 (1979)

This case held that SECTION 1983, TITLE 42, UNITED STATES CODE, does not abrogate the states' ELEVENTH AMENDMENT immunity from suit in federal court. The amendment therefore precludes retroactive damage awards against states. States, however, may be forced to bear the costs of future compliance with the Constitution and state officials may be enjoined to comply with the Constitution.

THEODORE EISENBERG

QUIRIN, EX PARTE
317 U.S. 1 (1942)

In 1942 President FRANKLIN D. ROOSEVELT issued a proclamation subjecting enemies entering the United States through the coastal defense zones to trial by military tribunal and denying them access to the civil courts. Seven German saboteurs, who had been set ashore in the United States from submarines and who had subsequently been captured, were tried under the terms of the proclamation. The saboteurs petitioned for a writ of HABEAS CORPUS, arguing that, so long as the regular courts were open and operating, they were entitled to TRIAL BY JURY, and citing as PRECEDENT the Civil War case EX PARTE MILLIGAN.

The Supreme Court, then in summer recess, met in extraordinary session to hear the petition. An 8–0 Court, speaking through Chief Justice HARLAN F. STONE, upheld the constitutionality of military trial for offenses against the law of war. But the Court also insisted upon the right of the civil courts to review the constitutionality or applicability of Roosevelt's proclamation in individual cases.

DENNIS J. MAHONEY

(SEE ALSO: *Cramer v. United States; Haupt v. United States.*)

Bibliography

BELKNAP, MICHAL R.   1980   The Supreme Court Goes to War: The Meaning and Implications of the Nazi Saboteur Case. *Military Law Review* 89:59–95.

QUOCK WALKER CASES

See: *Commonwealth v. Jennison*

QUOTAS, RACIAL

See: Racial Quotas

R

RABINOWITZ, UNITED STATES v.

See: Search Incident to Arrest

RACIAL BALANCE

The idea of racial balance is a product of the DESEGREGATION of public schools in the years since BROWN v. BOARD OF EDUCATION (1954–1955). The term refers to the racial distribution of students in particular schools in relation to the racial distribution of school children in an entire district. If a district's children are seventy percent white and thirty percent black, then a hypothetically perfect balance would produce these same percentages in each school. By extension, the notion of racial balance may be used in discussing other institutions: a housing project, a factory's work force, a state university's medical school. (See RACIAL QUOTAS; AFFIRMATIVE ACTION.)

In the school cases, the Supreme Court has held that racial balance is an appropriate "starting point" for a lower court to use in fashioning a remedy for de jure SEGREGATION. (See DE FACTO/DE JURE; SWANN V. CHARLOTTE-MECKLENBURG BOARD OF EDUCATION, 1971.) However, even where segregation has been deliberately caused by school board actions, there is no constitutional requirement of racial balance throughout the district's schools. Although one-race schools are presumptively to be eliminated, the school board will be allowed to prove that the racial distribution in those schools results from something other than the board's deliberate policy.

SCHOOL BUSING over very long distances, for example, would not be required under this approach; distance alone would be a racially neutral explanation for the board's failure to remedy racial imbalance.

In the absence of previous legislation commanding or authorizing school segregation, or school board actions with segregative intent, the fact of racial imbalance in a district's schools, standing alone, does not amount to a constitutional violation. However, intentional acts of segregation by the board in the remote past, coupled with current racial imbalance, will place on the board an almost impossible burden of proving that it has dismantled its "dual" (segregated) system. (See COLUMBUS BOARD OF EDUCATION V. PENICK, 1979.)

The term racial balance is sometimes used in a different sense. Some discussions of school segregation use the term to describe a school that includes a "critical mass" of students from each race. Social scientists disagree over the educational value to minority students of having a significant number of white students in the classroom. The suggestion that minority students learn better in the company of whites has roots in the Supreme Court's pre-*Brown* decisions on graduate education. (See SWEATT V. PAINTER, 1950.) And where segregation is imposed by official action, *Brown* itself takes the view that the resulting stigma impairs minority students' ability to learn. But the abstract proposition that minority students cannot learn effectively outside the presence of whites is more than a little patronizing. And the notion of racial balance in this sense is immensely complicated in a multiethnic community: is a school integrated if it contains significant numbers of both white and minority students, or should the category of minority students be broken down into its black, Hispanic, and other components? Merely to ask this question is to understand why the Supreme Court has avoided speaking of racial balance in this latter sense and has used the idea in its mechanical racial-percentages sense only as a "starting point."

KENNETH L. KARST

Bibliography

FISS, OWEN M. 1975 The Jurisprudence of Busing. *Law and Contemporary Problems* 1975:194–216.

RACIAL CLASSIFICATION

See: Benign Racial Classification; Invidious Discrimination; Racial Discrimination; Suspect Classification

RACIAL DISCRIMINATION

The nation was founded with the enslavement of blacks as an established and ongoing institution, and though we were not particularly proud of the institution, we were prepared to live with it. The Constitution did not mention the word "slave," and contemplated the eventual closing of the slave trade (referred to simply as the "importation of persons"), but, through similar circumlocutions, also created obligations to return fugitive slaves, and included a proportion of the slaves within the population base to be used for the apportionment of representatives and taxes. In DRED SCOTT V. SANDFORD (1857) the Supreme Court viewed slaves as property and declared that the right of slaveholders to take their slaves to the territories was protected by the DUE PROCESS CLAUSE of the Fifth Amendment.

The Civil War brought slavery to an end and reversed the basic commitment of the Constitution toward blacks. The law sought equality rather than enslavement, and it was through the elaboration of this egalitarian commitment that the concept of racial discrimination emerged. Prohibiting racial discrimination became the principal strategy of the American legal system for achieving equality for blacks. The laws against racial discrimination typically protect all racial minorities, not just blacks, and yet, for purely historical reasons, the development of those laws would be unimaginable apart from the struggle of blacks for equality in America. That struggle has been

the source both of the achievements of antidiscrimination law and of its recurrent dilemmas.

The three amendments adopted following the Civil War constitute the groundwork of this branch of the law, although only one—the FIFTEENTH AMENDMENT—actually speaks of racial discrimination. It provides that "the right . . . to vote shall not be denied or abridged . . . on account of race, color, or previous condition of servitude." The other Civil War amendments are not cast in terms of racial discrimination. The THIRTEENTH AMENDMENT prohibits slavery and involuntary servitude, and the FOURTEENTH AMENDMENT, in relevant aspect, prohibits states from denying "the EQUAL PROTECTION OF THE LAWS." But the Supreme Court has interpreted both these amendments to prohibit racial discrimination. With respect to the Thirteenth Amendment, the Court reasoned in JONES V. ALFRED H. MAYER CO. (1968) that racial discrimination is a badge or incident of slavery. (See BADGES OF SERVITUDE.) Similarly, in interpreting the Fourteenth Amendment, the Court, as early as STRAUDER V. WEST VIRGINIA (1880), declared racial discrimination to be the kind of unequal treatment that constitutes a denial of equal protection of the laws. Indeed, over the years, racial discrimination came to be seen as the paradigmatic denial of equal protection, and supplied the standard against which all other equal protection claims came to be measured, even when pressed by nonracial groups such as the poor or women. They too had to show that they were discriminated against on the basis of some impermissible criterion such as their wealth or sex. The promise of equal protection was thus transformed into a promise not to discriminate.

It was, moreover, through the enforcement of the Fourteenth Amendment that the prohibition against racial discrimination achieved its greatest prominence. Antidiscrimination was the instrument that finally put to an end the system of white supremacy that emerged in the late nineteenth and early twentieth centuries and that worked by separating whites and blacks—Jim Crow. The discrimination appeared on the very face of Jim Crow laws and a principle that condemned racial discrimination easily brought those laws within the sweep of the Fourteenth Amendment. All that was needed was an understanding of how the separatism of Jim Crow worked to the disadvantage of blacks; that was the burden of BROWN V. BOARD OF EDUCATION (1954) and the cases that followed. As the principle controlling the interpretation of the Fourteenth Amendment, antidiscrimination was a limitation only upon the actions of states, but once the step entailed in *Brown* was taken, the federal government was, in BOLLING V. SHARPE (1954), made subject to an identical prohibition by a construction of the due process clause of the Fifth Amendment. Racial discrimination was deemed as inconsistent with the constitutional guarantee of liberty as it was with equal protection.

Statutes, too, have been concerned with racial equality. In the years immediately following the Civil War, Congress passed a comprehensive program to protect the newly freed slaves, and defined the conduct it sought to prohibit in a variety of ways. In the CIVIL RIGHTS ACT OF 1866 Congress promised that blacks would enjoy the same rights as whites; in the FORCE ACTS (1870, 1871) it guaranteed all citizens the rights and privileges arising from the Constitution or laws of the United States. In the decades following *Brown v. Board of Education,* however, when the antidiscrimination principle of the Fourteenth Amendment received its most strenuous affirmation and the nation embarked on its Second Reconstruction, Congress cast the substantive standard in terms of a single idiom—do not discriminate. (See CIVIL RIGHTS ACT OF 1964; VOTING RIGHTS ACT OF 1965; CIVIL RIGHTS ACT OF 1968.)

During this period, Congress introduced new mechanisms to enforce the equal protection clause; for example, it authorized the attorney general to bring injunctive school desegregation suits, required federal administrative agencies to terminate financial assistance to segregated school systems, and provided for criminal prosecutions against those who forcibly interfered with desegregation. Congress also broadened the reach of federal antidiscrimination law beyond the scope of the Fourteenth Amendment by regulating, in the name of racial equality, activities of private agencies (for example, restaurants, employers, or landlords), which otherwise would not have been covered by that amendment because of its "state action" requirement. In each of these measures, Congress used the language of antidiscrimination. So did the President in promulgating EXECUTIVE ORDER 11246 (1965), which regulates government contractors. Many state legislatures also intervened on behalf of racial equality during the Second Reconstruction, and these enactments were also couched in terms of prohibiting discrimination.

Sometimes Congress and the state legislatures exempted certain discriminatory practices from the laws they enacted. One instance is the federal open housing law, which exempts discrimination by small residences ("Mrs. Murphy's roominghouse"); another is the federal fair employment statute, which exempts from its coverage small businesses (at first businesses with fewer than twenty-five employees, later reduced to fifteen). Apparently Congress viewed the interest in associational liberty present in these settings as sufficiently strong to justify limited exemptions to the ban on racial discrimination. Yet, putting these exemptions and a handful of others to one side, it is fair to say that today, primarily as a result of the Second Reconstruction, the prohibition against racial discrimination is all-encompassing. It has both constitutional and statutory bases and is the subject of an executive order. It is a pervasive feature of both federal and state law and calls forth a broad array of civil and criminal remedies. It almost has the status of a moral imperative, like the norm against theft or killing. The issue that divides Americans today is thus not whether the law should prohibit racial discrimination but what, precisely, doing so entails.

The antidiscrimination norm, as already noted, was largely fashioned at a time when the nation was swept by the SEPARATE-BUT-EQUAL DOCTRINE of Jim Crow and when blacks were disadvantaged in a rather open and crude manner. In such a context, the principle of antidiscrimination invites a color blindness: When allocating a scarce opportunity, such as a job or a place in a professional school, the decision maker should not prefer a white candidate over a black one on the basis of the individual's color or race. Here antidiscrimination requires that individuals be judged independently of race. This much is settled. Interpretive problems arise, however, when the social context changes—when we have moved beyond Jim Crow and blacks have come to be disadvantaged primarily in ways that are hidden and systematically entrenched. Then we confront two issues. One arises from the exclusion of blacks on the basis of a seemingly innocent criterion such as performance on a standardized test; the other from the preference given to blacks to correct for long-standing unequal distributional patterns.

To clarify the first issue, it should be understood that the appearance of innocence might be misleading. Although a black scores higher than a white on a test, the employer might manipulate or falsify the scores so that the white is given the job. In this case, the apparent use of an innocent criterion is simply a mask for racial discrimination. The decision is still directly based on race and would be deemed unlawful. The most straightforward remedy would be to set aside the decision and allow an honest application of the test.

There are, moreover, situations when a test is honestly administered and yet the very decision to use the test in the first place is based on an illegitimate concern, namely, a desire to exclude blacks. A highly sophisticated verbal aptitude test might be used, for example, to select employees for manual work because the employer, wanting to maintain a predominantly white work force, assumes that fewer whites than blacks will be screened out by the test. Here again, the "real" criterion of selection is race; a court would disallow the use of the irrelevant test, and require the employer to choose a criterion that serves a legitimate end. In both of these cases—the dishonest application of legitimate criteria and the honest application of illegitimate criteria—the appearance of color blindness is a sham and a court could use the simple, colorblind form of the antidiscrimination norm to void the results.

The more troublesome variant of the first issue arises when (1) the facially innocent criterion is adopted in order to serve a legitimate interest; (2) the criterion in fact furthers that interest; and (3) the application of the criterion disadvantages the racial minority in much the same way as would the use of race as the criterion of selection. The job may in fact require sophisticated verbal skills and the test that measures these skills may screen out more blacks than whites. The test is job-related but has a disparate adverse impact on blacks. The question then is whether an employment decision based on the test violates the antidiscrimination prohibition. This is a question of considerable difficulty because while the law, strictly speaking, prohibits distinctions based on race, this particular decision is based on a criterion other than race.

One school of thought answers this question in the negative. This view stresses process, and interprets antidiscrimination in terms of the integrity of the selection process: A selection process based on race is corrupt and cannot be allowed. A selection process free of racial influence might redound to the benefit of the racial minority, since it would allow them to compete on equal footing with other groups and thus give them a chance to alter the distributional inequalities that occurred under a regime such as Jim Crow, where they were penalized because of their race. Any actual effect on their material status as a group, however, would represent just an agreeable by-product, or a background assumption, not the purpose of antidiscrimination law. According to this school, the aims of antidiscrimination law are fulfilled when the process of selection is purified of all racial criteria or motivations.

Another viewpoint stresses results or effects, not process; it would find the use of the innocent criterion unlawful even if it serves legitimate ends. What is decisive, according to this school of thought, is the actual disadvantaging of blacks, not the way the disadvantage comes about. If the application of a criterion has a disproportionately adverse impact on the racial minority, in the sense that it excludes substantially more blacks than whites, the criterion should be treated as the functional equivalent of race.

At the heart of this interpretation of antidiscrimination is a concern for the social status of blacks. It is motivated by a desire to end all practices that would tend to perpetuate or aggravate their subordinate position. Admittedly, the costs of this program are real, for it is stipulated that the contested criterion serves some legitimate end; the test is job-related. But these costs are seen as a necessary price of justice. Only when the costs become extraordinarily large or achieve a special level of urgency, as when the criterion serves some "compelling" (and not just a "legitimate") interest, will the use of the criterion be allowed.

The theorist who so emphasizes effects rests his argument principally on the Fourteenth Amendment and ascribes to it the grandest and noblest of purposes—the elimination of caste structure. He insists that antidiscrimination, as the principle that controls the application of that amendment, be construed with this broad purpose in mind and if need be, that a new principle—the group-disadvantaging principle—be articulated in order to make this purpose even more explicit. He also insists that the various statutes that prohibit discrimination—the principal argumentative props of the process school—should be construed derivatively. These statutes, unlike the Fourteenth Amendment, may contain in so many words a specific ban on "discrimination based on race," but, so the effects theorist argues, these statutes should be seen as a legislative adoption of the prevailing constitutional principle. When that principle is interpreted to forbid the use of criteria that effectively disadvantage blacks, the statutes should be interpreted in a similar fashion.

The process school emphasizes not only the precise language in which the statutory norm is cast but also the traditional rule that conditions judicial intervention on a finding that the defendant is at fault. This fault exists when a white is given a job over a black even though the black scored higher on a test; the employer is said to be acting wrongfully because race is unrelated to any legitimate purpose and is a factor over which individuals have no control. But the requisite fault is said to be lacking when the selection is made on the basis of the individual's performance under some nonracial standard, such as a job-related test. On the other hand, those who subscribe to an effects test emphasize the prospective nature of the remedy typically sought in these cases (an injunction to forbid the use of the criterion in the future) and deny the need for a finding of fault. Such a finding may be necessary to justify damages or the criminal sanction, because these remedies require the defendant to pay for what he did in the past, and presumably such a burden can be placed only on someone who acted wrongfully. But an injunction simply directs that the defendant do what is just and does not presuppose that the defendant has acted wrongfully. Alternatively, the effects theorist might contend that if fault is necessary, it can be found in the defendant's willingness to persist in the use of the contested criterion with full knowledge of its consequences for the racial minority. Such persistence connotes a certain moral indifference.

The disadvantaging that the effects test seeks to avoid is usually defined in terms of the status of a group (for example, the criterion has a greater adverse impact on blacks than on whites and thus tends to perpetuate their subordinate position). Some see this group orientation as alien to our jurisprudence, and thus find a further reason for turning away from an effects test. Borrowing the Court's language in SHELLEY V. KRAEMER (1948), they insist that "[t]he rights created by the first section of the Fourteenth Amendment are, by its terms, guaranteed to the individual" and that "[t]he rights established are personal rights." But those who subscribe to the effects test see the well-being of individuals and of groups as inextricably linked: They believe that the status of an individual is determined in large part by the status of the group with which he is identified. Slavery itself was a group phenomenon, and any corrective strategy must be structured in group terms. Effects theorists also point to practices outside the racial context that display a concern for the welfare of groups such as religious minorities, women, the handicapped, labor, and consumers, and for that reason insist that a group orientation is thoroughly compatible with American legal principles.

In the late 1960s and early 1970s, the Supreme Court responded to these arguments and moved toward adopting an effects test in cases such as *Gaston County v. United States* (1969), GRIGGS V. DUKE POWER CO. (1971), and SWANN V. CHARLOTTE-MECKLENBURG BOARD OF EDUCATION (1971). There was, however, an element of ambiguity or hesitation in the Court's response. The Court prohibited the use of seemingly innocent criteria that disadvantaged blacks, even when their use served some legitimate interests, but the Court did not justify its decisions solely in terms of the adverse effects of the criteria. In addition, the Court characterized the adverse effect as a vestige of an earlier use of race. For example, a literacy test was disallowed as a qualification for voting not simply because it disqualified more blacks than whites but also because it perpetuated the disadvantages previously imposed on blacks in segregated schools. This insistence on analyzing the disadvantage as a vestige of past discrimination may have reflected a commitment to the process test insofar as the Court treated the earlier procedural imperfection (the assignment to schools on the basis of race) as the legally cognizable wrong and the present practice (the literacy test) as merely a device that perpetuates that wrong. But at the same time, the concern with past discrimination surely reflected some commitment to the effects test, for it resulted in the invalidation of facially innocent criteria that in fact served legitimate ends. Disallowing today's literacy test would avoid perpetuating yesterday's discrimination in the educational system, but only by compromising an interest the Court had previously deemed legitimate, namely, that of having a literate electorate. In fact, an interpretation of antidiscrimination law to forbid practices that perpetuate past discrimination could become functionally coextensive with an interpretation that makes effects decisive if some global practice such as slavery is taken as the relevant past discrimination, if the victims of past discrimination are identified in group terms, and if the remedial burden is placed on parties who had no direct role in the earlier discrimination. All disparate effects can be seen as a vestige of the special and unfortunate history of blacks in America.

By the mid-1970s, however, it became clear that the Court was not inclined to broaden its concern with past discrimination so as to make it the functional equivalent of the effects test. In fact, the Court turned in the opposite direction—away from effects and toward process. As Justice POTTER STEWART announced, "Reconstruction is over." The Court did not flatly repudiate its earlier decisions, but instead tried to limit them by confining the effects test to those antidiscrimination norms that were embodied in statutes. For constitutional claims of discrimination, the Court in cases such as WASHINGTON V. DAVIS (1976) and MOBILE V. BOLDEN (1980) required a showing that the process was flawed, or more precisely, that the defendant "intended to discriminate." The plaintiff had to show that the defendant's decision was based on race, or that he chose the seemingly innocent criterion not to further legitimate ends but to exclude or disadvantage blacks. The Court continued to honor claims of past discrimination, but by and large insisted that those claims be advanced by individually identifiable victims of the earlier discrimination, that past acts of discrimination be defined with a great deal of specificity, and that the causal links of those acts to the present racially disparate effects be manifest. No global claims of past discrimination have been allowed.

There is a certain irony in this distinction between statutory and constitutional claims, and in the Supreme Court's decision to confine the effects test to the statutory domain, for the statutes are couched in terms less congenial to such a test. The statutes speak specifically in terms of decisions based on race, while the Fourteenth Amendment speaks of equal protection. (Antidiscrimination is but the judicially constructed principle that is to guide the application of that provision.) Arguably, the distinction between statute and Constitution might reflect the Court's desire to find some way of limiting the practical impact of the effects test, for under the Fourteenth Amendment an effects test would have the widest scope and present the greatest possibilities of judicial intervention. The Fourteenth Amendment extends to all state practices and, because of its universality (it protects every "person"), could be used to protect even those groups that are not defined in racial terms. Indeed, in *Washington v. Davis* the Court expressed the fear that under the effects test the Fourteenth Amendment might even invalidate a sales tax because of its disproportionately adverse impact on the poor (never for a moment pausing to consider whether suitable limiting principles could be developed for avoiding such a result). The Court's distinction between statutory and constitutional claims might also stem from a desire to devise a means for sharing with other political institutions responsibility for the sacrifice of legitimate interests entailed in the application of an effects test. When attached to the statute, the effects test and its disruptive impact become the responsibility of both Court and Congress, since Congress remains free to repeal the statute or otherwise disavow the test.

In the mid-1970s, at the very moment the Court was struggling to identify the circumstances in which the use of a seemingly innocent criterion could be deemed a form of racial discrimination and was moving away from an effects test, it also had to confront the other major interpretive issue posed by antidiscrimination law, the issue of AFFIRMATIVE ACTION. The Court had to decide whether the norm against racial discrimination prohibits giving preference to blacks.

For much of our history, it was assumed that race-based action would be hostile to blacks and that therefore colorblindness would work to the advantage of blacks or at least shield them from hostile action. During the Second Reconstruction, however, as the drive for racial equality grew stronger, an assertedly "benign" use of race became more common. Many believed that even the honest application of legitimate criteria would not significantly alter the unequal distributional patterns that were produced among the races first under slavery and then under Jim Crow, and that it would be necessary, at least for the immediate or foreseeable future, to give blacks a preference in order to improve their status relative to other groups.

These affirmative action programs typically included other minorities, such as Hispanics, as beneficiaries, but were primarily seen as addressed to blacks and did not extend to all disadvantaged groups, such as the poor or white ethnic minorities. They had a distinctive racial cast and were sometimes described as a form of "reverse discrimination." These programs were also typically structured so as to require the decision maker to achieve a certain number of blacks or other minorities within the institution, say, as employees or students. Often that number equaled the percentage of blacks or other minorities in the general population, and was variously described as a goal or quota, depending on which side of the issue one was on. A "goal" was said to establish the minimum rather than the maximum and to be more flexible than a "quota." But more significantly, the term "goal" did not have the odious connotations of the term "quota," which had been used in the past to describe numerical limits on the admission of minorities, limits that were designed to preserve rather than eradicate the caste structure.

For the most part, these affirmative action programs were not treated as a constitutional or statutory requirement. Some of those who subscribed to an effects test argued that the failure to institute preferential programs would constitute a practice that perpetuated the subordinate position of blacks and thus would be itself a form of racial discrimination. But this argument equated inaction with action, and either for that reason or because the effects test was having difficulties of its own, this argument never established a toehold in the law. Equally unsuccessful were the arguments that emphasized those antidiscrimination laws, such as the federal fair employment statute or the executive order governing government contractors, that not only prohibited discrimination but also commanded in so many terms "affirmative action"; the inclusion of these two words were deemed insufficient to alter or add to the basic obligations of the law. The issue posed by affirmative action programs was therefore one of permissibility, rather than obligation: Were these programs consistent with the prohibition against racial discrimination?

Sometimes the purported beneficiaries of the programs (or people speaking on their behalf) objected to them on the theory that the use of race was not wholly benign. Affirmative action was premised on the view that the racial minorities would not fare well under a colorblind policy, thus implying that these minorities are not as well equipped as whites to compete under traditional meritocratic criteria. They are being told, as they were under Jim Crow, that they are inferior—nothing "reverse" about this distinction. This complaint forced those who ran affirmative action programs to be secretive or discreet about what they were doing, but it did not bring those programs to an end or even present an especially formidable obstacle. The proponents of affirmative action explained that the race-based preference was premised on an assessment of the group's history in America, on the wrongs it suffered, not on a belief about innate ability, and as such could not justifiably be seen as giving rise to a slight. The use of race is benign, they insisted, because it improves the status of blacks and other racial minorities by giving them positions, jobs, or other concrete material advantages that they otherwise would not enjoy, at least not in the foreseeable future.

Affirmative action programs have also been attacked by whites, especially when there are discernible differences in the applicants under standard nonracial criteria and when scarce goods, such as highly desired jobs or places in professional schools, are being allocated. In such circumstances favoring a black because of his race necessarily means disfavoring a white because of his race; a job given to one is necessarily denied another. The rejected white applicant cannot truly claim that he is stigmatized even in these circumstances; no one is suggesting he is inferior. His exclusion comes as the by-product or consequence of a program founded on other principles—not to hurt him or the members of his group, but to help the disadvantaged. On the other hand, the rejected white applicant does not rest his complaint solely on the fortuity of the general, racially unspecific language of the antidiscrimination norm, the fact that discrimi-

nation based on *any* race is prohibited. The white applicant can also claim that he is being treated unfairly, since he is being judged on the basis of a criterion over which he has no control and which is unrelated to any conception of merit. The rejected white applicant might not be stigmatized, but he can insist that he is being treated unfairly.

This claim of individual unfairness finds support in the process theory of antidiscrimination: If the purpose of antidiscrimination law is to preserve the integrity of a process, to insure that individuals are treated fairly and to prevent them from being judged on the basis of irrelevant criteria, then it would not seem to matter whether the color used in the process were white or black. In either instance, the selection process would be unfair. The program may be well-intentioned, but the intention is of little solace to the rejected white applicants who, as Justice LEWIS F. POWELL put it, are being forced "to bear the burdens of redressing grievances not of their making."

Some of the proponents of affirmative action deny that there is any unfairness to the rejected white applicant. They argue that the claim of unfairness presupposes a special moral status for certain nonracial or meritocratic standards of evaluation, such as grades or performance on a standardized test, and that the requisite moral status is in fact lacking. The white has no "right" to be judged on the meritocratic standard. The more widely shared view among the proponents of affirmative action, however, acknowledges the unfairness caused to individual whites by the preference for blacks but treats it as a necessary, yet regrettable cost of eliminating caste structure. As Justice HARRY A. BLACKMUN put it, "In order to get beyond race, we must first take account of race. There is no other way." Those who take this position, like those who support an effects test, argue that the purpose of antidiscrimination law is to guard against those practices that would perpetuate or aggravate the subordinate position of blacks and other racial minorities and that it would be a perversion of history now to use that law to stop programs designed to improve the status of these groups.

The Supreme Court confronted the issue of affirmative action and weighed these arguments in two different settings. In one, affirmative action was undertaken at the behest of a court order. The theory underlying such orders is not that affirmative action is directly required by an antidiscrimination statute or by the Constitution but rather that it is needed to remedy a pattern or practice of discrimination. Affirmative action is part of the court's corrective plan. A court might, for example, require a company to grant a preference in the seniority system to blacks who were previously excluded from the company and thus unable to earn seniority rights equal to those of whites. The Supreme Court has accepted such remedial uses of race, although it has insisted that this kind of preference be limited to identifiable victims of past discrimination and that some regard be given to the interests of the innocent whites who might be adversely affected by the preferences. For example, blacks might be preferred for vacancies, but will not necessarily be allowed to force the layoff of whites.

The second setting consists of the so-called voluntary affirmative action programs, which are adopted not under orders from a court but out of a sense of moral duty or a belief that the eradication of caste structure is a desirable social policy. These voluntary affirmative action programs have proved more troublesome than the remedial ones, in part because they are not limited to individually identifiable victims of past discriminations (they are truly group oriented), but also because they are not preceded by a judicial finding that the institution has previously discriminated and they are not carried out under the close supervision of a court. The Supreme Court approved these affirmative action programs, but its approval has not been a blanket one. By the mid-1980s, it was established that under certain circumstances color consciousness is permissible, but the Court has been divided in its effort to define or limit these circumstances.

These divisions have been especially pronounced when the voluntary programs were used in higher education. In the first case, DeFunis v. Odegaard (1974), involving admissions to a state law school, the Court heard arguments and then dismissed the case on grounds of MOOTNESS because the rejected white applicant had graduated by the time the Court came to decide the case—a disposition that underscored the difficulty of the issue and the internal divisions on the Court. A few years later, the Court took up the issue again, in REGENTS OF UNIVERSITY OF CALIFORNIA v. BAKKE (1978), this time at the insistence of a rejected white applicant to a state medical school. In this case the Court reached the merits, but the divisions were even more apparent. No single opinion commanded a majority.

Four Justices thought the preferential program in Bakke unlawful. They stressed an antidiscrimination statute, which prohibited, in so many terms, discrimination based on race. These Justices reasoned that a preference for blacks is as much a discrimination based on race as one for whites. No discrimination means no discrimination. Another Justice thought preferential programs could be justified as a means of diversifying the student body, but he objected to the manner in which the particular program before the Court had been implemented. He would allow race to be considered in the admissions process, but would not permit separate tracks for applicants according to race. The remaining four Justices joined in an opinion that would sustain the program as it was in fact implemented, but two of these Justices also wrote separate opinions.

These deep-seated divisions did not resolve themselves substantially in the years following Bakke. One voluntary program received a slightly more resolute acceptance by the Court, however, in FULLILOVE V. KLUTZNICK (1980). This program was established by Congress and required a preference for minority-owned businesses in awarding contracts for federally funded public works projects. Although, once again, no single opinion commanded a majority of the Court, the vote of the Justices shifted from 1–4–4 to 6–3, and Chief Justice WARREN E. BURGER, who had objected (without qualification) to the preferential program in Bakke, voted to uphold this one. He also wrote one of three opinions that supported the constitutionality of the program. The Chief Justice studiously avoided choosing among "the formulas of analysis" articulated in Bakke; that is, he refused to say whether the affirmative action program had to meet the "compelling" interest standard or whether it was sufficient if the corrective ends of the program were deemed "important" or just "legitimate" and the means substantially related to those ends. He simply said, whatever the standard, this program meets it. He did, however, specifically and repeatedly mention one factor that might be the key to the change in his position and the Court's attitude in general: "Here we pass, not on a choice made by a single judge or a school board, but on a considered decision of the Congress and the President."

With this emphasis on the role played by the coordinate branches of government in the affirmative action program, the Chief Justice returned to an idea that emerged in the analysis of the Court's treatment of facially innocent criteria, and that might well explain the Court's determination to confine the effects test to statutes: The Court is more prepared to accept the costs and dislocations that are entailed in the eradication of caste structure when it can share the responsibility for this project with the other branches of government. The Court does not want to go it alone. This suggests that the fate of equality will depend not only on the substantive commitments of the

Justices, on their determination to bring the subordination of blacks and other racial minorities to an end, but also on their views about the role of the Court. The content of antidiscrimination law will in good measure depend on the willingness of the Justices to use their power to lead the nation, or if that impulse is lacking, on the willingness of the other branches of government to participate aggressively in the reconstruction of a society disfigured by one century of slavery and another of Jim Crow.

OWEN M. FISS

Bibliography

BELL, DERRICK 1980 Race, Racism and American Law. Boston: Little, Brown.

BREST, PAUL 1976 In Defense of the Antidiscrimination Principle. Harvard Law Review 90:1–54.

COHEN, MARSHALL; NAGEL, THOMAS; and SCANLON, THOMAS 1977 Equality and Preferential Treatment. Princeton, N.J.: Princeton University Press.

EISENBERG, THEODORE 1981 Civil Rights Legislation. Charlottesville, Va.: Michie Co.

FISHKIN, JAMES 1983 Justice, Equal Opportunity and the Family. New Haven, Conn.: Yale University Press.

FISS, OWEN 1971 A Theory of Fair Employment Laws. University of Chicago Law Review 38:235–314.

———— 1976 Groups and the Equal Protection Clause. Philosophy and Public Affairs 5:107–177.

FREEMAN, ALAN 1978 Legitimizing Racial Discrimination through Antidiscrimination Law: A Critical Review of Supreme Court Doctrine. Minnesota Law Review 62:1049–1119.

GARET, RONALD 1983 Communality and Existence: The Rights of Groups. Southern California Law Review 56:1001–1075.

GUNTHER, GERALD 1972 In Search of Evolving Doctrine on a Changing Court: A Model for Newer Equal Protection. Harvard Law Review 86:1–48.

KARST, KENNETH and HOROWITZ, HAROLD 1974 Affirmative Action and Equal Protection. Virginia Law Review 60:955–974.

RAE, DOUGLAS 1981 Equalities. Cambridge, Mass.: Harvard University Press.

TUSSMAN, JOSEPH and TEN BROEK, JACOBUS 1949 The Equal Protection of the Laws. California Law Review 37:341–381.

RACIAL QUOTAS

Programs of AFFIRMATIVE ACTION, aimed at increasing opportunities for women and members of racial and ethnic minorities in employment and higher education, have sometimes taken the form of numerical quotas. In REGENTS OF UNIVERSITY OF CALIFORNIA V. BAKKE (1978) sixteen places in a state university medical school's entering class were reserved for minority applicants; in FULLILOVE V. KLUTZNICK (1980) ten percent of funds in a federal public works program were reserved for minority-owned businesses. Such quotas have been challenged as denials of the EQUAL PROTECTION OF THE LAWS, with mixed doctrinal results.

Opponents of racial quotas maintain that it is offensive to penalize or reward people on the basis of race—in short, that the Constitution is, or ought to be, colorblind. Opponents discern in quotas a subtle but pervasive racism, in the patronizing assumption that persons of particular colors or ethnic backgrounds cannot be expected to meet the standards that apply to others. This assumption, the opponents argue, is, in its own way, a BADGE OF SERVITUDE, stigmatizing the quotas' supposed beneficiaries. Some opponents see quotas as part of a general trend toward dehumanization, robbing individuals of both personal identity and human dignity, lumping them together in a collectivity based on other people's assumptions about racially defined traits.

Unfortunately for today's America, race has never been a neutral fact in this country. Those who defend affirmative action generally admit to some uneasiness about the potential abuse of racial distinctions. They argue, however, that there is no real neutrality in a system that first imposes on a racial group harsh disadvantages, readily transmitted through the generations, and then tells today's inheritors of disadvantages that from now on the rules prohibit playing favorites. If either compensation for past RACIAL DISCRIMINATION or the integration of American institutions is a legitimate social objective, the proponents argue, a government in pursuit of those objectives can hardly avoid taking race into account.

The recent attack on racial quotas draws fuel from an emotional reservoir filled two generations ago by universities that limited admission of racial and religious minorities—most notably Jews—to specified small quotas. This ugly form of discrimination was part of a systematic stigmatization and subordination of minority groups by the dominant majority. The recent quotas are designed to remedy the effects of past discrimination, and—when they serve the objective of compensation or integration—are not stigmatizing. They do, however, use race or ethnic status as a means of classifying persons, and thus come under fire for emphasizing group membership rather than "individual merit."

The right to equal protection is, indeed, an individual right. Yet the term "individual merit" misleads in two ways. The word "individual" misleads by obscuring the fact that every claim to equality is a claim made on behalf of the group of persons identified by some set of characteristics: race, for example, or high college grades and test scores. To argue against a racial preference is not to support individual merit as against a group claim, but to argue that some other group, defined by other attributes, is entitled to preference.

"Merit" misleads by conveying the idea of something wholly intrinsic to an individual, apart from some definition of community needs or purposes. When we reward achievement, we are not merely rewarding effort, but are also giving out prizes for native talents and environmental advantages. Mainly, we reward achievement because society wants the goods produced by the combination of talents, environment, and effort. But it is also reasonable to look to past harms and potential contributions to society in defining the characteristics that deserve reward. We admit college achievers to law schools not to reward winners but to serve society with good lawyers. If it be legitimate to seek to end a system of racial caste by integrating American society, nothing in the idea of individual merit stands in the way of treating race as one aspect of "merit."

Race-conscious remedies for past governmental discrimination were approved in decisions as early as SWANN v. CHARLOTTE-MECKLENBURG BOARD OF EDUCATION (1971). Affirmative action quotas pose another question: can government itself employ race-conscious remedies for the effects of past societal discrimination? In *Fullilove,* six Justices agreed on an affirmative answer to that question, at least when Congress prescribes the remedy. *Bakke* was complicated by a statutory claim; its result—and its practical effect in professional school admissions—was a distinction between racial or ethnic quotas, which are unlawful, and the use of racial or ethnic status as "one factor" in admission, which is lawful.

The distinction was a political success; it drew the fangs from a controversy that had turned venomous. But the distinction between a quota and a racial factor is more symbol than substance. If race is a factor, it will decide some cases. How many cases? The weight assigned to race surely will be determined by reference to the approximate number of minority admittees necessary to achieve the admitting university's goals of educational "diversity." The difference between saying "sixteen out of a hundred" and "around sixteen percent" is an exercise in constitutional cosmetics—but it seems to have saved affirmative action during a critical season.

KENNETH L. KARST

Bibliography
KARST, KENNETH L. and HOROWITZ, HAROLD W. 1974 Affirmative Action and Equal Protection. *Virginia Law Review* 60:955–974.
VAN ALSTYNE, WILLIAM W. 1979 Rites of Passage: Race, the Supreme Court, and the Constitution. *University of Chicago Law Review* 46:775–810.

RAILROAD COMMISSION OF TEXAS v. PULLMAN COMPANY

See: Abstention Doctrines

RAILROAD CONTROL ACT
40 Stat. 451 (1918)

Railroad service virtually ceased during the severe winter of 1917–1918. The extraordinary wartime volume of traffic and the railroads' fiscal and physical inability to meet its demands prompted President WOODROW WILSON to take control of all railway transport in the country on December 26, 1917. Congress ratified his proclamation in March 1918, by "emergency legislation enacted to meet conditions growing out of war."

The substance of the act concerned reimbursement of the owners for the use of their property while under government management. Congress set JUST COMPENSATION for this TAKING OF PROPERTY at the average operating income for the prior three years and also insured "adequate and appropriate [monies] for the maintenance, repair, renewals and depreciation of property." This legislation temporarily superseded much of the regulatory power of the Interstate Commerce Commission (ICC). It authorized the President to initiate "reasonable and just" rates which became effective without the ordinarily required wait and without ICC approval. That body could review the reasonableness of the rates but must give "due consideration" to the "unified and coordinated national control" and the stipulation that the roads "are not in competition." The constitutionality of the act as a whole was never challenged but separate sections were sustained under the WAR POWERS in a series of cases.

DAVID GORDON

RAILROAD REGULATION

See: Economic Regulation

RAILROAD RETIREMENT ACT
48 Stat. 1283 (1934)

This act established a retirement and pension plan for railroad employees engaged in INTERSTATE COMMERCE. Congress specified "promoting efficiency and safety in interstate transportation" among the purposes of the act. Each employee, whose participation was mandatory, would be required to retire after thirty years service or at sixty-five, receiving thereafter an annuity based upon his length of service. Contributions from both employee and the carrier would finance these payments. A Railroad Retirement Board would adjust the contributions, initially set at two percent of a worker's salary and doubled by the carrier, and would administer the act. Congress further authorized the board to make actuarial surveys and keep pertinent records and data. The act vested district courts with JURISDICTION to enforce board orders and to review administrative questions.

A 5–4 Supreme Court voided the law in RAILROAD RETIREMENT BOARD V. ALTON (1935) as a violation of DUE PROCESS OF LAW and outside the commerce power, a decision effectively nullified in STEWARD MACHINE CO. V. DAVIS (1937).

DAVID GORDON

RAILROAD RETIREMENT BOARD *v. ALTON RAILWAY COMPANY*
295 U.S. 330 (1935)

In the spring of 1935, as the FRANKLIN D. ROOSEVELT administration made plans for a general SOCIAL SECURITY ACT, the Supreme Court held unconstitutional the RAILROAD RETIREMENT ACT of 1934, which established a program of compulsory retirement and old age pensions for railroad workers engaged in INTERSTATE COMMERCE. Justice OWEN ROBERTS, for a five-member majority, found the act violative of DUE PROCESS OF LAW and unauthorized by the COMMERCE CLAUSE. By exacting a percentage of payrolls for a pension fund, the act, Roberts said, was a "naked appropriation of private property" for the benefit of workers. The act was also "bad" because no reasonable connection existed between the welfare of railroad workers and the efficiency or safety of interstate transportation.

Chief Justice CHARLES EVANS HUGHES, joined by Justice LOUIS D. BRANDEIS, BENJAMIN N. CARDOZO, and HARLAN FISKE STONE, dissented. The MAJORITY OPINION shocked Hughes because it went beyond the invalidation of this particular pension plan; the majority's "unwarranted limitation" on the commerce clause denied wholly and forever the power of Congress to enact any social welfare scheme. Relying on GIBBONS V. OGDEN (1824) for the scope of the commerce power, Hughes observed that its exercise had the widest range in dealing with interstate railroads. He accepted Congress's judgment that the plan enhanced efficiency and safety. Moreover, the precedents supported the constitutionality of the act, he argued; the act did not differ in principle from workmen's compensation acts for railroad employees, which the Court had sustained. It had also upheld a congressional enactment that empowered the Interstate Commerce Commission to take excess profits from some railroads for the benefit of others. (See DAYTON GOOSE CREEK RAILROAD CO. V. UNITED STATES, 1924.) The Court's opinion helped provoke the constitutional crisis of 1937.

LEONARD W. LEVY

RAILWAY EXPRESS AGENCY v. NEW YORK
336 U.S. 106 (1949)

Railway Express is a leading modern example of the Supreme Court's deference to legislative judgments in the field of ECONOMIC REGULATION. The Court unanimously upheld a New York City "traffic safety" ordinance forbidding advertisements on vehicles but exempting delivery vehicles advertising their owners' businesses. No one mentioned the FIRST AMENDMENT. (See COMMERCIAL SPEECH.) Justice WILLIAM O. DOUGLAS, for the Court, first waved away a DUE PROCESS attack on the ordinance. Turning to the companion EQUAL PROTECTION attack, Douglas said that the city "may well have concluded" that advertising vehicles presented a greater traffic hazard than did trucks carrying their owners' messages. "We cannot say that that judgment is not an allowable one." The opinion typifies the Court's use of the most deferential RATIONAL BASIS review of economic regulation.

Justice ROBERT H. JACKSON expressed some doubt as to the Court's reasoning but concurred, referring to the law's historic distinctions between "doing in self-interest and doing for hire." Along the way he uttered the decision's most memorable words: "there is no more effective practical guarantee against arbitrary and unreasonable government than to require that the principles of law which officials would impose on a minority must be imposed generally."

KENNETH L. KARST

RANDOLPH, EDMUND
(1753–1813)

In 1776 Edmund Jenings Randolph, lawyer, mayor of Williamsburg, and aide to General GEORGE WASHINGTON, was the youngest delegate to the convention that adopted the VIRGINIA DECLARATION OF RIGHTS AND CONSTITUTION. He became the state's first attorney general under the new constitution and was later a delegate to Congress, where he favored amending the ARTICLES OF CONFEDERATION to give Congress the power to levy import duties. He was a member of the Annapolis Convention of 1786 and later the same year defeated RICHARD HENRY LEE to become governor of Virginia.

Randolph led Virginia's delegation to the CONSTITUTIONAL CONVENTION OF 1787, where he introduced the VIRGINIA PLAN. He did not, however, sign the finished Constitution, which, he believed, gave too much power to the President and so tended toward monarchy. Nevertheless, in 1788 he argued and voted in the state convention for RATIFICATION OF THE CONSTITUTION. He argued that there was no alternative except disunion and that a second convention could be called to perfect the document.

President Washington appointed Randolph the first attorney general of the United States, making him a colleague of and mediator between THOMAS JEFFERSON and ALEXANDER HAMILTON. When Jefferson resigned in 1794, Randolph succeeded him as secretary of state, but he was himself forced to resign the next year when British publication of captured French dispatches led to charges of TREASON and bribery against Randolph. This disgrace ended his political career, but he remained an eminent lawyer. In 1807 he was chief defense counsel when AARON BURR was tried for and acquitted of treason.

DENNIS J. MAHONEY

RANDOLPH, JOHN
(1773–1833)

John Randolph of Roanoke, Virginia, congressman and sometime senator, advocated the constitutional doctrines of STATES' RIGHTS and STRICT CONSTRUCTION that became identified with southern opposition to the federal government and that eventuated in SECESSION. Excepting his support for the LOUISIANA PURCHASE, Randolph consistently preferred the claim of state to federal SOVEREIGNTY. A bitter critic of the Federalist federal judiciary, he managed or misman-

aged the IMPEACHMENT of Justice SAMUEL CHASE in 1804.

Breaking with THOMAS JEFFERSON in 1806, Randolph commenced a career of opposition to almost every sitting President and to most national policies. His principles were straightforward. He believed that the Constitution was a compact among sovereign states. Sovereignty did not inhere in the federal government, and the admission of new states was a device to weaken the original, compacting states. He espoused the southern view that regarded every attempt to expand federal power as an attack on SLAVERY, and he regarded democracy and nationalism as leveling and centralizing invasions of ancient state privileges and mores. He viewed with especial bitterness the rulings of the MARSHALL COURT.

ROBERT DAWIDOFF

Bibliography
DAWIDOFF, ROBERT 1979 *The Education of John Randolph.* New York: Norton.

RASMUSSEN v. UNITED STATES

See: Insular Cases

RATE REGULATION

See: Economic Regulation

RATIFICATION OF CONSTITUTIONAL AMENDMENTS

The delegates to the CONSTITUTIONAL CONVENTION OF 1789 decided upon the outlines of the AMENDING PROCESS after only a few hours of debate. The requirement that any proposed amendment be ratified by three-fourths of the states was adopted unanimously, but was, like so much of the Constitution, the result of a compromise. Initially the convention seems to have assumed that amendments to the federal charter would require ratification by all the states; but five state delegations were willing to set the requirement as low as two-thirds of the states. No form of ratification other than by the states as entities was proposed or discussed in the convention.

JAMES MADISON, writing in THE FEDERALIST # 39, described the method of ratifying amendments to the new Constitution as "partly federal, partly national." The method is [con]federal in that ratification is accomplished by the states as states, and not by a referendum of the people or a national majority. At the same time, the method is national in that it does not require the assent of all the constituent states to alter the terms of the federal union. A pure theory of FEDERALISM, as it was understood by the founding generation, would not have sanctioned imposition of an amended compact upon unconsenting parties.

Our first constitution, the ARTICLES OF CONFEDERATION, had required the unanimous consent of the states to any amendment. For that reason, during the "critical period" between 1781 and 1789 no amendments were adopted, even when decisive weaknesses in the confederal system were apparent. The requirement for unanimous ratification of amendments made the Constitutional Convention and the new Constitution necessary.

Article V in fact provides for state ratification of constitutional amendments in one or the other of two distinct modes, leaving the choice of mode to Congress. The first mode is ratification by state legislatures, the second is ratification by conventions. In two centuries of government under the Constitution Congress has proposed thirty-three constitutional amendments and in thirty-two cases has prescribed state legislatures as the agents of ratification. The single exception was ratification of the TWENTY-FIRST AMENDMENT, repealing PROHIBITION.

The constitutional provision relating to ratification is little more than an outline. The details have been filled in as the need has arisen. Although the state legislatures derive their authority to ratify amendments from the federal Constitution, the size of the majority required to effect ratification is determined by the constitution, statutes, or legislative rules of each state. Many, perhaps most, prescribe an extraordinary majority for that purpose.

An amendment automatically becomes part of the Constitution when it is ratified by the requisite number of states, but someone must be designated to receive the certificates of ratification, to count them, and to announce publicly that ratification is complete. Originally Congress delegated this task to the secretary of state, but it is now performed by a relatively minor official, the director of general services. Congress itself proclaimed the ratification of the FOURTEENTH AMENDMENT.

Article V sets no time limit within which the states must act on proposed amendments. The Framers supposed that the ratification process would occur at roughly the same time throughout the country. RATIFICATION OF THE CONSTITUTION itself took nine months; the BILL OF RIGHTS was ratified in just over two years. The convention provided no definite time period after which a proposal for amendment would lapse. Therefore, a recurring question has been how long the states have to ratify proposed amendments.

The principles of democracy and CONSTITUTIONALISM would be ill-served if ratification of constitutional amendments by the several states did not have to be accomplished roughly contemporaneously. This goal has been met in the case of every successful amendment. Although seven years has become the standard period for the states to consider ratification, no amendment has, in fact, required as long as four years for ratification. The TWENTY-SECOND AMENDMENT required the longest time, forty-seven and one-half months; the TWENTY-SIXTH AMENDMENT required the shortest period, four months. The average time for ratification of a constitutional amendment has been eighteen months.

As a legal matter, ratification must be accomplished within a "reasonable" time, but no statute or court decision has defined just how long a period that is. The CHILD LABOR AMENDMENT, proposed in 1924, was ratified by three state legislatures as late as 1937, and the Supreme Court declined to hold that those ratifications were ineffective. The Supreme Court, in *Dillon v. Gloss* (1920), upheld the power of Congress to set a seven-year limit on the ratification period; but in *Coleman v. Miller* (1939) the Court refused to set such a limit on its own account where Congress failed to exercise the power.

The EIGHTEENTH, TWENTIETH, Twenty-First, and Twenty-Second AMENDMENTS comprise the ratification time limit within their texts. In several other cases, Congress has prescribed the time limit (invariably seven years) in the JOINT RESOLUTION proposing the amendment. Only once did Congress attempt to extend the prescribed time limit: when the seven years allotted for ratification of the so-called EQUAL RIGHTS AMENDMENT (ERA) expired in 1979, Congress—by less than the two-thirds majority required for the original proposal—voted to extend the ratification period for an extra three and one-half years. The failure of the proposed amendment's supporters to garner sufficient ratifications even in the extended time period averted a constitutional crisis over the issue of time limits.

A matter frequently debated but never definitively resolved is whether the states, during the period for consideration of a proposed amendment, may alter a decision once one is taken. The question arose with regard to the Fourteenth Amendment and was revived during the controversy over the ERA. Indeed, there seems to be no doubt that a state, having declined to ratify a proposed amendment, may, within the allotted time, alter that decision and ratify the amendment. It is less certain whether a state that has voted to ratify a proposed amendment may subsequently rescind such a ratification. In 1868 Congress and Secretary of State WILLIAM H. SEWARD declared the Fourteenth Amendment ratified, apparently counting the ratifications of two states (New Jersey and Ohio) that had voted to rescind their ratifications. On the date of the declaration a sufficient number of states had ratified to render the disputed votes irrelevant. Expiration in 1983 of the extended time limit for ratification of the ERA made the question of rescinded ratifications of that proposal moot.

The requirement of state ratification presupposes that the state legislatures are free to choose whether or not to ratify a proposed amendment. But this is not always true. Ratification of the Fourteenth Amendment was secured, in part, because Congress made such ratification a condition for readmission of the states of the former Confederacy. Clearly Congress, amidst the crisis of Civil War and Reconstruction, stretched the limits of its authority by imposing that condition.

Controversies concerning the ratification of constitutional amendments are almost prototypically POLITICAL QUESTIONS. Only rarely has the Supreme Court decided such controversies. In *Hawke v. Smith* (1920) and *Leser v. Garnett* (1922) the Court rejected attempts to submit the question of ratification to a popular vote or to condition ratification on approval in a REFERENDUM. In *United States v. Sprague* (1931) the Court refused to impose any limit on Congress's freedom to choose between the two constitutional modes of ratification. The effect of the few cases the Court has decided has been, as in *Dillon* and *Coleman,* to reserve the power of final determination to Congress.

DENNIS J. MAHONEY

Bibliography

FREEDMAN, SAMUEL S. and NAUGHTON, PAMELA J. 1978 *ERA: May a State Change Its Vote?* Detroit, Mich.: Wayne State University Press.
ORFIELD, LESTER 1942 *The Amending of the Federal Constitution.* Ann Arbor: University of Michigan Press.

RATIFICATION OF THE CONSTITUTION

Plans for a convention to revise the ARTICLES OF CONFEDERATION were in fact a subterfuge, because the delegates in Philadelphia convened in May 1787 with no serious thought whatever of an attempt to keep that instrument in force. But a legal problem had to be resolved, for the Articles were a fact and their revision was to be made only by unanimous agreement of the Continental Congress which "the legislatures of every state" would later confirm. Delegates to the CONSTITUTIONAL CONVENTION OF 1787, including several lawyers who later became Supreme Court Justices, wasted little time in disposing of such restrictions, but they were wary of the manner in which the Constitution could be made acceptable to the people. The solution hit upon by JAMES MADISON in his VIRGINIA PLAN was to circumvent the state legislatures and ask Congress to send whatever plan they adopted in Philadelphia to "assemblies of Representatives . . . expressly chosen by the people, to consider & decide thereon." Frankly fearful of local officeholders who would see the new Constitution as a threat to "the importance they now hold," the Virginia delegates were united on this point. "Nine States had been required in all great cases under the Confederation & that number was on that account preferable," GEORGE MASON suggested, and his logic prevailed.

After some maneuvering, the expiring Continental Congress by unanimous resolution forwarded the Constitution to the states for their approbation, thus placing an implicit seal of congressional approval on Article VII. The principle of a two-thirds majority rather than unanimity was crucial. Ominously, Rhode Island had sent no delegate to the convention. To avoid embarrassing obstructions, prudence dictated a fair trial for the Constitution, provided key state conventions ratified the document. Rarely in American history has such a sweeping change moved so rapidly through the cumbersome machinery of disparate state governments, and the phenomenon can be explained only in the adroit handling of GEORGE WASHINGTON's implied endorsement along with the urgency which supporters of the Constitution preached in pamphlets and newspapers or wherever influential citizens congregated.

Much of the credit for the Federalists' strategy must go to James Madison. As a central figure at the convention and in the Continental Congress he carefully brought forward the accompanying documents which gave an impression of unanimity by the framers and the forwarders. Using his franking privilege (as a congressman), Madison maintained a correspondence with colleagues in the principal state capitals and coordinated plans to hold conventions at the proper tactical time. Ratification by the conventions in Pennsylvania, Massachusetts, and Virginia was essential, for these three states contained most of the nation's people and much of its wealth. In New York a surly band controlled the state government and was in no hurry to surrender its profitable customs collecting to a national government, but these men could not withstand pressure from the commercial community if all the other large states ratified. Rhode Island was doubtful, and New Jersey and Georgia were unnecessary, owing to the smallness of their populations and their geographic positions.

The Federalists had powerful allies in the newspapers, some ninety-eight in number, most of which printed the Constitution *in toto* shortly after September 17. In Philadelphia, Boston, and New York the leading journals soon printed essays favoring the Constitution and denouncing the opposition Anti-Federalists as obstinate "placemen" (state officeholders) fearful of losing their jobs or "wrongheaded" on other grounds. Pennsylvania Federalists moved swiftly but could not outrace their friends in Delaware, who hurriedly called a three-county convention and became the first ratifying state on December 7 (30–0). In Philadelphia, the first stirrings of Anti-Federalist activity included publication of attacks on the Constitution's lack of a BILL OF RIGHTS, but as that argument was picked up elsewhere the high-handed legislature called a convention that was heavily weighted with delegates from eastern counties favorable to the Federalist cause. Before farming communities in western counties could organize, the Pennsylvania convention ratified on December 12 (46–23). New Jersey fell in line on December 18 (38–0). Then word came that Georgia had also unanimously ratified on January 2, 1788 (26–0). After perfunctory debate, Connecticut ratified on January 9 (128–40).

Before they could enjoy these triumphs, the Federalists learned that the failure to include a bill of rights, the fears of an overbearing (and tax-hungry) "consolidated" government, and a variety of local circumstances would slow ratification and might jeopardize the whole process. Massachusetts became the focal point of Federalist efforts, for rumblings from town meetings indicated that opposition was greater than anticipated. A phalanx of Harvard-trained lawyers, supported by commercial and shipping interests, accepted a set of recommendatory amendments to weaken the major Anti-Federalist positions, and on February 6 the Federalists won, 187–168.

New York Anti-Federalists began to counterattack. They urged friends in New Hampshire to reject the Constitution, and there is some murky evidence that a quick vote would have gone against ratification. Both sides finally settled on a postponement until June.

Madison helped ALEXANDER HAMILTON write the essays of "Publius" (these became a classic treatise titled THE FEDERALIST) for the New York newspapers and continued to send his morale-building, organizing letters to friends in the South. An unexpected stumbling block to ratification came from Baptist ministers and congregations, who voiced concern that freedom of conscience was not safeguarded by the Constitution.

Meanwhile, Maryland Federalists lost patience with their long-winded opponents in the Annapolis convention and ratified on April 28 (63–11). The recommended amendments from Massachusetts Anti-Federalists were used as a talking point, but when the argument came to whether amendments could be part of a conditional ratification, the Federalists lost their tempers. Madison hurried back to Virginia, aware that PATRICK HENRY and Mason would form the most powerful Anti-Federal combination possible. New York seemed safely Anti-Federalist, for Governor George Clinton and his friends talked and printed venomous attacks on the Constitution and its Federalist drafters. Hamilton counted heads and asked Madison if a conditional ratification would suffice. No, Madison replied, a ratification with any strings attached would leave New York out of the Union. After slight Anti-Federal resistance, South Carolina ratified on May 23 (149–73). In Rhode Island, the people rejected ratification directly, 237 yeas to 2,708 nays.

Ratification by Virginia on June 25 was uncertain until a crucial ballot was won by Federalists, who captured the eight doubtful votes from western areas. Madison, JOHN MARSHALL, and EDMUND RANDOLPH led the charge against Henry and Mason, but they agreed to recommend amendments adding a bill of rights to preserve some good will on the final roll call (89–79). The ninth state, New Hampshire, had already ratified on June 21, 1788 (57–46). The news from Virginia, however, sent a thrill through the North. Diarist JOHN QUINCY ADAMS noted that jubilant Federalists fired muskets far into the night when the tidings from Richmond reached Boston. With ten states now committed, the Constitution was sure of a trial. Even so, a powerful, entrenched Anti-Federal faction prevented action by the North Carolina convention, which adjourned to await future developments and a possible second convention that diehard Anti-Federalists thought might patch up another version of the Constitution (with a bill of rights among the additions). A test vote on ratification lost, 184–84, but New York fooled everybody by ratifying on July 26 (30–27).

Within four months, all the states except North Carolina and Rhode Island had set in motion machinery to elect the new federal Congress and a President. The knowledge that Washington supported the Constitution and would be the first President tipped the balance in crucial situations. Washington's stature, the concession by Madison and others that amendments adding a bill of rights would be proposed forthwith, and the overwhelming support of the press were the chief reasons that ratification proceeded with relative speed. The new government was operating, and Madison had introduced a bill of rights by the time North Carolina ratified on November 21, 1789 (197–99). Rhode Island narrowly ratified on May 29, 1790 (34–32), to become a fully participating member of the Union. Few scars remained. The hastily drawn lines of the ratification battle soon faded, and the divergent political philosophies that emerged in the next decade had little to do with the intense struggle of 1787–1788.

ROBERT A. RUTLAND

Bibliography

FARRAND, MAX, ed. (1911)1966 *The Records of the Federal Convention of 1787,* 4 vols. New Haven, Conn.: Yale University Press.

MAIN, JACKSON TURNER 1961 *The Antifederalists: Critics of the Constitution, 1781–1788.* Chapel Hill: University of North Carolina Press.

RUTLAND, ROBERT A. 1966 *The Ordeal of the Constitution: The Antifederalists and the Ratification Struggle of 1787–1788.* Norman: University of Oklahoma Press.

WOOD, GORDON S. 1969 *The Creation of the American Republic, 1776–1787.* Pages 306–344. Chapel Hill: University of North Carolina Press.

RATIO DECIDENDI

(Latin: "Reason for being decided.") A statement made in an OPINION OF THE COURT is either *ratio decidendi* or OBITER DICTUM. *Ratio decidendi* refers to a statement that is a necessary part of the chain of reasoning leading to the DECISION of the case, while obiter dictum ("said by the way") refers to any other statement in the opinion. The distinction is clear in theory but, in practice, may be difficult to apply to any given case.

No federal court may properly pass on a legal or constitutional question that is not brought before it in a CASE OR CONTROVERSY, and a court properly resolves only those questions necessary to decide a case before it. The resolution of a particular question is the court's HOLDING on that question, and the reasoning necessary to the resolution of a question properly before the court is *ratio decidendi.* The *ratio decidendi* is thereafter binding as a rule of law when the case is cited as precedent. Although a judge may have a clear idea of what arguments were necessary to reach the decision in a case and may attempt to convey that idea in his opinion, it is the courts that apply the case as precedent in future decisions that finally establish which statements were obiter dicta and which *ratio decidendi.*

DENNIS J. MAHONEY

RATIONAL BASIS

The "rational basis" STANDARD OF REVIEW emerged in the late 1930s, as the Supreme Court retreated from its earlier activism in the defense of economic liberties. We owe the phrase to Justice HARLAN FISKE STONE, who used it in two 1938 opinions to signal a new judicial deference to legislative judgments. In UNITED STATES V. CAROLENE PRODUCTS CO. (1938), Stone said that an ECONOMIC REGULATION, challenged as a violation of SUBSTANTIVE DUE PROCESS or of EQUAL PROTECTION, would be upheld unless demonstrated facts should "preclude the assumption that it rests upon some rational basis within the knowledge and experience of the legislators." In *South Carolina State Highway Department v. Barnwell Brothers, Inc.* (1938), Stone proposed "rational basis" as the standard for reviewing STATE REGULATIONS OF COMMERCE. (Later, Stone would accept the necessity for more exacting judicial scrutiny of such laws.) To complete the process, the Court adopted the same deferential posture toward congressional judgments that local activities substantially affected INTERSTATE COMMERCE and thus might be regulated by Congress under the COMMERCE POWER. In all its uses, "rational basis" represents a strong presumption of the constitutionality of legislation.

Yet even so minimal a standard of JUDICIAL REVIEW does, in theory, call for some judicial scrutiny of the rationality of the relationship between legislative means and ends. And that scrutiny of means makes sense only if we assume that the ends themselves are constitutionally required to serve general, public aims; otherwise, every law would be self-justifying, as precisely apt for achieving the advantages and disadvantages it achieves. Although the Court has sometimes suggested in economic regulation cases that even a search for legislative rationality lies beyond the scope of the judicial function, some such judicial scrutiny is required if our courts are to give effect to generalized constitutional guarantees of liberty and equality. Today's assumption, therefore, is that a law depriving a person of liberty or of equal treatment is invalid unless, at a minimum, it is a rational means for achieving a legitimate legislative purpose.

Even so relaxed a standard of review appears to call for a judicial inquiry always beset by uncertainties and often dominated by fictitious assumptions. Hans Linde has demonstrated the unreality attendant on judicial efforts to identify the "purposes" served by a law adopted by legislators with diverse objectives, or objectives only tenuously connected to the public good. Lacking sure guidance as to those "purposes"—which may have changed in the years since the law was adopted—a court must rely on counsel's assertions and its own assumptions. But in its inception the rational basis standard was not so much a mode of inquiry as a formula for validating legislation. Thus, in McGOWAN v. MARYLAND (1961), the Supreme Court said, "A statutory discrimination will not be set aside if any state of facts reasonably may be conceived to justify it." Part of the reason why the rational basis standard survives in federal constitutional law is that it is normally taken seriously only in its permissive feature (*United States Railroad Retirement Board v. Fritz,* 1980). A number of state courts, interpreting STATE CONSTITUTIONAL LAW, do take the rational basis standard to require a serious judicial examination of the reasonableness of legislation. And the Supreme Court itself, in its late-1960s forays into the reaches of equal protection doctrine lying beyond racial equality, sometimes labeled legislative classifications as "irrational" even as it insisted that state-imposed inequalities be justified against more exacting standards of review. (See HARPER v. VIRGINIA STATE BOARD OF ELECTIONS, 1966; LEVY v. LOUISIANA, 1968; SHAPIRO v. THOMPSON, 1969.) Since that time, the explicit recognition of different levels of judicial scrutiny of legislation has allowed the Court to reserve the rhetoric of rational basis for occasions thought appropriate for judicial modesty, in particular its review of "economic and social regulation." Some substantive interests call for heightened judicial scrutiny of legislative incursions into them; absent such considerations, the starting point for constitutional analysis remains the rational basis standard.

KENNETH L. KARST

Bibliography

LINDE, HANS A. 1976 Due Process of Lawmaking. *Nebraska Law Review* 55:197–255.

RAWLE, WILLIAM
(1759–1836)

A Philadelphia lawyer and Federalist, Rawle declined GEORGE WASHINGTON's offer to become the first attorney general of the United States. As United States attorney for Pennsylvania, he was the government prosecutor in the cases arising from the WHISKEY REBELLION (1794) and FRIES' REBELLION (1798). Rawle also advocated the existence of a FEDERAL COMMON LAW OF CRIMES. He is best remembered as one of the earliest COMMENTATORS ON THE CONSTITUTION. His *New View of the Constitution* (1825) was widely used as a textbook. Although he was a nationalist, he was the first to advocate the right of state SECESSION.

LEONARD W. LEVY

RAYMOND MOTOR TRANSPORTATION COMPANY v. RICE
434 U.S. 429 (1978)

Continuing a line of decisions begun in SOUTHERN PACIFIC COMPANY v. ARIZONA (1945), an 8–0 Supreme Court struck down a state highway regulation as an unconstitutional burden on INTERSTATE COMMERCE. A Wisconsin statute barred trucks over fifty-five feet in length from state highways as a safety measure. Two trucking companies challenged the law under the COMMERCE CLAUSE. A strong demonstration that the law made, at best, a negligible contribution to highway safety combined with the state's failure to provide an adequate defense of the measure led the Court to override the strong presumption usually given such laws.

In *Kassel v. Consolidated Freightways Corp. of Delaware* (1981), Iowa made a "more serious effort to support the safety rationale of its [fifty-five foot limit] than did Wisconsin in *Raymond,*" but a 6–3 Court, relying on *Raymond,* struck down the Iowa statute on the same grounds.

DAVID GORDON

READ, GEORGE
(1733–1798)

George Read of Delaware was a signer of both the DECLARATION OF INDEPENDENCE and the Constitution. A frequent speaker at the CONSTITUTIONAL

CONVENTION OF 1787, he favored a consolidated national government and proposed abolition of state boundaries. He was a leader of the ratification movement in Delaware, and later he served as state chief justice and as a United States senator.

DENNIS J. MAHONEY

REAGAN, RONALD
(1911–)

Born in Tampico, Illinois, brought up in Dixon, Illinois, a graduate of Eureka College, Illinois, Ronald Reagan came from the American Midwest, while his adult life was largely spent in California, leading to a classic California combination of midwestern seriousness of purpose and California casualness of style. Coming to maturity in 1932, he was first a convinced follower of FRANKLIN D. ROOSEVELT, changing his political beliefs in response to his perceptions of communist infiltration in the late 1940s, and formally becoming a Republican only in 1962. A radio announcer as a young man, then an actor (playing in more than fifty motion pictures), then for three years an Army captain, then for five years president of the Screen Actors Guild, he became a spokesman for the General Electric Company, traveling nationally to speak to company employees and civic groups on domestic and patriotic themes. In 1966 he defeated five other candidates to win the Republican nomination for governor of California and was then elected over the incumbent Edmund Brown by a historic margin of nearly one million votes. He was easily reelected in 1970. His two terms as governor of the most populous state in the Union were marked by a dramatic reduction in the number of welfare recipients, a small increase in the number of state employees, and a large increase in the funding of higher education.

In 1976 he fell sixty votes short of defeating President GERALD R. FORD for the Republican nomination for the presidency. In 1980 he defeated five other candidates to capture the nomination, and he won the presidential election by a landslide of 489 electoral votes. In 1984 he was reelected, this time taking the votes of forty-nine of the fifty states and emerging in a position to put his stamp on the judiciary of the nation.

Three themes characterize President Reagan's approach to the Constitution. They are the necessity of moral virtue if American democracy is to work; the importance of FEDERALISM; and the guiding force of American practices approved by the Founding Fa-

thers. These themes run through Reagan's public pronouncements on a variety of specific topics bearing on constitutional law. For example, he has seen the solution to the problem of curbing crime in America as first restoring a sense of moral seriousness to the criminal trial, so that it is not seen as a bureaucratized bargaining process. At the same time, he has criticized courts for taking on tasks for which they are unfitted and so slighting their essential role of determining guilt or innocence; and he has proposed legislation limiting the use of HABEAS CORPUS review of state courts by federal judges.

Traditional functions for the courts, less federal supervision, an infusion of moral purpose—these are remedies that Reagan sees as congruent with the Constitution even as interpreted by the Supreme Court. For another example, he has opposed the imposition of RACIAL QUOTAS in EDUCATION, hiring, or housing, even when the quotas are disguised as AFFIRMATIVE ACTION. Belief in equality under the law does not in his view require reverse discrimination. Nothing in a Constitution he sees as colorblind supports a contrary conclusion. In other areas his views require constitutional amendment.

Religion is the foundation of morality, and morality is inseparable from government—this note in American politics is as old as WASHINGTON'S FAREWELL ADDRESS, which Reagan has frequently invoked. In Reagan's own words, "We poison our society when we remove its theological underpinnings," and again, "Without God there is no virtue because there is no prompting of conscience."

From this perspective, the Court-compelled exclusion of religious exercises from the public schools is disastrous and is unwarranted by the Constitution, which, Reagan has repeatedly remarked, says nothing about public education or prayer. In Reagan's words, the FIRST AMENDMENT "was not meant to exclude religion from our schools." Reagan has affirmed his belief in a "wall of separation" between church and state. In an American tradition as old as ROGER WILLIAMS, he sees the primary function of that wall as protecting religion from governmental intrusion. The Supreme Court, in his view, has been guilty of such intrusion.

Federalism influences this approach. The Supreme Court, interpreting the Constitution, often conceives of itself as though it were a superior, benign, and neutral agency that is not part of the national government. Reagan has cut through this position and identified the Court as the champion of a particular ideology, imposing uniform requirements in disregard of local custom. Justified where there was a national mandate to eliminate RACIAL DISCRIMINATION, the Court has acted in this way even, he believes, where it has discovered no national mandate. Reagan's criticism of the Court on RELIGION IN THE PUBLIC SCHOOLS not only affirms earlier American traditions; it also reflects attachment to the local autonomy that federalism fosters.

The religion Reagan refers to is biblical religion, described by him as "our Judaeo-Christian heritage." He quotes both Old and New Testaments in his public addresses. The Ten Commandments, he has observed, have not been improved upon by the millions of laws enacted since their promulgation. He issued a proclamation of National Bible Week and rejoiced that twenty-five states followed suit. He sees no constitutional barrier to a believer, as President, acknowledging the God of the Bible, speaking of the moral values he derives from his belief in God, and taking seriously such slogans as "one nation under God" and "in God we trust."

Public testimony to moral values based on religion has been conjoined with insistent rejection of religious intolerance. Reagan has consistently denounced bigotry, but he contends that those who have excluded biblical religion from the schools are themselves "intolerant of religion." They have denied a freedom to exercise religion as old as the practice of prayers in legislatures, the employment of chaplains by the military, and the invocation of God before opening any court. Such American traditions are his guide to the meaning of the Constitution in an area crucial for him in the formation of morality.

Critical of the Supreme Court's individual decisions in a manner sanctioned by the example of THOMAS JEFFERSON, ABRAHAM LINCOLN, and FRANKLIN D. ROOSEVELT, Reagan has not denied the Court's authority. He has favored correction of the prayer decision by the adoption of a constitutional amendment permitting voluntary group prayer in the schools. The government in his view should tolerate and accommodate the religious beliefs, speech, and conduct of the people; it should not direct their religious beliefs, speech, or conduct. For that reason, Reagan's school prayer amendment expressly prohibits any governmental role in composing the words of prayers to be said in the public schools.

The constitutional right to abortion, announced by the Supreme Court in ROE V. WADE (1973), has been the object of repeated criticism by Reagan. He has taken the extraordinary step, for a sitting President, of publishing a book, *Abortion and the Conscience of a Nation* (1984), in which he declares that "there is no cause more important than affirming the tran-

scendent right to life of all human beings, the right without which no other rights have any meaning." On January 22, 1985, the twelfth anniversary of *Roe v. Wade,* he addressed the prolife march in Washington as the marchers prepared once again to ask the Supreme Court to change its position, and told them that he was "proud to stand with you in the long march to protect life." No other constitutional decision of the Supreme Court has been so vigorously, persistently, and personally condemned by an American President.

Reagan has consciously used the presidency as "a bully pulpit" to proclaim that there is no proof that the child in the womb is *not* human; that the child in midterm and later abortion feels pain; and that over 4,000 such children are killed every day in America, 15,000,000 in the first decade since ROE V. WADE. Such facts alone, he believes, will make most people reconsider and seek reversal of *Roe.*

How the reversal is accomplished has not been a matter of great concern to Reagan. He endorsed reversal by amendment of the Constitution. He attempted to persuade the Senate to end a FILIBUSTER that killed the Helms Bill that would have used Congress's power under section 5 of the FOURTEENTH AMENDMENT to define life as including the unborn. Passage of the bill (itself without sanctions) would undoubtedly have led to state legislation on abortion that would have given the Supreme Court the opportunity of looking at abortion in the light of the congressional definition. It has been speculated that Reagan believes the most practical way of effecting the result he desires is by his appointments to the Supreme Court.

In the cases of abortion and of prayer, Reagan has sought amendments reversing Supreme Court decisions that upset traditional balances. In the case of the balanced BUDGET, he has asked for something new, a constitutional restraint that would prevent federal expenditures exceeding federal revenues. The desirability of such an amendment had, however, been voiced as early as 1798 by Thomas Jefferson. In Reagan's view, a balanced budget amendment could be a powerful tool for reducing the federal establishment and restoring economic power to the states. Federalism would be enhanced by its enactment. The traditional role of the states would very likely be increased. Reagan also perceives a moral element: habitual deficit spending by the federal government is an easy evasion of responsibility. In his second Inaugural Address, on January 21, 1985, Reagan called for passage of the Balanced Budget Amendment.

Citizens and Presidents must interpret the Constitution as well as lawyers and judges. President Reagan's approach to the Constitution is not dependent on the reasoning advanced by recent Justices of the Supreme Court to justify or rationalize their decisions. He has employed older and broader criteria. For him the Constitution does not mean the gloss put upon it by opinions of the Court but the original document illumined by tangible traditions and by reflection on its foundation in moral realities. He has evidenced a strong commitment to the essentials that the Constitution presupposes and at the same time preserves.

JOHN T. NOONAN, JR.

Bibliography

REAGAN, RONALD   1984   *Abortion and the Conscience of a Nation.* New York: Thomas Nelson.
REAGAN,   RONALD 1981–1985 *Presidential   Papers.* Washington, D.C.: Government Printing Office.
SMITH, HEDRICK; CLYMER, ADAM; SILK, LEONARD; LINDSEY, ROBERT; AND BURT, RICHARD   1980   *Reagan the Man, the President.* New York: Macmillan.
WHITE, F. CLIFTON   1980   *Why Reagan Won: A Narrative History of the Conservative Movement.* Chicago: Regnery Gateway.

REAGAN v. FARMERS' LOAN & TRUST CO.
154 U.S. 362 (1894)

In a grotesque opinion the Supreme Court unanimously held unconstitutional a rate schedule fixed by a state railroad commission. Justice DAVID BREWER for the Court had no doubt that the economic validity of rates was subject to JUDICIAL REVIEW, and he found that these rates were "unjust and unreasonable," meaning too low in the estimate of the Court. They resulted, he said with exaggeration, in "a practical destruction to rights of property." Four years later, in SMYTH V. AMES (1898), the Court finally adopted SUBSTANTIVE DUE PROCESS as the basis for such a ruling, but in this case the Court seemed unready to embrace such an extravagant position, despite previous flirtations with it. Here the Court cast about for something more familiar and found it in the concepts of EQUAL PROTECTION and JUST COMPENSATION, which it united. The difficulty was that the just compensation clause of the Fifth Amendment bound only the national government, not the states, and it applied only in cases of EMINENT DOMAIN, when private property was taken for a PUBLIC PURPOSE. Nothing of that sort had happened here. Brewer, however, declared that the commission's rates denied "equal protection which is the constitutional right of all owners of other property," and then he ruled that the equal protection clause "forbids legislation . . . by which the property of one individual is, without compensation, wrested from him for the benefit of another, or of the public." Thus the Court incorporated the substance of the just compensation clause of the Fifth Amendment into the Fourteenth for the benefit of railroads, though the Court refused in other cases of this period to incorporate into the FOURTEENTH AMENDMENT the rights that protected accused persons or victims of RACIAL DISCRIMINATION. (See INCORPORATION DOCTRINE.) Moreover, this was not a case of eminent domain and the property of the railroad was not "wrested" without compensation. More rationally, Brewer sought to devise an economic test for determining the reasonableness of a rate schedule: whether the rate was equivalent to the market value of the use of the property. That economists found such a test to be unsound was not so significant as the Court's arrogating to itself the power to determine reasonableness by economic criteria that thrust it into judgments better suited to legislative and administrative agencies. (See ECONOMIC REGULATION AND THE CONSTITUTION.)

LEONARD W. LEVY

REAL EVIDENCE

Real evidence is supplied by a thing that is inspected by the jury, or other trier of fact. (Statements by witnesses are called testimonial evidence.) The acquisition and use of real evidence in the criminal process intersects with constitutional doctrine in various ways. For example, the EXCLUSIONARY RULE may forbid the offering of evidence—such as a gun or a bag containing marijuana—that has been obtained in an unconstitutional SEARCH AND SEIZURE. Correspondingly, the probability that such real evidence will be found in a particular place may, under the doctrine of PROBABLE CAUSE, justify the issuance of a SEARCH WARRANT.

KENNETH L. KARST

REAPPORTIONMENT

Direct democracy is not possible in a nation as populous as the United States is now, or even as it was in 1787 when the Constitution of the United States was drafted. Accordingly, the objective was then, and is now, to devise and implement as fair and effective a plan of democratic REPRESENTATION as possible.

The idea of fair and effective representation at each level of government was not new in 1787. The search for such a formula lies at the center of Anglo-American political thought. In 1690 JOHN LOCKE sought to abolish England's rotten boroughs by urging that, "it being the interest as well as the intention of the people, to have a fair and equal representation, whoever brings it nearest to that is an undoubted friend to and establisher of the government, and cannot miss the consent and approbation of the community."

Although Britain did not put an end to its rotten boroughs until near the middle of the twentieth century, the issue of how best to structure a truly representative government was very much alive at the time the various proposals for the American Constitution were being debated. At last a compromise was struck in the CONSTITUTIONAL CONVENTION OF 1787, giving equal representation to each state in the Senate and representation based on population in the House of Representatives. Article I, section 2, of the Constitution provides that "Representatives . . . shall be apportioned among the several states . . . according to their respective numbers . . . ," with recomputation of the apportionment every ten years, and each state to have at least one representative regardless of population. But the task of fixing the formula for the apportioning process was left to Congress, and no directions at all were established to guide the states in the parallel function of allocating seats in the state legislature or in local governmental bodies. We are not, however, left entirely in doubt about what Congress thought appropriate for apportionment in the states. The NORTHWEST ORDINANCE of 1787 provided that representation in the territorial legislatures to be created in that area should be based on population. In general, the states accepted the principle of reasonably equal population among legislative districts, but the principle was often modified by assurances of at least one representative from each county or township or municipality. Departures from population equality may not have been egregious in this time of mostly rural dispersal; but by the late nineteenth and early twentieth centuries what had once been minor deviations became major divergences.

JOHN QUINCY ADAMS observed in 1839 that the division of sovereign powers between the states and the nation, as set out in the Constitution, gave us "the most complicated government on the face of the globe." The twentieth century has proved how right he was. The interaction between increasingly potent national and state governments, frequently aggravated by friction arising out of competition for power, has produced a delicately balanced division of power and a complexity of relationships probably unsurpassed in the history of governmental institutions.

Yet it is the proud boast of FEDERALISM in the United States that the governments of the fifty states and that of the nation can work together in common purpose rather than in a relationship of competition and mistrust. Moreover, it is a basic premise of representative democracy in the United States that the people are entitled to representation somewhat in proportion to their numbers, at every level of government. The tradition of majority rule cannot otherwise be attained. Neither the division of sovereign powers prescribed in the federal system nor the fairness of legislative representation formulas can long be left unattended. Vigilant superintendence by an informed electorate is essential.

Even the wisest political scientists have difficulty in defining the precise meaning of representative democracy. There is, however, general agreement that representative democracy in the United States includes something of liberty, equality, and majority rule. Even though these qualities are scarcely less abstract, it can surely be said that representative democracy relates to the processes by which citizens exert control over their leaders. From the time of the Constitutional Convention debate has centered on the extent to which, and the ways in which, majority control over leaders should be exercised. Congress has wrestled with the issue, with inconclusive results. In 1842, for example, Congress required each state to establish compact, contiguous, single-member congressional districts as nearly equal in population as possible. These criteria, however, lapsed in 1911. In any event, no enforcement method had been established, and the courts considered the issue none of their business.

Not until more than a hundred years after the RATIFICATION OF THE CONSTITUTION in 1789 did such states as California, Illinois, Michigan, New York, Ohio, and Pennsylvania, responding to new pressures, abandon the equal-population principle in one or both houses. So widespread had been the original acceptance of the equality concept that no fewer than thirty-six of the original state constitutions provided that representation in both houses of the state legislature would be based completely, or predominantly, on population. Between 1790 and 1889 no state was admitted to the Union in which its original constitution did not provide for representation principally based on population in both houses of the state legislature.

To speak of the equal-population principle as the basis for apportionment of those nineteenth-century legislatures is not to say that there was mathematically precise equality among the districts at that time. The western states, for example, commonly relied on county lines in drawing their apportionment formulas. The distortions that resulted from assuring each county at least one representative, for example, or from grouping whole counties to form election districts, were much less pronounced in agricultural and rural America than in present-day industrial and urban America. The population of the United States, outside the few great commercial centers in the East, was spread thinly across the face of the country.

The drift from relative equality to substantial inequality would have moved at about the same pace as the shift in population from rural to urban America; and that would have been bad enough. But some states accelerated the trend away from the equality principle by other devices as well. As state legislatures were enlarged, additional seats were granted to the areas of new growth without diminishing representation of the declining population areas. As the population of rural areas declined, state legislatures abandoned even the formal acceptance of equal population as a controlling principle, typically guaranteeing each county (or township) one representative. Some states, unable or unwilling to change the constitutional requirement for equality among districts, simply ignored the mandate for decennial change. (Tennessee is a good example; the state constitutional requirement of reapportionment every ten years was ignored between 1901 and 1961, giving rise in 1962 to BAKER v. CARR.)

The consequence of these factors, singly or in combination, was by the middle of the twentieth century a remarkable skewing of voter impact, ordinarily giving the less populated areas of a state a disproportionate influence in legislative representation. The impact was most marked at the state and local legislative levels, but not without considerable influence on congressional districting as well.

By the middle of the twentieth century the disparities in legislative representation were marked. Thus, in the then ninety-nine state legislative chambers (forty-nine bicameral legislatures plus the Nebraska unicameral legislature), thirty-two relied in large part on population; eight used population, but with weighted ratios; forty-five combined population and area considerations; eight granted representation to each unit; five had fixed constitutional apportionments; and one (the New Hampshire Senate) was based on state tax payments. These conclusions somewhat understate the actual disregard of population as the basis of representation because this summary is drawn exclusively from the state constitutional requirements, without adjustment for violation of those provisions.

The time has come to ask: what is (re)apportionment and what is (re)districting? The question is well put, for the terms are sometimes (confusingly) used interchangeably. But there is a difference. Apportionment is ordinarily described as the allocation of legislative seats by a legislative body to a subordinate unit of government, and districting as the process of drawing the final lines by which each legislative district is bounded. Thus, Congress apportions the number of congressional districts to which each state is entitled, based on population figures disclosed at each decennial census. Each state legislature then draws lines that divide the state into as many congressional districts as have been allocated to it by Congress.

State legislatures, on the other hand, both apportion the distribution of state legislative seats *and* draw the district lines that determine which voters will make each selection. Therein lies the problem, clearly rooted in the political ambition of each political group to overcome its opposition, before the voting begins, on the basis of the dispersion of voters eligible to vote for one candidate rather than another.

By the early 1960s the act and the impact of malapportionment were everywhere apparent, typically to the apparent disadvantage of individual voters in heavily populated districts and to the apparent advantage of voters in sparsely populated districts. Despite the fact that many state constitutions required reapportionment every ten years and included formulas requiring approximate population equality, no legislative chamber came closer to that goal than two to one, and the disparity between most populous to least populous district was in many states more than ten to one and in several more than one hundred to one. To put the matter another way, in twelve states fewer than twenty percent of the voters lived in districts that elected a majority of the state senators, and in seven states fewer than thirty percent of the voters lived in districts that elected a majority of the members of the lower house.

State courts occasionally acted to deal with the most egregious abuses, but the federal courts, until 1962, adamantly refused to intervene. Although the Supreme Court had long recognized the right of citizens to vote free of arbitrary impairment by STATE ACTION when such impairment resulted from dilution by false tally or by stuffing of the ballot box, the Court had declined to deal with apportionment and districting abuses on the grounds that the issue was not justiciable, that is, not appropriate for federal judicial intervention. As Justice FELIX FRANKFURTER said in COLE-GROVE V. GREEN (1946), "Courts ought not to enter this political thicket."

Finally, the case of interference with the exercise of the franchise was made so clearly that a majority of the Court was persuaded that only federal judicial intervention could put an end to this denial of equality. The case that triggered this change in attitude provided a dramatic illustration of flagrant abuse of voter rights by a state legislature that had openly flouted its own state constitution for more than half a century.

The Tennessee Constitution had required, since 1870, that the number of senators and representatives in the general assembly "be apportioned among the several counties or districts, according to the number of qualified electors in each. . . ." Moreover, the state constitution required reapportionment in accordance with the equal-population standard every ten years. Between 1901 and 1961, however, the legislature had not acted on the matter. As a result, thirty-seven percent of the Tennessee voters lived in districts that elected twenty of the thirty-three senators, and forty percent of the voters lived in districts that elected sixty-three of the ninety-nine members of the lower house. The federal court challenge was brought by voters in urban areas of the state, who invoked the Constitution of the United States and claimed that they had been denied the EQUAL PROTECTION OF THE LAWS, "by virtue of the debasement of their votes."

The resulting Supreme Court decision, *Baker v. Carr*, did not rule on the substance of the equality claim, but did hold that the issue was properly within the JURISDICTION OF THE FEDERAL COURTS and was justiciable. Only Justices Frankfurter and JOHN MAR-SHALL HARLAN dissented.

Within two years the Supreme Court signaled how it would decide the equality issue. GRAY V. SANDERS (1963), while not strictly an apportionment case, involved the closely related issue of voter discrimination. The election practice there challenged was the Georgia "county-unit" system, as it applied to state-wide primaries: a candidate for nomination who received the highest number of popular votes in a county was considered to have carried the county and to be entitled to two votes for each representative to which the county was entitled in the lower house of the general assembly. The majority of the county unit vote was required to nominate a candidate for United States senator or state governor, while a plurality was sufficient for nomination of candidates for other offices. Because the most populous county (Fulton, with a 1960 population of 556,326) had only six

unit votes, while the least populous county (Echols, with a 1960 population of 1,876) had two unit votes, "one resident in Echols County had an influence in the nomination of candidates equivalent to 99 residents of Fulton County."

Georgia argued that, because the ELECTORAL COL-LEGE permitted substantial inequalities in voter representation in a "winner-take-all" system, parallel systems should be permitted to the states. Moreover, the state argued that because United States senators represent widely divergent numbers of voters, the same should be permitted in one house of a state legislature. But the Supreme Court rejected all such analogies as inapposite: "The inclusion of the electoral college in the Constitution, as the result of specific historical concerns, validated the collegiate principle despite its inherent numerical inequality, but implied nothing about the use of an analogous system by a State in a statewide election. No such specific accommodation of the latter was ever undertaken, and therefore no validation of its numerical equality ensued."

While conceding that states "can within limits specify the qualifications of voters both in state and federal elections," the Court denied that a state is entitled to weight the votes "once the geographical unit for which a representative is to be chosen is designated. . . ." Accordingly, the Court concluded: "The conception of political equality from the DECLA-RATION OF INDEPENDENCE, to Lincoln's Gettysburg Address to the FIFTEENTH, SEVENTEENTH and NINETEENTH AMENDMENTS can mean only one thing—ONE PERSON, ONE VOTE." The fatal defect in the Georgia plan was that the votes were weighted on the basis of geography as an expression of legislative preference for rural over urban voters.

The next franchise case decided by the Supreme Court with full opinion, WESBERRY V. SANDERS (1964), was also not a state legislative apportionment case; it was a congressional districting case not very dissimilar from *Colegrove v. Green*—except in result. Plaintiffs were qualified voters of Fulton County, Georgia, entitled to vote in the state's fifth congressional district, which had a 1960 population of 823,680, as compared with the 272,154 residents of the ninth district.

After the decision in *Baker v. Carr*, the Court had little difficulty deciding that such issues were justiciable in federal courts. The substantive ruling, however, came as something of a surprise. Plaintiffs had argued principally that the gross population disparities violated the equal protection clause of the FOURTEENTH AMENDMENT. The Supreme Court, however, adopted what had been a subordinate contention, that the Georgia arrangement violated Article I, section 2, of the Constitution, which prescribed that representatives be chosen "by the People of the several States." Justice HUGO L. BLACK, writing for the majority of six, stated that this provision, when construed in its historical context, means "that as nearly as practicable one man's vote in a congressional election is to be worth as much as another's. . . . To say that a vote is worth more in one district than in another would not only run counter to our fundamental ideas of democratic government, it would cast aside the principle of a House of Representatives elected 'by the People,' a principle tenaciously fought for and established at the Constitutional Convention." That result, at first surprising in view of the nonspecific constitutional text, was well supported in the Court's review of the relevant history. For example, at the Constitutional Convention JAMES WILSON of Pennsylvania had said that "equal numbers of people ought to have an equal number of representatives," and representatives "of different districts ought clearly to hold the same proportion to each other, as their respective constituents hold to each other."

Reliance on section 2 of Article I rather than on the equal protection clause has had significant consequences. From that date forward the Court has been less tolerant of population variations among congressional districts than of those in state legislative districts, as to which the population-equality principle has, since REYNOLDS V. SIMS (1964), been based on the equal protection clause of the Fourteenth Amendment.

Reynolds v. Sims and its five companion cases completed the original round of apportionment and districting cases and constituted the foundation on which all subsequent litigation has built. On June 15, 1964, the Court invalidated the state legislative apportionment and districting structure in Alabama (the *Reynolds* case), Colorado, Delaware, Maryland, New York, and Virginia. One week later the Court struck down the formulas in nine additional states, foretelling a complete reapportionment revolution.

Reynolds v. Sims was illustrative. The complaint in that case alleged that the last legislative reapportionment in the state had been based on the 1900 federal census despite a state constitutional requirement for decennial reapportionment. Accordingly, because the population growth had been uneven, urban counties were severely disadvantaged by the state legislature's failure to reapportion every ten years and by the state constitution's provision requiring each of the sixty-seven counties to have at least one repre-

sentative in the lower house with a membership of 106. The Supreme Court of the United States ruled unequivocally in favor of the equal-population principle: "We hold that, as a basic constitutional standard, the Equal Protection Clause requires that the seats in both houses of a bicameral state legislature must be apportioned on a population basis. Simply stated, an individual's right to vote for state legislators is unconstitutionally impaired when its weight is in a substantial fashion diluted when compared with votes of citizens living in other parts of the state."

The decisions in *Wesberry* and *Reynolds* required adjustment of congressional districting practices in all states (except the few states with only one representative each) and of all state legislative districting practices. Despite considerable adverse reaction in the beginning and substantial litigation to determine the full significance of the decisions, by and large compliance was secured; and further adjustments were made after the results of the 1970 and 1980 censuses were determined.

Two principal types of questions remained to be worked out after the first decisions were announced: how equal is "equal" in congressional districting and in state legislative apportionment and districting? and to what extent does the equal-population principle apply to the thousands of local governmental units and the even larger number of special districts that serve multitudinous quasi-governmental purposes?

Despite criticism of the *Reynolds* decision based on an assumption that the Court had demanded mathematical exactness among election districts, the Court explicitly acknowledged the permissibility of some variation: "We realize that it is a practical impossibility to arrange legislative districts so that each one has an identical number of residents, or citizens, or voters. Mathematical exactness or precision is hardly a workable constitutional requirement." The important obligation is for each state to "make an honest and good faith effort to construct districts, in both houses of its legislature, as nearly of equal population as is practicable."

From the beginning the *Reynolds* Court acknowledged that states could continue to place some reliance on political subdivision lines, at least in drawing the lines for state legislative bodies. "Since almost invariably there is a significantly larger number of seats in state legislative bodies to be distributed within a state than congressional seats, it may be feasible to use political subdivision lines to a greater extent in establishing state legislative districts than in congressional districting while still affording adequate representation to all parts of the State." A further reason for at least limited adherence to local political subdivision lines is the highly pragmatic proposition that, to do otherwise, "[i]ndiscriminate districting, without any regard for political subdivisions, may be little more than an invitation to partisan gerrymandering."

Acknowledging the principle that population deviations are permissible in state districting implementation of rational state policy, the Supreme Court has recognized that de minimis numerical deviations are unavoidable. Maximum deviations in Connecticut of 7.83 percent among house districts and 1.81 percent among senate districts were upheld in *Gaffney v. Cummings* (1973). Texas deviations of 9.9 and 1.82 percent respectively among house and senate districts were similarly approved in *White v. Regester* (1973). In MAHAN V. HOWELL (1973) the Court upheld a Virginia plan despite a maximum deviation of 16.4 percent, on the grounds that the plan could "reasonably be said to advance the rational state policy of respecting the boundaries of political subdivisions," but cautioned that "this percentage may well approach tolerable limits."

The requirement of population equality is far more exacting in the drawing of congressional district lines. In *Kirkpatrick v. Preisler* (1969) the Court struck down Missouri's 1967 Redistricting Act despite the fact that the most populous district was 3.13 percent larger and the least populous 2.84 percent smaller than the average district. In explanation the Court stated, "Since 'equal representation for equal numbers of people [is] the fundamental goal for the House of Representatives,' the 'as nearly as practicable' standard requires that the State make a good faith effort to achieve precise mathematical equality. Unless population variances among congressional districts are shown to have resulted despite such effort, the State must justify each variance, no matter how small." In *Karcher v. Daggett* (1983) the Supreme Court invalidated a deviation of less than one percent among New Jersey congressional districts because the state had failed to make "a good-faith effort to achieve precise mathematical equality" in population among its congressional districts. In sum, because local units of government are less important as factors in the representation of relatively large numbers of persons in the Congress than for smaller numbers of persons in the state legislature, population deviations among congressional districts are strictly scrutinized, while a more tolerant review is accorded state districting. But even in state districting the excesses of the past are no longer tolerable; above the *de minimis* level deviations must be held within narrow limits and must be justified in terms of preservation of political subdivi-

sions, compactness and contiguity of districts, and respect for natural or historical boundaries.

No matter how close the judicial superintendence of population equality, one problem remains. In congressional and state legislative districting alike, even the most exact adherence to the equal-population principle does not assure protection against legislative line-drawers who seek partisan advantage out of the process. "Gerrymander" is the term used to describe such efforts to preserve partisan power or to extend such power through manipulative use of the process. The term originated in 1812 in Massachusetts, where political maneuvering had produced a salamander-shaped district which was named after ELBRIDGE GERRY, then governor. From that time forward the gerrymander has been an altogether too-common fact of American political life. Nevertheless, despite repeated attempts to persuade the Supreme Court to enter this new "political thicket," the Court has denied that there is any constitutional ground for superintending the apportionment and districting process other than the equal-population principle. Accordingly, the states remain free, so far as the United States Constitution is concerned, to construct congressional and state legislative districts that resemble salamanders or other equally peculiar creatures. And many state legislatures have done just that, particularly where one party is in secure control of the state legislative process. Where party control of the two houses of a bicameral legislature is divided, or where the governor is of a different party, the drawing of congressional and state legislative district lines is likely to be worked out by political compromise or, that failing, by the courts.

More seemly alternatives are possible, but they are not often adopted in the absence of JUDICIAL REVIEW over the process except as to population equality among districts. Congress has the authority to set standards of compactness and contiguity that would avoid the worst abuses and could be enforced in the courts. State legislatures could adopt similar standards to control the process within their own states, but few political leaders are willing to relinquish the prospect of present or future partisan advantage to be secured out of the districting process.

Like state legislative districting, the districting of counties, municipalities, or other local governmental units is constitutionally permitted to deviate to some extent from full equality if it can be demonstrated that the governmental unit has made "an honest and good faith effort" to construct districts "as nearly of equal population as practicable." Local governments may use MULTIMEMBER DISTRICTS if there is a history of such representation and if such plans are not part of a deliberate attempt to dilute or cancel the voting strength of racial or political elements in the governmental unit. Despite that limitation, local governments, like states, may use ethnic or minority population data in constructing districts designed to elect representatives of that minority or ethnic group. (See UNITED JEWISH ORGANIZATION V. CAREY, 1977.)

Supreme Court intervention in the apportionment and districting process has unquestionably restructured congressional and state legislative representation. Gross population disparities among election districts have been evened out so that the democratic promise of fair representation has been made possible of realization. But no court, even so powerful a body as the Supreme Court of the United States, can assure democratic representation. The ultimate test of the democratic process will depend upon the level of concern of the voters and their willingness to insist that their legislative representatives take whatever action is necessary to prevent excesses.

There are two principal types of gerrymandering, both of which should be controlled. The bipartisan or "incumbent survival" plan is designed to assure as far as possible the reelection of incumbents, sometimes regardless of party affiliation; the technique is to distribute party registration or proven party supporters to the legislators who will benefit most. The partisan plan is designed to maintain or increase the number of seats held by the majority party; the technique is to "waste" votes of the opposition party either by concentrating the voters loyal to that party in as few districts as possible, or by dispersing the opposition voting strength among a number of districts in which it cannot command majorities. Control of these abuses is not likely to come from party leadership. Voters concerned with the integrity of the process must demand an end to such practices, calling for state constitutional amendments or statutes requiring that districts be compact and contiguous.

Redistricting should be a matter of special concern for ethnic and racial minorities, many of whom are concentrated in urban centers. Typically, minority spokesmen claim that fair representation requires districts that will elect members of their own groups. When legislatures act to meet such demands, other groups are likely to feel disadvantaged. That issue was litigated to the Supreme Court in *United Jewish Organization v. Carey*. In that case a New York redistricting plan had been modified to bring it into compliance with the VOTING RIGHTS ACT OF 1965. In the process the act divided a community of Hasidic Jews in order to establish several substantially nonwhite districts.

The Court upheld the plan, ruling that such a use of racial criteria was justified in fulfillment of congressional legislative policy in the Voting Rights Act.

Somewhat related to the issue just discussed is the question whether municipalities and other local legislative bodies should be permitted to require at-large elections for all the seats in the legislative unit. Such a practice may make it impossible for a minority group in the community to secure representation, even though one or more members of that minority might be elected if single-member districts were used. The Supreme Court held, in MOBILE V. BOLDEN (1980), that multimember district elections would be tolerated, even where the impact on minority groups was demonstrated, unless it could be shown that the plan was adopted with racially discriminatory intent. However, the Voting Rights Act of 1982 overturned that ruling; under the act, invidious intent need not be shown if impact disadvantageous to identifiable minorities can be established.

In the era before the application of computer technology to politics, it was common for politicians and their staffs to spread out maps on office floors, using adding machines for their arithmetic, slowly building new districts from census tracts and precinct figures. Because most redistricting decisions must be made sequentially—one boundary change requires another, which requires yet another—the computer is perfectly designed to speed the process and allow for more sophisticated analysis. The computer not only makes available numerical population counts, voter history, and party registration, but also permits a graphic display of the areas represented.

These technical advances have resulted in what may be styled the second reapportionment revolution. They place in the hands of those responsible for redistricting a vast array of information for use in drawing district lines. It follows, for better or for worse, that the computer's twin features of speed and accuracy can advance the goal of "fair and effective representation" as well as engineer the nearly perfect gerrymander.

At the time of the reapportionment decisions of the early 1960s, commentators speculated about the decisions' likely impact on the representational process. The most common prediction was that the urban areas would dominate state legislatures, with a general tendency toward liberal legislative policies. It is by no means clear that this prediction has come true. Enlarged influence of the suburbs, often with a conservative representation and not infrequently allied with rural representatives, has been the more typical reality. The one thing that can be said with confidence is that adoption of the equal-population principle has ended the worst abuses and assured basic fairness in the most important features of the democratic process.

ROBERT B. MCKAY

Bibliography

ADAMS, BRUCE 1977 A Model State Reapportionment Process: The Continuing Quest for "Fair and Effective Representation." *Harvard Journal on Legislation* 14:825–904.
COMMON CAUSE 1977 *Reapportionment: A Better Way.* Washington, D.C.: Common Cause.
DIXON, ROBERT G. 1968 *Democratic Representation: Reapportionment in Law and Politics.* New York: Oxford University Press.
GROFMAN, BERNARD; LIJPHART, AREND; MCKAY, ROBERT B.; and SCARROW, HOWARD (EDS.) 1981 *Representation and Redistricting Issues.* Lexington, Mass.: D. C. Heath.
MCKAY, ROBERT B. 1965 *Reapportionment: The Law and Politics of Equal Representation.* New York: Twentieth Century Fund.
POLSBY, NELSON, ED. 1971 *Reapportionment in the 1970s.* Berkeley: University of California Press.

REASONABLE DOUBT

Proof beyond a reasonable doubt is the highest level of proof demanded in American courts. It is the usual standard for criminal cases, and in criminal litigation it has constitutional grounding in decisions of the United States Supreme Court. Although the reasonable doubt standard is not often used in noncriminal settings, there are exceptional situations, usually where liberty is placed in jeopardy, when a JURISDICTION will borrow the criminal standard of proof for a civil case.

Any standard of proof chosen by an American court recognizes that in all litigation there is the chance of a mistake. If opposing litigants agree on the various matters that constitute their case, usually the case is settled. There is little for a judge or a jury to do. Once a dispute arises, however, adversaries offer conflicting EVIDENCE and conflicting interpretations of evidence to decision makers. Rarely, if ever, is there a dispute in which every witness and every aspect of physical and scientific evidence presented by opposing parties point with perfect certainty to one specific conclusion. Witnesses may suffer from ordinary human frailties—they have memory problems; they sometimes confuse facts; they see events differently from each other; they have biases and prejudices that

call into question their judgment; and they may be frightened and have trouble communicating on the witness stand. Physical evidence might be damaged or destroyed and thus of minimal or no use at trial. Or, it might be difficult to connect physical evidence with the parties before the court. Even scientific tests often provide little more than probabilities concerning the relationship of evidence to the issues in a case.

Were judges and juries required to decide cases on the basis of absolute certainty about what occurred, it is doubtful that they ever would find the standard satisfied. Whoever was required to prove the case would always lose. Recognizing that absolute certainty is not reasonably possible, American courts have chosen to demand less. How much less determines the extent to which they are willing to accept the risk of error in the course of litigation.

In criminal cases the typical requirement is that the government must prove the essential elements of any offense it chooses to charge beyond a reasonable doubt. This means that, although the decision maker need not be certain that a defendant is guilty before convicting, any reasonable doubt requires that it find the defendant not guilty. Such a standard allocates most of the risk of error in criminal cases to the state. It cannot assure that no innocent person will ever be convicted, but the standard is demanding enough to make it most unlikely that someone who is actually innocent will be found guilty. It is more likely that truly guilty persons may go free, but that is the price American criminal justice pays to avoid mistakes that harm the innocent.

It is uncertain when this standard of proof was first used in criminal cases. In early England, whether or not a person would be convicted depended on his ability to produce compurgators or to avoid misfortune in an ordeal. Subsequently, success turned on whether or not a suspect could succeed in trial by combat. As trial by jury replaced other forms of proof, the jurors originally decided cases on the basis of their own knowledge, and even if they relied on informants, the jurors themselves were responsible for the accuracy of the facts. Not until the notion of an independent fact finder, typically a jury, developed was a standard of proof very meaningful. With the development of the independent and neutral fact finder, the "beyond a reasonable doubt" concept took on importance.

Although there is no mention of the proof beyond a reasonable doubt concept in the United States Constitution, trial by jury is in all but petty cases guaranteed by the Sixth Amendment, and with the Supreme Court's decision in DUNCAN V. LOUISIANA (1968), this right is now binding on the states. By the time the Sixth Amendment was adopted, proof beyond a reasonable doubt was closely associated with the right to an impartial jury guaranteed by the Constitution in criminal cases.

Thus, it is not surprising that the Supreme Court has found the proof beyond a reasonable doubt standard to be constitutionally required in criminal cases with respect to all essential elements of offenses charged, whether the criminal case is litigated in state or federal court (IN RE WINSHIP, 1970). The Court associated the high proof standard with the strong presumption of innocence in criminal cases and observed that before a defendant may be stigmatized by criminal conviction and punished for criminal wrongdoing, DUE PROCESS requires the state to prove guilt beyond a reasonable doubt. (See JACKSON V. VIRGINIA, 1979).

There is little agreement on exactly what a reasonable doubt is. No single definition of reasonable doubt has ever gained acceptance in American courts. There does seem to be some consensus that a decision maker should understand that a reasonable doubt is one based in reason as applied to the proof offered in a case. This elaboration of the standard is consistent with the oath that judges administer to jurors who are called upon to decide a case. Beyond this, it is difficult to define the term. Any language that is used is likely to be challenged as being either too demanding or not demanding enough.

Judges and juries have come to know that the proof beyond a reasonable doubt standard represents American regard for liberty and the dignity of the individual who stands against the state and who seeks to preserve his freedom and independence. A reasonable doubt will protect him.

STEPHEN A. SALTZBURG

(SEE ALSO: *Burden of Proof.*)

Bibliography

KALVEN, HARRY, JR. and ZEISEL, HANS   1966   *The American Jury.* Boston: Little, Brown.
TRIBE, LAURENCE H.   1971   Trial by Mathematics: Precision and Ritual in the Legal Process. *Harvard Law Review* 84:1329–1393.

REASONABLE SEARCH

See: Unreasonable Search

RECALL

Among the reforms introduced during the Progressive era was the recall, a device by which the people, at an election, can remove an official from office before his term expires. Unlike IMPEACHMENT, recall does not involve an accusation of criminality or misconduct, and it is commonly used when the official decides or acts contrary to the opinion of a significant segment of his constituency.

Although recall is widely used at the state and local levels, there is no provision for recall of national officials. Moreover, because senators and representatives hold office under the United States Constitution, they are not subject to recall under state law.

DENNIS J. MAHONEY

RECIPROCAL TAX IMMUNITIES

See: Intergovernmental Immunities

RECONSTRUCTION AMENDMENTS

See: Fifteenth Amendment; Fourteenth Amendment; Thirteenth Amendment

RED LION BROADCASTING CO. *v.* FEDERAL COMMUNICATIONS COMMISSION
395 U.S. 367 (1969)

The Federal Communications Commission promulgated fairness rules requiring balanced BROADCASTING on public issues. The Court answered FIRST AMENDMENT challenges by arguing that different media required different constitutional standards, and that the scarcity of frequencies both necessitated government allocation and justified requirements that allocatees insure balanced programming. Comparing *Red Lion* to MIAMI HERALD PUBLISHING CO. V. TORNILLO (1974) indicates that electronic media enjoy less editorial freedom than do the print media. As technological developments undercut the scarcity rationale, the Court shifted toward an intrusiveness-into-the-home rationale for greater regulation of broadcasters.

MARTIN SHAPIRO

(SEE ALSO: *Fairness Doctrine.*)

REED, STANLEY F.
(1884–1980)

Stanley Forman Reed, a descendant of Kentucky gentry, was educated at Kentucky Wesleyan College, Yale, Columbia, the University of Virginia, and the Sorbonne. He then returned to Maysville, Kentucky, where he entered private law practice and Democratic party politics. After serving two terms in the Kentucky General Assembly, he was called to Washington as counsel to the Federal Farm Board during HERBERT C. HOOVER's administration. His competence as a legal technician led to his promotion to general counsel to the Reconstruction Finance Corporation (RFC) and his retention at that post when FRANKLIN D. ROOSEVELT came to power. During the early years of the New Deal, Reed played an important role in the attempts at economic revival through the RFC and in the framing of new legislation by the Brain Trust. He defended New Deal measures before an unreconstructed Supreme Court, first as special counsel arguing the GOLD CLAUSE CASES and then as solicitor general from 1935 to 1938. Reed was Roosevelt's second appointee to the Supreme Court, taking office January 15, 1938, and replacing Justice GEORGE H. SUTHERLAND.

Reed was a moderate man in both personal style and constitutional views. He occupied a position of influence between the Court's liberal and conservative wings, between activists and advocates of judicial self-restraint. He was most comfortable with the majority and was willing to modify his views as the Court majority shifted. In a Court marked by strong personalities, Reed was able to maintain cordial relations with colleagues of different ideological persuasions.

Reed's opinions are not noted for ringing phrases or rigid insistence on principled positions. The discussion places great weight on the specifics of factual circumstances and often takes on a dialectic quality, a paragraph-by-paragraph dialogue between the Justice and a holder of divergent views whom Reed is trying to accommodate and coopt. The other voice may be internal; perhaps, if it is not that of the Justice himself it may belong to a defeated law clerk, echoing the heated in-chambers arguments Reed relished.

A central theme that runs through Reed's views on many constitutional issues is his willingness to uphold the exercise of governmental power by both the federal government and the states. He had faith in the good intentions of government officials, and was rarely willing to infer impermissible motives behind their actions. These attitudes are consistent with Reed's experience as the architect and legal manager of New Deal programs and as the advocate who defended these laws before a hostile Supreme Court. Justice Reed was a key part of the new majority of the Court that upheld federal regulation in the face of challenges under the DUE PROCESS clause. In dissent with Chief Justice FRED M. VINSON he was a staunch defender of presidential power in YOUNGSTOWN SHEET & TUBE COMPANY V. SAWYER (1952). Similarly, he was notably willing to defer to administrative fact-finding and interpretation of statutes.

These same attitudes can be seen in Reed's approach to CRIMINAL PROCEDURE, particularly in cases presenting claims of abusive police behavior. His deference to what he saw as another administrative agency was reinforced by the attitudes of a Mason County, Kentucky, landowner, whose experience led him to think of the police as a benevolent small-town constabulary. Beginning with his lone dissent in *United States v. McNabb* (1943), Reed deferred to the police and to state procedural rules in ways that led him to accept behavior that a majority of his colleagues found unacceptable. "I am opposed to broadening the possibilities of defendants escaping punishment by these more rigorous technical requirements on the administration of justice," he wrote in *McNabb*.

Reed occupied a pivotal position on the Court in CIVIL RIGHTS cases. He joined with and frequently wrote for the majority in vindication of the rights of blacks, including MORGAN V. VIRGINIA (1945), SMITH V. ALLWRIGHT (1943), and BROWN V. BOARD OF EDUCATION (1954). However, like a majority of his colleagues, he saw the treatment of Japanese Americans during World War II in a different light. (See JAPANESE AMERICAN CASES.)

Reed was slow to join the emerging majority during the 1940s that protected Jehovah's Witnesses in the exercise of their religion; his view on RELEASED TIME for religious instruction of public school pupils, expressed originally in his sole dissent in MCCOLLUM V. BOARD OF EDUCATION (1948), became substantially the majority position in ZORACH V. CLAUSEN (1952). He was relatively permissive of local time, place, and manner regulations of SOUNDTRUCKS in KOVACS V. COOPER (1948), but often voted with the absolutist position of Justices HUGO L. BLACK and WILLIAM O. DOUGLAS regarding other public speech issues, as he did in BEAUHARNAIS V. ILLINOIS (1952) and TERMINIELLO V. CHICAGO (1947). Nonetheless, Reed sided with the finding of necessity of police action against a public speaker in FEINER V. NEW YORK (1951).

A more consistent theme in Reed's positions was his opposition to what he saw as political radicalism. He upheld federal and state statutes as well as legislative and grand jury investigative powers and deportation aimed at the removal of "security risks." Writing for the Court majority, he also upheld the power of the federal government to limit the political activities of its employees in *United Public Workers v. Mitchell* (1947).

Justice Reed retired from active service on the Supreme Court in 1957, but continued to sit on the Court of Claims and Court of Appeals for the District of Columbia, as special master for the Supreme Court in original jurisdiction cases, and briefly as chairman of the CIVIL RIGHTS COMMISSION. He died in 1980 at the age of ninety-five, having lived longer than any other Justice in history.

ARTHUR ROSETT

Bibliography

PRITCHETT, C. HERMAN 1969 Stanley Reed. In Leon Friedman and Fred L. Israel, eds., *The Justices of the United States Supreme Court: 1789–1969*, Vol. 3:2373–2389. New York: Chelsea House.

REESE v. UNITED STATES
92 U.S. 214 (1876)

Reese was the first VOTING RIGHTS case under the FIFTEENTH AMENDMENT and, among the early decisions, the most consequential. The Supreme Court crippled the attempt of the federal government to protect the right to vote and made constitutionally possible the circumvention of the Fifteenth Amendment by formally nonracial state qualifications on the right to vote. Congress had made election officials subject to federal prosecution for refusing to qualify eligible voters or not allowing them to vote. Part of the statute specified denial on account of race, part did not. One section, for example, provided for the punishment of any person who prevented any citizen from voting or qualifying to vote. A black citizen offered to pay his POLL TAX to vote in a municipal election, but the election officials refused to receive his tax or to let him vote. The United States prosecuted the officials.

The Court, by an 8–1 vote, in an opinion by Chief Justice MORRISON R. WAITE, held the act of Congress unconstitutional because it swept too broadly: two sections did not "confine their operation to unlawful discriminations on account of race, etc." The Fifteenth Amendment provided that the right to vote should not be denied because of race, but Congress had overreached its powers by seeking to punish the denial on any ground. The Court voided the whole act because its sections were inseparable, yet refused to construe the broadly stated sections in terms of those sections that did refer to race. By its pinched interpretation of the amendment, the Court made it constitutionally possible for the states to deny the right to vote on any ground except race, thus allowing the use of poll taxes, LITERACY TESTS, good character tests, understanding clauses, and other devices to achieve black disfranchisement.

LEONARD W. LEVY

REFERENDUM

Among the political reforms introduced during the Progressive Era was the referendum, by which acts of the legislature are referred to the people for their approval or rejection at an election. Referenda may be initiated by the legislature itself or by petition of the people. The referendum is a check on such abuses as corrupt legislation or blatantly partisan gerrymandering of legislative districts (see GERRYMANDER); but it also provides a way for politicians to avoid responsibility for controversial measures.

Reformers have frequently advocated a national referendum procedure. However, legislation authorizing a national referendum would probably be unconstitutional, and an amendment authorizing it would almost certainly fail to receive congressional approval.

DENNIS J. MAHONEY

REGAN v. WALD
468 U.S. 222 (1984)

A 1982 Treasury Department regulation prohibited travel-related business transactions with Cuba. Persons who wished to travel to Cuba, but were inhibited from doing so by the regulation, sued to enjoin its enforcement. The Supreme Court, 5–4, followed ZEMEL V. RUSK (1965) and HAIG V. AGEE (1981) in rejecting claims based on the RIGHT TO TRAVEL protected by the Fifth Amendment's DUE PROCESS clause. The dissenters argued that Congress had not authorized the regulation.

KENNETH L. KARST

REGENTS OF UNIVERSITY OF CALIFORNIA v. BAKKE
438 U.S. 265 (1978)

Perhaps the Supreme Court's majority in DeFunis v. Odegaard (1974) thought a delay in deciding on the constitutionality of racial preferences in state university admissions would give time for development of a political consensus on the issue. The result was just the opposite; by the time *Bakke* was decided, the question of RACIAL QUOTAS and preferences had become bitterly divisive. Bakke, a nonminority applicant, had been denied admission to the university's medical school at Davis. His state court suit had challenged the school's program setting aside for minority applicants sixteen places in an entering class of 100. Bakke's test scores and grades exceeded those of most minority admittees. The California Supreme Court held that the racial preference denied Bakke the EQUAL PROTECTION OF THE LAWS guaranteed by the FOURTEENTH AMENDMENT.

A fragmented United States Supreme Court agreed, 5–4, that Bakke was entitled to admission, but concluded, in a different 5–4 alignment, that race could be taken into account in a state university's admissions. Four Justices thought the Davis quota violated Title VI of the CIVIL RIGHTS ACT OF 1964, which forbids the exclusion of anyone on account of race from any program aided by federal funds. This position was rejected, 5–4. Four other Justices argued that the Davis quota was constitutionally valid as a reasonable, nonstigmatizing remedy for past societal discrimination against racial and ethnic minorities. This view was rejected by Justice LEWIS F. POWELL, who concluded that the Davis quota was a denial of equal protection. His vote, along with the votes of the four Justices who found a Title VI violation, placed Bakke in Davis's 1978 entering class.

Justice Powell's opinion on the constitutional question began by rejecting the notion of a "BENIGN" RACIAL CLASSIFICATION. He concluded that the burden of remedying past societal discrimination could not constitutionally be placed on individuals who had no part in that discrimination—absent the sort of constitutional violation that had been found in school DESEGREGATION cases such as SWANN V. CHARLOTTE-MECKLENBURG BOARD OF EDUCATION (1971), where color-conscious remedies had been approved. While rejecting quotas, Justice Powell approved the use of race as one factor in a state university's admissions policy for the purpose of promoting diversity in its student body.

Race is relevant to "diversity," of course, mainly because past societal discrimination has made race relevant to a student's attitudes and experiences. And if one's membership in a racial group may be a factor in the admissions process, it may be the decisive factor in a particular case. The Powell opinion thus anticipates a preference for minority applicants; how much of a preference will depend, as he says, on "some attention to numbers"—that is, the number of minority students already admitted. The difference between such a system and a racial quota is mostly symbolic.

The press hailed Justice Powell's opinion as a judgment of Solomon. As a contribution to principled argument about equal protection doctrine, it failed. As a political solution, however, it was a triumph. The borders of preference became blurred, so that no future applicant could blame her rejection on the preference. At the same time, a university following a "diversity" approach to admissions was made safe from constitutional attack. AFFIRMATIVE ACTION was thus saved, even as Bakke was ushered into medical school and racial quotas ringingly denounced. Almost miraculously, the issue of racial preferences in higher education virtually disappeared from the political scene, and legislative proposals to abolish affirmative action were shelved. Solomon, it will be recalled, succeeded in saving the baby.

KENNETH L. KARST

Bibliography

BLASI, VINCENT 1979 Bakke as Precedent: Does Mr. Justice Powell Have a Theory? *California Law Review* 67:21–68.
KARST, KENNETH L. and HOROWITZ, HAROLD W. 1979 The Bakke Opinions and Equal Protection Doctrine. *Harvard Civil Rights–Civil Liberties Law Review* 14:7–29.
WILKINSON, J. HARVIE, III 1979 *From Brown to Bakke.* New York: Oxford University Press.

REGULATORY AGENCIES

Regulatory agencies are governmental bodies created by legislatures to carry out specified state or national policies. Such an agency is typically responsible for regulating one particular area of social or economic life; it is staffed by specialists who develop the knowledge and experience necessary to enforce complex regulatory laws. Regulatory agencies normally combine the powers to make rules, to adjudicate controversies, and to provide ordinary administrative services, functions corresponding to the legislative, judicial, and executive powers of the separate branches of government. They fill in the gaps of general policy by bringing order, method, and uniformity to the process of modern government.

Although administrative agencies are as old as the federal government, the national regulatory process as we know it today began with the creation of the Interstate Commerce Commission in 1887. Granted extensive authority over the booming railroad industry, the commission received broad rule-making and adjudicatory powers, broader than those of any previous agency. It set the trend, and the goal, for future agencies by being the first governmental unit "whose single concern was the well-being," as James Landis said, "in a broad public sense, of a vital and national industry."

Since the New Deal, regulatory agencies have become the most visible tool for the achievement of national policy. They provide a form of centralized supervision which in earlier periods of American history was deemed neither necessary nor desirable. Their proliferation paralleled the development of national industries and the emergence of Congress as a policymaking body unable to supervise the details of administration. At the same time, a growing welfare state has recognized new interests such as welfare entitlements and equal employment opportunity. New regulatory agencies have been created to provide sympathetic administration of the new national policy goals, and to resolve conflicts by procedures less formalized and adversarial—and far less costly—than those prevailing in courts of law.

The character and origin of a regulatory agency depend on the nature of its tasks. Generally, such agencies fall into three main categories: independent regulatory commissions; executive agencies; and government corporations. The independent commissions, so called because of their relative freedom from executive control, are the most important, and include such agencies as the Interstate Commerce Commission (ICC), Securities and Exchange Commission (SEC), Federal Trade Commission (FTC), National Labor Relations Board (NLRB), and Nuclear Regulatory Commission (NRC). Each independent commission is headed by a multimember board appointed by the President with the ADVICE AND CONSENT of the Senate. Congress has sought to guarantee the commissions' independence by establishing their governing boards on a bipartisan basis, providing fixed terms of office for board members, and authorizing the President to remove them only for reasons specified by statute.

The executive agency, an example of which is the Environmental Protection Agency, is one whose administrator and top assistants are appointed by the President, to whom they report directly and who may remove them freely. The executive agency lies squarely within the executive branch; its position within the constitutional framework of SEPARATION OF POWERS is thus more clearly defined than that of the independent regulatory agencies. The government corporation, an example of which is the Tennessee Valley Authority, is created by statute for a stated purpose and is wholly owned by the government. This model has been used when a project, because of its duration or its required investment, cannot easily be achieved through private development.

Regulatory agencies differ significantly in the range of their powers and their modes of operation. For example, the work of the NLRB is almost exclusively judicial in character. Although it has broad authority under the WAGNER ACT and TAFT-HARTLEY ACT, the NLRB has chosen to exercise only adjudicatory powers. The Equal Employment Opportunity Commission, on the other hand, has no formal power to adjudicate claims or impose administrative sanctions. The sensitive and highly controversial character of its mission—to carry out the antidiscrimination provisions of Title VII of the CIVIL RIGHTS ACT OF 1964—prompted Congress to limit EEOC's authority to "informal methods of conference, conciliation, and persuasion." If these methods fail the alleged victim of discrimination may sue in federal court. Even though EEOC itself may not issue final orders, its guidelines for dealing with patterns of discrimination in employment, together with its field investigations in particular cases, often induce compliance. The result is a significant regulatory effect.

An immense body of administrative law, found in the voluminous *Code of Federal Regulations* and in a multitude of specialized publications, has been created by these and other administrative agencies.

The development and structure of regulatory agencies have strained the constitutional theory of separation of powers, for the agencies typically blend functions of all three branches of government. Yet the Supreme Court has sought to accommodate the constitutional theory with the needs of effective government, and thus to preserve the constitutional balance underscored by the principle of separation of powers. The constitutional basis for Congress's power to create regulatory agencies is derived from Article I. Section 1 grants "[a]ll legislative powers" to Congress; section 8 enumerates these powers and vests Congress with the additional power to make laws NECESSARY AND PROPER for carrying them into effect. Regulatory agencies have always been regarded as necessary and proper means of achieving the ends of national policy.

Implicit in the theory of separation of powers is the doctrine that delegated authority cannot be redelegated. Under this principle Congress cannot constitutionally invest the executive (or, for that matter, the judiciary) with the power of legislation. How then is it possible to justify the rule-making power conferred on agencies? The Supreme Court's answer is that such authority is permissible if the authorizing statute embodies a policy and provides guidelines to channel administrative action. Of course, within these guidelines agencies exercise considerable discretion. In theory, however, they are not legislating in a constitutional sense when exercising their discretion; they are simply carrying out legislative policies established by Congress.

Reality, however, had not easily converged with theory. Despite its reiteration of the doctrine forbidding delegation, the Supreme Court has consistently allowed "directionless" delegations of legislative authority. Not until the 1930s did the Court actually invalidate congressional statutes for excessive delegation of legislative power. But these precedents soon fell from favor as the Court proceeded to uphold subsequent legislative mandates as vague as those previously nullified. Some delegations have been disturbingly broad. For example, the Federal Communications Commission is to use its licensing power in the "public convenience, interest, or necessity." The Court upheld this "supple instrument" of delegation as being "as concrete as the complicated factors for judgement in such a field" permit. Nevertheless, the doctrine forbidding delegation still lives in theory. As recently as 1974, in *National Cable Television v. United States*, the Supreme Court construed a federal statute narrowly so as to avoid the implication from a literal reading of the statute that taxing power—clearly a legislative function—had been conferred on the Federal Communications Commission.

The doctrine forbidding legislative delegation has had its corollary in challenges to the constitutionality of regulatory agencies' exercise of judicial functions. The contention is that these functions are inconsistent with Article III's grant of the JUDICIAL POWER to courts. Yet the Supreme Court has upheld the delegation of adjudicatory functions to regulatory agencies, so long as the courts retain power to determine whether the agencies have acted within their legislative mandates.

The obverse of the delegation issue concerns strategies by which Congress may take back authority it has granted. Despite congressional efforts to ensure their independence, regulatory agencies came under criticism of liberals who complained that, instead of regulating in the public interest, the agencies had become the clients of the special interest they were supposed to regulate. More recently, conservatives have attacked regulatory agencies for pervasive bureaucratization, for growing unaccountability, and for disregard of their legislative mandates. The congressional response to these criticisms has taken a number of forms, including attempts to deregulate certain industries and the effort to reserve a power of LEGISLATIVE VETO of agency actions.

The legislative veto, adopted by Congress with increasing frequency in the 1970s, when public criticism of regulatory agencies was at its zenith, poses serious constitutional issues. Congress required various executive agencies to report to it in advance of specified kinds of proposed action. Then, if Congress (or, in some cases, one house of Congress) should adopt a resolution of disapproval within a certain time, the proposed action was effectively "vetoed." The Supreme Court held this mechanism unconstitutional in IMMIGRATION AND NATURALIZATION SERVICE V. CHADHA (1983), as applied to the one-house veto of a deportation order. First, the Court held, the congressional veto was a legislative act requiring passage by both houses of Congress. Second, and more serious, the congressional veto offended Article II, which requires any legislative act to be presented to the President for his approval before it takes effect.

The President as chief executive is commanded by Article II of the Constitution to "take care that the Laws be faithfully executed." From an early time, Presidents claimed an inherent constitutional power to remove any executive official whom they or their predecessors had appointed. This claim was vindicated in MYERS V. UNITED STATES (1926). But in HUMPHREY'S EXECUTOR V. UNITED STATES (1935) the Supreme Court refused to apply this theory of inherent power to the removal of a member of an independent agency exercising quasi-legislative and quasi-judicial powers. Distinguishing between a "purely executive" officer and an officer of an independent agency, the Court sustained Congress's authority, when creating regulatory agencies, to fix the terms of commissioners and specify the exclusive grounds for their removal. In *Weiner v. United States* (1958) this principle was applied to the removal of a member of the War Claims Commission, whose organizing statute specified no grounds for removal. The Court noted the adjudicatory nature of the agency's work, and thus concluded that Congress had not made it part of the executive establishment under the political control of the President. The Supreme Court has recognized that independent agencies cannot exercise their statutory duties fairly or impartially, as Congress intended, unless they are free from executive control.

The combination of investigatory, prosecutorial, and adjudicatory functions within the same regulatory agency has also been the subject of constitutional litigation. In *Winthrop v. Larkin* (1975), however, the Supreme Court reaffirmed its long-standing view that the mixture of these functions within a single agency or person does not violate DUE PROCESS unless the presumption of honesty and integrity of officers exercising these functions is overcome by evidence of actual bias or prejudgment in a particular case. Even though the separation of these functions within the regulatory context is not constitutionally commanded, legislators have often concluded that the best mix of efficiency and impartiality is maintained when prosecutorial and judicial functions are performed by different officers within an agency.

All regulatory agencies are subject to the constitutional requirement of PROCEDURAL DUE PROCESS. The right to a hearing must be granted when an agency takes action directly affecting rights and obligations: those affected must be given NOTICE and an opportunity to present their case in a FAIR HEARING. The process due in any particular case depends on the nature of the liberty or property interest involved. If these interests are constitutionally recognized then notice and even a prior hearing may be required before agency action can be taken. Whether the RIGHT TO COUNSEL, cross-examination, and other trial-type procedures will be required depends on the importance of the private interest at stake when balanced against the government's interest and the risk of erroneous deprivation under an agency's normal operating procedures.

The extent to which agency determinations are subject to judicial review is governed by the Administrative Procedure Act. Generally, administrative action is unreviewable if committed by statute to agency discretion. Courts may, however, set aside even discretionary action when it is "arbitrary, capricious, an abuse of discretion, or otherwise not in accordance with law." Under the act, the courts are to sustain agency findings of fact if they are supported by substantial evidence. Although the definition of "substantial" may differ from court to court, the Supreme Court retains the final say on whether the rule has been properly applied in a given case.

DONALD P. KOMMERS

Bibliography

DAVIS, KENNETH C. 1969 *Discretionary Justice.* Baton Rouge: Louisiana State University Press.
FREEDMAN, JAMES O. 1978 *Crisis and Legitimacy.* Cambridge: At the University Press.
KOHLMEIER, LOUIS M. 1969 *The Regulators.* New York: Harper & Row.
LANDIS, JAMES 1938 *The Administrative Process.* New Haven, Conn.: Yale University Press.
REDORD, EMMETT S. 1969 *The Regulatory Process.* Austin: University of Texas Press.

REHABILITATION ACT
87 Stat. 355 (1973)

In addition to providing funding and research incentives for various programs to aid the handicapped, Congress incorporated antidiscrimination provisions into the Rehabilitation Act. In federally assisted programs, the act prohibits discrimination solely by reason of handicap against an "otherwise qualified handicapped individual." In addition, the act requires federal executive agencies to take AFFIRMATIVE ACTION to employ handicapped individuals. In *Southeastern Community College v. Davis* (1979) the Supreme Court held that the Rehabilitation Act does not forbid a nursing school from imposing relevant physical qualifications upon participants in its training programs.

THEODORE EISENBERG

Bibliography

BURGDORF, ROBERT L., JR. 1980 *The Legal Rights of Handicapped Persons.* Baltimore: Paul H. Brookes Publishing Co.

REHEARING

A party who is dissatisfied with the court's decision or opinion in a case may request the court to reconsider. The term "rehearing" refers to such a reconsideration, usually by an appellate court.

By statute, the Supreme Court's APPELLATE JURISDICTION over cases coming from the state courts is limited to questions of federal law that have been properly drawn in question in the lower courts. This requirement normally is not satisfied by a litigant who raises a federal question for the first time in a petition for rehearing after a state supreme court has decided the case. However, if the state court entertains the petition and actually considers the federal question, the question can be brought to the Supreme Court.

The Supreme Court itself receives between 100 and 200 petitions for rehearing each year, seeking reconsideration of its own decisions or opinions. Fewer than one percent of these petitions are granted. By rule, the Court has provided that a petition for rehearing will be granted only by the vote of a majority of the Justices, including at least one Justice who concurred in the decision. By custom, a Justice who did not participate in that decision does not vote on the petition for rehearing.

One occasion for granting a petition for rehearing is the case in which the Supreme Court has affirmed the lower court's decision by a 4–4 vote. If the missing Justice was ill and has recovered, or if a ninth Justice has been appointed to fill a vacancy, it may seem likely that a majority will be mustered once the Court returns to full strength. Absent such a circumstance, the typical petition for rehearing achieves little but delay and the chance for a parting shot.

KENNETH L. KARST

Bibliography
STERN, ROBERT L. and GRESSMAN, EUGENE 1978 Supreme Court Practice, 5th ed. Chap. 15. Washington, D.C.: Bureau of National Affairs.

REHNQUIST, WILLIAM H.
(1924–)

William Rehnquist joined the Supreme Court in 1971 at age forty-seven. He had been a clerk to Justice ROBERT H. JACKSON and a practitioner in Arizona. At the time of his appointment, he was the assistant attorney general for legal counsel—as President RICHARD M. NIXON described the post on appointing him, "the President's lawyer's lawyer."

Brilliant, charming, and deeply conservative, he has become the intellectual leader of the court—a fact that is not obvious from the statistics. Many terms he has dissented more than any other Justice, often alone. Rehnquist's influence lies in setting the terms of the debate. His dissents mark the path for future developments. His MAJORITY OPINIONS have been unusually influential, in part because Chief Justice WARREN E. BURGER regularly assigns him the most difficult and interesting cases, and in part because the opinions articulate approaches that have substantial general importance.

Rehnquist follows a structural approach in which the original understanding and the text of the Constitution assume great importance. The states play a substantial role in this structure, and a vision of an allocation of functions between state and federal governments lies at the center of Rehnquist's thought. He takes seriously the proposition that the federal government has limited powers and that the states hold sway over substantial fields. The Justice also has a view of the allocation of powers within the federal government in which judges play only a limited role. Judges may enforce some explicit guarantees, such as the right to FREEDOM OF SPEECH, but Rehnquist sees their more important function as enforcing the decisions of the political branches rather than questioning them. Judges must patrol the allocation of powers among other contending claimants, but once a political branch acts within its capacity, the decision, no matter how unwise, binds the courts.

This highly deferential approach follows from a belief that the Framers of the Constitution settled little but governmental structure, leaving the rest to future generations. Judges have no authority to restrict the powers of the political branches. They cannot invoke a decision by the Framers or political branches allocating power to the courts, and they cannot point to any other source of authority. Rehnquist is a moral skeptic and so rejects arguments that the Constitution authorizes judges to insist that other branches keep up with evolving notions of decent conduct; he believes that only the political process can define decency.

Justice Rehnquist outlined his approach in a solitary dissent to TRIMBLE V. GORDON (1977). The majority held that a statute discriminating against illegitimate children violated the EQUAL PROTECTION clause of the FOURTEENTH AMENDMENT. Calling that clause a "classic paradox" that "makes sense only in the context of a recently fought Civil War," Rehnquist continued:

In the case of equality and equal protection, the constitutional principle—the thing to be protected to a greater or lesser degree—is not even identifiable from within the four corners of the Constitution. For equal protection does not mean that all persons must be treated alike. Rather, its general principle is that persons similarly situated should be treated similarly. But that statement of the rule does little to determine whether or not a question of equality is even involved in a given case. For the crux of the problem is *whether persons are similarly situated* for purposes of the STATE ACTION in issue.

Rehnquist therefore finds the constitutional guarantee of equality empty and thus vulnerable to being made a mere vessel for the beliefs of modern judges about what things *should* count as the pertinent similarities and differences. In his view, however, the Constitution does not resolve that question, which is at root political, to be resolved by political processes. The equal protection clause is limited to the Civil War concern, race. Within that field the prohibition is absolute, and race is a forbidden classification. Rehnquist has opposed governmental racial distinctions of all sorts, preferential "set-asides" for construction work, which the majority approved in FULLILOVE V. KLUTZ- NICK (1980), and preferences for private employment, which were sustained in UNITED STEELWORKERS V. WEBER (1979), as well as those stigmatizing blacks.

He applies the same approach to almost every other aspect of the Constitution. The FIRST AMENDMENT disables government from stopping speech—the sub- ject debated by the Framers—but does not require government to facilitate speech, for example, by cre- ating rights of access to information. Judicial expan- sion of the amendment's core meaning is unauthor- ized. A judge may not properly pursue the principles or values that underlie the document, because every principle has its limit, and the Constitution left adjust- ments to the political branches. As Rehnquist wrote in an article published in 1976: "Even in the face of a conceded social evil, a reasonably competent and reasonably representative legislature may decide to do nothing. It may decide that the evil is not of suffi- cient magnitude to warrant any governmental inter- vention. It may decide that the financial cost of elimi- nating the evil is not worth the benefit which would result from its elimination. It may decide that the evils which might ensue from the proposed solution are worse than the evils which the solution would eliminate." The judge must accept the political an- swers to these problems.

This limitation does not imply judicial passivity. The judge must rigorously enforce any actual constitu- tional decisions to remove issues from the political process. The BILL OF RIGHTS contains some of these decisions, but the most important are those concern- ing the structure of government. Rehnquist is perhaps best known for his enforcement of principles of FED- ERALISM that cannot be found in the constitutional text. Writing for a bare majority in NATIONAL LEAGUE OF CITIES V. USERY (1976), he concluded that the structure of the Constitution withheld from Congress any power to regulate the operation of "states as states." As a result, the Court held, Congress could not require state and local governments to pay the minimum wages applicable to private parties. The Justice also has read into many statutes limits founded on a perceived need to maintain the role of states as coordinate centers of power.

But decisions based on the structure of the Consti- tution do not always favor the states. Often Rehnquist has joined holdings under the COMMERCE CLAUSE re- stricting the powers of states to levy discriminatory taxes or otherwise hinder INTERSTATE COMMERCE, even though neither legislation not any clear textual command prohibits this discrimination. He wrote the court's opinion in FITZPATRICK V. BITZER (1976), holding that in the exercise of its power under the Fourteenth Amendment, Congress may authorize suits against the states, even though the ELEVENTH AMENDMENT appears to deprive federal courts of JURISDICTION to entertain such suits.

The allocation of powers within the federal govern- ment also has been a theme of Rehnquist's work. He has attempted to revive the "antidelegation" doc- trine, arguing that Congress may not grant uncertain decision-making powers to the executive branch. He joined the Court's opinion in BUCKLEY V. VALEO (1976), invalidating Congress's effort to appoint offi- cers to administer the election laws, characterizing that effort as an intrusion on the executive power. And he supplied the theory and vote necessary to strike down in NORTHERN PIPELINE CONSTRUCTION CORP. V. MARATHON PIPE LINE CO. (1982) a grant of judicial power to BANKRUPTCY judges who lacked life tenure of office.

Part of Rehnquist's influence among the Justices comes from his distinctive style. Most judicial opinions come in shades of gray, following a dull formula nota- ble only for turgid prose and abundant footnotes. Jus- tice Rehnquist's opinions come closer to lavender than gray. They are relatively short and lively. One began with a limerick. Rehnquist often uses colorful (if strained) metaphors. The opinions are less copiously documented than those of his colleagues, but not be- cause he does not know the references—they appear in the appropriate quantities in his articles. The Justice has simply chosen to write in an entertaining style. His opinions are read, and being read is the first step in being influential.

Some critics, including David L. Shapiro, have ac- cused Rehnquist of intellectual dishonesty, because he is willing to distinguish a case on a marginally rele- vant basis, or to purport to honor PRECEDENT while disavowing the earlier case's rationale. Timid or weak Justices routinely treat precedents so, but Rehnquist is neither timid nor weak. That is why his nimble treatment of precedent is troubling. No one can at- tribute his conduct to inadvertence or to the work of a law clerk.

Justice Rehnquist is not always cavalier in distin- guishing or narrowing unpleasant precedents. He will attack earlier cases openly in separate or DISSENTING OPINIONS, only to distinguish them in opinions for the Court. His opinion in *National League of Cities* purported to preserve some cases he had attacked, in solitary dissent, a year before, in *Fry v. United States* (1975). Part of his approach to precedent arises from his understanding that the author of a majority opinion speaks not for himself but for the Court as institution. He therefore tries to preserve precedents with which he does not agree, by flimsy distinctions if necessary. The result may seem contrived, but it is often essential to the functioning of the Court.

The ultimate test of honesty is whether a Justice faithfully distinguishes his constitutional views from his personal ones. Most Justices see little difference, leading to the conclusion that the Constitution follows the personal view rather than the reverse. Yet Rehnquist, who generally opposes governmental control of economic affairs, believes that the Constitution allows the political branches to establish and maintain a welfare state with extensive ECONOMIC REGULATION. He follows his jurisprudence to its logical conclusions. Though he supports property rights, he wrote an opinion in PRUNEYARD SHOPPING CENTER V. ROBINS (1980) sustaining the authority of a state to restrict those rights in the interest of fostering political speech with which the property owner disagreed.

In 1986 President RONALD REAGAN nominated Rehnquist to succeed Warren Burger as Chief Justice of the United States. One may expect Chief Justice Rehnquist to retain the same coherent picture of a government in which judges police structure rather than substance.

FRANK H. EASTERBROOK

Bibliography

POWELL, JEFF 1982 The Compleat Jeffersonian: Justice Rehnquist and Federalism. *Yale Law Journal* 91:1317–1370.
REHNQUIST, WILLIAM H. 1976 The Notion of a Living Constitution. *Texas Law Review* 54:693–706.
SHAPIRO, DAVID L. 1976 Mr. Justice Rehnquist: A Preliminary View. *Harvard Law Review* 90:293–357.

REID v. COVERT
KINSELLA v. KRUEGER
354 U.S. 1 (1957)

In a 6–2 decision, the Supreme Court invalidated a provision making the Uniform Code of Military Justice applicable to civilians accompanying the armed forces abroad, and reversed the COURT-MARTIAL convictions of two women who had murdered their servicemen husbands on military bases overseas.

Justice HUGO L. BLACK, for a plurality, held that neither the power to make rules for governing the armed forces nor any international agreement could free the government from the procedural requirements of Article III, Section 2, and the Fifth and Sixth Amendments.

DENNIS J. MAHONEY

REITMAN v. MULKEY
387 U.S. 369 (1967)

By an overwhelming majority, California's voters adopted an INITIATIVE measure ("Proposition 14") adding to the state constitution a provision repealing existing OPEN HOUSING LAWS and forbidding the enactment of new ones. Following the lead of the state supreme court, the Supreme Court held, 5–4, that the circumstances of Proposition 14's adoption demonstrated state encouragement of private RACIAL DISCRIMINATION in the sale and rental of housing. Justice BYRON R. WHITE, for the majority, said this encouragement amounted to STATE ACTION in violation of the FOURTEENTH AMENDMENT. Justice JOHN MARSHALL HARLAN, for the dissenters, argued that Proposition 14 merely withdrew the state from regulation of private conduct; the state court determinations of "encouragement" were not fact findings, but mistaken readings of the Supreme Court's own precedents.

Taken seriously, the *Reitman* decision implies an affirmative state obligation to protect against private racial discrimination in housing. The Supreme Court, far from reading the decision in this manner, has consistently rejected litigants' efforts even to invoke the "encouragement" doctrine there announced. *Reitman* thus lies in isolation, awaiting resurrection. But the trumpet call announcing the end of the world of state action doctrine, seemingly so close in the final years of the WARREN COURT, now seems far away.

KENNETH L. KARST

RELEASED TIME

Twice, in MCCOLLUM V. BOARD OF EDUCATION (1948) and again in ZORACH V. CLAUSEN (1952), the Supreme Court considered FIRST AMENDMENT challenges to the practice of releasing public school pupils from their regular studies so that they might participate in programs for religious instruction.

The first such program, in Gary, Indiana, in 1914, provided that, with parental consent and cooperation of church authorities, children could be released for one or more periods each week to go to churches of their own faith and there participate in religious instruction, returning to the public school at the end of the period, or if the period was the last of the day, going home.

The idea spread to other communities, but, for a variety of reasons, quite slowly. In rural and small urban communities, such as Champaign, Illinois, it was found more effective to have the religious instruction take place within the public schools rather than in the church schools.

In Champaign in 1940, an interfaith council with Protestant, Roman Catholic, and Jewish representatives was formed to offer religious instruction within the public schools during regular school hours. Instructors of religion were to be hired and paid by or through the interfaith council, subject to the approval and supervision of the public school superintendent. Each term the public school teachers distributed to the children cards on which parents could indicate their consent to the enrollment of their children in the religion classes. Children who obtained such consent were released by the school authorities from the secular work for a period of thirty minutes weekly in the elementary schools and forty-five minutes in the junior high school. Only Protestant instruction was conducted within the regular classroom; children released for Roman Catholic or Jewish instruction left their classroom for other parts of the building. Nonparticipants were also relocated, sometimes accompanied by their regular teachers and sometimes not. At the end of each session, children who had participated in any religious instruction returned to the regular classroom, and regular class work was resumed.

McCollum v. Board of Education (1948) was a suit, brought in a state court by the mother of a fifth grader, challenging the constitutionality of Champaign's program. In the Supreme Court, counsel for the school authorities argued that the establishment clause did not apply to the states, and that the contrary HOLDING in EVERSON V. BOARD OF EDUCATION (1947) should be overruled. This the Court refused to do, reasserting *Everson*'s conclusion about the scope of the establishment clause.

No more successful was the argument that historically the establishment clause had been intended to forbid only preferential treatment of one faith over others, whereas the Champaign program was open equally to Protestants, Roman Catholics, and Jews. Here, too, the Court found no reason to reconsider its statement in *Everson* that the clause barred aid not only to one religion but equally to all religions.

Where, the Court said, pupils compelled by law to go to school for secular education are released in part from their legal duty if they attend religious classes, the tax-supported public school system's use to aid religious groups to spread their faiths falls squarely under the ban of the First Amendment. Not only are the public school buildings used for the dissemination of religious doctrines, but the state also affords sectarian groups an invaluable aid, helping to provide pupils for their religious classes through the use of the state's compulsory public school machinery. This, the Court concluded, was not SEPARATION OF CHURCH AND STATE.

Although the Court's language appeared to encompass in its determination of unconstitutionality released time plans providing for off-school religious instruction (and Justice HUGO L. BLACK who wrote the opinion so interpreted it), the majority reached a contrary conclusion in *Zorach v. Clausen* (1952).

Zorach involved New York City's program, which restricted public school participation to releasing children whose parents had signed consent cards and specifically forbade comment by any principal or teacher on the attendance or nonattendance of any pupil upon religious instruction. This situation, said the Court speaking through Justice WILLIAM O. DOUGLAS, differed from that presented in the *McCollum* case. There, the classrooms had been used for religious instruction and the influence of the public school used to promote that instruction. Here, the public schools did no more than accommodate their schedules to allow children, who so wished, to go elsewhere for religious instruction completely independent of public school operations. The situation, Douglas said, was not different from that presented when a Roman Catholic student asks his teacher to be excused to attend a mass on a Holy Day of Obligation or a Jewish student to attend synagogue on Yom Kippur.

Government, Justice Douglas said further, may not finance religious groups nor undertake religious instruction nor blend secular and sectarian education nor use secular institutions to force one or some religion on any person. Government, however, must be neutral in respect to religion, not hostile. "We are," he said, "a religious people whose institutions presuppose a Supreme Being. When the state encourages religious instruction or cooperates with religious authorities, it follows the best of our traditions. For it then respects the religious nature of our people and accommodates the public service to their spiritual needs."

On the basis of *McCollum* and *Zorach*, the present law is that released time programs are constitutional so long as the religious instruction is given off the public school premises and the public school teachers and authorities are involved in it only by releasing uncoerced children who choose to participate in it.

LEO PFEFFER

Bibliography

PFEFFER, LEO (1953)1967 *Church, State and Freedom.* Boston: Beacon Press.
Released Time for Religious Education in New York City Schools. 1949 Public Education Association.
STOKES, A. P. and PFEFFER, LEO 1964 *Church and State in the United States.* New York: Harper & Row.

RELIGION AND FRAUD

Few responsibilities are more sensitive and difficult to meet than drawing a line between punishable obtaining of property under false pretenses and constitutionally protected free exercise of religion. In the one major case to reach the Supreme Court, *United States v. Ballard* (1944), the Court split three ways in its decision.

Ballard involved the conviction of organizers of the "I Am" movement, indicted for using the mails to defraud because they falsely represented that they had supernatural powers to heal the incurably ill, and that as "Divine messengers" they had cured hundreds of afflicted persons through communication with Saint Germain, Jesus, and others. The trial court had instructed the jury that they should not decide whether these statements were literally true, but only whether the defendants honestly believed them to be true.

On appeal the majority of the Supreme Court agreed with the trial judge. Under the principles of SEPARATION OF CHURCH AND STATE and RELIGIOUS LIBERTY, it held, neither a jury nor any other organ of government had the competence to pass on whether certain religious experiences actually occurred. A jury could no more constitutionally decide that defendants had not shaken hands with Jesus, as they claimed, than they could determine that Jesus had not walked on the sea, as the Bible related. The limit of the jury's power was a determination whether defendants actually believed that what they recounted was true.

Chief Justice HARLAN FISKE STONE dissented on the ground that the prosecution should be allowed to prove that none of the alleged cures had been effected. On the other extreme Justice ROBERT H. JACKSON urged that the prosecution should not have been instituted in the first place, for few juries would find that the defendants honestly believed in something that was unbelievable. Nevertheless the majority decision remains the law, and is not likely to be OVERRULED after a half-century of acceptance.

LEO PFEFFER

Bibliography

PFEFFER, LEO (1953)1967 *Church, State and Freedom.* Boston: Beacon Press.

RELIGION IN PUBLIC SCHOOLS

For centuries in the Western world, organized education was church education; colonial schools established on the American shores therefore naturally reflected a religious orientation. Prior to the early nineteenth-century migration of Irish to this country, the orientation of these schools was Protestant—a fact that contributed to the establishment and growth of the Roman Catholic parochial school system. Nevertheless, when the RELEASED TIME plan for religious instruction was initiated in 1914, the majority of Roman Catholic children still attended public schools. The plan thus provided for separate religious instruction classes for Protestants, Roman Catholics, and Jews. Roman Catholic Church spokesmen condemned the Supreme Court's decision in MCCOLLUM V. BOARD OF EDUCATION (1948) invalidating the program. Previously, however, Roman Catholics had protested against public school religious instruction with a Protestant orientation, and had instituted lawsuits challenging such programs' constitutionality. Public school authorities in New York chose to formulate their own "non-sectarian" prayer, which was submitted to and received the approval of prominent religious spokesmen of the three major faiths. The twenty-two-word prayer read: "Almighty God, we acknowledge our dependence upon Thee, and beg Thy blessings upon us, our parents, our teachers and our country."

The denominational neutrality of the prayer, the Supreme Court held in ENGEL V. VITALE (1962), was immaterial. Nor was it relevant that observance on the part of students was voluntary (nonparticipating students were not even required to be in the classroom or assembly hall while the prayer was recited). Under the establishment clause, the Court said, aid to all religions was as impermissible as aid to one religion, even if the aid was noncoercive. The constitutional prohibition against laws respecting an ESTABLISHMENT OF RELIGION means at least that it is "no part of the business of government to compose official prayers for any group of the American people to recite as part of a religious program carried on by government."

One year after *Engel*, the Court, in ABINGTON SCHOOL DISTRICT v. SCHEMPP, was called upon to rule on the constitutionality of two practices in the public schools common throughout the nation, prayer recitation and devotional Bible reading. In respect to the former it ruled immaterial the fact that, unlike *Engel*, the recited prayer had not been formulated by public school authorities, but was the Lord's Prayer taken from the Bible. The fatal flaw in the *Engel* regulation lay not in the authorship of the prayer but in the fact that its purpose and primary effect were the advancement of religion. This fact mandated invalidation of both Lord's Prayer recitation and devotional Bible reading. The Court rejected the claim that the purposes of the challenged program were the secular ones of promoting moral values, contradicting the materialistic trends of our time, perpetuating our institutions, and teaching literature. None of these factors, the Court said, justified use of the Bible as an instrument of religion or resort to a ceremony of pervasive religious character. Nothing in its decision, it concluded, was intended to cast doubt on the study of comparative religion or the study of the Bible for its literary and historic qualities, so long as these were presented as part of a secular program of education.

McCollum, Engel, and *Schempp* involved efforts to introduce religious teachings or practices into the public schools. EPPERSON V. ARKANSAS (1968) presented the converse, that is, religiously motivated exclusion of secular instruction from the public school curriculum. A statute forbade teaching "the theory or doctrine that mankind ascended or descended from a lower order of animals." The Court held that the statute violated the establishment clause, because its purpose was to protect religious orthodoxy from inconsistent secular teaching of evolution.

In *Stone v. Graham* (1980) the Court struck down a Kentucky statute requiring the posting of copies of the Ten Commandments (purchased with private contributions) on the walls of all the public school classrooms in the state. The statute, it held, had no secular purpose; unlike the second part of the Commandments, the first (worshiping God, avoiding idolatry, not taking the Lord's name in vain, and observing the Sabbath) concerned religious rather than secular duties.

WIDMAR V. VINCENT (1981) manifests a more tolerant approach in respect to colleges than to elementary and secondary schools. With but one dissent, the Court held that where state university facilities were open to groups and speakers of all kinds, they must also be open for use by an organization of evangelical Christian students for prayer, hymns, Bible commentary, and discussion of religious views and experience. As construed by the Court, the establishment clause did not mandate such exclusion; on the contrary, the state's interest in enforcing its own constitution's church–state separation clause was not sufficiently "compelling" to justify content-barred discrimination forbidden by the FREEDOM OF SPEECH clause.

However, in *Jaffree v. Board of School Commissioners* (1984) the Court affirmed without opinion a Court of Appeals decision ruling unconstitutional an Alabama law authorizing voluntary participation in a prayer formulated by the legislators; and a year later, in WALLACE V. JAFFREE (1985) it invalidated another section of the statute that required a one-minute period of silence for "meditation or voluntary prayer." The provision, the Court said, did not have a valid secular purpose, but rather one that sought to return prayer to the public schools.

LEO PFEFFER

Bibliography
PFEFFER, LEO (1953)1967 *Church, State and Freedom.* Boston: Beacon Press.
STOKES, A. P. and PFEFFER, LEO 1964 *Church and State in the United States.* New York: Harper & Row.
TRIBE, LAURENCE H. 1984 *American Constitutional Law.* Chap. 14. Mineola, N.Y.: Foundation Press.

RELIGIOUS LIBERTY

Although the FIRST AMENDMENT's mandate that "Congress shall make no law respecting an ESTABLISHMENT OF RELIGION, or prohibiting the free exercise thereof" is expressed in unconditional language, religious liberty, insofar as it extends beyond belief, is not an absolute right. The First Amendment, the Supreme Court said in CANTWELL v. CONNECTICUT (1940), "embraces two concepts—freedom to believe and freedom to act. The first is absolute but, in the nature of things, the second cannot be. Conduct remains subject to regulation of society."

Although the Court has repeated this dualism many times, it does not explain what the free exercise clause means. There is no need for a constitutional guarantee protecting freedom to believe, for, as the COMMON LAW had it, "the devil himself knows not the thoughts of man." Even if freedom to believe encompasses freedom to express what one believes, the clause adds nothing, since FREEDOM OF SPEECH and FREEDOM OF THE PRESS are specifically guaranteed in the amendment. Indeed, before *Cantwell* was decided, the Court applied the free speech rather than free exercise guarantee to challenges against state laws allegedly impinging upon religious liberty. Moreover, the word "exercise" connotes action or conduct, thus indicating that the framers had in mind something beyond the mere expression of a belief even if uttered in missionary activities.

In America the roots of religious liberty can be traced to ROGER WILLIAMS, whose pamphlet, "The Bloudy Tenent of Persecution for cause of Conscience, discussed in a Conference between Truth and Peace," asserted that it was God's command that "a permission of the most Paganish, Jewish, Turkish, or Antichristian consciences and worships, be granted to all men in all Nations and Countries." Another source was THOMAS JEFFERSON's VIRGINIA STATUTE OF RELIGIOUS LIBERTY, adopted in 1786, which declared that no person should be compelled to frequent or support any religious worship nor suffer on account of religious opinions and beliefs.

By the time the First Amendment became part of the Constitution in 1791, practically every state in the Union, to a greater or lesser degree, had enacted constitutional or statutory provisions securing the free exercise of religion. Indeed, it was the absence of a BILL OF RIGHTS whose proponents invariably called for a guarantee of religious freedom, that was the most frequently asserted objection to the Constitution presented to the states for approval. The necessary approval was obtained only because the Constitution's advocates promised that such a bill would be added by amendment after the Constitution was adopted.

Although the First Amendment was framed as a limitation of congressional powers, Supreme Court decisions have made it clear that executive and judicial action were likewise restricted by the amendment. Thus in *Anderson v. Laird* (1971) the Supreme Court refused to review a decision that the secretary of defense violated the First Amendment in requiring cadets in governmental military academies to attend chapel. As to the judiciary, unquestionably a federal court could not constitutionally disqualify a person from testifying as a witness because he was an atheist. (See TORCASO V. WATKINS, 1961.)

Since the Court's decision in *Cantwell* the states are subject to the restrictions of the free exercise clause no less than the federal government. Because our federal system leaves to the states what is generally called the POLICE POWER, there were few occasions, prior to *Cantwell*, when the Supreme Court was called upon to define the meaning of the clause. The few that did arise involved actions in the TERRITORIES, which were subject to federal laws and thus to the First Amendment. Most significant of these was REYNOLDS V. UNITED STATES (1879), wherein the Supreme Court upheld the constitutionality of an act of Congress criminalizing POLYGAMY in any American territory. In rejecting the defense that polygamy was mandated by doctrines of the Holy Church of Latter-Day Saints (Mormons) and thus was protected by the free exercise clause, the Court stated what was later echoed in *Cantwell*, that although laws "cannot interfere with mere religious belief, they may with practice." It could hardly be contended, the Court continued, that the free exercise clause barred prosecution of persons who engaged in human sacrifice as a necessary part of their religious worship.

Since Reynolds was charged with practicing polygamy, the Court's decision did not pass upon the question whether teaching it as a God-mandated duty was "mere religious belief" and therefore beyond governmental interference. In DAVIS V. BEASON (1890) the Court decided that such teaching was "practice," and therefore constitutionally subject to governmental restrictions.

Teaching or preaching, even if deemed action, is however not beyond all First Amendment protection, which encompasses freedom of speech as well as religion. In GITLOW V. NEW YORK (1925) the Supreme Court declared for the first time that the free speech guarantee of the First Amendment was incorporated into the FOURTEENTH AMENDMENT by virtue of the DUE PROCESS clause in the latter and thus was applicable to the states. Accordingly, the Jehovah's Witnesses cases that first came to the Court in the 1930s were initially decided under the speech rather than the religion clause (LOVELL V. GRIFFIN, 1938; *Schneider v. Irvington*, 1939). It was, therefore, natural for the Court to decide the cases under the CLEAR AND PRESENT DANGER test that had first been announced in SCHENCK V. UNITED STATES (1919), a case involving prosecution for speaking against United States involvement in World War I.

In another sense, this too was quite natural since, like Schenck, the Witnesses were pacifists, at least in respect to wars in this world. (In *Sicurella v. United States,* the Court in 1955 ruled that a member of the sect was not disqualified from conscientious objector exemption because the sect's doctrines encompassed participation by believers in serving as soldiers in the Army of Christ Jesus at Armageddon.) Nevertheless, unlike Schenck and other opponents to American entry in World War I, the Witnesses (like the Friends) did not vocally oppose American entry into the war but limited themselves to claiming CONSCIENTIOUS OBJECTION status.

The Court did not apply the clear and present danger test in a case involving a member of the Jehovah's Witnesses whose child was expelled from public school for refusing to participate in the patriotic program of flag salute. In that case, *Minersville School District v. Gobitis* (1940), the Court, in an opinion by Justice FELIX FRANKFURTER, rejected the assertion as a defense of religious freedom. (See FLAG SALUTE CASES.) The antipolygamy law, he stated, was upheld in *Reynolds* not because it concerned action rather than belief, but because it was a valid general law, regulating the secular practice of marriage.

The majority of the Court, however, soon concluded that *Gobitis* had been incorrectly decided, and three years later the Court overruled it in *West Virginia State Board of Education v. Barnette* (1943). There the Court treated the Witnesses' refusal to salute the flag as a form of speech and therefore subject to the clear and present danger test. In later decisions, the Court returned to *Cantwell* and treated religious freedom cases under the free exercise rather than free speech clause, although it continued to apply the clear and present danger test.

Unsatisfied with that test, Justice Frankfurter prevailed upon his colleagues to accept a differently worded rule, that of BALANCING competing interests, also taken from Court decisions relating to other freedoms secured in the Bill of Rights. When a person complains that his constitutional rights have been infringed by some law or action of the state, it is the responsibility of the courts to weigh the importance of the particular right in issue as against the state's interest upon which its law or action is based. For example, the right of an objector not to violate his religious conscience by engaging in war must be weighed against the nation's interest in defending itself against foreign enemies, and, in such weighing, the latter interest may be adjudged the weightier.

The majority of the Court accepted this rule, but in recent years it has added an element that has almost turned it around. Justice Frankfurter believed that a citizen who challenged the constitutionality of state action had the burden of convincing the court that his interest was more important than the state's and should therefore be adjudged paramount. Establishing an individual's right superior to the state's interest was a particularly heavy burden to carry, but it was made even heavier by Justice Frankfurter's insistence that any doubt as to relative weights must be resolved in favor of the state, which would prevail unless its action were patently unreasonable. Recently, however, the Court has taken a more libertarian approach, requiring the state to persuade the courts that the values it seeks to protect are weightier. In the language of the decisions, the state must establish that there is a COMPELLING STATE INTEREST that justifies infringement of the citizen's right to the free exercise of his religion. If it fails to do so, its law or action will be adjudged unconstitutional. (See THOMAS V. REVIEW BOARD OF INDIANA, 1981; UNITED STATES V. LEE, 1982.)

In accord with this rule, the Court, in the 1972 case of WISCONSIN V. YODER, expressly rejected the belief–action test, holding that Amish parents could not be prosecuted for refusing to send their children to school after they had reached the age of fourteen. "Only those interests of the highest order," the Court said, "and those not otherwise served can overbalance the legitimate claim to the free exercise of religion."

Religious liberty is protected not only by the free exercise clause but also by the clause against ESTABLISHMENTS OF RELIGION. In EVERSON V. BOARD OF EDUCATION (1947) and later cases, the Court has stated that under the establishment clause, government cannot force a person to go to church or profess a belief in any religion. In later decisions, the Court has applied a three-pronged purpose–effect–entanglement test as a standard of constitutionality under the establishment clause. The Court has held, in *Committee for Public Education and Religious Liberty v. Nyquist* (1973), for example, that a challenged statute must have a primary effect that neither advances nor inhibits religion, and must avoid government entanglement with religion. (See SEPARATION OF CHURCH AND STATE.)

The Supreme Court's decisions in the arena of conflict between governmental concerns and individuals' claims to religious liberty can be considered in relation to the four categories suggested by the PREAMBLE to the Constitution: national defense, domestic tranquillity, the establishment of justice, and GENERAL WELFARE. In resolving the issues before it in these decisions the Court has spoken in terms of clear and present danger, balancing of competing interests, or determination of compelling governmental interests, depending upon the date of the decision rendered.

Probably no interest of the government is deemed more important than defense against a foreign enemy. Individual liberties secured by the Constitution must yield when the nation's safety is in peril. As the Court ruled in the SELECTIVE DRAFT LAW CASES (1918), the prohibition by the THIRTEENTH AMENDMENT of involuntary servitude was not intended to override the nation's power to conscript an army of—if necessary—unwilling soldiers, without which even the most just and defensive war cannot be waged.

By the same token, exemption of Quakers and others whose religious conscience forbids them to engage in military service cannot be deemed a constitutional right but only a privilege accorded by Congress and thus subject to revocation at any time Congress deems that to be necessary for national defense. However, even in such a case, Congress must exercise its power within the limitations prescribed by the First Amendment's mandate of neutrality among religions and by the EQUAL PROTECTION component of the Fifth Amendment's due process clause. Hence, in exercising its discretion, Congress could not constitutionally prefer some long-standing pacifist religions over others more recently established.

Exemption of specific classes—the newly betrothed, the newly married, the fainthearted, and others—goes back as far as Mosaic times (Deuteronomy 20:1–8). Since all biblical wars were theocratic, there was no such thing as religious exemption. In England, Oliver Cromwell believed that those whose religious doctrine forbade participation in armed conflict should constitute an exempt class. So too did the legislatures in some of the American colonies, the Continental Congress, and a number of the members of the Congress established under the Constitution. Madison's original draft of what became the SECOND AMENDMENT included a provision exempting religious objectors from compulsory militia duty; but that provision was deleted before Congress proposed the amendment to the states. The first national measure exempting conscientious objectors was adopted by Congress during the Civil War; like its colonial and state precedents, it was limited to members of well-recognized religious denominations whose articles of faith forbade the bearing of arms.

The SELECTIVE SERVICE ACT of 1917 exempted members of recognized denominations or sects, such as the Friends, Mennonites, and Seventh-Day Adventists, whose doctrine and discipline declared military service sinful. The 1940 act liberalized the requirements for exemption to encompass anyone who by "reason of religious training and belief" possessed conscientious scruples against "participation in war in any form." In 1948, however, the 1940 act was further amended, first, to exclude those whose objection to war was based on "essentially political, sociological or philosophical views or a mere personal code," and second, to define religion as a belief in a "Supreme Being."

In view of the Court's holding in *Torcaso v. Watkins* (1961) that the Constitution did not sanction preferential treatment of theistic religions over other faiths, limitation of exemption to persons who believe in a "Supreme Being" raised establishment clause issues. In UNITED STATES V. SEEGER (1965) the Court avoided these issues by interpreting the statute to encompass a person who possessed a sincere belief occupying a place in the life of its possessor parallel to that filled by the orthodox belief in God of one who clearly qualified for the exemption. Applying this definition to the three cases before it, the Court held that Selective Service boards had erroneously denied exemption: to one who expressed a "belief in and devotion to goodness and virtues for their own sakes, and a religious faith in a purely ethical creed"; to another who rejected a relationship "vertically towards Godness directly," but was committed to relationship "horizontally towards Godness through Mankind and the World"; and to a third who defined religion as "the supreme expression of human nature," encompassing "man thinking his highest, feeling his deepest, and living his best."

Because exemption of conscientious exemption is of legislative rather than constitutional origin, Congress may condition exemption on possession of belief forbidding participation in all wars, excluding those whose objection is selective and forbids participation only in what they personally deem unjust wars, such as that in Vietnam. The Court sustained such an act of Congress in *Gillette v. United States* (1971). However, independent of any statutory exemption, the Court held in *Thomas* that, at least in peacetime, disqualification of a person from unemployment insurance benefits for conscientious refusal to accept an offered job in a plant that manufactured arms violated the free exercise clause.

Closely related to military service as an aspect of national defense is national unity, cultural as well as political. The relevant constitutional issues reached the Supreme Court in 1923 in three cases involving Lutheran and Reformed schools, and, two years later, in two cases involving a Roman Catholic parochial and a nonsectarian private school. The former cases, reflecting post-World War I hostility to German-speaking Americans, were decided by the Court in MEYER V. NEBRASKA (1923) and two companion cases. These involved the conviction of teachers of German who violated statutes forbidding the teaching of a foreign language to pupils before they had completed eight grades of elementary schooling. The Court, in reversing the convictions, relied not only on the constitutional right of German teachers to pursue a gainful occupation not inherently evil or dangerous to the welfare of the community, but also the right of parents to have their children taught "Martin Luther's language" so that they might better understand "Martin Luther's dogma." The cases were decided long before the Court held that the free exercise clause was incorporated in the Fourteenth Amendment's due process clause and therefore were technically based upon the teachers' due process right to earn a livelihood and the parents' due process right to govern the upbringing of their children.

In PIERCE V. SOCIETY OF SISTERS and its companion case, *Pierce v. Hill Military Academy* (1925), the Court invalidated a compulsory education act that required all children, with limited exceptions, to attend only public schools. A single opinion, governing both cases, relied upon *Meyer v. Nebraska* and based the decision invalidating the law on the due process clause as it related to the school owners' contractual rights and the parents' right to control their children's education, rather than to the free exercise rights of teachers, parents, or pupils. Nevertheless, since the Court's ruling in *Cantwell* that the free exercise clause was applicable to the states, *Pierce* has often been cited by lawyers, scholars, and courts as a free exercise case, and particularly one establishing the constitutional rights of churches to operate parochial schools. Had *Pierce* been decided after *Cantwell* it is probable that free exercise would have been invoked as an additional ground in respect to the Society of Sisters' claim; the opinion as written did note that the child was not the mere creature of the state and that those who nurtured him and directed his destiny had the right, coupled with the high duty, to recognize and prepare him for additional obligations.

Reference has already been made to the Supreme Court's decision in *West Virginia State Board of Education v. Barnette* upholding the First Amendment right of Jehovah's Witnesses public school pupils to refrain from participating in flag salute exercises, although there the Court predicated its decision on the free speech rather than the free exercise mandate of the Amendment.

Jehovah's Witnesses' creed and conduct affected not only national defense through pacifism and alleged failure to pay respect to the flag but also governmental concern with domestic tranquillity. What aggravated hostility to the sect beyond its supposed lack of patriotism were its militant proselytizing methods, encompassing verbal attacks on organized religion in general and Roman Catholicism in particular. In their 1931 convention the Witnesses declared their mission to be "to inform the rulers and the people of and concerning Satan's cruel and oppressive organization, and particularly with reference to Christiandom, which is the most visible part of that visible organization." God's purpose was to destroy Satan's organization and bring quickly "to the obedient peoples of the earth peace and prosperity, liberty and health, happiness and life."

This is hardly new or surprising. Practically every new religion, from Judaism through Christianity and Islam to the present, has been predicated upon attacks against existing faiths; indeed, this is implied in the very term "Protestant." Clearly, those who wrote the First Amendment intended it to encompass attacks upon existing religions. (In BURSTYN V. WILSON, 1952, the Court invalidated a statute banning "sacrilegious" films.) Attacks on existing religions are almost invariably met with counterattacks, physical as well as verbal, by defenders of the accepted faiths.

The assaults upon the Jehovah's Witnesses were particularly widespread and intense for a number of reasons. Their conduct enraged many who felt that their refusal to salute the flag was unpatriotic, if not treasonous. Their attacks upon the Christian religion infuriated many others. The evidence in *Taylor v. Mississippi* (1943), for example, included a pamphlet suggesting that the Roman Catholic Church was responsible for flag saluting. The book *Religion,* by the Witnesses' first leader, Charles T. Russell, described their operations: "God's faithful servants go from house to house to bring the message of the kingdom to those who reside there, omitting none, not even the houses of the Roman Catholic hierarchy, and there they give witness to the kingdom because they are commanded by the Most High to do so. . . . They do not loot nor break into the houses, but they set up their phonographs before the doors and windows and send the message of the kingdom right into the ears of those who might wish to hear; and while those desiring to hear are hearing, some of the 'sourpusses' are compelled to hear."

The predictably resulting resort to violence and to law for the suppression of the Witnesses' activities gave rise to a host of Supreme Court decisions defining for the first time both the breadth and the limitations of the free exercise clause (and also, to some extent, the free speech clause). Most of the Jehovah's Witnesses cases were argued before the Supreme Court by Hayden Covington; his perseverance, as well as that of his client, was manifested by the fact that before *Minersville School District v. Gobitis* was decided, the Court had rejected his appeals in flag salute cases four times. The Court had accepted JURISDICTION in *Gobitis*, as well as its successor, *Barnette*, because, notwithstanding these previous rejections, the lower courts had decided both cases in the Witnesses' favor.

The Witnesses were not the only persons whose aggressive missionary endeavors and verbal attacks upon other faiths led to governmental actions that were challenged as a violation of the free exercise clause and were defended as necessary to secure domestic tranquillity. In KUNZ V. NEW YORK (1951), the Court held that a Baptist preacher could not be denied renewal of a permit for evangelical street meetings because his preachings, scurrilously attacking Roman Catholicism and Judaism, had led to disorder in the streets. The Court said that appropriate public remedies existed to protect the peace and order of the communities if the sermons should result in violence, but it held that these remedies did not include prior restraint under an ordinance that provided no standards for the licensing official.

Jehovah's Witnesses were the major claimants to religious liberty in the two decades between 1935 and 1955. During that period they brought to the Supreme Court a large number of cases challenging the application to them of a variety of laws forbidding disturbing the peace, peddling, the use of SOUND-TRUCKS, as well as traffic regulations, child labor laws, and revenue laws.

In *Cantwell v. Connecticut* (1940) the Court held that the First Amendment guaranteed the right to teach and preach religion in the public streets and parks and to solicit contributions or purchases of religious materials. Although a prior municipal permit might be required, its grant or denial might not be based upon the substance of what is taught, preached, or distributed but only upon the need to regulate, in the interests of traffic control, the time, place, and manner of public meetings. In COX V. NEW HAMPSHIRE (1940) the Court ruled that religious liberty encompassed the right to engage in religious processions, although a fee might be imposed to cover the expenses of administration and maintenance of public order. The Constitution, however, does not immunize from prosecution persons who in their missionary efforts use expressions that are lewd, obscene, libelous,

insulting, or that contain "fighting" words which by their very utterance, the Court declared in CHAPLINSKY V. NEW HAMPSHIRE (1942), inflict injury or tend to incite an immediate breach of the peace. The Constitution also secures the right to distribute religious handbills in streets and at publicly owned railroad or bus terminals, according to the decision in *Jamison v. Texas* (1943), and, according to *Martin v. City of Struthers* (1943), to ring doorbells in order to offer house occupants religious literature although, of course, not to force oneself into the house for that purpose.

Related to the domestic tranquillity aspects of Jehovah's Witnesses claims to use public streets and parks are the claims of other feared or unpopular minority religious groups (often referred to as "sects" or, more recently, "CULTS") to free exercise in publicly owned areas. In HEFFRON V. INTERNATIONAL SOCIETY FOR KRISHNA CONSCIOUSNESS (ISKCON) (1981) the Court held that a state rule limiting to specific booths the sale or distribution of merchandise, including printed material, on public fair grounds did not violate the free exercise clause when applied to members of ISKCON whose ritual required its members to go into all public places to distribute or sell its religious literature and to solicit donations.

Discriminatory treatment, however, is not constitutionally permissible. Thus, in *Cruz v. Beto* (1972) the Supreme Court upheld the claim of a Buddhist prisoner in Texas that his constitutional rights were violated by denying him use of the prison chapel, punishing him for sharing his Buddhist religious materials with other prisoners, and denying him other privileges, such as receiving points for attendance at religious services, which enhanced a prisoner's eligibility for early parole consideration. While a prisoner obviously cannot enjoy the free exercise of religion to the same extent as nonprisoners, the Court said, he is protected by the free exercise clause subject only to the necessities of prison security and discipline, and he may not be discriminated against simply because his religious belief is unorthodox. This does not mean that every sect within a prison, no matter how few in number, must have identical facilities or personnel; but reasonable opportunities must be afforded to all persons to exercise their religion without penalty.

One of the most difficult problems facing a court arises when it is called upon to decide between free exercise and the state's interest in preventing fraud. The leading case on the subject is *United States v. Ballard* (1944), which involved a prosecution for mail fraud. The INDICTMENT charged that the defendants, organizers of the "I Am" cult, had mulcted money from elderly and ill people by falsely representing that they had supernatural powers to heal and that they themselves had communicated personally with Heaven and with Jesus Christ.

The Court held that the free exercise clause would be violated if the state were allowed to seek to prove to a jury that the defendants' representations were false. Neither a jury nor any other organ of government had power to decide whether asserted religious experiences actually occurred. Courts, however, could constitutionally determine whether the defendant himself believed that what he recounted was true, and if a jury determined that he did not, they could convict him of obtaining money under false pretenses. The difficulty with this test, as Justice ROBERT H. JACKSON noted in his dissenting opinion, is that prosecutions in cases such as *Ballard* could easily degenerate into religious persecution; juries would find it difficult to accept as believed that which, by reason of their own religious upbringing, they deemed unbelievable.

In providing for "affirmation" as an alternative to "oath" in Article II, section 1, and Article VI, section 3, the framers of the Constitution, recognizing that religious convictions might forbid some persons (specifically Quakers) to take oaths, manifested their intention that no person in the judicial system—judge, lawyer, court official, or juryman—should be disqualified from governmental service on the ground of religion. In *Torcaso v. Watkins* (1961) the Court reached the same conclusion under the First Amendment as to state officials (for example, notaries public), and in *In re Jenison* (1963), the Court refused to uphold a conviction for contempt of court of a woman who would not serve on a jury because of the biblical command "Judge not that ye not be judged."

Resort to secular courts for resolution of intrachurch disputes (generally involving ownership and control of church assets) raises free exercise as well as establishment problems. As early as 1872 the Court held in *Watson v. Jones* that judicial intervention in such controversies was narrowly limited: a court could do no more than determine and enforce the decision of that body within the church that was the highest judicatory body according to appropriate church law. If a religious group (such as Baptist and Jewish) were congregational in structure, that body would be the majority of the congregation; if it were hierarchical (such as Roman Catholic or Russian Orthodox), the authority would generally be the diocesan bishop.

That principle was applied by the Supreme Court consistently until *Jones v. Wolf* (1979). There the court held that "neutral principles of law developed for use in all property disputes" could constitutionally be applied in church schism litigation. This means that unless the corporate charter or deeds of title provide that the faction loyal to the hierarchical church will retain ownership of the property, such a controversy must be adjudicated in accordance with the laws applicable to corporations generally, so that if recorded title is in the name of the local church, the majority of that body is entitled to control its use and disposition. The Court rejected the assertion in the dissenting opinion that a rule of compulsory deference to the highest ecclesiastical tribunal is necessary in order to protect the free exercise of those who formed the association and submitted themselves to its authority.

Where a conflict exists between the health of the community and the religious conscience of an individual or group, there is little doubt that the free exercise clause does not mandate risk to the community. Thus, as the Court held in JACOBSON V. MASSACHUSETTS (1905), compulsory VACCINATION against communicable diseases is enforceable notwithstanding religious objections to the procedure. So, too, fluoridation of municipal water supplies to prevent tooth cavities cannot be enjoined because of objection by some that drinking fluoridated water is sinful.

Where the life, health, or safety of individuals, rather than communities at large, is involved the constitutional principles are also fairly clear. When the individuals are children, a court may authorize blood transfusions to save their lives notwithstanding objection by parents (such as Jehovah's Witnesses) who believe that the procedure violates the biblical command against the drinking of blood. The underlying principle was stated by the Court in PRINCE V. MASSACHUSETTS (1944) upholding the conviction of a Jehovah's Witness for violating the state's child labor law in allowing her nine-year-old niece to accompany and help her while she sold the sect's religious literature on the city's streets. "Parents," the Court said, "may be free to become martyrs themselves. But it does not follow that they are free, in identical circumstances, to make martyrs of their children before they have reached the age of full and legal discretion when they can make that choice for themselves." It follows from this that unless mental incompetence is proved, a court may not authorize a blood transfusion upon an unconsenting adult.

The Court also balances competing interests in determining the constitutionality of enforcing compulsory Sunday laws against those whom religious conscience forbids labor or trade on the seventh rather than the first day of the week. In McGOWAN V. MARYland and *Two Guys from Harrison-Allentown v. McGinley* (1961) the Court upheld the general validity of such laws against an establishment clause attack. Although their origin may have been religious, the Court said, the laws' present purpose was secular: to assure a weekly day for rest, relaxation, and family companionship.

Two other cases, *Gallagher v. Crown Kosher Super Market* (1961) and *Braunfeld v. Brown* (1961), decided at the same time, involved Orthodox Jews who observed Saturday as their day of rest and refrained from business on that day. In these cases the Court rejected the argument that requiring a Sabbatarian either to abstain from engaging in his trade or business two days weekly or to sacrifice his religious conscience, while requiring his Sunday-observing competitors to abstain only one day, imposed upon the Sabbatarian a competitive disadvantage, thereby penalizing him for his religious beliefs in violation of the free exercise clause. Exempting Sabbatarians, the Court held, might be administratively difficult, might benefit non-Sabbatarians motivated only by a desire for a competitive advantage over merchants closing on Sundays, and might frustrate the legitimate legislative goal of assuring a uniform day of rest. Although state legislatures could constitutionally elect to grant an exemption to Sabbatarians, the free exercise clause does not require them to do so.

In SHERBERT V. VERNER (1963), however, the Court reached a conclusion difficult to reconcile with that in *Gallagher* and *Braunfeld.* Denial of unemployment insurance benefits to a Seventh-Day Adventist who refused to accept tendered employment that required working on Saturday, the Court held, imposed an impermissible burden on the free exercise of religion. The First Amendment, it said, forbids forcing an applicant to choose between following religious precepts and forfeiting government benefits on the one hand, or, on the other, abandoning the precepts by accepting Sabbath work. Governmental imposition of such a choice, the Court said, puts the same kind of burden upon the free exercise of religion as would a fine imposed for Saturday worship.

The Court upheld statutory tax exemptions for church-owned real estate used exclusively for religious purposes in WALZ V. TAX COMMISSION (1970), rejecting an establishment clause attack. In *Murdock v. Pennsylvania* (1943) and *Follett v. Town of McCormack* (1944), however, the Court ruled that under the free exercise clause a revenue-raising tax on the privilege of canvassing or soliciting orders for articles could not be applied to Jehovah's Witnesses who sold their religious literature from door to door; in the same cases, the Court stated that an income tax statute could constitutionally be applied to clergymen's salaries for performing their clerical duties.

In *United States v. Lee* (1982) the Court upheld the exaction of social security and unemployment insurance contributions from Amish employers. The employers argued that their free exercise rights had been violated, citing 1 Timothy 5:8: "But if any provide not . . . for those of his own house, he hath denied the faith, and is worse than an infidel." Compulsory contribution, the Court said, was nonetheless justified; it was essential to accomplish the overriding governmental interest in the effective operation of the social security system.

To sum up, the Supreme Court's decisions in the arena of religious liberty manifest a number of approaches toward defining its meaning, specifically clear and present danger, the balancing of competing interests, and the establishment of a compelling state interest justifying intrusion on free exercise. On the whole, the Court has been loyal to the original intent of the generation that wrote the First Amendment to accord the greatest degree of liberty feasible in our society.

LEO PFEFFER

(SEE ALSO: *Widmar v. Vincent, 1981.*)

Bibliography

GIANELLA, DONALD 1968 Religious Liberty: Non-Establishment and Doctrinal Development: Part I, The Religious Liberty Guarantee. *Harvard Law Review* 80:1381–1431.

HOWE, MARK DEWOLFE 1965 *The Garden and the Wilderness: Religion and Government in American Constitutional History.* Chicago: University of Chicago Press.

KAUPER, PAUL G. 1964 *Religion and the Constitution.* Baton Rouge: Louisiana State University Press.

MANWARING, DAVID R. 1962 *Render unto Caesar: The Flag Salute Controversy.* Chicago: University of Chicago Press.

PFEFFER, LEO (1953) 1967 *Church, State and Freedom.* Boston: Beacon Press.

STOKES, ANSON P. 1950 *Church and State in the United States.* New York: Harper & Brothers.

———— and PFEFFER, LEO 1965 *Church and State in the United States.* New York: Harper & Row.

TRIBE, LAWRENCE H. 1978 *American Constitutional Law.* Mineola, N.Y.: Foundation Press.

RELIGIOUS SCHOOLS

See: Government Aid to Religious Institutions

RELIGIOUS TEST FOR PUBLIC OFFICE

As early as the seventeenth century ROGER WILLIAMS expressed his dissent from the common practice, inherited from England, of imposing a religious test for public office. However, by the beginning of the eighteenth century even Rhode Island had adopted the pattern prevailing among the other colonies and had enacted a law that limited CITIZENSHIP and eligibility for public office to Protestants.

Most liberal of these was Pennsylvania's law, which required a belief that God was "the rewarder of the good and punisher of the wicked." At the other extreme was that of North Carolina, which disqualified from office any one who denied "the being of God or the truth of the Protestant religion, or the divine authority of either the Old or New Testament."

After the Revolutionary War, however, the states began the process of disestablishment, including the elimination of religious tests. The 1786 VIRGINIA STATUTE OF RELIGIOUS LIBERTY, for example, asserted that "our CIVIL RIGHTS have no dependence on our religious opinions," and "the proscribing of any citizen as unworthy of being called to office of trust and emolument, unless he profess or renounce this or that religious opinion, is depriving him injuriously of those privileges and advantages to which in common with his fellow citizens he has a NATURAL RIGHT." The CONSTITUTIONAL CONVENTION OF 1787 unanimously adopted the clause of Article VI providing that "no religious Test shall ever be required as a qualification to any Office or public Trust under the United States."

The prohibition applies only to federal offices, and some states having religious tests in their constitutions or laws did not repeal them but contented themselves with limiting them to belief in the existence of God. One of these was Maryland, where an otherwise fully qualified appointee to the office of notary public was denied his commission for the office for refusing to sign the oath.

In TORCASO V. WATKINS (1961) the Supreme Court ruled the denial unconstitutional, relying upon both the no-establishment and the free exercise clauses of the FIRST AMENDMENT. As to the former, it asserted that the clause does not bar merely preferential treatment of one religion over others (although even such limited interpretation would require invalidation since the oath preferred theistic over nontheistic faiths such as "Buddhism, Taoism, Ethical Culture and Secular Humanism and others") but also preferential treatment of religion as against nonreligion. The opinion also invoked the free exercise clause in concluding that the provision invades "freedom of religion and belief."

The converse of religious tests for public office, reflecting a prevalent anticlericalism, was the disqualification of clergymen from serving in public office. A majority of the states had such provisions when the Constitution was written, but in *McDaniel v. Paty* (1978) the Supreme Court held such laws violative of the First Amendment's free exercise clause.

LEO PFEFFER

Bibliography

PFEFFER, LEO (1953)1967 *Church, State and Freedom.* Boston: Beacon Press.
——— 1975 *God, Caesar and the Constitution.* Boston: Beacon Press.

RELIGIOUS USE OF STATE PROPERTY

In WIDMAR V. VINCENT (1981) the Supreme Court ruled that a state university's exclusionary policy in respect to students' use for prayer or religious instruction of premises generally available to students for nonreligious use violated the FIRST AMENDMENT's guarantee of FREEDOM OF SPEECH.

Earlier, relevant decisions, mostly involving Jehovah's Witnesses, were handed down before the Court ruled in CANTWELL V. CONNECTICUT (1940) that the free exercise of religion clause, like the free speech clause, was applicable to the states no less than to the federal government. Quite naturally, therefore, it applied to religious meetings and conversionary efforts the CLEAR AND PRESENT DANGER (later COMPELLING STATE INTEREST) test formulated in SCHENCK V. UNITED STATES (1919) in respect to political speech and meetings and continued to do so after *Cantwell.*

In *Jamison v. Texas* (1943) the Court rejected a contention that a city's power over streets and parks is not limited to making reasonable regulations for the control of traffic and maintenance of order, but encompasses power absolutely to prohibit use for communication of ideas, including religious ones. No doubt, it ruled in NIEMOTKO V. MARYLAND (1951), a municipality may require a permit to hold religious meetings or, as in *Cox v. New Hampshire* (1941), public parades or processions, in streets and parks, but only to regulate time and place, and it may not refuse a permit by reason of the meeting's content, even if it includes verbal attacks upon some religions. This is so, the Court ruled in KUNZ V. NEW YORK (1941), even where prior missionary meetings had resulted in disorder because of the minister's scurrilous attacks on Roman Catholicism and Judaism, because the added cost of providing police to prevent possible violence does not justify infringement upon First Amendment rights.

Nor, as the Court held in *Schneider v. Irvington* (1939), may a municipality prohibit distribution of leaflets, including religious ones, on public streets and parks in order to prevent littering; the constitutional way to avoid littering is by arresting litterers, rather than restricting rights secured by the amendment. For the same reason, it reversed the conviction of a Jehovah's Witness who rang door bells to distribute religious handbills, in violation of an ordinance (enacted in part to prevent criminal entry) prohibiting ringing of doorbells or knocking on doors to distribute handbills.

The Court, in *Widmar*, did not hold that a state university must provide premises for student prayer and religious instruction, but only that it may not exclude such use if premises are provided for other non-curricular purposes. It is hardly likely that it intended thereby to overrule MCCOLLUM V. BOARD OF EDUCATION (1948), wherein it outlawed religious instruction in public schools even where limited to pupils whose parents consent thereto. The distinction between the two situations lies in the fact that *McCollum* involved students of elementary and secondary school ages, whereas *Widmar* concerned students of college age who are generally less likely to be unduly influenced by on-premises prayer meetings.

In LYNCH V. DONNELLY (1984) the Court upheld the use of municipal funds to finance the cost of erecting and illuminating a life-size nativity scene in Pawtucket, Rhode Island, as part of an annual Christmas display. (Although the display was on private property, the Court made it clear that the result would have been the same had it been on town-owned property.) The Court based its decision on the recognition that Christmas had become a national secular holiday in American culture.

LEO PFEFFER

Bibliography
PFEFFER, LEO 1985 *Religion, State and the Burger Court.* Buffalo, N.Y.: Prometheus.

REMAND

A remand is an appellate court's act in returning a case to a lower court, usually unnecessary when the appellate court affirms the lower court's judgment.

When the Supreme Court reverses or vacates a state court judgment, it customarily remands for "proceedings not inconsistent" with the Court's decision.

KENNETH L. KARST

REMEDIES

See: Constitutional Remedies; Exhaustion of Remedies

REMOVAL OF CASES

When a civil or criminal case within CONCURRENT federal and state JURISDICTION is filed in state court, Congress may choose to offer the parties the right to remove it from state to federal court. Indeed, removal is the only way to provide for ORIGINAL federal JURISDICTION in some cases, such as those in which a FEDERAL QUESTION appears for the first time in the defendant's answer to the complaint. Because federal removal jurisdiction is treated as derivative from state jurisdiction, a suit improperly filed in state court may not be removed.

Congress has employed removal ever since the JUDICIARY ACT OF 1789. The device serves two principal purposes. First, removal can equalize the position of plaintiffs and defendants with respect to choice of forum. For example, federal statutes allow defendants to remove most DIVERSITY JURISDICTION and federal question cases that the plaintiff could have brought initially in federal court. Second, removal can provide access to a more sympathetic federal forum for defendants who are asserting federal rights as defenses. For example, statutes permit federal officers and others acting under federal authority to remove suits brought against them for conduct within the scope of that authority. Another statute authorizes removal of suits by individuals whose rights under federal equal rights laws cannot be enforced in state court. (See CIVIL RIGHTS REMOVAL.)

Federal statutory law provides that if a removable claim is joined in the same suit with a nonremovable claim, the entire suit may be removed if the two claims are "separate and independent." If the nonremovable claim is sufficiently separate to satisfy the statutory requirement, however, it may not be within the federal court's PENDENT or ANCILLARY JURISDICTION. In such cases, the statute resolves the constitutional problem by granting the federal court discretion to remand the nonremovable claim to state court.

CAROLE E. GOLDBERG-AMBROSE

Bibliography

COHEN, W.   1961   Problems in the Removal of a "Separate and Independent Claim or Cause of Action." *Minnesota Law Review* 46:1–41.

REMOVAL POWER (PRESIDENTIAL)

See: Appointing and Removal Power, Presidential

RENDELL-BAKER v. KOHN

See: *Blum v. Yaretsky*

RENDITION

See: Fugitive from Justice; Fugitive Slavery

REPEAL ACT (1894)

See: Civil Rights Repeal Act

REPORTER'S PRIVILEGE

The reporter's privilege issue posed in BRANZBURG V. HAYES (1972) is a microcosm of the difficulties of both journalism and law in accommodating traditional procedures and principles to the development of widespread disenchantment and disobedience in American society. For knowledge about dissident groups we must depend on the efforts of journalists, efforts that will be impeded if the subjects believe that reporters' information will become available to law enforcement agencies. Yet the legal system has important interests in prompt detection and prosecution of crimes. Anglo-American judges have long boasted that no person is too high to escape the obligation of testifying to a GRAND JURY. This obligation is an important guarantee of equality in the operation of criminal law. Thus, courts have historically been unsympathetic to claims that certain kinds of information should be privileged from disclosure before the grand jury. Only the RIGHT AGAINST SELF-INCRIMINATION and the attorney–client privilege have achieved general recognition from American courts.

In *Branzburg,* three cases joined for decision, three reporters had declined to provide requested information to a grand jury. The reporters argued for a special privilege, arguing that compulsory testimony would significantly diminish the flow of information from news sources.

The opinions of a closely divided Supreme Court spanned the spectrum of possible FIRST AMENDMENT responses. Justice BYRON R. WHITE's majority opinion rejected the notion of a journalist's claim of privilege, calling the journalists' fear speculative. Even assuming some constriction in the flow of news, White argued, the public interest in investigating and prosecuting crimes reported to the press outweighs that in the dissemination of news about those activities when the dissemination rests upon confidentiality.

After seemingly rejecting both the theoretical and the empirical arguments for a journalist's privilege, the majority opinion concluded with an enigmatic suggestion that the door to the privilege might not be completely closed. "Newsgathering," the majority noted obliquely, "is not without its First Amendment protection": "[G]rand jury investigations if instituted or conducted other than in good faith, would pose wholly different issues for resolution under the First Amendment. Official harassment of the press undertaken not for purposes of law enforcement but to disrupt a reporter's relationship with his news sources would have no justification."

Moreover, the majority opinion made clear that the subject of reporter's privilege is an appropriate one for legislative or executive consideration. It noted that several states already had passed SHIELD LAWS embodying a journalist's privilege of the kind sought.

In a brief but important concurring opinion, Justice LEWIS F. POWELL emphasized that "we do not hold that . . . state and federal authorities are free to 'annex' the news media as an investigative arm of government." No "harassment" of newsmen will be tolerated, Powell continued, if a reporter can show that the grand jury investigation is "not being conducted in good faith" or if he is called upon for information "bearing only a remote and tenuous relationship to the subject of the investigation." Lower courts have generally followed the Powell approach to claims of reporter's privilege.

Four Justices dissented. For Justice WILLIAM O. DOUGLAS, the First Amendment offered immunity from appearing or testifying before a grand jury unless the reporter were implicated in a crime. Justice POTTER J. STEWART, for himself and Justices WILLIAM J. BRENNAN and THURGOOD MARSHALL, wrote a careful but impassioned dissent. From the right to publish Stewart deduced corollary right to gather news. This right, in turn, required protection of confidential sources. Stewart recognized that the interest of the government in investigating crime could properly outweigh the journalist's privilege if the government could show that the information sought were "clearly relevant to a precisely defined subject of governmental inquiry"; that the reporter probably had the relevant information; and that there were no other available source for the information.

Later decisions have uniformly rejected claims of special privilege for reporters in other factual settings. In ZURCHER V. STANFORD DAILY (1978) the Supreme Court denied that the First Amendment gave any special protection to newsrooms against police searches and seizures. And in HERBERT V. LANDO (1979) the Court rejected a claim that journalists should be privileged not to respond to questions about the editorial processes or their subjective state of mind concerning stories involved in libel actions. Thus the Court has left the question of reporter's privilege to legislative treatment through shield laws and to prosecutorial discretion.

BENNO C. SCHMIDT, JR.

Bibliography

BLASI, VINCENT 1971 The Newsman's Privilege: An Empirical Study. *Michigan Law Review* 70:229.

REPORT OF THE CONFERENCE OF CHIEF JUSTICES ON FEDERAL–STATE RELATIONSHIPS
(August 23, 1958)

By the late 1950s resentment grew among many state officials over the Supreme Court's increasing monitoring of state policies and activities. The Conference of State Chief Justices, with Southerners among the prime movers, issued a long critique of the Supreme Court's rulings, condemning the body's activism, "policy making," and departures from STARE DECISIS. The report chiefly criticized the Court for: increasing national power at the expense of the states through the use of the GENERAL WELFARE CLAUSE, FEDERAL GRANTS-IN-AID, and the doctrine of PREEMPTION; and curtailing state authority in state LEGISLATIVE INVESTIGATIONS, public employment, admission to the bar, and administration of the criminal law. The report called for rebuilding a strong FEDERALISM; the Court's curtailment of its own policymaking; and restoration of the "great principle of distribution of powers among the various branches of government and be-

tween levels of government—the crucial base of our democracy." Court defenders responded by pointing to the need for uniform national constitutional standards, particularly in THE CIVIL RIGHTS area, maintaining the "democracy" of JUDICIAL REVIEW.

PAUL L. MURPHY

Bibliography

PRITCHETT, C. HERMAN 1961 *Congress versus the Supreme Court, 1957–1961.* Minneapolis: University of Minnesota Press.

REPRESENTATION

Representation is standing or acting in the place of another, normally because a group is too large, dispersed, or uninformed for its members to act on their own. It is not necessarily democratic; nor is it necessarily connected to the idea of government by consent. Democratic representation, based on the concept that governmental legitimacy rests on the reasoned assent of individual citizens, dates from the seventeenth century.

This concept has long been taken seriously in the United States. Colonial assemblies won as much domestic legislative power in the fifty years before the American Revolution as Parliament had won in 500, with broader voting constituencies than Parliament's and more conviction that the representatives should speak for their local constituencies rather than for the nation at large. Both this "inner revolution" and the outward break with England asserted a NATURAL RIGHT to government by consent of the governed and treated consent as more than a legal fiction. "No TAXATION WITHOUT REPRESENTATION" was the slogan asserting this right. A guarded commitment to majority rule has helped put the right into practice. As THOMAS JEFFERSON declared in his first inaugural address, "though the will of the majority is in all cases to prevail, that will to be rightful must be reasonable."

The Constitution put certain restraints on majority rule: it banned some acts outright; it divided its majorities by SEPARATION OF POWERS and FEDERALISM; and it permitted an electorate that was restricted mostly to white male landowners. Yet the Constitution was democratic for its day; it has since expanded both the number of elective offices and the franchise; and its very barriers to majority whim, requiring the creation of broad, stable coalitions to rule, have brought about a majority rule stronger and more reasonable than might have evolved from a less fettered regime. JAMES MADISON, explaining and defending the Constitution in THE FEDERALIST, extolled the principle of representation as the device that made majority rule compatible with good government. Representation made possible the extended republic, embracing a large enough territory and population to be safe from foreign aggression and a great enough diversity of economic and other interests to minimize the danger of majority faction. Indirect self-government through a limited number of representatives required coalition-building, with diverse factions compromising their antagonistic goals. Representation also facilitated deliberation: direct democracy (exemplified by the Athenian Assembly) smacked too much of mob rule.

But the Constitution left many questions of representation unsettled. Whom, exactly, do the representatives represent? Does the representative speak for his district, state, or nation? Does he speak only for his supporters and his party, or for opponents, nonvoters, and the unfranchised as well? Does he speak for the whole people or for a coalition of interests? Answers depend on what representation is expected to accomplish and how it is structured.

There has been little agreement in American history about the goals of representation. Some, such as Jefferson and ABRAHAM LINCOLN, have argued that the purpose of the regime is to protect individual rights of liberty and equality. Others, such as JOHN C. CALHOUN, with his doctrine of concurrent majorities, have argued that protection of STATES' RIGHTS or property rights is the basic goal. Still others, such as ALEXANDER HAMILTON and STEPHEN A. DOUGLAS, have emphasized institutional stability and regularity.

Structural variation can drastically affect the quality of representation. A representative can be a symbol, a sample, an agent, or a trustee, elected directly or through intermediaries, individually or jointly accountable to a territorial or an ideological constituency. The American system, with two-party competition for single-member districts, bicameral legislatures, and separate executive branch, has had accessible representatives who speak for their local constituencies (though they are more than agents and are not bound by detailed constituent "instruction") but may be hard to unite on national issues. The British system, combining legislative and executive powers, and with disciplined national parties, has produced representatives who speak for the nation and coalesce easily on national issues but are much less accessible and attentive to district interests than American representatives. Proportional representation, used by several European governments since World War I, usually has MULTIMEMBER DISTRICTS,

with seats divided by proportion of vote for each party. Proportional representation reflects public ideological variety, often with a small party for every view. By focusing on ideological issues, it tends to discourage compromise and produce weak, volatile coalitions, such as those of Weimar Germany and the Fourth French Republic.

American reformers have greatly extended the franchise without greatly changing the structure or working of government. In the Progressive Era, 1880–1920, they also sought to cleanse elections of control by party and financial bosses with "good government" reforms: Australian ballot; PRIMARY ELECTIONS, INITIATIVE, REFERENDUM, and RECALL; nonpartisan civil service; nonpartisan local elections, corrupt practices acts, and weakening of the speaker's control over the House of Representatives. These reforms reduced corruption but also undermined party discipline and lowered voter turnout.

Academic reformers responded to these changes in three different ways. Some called for less separation of powers and more disciplined national parties on the British model. Others wanted to make every office elective, including party, cabinet, and corporate leaders, and to make elections more "representative" with public funding, REAPPORTIONMENT, proportional representation, or quotas. Yet others called for councils of experts to take over problems that elected representatives had failed to solve.

These prescriptions have been partially fulfilled in the adoption of structural change but less so in the delivery of promised results. National power has been enlarged over state, public over private, expert over amateur, and judicial over legislative. Blacks have the right to political equality; legislative districts are equalized; public funding of presidential campaigns has been increased; presidential nomination has been made almost plebiscitary. But these reforms did not still complaints that the system was producing unrepresentative leadership. Reformers deplored most of the candidates in the reformed presidential elections of the 1970s and public turnout sank to new lows. The winning candidate in 1980 and 1984 argued that private consumer sovereignty was the truest form of democracy.

Over the years the Supreme Court, though once reluctant to take sides on POLITICAL QUESTIONS, has become an important player in the game of reform. Chief Justice JOHN MARSHALL first laid down the political question doctrine in OBITER DICTUM in MARBURY V. MADISON (1803), forbearing to "intermeddle with the prerogatives of the executive." "Questions, in their nature political," he wrote, "can never be made in this court." Chief Justice ROGER B. TANEY, in LUTHER V. BORDEN (1849), declared that the republican or representative character of state domestic government was "political in its nature" and reserved by judicial prudence—and perhaps also by constitutional mandate under the GUARANTEE CLAUSE—for resolution by the "political branches, not the judiciary." The Dorr controversy in *Luther* involved many of the same issues as BAKER V. CARR (1962), but the Court lacked the political strength, the appearance of constitutional authority, and the enforcement technique to intervene effectively.

Against the disfranchisement of blacks, prohibited on paper after 1870 by the FIFTEENTH AMENDMENT, the Court provided no lasting protection until 1944, when it ended the white primary—although it had intervened against some administrative abuses and would later intervene aggressively against franchise restrictions under both the Fourteenth and Fifteenth Amendments. Almost all other state representation questions—validity of delegations of authority, of legislative enactments, of party nomination decisions, and of initiatives and referenda—the Court found nonjusticiable.

The Court's list of nonjusticiable political questions appeared to include unequal or "malapportioned" electoral districts, especially after COLEGROVE V. GREEN (1946). But in *Baker v. Carr*, over objections from Justices FELIX FRANKFURTER and JOHN MARSHALL HARLAN that the Court was entering a "quagmire" of insoluble questions, the majority held that apportionment was not a political question and was "within the reach of judicial protection under the FOURTEENTH AMENDMENT." In REYNOLDS V. SIMS (1964), the Court proclaimed that "ONE PERSON, ONE VOTE" is the "fundamental principle" of the Constitution, applicable to both houses of state legislatures and to local and special-purpose elections—even if most of the voters involved opposed it. The principle does not, however, apply to the United States Senate, the ELECTORAL COLLEGE, or most aspects of party organization. Nor does it seem to apply to the manipulation of effective votes through gerrymandering (see GERRYMANDER) and multimember districting unless these are surgically exclusive of a protectable minority, as in GOMILLION V. LIGHTFOOT (1960). *Gomillion* invalidated a law excluding from the city limits of Tuskegee, Alabama, all but four or five black voters while keeping every white voter. In a series of cases beginning with *Wright v. Rockefeller* (1965) and highlighted by UNITED JEWISH ORGANIZATIONS V. CAREY (1977) and MOBILE V. BOLDEN (1980), the Court has repeatedly refused to interfere with nonsurgical dis-

tricting to the obvious disadvantage of racial or religious minorities who as individuals would have been eminently protectable against franchise discrimination. The difference between districting discrimination against groups and franchise discrimination against individuals is that franchise discrimination is easy to remedy, but districting discrimination is not. Courts have equalized nominal votes by equal apportionment but not effective votes—votes that actually elect the voter's candidate—because there is no way short of proportional representation to equalize every group's effective vote.

Besides holding apportionment justiciable, the reapportionment cases did something more radical: they treated districting discrimination and franchise discrimination as if they were virtually interchangeable, and they invoked the EQUAL PROTECTION clause of the Fourteenth Amendment to protect a "right to vote" against "dilution" by unequal districts. But the framers of the Fourteenth Amendment had insisted that it left suffrage "exclusively under the control of the states"; construing it to grant a federal right to vote would seem to render at least five subsequent voting rights amendments, including section 2 of the Fourteenth Amendment, superfluous. This "parthenogenesis of a VOTING RIGHT," combined with an aggressive application of STRICT SCRUTINY, led to the judicial abolition of POLL TAX, property, and taxpayer qualifications on voting, and all but the shortest RESIDENCY REQUIREMENTS. It also cleared the way for the passage of the VOTING RIGHTS ACT of 1965 and, paradoxically, gave a boost to the TWENTY-SIXTH AMENDMENT (eighteen-year-old vote)—and, possibly, to the proposed DISTRICT OF COLUMBIA REPRESENTATION AMENDMENT.

These voting rights decisions substantially aided the "inclusion process" in a formal sense. Some critics feel that this aid was a desirable end in itself; others argue that, by overriding the choices of elected representatives and creating constitutional authority *ex nihilo*, the Court has debased the vote in substance more than it has enlarged it in form. As the nation enters its third century under the Constitution, the inclusion process has been judicialized but hardly completed—and the same may be said of the ancient debate over political representation.

WARD E. Y. ELLIOTT

Bibliography

ELLIOTT, WARD E. Y. 1975 *The Rise of Guardian Democracy: The Supreme Court's Role in Voting Rights Disputes, 1845–1969.* Cambridge, Mass.: Harvard University Press.

REPRODUCTIVE AUTONOMY

Commencing in 1942 in SKINNER V. OKLAHOMA, and most intrepidly in 1973 in ROE V. WADE, the Supreme Court has secured against unwarranted governmental intrusion a decision fundamental to the course of an individual's life—the decision whether to beget or bear a child. Government action in this area bears significantly on the ability of women, particularly, to plan and control their lives. Official policy on reproductive choice may effectively facilitate or retard women's opportunities to participate in full partnership with men in the nation's social, political, and economic life. Supreme Court decisions concerning BIRTH CONTROL, however, have not yet adverted to evolving sex equality-equal protection doctrine. Instead, high court opinions rest dominantly on SUBSTANTIVE DUE PROCESS analysis; they invoke basic liberty-autonomy values difficult to tie directly to the Constitution's text, history, or structure.

Skinner marked the first occasion on which the Court referred to an individual's procreative choice as "a basic liberty." The Court invalidated a state statute providing for compulsory STERILIZATION of habitual offenders. The statute applied after a third conviction for a FELONY "involving moral turpitude," defined to include grand larceny but exclude embezzlement. The decision ultimately rested on an EQUAL PROTECTION ground: "Sterilization of those who have thrice committed grand larceny, with immunity for those who are embezzlers, is a clear, pointed, unmistakable discrimination." Justice WILLIAM O. DOUGLAS's opinion for the Court, however, is infused with substantive due process tones: "We are dealing here with legislation which involves one of the basic CIVIL RIGHTS of man. Marriage and procreation are fundamental to the very existence and survival of the race." Gerald Gunther has noted that, in a period marked by a judicial hands-off approach to economic and social legislation, *Skinner* stood virtually alone in applying a stringent review standard favoring a "basic liberty" unconnected to a particular constitutional guarantee.

Over two decades later, in GRISWOLD V. CONNECTICUT (1965), the Court grappled with a state law banning the use of contraceptives. The Court condemned the statute's application to married persons. Justice Douglas's opinion for the Court located protected "zones of privacy" in the penumbras of several specific BILL OF RIGHTS guarantees. The law in question impermissibly intruded on the marriage relationship, a privacy zone "older than the Bill of Rights" and "intimate to the degree of being sacred."

In EISENSTADT V. BAIRD (1972) the Court confronted a Massachusetts law prohibiting the distribution of contraceptives, except by a registered pharmacist on a doctor's prescription to a married person. The Court avoided explicitly extending the right announced in *Griswold* beyond use to distribution. Writing for the majority, Justice WILLIAM J. BRENNAN rested the decision on an equal protection ground: "whatever the rights of the individual to access to contraceptives may be," the Court said, "the right must be the same for the unmarried and the married alike." *Eisenstadt* thus carried constitutional doctrine a considerable distance from "the sacred precincts of marital bedrooms" featured in *Griswold.*

The Court's reasoning in *Eisenstadt* did not imply that laws prohibiting fornication, because they treat married and unmarried persons dissimilarly, were in immediate jeopardy. Rather, Justice Brennan declined to attribute to Massachusetts the base purpose of "prescrib[ing] pregnancy and the birth of an unwanted child as punishment for fornication."

In 1977, in CAREY V. POPULATION SERVICES INTERNATIONAL, the Court invalidated a New York law prohibiting the sale of contraceptives to minors under age sixteen and forbidding commercial distribution of even nonprescription contraceptives by anyone other than a licensed pharmacist. Justice Brennan reinterpreted the pathmarking precedent. *Griswold,* he noted, addressed a "particularly 'repulsive' " intrusion, but "subsequent decisions have made clear that the constitutional protection of individual autonomy in matters of childbearing is not dependent on [the marital privacy] element." Accordingly, "*Griswold* may no longer be read as holding only that a State may not prohibit a married couple's use of contraceptives. Read in light of [*Eisenstadt* and *Roe v. Wade*], the teaching of *Griswold* is that the Constitution protects individual decisions in matters of childbearing from unjustified intrusion by the State."

Roe v. Wade declared that a woman, guided by the medical judgment of her physician, has a FUNDAMENTAL RIGHT to abort her pregnancy, a right subject to state interference only upon demonstration of a COMPELLING STATE INTEREST. The right so recognized, Justice HARRY L. BLACKMUN wrote for the Court, falls within the sphere of personal privacy recognized or suggested in prior decisions relating to marriage, procreation, contraception, family relationships, child-rearing and education. The "privacy" or individual autonomy right advanced in *Roe v. Wade* is not explicit in our fundamental instrument of government, Justice Blackmun acknowledged; however, the Court viewed it as "founded in the FOURTEENTH AMENDMENT's [and presumably the FIFTH AMEND-

MENT's] concept of personal liberty and restrictions upon state action." Justice Blackmun mentioned, too, the district court's view, derived from Justice ARTHUR J. GOLDBERG's concurring opinion in *Griswold*, that the liberty at stake could be located in the NINTH AMENDMENT's reservation of rights to the people.

The Texas criminal abortion law at issue in ROE V. WADE was severely restrictive; it excepted from criminality "only a *lifesaving* procedure on behalf of the mother, without regard to pregnancy stage and without recognition of the other interests involved." In the several years immediately preceding the *Roe v. Wade* decision, the Court noted, the trend in the states had been "toward liberalization of abortion statutes." Nonetheless, the Court's rulings in *Roe v. Wade* and in a companion case decided the same day, *Doe v. Bolton* (1973), called into question the validity of the criminal abortion statutes of every state, even those with the least restrictive provisions.

The sweeping impact of the 1973 rulings on state laws resulted from the precision with which Justice Blackmun defined the state interests that the Court would recognize as compelling. In the first two trimesters of a pregnancy, the state's interest was confined to protecting the woman's health: during the first trimester, "the abortion decision and its effectuation must be left to the medical judgment of the pregnant woman's attending physician"; in the next three-month stage, the state may, if it chooses, require other measures protective of the woman's health. During "the stage subsequent to viability" (roughly, the third trimester), the state may protect the "potentiality of human life"; at that stage, the state "may, if it chooses, regulate, and even proscribe, abortion except where it is necessary, in appropriate medical judgment, for the preservation of the life or health of the mother."

Sylvia Law has commented that no Supreme Court decision has meant more to women. Wendy Williams has noted that a society intent on holding women in their traditional role would attempt to deny them reproductive autonomy. Justice Blackmun's opinion indicates sensitivity to the severe burdens, mental and physical, immediately carried by a woman unable to terminate an unwanted pregnancy, and the distressful life she and others in her household may suffer when she lacks the physical or psychological ability or financial resources necessary for child-rearing. But *Roe v. Wade* bypassed the equal protection argument presented for the female plaintiffs. Instead, the Court anchored stringent review to the personal autonomy concept found in *Griswold*. Moreover, *Roe v. Wade* did not declare an individual right; in the Court's words, the decision stated a joint right of "the woman

and her responsible physician . . . in consultation."

The 1973 abortion rulings have been called aberrational, extraordinarily activist interventions by a Court reputedly deferential to STATES' RIGHTS and legislative judgments. John Hart Ely criticized *Roe v. Wade* as a decision the Court had no business making because freedom to have an abortion "lacks connection with any value the Constitution marks as special."

Archibald Cox described his own view of *Roe v. Wade* as "less rigid" then Ely's. He said in a 1975 lecture: "The Court's persistent resort to notions of substantive due process for almost a century attests the strength of our natural law inheritance in constitutional adjudication." Cox considered it "unwise as well as hopeless to resist" that strong tradition. *Roe v. Wade* nevertheless foundered, in his judgment, because the Court did not (and, he believed, could not) articulate an acceptable "precept of sufficient abstractness." The critical parts of the opinion, he commented, "read like a set of hospital rules and regulations."

Paul Freund expressed a similar concern in 1982. He thought *Roe v. Wade* epitomized a tendency of the modern Supreme Court (under Chief Justice WARREN E. BURGER as well as Chief Justice EARL WARREN) "to specify by a kind of legislative code the one alternative pattern which will satisfy the Constitution, foreclosing further experimentation by Congress or the states." In his view, "a law which absolutely made criminal all kinds and forms of abortion could not stand up; it is not a reasonable accommodation of interests." But the Court "adopted what could be called the medical point of view—making distinctions that turn on trimesters." The Court might have drawn other lines, Freund suggested; it might have adopted an ethical rather than a medical approach, for example, by immunizing abortions, in a manner resembling the American Law Institute proposal, "where the pregnancy was the result of rape or incest, where the fetus was severely abnormal, or where the mother's health, physical or mental, would be seriously impaired by bringing the fetus to term." (The Georgia statutes struck down in *Doe v. Bolton,* companion case to *Roe v. Wade,* were patterned on the American Law Institute's model.) If the Court had proceeded that way, Freund commented, perhaps "some of the bitter debate on the issue might . . . have been averted; at any rate the animus against the Court might have been diverted to the legislative halls."

Animus there has been, in the form of anti-abortion constitutional amendments introduced in Congress in 1973 and each session thereafter; proposals for "human life" legislation, in which Congress, upon the vote of a simple majority, would declare that the Fourteenth Amendment protects the life of "persons" from the moment of conception; and bills to strip the Supreme Court of JURISDICTION to decide abortion cases. State legislatures reacted as well, adopting measures aimed at minimizing the impact of the 1973 ruling, including notice and consent requirements, prescriptions for the protection of fetal life, and bans on public expenditures or access to public facilities for abortion.

Some speculated that the 7–2 judgments in the 1973 cases (Justices BYRON R. WHITE and WILLIAM H. REHNQUIST dissented) were motivated in part by population concerns and the specter of unwanted children born to women living in grinding poverty. But in 1977, the Court voted 6–3 against pleas to extend the 1973 rulings to require public assistance for an indigent woman's elective (not medically necessary) abortion. First, in *Beal v. Doe*, the Court held that the federally established Medicaid program did not require Pennsylvania, as a condition of participation, to fund elective abortions. Second, in MAHER V. ROE the Court ruled that the equal protection clause did not command Connecticut, which furnished Medicaid funds for childbirth, to pay as well for elective abortions. Finally, *Poelker v. Doe* held that the city of St. Louis did not violate the equal protection clause by providing publicly financed hospital services for childbirth but not for elective abortions.

The impoverished Connecticut women who sought Medicaid assistance in *Maher* maintained that, so long as their state subsidized childbirth, it could not withhold subsidy for abortion, a far less expensive and, at least in the first trimester, less risky procedure. Stringent equal protection review was required, they urged, because the state had intruded on the "fundamental right" declared in *Roe v. Wade*. Justice LEWIS F. POWELL, writing for the Court, responded that the right recognized in *Roe* did not require government neutrality as to the abortion decision; it was not a right to make a choice unchecked by substantive government control. Rather, it was a right restraining government from obstructing a woman's access to private sources to effectuate her decision. Because the right *Roe v. Wade* secured, as explained in *Maher*, was not impinged upon (and because disadvantageous treatment of needy persons does not alone identify SUSPECT CLASSIFICATION requiring close scrutiny), Connecticut's funding refusal could be sustained if it related "rationally" to a "constitutionally permissible" purpose. The policies to encourage childbirth in preference to abortion and to protect potential life

supported the *Maher* regulation. There was, in the Court's view, no issue here, as there had been in *Roe v. Wade*, of an attempt "to impose [the state's] will by force of law."

Although criticized as irrational in the reproductive choice context, the distinction Justice Powell drew between government carrot and government stick had been made previously in other settings. But in *Maher*, unlike other cases in which the carrot/stick distinction had figured, the state could not justify its funding bar as an attempt to conserve public funds. In comparison to the medical costs of childbirth and the subsequent costs of child-rearing borne by public welfare programs, the costs of elective abortions are insubstantial.

The *Maher* logic was carried further in HARRIS V. MCRAE (1980). The federal law at issue, known as the HYDE AMENDMENT, excluded even therapeutic (medically needed) abortions from the Medicaid program. In holding, 5–4, that the Hyde Amendment survived constitutional review, the Court reiterated the distinction drawn in *Maher*. Justice JOHN PAUL STEVENS, who had joined the majority in *Maher*, switched sides in *McRae* because he discerned a critical difference between elective and therapeutic abortions in the context of the Medicaid program. Congress had established two neutral criteria for Medicaid benefits—financial need and medical need. The pregnant women who challenged the Hyde Amendment met both criteria. By creating an exception to the medical need criterion for the sole purpose of deterring exercise of the right declared "fundamental" in *Roe v. Wade*, Justice Stevens reasoned, the sovereign had violated its "duty to govern impartially."

Following the bold step in the 1973 abortion rulings, the public funding rulings appear incongruous. The direct, practical effect of the funding rulings will not endure, however, if the legislative trend again turns in the direction discernible at the time of the *Roe v. Wade* decision. National and state legislators may come to question the wisdom of a childbirth-encouragement policy trained on Medicaid-eligible women, and to comprehend more completely the centrality of reproductive autonomy to a woman's control of her life's course.

May the state require spousal consent to the abortion decision of a woman and her physician when the state itself may not override that decision? In PLANNED PARENTHOOD V. DANFORTH (1976) the Court held unconstitutional Missouri's requirement of spousal consent to a first-trimester abortion. Justice Blackmun, for the six-member majority, declared that the state may not delegate authority to any person, even a spouse, to veto abortions which the state may not proscribe or regulate. A husband, of course, has a vital interest in his wife's pregnancy, Justice Blackmun acknowledged. But the woman's stake is more compelling; therefore the final decision must rest with her.

Although government may not remove the abortion decision from the woman and her physician unless its action demonstrably serves a compelling interest in the woman's health or in potential life, a state may act to ensure the quality of the decision. In *Danforth* the Court unanimously upheld Missouri's requirement that, prior to a first-trimester abortion, a woman certify that she has given her informed, uncoerced consent. The abortion decision is stressful, the Court observed; it should be made with "full knowledge of its nature and consequences." A state's authority in this regard, however, is limited. Regulations must be genuinely necessary to secure enlightened consent; they must be designed to inform rather than persuade; and they must not interfere with the physician's counseling discretion.

In *Akron v. Akron Center for Reproductive Health* (1983) the Court, 6–3, speaking through Justice Powell, struck down a series of regulations that exceeded these limits. One regulation required the physician to tell any woman contemplating an abortion that the unborn child is a human life from conception; to tell her the details of the anatomical characteristics of the fetus; and to enumerate the physical and psychological risks of abortion. The Court held this regulation invalid because it was designed to persuade women to forgo abortions, and because it encroached upon the physician's discretion to decide how best to advise the patient. The Court also invalidated as unnecessary to secure informed, uncoerced consent a twenty-four-hour waiting period between consent and abortion and a requirement that the physician personally convey information to the woman.

The Court has not yet had occasion to pass upon a regulation designed to render the birth-control-through-contraception decision an informed one. In *Bolger v. Youngs Drug Product Corporation* (1983), however, a majority held that government may not block dissemination of information relevant to that decision. At issue was a federal statute (the Comstock Act) prohibiting the mailing of contraceptive advertisements. All eight participating Justices held the statute unconstitutional as applied to the promotional and informational literature in question because the legislation impermissibly regulated COMMERCIAL SPEECH. (Earlier, in *Carey,* the Court had invalidated an analogous state regulation on the same ground.) Five Jus-

tices joined in a further ruling that the federal statute violated the right to reproductive autonomy because it denied adults truthful information relevant to informed contraception decisions.

The trimester scheme established in *Roe v. Wade* has guided the Court's ruling on state regulation of abortion procedures. Under that scheme, the state may not interfere with a physician's medical judgment concerning the place and manner of first-trimester abortions because abortions performed at that stage are less risky than childbirth. Thus in *Doe v. Bolton* (1973), the companion case to *Roe v. Wade,* the Court invalidated a Georgia requirement that even first-trimester abortions be performed in a full-service hospital. In *Connecticut v. Menillo* (1975), however, the Court, per curiam, explicitly relied upon one of the underpinnings of *Roe v. Wade,* the need for a physician's medical judgment, to uphold a state's conviction of a nonphysician for performing an abortion.

The ban on state regulation of a physician's performance of first-trimester abortions is not absolute; it does not exclude regulation serving an important state health interest without significantly affecting the abortion decision. A unanimous bench in *Danforth* so indicated in upholding a Missouri regulation requiring maintenance of records of all abortions, for disclosure only to public health officials, for seven years.

Roe v. Wade declared that after the first trimester, because an abortion entails greater risks, the state's interest in women's health could justify "place and manner" regulations even if the abortion decision itself might be affected. However, the Court has attentively scrutinized procedural regulations applicable after the first trimester to determine whether, in fact, they are reasonably related to the protection of the patient's health in light of current medical knowledge. Several regulations have failed to survive the court's scrutiny. In *Doe v. Bolton,* for example, the Court struck down Georgia's requirement that a hospital committee and two doctors, in addition to the woman's physician, concur in the abortion decision. And in *Danforth,* the Court struck down a Missouri ban on use, after the first trimester, of saline amniocentesis, then the most widely used second-trimester abortion procedure. Justice Blackmun, for the majority, observed that although safer procedures existed, they were not generally available. Consequently, the regulation in practice would either require the use of more dangerous techniques or compel women to forgo abortions.

The Court had three 1983 encounters with regulations alleged to connect sufficiently with a women's health: *Akron, Planned Parenthood Association v. Ashcroft,* and *Simopoulos v. Virginia.* In *Akron* and *Ashcroft,* the Court invalidated regulations requiring that abortions, after the first trimester, be performed in licensed acute-care hospitals. Justice Powell, for the majority, said that although current medical knowledge justified this requirement during much of the relevant period, it was unnecessary during the first four weeks of the second trimester; medical advances had rendered abortions safe at that stage even when performed in less elaborate facilities. The hospital requirement significantly burdened a woman's access to an abortion by raising costs substantially; therefore it must be tied more precisely to the period in which it was necessary. In *Simopoulos,* on the other hand, the Court upheld the limitation of second-trimester abortions to licensed facilities (including nonacute care facilities licensed to perform abortions during the first four to six weeks of the second trimester).

These three decisions indicate the Court's readiness to test specific second-trimester regulations that increase the cost of abortions against advances in medical technology. However, the majority in *Akron,* although aware that medical advances had rendered early second-trimester abortions safer than childbirth, explicitly refused to extend beyond the first trimester an across-the-board proscription of burdensome "place and manner" regulations.

Only in the last stage of pregnancy, after viability, does the state's interest in potential life become sufficiently compelling to allow the state to forbid all abortions except those necessary to preserve the woman's health. The point at which viability occurs is a medical judgment, the Court said in *Roe v. Wade, Danforth,* and *Colautti v. Franklin* (1979); the state may not establish a fixed measure of that point after which nontherapeutic abortions are illegal.

When postviability abortions occur, may the state impose manner requirements in the interest of preserving a viable fetus? The answer appears to be yes, if the regulations are not overbroad. In *Danforth* the Court invalidated a regulation requiring the physician to exercise due care to preserve the fetus; the regulation was not limited to postviability abortions. In *Ashcroft,* however, a 5–4 majority sustained a law requiring a second physician to attend a postviability abortion and attempt to preserve the life of the fetus. Even the dissenters agreed that such a regulation could stand if trimmed; they objected to Missouri's regulation because it required a second physician even at abortions using techniques that eliminated any possibility of fetal survival.

Dissenting in *Akron,* Justice SANDRA DAY O'CONNOR, joined by Justices White and Rehnquist, strongly criticized the Court's trimester approach to the regulation of abortion procedures. *Roe v. Wade's* medical model, she maintained, had been revealed as unworkable in subsequent cases. Advances in medical technology would continue to move forward the point during pregnancy when regulation could be justified as protective of a woman's health, and to move backward the point of viability, when the state could forbid abortions unless they were necessary to preserve the patient's life or health. The *Roe v. Wade* framework thus impelled legislatures to adjust their laws to changing medical practices, and called upon courts to examine legislative judgments, not as jurists applying "neutral principles" but as "science review boards."

More fundamentally, Justice O'Connor disapproved the interest balancing exhibited by the Court in the 1973 decisions. Throughout pregnancy, she said, the state has "compelling interests in the protection of potential human life and in maternal health." (In *Beal* the Court had said that the state does have an interest in potential life throughout a pregnancy, but that the interest becomes *compelling* only in the postviability stage.) Justice O'Connor's analysis, it appears, would permit from the beginning of pregnancy the regulation *Roe v. Wade* permits only in the final trimester: state proscription of abortion except to preserve a woman's health.

Vagueness doctrine has occasionally figured in the Court's review of state regulation of abortion procedures. In *Colautti,* the Court invalidated as too vague to supply adequate notice a statute attaching a criminal sanction to a physician's failure to exercise due care to preserve a fetus when there is "sufficient reason to believe that the fetus may be viable." And in *Akron,* a vagueness handle was employed to strike down a provision mandating the sanitary and "humane" disposal of aborted fetuses.

Minors have constitutional rights, but state authority over CHILDREN'S RIGHTS is greater than over adults'; the state may protect minors because of their immaturity and "peculiar vulnerability," and in recognition of "the importance of the parental role in child rearing." Justice Powell so observed in his plurality opinion in *Bellotti v. Baird* (1979), and no Justice has disagreed with these general statements. In concrete cases concerning the reproductive autonomy of minors, however, the Court has been splintered.

In *Danforth,* the Court invalidated, 5–4, a law requiring a parent's consent for most abortions performed on unmarried women under the age of eighteen. The majority did not foreclose a parental consent requirement for minors unable to make the abortion decision in an informed, mature manner.

The Court "continue[d] the inquiry" in *Bellotti*. Massachusetts required unmarried minors to obtain the consent of both parents or, failing that, the authorization of a state judge "for good cause shown." The Court voted 8–1 to invalidate the law, but split 4–4 on the rationale. Justice Stevens, writing for four Justices, thought the case governed by *Danforth*. Justice Powell, writing for four other Justices, attempted to provide guidance for state legislators. The abortion decision is unique among decisions facing a minor, he observed; it cannot be postponed until attainment of majority, and if the fetus is carried to term, the new mother will immediately face adult responsibilities. A blanket requirement of parental consent, using age as a proxy for maturity, was too sweeping. Yet the state's interest in ensuring the quality of a minor's abortion decision and in encouraging family participation in that decision would justify a law requiring either parental consent or the determination of an independent decision maker that abortion is in the minor's best interest, or that she is mature enough to decide for herself.

Justice Powell's *Bellotti* framework, although by 1983 only a two-member view, became, in *Akron* and *Ashcroft*, the de facto standard governing consent statutes. In *Ashcroft*, the Court upheld, 5–4, a statute conditioning a minor's abortion on either parental consent or a juvenile court order. Justice Powell and Chief Justice Burger voted to uphold the provision because, as indicated in *Bellotti*, the juvenile court must authorize an abortion upon finding that the abortion is in the minor's best interest or that the minor is mature enough to make her own decision. Three other Justices viewed the consent requirement as imposing "no undue burden on any right that a minor [arguably] may have to undergo an abortion." Four Justices dissented because the statute permitted an absolute veto, by parent or judge, "over the decision of the physician and his patient."

In *Akron*, however, the Court struck down, 6–3, an ordinance requiring all minors under age fifteen to have either parental or judicial consent. Because *Akron* failed to provide explicitly for a judicial determination of the minor's maturity, Justice Powell and the Chief Justice joined the four *Ashcroft* dissenters in condemning the consent provision.

With respect to contraception, no clear statement has emerged from the Court on the extent of state and parental authority over minors. In *Carey* the Court, 7–2, struck down a ban on the distribution of contraceptives to persons under age sixteen. The state sought to justify the measure as a means of deterring sexual activity by minors. There was no majority decision, but six Justices recognized that banning birth control would not in fact deter sexual activity.

May the state require parental consent to the minor's use of contraceptives? At least five Justices, it appears from the *Carey* decision, would state unequivocally that minors have no right to engage in sexual activity in face of disapproval of the state and of their parents. But it is hardly apparent that any minor-protective interest supports stopping the young from effectuating a decision to use nonhazardous contraceptives when, despite the views or commands of the state and their parents, they do engage in sexual activity.

Arguably, such a provision would serve to preserve parental authority over a decision many people consider a moral one. *Danforth* indicated that this end is insufficient to justify requiring parental consent for an abortion. Yet, as Justice Powell's *Bellotti* opinion illustrates, at least some Justices consider the abortion decision unique. Perhaps the issue will remain undecided. For practical reasons, lawmakers may be deterred from conditioning a minor's access to contraceptives on parental consent or notification. Many minors whose parents would wish them to use birth control if they engaged in sexual activity would nevertheless fail to seek parental consent for fear of disclosing their sexual activities. As five Justices indicated in *Carey*, deliberate state policy exposing minors to the risk of unwanted pregnancies is of questionable rationality.

In *Akron*, which came to the Court a decade after *Roe v. Wade*, Justice Powell acknowledged the continuing argument that the Court "erred in interpreting the Constitution." Nevertheless, *Akron* commenced with a reaffirmation of the 1973 precedent. As *Akron* itself illustrates, the Court typically has applied *Roe v. Wade* to restrict state efforts to impede privately financed access to contraceptives and abortions.

It appears safe to predict continued "adher[ence] to STARE DECISIS in applying the principles of *Roe v. Wade*." But other issues remain beyond the zone of secure prediction. Current opinions do not indicate whether the Court eventually will relate its reproductive autonomy decisions to evolving law on the equal status of men and women. Nor can one forecast reliably how science and population will influence the next decades' legislative and judicial decisions in this area.

The development of a safe, efficient, inexpensive

morning-after pill, for example, may alter the reproductive autonomy debate by further blurring distinctions between contraceptives and abortifacients, and by sharply reducing occasions for resort to clinical procedures. A development of this order may diminish in incidence and detail both legislative activity and constitutional review of the kind sparked in the decade following *Roe v. Wade.* Moreover, it is at least possible that a different question will confront the Court by the turn of the century: If population size becomes a larger governmental concern, legislators may change course, and measures designed to limit childbirth may become the focus of constitutional controversy.

RUTH BADER GINSBURG

Bibliography

BREST, PAUL 1981 The Fundamental Rights Controversy: The Essential Contradictions of Normative Constitutional Scholarship. *Yale Law Journal* 90:1063–1112.

BYRN, ROBERT 1973 An American Tragedy: The Supreme Court on Abortion. *Fordham Law Review* 41:807–862.

COX, ARCHIBALD 1976 *The Role of the Supreme Court in American Government.* New York: Oxford University Press.

DEMBITZ, NANETTE 1980 The Supreme Court and a Minor's Abortion Decision. *Columbia Law Review* 80:1251–1263.

DESTRO, ROBERT 1975 Abortion and the Constitution: The Need for a Life Protective Amendment. *California Law Review* 63:1250–1351.

ELY, JOHN HART 1973 The Wages of Crying Wolf: A Comment on *Roe v. Wade. Yale Law Journal* 82:920–949.

ESTREICHER, SAMUEL 1982 Congressional Power and Constitutional Rights: Reflections on Proposed "Human Life" Legislation. *Virginia Law Review* 68:333–458.

FREUND, PAUL 1983 Storms over the Supreme Court. *American Bar Association Journal* 69:1474–1480.

HEYMANN, PHILIP and BARZELAY, DOUGLAS 1973 The Forest and the Trees: *Roe v. Wade* and its Critics. *Boston University Law Review* 53:765–784.

LAW, SYLVIA 1984 Rethinking Sex and the Constitution. *University of Pennsylvania Law Review* 132:955–1040.

PERRY, MICHAEL 1976 Abortion, the Public Morals, and the Police Power: The Ethical Function of Substantive Due Process. *UCLA Law Review* 23:689–736.

——— 1978 The Abortion Funding Cases: A Comment on the Supreme Court's Role in American Government. *Georgetown Law Journal* 66:1191–1245.

REGAN, DONALD 1979 Rewriting *Roe v. Wade. Michigan Law Review* 77:1569–1646.

TRIBE, LAURENCE H. 1978 *American Constitutional Law* Pages 921–934. Mineola, N.Y.: Foundation Press.

REPUBLICAN FORM OF GOVERNMENT

The Constitution requires that "The United States shall guarantee to every State in this Union a Republican Form of Government" (Article IV, section 4). The ideal of republican government antedated the Constitution and supplied some substantive criteria for the guarantee. The concept of republican government has changed and expanded over time, but it has influenced constitutional development only indirectly.

THOMAS JEFFERSON's 1776 draft constitution for Virginia, various Revolutionary-era state constitutions, and the NORTHWEST ORDINANCE (1787) mandated republican government in the states or TERRITORIES. When the GUARANTEE CLAUSE was adopted at the CONSTITUTIONAL CONVENTION OF 1787, the concept of republican government had identifiable connotations to the Revolutionary generation. In a negative sense, it excluded monarchical government and the creation of nobility. Because the Framers believed that internal disorder threatened republican institutions, they fused the guarantee clause with the clause in Article IV authorizing the federal government to suppress domestic violence. But in its positive connotations, republican government implied popular SOVEREIGNTY, a balance and SEPARATION OF POWERS, and LIMITED GOVERNMENT.

The contributions of ALEXANDER HAMILTON and JAMES MADISON in THE FEDERALIST reflected these negative and positive emphases. In numbers 6, 21, 22, 25, 34, and 84, Hamilton stressed the nonmonarchical character of republican governments and the need for a central authority powerful enough to suppress insurrections so as to forestall republican degeneration into absolutism. Madison, however, in numbers 10, 14, 39, and 43, emphasized the representative and majoritarian nature of republican government, contrasting it with direct democracies. SHAYS' REBELLION in central Massachusetts (1786–1787), rumors of monarchical plots and overtures late in the Confederation period, and federal response to the WHISKEY REBELLION (western Pennsylvania, 1794) lent weight to the emphasis that Hamilton reflected.

Conservative judges in the antebellum period insisted that statutes must conform to "certain vital principles in our free republican governments," in the words of Justice SAMUEL CHASE in CALDER V. BULL (1798) (SERIATIM OPINION). He claimed that "the genius, the nature, and the spirit of our state governments" voided unconstitutional legislation even without specific constraints in the state constitutions. Thus the concept of republican government became a fecund source of authority for judges seeking to restrain legislative innovation that affected property in such matters as liquor PROHIBITION and the Married Women's Property Acts.

In Rhode Island's Dorr Rebellion (1842), frustrated suffrage reformers abandoned hope that the state's conservative political leadership (called the "Freeholders' Government") would rectify the severe malapportionment and disfranchisement that existed under the royal charter of 1662, which still served as the state's constitution. They therefore applied the DECLARATION OF INDEPENDENCE literally to write a new constitution at a convention elected by the votes of all adult males, including those not entitled by existing law to vote. They then elected a government under the new constitution, including the "People's Governor," Thomas Wilson Dorr. The Freeholders, relying on Hamilton's nonmonarchic conception of republican government, insisted that a government was republican if it enjoyed the support of the enfranchised voters. By imposing martial law, the Freeholders crushed the Dorrite government. They then instituted suffrage reforms under a new state constitution.

The Dorr Rebellion was the matrix for LUTHER V. BORDEN (1849), where Chief Justice ROGER B. TANEY provided the first significant judicial hints about the meaning of republican government. Though Taney rebuffed Dorrite efforts to have the Court declare the Freeholder and subsequent regimes illegitimate, he conceded that "according to the institutions of this country, the sovereignty in every State resides in the people of the State, and . . . they may alter and change their form of government at their own pleasure." But he nullified this concession by applying the POLITICAL QUESTION doctrine: whether the people have altered their government is a question to be decided by the political branches of the national government (Congress and the President), whose determination is binding on the courts.

The constitutional controversy over slavery turned partly on the nature of republican forms of government. In the debates over the admission of Missouri in 1819–1821, antislavery congressmen asserted that slavery was inconsistent with republican government. ABOLITIONISTS later maintained that slavery violated natural law by depriving slaves of the right to their liberty, their persons, and their labor. Southern spokesmen after 1835 developed the position that slavery was not only compatible with republicanism, but actually conducive to it, creating a leisured master class freed for the disinterested pursuit of civic responsibilities.

The slavery controversy echoed in debates on Reconstruction between 1862 and 1875. Many Republicans supported policies that would have given blacks the vote, assured equal rights for all, and excluded southern states from representation in Congress until they had eradicated the vestiges of slavery and secessionist sentiment. They demanded that Congress force these improvements on the southern state governments. Democrats and other conservatives, on the other hand, identified the essence of republicanism with self-government—for whites only. Though adoption of the MILITARY RECONSTRUCTION ACTS (1867–1868) evidenced a Republican willingness to exact certain minima from the southern states, such as the program reflected in sections 1 through 4 of the FOURTEENTH AMENDMENT, the party soon fell back to a more compromising position. Senator JACOB HOWARD of Michigan reflected a Republican consensus late in Reconstruction when he defined a republican form of government as one "in which the laws of the community are made by their representatives, freely chosen by the people. . . . [I]t is popular government; it is the voice of the people expressed through their representatives." He was echoed by Chief Justice MELVILLE W. FULLER in *In re Duncan* (1891): the "distinguishing feature of [the republican] form is the right of the people to choose their own officers for governmental administration, and pass their own laws in virtue of the legislative power reposed in representative bodies."

However, the Supreme Court has otherwise consistently declined to specify substantive characteristics of a republican form of government, sometimes using the political-question doctrine to avoid doing so. Chief Justice MORRISON R. WAITE observed in MINOR V. HAPPERSETT (1875) that "no particular government is designated as republican, neither is the exact form to be guaranteed, in any manner especially designated." In *Pacific States Telephone and Telegraph Co. v. Oregon* (1912) Chief Justice EDWARD D. WHITE refused to declare that direct-democracy innovations such as the REFERENDUM or the INITIATIVE fell afoul of the constitutional guarantee. In the previous year, though, President WILLIAM HOWARD TAFT vetoed the Arizona/New Mexico admissions bill because it provided for judicial RECALL. Taft condemned the "possible tyranny of a popular majority." In BAKER V. CARR (1962) Justice WILLIAM J. BRENNAN refused to use the guarantee clause as a basis for requiring REAPPORTIONMENT, relying instead on the EQUAL PROTECTION clause. But he trimmed back the breadth of the political question DOCTRINE, leaving open the remote possibility that the Supreme Court might someday take on a more active role in delineating the substantive content of republican forms of government.

Unless it does so, however, the nature of republican government will be determined largely outside judicial forums, and the constitutional guarantee of republican government in the states will be enforced, as it has been consistently since before the Civil War, by Congress and, derivatively, the President.

WILLIAM M. WIECEK

Bibliography

BONFIELD, ARTHUR   1962   Baker v. Carr: New Light on the Constitutional Guarantee of Republican Government. *California Law Review* 1962:245–263.

——— 1962   The Guarantee Clause of Article IV Section 4: A Study in Constitutional Desuetude. *Minnesota Law Review* 46:513–572.

WIECEK, WILLIAM M.   1972   *The Guarantee Clause of the U.S. Constitution*. Ithaca, N.Y.: Cornell University Press.

WOOD, GORDON S.   1969   *The Creation of the American Republic, 1776–1787*. Chapel Hill: University of North Carolina Press.

RESERVED POLICE POWER

If a state reserves a power to alter, amend, or repeal a charter of incorporation before or when granting that charter, the CONTRACT CLAUSE is not necessarily a bar to the exercise of the state police power. In HOME BUILDING AND LOAN ASSOCIATION V. BLAISDELL (1934), the Court ruled that a state may modify or abrogate contracts because existing laws, by becoming part of the contracts, limit their obligations and because "the reservation of essential attributes of sovereign power is also read into contracts." That principle had originated in the concurring opinion of Justice JOSEPH STORY in DARTMOUTH COLLEGE V. WOODWARD (1819), when he declared that a corporate charter could not be changed unless a power for that purpose were reserved in the charter itself. Thereafter the states began to reserve such a power not only in charters, but in general acts of incorporation and in state constitutions, which applied to all charters subsequently granted. In 1877, when the court sustained a rate-fixing statute enacted under the reserved police power, it declared that the power must be reasonably exercised, consistent with the objects of the charter, and must not violate VESTED RIGHTS. In a 1936 case in which the Court repeated that formulation, as it had many times before, it stated that the reserved power prevented reliance on the contract clause. Never has the Court clarified its standards to explain why it has struck down some regulations

under the reserved power yet has sustained others.

The reserved power nevertheless weakened the contract clause's service as a bastion of inviolable corporate charters. In 1884, for example, the Court held that because a private water works company was a public utility, its rates could be fixed by government authority under a reservation clause enacted after the state granted a charter giving the company an equal voice in the fixing of rates. The rise of the DOCTRINE of the reserved police power and the related doctrine of the INALIENABLE POLICE POWER forced the defenders of property rights to seek a more secure constitutional base than the contract clause, thus contributing to the emergence of SUBSTANTIVE DUE PROCESS OF LAW in the 1890s. Dozens of cases involved the application of the reserved police power even after the FOURTEENTH AMENDMENT replaced the contract clause as the main basis for invalidating state regulations. These cases did not, however, produce consistent principles that fixed ascertainable limits on the reserved power. The Court reserved to itself the final power to decide when it will enforce constitutional limitations on the reserved police power. Today the Court speaks of "the reserved powers doctrine" without making the "formalistic distinction" between powers that are reserved and those that are inalienable. *Home Building and Loan Association v. Blaisdell* (1934) obliterated a distinction between the reserved police power and the inalienable police power.

LEONARD W. LEVY

Bibliography

WRIGHT, BENJAMIN F.   1938   *The Contract Clause of the Constitution*. Pages 195–213. Cambridge, Mass.: Harvard University Press.

RESERVED POWERS (OF STATES AND PEOPLE)

See: Tenth Amendment

RESIDENCE REQUIREMENTS

Most states limit some benefits, such as welfare payments or free medical care for indigents, to state residents; all states limit voting to residents. Legislative classifications based on nonresidence or out-of-state CITIZENSHIP are not subjected to heightened judicial scrutiny under the EQUAL PROTECTION clause, and these residence requirements consistently pass the relaxed RATIONAL BASIS test.

Because state citizenship and residence are "essentially interchangeable" for purposes of the PRIVILEGES AND IMMUNITIES clause of Article IV, however, discriminations against nonresidents are scrutinized more carefully under that provision. The state must justify such discriminations by showing that they are substantially related to dealing with some special problem or condition caused by nonresidents. A state might constitutionally charge out-of-staters more than residents for a license to cut timber, if the increased charge bore some fair relation to increased costs of enforcing conservation laws against nonresidents. Similarly, nonresidents might constitutionally be denied WELFARE BENEFITS or charged higher tuition for attending a state university, because residents have supported the welfare system and the university out of general tax revenues. The notion of a "political community" justifies limiting the vote to residents.

Discriminations not so justified, however, violate Article IV's privileges and immunities clause when they touch privileges that are deemed "fundamental" to interstate harmony. (See TOOMER V. WITSELL, 1948, commercial shrimping; HICKLIN V. ORBECK, 1978, employment; DOE V. BOLTON, 1973, abortion; NEW HAMPSHIRE SUPREME COURT V. PIPER, 1985, practice of law.)

Requirements of residence for a specified period raise an additional constitutional problem. The Court has invalidated a number of these durational residence requirements on EQUAL PROTECTION grounds, also invoking the RIGHT TO TRAVEL or migrate interstate. (See SHAPIRO V. THOMPSON, 1969, welfare benefits; DUNN V. BLUMSTEIN, 1972, one-year requirement for voting invalid; later decisions allow fifty-day residence qualification; *Memorial Hospital v. Maricopa County*, 1974, nonemergency medical care for indigents; *Zobel v. Williams*, 1982, payment of bonuses apportioned to length of residence in the state. But see SOSNA V. IOWA, 1975, one year's residence a valid requirement for access to divorce court.) William Cohen has argued persuasively that these decisions are consistent with a theory that validates a state's durational residence requirement only when the requirement is a reasonable test of a newcomer's intent to remain a resident of the state. The Supreme Court has not yet embraced this theory—or, indeed, any coherent theory explaining its decisions concerning durational residence requirements.

KENNETH L. KARST

Bibliography

COHEN, WILLIAM 1984 Equal Treatment for Newcomers: The Core Meaning of National and State Citizenship. *Constitutional Commentary* 1:9–19.

VARAT, JONATHAN D. 1984 "Citizenship" and Interstate Equality. *University of Chicago Law Review* 48:487–572.

RES JUDICATA

(Latin: "The thing has been adjudicated.") The term is used broadly to refer to two kinds of effect given to a court's judgment: extinguishing claims and thus barring future litigation ("claim preclusion"), or conclusively determining certain issues that might arise in future litigation ("issue preclusion").

KENNETH L. KARST

(SEE ALSO: *Collateral Attack; Full Faith and Credit; Habeas Corpus.*)

RESOLUTIONS OF STAMP ACT CONGRESS

See: Stamp Act Congress

RESTRAINT OF TRADE

See: Antitrust Law and the Constitution

RESTRICTIVE COVENANT

Until the Supreme Court ruled their judicial enforcement unconstitutional in SHELLEY V. KRAEMER (1948), restrictive covenants were widely employed to achieve the racial SEGREGATION of urban neighborhoods in America. A restrictive covenant is a contract among owners of land, mutually limiting the uses of land covered by the covenant. Many such covenants have benign purposes: all the owners on a residential block, for example, might agree that houses will be set back thirty feet from the street. Racial covenants, however, limited the occupancy of homes on the basis of the occupants' race. They rested on an ugly premise: excluding blacks or Asians would, as one Louisiana court put it, make a neighborhood "more attractive to white people."

Such covenants were commonly adopted by landowners, or written into deeds of newly developed land, beginning in the late nineteenth century. Under existing property law, they were enforceable not only against their signers, but against the signers' heirs, assignees, and purchasers—at least so long as "conditions" had not changed. The use of the covenants accelerated after the Supreme Court decided, in BUCHANAN V. WARLEY (1917), that municipal ZONING ordinances specifying where persons of one race or another might live were unconstitutional. The typical covenant ran for twenty-five years, but some ran for fifty years or even in perpetuity.

Restrictive covenants cannot be said to be the sole cause, or even the primary cause, of residential segregation before 1948. The poverty of most blacks was itself a severe restriction on the purchase of homes; and middle-class blacks who could afford to buy were steered to "colored sections" by real estate brokers and lenders. (The latter practices became violations of federal law only in 1968.) Yet the covenants surely played their part in the segregative process, a part they could play only because they were enforceable in court.

If an owner started to build a house too close to the street, in violation of a restrictive covenant, the neighbors would be entitled to an INJUNCTION ordering the owner to stop. They might also be entitled to damages, if they could demonstrate some loss. But, subject to the covenant's limitations, the owner would be entitled to occupy the property, or sell it to any purchaser. The owner of property subject to a racial covenant, however, could not—so long as the covenant was enforceable—sell it to blacks for their use as a residence. The racial covenants, then, not only restricted black would-be buyers but also restricted the owners' free alienation of property—an interest recognized in the COMMON LAW since the thirteenth century. Yet the state courts regularly enforced the covenants.

The Supreme Court lent its approval in 1926, in CORRIGAN V. BUCKLEY, holding that judicial enforcement of a racial covenant did not even raise a substantial federal question; any discrimination was private action, not STATE ACTION. (The case arose not in a state, covered by the FOURTEENTH AMENDMENT, but in the DISTRICT OF COLUMBIA. The Court correctly sensed, however, that a similar problem would arise if an EQUAL PROTECTION guarantee were found applicable to governmental action in the District.)

Over the next two decades, the NAACP searched for opportunities to bring to the Court new challenges to the judicial enforcement of racially restrictive covenants. They finally succeeded in *Shelley*, where the Court did find state action in a state court's injunctive relief to enforce a covenant against black buyers of a home. On the same day, in *Hurd v. Hodge* (1948), the Court reached a comparable result in an attack on judicial enforcement of a covenant in the District of Columbia. No constitutional issue was decided in *Hurd*; the Court based its decision on "the public policy of the United States."

Five years later, the Court took away the last remaining weapon of persons who would seek to use racial covenants as a way of keeping their neighborhoods white. In BARROWS V. JACKSON (1953) the Court held that a state court violated the Fourteenth Amendment by using a covenant as a basis for awarding damages against persons who sold their house to black buyers.

One of the worst features of the racial covenants was their contribution to the symbolism of black inferiority. The removal of that symbolism, wherever it may be found, is necessary if the Fourteenth Amendment's promise of equal CITIZENSHIP is to be fulfilled. But ending the judicial enforcement of racial covenants did not end residential segregation, a phenomenon that has declined only slightly since 1940.

KENNETH L. KARST

Bibliography

HENKIN, LOUIS 1962 Shelley v. Kraemer: Notes for a Revised Opinion. *University of Pennsylvania Law Review* 110:473–505.
VOSE, CLEMENT E. 1959 *Caucasians Only.* Berkeley: University of California Press.

RETROACTIVITY OF JUDICIAL DECISIONS

LEGISLATION ordinarily does not apply retroactively to conduct occurring prior to its adoption but only to actions taking place after enactment. Indeed, the potential unfairness of some retroactive legislation is so great that certain forms of legislative retroactivity are specifically prohibited by the Constitution. The EX POST FACTO clauses of the Constitution prohibit retroactive criminal penalties, and the CONTRACT CLAUSE limits state legislation that would impair the obligation of pre-existing contracts. In addition, certain other fundamentally unfair forms of legislative retroactivity may violate constitutional due process guarantees.

Judicial decisions, on the other hand, ordinarily *are* retroactive in application. To some extent, such retroactivity is a consequence of the nature and function of the judicial decision-making process. Traditional lawsuits and criminal prosecutions concern the legal consequences of acts that have already taken place. If judicial decisions in such cases are to adjudicate the issues between the parties, those decisions necessarily must apply to prior events. The retroactive effect of judicial decisions, however, commonly extends beyond application to the particular parties involved in a case. To the extent that a judicial decision constitutes a new legal precedent, it will ordinarily be applied to all undecided cases that are subsequently litigated, regardless of whether the relevant events occurred before or after the new precedent was announced.

Although traditional judicial decisions are, in theory, completely retrospective in nature, two sets of legal doctrines place important practical limits on the actual breadth of decisional retroactivity. Statutes of limitations, which require suits to be brought within some specified period of time after the relevant events occur, limit the retrospective application of new precedents to the length of the prescribed limitations period; and the doctrines of RES JUDICATA and collateral estoppel prevent the relitigation of cases and issues that have been finally decided before the new precedent is announced. In addition, as in the case of retroactive legislation, there are some circumstances of fundamental unfairness in which constitutional principles may prevent the retroactive use of judicial decisions. By analogy to the constitutional prohibition of ex post facto laws, for example, the Supreme Court in *Bowie v. City of Columbia* (1964) held it unconstitutional to apply a new expansive judicial interpretation of a criminal statute to prior conduct.

The principal theoretical basis supporting the broad traditional retroactivity of judicial decisions is the abstract idea that courts (unlike legislatures) do not make, but merely find, the law. This theory in effect denies the existence of retroactivity; under the theory the events in question were always subject to the newly announced rule, although that rule had not been authoritatively articulated.

The theory that judicial decisions do not make law does not always reflect reality. Perhaps the clearest example of apparent judicial lawmaking is a court's overruling of an earlier judicial decision regarding the meaning of the COMMON LAW, a statute, or a constitutional provision. Even when no earlier decision is overruled, judicial decisions or interpretations may announce genuinely new principles. When judicial decisions thus create new law, it is plausible to argue that the new principles should not be given the retroactive effect normally accorded to judicial decisions, but should instead be treated more like new legislation and given prospective effect only. These arguments are strongest when individuals or governments have relied (perhaps irrevocably) upon earlier decisions in shaping their conduct. In such circumstances, retroactive application may cause unanticipated and harmful results.

In response to these and similar considerations, some courts have used the practice of PROSPECTIVE OVERRULING of prior decisions. Such a court, in overruling a precedent upon which substantial reliance may have been placed, may announce in OBITER DICTUM its intention to reject the old doctrine for the future, but nevertheless apply the old rule to the case at hand and to other conduct prior to the new decision. Alternatively, the court may apply the new rule to the parties before it, thus making the announcement of the new rule HOLDING rather than "dictum," but may otherwise reserve the rule for future application. In *Great Northern Railway Company v. Sunburst Oil and Refining Company* (1932) the Supreme Court held that the Constitution permits either of these forms of prospective overruling. The *Sunburst* decision gave constitutional approval to prospective judicial overruling of common law precedents and of decisions interpreting statutes. Such prospective overruling has primarily been used in two kinds of cases: new interpretations of statutes relating to property and contract rights, and the overruling of doctrines of municipal and charitable immunity from tort liability.

The most prominent and controversial recent issue concerning prospective overruling, however, has involved the retroactivity of new Supreme Court decisions enlarging the constitutional rights of defendents in criminal proceedings. During the 1950s and 1960s, the Court significantly broadened the rights of criminal defendants with respect to unconstitutional SEARCHES AND SEIZURES, POLICE INTERROGATION AND CONFESSIONS, the scope of the RIGHT AGAINST SELF-INCRIMINATION, and the inadmissibility of unconstitutionally obtained evidence. The Court has ruled that some of these new constitutional interpretations should not be given general retrospective application.

The extent of the possible retroactive application of new doctrines affecting the constitutionality of criminal convictions is greater than in most other areas of law because of the potential availability of postconviction relief to prisoners whose convictions might be effectively challenged if the newly announced rules were applicable to prior convictions. Petitions for HABEAS CORPUS are not subject to statutes of limitations or to the ordinary operation of the doctrine of *res judicata*. Thus, in 1961, when the Supreme Court decided in MAPP V. OHIO that the Constitution prohibits states from basing criminal convictions upon EVIDENCE obtained in violation of the FOURTH and FOURTEENTH AMENDMENTS, full retroactivity of that decision would have permitted a great many prisoners to challenge their convictions, no matter when their trials had occurred. Because the *Mapp* decision was based upon the interpretation of constitutional provisions dating from 1791 and 1868, the theoretical arguments for full retroactivity were strong. However, *Mapp* overruled the opinion of the Court in WOLF v. COLORADO (1949), which had held, directly contrary to *Mapp,* that the states were free to use unconstitutionally obtained evidence in most circumstances. Although police could hardly have legitimately relied upon *Wolf* in engaging in unconstitutional searches, state prosecutors and courts might have relied upon *Wolf* in using unconstitutionally obtained evidence. The primary reason given by the Court for the *Mapp* decision, moreover, was to deter police misconduct; the *Mapp* EXCLUSIONARY RULE is not a safeguard against conviction of the innocent. Retroactive application of *Mapp* to nullify pre-existing convictions would thus arguably contribute little to the main purpose of the *Mapp* rule while permitting guilty defendants to escape their just punishment. Similar issues have surrounded the potential retroactivity of other new Supreme Court decisions enlarging the constitutional rights of criminal defendants.

The Supreme Court has resolved these retroactivity issues by employing a test focusing on three main criteria: whether the purpose of the new rule would be furthered by its retroactive application; the extent of the reliance by law enforcement authorities and courts on prior decisions and understandings; and the likely effect of retroactive application on the administration of justice. Using this approach the Court held, in *Linkletter v. Walker (1965),* that the *Mapp* decision would be applied to trials and direct APPEALS pending at the time of the *Mapp* decision, but not to state court convictions where the appeal process had been completed prior to announcement of the *Mapp* opinion. The same rule of general nonretroactivity has been applied to new constitutional interpretations prohibiting comment on a defendant's failure to take the witness stand at trial; establishing the MIRANDA RULES for police warnings to persons interrogated; prohibiting WIRETAPPING without judicial SEARCH WARRANTS; and limiting the permissible scope of SEARCHES INCIDENT TO ARRESTS. On the other hand, full retroactivity has been accorded to new decisions requiring provision of free counsel for INDIGENTS in criminal trials; requiring proof beyond a REASONABLE DOUBT in state criminal proceedings; and broadening the definition of constitutionally prohibited DOUBLE JEOPARDY. In general, rules designed to protect innocent persons from conviction have been given full retroactive application, while rules primarily intended to correct police and prosecutorial abuses that do not implicate guilt have been given limited retroactivity. The practical significance of these retroactivity decisions has been diminished in recent years by Supreme Court decisions that limit the availability of post-conviction relief to incarcerated persons (for example, STONE V. POWELL, 1976) and by the current Supreme Court's general opposition to continued expansion of defendants' constitutional rights in criminal proceedings.

PAUL BENDER

Bibliography

FIELD, OLIVER P. 1935 *The Effect of an Unconstitutional Statute.* Minneapolis: University of Minnesota Press.

RETROACTIVITY OF LEGISLATION

A characteristic of arbitrary government is that the state can alter retroactively the legal status of acts already done. Therefore, proposals to prohibit various types of retroactive LEGISLATION encountered the opposition of those delegates to the CONSTITUTIONAL CONVENTION OF 1787 who believed such laws were "void of themselves" and that a formal prohibition would "proclaim that we are ignorant of the first principles of legislation." There are, nevertheless, three such prohibitions in the Constitution: Congress may not pass EX POST FACTO laws and the states may not pass ex post facto laws or laws impairing the OBLIGATION OF CONTRACTS.

There are sound historical reasons for supposing that the Framers meant to proscribe both criminal and civil legislation with retrospective application. But JOHN DICKINSON had warned the convention that WILLIAM BLACKSTONE's commentaries treated "ex post facto" as a technical term applying only to criminal law. In CALDER V. BULL (1798), the Supreme Court relied on Blackstone's authority to confine the constitutional prohibition to criminal laws.

The CONTRACT CLAUSE ultimately proved a mere parchment barrier to retroactive legislation. It does not apply to the federal government and the courts have so interpreted it as to make it a weak defense against retroactive state laws.

DENNIS J. MAHONEY

REVENUE SHARING

One consequence of the massive increase in the size and power of the federal government that began in the 1930s was the preemption by the federal government of the sources of revenue that had previously supported the state and local governments. The inability of such governments to find adequate stable sources of income seemed to pose grave problems for American FEDERALISM.

Funds appropriated by the federal government already flowed to state and local governments in the form of FEDERAL GRANTS-IN-AID, often with the effect of coopting those governments as administrators of federally mandated programs. The federal grants brought with them various restrictions as well as burdensome paperwork requirements.

One solution was to return to the state and local governments a share of the tax revenues collected by the federal government, not in support of particular federal programs but as general revenue to be spent for local purposes, with a minimum of restrictions. In the late 1960s, the idea of general revenue sharing was adopted by the Republican party as part of its proposal for a "new federalism." In 1972, Congress, at the urging of President RICHARD M. NIXON, enacted the State and Local Fiscal Assistance Act. The act authorized the distribution of $30 billion to state and local governments over a five-year period. Of that sum, one-third was allocated to the states and two-thirds to counties, cities, and other local governments to be distributed according to a flexible formula taking into account population, locally generated revenues, and other factors. The major restriction was a ban on RACIAL DISCRIMINATION in funded activities.

The program was extended in 1976; in 1980, a revised version was enacted that eliminated the states from the distribution scheme. Any revitalization of federalism as a result of revenue sharing has been less than apparent.

DENNIS J. MAHONEY

Bibliography

SCHEFFER, WALTER F., ed. 1976 *General Revenue Sharing and Decentralization.* Norman: University of Oklahoma Press.

REVISED STATUTES OF THE UNITED STATES
18 Stat. 1 (1875)

In 1866, Congress authorized the President to appoint a commission "to revise, simplify, arrange, and consolidate all statutes of the United States." The revision, completed in 1874 and modified in 1878, constituted the first official codification of the general and permanent laws of the United States. The revision super-

sedes the original public laws it consolidated. Except for those portions of the revision that have been repealed, amended, or superseded by subsequent compilations of federal statutes, the revision remains the authoritative statement of federal statutes enacted prior to 1874.

The revision was not supposed to work substantive changes in the code. But some relatively straightforward statutes became hopelessly confused as a result of the revision. Its most drastic effects may have been upon CIVIL RIGHTS statutes designed to enhance and protect constitutional rights. The revision's treatment of the JURISDICTION of the federal courts to hear civil rights cases brought under SECTION 1983, TITLE 42, UNITED STATES CODE, generated a century of confusion that was furthered by Justice HARLAN FISKE STONE's opinion in HAGUE V. CIO (1939) and that culminated in *Lynch v. Household Finance Corporation* (1972), *Chapman v. Houston Welfare Rights Organization* (1979), and a 1980 amendment providing for jurisdiction in all such cases. The revision's scattering of the CIVIL RIGHTS ACT OF 1866 throughout the Code contributed to that provision's century of near dormancy, to the Court's questionable reading of the 1866 act's intended scope in JONES V. ALFRED H. MAYER CO. (1968) and RUNYON V. MCCRARY (1976), to a confusing of CIVIL RIGHTS REMOVAL statutes that the Court only slightly illuminated in *Georgia v. Rachel* (1966) and *City of Greenwood v. Peacock* (1966), and to a misunderstanding, manifested in *Robertson v. Wegmann* (1978) and *Board of Regents v. Tomanio* (1980), of Congress's intent with respect to the role of state law in federal civil rights cases.

THEODORE EISENBERG

Bibliography

SUNSTEIN, CASS 1982 Section 1983 and the Private Enforcement of Federal Law. *University of Chicago Law Review* 49:401–409.

REYNOLDS v. SIMS
377 U.S. 533 (1964)

Once the Supreme Court declared in BAKER V. CARR (1962) that legislative districting presented a justiciable controversy, lawsuits were filed in more than thirty states challenging existing legislative apportionments. Six of these cases were decided by the Court on the same day, and the Court held all six states' apportionments unconstitutional. The main opinion was written in *Reynolds v. Sims,* the Alabama case; all six opinions of the Court were by Chief Justice

EARL WARREN, who believed until his death that *Reynolds* was the most important decision rendered by the Court during his tenure. The vote in four of the cases was 8–1, and in the other two, 6–3. Justice JOHN MARSHALL HARLAN dissented in all six cases, joined in two of them by Justices POTTER STEWART and TOM C. CLARK.

Baker v. Carr had been a response to decades of stalemate in the political process. Population shifts from rural areas to cities in the twentieth century had not been accompanied by changes in the electoral maps of most states. As a result, vast disparities in district populations permitted control of both houses of the typical state legislature to be dictated by rural voters. In Alabama, for example, Mobile County, with a population over 300,000, had three seats in the lower house, while Bullock County's two representatives served a population under 14,000. If JUDICIAL REVIEW normally defers to majoritarian democracy, here the premise for that deference was lacking; legislators favored by these apportionment inequalities were not apt to remedy them.

Baker had rested decision not on the GUARANTEE CLAUSE but on the EQUAL PROTECTION clause of the FOURTEENTH AMENDMENT. In the early 1960s, the Court had heightened the STANDARD OF REVIEW in equal protection cases only when RACIAL DISCRIMINATION was present; for other cases, the relaxed RATIONAL BASIS standard prevailed. Some Justices in the *Baker* majority had based their concurrence on the total arbitrariness of the Tennessee apportionment scheme there challenged. Justice WILLIAM O. DOUGLAS, concurring, had even said, "Universal equality is not the test; there is room for weighting." The *Baker* dissenters and academic critics had argued that the apportionment problem was unsuitable for judicial determination because courts would be unable to devise principled standards to test the reasonableness of the "weighting" Justice Douglas had anticipated; the problem belonged, they had said, in the category of POLITICAL QUESTIONS. The *Baker* majority had replied blandly: "Judicial standards under the Equal Protection Clause are well developed and familiar," and courts could determine that malapportionment represented "*no* policy, but simply arbitrary and capricious action." The suggestion was plain: departures from district population equality would be valid if they rested on legitimate policies.

Reynolds belied this suggestion. In a sweeping opinion that Archibald Cox called a *coup de main,* the Court discarded almost all possible justifications for departing from a strict principle of equal district populations and established for state legislative dis-

tricts the ONE PERSON, ONE VOTE formula it had recently used in other electoral contexts. (See GRAY V. SANDERS 1963; WESBERRY V. SANDERS, 1964.) The Court thus solved *Baker*'s problem of judicially manageable standards by resort to a mechanical test that left no "room for weighting"—and, not incidentally, no room for legislative evasion. The companion cases to *Reynolds* demonstrated the strength of the majority's conviction. *Maryland Committee for Fair Representation v. Tawes* (1964) rejected the "federal analogy" and imposed the population equality principle on both houses of a bicameral legislature, and LUCAS V. FORTY-FOURTH GENERAL ASSEMBLY OF STATE OF COLORADO (1964) insisted on the principle in the face of a popular REFERENDUM approving an apportionment that departed from it. In *Reynolds* itself the Court made clear that the states must keep their legislative apportionments abreast of population shifts as reported in the nation's decennial census.

In short, numbers were in, and a political theory of interest representation was out: "Citizens, not history or economic interests, cast votes." Justice Stewart, dissenting in two of the cases, took another view: "Representative government is a process of accommodating group interests through democratic institutional arrangements." Fairness in apportionment thus requires effective representation of the various interests in a state, a concern that the principle of district population equality either ignored or defeated. But Justice Stewart's premise—that equal protection required only an apportionment scheme that was rationally based and did not systematically frustrate majority rule—was rejected by the Court. Because voting "is a fundamental matter in a free society," the Chief Justice said, the dilution of the strength of a citizen's vote "must be carefully and meticulously scrutinized." *Reynolds* was the crucial decision in the line of equal protection cases developing the doctrine that voting is a FUNDAMENTAL INTEREST, whose impairment calls for STRICT SCRUTINY. (See HARPER V. VIRGINIA BOARD OF ELECTIONS, 1966; KRAMER V. UNION FREE SCHOOL DISTRICT NO. 15, 1969.)

The Court's disposition of the six REAPPORTIONMENT cases, and its memorandum orders in other cases in succeeding months, left little doubt that the Justices had learned a lesson from their experience in BROWN V. BOARD OF EDUCATION (1954–1955). Here there would be no ALL DELIBERATE SPEED formula to extend the time for compliance with the decision. Lower courts were expected to move quickly—and did move quickly—to implement the doctrine announced in *Reynolds.* Even so, politicians had some time to mount a counterattack. Thirty-two state legislatures requested the calling of a CONSTITUTIONAL CONVENTION to overturn *Reynolds.* Senator Everett Dirksen gained substantial support when he introduced a proposed constitutional amendment to the same end. Bills were offered in both houses of Congress to withdraw the federal courts' JURISDICTION over reapportionment cases. But all these efforts came to nothing. The jurisdictional bills failed; the Dirksen proposal did not pass either house; the constitutional convention proposal, which had been carried forward with little publicity, withered in the remaining state legislatures when it was exposed to political sunlight.

The reason for the politicians' protest was obvious to all: many of them anticipated losing their own seats, and many others foresaw reduced influence for certain interests that rural representatives had favored. The public, however, overwhelmingly approved the principle of "one person, one vote" when the issue was tested in opinion polls; the politicians' counterattack failed because the people sided with the Court.

Academic criticism of the WARREN COURT has prominently featured *Reynolds* as a horrible example. The Court, the critics say, failed to write an opinion that reasoned from generally accepted premise to logically compelled conclusion. That is a telling criticism if, as HENRY HART was fond of saying, "reason is the life of the law." But reason is not the *life* of the law, or of anything else. It is a mental instrument to be used by judges and other humans along with their capacities for other ways of knowing: recognizing textures, patterns, analogies, relations that are not demonstrated by "if . . . then" syllogisms but grasped intuitively and at once. Perhaps the public was more ready to accept "one person, one vote" than were the Warren Court's critics because people who are not lawyers understand that the Supreme Court's most important product is justice. Surely they understood that the *Reynolds* formula, for all its inflexibility, more truly reflected our national sense of political justice than did the "cancer of malapportionment"— the term is Professor Cox's—that preceded it.

It is, by definition, hard to justify innovation by reference to the conventional wisdom. The beginnings of judicial DOCTRINE, like other beginnings, may be more easily felt than syllogized. Ultimately, if constitutional intuitions are to be translated into constitutional law, coherent explanation must come to replace the vague sense of doing the right thing; consolidation is an essential part of the Supreme Court's task. Yet to deny the legitimacy of a decision whose underlying value premises are clear, on the ground that the decision does not follow deductively from what has gone before, is to deny the legitimacy of judicial creativ-

ity—and it is our creative judges whom we honor most.

Reynolds v. Sims did not remake the political world; it mostly transferred power from rural areas to the conservative suburbs of large cities. But the decision touched a deep vein of American political egalitarianism and gave impetus to a doctrinal development as important as any in our time: recognition of the values of equal citizenship as the substantive core of the Fourteenth Amendment.

KENNETH L. KARST

Bibliography

CASPER, GERHARD 1973 Apportionment and the Right to Vote: Standards of Judicial Scrutiny. *Supreme Court Review* 1973:1–32.

DIXON, ROBERT G., JR. 1968 *Democratic Representation: Reapportionment in Law and Politics.* New York: Oxford University Press.

MCKAY, ROBERT B. 1965 *Reapportionment: The Law and Politics of Equal Representation.* New York: Twentieth Century Fund.

REYNOLDS v. UNITED STATES
98 U.S. 145 (1879)

This case established the principle that under the guarantee of RELIGIOUS LIBERTY, government may not punish religious beliefs but may punish religiously motivated practices that injure the public interest. Reynolds violated a congressional prohibition on bigamy in the territories and appealed his conviction in Utah on FIRST AMENDMENT grounds, alleging that as a Mormon he had a religious duty to practice POLYGAMY. Chief Justice MORRISON R. WAITE for a unanimous Supreme Court ruled that although government might not reach opinions, it could constitutionally punish criminal activity. The question, Waite declared, was whether religious belief could be accepted as justification of an overt act made criminal by the law of the land. Every government, he answered, had the power to decide whether polygamy or monogamy should be the basis of social life. Those who made polygamy part of their religion could no more be exempt from the law than those who believe that human sacrifice was a necessary part of religious worship. Unless the law were superior to religious belief, Waite reasoned, every citizen might become a law unto himself and government would exist in name only. He did not explain why polygamy and human sacrifice were analogous, nor did he, in his simplified exposition, confront the problem whether an uncontrollable freedom of belief had much substance if the state could punish the dictates of conscience: belief without practice is an empty right. Moreover, Waite did not consider whether belief should be as absolutely free as he suggested; if polygamy was a crime, its advocacy had limits.

LEONARD W. LEVY

RHODE ISLAND v. INNES
446 U.S. 291 (1980)

Innes explained the meaning of "interrogation" under MIRANDA V. ARIZONA (1966). *Miranda* declared, "If the individual states that he wants an attorney, the interrogation must cease until an attorney is present." Everyone agreed that the suspect in *Innes* had received his *Miranda* warnings and invoked his RIGHT TO COUNSEL, and that he was in custody. The question was whether he had been interrogated.

Police arrested a man suspected of a shotgun murder. Repeatedly they advised him of his *Miranda* rights, and a captain instructed officers about to transport him to the stationhouse not to question him in any way. During a brief automobile ride, one officer said to another, within the suspect's hearing, that they ought to try to find the shotgun because a child might discover it and kill herself. The suspect promptly volunteered to take the police to the shotgun. Again the police gave the *Miranda* warnings. The suspect replied that he understood his rights but wanted the gun removed from the reach of children. His statements and the gun were introduced in EVIDENCE at his trial, over his objection. The state supreme court reversed his conviction, finding a violation of *Miranda*.

A 6–3 Supreme Court decided that the police had not interrogated the suspect. Justice POTTER STEWART for the majority construed *Miranda* broadly to mean that interrogation includes questioning or a "functional equivalent"—any words or actions by the police reasonably likely to elicit any response from their suspect. Here there was no interrogation, only a spontaneous admission. The dissenters believed that an officer deliberately referred to the missing gun as a danger to innocent children in the hope of eliciting from the suspect an incriminating statement; whether that happened cannot be known. If the Court majority had believed that the officer making the remark had understood the suspect's psychological makeup and that an appeal to his conscience might have worked, that majority would have decided that the suspect

had been interrogated. Contrary to the view of Justice JOHN PAUL STEVENS, dissenting, *Miranda* was not narrowed.

LEONARD W. LEVY

(SEE ALSO: *Police Interrogations and Confessions.*)

RHODE ISLAND AND PROVIDENCE PLANTATIONS, CHARTER OF
(July 8, 1663)

ROGER WILLIAMS founded Providence in 1636 as a shelter for anyone "distressed in conscience." His covenant was the first anywhere to exclude the civil government from religious matters. From the beginning the towns that became Rhode Island practiced RELIGIOUS LIBERTY, welcoming Quakers and Jews, and enjoyed SEPARATION OF CHURCH AND STATE. John Clarke, a Baptist minister who was Williams's friend and co-worker, was influential in the framing of the code of laws of 1647 establishing a "democratical" government. The restoration of the Stuarts in 1660 forced Rhode Island to secure a charter; Clarke was Williams's emissary to Charles II, who granted the first American charter guaranteeing religious liberty. The MARYLAND ACT OF TOLERATION (1649) was a statute; the charter of Rhode Island, which remained its constitution until 1842, made the guarantee a part of FUNDAMENTAL LAW. The language of the charter on this key provision was Clarke's. It referred to the colony's "livlie experiment" to show that a civil state could best be maintained if the inhabitants were secured "in the free exercise and enjoyment of all theire civill and religious rights." All peaceable persons might "freelye and fullye hav and enjoye his and theire owne judgments."

LEONARD W. LEVY

Bibliography
PERRY, RICHARD L., ed. 1959 *Sources of Our Liberties.* Pages 162–179. New York: American Bar Foundation.

RIBNIK v. MCBRIDE
277 U.S. 350 (1928)

Guided by TYSON AND BROTHER V. BANTON (1927), the Supreme Court voided a New Jersey statute regulating fees charged by employment agencies. The majority held that although widespread evils existed which were subject to regulation, the establishment of prices for a private business was outside legislative power. Justice HARLAN FISKE STONE'S dissent, joined by Justices OLIVER WENDELL HOLMES and LOUIS D. BRANDEIS, denied any distinction between illegal price controls and other, acceptable regulations. (See OLSEN V. NEBRASKA EX REL. REFERENCE & BOND ASSOCIATION, 1941; ADAMS V. TANNER, 1917.)

DAVID GORDON

RICHMOND NEWSPAPERS, INC. v. VIRGINIA
448 U.S. 555 (1980)

Richmond Newspapers recognized a constitutional right of access to criminal trials. It marked the first time a majority embraced any such FIRST AMENDMENT claim. Yet division and bitterness obviously remained from the splintered decision a year earlier in GANNETT V. DEPASQUALE, which had held that the Sixth Amendment did not preclude closing a pretrial suppression hearing to the press and public.

In *Richmond Newspapers*, a 7–1 majority distinguished *Gannett* and held that the press and public share a right of access to actual criminal trials, though the press may enjoy some preference. In the PLURALITY OPINION, Chief Justice WARREN E. BURGER found a right to attend criminal trials within "unarticulated rights" implicit in the First Amendment rights of speech, press, and assembly, as well as within other constitutional language and the uninterrupted Anglo-American tradition of open trials. This right to an open trial prevailed over efforts by Virginia courts to close a murder trial, premised on the defendant's request to do so. The trial judge had made no particularized finding that a FAIR TRIAL could not be guaranteed by means less drastic than total closure.

Justice WILLIAM H. REHNQUIST was alone in dissent, but only Justices BYRON R. WHITE and JOHN PAUL STEVENS concurred in Burger's opinion. Justice LEWIS F. POWELL took no part in the decision. Four Justices concurred separately in the JUDGMENT. They differed about whether *Gannett* actually was distinguishable, what weight to give history, and what particular constitutional basis mandated the result.

Richmond Newspapers decided only the UNCONSTITUTIONALITY of a total ban on public access to actual criminal trials when there is no demonstration that alternative means could not guarantee a fair trial. Yet the decision is significant for its recognition of a First Amendment right to gather newsworthy infor-

mation; moreover, some Justices identified a broad right to receive information about government, including the activities of the judicial branch.

AVIAM SOIFER

RIGHT . . .

See also: Freedom of . . .

RIGHT AGAINST SELF-INCRIMINATION

The Fifth Amendment is virtually synonymous with the right against self-incrimination. One who "pleads the Fifth" is not insisting on grand jury INDICTMENT, freedom from DOUBLE JEOPARDY, or JUST COMPENSATION for property taken by the government—all safeguarded in the same amendment. He is saying that he will not reply to an official query because his truthful answer might expose him to criminal jeopardy. He seems to be saying that he has something to hide, making the Fifth appear to be a protection of the guilty; it is, but probably no more so than other rights of the criminally accused. The right against self-incrimination is the most misunderstood, unrespected, and controversial of all constitutional rights.

Its very name is a problem. It is customarily referred to as "the privilege" against self-incrimination, following the usage of lawyers in discussing evidentiary privileges (for example, the husband–wife privilege, the attorney–client privilege). Popular usage, however, contrasts "privilege" with "rights," and the Fifth Amendment's clause on self-incrimination creates a constitutional right with the same status as other rights. Its "name" is unknown to the Constitution, whose words cover more than merely a right or privilege against self-incrimination: "no person . . . shall be compelled in any criminal case to be a witness against himself." What does the text mean?

The protection of the clause extends only to natural persons, not organizations like corporations or unions. A member of an organization cannot claim its benefits if the inquiry would incriminate the organization but not him personally. He can claim its benefits only for himself, not for others. The text also suggests that a prime purpose of the clause is to protect against government coercion; one may voluntarily answer any incriminating question or confess to any crime—subject to the requirements for WAIVER OF CONSTITUTIONAL RIGHTS. In some respects the text is broad, because a person can be a witness against himself in ways that do not incriminate him. He can, in a criminal case, injure his civil interests or disgrace himself in the public mind. Thus the Fifth can be construed on its face to protect against disclosures that expose one to either civil liability or INFAMY. The Fifth can also be construed to apply to an ordinary witness as well as the criminal defendant himself. In Virginia, where the right against self-incrimination first received constitutional status, it appeared in a paragraph relating to the accused only. The Fifth Amendment is not similarly restrictive, unlike the Sixth Amendment which explicitly refers to the accused, protecting him alone. The location of the clause in the Fifth, rather than in the Sixth, and its reference to "no person" makes it applicable to witnesses as well as to the accused.

On the other hand, the clause has a distinctively limiting factor: it is restricted on its face to criminal cases. The phrase "criminal case" seems to exclude civil cases. Some judges have argued that no criminal case exists until a formal charge has been made against the accused. Under such an interpretation the right would have no existence until the accused is put on trial; before that, when he is taken into custody, interrogated by the police, or examined by a GRAND JURY, he would not have the benefit of the right. Nor would he have its benefit in a nonjudicial proceeding such as a LEGISLATIVE INVESTIGATION or an administrative hearing. The Supreme Court has given the impression that the clause, if taken literally, would be so restricted; but the Court refuses to take the clause literally. Thus, in COUNSELMAN V. HITCHCOCK (1892), the Court held that the Fifth does protect ordinary witnesses, even in federal grand jury proceedings. Unanimously the Court declared, "It is impossible that the meaning of the constitutional provision can only be that a person shall not be compelled to be a witness against himself in a criminal prosecution against himself." Although the Court did not explain why it was "impossible," the Court was right. Had the framers of the Fifth intended the literal, restrictive meaning, their constitutional provision would have been a meaningless gesture. There was no need to protect the accused at his trial; he was not permitted to give testimony, whether for or against himself, at the time of the framing of the Fifth. Making the criminal defendant competent to be a witness in his own case was a reform of the later nineteenth century, beginning in the state courts with Maine in 1864, in the federal courts by an act of Congress in 1878.

Illumination from the face of a text that does not mean what it says is necessarily faint. Occasionally the Court will display its wretched knowledge of history in an effort to explain the right against self-incrimination. Justice FELIX FRANKFURTER for the Court, in ULLMANN V. UNITED STATES (1956), drew lessons from the "name" of "the privilege against self-incrimination," but conceded that it is a provision of the Constitution "of which it is peculiarly true that 'a page of history is worth a volume of logic.' " TWINING V. NEW JERSEY (1908), the most historically minded opinion ever delivered for the Court on the right, was misleading and shallow when it was not inaccurate on the question whether the right was "a fundamental principle of liberty and justice which inheres in the very idea of free government."

The American origins of the right derive largely from the inherited English COMMON LAW system of criminal justice. But the English origins, so much more complex, spill over legal boundaries and reflect the many-sided religious, political, and constitutional issues that racked England during the sixteenth and seventeenth centuries: the struggles between Anglicanism and Puritanism, between Parliament and king, between limited government and arbitrary rule, and between freedom of conscience and suppression of heresy and SEDITION. Even within the more immediate confines of law, the history of the right against self-incrimination is enmeshed in broad issues: the contests for supremacy between the accusatory and the inquisitional systems of procedure, the common law and the royal prerogative, and the common law and its canon and civil law rivals. Against this broad background the origins of the concept that "no man is bound to accuse himself" (*nemo tenetur seipsum accusare*) must be understood and the concept's legal development traced.

The right against self-incrimination originated as an indirect product of the common law's accusatory system and of its opposition to rival systems which employed inquisitorial procedures. Toward the close of the sixteenth century, just before the concept first appeared in England on a sustained basis, all courts of criminal jurisdiction habitually sought to exact self-incriminatory admissions from persons suspected of or charged with crime. Although defendants in crown cases suffered from this and many other harsh procedures, even in common law courts, the accusatory system afforded a degree of fair play not available under the inquisitional system. Moreover, torture was never sanctioned by the common law, although it was employed as an instrument of royal prerogative until 1641.

By contrast, torture for the purpose of detecting crime and inducing confession was regularly authorized by the Roman codes of the canon and civil law. "Abandon all hope, ye who enter here" well describes the chances of an accused person under inquisitorial procedures characterized by PRESENTMENT based on mere rumor or suspicion, indefiniteness of accusation, the oath *ex officio*, secrecy, lack of CONFRONTATION, coerced confessions, and magistrates acting as accusers and prosecutors as well as "judges." This system of procedure, by which heresy was most efficiently combated, was introduced into England by ecclesiastical courts.

The use of the oath *ex officio* by prerogative courts, particularly by the ecclesiastical Court of High Commission, which Elizabeth I reconstituted, resulted in the defensive claim that "no man is bound to accuse himself." The High Commission, an instrument of the Crown for maintaining religious uniformity under the Anglican establishment, used the canon law inquisitorial process, but made the oath *ex officio,* rather than torture, the crux of its procedure. Men suspected of "heretical opinions," "seditious books," or "conspiracies" were summoned before the High Commission without being informed of the accusation against them or the identity of their accusers. Denied DUE PROCESS OF LAW by common law standards, suspects were required to take an oath to answer truthfully to interrogatories which sought to establish guilt for crimes neither charged nor disclosed.

A nonconformist victim of the High Commission found himself thrust between hammer and anvil: refusal to take the oath or, having taken it, refusal to answer the interrogatories meant a sentence for contempt and invited Star Chamber proceedings; to take the oath and respond truthfully to questioning often meant to convict oneself of religious or political crimes and, moreover, to supply evidence against nonconformist accomplices; to take the oath and then lie meant to sin against the Scriptures and risk conviction for perjury. Common lawyers of the Puritan party developed the daring argument that the oath, although sanctioned by the Crown, was unconstitutional because it violated MAGNA CARTA, which limited even the royal prerogative.

The argument had myth-making qualities, for it was one of the earliest to exalt Magna Carta as the symbol and source of English constitutional liberty. As yet there was no contention that one need not answer incriminating questions after accusation by due process according to common law. But a later generation would use substantially the same argument—"that by the Statutes of Magna Charta . . . for a man to accuse himself was and is utterlie inhibited"—on behalf of the contention that one need not

involuntarily answer questions even after one had been properly accused.

Under Chief Justice EDWARD COKE the common law courts, with the sympathy of Commons, vindicated the Puritan tactic of litigious opposition to the High Commission. The deep hostility between the canon and common law systems expressed itself in a series of writs of prohibition issued by Coke and his colleagues, staying the Commission's proceedings. Coke, adept at creating legal fictions which he clothed with the authority of resurrected "precedents" and inferences from Magna Carta, grounded twenty of these prohibitions on the allegedly ancient common law rule that no man is bound to accuse himself criminally.

In the 1630s the High Commission and the Star Chamber, which employed similar procedures, reached the zenith of their powers. But in 1637 a flinty Puritan agitator, JOHN LILBURNE, refused the oath. His well-publicized opposition to incriminatory questioning focused England's attention upon the injustice and illegality of such practices. In 1641 the Long Parliament, dominated by the Puritan party and common lawyers, condemned the sentences against Lilburne and others, abolished the Star Chamber and the High Commission, and prohibited ecclesiastical authorities from administering any oath obliging one "to confess or to accuse himself or herself of any crime."

Common law courts, however, continued to ask incriminating questions and to bully witnesses into answering them. The rudimentary idea of a right against self-incrimination was nevertheless lodged in the imperishable opinions of Coke, publicized by Lilburne and the Levellers, and firmly associated with Magna Carta. The idea was beginning to take hold of men's minds. Lilburne was again the catalytic agent. At his various trials for his life, in his testimony before investigating committees of Parliament, and in his ceaseless tracts, he dramatically popularized the demand that a right against self-incrimination be accorded general legal recognition. His career illustrates how the right against self-incrimination developed not only in conjunction with a whole gamut of fair procedures associated with "due process of law" but also with demands for freedom of conscience and expression. After Lilburne's time the right became entrenched in English jurisprudence, even under the judicial tyrants of the Restoration. As the state became more secure and as fairer treatment of the criminally accused became possible, the old practice of bullying the prisoner for answers gradually died out. By the early eighteenth century the accused was no longer put on the stand at all; he could not give evidence in his own behalf even if he wished to, although he was permitted to tell his story, unsworn. The prisoner was regarded as incompetent to be a witness for himself.

After the first quarter of the eighteenth century, the English history of the right centered primarily upon the preliminary examination of the suspect and the legality of placing in evidence various types of involuntary confessions. Incriminating statements made by suspects at the preliminary examination could be used against them at their trials; a confession, even though not made under oath, sufficed to convict. Yet suspects could not be interrogated under oath. One might be ensnared into a confession by the sharp and intimidating tactics of the examining magistrate; but there was no legal obligation to answer an incriminating question—nor, until 1848, to notify the suspect or prisoner of his right to refuse answer. One's answers, given in ignorance of his right, might be used against him. However, the courts excluded confessions that had been made under duress. Only involuntary confessions were seen as a violation of the right. Lord Chief Baron Geoffrey Gilbert in his *Law of Evidence* (1756) declared that although a confession was the best evidence of guilt, "this Confession must be voluntary and without compulsion; for our Law . . . will not force any Man to accuse himself; and in this we do certainly follow that Law of Nature" that commands self-preservation.

Thus, opposition to the oath *ex officio* ended in the common law right to refuse to furnish incriminating evidence against oneself even when all formalities of common law accusation had first been fulfilled. The prisoner demanded that the state prove its case against him, and he confronted the witnesses who testified against him. The Levellers, led by Lilburne, even claimed a right not to answer any questions concerning themselves, if life, liberty, or property might be jeopardized, regardless of the tribunal or government agency directing the examination, be it judicial, legislative, or executive. The Leveller claim to a right against self-incrimination raised the generic problem of the nature of SOVEREIGNTY in England and spurred the transmutation of Magna Carta from a feudal relic of baronial reaction into a modern bulwark of the RULE OF LAW and regularized restraints upon government power.

The claim to this right also emerged in the context of a cluster of criminal procedures whose object was to ensure fair play for the criminally accused. It harmonized with the principles that the accused was innocent until proved guilty and that the BURDEN OF PROOF was on the prosecution. It was related to the idea that a man's home should not be promiscuously broken into and rifled for evidence of his reading and writing. It was intimately connected to the belief that torture or any cruelty in forcing a man to expose his guilt was unfair and illegal. It was indirectly associated with the RIGHT TO COUNSEL and the right to have witnesses on behalf of the defendant, so that his lips could remain sealed against the government's questions or accusations. It was at first a privilege of the guilty, given the nature of the substantive law of religious and political crimes. But the right became neither a privilege of the guilty nor a protection of the innocent. It became merely one of the ways of fairly determining guilt or innocence, like TRIAL BY JURY itself; it became part of due process of the law, a fundamental principle of the accusatorial system. It reflected the view that society benefited by seeking the defendant's conviction without the aid of his involuntary admissions. Forcing self-incrimination was thought to brutalize the system of criminal justice and to produce untrustworthy evidence.

Above all, the right was closely linked to FREEDOM OF SPEECH and RELIGIOUS LIBERTY. It was, in its origins, unquestionably the invention of those who were guilty of religious crimes such as heresy, schism, and nonconformity, and later, of political crimes such as TREASON, SEDITIOUS LIBEL, and breach of PARLIAMENTARY PRIVILEGE. More often than not, the offense was merely criticism of the government, its policies, or its officers. The right was associated, then, with guilt for crimes of conscience, of belief, and of association. In the broadest sense it was not so much a protection of the guilty, or even the innocent, but a protection of freedom of expression, of political liberty, and of the right to worship as one pleased. The symbolic importance and practical function of the right certainly settled matters, taken for granted, in the eighteenth century. And it was part of the heritage of liberty that the common law bequeathed to the English settlers in America.

Yet, the right had to be won in every colony, invariably under conditions similar to those that generated it in England. The first glimmer of the right in America was evident in the heresy case of John Wheelwright, tried in 1637 in Massachusetts. In colony after colony, people exposed to the inquisitorial tactics of the prerogative court of the governor and council refused to answer to incriminating interrogatories in cases heavy with political implications. By the end of the seventeenth century the right was unevenly recognized in the colonies. As the English common law increasingly became American law and the legal profession grew in size, competence, and influence,

Americans developed a greater familiarity with the right. English law books and English criminal procedure provided a model. From Edmond Wingate's *Maxims of Reason* (1658), which included the earliest discussion of the maxim, *"Nemo tenetur accusare seipsum,"* to Gilbert's *Evidence,* law books praised the right. It grew so in popularity that in 1735 BENJAMIN FRANKLIN, hearing that a church wanted to examine the sermons of an unorthodox minister, could declare: "It was contrary to the common Rights of Mankind, no Man being obliged to furnish Matter of Accusation against himself." In 1754 a witness parried a Massachusetts legislative investigation into seditious libel by quoting the well-known Latin maxim, which he freely translated as "A Right of Silence as the Priviledge of every Englishman." In 1770 the attorney general of Pennsylvania ruled that an admiralty court could not oblige people to answer interrogatories "which may have a tendency to criminate themselves, or subject them to a penalty, it being contrary to any principle of Reason and the Laws of England." When, in 1770, New York's legislature jailed Alexander McDougall, a popular patriot leader who refused answer to incriminating queries about a seditious broadside, the public associated the right with the patriot cause, and the press printed the toast, "No Answer to Interrogatories, when tending to accuse the Person interrogated." Thereafter the New York legislature granted absolute immunity to recalcitrant malefactors whose testimony was required in trials or investigations.

In 1776 the VIRGINIA CONSTITUTION AND DECLARATION OF RIGHTS provided that in criminal prosecutions the accused party cannot "be compelled to give evidence against himself." Every state (eight including Vermont) that prefaced its constitution with a bill of rights imitated Virginia's phrasing, although two, by placing the clause in a section apart from the rights of the accused, extended the right to third parties or witnesses. Whether the right was constitutionally secured or was protected by common law made little difference, because the early decisions, even in states that constitutionally secured the right, followed the common law rather than the narrower phrasing of their constitutions. For example, the PENNSYLVANIA CONSTITUTION of 1776 had a self-incrimination clause that referred to "no man," which the 1790 constitution narrowed to "the accused." Nevertheless, in the first case on this clause the state supreme court applied it to the production of papers in civil cases and to questions involving exposure to "shame or reproach."

During the controversy over the RATIFICATION OF THE CONSTITUTION of 1787, only four states recommended that a comprehensive bill of rights should be added to the new document, but those four demanded a self-incrimination clause modeled on the conventional phrasing that no person should be compelled to give evidence against himself. JAMES MADISON, in framing what became the Fifth Amendment, urged in sweeping language that no person should be "compelled to be a witness against himself." That phrasing was amended to apply only to criminal cases, thereby permitting courts to compel a civil defendant to produce documents against himself, injuring his civil interest without infringing his traditional rights not to produce them if they could harm him criminally. Whether the framers of the clause in the Fifth meant it to be fully coextensive with the still expanding common law principle is unknown. The language of the clause and its framers' understanding may not have been synonymous, especially because a criminal defendant could not testify under oath even in the absence of the self-incrimination clause. It was intended as a ban on torture, but it also represented the opinion of the framers that the right against self-incrimination was a legitimate defense possessed by every individual against government. The framers were tough-minded revolutionaries who risked everything in support of their belief that legitimate government exercises its powers in subordination to personal rights. The framers were not soft, naive, or disregardful of the claims of law and order. They were mindful that the enduring interests of the community required justice to be done as fairly as possible: that no one should have to be a witness against himself in a criminal case was a central feature of the accusatory system of criminal justice, which the framers identified with fairness. Deeply committed to a system of criminal justice that minimized the possibilities of convicting the innocent, they were not less concerned about the humanity that the law should show even to the offender. The Fifth Amendment reflected their judgment that in a society based on respect for the individual, the government shouldered the entire burden of proving guilt and the accused need make no unwilling contribution to his conviction.

What is the present scope of the right and how have the Supreme Court's interpretations compared with the history of the right? Generally the Court has construed the clause of the Fifth as if the letter killeth. Seeking the spirit and policies of the clause, the Court has tended to give it an ever widening meaning, on the principle that "it is as broad as the mischief against which it seeks to guard," as the Court said in *Counselman.* In effect the Court has taken the position that the Fifth embodied the still evolving common law of the matter rather than a rule of fixed meaning. Often the Court has had history on its side without knowing it, with the result that many apparent innovations could have rested on old practices and precedents.

History supported the decision in BOYD V. UNITED STATES (1886) connecting the Fifth and FOURTH AMENDMENTS and holding that the seizure of one's records for use as evidence against him compels him to be a witness against himself. Beginning in the early eighteenth century the English courts had widened the right against self-incrimination to include protection against the compulsory production of books and papers that might incriminate the accused. In a 1744 case a rule emerged that to compel a defendant to turn over the records of his corporation would be forcing him to "furnish evidence against himself." In the 1760s in WILKES'S CASES, the English courts extended the right to prevent the use of GENERAL WARRANTS to seize private papers in seditious libel cases. Thus the right against self-incrimination and FREEDOM OF THE PRESS, closely allied in their origins, were linked to freedom from unreasonable SEARCHES AND SEIZURES. In *Entick v. Carrington* (1765), Lord Camden (CHARLES PRATT) declared that the law obliged no one to give evidence against himself "because the necessary means of compelling self-accusation, falling upon the innocent as well as the guilty, would be both cruel and unjust; and it should seem that search for evidence is disallowed upon the same principle." American colonists made similar arguments against WRITS OF ASSISTANCE, linking the right against UNREASONABLE SEARCH to the right against self-incrimination. UNITED STATES V. WHITE (1944), which required the production of an organization's records even if they incriminated the witness who held them as custodian, was a departure from history.

That the right extends to witnesses as well as the accused is the command of the text of the Fifth. Protection of witnesses, which can be traced to English cases of the mid-seventeenth century, was invariably accepted in American manuals of practice as well as in leading English treatises throughout the eighteenth century. The Supreme Court's decision in *McCarthy v. Arndstein* (1924), extending the right to witnesses even in civil cases if a truthful answer might result in a forfeiture, penalty, or criminal prosecution, rested on dozens of English decisions going back to 1658 and to American precedents beginning in 1767. In a little known aspect of MARBURY V. MADISON (1803), Chief Justice JOHN MARSHALL asked Attorney General LEVI LINCOLN what he had done with Marbury's missing commission. Lincoln, who probably had burned the commission, refused to incriminate himself by answering, and Marshall conceded that he need not reply, though he was a witness in a civil suit.

Many early state decisions held that neither witnesses nor parties were required to answer against themselves if to do so would expose them to public disgrace or infamy. The origins of so broad a right of silence can be traced as far back as sixteenth-century claims by Protestant reformers such as William Tyndale and Thomas Cartwright in connection with their argument that no one should be compelled to accuse himself. The idea passed to the common lawyers and Coke, was completely accepted in English case law, and found expression in WILLIAM BLACKSTONE's *Commentaries* as well as American manuals of practice. Yet the Supreme Court in BROWN V. WALKER (1896) restricted the scope of the historical right when ruling that the Fifth did not protect against compulsory self-infamy. Its decision was oblivious to history as was its reaffirmation of that decision in *Ullmann v. United States* (1956).

From the standpoint of history that 1896 holding and its 1956 reaffirmation correctly decided the main question whether a grant of full immunity supersedes the witness's right to refuse answer on Fifth Amendment grounds. Colonial precedents support absolute or transactional immunity, as did the IMMUNITY GRANT decisions in 1896 and 1956. The Court departed from its own precedents and history when ruling in KASTIGAR V. UNITED STATES (1972) that limiting the right to use and derived-use immunity does not violate the right not to be a witness against oneself.

History supports the decisions made by the Court for the first time in *Quinn v. United States* (1955) and WATKINS V. UNITED STATES (1957) that the right extends to legislative investigations. As early as 1645 John Lilburne, relying on his own reading of Magna Carta and the PETITION OF RIGHT, claimed the right, unsuccessfully, before a parliamentary committee. In 1688 the Pennsylvania legislature recognized an uncooperative witness's right against self-incrimination. Other colonial assemblies followed suit though New York's did not do so until forced by public opinion after McDougall's case. That Parliament also altered its practice is clear from the debates in 1742 following the refusal of a witness to answer incriminatory questions before an investigating committee. The Commons immunized his testimony against prosecution, but the bill failed in the Lords in part because it violated one of the "first principles of English law," that no person is obliged to accuse himself or answer any questions that tend to reveal what the nature of his defense requires to be concealed. In 1778 the Continental Congress investigated the corrupt schemes of Silas Deane, who invoked his right against self-incrimination, and Congress, it seems, voted that it was lawful for him to do so.

History belies the TWO-SOVEREIGNTIES RULE, a stunting restriction upon the Fifth introduced by the Court in 1931 but abandoned in MURPHY V. WATERFRONT COMMISSION (1964). The rule was that a person could not refuse to testify on the grounds that his disclosures would expose him to prosecution in another jurisdiction. The Court mistakenly claimed that the rule had the support of historical precedents; history clearly contradicted that rule as the Court belatedly confessed in 1964.

History supports the rule of *Bram v. United States* (1897) that in criminal cases in the federal courts—this was extended by MALLOY V. HOGAN (1964) to the state courts, too—whenever a question arises whether a confession is incompetent because it is involuntary or coerced, the issue is controlled by the self-incrimination clause of the Fifth. Partly because of JOHN H. WIGMORE's intimidating influence and partly because of the rule of *Twining* denying that the FOURTEENTH AMENDMENT extended the Fifth to the states, the Court until 1964 held that the coercion of a confession by state or local authorities violated due process of law rather than the right against self-incrimination. Wigmore, the master of evidence, claimed that the rule against coerced confessions and the right against self-incrimination had "no connection," the two being different in history, time or origin, principle, and practice.

Wigmore was wrong. From the fact that a separate rule against coerced confessions emerged in English decisions of the eighteenth century, nearly a century after the right against self-incrimination had become established, he concluded that the two rules had *no* connection. That the two operated differently in some respects and had differing rationales in other respects led him to the same conclusion. But he focused on their differences only and so exaggerated those differences that he fell into numerous errors and inconsistencies of statement. The relationship of the two rules is apparent from the fact that the shadow of the rack was part of the background from which each rule emerged. The disappearance of torture and the recognition of the right against compulsory self-incrimination were victories in the same political struggle. The

connections among torture, *compulsory* self-incrimination, and *coerced* confessions was a historical fact as well as a physical and psychological one. In the sixteenth and seventeenth centuries, the argument against the three, resulting in the rules that Wigmore said had no connection, overlapped. Compulsory self-incrimination was always regarded by its opponents as a species of torture. An act of 1696 regulating treason trials required that confessions be made willingly, without violence, and in open court. The quotation above from Geoffrey Gilbert disproves Wigmore's position. When the separate rule against coerced confessions emerged, its rationale was that a coerced confession is untrustworthy evidence. There remained, however, an indissoluble and crucial nexus with the right against self-incrimination because both rules involved coercion or the involuntary acknowledgment of guilt. Significantly the few references to the right against self-incrimination, in the debates on the ratification of the Constitution, identified the right with a protection against torture and inquisition, that is, against coerced confessions. Wigmore fell into error by assuming that the right against self-incrimination had a single rationale and a static meaning. In fact it always had several rationales, was an expanding principle of law, and spun off into different directions. One spin-off was the development of a separate rule against coerced confessions. If there was "an historical blunder," it was made by the English courts of the eighteenth century when they divorced the confessions rule from the self-incrimination rule.

History is not clear on the Court's distinction between TESTIMONIAL COMPULSION, which the Fifth prohibits, and nontestimonial compulsion, which it does not prohibit. Blood samples, photographs, fingerprints, voice exemplars, and most other forms of nontestimonial compulsion are of modern origin. The fact that the Fifth refers to the right not to be a witness against oneself seems to imply the giving of testimony rather than keeping records or revealing body characteristics for identification purposes. The distinction made by the Court in SCHMERBER V. CALIFORNIA (1966) was reasonable. Yet, limiting the Fifth to prohibit only testimonial compulsion poses problems. The accused originally could not testify at all, and the history of the right does not suggest the *Schmerber* limitations. The common law decisions and the wording of the first state bills of rights explicitly protected against compelling anyone to give or furnish "evidence" against himself, not just testimony.

The fact that history does not support some of the modern decisions limiting the scope of the right hardly means that history always substantiates decisions expanding it. Decisions like *Slochower v. Board of Education* (1956) and GARRITY V. NEW JERSEY (1967), which protect against penalizing the invocation of the right or chilling its use, draw no clear support from the past. Indeed, the decision in GRIFFIN V. CALIFORNIA (1965) which prohibited comment on the failure of a criminal defendant to testify on ground that such comment "is a remnant of the inquisitorial system" is historically farfetched.

Finally, history is ambiguous on the controversial issue whether the right against self-incrimination extends to the police station. When justices of the peace performed police functions and conducted the preliminary examination of suspects, their interrogation was inquisitorial in character (as it is in the interrogation rooms of modern police stations) and it usually had as its object the incrimination of the suspect. Yet he could not be examined under oath, and he did have a right to withhold the answer to incriminating questions. On the other hand, he had no right to be told that he need not answer or be cautioned that his answers could be used against him. However, the right against self-incrimination grew out of a protest against incriminating interrogation *prior to* formal accusation. That is, the maxim *nemo tenetur seipsum prodere* originally meant that no one was obligated to supply the evidence that could be used to indict him. Thus, from the very inception of the right, a suspect could invoke it at the earliest stages of his interrogation.

In MIRANDA V. ARIZONA (1966) the Supreme Court expanded the right beyond all precedent, yet not beyond its historical spirit. *Miranda's* purpose was to eliminate the inherently coercive and inquisitional atmosphere of the interrogation room and to guarantee that any incriminating admissions are made voluntarily. That purpose was, historically, the heart of the Fifth, the basis of its policy. Even the guarantee of counsel to effectuate that purpose has precedent in a historical analogy: the development of the right to counsel originally safeguarded the right against self-incrimination at the trial stage of prosecution. When the defendant lacked counsel, he had to conduct his own case, and although he was not put on the stand and did not have to answer incriminating questions, his failure to rebut accusations and insinuations by the prosecution prejudiced the jury, vitiating the right to silence. The right to counsel permitted the defendant's lips to remain sealed; his "mouthpiece" spoke for him. In *Miranda* the Court extended the protection of counsel to the earliest stage of a criminal action,

when the need is the greatest because the suspect is most vulnerable.

Nevertheless, the *Miranda* warnings were an invention of the Court, devoid of historical support. Excepting rare occasions when judges intervened to protect a witness against incriminatory interrogatories, the right had to be claimed or invoked by the person seeking its protection. Historically it was a fighting right; unless invoked it offered no protection. It did not bar interrogation or taint an uncoerced confession as improper evidence. Incriminating statements made by a suspect could always be used at his trial. That a person might unwittingly incriminate himself when questioned in no way impaired his legal right to refuse answer. He lacked the right to be warned that he need not answer; he lacked the right to have a lawyer present at his interrogation; and he lacked the protection of the strict waiver requirements that now accompany the MIRANDA RULES. From a historical view, the decision in BREWER V. WILLIAMS (1977) and the limits on interrogation imposed by RHODE ISLAND V. INNES (1980) extraordinarily inflate the right. What was once a fighting right has become a pampered one. Law should encourage, not thwart, voluntary confessions. The Fifth should be liberally construed to serve as a check on modern versions of the "third degree" and the spirit of McCarthyism, but the Court should distinguish rapists and murderers from John Lilburne and realize that law enforcement agencies today are light years away from the behavior revealed in BROWN V. MISSISSIPPI (1936) and CHAMBERS V. FLORIDA (1940).

The Court said in PALKO V. CONNECTICUT (1937) that the right against compulsory self-incrimination was not a fundamental right; it might be lost, and justice might still be done if the accused "were subject to a duty to respond to orderly inquiry." Few would endorse that judgment today, but it is a yardstick for measuring how radically different the constitutional law of the Fifth became in half a century.

History surely exalts the right if precedence be our guide. It won acceptance earlier than did the freedoms of speech, press, and religion. It preceded a cluster of procedural rights such as benefit of counsel. It is older, too, than immunities against BILLS OF ATTAINDER, EX POST FACTO laws, and unreasonable searches and seizures. History also exalts the origins of the right against self-incrimination, for they are related to the development of the accusatorial system of criminal justice and the concept of FAIR TRIAL; to the principle that FUNDAMENTAL LAW limits government—the very foundation of CONSTITUTIONAL-

ISM; and to the heroic struggles for the freedoms of the FIRST AMENDMENT. History does not, however, exalt the right against the claims of justice.

LEONARD W. LEVY

Bibliography

FRIENDLY, HENRY J. 1968 The Fifth Amendment Tomorrow: The Case for Constitutional Change. *University of Cincinnati Law Review* 37:671–726.

GRISWOLD, ERWIN 1955 *The 5th Amendment Today.* Cambridge, Mass.: Harvard University Press.

HOOK, SIDNEY 1957 *Common Sense and the Fifth Amendment.* New York: Criterion.

KAMISAR, YALE 1980 *Police Interrogation and Confessions: Essays in Law and Policy.* Ann Arbor: University of Michigan Press.

LEVY, LEONARD W. 1968 *Origins of the Fifth Amendment: The Right against Self-Incrimination.* New York: Oxford University Press.

MAYERS, LEWIS 1959 *Shall We Amend the Fifth Amendment?* New York: Harper & Row.

MORGAN, EDMUND M. 1949 The Privilege against Self-Incrimination. *Minnesota Law Review* 34:1–37.

WIGMORE, JOHN HENRY 1961 *Evidence in Trials at Common Law,* vol. 8, rev. by John T. McNaughton. Boston: Little, Brown.

RIGHT OF PRIVACY

Long before anyone spoke of privacy as a constitutional right, American law had developed a "right of privacy," invasion of which was a tort, justifying the award of money damages. One such invasion would be a newspaper's embarrassing publication of intimate facts about a person, or a statement placing someone in a "false light," when the story was not newsworthy. Other invasions of this right were found in various forms of physical intrusion, or surveillance, or interception of private communications. The Constitution, too, protected some interests in privacy: the FOURTH AMENDMENT forbade unreasonable SEARCHES AND SEIZURES; the Fifth Amendment offered a RIGHT AGAINST SELF-INCRIMINATION; the THIRD AMENDMENT, a relic of the Revolutionary War, forbade the government to quarter troops in a private house in peacetime without the owner's consent. Even so, despite Justice LOUIS D. BRANDEIS's famous statement in the WIRETAPPING case of OLMSTEAD V. UNITED STATES (1928), there was no general constitutional "right to be let alone." Nor does any such sweeping constitutional right exist today. Beginning with GRISWOLD V. CONNECTICUT (1965), the Su-

preme Court has recognized a constitutional right of privacy, but the potentially broad scope of that right remains constricted by the Court's current interpretations of it.

Griswold held invalid a Connecticut law forbidding the use of contraceptives, in application to the operators of a BIRTH CONTROL clinic who were aiding married couples to violate the law, offering them advice and contraceptive devices. Justice WILLIAM O. DOUGLAS, writing for the Court, disavowed any reliance on SUBSTANTIVE DUE PROCESS to support the decision. Although the statute did not violate the terms of any specific guarantee of the BILL OF RIGHTS, said Douglas, the Court's decisions had recognized that "specific guarantees in the Bill of Rights have penumbras, formed by emanations from those guarantees that help give them life and substance." The FREEDOM OF ASSOCIATION, although not mentioned in the FIRST AMENDMENT, had been protected against intrusions on the privacy of political association. The Third, Fourth, and Fifth Amendments also created "zones of privacy." The *Griswold* case concerned "a relationship lying within the zone of privacy created by several fundamental constitutional guarantees." Furthermore, the idea of allowing police to enforce a ban on contraceptives by searching the marital bedroom was "repulsive to the notions of privacy surrounding the marriage relationship."

Connecticut had not been enforcing its law even against drugstore sales of contraceptives; the governmental prying conjured up in the *Griswold* opinion was not really threatened. What *Griswold* was protecting was not so much the privacy of the marital bedroom as a married couple's control over the intimacies of their relationship. This point emerged clearly in EISENSTADT V. BAIRD (1972), which extended the right to practice contraception to unmarried persons, and in CAREY V. POPULATION SERVICES INTERNATIONAL (1977), which struck down three laws restricting the sale and advertisement of contraceptives.

In *Eisenstadt* the Court characterized the right of privacy as the right of an individual "to be free from unwarranted intrusion into matters so fundamentally affecting a person as the decision whether to bear or beget a child." The prophecy in those words came true the following year when the Court, in ROE V. WADE (1973), held that the constitutional right of privacy recognized in *Griswold* was "broad enough to encompass a woman's decision whether or not to terminate her pregnancy." This right to decide whether to have an abortion was qualified only in the later stages of pregnancy; during the first trimester of pregnancy it was absolute. Abandoning *Griswold*'s PENUMBRA THEORY, the Court placed the right of privacy within the liberty protected by the DUE PROCESS clause of the FOURTEENTH AMENDMENT. (See ABORTION AND THE CONSTITUTION.)

As the *Roe* dissenters pointed out, an abortion operation "is not 'private' in the ordinary usage of that word." Liberty, not privacy, was the chief constitutional value at stake in *Roe*. In later years various Justices have echoed the words of Justice POTTER STEWART, concurring in *Roe*, that "freedom of personal choice in matters of marriage and family life" is a due process liberty. Indeed, Justice Stewart's formulation was too narrow; the Court's decisions have gone well beyond formal marriage and the traditional family to protect a much broader FREEDOM OF INTIMATE ASSOCIATION. Yet that freedom is often defended in the name of the constitutional right of privacy.

From the time of the *Griswold* decision forward, privacy became the subject of a body of legal and philosophical literature notable for both analytical quality and rapid growth. The term "privacy" cried out for definition—not merely as a feature of constitutional law, where the Supreme Court had offered no more than doctrinal impressionism, but more fundamentally as a category of thought. Is privacy a situation, or a value, or a claim of right? Is privacy itself the subject of our moral and legal claims, or is it a code word that always stands for some other interest? However these initial questions be answered, what are the functions of privacy in our society? These are not merely philosophers' inquiries; in deciding "right of privacy" cases judges also answer them, even if the answers are buried in assumptions never articulated.

Not until 1977 did the Supreme Court begin to map out the territory occupied by the constitutional right of privacy. In WHALEN V. ROE the Court upheld a state law requiring the maintenance of computerized records of persons who obtained various drugs by medical prescription. "The cases sometimes characterized as protecting 'privacy,'" said the Court, "have in fact involved at least two different kinds of interests. One is the individual interest in avoiding disclosure of personal matters, and another is the interest in independence in making certain kinds of important decisions." This passage is noteworthy in two respects: first, its opening words suggest a new awareness that "privacy" may not be the most informative label for an interest in freedom of choice whether to marry, or procreate, or have an abortion,

or send one's child to a private school. Second, the passage strongly hints that some interests in informational privacy—freedom from disclosure—are constitutionally protected not only by the First, Fourth, and Fifth Amendments but also by a more general right of privacy.

The *Whalen* opinion was written by Justice JOHN PAUL STEVENS, who has consistently urged an expansive reading of the "liberty" protected by the due process clauses. As if to emphasize that the right of privacy is merely one aspect of a broadly defined right of substantive due process, Justice Stevens cited, to support his reference to the interest in independence in making important decisions, ALLGEYER V. LOUISIANA (1897), which established the FREEDOM OF CONTRACT as a due process right. If the "important decisions" part of the right of privacy is to be absorbed back into the body of substantive due process, and if informational privacy is to become part of a redefined constitutional right of privacy, the contours of this new right will for the first time approach the meanings of "privacy" in common speech. Before *Whalen*, it was possible to say that the one interest most conspicuously left unprotected by the constitutional right of privacy was privacy itself. In any event, even after *Whalen*'s suggestive analysis, the Supreme Court has continued to speak of "the" constitutional right of privacy.

There is a sense in which personal decisions about sex and marriage and procreation are private decisions. Indeed, the word "private" serves better than "privacy" to indicate the interests in personal autonomy at stake in such cases. Both words can refer to such forms of privacy as seclusion and secrecy; to do something in private is to do it free from public or general observance, and private information consists of facts not publicly or generally known. But "private" has another meaning that lacks any similar analogue in the idea of privacy. Private property, for example, is property that is one's own, subject to one's control, from which one has the right to exclude others if one chooses to do so. It makes perfect sense to speak of a power of decision as private in this sense. From this perspective the line of "privacy" opinions from *Griswold* to *Roe* and beyond can be seen as seeking to identify the circumstances in which the decision "to bear or beget a child" is one that "belongs" to the individual, one from which the public—even the state—can be excluded. Calling such an interest "privacy," however, is a play on words; any freedom from governmental regulation might just as easily be called "privacy." Perhaps Justice Stevens was making this point in his *Whalen* opinion when he cited *Allgeyer*, a case in which the liberty at stake was freedom to buy insurance from an out-of-state company.

Much of what government does in the way of regulating behavior intrudes on privacy in its commonly understood senses of solitude and nondisclosure. Yet even when these forms of privacy are assimilated to the constitutional right of privacy, the result is not wholesale invalidation of governmental action. The *Whalen* decision itself is illustrative. Recognizing that the drug records law threatened some impairment of both the interest in nondisclosure and the interest in making personal decisions, the Court nonetheless concluded that the law's informational security safeguards minimized the chances of serious harm to those interests and that the law was a reasonable means of minimizing drug abuse. More serious threats of disclosure of accumulated personal information, the Court said, might exceed constitutional limitations. The clear implication is that future claims to a constitutional right of privacy in the form of nondisclosure will be evaluated through a process of judicial interest balancing.

Even a judge who regards privacy as a constitutional value in itself, something more than a label for other interests, will be pressed to consider why privacy is important, in order to place the proper weights in a given case's decisional balance. The commentary on privacy regularly identifies several overlapping values. If governmental "brainwashing" would be unconstitutional, as all observers assume, the reason surely lies in the widely shared sense that the essentials of due process "liberty" include a healthy measure of control over the development of one's own individuality. That control undoubtedly requires some amount of privacy in the form of nondisclosure and seclusion. To have the sense of being a person, an individual needs some degree of control over the roles she may play in various social settings; control over the disclosure of personal information contributes to this process. Similarly, both learning and creative activity require a measure of relaxation and refuge from the world's intrusions.

A closely related function of informational privacy is its value as a foundation for friendship and intimacy. Although a cynic might say that the most effective way for an individual to preserve the privacy of his thoughts and feelings would be never to disclose them, that course would sacrifice the sort of sharing that constitutes a central value of intimate association—which, in turn, is crucial to the development of individuality. It is here that we can see clearly the overlap between privacy as selective nondisclosure and "privacy" as autonomy in intimate personal deci-

sions. Justice Douglas's *Griswold* opinion spoke to both concerns: he sought to defend the privacy of the marital bedroom against hypothetical government snooping and to defend a married couple's autonomy over the intimacies of their relationship. The special constitutional status of the home, recognized in decisions ranging from search and seizure doctrines to the "private" possession of OBSCENITY protected in STANLEY V. ILLINOIS (1969), draws not only on the notion of the home as a sanctuary and place of repose but also on the home's status as the main locus of intimate associations.

Finally, privacy in the sense of seclusion or nondisclosure serves to encourage freedom, both in the sense of political liberty and in the sense of moral autonomy. The political privacy cases from NAACP V. ALABAMA (1958) to GIBSON V. FLORIDA LEGISLATIVE INVESTIGATION COMMITTEE (1963) and beyond rest on the premise that disclosure of political associations is especially harmful to members of political groups that are unpopular or unorthodox. When the Army engaged in the domestic political surveillance that produced the Supreme Court's 5–4 nondecision in LAIRD V. TATUM (1972), its files were filled with the names of those who "were thought to have at least some potential for civil disorder," not with the names of Rotarians and Job's Daughters. A similar threat is posed by disclosure of one's homosexual associations or other intimate associations outside the mainstream of conventional morality. Such a case, like *Griswold*, implicates both privacy as nondisclosure or seclusion and "privacy" as associational autonomy.

On the other side of the constitutional balance, opposed to the interest in informational privacy, may be ranged any of the interests commonly advanced to support the free exchange of information. To further many of those interests, the common law of defamation erected an elaborate structure of "privileges," designed to protect from liability persons who made defamatory statements in the course of exchanging information for legitimate purposes: a former employer might give a servant a bad reference; a newspaper might criticize the town mayor. As these examples show, informational privacy is by no means the only constitutional interest that may be raised in such cases. Not only has the law of defamation been hedged in with First Amendment limitations; liability for the tort of invasion of privacy must also pass judicial scrutiny aimed at avoiding violations of the FREEDOM OF THE PRESS. Although the Supreme Court has not ruled on the matter, undoubtedly the First Amendment will be read to include a "newsworthiness" defense to an action for damages for invasion of privacy by publication of intimate facts. Even where the First Amendment is not involved directly as a constitutional limit on the award of damages or the imposition of punishment under state law, that amendment's values must be taken into account in evaluating any claim that a state has violated an individual's constitutional right of informational privacy. (See GOVERNMENT SPEECH.) Perhaps for this reason, most lower federal courts have been reluctant to find in Justice Stevens's *Whalen* opinion a general invitation to expand the constitutional right of privacy's protections against disclosure of information.

Nor has the Supreme Court been ready, in the years since ROE V. WADE, to extend either branch of the constitutional right of privacy. The Court's best-known opportunities for widening the scope of the right have come in "important decisions" cases involving nonmarital intimate relationships (including homosexual ones; see SEXUAL PREFERENCE AND THE CONSTITUTION) and the asserted right to control one's own personal appearance (including dress and hair length). In some of these cases the Court has avoided deciding cases on their constitutional merits; in no case has the Court validated the claim of a right of privacy. On principle, the intimate association cases seem clearly enough to be governed by *Griswold* and its successor decisions. Yet the Court has temporized, displaying what ALEXANDER BICKEL once called "the passive virtues," evidently awaiting the formation of a sufficient political consensus before extending constitutional protection to unconventional intimate associations.

One factual context in which the Court seems likely to continue its hospitality to "privacy" claims touching intimate personal decisions is that of governmental intrusions into the body. The abortion decisions, of course, are the modern starting point. Compulsory smallpox VACCINATION, once upheld as a health measure, stands on shakier constitutional ground now that smallpox has been virtually eradicated. Compulsory STERILIZATION, too, is unconstitutional in the absence of justification by some COMPELLING STATE INTEREST. The Supreme Court has explicitly redescribed SKINNER V. OKLAHOMA (1942) as a "privacy" case. By analogy, the right of a competent adult to refuse medical treatment seems secure, even when that choice will probably lead to death. (See EUTHANASIA.)

If the Supreme Court comes to accept Justice Stevens's broad reading of due process "liberty," it makes little difference whether the bodily intrusion cases be seen as raising "privacy" issues. There are occasions, however, when governmental invasions of the body implicate not only the interest in autonomy over one's own body but also privacy in its true sense of nondisclosure and seclusion. An appalling case in point is *Bell v. Wolfish* (1979). Inmates of a federal detention center, held in custody before being tried on criminal charges, sued to challenge the constitutionality of various conditions of their confinement. One challenged practice was the systematic subjection of every inmate to visual inspection of his or her body cavities after every "contact visit" with a person from outside the center, whether or not anyone had any suspicion that contraband was being smuggled into the center. A 5–4 Supreme Court held that the searches were not unreasonable and thus presented no Fourth Amendment problem; the majority did not separately consider any constitutional right of privacy founded on due process. The two main dissenting opinions, emphasizing substantive due process, insisted that the government must offer substantial justification for such a degrading invasion of privacy. (See ROCHIN V. CALIFORNIA, 1952.) Justification was lacking: the lower court had found that the searches were ineffective in detecting smuggled goods, and the government's argument that the searches deterred smuggling was an obvious makeweight.

There was no significant physical invasion of the body in the *Wolfish* case. Yet the privacy interests of the individuals searched were not far removed from those involved in the abortion and sterilization cases. The detainees sought vindication of their right to be afforded the dignity of respect, not just for their bodies but for their persons. The very pointlessness of the searches in cases where suspicion was lacking heightened the humiliation, to the point that many inmates had given up visits by family members. The case illustrates perfectly the convergence of the interests in personal autonomy and informational privacy in an individual's control over his own personality. When government seriously invades that sphere, due process demands important justification.

Several states guarantee a right of privacy in their state constitutions. The various state supreme courts have relied on these provisions to hold unconstitutional not only invasions of informational privacy, such as police surveillance, but also invasions of personal autonomy, such as laws limiting the occupancy of a house to members of a family, or forbidding the possession of marijuana for personal use. If the Supreme Court were to follow the doctrinal leadership of these courts, it would not be the first time. (See INCORPORATION DOCTRINE.)

Both types of interests protected by the federal constitutional right of privacy are susceptible to either broad or narrow interpretation. A generalized "privacy" right to make important decisions, like a generalized right of informational privacy, resists clear-cut definition. Every extension of a constitutional right of personal autonomy detracts from the power of government to regulate behavior in the public interest (as government defines that interest); and every extension of a constitutional right of informational privacy detracts from the free flow of communication. The problem for the courts, here as in EQUAL PROTECTION and other areas of constitutional growth, is the stopping-place problem. It is no accident that most discussions of the newer constitutional right of privacy turn to questions about the proper role of the judiciary—a theme that has dominated discussion of substantive due process since it appeared on the constitutional scene a century ago. The problem of defining a constitutional right and the problem of establishing the courts' proper constitutional role are two faces of the same inquiry. A constitutional right that defies description not only fails to protect its intended beneficiaries but also undermines the position of the courts in the governmental system.

Justice Stevens's opinion in WHALEN V. ROE begins to point the way toward the resolution of the uncertainties that have surrounded the constitutional right of privacy ever since the *Griswold* decision. It does aid constitutional analysis to separate the right into the two strands of personal autonomy and informational privacy. Yet it remains useful to recognize, as Justice Stevens has continued to remind us, that both strands remain part of a single substantive due process principle: significant governmental invasions of individual liberty require justification, scaled in importance according to the severity of the invasions. The right of privacy, then, is no more susceptible to precise definition than are such rights as due process or equal protection. What can be identified are the substantive values that inform the right of privacy. These values, as the Supreme Court's decisions show, are centered in the respect owed by the organized society to each individual as a person and as a member of a community. When governmental officers invade a person's control over her own body, or development of individual identity, or intimate associations—either by restricting decisional autonomy or by intruding on privacy in the sense of nondisclosure or solitude—then the Constitution demands that they be called to account and made to justify their actions.

For the future, the fate of the right of privacy, like that of all constitutional rights, will depend on the courts only secondarily. In the long run, the crucial questions will be how much privacy and what kinds of privacy we value. Total privacy—that is, isolation

from others—is not merely unattainable; hardly anyone could stand it for long. In some societies people neither have nor want much of what we call privacy. Yet even among Australian aborigines who eke out their precarious living in a desert that often fails to provide walls, there are rules of restraint and social distance, and, when all else fails, the magic of secret names. Our own constitutional right of privacy will grow or wither as our own society's rules of restraint and social distance form and dissolve.

KENNETH L. KARST

(SEE ALSO: *Privacy and the First Amendment.*)

Bibliography
BOSTWICK, GARY L. 1976 A Taxonomy of Privacy: Repose, Sanctuary, and Intimate Decision. *California Law Review* 64:1447–83.
GAVISON, RUTH 1980 Privacy and the Limits of Law. *Yale Law Journal* 89:421–71.
GERETY, TOM 1977 Redefining Privacy. *Harvard Civil Rights–Civil Liberties Law Review* 12:233–96.
GREENAWALT, KENT 1974 Privacy and Its Legal Protections. *Hastings Center Studies* 2:45–68.
HENKIN, LOUIS 1974 Privacy and Autonomy. *Columbia Law Review* 74:1410–33.
PENNOCK, J. ROLAND and CHAPMAN, JOHN W., eds. 1971 *Privacy.* NOMOS XIII. New York: Atherton Press.
Symposium on Privacy 1966 *Law and Contemporary Problems* 31:251–435.
TRIBE, LAURENCE H. 1978 *American Constitutional Law.* Chap. 15. Mineola, N.Y.: The Foundation Press.
WESTIN, ALAN F. 1967 *Privacy and Freedom.* New York: Atheneum.

RIGHT OF REVOLUTION

The right of revolution is not a right that is defined and protected by the Constitution but a NATURAL RIGHT. It would be absurd for a constitution to authorize revolutionary challenges to its authority. However, it would not have been absurd for the preamble to the Constitution to have acknowledged the right of revolution, as, for example, the preamble to the PENNSYLVANIA CONSTITUTION of 1776 had done. It was unnecessary to include such an acknowledgment in the Constitution of 1787, for the Constitution did not supplant the DECLARATION OF INDEPENDENCE of 1776, which remained the first organic law of the United States. The "people" who "ordain and establish this Constitution" are the same "people" who in 1776 "assume among the powers of the earth, the separate and equal station to which the Laws of Nature and of Nature's God entitle them." The Declaration, borrowing the reasoning of JOHN LOCKE, succinctly states the American doctrine of the right of revolution:

We hold these truths to be self-evident, that all men are created equal, that they are endowed by their Creator with certain unalienable Rights, that among these are Life, Liberty and the pursuit of Happiness. That to secure these rights, Governments are instituted among Men, deriving their just powers from the consent of the governed, That whenever any Form of Government becomes destructive of these ends, it is the Right of the People to alter or abolish it, and to institute new Government, laying its foundation on such principles and organizing its powers in such form, as to them shall seem most likely to effect their Safety and Happiness. Prudence, indeed, will dictate that Governments long established should not be changed for light and transient causes; and accordingly all experience hath shown, that mankind are more disposed to suffer, while evils are sufferable, than to right themselves by abolishing the forms to which they are accustomed. But when a long train of abuses and usurpations, pursuing invariably the same Object evinces a design to reduce them under absolute Despotism, it is their right, it is their duty, to throw off such Government, and to provide new Guards for their future security.

Recognition of the right of revolution is, in this view, implicit in the recognition of human equality. A people who recognize that they are equal members of the same species—that no human being is the natural ruler of another—accept that the inequalities necessarily involved in government are not natural but must be "instituted" and operated by "consent"; and that the primary end of government is not the promotion of the interests of one allegedly superior class of human beings but the security of all citizens' equal rights to "life, liberty, and the pursuit of happiness." It follows that it is the right and the duty of such a people to change their government when it persistently fails to effect this end. This right and duty, the Declaration says, belongs not to all peoples but only to those enlightened peoples who recognize human equality and natural rights, and who will therefore exercise their revolutionary right to establish right-securing government by consent.

Not only the revolutionaries of 1776 but also the Framers of the Constitution of 1787 justified their actions on this basis. In THE FEDERALIST #40 and #43 JAMES MADISON cites the Declaration's right of revolution to explain and to support the revolutionary proposals of the CONSTITUTIONAL CONVENTION. Madison argues that political leadership (by patriots like those assembled in Philadelphia) is needed in a revolution because "it is impossible for the people spontaneously and universally to move in concert towards their object." Thus, while the right of revolution

is justly exercised when an enlightened people feel and judge that their government threatens to lead them back into an anarchical state of nature by failing to fulfill the duties they have entrusted to it, a revolution need neither wait for nor involve an anarchical disruption of society. However, exercise of the right of revolution (in contrast to mere CIVIL DISOBEDIENCE) can well necessitate and justify war. Those who exercise the right of revolution must prudently measure their forces.

ALEXANDER HAMILTON, in *The Federalist* #16, acknowledged that no constitution can guarantee that a widespread revolutionary opposition to the government will never occur; such opposition might well proceed "from weighty causes of discontent given by the government" itself. In contrast to Marxist doctrines of revolution, the American doctrine does not anticipate a future in which the right of revolution can safely disappear. It is therefore a cause for concern that today the right of revolution is obscured not only because it is a natural rather than a constitutional right but also because natural rights are no longer generally recognized by political theorists and jurists.

JOHN ZVESPER

Bibliography

MANSFIELD, HARVEY C., JR. 1978 *The Spirit of Liberalism*. Cambridge, Mass.: Harvard University Press.
STOURZH, GERALD 1970 *Alexander Hamilton and the Idea of Republican Government*. Stanford, Calif.: Stanford University Press.

RIGHT–PRIVILEGE DISTINCTION

There are at least two ways of distinguishing between "privileges" and "rights" in the context of American constitutional law and history, and careful analysis does not confound the two. The text of the Constitution refers to both privileges and rights, and uses "privileges" as a term of art denoting a class of rights that may be invoked defensively, to excuse one from a legal restraint or obligation. In another usage, privileges have both an inferior status to and a less permanent existence than rights, being subject to revocation by the government or to the imposition of conditions on their exercise. There is no foundation in the Constitution for the latter distinction.

In the Constitution, a privilege is one kind of right. The word privilege appears four times. The first appearance is in the PRIVILEGE FROM ARREST in civil cases enjoyed by members of Congress during congressional sessions. The second appearance is the guarantee of the "privilege of the writ of HABEAS CORPUS," yet that "privilege" has at least as great a degree of status and permanence as any right in the Constitution. The other appearances are in the PRIVILEGES AND IMMUNITIES clauses of Article IV and of the FOURTEENTH AMENDMENT: the citizens of each state are entitled to the privileges and immunities of citizens in the several states; and no state may abridge the privileges or immunities of citizens of the United States.

Privileges are associated with, but are distinct from, immunities. A privilege is an exemption from a legal restraint or duty (such as the duty to testify in court), while an immunity is an exemption from liability (usually civil liability). Thus members of Congress are privileged from arrest and immune from having to answer in another place for their SPEECH OR DEBATE. The way in which the word is used in the Constitution suggests that a privilege is a kind of right distinguished not by revocability or conditionability but by the fact that it cannot be asserted until some authority has taken action against one. One can exercise the right of RELIGIOUS LIBERTY or the right of peaceable assembly on one's own initiative; but one cannot demand that the state show cause for holding one in jail until one is actually held, and one cannot refuse to answer questions until questions are asked. A constitutional privilege is defensive, but it may be asserted as of right. Thus there is not necessarily a diminution of the RIGHT AGAINST SELF-INCRIMINATION when that right is called a privilege.

The word "right," standing alone, along with the word "freedom" and the phrase "right of the people," is used in the Constitution to designate a right that one may assert affirmatively and which the government is precluded from invading. Among these are NATURAL RIGHTS, which antedate the Constitution, such as the FREEDOM OF SPEECH, the right of the people to keep and bear arms, and the right of the people to be secure in their persons, houses, papers, and effects. Another category of constitutional rights comprises procedural rights, both civil and criminal.

Precise usage of constitutional terms is hampered by an unfortunate rhetorical use of the terms "right" and "privilege." Even JAMES MADISON seems, on occasion, to have used "privilege" to mean a special boon conferred by authority and subject to revocation at the pleasure of the grantor. Subsequently, because the power to revoke a right includes the power to impose conditions upon its exercise, "privilege" came, in certain rhetorical circumstances, to stand for rights that were conditionable.

This rhetorical use of "right" and "privilege" was introduced into American public law by OLIVER WENDELL HOLMES. Writing as a justice of the Massachusetts Supreme Judicial Court, Holmes commented in 1892 on the freedom of speech of PUBLIC EMPLOYEES: "The petitioner may have the constitutional right to talk politics, but he has no constitutional right to be a policeman." Public employment was, for Holmes, not a right but a privilege. In GOLDBERG V. KELLY (1970) the Supreme Court stated that it had abandoned the right–privilege distinction. WELFARE BENEFITS might be a privilege, in the sense that the state could constitutionally abolish a welfare program, but a particular beneficiary's benefits could not be terminated except by procedures that satisfied the requirements of PROCEDURAL DUE PROCESS.

Similarly, the federal courts today interpret the FIRST AMENDMENT to protect public employees against at least some restrictions on their constitutional freedoms. Government, the Court has said, "may not deny a benefit to a person because he exercises a Constitutional right." Yet rights—even First Amendment rights—are defined more narrowly for public employees than they are for others, as the validation of the HATCH ACT demonstrated. (See UNCONSTITUTIONAL CONDITIONS.)

In recent years the Court has erected new barriers to the invocation of the right to procedural due process, requiring that a claimant establish deprivation of a liberty or property interest before due process even becomes an issue and paying considerable deference to state law in defining both types of interest. In refusing to characterize some important interests as liberty or property, the Court has relegated those interests to an inferior status. Thus the Holmesian right–privilege distinction, once abandoned, has been welcomed home in new clothes.

DENNIS J. MAHONEY
KENNETH L. KARST

Bibliography

HOHFELD, WESLEY N. 1923 *Fundamental Legal Conceptions.* New Haven, Conn.: Yale University Press.
MONAGHAN, HENRY P. 1977 Of "Liberty" and "Property." *Cornell Law Review* 62:401–444.
VAN ALSTYNE, WILLIAM W. 1968 The Demise of the Right–Privilege Distinction in Constitutional Law. *Harvard Law Review* 81:1439–1464.
———— 1977 Cracks in "The New Property": Adjudicative Due Process in the Administrative State. *Cornell Law Review* 62:445–493.

RIGHT TO BAIL

See: Bail

RIGHT TO BEAR ARMS

See: Second Amendment

RIGHT TO BE INFORMED OF ACCUSATION

The Sixth Amendment provides that "[i]n all criminal prosecutions, the accused shall enjoy the right . . . to be informed of the nature and cause of the accusation. . . ." The right was recognized in English law prior to adoption of the Constitution and exists today in every state, under state law and through judicial interpretation of the DUE PROCESS clause of the FOURTEENTH AMENDMENT. The notice of accusation contemplated by the Sixth Amendment is the formal charge of crime to which the accused must respond by pleading guilty or not guilty; it does not include the notice issues that may arise in the investigative phase of a criminal proceeding.

The "notice clause" makes no reference to the institution that must produce the charge, the instrument through which notice must be given, or the precise function of the notice. But these details are supplied by other provisions of the Constitution, by history, and by judicial opinions. Where the accused is charged with an infamous federal crime, usually a FELONY, the Fifth Amendment requires that the accusation must be made by the INDICTMENT of a GRAND JURY. For lesser federal crimes, an INFORMATION drafted by a prosecutor or even a complaint will suffice. In the states, any of these processes may be used because indictment by grand jury is not required by the Fourteenth Amendment.

Over the years, the charging instrument has been assigned several roles by the courts. It provides the notice required by the Sixth Amendment, and it assists in enforcing the provisions of the Fifth Amendment dealing with the grand jury, DOUBLE JEOPARDY, and due process. For example, indictments and informations must demonstrate that the offense charged is not the same as one for which the accused has already been placed in jeopardy. And indictments must reflect the decisions of the grand juries that returned them.

The unique function of the Sixth Amendment's notice clause—as distinct from the facilitative role it plays for the Fifth Amendment—is to require advice to the accused of the charge against him so that he may decide whether to concede his guilt or, if he does not, so that he may prepare to defend himself at trial. The notice must also contain enough detail to enable the court to determine whether the charge is sufficient in law to support a conviction. To perform these functions, the notice must state the basic facts regarding each element of the offense with "reasonable particularity of time, place and circumstances." Such notice is especially important in an adversary system that contemplates a trial as a climactic event. Without notice, defendants would find it difficult to proceed expeditiously, and frequent continuances might be necessary; trial judges would have no manageable criterion for determining the relevance of EVIDENCE or the instructions to be given to juries; and appellate courts would have inadequate standards for review.

Few cases have tested the limits of the notice clause, for both the federal government and the states now have statutes or rules of court that define what must appear in the charging instrument and these requirements usually reflect the constitutional standard. For example, Rule 7 of the FEDERAL RULES OF CRIMINAL PROCEDURE requires a "plain, concise and definite written statement of the essential facts constituting the offense charged." There are state decisions, however, that suggest how little might now be constitutionally required of the initial charge in a criminal case. In these cases, state laws authorized indictments that informed defendants only of the names or citations of the statutes they were accused of violating. In *People v. Bogdanoff* (1930) New York's high court upheld the constitutionality of such a "short form indictment." Although the New York statute involved in that case has not survived, the opinion called attention in dramatic fashion to changes that may have made the law of "notice" partially obsolete. The routine maintenance of trial records was said to provide a basis for determining whether a prior proceeding involved the same offense as the one charged in the indictment. And the availability of grand jury minutes made it possible to determine whether the offense charged at trial was the same as the one contemplated by the grand jury. The only interest of the accused remaining to be protected by the charging instrument itself, said the court, was an adequate opportunity to prepare for trial; that interest could be served by a bill of particulars, continuances, and other measures. In sum, the notice clause—stripped of its relation to the jeopardy and grand jury provisions—may be satisfied not only by a single charging document but also by a process of notice that enables the defendant to understand the charge and defend against it.

The logic of a flexible conception of notice, rooted less in form than in concern for the defendant's need to prepare for trial, led inevitably to the position that many defects in the indictment or information—which might have led to dismissal in an earlier, more formalistic period—were now regarded as merely technical. For example, the doctrine of "fatal variance" had prohibited any departure in the course of trial from the offense charged. Such variances are now held to be HARMLESS ERROR so long as the defendant has not been materially prejudiced in making his defense and, if an indictment is involved, the trial falls fairly within the scope of the grand jury's charge.

As the specificity demanded of indictments and informations declined, defendants lost one of the principal means for learning about the prosecution's case in advance of trial. Pleadings in criminal cases had been assimilated to an increasingly liberal law of civil procedure, but those changes had not been accompanied in CRIMINAL PROCEDURE by the pretrial DISCOVERY which had emerged to compensate for looser pleadings in civil cases. Beginning in the 1960s, however, pretrial disclosure of the prosecution's case has become more available to the defendant, some of it mandated by the due process clause. This expansion of the process of notice before and during trial has minimized the problems of law and policy which relatively spare charges might otherwise have presented under the notice clause of the Sixth Amendment.

ABRAHAM S. GOLDSTEIN

Bibliography

GOLDSTEIN, ABRAHAM S. 1960 The State and the Accused: Balance of Advantage in Criminal Procedure. *Yale Law Journal* 69:1149, 1172–1180.
SCOTT, AUSTIN, JR. 1982 Fairness in Accusation of Crime. *Minnesota Law Review* 41:509–546.
WRIGHT, CHARLES ALAN 1982 *Federal Practice and Procedure, Criminal*, 2nd ed. Vol. 1, Sections 125–126. St. Paul, Minn.: West Publishing Co.

RIGHT TO CONFRONT WITNESSES

See: Confrontation, Right of

RIGHT TO COUNSEL

The constitutional right to counsel in American law encompasses two broad categories of rights: first, rights of persons to retain and employ counsel in official proceedings and, second, rights of persons who because of financial incapacity or other reasons are unable to procure the assistance of lawyers, to have counsel appointed in their behalf.

The modern rights to counsel are the product of a historical evolution extending over a half-millennium. English criminal procedure in the early modern era diverged sharply from today's institutions of adversary criminal justice. In the Tudor and Stuart regimes, legal proceedings in which the crown's interests were strongly implicated were heavily tilted in favor of the state and against the accused. Thus it was only in the least serious cases, those involving MISDEMEANORS, that the privilege of the accused to present his defense by counsel was recognized. Not until the end of the seventeenth century was a similar right granted defendants in TREASON trials (along with the right to have counsel appointed by the court when requested). Over 140 years were to elapse before Parliament recognized the right of the accused to retain and employ counsel in FELONY trials. The earlier recognition of the right to counsel in treason cases reflects the fact that members of Parliament were themselves frequent targets of treason prosecutions launched by the crown. Throughout the eighteenth century the incongruity of a system that recognized counsel rights in misdemeanor and treason cases but withheld them in felony cases at a time when as many as 150 felonies were punishable by death was widely perceived and sometimes protested.

In the American colonies there was great variation in practices and statutory provisions relating to rights of counsel in criminal cases. By 1776, however, the right of attorneys retained by the accused to perform defense functions in courts appears to have been widely conceded, and in several of the colonies practices were considerably in advance of those then prevailing in England. In Pennsylvania, for example, the appointment of counsel for impoverished defendants in capital cases was mandated by statute; and in Connecticut even more liberal practices of appointment were established in the quarter-century before the American revolution.

Rights to counsel entered American constitutional law through provisions included in the early state constitutions and with the ratification of the Sixth Amendment to the federal Constitution in 1791. Seven of the original states and Vermont adopted constitutional provisions relating to the rights to counsel, and the right so protected was that to retain and employ lawyers in criminal trials. By the beginning of the nineteenth century only two states, Connecticut and

New Jersey, appear clearly to have recognized a right in the accused to request appointment of counsel in all serious cases; and in neither was the privilege created by a constitutional provision.

Included in the Sixth Amendment, upon which most of the modern law of counsel rights depends, is the following clause: "In all criminal prosecutions, the accused shall enjoy the right . . . to have the Assistance of Counsel for his defense." There is no direct evidence of the framers' intentions in drafting the language or of the understanding of those who ratified the amendment. Yet the general assumption until well into the present century was that the right constitutionally protected was one to employ counsel, not to have counsel assigned.

One of the most remarkable features of Sixth Amendment history is the paucity of judicial authority on the counsel clause for nearly a century and a half after the amendment's ratification. There was no comprehensive exegesis in the Supreme Court, and only a scattering of holdings in the lower federal courts. The relative absence of authoritative interpretation may be explained in part by the long delay in establishing a system of federal criminal APPEALS and the strict limitations applied to the HABEAS CORPUS remedy in the federal courts. The landmark decision in JOHNSON V. ZERBST was not handed down until 1938, six years after the Court had begun its delineation of the rights to counsel protected by the DUE PROCESS clause of the FOURTEENTH AMENDMENT in state criminal prosecutions. (See POWELL V. ALABAMA, 1932.) *Johnson* was comprehensive and far-reaching. The Court, through Justice HUGO L. BLACK, without pausing to canvass the historical understanding of the counsel clause, held that a federal trial court lacked power "to deprive an accused of his life and liberty unless he has or waives the assistance of counsel." Second, the assistance of counsel "is an essential jurisdictional prerequisite" to a federal court's power to try and sentence a criminal defendant. Hence the habeas corpus remedy may be invoked by a prisoner to set aside his conviction if the Sixth Amendment right to counsel was withheld at his trial. Third, although the right to have counsel assigned may be waived, allegations of waiver will be closely scrutinized. WAIVER OF CONSTITUTIONAL RIGHTS involves "an intentional relinquishment of a known right or privilege." The trial judge has a "protecting duty" to see that the accused understands his rights to legal assistance, and if the judge determines that the defendant has waived his rights, the record of the trial should clearly reveal the judge's determination and the basis for it.

In holding that the counsel clause not only creates a right to make use of a retained lawyer in federal criminal proceedings but also mandates the assignment of counsel for an accused otherwise unable to procure legal assistance, *Johnson v. Zerbst* upset the long-prevailing understanding to the contrary. Yet the decision did not immediately produce a major alteration in the actual practices of federal criminal justice. Many federal district courts before 1938, with the active encouragement of the Department of Justice, had been assigning counsel to indigent defendants in felony cases. The lawyers so appointed typically received no compensation for their services and were hampered in having no resources for pretrial investigations of their cases or for many other incidents of trial. *Johnson v. Zerbst* did little to improve this situation. It was not until a quarter-century later that Congress enacted the Criminal Justice Act of 1964 and for the first time provided, however inadequately, a system of compensated legal assistance in the federal courts.

In the celebrated case of *Powell v. Alabama,* decided in 1932, the Supreme Court made its first significant contribution to the constitutional law of counsel rights in Fourteenth Amendment cases. *Powell,* in addition, was one of the great seminal decisions in the Court's history and strongly influenced the development of the entire modern constitutional law of CRIMINAL PROCEDURE. The decision arose out of one of the most famous of twentieth-century criminal prosecutions, that of the Scottsboro defendants. Seven illiterate young blacks were arrested on the charge of raping two white women. After INDICTMENT the accused were divided into groups and tried in three separate trials. No lawyer having come forward to represent the defendants, the trial judge appointed "all the members of the bar" to assist in the arraignment, an act later described by the Supreme Court as merely "an expansive gesture." At the trial no lawyer was designated to assume personal responsibility for protecting the defendants' interests. Each trial was completed in a single day, and in each the jury convicted the accused and sentenced them to death. The convictions were affirmed in the Alabama Supreme Court, the chief justice vigorously dissenting.

At the time of the *Powell* decision, the Supreme Court had rarely employed the federal judicial power to upset state criminal prosecutions. (See MOORE V. DEMPSEY, 1923.) The determination of the Court that the procedures in the Alabama trial had violated the accused's rights to due process of law protected by the Fourteenth Amendment was, therefore, an event of portentous significance. The Court held that both the right of the defendants to retain counsel and the right to have counsel assigned in their behalf had been nullified. The speed with which the Scottsboro defendants had been rushed to trial and conviction deprived them of an opportunity to secure legal assistance, and the arrival of lawyers eager to provide representation for the defendants shortly thereafter indicated that the haste was seriously prejudicial. Beyond this, the Court found that the failure to make an effective appointment of counsel in behalf of the accused, given the circumstances of the case, constituted a denial of due process.

The constitutional theory of Justice GEORGE SUTHERLAND's opinion for the court is important, for it dominated thought about the rights of counsel for the next three decades. Whatever else the protean phrase "due process of law" contemplates, argued the Court, it encompasses the requirement of NOTICE and hearing in criminal cases. A FAIR HEARING, in turn, encompasses the right to counsel. In one of the Court's best-known OBITER DICTA, Justice Sutherland wrote: "The right to be heard would be, in many cases, of little avail if it did not comprehend the right to be heard by counsel. [Even the intelligent and educated layman] requires the guiding hand of counsel at every step of the proceedings against him. Without it, though he be not guilty, he faces the danger of conviction because he does not know how to establish his innocence."

Although the *Powell* decision was placed on a broad constitutional base, one susceptible of future doctrinal development, the actual HOLDING of the case was narrowly drawn. Thus the right of the accused to receive an assignment of counsel in *Powell* was made to rest on such considerations as that the charge was a capital offense, that the defendants were young, inexperienced, illiterate, and the like. The question that immediately became pressing was how far the *Powell* precedent would be extended when one or more of the circumstances in that case were absent. It was widely assumed that the Fourteenth Amendment might require the state to appoint counsel for an INDIGENT defendant in any capital case, even though a considerable interval elapsed before the proposition was authoritatively stated in *Bute v. Illinois* (1948). The more important question, however, was whether a "flat requirement" of counsel similar to the Sixth Amendment rule imposed on the federal courts in *Johnson v. Zerbst* would also be found applicable to state prosecutions by reason of the Fourteenth Amendment. A definitive negative answer came in BETTS V. BRADY (1942).

In *Betts* the defendant was convicted of robbery,

a noncapital felony. At his trial in the state court, the accused, an unemployed farm hand said by the Supreme Court to be "of ordinary intelligence," requested the appointment of counsel to assist in his defense. The request was denied by the trial judge, and the accused participated in the defense by examining his own witnesses and cross-examining those of the prosecution. When, after conviction, defendant was denied *habeas corpus* relief in the state courts, he took his case to the Supreme Court alleging that the denial of counsel at his trial violated due process of law. Justice OWEN ROBERTS for the Court denied that due process required the assignment of counsel for indigent defendants in every state felony case. There was, in the view of the Court's majority, nothing in historical or contemporary practice to validate the claim. Rather, the question in each case was whether in the totality of circumstances presented, appointment of counsel was required to insure the accused a fair hearing. In the present case, the Court said, there was no such necessity. The issue upon which the defense rested, that of alibi, was simple and straightforward. There were no special circumstances of mental incapacity or inexperience that placed defendant at a serious disadvantage in maintaining his defense.

Criticism of the *Betts* decision began with Justice Black's vigorous dissent in that case and was promptly amplified in the press and the writings of legal commentators. Two principal reasons for the reluctance of the Court's majority to impose the obligation of assigning counsel in all state felony prosecutions can be identified. First, the prevailing opinion in *Betts* reflected the Court's deference to state autonomy, a deference widely believed at the time to be mandated by the nature of American FEDERALISM. The administration of criminal justice was an area in which state powers of self-determination were thought to be particularly broad. Second, there was the related concern that the states were poorly prepared suddenly to assume the obligation of providing legal aid for unrepresented defendants in all state felony cases. The problem was not only that lawyers and resources would have to be supplied in pending and future cases, but also that hundreds of state prisoners had been convicted in trials in which no assistance of counsel was received. The concern was freely articulated by Justice FELIX FRANKFURTER when in *Foster v. Illinois* (1947) he wrote: "Such an abrupt innovation . . . would furnish opportunities hitherto uncontemplated for opening wide the prison doors of the land."

Nevertheless, with the passage of time opinion increasingly supported the overturning of *Betts* and recognition of a "flat requirement" of counsel in state as well as federal prosecutions. The *Betts* rule, far from strengthening federalism, exacerbated the relations of state and federal courts. Because under *Betts* the requirement of appointing counsel depended on the unique circumstances of the particular case, the resulting decision often provided little guidance to state judges dealing with cases in which the facts were significantly different. Many state judges came to favor the broader rule of *Johnson v. Zerbst* because of its greater certainty. It became apparent to many state officials that ultimately *Betts v. Brady* would be overruled, and in anticipation of the event they created systems of legal aid on their own initiative, supplying counsel for unrepresented defendants in all serious state cases. Meanwhile it had become increasingly difficult for the states to protect convictions in the Supreme Court when defendants argued that "special circumstances" had required appointment of counsel at the trial. In the thirteen years before *Betts* was overruled in GIDEON V. WAINWRIGHT (1963), no state conviction was upheld by the Court against a claim of special circumstances. It is significant also that when the *Gideon* case was pending before the Court, the attorneys general of twenty-two states filed AMICUS CURIAE briefs asking that *Betts* be overruled and the broader rule of appointment recognized.

Although the opinion of Justice Black for the court is unprepossessing, *Gideon v. Wainwright* marked a new era in the constitutional law of counsel rights. Portions of the opinion appear to pay deference to the older theories of fair hearing, and others seem to suggest that counsel must be assigned to unrepresented defendants on grounds of equality. Ultimately, however, *Gideon's* constitutional basis is the Sixth Amendment: the Sixth Amendment is "subsumed" in the provisions of the Fourteenth Amendment, and hence the same obligations relating to assignment of counsel for the indigent accused in federal courts are also owed in state prosecutions. Since the *Gideon* case there has been a flowering of constitutional doctrine relating to counsel rights in many important areas of the criminal process.

Although the prevailing opinion in the *Gideon* case did not specifically limit its holding to felony trials, most observers believed that the right to counsel for indigent defendants would not apply in all misdemeanor cases. Following *Gideon*, state and lower federal courts devised various formulas for dealing with counsel rights in small-crime prosecutions. The state of Florida, borrowing from cases involving the constitutional right to jury trial, provided that counsel rights should not attach in prosecutions for "petty offenses," *i.e.*, crimes punishable by not more than six months' imprisonment. (Cf. BALDWIN V. NEW YORK, 1970.) In ARGERSINGER V. HAMLIN (1972), nine years after *Gideon*, the Supreme Court rejected Florida's use of the petty-offense concept. In effect, the Court ruled that any deprivation of liberty, even for a few days, is a sanction of significant gravity. Accordingly, no unrepresented defendant may be jailed for any term unless he has waived counsel at the trial. The *Argersinger* holding dramatically expanded the legal aid obligations of state systems of criminal justice. Adequate practical implementation of counsel rights in small-crimes courts is yet to be fully attained in many jurisdictions.

The right recognized in *Argersinger* was defined further in *Scott v. Illinois* (1979). In the latter case an unrepresented defendant was sentenced for an offense which under state law was punishable by both fines and imprisonment. The sentence actually imposed, however, was a monetary fine. The Court, through Justice WILLIAM H. REHNQUIST, ruled that because the unrepresented accused was not actually sentenced to jail, his constitutional rights had not been denied. Ironically, Scott's rights were given less protection than he would have received if the Court had adopted the petty-offense formula in *Argersinger;* that formula would have looked to the penalties authorized by a statute, not solely to those actually imposed.

Because of the comparative modernity of criminal appeals in Anglo-American legal history, the Supreme Court's consideration of constitutional rights of representation in appellate proceedings was not preceded by extensive COMMON LAW experience. The first substantial discussion of constitutional rights to counsel on appeal occurred in DOUGLAS V. CALIFORNIA (1963) decided on the same day as the *Gideon* case. A California rule of court authorized the state intermediate appellate court to scrutinize the record in a pauper's appeal "to determine whether it would be of advantage to the defendant or helpful to the appellate court to have counsel appointed." Pursuant to this authority the court denied counsel to defendant, adjudicated his appeal, and affirmed his criminal conviction. In the Supreme Court the defendant successfully asserted that the California procedures violated his Fourteenth Amendment rights.

In reaching its result the Court relied primarily on an obligation in the state to accord equal treatment to rich and poor appellants and revived an earlier dictum of Justice Black in GRIFFIN V. ILLINOIS (1956): "There can be no equal justice where the kind of trial a man gets depends on the amount of money he has." Here the obligation of equal treatment was not met. Had defendant been able to retain his own lawyer, his appeal, regardless of its merits, would have been presented by counsel. Because of his poverty and the decision of the appellate court not to assign a lawyer to him, he was unrepresented on appeal. Whatever the implications of the Court's theory, the obligation of the state to provide "equal treatment" to the poor does not necessarily mean that the treatment must be identical to that meted out to appellants able to hire their own lawyers. Thus, the opinion asserts, "absolute equality is not required." In illustrating this possibility, the Court strongly implied that the constitutional obligation to assign counsel involved in *Douglas* may apply only to the first appeal. If an indigent represented by an assigned counsel is unsuccessful in the intermediate appellate court and decides to seek further review in the state's highest court, he may submit to the latter the brief prepared by counsel in the intermediate court, but the highest court may not be under obligation to assign a lawyer to conduct the second appeal. A decade later the Court made explicit what had been suggested in the *Douglas* case. In ROSS V. MOFFITT (1974) the Court sustained the validity of North Carolina procedures that provided the indigent with counsel in the first appeal but denied his requests for representation when he sought a discretionary review in the state supreme court and later, when seeking a WRIT OF CERTIORARI in the United States Supreme Court.

The limitations recognized by the Court, however, do not appear to have seriously inhibited the availability of appellate remedies to indigent defendants. Arguably, this may be true in part because the Court was essentially correct in concluding that the decencies of fair hearing and reasonable equality of treatment can be accorded such appellants without offering counsel in all stages of the appellate procedure. Also, many jurisdictions have gone beyond the constitutional minima and supply counsel throughout the review process. Perhaps of equal importance is a series of cases that have overcome many of the difficulties that earlier confronted impoverished criminal litigants in the appellate courts. As early as 1956, the Court in *Griffin v. Illinois* held that a convicted defendant may not be denied access to an appellate remedy because of his poverty. Under state law the appellant could perfect his appeal only by use of a stenographic transcript of the trial proceedings, the latter being unavailable to him because he had no funds to purchase it. Under these circumstances, the Court ruled,

the state must furnish the prisoner with a transcript. In the years following, the *Griffin* principle was broadly applied. (For example, *Burns v. Ohio*, 1950; see WEALTH DISCRIMINATION.)

Recognition of counsel rights and the removal of obstacles to review for indigent prisoners have greatly widened opportunities for appellate regulation of the trial process. They have, at the same time, created substantial problems for the administration of justice in the appellate courts. Economic constraints may operate on appellants "paying their own way" so as to deter the filing of frivolous appeals. No such constraints influence the indigent prisoner. The resulting problems go beyond the swelling of the dockets of appellate courts and also include certain difficulties for lawyers assigned by the courts to represent indigent appellants. Many such attorneys believe, often rightly, that the appeals of their clients cannot be supported on any substantial legal grounds. Yet efforts by the lawyers to withdraw from representation may, on occasion, prejudice the interests of their clients and, in some instances, may be motivated by the lawyers' design to escape onerous and unprofitable obligations. Efforts to balance such considerations have not as yet resulted in a satisfactory resolution. The rule announced by the Supreme Court requires the appointed lawyer seeking to be relieved of the case to allege that it is "wholly frivolous." The motion must be accompanied by a brief referring to anything in the record that might arguably support the appeal. How matters may be both "arguable" and "wholly frivolous" is not explained, and the effect of the rule must be to induce the lawyer to remain in the case regardless of his professional judgment of frivolity. The Massachusetts Supreme Judicial Court, in *Commonwealth v. Moffett* (1981) recognizing this effect, simply refused to permit counsel to withdraw solely on grounds of absence of merit in the appeal.

Other questions relating to counsel rights have arisen in the postconviction criminal process. As early as *Mempa v. Ray* (1967) a unanimous Court held that an indigent defendant, who had been placed on probation after conviction and given a deferred sentence, was entitled to be represented by counsel when his probation was revoked and he was sentenced to imprisonment. In *Gagnon v. Scarpelli* (1973), however, the Court ruled that although due process requires a hearing whenever a probation or parole is revoked, counsel need not be appointed unless special circumstances dictate the need for legal representation. This dubious resurrection of the *Betts v. Brady* doctrine, long since rejected at the criminal trial, was justified in part by the need to preserve "flexibility" in procedures leading to revocation. The American Bar Association in its *Standards of Criminal Justice* repudiated the *Gagnon* rule and called for appointment of counsel in such cases.

One of the most striking characteristics of the WARREN COURT was its allegiance to the adversarial system of criminal justice. This dedication inevitably resulted in the expansion of constitutional rights to counsel. Thus, the adversary system was strengthened in areas where it already existed, such as the criminal trial, and also extended to other areas where it had had little or no operation, such as pretrial police interrogations. Clearly the Court's attitudes toward a rejuvenated adversarial process reflected some of its deepest convictions about the proper containment of state power in the administration of criminal justice. Introducing lawyers into the interrogation rooms of police stations, for example, was intended to achieve values going beyond those ordinarily associated with counsel rights. In addition to advising his client, the lawyer could serve as a witness to police interrogatory activity and a deterrent to police abuse. His presence might often be indispensable to the preservation of the suspect's RIGHT AGAINST SELF-INCRIMINATION and other constitutional rights.

Concern with proper representation of defendants' interests in the pretrial phases of the criminal process was expressed by the Supreme Court in its earliest cases involving rights to counsel. Even in *Powell v. Alabama* (1932) the Court had referred to the pretrial preparation of the defense as "the most critical" period in the criminal proceedings. Before the decision of *Gideon v. Wainwright* (1963) the Court had begun mandating the appointment of counsel for unrepresented accused persons at various "critical stages of the proceedings." Thus in *Hamilton v. Alabama* (1961) the murder conviction of the indigent accused was reversed because of the absence of defense counsel at the pretrial arraignment.

The more difficult problems, however, were those of the accused's rights after ARREST but before formal commencement of the judicial proceedings by bringing the accused into court for preliminary hearing or arraignment. The issues were squarely drawn in the companion cases of *Crooker v. California* and *Cicenia v. La Gay* (1958). In the former, petitioner, who was under sentence of death, complained that the confession introduced against him at his trial had been obtained in a period of incommunicado questioning during which time he was denied the opportunity to confer with his own attorney. A narrowly divided Court affirmed the conviction, Justice TOM C.

CLARK emphasizing the "devastating effect" of the presence of counsel in the interrogation room on criminal law enforcement.

Crooker and *Cicenia* were overruled in ESCOBEDO V. ILLINOIS (1964) which represented the high-water mark of judicial protection of Sixth Amendment counsel rights in the pretrial interrogatory process. In a 5–4 decision the Court ruled that at the point in questioning when suspicions of the police have "focused" on the party being interrogated, even if this occurs before defendant is indicted for a criminal offense, the right of the party to consult with an attorney cannot constitutionally be denied. Two years later the Court decided the famous case of MIRANDA V. ARIZONA (1966), holding that whenever a suspect has been taken into custody he may not be interrogated until he has been given the "fourfold" warning: the arrested party must be advised that he has a right to remain silent, that he is entitled to consult with a lawyer, that the lawyer may be present at the interrogation, and that if he is unable to hire an attorney, counsel will be supplied. (See MIRANDA RULES.)

Although the prevailing opinion in *Miranda* reaffirmed the holding of the *Escobedo* case, the impact of the latter was considerably modified. Thus, use of the "focus" concept, while not expressly rejected, was for practical purposes abandoned. Again, although the *Miranda* opinion reaffirmed the existence of Sixth Amendment counsel rights in pretrial interrogation, the emphasis of the opinion is significantly different. The dominant view regarded the right to counsel in the interrogation situation as an incident to and a necessary means for protection of the Fifth Amendment's right against self-incrimination. The emphasis on that right is so dominant that the rights to representation recognized in *Miranda* have sometimes been referred to as Fifth Amendment rights to counsel.

The *Miranda* case did not bring lawyers into interrogation rooms so frequently as was hoped or feared at the time the decision was handed down. One principal weakness of the prevailing opinion was its failure to insist that a suspect's decision to waive the presence of counsel must itself be made only with the advice of a lawyer. In consequence, rights to counsel are frequently waived by persons in police custody. One study published shortly after the *Miranda* ruling revealed as few as seven percent of the suspects requesting stationhouse counsel. The tendency toward widespread waiver of *Miranda* rights appears to have continued in the intervening years.

Even before *Escobedo*, the Court had contributed another important strand to counsel doctrine in MASSIAH V. UNITED STATES (1964). After the defendant in that case had been indicted for a narcotics offense, government agents induced an accomplice of Massiah to draw him into conversation in an electronically "bugged" automobile. Incriminating admissions made by the defendant were overheard by the agents and introduced against him at the trial. In reversing Massiah's conviction, the Court ruled that the ELECTRONIC EAVESDROPPING violated defendant's rights to counsel, which rights had "attached" when the INDICTMENT against him was returned. Contemporary reaction to the *Massiah* decision was generally critical. Many commentators believed that if a wrong had been done to Massiah it consisted not of a denial of counsel rights, but rather an invasion of his Fourth Amendment RIGHT TO PRIVACY, or perhaps of the introduction of an "involuntary" confession against him. Again, to conceive of the rights to counsel attaching only at the return of the indictment leaves open to police officials an opportunity of frustrating the rule by simply delaying the indictment or INFORMATION.

After the decision of *Escobedo* it was widely assumed that the *Massiah* precedent had been drained of vitality. Yet in the widely noted case of BREWER V. WILLIAMS (1977) *Massiah* was invested with renewed significance. Although *Brewer* might readily have been decided by an application of the *Miranda* rule, the Court chose instead to reverse the conviction on the grounds of denial of counsel, reliance being placed on the *Massiah* precedent. Later decisions, building on *Massiah*, appear to assert a right in the defendant not to be approached by the government for evidence of his own guilt in the absence of counsel, once judicial proceedings are initiated by return of an indictment or other in-court proceedings (*United States v. Henry*, 1980). In New York the state courts have transcended the *Massiah* precedent by interpreting state law to mean that whenever a lawyer enters a case in behalf of the defendant, even when this occurs before indictment, the accused in custody may not waive his right to counsel in the absence of his lawyer (*People v. Hobson*, 1976). Although the New York rule alleviates the restrictions imposed by the Supreme Court on the *Massiah* doctrine, it is of limited value to indigent defendants, who ordinarily do not acquire counsel before the commencement of judicial proceedings.

A final area of pretrial counsel rights involves LINE-UPS. Misidentification of the accused by prosecution witnesses constitutes perhaps the most prolific source of erroneous convictions; police lineups and other identification procedures often spawn such errors. In UNITED STATES V. WADE (1967) the Court responded to these problems by designating the pretrial identifi-

cation confrontation between witnesses and the accused as a "critical stage" of the proceedings and hence one requiring the presence of the accused's attorney. An identification made at a lineup in which the suspect's right to counsel was not honored may not be introduced at the criminal trial. An in-court identification is not summarily barred, but before it can be employed as evidence, the prosecution must establish by "clear and convincing evidence" that it was based on observations other than those made at the flawed lineup. After this promising beginning the Court backed away, and the view appears established that unless the identification evidence was obtained by methods so defective as to deny due process of law, an identification obtained in the absence of counsel may be introduced in court if the lineup occurred before return of an indictment. (See KIRBY V. ILLINOIS, 1972.) Limiting rights of counsel to the post-indictment period is especially devastating in these areas because identification efforts are typically undertaken before formal charges are made. In UNITED STATES V. ASH (1973) the Court has also refused to supervise other identification procedures, such as those involving the use of photographic files. The problems of convicting the innocent through misidentification persist, and the Court has relegated their solutions largely to administrative and legislative action.

Basic to the rights of counsel is the quality of the legal representation supplied the criminal accused. Yet growth of the law in this area is inhibited by the fear that close judicial scrutiny of the competency of such representation will provide numerous and unwarranted opportunities for disappointed criminal litigants to attack their convictions. Such administrative concerns resulted in the once widely recognized rule that convictions were not to be reversed on incompetency grounds unless the performance of defense counsel constituted a "mockery of justice." The formula employed in the Supreme Court today is considerably more demanding: counsel's advice must not fall "outside the range of competence demanded of attorneys in criminal cases" (*Tollet v. Henderson*, 1953). The application of the "ordinary competence" test, however, results in the reversal of comparatively few criminal convictions. Thus in *United States v. Decoster* (1979) the District of Columbia Court of Appeals refused to upset a conviction in which a court-appointed lawyer failed to interview his client's co-defendants or any other witnesses before trial. Failures to achieve the objective of adequate defense in criminal cases are often not the product of the professional incompetence of lawyers. In many cases the court-appointed lawyer is on the staff of an inadequately funded legal aid agency that must impose wholly unrealistic case loads on its attorneys. Similar problems also often affect the privately retained lawyer who because of the economics of criminal law practice may be under pressure to accept more cases than he can adequately handle. The courts alone cannot be expected to solve problems of this sort, but it is doubtful that instances of inadequate defense will be significantly abated until the courts articulate and apply specific minimum standards of counsel performance.

The right of an indigent litigant to demand appointment of counsel from the state in noncriminal proceedings has received comparatively little judicial consideration or development. In the famous case of IN RE GAULT (1967) the Court recognized a right to counsel in a state juvenile court delinquency proceeding. Some courts have held that, where necessary to a fair hearing, a similar right is possessed by an indigent petitioner in an habeas corpus action. Since juvenile court and habeas corpus proceedings, although "civil" in form, are analogous or intimately related to the criminal process, the precedents in neither category represent a significant expansion of counsel rights into noncriminal areas.

In *Lassiter v. Department of Social Services* (1981) the question was whether counsel must be appointed to represent an indigent mother in a proceeding brought by the state to terminate her parental rights. In such a proceeding the defendant faces a sanction often considered more severe than a sentence of imprisonment, and, given the nature of the issues, the defendant's need for professional assistance is at least as great as that of the accused in many criminal cases. Although recognizing these considerations, the Court's majority limited the right to counsel to the situation in which all the circumstances in a particular case make legal representation necessary for a fair hearing, and it concluded that such considerations were not shown to be present in the *Lassiter* case. This latter-day revival of the *Betts v. Brady* precedent is regrettable in view of the needs for counsel in these proceedings and the comparatively small social costs involved in making counsel available routinely in all such cases. Like *Betts*, however, the *Lassiter* holding may represent a step toward a more satisfactory ultimate result.

In the development of the modern constitutional law of criminal procedure, questions of the rights of counsel have held a central position. This centrality is not surprising; counsel rights are integral to an adversarial system of justice, and the expansion and re-furbishing of that system have been a dominant objective of constitutional procedural law from the decision of *Powell v. Alabama* in 1932 to the present. In the intervening years, issues of counsel rights have continued to emerge in a variety of contexts. It may be anticipated that this course of constitutional events will continue so long as the Supreme Court places significant reliance on the adversarial system as the principal mechanism to control and order the applications of state power in the criminal process.

FRANCIS A. ALLEN

(SEE ALSO: *Nix v. Williams, 1986.*)

Bibliography

ALLEN, FRANCIS A. 1975 The Judicial Quest for Penal Justice: The Warren Court and the Criminal Cases. *Illinois Law Forum* 1975:518–542.

ATTORNEY GENERAL'S COMMITTEE 1963 *Poverty and the Administration of Federal Criminal Justice.* Washington: Government Printing Office.

BEANEY, WILLIAM A. 1955 *The Right to Counsel in American Courts.* Ann Arbor: University of Michigan Press.

HOLTZOFF, A. 1944 Right to Counsel under the Sixth Amendment. *New York University Law Review* 20:1–22.

KAMISAR, YALE 1962 Betts v. Brady Twenty Years Later. *Michigan Law Review* 61:219–282.

———— 1978 Brewer v. Williams, Massiah and Miranda: What Is Interrogation? When Does It Matter? *Georgetown Law Journal* 67:1–101.

LEVINE, F. and TAPP, J. 1973 The Psychology of Criminal Identification: The Gap from Wade to Korley. *University of Pennsylvania Law Review* 121:1079–1131.

RIGHT TO JURY TRIAL

See: Trial by Jury

RIGHT TO KNOW

The phrase "right to know" does not appear in the text of the FIRST AMENDMENT, nor has it been used as an organizing category in Supreme Court opinions. Nonetheless, the phrase captures several major themes in First Amendment law, and its frequent appearance in editorials concerning FREEDOM OF THE PRESS attests to its rhetorical appeal. The phrase conjures up the citizen critic responsible for democratic decision making and a vigilant press acting as public trustee in gathering and disseminating vital information. It recalls the companion ideas of LISTENERS' RIGHTS and the MARKETPLACE OF IDEAS.

The "right to know" is a slogan, but it is not empty and its content is not exhausted by conceptions of self-government, the marketplace of ideas, or listeners' rights. To be sure, such conceptions provide rationales for a right to know. Most court decisions preventing government from interfering with speakers' liberty have the effect of protecting the right to know. Some decisions are explicitly founded upon theories of listeners' rights, and, indeed, listeners have occasionally been the plaintiffs challenging the offending government action. Not every decision protecting a speaker's liberty, however, is appropriately characterized as protecting a right to know. For example, opinions in which the court has used the OVERBREADTH DOCTRINE to invalidate convictions for using fighting words find little support in any claim of a right to know. A police officer may learn something by being exposed to insulting language, but protection of speech in such decisions rests on a defense of speaker liberty for its own sake, wholly apart from anything the audience may learn.

If decisions protecting speaker's liberty are not always premised upon a right to know, neither are claims of the right to know limited to assertions of speaker's liberty. Indeed, the most intriguing question begged by the expression "right to know" is the scope of such a right. Does the public have a constitutional right to know anything that speakers themselves are unwilling to provide? To date, there is no judicial authority for the proposition that the public or the press has any First Amendment right to information voluntarily withheld by private actors. Indeed, even though the press is sometimes said to act as trustee for the public in getting information, the public has no constitutional right to compel the press to disclose any information it may choose to withhold.

The fighting issue is the extent to which the public or press has a constitutional right to know information that government officials wish to withhold. For a long time it appeared there was no such right. By 1978, no Supreme Court holding contradicted Chief Justice WARREN E. BURGER'S contention in *Houchins v. KOED* that "neither the First not Fourteenth Amendment mandates a right of access to government information or sources of information within the government's control." Or, as Justice POTTER STEWART put it in an often-quoted statement, "[T]he First Amendment is neither a Freedom of Information Act nor an Official Secrets Act."

RICHMOND NEWSPAPERS, INC. V. VIRGINIA (1980) constituted the Court's first break with its past denials of constitutional rights of access to information within government control. The Court held that in the ab-

sence of some overriding consideration requiring closure, the public possessed a First Amendment right to be present at a criminal trial. Some of the Justices in *Richmond Newspapers* would have opted for a general right of access to governmental information subject to a degree of restraint dictated by the nature of the information and the strength of the government's interests in nondisclosure. Other Justices would have confined the right of access to places traditionally open to the public. What *Richmond Newspapers* makes clear, however, is that the First Amendment is a sword as well as a shield and that the right to know promises to be a developing area of First Amendment law.

STEVEN SHIFFRIN

Bibliography

BeVier, Lillian 1980 An Informed Public, an Informing Press: The Search for a Constitutional Principle. *Stanford Law Review* 68:482–517.

Emerson, Thomas I. 1976 Legal Foundations of the Right to Know. *Washington University Law Quarterly* 1976:1–24.

RIGHT TO TRAVEL

The right to travel is a doctrinal orphan grown to vigorous adulthood. As the ARTICLES OF CONFEDERATION (1781) recognized expressly, the freedom of interstate movement follows logically from the recognition of our nationhood. The Constitution contains no similarly explicit guarantee, but the logic of nationhood remains, reinforced by two centuries of nationalizing experience. The modern right to travel may still be searching for its doctrinal sources, but its historical base is secure.

Personal mobility is a value Americans have always prized. FRANKLIN D. ROOSEVELT brushed the edges of this idea when he greeted the Daughters of the American Revolution as fellow "immigrants." The nineteenth century, the formative era for our constitutional law, was also the century of the frontier. The twentieth century brought the automobile—and the moving van; each year nearly one family in five changes residence.

The power of Congress to protect the freedom of interstate movement is a theme both old and new. The great decision in GIBBONS V. OGDEN (1824) recognized that the COMMERCE CLAUSE authorized congressional regulation of the interstate transportation of persons as well as goods. The modern reach of congressional power is illustrated by the holding in GRIF-

FIN V. BRECKINRIDGE (1971) that Congress can protect CIVIL RIGHTS by prohibiting private interferences with the right of black persons or civil rights workers to travel interstate.

The commerce power of Congress has long been held to imply limits on STATE REGULATION OF COMMERCE. When a state interferes with the interstate movement of persons, it must provide weighty justification for so burdening commerce. EDWARDS V. CALIFORNIA (1941) shows how difficult it is for a state to justify this sort of regulation.

The *Edwards* majority, resting decision on the commerce clause, said nothing about the right to travel. Four Justices, while not disputing the commerce ground, preferred to base decision on the PRIVILEGES AND IMMUNITIES clause of Article IV. This clause, which superseded the Articles of Confederation provision guaranteeing "free ingress and egress" from one state to another, had been interpreted early in the nineteenth century (in CORFIELD V. CORYELL, 1823) to include the "fundamental" right of a citizen of one state to travel through or migrate to another.

The Constitution's other privileges and immunities clause—that of the Fourteenth Amendment—is yet another potential source for a right of interstate travel. The concurring Justices in *Edwards* echoed the words of Chief Justice ROGER B. TANEY, dissenting in the PASSENGER CASES (1849), when they said that the freedom of interstate travel was one of the privileges of national citizenship. (See CRANDALL V. NEVADA, 1868; SLAUGHTERHOUSE CASES, 1873.)

This doctrinal untidiness has the blessing of the Supreme Court. Speaking for the Court in UNITED STATES V. GUEST (1966), Justice POTTER STEWART, who yielded to no one in expressing his affection for the right to travel, said: "The constitutional right to travel from one State to another . . . occupies a position so fundamental to the concept of our Federal Union. It is a right that has been firmly established and repeatedly recognized. . . . Although there have been recurring differences in emphasis within the Court as to the source of the constitutional right to travel, there is no need to canvas those differences further. All have agreed that the right exists. . . . We reaffirm it now."

Guest involved the power of Congress to protect interstate travel, a power easily inferable from the commerce clause. When the WARREN COURT expanded the reach of the right to travel as a limit on the states, the Court selected still another constitutional weapon: the EQUAL PROTECTION clause. SHAPIRO V. THOMPSON (1969) established the modern pattern. The Court invalidated state laws limiting WELFARE BENEFITS to persons who had been residents for a year. Such a durational RESIDENCE REQUIREMENT impaired the right to travel, which was a FUNDAMENTAL INTEREST; accordingly, the states must justify the impairment by showing its necessity as a means for achieving a COMPELLING STATE INTEREST. The justifications offered in *Shapiro* failed this STRICT SCRUTINY standard of review.

In two decisions following *Shapiro,* the Court refined its analytical style for cases implicating the right to travel interstate. Both opinions were written by Justice THURGOOD MARSHALL. DUNN V. BLUMSTEIN (1972) held unconstitutional a state law limiting voting to persons with one year of residence in the state and three months in the county. Justice Marshall elaborated on *Shapiro:* That opinion had emphasized the illegitimacy of a state's purpose to deter interstate migration, but had not insisted on a showing that any welfare applicants had, in fact, been deterred from migrating. Strict judicial scrutiny was required, irrespective of any such showing, whenever a state law penalized interstate migration, and here the durational residence qualifications for voting amounted to a penalty. Failing the test of strict scrutiny, they must be invalidated. A year later, in MARSTON V. LEWIS (1973) and BURNS V. FORTSON (1973), the Court upheld fifty-day residence qualifications for voting, remarking that "the 50-day registration period approaches the outer constitutional limits in this area."

The "penalty" analysis was fully developed in MEMORIAL HOSPITAL V. MARICOPA COUNTY (1974), when the Court struck down a one-year county residence qualification for an indigent to receive free nonemergency hospital or health care. Denial to new residents of "a basic necessity of life" amounted to a "penalty" on interstate migration and medical care was as much a necessity as welfare subsistence. This analysis allowed Justice Marshall to distinguish STARNS V. MALKERSON (1971), in which the Court had summarily affirmed a lower court's decision upholding a one-year durational requirement for receiving state higher education at reduced tuition rates.

Beyond elucidating the sort of penalty on interstate travel that would require strict judicial scrutiny, the *Dunn* and *Memorial Hospital* opinions also emphasized the right to migrate to another state for the purpose of settling there, as differentiated from the right merely to travel. Commentators have made much of this distinction, but little turns on it in practice, and any serious effort to reduce the right to travel to a right of migration would turn away from the right's historical sources in national citizenship.

By 1975, the right to travel's doctrinal state was cluttered with furniture. The stage direction for the next event might read: "Enter Justice WILLIAM H. REHNQUIST, bearing an axe." SOSNA V. IOWA (1975) confronted the Court with a one-year residence qualification for access to the state's divorce court. Writing for the majority, Justice Rehnquist (the only dissenter in *Memorial Hospital*) not only concluded that the limitation was valid; he reached that conclusion without discussing "penalties" or even the equal protection clause. Indeed, the only doctrinal reference in his whole treatment of the merits of the case was a summary rejection of a marginal argument addressed to the short-lived doctrine of IRREBUTTABLE PRESUMPTIONS.

Doctrinal demolition seems to have been Justice Rehnquist's aim; throughout his opinion he referred abstractly to "the constitutional issue," without saying what the issue was, and he concluded by saying that the one-year qualification was "consistent with the provisions of the United States Constitution." Distinguishing *Shapiro* and the other recent precedents, he remarked that the states' interests in those cases had touched nothing more than budgetary or record-keeping considerations. In *Sosna*, the state was concerned to protect the interests of defendant spouses and possible minor children, and also to make its divorce decrees safe from COLLATERAL ATTACK. Thus the state might "quite reasonably" choose not to be a divorce mill. Predictably, the *Sosna* dissenters were led by Justice Marshall, who expressed his dismay over the dismantling of the only theory yet constructed to explain the modern right to travel decisions. What had happened to strict scrutiny, to the notion of penalties on interstate travel, to the link between the right to travel and the equal protection clause? The majority's silence on all these questions persisted for seven years.

In ZOBEL V. WILLIAMS (1982) an 8–1 Supreme Court struck down an Alaska law that would have distributed much of the state's vast oil revenues to its adult residents, apportioning distributions on the basis of length of residence in the state. For the Court, Chief Justice WARREN E. BURGER rested decision on the equal protection clause, remarking that "right to travel analysis" was "little more than a particular application of equal protection analysis." The state's purpose to reward citizens for past contributions was ruled out by SHAPIRO V. THOMPSON; to uphold Alaska's law would invite apportionment of all manner of taxes and benefits according to length of residence, a result that was "clearly impermissible." Concurring, Justice SANDRA DAY O'CONNOR rejected the equal

protection ground, but argued that requiring nonresidents settling in the state "to accept a status inferior to that of old-timers" would impose one of the "disabilities of alienage" prohibited by the privileges and immunities clause of Article IV. In a separate concurrence, Justice WILLIAM J. BRENNAN returned to the origins of the right to travel; even if no specific provision of the Constitution were available, he found that right's "unmistakable essence in that document that transformed a loose confederation of States into one Nation."

William Cohen has suggested a sensible rule of thumb for the durational residence decisions: Equality of treatment for newcomers is required, but durational residence requirements are permitted as tests for residents' intention to remain in the state, that is, tests for state citizenship. Until the Court accepts this view, constitutional doctrine concerning the right to interstate travel remains where it was in the mid-1960s: "All are agreed that the right exists," but it has itself become a rootless wanderer.

The right to international travel is quite another matter. Its doctrinal location is clear: the Fifth Amendment's due process clause. Congressional power to regulate this liberty is wide-ranging. ZEMEL V. RUSK (1966) sustained the government's refusal to issue a passport valid for travel to Cuba, and CALIFANO V. AZNAVORIAN (1978) upheld the withholding of social security benefits during months when beneficiaries are out of the country. In the latter case, the Court remarked that "indirect" congressional burdens on the right of international travel should not be tested by the strictness attending penalties on interstate travel, but were valid unless they were "wholly irrational." Direct restrictions on travel, such as the denial of a passport, are undoubtedly to be tested against a somewhat higher—but as yet unspecified—level of judicial scrutiny. And when Congress regulates foreign travel in a way that discriminates against the exercise of FIRST AMENDMENT freedoms, strict scrutiny is called for. Thus APTHEKER V. SECRETARY OF STATE (1964) held unconstitutional the denial of passports to members of the Communist party.

The decisions recognizing a right to travel abroad have been concerned with travel itself, and not with a more limited right to migrate. The reasoning of those decisions is readily extended to congressional regulation of interstate travel. The commerce clause unquestionably empowers Congress to control the interstate movement of persons, but, like all the powers of Congress, that clause is subject to the provisions of the BILL OF RIGHTS. Congress obviously could not constitutionally forbid members of the Communist party to travel interstate. First Amendment considerations aside, the liberty protected by the Fifth Amendment's due process clause bars Congress from any arbitrary restrictions on interstate travel. The point has practical importance, for the broad sweep of the commerce power has made the prohibition of interstate movement one of the favorite regulatory techniques of Congress. Almost certainly the extremely permissive standard of the *Aznavorian* decision (upholding restrictions unless they are "wholly irrational") would apply to "indirect" congressional regulations of interstate travel. A direct prohibition, however, very likely would encounter a judiciary ready to insist on a more substantial justification.

The notion that the freedom to travel is a liberty protected by the guarantee of due process need not be limited to congressional restrictions on travel. The Fourteenth Amendment's due process clause surely is equally capable of absorbing the right to travel as a limitation on the states. The main barrier to recognizing the right to travel as an aspect of SUBSTANTIVE DUE PROCESS, no doubt, is the Supreme Court's reluctance to contribute further to the development of substantive due process as a vehicle for active judicial intervention in legislative policymaking.

For a season, then, the right of interstate travel is left without certain doctrinal underpinnings. Its capacity to survive on its own, cut off from the usual doctrinal supports, indicates that it draws nourishment from something else. The something else is our strong sense that we are not only a collection of states but a nation.

KENNETH L. KARST

Bibliography

BAKER, STEWART A. 1975 A Strict Scrutiny of the Right to Travel. *UCLA Law Review* 22:1129–1160.

BARRETT, EDWARD L., JR. 1976 Judicial Supervision of Legislative Classification—A More Modest Role for Equal Protection? *Brigham Young University Law Review* 1976:89–130.

BLACK, CHARLES L., JR. 1969 *Structure and Relationship in Constitutional Law.* Pages 27–30. Baton Rouge: Louisiana State University Press.

COHEN, WILLIAM 1984 Equal Treatment for Newcomers: The Core Meaning of National and State Citizenship. *Constitutional Commentary* 1:9–19.

RIGHT TO VOTE

RIGHT-TO-WORK LAWS

Union security provisions in labor contracts have required membership in, or financial support of, the signatory union by employees, as a condition of employment by the signatory employer. Concern that such provisions could be used to restrict employment unduly, to penalize dissent, and to infringe on employees' associational interests, stimulated the enactment of state right-to-work laws. Such laws, now operative in approximately twenty states, prohibit conditioning of employment on union membership or, generally, on financial support of a union.

The TAFT-HARTLEY ACT (1947) amended the National Labor Relations Act (NLRA) (1935) and imposed new restrictions on union security provisions, barring requirements of full-fledged union membership before or after employment and limiting compulsory membership to payment of uniform dues and initiation fees. Congress's approach appeared responsive to the argument that unions should be permitted, through collective bargaining, to secure financial support from all members of a bargaining unit, including those not members of the union, because the union's duty of fair representation encompasses all of them. Nonetheless, section 14(b), enacted by the Taft-Hartley Act, permitted states to prohibit union security provisions otherwise legal under the NLRA. This extraordinary deference to state labor law contrasts sharply with the preemption of more restrictive state laws by the 1951 Railway Labor Act amendments (now applicable to both airline and railway employees).

The Supreme Court, in *Lincoln Federal Labor Union v. Northwestern Iron & Metal Co.* (1949) and a companion case, *American Federation of Labor v. American Sash Co.*, upheld state right-to-work laws against challenges based on the CONTRACT CLAUSE and constitutional guarantees of FREEDOM OF SPEECH, FREEDOM OF PETITION and assembly, EQUAL PROTECTION, and DUE PROCESS OF LAW. The Court, moreover, negated any equal protection requirement that state remedies for discrimination against union members and nonmembers, respectively, be coextensive. The Court wryly observed that the unions' due process contentions were a reversion to the doctrines of LOCHNER V. NEW YORK (1905), ADAIR V. UNITED STATES (1908), and COPPAGE V. KANSAS (1915), which the Court had discarded—after having used them to invalidate prohibitions of YELLOW DOG CONTRACTS and other measures designed to protect workers' associational interests.

In *Retail Clerks v. Schermerhorn* (1963) the Supreme Court upheld state power "to enforce their laws restricting the execution and enforcement of union-security agreements." The Court, however, significantly limited state authority, stating that "[it] begins only with the actual negotiation and execution of the type of agreement described by §14(b)." Consequently, under section 14(b), a state could not properly enjoin PICKETING for an agreement proscribed by state law. The Court did not explain the reasoning behind the apparent anomaly of permitting a state to prohibit a completed agreement but not economic pressure to secure it. The Court may, however, have feared that state authority over such antecedent pressures would too often be used to restrict activity protected by the NLRA, such as peaceful picketing that publicizes substandard working conditions.

Otherwise valid union security agreements raise questions under the FIRST AMENDMENT when dissidents object to the use of compulsory financial exactions for political and other purposes not central to collective bargaining.

BERNARD D. MELTZER

Bibliography

HAGGARD, T. 1977 *Compulsory Unionism, the NLRB and the Courts: A Legal Analysis of Union Security Agreements.* Philadelphia: Industrial Research Unit, Wharton School, University of Pennsylvania.

RIPENESS

People who anticipate harm occasionally attack a law's constitutionality before it is applied to them, or even before the law takes effect. A federal court may decline to decide such a case for lack of ripeness if it is unclear that adjudication is needed to protect the challengers, or if information sufficient to permit intelligent resolution is not yet available. A matter of timing and degree, ripeness is grounded both in Article III's CASE OR CONTROVERSY requirement and the federal courts' reluctance to issue constitutional decisions needlessly or prematurely. Delaying decision may cause interim hardship and allow unconstitutional harm to occur, but further developments may narrow the issues, or produce important information, or even establish that no decision is needed.

The Supreme Court's ripeness decisions display varying sensitivity to these sometimes conflicting factors. Normally, a court is more likely to defer resolution of fact-dependent issues, like those based on a particular application of a law, than it is to defer adjudication of strictly legal issues. A single case may present some issues ripe for adjudication, but others not ripe. Ripeness decisions mainly respond, however, to the degree of contingency or uncertainty of the law's expected effect on the challenger.

Where leeway exists, the court may be influenced by determining whose interests a quicker decision would serve. Thus, when federal civil servants fearing dismissal for violation of the HATCH ACT asked that the political activities they were contemplating be declared constitutionally protected in *United Public Workers v. Mitchell* (1947), the Court found the case unripe absent enforcement of the act against some particular employee behavior. Similarly, a challenge to IMMIGRATION policy was held unripe in *International Longshoremen's Union v. Boyd* (1954) despite a strong indication that, without a ruling, resident ALIENS risked jeopardizing their right to return to the United States. With little doubt that the laws would be applied, the challengers nonetheless were forced to act at their peril. By contrast, when a delay in decision has threatened to frustrate government policy, the Court has resolved anticipatory challenges to laws whose future application appeared inevitable, including legislation restructuring some of the nation's railroads in the *Regional Rail Reorganization Act Cases* (1974) and the FEDERAL ELECTION CAMPAIGN ACTS in BUCKLEY V. VALEO (1976).

Sensitivity to the government's interest in quick resolution even led the Court to uphold a federal statute limiting aggregate operator liability for nuclear power plant explosions in *Duke Power Co. v. Carolina Environmental Study Group, Inc.* (1978), despite evidence that explosions are unlikely and serious doubt that this statute would ever be applied. Because injury to the asserted right of unlimited recovery for nuclear disaster was unlikely to occur soon, if at all, the constitutional issues did not seem ripe; yet the Court concluded that the case was ripe, because the normal operation of nearby nuclear plants (whose development the statute had facilitated) threatened imminent pollution—even though the suit had not questioned the pollution's legality.

As the *Duke Power* case illustrates, the inherent policy choice in ripeness decisions—between finding constitutional adjudication premature and finding prevention of harm or validation of government policy timely—embodies important perceptions of judicial role in a regime characterized by the SEPARATION OF POWERS.

JONATHAN D. VARAT

Bibliography

WRIGHT, CHARLES A.; MILLER, ARTHUR R.; and COOPER, EDWARD H. 1984 *Federal Practice and Procedure.* Vol. 13A:112–214. St. Paul, Minn.: West Publishing Co.

RIZZO v. GOODE
423 U.S. 362 (1978)

Rizzo exemplifies the BURGER COURT's inhospitability to INSTITUTIONAL LITIGATION aimed at broad structural reform. Philadelphia citizens sued the mayor and other officials in federal court, alleging condonation of a pattern of police mistreatment of minority residents and others. The district court held long hearings, validated the plaintiffs' charges, and ordered the defendants to submit a comprehensive plan to improve complaint procedures and police discipline.

The Supreme Court, 5–3, held this order improper. The Court implied that the controversy lacked RIPENESS, and suggested that YOUNGER V. HARRIS (1971) might protect the action of state executives as well as state courts. The decision, however, rested on the ground that police supervisors had been insufficiently involved in the proved misconduct to justify the court's systemwide order.

KENNETH L. KARST

ROANE, SPENCER
(1762–1822)

Spencer Roane, a Virginian, was the foremost judicial exponent of STATES' RIGHTS in the era of the MARSHALL COURT, and President THOMAS JEFFERSON would have made him Chief Justice of the United States had the opportunity arisen. Roane served for twenty-eight years (1794–1822) on Virginia's highest court. Before then he was a state legislator. He opposed RATIFICATION OF THE CONSTITUTION and never abandoned his belief that the national government possessed powers dangerous to the states.

Roane supported the authority of his court to hold unconstitutional a state act and even a congressional act, but he denied the authority of the Supreme Court to hold a state act unconstitutional. As leader of the nation's most influential state court he regarded the Supreme Court as a rival, and his words carried extrajudicial influence. He founded the Richmond *Enquirer* and ran Virginia politics. By the close of his life he headed an organization that controlled Virginia's press, its banks, its congressional delegation, and all three branches of its state government. He was JOHN MARSHALL's most formidable foe and outspoken opponent.

In the controversy leading to MARTIN V. HUNTER'S LESSEE (1816), Roane's court held unconstitutional section 25 of the JUDICIARY ACT OF 1789. In 1815 he described the United States as "a confederation of distinct sovereignties." His constitutional decisions differed from the Marshall Court's even on matters not involving the nature of the Union. He sustained the act later held void in TERRETT V. TAYLOR (1815) and supported the state in a case similar to DARTMOUTH COLLEGE V. WOODWARD (1819).

His vehement opposition to the nationalist doctrines of MCCULLOCH V. MARYLAND (1819) and COHENS V. VIRGINIA (1821) led him to denounce the Marshall Court in a series of essays in the Richmond *Enquirer,* which Jefferson warmly acclaimed and even JAMES MADISON tentatively endorsed. Roane's views on the Union were probably closer to those of 1787 than Marshall's. Doubtlessly Roane loved the "federal union" as he understood it, although Marshall called him "the champion of dismemberment." Roane was an able, orthodox judge who died a sectional advocate.

LEONARD W. LEVY

Bibliography

MAYS, DAVID J. 1928 Judge Spencer Roane. *Proceedings of the Thirty-Ninth Annual Meeting of The Virginia State Bar Association* 39:446–464.

ROBBINS v. CALIFORNIA

See: *Ross, United States v.*

ROBEL v. UNITED STATES
389 U.S. 258 (1967)

Over two dissents, the WARREN COURT struck down on FIRST AMENDMENT grounds a section of the SUBVERSIVE ACTIVITIES CONTROL ACT of 1950 that prohibited the employment of members of the Communist party in "defense facilities" designated by the secretary of defense. Because the statute failed to distinguish between those who supported the unlawful goals of the party and those who did not, wrote Chief Justice EARL WARREN, its OVERBREADTH violated the right of association protected by the FIRST AMENDMENT. Warren rejected government arguments seeking to justify the provision by the WAR POWER and national security interests. "It would indeed be ironic if, in the name of national defense, we would sanction the subversion of one of those liberties—the freedom of association—which makes the defense of the Nation worthwhile." Justices BYRON R. WHITE and JOHN MARSHALL HARLAN dissented, observing that the majority "arrogates to itself an independent judgement of the requirements of national security."

MICHAEL E. PARRISH

ROBERTS, OWEN J.
(1875–1955)

Best known as an Associate Justice of the United States Supreme Court, Owen Josephus Roberts had a varied preliminary career—law practice and teaching, administration, and public service. In 1930, after the Senate Judiciary Committee rejected the nomination of Circuit Judge John J. Parker, President HERBERT C. HOOVER appointed Roberts, a Philadelphia Republican, who was approved without a dissenting vote. That same year, CHARLES EVANS HUGHES returned to the Court as Chief Justice of the United States.

Roberts and Hughes came to the Court in a period of sharp disagreement concerning not only the role of government in economic and social affairs but also the nature and scope of the judicial function itself. Both men were destined to play significant roles. Examples abound, and Hughes and Roberts were often joined. They agreed, for example, in sustaining Minnesota's moratorium on mortgage foreclosures in HOME BUILDING AND LOAN ASSOCIATION V. BLAISDELL (1934).

In NEBBIA V. NEW YORK (1934) Roberts, without using the word "emergency," upheld a New York statute regulating the price of milk. In WOLFF PACKING COMPANY V. COURT OF INDUSTRIAL RELATIONS (1923) Chief Justice WILLIAM HOWARD TAFT had invoked the concept of business AFFECTED WITH A PUBLIC INTEREST as a test of legitimate government power. Rejecting this test, Roberts observed: "The phrase can mean no more than that an industry for adequate reason is subject to control for the public good." Roberts also opposed the judicial notion that prices and wages were constitutionally immune from regulation. Thus the constitutional barriers Justice GEORGE H. SUTHERLAND had erected in ADKINS V. CHILDREN'S HOSPITAL (1923) against the District of Columbia minimum wage for women as the "heart of a contract" were weakened. Citing *Munn v. Illinois* (1877), Roberts recalled: "The DUE PROCESS clause makes no mention of sales or prices. . . . The thought seems, nevertheless, to have persisted that there is something peculiarly sacrosanct about prices and wages."

Roberts's *Nebbia* opinion also disavowed a broad scope of judicial power. Here, as in UNITED STATES

V. BUTLER (1936), the judicial function involved "only one duty, to lay the article of the Constitution which is involved beside the statute which is challenged and to decide whether the latter squares with the former." The *Nebbia* opinion was thus hailed as indicating fair weather for FRANKLIN D. ROOSEVELT's New Deal legislation. Without specifying any particular level of government, Roberts declared: "This Court from the early days affirmed that the power to promote the general welfare is inherent in government." Yet, speaking for the Court in RAILROAD RETIREMENT BOARD V. ALTON RAILWAY COMPANY (1935), Roberts argued that Congress lacked power under the COMMERCE CLAUSE to pass any compulsory pension act for railroad workers. Hughes, LOUIS D. BRANDEIS, BENJAMIN N. CARDOZO, and HARLAN F. STONE dissented, the last rating this decision "the worst performance of the Court in my time."

UNITED STATES V. BUTLER apparently put the New Deal's legislative program beyond the scope of the TAXING AND SPENDING POWER. Roberts, invoking the TENTH AMENDMENT, argued that judicial endorsement of the AGRICULTURAL ADJUSTMENT ACT would "sanction legislative power without restriction or limitation" and convert Congress into a "parliament of the whole people, subject to no restrictions save such as are self-imposed." Roberts also voted with the conservatives in CARTER V. CARTER COAL COMPANY (1936), which set aside the Coal Conservation Act. Again the stumbling block was the Tenth Amendment. Coal mining, like agriculture, was local and therefore beyond the reach of national authority.

Meanwhile, overwhelming popular approval of the New Deal in the 1936 presidential election and the continuing high level of unemployment made it apparent that reliance on the states to cope with the economic emergency was misplaced. Blocking national action were four Supreme Court Justices, sometimes joined by Hughes and Roberts.

Roberts's judicial record appears inconsistent. Although the cases involved different issues, the shift between *Nebbia* on the one hand and *Alton* and *Butler* on the other is a clear instance of change. Some observers charged that Roberts, alarmed by Roosevelt's court-packing proposal of February 1937, shifted from a vote against the minimum wage in MOREHEAD V. NEW YORK EX REL. TIPALDO (1936) to one in favor of it in WEST COAST HOTEL COMPANY V. PARRISH (1937). Thus Roberts became famous as "a man of many minds."

In the personal rights area Roberts was, on occasion, conspicuously on the liberal side. Joined by Brandeis, Sutherland, and Butler, he dissented in *Snyder v.*

Massachusetts (1934), insisting that when a jury visits the scene of a crime, the defendant and counsel must be present. In *Schneider v. Irvington* (1939) he voted to set aside a city ordinance restricting FREEDOM OF THE PRESS and distribution of nonadvertising circulars and pamphlets.

In HERNDON V. LOWRY (1937) Roberts wrote for the Court, which reversed the conviction of Angelo Herndon, a black organizer for the Communist party, who had been found guilty of inciting insurrection by trying to enlist other blacks in that organization. The Georgia courts sentenced Herndon to eighteen years in prison. Said Roberts of the state act that penalized any attempt to incite an insurrection against the state: "The statute, as construed and applied, amounts merely to a dragnet which may enmesh anyone who agitates for a change of government if a jury can be persuaded that he ought to have foreseen his words would have some effect in the future conduct of others. No reasonably ascertainable standard of guilt is prescribed. So vague and indeterminate are the boundaries thus set to the FREEDOM OF SPEECH and assembly that the law necessarily violates the guarantees of liberty embodied in the FOURTEENTH AMENDMENT." In BETTS V. BRADY (1942), however, Roberts for the Court held that the right to be represented by counsel in a noncapital felony case was not essential to due process of law (overruled in GIDEON V. WAINRIGHT, 1961).

During World War II, when the Court, speaking through Justice HUGO L. BLACK in *Korematsu v. United States* (1944), upheld the compulsory transfer of Japanese American citizens to relocation centers, Roberts wrote an eloquent dissent. Joined by FRANK MURPHY and ROBERT H. JACKSON, he challenged Black's majority opinion, then the prevailing public view. He wrote: "[This] is the case of convicting a citizen as a punishment for not submitting to imprisonment in a concentration camp, based on his ancestry, and solely because of his ancestry, without evidence or inquiry concerning his loyalty and good disposition towards the United States. . . . I need hardly labor the conclusion that constitutional rights have been violated."

Roberts and all his colleagues, including Stone, had held in GROVEY V. TOWNSEND (1935) that voting in PRIMARY ELECTIONS was not a constitutional prerogative but a privilege of party membership. In the famous case of UNITED STATES V. CLASSIC (1941) the Court, again speaking through Stone, without mentioning *Grovey*, ruled that participation in primaries was a right secured by the Constitution. Thus, with the adherence of Roberts, but without discussing *Gro-*

vey, Stone brought traditional southern election customs to the brink of destruction. More alert than Roberts, commentators knew that another precedent had been broken. In 1944, when the Court overruled *Grovey*, Roberts exploded. "Not a fact differentiates that case (*Grovey*) from this, except the names of the parties. . . . If this Court's opinion in the *Classic* case discloses its method of overruling earlier decisions, I can protest that in 'fairness,' it should rather have adopted the open and frank way of saying what it was doing. . . ." "The instant decision," Roberts fumed in SMITH V. ALLWRIGHT (1944), "tends to bring the adjudication of this tribunal into the same class as a restricted railroad ticket, good for this day and train only."

New trends and new judicial personnel in a rapidly changing world disturbed Roberts. He asserted that law had become not a chart to govern but a game of chance. By 1941 the cordial relations he had previously enjoyed with his colleagues became strained. When Roberts retired in 1945, Chief Justice Stone drafted the customary letter to a departing colleague commenting: "You have made fidelity to principle your guide to decision." Black and WILLIAM O. DOUGLAS strongly objected, contending that this was precisely the quality Roberts lacked. Consequently no farewell letter was sent.

Roberts was a modest man, sensitive to his shortcomings. On leaving the bench he commented: "I have no illusion about my judicial career. . . . Who am I to revile the good God that did not make me a Marshall, a Taney, a Bradley, a Holmes, a Brandeis, or a Cardozo?"

ALPHEUS THOMAS MASON

Bibliography

LEONARD, CHARLES A. 1971 *A Search for Judicial Philosophy: Mr. Justice Roberts.* Port Washington, N.Y.: Kennikat Press.

MASON, ALPHEUS T. 1956 *Harlan Fiske Stone: Pillar of the Law.* New York: Viking.

NOTE 1955 Owen J. Roberts—In Memoriam. *University of Pennsylvania Law Review* 104:311–317.

ROBERTS v. CITY OF BOSTON
5 Cush. (Mass.) 198 (1850)

In BROWN V. BOARD OF EDUCATION (1954) the Court observed that the SEPARATE BUT EQUAL DOCTRINE "apparently originated in *Roberts v. City of Boston.*" Chief Justice LEMUEL SHAW's opinion in that case had an extraordinary influence. The courts of at least ten states relied on it as a precedent for upholding segregated education. In HALL v. DeCUIR (1878) the Supreme Court cited it as an authority for the rule that "equality does not mean identity." In PLESSY v. FERGUSON (1896) the Court relied on it as the leading precedent for the validity of state legislation requiring racial SEGREGATION in places where whites and blacks "are liable to be brought in to contact," and in GONG LUM v. RICE (1927) the Court explained *Roberts* as having sustained "the separation of colored and white schools under a state constitutional injunction of EQUAL PROTECTION, the same as the FOURTEENTH AMENDMENT. . . ."

Roberts arose as a TEST CASE to determine the validity of Boston's requirement that black children attend segregated schools. CHARLES SUMNER, attacking that requirement, denied that a racially separate school could be equal, because it imposed a stigma of caste and fostered prejudice.

Shaw, for a unanimous Supreme Judicial Court, agreed that the case presented the question whether the separate schools for blacks violated their constitutional right to equality. But he reasoned that all rights must depend on laws adapted to the "respective relations and conditions" of individuals. He believed that the school committee had exercised "a discriminating and honest judgment" in deciding that the good of both races was best promoted by the separate education of their children. The law, Shaw said in reply to Sumner, did not create prejudice, probably could not change it, and might only foster it by "compelling" both races to attend "the same schools." Thus, by a singular absence of considered judgment, the court found no constitutional violation of equal protection in compulsory racial segregation as long as blacks had an equal right to attend public schools.

LEONARD W. LEVY

ROBERTS v. LOUISIANA

See: Capital Punishment Cases, 1976

ROBINSON, UNITED STATES v.
414 U.S. 218 (1973)

The Supreme Court here resolved the question whether the FOURTH AMENDMENT permits a full search of the person INCIDENT TO ARREST for a minor offense. This question is particularly acute in cases of traffic offenses, where police commonly make ar-

rests in order to search drivers and their automobiles.

In *Robinson* the police stopped an automobile and arrested its driver for operating the vehicle without a license. A search of his clothing uncovered heroin. Because searches incident to arrest are allowed for the purpose of discovering concealed weapons and evidence, Robinson's counsel argued that such searches are unjustified in connection with routine traffic arrests: they will seldom yield evidence related to the traffic offense itself, and the chances of the driver's being armed are usually minimal.

The Supreme Court ruled, however, that a search incident to a custodial arrest requires no justification beyond the arrest; it is not an exception to the warrant requirement, but rather is itself a reasonable search. It was "speculative" to believe that those arrested for driving without a license "are less likely to be armed than those arrested for other crimes." Any lawful arrest justifies "a full search of the person."

JACOB W. LANDYNSKI

ROBINSON-PATMAN ACT
49 Stat. 1526 (1936)

The rapid growth of chain stores during the Depression effectively bypassed the price discrimination prohibitions of the CLAYTON ACT by altering the basic lines of competition which that act addressed. Shortly after the Supreme Court invalidated the NATIONAL INDUSTRIAL RECOVERY ACT's codes of fair competition (beginning in SCHECHTER POULTRY CORPORATION v. UNITED STATES, 1935), Representative Wright Patman introduced a corrective bill into the House designed to regulate chain stores' use of economies of scale. As finally passed, the act amended section 2 of the Clayton Act. Although one section of the new act allowed price discrimination made "in good faith" to match a competitor's price, the act generally outlawed discrimination that "substantially lessened" competition or tended to create a monopoly. Other provisions prohibited the taking or making of allowances or commissions to buyers if not made proportionally. Buyers were also forbidden from "knowingly receiving" or inducing any discrimination. Although the act provided for suits by the Department of Justice and private individuals, the burden of enforcement fell on the FEDERAL TRADE COMMISSION. By tightening and narrowing section 2 of the Clayton Act, this legislation protected smaller firms by reducing the competitive advantages of large chains.

DAVID GORDON

Bibliography
HANSEN, HUGH C. 1983 Robinson Patman Law: A Review and Analysis. *Fordham Law Review* 51:1113.

ROCHIN v. CALIFORNIA
342 U.S. 165 (1952)

To dispose of evidence, Rochin swallowed drug capsules. Officers pummeled his stomach and jumped on him in an effort to make him throw up the evidence. That failing, they rushed him to a hospital where a doctor, on police instructions, pumped an emetic solution through a tube into Rochin's stomach, forcing him to vomit the capsules. With that evidence the state convicted Rochin as a drug pusher. The Supreme Court unanimously reversed his conviction. Justice FELIX FRANKFURTER, for the Court, held that the state had violated Rochin's right to DUE PROCESS OF LAW. Due process, said Frankfurter, however "indefinite and vague," outlawed "conduct that shocks the conscience." State prosecutions must not, at the risk of violating due process, offend the "sense of justice" or of "fair play." Due process enjoined a respect for the "decencies of civilized conduct."

Justices HUGO L. BLACK and WILLIAM O. DOUGLAS, concurring separately, repudiated Frankfurter's reasoning as excessively subjective. His "nebulous" standard of due process, they believed, allowed the Court to draw upon undefinable notions of justice or decency or fairness. They would have ruled that the state violated Rochin's Fifth Amendment RIGHT AGAINST SELF-INCRIMINATION, which the FOURTEENTH AMENDMENT incorporated.

LEONARD W. LEVY

ROCK ROYAL CO-OPERATIVE, UNITED STATES v.

See: *Wrightwood Dairy, United States v.*

RODNEY, CAESAR A.
(1772–1824)

Elected to the House of Representatives in 1802, Jeffersonian Congressman Caesar Augustus Rodney became one of the managers of the IMPEACHMENT of Justice SAMUEL CHASE. In that capacity he argued that any deviation from GOOD BEHAVIOR on the part of a judge constituted a MISDEMEANOR in the constitu-

tional sense and was, therefore, an impeachable offense even if not an indictable crime.

As attorney general of the United States (1807–1811), Rodney asserted President THOMAS JEFFERSON's right to overrule a federal court decision on enforcement of the EMBARGO ACTS and defended, in EX PARTE BOLLMAN AND SWARTWOUT (1807), prosecutions for constructive TREASON.

DENNIS J. MAHONEY

ROE v. WADE
410 U.S. 113 (1973)
DOE v. BOLTON
410 U.S. 179 (1973)

In these cases the Supreme Court confronted the emotionally charged issue of abortion. The decisions invalidated two states' abortion laws—and, by inference, similar laws in a majority of states. As a result, the Court was plunged into prolonged and intense controversy, ranging from questions about the bearing of morality on constitutional law to questions about the proper role of the judiciary in the American system of government. The Court held unconstitutional a Texas law forbidding abortion except to save the pregnant woman's life and also invalidated several features of a Georgia law regulating abortion procedures and limiting abortion to Georgia residents.

The two women whose fictitious names grace the cases' titles were pregnant when they filed their actions in 1970, but not at the time of the Supreme Court's decision. The Court nonetheless held that their cases were not moot; rigid application of the MOOTNESS doctrine would prevent appellate review of an important issue that was capable of repetition. Nine doctors were also held to have STANDING to challenge the Georgia law; the intervention of a doctor under prosecution in Texas was held improper under the equitable ABSTENTION principle of YOUNGER V. HARRIS (1971); and a Texas married couple was denied standing because the woman had not been pregnant. The Court thus proceeded to the constitutional merits.

The *Roe* opinion, by Justice HARRY A. BLACKMUN, reviewed the history of abortion laws and the recent positions on abortion taken by medical groups and the American Bar Association, but the Court grounded its decision on neither history nor current professional opinion. Instead, the Court relied on a constitutional right of PRIVACY previously recognized in GRISWOLD V. CONNECTICUT (1965) and now relocated in the "liberty" protected by the DUE PROCESS clause of the FOURTEENTH AMENDMENT. This right included "a woman's decision whether or not to terminate her pregnancy," which decision was a FUNDAMENTAL INTEREST that could be restricted only on a showing of a COMPELLING STATE INTEREST.

The Court identified two state interests that would qualify as "compelling" at different stages in pregnancy: protection of maternal health and protection of potential life. Before discussing these interests, however, the Court dealt with a preliminary question: whether a fetus was a PERSON within the meaning of the Fourteenth Amendment. In an abortion, of course, it is not the state that denies life to a fetus; presumably the point of the Court's question was that if a fetus were a "person," the amendment should not be read to bar a state from protecting it against being aborted. The Court concluded, however, that a fetus was not a "person" in the amendment's contemplation. In reaching this conclusion, Justice Blackmun said: "We need not resolve the difficult question of when life begins." Absent a consensus among doctors, philosophers, or theologians on the issue, "the judiciary, at this point in the development of man's knowledge, is not in a position to speculate as to the answer." In any event, the law had never recognized the unborn "as persons in the whole sense." That conclusion alone, however, could not dispose of the question of the state's power. A state can constitutionally protect beings (or even things) that are not persons—including fetuses, which surely can be protected by law against certain kinds of experimentation or disposal, even though the law may be motivated by a feeling that fetuses share our common humanity.

The Court did recognize the state's interests in protecting maternal health and potential life; each would become "compelling" at successive stages of pregnancy. During the first trimester of pregnancy, neither interest is compelling; the abortion decision and its implementation must be left to the woman and her doctor. During the second trimester, the interest in maternal health becomes sufficiently compelling to justify some state regulations of the abortion procedure. When the fetus becomes "viable"—capable of life outside the womb, around the beginning of the third trimester of pregnancy—the state's interest in potential life becomes sufficiently compelling to justify prohibiting abortion except to preserve the "life or health" of the mother.

This scheme of constitutional rights has the look of a statute and evidently was influenced by New York's liberal law and the American Bar Association's model abortion law. Investigative reporters tell us that the three-part scheme resulted from negotiation among the Justices, and it is hard to see it as anything but a compromise between banning abortion altogether and turning over the entire abortion decision to the pregnant woman.

Justice BYRON R. WHITE, dissenting, complained that the Court had permitted abortion to satisfy "the convenience, whim or caprice of the putative mother." Chief Justice WARREN E. BURGER, concurring, responded that the Court had rejected "any claim that the Constitution requires abortion on demand" in favor of a scheme relying on doctors' "medical judgments relating to life and health." The Court's opinion deals ambiguously with the doctor's decisional role. At one point it states that the abortion decision "must be left to the medical judgment of the pregnant woman's attending physician." Yet the Court's decision rests on the constitutional right to privacy, which includes "a woman's decision whether or not to terminate her pregnancy." Very likely Justice Blackmun, a former general counsel of the Mayo Clinic, was influenced by the medical authorities he cited. Indeed, the Blackmun and Burger opinions both convey an inclination to convert abortion issues into medical questions. Linking the state's power to forbid abortions with "viability" is one example—although it is unclear how the Court will respond when medical technology permits the preservation of very young fetuses outside the womb. Similarly, a supposed lack of medical consensus made the Court reluctant to decide when life begins.

The issues in *Roe*, however, were not medical issues. First, there is no medically correct decision concerning an abortion when the pregnant woman's health is not endangered. Second, there is no lack of medical consensus about what happens in the normal process of reproduction from insemination to birth. In some sense "life" begins at conception; to say otherwise is not to make a medical judgment but to decide a question of law or morality. The problem before the Court in *Roe* was to determine whether (or when) a state could constitutionally protect a fetus. The state's interest in potential life surely begins at the time of conception, and arguably before. Yet if *Griswold* and EISENSTADT V. BAIRD (1972) remained good law, the state could not constitutionally protect that interest by forbidding contraception. Most people do not equate the use of "morning after" pills or intrauterine devices with murder, although these forms of "contraception" are really ways of effecting abortion after conception. In 1973 no state was enforcing its abortion laws against such practices. Yet the argument that "life" begins at conception, for purposes of defining legal or moral rights, embraced the claims of both the newest embryo and the eight-month fetus. There was evident artificiality in the Court's selection of "viability" as the time when the state's concerns for potential life became "compelling," but there would have been artificiality in any resolution of the issue of state power other than an all-or-nothing decision.

In *Roe*'s companion case, *Doe v. Bolton,* the Court held invalid four provisions of Georgia law, requiring that abortions be: (1) performed in hospitals accredited by the Joint Commission on Accreditation of Hospitals; (2) approved by hospital staff committees; (3) approved in each case by two physicians other than the pregnant woman's doctor; and (4) limited to Georgia residents. The latter requirement was an obvious violation of Article IV's PRIVILEGES AND IMMUNITIES clause, and the other three were held to impose unreasonable restrictions on the constitutional right recognized in *Roe.*

The *Roe* opinion has found few defenders; even the decision's supporters are inclined to offer substitute justifications. *Roe*'s critics divide roughly into two groups: those who regard abortion as murder, and those who think the Supreme Court exceeded its proper institutional bounds, failing to ground its decision in the Constitution and merely substituting its own policy judgment for that of the people's elected representatives.

The latter criticism touched off an impressive succession of essays on JUDICIAL REVIEW. It was the former group of critics, however, who dominated the politics of abortion. The "right to life" movement was, for a time, one of the nation's most effective "single issue" groups, achieving enough respect from legislators to permit the adoption of laws withdrawing governmental financial aid to poor women who seek abortions. (See MAHER V. ROE, 1977; HARRIS V. MCRAE, 1980.) Various constitutional amendments to overturn *Roe* were proposed in Congress, but none was submitted to the states for ratification. In the early 1980s Congress considered, but did not adopt, a bill declaring that "human life begins from the moment of conception." Congress also heard proposals to withdraw federal court jurisdiction over abortion cases. (See JUDICIAL SYSTEM.) Yet the *Roe* decision has weathered all these political storms.

Roe's stability as a precedent is founded on the same social and political base that initially supported the decision. It was no accident that *Roe* was decided in the 1970s, when the movement against SEX DISCRIMINATION was winning its most important constitutional and political victories. The abortion question was not merely an issue between pregnant women and their unwanted fetuses; it was also a feminist issue, going to women's position in society in relation to men. Even today American society imposes a greater stigma on unmarried women who become pregnant than on the men who father their children, and society still expects women to take the major responsibility for contraception and child care. The implications of an unwanted pregnancy or parenthood for a woman's opportunities in education, employment, and personal association—indeed, for the woman's definition of self—are enormous. Justice White's dissenting remark, that abortion regulation is an issue about which "reasonable men may easily and heatedly differ," perhaps said more than he intended to say.

KENNETH L. KARST

(SEE ALSO: *Abortion and the Constitution; Reproductive Autonomy.*)

Bibliography

ELY, JOHN HART 1973 The Wages of Crying Wolf: A Comment on *Roe v. Wade. Yale Law Journal* 82:920–949.

HENKIN, LOUIS 1974 Privacy and Autonomy. *Columbia Law Review* 74:1410–1433.

Symposium on the Law and Politics of Abortion. 1979 *Michigan Law Review* 77:1569–1646.

TRIBE, LAURENCE H. 1978 *American Constitutional Law.* Pages 923–934. Mineola, N.Y.: Foundation Press.

WOODWARD, BOB and ARMSTRONG, SCOTT 1979 *The Brethren: Inside the Supreme Court.* Pages 165–189, 229–240. New York: Simon & Schuster.

ROGERS v. LODGE
458 U.S. 613 (1982)

Rogers v. Lodge involved a successful challenge to an at-large electoral scheme for county commissioners in Burke County, Georgia. The Supreme Court noted that at-large systems are not unconstitutional per se and that a challenge could succeed only upon a showing that the system was established or maintained for a discriminatory purpose. All sides conceded that blacks in Burke County had free access to registration, voting, and candidacy for office. The issue was not, therefore, equal participation in the electoral process but "effective" participation. The Court held that where there was evidence of the lingering effects of past RACIAL DISCRIMINATION that had limited "the ability of blacks to participate effectively in the political process," the district court was justified in finding that an electoral scheme that did not hold at least the potential of electing minority members to office in proportion to their numbers was maintained for discriminatory purposes in violation of the EQUAL PROTECTION clause. Thus the Court, while not requiring proportional representation, nevertheless permitted it to be used as the test in determining whether an electoral system worked to "diminish or dilute the political efficacy" of minorities.

EDWARD J. ERLER

ROGERS v. RICHMOND
365 U.S. 534 (1961)

This is one of numerous cases prior to MALLOY V. HOGAN (1964) dealing with the question whether a confession was voluntary under a DUE PROCESS standard or coercive in violation of that standard. *Rogers* is significant because it was the first case in which the Court repudiated the test of trustworthiness as an element of the due process standard. Justice FELIX FRANKFURTER, for a 7–2 Court, declared that even if a confession were true or reliable, it should be excluded from admission in evidence if involuntary. Our system is accusatorial, not inquisitorial, Frankfurter said, and therefore the state must establish guilt by evidence not coerced from the accused.

LEONARD W. LEVY

ROOSEVELT, FRANKLIN D.
(1882–1945)

Franklin Delano Roosevelt, four-time President of the United States, received his formal instruction in the constitutional system at Harvard College (1900–1904) and Columbia Law School (1904–1907). The mood of the Progressive period, however, was more potent than academic doctrine in shaping his understanding of the constitutional process.

His kinsman Theodore Roosevelt, for whom he cast his first presidential vote in 1904, saw the Constitution "not as a straitjacket . . . but as an instrument designed for the life and healthy growth of the Nation." T. R. further saw the courts as "agents of reaction" and the President as the "steward of the people." If necessary, the President must be prepared to act as the savior of the Constitution against the courts, a role in which T. R. cast himself when he proposed the recall of judicial decisions in 1912. Service under WOODROW WILSON confirmed the young Franklin Roosevelt's belief in a spacious reading of executive

authority, and experience as assistant secretary of the navy in wartime Washington showed him how emergency expanded presidential initiative.

After the Wilson administration, Roosevelt's return to legal practice was interrupted when he was crippled in 1921 by poliomyelitis. Elected governor of New York in 1928, he soon confronted the consequences of the Wall Street crash of 1929. He foresaw no constitutional objections to his state programs of unemployment relief, public power development, and land planning. "The United States Constitution," he said in a 1930 speech, "has proved itself the most marvelously elastic compilation of rules of government ever written." Though Roosevelt's purpose in that speech was to vindicate STATES' RIGHTS, he proved marvelously elastic himself when elected President in 1932. Favoring the concentration of power at whatever level of government he happened to be serving, he became thereafter a resolute champion of federal authority.

"Our Constitution," he said in his first inaugural address, "is so simple and practical that it is possible always to meet extraordinary needs by changes in emphasis and arrangement without loss of essential form." He hoped, he continued, to preserve the normal balance between executive and legislative authority. However, if the national emergency remained critical, "I shall ask the Congress for the one remaining instrument to meet the crisis—broad Executive power to wage a war against the emergency." He thus combined optimism about the essential elasticity of the Constitution with an understanding that extraordinary executive initiative must rest, not on inherent presidential power, but on the delegation to the President of powers possessed by Congress. To this he added a certain pessimism about the federal courts, assuming, as he had said during the 1932 campaign, that the Republican party had been in "complete control of all branches of the Federal Government . . . the Supreme Court as well."

For this last reason he was in no hurry to send New Deal legislation through the gantlet of the Supreme Court. The first major test came in February 1935 over the constitutionality of the congressional JOINT RESOLUTION of June 1933 abrogating the so-called gold clause in public and private contracts. If the Court invalidated the resolution, the result would increase the country's total debt by nearly $70 billion. Roosevelt prepared a radio speech attacking an adverse decision and planned to invoke EMERGENCY POWERS to mitigate the effects. But while the Court, in PERRY V. UNITED STATES (1935), held the repudiation of the gold clause unconstitutional with regard to government bonds (though not to private obligations), it also held that, because the plaintiff had suffered no losses, he was not entitled to compensation. The administration's monetary policy remained precariously intact. (See GOLD CLAUSE CASES.)

But three months later in a 5–4 decision the Court nullified the Railroad Retirement Act as an invalid use of the commerce power. Then on May 27, in SCHECHTER POULTRY CORP. V. UNITED STATES it struck down the NATIONAL INDUSTRIAL RECOVERY ACT on two grounds: that the act involved excessive DELEGATION OF POWER by Congress, and that it exceeded the reach of congressional power under the COMMERCE CLAUSE. The vote against the National Recovery Administration was unanimous, as were two other decisions the same day—"Black Monday" in the eyes of New Dealers—one holding the FRAZIER-LEMKE FARM BANKRUPTCY ACT unconstitutional, the other denying the President the power to remove a member of a regulatory commission without congressional consent. If the Court was warning Roosevelt not to go to extremes, Roosevelt responded by warning the Court not to go to extremes either. Calling the SCHECHTER decision "more important probably than any decision since [DRED SCOTT V. SANFORD (1857)]," he said that it carried the Constitution back to "the horse-and-buggy definition of INTERSTATE COMMERCE."

Undeterred, the Court majority prosecuted its attack. In January 1936 six Justices in UNITED STATES V. BUTLER pronounced agriculture a "local" subject, beyond Congress's power, and set aside the AGRICULTURAL ADJUSTMENT ACT. Justice HARLAN F. STONE protested a "tortured construction of the Constitution" in an eloquent dissent. The Court majority, however, proceeded to strike down the Guffey Bituminous Coal Conservation Act, the Municipal Bankruptcy Act, and, finally, in MOREHEAD V. NEW YORK EX REL. TIPALDO (1936), a New York minimum wage law. The Court, Roosevelt now said, had thereby created a " 'no-man's-land' where no Government—State or Federal—can function." Between 1789 and 1865 the Court had declared only two acts of Congress unconstitutional; now, between 1934 and 1936, it invalidated thirteen. Doctrines propounded by the Court majority held out small hope for the SOCIAL SECURITY ACT, the WAGNER NATIONAL LABOR RELATIONS ACT, and other New Deal laws awaiting the judicial test. Roosevelt concluded that "[JOHN] MARSHALL's conception of our Constitution as a flexible instrument—adequate for all times, and, therefore, able to adjust itself as the new needs of new generations arose—had been repudiated."

By 1936 apprehension was spreading about the destruction of the New Deal by the unelected "Nine Old Men." Congress and the law schools were astir with proposals to rein in the Court. Roosevelt outlined three possibilities to his cabinet: limiting the power of the Court to invalidate congressional legislation; making an explicit grant to Congress of powers now in dispute; or ("a distasteful idea") packing the Court by appointing new judges. The first two courses required constitutional amendments. Roosevelt soon decided that an amendment would be difficult to frame, even more difficult to ratify, and in any event subject to judicial interpretation. The problem lay not in the Constitution but in the Court. In early 1936 he instructed Attorney General HOMER CUMMINGS to prepare in utmost secrecy a plan, short of amendment, that would overcome the Court's resistance.

Roosevelt did not make the Court an issue in the 1936 campaign. But his smashing victory in November convinced him that the moment had arrived. Cummings proposed legislation providing for the appointment of new Justices when sitting Justices failed to retire at the age of seventy. Roosevelt sprang the plan in a message to Congress on February 5, 1937. Claiming overcrowded dockets and overworked and overage judges, Roosevelt requested legislation that would enable him to appoint as many as six new Justices.

Postelection euphoria had evidently marred Roosevelt's usually astute political judgment. Wider consultation might at least have persuaded him to make his case as an honest confrontation of power. The pretense that he was seeking merely to ease the burdens of the Court relied on arguments that Chief Justice CHARLES EVANS HUGHES soon demolished in a letter to the Senate Judiciary Committee. By the time Roosevelt began to present the true issue—"We must take action to save the Constitution from the Court and the Court from itself"—his initial trickiness had lost the court plan valuable momentum.

The Chief Justice had further resources. On March 29, in WEST COAST HOTEL V. PARRISH, a 5–4 Court upheld a Washington minimum wage law, thereby in effect overruling the Tipaldo decision taken the preceding term. The "switch in time" that "saved nine" was provided by Justice OWEN J. ROBERTS; because Parrish had been argued in December, Roberts's second thoughts, if affected by external circumstances, responded to the election, not to the Court plan. In March, the Court also upheld a slightly modified version of the Farm Bankruptcy Act rejected two years earlier. In April, in National Labor Relations Board v. Jones & Laughlin Steel Corporation, the

Court approved the National Labor Relations Act in a 5–4 decision in which, as Roberts later conceded, both he and Hughes reversed the position they had taken in condemning the Guffey Act the year before. In May the Court upheld the Social Security Act.

In two months, the Court, under the pressure of the election and the Roosevelt plan, wrought a constitutional revolution, recognizing in both federal and state governments powers it had solemnly denied them in the two previous years as contrary to the Constitution. It greatly enlarged the federal commerce power and the TAXING AND SPENDING POWER, gave new force to the GENERAL WELFARE CLAUSE, altered the application of the DUE PROCESS clause to the states, and abandoned the doctrine of excessive delegation as a means of invalidating federal legislation.

The Court's revisionism, by lessening the felt need for reform, strengthened opposition, already vehement, to the President's plan for the Court. Democrats joined Republicans in denouncing "court-packing." In May the decision of Justice WILLIS VAN DEVANTER to resign, opening the way for Roosevelt's first Supreme Court appointment, further weakened pressure for the plan. In the interests of Senate passage, Roosevelt promised the vacancy to the majority leader Senator Joseph T. Robinson. As Robinson was both old and conservative, he was an anomalous reform choice. By summer Roosevelt was belatedly ready to entertain compromise. But Robinson's death in July brought the bitter struggle to an end.

The insouciance with which Roosevelt presented the Court plan exacted heavy costs in the future of his domestic program, the unity of his party, the confidence of the electorate, and his own self-confidence. Still, the plan attained its objective. As ROBERT H. JACKSON summed it up, "The President's enemies defeated the court reform bill—the President achieved court reform." The plan forced the Court to abandon rigid and restrictive constitutional views; at the same time, the plan's rejection eliminated Court packing as a precedent for the future. History may well conclude both that Roosevelt was right to propose the plan and that the opposition was right to beat it.

In the next half dozen years Roosevelt made the Court his own, appointing HUGO L. BLACK (1937), STANLEY F. REED (1938), FELIX FRANKFURTER (1939), WILLIAM O. DOUGLAS (1939), FRANK MURPHY (1940), JAMES F. BYRNES (1941), Robert H. Jackson (1941), and WILEY B. RUTLEDGE (1943) as Associate Justices and Harlan F. Stone as Chief Justice (1941). In time the Roosevelt Court itself split between the apostles of judicial restraint, who had objected to the methods of the "Nine Old Men," and the activists, who had objected only to their results. But the new Court was united in affirming the reach of the national government's constitutional power to meet the social and economic problems created by the Great Depression.

With the status of New Deal legislation thus assured, Roosevelt's next tangle with constitutional issues took place in FOREIGN AFFAIRS. The Court in UNITED STATES V. CURTISS-WRIGHT EXPORT CORPORATION (1936) had unanimously endorsed the propositions that "the powers of external SOVEREIGNTY did not depend upon the affirmative grants of the Constitution" and that the President had in foreign affairs "a degree of discretion and freedom from statutory restriction which would not be admissible were domestic affairs alone involved." But Congress still had statutory control over vital areas of foreign policy. Neutrality, for example, had been a congressional prerogative since 1794. While Roosevelt requested discretionary neutrality legislation, he saw no practical choice but to accept mandatory laws passed by a stubbornly isolationist Congress. These laws placed the administration in a foreign policy straitjacket from which it sought to wriggle free to the very eve of Pearl Harbor.

Congress, too, retained the constitutional power to declare war. As Roosevelt reminded the French prime minister during the fall of France in 1940, assurance of aid did not imply military commitments; "only the Congress can make such commitments." And legislative power extended to a variety of defense questions. When Winston S. Churchill asked for the loan of old American destroyers, Roosevelt initially responded that "a step of that kind could not be taken except with the specific authorization of the Congress." Later Roosevelt was persuaded that he could make the transfer through executive action. Attorney General Robert H. Jackson's official opinion to this effect rested not on claims of inherent power as President or COMMANDER-IN-CHIEF but on the construction of laws passed by Congress. Critics found the argument strained, but public opinion supported the action.

The decisive step marking the end of American neutrality was the Lend-Lease Act, passed after full and vigorous debate in March 1941. Once Congress had authorized the lending and leasing of goods to keep Britain in the war, did this authority not imply an effort to make sure that the goods arrived? So Roosevelt evidently assumed, trusting that a murky proclamation of "unlimited national emergency" in May 1941 and the impact of Nazi aggression on public opinion would justify his policy. When Grenville Clark urged a joint resolution by which Congress would explicitly approve measures necessary to assure the delivery of supplies, Roosevelt replied in July that the time was not "quite right." The renewal of the draft the next month by a single-vote majority in the House of Representatives showed the fragility of congressional support. By autumn the navy, on presidential orders and without congressional authorization (until Neutrality Act revision in November), was fighting an undeclared war against Germany to protect convoys in the North Atlantic.

Roosevelt's actions in the latter part of 1941, like ABRAHAM LINCOLN'S after the fall of Fort Sumter, were arguably unconstitutional, though not without historical precedent. He did not seek to justify the commitment of American forces to combat by pleas of inherent power as President or as Commander in Chief, and thereby proposed no constitutional novelties. If pressed, he perhaps would have associated himself with JOHN LOCKE, THOMAS JEFFERSON, and Abraham Lincoln in asserting not continuing presidential power but emergency prerogative to be exercised only when the life of the nation was at stake.

Entry into war, as always, increased unilateral presidential authority. When under the New Deal Roosevelt had acted most of the time on the basis of specific statutes, as a war President he acted very often on the basis of general powers claimed as "Commander in Chief in wartime" and on emergency powers activated by proclamation and conferred on an all-purpose agency, the Office of Emergency Management. Of the agencies established in 1940–1943 to control the war economy, only one, the Office of Price Administration, rested on a specific statute.

This statute ironically provoked Roosevelt's most notorious assertion of unilateral authority. The Price Control Act contained a farm parity provision deemed threatening to the anti-inflation program. Roosevelt told Congress in September 1942 that, if it did not repeal the provision within three weeks, he would refuse to execute it. "The President has the powers, under the Constitution and under Congressional Acts," he declared, "to take measures necessary to avert a disaster which would interfere with the winning of the war." He added, "When the war is won, the powers under which I act automatically revert to the people—to whom they belong."

The international threat, as always, increased pressure on CIVIL LIBERTIES. In 1940, while protesting his sympathy with OLIVER WENDELL HOLMES's condemnation of wiretapping in OLMSTEAD V. UNITED STATES (1928), Roosevelt granted his attorney general

qualified permission to wiretap "persons suspected of SUBVERSIVE ACTIVITIES against the United States." Given the conviction Roosevelt shared with most Americans that a Nazi victory in Europe would have endangered the United States, he would have been delinquent in his duty had he not taken precautionary measures. Though we know now that the internal menace was exaggerated, no one could be sure of that at the time.

Roosevelt, however, extended his concern to include Americans honestly opposed to intervention, directing the Federal Bureau of Investigation to investigate isolationists and their organizations. There was so little government follow-up of Roosevelt's prodding, however, that the prods were evidently taken by his subordinates as expressions of passing irritation rather than constant purpose. In 1941 Roosevelt appointed FRANCIS BIDDLE, a distinguished civil libertarian, as attorney general and kept him on the job throughout the war despite Biddle's repeated resistance to presidential requests that threatened the BILL OF RIGHTS.

Roosevelt's preoccupation with pro-Nazi agitation increased after Pearl Harbor. "He was not much interested in the theory of SEDITION," Biddle later recalled, "or in the constitutional right to criticize the government in wartime. He wanted this anti-war talk stopped." In time, his prods forced a reluctant Biddle to approve the indictment of twenty-six pro-Fascist Americans under a dubious application of the law of CRIMINAL CONSPIRACY. A chaotic trial ended with the death of the judge, and the case was dropped.

Biddle also resisted the most shameful abuse of power within the United States during the war—the relocation of Americans of Japanese descent. Here Roosevelt responded both to local pressure, including that of Attorney General EARL WARREN of California, and to the War Department, where such respected lawyers as Henry L. Stimson and John J. McCloy demanded action. Congress ratified Roosevelt's EXECUTIVE ORDER before it was put into effect, so the relocation did not represent a unilateral exercise of presidential power. The Supreme Court upheld the program in the JAPANESE AMERICAN CASES (1943–1944).

Still, despite Roosevelt's moments of impatience and exasperation, his administration's civil liberties record during World War II was conspicuously better than that of the Lincoln administration during the Civil War or of the Wilson administration during World War I. In 1944 the AMERICAN CIVIL LIBERTIES UNION saluted "the extraordinary and unexpected record . . . in freedom of debate and dissent on all public issues and in the comparatively slight resort to war-time measures of control or repression of opinion."

Roosevelt's presidency vindicated his conviction that social reform and military victory could be achieved without breaching the Constitution. A believer in a strong presidency, he was himself a strong President within, on the whole, constitutional bounds. His deviations from strict constitutional propriety were mostly under impressions, sometimes mistaken, of clear and present international danger. Those of his successors who claimed inherent presidential WAR POWERS went further than he ever did.

Roosevelt was a political leader, not a constitutional lawyer, and he correctly saw that in its major phase constitutional law is often a question of political and economic philosophy. No doubt his understanding of the practical necessity of consent was more important than technical appreciation of constitutional limitations in keeping his actions within the frame of the basic charter. But his presidency justified his inaugural assertion that the Constitution could meet extraordinary needs by changes in emphasis and arrangement without loss of essential form. His legacy was a revivified faith in the adequacy of the Constitution as a progressive document, equal to domestic and foreign emergency and "capable of meeting evolution and change."

ARTHUR M. SCHLESINGER, JR.

Bibliography

ALSOP, JOSEPH and CATLEDGE, TURNER 1938 *The 168 Days.* Garden City, N.Y.: Doubleday.
BIDDLE, FRANCIS 1962 *In Brief Authority.* Garden City, N.Y.: Doubleday.
FREEDMAN, MAX, ed. 1967 *Roosevelt and Frankfurter: Their Correspondence, 1928–1945.* Boston: Little, Brown.
JACKSON, ROBERT H. 1941 *The Struggle for Judicial Supremacy: A Study of a Crisis in American Power Politics.* New York: Knopf.
MASON, A. T. 1956 *Harlan Fiske Stone: Pillar of the Law.* New York: Viking.
SCHLESINGER, ARTHUR M., JR. 1957–1960 *The Age of Roosevelt,* vols. I–III. Boston: Houghton Mifflin.

ROOSEVELT, THEODORE
(1858–1919)

The son of a New York City merchant and philanthropist and a descendant of the original Dutch settlers of New Amsterdam, Theodore Roosevelt was graduated magna cum laude from Harvard College in 1879. He studied law for one year at Columbia University, but never completed law school or practiced law. When he was twenty-three years old he published his first book (the influential *Naval War of 1812*) and was elected to the New York state legislature on the Republican ticket. In his second term, having successfully campaigned for a LEGISLATIVE INVESTIGATION of statewide corruption, he was chosen minority leader of the state Assembly, and from that position he engineered passage of the state civil service reform measures proposed by Democratic Governor GROVER CLEVELAND.

In 1886, after two years of ranching in the Dakota badlands, Roosevelt returned to New York City and attempted to resume his political career, but he was defeated in his race for mayor. He held no political office until 1889, when President BENJAMIN HARRISON appointed him to the United States Civil Service Commission, a post in which he was retained when Cleveland returned to the presidency. In 1895, Roosevelt became president of the New York City Police Commission; for more than two years he did public battle with police corruption and demon rum.

When William McKinley was elected President, Roosevelt went back to Washington as the vigorous assistant secretary of the Navy. At the beginning of the Spanish-American War in 1898, Roosevelt resigned his office in the Navy Department and raised a regiment of volunteer cavalry, which he subsequently led in combat in Cuba. Riding the crest of fame from his wartime exploits, Roosevelt was elected governor of New York in 1898 and vice-president of the United States in 1900.

Roosevelt succeeded to the presidency when McKinley was assassinated in September 1901. He immediately pledged that his aim was "to continue, absolutely unbroken, the policy of President McKinley." But neither his love of fame nor his reformist impulses would permit him to redeem that pledge. Having reached the highest office in the land at a younger age than anyone before or since, he displayed a degree of vigor and impatience far greater than his predecessors had done. He also had a more expansive view of the powers and duties of the President than any of his predecessors since ABRAHAM LINCOLN. Not only did he think of the presidency as a "bully pulpit" from which one might lead, rather than follow, public opinion, but he also conceived of the office as having a roving commission to do anything the public weal might require so long as the Constitution did not by its terms prohibit the proposed course of action.

In FOREIGN AFFAIRS, Roosevelt acted with particular energy. On his own initiative he imposed a form of government in the Philippines (a commission headed by WILLIAM HOWARD TAFT) that Congress subsequently confirmed in the Philippine Organic Act (1902). He arranged by treaty for America to take over the British interest in construction of a canal across the Isthmus of Panama and subsequently fomented a revolt of Panamanians against the government of Colombia so that a favorable PANAMA CANAL TREATY could be negotiated (1903) and work on the canal begun. When the Latin American countries of Venezuela and Santo Domingo (now the Dominican Republic) defaulted on loans from European banks, Roosevelt put those countries under American occupation and receivership rather than risk military intervention by Europeans in the Western Hemisphere. This policy he called his "corollary" to the MONROE DOCTRINE. When an American citizen was kidnapped in 1904 by a band of Moroccan brigands, Roosevelt ordered a force of sailors and marines to invade a neutral and sovereign state to secure the citizen's release. Roosevelt also personally mediated the settlement of the Russo-Japanese War in 1905 (thereby earning the Nobel Peace Prize), and his administration was instrumental in achieving agreements to guarantee the independence of Morocco (1906) and to settle disputes among the Central American republics (1907). When Congress refused to appropriate funds so that the United States fleet could make a round-the-world show-the-flag cruise, Roosevelt used his power as COMMANDER-IN-CHIEF to order the ships to go as far as they could, confident that Congress would appropriate the funds to bring them home.

In domestic policy, Roosevelt's administration was both nationalist and interventionist. Roosevelt resumed prosecutions under the SHERMAN ANTITRUST ACT (albeit not so vigorously as his later critics would have liked) and proposed what became the HEPBURN ACT (1906), giving the Interstate Commerce Commission authority to set railroad rates nationwide. He put the federal government into the business of conserving America's wild places and natural resources, creating the Inland Waterways Commission (1907) and the National Conservation Commission (1908).

Roosevelt was generally critical of the constitutional jurisprudence of his day, and especially of the Supreme Court's protection of SUBSTANTIVE DUE PROCESS OF LAW in cases relating to ECONOMIC REGULATION. He emphatically rejected the contention that criticism of the judiciary weakens respect for law and undermines the independence of the judiciary. In his sixth state-of-the-Union message, he said: "The judge has a power over which no review can be exercised; he himself sits in review upon the acts of both the executive and legislative branches of the government; save in the most extraordinary cases he is amenable only at the bar of public opinion; and it is unwise to maintain that public opinion in reference to a man with such power shall neither be exprest nor led." Influenced by some of the more radical strains of PROGRESSIVE CONSTITUTIONAL THOUGHT, he favored a right of popular "recall" of state judicial decisions, that is, of allowing decisions to be overturned by a vote of the people. His first appointee to the Supreme Court, OLIVER WENDELL HOLMES of Massachusetts, initially so disappointed Roosevelt that the President remarked that he could "carve a judge with more backbone from a banana." Roosevelt's two other appointees, WILLIAM R. DAY and WILLIAM MOODY, both generally provided judicial support for state and federal regulation of business enterprise.

In 1908, Roosevelt did not seek reelection, but hand-picked as his successor William Howard Taft. He then retired from politics to a life of writing and adventuring. But Roosevelt disapproved of the conservative tone assumed by the Taft administration and attempted to wrest the 1912 Republican nomination for himself. When Taft was renominated, Roosevelt formed his own party, the Progressive party, and ran for President anyway. Roosevelt's candidacy split the Republican vote and permitted the election of WOODROW WILSON.

Roosevelt was later reconciled to the Republican party and in 1916 campaigned for the Republican presidential candidate, CHARLES EVANS HUGHES. When the United States entered World War I, Roosevelt asked President Wilson to authorize him to raise and command a volunteer division to serve in the expeditionary force; Wilson refused. After the war, Roosevelt opposed Wilson's plan for a League of Nations, preferring that the postwar world be dominated by an Anglo-American alliance. When he died, in 1919, Roosevelt was beginning to plan for yet another attempt at reelection to the presidency.

DENNIS J. MAHONEY

Bibliography

BLUM, JOHN MORTON 1954 *The Republican Roosevelt.* Cambridge, Mass.: Harvard University Press.
MORRIS, EDMUND 1979 *The Rise of Theodore Roosevelt.* New York: Coward, McCann & Geohegan.
MOWRY, GEORGE E. 1958 *The Era of Theodore Roosevelt: 1900–1912.* New York: Harper & Brothers.

ROSENBERG v. UNITED STATES
346 U.S. 273 (1953)

Over the vehement protests of three of its members (HUGO BLACK, FELIX FRANKFURTER, and WILLIAM O. DOUGLAS), the VINSON COURT vacated a STAY OF EXECUTION issued by Douglas that had halted the scheduled electrocution of Julius and Ethel Rosenberg. The Rosenbergs had been convicted and sentenced to death in 1951 for allegedly violating the 1917 ESPIONAGE ACT by passing secret information about the atomic bomb to the Soviet Union. Douglas had refused to join Black, Frankfurter, and HAROLD BURTON in earlier efforts to review the case by means of CERTIORARI and HABEAS CORPUS, but on June 17, 1953, after the Court had recessed for the term, he stayed the Rosenbergs' execution on the ground that their lawyers had raised a new argument deserving judicial scrutiny—the couple should have been tried under the Atomic Energy Act of 1946 rather than the earlier statute.

Responding to intense pressure from the Eisenhower administration, Chief Justice FRED VINSON recalled the Justices to Washington for special session. On June 19, a 6–3 majority overturned the stay and rejected Douglas's interpretation of the Atomic Energy Act. The Rosenbergs were executed that same evening. Frankfurter, who, with Black, had urged a full review of the case since the earliest appeals, later wrote that this last act of the Vinson Court was "the most disturbing single experience I have had during my term of service on the Court."

MICHAEL E. PARRISH

Bibliography

RADOSH, RONALD and MILTON, JOYCE 1983 *The Rosenberg File: A Search for the Truth.* New York: Holt, Rinehart & Winston.

ROSS, UNITED STATES v.
456 U.S. 798 (1982)

Ross altered the constitutional law of AUTOMOBILE SEARCHES. A UNITED STATES COURT OF APPEALS, following Supreme Court precedents, had held that although police had PROBABLE CAUSE to stop an automobile and make a WARRANTLESS SEARCH of its interior, including its closed areas, they should have had a SEARCH WARRANT before opening closed containers that they had searched for evidence. And in *Robbins v. California* (1981) the Court had declared that unless a closed container, by its shape or transparency, revealed contraband, it might not be opened without a warrant. The rationale of requiring a warrant for such a search turned on the reasonable expectation of privacy protected by the FOURTH AMENDMENT. *Ross,* however, substantially expanded the automobile exception to the warrant requirement.

Justice JOHN PAUL STEVENS for a 6–3 Court declared that the question for decision was whether the police, making a warrantless search with probable cause, had a right to open containers found in a vehicle. A lawful search of any premises extended to the whole area where the object of the search might be found. Thus a warrant to search a vehicle authorizes the search of all closed areas within it, including containers. "The scope of a warrantless search based on probable cause," Stevens said, "is no narrower—and no broader—than the scope of a search authorized by a warrant supported by probable cause." Accordingly, the scope of the search depended on the EVIDENCE sought for, not on the objects containing that evidence. Having so reasoned, the Court necessarily overruled the *Robbins* holding.

Justices THURGOOD MARSHALL, WILLIAM J. BRENNAN, and BYRON R. WHITE, dissenting, lamented that "the majority today not only repeals all realistic limits on warrantless automobile searches, it repeals the Fourth Amendment warrant requirement itself"—patently an exaggeration. *Ross* did make a shambles of the reasoning in earlier cases on searching closed containers in automobiles, but the Court finally delivered an unambiguous opinion for the guidance of law enforcement officers. Whether or not the Court based the new rule on expediency for the purpose of assisting prosecutorial forces, it will likely have serious implications for the privacy of Americans using their vehicles.

LEONARD W. LEVY

ROSS v. MOFFITT
417 U.S. 600 (1974)

Ross sharply limited the requirement of DOUGLAS V. CALIFORNIA (1963) that counsel be provided, free of charge, to INDIGENTS seeking to appeal from state convictions. The *Douglas* opinion had referred only to the "first appeal as of right," and here the Supreme Court's 6–3 majority drew the line defining the state's constitutional responsibility at precisely that point. There was no obligation to furnish counsel to pursue discretionary appeals or applications for Supreme Court review. Justice WILLIAM H. REHNQUIST's majority opinion did distinguish *Douglas,* but its reasoning drew heavily on the *Douglas* dissent of Justice JOHN MARSHALL HARLAN.

KENNETH L. KARST

ROSSITER, CLINTON
(1917–1970)

Clinton Lawrence Rossiter III was a political scientist, constitutional scholar, and historian. His fascination with the response of constitutional government to the exigencies of crisis and war led to his first two books, *Constitutional Dictatorship* (1948) and *The Supreme Court and the Commander in Chief* (1951). His most widely read work, *The American Presidency* (1956, rev. ed. 1960), a deft and approving account of the Presidency's growth in power, influence, and responsibility, was perhaps the most influential study of that institution before Watergate. *Seedtime of the Republic,* a monumental intellectual history of the American Revolution, traced the roots of the Revolutionary generation's political ideas to seventeenth-century English republican thought. Rossiter's other works include *Parties and Politics in America* (1960), *Conservatism in America* (1955, rev. ed. 1962), *Alexander Hamilton and the Constitution* (1964), *1787: The Grand Convention* (1966), and the posthumously published *The American Quest, 1790–1860* (1971).

RICHARD B. BERNSTEIN

ROSTKER v. GOLDBERG
453 U.S. 57 (1981)

Men subject to registration for possible military CONSCRIPTION challenged the exclusion of women from the registration requirement as a denial of EQUAL PROTECTION. The Supreme Court, 6–3, rejected this claim. Justice WILLIAM H. REHNQUIST, for the majority, paid great deference to Congress's authority over military affairs; with the most minimal judicial second-guessing of the congressional judgment, he concluded that men and women were "not similarly situated," because any draft would be designed to produce combat troops, and women were ineligible for combat. SEX DISCRIMINATION, in other words, was its own justification.

As the dissenters demonstrated, the exclusion of women from draft registration had resulted from no military judgment at all; the President and the Joint Chiefs of Staff had urged that women be registered. Rather, Congress had heard the voice of public opin-

ion. It is not impossible that the Court itself heard that voice. Thus do sex-role stereotypes perpetuate themselves.

KENNETH L. KARST

ROTH v. UNITED STATES
354 U.S. 476 (1957)
ALBERTS v. CALIFORNIA
354 U.S. 476 (1957)

Until *Roth* and *Alberts,* argued and decided on the same days, the Supreme Court had assumed that the FIRST AMENDMENT did not protect OBSCENITY. Squarely confronted with the issue by appeals from convictions under the federal obscenity statute (in *Roth*) and a California law outlawing the sale and advertising of obscene books (in *Alberts*), the Court held that obscenity was not constitutionally protected speech.

Justice WILLIAM J. BRENNAN, for the majority, relied on historical evidence that the Framers of the First Amendment had not intended to protect all speech, but only speech with some redeeming social value. Thus, the First Amendment protected even hateful ideas that contributed toward the unfettered exchange of information that might result in desired political and social change. Obscenity, however, was utterly without redeeming social importance, and was not constitutionally protected.

Neither statute before the Court defined obscenity; nor did the Court examine the materials to determine whether they were obscene. The Court nevertheless rejected the appellants' due process objections on the grounds that the statutes had given sufficient warning as to the proscribed conduct and the trial courts had applied the proper standard for judging obscenity.

The Court rejected the widely used test based on *Queen v. Hicklin* (1868) which judged a work's obscenity by the effect of an isolated excerpt upon particularly susceptible persons. The proper standard was "whether to the average person, applying contemporary community standards, the dominant theme taken as a whole appeals to prurient interest," that is, has a tendency to excite lustful thoughts. Because the obscenity of the materials involved in *Roth* was not at issue, the Court escaped the task of applying its definition. Ironically, the definition of obscenity was to preoccupy the Court for the next sixteen years. The Court, having designated a category of speech that could be criminally proscribed, now confronted the critical task of delineating that category.

Chief Justice EARL WARREN and Justice JOHN MARSHALL HARLAN, separately concurring, sought to limit the scope of the majority opinion. Warren, concurring in the result, agreed that the defendants' conduct in commercially exploiting material for its appeal to prurient interest was constitutionally punishable. Harlan, concurring in *Alberts* and dissenting in *Roth*, believed the Court was required to examine each work individually to determine its obscene character, and argued that the Constitution restricted the federal government in this field more severely than it restricted the states. Justices WILLIAM O. DOUGLAS and HUGO L. BLACK, dissenting in both cases, enunciated the positions they were to take in the wave of obscenity cases soon to overwhelm the Court: obscenity, like every other form of speech, is absolutely protected by the First Amendment.

KIM MCLANE WARDLAW

RULE OF FOUR

Even before Congress expanded the Supreme Court's discretionary CERTIORARI jurisdiction in 1925, the Court had adopted the practice of granting certiorari whenever four of the nine Justices agreed that a case should be heard. This "rule of four" was first made public in testimony concerning the bill that became the 1925 act. Some commentators have seen the adoption of that act as a congressional ratification of the practice; in any case, the rule is well established. In *Rogers v. Missouri Pacific R.R.* (1957) a majority agreed that the rule required the Court to hear a petition granted on the vote of four Justices, even though the other five might still think the case unworthy of review, unless new considerations had come to light in the meanwhile. As *New York v. Uplinger* (1984) makes clear, however, the vote of four Justices to *hear* a case does not require the Court to *decide* it if the other five Judges think a decision inappropriate.

The Court follows a similar practice in APPEAL cases coming from the state courts. The Court has even dismissed such an appeal "for want of a substantial FEDERAL QUESTION" over the expressed dissent of three Justices. When three members of the Court argue that a question is a substantial one, it probably is. The dismissal of an appeal under these circumstances reinforces the view that appeal, despite its theoretically obligatory nature as defined by Congress, has taken on much of the discretionary quality of the Court's certiorari policy.

KENNETH L. KARST

Bibliography

LEIMAN, JOAN MEISEL 1957 The Rule of Four. *Columbia Law Review* 57:975–992.

RULE OF LAW

The rule of law is the general principle that government and the governed alike are subject to law, as regularly adopted and applied. The principle is nowhere express in the United States Constitution, but it is a concept of basic importance in Anglo-American constitutional law. In that context, it is not merely a positivist doctrine of legality, requiring obedience to any duly adopted doctrine, but a means to assure that the actions of all branches of government are measured against the fundamental values enshrined in the COMMON LAW and the Constitution.

The rule of law has its roots in classical antiquity, in the *Politics* of Aristotle and the works of Cicero. As an Anglo-American legal principle, the concept may be traced to MAGNA CARTA (1215). In the thirty-ninth clause of that instrument, King John promised the barons that "No free man shall be taken, imprisoned, disseized, outlawed, or banished, or in any way destroyed, nor will we proceed against or prosecute him, except by the lawful judgment of his peers and the LAW OF THE LAND." Four centuries later, with the principle well entrenched in the theory and practice of the English common law, EDWARD COKE challenged James I's assertion of the right to exercise an independent judicial power with the words of Henry Bracton: "Quod Rex non debet esse sub homine, sed sub Deo et lege" [The King ought not to be under man, but under God and the law.] After the chaos of revolution, commonwealth, and restoration, the Glorious Revolution of 1688 established the permanent subjection of the king to the law, both of the common law courts and of Parliament.

Coke's *Reports* and *Institutes,* JOHN LOCKE's *Second Treatise of Government* (1691), and the flood of English radical political writing that accompanied the events of the seventeenth and eighteenth centuries carried these ideas to the American colonies. They became a key element in the ideology of the American Revolution. THOMAS PAINE's *Common Sense* (1776) proclaimed, "that in America, *the law is king.* For as in absolute governments, the king is law, so in free countries the law ought to be king; and there ought to be no other." As the unprecedented era of constitution making that succeeded the American Revolution provoked more sophisticated analysis of the structure of government, it became clear that not only the executive but also the legislature must be subject to law. Thus, JOHN ADAMS more temperately but more tellingly expressed the principle of the rule of law in drafting the MASSACHUSETTS CONSTITUTION of 1780. The Declaration of Rights in that instrument called for the SEPARATION OF POWERS, "to the end it may be a government of laws and not of men." Chief Justice JOHN MARSHALL gave practical effect to Adams's words in the actual application of the new federal Constitution, using them in MARBURY V. MADISON (1803) to bolster his argument that William Marbury had a judicial remedy for the withholding of his commission by the secretary of state.

The principle was elaborated and definitively labeled "the Rule of Law" by the leading nineteenth-century English constitutional theorist Albert Venn Dicey (1835–1922). In his influential work, *Introduction to the Study of Law of the Constitution* (1885), Dicey ranked the rule of law with parliamentary SOVEREIGNTY and constitutional conventions as one of the three fundamental elements of the unwritten British constitution. He gave the term "rule of law" three meanings: a requirement that government act against the citizen only in accordance with "regular law" enforced in the "ordinary courts" and not arbitrarily or in the exercise of "wide discretionary authority"; a requirement that the government and all citizens be equal before the law and equally subject to the ordinary courts; and a formulation reflecting the fact that constitutional rights were grounded not in abstract principles but in "the ordinary law of the land" as enforced in the courts.

Dicey's views of the rule of law have been rigorously elaborated by later political theorists, notably Friedrich Hayek in his *Constitution of Liberty* (1960) and other works. The fundamental nature of the rule of law as the basis of a moral and just social order has been recognized in more general terms in works such as Lon Fuller's *The Morality of Law* (1964) and John Rawls's *A Theory of Justice* (1971). It is also seen in the efforts of internationalists in the 1960s to establish international doctrines of world peace and human rights through a "world rule of law." More recently, critics have challenged the legitimacy of the rule of law, characterizing it as simply a cover for the maintenance of power by privileged social classes. Roberto Unger, in *Law and Modern Society* (1976), questioned the viability of the rule of law in the modern welfare/corporate state as the liberal premises upon which it is based decline.

Dicey's elaboration of the rule of law has also been forcefully criticized in England and the United States because its prohibition of discretionary action is inconsistent with the widespread use of the administrative process that has become characteristic of modern democratic government. Kenneth Culp Davis, a leading American critic, attributed the virtual nonuse of the phrase in American judicial opinions to the unreality of Dicey's "extravagant version" of the doctrine. Its occasional appearance to highlight a discussion of fairness or legality reflects, according to Davis, only the tendency of some judges "to add the touch of poetry" to their work.

Nevertheless, the concept of the rule of law remains fundamental to Anglo-American constitutional jurisprudence. In Britain, it remains a device for calling upon the protections of the common law against legislative and executive intrusion. In the United States, at the most general level, the rule of law is invoked by judges as they seek to assure compliance by the federal and state governments with the guarantees of the BILL OF RIGHTS. Those guarantees, as interpreted by the courts, are binding upon the governments and individuals to whom they are addressed. The Supreme Court made this point clear in COOPER V. AARON (1958), rejecting the position of defiance toward a federal court's school desegregation order taken by the governor and legislature of Arkansas.

More specifically, the concept of the rule of law embodies what Laurence H. Tribe has characterized as "the Model of Governmental Regularity." This model describes requirements of generality and prospectivity of legislation and procedural regularity in administration and adjudication that are articulated in and enforced through the EX POST FACTO and BILL OF ATTAINDER clauses of the Constitution and the DUE PROCESS clauses of the Fifth and FOURTEENTH AMENDMENTS. Finally, the element of equality in Dicey's rule of law has received fundamental expression in the development of the EQUAL PROTECTION clause of the Fourteenth Amendment. That clause, as interpreted and applied by the Supreme Court in the second half of the twentieth century, has provided constitutional support for the most profound changes that our society has seen, short of revolution or civil war.

L. KINVIN WROTH

Bibliography

ALLAN, T. R. S. 1985 Legislative Supremacy and the Rule of Law. *Cambridge Law Journal* 44:111–143.
DICEY, ALBERT VENN 1885 *Introduction to the Study of the Law of the Constitution.* London: Macmillan.
TRIBE, LAURENCE H. 1978 *American Constitutional Law.* Mineola, N.Y.: Foundation Press.

RULE OF REASON

The rule of reason was a statutory construction of the SHERMAN ANTITRUST ACT by the Supreme Court. Nothing better illustrated JUDICIAL POLICYMAKING than the rule of reason, which held that the Sherman Act excepted from its scope "good trusts" or "reasonable restraints of trade." The statute expressly declared illegal "every" contract, combination, and conspiracy in restraint of trade, and as a result the Court in several early cases rejected the argument that "every" did not mean what it said. The Court also denied that the statute should be construed in the light of the COMMON LAW, which had recognized the legality of certain ancillary restraints of trade on the ground that they were reasonable. For example, in UNITED STATES V. TRANS-MISSOURI FREIGHT ASSOCIATION (1897) the Court rejected the proposition that "Congress, notwithstanding the language of the [Sherman] act, could not have intended to embrace all contracts, but only such contracts as were in unreasonable restraint of trade." Said Justice RUFUS PECKHAM for the Court: "[w]e are, therefore, asked to hold that the act of Congress excepts contracts which are not in unreasonable restraint of trade." To read that rule of reason into the statute, Peckham answered, would be an exercise of JUDICIAL LEGISLATION.

That remained the Court's view until 1911, when it ignored its PRECEDENTS, the text of the statute, and the views of the Senate and the President. In 1909 the Senate had rejected a bill that proposed to amend the Sherman Act by incorporating the rule of reason. "To amend the antitrust act, as suggested by this bill," declared a subcommittee of the Senate Judiciary Committee, "would be to entirely emasculate it, and for all practical purposes render it nugatory as a remedial statute." In 1910 President WILLIAM HOWARD TAFT in a message to Congress had argued that no need existed to amend the scope of the Sherman Act. Yet in 1911, in two major antitrust cases, UNITED STATES V. STANDARD OIL COMPANY OF NEW JERSEY and *United States v. American Tobacco Co.*, Chief Justice EDWARD D. WHITE, who had dissented from earlier opinions repudiating the rule of reason, explicitly adopted it for an 8–1 Court. The sole dissenter, Justice JOHN MARSHALL HARLAN, echoing the *Trans-Missouri Freight* case, assaulted "judicial legislation"—the usurpation by the Court of a congressional function. The Sherman Act, Harlan insisted, included "every" restraint of trade, even a reasonable one. But Congress, in its 1914 antitrust legislation of the CLAYTON ACT and the FEDERAL TRADE COMMIS-SION ACT, by failing to attack the rule of reason acquiesced in it.

As a result of its rule of reason, the Supreme Court prevented effective use of the Sherman Act to prevent industrial consolidations of a monopolistic character. Thus, in *United States v. United Shoe Machinery Company* (1918), the Court held that the antitrust act did not apply to the company even though its dominating position in the industry approached that of an absolute monopoly which had restrained trade by its use of exclusive PATENT rights. In UNITED STATES V. UNITED STATES STEEL CORPORATION (1920) the Court held that the nation's largest industrial enterprise had reasonably restrained trade despite its "attempt to monopolize" in violation of the act. Similarly, in *United States v. International Harvester Company* (1927) the rule of reason defeated the government's case once again even though the company controlled a big proportion of the market and used exclusive dealer contracts to eliminate competition. Although the Court ruled that trade union activities came within the scope of the antitrust act, no union ever benefited from a Court finding that its restraint of trade was reasonable. The rule of reason, in short, proved to be of considerable importance in the history of JUDICIAL REVIEW, of the economy, and of government efforts to regulate monopolistic practices.

LEONARD W. LEVY

(SEE ALSO: *Antitrust Law and the Constitution.*)

Bibliography
NEALE, A. D. 1970 *The Antitrust Laws of the United States of America.* Cambridge: At the University Press.

RUMMEL v. ESTELLE
445 U.S. 263 (1980)

OLIVER WENDELL HOLMES once said that the Supreme Court sits to expound law, not do justice. This case is proof. On the premise that the length of a sentence is "purely a matter of legislative judgment," Justice WILLIAM H. REHNQUIST for a 5–4 Court found no CRUEL AND UNUSUAL PUNISHMENT in Rummel's mandatory life sentence after his third felony conviction for obtaining $120.75 by false pretenses. Rummel argued that his sentence was disproportionate to his crime. Rehnquist replied that the possibility of a parole in twelve years and the right of a state legislature to fix penalties against recidivists overcame Rummel's argument. Rehnquist declared that the state legislature was acting within its competence in prescribing punishment and that the state has a legitimate interest in requiring extended incarceration of habitual criminals. The Court would not substitute its judgment for the legislature's and overturn a sentence which was neither inherently barbarous nor grossly disproportionate to the offense.

Justice LEWIS F. POWELL for the dissenters believed that Rummel's life sentence "would be viewed as grossly unjust by virtually every layman and lawyer." The cruel and unusual punishment clause of the Eighth Amendment, extended by the FOURTEENTH AMENDMENT to the states, Powell argued, prohibited grossly disproportionate punishments as well as barbarous ones. Rummel's three felonies netted him about $230 in frauds. He never used violence, threatened anyone, or endangered the peace of society. Texas treated his crimes as no different from those of a three-time murderer. The Court's decision weakened the use of the cruel and unusual punishment clause in noncapital cases.

LEONARD W. LEVY

RUNYON v. MCCRARY
427 U.S. 160 (1976)

The CIVIL RIGHTS ACT OF 1866 gives all persons "the same right . . . to make and enforce contracts . . . as is enjoyed by white persons." In the *Runyon* case the Supreme Court, following its 1968 decision in JONES V. ALFRED H. MAYER CO., relied on the THIRTEENTH AMENDMENT as a source of congressional power and upheld the application of this provision to two private schools' exclusion of qualified black applicants.

Justice POTTER STEWART, writing for the Court, made clear that several issues concerning the act's coverage were being left open. The Court was not deciding whether the act forbade a private social organization to impose a racial limitation on its membership; nor was it deciding whether a private school might limit its students to boys or girls, or to members of some religious faith. *Runyon* itself involved "private, commercially operated, non-sectarian schools."

Although Congress is empowered to enforce the Thirteenth Amendment, the provisions of the BILL OF RIGHTS limit congressional power here as elsewhere. The school operators argued unsuccessfully that the application of the 1866 act to their admissions practices violated rights of association, parental rights, and the RIGHT OF PRIVACY.

In responding to the associational freedom claim,

Justice Stewart came close to saying that the freedom to practice racial discrimination in the choice of one's associates is not entitled to constitutional protection—a view that surely would not survive in the context of marriage or other intimate association. Concurring specially, Justice LEWIS F. POWELL remarked on the strength of the associational freedoms that would be involved if the 1866 Act were applied to a racially discriminatory selection of a home tutor or babysitter.

The Court dismissed the parental rights claim with the comment that parents and school operators retained the right to use the schools to inculcate the values of their choice. The privacy claim was similarly rejected; parents had a right to send their children to private schools, but the schools remained subject to reasonable government regulation.

Justices BYRON R. WHITE and WILLIAM H. REHNQUIST dissented, arguing that *Jones* was wrongly decided and that the 1866 act had not been intended to forbid a private, racially motivated refusal to contract. Justice JOHN PAUL STEVENS, in a special concurrence, agreed with the dissenters' view of the 1866 act's purposes. However, he concluded, "for the Court now to overrule *Jones* would be a significant step backwards" in the process of eliminating RACIAL DISCRIMINATION; thus he joined the Court's opinion. It was ever so; today's history almost always prevails in a contest with yesterday's.

KENNETH L. KARST

RUTGERS v. WADDINGTON
(New York Mayor's Court, 1784)

Decided in 1784 by the Mayor's Court of New York City, this was an early state precedent for JUDICIAL REVIEW and the first reported case in which the constitutionality of a state act was attacked on the ground that it violated a treaty of the United States. The state's Trespass Act allowed Rutgers, who had fled New York when the British occupied the city, to sue for the value of rents lost while her property was held by British merchants under military authority. The statute barred defendants from pleading that military authority justified the "trespass" under acts of war and the law of nations. The Treaty of Peace, however, canceled claims for injuries to property during the war. ALEXANDER HAMILTON, representing the defendants, expressly argued that the court should hold the Trespass Act unconstitutional.

Chief Judge JAMES DUANE, for the court, declared that the state constitution embodied the COMMON

LAW and that the common law recognized the law of nations. Duane also declared that the union of the states under the ARTICLES OF CONFEDERATION constituted "a FUNDAMENTAL LAW," according to which Congress had exclusive powers of making war and peace: "no state in this union can alter or abridge, in a single point, the federal articles or the treaty." His logic having led him to the brink of holding the Trespass Act void, Duane abruptly endorsed the prevailing Blackstonian theory of legislative supremacy. When the legislature enacted a law, "there is no power which can controul them . . . the Judges are not at liberty, altho' it appear to them to be unreasonable, to reject it: for this were to set the judicial above the legislative, which would be subversive of all government." Duane then declared that the legislature had not intended to revoke the law of nations and that the court had to expound the statute to give the legislature's intention its effect, whereupon the court emasculated the statute. The judgment was that for the time the property was held under military order, acts done according to the law of nations and "buried in oblivion" by the treaty could not be redressed by the statute; Rutgers could not recover for trespass.

Technically the court had construed the act to conform to the treaty and the law of nations, but the legislature angrily resolved that the adjudication was "subversive of all law and good order" and that if a court could "dispense with" state law, "Legislatures become useless." Although a motion to remove the judges failed, a public protest meeting adopted "An Address to the People," angrily accusing the court of having "assumed and exercised a power to set aside an Act of the State." The "Address," severely condemning judicial review, was widely circulated, as was the pamphlet report of the case.

LEONARD W. LEVY

RUTLEDGE, JOHN
(1739–1800)

John Rutledge, a wealthy lawyer, represented South Carolina in the STAMP ACT Congress (1765) and chaired that state's delegations to the First and Second Continental Congresses. He was a member of the committee that drafted the South Carolina Constitution (1776) and was elected the state's first president (1776–1778) and second governor (1779). He led his state's delegation to the CONSTITUTIONAL CONVENTION OF 1787, where he used his oratorical skill to advance a moderate STATES' RIGHTS position and to

defend the interests of the southern slaveholding aristocracy. He opposed creation of a separate federal judiciary, but favored a provision making the federal Constitution and laws binding on state courts. After signing the Constitution, he served as a member of the South Carolina ratifying convention.

In 1789, President GEORGE WASHINGTON appointed Rutledge one of the original associate justices of the Supreme Court, but he resigned in 1791—having done only circuit duty—to become Chief Justice of South Carolina. In 1795, Washington appointed him Chief Justice of the United States, and he presided over the August 1795 term of the Court; but an intemperate speech against JAY'S TREATY alienated the Federalists, and the Senate refused to confirm his nomination. (See SUPREME COURT, 1789–1801.)

DENNIS J. MAHONEY

RUTLEDGE, WILEY B.
(1894–1949)

When Wiley B. Rutledge joined the Supreme Court in January 1943, succeeding JAMES F. BYRNES, he helped to forge a liberal coalition that substantially redirected constitutional developments for the next six years. His sudden death in the summer of 1949, two months after the passing of Justice FRANK MURPHY, ended a brief era of liberal activism and ushered in the bleakest period for CIVIL LIBERTIES in the Court's history. President FRANKLIN D. ROOSEVELT's eighth and last appointment to the high bench, Rutledge remained, with the exception of Murphy, the most consistently liberal member of the STONE and VINSON COURTS.

When dean of the law school of the University of Iowa, Rutledge's support for FDR's New Deal, including the "court-packing" proposal, earned him an appointment to the Circuit Court of Appeals for the District of Columbia in 1939. There he consistently endorsed the social and economic reforms of the Roosevelt administration and also compiled a strong record on civil liberties. In one opinion Rutledge dissented on FIRST AMENDMENT grounds when the judges upheld a local license tax levied against itinerant religious preachers.

A year later, as the newest member of the Stone Court, Rutledge provided the fifth and crucial vote in a coalition including HUGO L. BLACK, WILLIAM O. DOUGLAS, Murphy, and Chief Justice HARLAN FISKE STONE that overturned the Supreme Court's own ruling in a similar case decided six months earlier

(*Jones v. Opelika*, 1943; MURDOCK V. PENNSYLVANIA, 1943). He also joined Justice ROBERT H. JACKSON's opinion in *West Virginia State Board of Education v. Barnette* (1943). (See FLAG SALUTE CASES.)

Rutledge's jurisprudence blended economic nationalism with compassion for the economically disadvantaged and extreme sensitivity to individual rights. He endorsed, for example, interpretation of the WAGNER ACT to cover local newspaper carriers and believed that the minimum wage provisions of the FAIR LABOR STANDARDS ACT benefited all employees "throughout the farthest reaches of the channels of INTERSTATE COMMERCE."

To protect workers from exploitation, Rutledge believed, the federal government could prohibit entirely homework in the embroidery industry. To protect consumers from abuses, the federal government could prosecute insurance companies under the SHERMAN ANTITRUST ACT, despite more than a half century of precedent to the contrary. (See UNITED STATES V. SOUTH-EASTERN UNDERWRITERS ASSOCIATION, 1944.) He consistently supported the constitutional and statutory rights of working-class Americans, even when the legislative history of the particular law under discussion appeared in doubt (UNITED STATES V. UNITED MINE WORKERS, 1947).

At the same time, Rutledge's concern for individual rights extended even to corporations and capitalists, two groups which often lay beyond the constitutional protection offered by other New Deal liberals on the Court. Unlike Justice FELIX FRANKFURTER, for example, he did not believe that Congress had intended in the pure FOOD AND DRUG LAWS to impose criminal liability upon corporate executives without a finding of personal culpability or negligence. Nor did he believe that Congress could punish violators of wartime price regulations without jury trials and without opportunity to contest the regulations' legality in enforcement proceedings. (See YAKUS V. UNITED STATES, 1944; JUDICIAL SYSTEM.)

Rutledge endorsed without hesitation the concept of PREFERRED FREEDOMS articulated by Justice Stone in UNITED STATES V. CAROLENE PRODUCTS CO. (1938). FREEDOM OF SPEECH and PRESS, RELIGIOUS LIBERTY, the right to vote, and judicial protection for "discrete and insular minorities" served as the cornerstones of his philosophy. Like Stone, he, too, failed

to implement these ideals in the infamous JAPANESE AMERICAN CASES, but, those apart, his civil liberties record remained impeccable. His most memorable CIVIL LIBERTIES opinions came in *Thomas v. Collins* (1944), where he wrote for a five-man majority that reversed the conviction of a labor organizer who had been convicted of contempt for speaking at a union rally without a permit; in EVERSON V. BOARD OF EDUCATION (1947), where he dissented against an opinion that sustained the constitutionality of state aid to the parents of children in parochical schools for bus transportation; and IN RE YAMASHITA (1946), where he and Murphy alone dissented against the drumhead trial of a vanquished Japanese general before an American military commission. With eloquence, heat, and sarcasm, Rutledge denounced the proceedings as "the most flagrant . . . departure . . . from the whole British-American tradition of the COMMON LAW and the Constitution."

He subscribed as well to Justice Black's notion that the DUE PROCESS clause of the FOURTEENTH AMENDMENT "incorporated" the specific protections of the BILL OF RIGHTS, but in the case of ADAMSON V. CALIFORNIA (1947), Rutledge and Murphy were also prepared to go far beyond Black's reasoning to hold that "occasions may arise where a proceeding falls so far short of conforming to fundamental standards of procedure as to warrant constitutional condemnation in terms of a lack of due process despite the absence of a specific provision in the Bill of Rights." (See INCORPORATION DOCTRINE.)

Had Rutledge and Murphy lived, the course of constitutional development in the McCarthy era of the early 1950s might have been healthier for both the Court and the country.

MICHAEL E. PARRISH

Bibliography

HARPER, FOWLER 1965 *Justice Rutledge and the Bright Constellation.* Indianapolis: Bobbs-Merrill.
MANN, W. HOWARD 1950 Rutledge and Civil Liberties. *Indiana Law Journal* 25:532–558.

RUTLEDGE COURT

See: Supreme Court, 1789–1801